Cases and Materials on

Company Law

Sixth Edition

Andrew Hicks, LLB, LLM

Solicitor (England and Wales and Hong Kong)

Former Senior Lecturer in Law, University of Exeter, National University of Singapore and University of Hong Kong

S. H. Goo, LLB, LLM

Associate Professor, Faculty of Law, University of Hong Kong

OXFORD
UNIVERSITY PRESS

OXFORD
UNIVERSITY PRESS

Great Clarendon Street, Oxford OX2 6DP

Oxford University Press is a department of the University of Oxford.
It furthers the University's objective of excellence in research, scholarship,
and education by publishing worldwide in

Oxford New York

Auckland Cape Town Dar es Salaam Hong Kong Karachi
Kuala Lumpur Madrid Melbourne Mexico City Nairobi
New Delhi Shanghai Taipei Toronto

With offices in

Argentina Austria Brazil Chile Czech Republic France Greece
Guatemala Hungary Italy Japan Poland Portugal Singapore
South Korea Switzerland Thailand Turkey Ukraine Vietnam

Oxford is a registered trade mark of Oxford University Press
in the UK and in certain other countries

Published in the United States
by Oxford University Press Inc., New York

© A. Hicks and S. H. Goo, 2008

First published by Blackstone Press Limited, 1994
Second edition, 1997
Third edition, 2001
Fourth edition, 2003
Fifth edition, 2004
Sixth edition, 2008

British Library Cataloguing in Publication Data
Data available

Library of Congress Cataloging in Publication Data
Data available

Typeset by Newgen Imaging Systems (P) Ltd., Chennai, India
Printed in Great Britain
on acid-free paper by
Ashford Colour Press Ltd, Gosport, Hampshire

ISBN 978-0-19-928985-1

3 5 7 9 10 8 6 4

OUTLINE CONTENTS

DETAILED CONTENTS

PREFACE

This book is meant for anyone who, for any purpose, has the pleasure of studying company law. It is a mini-library of original sources distilled into a single volume which introduces you, the reader, systematically to one of the most exciting and challenging of legal subjects and puts you one step ahead in the exam stakes. Not only is it a careful selection of key cases and statutory provisions, it also includes all the delights of European directives, authentic company documents, law reform reports, non-statutory codes of practice and academic writings by leading authors, none of which are generally found in a traditional 'casebook'.

For each chapter, section and reading there are full introductions and commentary that will help you to understand the material you are about to read. In this way, the study of the original sources should be more interesting and instructive than merely reading a conventional student text. Also, we hope, the book will inspire you to explore further if you have access to a law library.

This sixth edition now covers the Companies Act 2006, the blockbuster statute of 1,300 bewildering sections that puts into effect the first comprehensive reform of company law in its century and a half of history. Getting a handle on legislation of this scale and complexity is challenging even for experienced lawyers and for a student the prospect is nothing less than daunting. The aim of the book is thus to help you find your way through the most important aspects of the new law with clear explanation of how the reforms were arrived at. There are many carefully selected readings from the extensive Company Law Review reports and papers prior to the reforms and these are then followed by the provisions of the Act itself, setting out the main principles and outlines of the law. We therefore hope that the book helps you to look beyond the detail and to see both the broad themes of the subject and also the human reality of companies, large and small, that are such major players in all our lives.

You will quickly appreciate that company law is an enormous subject and you should never try to learn its whole content; if you cannot see the wood from the trees you will soon get hopelessly bogged down in detail. Nor should you ever be misled by the polished performance your lecturers put on for you each week, effortlessly analysing a difficult academic issue. Either it's their favourite topic, many times revisited, or they read it up the night before, burning the midnight oil. Like you, they can never unravel and absorb all the intricacies of company law.

With all that in mind, this book aims to help you to understand company law's essential principles, to achieve an overview of its terminology and content and to develop the necessary skills to research and master specific details of the subject. As reading and understanding a complex modern statute is an important skill, the book reproduces many sections from the new Act. Though this is called a case book, company law is nonetheless still a statutory subject and the legislation is always paramount.

As was said by Lady Justice Arden at a meeting of the DTI law reform committee of which I (Andrew Hicks) was a member, when it comes to reforming the law, 'the devil is in the detail'. We have tried not to sup with that particular devil as company law is a mass of technicalities, but instead aim to explain and illustrate the main principles of the law. The full details of company law can be comprehensively studied in texts such as Mayson, French and Ryan, *Company Law*, OUP, which is updated annually.

We believe therefore that the best way for students to cope with the challenge of company law is by reading its original sources. A core selection of these is now presented to you in this book as being the most efficient, stimulating and enjoyable way to absorb its essential principles.

Andrew Hicks prepared Chapters 1, 2, 3, 4, 7, 9, 10, 11, 14, 15, 16, 17, 18, 19 and 20 and Say Goo prepared Chapters 5, 6, 8, 12 and 13.

Andrew Hicks, Surin, Thailand
S. H. Goo, Hong Kong
October 2007

CASEBOOKS AS COURSE BOOKS—A NOTE FOR LECTURERS

This note is to raise the question, what are casebooks for? Why should a student buy a casebook? A possible answer may be convenience, that the student does not have ready access to a library and this is a useful substitute in concentrated form. Ideally one hopes that reading a casebook is not generally a substitute but a stimulus to the use of the library, a convenient expander of horizons. This book especially aims to achieve that stimulus in offering extracts from many diverse sources not always consulted such as law reform reports, academic writings, directives, statutory provisions, non-statutory codes and regulations. Students who read only a textbook receive a distilled and derivative personal account of all these sources. Reading the original source as a matter of first priority is infinitely more exciting and constructive in itself and invites further exploration in the library.

The other use for the book is its original American purpose as a 'casebook'. It can be used as a convenient diet of reading to support 'lectures' or seminars that are wholly or partly interactive. With so many excellent texts, lectures need no longer be a process of relaying basic information to a sea of passive faces. A course can be structured around the casebook, with some chapters omitted if desired. By asking students to study specified readings from it ahead of the 'lecture' it becomes possible to cover twice the ground. It enables the lecturer to engage the students in an open debate and to stimulate them actively to process the information and issues before them, rather than merely being passive receptors of knowledge. The quality of learning can be greatly enhanced and extended, facilitated primarily by prescribing a casebook as the course text. This book is specifically designed for that purpose.

ACKNOWLEDGMENTS

Grateful acknowledgement is made to all the authors and publishers of copyright material which appears in this book, and in particular to the following for permission to reprint material from the sources indicated:

Extracts from *Law Commission Reports* and Consultation papers are Crown copyright material and are reproduced under Class Licence Number C01P0000148 with the permission of the Controller of HMSO and the Queen's Printer for Scotland.

Association of British Insurers: extract from *Risk, Returns and Responsibility* by Roger Cowe (2004).

Association of Chartered Certified Accountants and the authors: extracts from Andrew Hicks: *Disqualification of Directors: No Hiding Place for the Unfit?* (ACCA Research Report No. 59, 1998); and Andrew Hicks, Robert Drury and Dr Jeff Smallcombe: *Alternative Company Structures for the Small Business* (ACCA Research Report No. 42, 1995).

Barclays Bank plc: Barclays Bank Debenture document.

Butterworths Asia: extract from case report in 2 *Malayan Law Journal* 53 (1980).

Cambridge Law Review Association and the authors: extracts from *Cambridge Law Journal*: L S Sealy: 'The Director as Trustee', extract from *CLJ* 83 (1967); and K W Wedderburn: 'Shareholders' rights and the rule in *Foss and Harbottle*', *CLJ* 194 (1957), and *CLJ* 93 (1958).

Caritas Data and the London Stock Exchange: extract from Stock Exchange Official Yearbook 1992–1993.

Department of Trade & Industry: extracts from A L Diamond: *A Review of Security Interests in Property* (1981); Steering Group's Final Report: *Modern Company Law for a Competitive Economy* (1998); *Modern Company Law for a Competitive Economy: The Strategic Framework* (1999); and *Modernising Company Law: The White Paper* (2002). *The Higgs Report* (pp 5–10) 2003.

Exeter University School of Law: extract from Robert Drury: 'A review of the European Community's company law harmonisation programme', 24 *Bracton Law Journal* 45 (1992).

Financial Reporting Council: extracts from *The Combined Code on Corporate Governance* (June 2006) (pp 3–20), *Guidance on Audit Committees* (The Smith Guidance) (pp 3–16) 2005, *Internal Control: Revised Guidance For Directors on the Cobined Code (The Turnbull Guidance)* (pp 3–15) 2005. Adapted and reproduced with the kind permission of the Financial Reporting Council. All rights reserved. For further information, please call 0207492 2300 or visit www.frc.org.uk.

Green, W., & Son: extract from case report from *Scots Law Times* 159 (1978).

De Gruyter, W.: extracts from Dan D Prentice: 'A survey of the law relating to corporate groups in the United Kingdom', in *Groups of Companies in the EC: a survey report to the European Commission on the law relating to corporate groups in various member states:* edited by Eddy Wymeersch (W de Gruyter, 1993).

Incorporated Council of Law Reporting for England and Wales, Megarry House, 119 Chancery Lane, London WC2A 1PP: extracts from *Queen's Bench Reports* (QB), *Appeal Court Reports* (AC), *Weekly Law Reports* (WLR), and *Chancery Reports* (Ch); www.lawreports.co.uk.

Jordan Publishing Ltd: extracts from Barry Rider and Michael Ashe: *Insider Crime: The New Law* (Jordans, 1993); and example of Memorandum and Articles of Association.

Kluwer Law International, www.kluwerlaw.com: extract from Andrew Hicks: 'Limiting the rise of limited liability', originally delivered at the 1995 W G Hart Legal Workshop at the Institute of Advanced Legal Studies, London, and published in R Baldwin and P Cane (Eds): *Law and Uncertainty: risks and legal processes* (Kluwer, 1997).

LexisNexis UK: extracts from *Insolvency Law and Practice*: Andrew Hicks: 'Wrongful Trading—has it been a failure?' (1993) 8 *Ins L & P* 134; and from *All England Law Reports* (All ER), and *Butterworths Company Law Cases* (BCLC).

Oxford University Press: extracts from *Current Issues in Insolvency Law*: edited by Alison Clarke (1991); Vanessa Finch: 'Directors' duties: insolvency and the unsecured creditor'; and David Milman: 'Priority rights on corporate insolvency'.

Pearson Education: extracts from *Company Lawyer*: David Calcutt: 'The work of the Takeover Panel', 11 *Co Law* 203 (1990); Andrew Hicks: 'Advising on wrongful trading', 14 *Co Law* 16 (1993); and Robert Pennington: 'Can shares in companies be defined?', 10 *Co Law* 140 (1989).

Shell International Limited: extract from Shell Group Annual Report 1987.

Sweet & Maxwell Ltd: extracts from *Law Quarterly Review*: Andrew Hicks: 'Directors' Liability for management errors', 110 LQR 390 (1994); and F G Rixon: 'Limiting the veil between holding and subsidiary companies', 102 *LQR* 415 (1986); and from *Journal of Business Law*: Andrew Hicks and Alan Gregory: Valuation of shares: a legal and accounting conundrum', *JBL* 56 (1995); and Lord Alexander of Weedon QC: 'Takeovers: the regulatory scene', *JBL* 203 (1990). Extracts from *Criminal Appeal Reports* (Cr App R), and *British Company Cases* (CcH Editions); and extracts from 'The Cadbury Code'—*Report of the Committee on the Financial Aspects of Corporate Governance* (Gee Publishing, 1992) and from *Committee on Corporate Governance: The Combined Code* (Gee Publishing, 1998).

The Takeover Panel: extracts from City Code on Takeovers and Mergers.

Every effort has been made to trace and contact copyright holders prior to going to press. Although we are continuing to seek the necessary permissions up to publication, if notified, the publisher will undertake to rectify any errors or omissions at the earliest opportunity.

Table of Cases

Cases reported in full are shown in **bold** type. The page at which the report is printed is shown in **bold** type.

Table of Statutes

Material reported in full is shown in **bold** type. The page at which the report is printed is shown in **bold** type.

Table of Statutory Instruments

Material reported in full is shown in bold type. The page at which the report is printed is shown in bold type

1

Sources of Company Law

For the last century and a half a complex body of legislation called the Companies Acts has declared that if anyone presents to Companies House the documents required to form a 'company', the Registrar of Companies will issue a Certificate of Incorporation stating, like a birth certificate, that a new person, a 'limited company', has that day come into being. This robotic person, 'owned' by its shareholders, has no arms or legs, nor even a brain, but it is recognised by the law as being capable of doing all the things necessary to own and run a business. Those dealing with the company make contracts directly with the company itself and the shareholders who formed it are not liable if it defaults on its obligations. They are not party to its contracts and the law allows them the privilege of 'limited liability'. Thus, even if it was they who set up the company and have themselves been running it for their own benefit, in principle they have no liability at all.

It is the function of the legislation as interpreted by the courts to determine how this new person, the company, though artificial and abstract, can have an existence and perform its functions. Thus companies have their own bye-laws called the memorandum and articles of association, the members in general meeting (i.e., the shareholders) elect directors, and the board of directors sees to or delegates the day-to-day running of the business. In addition, the law has to deal with the risk that the extraordinary privilege of limited liability could so easily be unfair and cause harm to creditors. In the final analysis, however, the law cannot protect creditors against limited companies that are not credit worthy. All it can do is to ensure that companies 'disclose' sufficient information to enable alert creditors to look after themselves by making informed decisions when dealing with them.

Core company law has been found in 'the Companies Acts', a constantly changing morass of legislation that has recently undergone the first comprehensive reform ever attempted, culminating in a massive new statute, the Companies Act 2006. For students of the subject, developing expertise in reading detailed modern legislation such as this is a major challenge and for this purpose many key sections are included in these pages. The law relating to companies is also demanding because it requires you to have some understanding of other areas of the law such as contract and tort, equity and trusts, aspects of property and commercial law and the law of the European Union. No longer can you expect to be spoon fed in bite-sized nuggets but must use your maturing expertise to absorb and digest a broad-based diet of law and practice.

The expansive nature of company law also poses particular problems for the authors of this book because many gallons of rich source material must necessarily be distilled into a manageable pint pot. This task is made more difficult as the law relating to companies also includes laws on the public issue of shares and the stock markets, of winding up and insolvency, both huge bodies of law in themselves. In addition, many other disciplines are of direct relevance and cannot be ignored, such as economics, accounting and business management. Recent years have also seen the emergence of new areas of concern and regulation such as financial services and investor protection, financial reporting and corporate governance, business ethics and corporate social responsibility. New buzz words abound such as competitiveness and deregulation, stakeholders and shareholder value and each of these areas of concern has spawned thriving industries, built around growing bodies of rules and regulation which this book can do little more than mention in passing. Nonetheless, while the essential content of the Companies Acts at first glance may seem somewhat dry, the overall breadth and context of company law makes it an exciting, relevant and enjoyable topic of study. Thus, it is the aim of this book to present to you some of the primary materials of company law to help you to grasp the basic principles, terminology and content of a subject that is living and vibrant and whose direct influence reaches into every high street and home throughout the land.

This first chapter now introduces the legislation relating to companies and describes how the companies legislation has been enacted and reformed over the years, culminating in the new Companies Act 2006, which you will soon come to know and love. Included are some extracts from the recent official reports that led to the enactment of the Act which give a readable account of how company law has developed over the years and how it is being reformed and modernised in the interests of promoting a competitive economy. There then follow some readings on how our company law has been amended to 'harmonise' it with the company laws of the other member states of the European Union.

Finally a case study of the life of a fictitious company describes in detail how a typical small company expands and prospers and then falls on hard times. This realistic scenario introduces you to most of the legal processes and problems that small companies encounter and gives you insight into the practical context within which company law generally operates. It will also introduce most of the terminology and give you an instant overview of the essential content of company law. Following this scenario are some examples of the main documents used by the company described in the scenario. Much of the company law that you will go on to study relates to these standard form documents, so it is important that you have some familiarity with them from the very beginning of your study of the subject.

First of all there now follows a brief extract from the beginning of the 'Explanatory Notes' to the Companies Act 2006. This will give you a quick overview of how the Act was contrived and of its structure, though a wider purpose for printing it here is to draw your attention to the fact that new legislation includes such Explanatory Notes. Go to www.opsi.gov.uk/acts.htm, click on 'Public Acts 2006' and scroll down to the 'Companies Act 2006', where you will find the text of the Act and the Notes which should prove helpful when you need to learn more about a particular section.

In reading this first extract you can quickly skim the second part on the structure of the Act at this stage and come back to it later when looking at the Act in more detail.

COMPANIES ACT 2006, EXPLANATORY NOTES

(London: DTI, 2006)

INTRODUCTION

1. These explanatory notes relate to the Companies Act 2006 (c.46) which received Royal Assent on 8 November 2006. They have been prepared by the Department of Trade and Industry (DTI) in order to assist the reader in understanding the Act. They do not form part of the Act and have not been endorsed by Parliament.

2. The notes need to be read in conjunction with the Act. They are not, and are not meant to be, a comprehensive description of the Act. So where a section or part of a section does not seem to require any explanation or comment, none is given. Further, where provisions in the Act restate what was in the Companies Act 1985 (the 1985 Act) an explanation is not always given, except to the extent required to explain changes to associated provisions.

BACKGROUND

3. The UK was one of the first nations to establish rules for the operation of companies. Today our system of company law and corporate governance, setting out the legal basis on which companies are formed and run, is a vital part of the legal framework within which business is conducted. As the business environment evolves, there is a risk that the legal framework can become gradually divorced from the needs of companies, in particular the needs of smaller private businesses, creating obstacles to ways that companies want and need to operate.

4. In March 1998, the DTI commissioned a fundamental review of company law. An independent Steering Group led the "Company Law Review" (CLR) whose terms of reference required them to consider how core company law could be modernised in order to provide a simple, efficient and cost effective framework for British business in the twenty-first century. After extensive consultation with interested parties, the CLR presented its Final Report to the Secretary of State for Trade and Industry on 26 July 2001. The report contained a range of recommendations for substantive changes to many areas of company law, and a set of principles to guide the development of the law more generally, most notably that it should be as simple and as accessible as possible for smaller firms and their advisers and should avoid imposing unnecessary burdens on the ways companies operate.

5. Many of the provisions of the Act implement CLR recommendations. The Government set out and consulted on its intentions in this regard in the White Papers "Modernising Company Law" (July 2002) and "Company Law Reform" (March 2005). The 2005 White Paper included approximately 300 draft clauses and described in detail the policy intention for other areas. Further clauses were made publicly available for comment in July, September and October 2005. The Companies Bill, then titled the Company Law Reform Bill, was introduced to the House of Lords on 4 November 2005.

OVERVIEW OF THE STRUCTURE OF THE ACT

6. The general arrangement of the Act is as follows:

PART	SUMMARY
Parts 1 to 7	The fundamentals of what a company is, how it can be formed and what it can be called.
Parts 8 to 12	The members (shareholders) and officers (management) of a company
Parts 13 and 14	How companies may take decisions
Parts 15 and 16	The safeguards for ensuring that the officers of a company are accountable to its members
Parts 17 to 25	Raising share capital, capital maintenance, annual returns, and company charges
Parts 26 to 28	Company reconstructions, mergers and takeovers
Parts 29 to 39	The regulatory framework, application to companies not formed under the Companies Acts and other company law provisions
Parts 40 to 42	Overseas disqualification of directors, business names and statutory auditors
Part 43	Transparency obligations
Parts 44 to 47	Miscellaneous and general

SUMMARY OF LEGISLATIVE CHANGES

7. The company law provisions of the 2006 Act (Parts 1 to 39) restate almost all of the provisions of the [Companies Act] 1985 Act, together with the company law provisions of the Companies Act 1989 (the 1989 Act) and the Companies (Audit, Investigations and Community Enterprise) Act 2004 (C(AICE) Act 2004). Paragraphs 9 and 10 below contain details of the provisions that remain in those Acts. The company law provisions also codify certain aspects of the case law.

8. Tables of origins and destinations are available that show the origins of the company law provisions of the Act by reference to enactments in force on 8 November 2006. The tables identify where provisions of the existing law have been re-enacted with or without changes and where provisions of the new law have no predecessor or are fundamentally different from their predecessors.

9. Of company law provisions in the Acts referred to in paragraph 7, the only ones that remain are those on investigations that go wider than companies (Part 14 of the 1985 Act) and the provisions on community interest companies in Part 2 of the C(AICE) Act 2004.

10. The non-company law provisions in those Acts that remain are:
a) Part 18 of the 1985 Act (floating charges and receivers (Scotland)),
b) Part 3 of the 1989 Act (powers to require information and documents to assist overseas regulatory authorities),
c) Section 112 to 116 of the 1989 Act (provisions about Scottish incorporated charities)
d) Part 7 of the 1989 Act (provisions about financial markets and insolvency)
e) Schedule 18 of the 1989 Act (amendments and savings consequential upon changes in the law made by the 1989 Act)
f) Sections 14 and 15 of the C(AICE) Act 2004 (supervision of accounts and reports), and
g) Sections 16 and 17 of the C(AICE) Act 2004 (bodies concerned with accounting standards etc).

11. In non-company law areas the Act makes amendments to other legislation, in particular the Financial Services and Markets Act 2000, and also makes new provision of various kinds. The main areas in which provision of this kind is made are:
- overseas disqualification of company directors (Part 40),
- business names (Part 41)—replacing the Business Names Act 1985,
- statutory auditors (Part 42)—replacing Part 2 of the Companies Act 1989, and
- transparency obligations (Part 43)—amending Part 6 of the Financial Services and Markets Act 2000.

1.2 THE REFORM OF COMPANY LAW

Your own first foray into company law has in some ways been made easier, though in others more difficult, by the Companies Act 2006 which enacts the first ever comprehensive review of company law.

Until now, the reform of company law has been criticised for being haphazard and piecemeal. From time to time when there were problems or scandals in the City, the usual response of governments was to appoint law reform committees or specialist consultants to produce a report. Some of their key recommendations might be passed into law but often their detailed proposals lay dormant, thwarted by the low political priority of company law and the shortage of parliamentary time. Nonetheless the Acts have regularly been tinkered with, including reforms implementing complex directives from Europe. In consequence company law had become a tangled mass of legislation, accumulating like barnacles on the hull of a ship. Furthermore, while the original purpose of limited liability companies had been to enable the raising of capital for big public enterprises such as railways, water companies, banks and insurers, throughout the twentieth century large numbers of small business were now being incorporated as limited companies. The need to reduce the burden of regulation for small companies then became one of the aims of reform, adding further to the law's bulk and complexity.

In March 1998 company law was at last moved higher up the political priorities with the announcement of a major project for its comprehensive reform. A consultative document entitled *Modern Company Law for a Competitive Economy* was issued stating that a fundamental review of company law was to be undertaken, directed at modernisation and economic competitiveness in a globalised world. The focus was moving away from regulation and towards facilitation; how best could company law more efficiently promote economic activity and enterprise. While the original aim of company law was to enable major public companies to raise large amounts of capital by offering shares to investors, the new approach to drafting the law had become, 'think small first'. This appropriately recognised the reality that the vast majority of limited companies are small businesses and refocuses the legislation with their needs primarily in mind.

The current reform process took a decade during which many trees were felled and quantities of consultation documents and reports issued. The principle documents are listed below at 1.2.1 and some key extracts from them appear throughout this book.

The Companies Act 2006 that resulted has thus now made your study of the subject a little easier as the statute has been comprehensively redrafted within a single Act and with a clearer style of language than was previously the case.

However, the old law was not swept away in one fell swoop when the Act received the Royal Assent on 8 November 2006. As appears from s. 1300 of the Act, a few of its sections have immediate effect, while the Government's present intention is to bring the rest of the Act into force in stages on days to be appointed by the Secretary of State by statutory instrument. It was hoped to complete implementation by the end of 2008 but this deadline was extended to 1 October 2009 to give Companies House more time to prepare for the changes. The day chosen for commencement of particular parts is determined by factors such as the need to implement EU directives (e.g., the takeovers and transparency directives), to have time to draft and enact the necessary subsidiary regulations and for Companies House to gear up to handle new procedures. Only by consulting these commencement orders therefore, can a lawyer determine the current state of the law.

Furthermore, even when the new law is fully in force, elements of the old law may still remain relevant. For example, transactions conducted before repeal will still be governed by the old provisions, and while, for example, the new law will streamline the formation of companies with new style memorandum and articles of association, all existing companies retain their traditional style constitutions unless and until the members choose to adopt new ones. The old ones which are the foundation on which company practice has developed over the decades will thus be in use for many years to come and accordingly this book continues to reproduce the so-called 'Table A' model articles of 1985 at 1.7 below and to refer to them from time to time throughout. The new order will thus emerge only gradually with time.

Finally, although the new law represents a major reform, it is not a revolution. It is a major blip in the long conservative continuum of company law, but it reflects organic growth with few fundamental changes. Lawyers always tend to cast an eye over their shoulder as they move forward and the experience of the law over many decades will continue to explain and influence interpretation of the new legislation.

Loath to abandon their favourite topics, your company law lecturers may also quite properly take an historical approach to their teaching of the subject, explaining the new law in the light of past problems and experience. In any event, elements of the 'old' law may still apply in some circumstances and will also influence the courts in how they interpret the new provisions For example, the traditional law of *ultra vires* has not been fully 'abolished' in the case of charitable companies (CA 2006, ss. 39 and 42), and the newly codified duties of directors are to be interpreted and applied with regard to the old common law rules and equitable principles (CA 2006, s. 170), which should thus still be studied in the initial absence of any new case law. Thus the book retains many older sources that are still of relevance, including extracts from the less accessible law reform reports that are not available online.

The following extracts from the first consultative document issued for public comment in 1988, and from 'The Strategic Framework' document of 1999 (which analysed the public response to the earlier one and proposed some guiding strategies), are a clear and authoritative statement of how company law has developed in the past, of its perceived weaknesses and of the proposed objectives and approach of the most major reform of company law ever undertaken. These are then followed by extracts from the White Papers of 2002 and 2005 indicating the Government's views on the way ahead. Though written in a style for non-lawyers to read, some of this inevitably may go over your head. Nonetheless, a first reading will begin the slow osmotic process of absorbing this challenging subject into a reluctant brain and you should later return for a re-read when you are no longer quite so novice a company lawyer.

Modern Company Law for a Competitive Economy

(London: DTI, 1998)

Chapter 1 Introduction

1.1 The Government has decided that the time is now right to embark on a fundamental review of the framework of core company law. Many of the key features of our current arrangements were put in place in the middle of the last century; and although there have been numerous changes and additions through the years, it is nearly 40 years since the last broad review of company law. The current framework has as a result become seriously outdated in key respects, not least as the economy has become more globalised. In addition, the current pace of change in areas such as information technology means that in a number of areas the present arrangements are holding back rather than facilitating competitiveness, growth and investment.

1.2 The object of the review will be to bring forward proposals for a modern law for the modern world. The Government is determined that the nation should have an up-to-date framework which promotes the competitiveness of UK companies and so contributes to national competitiveness and increased prosperity.

1.3 The Government is committed to ensuring that the review proceeds on the basis of the widest possible consultation with all interested parties. This Consultation Paper outlines plans for the handling of the review; these envisage the establishment of a Steering Group and Working Groups with broad representation, a Consultative Committee, and the publication for comment of key documents from time to time. The Government is keen to ensure that the new arrangements which result from the review enjoy wide support not simply from business and industry but also in the community at large. This Consultation Paper is therefore directed at the non-specialist reader, not simply at experts in company law.

1.4 The proposed review will be wide ranging; but business should not fear large-scale upheaval of familiar requirements. There is rightly a premium on stability, and the Government is conscious of the need to avoid gratuitous and unnecessary change and the cost this would impose. There will be no change for its own sake. Where change does result, careful thought will be given to transitional arrangements.

1.5 The review outlined in this Consultation Paper is necessarily a substantial undertaking. Given that major reviews of this sort are—for good reason—infrequent events, it is right to take the time to do it properly, and to ensure that the resulting arrangements will stand the test of time.

. . .

Chapter 2 Background

2.1 There are about 1.14 million UK companies registered at Companies House. They range from the smallest of start-up businesses to large long-established companies operating internationally. There are relatively few companies at the larger end of the scale—only 2,450 or so have their shares publicly traded on the London Stock Exchange.

2.2 All companies are subject to the same broad framework of company law. The main piece of legislation is the Companies Act 1985, which brought together or 'consolidated' previous legislation. Although some requirements vary according to the type and size of company, the same basic principles apply to all companies.

2.3 Many of the principles of key importance (such as limited liability, registration on a public register, and disclosure of information about the financial state of the business) were put in place in the middle of the last century, and some mention of the historical background is helpful for an understanding of the present arrangements. Two reforms were especially significant:

- The Joint Stock Companies Act of 1844. This required all new businesses with more than 25 participants to be 'incorporated'—that is, to be set up as companies with a legal status and personality of their own, rather than as conventional partnerships. Second, the Act said that such companies should be set up by the simple process of registration (rather than by Act of Parliament or royal charter), and created the post of Registrar of Companies which continues to this day. Third, it provided for 'publicity'—or, as we would say today, *disclosure*—in particular through companies' constitutions and annual accounts being filed with the Registrar of Companies.

- The Limited Liability Act of 1855. This introduced the concept of general limited liability for shareholders—i.e. their liability for the company's debts, if it became bankrupt, was limited to the amount of share capital which they had invested. It was felt important that the company's creditors should be aware of the limited liability status of the company, and the requirement for companies to have 'limited' or 'ltd' in their name dates from this time. It was the 1855 Act which, in the words of the late Professor Gower, 'finally established companies as the major instrument in economic development'.

2.4 After this legislation, businesses mostly fell into two categories: incorporated companies and conventional partnerships. The numbers of incorporated companies increased steadily, in particular towards the end of the nineteenth century. By 1914 around 65,000 were registered; by 1945 about 200,000. Since the last war the number has increased greatly to the present level. The principal rules for partnerships were brought together in the Partnership Act 1890 and continue to govern partnerships to this day.

2.5 Development of company law in this century comes mostly from reactions to scandals and mischiefs arising from the wide scope allowed by the Victorian legislation, which in general had only a light regulatory touch. The pattern was that the Board of Trade appointed a Committee at intervals of around 20 years to review company law. The resulting recommendations were introduced in an amending Companies Act. The old and the new law were then 'consolidated' into a new comprehensive Companies Act. Such consolidations took place in 1908, 1929 and 1948. The most recent major review was that of the Company Law Committee—the 'Jenkins Committee'—which was appointed in 1960 and reported in 1962. A number of its recommendations were enacted piecemeal in the companies legislation of 1967, 1980 and 1981. As already pointed out, these reviews concentrated on current scandals and perceived deficiencies in protecting investors or preventing fraud. The net result was a constant addition of new rules and regulations to companies legislation without any re-examination of its fundamental principles. Company law thus grew in bulk and complexity, but there was no attempt to slim down the basic structure and remove sections designed to deal with practices and situations which, often, no longer happened.

2.6 The complexity grew even more rapidly from 1972 as a result of the need to reflect in UK companies legislation EC Directives adopted under the EC company law harmonisation programme. This left the legislation, in the view of the late Professor Gower, 'in a worse state than at any time this century'.

2.7 As noted in paragraph 2.2, the legislation up to 1985 was consolidated in the form of the Companies Act 1985. This was quickly followed by the Insolvency Acts of 1985 and 1986, and by the Financial Services Act 1986. These latter acts represented a major structural change in the legislation by removing insolvency law and securities regulation from companies legislation and establishing them as distinct areas of law. This may be said to be the only major simplification, if that is the correct word, of companies legislation this century.

2.8 A further Companies Act was passed in 1989. Its main aim was to implement the 7th EC Company Law Directive on Consolidated Accounts, and the 8th on Audits; but it also included some domestic reforms. The 1989 Act is the most recent Act in company law, though a number of parts of this Act and the 1985 Act have since been modified by the use of Order-making powers (i.e. powers to make minor changes without a new Act of Parliament). In addition the DTI has in recent years reviewed a number of those areas of current legislation which frequently give rise to difficulty, and has developed proposals to amend the present law when there is an opportunity.

2.9 The history of company law since the great reforms of the last century can thus be seen as a series of additions to the existing legal framework resulting from the need to tackle perceived deficiencies and shortcomings. For long periods this process may be enough. But recent years have seen increasing concern that the framework is becoming obsolescent; and it is clear that piecemeal reform cannot significantly reduce the amount and complexity of current arrangements.

Modern Company Law for a Competitive Economy: The Strategic Framework
(London: DTI: 1999)

Chapter 1 Introduction and background responses to the Consultation Paper

1.11 In so far as it is possible to draw consistent messages from such a large number of responses covering such a wide range of issues, the themes that seemed to be emerging from the comments made in response to the Consultation Paper were these:

- there was a considerable degree of support for making company law more accessible;
- there was a strong view that company law should make greater use of civil as opposed to criminal remedies;
- there was a wide view that a differential approach needed to be adopted to cater for the needs of different types of company, especially the small private firm;
- there were real doubts about the usefulness of the Annual General Meeting as currently provided for in company law;
- there was wide agreement that company law needed to be amended to allow greater use of electronic means of communication and storage of information;
- there was wide agreement on the case for revision of the provisions relating to a company's objects and powers;
- there was widespread concern that the capital maintenance regime was in need of thorough re-examination;
- there was agreement that the 'stakeholder' issue lay at the heart of the Review, though no consensus on the most appropriate approach;
- issues surrounding directors, and especially their duties and their pay, were the areas to attract most comment; and
- there was concern that company law is not well suited to groups of companies.

The Review's terms of reference

1.12 The Department of Trade and Industry ('the Department') Consultation Paper proposed (in paragraph 5.2) the following terms of reference for the Review:

(i) To consider how core company law can be modernised in order to provide a simple, efficient and cost-effective framework for carrying out business activity which:

    (a) permits the maximum amount of freedom and flexibility to those organising and directing the enterprise;

    (b) at the same time protects, through regulation where necessary, the interests of those involved with the enterprise, including shareholders, creditors and employees; and

    (c) is drafted in clear, concise and unambiguous language which can be readily understood by those involved in business enterprise.

(ii) To consider whether company law, partnership law, and other legislation which establishes a legal form of business activity together provide an adequate choice of legal vehicle for business at all levels.

(iii) To consider the proper relationship between company law and non-statutory standards of corporate behaviour.

(iv) To review the extent to which foreign companies operating in Great Britain should be regulated under British company law.

(v) To make recommendations accordingly.

The proposed terms of reference support, in turn, the objectives of the Review which were set out in paragraph 5.1 of the Paper: the competitiveness of British companies, an attractive regime for overseas companies, a proper balance of the interests of those concerned with companies in the context of straightforward, cost effective and fair regulation, and the promotion of consistency, predictability and transparency in company law. The Paper specifically sought comments on the proposed terms of reference.

Chapter 2 The overall approach

A. Objectives

Modern law

2.3 We believe 'modern' law means law well fitted to meet current, and foreseeable future, needs. This may involve deregulation, but it is not restricted to deregulation; the objective is to suit the law to the needs of all participants. and of other relevant interests, rather than to reduce regulatory safeguards. Our focus is therefore on provisions which, in form or substance, no longer serve their proper purpose or which can be adjusted better to do so, and on needs for which there is currently no provision.

Law for a competitive economy

2.4 This is the predominant objective. We shall pursue policies to facilitate productive and creative activity in the economy in the most competitive and efficient way possible for the benefit of everyone, with appropriate freedom for managers and others controlling companies, ensuring that in order to maximise wealth and welfare, they are enabled to exercise their proper function in managing resources. It is not for the law to substitute for the business judgements involved, but to provide optimal conditions for their proper exercise. The importance of the law should be kept in perspective—companies should not, and typically do not, operate at the legal boundary but adopt a wide range of non-legal standards, including best practice. A competitive economy will rely as little as possible on costly and inflexible legal mechanisms. The most efficient law will often derive from well tried best practice or provide the best conditions for its development. We recognise that the limited company form has proved over the last 150 years an outstandingly successful means for organising productive activity, deploying and protecting investment and allocating risks. It is critically important that that success should be preserved, and indeed enhanced, in the modern context. But it also needs to be recognised that a variety of forms work well in different jurisdictions. There is clearly room for improvement.

2.5 We would stress in this context that we interpret our terms of reference as requiring us to propose reforms which promote a competitive economy by facilitating the operations of companies so as to maximise wealth and welfare as a whole. We have not regarded it as our function to make proposals as to how such benefits should be shared or allocated between different participants in the economy, on grounds of fairness, social justice or any similar criteria. Such questions are, of course, extremely important but we do not consider that they fall within the scope of this Review. It may well be the case (and indeed we believe it is likely to be) that our proposals will have the effect of creating fairer outcomes. But if that is so it will be because that is the result of our adopting the objective of achieving wealth and welfare creation overall, and not because fairness in itself is an objective for us.

Freedom and abuse

2.6 This does not mean that the law should merely facilitate and secure freedom for management and controllers of companies. There is a trade-off between freedom and abuse, and between freedom and efficiency. Indeed abuse damages efficiency and the credibility of business and of the productive system. The optimal balance between freedom and risk of abuse is clearly a matter of judgement, to be worked out in the context of particular provisions. We also seek to ensure that appropriate high standards of conduct are maintained. Such standards are important components in promoting competitiveness and efficiency. They give rise to demands on management which must be recognised—both internal, from shareholders and others, and external—ensuring corporate activity responds also, to the maximum extent it efficiently can, to wider economic, environmental and social needs.

2.7 Some respondents have stressed that wider considerations, beyond relations between members, creditors and directors, ('externalities') are already properly and rightly dealt with by specialised legislation bearing equally on all businesses, companies or not (e.g. employment, health and safety, consumer protection and environmental laws, the weight of which has increased substantially in recent years). We recognise the concern that introduction of extraneous considerations into rules governing continuing relationships within companies may prevent management from focusing on the key business of managing to generate wealth. But we also recognise that the corporate sector remains the most important component of the productive economy; the laws governing its constitution, management and accountability already recognise wider interests. Best practice often goes further. Companies can be viewed largely as contractual entities, created and controlled under agreements entered into by members and directors; but we do not accept that it follows that the law has no place in securing that they are operated so that a wider range of interests are met. It is a proper question of public policy whether company law is an appropriate vehicle to achieve this, and what constraints and conditions should be attached to corporate status and limited liability. But we believe that, in designing a legislative and broader framework to enable companies properly to respond, we should ensure wherever possible that the law enables both internal and external interests to be satisfied.

Comprehensive, coherent reform

2.8 Our task is also to ensure a comprehensive reform to produce a coherent framework. This contrasts with the current patchwork of largely facilitative core and prescriptive additions, accumulated as a result of episodic and reactive reform. Comprehensive reform is, in fact, essential to produce a competitive and efficient outcome.

2.9 The present law has many strengths and benefits, but does not measure up well against the objectives outlined above. Detailed examples emerge in Chapter 5. It fails in terms of responsiveness to the shape of modern businesses, and in the accessibility of the language in which it is expressed—relevant provisions sometimes being hard to find and understand and expensive to administer. Anti-abuse provisions may take the form of an unduly wide prohibition, sometimes introduced for broad or now superseded reasons, overlaid with complex exemptions, to which are attached a further layer of conditions and safeguards. The purpose may be reasonably clear in theory but may bear little relationship to modern commercial reality, particularly in the context of the wide range of purposes to which the law is put. Elaborate prescriptive structures, such as the capital maintenance doctrine, have been built up on the back of theories which may now have only limited relevance. Legal obscurity may also lend support to outdated views, for example about the proper scope of managerial discretion.

The importance of change

2.10 These problems are exacerbated by more general changes. Today's markets and businesses are characterised by the following key trends.

Globalisation

2.11 The UK's economy is less and less insulated from wider influences. Inward investment has been of great importance. The increasing openness of regional and international trading relationships reinforces the need for a low cost, speedy and efficient method of organisation of commercial activity, attractive to foreign undertakings and providing an optimal infrastructure for indigenous ones. The increasing international mobility of business and capital, the globalisation of brands and the ability of firms to operate internationally, without local incorporation, also raise the need to review systems for regulating overseas businesses operating in Great Britain. We have to recognise that it is increasingly possible that, if we make our law unduly prescriptive, inflexible, inaccessible or onerous, businesses will choose to incorporate elsewhere.

Europe

2.12 The UK's membership of the European Union has had two relevant consequences. The first, the increasing openness of the UK market and that of its EU partners, is part of the globalisation process. The second is that the UK has become party to the Community legal harmonisation programme, which is part of the single market enterprise. Continental European traditions are typically more prescriptive and regulatory than the UK's. This has led to some difficulties in adjusting domestic British law, and the harmonisation programme does create some special problems in considering reforms. However, there has been some movement in the direction of the more open, contractual and transparency-based British approach, and there are indications of an increasing recognition of its value. We respect the objectives of the harmonisation programme and will pay careful regard to the experience of continental partners in developing proposals for reform.

Changing patterns of regulation

2.13 Companies are now subject to a range of regulatory control beyond traditional company law. The Stock Exchange, Financial Services Authority, Takeover Panel, and accountancy bodies, all issue rules and exercise enforcement powers. Much of this has come about since the last major review of company law in the early 1960s. All these bodies are specialised and bring particular skills, but the resulting picture is inevitably more complex.

Information technologies

2.14 Company law depends on, and in ultimate output very largely consists of, the accumulation and communication of information. The new systems for electronic communication and information management have the potential to transform the processes, and the substantive relationships, involved.

Changing patterns of ownership

2.15 The overwhelming majority of registered companies are small owner-managed businesses; of companies on the Companies House register, only 1% are public companies. In large companies, ownership (or at least control) has become increasingly concentrated, with institutional investors holding around 80% of shares in UK companies The top institutions in 1996 accounted for approximately 25 per cent of stock market value, the top 20 for one-third, and top 50 institutions for half of stock market value. Across the market, the largest institutional investors are consistently companies' largest shareholders. The growth in the influence of institutional investors has led in turn to the development of a more effective market in corporate control—a further non-legal constraint on the powers of managers. At the same time, over the last 15 years there has been significant growth in personal share ownership, much of it attributable to factors such as privatisations, demutualisations and employee share ownership schemes. The number of individuals in Great Britain holding shares directly rose from approximately 3 million in 1979 to 10 million in 1993; a more recent estimate is that there were 15 million shareholders in Britain in October 1997. . . .

The importance of small and closely held companies

2.19 Small and closely-held firms play a major role in the UK economy. . . . The evidence suggests that small firms are the main job creators. For instance, statistics available to the Department show that between 1989 and 1991 over 90% of additional jobs created were in firms with fewer that 10 employees even though they accounted for only 18% of total employment in 1989. Government has often expressed the view that small businesses are crucial to UK's competitiveness and lie at the heart of its economic strategy. Company law, however, makes little attempt to respond to the peculiar needs of small firms, either in accessibility and simplicity of operation or in substantive provision. The start up and development of such businesses is a particularly important process for which the law should provide an optimal climate.

B. Guiding principles

2.20 With these points in mind, we have sought to develop guiding principles for the Review.

Facilitation of transactions—a presumption against prescription

2.21 First, the need for companies to be responsive to change, to leave space for developing best practice and to enable competitive efficiency leads us to seek maximum scope for freedom of activity for participants. A key role of company law is as a means of facilitating the operation of market forces, through contractual and other mutual relationships. These operate in markets and other arenas where accountability ('transparency') enables effective assertion of claims by external interests and appropriate response by managements and members (or shareholders). The key markets include capital markets and markets for managerial skills and corporate control. Other arenas of accountability are those where a broader range of influences is brought to bear, informed by company law reporting requirements and other information. Companies respond to such pressures, expressed typically through pressure groups and the media, in order to sustain the reputation and credibility on which commercial success depends. A range of interrelated contracts and other relationships thus enables demands and claims to be efficiently met. This process however depends critically on adequacy of information through transparency in relationships, between all participants and parties concerned.

2.22 We therefore conclude that freedom of contract and exchange in the broadest sense, supported by transparency requirements, should be the approach wherever possible. The law should acknowledge the diversity of economic activity and provide participants with the means to devise the best legal solution for themselves exercising their own commercial and other judgement and freedom of choice within the network of non-legal constraints and pressures described.

2.23 This presumption must yield, however, where markets and informal pressures combined with transparency cannot be expected to work; this may happen because participants lack the market power, skill or resources to contract effectively. Such prescriptive intervention must of course be justified in terms of the costs and benefits and the effectiveness of the protections conferred. In this context the flexibility of civil enforcement, with costs borne by the wrong-doer, has great advantages over criminal sanctions, which require public resource which is already overstretched. However even civil enforcement may be expensive and inefficient. This suggests that where detailed prescription is nevertheless justified the sensitive application of 'self regulatory' rules will often be a preferable approach where available in effective form.

Accessibility—ease of use and identification of the law

2.24 The complexity and inaccessibility of the law mean that even elementary issues are often regarded as material for experts, and even non-specialist lawyers and other professionals cannot always find their way around. Competitiveness requires the minimum complexity and maximum accessibility, both in terms of the substance of the law and the way in which it is communicated. The final output of reform is words on paper. It must be as easy as possible to find out which requirements apply and what they mean. This has implications both for substance and language used and for the way in which it is assembled and arranged. Sometimes the law must provide for complex situations (many company transactions are inevitably subtle and complicated). But this legitimate need of the few should not result in cost and confusion to the majority. In addition, sensitive use of a variety of communications media may help to reduce the difficulties.

2.25 The current structure of the law is essentially based on the needs of the large company with a wide shareholding. Special exemptions and derogations are allowed for smaller and more informally managed entities. In general however the same law (aggregated by reference to broad topics, such as share capital, accounts and audit, or meetings and resolutions) applies to all companies whether large or small, public or private. The fact that most company law is irrelevant to the vast majority of users leads us, like many respondents to the document in March 1998, to incline to favour radical restructuring of the legislation, treating the small company as the basic entity and adding on the relevant requirements for exceptional, larger and more sophisticated entities in further discrete layers. The work of the Working Group on small firms supports this view.

Modernising Company Law: The White Paper

(London: DTI: July 2002. Cm 5553)

PART II—THE GOVERNMENT'S POLICY

1 Introduction

1.1 This part of the White Paper sets out the Government's response to the key recommendations made by the Company Law Review and its proposals for modernising the main elements of company law. The detailed implementation of our policies is covered in the draft clauses in Volume II and the notes commenting on them in Part III below (or will be covered in clauses and notes in later documents).

The Right Approach to Small Companies

1.2   Current company law is designed around the needs of big public companies, with additional provisions for other companies. This reflects the origins of company law in the mid-nineteenth century, when the joint-stock company was seen as an ideal model for raising money for large capital projects, such as railway building. However, since then small businesses have increasingly sought the advantages of corporate status and limited liability. There are now 1.5 million companies in Great Britain. Some have existed for over a century, but two thirds are less than 10 years old. A few are household names, employing many thousands and with shares traded internationally, but most are small private companies with relatively few employees.

1.3   The Government agrees with the Review that the starting point for company law should be the small firm, with additional or different provisions for larger companies where necessary. The law needs to balance various interests, including those of shareholders, directors, employees, creditors and customers, but it should avoid imposing unnecessary or inappropriate burdens. Company law should make it easy to start and run businesses. In drawing up these proposals, the Government has examined carefully the scope for simplification of the current law.

1.4   At present much of company law draws an important distinction between public and private companies. A public company is so called because it can offer its shares direct to the general public. In general, public companies have to meet higher disclosure requirements than private companies. Although some private companies are large, and some public companies are small, the very largest companies are likely to be public and the smallest more likely to be private.

1.5   The Review considered whether there should be a special and distinct corporate structure for small businesses. The problem with this approach is that it requires a definition of small, for example a maximum number of shareholders, number of employees, turnover or assets. Once a company passed the threshold, it would no longer qualify for the special regime. Such a threshold would therefore be likely to act as a barrier to growth, and could create problems were it to be crossed inadvertently or re-crossed several times by a company.

1.6   The Government agrees with the Review that a more appropriate way forward is to tailor the core of company law to fit the smallest companies, which are mostly private companies. Additional safeguards can be added as necessary, for example for public companies which offer their shares to the public. In general therefore the Bill will, like the present Act, distinguish between private and public companies. But it will put private companies first.

1.7   In the specific areas of accounting and auditing the Government intends to continue with the present approach of monetary thresholds. The current ceilings for preparation of different types of account will be raised to the maximum permitted by the relevant EC directives, as described in paragraph 4.19 below. In the case of audit thresholds the Government intends to assess the impact of the substantial July 2000 increase in the threshold before making a final decision on whether to increase the threshold further (see paragraph 4.23 below).

Looking to the Future

1.8   This Companies Bill will be the most extensive reform in this area for 150 years. If it is not itself to become quickly outdated, it must look forward as far as possible. It is important too that it is sufficiently flexible to react to future developments. The Government has therefore accepted the Review's proposals that:

— while basic principles are anchored in primary legislation, technical matters which are likely to require amendment as business practices develop should be able to be amended by secondary legislation; and

— certain implementing legislation on accounting standards and disclosure should be made by a suitable expert body (see section 5 below).

1.9 Previous legislation made no allowance for changing technology. Thus it had to be amended to allow records to be kept in loose-leaf books (in 1948), then to allow certain records to be kept on computers (in 1976, 1980 and 1989), and then again for the further use of electronic communications in 2000. The Government proposes that companies legislation should, as far as possible, allow the maximum flexibility to use future technology without the need to amend legislation.

Company Law Reform: The White Paper

(London: DTI, March 2005, Cm 6456)

I Summary

This White Paper builds closely on the work of the Company Law Review (CLR), and of the Government's subsequent White Paper of 2002. The CLR itself conducted a series of public consultations before publishing its final report, and the Government has taken full account of that process, of responses to the White Paper, and of subsequent consultations, both formal and informal, in determining the policy measures now set out in this document. Draft clauses are included for a number of the areas.

Company law can be very complex, and there will be some interested parties (perhaps particularly smaller firms and their advisors) who will want to gain some understanding of the central measures proposed, but who may not wish to investigate the technical minutiae of how they will be delivered in legislation. Set out below, therefore, is a list of the key legislative changes. A separate small business summary has also been prepared, highlighting the measures likely to be of most interest to smaller firms and their advisors.

Summary of Legislative Changes

Enhancing shareholder engagement and a long-term investment culture

Shareholders are the lifeblood of a company, whatever its size. We want to promote wide participation of shareholders, ensuring that they are informed and involved, as they should be. And we want decisions to be made based on the longer-term view and not just immediate return. We will:

- embed in statute the concept of Enlightened Shareholder Value by making clear that directors must promote the success of the company for the benefit of its shareholders, and this can only be achieved by taking due account of both the tong-term and short-term, and wider factors such as employees, effects on the environment, suppliers and customers;
- introduce a statutory statement of directors' duties to clarify their responsibilities and improve the law regulating directors' conflicts of interest;
- relax the prohibition on provisions which prevent auditors from limiting their liability, while delivering further improvements in the quality of the audit;
- enhance the rights of proxies and make it easier for companies to enfranchise indirect owners of shares:
- remove the requirement for paper share certificates and facilitate the use by companies of e-communications where their shareholders want this;
- implement the Takeovers Directive that will facilitate takeover activity in the EU through improved shareholder protection and access to capital markets.

Ensuring better regulation and a "Think Small First" approach

Although the vast majority of UK companies are small, company law has been written traditionally with the large company in mind. We want to reset the balance and make the law easier for all to understand and use. We will:

- provide separate and better-adapted default articles (the current "Table A") for private companies;
- simplify decision-making for private companies, for example by making it easier for decisions to be taken by written resolution, and making Annual General Meetings (AGMs) opt-in rather than opt-out;

- abolish the requirement for private companies to have a company secretary;
- update company financial and narrative reports;
- simplify the rules about company share capital in particular for private companies;
- implement some aspects of the European Transparency Directive;
- introduce a power to allow the law to be restated where necessary in future to make it accessible.

In addition to the changes in the law itself, the Government will be ensuring that there is appropriate advice and guidance available to users of company law, particularly smaller firms and their advisors, so that all can understand the options available to them and the requirements placed upon them.

Making it easier to set up and run a company

We want to remove unnecessary burdens to directors and preserve Britain's reputation as a favoured country in which to incorporate. We will:

- remove the requirement on most directors to disclose publicly their home address;
- abolish the requirement for a company to have authorised share capital;
- enable a single person to form a public company;
- streamline the rules on company names and trading disclosures;
- make deregulatory changes to the register of past and present members which companies are obliged to maintain.

Providing flexibility for the future

Company law is not static. We intend to introduce a new reform power to allow updating and amendment as circumstances dictate, subject to rigorous safeguards for full consultation and appropriate Parliamentary scrutiny.

Benefits to business

The Government believes that the measures above, by making company law better fitted to today's realities, should create improved performance across the economy as a whole, as well as reducing direct compliance costs for business and producing cost savings which could amount to some £250m a year.

2 Setting the Scene

The Government is committed to ensuring that the legal and regulatory framework within which business operates promotes enterprise, growth and the right conditions for investment and employment.

Our system of company law and corporate governance is a critical part of this framework. It sets out the legal basis on which companies are formed, operated and managed. It provides the corporate vehicle which enables people to collaborate in business, and the legal structure through which companies are financed, ultimately by millions of savers and pensioners. It sets the rules for company boards and shareholders and for the exercise of decisions on business growth and investment. And it is the means by which people are held to account for the exercise of corporate economic power.

For these reasons, an effective framework of company law and corporate governance is a key building block of a modern economy. A genuinely modern and effective framework can promote enterprise, enhance competitiveness and stimulate investment. Conversely, an ineffective or outmoded framework can inhibit productivity and growth and undermine investment confidence. The high profile corporate collapses of recent years—including Enron, Worldcom and Parmalat—have demonstrated the critical importance to the modern global economy of robust frameworks for corporate activity, and the farreaching economic consequences when these fail.

Our objectives

That is why we are committed to creating a modern, enabling and robust framework for our companies. We are determined to ensure that our system of company law and corporate governance is one which:

- facilitates enterprise by making it easy to set up and grow a business;
- encourages the efficient allocation of capital by giving confidence to investors;
- promotes long-term company performance through shareholder engagement and effective dialogue between business and investors; and
- maintains the UK's position as one of the most attractive places in the world to set up and run a business.

Global challenge

This last point is critical. Our framework must reflect the challenges of modern capital markets in which business and investment decisions are increasingly determined by global conditions. More and more companies are operating internationally. Increasingly, businesses can make choices as to where to incorporate, and recent legal judgments are tending to make such cross-border incorporations easier. Similarly, investors can choose where to put their money—around a third of stock in listed UK companies is now held by overseas owners, more than twice the level in 1993.

This increasingly global marketplace is reflected in changes in regulatory conditions—for example the move towards global convergence of accounting standards, so that ultimately companies should be able to prepare their accounts on the same basis, wherever in the world they are listed. It is also reflected in developments at European level, where there is already a large body of European law and where the Commission's Company Law and Corporate Governance Action Plan is focused on fostering the global efficiency and competitiveness of EU businesses, strengthening shareholders' rights and third party protection and rebuilding the confidence of investors.

The Government supports the Action Plan as a platform for action to remove barriers to the efficient operation of markets, make it easier for companies to set up cross-border operations, extend investment opportunities for investors and improve access to, and the availability of, capital across Europe. As in the UK, it believes that EU action should be facilitative and enable enterprise and entrepreneurship to flourish. The aim must be to promote growth, competitiveness and jobs, not put new barriers in the way of economic activity.

The recent Sarbanes-Oxley legislation in the US, enacted in response to the Enron and Worldcom collapses, has also had important consequences for companies and investors around the world.

1.2.1 Sources on company law reform

A list of some of the principal law reform reports on company law and related matters appears below. Some of these reports, including, for example, the Jenkins and Cork Committees, the Law Commission and recent DTI reports, are remarkable for their scholarship and insight on the subject-matter. Despite such careful consideration by the committees, elements of some of these were not always promptly enacted, the Jenkins recommendations in particular languishing for many years before enactment or being ignored entirely.

Such works preparatory to law reform have long been referred to by the courts in analysing the purpose of provisions enacted in response to their recommendations. Looking behind the statute will become increasingly common as Parliamentary materials may also be used as an aid to statutory interpretation in the light of the recent House of Lords case of *Pepper* v *Hart* [1993] AC 593. See 1.5 below.

In addition to domestic initiatives for law reform, as has been mentioned, the EC harmonisation programme, referred to more fully in 1.4 below, is of enormous importance.

Davey Committee, 1895, C 7779 (company charges etc.)
Loreburn Committee, 1906, Cmnd 405, implemented in Companies Act 1908

Wrenbury Committee, 1918, Cmnd 9138

Greene Committee, 1926, Cmnd 2657, implemented in Companies Act 1929

Bodkin Committee, 1937 (sharepushing), implemented in Prevention of Fraud (Investments) Act 1939

Anderson Committee, 1936 (unit trusts)

Cohen Committee, 1945, Cmnd 6659, implemented in Companies Act 1948

Gedge Committee, 1954 (no par value shares)

Jenkins Committee, 1962, Cmnd 1749, partially implemented in subsequent Companies Acts

Bolton Committee, Small Firms, 1971, Cmnd 4811

Bullock Committee, 1977, Cmnd 6706 (employee representation)

Wilson Committee, 1980, Cmnd 7937 (financial institutions)

Cork Committee, 1982, Cmnd 8558 (insolvency law and practice), implemented in part in Insolvency Act 1986

Gower, *Review of Investor Protection*, Cmnd 9125, implemented in Financial Services Act 1986

Prentice, *Reform of the* Ultra Vires *Rule*, 1986

Dearing, *The Making of Accounting Standards*, 1988

Diamond, *A Review of Security Interests in Property*, 1989 (company charges)

Shareholder Remedies, Law Commission Consultation Paper No. 142 and Report No. 246

Company Directors: Regulating Conflicts of Interests and Formulating a Statement of Duties, Law Commission Consultation Paper No. 153, and Report No. 261/173, September 1999

Partnership Law, A Joint Law Commission Consultation Paper No. 159/111

Partnership Law, Final Report, No. 283, Cm 6015, November 2003

The 'Company Law Review', (CLR) the recent DTI programme for the comprehensive reform of company law entitled *Modern Company Law for a Competitive Economy* has issued the following documents.

Modern Company Law for a Competitive Economy, March 1998

The Strategic Framework, February 1999

Company General Meetings and Shareholder Communication, October 1999

Company Formation and Capital Maintenance, October 1999

Reforming the Law Concerning Oversea Companies, October 1999

Developing the Framework, March 2000

Capital Maintenance: Other Issues, June 2000

Registration of Company Charges, October 2000

Completing the Structure, November 2000

Trading Disclosures, January 2001

Final Report, July 2001

Modernising Company Law (White Paper), July 2002, Cm 5553

Flexibility and Accessibility, May 2004

Law Commission documents and the CLR documents listed above are available respectively on the following web sites:

http://www.lawcom.gov.uk

http://www.dti.gov.uk

The text of the Companies Act 2006 can be found on http://www.opsi.gov.uk/acts.htm.

For current information on the Companies Act 2006 and its implementation etc, see http://www.dti.gov.uk/bbf/co-act-2006/index/html. You can also go to the Site Map and click on Companies Act 2006 to bring up a page called 'Better Business Framework: Companies Act 2006'. Then click on 'Related Documents: Company Law Review' which should take you to www.dti.gov.uk/bbf/co-act-2006/clr-review/page22794.html where the above CLR documents are available.

1.3 STATUTES AND REGULATIONS

The following are being repealed or substantially repealed by the Companies Act 2006 (further detail on former legislation and the extent of repeals appears in the first reading at 1.1 above):

Companies Act 1985
Companies Act 1989 (amending the Companies Act 1985)
Business Names Act 1985

The following laws are current:

Companies Act 2006
Criminal Justice Act 1993, part V (replacing the repealed Company Securities (Insider Dealing) Act 1985)
Insolvency Act 1986
Company Directors Disqualification Act 1986
Financial Services and Markets Act 2000 (repealing Financial Services Act 1986)
Limited Liability Partnerships Act 2000
Enterprise Act 2002

In addition to the primary legislation there is a mass of delegated legislation in the form of orders, regulations and other statutory instruments. These have included, for example, the Companies (Tables A to F) Regulations 1985 (SI 1985/805) which set out the standard-form 'Table A' articles of association, at the time of writing to be replaced by two new sets of model articles, one for public companies and one for private companies. The Companies (Forms) Regulations 1985 (SI 1985/854) regulate the form of the various documents that are to be returned to Companies House such as the annual return and the declaration of compliance. An example of substantive reform is that the Companies (Single Member Private Limited Companies) Regulations 1992 (SI 1992/1699) first authorised the formation of a company by one subscriber. As a final example, the Insolvency Rules 1986 (SI 1986/1925) hugely add to the detail and complexity of the Insolvency Act 1985. The shortage of Parliamentary time and the complexity and detail of modern legislation now means that much of company legislation is to be found in this delegated legislation rather than in the primary statutes.

Another category of statutory instrument of enormous importance to company lawyers is the commencement order. Statutes do not always come into force on the date of royal assent. As has been mentioned above for example, Companies Act s. 1300 brings a few sections into force on the day the Act is passed but the rest come into force at different times on days appointed by the Secretary of State by commencement orders.

In a particular case it is therefore crucial for a legal practitioner to ascertain which statutory provisions are in force at the relevant time. This is done by checking the commencement orders enacted by the Secretary of State as statutory instruments. On the day of the exam, students also have to be aware that as the new law is being brought into force incrementally, they should ask themselves what law they are supposed to be applying to their answers.

1.4 THE HARMONISATION OF EUROPEAN COMPANY LAW

1.4.1 The scope and purpose of harmonisation

The programme for the 'harmonisation' of the company laws of the member states of the EC has had a considerable impact on our company laws. These reforms implementing detailed directives have led to a number of important changes to technical company law such as making promoters liable on pre-incorporation contracts, abolishing the external effect of the *ultra vires* rule and redefining public and private companies. Some of the most voluminous reforms have been in the areas of accounting and audit requirements, legislation which is detailed and technical. The following readings now introduce the principal objectives of the harmonisation programme, review progress made and indicate the direction of the forthcoming company law harmonisation plans. The extract from the Commission's 1997 consultation paper usefully summarises the initial achievements of the harmonisation programme, though progress has been made since then. For example as from 8 October 2004 it has been possible within each member state to register a 'European Company' (Council Regulation (EC) No. 2157/2001). The paper of 2005 that follows indicates that the Commission is still ambitious for further harmonisation in modernising company laws throughout the member states. For full texts of directives etc see http://eur-lex.europa.eu/en/index.htm.

While the article that now follows is a readable introduction, you may prefer to skim the European Commission documents at this stage to get a sense of the scale and impact of this programme and then return to them later for a fuller reading when you know a little more company law and can understand them a little better.

Robert Drury, 'A review of the European Community's company law harmonisation programme'
(1992) 24 Bracton Law J 45

1. Why harmonise and not introduce a uniform law?   In reviewing the European Community's harmonisation programme in the field of company law, it is permissible perhaps to pose the question, 'Why are we trying to harmonise disparate company laws, and not simply to introduce one uniform law?' The overall object of the exercise, as set out in art. 2 of the Treaty establishing the European Economic Community is, 'by establishing a common market and progressively approximating the economic policies of Member States, to promote throughout the Community a harmonious devel-opment of economic activities, a continuous and balanced expansion, an increase in stability, an accelerated raising of the standard of living and closer relations between the States belonging to it'. These are objects which, though laudable, are vague in the extreme. Slightly sharper focus is given in art. 3 which refers to abolition of obstacles to freedom of movement for persons, services and capital, and to the approximation of laws to the extent required for the proper functioning of the common market.

If we want to create a common market within which corporate and other persons, and their cap-ital can move freely, then it has been argued that we need to have a situation in which national laws are synchronised to a very considerable extent. The programme for the harmonisation of company and capital market laws seems to have been based, at least initially on two premises. The first is that companies are the most important economic actors within the Member States, and that they are becoming increasingly active on a wider transnational stage. The second premise assumes the existence of a substantial connection between the harmonisation of company and capital mar-ket laws on the one hand, and the advancement of economic integration on the other. One can readily subscribe to the first premise without much convincing, however, the second does perhaps become something of an article of faith, and with our theatrical analogy in mind, requires maybe a willing suspension of disbelief.

. . . European systems of company law had diverged over the years, and the position at the end of the 60s, when the harmonisation programme took off, was that there were a number of diverse groupings of systems, with some countries having strong features of one particular law and others with elements of several. The most numerous grouping was French related, and France, Belgium, Luxembourg, Spain and to a slightly lesser extent Italy, all having reasonably strong elements of this approach. In Greece the impact was somewhat less, but still quite clearly discernible. Another influ-ential system was the German one, and while no other community system resembled it in fine detail, elements of the German approach are found in the Netherlands, Greece, Denmark and Portugal (e.g. law of groups). The third system was the common law approach of UK and Ireland—which in turn had some influence in terms of approach in the Netherlands. Although the Netherlands has been influenced by other systems, it has developed quite a few outstandingly original ideas of its own, and these have in turn been fed back into the other countries by the harmonisation process which we are examining.

At the onset of harmonisation, these systems diverged in many important respects. However, the harmonisation programme was influential even before the first of the Directives came into operation. In 1965 Germany and in 1966 France introduced fairly fundamental bodies of legislation reforming their company laws, and while they have been subsequently amended, some of the ideas from the harmonisation programme found their way into these new 'company codes' in advance of the obligations arising from the First Directive of 1968. Many examples of the divergence can be given—a few will be selected here, just to illustrate the problems faced by the harmonisers.

Let us look firstly at the types of company permitted in the field of the commercial company with limited liability. Most States had public and private company types, and most of these were regu-lated by separate blocks of legislation if not by separate statutes. The Netherlands though did not initially have the private company form, introducing it only in 1971. The UK had both public and private companies, but its single-theme legislation did not greatly discriminate between them, and the majority of its provisions applied equally to both types. There was no way of telling from its name alone whether you were dealing with a public or with a private company.

Provision for capital and its function was very different. All of the original six members, except Netherlands, had a requirement of a minimum capital on the formation of a company. The role of this was in theory the protection of persons doing business with the company. Hence the import-ance which these countries, especially France, placed on getting the right amount of money in at the outset, and on the valuation of contributions in kind. Netherlands, UK and Ireland did not have a minimum capital and preferred to rely on the disclosure philosophy (see below) rather than min-imum capital to protect those dealing with the company. . . .

Management structure has been and remains a bone of contention. Generally most systems have a single-tier board like the British, with a board of directors (*conseil d'administration* in France) and a managing director (*président*). However, the German position has a two-tier structure with an executive board (*Vorstand*) which does not normally have a chairman with executive powers on the British or French model—the chairman in Germany being only *primus inter pares*. The *Vorstand* is appointed by a supervisory board (*Aufsichtsrat*) whose function is limited to informing itself, advising and consenting, but which may not play any part in the management of the business. The Netherlands and Denmark now have a mandatory two-tier board for larger companies, and the structure is optional for smaller ones. In France there has been an optional two-tier structure available since 1966, but not a great deal of use has been made of it.

Auditing requirements apply everywhere to public companies and often to private ones, but their rigour and importance varied greatly—being strongest in the UK.

The *disclosure philosophy* has long been an important part of the UK approach—you inform those persons dealing with the company fairly fully—you can leave it to them or their professional advisers to decide whether that company is a good 'risk' and therefore you do not have to build so many protective measures such as minimum capital into the system. Other countries have followed this lead, but in the late 60s only very feebly . . . [See chapter 4.]

Hence, while ideally one might have liked to have wiped the slate clean and started again to develop a uniform system of company law, this was just not feasible. The political problems of persuading and cajoling States to form the common market did not (perhaps until the present day) leave any surplus of political initiative to devote to the purpose of creating this *tabula rasa*.

The draftsmen were therefore compelled to work with what they had got, first six then nine then 12 disparate legal systems, harmonising by way of a series of Directives, whittling away at the differences, rather than by the forcible imposition of a grandiose master plan—a uniform European company law.

Commission Consultation Paper on Company Law
European Commission 1997

I. INTRODUCTION

The purpose of this consultation exercise is to help the Commission draw up a work programme for the European Union in the field of company law based on a broad consensus about the changes that are needed to meet today's needs. What action must be taken to complete the single market in the company law sphere? Should the EU play a part in resolving the questions raised in the course of the corporate governance debate and, if so, what part and in response to what questions? Do the requests for simplification and deregulation concern company law (as opposed to, say, tax law, environment law and labour law) and, if so, what improvements, in particular, may be made and by whom (EU or member States)? This questionnaire is being sent to a wide range of interested parties . . .

II. BACKGROUND

Company law is one of the few branches of private law to be directly referred to by the Treaty of Rome. The main provisions on the subject are to be found in the chapter on freedom of establishment, namely arts 52, 54 and 58. To these may be added arts 220, 235 and 100a.

The Treaty of Rome confers on Community companies, i.e. companies or firms formed in accordance with the law of a member State and having their registered office, central administration or principal place of business within the Community, the right of establishment (art. 58). This right means that companies may carry on any economic and financial activity in the Community, either directly or through the creation of subsidiaries or branches. Companies from one member State establishing themselves in another member State rnay not be subjected to formalities other than those which are applicable to national companies.

It would be a mistake to think, however, that all one needs to do in order to ensure true freedom of movement for companies in the Community is to assert the right of establishment: one must at the same time embark on a process of harmonising the relevant national laws. There were (and still are) clear differences between national laws. Without—at least partial—harmonisation, this would form a veritable barrier to intra-Community activities, both for those who might have dealings with companies and for companies themselves. What is more, where the differences between laws are too great, exercise of the right of establishment may bring with it the risk that companies might relocate to countries with less stringent provisions. Such an outcome would be unacceptable to member States.

Moreover, there are considerable obstacles in the way of a rational restructuring of companies such as would enable them to benefit from a market operating henceforth on a Community or world, and no longer on a national, scale. It is, for example, virtually impossible for a company to transfer its registered office from one member State to another or to merge with another company across intra-Community borders.

The architects of the Treaty of Rome, who were aware of these difficulties and wished to resolve them, gave the Community institutions the power to harmonise national company laws by means of Directives (art. 54). This harmonising power is fairly limited, being intended to render equivalent to the extent necessary member States' provisions laid down with a view to protecting shareholders and others.

Subsequently, as economic integration progressed, harmonisation has ceased to suffice and it has become necessary to create uniform legal instruments of cooperation and integration between European businesses so as to enable them to derive the greatest possible benefit from the establishment of a single market and thus face up to world competition. The Commission has proposed that these uniform instruments be drawn up on the basis of arts 235 and 100a.

RESULTS OBTAINED

The harmonisation process has to some extent been a success. Nine major Directives have been adopted, as have four amending Directives.

The First Directive (OJ No. L 68, 14 March 1968) lays down a system of disclosure applicable to all companies. Member States must keep a companies register, which must be open to the public. Registration is followed by publication in a national gazette. This system ensures that access may be had throughout the Community to information on the same matters, namely the company's articles of association, the identity of persons who have the power to bind the company either jointly or severally, the procedures for winding the company up, etc. Within their particular ambit, all subsequent Directives also refer to this system of disclosure of essential information.

The First Directive also deals with the validity of a company's commitments. Thus, a company may not, in principle, rely as against third parties on the fact that it has acted *ultra vires;* member States may grant it the right to do so only on condition that it can prove that the third party was himself aware of that circumstance. Likewise in the interests of enhancing the protection of third parties, the Directive drastically limits the grounds for nullity of companies.

The Second Directive (OJ No. L 26, 31 January 1977) concerns the formation, maintenance and alteration of the capital of public limited liability companies. The articles or memorandum of association of a company must furnish essential information in this respect. In order to preserve the capital, which serves as security for creditors, the making of undue distributions to shareholders is prohibited and the opportunities for a company to acquire its own shares are limited.

In the event of an increase or a reduction in capital, shareholders who are in the same position must be treated equally and creditors whose claims antedate the decision to make the reduction must be protected. The part of the Directive which relates to the purchase by a company of its own shares was amended in 1992 (OJ No. L 347, 28 November 1992).

The Third and Sixth Directives (OJ No. L 295, 20 October 1978; OJ No. L 318, 17 December 1982) deal respectively with mergers and divisions of public limited liability companies on a national level. These are the main types of company restructuring measure. The principles underlying both Directives are the same. Shareholders of the companies concerned must be provided with adequate information which is as objective as possible and they must be afforded appropriate protection of their rights. Creditors and the holders of other securities of the merging companies must be protected lest the merger or division operation causes them loss or damage. In order that third parties might be kept sufficiently informed, such operations must be publicised. To ensure legal certainty in the event of a merger or division, cases of nullity are limited and the principle of regularisation is applied whenever possible. Moreover, nullity may only be invoked during a short period.

The Eleventh Directive provides for a system of disclosure for branches based on that of the First Directive (OJ No. L 395, 21 December 1989).

The Twelfth Directive requires those member States which have not yet done so to introduce the single member private limited liability form of company (OJ No. L 395, 21 December 1989).

The Fourth, Seventh and Eighth Directives concern respectively the drawing up, auditing and publication of annual and consolidated accounts, and the approval and qualifications of persons who audit accounts (OJ No. L 222, 14 August 1978; OJ No. L 193, 18 July 1983; OJ No. L 126, 10 April 1984). The threshold in the Fourth Directive which makes it possible to identify those SMEs for which member States may provide derogations has been adapted periodically to allow for inflation, the most recent occasion being in 1994 (OJ No. L 82, 25 August 1994, p. 94). The same Directive has also been amended in order to make its application to GmbHs in Germany more explicit (OJ No. L 317, 16 November 1990, p. 90).

On the other hand, most of the proposals aimed at creating uniform legal instruments of cooperation and integration have run into difficulties, including that of the role of employees. Only the Regulation on the European Economic Interest Grouping (EEIG) has been adopted. This Regulation introduces into member States a new legal instrument designed to facilitate cooperation between enterprises from different member States (OJ No. L 199, 25 July 1985). So far, 722 EEIGs have been set up.

Press Release issued by The High Level Group of Company Law Experts on A Modern Regulatory Framework for Company Law in Europe
(European Commission 2002)

KEY RECOMMENDATIONS AND PRIORITIES

The Group recommends that the priorities on the short term for the EU should be to:

- improve the EU framework for corporate governance, specifically through:
  - enhanced corporate governance disclosure requirements;
  - providing for a strong and effective role for independent non-executive or supervisory directors, particularly in three areas where executive directors have conflicts of interests, i.e. nomination and remuneration of directors and supervision of the audit of the company's accounts;
  - an appropriate regime for directors' remuneration, requiring disclosure of the company's remuneration policy and individual directors' remuneration, as well as prior shareholder approval of share and share option schemes in which directors participate, and accounting for the costs of those schemes to the company;
  - confirming as a matter of EU law the collective responsibility of directors for financial and key non-financial statements of the company;
  - an integrated legal framework to facilitate efficient shareholder information, communication and decision-making on a cross-border basis, using where possible modern technology, in particular the company's website;
  - setting up a structure to co-ordinate the corporate governance efforts of Member States;
- offer efficient mechanisms for cross-border restructuring and mobility of companies, specifically by adopting proposals for the 10th and 14th Company Law Directives on cross-border mergers and transfers of seat;
- simplify the 2nd Company Law Directive on capital formation and maintenance rules on the basis of the SLIM Group recommendations as supplemented in the Final Report of the Group.

Modernising Company Law and Enhancing Corporate Governance in the European Union—A Plan to Move Forward

(European Commission 2003)

INTRODUCTION

A dynamic and flexible company law and corporate governance framework is essential for a modern, dynamic, interconnected industrialised society. Essential for millions of investors. Essential for deepening the internal market and building an integrated European capital market. Essential for maximising the benefits of enlargement for all the Member States, new and existing.

Good company law, good corporate governance practices throughout the EU will enhance the real economy:

— An effective approach will foster the global efficiency and competitiveness of businesses in the EU. Well managed companies, with strong corporate governance records and sensitive social and environmental performance, outperform their competitors. Europe needs more of them to generate employment and higher long term sustainable growth.

— An effective approach will help to strengthen shareholders rights and third parties protection. In particular, it will contribute to rebuilding European investor confidence in the wake of a wave of recent corporate governance scandals. The livelihood of millions of Europeans, their pensions, their investments are tied up in the proper, responsible performance and governance of listed companies in which they invest.

Scope

This Communication outlines the approach that the Commission intends to follow specifically in the area of company law and corporate governance.

Achieving the objectives pursued (fostering efficiency and competitiveness of business, and strengthening shareholders rights and third parties protection) requires a fully integrated approach.

Related initiatives, forming part of this integrated approach but not part of this Action Plan, include:

— The Financial Services Action Plan of 1999, which confirmed the overall objectives which should guide the financial services policy at EU level and set out a framework for an integrated capital market by 2005;

— The Financial Reporting Strategy of 2000, which seeks to achieve high quality financial reporting through the adoption of a common set of accounting standards and the development of a proper enforcement system, which led to the adoption in 2002 of the Regulation on the application of the international accounting standards;

— The Communication on Corporate Social Responsibility of 2002, which addresses the social and environmental dimension of business in a global economy and led to the setting up of a European Multi-Stakeholder Forum with a view to promoting voluntary social and environmental practices of business, linked to their core activities, which go beyond their existing legal obligations;

— The Communication on Industrial Policy in an Enlarged Europe of 2002, which addresses the need for EU industry to achieve a more sustainable production structure as a driver of growth and productivity.

— The Communication on the priorities for the statutory audit in the EU, which is published together with the present Communication and which covers an EU policy approach aimed at ensuring audit quality and public confidence in the audit profession. It covers issues like the use of ISA's (International Standards on Auditing), public oversight of auditors, and the modernisation of the Eighth Company Law Directive into a comprehensive principles-based approach.

Responding to the High Level Group's report

On 4 November 2002, a High Level Group of Company Law Experts appointed by Commissioner Bolkestein in September 2001 and chaired by Jaap Winter presented its Final Report on "A modern regulatory framework for company law in Europe". This report focused on corporate governance in the EU and the modernisation of European Company Law. The Competitiveness Council (30 September 2002) invited the Commission to organise an in-depth discussion on the forthcoming report and to develop—in co-ordination with Member States—an Action Plan for Company Law, including Corporate Governance, as soon as is feasible, declaring its intention to deal with the Action Plan as a matter of priority. The Ecofin Council has also shown a major interest in this work.

This Communication is the Commission's response. It explains why the European regulatory framework for company law and corporate governance needs to be modernised. It defines the key policy objectives which should inspire any future action to be taken at EU level in these areas. It includes an action plan, prioritised, over the short, medium and long term. It indicates which type of regulatory instrument should be used, and by when.

Guiding political criteria

In developing this Action Plan, the Commission has paid particular attention to the need for any regulatory response at European level to respect a number of guiding criteria:

— It should fully respect the subsidiarity and proportionality principles of the Treaty and the diversity of many different approaches to the same questions in the Member States, while at the same time pursuing clear ambitions (strengthening the single market and enhancing the rights of shareholders and third parties);

— It should be flexible in application, but firm in the principles. It should concentrate on priorities; be transparent; and subject to proper due process and consultation;

— It should help shape international regulatory developments. The EU must define its own European corporate governance approach, tailored to its own cultural and business traditions. Indeed, this is an opportunity for the Union to strengthen its influence in the world with good, sensible corporate governance rules. Corporate governance is indeed an area where standards are increasingly being set at international level, as evidenced by the recent developments observed in the United States. The Sarbanes-Oxley Act, adopted on 30 July 2002 in the wave of a series of scandals, delivered a rapid response. The Act unfortunately creates a series of problems due to its outreach effects on European companies and auditors, and the Commission is engaged in an intense regulatory dialogue with a view to negotiating acceptable solutions with the US authorities (in particular the Securities and Exchange Commission). In many areas, the EU shares the same broad objectives and principles of the Sarbanes-Oxley Act and in some areas robust, equivalent regulatory approaches already exist in the EU. In some other areas, new initiatives are necessary. Earning the right to be recognised as at least "equivalent" alongside other national and international rules is a legitimate and useful end in itself.

1. MODERNISING COMPANY LAW AND ENHANCING CORPORATE GOVERNANCE: THE EU ACQUIS AND THE NEED FOR NEW INITIATIVES

1.1. The EU Company Law Acquis

Historically, most of the initiatives taken at EU level in the area of company law have been based on Article 44 (2) g (ex 54) of the Treaty establishing the European Community. This Article, which appears in the Chapter devoted to the right of establishment, requires the European institutions to attain freedom of establishment, "by co-ordinating to the necessary extent the safeguards which, for the protection of the interests of members and others, are required by Member States of companies or firms within the meaning of the second paragraph of Article 48 (ex 58), with a view to making such safeguards equivalent throughout the Community".

This Article has been interpreted to include two important grounds for the adoption of EU initiatives in the area of company law:

a) facilitating freedom of establishment of companies: the harmonisation of a number of minimum requirements makes it easier for companies to establish themselves in other Member States where the regulatory framework is similar;

b) guaranteeing legal certainty in intra-Community operations, where the presence of a number of common safeguards is key for the creation of trust in cross-border economic relationships.

Over the years, the EU institutions have taken a number of initiatives in the area of company law, many leading to impressive achievements. Between 1968 (adoption of the First Company Law Directive) and 1989 (adoption of the Twelfth Company Law Directive), nine Directives and one Regulation were adopted. Although the exact situation may differ from one Member State to the other, these European measures have had an important impact on national company law. Moreover, their influence was not limited to the types of companies expressly covered in the Directives, because many Member States decided to extend their provisions to other legal forms.

Over the last ten years, the EU company law legislative process has been characterised, in the wake of the Maastricht Treaty of 1992, by more political deference to national law (with a higher number of references to national rules in the legislative proposals). This more flexible approach to harmonisation made possible, in particular, the adoption of the European Company Statute (Societas Europaea), in October 2001.

1.2. Reasons for new initiatives at EU level

Now is the right time to give a fresh and ambitious impetus to the EU company law harmonisation process. New initiatives, aiming either at modernising the existing EU company law instruments or at completing the EU framework with a limited number of new, tailored instruments, are needed for the following reasons:

— Making the most of the Internal Market: the growing trend of European companies to operate cross-border in the Internal Market calls for common European company law mechanisms, inter alia, to facilitate freedom of establishment and cross-border restructuring.

— Integration of capital markets: dynamic securities markets are vital to Europe's economic future. This requires giving both issuers and investors the opportunity to be far more active on other EU capital markets and to have confidence that the companies they invest in have equivalent corporate governance frameworks. Listed companies want a more coherent, dynamic and responsive European legislative framework.

— To maximise the benefits of modern technologies : the rapid development of new information and communication technology (video conferencing, electronic mail and above all the Internet) is affecting the way company information is stored and disseminated, as well as the way corporate life is conducted (e.g. virtual general meetings, video-link board meetings, exercise of cross-border voting rights).

— Enlargement: the forthcoming enlargement of the EU to 10 new Member States is another gilt-edged reason to revisit the scope of EU company law. The new member countries will increase the diversity of the national regulatory frameworks in the EU, underlying further the importance of a principles-based approach able to maintain a high level of legal certainty in intra-Community operations. In addition to that, initiatives to modernise the EU Acquis will become more urgent than ever to ease the rapid and full transition of these countries to becoming fully competitive modern market economies.

— Addressing the challenges raised by recent events: Recent financial scandals have prompted a new, active debate on corporate governance, and the necessary restoration of confidence is one more reason for new initiatives at EU level. Investors, large and small, are demanding more transparency and better information on companies, and are seeking to gain more influence on the way the public companies they own operate. Shareholders own companies, not management—yet far too frequently their rights have been trampled on by shoddy, greedy and occasionally fraudulent corporate behaviour. A new sense of proportion and fairness is necessary.

1.4.2 Interpretation of EC derived legislation

The style of English legislation is to draft highly detailed and specific provisions, rather than stating general principles in broad brush strokes. The courts then interpret this legislation literally according to the strict wording of the statute rather than by reaching a conclusion based on a general principle or on the presumed spirit or intention of the provision. From this flows the English tendency to be satisfied with the form rather than looking to the substance of the matter in question. However, with regard to legislation derived from EC Directives a major change has occurred.

Of fundamental importance to company law is the recent line of cases exemplified by the *Litster* case in 1990 extracted below, which requires English legislation implementing a Directive to be interpreted in the light of the Directive. The English courts have taken it that as Parliament intended to implement the Directive, the legislation must be interpreted so as to give effect to that Directive. The courts may therefore in effect rewrite the domestic legislation even when there is no ambiguity in its wording. Whether the obligation of the domestic court in interpreting such legislation goes further than this is not yet clear. It could be that the obligation is to strike down domestic legislation where the legislature has not implemented the Directive properly and to substitute the appropriate provision. This would go beyond the current approach in English courts which seems to have dealt with the matter more conservatively as a question of interpretation. The principles of interpreting EC derived company legislation have been considered in a number of earlier company law cases (including *Phonogram Ltd* v *Lane* [1982] QB 938, CA; *International Sales and Agencies Ltd* v *Marcus* [1982] 3 All ER 551; *Official Custodian for Charities* v *Parway Estates Developments Ltd* [1985] Ch 151; *Barclays Bank Ltd* v *TOSG Trust Fund Ltd* [1984] BCLC 1; *TCB Ltd* v *Gray* [1986] Ch 621), which should now be read with caution.

Litster v Forth Dry Dock & Engineering Co. Ltd
Rewriting the rules as Brussels intended
[1990] 1 AC 546, House of Lords

This case confirms that as a matter of statutory interpretation, where a domestic statute implements a Directive, the court will if necessary imply words into the domestic statute to enable it to comply with the Directive, even though the statute is not ambiguous.

The substantive issue in the case is also of relevance to company lawyers. The following attempts to explain the background. If a company becomes insolvent, its administrative receivers may sell the business assets as a going concern, i.e., buildings, stock, plant, contracts, goodwill etc. (On administrative receivership see 15.4 below.) Overmanning is often a problem. Cutting the workforce is expensive as workers may be entitled to claims for unfair dismissal, accrued wages and redundancy pay. If the administrative receiver of the insolvent company can dismiss the surplus workers, their claims will not all be enforceable if the company has no free assets to pay its unsecured creditors. To implement a Directive intended to protect workers where the 'undertaking' or business they work for is transferred by sale or otherwise, the Transfer of Undertakings (Protection of Employment) Regulations

1981 (SI 1981/1794) were made. By reg. 5(3) those employed 'immediately before the transfer' automatically have their employment transferred (with all accrued rights as if employment were continuous) to the buyer of the business. If the buyer then wishes to shed surplus employees, their claims on dismissal will have to be paid, the buyer being solvent. (Incidentally the obligation of the government's National Insurance fund to pick up the liability to pay them is also relieved.) To avoid the Regulations, the obvious ploy was for the administrative receiver of the insolvent company to dismiss the workers so that they are not in employment 'immediately before the transfer'. With the excess employees disposed of, the business will then be worth more on sale. However, the House of Lords in effect amended the literal meaning of the regulation to enable it to carry out the intention of the directive.

Facts   Litster and 11 others were dismissed an hour before a transfer by the administrative receiver of the insolvent company's business assets took place. The transferee company then took on other workers at lower wages. Litster successfully claimed for unfair dismissal against the transferee.

LORD OLIVER OF AYLMERTON: My lords, this appeal raises, not for the first time, the broad question of the approach to be adopted by courts in the United Kingdom to domestic legislation enacted in order to give effect to this country's obligations under the EEC Treaty (Cmnd 5179-II). The legislation with which the appeal is concerned is a statutory instrument made on 14 December 1981 pursuant to para. 2(2) of sch. 2 to the European Communities Act 1972 and entitled 'The Transfer of Undertakings (Protection of Employment) Regulations 1981'. The Regulations were made by the Secretary of State—and this is common ground—in order to give effect to a Directive (77/187/EEC) adopted by the Council of the European Communities on 14 February 1977 to provide for the approximation of the laws of the Member States relating to the safeguarding of employees' rights in the event of transfers of undertakings, businesses or parts of businesses. The question which arises is whether it has achieved this object.

The approach to the construction of primary and subordinate legislation enacted to give effect to the United Kingdom's obligations under the EEC Treaty have been the subject matter of recent authority in this House (see *Pickstone* v *Freemans plc* [1989] AC 66) and is not in doubt. If the legislation can reasonably be construed so as to conform with those obligations—obligations which are to be ascertained not only from the wording of the relevant Directive but from the interpretation placed upon it by the European Court of Justice at Luxembourg—such a purposive construction will be applied even though, perhaps, it may involve some departure from the strict and literal application of the words which the legislature has elected to use.

It will, I think, be convenient to consider the terms of the Directive and the Regulations before outlining the circumstances in which the instant appeal arises. The broad scope of the Directive appears from the following two recitals:

> Whereas economic trends are bringing in their wake, at both national and Community level, changes in the structure of undertakings, through transfers of undertakings, businesses or parts of businesses to other employers as a result of legal transfers or mergers;
>
> Whereas it is necessary to provide for the protection of employees in the event of a change of employer, in particular, to ensure that their rights are safeguarded. . . .

[His lordship considered the issues at length. On the statutory interpretation point, referring to the Regulations, he continued:] If this provision fell to be construed by reference to the ordinary rules of construction applicable to a purely domestic statute and without reference to Treaty obligations, it would, I think, be quite impermissible to regard it as having the same prohibitory effect as that attributed by the European Court to art. 4 of the Directive. But it has always to be borne in mind that the purpose of the Directive and of the Regulations was and is to 'safeguard' the rights of employees on a transfer and that there is a mandatory obligation to provide remedies which are effective and not merely symbolic to which the Regulations were intended to give effect. The remedies provided by the Act of 1978 [the Employment Protection (Consolidation) Act 1978, protecting against unfair dismissal] in the case of an insolvent transferor are largely illusory unless they can be exerted against the transferee as the Directive contemplates and I do not find it conceivable that, in framing Regulations intending to give effect to the Directive, the Secretary of State could have envisaged that its purpose should be capable of being avoided by the transparent device to which resort was had in the instant case. *Pickstone* v *Freemans plc* [1989] AC 66, has established that the greater flexibility available to the court in applying a purposive construction to legislation designed to give effect to the United Kingdom's Treaty obligations to the Community enables the court, where necessary, to supply by implication words appropriate to comply with those obligations: see particularly the speech of Lord Templeman, at pp. 120–1. Having regard to the manifest purpose of the Regulations, I do not, for my part, feel inhibited from making such an implication in the instant case. The provision in reg. 8(1) that a dismissal by reason of a transfer is to be treated as an unfair dismissal, is merely a different way of saying that the transfer is not to 'constitute a ground for dismissal' as contemplated by art. 4 of the Directive and there is no good reason for denying to it the same effect as that attributed to that article. In effect this involves reading reg. 5(3) as if there were inserted after the words 'immediately before the transfer' the words 'or would have been so employed if he had not been unfairly dismissed in the circumstances described in reg. 8(1)'. For my part, I would make such an implication which is entirely consistent with the general scheme of the Regulations and which is necessary if they are effectively to fulfil the purpose for which they were made of giving effect to the provisions of the Directive. This does not involve any disapproval of the reasoning of the Court of Appeal in *Secretary of State for Employment* v *Spence* [1987] QB 179 which, on the facts there found by the industrial tribunal, did not involve a dismissal attracting the consequences provided in reg. 8(1). . . .

It follows from the construction that I attach to reg. 5(3) that where an employee is dismissed before and by reason of the transfer the employment is statutorily continued with the transferee by virtue of the Regulations. . . .

1.5 STATUTORY INTERPRETATION

The European influence in interpretation of statutes indicated in the *Litster* case above may also have been influential in a major change of policy decided upon by the House of Lords in *Pepper* v *Hart* [1993] AC 593. This case on taxation of employee benefits, held that where a statutory provision is ambiguous, in order to give effect to the true intention of the legislature, the court may permit reference to Parliamentary materials. Primarily this means that *Hansard* may be referred to for a transcript of full Parliamentary debates and committee proceedings to ascertain the intention of Parliament. However, the material relied on may consist of statements by a Minister or other promoter of a Bill together if necessary with such other Parliamentary material as is necessary to understand the statements and their effect.

1.6 COMPANY DOCUMENTS

The typical form of company documents can be regarded as a major source of law and practice. Of particular importance has been the memorandum and articles of association, the constitution of the company. The 'Table A' articles, a standard set of statutory articles which apply by default unless expressly excluded (see chapter 6), are the usual form of bye-laws for most private companies. It is therefore essential to be familiar with the content of traditional memorandum and articles. In studying the law of *ultra vires*, for example, it is useful to read a typical objects clause. It is also important to be aware of the contents of the usual articles of association. For instance, in studying the division of powers between the board and general meeting it is essential to be familiar with the content of 1985 Table A, art. 70 which is part of most articles of association and establishes that the directors conduct the business of the company by resolution of the board. It is again valuable, in order to grasp this concept, to see specimen minutes of the board of a company. Samples of all these documents are reproduced below.

Similarly the full significance of floating charges and receivership is not easily appreciated without reading a typical bank debenture document. The specimen debenture reproduced below at 1.7 shows the brief wording that was necessary to create a floating charge, and the contractual nature of this security device. In all cases traditional forms of documents have been selected as these illustrate the basis of company practice during the twentieth century and beyond.

For this reason, although new 'Table A' articles are being prescribed by statutory instrument, the articles of all companies incorporated prior to their introduction use the traditional style of articles and will continue to do so unless and until they pass a resolution adopting the new ones. Thus the documents that follow at 1.7 are based on the old 1985 Table A in order to illustrate the basis of company law and practice during the twentieth century and beyond. Likewise, throughout the book, the traditional Table A of 1985 is regularly referred to as, though obsolescent, it will remain the most widely used form for many years.

The White Paper of 2005 indicated that new articles would be prescribed by the Secretary of State in particular so as to provide a form of articles more suited to the needs of small companies. A draft of default articles intended for small owner-managed companies was thus included in the White Paper and a draft of default articles for public companies was later published for public consultation and comment.

There now follows an extract from the White Paper which briefly explains the background to the existing model default articles and gives reasons why the existing Table A is no longer appropriate and why new forms should be prescribed.

COMPANY LAW REFORM: THE WHITE PAPER
(London: DTI, March 2005. Cm 6456)

4.3 Company constitutions
A feature of GB company law is that the members are free, subject to certain legal constraints, to make their own rules about the internal affairs of their company. These rules are a key part of a company's constitution and can generally be found in a company's articles of association ("articles").

Although companies have considerable freedom to include whatever rules they see fit in their articles, in practice the articles tend to contain provisions on a relatively restricted range of matters, for example rules on decision taking by the members and directors and various matters connected with shares (such as the payment of dividends).

Since 1856, model articles have been provided for certain types of companies by law, for example, Companies Act 1985 Table A ("Table A") provides model articles for companies limited by shares. Table A operates as a "default" set of articles for all such companies: that is, the articles of a company limited by shares will be set out in Table A if the company does not register articles at Companies House, or to the extent that any articles which it does register do not exclude or modify the provisions of Table A.

Table A—reasons why this is no longer an appropriate form of model articles

Table A has been revised several times over the past 150 years or so, but it remains a product of the mid-19th Century both in terms of the language that it uses and in substance. It is drafted with what we would today think of as "public" rather than "private" companies in mind and successive revisions to Table A have tended to include increasingly elaborate provisions, designed to cover every conceivable event or set of circumstances that a company may find itself in (however unlikely it is that the majority of companies who are using Table A would ever find themselves in those circumstances).

The result is that the vast majority of the provisions in Table A are irrelevant to the vast majority of companies who are using Table A as their articles. In addition, whilst many new provisions have been added to Table A over the years, redundant provisions have rarely, if ever, been removed.

We are left with a "one size fits all" approach to the model articles, which has a number of problems:

- Table A is user-unfriendly, poorly laid out and often unintelligible to nonspecialists;
- much of Table A is taken up with matters which are remote from the concerns of smaller companies (so that it is not unusual for private companies to have articles which are completely irrelevant to the owners and managers of such companies);
- Table A does not take account of relatively recent changes in the law, for example, the introduction of single member companies, and will need also to reflect further changes which are proposed in this White Paper.

Following the recommendations of the CLR, the Government considers that reform of Table A is an important part of making our company law fit for purpose in the modern economy. The Government proposes that in future there should be:

- a radically simplified set of model articles for private companies limited by shares, reflecting the way that small companies operate;
- a separate set of model articles for public companies limited by shares (similar in scope to the current Table A, but with clearer layout and drafting);
- (for the first time) a full set of model articles for private companies limited by guarantee; and
- comprehensive, clear and concise guidance for small companies who are using, or thinking of using, model articles.

For companies set up under the new legislation, the new sets of model articles will operate as default provisions for the types of company for which they are prescribed, in the same way as Table A now does. Existing companies will be able to replace their current articles (whether or not these are as set out in Table A) with the new model articles, if their members pass a special resolution to do so.

The private company articles

The Bill will contain a power for the Secretary of State to prescribe, by secondary legislation, stand alone model articles for public companies, private companies limited by shares and private companies limited by guarantee. Draft model articles for private companies limited by shares (the "private company articles") are set out in the White Paper.

The private company articles will replace Table A for those private companies limited by shares which are in future formed under the new Act and will play an important role in the simplification of the law for small companies. Like Table A the private company articles will apply by default where a company does not register its own articles at Companies House (to the extent that the company in question has not specifically excluded or modified the model articles). Table A will continue to provide the model articles for companies formed before the new model articles come into force.

The text of the private company articles follows the principles set out in the CLR's Final Report, for example, archaic and legalistic language has been avoided. In the interests of producing a "leaner" set of model articles and making the model articles more accessible to the directors and shareholders of small companies, we have omitted model articles on areas of law for which there are already procedural rules in the Companies Act (for example, the draft model articles do not contain any provisions on decision-taking by shareholders—see below).

Will the private company articles be suitable for all private companies?

The private company articles contain the minimum number of rules which it is envisaged that a typical private company limited by shares will need and which the shareholders will want to have. (There is little point having a default rule if the majority of companies will want to disapply it). They are primarily aimed at small, owner-managed companies.

Some or all of these rules may be suitable for less typical private companies, but if they are not, it will be open to any private company limited by shares which is using, or intends to use, the private company articles to add to, amend, or delete rules from the model articles as they see fit (as is the case with Table A), or to adopt completely different "bespoke" articles of their own.

The public company articles

Separate model articles will be provided for public companies (the "public company articles"). In terms of content, these will be similar to the existing Table A (that is, the public company articles will include more detailed rules to cater for more complex circumstances), but will be drafted in plainer English and updated to reflect changes in the law. Private companies which find that the new private company articles fail to address their needs will be able to import provisions from the public company model on a voluntary basis.

1.7 THE LIFE OF A COMPANY

In studying company law it has to be remembered that no company is typical. The economic realities and the legal problems of a nationally known public company and the local corner shop or garage are fundamentally different, even though the basic company structure is the same. Small companies are by far the most numerous and are the type that the practitioner, whether lawyer or accountant, will most often meet in practice.

The following account now sketches out the life of an ordinary firm of builders. The purpose is to help readers to understand the context of the law of private companies, to introduce some of the main legal issues that may face such companies, to introduce much of the principal terminology of company law, and to set the typical company documentation that follows in context.

As the new law of 2006 has not yet been applied in practice and as our fictitious company was trading when the Companies Act 1985 was in force, most references that follow are to the old law prior to its reform.

(a) Trading as a partnership

The four Baker brothers carry on business as partners in a firm, J. B. Baker & Co., sharing profits and losses equally. They are John, Fred, Michael and Charlie. They have the balance of an 18-year lease on a builder's yard, a stock of building materials, vehicles, contracts in the course of execution for various building and construction work, some unpaid debts owed to them, a freehold site on which they are building four houses, an overdraft at the bank and various insurance policies covering assets and liabilities. As a partnership, contracts are made in their names personally, 'trading as J. B. Baker & Co.' and signed by one or more of the partners 'for and on behalf of J. B. Baker & Co.'. If the business fails financially, each one of them is fully liable to the full extent of his personal assets for all of the debts of the firm. Their relationship is regulated by the Partnership Act 1890 and a simple partnership agreement. Consequently each one is agent of the firm for the purpose of making contracts relating to the business. Each one of them also has the right to participate in running the business.

(b) Setting up a limited company

The business prospers and the brothers wish to expand its operation. They are recommended by their accountants to incorporate and trade as a limited company in order to obtain limited liability, and to facilitate bank borrowing. Their solicitor advises them to buy a ready-made company 'off the shelf'. The solicitor telephones a company formation agent, and the next day receives in the mail company documents, including a certificate of incorporation, memorandum and articles of association, and blank share transfer forms signed by the subscribers. Buying a company 'off the shelf', which is of course dormant and has not traded, is a quick and convenient means of obtaining a company. If necessary the name, the objects, the capital and the articles can be altered to coincide with the wishes of the shareholders. Thus the name of the company is changed by special resolution to J. B. Baker & Co. Ltd. The one share held by each of the subscribers to the memorandum of the company will be transferred to two of the brothers. An equal proportion of shares will be issued to each of the brothers, who will all become directors to enable them to participate in management.

(c) At this stage, the brothers still own the assets of the partnership business, while two of them hold the shares in the dormant company. If the company is to run the business, the company will have to acquire or take possession of the assets of the business. The assets will therefore all be transferred to the company by sale or lease, including vehicle registrations, licences, contracts and insurance policies. The lease of the builder's yard may either be subleased or assigned to the company. (The choice may be decided by tax considerations. If assets are transferred to the company rather than leased to it, an immediate capital gains tax liability may arise. However, 'roll-over relief', postponing payment of tax, is available if *all* the assets of the business are transferred to the company and in return for shares and not for cash.)

The partners will not, of course, be *giving* their business to the company. Nor does the company at present have any cash to pay for it. In this case the brothers estimate the business assets as a going concern at £160,000. As partners holding an equal share of the business which they are transferring to the company they will each therefore expect to receive a consideration of £40,000. The company can give consideration by issuing shares to them or by acknowledging indebtedness to pay them in cash. In this case a mixture of each is chosen, each partner being shown as owed £15,000 by the company to remain on loan indefinitely and as having issued to him 25,000 £1 ordinary shares credited as fully paid up. Thus the company will have an issued capital of £100,000 paid up in kind, rather than in cash.

The brothers through their shareholdings now own the company, while the company owns and will run the business. If the brothers' valuation is correct, the business is worth £160,000, while the company, or the whole issued share capital, is (in very crude terms) worth £100,000 (that is the value of the company's business assets, less outstanding liabilities to the brothers of £60,000). At present, on an assets valuation, the pro rata market value of each share is £1. If the company trades successfully and retains profits, or its assets appreciate so that its net worth becomes £200,000, each share on an assets valuation will be worth £2. If, on the other hand, it does badly so that the net worth falls to £50,000, the market value of each share will fall to 50 pence. The nominal value of each share remains at £1, and the issued capital of the company, a purely historical accounting entry, remains at £100,000. Valuation of shares in private companies is in fact more complex than this. Profitability as well as assets is relevant and shares in a minority holding are generally worth less pro rata than in a block of shares carrying control. (On valuation see para. 9.5 below.)

The partnership account with the bank is closed, and a new account opened in the name of the company. As the account is overdrawn and the bank can now only look to the assets of the business as a basis for credit, the bank asks the brothers to sign unlimited personal guarantees of the liability to the bank of the company. Thus if the company gets into financial difficulty and is unable to pay its debts, the bank may require each of the brothers to pay off to the bank what the company owes on the overdraft. The effect of this is immediately to destroy the benefit of limited liability in respect of liability to the company's principal creditor.

(d) How the brothers run the company
In practice the style of management of the business probably changes very little. The legal position is that the brothers meet in annual general meeting to appoint the directors. In reality they probably do not bother to hold formal general meetings as shareholders, but merely draw up (or rely on their professional advisers to draw up) minutes of the general meetings which they all sign. As directors they manage the business from day to day. While theoretically they manage the company by board resolution, in reality they run it informally as they always did and keep no formal minutes, except for particular circumstances when their advisers tell them that they should. In this case, as with the minutes of the first meeting of the board of directors reproduced below, these are merely standard-form minutes produced by the solicitor and signed by the directors. They do not actually hold a formal meeting. They just pass the papers around the table for signature by each of them.

(e) One of the brothers asks his lawyer to advise him how secure he is as a minority shareholder. Previously as a partner he was entitled to a role in management. His solicitor confirms that, like each of his brothers, he is a minority shareholder, holding only 25 per cent of the shares. By demanding a poll at a general meeting, he is entitled to 25,000 votes out of a total of 100,000 votes, which means that he may be voted down by his brothers. Thus in a vote for appointment of directors he cannot on his own ensure that he will be elected on to the board and take part in management. He has no right to be a director and to a role in management, and his brothers may refuse to elect him, or may remove him from the board. This represents a deterioration from his earlier position as a partner, and makes him and each of his brothers potentially vulnerable to being squeezed out by the others. The solicitor therefore recommends that a shareholders' agreement is drawn up which is effectively like a partnership agreement supplementing the constitution of the company. The shareholders' agreement states that each of the members agrees to vote in general meeting in favour of electing each of the others as a director and will not vote to remove any of them from the board. To ensure a collective role for each of them in management and to ensure that none of them is overridden, they also agree that major transactions such as the purchase of land, the commencement of major building work, and the hiring and firing of employees may be done only on the unanimous resolution of the four brothers in a board meeting. They also provide pre-emption rights on transfer of shares. Under these, if any one of them wishes to sell his shares, he must offer them pro rata to each of the others at a valuation to be decided by the company's auditors. There are thus two parallel agreements between the shareholders, the articles of association and the shareholders' agreement. The shareholders' agreement is easier to alter than the articles of association but if a new shareholder is introduced, that shareholder will be bound by the terms of the articles of association but not by the shareholders' agreement. A new shareholders' agreement would be required.

(f) The company borrows from the bank

One of the purposes of incorporating was to increase bank borrowing. The bank has agreed to give a further term loan in return for security. The directors, on behalf of the company, therefore execute the bank's standard-form debenture document, a copy of which is reproduced below. This gives the bank a fixed mortgage on the company's land, and also a floating charge on all the undertaking and assets of the company. This entitles the company to deal with its assets in the ordinary course of business. It is thus free to buy and sell in the usual way. If, however, the company is in default under the terms of the debenture document, for example, by failing to pay capital or interest, the bank may make a demand for repayment and if, as is probable, the company is unable to repay immediately, the bank may appoint an administrative receiver. The receiver is an insolvency practitioner, generally a qualified accountant. The receiver's task will be to take control of the business, possibly to run it and to sell it as a going concern, or to sell off the assets. The proceeds will be used to pay the receiver's own costs and expenses, to pay off the employees as preferential creditors up to specified limits, and finally to pay off the capital, interest and charges that are due to the bank. The surplus, if any (and often there is no surplus), remains the property of the company. At this point the company would be beyond recovery and a formal liquidation or informal liquidation and striking off would occur. The right of a lender holding a floating charge created before the Enterprise Act 2002 to appropriate all the assets of the company to recover its debt has been a significant feature of English company law. It must be clearly distinguished from liquidation where the liquidator's objective is not merely to pay off one secured creditor, but to liquidate all the assets and distribute them pro rata to the ordinary creditors, and then to dissolve the company.

(g) Holding an AGM

At one time all companies were required to hold an annual general meeting of members, though under CA 2006, s. 336, only public companies now have to hold one. At the AGM the directors report to the members as to the financial year just past, present the accounts and their reports to the members for approval and obtain approval for any dividend to be declared on the shares. Directors are reappointed and auditors (professional accountants) appointed where required by the law. In addition, all companies have to file at the Companies Registry an annual return in a standard form (see now CA 2006, s. 854), which includes brief formal details of the company's business, its directors, members, issued share capital etc. Further, the directors' reports and the annual accounts (audited where required) have to be filed (see now CA 2006, s. 441), and this was often done following the AGM.

For the Baker brothers as directors to have to report to themselves as members was a bit of a farce so they got together at the White Hart after work and signed the necessary minutes and papers their accountant had prepared for them, before celebrating a good year in a strong property market with steaks and ale. (Because it was sometimes a charade, the law later allowed a private company to opt out of holding an AGM and now they are wholly exempt, though they still have to file an annual return and accounts.)

(h) The company is doing well, and the brothers take their income by way of salary. As a result, the company, to begin with, makes no profits. After a while the accounts show that the company has made a profit, though no dividends are declared as there is no cash available to pay a dividend, all of the paper profits being retained in the business as working capital.

(i) The younger generation moves in
John Baker has a heart attack and decides to retire from the company. He proposes to resign as a director, to stop working and to dispose of his 25 per cent of the shares. Under the pre-emption rights in the articles, and the shareholders' agreement, he is required first to offer his shares at valuation to the other shareholders. However, his brothers do not have the available funds to buy his shares. The outcome is that Fred Baker's sons, Simon and Stephen, who are both working full time for the company, buy from John a 5 per cent shareholding each. They are all well aware that no outside purchaser will be found for the remaining 15 per cent of the shares. While John would like to be able to get his investment out of the company, in principle a company may not buy its own shares or return capital to a member. However, the law (now CA 2006, s. 692) permits a private company to buy its shares out of profits, subject to strict conditions. The accounts do show sufficient undistributed profits available to pay John for the purchase and cancellation of his shares but as there is not sufficient cash in the company to pay him, the company obtains a loan from the bank to pay John for the shares. Paying one of the shareholders for his 15 per cent shareholding has the effect that the net assets of the company contract by approximately 15 per cent.

(j) Fred's sons, Simon and Stephen, are appointed directors. Michael is appointed managing director as well as his present position as chairman. The procedures necessary to achieve this are found in the articles. The precise authority of the managing director and how his powers relate to any powers retained by the board or the other directors should be laid down precisely by a resolution of the board. As is often the case, this relationship is not in fact clearly defined by the brothers. Michael just gets on with the job of running the business.

(k) The business expands
Michael is aggressively promoting expansion of the business and he is planning a number of new major property developments. On advice it is decided to adopt a group structure to shelter the assets of the company and to spread the risks among different subsidiaries. The name of the company is altered by special resolution to J. B. Baker (Holdings) Ltd. A number of wholly owned subsidiaries are formed. These are J. B. Baker (Builders) Ltd offering general building services, JBB Builders

Merchants Ltd selling building materials, JBB (Heavitree) Ltd, which is to buy and develop a particular site in Exeter, and JBB (Cullompton) Ltd, which is to carry out a major housing development in Cullompton. The holding company ('Holdings') subscribes for 999 shares in each of the companies, while Michael holds the remaining share in each. The existing directors of Holdings are appointed directors of each subsidiary. The subsidiaries have no separate premises, no employees or assets, and services provided to them by Holdings are billed at cost monthly. The intention of the new group structure is that if any one business is unsuccessful and becomes insolvent, that company being a separate entity may be left to go into liquidation and the rest of the group will not be obliged to support it. This is so unless, as is often the case, lenders have demanded cross-guarantees or the provision of collateral security from other members of the group.

(l) The board of Holdings decides to take over another company called Rex Plant Hire Ltd. The group has been hiring plant and equipment from this company which is wholly owned by Rex Williams, its managing director. Rex is having difficulty financing its next generation of bulldozers, and the brothers would like to acquire the plant-hire business. The group does not have cash available to pay for Rex's shares, but issues shares in Holdings to him in return for the shares in his company which he transfers to Holdings. Rex remains as managing director of his former company with a five-year contract of employment.

(m) Michael is ambitious to expand further as the property market is booming. He therefore is keen to obtain cheap capital for the company and to make a killing for himself by offering some of the company's shares to the public. He takes full advice from his solicitors, and discovers that it will be necessary to obtain a listing of the shares on the Stock Exchange, that this is an extremely expensive process, and that the company would not yet satisfy the rules for listing of securities. The idea is dropped. As a private company it is in any case illegal to offer shares to the public.

(n) Tensions in the family

Michael, as managing director, is consolidating his power within the group. Fred and Charlie are ageing and are becoming less active in management. Of the two sons, Stephen is Michael's protégé, while Simon finds himself increasingly excluded from essential decision-making. Simon becomes increasingly disillusioned with Michael's behaviour. For example, Michael sells a company building plot at a loss, saying that the market is going to fall. He did not first obtain a valuation of the land. Simon says that the land was worth much more than Michael obtained for it, that he was grossly negligent and should be made accountable to the company. He hears that Michael proposes to sign a contract for Holdings to buy an expensive plot of land for development. Simon is against this, and so has a look at the shareholders' agreement to see whether Michael can buy the land without consulting the others. He wants to know what he can do to stop the deal going ahead and to obtain any remedies for the company.

Michael and Stephen, from their expertise in planning development projects, are generating a healthy business spin-off in ancillary services. They set up their own company called Architectural and Planning Services Ltd, and employ a town planner. The group's connections ensure a flow of work to the new company, and the group also places work with it. A general meeting of Holdings is called which ratifies Michael and Stephen's role in the company. Simon thinks they should be accountable to the group for the profits they are making.

Michael, who is near retirement, procures a substantial company pension for himself and his widow, and buys from the company's present stock of houses a retirement house for himself at well below list price. Both these arrangements were approved by the general meeting, but Simon says that no proper notice of the meeting was given and no quorum was present. Simon then has his ultimate argument with Michael and Stephen. The board resolves to terminate Simon's contract of employment by giving notice. He is also removed from the board of directors by ordinary resolution. No dividends are paid on the shares, so he receives no income on his capital. The others refuse to buy out his shares, and when he demands that they do so, they offer a derisory price for them. At this point Simon seeks advice as to any remedies that may be available to him. (See for example CA 2006, s. 994, and Insolvency Act 1986, s. 122(1)(g).)

(o) The good times come to an end

JBB (Heavitree) Ltd has completed a development which has gone disastrously wrong. House prices have fallen, only two of the houses have been sold and substantial finance is outstanding. An unpaid supplier of bricks has obtained a winding-up order from the court. Although Holdings has not guaranteed its subsidiary's debts, the liquidator is arguing that the subsidiary is a sham, or a façade. It had no employees, no premises, no separate economic existence and, insofar as it carried on business, it did so as agent for Holdings. Holdings resists the claim which is soon dropped, and the subsidiary is liquidated. The properties are sold by auction and the proceeds are distributed pro rata to the creditors.

(p) Holdings is becoming slow in paying interest on its various loans from the bank, and is becoming a slow payer of its general trading debts. It becomes apparent to the bank that the group is suffering a cash flow crisis. The directors are worried that with high interest rates and no upturn in the property market in sight, the company and group may be in difficulty. Nonetheless they continue to buy supplies on 30 days' credit. Stephen is beginning to have qualms that the company may become unable to pay some of these suppliers which are small businesses whose proprietors he knows personally. He is also concerned as to whether he, and the other directors, might be made personally liable if the company goes on trading. (See, for example, Insolvency Act 1986, s. 214, the 'wrongful trading' provision. This empowers the court to make an order that the directors pay a contribution to the assets of a company in liquidation where they ought to have realised that the company would not avoid going into insolvent liquidation, but did not take all necessary steps to avoid further losses to the creditors.)

(q) The bank realises that with the property market slack it will probably be impossible for the group to sell any more houses to relieve its cash-flow problems. The bank therefore demands repayment of the finance, and as the group is of course unable to repay immediately, the bank declares it in default and appoints a partner in a local firm of chartered accountants as administrative receiver. (This remedy is only available if the floating charge was created before the Enterprise Act 2002 was brought into force.) The administrative receiver takes over the running of the business from the directors, changing the locks on all the premises, taking inventories of goods and dismissing most of the staff. He sees no prospect of selling any part of the business as a going concern, and so decides to close the business down, retaining only sufficient employees to complete a number of houses that are in course of construction. The administrative receiver sells properties by auction and uses the proceeds to pay to the employees a limited amount of unpaid wages. (As required by Insolvency Act 1986, s. 175 these 'preferential debts' are paid first.) Holdings has debts exceeding its assets, largely comprising liabilities under guarantees of its subsidiaries' debts. Once the administrative receiver has paid off his own costs and what is owed to the bank in respect of outstanding interest, capital and charges, there are insufficient assets remaining to justify an ordinary creditor petitioning the court to wind up the company. The consequence is that the bank as a secured creditor under a floating charge, is paid off in full, while the ordinary creditors such as suppliers of goods consumed in the business are unable to recover any part of their unpaid debts.

The documents that now follow are those used by J. B. Baker & Co. Ltd. during the life of the company. These documents are the memorandum and articles of association of the company as bought 'off the shelf'. (Note that Article 6 incorporates Table A with exclusions and variations.) Then follows the 1985 Table A model articles, minutes of the first meeting of the board of directors and the bank's standard form debenture (a secured loan agreement).

Memorandum and articles of association of Shelfco Ltd

The Companies Acts 1985 to 1989

Private Company Limited by Shares

Company Number: 9999999

MEMORANDUM
AND ARTICLES
OF ASSOCIATION

SHELFCO LIMITED

Incorporated the 24th October, 1994

Jordan & Sons Limited
Company Formation and Information Specialists
Legal Stationers and Publishers
Branches throughout the United Kingdom
Telephone 071-253-3030 Telex 261010

© This is kindly reproduced courtesy of Jordans Limited.

THE COMPANIES ACTS 1985 to 1989

PRIVATE COMPANY LIMITED BY SHARES

MEMORANDUM OF ASSOCIATION OF

SHELFCO LIMITED

1. The Company's name is 'SHELFCO LIMITED'.

2. The Company's registered office is to be situated in England & Wales.

3. The Company's objects are:

   (a) To carry on all or any of the businesses of advertising agents, consultants and contractors, commercial artists, lay-out specialists, designers, illustrators and draughtsmen, inventors, designers and printers of publicity and advertising media of every description, to initiate and purchase art work, photographs and printing blocks and to make all arrangements for type-setting and the insertion of advertisements, to book space in press and on television programmes, films and the like; proprietors and organisers of editorial and other public relations services, printers, tracers and engravers, studio proprietors, portrait, technical, commercial and general photographers, publishers, producers and editors of display materials, trade publications and commercial and other undertakings, exhibition contractors, sales promotion specialists and demonstrators, market research specialists, marketing consultants and advisers, manufacturers' agents and representatives and importers, exporters, distributors and factors of, and dealers in goods, wares and merchandise of every description, business system organisers, business transfer agents, general printers and publishers; and to undertake and arrange the employment, training, instruction and engagement of demonstrators, salesmen, personalities, staff and personnel of all kinds; designers, merchants of, and dealers in advertising and commercial screens, models, figures, signs, signals, tablets and novelties of every description and in cabinets, boxes, stands and decorative and ornamental goods, articles and materials required in connection therewith; and dealers in cameras, films and photographic materials and requisites of all kinds, electrical goods of every description, joiners, carpenters, painters and decorators, furniture removers and storers, warehousemen, carriers and general storage contractors, insurance brokers and agents, hire purchase financiers, general merchants and traders; and to buy, sell and generally deal in materials, apparatus, machinery, plant, articles and things of every kind and description capable of being used for the purpose of any of the above-mentioned businesses, or commonly supplied by persons engaged therein, or likely to be required by any of the customers of the Company.
   (b) To carry on any other trade or business whatever which can in the opinion of the Board of Directors be advantageously carried on in connection with or ancillary to any of the businesses of the Company.
   (c) To purchase or by any other means acquire and take options over any property whatever, and any rights or privileges of any kind over or in respect of any property.

(d) To apply for, register, purchase, or by other means acquire and protect, prolong and renew, whether in the United Kingdom or elsewhere any patents, patent rights, brevets d'invention, licences, secret processes, trade marks, designs, protections and concessions and to disclaim, alter, modify, use and turn to account and to manufacture under or grant licences or privileges in respect of the same, and to expend money in experimenting upon, testing and improving any patents, inventions or rights which the Company may acquire or propose to acquire.

(e) To acquire or undertake the whole or any part of the business, goodwill and assets of any person, firm, or company carrying on or proposing to carry on any of the businesses which the Company is authorised to carry on and as part of the consideration for such acquisition to undertake all or any of the liabilities of such person, firm or company, or to acquire an interest in, amalgamate with, or enter into partnership or into any arrangement for sharing profits, or for co-operation, or for mutual assistance with any such person, firm or company, or for subsidising or otherwise assisting any such person, firm or company, and to give or accept, by way of consideration for any of the acts or things aforesaid or property acquired, any shares, debentures, debenture stock or securities that may be agreed upon, and to hold and retain, or sell, mortgage and deal with any shares, debentures, debenture stock or securities so received.

(f) To improve, manage, construct, repair, develop, exchange, let on lease or otherwise, mortgage, charge, sell, dispose of, turn to account, grant licences, options, rights and privileges in respect of, or otherwise deal with all or any part of the property and rights of the Company.

(g) To invest and deal with the moneys of the Company not immediately required in such manner as may from time to time be determined and to hold or otherwise deal with any investments made.

(h) To lend and advance money or give credit on any terms and with or without security to any person, firm or company (including without prejudice to the generality of the foregoing any holding company, subsidiary or fellow subsidiary of, or any other company associated in any way with, the Company), to enter into guarantees, contracts of indemnity and suretyships of all kinds, to receive money on deposit or loan upon any terms, and to secure or guarantee in any manner and upon any terms the payment of any sum of money or the performance of any obligation by any person, firm or company (including without prejudice to the generality of the foregoing any such holding company, subsidiary, fellow subsidiary or associated company as aforesaid).

(i) To borrow and raise money in any manner and to secure the repayment of any money borrowed, raised or owing by mortgage, charge, standard security, lien or other security upon the whole or any part of the Company's property or assets (whether present or future), including its uncalled capital, and also by a similar mortgage, charge, standard security, lien or security to secure and guarantee the performance by the Company of any obligation or liability it may undertake or which may become bindng on it.

(j) To draw, make, accept, endorse, discount, negotiate, execute and issue cheques, bills of exchange, promissory notes, bills of lading, warrants, debentures, and other negotiable or transferable instruments.

(k) To apply for, promote, and obtain any Act of Parliament, order, or licence of the Department of Trade or other authority for enabling the Company to carry any of its objects into effect, or for effecting any modification of the Company's constitution, or for any other purpose which may seem calculated directly or indirectly to promote the Company's interests, and to oppose any proceedings or applications which may seem calculated directly or indirectly to prejudice the Company's interests.

(l) To enter into any arrangements with any government or authority (supreme, municipal, local, or otherwise) that may seem conducive to the attainment of the Company's objects or any of them, and to obtain from any such government or authority any charters, decrees, rights, privileges or concessions which the Company may think desirable and to carry out, exercise, and comply with any such charters, decrees, rights, privileges, and concessions.

(m) To subscribe for, take, purchase, or otherwise acquire, hold, sell, deal with and dispose of, place and underwrite shares, stocks, debentures, debenture stocks, bonds, obligations or securities issued or guaranteed by any other company constituted or carrying on business in any part of the world, and debentures, debenture stocks, bonds, obligations or securities issued or guaranteed by any government or authority, municipal local or otherwise, in any part of the world.

(n) To control, manage, finance, subsidise, co-ordinate or otherwise assist any company or companies in which the Company has a direct or indirect financial interest, to provide secretarial, administrative, technical, commercial and other services and facilities of all kinds for any such company or companies and to make payments by way of subvention or otherwise and any other arrangements which may seem desirable with respect to any business or operations of or generally with respect to any such company or companies.

(o) To promote any other company for the purpose of acquiring the whole or any part of the business or property or undertaking or any of the liabilities of the Company, or of undertaking any business or operations which may appear likely to assist or benefit the Company or to enhance the value of any property or business of the Company, and to place or guarantee the placing of, underwrite, subscribe for, or otherwise acquire all or any part of the shares or securities of any such company as aforesaid.

(p) To sell or otherwise dispose of the whole or any part of the business or property of the Company, either together or in portions, for such consideration as the Company may think fit, and in particular for shares, debentures, or securities of any company purchasing the same.

(q) To act as agents or brokers and as trustees for any person, firm or company, and to undertake and perform sub-contracts.

(r) To remunerate any person, firm or company rendering services to the Company either by cash payment or by the allotment to him or them of shares or other securities of the Company credited as paid up in full or in part or otherwise as may be thought expedient.

(s) To pay all or any expenses incurred in connection with the promotion, formation and incorporation of the Company, or to contract with any person, firm or company to pay the same, and to pay commissions to brokers and others for underwriting, placing, selling, or guaranteeing the subscription of any shares or other securities of the Company.

(t) To support and subscribe to any charitable or public object and to support and subscribe to any institution, society, or club which may be for the benefit of the Company or its Directors or employees, or may be connected with any town or place where the Company carries on business: to give or award pensions, annuities, gratuities, and superannuation or other allowances or benefits or charitable aid and generally to provide advantages, facilities and services for any persons who are or have been Directors of, or who are or have been employed by, or who are serving or have served the Company, or any company which is a subsidiary of the Company or the holding company of the Company or a fellow subsidiary of the Company or the predecessors in business of the Company or of any such subsidiary, holding or fellow subsidiary company and to the wives, widows, children and other relatives and dependants of such persons; to make payments towards insurance; and to set up, establish, support and maintain superannuation and other funds or schemes (whether contributory or non-contributory) for the benefit of any of such persons and of their wives, widows, children and other relatives and dependants; and to set up, establish, support and maintain profit sharing or share purchase schemes for the benefit of any of the employees of the Company or of any such subsidiary, holding or fellow subsidiary company and to lend money to any such employees or to trustees on their behalf to enable any such purchase schemes to be established or maintained.

(u) Subject to and in accordance with a due compliance with the provisions of ss. 155 to 158 (inclusive) of the Act (if and so far as such provisions shall be applicable), to give, whether directly or indirectly, any kind of financial assistance (as defined in s. 152(1)(a) of the Act) for any such purpose as is specified in s. 151(1) and/or s. 151(2) of the Act.

(v) To distribute among the Members of the Company in kind any property of the Company of whatever nature.

(w) To procure the Company to be registered or recognised in any part of the world.

(x) To do all or any of the things or matters aforesaid in any part of the world and either as principals, agents, contractors or otherwise, and by or through agents, brokers, sub-contractors or otherwise and either alone or in conjunction with others.

(y) To do all such other things as may be deemed incidental or conducive to the attainment of the Company's objects or any of them.

AND so that:

(1) None of the objects set forth in any sub-clause of this Clause shall be restrictively construed but the widest interpretation shall be given to each such object, and none of such objects shall, except where the context expressly so requires, be in any way limited or restricted by reference to or inference from any other object or objects set forth in such sub-clause, or by reference to or inference from the terms of any other sub-clause of this Clause, or by reference to or inference from the name of the Company.

(2) None of the sub-clauses of this clause and none of the objects therein specified shall be deemed subsidiary or ancillary to any of the objects specified in any other such sub-clause, and the Company shall have as full a power to exercise each and every one of the objects specified in each sub-clause of this Clause as though each such sub-clause contained the objects of a separate Company.

(3) The word 'Company' in this Clause, except where used in reference to the Company, shall be deemed to include any partnership or other body of persons,

whether incorporated or unincorporated and whether domiciled in the United Kingdom or elsewhere.

(4) In this Clause the expression 'the Act' means the Companies Act 1985, but so that any reference in this Clause to any provision of the Act shall be deemed to include a reference to any statutory modification or re-enactment of that provision for the time being in force.

4. The liability of the Members is limited.

5. The Company's share capital is £100 divided into 100 shares of £1 each.

We, the subscribers to this Memorandum of Association, wish to be formed into a Company pursuant to this Memorandum; and we agree to take the number of shares shown opposite our respective names.

Names and addresses of Subscribers	Number of shares taken by each Subscriber
1. Instant Companies Limited, 2, Baches Street, London N1 6U8	—One
2. Swift Incorporations limited 2, Baches Street London N1 6U8	—One
Total shares taken	—Two

Dated The 7th day of October, 1994.
Witness to the above Signatures: Terry Jayne,
2, Baches Street
London N1 6U8

THE COMPANIES ACTS 1985 to 1989

PRIVATE COMPANY LIMITED BY SHARES

ARTICLES OF ASSOCIATION OF SHELFCO LIMITED

PRELIMINARY

1. (a) The Regulations contained in Table A in the Schedule to the Companies (Tables A to F) Regulations 1985 (SI 1985 No. 805) as amended by the Companies (Tables A to F) (Amendment) Regulations 1985 (SI 1985 No. 1052) (such Table being hereinafter called 'Table A') shall apply to the Company save in so far as they are excluded or varied hereby and such Regulations (save as so excluded or varied) and the Articles hereinafter contained shall be the regulations of the Company.

(b) In these Articles the expression 'the Act' means the Companies Act 1985, but so that any reference in these Articles to any provision of the Act shall be deemed to include a reference to any statutory modification or re-enactment of that provision for the time being in force.

ALLOTMENT OF SHARES

2. (a) Shares which are comprised in the authorised share capital with which the Company is incorporated shall be under the control of the Directors who may (subject to Section 80 of the Act and to paragraph (d) below) allot, grant options over or otherwise dispose of the same, to such persons, on such terms and in such manner as they think fit.

(b) All shares which are not comprised in the authorised share capital with which the Company is incorporated and which the Directors propose to issue shall first be offered to the Members in proportion as nearly as may be to the number of the existing shares held by them respectively unless the Company in General Meeting shall by Special Resolution otherwise direct. The offer shall be made by notice specifying the number of shares offered, and limiting a period (not being less than fourteen days) within which the offer, if not accepted, will be deemed to be declined. After the expiration of that period, those shares so deemed to be declined shall be offered in the proportion aforesaid to the persons who have, within the said period, accepted all the shares offered to them; such further offer shall be made in like terms in the same manner and limited by a like period as the original offer. Any shares not accepted pursuant to such offer or further offer as aforesaid or not capable of being offered as aforesaid except by way of fractions and any shares released from the provisions of this Article by any such Special Resolution as aforesaid shall be under the control of the Directors, who may allot, grant options over or otherwise dispose of the same to such persons, on such terms, and in such manner as they think fit, provided that, in the case of shares not accepted as aforesaid, such shares shall not be disposed of on terms which are more favourable to the subscribers therefor than the terms on which they were offered to the Members. The foregoing provisions of this paragraph (b) shall have effect subject to Section 80 of the Act.

(c) In accordance with Section 91(1) of the Act Sections 89(1) and 90(1) to (6) (inclusive) of the Act shall not apply to the Company.

(d) The Directors are generally and unconditionally authorised for the purposes of Section 80 of the Act, to exercise any power of the Company to allot and grant rights to subscribe for or convert securities into shares of the Company up to the amount of the authorised share capital with which the Company is incorporated at any time or times during the period of five years from the date of incorporation and the Directors may, after that period, allot any shares or grant any such rights under this authority in pursuance of an offer or agreement so to do made by the Company within that period. The authority hereby given may at any time (subject to the said Section 80) be renewed, revoked or varied by Ordinary Resolution of the Company in General Meeting.

SHARES

3. The lien conferred by Clause 8 in Table A shall attach also to fully paid-up shares, and the Company shall also have a first and paramount lien on all shares, whether fully paid or not, standing registered in the name of any person indebted or under liability to the Company, whether he shall be the sole registered holder thereof or shall be one of two or more joint holders, for all moneys presently payable by him or his estate to the Company. Clause 8 in Table A shall be modified accordingly.

4. The liability of any Member in default in respect of a call shall be increased by the addition at the end of the first sentence of Clause 18 in Table A of the words 'and all expenses that may have been incurred by the Company by reason of such non-payment'.

GENERAL MEETINGS AND RESOLUTIONS

5. Every notice convening a General Meeting shall comply with the provisions of Section 372(3) of the Act as to giving information to Members in regard to their right to appoint proxies; and notices of and other communications relating to any General Meeting which any Member is entitled to receive shall be sent to the Directors and to the Auditors for the time being of the Company.

6. (a) If a quorum is not present within half an hour from the time appointed for a General Meeting the General Meeting shall stand adjourned to the same day in the next week at the same time and place or to such other day and at such other time and place as the Directors may determine; and if at the adjourned General Meeting a quorum is not present within half an hour from the time appointed therefor such adjourned General Meeting shall be dissolved.

(b) Clause 41 in Table A shall not apply to the Company.

APPOINTMENT OF DIRECTORS

7. (a) Clause 64 in Table A shall not apply to the Company.

(b) The maximum number and minimum number respectively of the Directors may be determined from time to time by Ordinary Resolution in General Meeting of the Company. Subject to and in default of any such determination there shall be no maximum number of Directors and the minimum number of Directors shall be one. Whensoever the minimum number of Directors shall be one, a sole Director shall have authority to exercise all the powers and discretions by Table A and by these Articles expressed to be vested in the Directors generally, and Clause 89 in Table A shall be modified accordingly.

(c) The Directors shall not be required to retire by rotation and Clauses 73 to 80 (inclusive) in Table A shall not apply to the Company.

(d) No person shall be appointed a Director at any General Meeting unless either:

(i) he is recommended by the Directors; or

(ii) not less than fourteen nor more than thirty-five clear days before the date appointed for the General Meeting, notice signed by a Member qualified to vote at the General Meeting has been given to the Company of the intention to propose that person for appointment, together with notice signed by that person of his willingness to be appointed.

(e) Subject to paragraph (d) above, the Company may by Ordinary Resolution in General Meeting appoint any person who is willing to act to be a Director, either to fill a vacancy or as an additional Director.

(f) The Directors may appoint a person who is willing to act to be a Director, either to fill a vacancy or as an additional Director, provided that the appointment does not cause the number of Directors to exceed any number determined in accordance with paragraph (b) above as the maximum number of Directors and for the time being in force.

BORROWING POWERS

8. The Directors may exercise all the powers of the Company to borrow money without limit as to amount and upon such terms and in such manner as they think fit, and subject (in the case of any security convertible into shares) to Section 80 of the Act to grant any mortgage, charge or standard security over its undertaking, property and uncalled capital, or any part thereof, and to issue debentures, debenture stock, and other securities whether outright or as security for any debt, liability or obligation of the Company or of any third party.

ALTERNATE DIRECTORS

9. (a) An alternate Director shall not be entitled as such to receive any remuneration from the Company, save that he may be paid by the Company such part (if any) of the remuneration otherwise payable to his appointor as such appointor may by notice in writing to the Company from time to time direct, and the first sentence of Clause 66 in Table A shall be modified accordingly.

(b) A Director, or any such other person as is mentioned in Clause 65 in Table A, may act as an alternate Director to represent more than one Director, and an alternate Director shall be entitled at any meeting of the Directors or of any committee of the Directors to one vote for every Director whom he represents in addition to his own vote (if any) as a Director, but he shall count as only one for the purpose of determining whether a quorum is present.

GRATUITIES AND PENSIONS

10. (a) The Directors may exercise the powers of the Company conferred by Clause 3(t) of the Memorandum of Association of the Company and shall be entitled to retain any benefits received by them or any of them by reason of the exercise of any such powers.

(b) Clause 87 in Table A shall not apply to the Company.

PROCEEDINGS OF DIRECTORS

11. (a) A Director may vote, at any meeting of the Directors or of any committee of the Directors, on any resolution, notwithstanding that it in any way concerns or relates to a matter in which he has, directly or indirectly, any kind of interest whatsoever, and if he shall vote on any such resolution as aforesaid his vote shall be counted; and in relation to any such resolution as aforesaid he shall (whether or not he shall vote on the same) be taken into account in calculating the quorum present at the meeting.

(b) Clauses 94 to 97 (inclusive) in Table A shall not apply to the Company.

THE SEAL

12. (a) If the Company has a seal it shall only be used with the authority of the Directors or of a committee of Directors. The Directors may determine who shall sign any instrument to which the seal is affixed and unless otherwise so determined it shall be signed by a Director and by the Secretary or second Director. The obligation under Clause 6 of Table A relating to the sealing of share certificates shall apply only if the Company has a seal. Clause 101 of Table A shall not apply to the Company.

(b) The Company may exercise the powers conferred by Section 39 of the Act with regard to having an official seal for use abroad, and such powers shall be vested in the Directors.

INDEMNITY

13. (a) Every Director or other officer or Auditor of the Company shall be indemnified out of the assets of the Company against all losses or liabilities which he may sustain or incur in or about the execution of the duties of his office or otherwise in relation thereto, including any liability incurred by him in defending any proceedings, whether civil or criminal, in which judgment is given in his favour or in which he is acquitted or in connection with any application under Section 144 or Section 727 of the Act in which relief is granted to him by the Court, and no Director or other officer shall be liable for any loss, damage or misfortune which may happen to or be incurred by the Company in the execution of the duties of his office or in relation thereto. But this Article shall only have effect in so far as its provisions are not avoided by Section 310 of the Act.

(b) The Directors shall have power to purchase and maintain for any Director, officer or Auditor of the Company insurance against any such liability as is referred to in Section 310(1) of the Act from and after the bringing in to force of Section 137 of the Companies Act 1989.

(c) Clause 118 in Table A shall not apply to the Company.

TRANSFER OF SHARES

14. (a) Any person (hereinafter called 'the proposing transferor') proposing to transfer any shares shall give notice in writing (hereinafter called 'the transfer notice') to the Company that he desires to transfer the same and specifying the price per share which in his opinion constitutes the fair value thereof. The transfer notice shall constitute the Company the agent of the proposing transferor for the sale of all (but not some of) the shares comprised in the transfer notice to any Member or Members willing to purchase the same (hereinafter called 'the

purchasing Member') at the price specified therein or at the fair value certified in accordance with paragraph (c) below (whichever shall be the lower). A transfer notice shall not be revocable except with the sanction of the Directors.

(b) The shares comprised in any transfer notice shall be offered to the Members (other than the proposing transferor) as nearly as may be in proportion to the number of shares held by them respectively. Such offer shall be made by notice in writing (hereinafter called 'the offer notice') within seven days after the receipt by the Company of the transfer notice. The offer notice shall state the price per share specified in the transfer notice and shall limit the time in which the offer may be accepted, not being less than twenty-one days nor more than forty-two days after, the date of the offer notice, provided that if a certificate of fair value is requested under paragraph (c) below the offer shall remain open for acceptance for a period of fourteen days after the date on which notice of the fair value certified in accordance with that paragraph shall have been given by the Company to the Members or until the expiry of the period specified in the offer notice whichever is the later. For the purpose of this Article an offer shall be deemed to be accepted on the day on which the acceptance is received by the Company. The offer notice shall further invite each Member to state in his reply the number of additional shares (if any) in excess of his proportion which he desires to purchase and if all the Members do not accept the offer in respect of their respective proportions in full the shares not so accepted shall be used to satisfy the claims for additional shares as nearly as may be in proportion to the number of shares already held by them respectively, provided that no Member shall be obliged to take more shares than he shall have applied for. If any shares shall not be capable without fractions of being offered to the Members in proportion to their existing holdings, the same shall be offered to the Members, or some of them, in such proportions or in such manner as may be determined by lots drawn in regard thereto, and the lots shall be drawn in such manner as the Directors may think fit.

(c) Any Member may, not later than eight days after the date of the offer notice, serve on the Company a notice in writing requesting that the Auditor for the time being of the Company (or at the discretion of the Auditor, a person nominated by the President for the time being of the Institute of Chartered Accountants in the Country of the situation of its Registered Office) certify in writing the sum which in his opinion represents the fair value of the shares comprised in the transfer notice as at the date of the transfer notice and for the purpose of this Article reference to the Auditor shall include any person so nominated. Upon receipt of such notice the Company shall instruct the Auditor to certify as aforesaid and the costs of such valuation shall be apportioned among the proposing transferor and the purchasing Members or borne by any one or more of them as the Auditor in his absolute discretion shall decide. In certifying the fair value as aforesaid the Auditor shall be considered to be acting as an expert and not as an arbitrator or arbiter and accordingly any provisions of law or statute relating to arbitration shall not apply. Upon receipt of the certificate of the Auditor, the Company shall by notice in writing inform all Members of the fair value of each share and of the price per share (being the lower of the price specified in the transfer notice and the fair value of each share) at which the shares comprised in the transfer notice are offered for sale. For the purpose of this Article the fair value of each share comprised in the transfer notice shall be its value as a rateable proportion of the total value of all the issued shares of the Company and shall not be discounted or enhanced by reference to the number of shares referred to in the transfer notice.

(d) If purchasing Members shall be found for all the shares comprised in the transfer notice within the appropriate period specified in paragraph (b) above, the Company shall not later than seven days after the expiry of such appropriate period give notice in writing (hereinafter called 'the sale notice') to the proposing transferor specifying the purchasing Members and the proposing transferor shall be bound upon payment of the price due in respect of all the shares comprised in the transfer notice to transfer the shares to the purchasing Members.

(e) If in any case the proposing transferor after having become bound as aforesaid makes default in transferring any shares the Company may receive the purchase money on his behalf, and may authorise some person to execute a transfer of such shares in favour of the purchasing Member. The receipt of the Company for the purchase money shall be a good discharge to the purchasing Members. The Company shall pay the purchase money into a separate bank account.

(f) If the Company shall not give a sale notice to the proposing transferor within the time specified in paragraph (d) above, he shall, during the period of thirty days next following the expiry of the time so specified, be at liberty to transfer all or any of the shares comprised in the transfer notice to any person or persons but in that event the Directors may, in their absolute discretion, and witbout assigning any reason therefor, decline to register any such transfer and Clause 24 in Table A shall, for these purposes, be modified accordingly.

(g) In the application of Clauses 29 to 31 (inclusive) in Table A to the Company:

(i) any person becoming entitled to a share in consequence of the death or bankruptcy of a Member shall give a transfer notice before he elects in respect of any share to be registered himself or to execute a transfer;

(ii) if a person so becoming entitled shall not have given a transfer notice in respect of any share within six months of the death or bankruptcy, the Directors may at any time thereafter upon resolution passed by them give notice requiring such person within thirty days of such notice to give a transfer notice in respect of all the shares to which he has so become entitled and for which he has not previously given a transfer notice and if he does not do so he shall at the end of such thirty days be deemed to have given a transfer notice pursuant to paragraph (a) of this Article relating to those shares in respect of which he has still not done so:

(iii) where a transfer notice is given or deemed to be given under this paragraph (g) and no price per share is specified therein the transfer notice shall be deemed to specify the sum which shall, on the application of the Directors, be certified in writing by the Auditors in accordance with paragraph (c) of this Article as the fair value thereof.

(h) Whenever any Member of the Company who is employed by the Company in any capacity (whether or not he is also a Director) ceases to be employed by the Company otherwise than by reason of his death the Directors may at any time not later than six months after his ceasing to be employed resolve that such Member do retire, and thereupon he shall (unless he has already served a transfer notice) be deemed to have served a transfer notice pursuant to paragraph (a) of this Article and to have specified therein the fair value to be certified in accordance with paragraph (c) of this Article. Notice of the passing of any such resolution shall forthwith be given to the Member affected thereby.

Names and addresses of Subscribers
1. Instant Companies Limited, 2 Baches Street London N1 6UB
2. Swift Incorporations Limited, 2 Baches Street London N1 6UB

Dated the 7th day of October, 1994.
Witness to the above signatures, Terry Jayne
2 Baches Street
London N1 6UB

COMPANIES (TABLES A TO F) REGULATIONS 1985 (SI 1985/805), TABLE A

Regulations for Management of a Company Limited by Shares

Interpretation

1. In these regulations—

    'the Act' means the Companies Act 1985 including any statutory modification or re-enactment thereof for the time being in force.

    'the articles' means the articles of the company.

    'clear days' in relation to the period of a notice means that period excluding the day when the notice is given or deemed to be given and the day for which it is given or on which it is to take effect.

    'communication' means the same as in the Electronic Communications Act 2000.

    'electronic communication' means the same as in the Electronic Communications Act 2000.

    'executed' includes any mode of execution.

    'office' means the registered office of the company.

    'the holder' in relation to shares means the member whose name is entered in the register of members as the holder of the shares.

    'the seal' means the common seal of the company.

    'secretary' means the secretary of the company or any other person appointed to perform the duties of the secretary of the company, including a joint, assistant or deputy secretary.

    'the United Kingdom' means Great Britain and Northern Ireland.

Unless the context otherwise requires, words or expressions contained in these regulations bear the same meaning as in the Act but excluding any statutory modification thereof not in force when these regulations become binding on the company.

Share capital

2. Subject to the provisions of the Act and without prejudice to any rights attached to any existing shares, any share may be issued with such rights or restrictions as the company may by ordinary resolution determine.

3. Subject to the provisions of the Act, shares may be issued which are to be redeemed or are to be liable to be redeemed at the option of the company or the holder on such terms and in such manner as may be provided by the articles.

4. The company may exercise the powers of paying commissions conferred by the Act. Subject to the provisions of the Act, any such commission may be satisfied by the payment of cash or by the allotment of fully or partly paid shares or partly in one way and partly in the other.

5. Except as required by law, no person shall be recognised by the company as holding any share upon any trust and (except as otherwise provided by the articles or by law) the company shall not be bound by or recognise any interest in any share except an absolute right to the entirety thereof in the holder.

Share certificates

6. Every member, upon becoming the holder of any shares, shall be entitled without payment to one certificate for all the shares of each class held by him (and, upon transferring a part of his holding of shares of any class, to a certificate for the balance of such holding) or several certificates each for one or more of his shares upon payment for every certificate after the first of such reasonable sum as the directors may determine. Every certificate shall be sealed with the seal and shall specify the number, class and distinguishing numbers (if any) of the shares to which it relates and the amount or respective amounts paid up thereon. The company shall not be bound to issue more than one certificate for shares held jointly by several persons and delivery of a certificate to one joint holder shall be a sufficient delivery to all of them.

7. If a share certificate is defaced, worn-out, lost or destroyed, it may be renewed on such terms (if any) as to evidence and indemnity and payment of the expenses reasonably incurred by the company in investigating evidence as the directors may determine but otherwise free of charge, and (in the case of defacement or wearing-out) on delivery up of the old certificate.

Lien

8. The company shall have a first and paramount lien on every share (not being a fully paid share) for all moneys (whether presently payable or not) payable at a fixed time or called in respect of that share. The directors may at any time declare any share to be wholly or in part exempt from the provisions of this regulation. The company's lien on a share shall extend to any amount payable in respect of it.

9. The company may sell in such manner as the directors determine any shares on which the company has a lien if a sum in respect of which the lien exists is presently payable and is not paid within fourteen clear days after notice has been given to the holder of the share or to the person entitled to it in consequence of the death or bankruptcy of the holder, demanding payment and stating that if the notice is not complied with the shares may be sold.

10. To give effect to a sale the directors may authorise some person to execute an instrument of transfer of the shares sold to, or in accordance with the directions of, the purchaser. The title of the transferee to the shares shall not be affected by any irregularity in or invalidity of the proceedings in reference to the sale.

11. The net proceeds of the sale, after payment of the costs, shall be applied in payment of so much of the sum for which the lien exists as is presently payable, and any residue shall (upon surrender to the company for cancellation of the certificate for the shares sold and subject to a like lien for any moneys not presently payable as existed upon the shares before the sale) be paid to the person entitled to the shares at the date of the sale.

Calls on shares and forfeiture

12. Subject to the terms of allotment, the directors may make calls upon the members in respect of any moneys unpaid on their shares (whether in respect of nominal value or premium) and each member shall (subject to receiving at least fourteen clear days' notice specifying when and where payment is to be made) pay to the company as required by the notice the amount called on his shares. A call may be required to be paid by instalments. A call may, before receipt by the company of any sum due thereunder, be revoked in whole or part and payment of a call may be postponed in whole or part. A person upon whom a call is made shall remain liable for calls made upon him notwithstanding the subsequent transfer of the shares in respect whereof the call was made.

13. A call shall be deemed to have been made at the time when the resolution of the directors authorising the call was passed.

14. The joint holders of a share shall be jointly and severally liable to pay all calls in respect thereof.

15. If a call remains unpaid after it has become due and payable the person from whom it is due and payable shall pay interest on the amount unpaid from the day it became due and payable until it is paid at the rate fixed by the terms of allotment of the share or in the notice of the call or, if no rate is fixed, at the appropriate rate (as defined by the Act) but the directors may waive payment of the interest wholly or in part.

16. An amount payable in respect of a share on allotment or at any fixed date, whether in respect of nominal value or premium or as an instalment of a call, shall be deemed to be a call and if it is not paid the provisions of the articles shall apply as if that amount had become due and payable by virtue of a call.

17. Subject to the terms of allotment, the directors may make arrangements on the issue of shares for a difference between the holders in the amounts and times of payment of calls on their shares.

18. If a call remains unpaid after it has become due and payable the directors may give to the person from whom it is due not less than fourteen clear days' notice requiring payment of the amount unpaid together with any interest which may have accrued. The notice shall name the place where payment is to be made and shall state that if the notice is not complied with the shares in respect of which the call was made will be liable to be forfeited.

19. If the notice is not complied with any share in respect of which it was given may, before the payment required by the notice has been made, be forfeited by a resolution of the directors and the forfeiture shall include all dividends or other moneys payable in respect of the forfeited shares and not paid before the forfeiture.

20. Subject to the provisions of the Act, a forfeited share may be sold, re-allotted or otherwise disposed of on such terms and in such manner as the directors determine either to the person who was before the forfeiture the holder or to any other person and at any time before sale, re-allotment or other disposition, the forfeiture may be cancelled on such terms as the directors think fit. Where for the purposes of its disposal a forfeited share is to be transferred to any person the directors may authorise some person to execute an instrument of transfer of the share to that person.

21. A person any of whose shares have been forfeited shall cease to be a member in respect of them and shall surrender to the company for cancellation the certificate for the shares forfeited but shall remain liable to the company for all moneys which at the date of forfeiture were presently payable by him to the company in respect of those shares with interest at the rate at which interest was payable on those moneys before the forfeiture or, if no interest was so payable, at the appropriate rate (as defined in the Act) from the date of forfeiture until payment but the directors may waive payment wholly or in part or enforce payment without any allowance for the value of the shares at the time of forfeiture or for any consideration received on their disposal.

22. A statutory declaration by a director or the secretary that a share has been forfeited on a specified date shall be conclusive evidence of the facts stated in it as against all persons claiming to be entitled to the share and the declaration shall (subject to the execution of an instrument of transfer if necessary) constitute a good title to the share and the person to whom the share is disposed of shall not be bound to see to the application of the consideration, if any, nor shall his title to the share be affected by any irregularity in or invalidity of the proceedings in reference to the forfeiture or disposal of the share.

Transfer of shares

23. The instrument of transfer of a share may be in any usual form or in any other form which the directors may approve and shall be executed by or on behalf of the transferor and, unless the share is fully paid, by or on behalf of the transferee.

24. The directors may refuse to register the transfer of a share which is not fully paid to a person of whom they do not approve and they may refuse to register the transfer of a share on which the company has a lien. They may also refuse to register a transfer unless—

    (a) it is lodged at the office or at such other place as the directors may appoint and is accompanied by the certificate for the shares to which it relates and such other evidence as the directors may reasonably require to show the right of the transferor to make the transfer;

    (b) it is in respect of only one class of shares; and

    (c) it is in favour of not more than four transferees.

25. If the directors refuse to register a transfer of a share, they shall within two months after the date on which the transfer was lodged with the company send to the transferee notice of the refusal.

26. The registration of transfers of shares or of transfers of any class of shares may be suspended at such times and for such periods (not exceeding thirty days in any year) as the directors may determine.

27. No fee shall be charged for the registration of any instrument of transfer or other document relating to or affecting the title to any share.

28. The company shall be entitled to retain any instrument of transfer which is registered, but any instrument of transfer which the directors refuse to register shall be returned to the person lodging it when notice of the refusal is given.

Transmission of shares

29. If a member dies the survivor or survivors where he was a joint holder, and his personal representatives where he was a sole holder or the only survivor of joint holders, shall be the only persons recognised by the company as having any title to his interest; but nothing herein contained shall release the estate of a deceased member from any liability in respect of any share which had been jointly held by him.

30. A person becoming entitled to a share in consequence of the death or bankruptcy of a member may, upon such evidence being produced as the directors may properly require, elect either to become the holder of the share or to have some person nominated by him registered as the transferee. If he elects to become the holder he shall give notice to the company to that effect. If he elects to have another person registered he shall execute an instrument of transfer of the share to that person. All the articles relating to the transfer of shares shall apply to the notice or instrument of transfer as if it were an instrument of transfer executed by the member and the death or bankruptcy of the member had not occurred.

31. A person becoming entitled to a share in consequence of the death or bankruptcy of a member shall have the rights to which he would be entitled if he were the holder of the share, except that he shall not, before being registered as the holder of the share, be entitled in respect of it to attend or vote at any meeting of the company or at any separate meeting of the holders of any class of shares in the company.

Alteration of share capital

32. The company may by ordinary resolution—

(a) increase its share capital by new shares of such amount as the resolution prescribes;

(b) consolidate and divide all or any of its share capital into shares of larger amount than its existing shares;

(c) subject to the provisions of the Act, sub-divide its shares, or any of them, into shares of smaller amount and the resolution may determine that, as between the shares resulting from the sub-division, any of them may have any preference or advantage as compared with the others; and

(d) cancel shares which, at the date of the passing of the resolution, have not been taken or agreed to be taken by any person and diminish the amount of its share capital by the amount of the shares so cancelled.

33. Whenever as a result of a consolidation of shares any members would become entitled to fractions of a share, the directors may, on behalf of those members, sell the shares representing the fractions for the best price reasonably obtainable to any person (including, subject to the provisions of the Act, the company) and distribute the net proceeds of sale in due proportion among those members, and the directors may authorise some person to execute an instrument of transfer of the shares to, or in accordance with the directions of, the purchaser. The transferee shall not be bound to see to the application of the purchase money nor shall his title to the shares be affected by any irregularity in or invalidity of the proceedings in reference to the sale.

34. Subject to the provisions of the Act, the company may by special resolution reduce its share capital, any capital redemption reserve and any share premium account in any way.

Purchase of own shares

35. Subject to the provisions of the Act, the company may purchase its own shares (including any redeemable shares) and, if it is a private company, make a payment in respect of the redemption or purchase of its own shares otherwise than out of distributable profits of the company or the proceeds of a fresh issue of shares.

General meetings

36. All general meetings other than annual general meetings shall be called extraordinary general meetings.

37. The directors may call general meetings and, on the requisition of members pursuant to the provisions of the Act, shall forthwith proceed to convene an extraordinary general meeting for a date not later than eight weeks after receipt of the requisition. If there are not within the United Kingdom sufficient directors to call a general meeting, any director or any member of the company may call a general meeting.

Notice of general meetings

38. An annual general meeting and an extraordinary general meeting called for the passing of a special resolution or a resolution appointing a person as a director shall be called by at least twenty-one clear days' notice. All other extraordinary general meetings shall be called by at least fourteen clear days' notice but a general meeting may be called by shorter notice if it is so agreed—

(a) in the case of an annual general meeting, by all the members entitled to attend and vote thereat; and

(b) in the case of any other meeting by a majority in number of the members having a right to attend and vote being a majority together holding not less than ninety-five per cent in nominal value of the shares giving that right.

The notice shall specify the time and place of the meeting and the general nature of the business to be transacted and, in the case of an annual general meeting, shall specify the meeting as such.

Subject to the provisions of the articles and to any restrictions imposed on any shares, the notice shall be given to all the members, to all persons entitled to a share in consequence of the death or bankruptcy of a member and to the directors and auditors.

39. The accidental omission to give notice of a meeting to, or the non-receipt of notice of a meeting by, any person entitled to receive notice shall not invalidate the proceedings at that meeting.

Proceedings at general meetings

40. No business shall be transacted at any meeting unless a quorum is present. Two persons entitled to vote upon the business to be transacted, each being a member or a proxy for a member or a duly authorised representative of a corporation, shall be a quorum.

41. If such a quorum is not present within half an hour from the time appointed for the meeting, or if during a meeting such a quorum ceases to be present, the meeting shall stand adjourned to the same day in the next week at the same time and place or to such time and place as the directors may determine.

42. The chairman, if any, of the board of directors or in his absence some other director nominated by the directors shall preside as chairman of the meeting, but if neither the chairman nor such other director (if any) be present within fifteen minutes after the time appointed for holding the meeting and willing to act, the directors present shall elect one of their number to be chairman and, if there is only one director present and willing to act, he shall be chairman.

43. If no director is willing to act as chairman, or if no director is present within fifteen minutes after the time appointed for holding the meeting, the members present and entitled to vote shall choose one of their number to be chairman.

44. A director shall, notwithstanding that he is not a member, be entitled to attend and speak at any general meeting and at any separate meeting of the holders of any class of shares in the company.

45. The chairman may, with the consent of a meeting at which a quorum is present (and shall if so directed by the meeting), adjourn the meeting from time to time and from place to place, but no business shall be transacted at an adjourned meeting other than business which might properly have been transacted at the meeting had the adjournment not taken place. When a meeting is adjourned for fourteen days or more, at least seven clear days' notice shall be given specifying the time and place of the adjourned meeting and the general nature of the business to be transacted. Otherwise it shall not be necessary to give any such notice.

46. A resolution put to the vote of a meeting shall be decided on a show of hands unless before, or on the declaration of the result of, the show of hands a poll is duly demanded. Subject to the provisions of the Act, a poll may be demanded—

(a) by the chairman; or

(b) by at least two members having the right to vote at the meeting; or

(c) by a member or members representing not less than one-tenth of the total voting rights of all the members having the right to vote at the meeting; or

(d) by a member or members holding shares conferring a right to vote at the meeting being shares on which an aggregate sum has been paid up equal to not less than one-tenth of the total sum paid up on all the shares conferring that right;

and a demand by a person as proxy for a member shall be the same as a demand by the member.

47. Unless a poll is duly demanded a declaration by the chairman that a resolution has been carried or carried unanimously, or by a particular majority, or lost, or not carried by a particular majority and an entry to that effect in the minutes of the meeting shall be conclusive evidence of the fact without proof of the number or proportion of the votes recorded in favour of or against the resolution.

48. The demand for a poll may, before the poll is taken, be withdrawn but only with the consent of the chairman and a demand so withdrawn shall not be taken to have invalidated the result of a show of hands declared before the demand was made.

49. A poll shall be taken as the chairman directs and he may appoint scrutineers (who need not be members) and fix a time and place for declaring the result of the poll. The result of the poll shall be deemed to be the resolution of the meeting at which the poll was demanded.

50. In the case of an equality of votes, whether on a show of hands or on a poll, the chairman shall be entitled to a casting vote in addition to any other vote he may have.

51. A poll demanded on the election of a chairman or on a question of adjournment shall be taken forthwith. A poll demanded on any other question shall be taken either forthwith or at such time and place as the chairman directs not being more than thirty days after the poll is demanded. The demand for a poll shall not prevent the continuance of a meeting for the transaction of any business other than the question on which the poll was demanded. If a poll is demanded before the declaration of the result of a show of hands and the demand is duly withdrawn, the meeting shall continue as if the demand had not been made.

52. No notice need be given of a poll not taken forthwith if the time and place at which it is to be taken are announced at the meeting at which it is demanded. In any other case at least seven clear days' notice shall be given specifying the time and place at which the poll is to be taken.

53. A resolution in writing executed by or on behalf of each member who would have been entitled to vote upon it if it had been proposed at a general meeting at which he was present shall be as effectual as if it had been passed at a general meeting duly convened and held and may consist of several instruments in the like form each executed by or on behalf of one or more members.

Votes of members

54. Subject to any rights or restrictions attached to any shares, on a show of hands every member who (being an individual) is present in person or (being a corporation) is present by a duly authorised representative, not being himself a member entitled to vote, shall have one vote and on a poll every member shall have one vote for every share of which he is the holder.

55. In the case of joint holders the vote of the senior who tenders a vote, whether in person or by proxy, shall be accepted to the exclusion of the votes of the other joint holders; and seniority shall be determined by the order in which the names of the holders stand in the register of members.

56. A member in respect of whom an order has been made by any court having jurisdiction (whether in the United Kingdom or elsewhere) in matters concerning mental disorder may vote, whether on a show of hands or on a poll, by his receiver, curator bonis or other person authorised in that behalf appointed by that court, and any such receiver, curator bonis or other person may, on a poll, vote by proxy. Evidence to the satisfaction of the directors of the authority of the person claiming to exercise the right to vote shall be deposited at the office, or at such other place as is specified in accordance with the articles for the deposit of instruments of proxy, not less than 48 hours before the time appointed for holding the meeting or adjourned meeting at which the right to vote is to be exercised and in default the right to vote shall not be exercisable.

57. No member shall vote at any general meeting or at any separate meeting of the holders of any class of shares in the company, either in person or by proxy, in respect of any share held by him unless all moneys presently payable by him in respect of that share have been paid.

58. No objection shall be raised to the qualification of any voter except at the meeting or adjourned meeting at which the vote objected to is tendered, and every vote not disallowed at the meeting shall be valid. Any objection made in due time shall be referred to the chairman whose decision shall be final and conclusive.

59. On a poll votes may be given either personally or by proxy. A member may appoint more than one proxy to attend on the same occasion.

60. The appointment of a proxy shall be executed by or on behalf of the appointor and shall be in the following form (or in a form as near thereto as circumstances allow or in any other form which is usual or which the directors may approve)—

'   PLC/Limited
              I/We,   , of
                                                                      , being a
member/members of the above-named company, hereby appoint
              of
              , of failing him
of   , as my/our proxy to vote in my/our name[s] and on my/our
behalf at the annual/extraordinary general meeting of the company, to be held on
              19 , and at any adjournment thereof.
Signed on   19   .'

61. Where it is desired to afford members an opportunity of instructing the proxy how he shall act the appointment of a proxy shall be in the following form (or in a form as near thereto as circumstances allow or in any other form which is usual or which the directors may approve)—

'   PLC/Limited
              I/We,   ,of
                                                                    , being a
member/members of the above-named company, hereby appoint
              of
              , or failing him,
of   , as my/our proxy to vote in my/our name[s] and on my/our
behalf at the annual/extraordinary general meeting of the company to be held on
              19   , and at any adjournment thereof.
This form is to be used in respect of the resolutions mentioned below as follows:
     Resolution No. 1   *for * against
     Resolution No. 2   *for * against.
     *Strike out whichever is not desired.
Unless otherwise instructed, the proxy may vote as he thinks fit or abstain from voting.
Signed this   day of   19   ."

62. The appointment of a proxy and any authority under which it is executed or a copy of such authority certified notarially or in some other way approved by the directors may—

(a) in the case of an instrument in writing deposited at the office or at such other place within the United Kingdom as is specified in the notice convening the meeting or in any instrument of proxy sent out by the company in relation to the meeting not less than 48 hours before the time for holding the meeting or adjourned meeting at which the person named in the instrument proposes to vote; or

(aa) in the case of an appointment contained in an electronic communication, where an address has been specified for the purpose of receiving electronic communications—

(i) in the notice convening the meeting, or

(ii) in any instrument of proxy sent out by the company in relation to the meeting, or

(iii) in any invitation contained in an electronic communication to appoint a proxy issued by the company in relation to the meeting,

be received at such address not less than 48 hours before the time for holding the meeting or adjourned meeting at which the person named in the appointment proposes to vote;

(b) in the case of a poll taken more than 48 hours after it is demanded, be deposited or received as aforesaid after the poll has been demanded and not less than 24 hours before the time appointed for the taking of the poll; or

(c) where the poll is not taken forthwith but is taken not more than 48 hours after it was demanded, be delivered at the meeting at which the poll was demanded to the chairman or to the secretary or to any director;

and an appointment of proxy which is not deposited, delivered or received in a manner so permitted shall be invalid.

In this regulation and the next, 'address', in relation to electronic communications, includes any number or address used for the purposes of such communications.

63. A vote given or poll demanded by proxy or by the duly authorised representative of a corporation shall be valid notwithstanding the previous determination of the authority of the person voting or demanding a poll unless notice of the determination was received by the company at the office or at such other place at which the instrument of proxy was duly deposited or, where the appointment of the proxy was contained in an electronic communication, at the address at which such appointment was duly received before the commencement of the meeting or adjourned meeting at which the vote is given or the poll demanded or (in the case of a poll taken otherwise than on the same day as the meeting or adjourned meeting) the time appointed for taking the poll.

Number of directors

64. Unless otherwise determined by ordinary resolution, the number of directors (other than alternate directors) shall not be subject to any maximum but shall be not less than two.

Alternate directors

65. Any director (other than an alternate director) may appoint any other director, of any other person approved by resolution of the directors and willing to act, to be an alternate director and may remove from office an alternate director so appointed by him.

66. An alternate director shall be entitled to receive notice of all meetings of directors and of all meetings of committees of directors of which his appointor is a member, to attend and vote at any such meeting at which the director appointing him is not personally present, and generally to perform all the functions of his appointor as a director in his absence but shall not be entitled to receive any remuneration from the company for his services as an alternate director. But it shall not be necessary to give notice of such a meeting to an alternate director who is absent from the United Kingdom.

67. An alternate director shall cease to be an alternate director if his appointor ceases to be a director; but, if a director retires by rotation or otherwise but is reappointed or deemed to have been reappointed at the meeting at which he retires, any appointment of an alternate director made by him which was in force immediately prior to his retirement shall continue after his reappointment.

68. Any appointment or removal of an alternate director shall be by notice to the company signed by the director making or revoking the appointment or in any other manner approved by the directors.

69. Save as otherwise provided in the articles, an alternate director shall be deemed for all purposes to be a director and shall alone be responsible for his own acts and defaults and he shall not be deemed to be the agent of the director appointing him.

Powers of directors

70. Subject to the provisions of the Act, the memorandum and the articles and to any directions given by special resolution, the business of the company shall be managed by the directors who may exercise all the powers of the company. No alteration of the memorandum or articles and no such direction shall invalidate any prior act of the directors which would have been valid if that alteration had not been made or that direction had not been given. The powers given by this regulation shall not be limited by any special power given to the directors by the articles and a meeting of directors at which a quorum is present may exercise all powers exercisable by the directors.

71. The directors may, by power of attorney or otherwise, appoint any person to be the agent of the company for such purposes and on such conditions as they determine, including authority for the agent to delegate all or any of his powers.

Delegation of directors' powers

72. The directors may delegate any of their powers to any committee consisting of one or more directors. They may also delegate to any managing director or any director holding any other executive office such of their powers as they consider desirable to be exercised by him. Any such delegation may be made subject to any conditions the directors may impose, and either collaterally with or to the exclusion of their own powers and may be revoked or altered. Subject to any such conditions, the proceedings of a committee with two or more members shall be governed by the articles regulating the proceedings of directors so far as they are capable of applying.

Appointment and retirement of directors

73. At the first annual general meeting all the directors shall retire from office, and at every subsequent annual general meeting one-third of the directors who are subject to retirement by rotation or, if their number is not three or a multiple of three, the number nearest to one-third shall retire from office; but, if there is only one director who is subject to retirement by rotation, he shall retire.

74. Subject to the provisions of the Act, the directors to retire by rotation shall be those who have been longest in office since their last appointment or reappointment, but as between persons who became or were last reappointed directors on the same day those to retire shall (unless they otherwise agree among themselves) be determined by lot.

75. If the company, at the meeting at which a director retires by rotation, does not fill the vacancy the retiring director shall, if willing to act, be deemed to have been reappointed unless at the meeting it is resolved not to fill the vacancy or unless a resolution for the reappointment of the director is put to the meeting and lost.

76. No person other than a director retiring by rotation shall be appointed or reappointed a director at any general meeting unless—

(a) he is recommended by the directors; or

(b) not less than fourteen nor more than thirty-five clear days before the date appointed for the meeting , notice executed by a member qualified to vote at the meeting has been given to the company of the intention to propose that person for appointment or reappointment stating the particulars which would, if he were so appointed or reappointed, be required to be included in the company's register of directors together with notice executed by that person of his willingness to be appointed or reappointed.

77. Not less than seven nor more than twenty-eight clear days before the date appointed for holding a general meeting notice shall be given to all who are entitled to receive notice of the meeting of any person (other than a director retiring by rotation at the meeting) who is recommended by the directors for appointment or reappointment as a director at the meeting or in respect of whom notice has been duly given to the company of the intention to propose him at the meeting for appointment or reappointment as a director. The notice shall give the particulars of that person which would, if he were so appointed or reappointed, be required to be included in the company's register of directors.

78. Subject as aforesaid, the company may by ordinary resolution appoint a person who is willing to act to be a director either to fill a vacancy or as an additional director and may also determine the rotation in which any additional directors are to retire.

79. The directors may appoint a person who is willing to act to be a director, either to fill a vacancy or as an additional director, provided that the appointment does not cause the number of directors to exceed any number fixed by or in accordance with the articles as the maximum number of directors. A director so appointed shall hold office only until the next following annual general meeting and shall not be taken into account in determining the directors who are to retire by rotation at the meeting. If not reappointed at such annual general meeting, he shall vacate office at the conclusion thereof.

80. Subject as aforesaid, a director who retires at an annual general meeting may, if willing to act, be reappointed. If he is not reappointed, he shall retain office until the meeting appoints someone in his place, or if it does not do so, until the end of the meeting.

Disqualification and removal of directors
81. The office of a director shall be vacated if—

(a) he ceases to be a director by virtue of any provision of the Act or he becomes prohibited by law from being a director; or
(b) he becomes bankrupt or makes any arrangement or composition with his creditors generally; or
(c) he is, or may be, suffering from mental disorder and either—
   (i) he is admitted to hospital in pursuance of an application for admission for treatment under the Mental Health Act 1983 or, in Scotland, an application for admission under the Mental Health (Scotland) Act 1960, or
   (ii) an order is made by a court having jurisdiction (whether in the United Kingdom or elsewhere) in matters concerning mental disorder for his detention or for the appointment of a receiver, curator bonis or other person to exercise powers with respect to his property or affairs; or
(d) he resigns his office by notice to the company; or
(e) he shall for more than six consecutive months have been absent without permission of the directors from meetings of directors held during that period and the directors resolve that his office be vacated.

Remuneration of directors
82. The directors shall be entitled to such remuneration as the company may by ordinary resolution determine and, unless the resolution provides otherwise, the remuneration shall be deemed to accrue from day to day.

Directors' expenses
83. The directors may be paid all travelling, hotel, and other expenses properly incurred by them in connection with their attendance at meetings of directors or committees of directors or general meetings or separate meetings of the holders of any class of shares or of debentures of the company or otherwise in connection with the discharge of their duties.

Directors' appointments and interests
84. Subject to the provisions of the Act, the directors may appoint one or more of their number to the office of managing director or to any other executive office under the company and may enter

into an agreement or arrangement with any director for his employment by the company or for the provision by him of any services outside the scope of the ordinary duties of a director. Any such appointment, agreement or arrangement may be made upon such terms as the directors determine and they may remunerate any such director for his services as they think fit. Any appointment of a director to an executive office shall terminate if he ceases to be a director but without prejudice to any claim to damages for breach of the contract of service between the director and the company. A managing director and a director holding any other executive office shall not be subject to retirement by rotation.

85. Subject to the provisions of the Act, and provided that he has disclosed to the directors the nature and extent of any material interest of his, a director notwithstanding his office—

(a) may be a party to, or otherwise interested in, any transaction or arrangement with the company or in which the company is otherwise interested;

(b) may be a director or other officer of, or employed by, or a party to any transaction or arrangement with, or otherwise interested in, any body corporate promoted by the company or in which the company is otherwise interested; and

(c) shall not, by reason of his office, be accountable to the company for any benefit which he derives from any such office or employment or from any such transaction or arrangement or from any interest in any such body corporate and no such transaction or arrangement shall be liable to be avoided on the ground of any such interest or benefit.

86. For the purposes of regulation 85—

(a) a general notice given to the directors that a director is to be regarded as having an interest of the nature and extent specified in the notice in any transaction or arrangement in which a specified person or class of persons is interested shall be deemed to be a disclosure that the director has an interest in any such transaction of the nature and extent so specified; and

(b) an interest of which a director has no knowledge and of which it is unreasonable to expect him to have knowledge shall not be treated as an interest of his.

Directors' gratuities and pensions

87. The directors may provide benefits, whether by the payment of gratuities or pensions or by insurance or otherwise, for any director who has held but no longer holds any executive office or employment with the company or with any body corporate which is or has been a subsidiary of the company or a predecessor in business of the company or of any such subsidiary, and for any member of his family (including a spouse and a former spouse) or any person who is or was dependent on him, and may (as well before as after he ceases to hold such office or employment) contribute to any fund and pay premiums for the purchase or provision of any such benefit.

Proceedings of directors

88. Subject to the provisions of the articles, the directors may regulate their proceedings as they think fit. A director may, and the secretary at the request of a director shall, call a meeting of the directors. It shall not be necessary to give notice of a meeting to a director who is absent from the United Kingdom. Questions arising at a meeting shall be decided by a majority of votes. In the case of an equality of votes, the chairman shall have a second or casting vote. A director who is also an alternate director shall be entitled in the absence of his appointor to a separate vote on behalf of his appointor in addition to his own vote.

89. The quorum for the transaction of the business of the directors may be fixed by the directors and unless so fixed at any other number shall be two. A person who holds office only as an alternate director shall, if his appointor is not present, be counted in the quorum.

90. The continuing directors or a sole continuing director may act notwithstanding any vacancies in their number, but, if the number of directors is less than the number fixed as the quorum, the continuing directors or director may act only for the purpose of filling vacancies or of calling a general meeting.

91. The directors may appoint one of their number to be the chairman of the board of directors and may at any time remove him from that office. Unless he is unwilling to do so, the director so appointed shall preside at every meeting of directors at which he is present. But if there is no director holding that office, or if the director holding it is unwilling to preside or is not present within five minutes after the time appointed for the meeting, the directors present may appoint one of their number to be chairman of the meeting.

92. All acts done by a meeting of directors, or of a committee of directors, or by a person acting as a director shall, notwithstanding that it be afterwards discovered that there was a defect in the appointment of any director or that any of them were disqualified from holding office, or had vacated office, or were not entitled to vote, be as valid as if every such person had been duly appointed and was qualified and had continued to be a director and had been entitled to vote.

93. A resolution in writing signed by all the directors entitled to receive notice of a meeting of directors or of a committee of directors shall be as valid and effectual as if it had been passed at a meeting of directors or (as the case may be) a committee of directors duly convened and held and may consist of several documents in the like form each signed by one or more directors; but a resolution signed by an alternate director need not also be signed by his appointor and, if it is signed by a director who has appointed an alternate director, it need not be signed by the alternate director in that capacity.

94. Save as otherwise provided by the articles, a director shall not vote at a meeting of directors or of a committee of directors on any resolution concerning a matter in which he has, directly or indirectly, an interest or duty which is material and which conflicts or may conflict with the interests of the company unless his interest or duty arises only because the case falls within one or more of the following paragraphs—

(a) the resolution relates to the giving to him of a guarantee, security, or indemnity in respect of money lent to, or an obligation incurred by him for the benefit of, the company or any of its subsidiaries;

(b) the resolution relates to the giving to a third party of a guarantee, security, or indemnity in respect of an obligation of the company or any of its subsidiaries for which the director has assumed responsibility in whole or part and whether alone or jointly with others under a guarantee or indemnity or by the giving of security;

(c) his interest arises by virtue of his subscribing or agreeing to subscribe for any shares, debentures or other securities of the company or any of its subsidiaries, or by virtue of his being, or intending to become, a participant in the underwriting or sub-underwriting of an offer of any such shares, debentures, or other securities by the company or any of its subsidiaries for subscription, purchase or exchange;

(d) the resolution relates in any way to a retirement benefits scheme which has been approved, or is conditional upon approval, by the Board of Inland Revenue for taxation purposes.

For the purposes of this regulation, an interest of a person who is, for any purpose of the Act (excluding any statutory modification thereof not in force when this regulation becomes binding on the company), connected with a director shall be treated as an interest of the director and, in relation to an alternate director, an interest of his appointor shall be treated as an interest of the alternate director without prejudice to any interest which the alternate director has otherwise.

95. A director shall not be counted in the quorum present at a meeting in relation to a resolution on which he is not entitled to vote.

96. The company may by ordinary resolution suspend or relax to any extent, either generally or in respect of any particular matter, any provision of the articles prohibiting a director from voting at a meeting of directors or of a committee of directors.

97. Where proposals are under consideration concerning the appointment of two or more directors to offices or employments with the company or any body corporate in which the company is interested the proposals may be divided and considered in relation to each director separately and (provided he is not for another reason precluded from voting) each of the directors concerned shall be entitled to vote and be counted in the quorum in respect of each resolution except that concerning his own appointment.

98. If a question arises at a meeting of directors or of a committee of directors as to the right of a director to vote, the question may, before the conclusion of the meeting, be referred to the chairman of the meeting and his ruling in relation to any director other than himself shall be final and conclusive.

Secretary

99. Subject to the provisions of the Act, the secretary shall be appointed by the directors for such term, at such remuneration and upon such conditions as they may think fit; and any secretary so appointed may be removed by them.

Minutes

100. The directors shall cause minutes to be made in books kept for the purpose—

(a) of all appointments of officers made by the directors; and

(b) of all proceedings at meetings of the company, of the holders of any class of shares in the company, and of the directors, and of committees of directors, including the names of the directors present at each such meeting.

The seal

101. The seal shall only be used by the authority of the directors or of a committee of directors authorised by the directors. The directors may determine who shall sign any instrument to which the seal is affixed and unless otherwise so determined it shall be signed by a director and by the secretary or by a second director.

Dividends

102. Subject to the provisions of the Act, the company may by ordinary resolution declare dividends in accordance with the respective rights of the members, but no dividend shall exceed the amount recommended by the directors.

103. Subject to the provisions of the Act, the directors may pay interim dividends if it appears to them that they are justified by the profits of the company available for distribution. If the share capital is divided into different classes, the directors may pay interim dividends on shares which confer deferred or non-preferred rights with regard to dividend as well as on shares which confer preferential rights with regard to dividend, but no interim dividend shall be paid on shares carrying deferred or non-preferred rights if, at the time of payment, any preferential dividend is in arrear. The directors may also pay at intervals settled by them any dividend payable at a fixed rate if it appears to them that the profits available for distribution justify the payment. Provided the directors act in good faith they shall not incur any liability to the holders of shares conferring preferred rights for any loss they may suffer by the lawful payment of an interim dividend on any shares having deferred or non-preferred rights.

104. Except as otherwise provided by the rights attached to shares, all dividends shall be declared and paid according to the amounts paid up on the shares on which the dividend is paid. All dividends shall be apportioned and paid proportionately to the amounts paid up on the shares during any portion or portions of the period in respect of which the dividend is paid; but, if any share is issued on terms providing that it shall rank for dividend as from a particular date, that share shall rank for dividend accordingly.

105. A general meeting declaring a dividend may, upon the recommendation of the directors, direct that it shall be satisfied wholly or partly by the distribution of assets and, where any difficulty arises in regard to the distribution, the directors may settle the same and in particular may issue fractional certificates and fix the value for distribution of any assets and may determine that cash shall be paid to any member upon the footing of the value so fixed in order to adjust the rights of members and may vest any assets in trustees.

106. Any dividend or other moneys payable in respect of a share may be paid by cheque sent by post to the registered address of the person entitled or, if two or more persons are the holders of the share or are jointly entitled to it by reason of the death or bankruptcy of the holder, to the registered address of that one of those persons who is first named in the register of members or to such person and to such address as the person or persons entitled may in writing direct. Every cheque shall be made payable to the order of the person or persons entitled or to such other person as the person or persons entitled may in writing direct and payment of the cheque shall be a good discharge to the company. Any joint holder or other person jointly entitled to a share as aforesaid may give receipts for any dividend or other moneys payable in respect of the share.

107. No dividend or other moneys payable in respect of a share shall bear interest against the company unless otherwise provided by the rights attached to the share.

108. Any dividend which has remained unclaimed for twelve years from the date when it became due for payment shall, if the directors so resolve, be forfeited and cease to remain owing by the company.

Accounts
109. No member shall (as such) have any right of inspecting any accounting records or other book or document of the company except as conferred by statute or authorised by the directors or by ordinary resolution of the company.

Capitalisation of profits
110. The directors may with the authority of an ordinary resolution of the company—

(a) subject as hereinafter provided, resolve to capitalise any undivided profits of the company not required for paying any preferential dividend (whether or not they are available for distribution) or any sum standing to the credit of the company's share premium account or capital redemption reserve;

(b) appropriate the sum resolved to be capitalised to the members who would have been entitled to it if it were distributed by way of dividend and in the same proportions and apply such sum on their behalf either in or towards paying up the amounts, if any, for the time being unpaid on any shares held by them respectively, or in paying up in full unissued shares or debentures of the company of a nominal amount equal to that sum, and allot the shares or debentures credited as fully paid to those members, or as they may direct, in those proportions, or partly in one way and partly in the other: but the share premium account, the capital redemption reserve, and any profits which are not available for distribution may, for the purposes of this regulation, only be applied in paying up unissued shares to be allotted to members credited as fully paid;

(c) make such provision by the issue of fractional certificates or by payment in cash or otherwise as they determine in the case of shares or debentures becoming distributable under this regulation in fractions; and

(d) authorise any person to enter on behalf of all the members concerned into an agreement with the company providing for the allotment to them respectively, credited as fully paid, of any shares or debentures to which they are entitled upon such capitalisation, any agreement made under such authority being binding on all such members.

Notices
111. Any notice to be given to or by any person pursuant to the articles (other than a notice calling a meeting of the directors) shall be in writing or shall be given using electronic communications to an address for the time being notified for that purpose to the person giving the notice.

In this regulation, 'address', in relation to electronic communications, includes any number or address used for the purposes of such communications.

112. The company may give any notice to a member either personally or by sending it by post in a prepaid envelope addressed to the member at his registered address or by leaving it at that address or by giving it using electronic communications to an address for the time being notified to the company by the member. In the case of joint holders of a share, all notices shall be given to the joint holder whose name stands first in the register of members in respect of the joint holding and notice so given shall be sufficient notice to all the joint holders. A member whose registered address is not within the United Kingdom and who gives to the company an address within the United Kingdom at which notices may be given to him, or an address to which notices may be sent using electronic communications, shall be entitled to have notices given to him at that address, but otherwise no such member shall be entitled to receive any notice from the company.

In this regulation and the next, 'address', in relation to electronic communications, includes any number or address used for the purposes of such communications.

113. A member present, either in person or by proxy, at any meeting of the company or of the holders of any class of shares in the company shall be deemed to have received notice of the meeting and, where requisite, of the purposes for which it was called.

114. Every person who becomes entitled to a share shall be bound by any notice in respect of that share which, before his name is entered in the register of members, has been duly given to a person from whom he derives his title.

115. Proof that an envelope containing a notice was properly addressed, prepaid and posted shall be conclusive evidence that the notice was given. Proof that a notice contained in an electronic communication was sent in accordance with guidance issued by the Institute of Chartered Secretaries and Administrators shall be conclusive evidence that the notice was given. A notice shall be deemed to be given at the expiration of 48 hours after the envelope containing it was posted or, in the case of a notice contained in an electronic communication, at the expiration of 48 hours after the time it was sent.

116. A notice may be given by the company to the persons entitled to a share in consequence of the death or bankruptcy of a member by sending or delivering it, in any manner authorised by the articles for the giving of notice to a member, addressed to them by name, or by the title of representatives of the deceased, or trustee of the bankrupt or by any like description at the address, if any, within the United Kingdom supplied for that purpose by the persons claiming to be so entitled. Until such an address has been supplied, a notice may be given in any manner in which it might have been given if the death or bankruptcy had not occurred.

Winding up

117. If the company is wound up, the liquidator may, with the sanction of an extraordinary resolution of the company and any other sanction required by the Act, divide among the members in specie the whole or any part of the assets of the company and may, for that purpose, value any assets and determine how the division shall be carried out as between the members or different classes of members. The liquidator may, with the like sanction, vest the whole or any part of the assets in trustees upon such trusts for the benefit of the members as he with the like sanction determines, but no member shall be compelled to accept any assets upon which there is a liability.

Indemnity

118. Subject to the provisions of the Act but without prejudice to any indemnity to which a director may otherwise be entitled, every director or other officer or auditor of the company shall be indemnified out of the assets of the company against any liability incurred by him in defending any proceedings, whether civil or criminal, in which judgment is given in his favour or in which he is acquitted or in connection with any application in which relief is granted to him by the court from liability for negligence, default, breach of duty or breach of trust in relation to the affairs of the company.

NOTE
The above text of Table A incorporates the amendments made by the Companies Act 1985 (Electronic Communications) Order 2000, which came into force on 22 December 2000.

It should also be reiterated that though the above 'traditional' 1985 form of Table A is currently used by many hundreds of thousands of existing companies, the reforms of 2006 will include a new plain English short form of articles suitable for small companies that can be used from the time they are put into effect by statutory instrument.

MINUTES OF FIRST BOARD MEETING OF SHELFCO LTD
SHELFCO LIMITED

Minutes of the first meeting of the directors of the Company held on 8th November 1994 at 10.00 am.

Present:	John Baker	Director
	Frederick Baker	"
	Michael Baker	"
	Charles Baker	"
In Attendance:	Richard Thomas	Secretary

1. Documents tabled

Copies of the following documents were tabled before the meeting:

1.1 Companies Forms 10 and 12 as submitted to the Registrar of Companies on incorporation;

1.2 the certificate of incorporation of the Company; and

1.3 the Memorandum and Articles of Association of the Company as registered.

2. First directors

It was noted that the following, each of whom had indicated a willingness to act by signing a Companies Form 10, were to be the first directors of the Company:

John Richard Baker

Frederick Maxwell Baker

Michael George Baker

Charles Guy Baker

3. Chairman

It was unanimously resolved that John Richard Baker be elected chairman of the Company, whereupon he took the chair of the meeting.

4. Directors' interests

Frederick Baker stated that he was a shareholder of BZ Building Services Limited and was to be considered as interested in any contracts, arrangements or dealings between the Company and BZ Building Services Limited.

5. Secretary

It was resolved that Richard Thomas, who had indicated his willingness to act by signing a Companies Form 288, be appointed as the secretary of the Company.

6. Common seal

It was resolved that the common seal, an impression of which is affixed below, be adopted as the common seal of the Company.

7. Registered office

It was resolved that the situation of the registered office of the Company as stated in the Companies Form 10 be ratified and confirmed.

8. Auditors

It was resolved that Bell, Cartwright & Co. be appointed auditors of the Company until the Company's first annual general meeting at a fee to be agreed with the directors.

9. Accounting reference date

It was resolved that the accounting reference date of the Company be fixed at 31 July and that the first accounts be made up to 31 July 1991.

10. Accounting records

It was resolved that the books of account of the Company be kept at the offices of Bell, Cartwright & Co. in compliance with the Companies Act 1985.

11. Bank account

11.1 It was resolved that a current account be opened with Barclays Bank PLC ('the Bank') at its branch at 27 High Street, Exeter, and that the account be operated by any two directors signing jointly for any amounts.

11.2 It was further resolved that the Bank's account opening forms, mandate and resolutions as tabled be executed and deemed to be an integral part of this resolution and incorporated herein.

12. Transfers of shares

It was resolved that, subject to stock transfer forms in respect thereof being duty stamped and presented to the Company for registration, the following transfers of ordinary shares of £1 each be approved:

Transferor	Transferee	Number of shares
Instant Companies Limited	John Richard Baker	1
Swift Incorporations Limited	Frederick Maxwell Baker	1

13. Acquisition of business

A draft agreement was produced to the meeting (for the purpose of identification initialled by the chairman) providing for the acquisition by the company of the existing business owned by J.R. Baker, F.M. Baker, M.G. Baker and C.G. Baker. It was resolved that the company enter into the agreement without amendment, subject to prior approval by a resolution of the company in general meeting under Companies Act 1985 s. 320.

14. It was resolved to call an extraordinary general meeting of the company to change its name to J.B. Baker & Co. Ltd., to increase the capital of the company and to propose the resolution referred to in minute 13 above.

15. Allotment of shares

15.1 The following letters of application for the number of shares indicated were tabled:

Applicant	No. and type of shares	Consideration
John Richard Baker	25,000 ordinary shares of £1	£25,000
Frederick Maxwell Baker	" " "	"
Michael George Baker	" " "	"
Charles Guy Baker	" " "	"

15.2 It was resolved that such applications be accepted and that, subject to increase of the company's authorised capital and to prior approval by the general meeting of the agreement referred to in minute 13 above for the transfer of the business to the company as consideration in kind for the issue of the shares, the names of the applicants be entered in the register of members for the number of shares stated.

16. Share certificates

Subject to the above conditions in respect of transfers and allotment being satisfied, it was resolved that the common seal be affixed to share certificates for the appropriate numbers of shares, that the same be signed by any one director and countersigned by the secretary and they be issued to the relevant transferees and allottees.

17. Numbering of shares

All shares in the Company presently in issue being fully paid up, it was resolved that, in accordance with Companies Act 1985, s. 182(2), none of the said shares in the Company need have a distinguishing number.

18. It was resolved to enter into the standard form Debenture with Barclays Bank, a copy of which was produced to the meeting for approval, providing security for the Company's overdraft and all indebtedness. It was resolved to affix the Company Seal to the Debenture and J.R. Baker and Richard Thomas were authorised to witness the affixture of the seal.

19. Conclusion

The secretary was instructed to file the necessary papers with the Registrar of Companies relating to the above and there being no further business, the meeting terminated.

J. R. Baker

Chairman of the meeting.

BANK DEBENTURE
DEBENTURE

Insert company's name as registered

1. J.B. Baker & Co. Limited

(hereinafter called 'the Company') whose registered office is at 73 Tiverton Road, Exeter EX7 5BZ.

will on demand in writing made to the Company pay or discharge to Barclays Bank PLC (hereinafter called 'the Bank') all moneys and liabilities which shall for the time being (and whether on or at any time after such demand) be due owing or incurred to the Bank by the Company whether actually or contingently and whether solely or jointly with any other person and whether as principal or surety and including interest discount commission or other lawful charges and expenses which the Bank may in the course of its business charge in respect of any of the matters aforesaid or for keeping the Company's account and so that interest shall be computed and compounded according to the usual mode of the Bank as well after as before any demand made or judgment obtained hereunder.

2. A demand for payment or any other demand or notice under this Debenture may be made or given by any manager or officer of the Bank or of any branch thereof by letter addressed to the Company and sent by post to or left at the registered office of the Company or its last known place of business and if sent by post shall be deemed to have been made or given at noon on the day following the day the letter was posted.

3. The Company as beneficial owner hereby charges with the payment or discharge of all moneys and liabilities hereby covenanted to be paid or discharged by the Company:—

(a) by way of legal mortgage all the freehold and leasehold property of the Company the title to which is registered at H.M. Land Registry and which is described in the Schedule hereto together with all buildings fixtures (including trade fixtures) and fixed plant and machinery from time to time thereon;

(b) by way of legal mortgage all other freehold and leasehold property of the Company now vested in it (whether or not registered at H.M. Land Registry) together with all buildings fixtures (including trade fixtures) and fixed plant and machinery from time to time thereon;

(c) by way of first fixed charge all future freehold and leasehold property of the Company together with all buildings fixtures (including trade fixtures) and faxed plant and machinery from time to time thereon and all the goodwill and uncalled capital for the time being of the Company;

(d) by way of first fixed charge all book debts and other debts now and from time to time due or owing to the Company;

(e) by way of a first floating charge all other the undertaking and assets of the Company whatsoever and wheresoever both present and future but so that the Company is not to be at liberty to create any mortgage or charge upon and so that no lien shall in any case or in any manner arise on or affect any part of the said premises either in priority to or *pari passu* with the charge hereby created and further that the Company shall have no power without the consent of the Bank to part with or dispose of any part of such premises except by way of sale in the ordinary course of its business.

Any debentures mortgages or charges hereafter created by the Company (otherwise than in favour of the Bank) shall be expressed to be subject to this Debenture. The Company shall subject to the rights of any prior mortgagee deposit with the Bank and the Bank during the continuance of this security shall be entitled to hold all deeds and documents of title relating to the Company's freehold and leasehold property for the time being and the Company shall on demand in writing made to the Company by the Bank at the cost of the Company execute a valid legal mortgage of any freehold and leasehold properties acquired by it after the date hereof and the fixed plant and machinery thereon to secure the payment or discharge to the Bank of the moneys and liabilities hereby secured such legal mortgage to be in such form as the Bank may require.

4. This security shall be a continuing security to the Bank notwithstanding any settlement of account or other matter or thing whatsoever and shall be without prejudice and in addition to any other security whether by way of mortgage equitable charge or otherwise howsoever which the Bank may now or any time hereafter hold on the property of the Company or any part thereof for or in respect of the moneys hereby secured or any of them or any part thereof respectively.

5. During the continuance of this security the Company:—

(a) shall furnish to the Bank copies of the trading and profit and loss account and audited balance sheet in respect of each financial year of the Company and of every subsidiary thereof forthwith upon the same becoming available and not in any event later than the expiration of three months from the end of such financial year and also from time to time such other financial statements and information respecting the assets and liabilities of the Company as the Bank may reasonably require;

(b) shall maintain the aggregate value of the Company's book debts (excluding debts owing by any subsidiary of the Company) and cash in hand as appearing in the Company's books and of its stock according to the best estimate that can be formed without it being necessary to take stock for the purpose at a sum to be fixed by the Bank from time to time and whenever required by the Bank obtain from the Managing Director of the Company for the time being or if there shall be no Managing Director then from one of the Directors of the Company and furnish to the Bank a certificate showing the said aggregate value;

(c) shall pay into the Company's account with the Bank all moneys which it may receive in respect of the book debts and other debts hereby charged and shall not without the prior consent of the Bank in writing purport to charge or assign the same in favour of any other person and shall if called upon to do so by the Bank execute a legal assignment of such book debts and other debts to the Bank;

(d) shall insure and keep insured with an insurance office or underwriters to be approved by the Bank in writing from time to time and if so required by the Bank in the joint names of the Company and the Bank such of its property as is insurable against loss or damage by fire and such other risks as the Bank may from time to time require to the full replacement value thereof and shall maintain such other insurances as are normally maintained by prudent companies carrying on similar businesses and will duly pay all premiums and other moneys necessary for effecting and keeping up such insurances within one week of the same becoming due and will on demand produce to the Bank thc policies of such insurance and the receipts for such payments and if default shall at any time be made by the Company in effecting or keeping up such insurance as aforesaid or in producing any such policy or receipt to the Bank on demand the Bank may take out or renew such insurances in any sum which the Bank may think expedient And all moneys expended by the Bank under this provision shall be deemed to be properly paid by the Bank;

(e) shall keep all buildings and all plant machinery fixtures fittings and other effects; in or upon the same and every part thereof in good repair and in good working order and condition.

6. (a) At any time after the Bank shall have demanded payment of any moneys hereby secured or if a petition shall be presented to the court under section 9 of the Insolvency Act 1986 for the making of an administration order in respect of the Company or if requested by the Company the Bank may appoint by writing any person or persons (whether an officer of the Bank or not) to be a receiver and manager or receivers and managers (hereinafter called 'the Receiver' which expression shall where the context so admits include the plural and any substituted receiver and manager or receivers and managers) of all or any part of the property hereby charged.

(b) Where two or more persons are appointed to be the Receiver any act required or authorised under any enactment this Debenture (including the power of attorney in clause 7 hereof) or otherwise to be done by the Receiver may be done by any one or more of them unless the Bank shall in such appointment specify to the contrary.

(c) The Bank may from time to time determine the remuneration of the Receiver and may remove the Receiver and appoint another in his place.

(d) The Receiver shall be the agent of the Company (which subject to the provisions of the Insolvency Act 1986 shall alone be personally liable for his acts defaults and remuneration) and shall have and be entitled to exercise all powers conferred by the Law of Property Act 1925 in the same way as if the Receiver had been duly appointed thereunder and in particular by way of addition to but without hereby limiting any general powers hereinbefore referred to (and without prejudice to the Bank's power of sale) the Receiver shall have power to do the following things namely:—

(i) to take possession of collect and get in all or any part of the property hereby charged and for that purpose to take any proceedings in the name of the Company or otherwise as he shall think fit;

(ii) to carry on or concur in carrying on the business of the Company and to raise money from the Bank or others on the security of any property hereby charged;

    (iii)   to sell or concur in selling let or concur in letting and to terminate or to accept surrenders of leases or tenancies of any of the property hereby charged in such manner and generally on such terms and conditions as he shall think fit and to carry any such transactions into effect in the name of and on behalf of the Company;

    (iv)   to make any arrangement or compromise which the Bank or he shall think fit;

    (v)   to make and effect all repairs improvements and insurances;

    (vi)   to appoint managers officers and agents for the aforesaid purposes at such salaries as he may determine;

    (vii)   to call up all or any portion of the uncalled capital of the Company;

    (viii) to do all such other acts and things as may be considered to be incidental or conducive to any of the matters or powers aforesaid and which he lawfully may or can do.

7. The Company hereby irrevocably appoints the Bank and the Receiver jointly and also severally the Attorney and Attorneys of the Company for the Company and in its name and on its behalf and as its act and deed or otherwise to seal and deliver and otherwise perfect any deed assurance agreement instrument or act which may be required or may be deemed proper for any of the purposes aforesaid and the Company hereby declares that as and when the security hereby created shall become enforceable the Company will hold all the property hereby charged (subject to the Company's right of redemption) upon Trust to convey assign or otherwise deal with the same in such manner and to such person as the Bank shall direct and declares that it shall be lawful for the Bank by an instrument under its Common Seal to appoint a new trustee or new trustees of the said property and in particular at any time or times to appoint a new trustee or new trustee thereof in place of the Company as if the Company desired to be discharged from the trust or in place of any trustee or trustees appointed under this power as if he or they were dead.

8. Any moneys received under the powers hereby conferred shall subject to the repayment of any claims having priority to this Debenture be paid or applied in the following order of priority:—

    (a) in satisfaction of all costs charges and expenses properly incurred and payments properly made by the Bank or the Receiver and of the remuneration of the Receiver;

    (b) in or towards satisfaction of the moneys outstanding and secured by this Debenture;

    (c) as to the surplus (if any) to the person or persons entitled thereto.

9. During the continuance of this security no statutory or other power of granting or agreeing to grant or of accepting or agreeing to accept surrenders of leases or tenancies of the freehold and leasehold property hereby charged or any part thereof shall be capable of being exercised by the Company without the previous consent in writing of the Bank nor shall section 93 of the Law of Property Act 1925 dealing with the consolidation of mortgages apply to this security.

10. Section 103 of the said Act shall not apply to this security but the statutory power of sale shall as between the Bank and a purchaser from the Bank arise on

and be exercisable at any time after the execution of this security provided that the Bank shall not exercise the said power of sale until payment of the moneys hereby secured has been demanded or the Receiver has been appointed but this proviso shall not affect a purchaser or put him upon inquiry whether such demand or appointment has been made.

11. All costs charges and expenses incurred hereunder by the Bank and all other moneys paid by the Bank or by the Receiver in perfecting or otherwise in connection with this security or in respect of the property hereby charged including (without prejudice to the generality of the foregoing) all moneys expended by the Bank under clause 5 hereof and all costs of the Bank or of the Receiver of all proceedings for the enforcement of the security hereby constituted or for obtaining payment of the moneys hereby secured or arising out of or in connection with the acts authorised by clause 6 hereof (and so that any taxation of the Banks costs charges and expenses shall be on a full indemnity basis) shall be recoverable from the Company as a debt and may be debited to any account of the Company and shall bear interest accordingly and shall be charged on the premises comprised herein and the charge hereby conferred shall be in addition and without prejudice to any and every other remedy lien or security which the Bank may or but for the said charge would have for the moneys hereby secured or any part thereof.

12. In respect of any freehold or leasehold property hereby charged the title to which is registered at H.M. Land Registry it is hereby certified that the charge created by this Debenture does not contravene any of the provisions of the Memorandum and Articles of Association of the Company.

13. In this Debenture where the context so admits the expression 'the Bank' shall include persons deriving title under the Bank and any reference herein to any statute or any section of any statute shall be deemed to include reference to any statutory modification or re-enactment thereof for the time being in force.

IN WITNESS whereof the Company has executed these presents as a deed this Fifteenth day of November 1994

The Schedule above referred to
Details of registered land.

County/London Borough	Title No.	Address of Property
Mid-Devon	DS 4273	Land at West End Road, Silverton, Devon.

2

The Incorporation of Companies

2.1 TYPES OF COMPANY

The original objective of company law was to allow a group of 'promoters' wanting to raise money for a big business venture such as railway construction to incorporate a 'limited liability company' and then to invite wealthy members of the public to invest in the enterprise by subscribing for shares in the company. As passive investors, these shareholders would generally take no part in management but they could safely invest a limited sum as they would enjoy limited liability. To reflect the fact that this would be a collective or 'company' of people, companies were at first required to have a minimum of seven members, while 'private companies' were in later years allowed a minimum of two. It was the very nature of things that human proprietors of companies should not be solitary and reflecting Oscar Wilde, that two is company but one is none.

However, the leading case of *Salomon v A. Salomon and Co. Ltd.* (see chapter 3), held as early as 1897 that one person could in substance validly incorporate and solely 'own' a company by putting some of his shares into the names of nominees to make up the required minimum number of members. This device soon became commonplace as companies were increasingly used for smaller and smaller businesses. Things came full circle when in 1992 the Twelfth EC Company Law Directive was implemented allowing a single member to incorporate a private company. Now the new s. 7 of the Companies Act 2006 likewise says that one or more persons may form a company.

The types of company that can be formed appear from the following sections reproduced below. The typical company trading for profit is a company limited by shares, a tiny proportion of which are public companies. Public companies are required to have a minimum share capital and private companies are prohibited from raising capital by offering their shares to the public. (This prohibition is in CA 2006, s. 755, printed at 17.1 below.) It has been common for non-profit organisations such as charities to be companies limited by guarantee but they now may take the form of the new community enterprise company.

The following brief extracts from the Companies Act 2006 define the various types of companies.

COMPANIES ACT 2006, PARTS 1 AND 2

3. Limited and unlimited companies

(1) A company is a "limited company" if the liability of its members is limited by its constitution. It may be limited by shares or limited by guarantee.

(2) If their liability is limited to the amount, if any, unpaid on the shares held by them, the company is "limited by shares".

(3) If their liability is limited to such amount as the members undertake to contribute to the assets of the company in the event of its being wound up, the company is "limited by guarantee".

(4) If there is no limit on the liability of its members, the company is an "unlimited company".

4. Private and public companies

(1) A "private company" is any company that is not a public company.

(2) A "public company" is a company limited by shares or limited by guarantee and having a share capital—

(a) whose certificate of incorporation states that it is a public company, and

(b) in relation to which the requirements of this Act, or the former Companies Acts, as to registration or re-registration as a public company have been complied with on or after the relevant date.

(3) For the purposes of subsection (2)(b) the relevant date is—

(a) in relation to registration or re-registration in Great Britain, 22nd December 1980;

(b) in relation to registration or re-registration in Northern Ireland, 1st July 1983.

(4) For the two major differences between private and public companies, see Part 20.

5. Companies limited by guarantee and having share capital

(1) A company cannot be formed as, or become, a company limited by guarantee with a share capital.

6. Community interest companies

(1) In accordance with Part 2 of the Companies (Audit, Investigations and Community Enterprise) Act 2004 (c. 27)—

(a) a company limited by shares or a company limited by guarantee and not having a share capital may be formed as or become a community interest company, and

(b) a company limited by guarantee and having a share capital may become a community interest company.

(2) The other provisions of the Companies Acts have effect subject to that Part.

761. Public company: requirement as to minimum share capital

(1) A company that is a public company (otherwise than by virtue of reregistration as a public company) must not do business or exercise any borrowing powers unless the registrar has issued it with a certificate under this section (a "trading certificate").

(2) The registrar shall issue a trading certificate if, on an application made in accordance with section 762, he is satisfied that the nominal value of the company's allotted share capital is not less than the authorised minimum.

763. The authorised minimum

(1) "The authorised minimum", in relation to the nominal value of a public company's allotted share capital is—

(a) £50,000, or

(b) the prescribed euro equivalent.

(2) The Secretary of State may by order prescribe the amount in euros that is for the time being to be treated as equivalent to the sterling amount of the authorised minimum.

(3) This power may be exercised from time to time as appears to the Secretary of State to be appropriate.

(4) The amount prescribed shall be determined by applying an appropriate spot rate of exchange to the sterling amount and rounding to the nearest 100 euros.

(5) An order under this section is subject to negative resolution procedure.

(6) This section has effect subject to any exercise of the power conferred by section 764 (power to alter authorised minimum).

2.2 THE RIGHT TO INCORPORATE

The effect of the legislation is that if the documents required for incorporation of a lawful company together with the necessary fee are delivered to Companies House, the Registrar must incorporate the company. A certificate of incorporation is issued as the 'birth' certificate of the company, showing the date of incorporation, the company name and registered number. While the name can be changed at any time, the number is permanent. The certificate is conclusive evidence that the company is properly formed. In an exceptional case extracted below, registration of a company formed for the business of prostitution was quashed.

COMPANIES ACT 2006, PARTS 1 AND 2

7. Method of forming company

(1) A company is formed under this Act by one or more persons—
    (a) subscribing their names to a memorandum of association (see section 8), and
    (b) complying with the requirements of this Act as to registration (see sections 9 to 13).
(2) A company may not be so formed for an unlawful purpose.

8. Memorandum of association

(1) A memorandum of association is a memorandum stating that the subscribers—
    (a) wish to form a company under this Act, and
    (b) agree to become members of the company and, in the case of a company that is to have a share capital, to take at least one share each.
(2) The memorandum must be in the prescribed form and must be authenticated by each subscriber.

Requirements for registration

9. Registration documents

(1) The memorandum of association must be delivered to the registrar together with an application for registration of the company, the documents required by this section and a statement of compliance.
(2) The application for registration must state—
    (a) the company's proposed name,
    (b) whether the company's registered office is to be situated in England and Wales (or in Wales), in Scotland or in Northern Ireland,
    (c) whether the liability of the members of the company is to be limited, and if so whether it is to be limited by shares or by guarantee, and
    (d) whether the company is to be a private or a public company.
(3) If the application is delivered by a person as agent for the subscribers to the memorandum of association, it must state his name and address.
(4) The application must contain—
    (a) in the case of a company that is to have a share capital, a statement of capital and initial shareholdings (see section 10);
    (b) in the case of a company that is to be limited by guarantee, a statement of guarantee (see section 11);
    (c) a statement of the company's proposed officers (see section 12).
(5) The application must also contain—
    (a) a statement of the intended address of the company's registered office; and
    (b) a copy of any proposed articles of association (to the extent that these are not supplied by the default application of model articles: see section 20).

(6) The application must be delivered—
 (a) to the registrar of companies for England and Wales, if the registered office of the company is to be situated in England and Wales (or in Wales);
 (b) to the registrar of companies for Scotland, if the registered office of the company is to be situated in Scotland;
 (c) to the registrar of companies for Northern Ireland, if the registered office of the company is to be situated in Northern Ireland.

14. Registration

If the registrar is satisfied that the requirements of this Act as to registration are complied with, he shall register the documents delivered to him.

15. Issue of certificate of incorporation

(1) On the registration of a company, the registrar of companies shall give a certificate that the company is incorporated.
(2) The certificate must state—
 (a) the name and registered number of the company,
 (b) the date of its incorporation,
 (c) whether it is a limited or unlimited company, and if it is limited whether it is limited by shares or limited by guarantee,
 (d) whether it is a private or a public company, and
 (e) whether the company's registered office is situated in England and Wales (or in Wales), in Scotland or in Northern Ireland.
(3) The certificate must be signed by the registrar or authenticated by the registrar's official seal.
(4) The certificate is conclusive evidence that the requirements of this Act as to registration have been complied with and that the company is duly registered under this Act.

16. Effect of registration

(1) The registration of a company has the following effects as from the date of incorporation.
(2) The subscribers to the memorandum, together with such other persons as may from time to time become members of the company, are a body corporate by the name stated in the certificate of incorporation.
(3) That body corporate is capable of exercising all the functions of an incorporated company.
(4) The status and registered office of the company are as stated in, or in connection with, the application for registration.
(5) In the case of a company having a share capital, the subscribers to the memorandum become holders of the shares specified in the statement of capital and initial shareholdings.
(6) The persons named in the statement of proposed officers—
 (a) as director, or
 (b) as secretary or joint secretary of the company,
 are deemed to have been appointed to that office.

R v *Registrar of Companies, ex parte Attorney-General*

Miss Whiplash and Hookers Ltd

[1991] BCLC 476, Queen's Bench Divisional Court

Facts   In this application heard in 1980 (but not reported until 1991) the Attorney-General successfully applied for an order to quash the incorporation of Lindi St Claire (Personal Services) Ltd which had been set up 'to carry on the business of prostitution'.

ACKNER LJ: This application has many of the indicia that one might expect to find in a student's end-of-term moot. It appears indirectly to have been stimulated by the action of the Policy Division of the Inland Revenue.

The Attorney-General applies to quash the incorporation and registration by the Registrar of Companies nearly a year ago, that is on 18 December 1979, of Lindi St Claire (Personal Services) Ltd as a limited company under the provisions of the Companies Acts 1948 to 1976.

The grounds of the application, to state them quite briefly, are these. In certifying the incorporation of a company and in registering the same the Registrar of Companies acted *ultra vires* or misdirected himself or otherwise erred in law, in particular as to the proper construction and application of s. 1(1) of the Companies Act 1948 [see now CA 2006 s. 7(2)] in that the company was not formed for any lawful purpose but, on the contrary, was formed expressly with the primary object of carrying on the business of prostitution, such being an unlawful purpose involving the commission of acts which are immoral and contrary to public policy.

The first point to consider is the validity of the procedure which has been adopted in this case, that is by way of application for judicial review, such application being made by the Attorney-General.

Section 15 of the Companies Act 1948 [see now CA 2006, s.15(4)] provides:

> (1) A certificate of incorporation given by the registrar in respect of any association shall be conclusive evidence that all the requirements of this Act in respect of registration and of matters precedent and incidental thereto have been complied with, and that the association is a company authorised to be registered and duly registered under this Act.

That on the face of it would appear to be a difficulty in the way of this application, but the matter was dealt with in the case of *Bowman* v *Secular Society Ltd* [1917] AC 406. In that case the Secular Society was registered as a company limited by guarantee under the Companies Acts 1862 to 1893. The question which there had to be considered was whether its objects were legal, criminal or otherwise such that the company should not be registered.

The matter of procedure was dealt with by Lord Parker in his speech in these terms ([1917] AC 406 at p. 439):

> My lords, some stress was laid on the public danger, or at any rate the anomaly, of the courts recognising the corporate existence of a company all of whose objects, as specified in its memorandum of association, are transparently illegal. Such a case is not likely to occur, for the registrar fulfils a quasi-judicial function, and his duty is to determine whether an association applying for registration is authorised to be registered under the Acts. Only by misconduct or great carelessness on the part of the registrar could a company with objects wholly illegal obtain registration. If such a case did occur it would be open to the court to stay its hand until an opportunity had been given for taking the appropriate steps for the cancellation of the certificate of registration. It should be observed that neither s. 1 of the Companies Act 1900, nor the corresponding section of the Companies (Consolidation) Act 1908, is so expressed as to bind the Crown, and the Attorney-General, on behalf of the Crown, could institute proceedings by way of certiorari to cancel a registration which the registrar in affected discharge of his quasi-judicial duties had improperly or erroneously allowed.

Then he deals with the instant case.

That view was expressly accepted in his speech by Lord Dunedin and was referred to by Lord Buckmaster in shorter terms at the conclusion of his speech (see [1917] AC 406 at p. 478). So clearly the Attorney-General is entitled to bring these proceedings.

Now as to the facts, these come within a very short compass and they amount to the following. A firm of certified accountants, Gilson Clipp & Co., on 16 August 1979 wrote to the Registrar of Companies at Companies House, Crown Way, Maindy, Cardiff pointing out that they had received a letter from the Inland Revenue Policy Division, who stated that they considered prostitution to be a trade which is fully taxable, and that they, the certified accountants, saw no reason why their client should not be able to organise her business by way of a limited company. They asked whether the name 'Prostitute Ltd' was available for registration as a limited company, pointing out the main object of the company would be that of organising the services of a prostitute.

The registrar did not like that name and did not accept it, nor did he accept another name 'Hookers Ltd' which was offered. But subsequently two further names were offered, 'Lindi St Claire (Personal Services) Ltd' and 'Lindi St Claire (French Lessons) Ltd', and it was the former which he registered.

The memorandum of association said in terms that the first of the objects of the company was 'To carry on the business of prostitution'.

The only director of the company is Lindi St Claire, Miss St Claire describing herself specifically as 'prostitute'. The other person who owns also one share is a Miss Duggan, who is referred to as 'the cashier'.

Leave having been obtained to apply for judicial review, Miss St Claire wrote in these terms:

> I would like to say that prostitution is not at all unlawful, as you have stated, and I feel it is most unfair of you to take this view, especially when I am paying income tax on my earnings from prostitution to the government Inland Revenue.
>
> Furthermore, I feel it is most unfair of you to imply that I have acted wrongly, as I was most explicit to all concerned about the sole trade of the company to be that of prostitution and nothing more. If my company should not be deemed valid, then it should have not been granted in the first place by the Board of Trade. It is most unfair of the government to allow me to go ahead with my company one moment, then quash it the next.

In regard to that paragraph Miss St Claire is perfectly right that she was most explicit to all concerned as to the trade of the company, and in that paragraph she confirms that it was the sole trade of the company. Mr Simon Brown on behalf of the Attorney-General, concedes that, if the company should not be deemed valid, then it should not have been registered in the first place by the Board of Trade, and therefore the issue with which we are concerned is the validity of the registration.

That takes us to s. 1(1) of the Companies Act 1948, and I need only read that subsection:

> Any seven or more persons, or, where the company to be formed will be a private company, any two or more persons, associated for any lawful purpose may, by subscribing their names to a memorandum of association and otherwise complying with the requirements of this Act in respect of registration, form an incorporated company, with or without limited liability.

It is well settled that a contract which is made upon a sexually immoral consideration or for a sexually immoral purpose is against public policy and is illegal and unenforceable. The fact that it does not involve or may not involve the commission of a criminal offence in no way prevents the contract being illegal, being against public policy and therefore being unenforceable. Here, as the documents clearly indicate, the association is for the purpose of carrying on a trade which involves illegal contracts because the purpose is a sexually immoral purpose and as such against public policy.

Mr Simon Brown submits that if that is the position, as indeed it clearly is on the authorities, then the association of the two or more persons cannot be for 'any lawful purpose'.

To my mind this must follow. It is implicit in the speeches in the *Bowman* case to which I have just made reference. In my judgment, the contention of the Attorney-General is a valid one and I would order that the registration be therefore quashed.

2.3 PRE-INCORPORATION CONTRACTS

At common law a contract purported to be made by a company before the date of its incorporation is of no effect and the company cannot adopt or ratify that contract when it is actually incorporated. Implementing the First Company Law Directive, the European Communities Act 1972, s. 9(2), provided that an agent who purported to make the contract for the unformed company may be held liable on the contract. (See now CA 2006, s. 51 at 2.3.3 below.)

In practice today the problem is less acute because companies can be bought off the shelf from company incorporation agents and the time taken by the Companies Registry to process papers for incorporation is very quick. Nonetheless, the majority of companies are still bought off the shelf.

2.3.1 The old common law

Kelner v *Baxter*

Who pays for the wine?

(1866) LR 2 CP 174, Court of Common Pleas

A company before incorporation is non-existent and may not be a party to a contract either initially or by later adopting it, but the agent who acted may be liable on the contract.

Facts   Kelner sold wine to Baxter and others who were described as acting 'on behalf of the proposed Gravesend Royal Alexandra Hotel Company, Limited'. The wine was delivered and used but when the company failed, Kelner successfully sued Baxter personally.

ERLE CJ: I agree that if the Gravesend Royal Alexandra Hotel Company had been an existing company at this time, the persons who signed the agreement would have signed as agents of the company. But, as there was no company in existence at the time, the agreement would be wholly inoperative unless it were held to be binding on the defendants personally. The cases referred to in the course of the argument fully bear out the proposition that, where a contract is signed by one who professes to be signing 'as agent', but who has no principal existing at the time, and the contract would be altogether inoperative unless binding upon the person who signed it, he is bound thereby: and a stranger cannot by a subsequent ratification relieve him from that responsibility. When the company came afterwards into existence it was a totally new creature, having rights and obligations from that time, but no rights or obligations by reason of anything which might have been done before. It was once, indeed, thought that an inchoate liability might be incurred on behalf of a proposed company, which would become binding on it when subsequently formed: but that notion was manifestly contrary to the principles upon which the law of contract is founded. There must be two parties to a contract; and the rights and obligations which it creates cannot be transferred by one of them to a third person who was not in a condition to be bound by it at the time it was made. The history of this company makes this construction to my mind perfectly clear. It was no doubt the notion of all the parties that success was certain: but the plaintiff parted with his stock upon the faith of the defendants' engagement that the price agreed on should be paid on the day named. It cannot be supposed that he for a moment contemplated that the payment was to be contingent on the formation of the company by 28 February. The paper expresses in terms a contract to buy. And it is a cardinal rule that no oral evidence shall be admitted to show an intention different from that which appears on the face of the writing. I come, therefore, to the conclusion that the defendants, having no principal who was bound originally, or who could become so by a subsequent ratification, were themselves bound, and that the oral evidence offered is not admissible to contradict the written contract.

Newborne v *Sensolid (Great Britain) Ltd*

The unborn company

[1954] 1 QB 45, Court of Appeal

In this case an agent was held to have no right to sue personally under a contract made by him in the name of his unformed company.

Facts   Tinned ham was sold to Sensolid under a contract headed Leopold Newborne (London) Ltd, ending 'Yours faithfully, Leopold Newborne (London) Ltd' and illegibly signed by Leopold Newborne. Sensolid refused to take and pay for the ham arguing successfully that neither the then unincorporated company nor Mr Newborne personally could sue.

LORD GODDARD CJ: Mr Diplock, who has argued the case for the plaintiff, bringing to our attention every point which could possibly be taken, has contended that it is governed by well-known series of cases of which *Kelner* v *Baxter* (1866) LR 2 CP 174 is one of the earliest and perhaps the best known. That was a case in which one Kelner sold wine intending to sell it to a company which was to be formed. The contract showed that it was agreed to be sold to certain men who were the proposed directors of a company which was coming into existence. They agreed to buy. The potential directors intended to buy the wine on behalf of the company, but the company was not in existence at the time the contract was made or at the time when the goods were delivered. They took delivery of the goods and, therefore, it was held that as they had contracted on behalf of a principal who did not exist they must, having received the wine, pay for it. That decision seems to me to stop far short of holding that every time an alleged company purports to contract—when there is no company in existence—everybody who is signing for the company is making himself personally liable.

Mr Diplock has also relied strongly on *Schmaltz* v *Avery* (1851) 16 QB 655, which lays down a principle, which has been acted on in other cases, notably in *Harper & Co.* v *Vigers Bros* [1909] 2 KB 549, that where a person purports to contract as agent he may nevertheless disclose himself as being in truth a principal. If he entered into a contract as agent he can bring an action in his own name and show that he was in fact the principal. All those cases are well established and we are not departing in any way from those decisions any more than did Parker J. What we cannot find in this case is that Mr Newborne ever purported to contract to sell as agent or as principal. The contract was one which he was making for the company, and although Mr Diplock has argued that in signing as he did Mr Newborne must have signed as agent, since the company could only contract through agents, that was not really the true position.

The company makes the contract. No doubt the company must do its physical acts, and so forth, through the directors, but it is not the ordinary case of principal and agent. It is a case in which the company is contracting and the company's contract is authenticated by the signature of one of the directors. This contract purports to be a contract by the company; it does not purport to be a contract by Mr Newborne. He does not purport to be selling his goods but to be selling the company's goods. The only person who had any contract here was the company, and Mr Newborne's signature merely confirmed the company's signature. The document is signed 'Yours faithfully, Leopold Newborne (London) Ltd', and then the signature underneath is the signature of the person authorised to sign on behalf of the company.

In my opinion, unfortunate though it may be, as the company was not in existence when the contract was signed there never was a contract, and Mr Newborne cannot come forward and say: 'Well, it was my contract'. The fact is, he made a contract for a company which did not exist. It seems to me, therefore, that the defendants can avail themselves of the defence which they pleaded and the appeal must be dismissed.

2.3.2 Proposals for reform

The Jenkins Report of 1962 (para. 44 quoted below) recommended that the agent who acted for the unformed company should be liable personally on the contract. However, once incorporated the company should be able to adopt the contract unilaterally. At this point the agent would drop out. Such a proposal was inserted as clause 6 of the Companies Bill 1973, but the Bill fell with the defeat of the government. Under the current law the agent is now liable but the idea of allowing the company to adopt the contract has not been revived.

Report of the Company Law Committee
(Cmnd 1749) (London: HMSO, 1962)

Pre-incorporation contracts

44. It frequently happens that a person engaged in forming a company has the company's note-paper printed and orders supplies thereon prior to the incorporation of the company. Under the present law, the company when formed cannot unilaterally adopt the resulting contracts, but must make a new contract with the parties concerned (*Kelner* v *Baxter* (1866) LR 2 CP 174). The unsatisfactory position of a person contracting with another acting on behalf of a company not yet formed is shown by a recent decision in *Newborne* v *Sensolid (Great Britain) Ltd* [1954] 1 QB 45. According to this case if the order was signed (as it normally would be), in the name of the company, the individual concerned adding his name as 'director', he cannot sue or be sued on the contract, which is a complete nullity. This may enable either the supplier or the company and those engaged in its formation, to refuse to honour their undertakings should a change in market conditions make it profitable for them to do so. We regard this as obviously undesirable. We also consider it anomalous that the enforceability of the contract should depend on subtle differences in the terminology employed; for example, if the order is signed not 'X and Co. Ltd., X director' but 'X director as agent for X & Co. Ltd', it appears that X can sue or be sued on the contract (*Kelner* v *Baxter*). We think that the Act should provide, as do some Commonwealth Acts, that a company may unilaterally adopt contracts which purport to be made on its behalf or in its name prior to incorporation and thereby become a party to the same extent as if the contract had been entered into after incorporation. We also think that, unless and until the company does so adopt such contracts, the persons who purported to act for the company should be entitled to sue and liable to be sued thereon.

2.3.3 The new legislation

First EEC Company Law Directive, art. 7

If, before a company being formed has acquired legal personality, action has been carried out in its name and the company does not assume the obligations arising from such action, the persons who acted shall, without limit, be jointly and severally liable therefor unless otherwise agreed.

This was implemented by the European Communities Act 1972, s. 9(2) and is currently in effect as Companies Act 2006, s. 51.

Companies Act 2006, s. 51(1)

51. Pre-incorporation contracts

(1) A contract that purports to be made by or on behalf of a company at a time when the company has not been formed has effect, subject to any agreement to the contrary, as one made with the person purporting to act for the company or as agent for it, and he is personally liable on the contract accordingly.

2.3.4 Recent cases

Phonogram Ltd **v** *Lane*
Cheap, Mean and Nasty
[1982] QB 938, Court of Appeal

This case examined the apparent distinctions in earlier cases based on how the person acting for the company signs the contract documents. Can the form of signature alone decide whether the signer is personally liable or whether only the company is party to the contract? These distinctions are now discredited. Further, any exclusion of personal liability must be clearly expressed.

Facts   A group of pop artists intended to perform under the name 'Cheap Mean and Nasty' and to form a company for the purpose to be called Fragile Management Ltd. Mr Lane accepted a cheque from Phonogram for £6,000 signing his name 'for and on behalf of Fragile Management Ltd'. The money was to be used to finance production of an LP and was repayable if this was not achieved. When the LP was not produced, Phonogram sought to recover the money from Lane, the company being non-existent at the time of the contract.

LORD DENNING MR: That brings me to the second point. What does 'purports' mean in this context? Mr Thompson suggests that there must be a representation that the company is already in existence. I do not agree. A contract can purport to be made on behalf of a company, or by a company, even though that company is known by both parties not to be formed and that it is only about to be formed.

The third point made by Mr Thompson was that a company can be 'a person' within the second line of s. 9(2) [of the European Communities Act 1972]. Mr Thompson says that Jelly Music Ltd was 'a person' which was purporting to contract on behalf of Fragile Management Ltd. I do not agree. Jelly Music Ltd were not entering into a contract. Mr Lane was purporting to do so.

So all three of Mr Thompson's points fail.

But I would not leave the matter there. This is the first time the section has come before us. It will have much impact on the common law. I am afraid that before 1972 the common law had adopted some fine distinctions. As I understand *Kelner* v *Baxter* (1866) LR 2 CP 174 it decided that, if a person contracted on behalf of a company which was nonexistent, he himself would be liable on the contract. Just as, if a man signs a contract for and on behalf 'of his horses', he is personally liable. But, since that case was decided, a number of distinctions have been introduced by *Hollman* v *Pullin* (1884) Cab & Ell 254; *Newborne* v *Sensolid (Great Britain) Ltd* [1954] 1 QB 45 and *Black* v *Smallwood* (1965) 117 CLR 52 in the High Court of Australia. Those three cases seem to suggest that there is a distinction to be drawn according to the way in which an agent signs a contract. If he signs it as 'agent for "X" company'—or 'for and on behalf of "X" company'—and there is no such body as 'X' company, then he himself can be sued upon it. On the other hand, if he signs it as 'X' company *per pro.* himself the managing director, then the position may be different: because he is not contracting personally as an agent. It is the company which is contracting.

That distinction was disliked by Windeyer J in *Black* v *Smallwood*. It has been criticised by Professor Treitel in *The Law of Contract*, 5th ed. (1979), p. 559. In my opinion, the distinction has been obliterated by s. 9(2) of the European Communities Act 1972. We now have the clear words, 'Where a contract purports to be made by a company, or by a person as agent for a company, at a time when the company has not been formed . . .'. That applies whatever formula is adopted. The person who purports to contract for the company is personally liable.

There is one further point on s. 9(2) which I must mention. In the latest edition of *Cheshire and Fifoot's Law of Contract*, 9th ed. (1976), after reciting s. 9(2), it says, at p. 462:

How far it in fact does so will depend on the meaning given to the words 'subject to any agreement to the contrary' since it could be argued that words showing that A signs as agent express an agreement that he is not to be personally liable. If this were correct *Newborne* v

Sensolid (Great Britain) Ltd [1954] 1 QB 45 would still be decided the same way. But it may be suspected that the courts will try to give more content to the subsection.

We certainly will. The words 'subject to any agreement to the contrary' mean—as Shaw LJ suggested in the course of the argument—'unless otherwise agreed'. If there was an express agreement that the man who was signing was not to be liable, the section would not apply. But, unless there is a clear exclusion of personal liability, s. 9(2) should be given its full effect. It means that in all cases such as the present, where a person purports to contract on behalf of a company not yet formed, then however he expresses his signature he himself is personally liable on the contract.

I think that Phillips J was right on the s. 9(2) point. I would dismiss the appeal.

OLIVER LJ: I also agree. Speaking for myself, I am not convinced that the common law position apart from the European Communities Act 1972 depends upon the narrow distinction between a signature 'for and on behalf of' and a signature in the name of a company or an association. The question I think in each case is what is the real intent as revealed by the contract? Does the contract purport to be one which is directly between the supposed principal and the other party, or does it purport to be one between the agent himself—albeit acting for a supposed principal—and the other party? In other words, what you have to look at is whether the agent intended himself to be a party to the contract. So in *Kelner v Baxter* (1866) LR 2 CP 174 where the correspondence was directed to the agents and referred to 'the proposed company' which everybody knew was not yet in existence, there really was no room for the suggestion that the purchasers were acting in any other capacity than personally. On the other hand, in *Newborne v Sensolid (Great Britain) Ltd* [1954] 1 QB 45, where the contract was on the company's notepaper, it was clearly intended to be a company's contract (nobody realising that it had not yet been registered) and it could not be said that the individual plaintiff's signature in the company's name could possibly have been intended to make him a party to the contract.

The case, in my judgment, does not rest on any narrow point as to the way in which the contract was actually signed. The result would have been exactly the same, in my judgment, as if the signature there had been accompanied by some such formula as 'for and on behalf of' or *per pro*. The judgment of Parker J and the judgments in the Court of Appeal of Lord Goddard and Morris LJ show that the case turned on what the contract purported to do; and precisely the same applies I think in *Hollman v Pullin* (1884) Cab & Ell 254, where a contract, albeit signed by the plaintiff as chairman of the association, was clearly intended to be, and intended only to be, a contract directly with the association by which the defendant's services were intended to be retained. The same again I think applies to the Australian case of *Black v Smallwood* (1965) 117 CLR 52. The contract there on its face purported to be a contract between the vendor and the company as purchaser and nothing else, nobody then realising that the company had not been incorporated.

Whether that is right or not, any such subtle distinctions which might have been raised are rendered now irrelevant by s. 9(2) of the European Communities Act 1972 in a case where a contract is either with a company or with the agent of a company. It has been suggested that an agreement to the contrary may still be inferred by the fact that the contract was signed by a person acting as agent so as to exclude the section. That I am bound to say seems to me to be wholly unarguable when the section itself in terms provides 'Where a contract purports to be made . . . by a person as agent for a company', and to interpret it in the way suggested would defeat the whole purpose of the section.

For the reasons which Lord Denning MR and Shaw LJ have given in the instant case, I agree that the appeal should be dismissed.

Cotronic (UK) Ltd v *Dezonie*

The disappearing company

[1991] BCLC 721, Court of Appeal

This case raises the issue whether the section (at that time in force as CA 1985, s. 36(4)) not only makes the person acting for the nonexistent company liable, but also enables him to sue on the contract. It should be noted that the Directive refers only to the person acting being liable, its policy being to protect third parties against his error. The relevant section (currently CA 2006, s. 51) says that the contract has effect as one made with him, though again it only refers to him being personally liable. Unfortunately the case was unable to resolve the issue. See also A. Griffiths, 'Agents without principals: pre-incorporation contracts and section 36C of the Companies Act 1985' (1993) 13 LS 241.

Facts   Dezonie signed a contract relating to some building work at a residential home, signing for and on behalf of his company, Wendaland Builders Ltd. Unknown to him the company had been struck off the register about five years earlier (presumably because the Registrar thought the company was defunct). On learning this he incorporated a new company with the same name and unsuccessfully sought to rely on the section to claim the benefit of the contract.

DILLON LJ: The judge in his judgment referred to a passage in *Gore-Brown on Company Law,* 44th ed. (1986) where it is suggested that, if that section applies, then any person who is liable to be sued under a contract as having signed it on behalf of a company not yet formed can equally sue on it and he reached the view therefore that Mr Dezonie was able to enforce, in the right of the new Wendaland Builders Ltd (the second company) the terms of the contract. I do not agree with that approach since I do not regard s. 36(4) as applicable in this case. At the time of the 1986 building agreement no one had thought about forming a new company at all. Accordingly it is not possible to say that the contract purports to be made by the new company which was not actually formed until March 1988. No one thought of the new company because Mr Dezonie thought that the original company was still in being. The original company, however does not fit the wording 'where a contract purports to be made by a company or by a person as agent for a company at a time when the company has not been formed', because it had been formed long before. The problem was not one to which the European Communities Act 1972 was directed.

2.4 COMPANY PROMOTERS

It is a settled principle that a company promoter owes a fiduciary obligation to the company and may not make a secret profit. The promoter is accountable to the company or its liquidator for any profit unless it was disclosed to the appropriate organ of the company and the company consented to the promoter retaining it.

In the nineteenth and early twentieth century a huge and complex volume of case law on these issues was generated. The scenario was of specialist promoters forming public companies, selling assets to them (possibly existing businesses) at an overvalue, and then offering their shares in the company to a gullible public in a speculative market. In making the promoters potentially liable to the companies they had formed, the courts were constructing their own code of investor protection. Much of this law is now of historic interest as investor protection is now achieved through extensive legislation on financial services and markets and by Stock Exchange regulations.

The case law on promoters may remain relevant for private companies, though the promoters usually promote the company for themselves and do not intend to dispose of the shares. If assets are sold to the company at an overvalue, as in Mr Salomon's case, this is usually inadvertent rather than deliberate. The promoters are usually in a position to obtain the company's valid approval of the acquisition. If shares in private companies are issued in return for these assets, the courts will not review the adequacy of the consideration unless on the face of the contract this was inadequate or illusory. (See *Re Wragg Ltd* at 10.2.1 below.)

The following brief extract from lengthy judgments gives some of the flavour of a major issue of the period.

Gluckstein v Barnes
A nefarious plan forsooth
[1900] AC 240, House of Lords

Facts   Gluckstein was one of a syndicate of four who bought the exhibition hall, Olympia, nominally for £140,000 but actually for £120,000, and promoted a company of which they became directors, and which then bought the property for £180,000. A prospectus offering the shares to the public disclosed a profit of £40,000 but not the reality that they had made over £60,000 on the deal. The company later failed financially. The liquidator claimed from Gluckstein his share of the undisclosed profit. The House of Lords stridently upheld the claim.

EARL OF HALSBURY LC: The property was sold on February 8 by the chief clerk of North J for £140,000, and the syndicate purchased nominally for that sum, but, by reason of the arrangement to which I have referred, that sum was less by £20,734 6s 1d than what they appeared to give. On March 29 they completed as directors the purchase of the property for £180,000, and they as directors paid to themselves as members of the syndicate £171,000 in cash and £9,000 in fully paid-up shares—in all £180,000.

The prospectus by which money was to be obtained from the public disclosed the supposed profit which the vendors were making of £40,000, while in truth their profit was £60,734 6s 1d, and it is this undisclosed profit of £20,000, and the right to retain it, which is now in question.

My lords, I am wholly unable to understand any claim that these directors, vendors, syndicate, associates, have to retain this money. . . .

In order to protect themselves, as they supposed, they inserted in the prospectus, qualifying the statement that they had bought the property for £140,000, payable in cash, that they did not sell to the company, and did not intend to sell, any other profits made by the syndicate from interim investments. . . .

My lords, I decline to discuss the question of disclosure to the company. It is too absurd to suggest that a disclosure to the parties to this transaction is a disclosure to the company of which these directors were the proper guardians and trustees. They were there by the terms of the agreement to do the work of the syndicate, that is to say, to cheat the shareholders; and this, forsooth, is to be treated as a disclosure to the company, when they were really there to hoodwink the shareholders, and so far from protecting them, were to obtain from them the money, the produce of their nefarious plans.

I do not discuss either the sum sued for, or why Gluckstein alone is sued. The whole sum has been obtained by a very gross fraud, and all who were parties to it are responsible to make good what they have obtained and withheld from the shareholders.

I move your lordships that the appeal be dismissed with costs.

LORD MACNAGHTEN: My lords, Mr Swinfen Eady argued this appeal with his usual ability, but the case is far too clear for argument. The learned counsel for the appellant did not, I am sure, raise the slightest doubt in the mind of any of your lordships as to the propriety of the judgment under appeal; the only fault to be found with the learned judges of the Court of Appeal, if I may venture to criticise their judgment at all, is that they have treated the defences put forward on Mr Gluckstein's behalf with too much ceremony. For my part, I cannot see any ingenuity or any novelty in the trick which Mr Gluckstein and his associates practised on the persons whom they invited to take shares in Olympia Ltd. It is the old story. It has been done over and over again.

These gentlemen set about forming a company to pay them a handsome sum for taking off their hands a property which they had contracted to buy with that end in view. They bring the company into existence by means of the usual machinery. They appoint themselves sole guardians and protectors of this creature of theirs, half-fledged and just struggling into life, bound hand and foot while yet unborn by contracts tending to their private advantage, and so fashioned by its makers that it could only act by their hands and only see through their eyes. They issue a prospectus representing that they had agreed to purchase the property for a sum largely in excess of the amount which they had, in fact, to pay. On the faith of this prospectus they collect subscriptions from a confiding and credulous public. And then comes the last act. Secretly, and therefore dishonestly, they put into their own pockets the difference between the real and the pretended price. After a brief career the company is ordered to be wound up. In the course of the liquidation the trick is discovered. Mr. Gluckstein is called upon to make good a portion of the sum which he and his associates had misappropriated. Why Mr Gluckstein alone was selected for attack I do not know any more than I know why he was only asked to pay back a fraction of the money improperly withdrawn from the coffers of the company.

However that may be, Mr Gluckstein defends his conduct, or, rather I should say, resists the demand, on four grounds, which have been gravely argued at the bar. In the first place, he says that he was not in a fiduciary position towards Olympia Ltd before the company was formed. Well, for some purposes he was not. For others he was. A good deal might be said on the point. But to my mind the point is immaterial, for it is not necessary to go back beyond the formation of the company.

In the second place, he says, that if he was in a fiduciary position he did in fact make a proper disclosure. With all deference to the learned counsel for the appellant, that seems to me to be absurd. 'Disclosure' is not the most appropriate word to use when a person who plays many parts announces to himself in one character what he has done and is doing in another. To talk of disclosure to the thing called the company, when as yet there were no shareholders, is a mere farce. To the intended shareholders there was no disclosure at all. On them was practised an elaborate system of deception.

2.5 WHY INCORPORATE?

This chapter has shown that the law allows small businesses to incorporate with limited liability cheaply and easily and that this opportunity has been taken up in huge numbers. One may therefore ask precisely why do individual small businesses choose so complex a business form as the limited company which was originally structured for big public enterprises.

Is it desirable that they should do so in such large numbers? Does the universal availability of limited liability encourage risky businesses to operate, possibly causing prejudice to creditors? Could an alternative business form be devised?

The following extract from a research report considers these issues and concludes that while a large proportion of small businesses wish to incorporate, limited liability is not always desired by or available to many of them. Parliament, it is proposed, should therefore create a new 'business corporation' without limited liability for those who do not want the benefits or the burdens of limited liability. The authors of the report conducted their empirical research by extensive interviews of 180 small business proprietors and professional advisers.

Andrew Hicks, Robert Drury and Dr Jeff Smallcombe, *Alternative Company Structures for the Small Business* (ACCA Research Report No. 42)

(London: Association of Chartered Certified Accountants, 1995)

Background

An article in *The Times* recently concluded that, 'limited liability, introduced in 1855 to allow people to trade without committing their personal fortune to a venture, requires a fine legislative balance. The limited company is in danger of being too wide a protection for free enterprise, and of providing a veil for the unscrupulous' ('What a way to run the DTI', 1 November 1994).

The aim of company law should be, first, to facilitate enterprise, and secondly to regulate companies in the interests of investing shareholders, (especially minorities), creditors, the companies themselves and the commercial community at large.

The private company limited by shares is a remarkable success story. Told in the words of Companies House itself, (*The Register*, Spring 1993, p. 3), while in 1893 only 40 companies were incorporated a week,

> We now incorporate 2,000 weekly. In 1893 the cost of incorporating a limited company
> . . . in today's money would be about £370. . . . The incorporation fee remained unchanged
> between the Companies Act 1862 and a review of pricing in 1967.

On 1 October 1994 the incorporation fee was reduced from £50 to £20. Access to limited liability has therefore become cheaper and cheaper.

The edition for 3 November 1994 of *Exchange and Mart*, 'Britain's Bargain Book', advertised shelf companies with first minutes, all fees paid, and a registered office in St James's SW1 for £45. Among about 30 advertisements are offered public limited companies for £130. Names available include Imperial Financial Services Ltd, Kensington Property Co. Ltd, Trafalgar Corporate Ltd and Interlink International Ltd.

With nearly 2,800,000 companies having been registered altogether, 115,400 incorporated in the year to 31 March 1994, and just under a million on the register at that date (*Companies in 1993–94*, (London: HMSO, 1994), table A1), the private company is in numerical terms a success story.

While there is apparently a policy of seeking fiscal neutrality between companies and unincorporated businesses, it is clear that tax law has gradually drifted towards favouring companies. In conclusion, as *The Times* suggests, it is now appropriate to review whether the necessary 'fine legislative balance' is currently being achieved.

As regards facilitating enterprise, it has to be asked whether the considerable legal complexity of the limited company, developed primarily to encourage passive investment in publicly quoted companies, is entirely appropriate. Is this welter of regulation always necessary for small businesses and could compliance costs be reduced and efficiency increased? Why do small businesses trade as limited companies and what are the consequences? How could company law be streamlined to provide a more efficient vehicle for small businesses?

Further it has to be asked whether the regulatory aspects of company law are currently satisfactory. Is the considerable privilege of limited liability being given away at too low a cost without due regard to the impact of its possible abuse on the commercial community? While large numbers of company start-ups may be politically appealing, irresponsible commercial risk taking may be particularly damaging especially to third parties such as creditors. Ironically, while limited liability, generously bestowed, is regarded as essential for the small business sector, it may be precisely the many well-managed small companies that are the most vulnerable to losses when their under-capitalised, irresponsibly run customers go into insolvent liquidation. Limited liability may be as much a curse for the small business sector as a benefit. While we cannot answer this question, we can at least raise it, and consider how the problem, if there is one, could be relieved.

The problem may range from ill-considered to dishonest incorporations. The article in *The Times* is only one of the many to suggest that the reforms of the 1980s intended to limit abuse of limited liability have not been a success. Only a handful of court orders that directors compensate creditors for wrongful trading have been reported. Disqualifying unfit directors hardly touches the problem.

The issues are many and complex, but perhaps a less generous bestowal of limited liability could be considered, perhaps by proposing an alternative business form. . . .

Why do small businesses choose to incorporate or not to do so?

Our sample [of small business proprietors interviewed] showed that small companies are rarely if ever incorporated to attract capital from outside investors not involved in running the business. The other advantage of company status, being able to borrow against the security of a floating charge, was also not often taken advantage of. Only 16 per cent of the companies interviewed had granted floating charges to their bankers. Indeed the supposed enhanced ability of companies to borrow was not apparent. Almost exactly half of both companies and partnerships had borrowed from the bank and 44 per cent of sole traders. As one would expect, amounts borrowed by companies were larger, though as a proportion of their balance sheet total, they had generally not borrowed proportionately more. Banks appeared to rely for creditworthiness not on corporate form or floating charges but on fixed security, land being mortgaged in a majority of all cases. All borrowings by companies and partnerships were secured in one way or another and 79 per cent in the case of sole traders. The banks are therefore risk averse demanding fixed security, a matter of concern for the financing of small businesses.

Asked about reasons given for incorporating a majority of advisers (56 per cent) and of companies who were not advised (61 per cent) mentioned limited liability. Some of these were among the third of all companies that substantially gave up the benefit of limited liability by signing personal guarantees. The figures therefore suggest that almost half of company founders did not incorporate principally to obtain limited liability. Of those asked about incorporating a new business today, 60 per cent said limited liability would be irrelevant. A significant proportion of small company proprietors might therefore be attracted to an unlimited corporate form that offered compensating advantages. Company proprietors also incorporated for prestige or credibility (14 per cent) and 22 per cent of advisers cited tax reasons.

Partnerships chose not to incorporate to obtain legal informality and simplicity. There was almost no perception that absence of limited liability was a problem. It was widely regarded as unimportant.

Sole traders again desired absence of legal and accounting regulation. Management autonomy was seen as very important, though this is a state of affairs rather than a legal issue, as a single member private company is also run by its single member. Again, lack of limited liability was not perceived as a significant disadvantage.

In conclusion, limited liability was a reason to incorporate for a little over a half of businesses that incorporated. Its absence also did not bother most partnerships or sole traders. . . .

What are the consequences of incorporation for small businesses?

A high level of satisfaction with the company form was indicated, only 6 per cent regarding the decision as a mistake. Some concern was expressed at the cost of accounting and audit and the burden of legal formalities generally. Existing relaxation of audit requirements will of course relieve these complaints to some extent. More irritation is expressed with other regulations such as administering VAT returns.

Though there is not a high level of complaint about the existing corporate form, it is self-evident that any reduction of excess regulation is desirable. In any event, small business proprietors are not legal specialists able to assess the needs for the fine tuning of company law.

It has to be remembered that companies are the minority form of business. Partnerships and sole traders comprise about 70 per cent of all business. Again in these cases proprietors were generally satisfied with their choice. However, an overall conclusion is that proprietors are not particularly aware of or concerned about the legal form of business. They cannot be expected to take a lead as opinion formers. It is for law reformers to offer them improved legal forms. Reformers, however, tend to concentrate on pure company law, though corporate form has been chosen by about 30 per cent of businesses only. Judging from the responses, a company with limited liability is not essential for some of them. Add to these the 70 per cent of businesses which are not presently incorporated and one has to conclude that providing a suitable business form for those that do not need limited liability is of utmost importance. Proposals for a 'business corporation' without limited liability for both sole traders and partnerships are outlined below. . . .

Conclusions

The incorporated company offering limited liability to its members is a success story which has been of immense significance to Western economies. In the United Kingdom dating from 1855, limited liability companies were intended to provide a vehicle for attracting public capital, to offer limited liability to passive investors not involved in running the business, to enable their investments to be freely marketable and to provide continuity. The capital raising public company was to be the norm. However, from the *Salomon* case in 1897 onwards the courts have permitted sole traders to become companies. The public company is now no longer the norm. Private companies most of them very small, constitute about 99 per cent of all companies.

It has been widely assumed that the predominant reasons why these small businesses incorporate is to achieve limited liability and to be able to borrow from the banks on the strength of floating security. Our empirical research, based on in-depth face-to-face interviews with small businesses and professional advisers, suggests that limited liability, while sometimes important, is not always so. Small business people can often live without it, and indeed do live without it in the many cases where personal guarantees are given to a lender. Also, the survey shows that the ability to offer floating charges is almost never a major issue behind incorporation.

The debate about small companies has often concentrated on how to provide more inducements to as many people as possible to form limited companies. However, limited liability is a very special privilege and only responsible incorporations should be deemed desirable. Company failure has a domino effect damaging to creditors which, ironically, are generally small businesses. In addition, the debate on company law reform should reflect the fact that about 70 per cent of businesses are not companies. It cannot simply be assumed that the best solution is to offer more and more business proprietors a company with limited liability. . . .

Finally, we might ask ourselves the question, 'Is the purpose of forming a limited company to enable the raising of share capital, to raise loans on floating charges and to trade with limited liability?' We would now answer that in the small business sector the first two of these are rarely relevant. Even the third is surprisingly often relatively unimportant. Small business people often use limited companies simply because they are there and are cheap to acquire; in our opinion too cheap. . . .

The business corporation

Many of the advantages of incorporation sought by businesses (such as prestige and credibility; protection of the business name; perpetual succession) can be conferred without limited liability. It is the element of limited liability which creates much of the legislative complexity and burdens of compliance for small businesses. It is therefore recommended that legislation is introduced to allow both partnerships and sole traders (and possibly companies) to incorporate in the form of a 'business corporation'. The members would have unlimited liability and, to the extent that there is more than one member, the law would build on the well-settled principles of partnership law.

The option of a business corporation without limited liability could be attractive to many small businesses, offering considerable potential advantages for about 85 per cent of the business population which our study suggests do not require or value limited liability. The need to make the limited company as seductive as possible to small businesses, and thereby causing possible risk to creditors, would then recede.

3

Separate Legal Personality

The Partnership Act 1890 is still the statute regulating the law of partnership. Section 1 defines a partnership as, 'the relation which subsists between persons carrying on a business in common with a view of profit'. An English partnership is thus a mere relationship between individuals participating in a business. No legal formality or public registration is required. The firm is not an entity separate from its members. Thus partnership property is owned in the names of the partners, and the partners personally are party to partnership contracts. These are sometimes made in the names of the individual partners, for example, 'trading as J. B. Baker & Co.'. The partners have unlimited joint liability for the firm's debts (Partnership Act 1890, s. 9), and so one wealthy partner will be obliged to satisfy the whole of a partnership debt if the creditor chooses to enforce it against him; if he pays more than his share he may seek a contribution from the other partners. The whole of a partner's personal assets are at risk to enforcement procedures such as the levy of execution (i.e., sending the bailiffs into his home) or personal bankruptcy proceedings. (On the nature of a partner's joint liability see Morse, *Partnership Law*, 6th ed., Oxford: Oxford University Press, 2006.)

The Rules of the Supreme Court as a convenience allow partners to sue or be sued in the name of the firm without naming them individually. However, a Scottish partnership under the Partnership Act 1890, s. 4(2), is a legal person distinct from the partners, thus establishing corporate capacity but not limited liability.

In contrast to a partnership, a company is a corporate body, a separate legal entity with corporate capacity to hold property, to sue and be sued in its own name. As a separate legal entity it also contracts in its own name. Its members are not liable for its debts, and enjoy limited liability.

Corporate personality and limited liability do not necessarily go together, however. For example, the following are separate legal entities without conferring limited liability: unlimited companies formed under CA 2006, s. 3(4), and a number of business entities under civil law systems, including Scottish partnerships under Partnership Act 1890, s. 4(2), and the French partnership, the *société en nom collectif*.

The possibility that the law may be changed to give partnerships separate legal personality was proposed in the Law Commission's report of November 2003 (Law Com. No. 283, Com 6015). However, in July 2006 the Government announced that it had decided not to take these proposals forward 'at this time'.

3.2 THE *SALOMON* PRINCIPLE

The *Salomon* case was a struggle between form and substance; whether to interpret the law literally or whether to consider more its presumed spirit and intention. Was a genuine association of seven proprietors really necessary to form a company, or would six nominees holding shares for the seventh suffice? Could a paper company really transact with the beneficial owner of all its shares? The Lords accepted that if the form of the company was within the letter of the law they would not look behind it to the substance.

Since the *Salomon* case, the company as a vehicle for business enterprise has grown from strength to strength. The one-man private company (i.e., with two shareholders, one a nominee) became a commonplace and has been accepted without further question. However, since the company is a separate person, the sole shareholder may still owe common law duties to it, even if these are in reality enforceable only when a controlling interest is sold or the company goes into liquidation (and assuming there to have been no effective ratification). The legislature has, however, been astute to enact provisions protecting the company (or more often the mass of ordinary creditors when the company fails) from unfair dealings with a 'connected person', i.e., directors and their families. Thus, for example, under Insolvency Act 1986, transactions by directors and other connected persons with the company at an undervalue (s. 238), 'preferences' such as selectively paying off a particular debt shortly before insolvency (s. 239), and giving a floating charge to secure an existing debt within two years before the onset of insolvency (s. 245) may all be overturned by the company's liquidator. In the case of public companies, assets transferred to the company in return for shares must be formally valued (CA 2006, Part 17, Chapter 6).

Whether it was appropriate that incorporation with limited liability should have become so freely available to a multitude of small businesses in consequence of the *Salomon* decision is discussed below in an extract from a chapter by Andrew Hicks. (See also Hicks, 'Corporate form: questioning the unsung hero' [1997] JBL 306.)

Salomon v A. Salomon and Co. Ltd
Depression in the boot trade
[1897] AC 22, House of Lords

In reading the following extracts from this case it has to be remembered that the original purpose of limited liability was to enable passive investors to put a limited sum of money into a business without further risk. It was not the original intention that partners participating actively in a business should incorporate, let alone to permit a 'one-man company'. The legislation required seven members to form a company. Could a single person evade the apparent intention of the legislation by transferring a share to each of six nominees holding them for him? Was it enough merely to comply with the formal requirement or was it necessary to comply in substance as well? The judge at first instance and the Court of Appeal accepted that the company was validly incorporated but sought ways to invalidate the deals that Salomon as director of the company had concluded with himself. The facts (which are difficult to follow) and the findings in the courts below are summarised in the judgment of Lord Herschell. (The reports refer to the issue of debentures.

A debenture is a document acknowledging a loan to a company and giving the lender security over the assets of the company. Thus on insolvency the lender can take the assets and so recover payment ahead of the unsecured creditors who may consequently receive nothing. See 15.3 and 15.4 below.)

LORD HERSCHELL: My lords, by an order of the High Court, which was affirmed by the Court of Appeal, it was declared that the respondent company [A. Salomon & Co. Ltd], or the liquidator of that company was entitled to be indemnified by the appellant [Aron Salomon] against the sum of £7,733 8s 3d, and it was ordered that the respondent company should recover that sum against the appellant.

On July 28, 1892, the respondent company was incorporated with a capital of £40,000 divided into 40,000 shares of £1 each. One of the objects for which the company was incorporated was to carry out an agreement, with such modifications therein as might be agreed to, of July 20, 1892, which had been entered into between the appellant and a trustee for a company intended to be formed, for the acquisition by the company of the business then carried on by the appellant. The company was, in fact, formed for the purpose of taking over the appellant's business of leather merchant and boot manufacturer, which he had carried on for many years. The business had been a prosperous one, and, as the learned judge who tried the action found, was solvent at the time when the company was incorporated. The memorandum of association of the company was subscribed by the appellant, his wife and daughter, and his four sons, each subscribing for one share. The appellant afterwards had 20,000 shares allotted to him. For these he paid £1 per share out of the purchase-money which by agreement he was to receive for the transfer of his business to the company. The company afterwards became insolvent and went into liquidation.

In an action brought by a debenture-holder on behalf of himself and all the other debenture-holders, including the appellant, the respondent company set up by way of counterclaim that the company was formed by Aron Salomon, and the debentures were issued in order that he might carry on the said business, and take all the profits without risk to himself; that the company was the mere nominee and agent of Aron Salomon; and that the company or the liquidator thereof was entitled to be indemnified by Aron Salomon against all the debts owing by the company to creditors other than Aron Salomon. This counterclaim was not in the pleading as originally delivered; it was inserted by way of amendment at the suggestion of Vaughan Williams J, before whom the action came on for trial. The learned judge thought the liquidator entitled to the relief asked for, and made the order complained of. He was of opinion that the company was only an 'alias' for Salomon; that, the intention being that he should take the profits without running the risk of the debts, the company was merely an agent for him, and, having incurred liabilities at his instance, was, like any other agent under such circumstances, entitled to be indemnified by him against them. On appeal the judgment of Vaughan Williams J was affirmed by the Court of Appeal, that court 'being of opinion that the formation of the company, the agreement of August, 1892, and the issue of debentures to Aron Salomon pursuant to such agreement were a mere scheme to enable him to carry on business in the name of the company with limited liability contrary to the true intent and meaning of the Companies Act 1862, and further to enable him to obtain a preference over other creditors of the company by procuring a first charge on the assets of the company by means of such debentures'.

The learned judges in the Court of Appeal dissented from the view taken by Vaughan Williams J, that the company was to be regarded as the agent of the appellant. They considered the relation between them to be that of trustee and cestui que trust; but this difference of view, of course, did not affect the conclusion that the right to the indemnity claimed had been established.

It is to be observed that both courts treated the company as a legal entity distinct from Salomon and the then members who composed it, and therefore as a validly constituted corporation. This is, indeed, necessarily involved in the judgment which declared that the company was entitled to certain rights as against Salomon. Under these circumstances, I am at a loss to understand what is meant by saying that A. Salomon & Co., Limited, is but an 'alias' for A. Salomon. It is not another name for the same person; the company is *ex hypothesi* a distinct legal persona. As little am I able to adopt the view that the company was the agent of Salomon to carry on his business for him. In a popular sense, a company may in every case be said to carry on business for and on behalf of its shareholders; but this certainly does not in point of law constitute the relation of principal and agent between them or render the shareholders liable to indemnify the company against the debts which it incurs. Here, it is true, Salomon owned all the shares except six, so that if the business were profitable he would be entitled, substantially, to the whole of the profits. The other shareholders, too, are said to have been 'dummies', the nominees of Salomon. But when once it is conceded that they were individual members of the company distinct from Salomon, and sufficiently so to bring into existence in conjunction with him a validly constituted corporation, I am unable to see how the facts to which I have just referred can affect the legal position of the company, or give it rights as against its members which it would not otherwise possess. . . .

LORD HALSBURY LC: My Lords, the important question in this case, I am not certain it is not the only question, is whether the respondent company was a company at all—whether in truth that artificial creation of the legislature had been validly constituted in this instance; and in order to determine that question it is necessary to look at what the statute itself has determined in that respect. I have no right to add to the requirements of the statute, nor to take from the requirements thus enacted. The sole guide must be the statute itself.

Now, that there were seven actual living persons who held shares in the company has not been doubted. As to the proportionate amounts held by each I will deal presently; but it is important to observe that this first condition of the statute is satisfied, and it follows as a consequence that it would not be competent to any one—and certainly not to these persons themselves—to deny that they were shareholders.

I must pause here to point out that the statute enacts nothing as to the extent or degree of interest which may be held by each of the seven, or as to the proportion of interest or influence possessed by one or the majority of the shareholders over the others. One share is enough. Still less is it possible to contend that the motive of becoming shareholders or of making them shareholders is a field of inquiry which the statute itself recognises as legitimate. If they are shareholders, they are shareholders for all purposes; and even if the statute was silent as to the recognition of trusts, I should be prepared to hold that if six of them were the cestuis que trust of the seventh, whatever might be their rights *inter se*, the statute would have made them shareholders to all intents and purposes with their respective rights and liabilities, and, dealing with them in their relation to the company, the only relations which I believe the law would sanction would be that they were corporators of the corporate body.

I am simply here dealing with the provisions of the statute, and it seems to me to be essential to the artificial creation that the law should recognise only that artificial existence—quite apart from the motives or conduct of individual corporators. In saying this, I do not at all mean to suggest that if it could be established that this provision of the statute to which I am adverting had not been complied with, you could not go behind the certificate of incorporation to shew that a fraud had been committed upon the officer entrusted with the duty of giving the certificate, and that by some proceeding in the nature of *scire facias* you could not prove the fact that the company had no real legal existence. But short of such proof it seems to me impossible to dispute that once the company is legally incorporated it must be treated like any other independent person with its rights and liabilities appropriate to itself, and that the motives of those who took part in the promotion of the company are absolutely irrelevant in discussing what those rights and liabilities are.

I will for the sake of argument assume the proposition that the Court of Appeal lays down—that the formation of the company was a mere scheme to enable Aron Salomon to carry on business in the name of the company. I am wholly unable to follow the proposition that this was contrary to the true intent and meaning of the Companies Act. I can only find the true intent and meaning of the Act from the Act itself; and the Act appears to me to give a company a legal existence with, as I have said, rights and liabilities of its own, whatever may have been the ideas or schemes of those who brought it into existence.

I observe that the learned judge (Vaughan Williams J) held that the business was Mr Salomon's business, and no one else's, and that he chose to employ as agent a limited company; and he proceeded to argue that he was employing that limited company as agent, and that he was bound to indemnify that agent (the company). I confess it seems to me that that very learned judge becomes involved by this argument in a very singular contradiction. Either the limited company was a legal entity or it was not. If it was, the business belonged to it and not to Mr Salomon. If it was not, there was no person and no thing to be an agent at all; and it is impossible to say at the same time that there is a company and there is not....

LORD MACNAGHTEN: When the trial came on before Vaughan Williams J, the validity of [the debenture holder,] Mr Broderip's claim was admitted, and it was not disputed that the 20,000 shares were fully paid up. The case presented by the liquidator broke down completely; but the learned judge suggested that the company had a right of indemnity against Mr Salomon. The signatories of the memorandum of association were, he said, mere nominees of Mr Salomon—mere dummies. The company was Mr Salomon in another form. He used the name of the company as an alias. He employed the company as his agent; so the company, he thought, was entitled to indemnity against its principal. The counterclaim was accordingly amended to raise this point; and on the amendment being made the learned judge pronounced an order in accordance with the view he had expressed.

The order of the learned judge appears to me to be founded on a misconception of the scope and effect of the Companies Act 1862. In order to form a company limited by shares, the Act requires that a memorandum of association should be signed by seven persons, who are each to take one share at least. If those conditions are complied with, what can it matter whether the signatories are relations or strangers? There is nothing in the Act requiring that the subscribers to the memorandum should be independent or unconnected, or that they or any one of them should take a substantial interest in the undertaking, or that they should have a mind and will of their own, as one of the learned Lords Justices seems to think, or that there should be anything like a balance of power in the constitution of the company. In almost every company that is formed the statutory number is eked out by clerks or friends, who sign their names at the request of the promoter or promoters without intending to take any further part or interest in the matter.

When the memorandum is duly signed and registered, though there be only seven shares taken, the subscribers are a body corporate 'capable forthwith', to use the words of the enactment, 'of exercising all the functions of an incorporated company.' Those are strong words. The company attains maturity on its birth. There is no period of minority—no interval of incapacity. I cannot understand how a body corporate thus made 'capable' by statute can lose its individuality by issuing the bulk of its capital to one person, whether he be a subscriber to the memorandum or not. The company is at law a different person altogether from the subscribers to the memorandum; and, though it may be that after incorporation the business is precisely the same as it was before, and the same persons are managers, and the same hands receive the profits, the company is not in law the agent of the subscribers or trustee for them. Nor are the subscribers as members liable, in any shape or form, except to the extent and in the manner provided by the Act. That is, I think, the declared intention of the enactment. If the view of the learned judge were sound, it would follow that no common law partnership could register as a company limited by shares without remaining subject to unlimited liability.

Mr Salomon appealed; but his appeal was dismissed with costs, though the appellate court did not entirely accept the view of the court below. The decision of the Court of Appeal proceeds on a declaration of opinion embodied in the order which has been already read.

I must say that I, too, have great difficulty in understanding this declaration. If it only means that Mr Salomon availed himself to the full of the advantages offered by the Act of 1862, what is there wrong in that? Leave out the words 'contrary to the true intent and meaning of the Companies Act 1862' and bear in mind that 'the creditors of the company' are not the creditors of Mr Salomon, and the declaration is perfectly innocent : it has no sting in it....

Among the principal reasons which induce persons to form private companies, as is stated very clearly by Mr Palmer in his treatise on the subject, are the desire to avoid the risk of bankruptcy, and the increased facility afforded for borrowing money. By means of a private company, as Mr Palmer observes, a trade can be carried on with limited liability, and without exposing the persons interested in it in the event of failure to the harsh provisions of the bankruptcy law. A company, too, can raise money on debentures, which an ordinary trader cannot do. Any member of a company, acting in good faith, is as much entitled to take and hold the company's debentures as any outside creditor. Every creditor is entitled to get and to hold the best security the law allows him to take.

If, however, the declaration of the Court of Appeal means that Mr Salomon acted fraudulently or dishonestly, I must say I can find nothing in the evidence to support such an imputation. The purpose for which Mr Salomon and the other subscribers to the memorandum were associated was 'lawful'. The fact that Mr Salomon raised £5,000 for the company on debentures that belonged to him seems to me strong evidence of his good faith and of his confidence in the company. The unsecured creditors of A. Salomon and Company, Limited, may be entitled to sympathy, but they have only themselves to blame for their misfortunes. They trusted the company, I suppose, because they had long dealt with Mr Salomon, and he had always paid his way; but they had full notice that they were no longer dealing with an individual, and they must be taken to have been cognisant of the memorandum and of the articles of association. For such a catastrophe as has occurred in this case some would blame the law that allows the creation of a floating charge. But a floating charge is too convenient a form of security to be lightly abolished. . . .

Macaura v Northern Assurance Co. Ltd
The fire at Killymoon
[1925] AC 619, House of Lords

A shareholder has no proprietary interest in the assets of the company. If he insures the company's assets in his own name he cannot make a claim on the insurance policy as he has no insurable interest in them.

Facts   Macaura owned the Killymoon estate in Ireland. He insured some timber on the estate. He transferred the estate and timber to a company in return for shares but did not apparently have the insurance reissued in the name of the company. The timber was substantially destroyed by fire. The insurance company successfully resisted his claim on the policy, arguing that the timber was not his to insure.

LORD BUCKMASTER: Turning now to his position as shareholder, this must be independent of the extent of his share interest. If he were entitled to insure, holding all the shares in the company, each shareholder would be equally entitled, if the shares were all in separate hands. Now, no shareholder has any right to any item of property owned by the company, for he has no legal or equitable interest therein. He is entitled to a share in the profits while the company continues to carry on business and a share in the distribution of the surplus assets when the company is wound up. If he were at liberty to effect an insurance against loss by fire of any item of the company's property, the extent of his insurable interest could only be measured by determining the extent to which his share in the ultimate distribution would be diminished by the loss of the asset—a calculation almost impossible to make. There is no means by which such an nterest can be definitely measured and no standard which can be fixed of the loss against which the contract of insurance could be regarded as an indemnity. . . .

LORD WRENBURY: My lords, this appeal may be disposed of by saying that the corporator even if he holds all the shares is not the corporation, and that neither he nor any creditor of the company has any property legal or equitable in the assets of the corporation. . . . I think the appeal should be dismissed.

Andrew Hicks, 'Limiting the rise of limited liability'
in R. Baldwin and P. Cane (eds), *Law and Uncertainty* (Kluwer, 1997)

'The limited liability corporation is the greatest single discovery of modern times . . . Even steam and electricity are far less important than the limited liability corporation'. This memorable comment from early in the century is much quoted. Another version in 1926 proclaims, 'The economic historian of the future may assign to the nameless inventor of the principle of limited liability, as applied to trading corporations, a place of honour with Watt and Stephenson, and other pioneers of the Industrial Revolution. . . . the limited liability company was the means by which huge aggregations of capital required to give effect to their discoveries were collected, organised and efficiently administered.' Is it too extravagant to suggest therefore that the limited company is the keystone of the capitalist system? But is the privilege of limited liability now too generously conceded to all-comers, no matter how insubstantial they may be? . . .

The necessity which led to the invention of the limited liability company was the increasing capital sums required for construction and other major business projects. Way beyond their means or too speculative for a small group of partners, these enterprises required limited contributions by a wide range of passive investors not actively involved in the business. Yet individuals contributing a modest stake for a proportionally modest return would not stake their all in such a project. If they were to make their investment they would require limited liability. Not being practicable for it to be agreed between contracting parties and a large number of members that their liability be limited, a statutory form of limited liability was required.

The seed was sown by the Joint Stock Companies Act 1844 providing for incorporation of companies by registration, together with the beginnings of the system of disclosure of information on a public register. The debate on limited liability was hard fought, being achieved in the Limited Liability Act 1855. Adam Smith earlier in 1776 had expressed a restrictive view that, incorporation with limited liability could only be justified if the capital was so great that private ventures would not otherwise provide it and the industry was of the greatest public utility. Smith identified four industries as coming into this category: insurance, water supply, banking, and canal construction. Nonetheless, the free availability of universal limited liability for registered companies was ultimately conceded. Gower expresses surprise at the 'almost indecent haste' with which the Bill was pushed through, 'particularly as the official view still seemed to be that it [limited liability] was a question of abstract principle rather than of practical importance'. The Act required at least 25 members and a minimum subscribed capital and the company had to wind up if three quarters of its capital was lost. Many of the creditor safeguards were removed and the requisite number of members reduced to seven the following year by the Joint Stock Companies Act 1856.

The well-known lawyer (and operatic versifier), W.S. Gilbert, was of the view that incorporation with limited liability tended to have the adverse effect of transferring uncompensated trading risks to creditors. However, he expressed his views in different terms, perhaps more clearly than the transatlantic economic school of legal academics. He commented that in promoting a company, seven men make a public declaration as to what extent they mean to pay their debts. 'That's called their capital. . . . When it's left to you to say what amount you mean to pay, why the lower you can put it at the better'. Undercapitalisation remains a major issue, and the £100 company is still very common in the 1990s.

Gower notes that up to 1856, 956 companies were registered under the Joint Stock Companies Act 1844. In the six years following the 1856 Act no fewer than 2,479 were registered, now with limited liability. In 1893 the incorporation rate appears to have been a little higher, 10 companies being incorporated a week (in contrast to 2,000 a week currently).

It was of course the pivotal House of Lords case of *Salomon* v *A. Salomon & Co. Ltd* [1897] AC 22 which confirmed that limited companies may be used not only for their original purpose as a means for a wide range of passive investors to pool their capital. They may also be used as a business vehicle for partners or even sole traders who take the full benefit of limited liability. This has never since been seriously questioned or reviewed by the legislature and has been vigorously affirmed by the courts as an invariable principle, even where the sole shareholder is a company and the subsidiary undercapitalised. The popularity of limited liability companies for small businesses has only been moderated by the significant burden of complying with the disclosure of accounts and the consequential loss of privacy. However the Companies Acts of 1900 and 1907 began to favour the 'private company' by exempting them from some of the publicity requirements. The pendulum of opinion for and against relieving private companies of the burdens accompanying the privilege of limited liability has continued to swing, the current urge to 'deregulate' being particularly pronounced.

Hadden comments, 'By 1911, when accurate figures for the division into public and private companies introduced in 1907, were published, almost two thirds of the total of 50,000 registered companies were private companies'. Figures he presents indicate that after the Second World War in 1946, 92 per cent of companies were private and by 1975, 97 per cent. Today the figure is almost 99 per cent. The economy is therefore apparently dominated by private companies, though also by the 2,075 public companies currently listed on the London Stock Exchange.

The rise of the private limited company is numerically a huge success story. Some academics, however, bewail its success. Kahn-Freund blamed their proliferation on the courts. Owing to the ease with which companies can be formed in this country, and owing to the rigidity with which the courts applied the corporate entity concept ever since the calamitous decision in *Salomon v A. Salomon & Co. Ltd* a sole trader may trade as a limited company. Further, 'the courts have failed to give that protection to the business creditors which should be the corollary of the privilege of limited liability.... The company has often been a means of evading liabilities and of concealing the real interests behind the business' ((1944) 7MLR54). Another writer refers to the 'jurisprudential ineptitude' of the House of Lords in rejecting 'the clear intention of the legislature in favour of the application of the so-called literal rule of interpretation'. The decision has done much 'to undermine commercial integrity'. These are hard words. While the English company is contract-based, the continental requirement of *affectio societatis* is not nearly so strong in this jurisdiction. The formality of six nominees holding shares for the seventh member has never been a problem for the formalistic style of English law. If the legal form is satisfied it does not matter if there is abuse of the substance. It is ironic that the statutory single member private company has now crossed the Channel from Brussels, to legitimate what in substance has been possible at common law for more than a century.

In defence of the courts, it was perhaps for the House of Lords to interpret the law as expressed by Parliament without anticipating the long-term consequences of its decisions. Indeed the refusal of the courts then and subsequently to 'lift the veil' and not thereby to compromise the principle of limited liability has preserved the essential certainty of separate corporate personality as the fundamental principle of company law. The primary policy makers responsible for reviewing (or for failing to review) the overall impact of the law are of course governments and the legislature.

3.3 LIFTING THE VEIL

The textbooks generally deal with a bewildering range of cases under the fanciful title of 'lifting the veil'. There is a small number of exceptional cases where the courts have lifted the veil of incorporation to recognise the substance or practical realities of a situation rather than the form.

It should be remembered that a principal feature of the separate legal personality of companies is that the company itself enters into contracts and is liable for them. The members are not party to these contracts: they enjoy limited liability and are not liable on them. This was so in the *Salomon* case even where the company was a one-man company and Mr Salomon in substance a sole trader. Despite the lifting-of-the-veil cases this principle remains extremely strong and almost without exception. Even incorporated companies may achieve limited liability by incorporating subsidiaries, thus giving the individual shareholders of the holding company in effect a double tier of limited liability. Just as an individual shareholder is not liable for the debts of the company, so a holding company is not liable for the debts of its subsidiaries.

In a group of companies, where there is an undercapitalised subsidiary with no independent economic existence, it is arguable that the subsidiary is merely carrying on as agent the business of the holding company. If there were a finding of agency in these circumstances the holding company could be liable for the debts of the subsidiaries. This is theoretically possible, but it seems that the courts will not imply an agency merely from the surrounding circumstances. Only if there is an actual express agency agreement that the subsidiary is carrying on the business of the holding company as its agent will the holding company be held liable as principal. The agency argument may possibly be used in other circumstances of lifting the veil. But the courts are reluctant to use it to impose liability for the company's debts on a holding company or other shareholder, just as they refused to find agency in the *Salomon* case.

Most of the cases where the courts have lifted the veil concern instances where the shareholders are using the company, deliberately or otherwise, as a device to achieve certain benefits or to avoid obligations. Where there is possibly an abuse of the corporate form, the courts may regard the company for this purpose only as a mere cloak or sham and lift the veil. Precisely when the courts will do this is very difficult to define. Sometimes the courts justify their decision by saying that they are interpreting different statute laws. Sometimes they justify it by the agency argument, holding that the subsidiary is merely the agent of the principal.

Thus, despite the formalistic nature of the concept of separate corporate personality, the courts on rare occasions will deny the corporators the advantage of hiding behind the corporate veil. If on the other hand corporate status may prove disadvantageous, it is unlikely that the members would persuade the court to lift the veil. However, exceptionally in the case of *DHN Food Distributors Ltd* v *Tower Hamlets London Borough Council* [1976] 1 WLR 852 the Court of Appeal treated a group of companies as a single economic entity so as to enable compensation for compulsory purchase of land to be paid. Lord Denning MR, who gave judgment in the *DHN* case was a notable enthusiast for lifting of veils, as some of the cases that follow suggest. However, the *DHN* case has since been doubted in a number of subsequent cases including *Woolfson* v *Strathclyde Regional Council* 1978 SLT 159 in the House of Lords.

If it is possible to summarise in a few lines, it is probably fair to say that the courts will not lift the veil to impose liability on a shareholder for the company's debts. Nor will they lift the veil to benefit shareholders who discover that trading as a company is a disadvantage. In rare instances the courts will look to the substance rather than the form to deny benefits of corporate status which they think should not be enjoyed. It is difficult to predict precisely when this will occur as the reasons are probably the judges' somewhat subjective perception of fairness or policy, or of how a statute should be interpreted. But a court may lift the veil and regard the receipt of money by a company as receipt by its controlling shareholder if the company was improperly used as a device or facade in order to evade liability (see *Trustor* v *Smallbone* [2002] BCC 795).

However, in conclusion, the courts do not lift the veil to impose personal liability on the shareholders for the debts of the company. The principle of limited liability is not threatened and remains as solid as a rock. As Professor Sealy has put it, the courts have refused to 'violate the sacred canon of limited liability'.

> ... one will search the reports in vain for a single English case where the principle of limited liability, as distinct from that of corporate personality, has not been respected—statute apart. This is true of cases brought against directors and dominant shareholders alike. Those cases where the corporate veil has been pierced on the basis that the company was a façade or sham, or was the agent of its controllers, turn out on examination to have been concerned with the evasion of a statutory provision or a contractual obligation, or some similar issue, and not with imposing personal liability on the directors or shareholders for the company's debts. ('Personal liability of directors and officers for debts of an insolvent company' in Ziegel (ed.), *Current Developments in International and Comparative Corporate Insolvency Law* (1994), p. 485.)

However, the textbooks usually list numerous examples of lifting the veil by statute. Tax law is one example; Parliament is free to legislate for the income of a subsidiary to be treated as that of the holding company if it thinks fit. Secondly, the requirement for groups to produce consolidated accounts recognises the single economic entity of the group, though it does not in any way deny the separate legal entity of each group company. (See 16.1 below.) Thirdly, Insolvency Act 1986, s. 214, empowers the court to order directors to make a contribution to an insolvent company's assets if (to oversimplify) they continued to increase the company's liabilities at a time when it should have been apparent to them that the company would not avoid insolvent liquidation. While this may in a particular case amount to a suspension of limited liability, it is the directors who suffer liability as a penalty for mismanagement and not the shareholders. (See 20.12 below.)

Another example where statute law attempted to have regard to the substance rather than the form was the case of the 'quota hopping' Spanish fishermen who incorporated English companies in order to take advantage of English fishing quotas. Regulations made under the Merchant Shipping Act 1988 lifted the veil and stated that companies could only be entered on the register of British fishing vessels if their shareholders were British citizens or domiciled in Britain. Valid under English law, the legislation was of course struck down in *R* v *Secretary of State for Transport, ex parte Factortame Ltd (No. 3)* (case C-221/89) [1992] QB 680 as being contrary to EU law.

The cases extracted start with some examples of where the courts have recognised the substance rather than the form of the matter. These are followed by a number of cases suggesting that the rigid formality of separate corporate personality is still alive and well, even in the context of groups with undercapitalised subsidiaries.

3.3.1 Abuse of the corporate form

Jones v Lipman

A device, a sham and a mask

[1962] 1 All ER 442, [1962] 1 WLR 832, Chancery Division

Facts   Lipman sold to Jones a house, 3 Fairlawns Avenue, Acton by a written contract but refused to complete the sale, offering damages for breach. To put the house beyond the reach of Jones, Lipman bought a shelf company and conveyed the house to it. Jones nonetheless succeeded in an action for specific performance against Lipman and the company.

RUSSELL J: When the matter came on again in chambers the affidavit evidence by the first defendant made it plain (i) that the defendant company was, and at all material times had been, under the complete control of the first defendant, and (ii) that the acquisition of the defendant company by the first defendant and the transfer to it of the real property comprised in the contract with the plaintiffs (for the chattels remained in the ownership of the first defendant) was carried through solely for the purpose of defeating the plaintiffs' rights to specific performance and in order to leave them to claim such damages, if any, as they might establish. So much was, quite rightly, admitted by counsel for the defendants.

For the plaintiffs the argument was twofold. First, that specific performance would be ordered against a party to a contract who has it in his power to compel another person to convey the property in question; and that admittedly the first defendant had this power over the defendant company. Second, that specific performance would also, in circumstances such as the present, be ordered against the defendant company. For the first proposition reference was made to *Elliott* v *Pierson* [1948] Ch 452. In that case resistance to specific performance at the suit of a vendor was grounded on the fact that the property was vested in a limited company and not in the vendor. The company, however, was wholly owned and controlled by the vendor, who could compel it to transfer the property, and on this ground the defence to the claim for specific performance failed. It seems to me, not only from dicta of the learned judge but also on principle, that it necessarily follows that specific performance cannot be resisted by a vendor who, by his absolute ownership and control of a limited company in which the property is vested, is in a position to cause the contract to be completed.

For the second proposition reference was made to *Gilford Motor Co. Ltd* v *Horne* [1933] Ch 935. In that case the individual defendant had entered into covenants restricting his trading activities. [He] caused the defendant company in that case to be formed. This company was under his control and did things which, if they had been done by him, would have been a breach of the covenants. An injunction was granted not only against him but also against the company. In that case Lord Hanworth MR, after referring to *Smith* v *Hancock* [1894] 2 Ch 377, said (at p. 961):

> Lindley LJ ([1894] 2 Ch at p. 385) indicated the rule which ought to be followed by the court: 'If the evidence admitted of the conclusion that what was being done was a mere cloak or sham, and that in truth the business was being carried on by the wife and Kerr for the defendant, or by the defendant through his wife for Kerr, I certainly should not hesitate to draw that conclusion, and to grant the plaintiff relief accordingly'. I do draw that conclusion. I do hold that the company was 'a mere cloak or sham'; I do hold that it was a mere device for enabling Mr E.B. Horne to continue to commit breaches of [the covenant], and in those circumstances the injunction must go against both defendants.

Lawrence LJ in his judgment, said (at p. 965):

> ...I agree with the finding by the learned judge that the defendant company was a mere channel used by the defendant Horne for the purpose of enabling him, for his own benefit, to obtain the advantage of the customers of the plaintiff company, and that therefore the defendant company ought to be restrained as well as the defendant Horne.

Similarly, Romer LJ said (at p. 969):

> In my opinion, Farwell J was perfectly right in the conclusion to which he came...that this defendant company was formed and was carrying on business merely as a cloak or sham for the purpose of enabling the defendant Horne to commit the breach of the covenant that he entered into deliberately with the plaintiffs on the occasion of and as consideration for his employment as managing director. For this reason, in addition to the reasons given by my lords, I agree that the appeal must be allowed with the consequences which have been indicated by the Master of the Rolls.

Those comments on the relationship between the individual and the company apply even more forcibly to the present case. The defendant company is the creature of the first defendant, a device and a sham, a mask which he holds before his face in an attempt to avoid recognition by the eye of equity. The case cited [*Gilford Motor Co. Ltd* v *Horne*] illustrates that an equitable remedy is rightly to be granted directly against the creature in such circumstances.

3.3.2 Lord Denning rending veils

Littlewoods Mail Order Stores Ltd v Inland Revenue Commissioners
The Oddfellows and Fork
[1969] 3 All ER 442, [1969] 1 WLR 1241, Court of Appeal

Facts   Littlewoods and its landlords, the Oddfellows (a friendly society), entered into an arrange-ment for a wholly owned subsidiary of Littlewoods called Fork Manufacturing Co. Ltd to acquire the freehold of the building in such a way that the purchase price could be treated, for tax purposes, as an operating expense, which could be deducted from Littlewoods' income, rather than as pay-ment for a fixed asset, which could not. The method was that Littlewoods assigned its lease to Fork Manufacturing which then granted a sublease to Littlewoods at a greatly increased rent (calcu-lated so that the total payments would equal the purchase price of the bulding). Fork then bought the freehold from the Oddfellows, paying for it by assigning the lease (with the benefit of the right to receive rent under the sublease) to the Oddfellows. The issue was whether Littlewoods could deduct the increased element of the rent in computing its taxable profits. The court held that Fork was not a separate and independent entity, the extra rent was to enable Littlewoods to acquire the freehold, and so the rent was not deductible (thus increasing the tax payable).

LORD DENNING MR: The taxpayers, Littlewoods Mail Order Stores Ltd, carry on a big business at Jubilee House in Oxford Street. In 1947 the building was bought by Oddfellows Friendly Society for £605,000. The Oddfellows let it to the taxpayer on a 99-years lease at a rent of £23,444 a year. That rent gave the Oddfellows a return of only $3\frac{7}{8}$ per cent on their outlay. During the next 11 years the value of money got much less. In 1958 the building was worth about £2,000,000 if sold with vacant possession. And the rent obtainable on a tenancy from year to year granted in 1958 would be £60,000 a year. Yet the taxpayers had a lease with another 88 years to go at a rent of £23,444.

Such being the position, in 1958 the advisers of Oddfellows and the taxpayers carried through a deal which was designed to confer a considerable advantage on both of them...[The deal is then described.]

The deal was designed to the advantage of both in this way; on the one hand Oddfellows would receive a rent of £42,450 a year for 22 years, which would be clear of tax as they were a charity. On the other hand, the taxpayers would claim to deduct the full rent of £42,450 from their profits instead of the smaller sum of £23,444. So they would escape a lot of tax. The deal would be to the advantage of both sides, at the expense of the Revenue.

...Counsel for the taxpayers...said that the interposition of the Fork company made all the dif-ference albeit it was a wholly owned subsidiary of the taxpayers. He said that the Fork company was to be regarded as a separate and independent entity, just as if shares were owned by someone quite unconnected with the taxpayers. In the case the freehold of Jubilee House would be acquired by the Fork company. The taxpayers would have acquired no capital asset at all. They would be able to deduct the whole £42,450 a year.

I cannot accept this argument. I decline to treat the Fork company as a separate and independent entity. The doctrine laid down in *Salomon v A. Salomon & Co. Ltd* [1897] AC 22 has to be watched very carefully. It has often been supposed to cast a veil over the personality of a limited company through which the courts cannot see. But that is not true. The courts can and often do draw aside the veil. They can, and often do, pull off the mask. They look to see what really lies behind. The legis-lature has shown the way with group accounts and the rest. And the courts should follow suit. I think that we should look at the Fork company and see it as it really is—the wholly owned subsidiary of the taxpayers. It is the creature, the puppet, of the taxpayers in point of *fact*; and it should be so regarded in point of *law*. The basic fact here is that the taxpayers, through their wholly owned sub-sidiary, have acquired a capital asset—the freehold of Jubilee House, and they have acquired it by paying an extra £19,006 a year. So regarded, the case is indistinguishable from the *Land Securities* case [*Commissioners of Inland Revenue v Land Securities Investment Trust Ltd* [1969] 1 WLR 604]. The taxpayers are not entitled to deduct this extra £19,006 in computing their profits.

Wallersteiner v *Moir*

Of David and Goliath

[1974] 3 All ER 217, [1974] 1 WLR 991, Court of Appeal

This case is but one episode in an epic battle through the courts waged by Mr Moir, a modest minority shareholder, against Dr Wallersteiner, the majority shareholder and managing director of Hartley Baird Ltd, a substantial public company. The issues were many and complex. The story line appears below in Lord Denning's unique style, richly populated with goodies and baddies. The extract gives a fla- vour of Lord Denning's response, a judge more inclined to recognise the substance of a situation and the broad principles of the law rather than be constrained by its narrow formality. His views are extreme, however, and do not necessarily state the law as it is currently perceived.

LORD DENNING MR:

I. The story in outline   Mr Moir works in a stockbroker's office. He has taken on a big fight. He has challenged Dr Wallersteiner, a man of influence in the City of London. Mr Moir issued a circular in March 1967 criticising Dr Wallersteiner up hill and down dale. He sent it to the shareholders of Hartley Baird Ltd. That was a substantial public company. Dr Wallersteiner had gained control of it in 1962. He had charge of 80 per cent of the shares. The other 20 per cent were held by members of the public. Mr Moir was one of them. In the circular Mr Moir accused Dr Wallersteiner of fraud, misfeasance and breach of trust. Dr Wallersteiner hit back at once. He issued a writ for libel claim- ing damages. He sought an injunction to stop Mr Moir saying such things. Mr Moir put up a spirited defence. He had, he said, only stated in the circular what he believed to be true. Dr Wallersteiner launched a vigorous counter-attack. Mr Moir, he said, was actuated by express malice. He made a business of this sort of thing. He got a few shares in a public company and then harassed those in control of it. He was, according to Dr Wallersteiner, a professional agitator.

The battle was long. Mr Moir got the support of other minority shareholders. He said that they had been unjustly oppressed. He brought in the company—Hartley Baird—itself. On its behalf, he made a considerable counterclaim. He alleged that Dr Wallersteiner had acquired the 80 per cent majority by a cheat. He had not paid a penny in hard cash for the shares. Having got control, he denuded the company of its resources. He never paid anything back, or at any rate very little. . . .

[The story continues at length, followed by legal arguments.]

II. The corporate veil   It is plain that Dr Wallersteiner used many companies, trusts, or other legal entities as if they belonged to him. He was in control of them as much as any 'one-man company' is under the control of the one man who owns all the shares and is the chairman and managing dir- ector. He made contracts of enormous magnitude on their behalf on a sheet of notepaper without reference to anyone else. Such as a contract on behalf of the Rothschild Trust to buy shares for £518,786 15s or to vary it; or a contract on behalf of Stawa AG for a commission of £235,000. He used their moneys as if they were his own. When money was paid to him for shares which he himself owned beneficially, he banked it in the name of IFT of Nassau. Such as the £50,000 for the shares in Watford Chemical Co. Ltd. When he paid out money on personal loans by himself, he drew the cheques on the account in the name of IFT of Nassau. Such as the £125,000 lent to Camp Bird to pay off the Pearl charge. His concerns always used as their bankers the Anglo-Continental Exchange Ltd. That was a merchant bank in the City of London of which he was chairman and which he effect- ively controlled.

Counsel as *amicus curiae* suggested that all these various concerns were used by Dr Wallersteiner as a facade, so that each could be treated as his *alter ego*. Each was in reality Dr Wallersteiner wear- ing another hat. Counsel for Dr Wallersteiner repudiated this suggestion. It was quite wrong, he said, to pierce the corporate veil. The principle enunciated in *Salomon* v *A. Salomon & Co. Ltd* [1897] AC 22 was sacrosanct. If we were to treat each of these concerns as being Dr Wallersteiner himself under another hat, we should not, he said, be lifting a corner of the corporate veil. We should be sending it up in flames.

I am prepared to accept that the English concerns—those governed by English company law or its counterparts in Nassau or Nigeria—were distinct legal entities. I am not so sure about the Liechtenstein concerns—such as the Rothschild Trust, the Cellpa Trust or Stawa AG. There was no evidence before us of Liechtenstein law. I will assume, too, that they were distinct legal entities, similar to an English limited company. Even so, I am quite clear that they were just the puppets of Dr Wallersteiner. He controlled their every movement. Each danced to his bidding. He pulled the strings. No one else got within reach of them. Transformed into legal language, they were his agents to do as he commanded. He was the principal behind them. I am of the opinion that the court should pull aside the corporate veil and treat these concerns as being his creatures—for whose doings he should be, and is, responsible. At any rate, it was up to him to show that any one else had a say in their affairs and he never did so: cf. *Gilford Motor Co. Ltd* v *Horne* [1933] Ch 935 at pp. 943 and 957.

3.3.3 The tide turns against the lifting of veils

The two previous extracts from judgments of Lord Denning represent the views of a judge inclined to look to the substance rather than the form and therefore to be ready to lift the veil. However, the following extracts from more recent cases suggest a formalistic approach more reluctant to lift the veil. As Slade LJ later pointed out in *Adams* v *Cape Industries plc* (below) two of Lord Denning's brother judges in the *Wallersteiner* case expressly declined to tear away the corporate veil and in the *Littlewoods* case refused to deny that the subsidiary was not a separate legal entity. Slade LJ's view that little support could be derived from the broad and flexible views of Lord Denning more accurately reflects the current state of the law.

Dimbleby & Sons Ltd v *National Union of Journalists*
A political case?
[1984] 1 All ER 751, [1984] 1 WLR 427, House of Lords

Facts   *The case concerned whether certain industrial action amounted to unlawful secondary picketing. The point of relevance here was whether TBF Ltd and TBF Printers Ltd which were both subsidiaries of the same holding company were separate entities. If they were considered to be one entity the industrial action would have been lawful. The court took a formalistic line and held against the union on grounds that the companies were separate entities.*

LORD DIPLOCK: Little time needs to be spent on the argument on behalf of the NUJ, which is purely one of statutory construction, that TBF Printers, although a separate corporate entity from T. Bailey Forman Ltd, was nevertheless a party to the trade dispute between the NUJ and the latter company.

My lords, the reason why English statutory law, and that of all other trading countries, has long permitted the creation of corporations as artificial persons distinct from their individual shareholders and from that of any other corporation even though the shareholders of both corporations are identical is to enable business to be undertaken with limited financial liability in the event of the business proving to be a failure. The 'corporate veil' in the case of companies incorporated under the Companies Acts is drawn by statute and it can be pierced by some other statute if such other statute so provides; but, in view of its *raison d'être* and its consistent recognition by the courts since *Salomon* v *A. Salomon & Co. Ltd* [1897] AC 22, one would expect that any Parliamentary intention to pierce the corporate veil would be expressed in clear and unequivocal language. I do not wholly exclude the possibility that even in the absence of express words stating that in specified circumstances one company, although separately incorporated, is to be treated as sharing the same legal personality of another, a purposive construction of the statute may nevertheless lead inexorably to the conclusion that such must have been the intention of Parliament. It was argued for the NUJ in the instant case that, because TBF Printers and T. Bailey Forman Ltd were operating companies with identical shareholding and were companies of which a single holding company had control, TBF Printers as well as T. Bailey Forman Ltd were 'an employer who is a party to the dispute' between the NUJ and T. Bailey Forman Ltd within the meaning of that phrase where it is used in s. 17(3) of the [Employment Act 1980].

My lords, this seems to me to be a quite impossible construction to put on the phrase 'an employer who is a party to the dispute' in the context in which it appears in subs. (3).

J. H. Rayner (Mincing Lane) Ltd v Department of Trade & Industry
The International Tin Council litigation
[1989] Ch 72, Court of Appeal

This case stridently upholds the *Salomon* principle. Agency cannot be inferred from the mere fact that the members control the company either as directors or shareholders, nor from the fact that the sole purpose of the company is to benefit the members.

Facts   *The case arises out of the collapse of the International Tin Council which left behind massive debts and a bonanza of litigation. (About half of the Chancery section of the Law Reports for 1989 is taken up with this and two other related cases.) Though not a registered company, the ITC had been given the legal capacities of a body corporate by order in council. The question was whether its members (which were sovereign States) were individually liable for its debts. It was held that they were not.*

KERR LJ: *Submission C: agency*
This is the plaintiffs' third alternative submission. It proceeds on the basis that, contrary to submissions A and B, the ITC falls to be treated as a legal entity which is distinct from its members in the same way as a body corporate, and that the ITC alone is accordingly liable on the contracts made by it unless it also contracted on behalf of its members as undisclosed principals. . . .

But it must be remembered that we are not now dealing with submission A, to the effect that the council is merely a collective name for the members themselves. We are dealing with submission C based on the contrary assumption that the ITC is a legal entity wholly distinct from its members. Its contracts are therefore prima facie made on its own behalf alone, without engaging the liability of its members, in the same way as contracts made by a company subject to the Companies Acts. In submitting that when entering into contracts the ITC nevertheless contracted as agent for its own members, the plaintiffs are therefore faced with the fundamental jurisprudence enshrined in the decision of the House of Lords in *Salomon* v *A. Salomon & Co. Ltd* [1897] AC 22. The crucial point on which the House of Lords overruled the Court of Appeal in that landmark case was precisely the rejection of the doctrine that agency between a corporation and its members in relation to the corporation's contracts can be inferred from the control exercisable by the members over the corporation or from the fact that the sole objective of the corporation's contracts was to benefit the members. That rejection of the doctrine of agency to impugn the non-liability of the members for the acts of the corporation is the foundation of our modern company law. The fallacy of the existence of any such agency relationship is particularly clearly exposed in the speech of Lord Herschell, at pp. 42–3, but there is no need to cite from it. . . .

Finally, Mr Sumption relied on two cases by way of analogy in order to show that there was an agent/principal relationship between the ITC and its members. These were *Gramophone and Typewriter Ltd* v *Stanley* [1908] 2 KB 89 and the decision of Atkinson J in *Smith, Stone and Knight Ltd* v *Birmingham Corporation* [1939] 4 All ER 116. But neither of these cases is of any assistance to the plaintiffs. In the first it was held that there was no principal/agent relationship between a parent company and its wholly owned subsidiary even though the business of the subsidiary was wholly under the control of the parent. Buckley LJ pointed out expressly, at p. 106, that 'obviously' only the German company, and not its English shareholders, would be liable on the German company's contracts. If anything, the decision runs counter to Mr Sumption's submission. In the second case the facts were so unusual that they cannot form any basis of principle. A company acquired a partnership concern, registered it as a subsidiary company but carried on its business as part of the parent company's own business exactly as if the subsidiary were still a partnership. The profits of the subsidiary were treated as the profits of the parent company. When the premises of the subsidiary were compulsorily acquired it was held that the parent—and not merely the subsidiary—was entitled to claim compensation, on the ground that the subsidiary had in fact been operating on behalf of the parent. In my view no conclusion of principle can be derived from that case.

3.3.4 Groups and the rock of limited liability

At 3.3 some comments have already been made about groups of companies. The following cases illustrate how strong is the principle of separate corporate personality and that the courts regard members of a group as separate entities perhaps without exception. On groups of companies generally see also chapter 14.

Re Southard & Co. Ltd
When the runt of the litter goes to the wall!
[1979] 3 All ER 556, [1979] 1 WLR 1198, Court of Appeal

TEMPLEMAN LJ: English company law possesses some curious features, which may generate curious results. A parent company may spawn a number of subsidiary companies, all controlled directly or indirectly by the shareholders of the parent company. If one of the subsidiary companies, to change the metaphor, turns out to be the runt of the litter and declines into insolvency to the dismay of its creditors, the parent company and the other subsidiary companies may prosper to the joy of the shareholders without any liability for the debts of the insolvent subsidiary. It is not surprising that, when a subsidiary company collapses, the unsecured creditors wish the finances of the company and its relationship with other members of the group to be narrowly examined, to ensure that no assets of the subsidiary company have leaked away, that no liabilities of the subsidiary company ought to be laid at the door of other members of the group, and that no indemnity from or right of action against any other company, or against any individual, is by some mischance overlooked.

The anxiety of the creditors will be increased where, as in the present case, all the assets of the subsidiary company are claimed by another member of the group in right of a debenture.

Woolfson v Strathclyde Regional Council
The downside of a group structure
1978 SLT 159, 1978 SC (HL) 90, House of Lords

Facts Mr Woolfson ran a shop in Glasgow specialising in wedding garments. In 1966 the shop premises were compulsorily purchased for road development. Part of the shop premises (57 and 59/61 St George's Road) were owned by Woolfson. The remainder (Nos 53/55) were owned by Solfred Holdings Ltd ('Solfred'), whose shares were owned by Mr and Mrs Woolfson. Woolfson and Solfred apparently received compensation for the value of the land. However, the claim for compensation for disturbance of the business (loss of profits etc.) was refused. This was because the business was operated by M. & L. Campbell (Glasgow) Ltd ('Campbell'), a company again owned by Mr and Mrs Woolfson. Though Campbell occupied the premises, it had no interest in the land. For a successful claim for disturbance, the regulations required that occupation and a legal interest in the land coincide. So Woolfson, as appellant, pursued a series of arguments to establish this *coincidence of occupation and ownership, finally failing to persuade the House of Lords that he and his two companies were in reality a single entity both owning and occupying the land.*

LORD KEITH OF KINKEL: The appellants' argument before the lands tribunal proceeded on the lines that the business carried on in the premises was truly that of the appellants, which Campbell conducted as their agents, so that the appellants were the true occupiers of the premises and entitled as such to compensation for disturbance. Reliance was placed on the decision of Atkinson J in *Smith, Stone & Knight Ltd* v *Birmingham Corporation* [1939] 4 All ER 116. Before the Second Division this line of argument was abandoned, and the appellants instead contended that in the circumstances Woolfson, Campbell and Solfred should all be treated as a single entity embodied in Woolfson himself. This followed the refusal by the court to allow Campbell and Mrs Woolfson to be joined as additional claimants in the proceedings. It was argued, with reliance on *DHN Food Distributors Ltd* v *Tower Hamlets London Borough Council* [1976] 1 WLR 852, that the court should set aside the legalistic view that Woolfson, Solfred and Campbell were each a separate legal persona, and concentrate attention upon the 'realities' of the situation, to the effect of finding that Woolfson was the occupier as well as the owner of the whole premises. This argument was rejected by the court for the reasons given in the opinion of the Lord Justice-Clerk. He approached the matter from the point of view of the principles upon which a court may be entitled to ignore the separate legal status of a limited company and its incorporators, which as held in *Salomon* v *A. Salomon & Co. Ltd* [1897] AC 22 must normally receive full effect in relations between the company and persons dealing with it. He referred to a passage in the judgment of Ormerod LJ in *Tunstall* v *Steigmann* [1962] 2 QB 593, at p. 601, to the effect that any departure from a strict observance of the principles laid down in *Salomon* has been made to deal with special circumstances when a limited company might well be a façade concealing the true facts. Having examined the facts of the instant case, the Lord Justice-Clerk reached the conclusion that they did not substantiate but negatived the argument advanced in support of the 'unity' proposition and that the decision in the *DHN Food Distributors* case was distinguishable.

It was maintained before this House that the conclusion of the Lord Justice-Clerk was erroneous. In my opinion the conclusion was correct, and I regard as unimpeachable the process of reasoning by which it was reached. I can see no grounds whatever, upon the facts found in the special case, for treating the company structure as a mere façade, nor do I consider that the *DHN Food Distributors* case is, on a proper analysis, of assistance to the appellants' argument. The position there was that compensation for disturbance was claimed by a group of three limited companies associated in a wholesale grocery business. The parent company, DHN, carried on the business in the premises which were the subject of compulsory purchase. These premises were owned by Bronze, which had originally been the wholly owned subsidiary of a bank which had advanced money for the purchase of the premises, but which had later become the wholly owned subsidiary of DHN. Bronze had the same directors as DHN and the premises were its only asset. It carried on no activities whatever. The third company, also a wholly owned subsidiary of DHN, owned as its only asset the vehicles used in the grocery business, and it too carried on no operations. The compulsory acquisition resulted in the extinction of the grocery business, since no suitable alternative premises could be found. It was held by the Court of Appeal (Lord Denning MR, Goff and Shaw LJJ), that the group was entitled to compensation for disturbance as owners of the business. The grounds for the decision were (1) that since DHN was in a position to control its subsidiaries in every respect, it was proper to pierce the corporate veil and treat the group as a single economic entity for the purpose of awarding compensation for disturbance; (2) that if the companies were to be treated as separate entities, there was by necessary implication from the circumstances an agreement between DHN and Bronze under which the former had an irrevocable licence to occupy the premises for as long as it wished, and that this gave DHN a sufficient interest in the land to found a claim to compensation for disturbance; and (3) (per Goff and Shaw LJJ) that in the circumstances Bronze held the legal title to the premises in trust for DHN, which also sufficed to entitle DHN to compensation for disturbance. It is the first of those grounds which alone is relevant for present purposes. I have some doubts whether in this respect the Court of Appeal properly applied the principle that it is appropriate to pierce the corporate veil only where special circumstances exist indicating that it is a mere façade concealing the true facts. Further, the decisions of this House in *Harold Holdsworth*

& Co. (Wakefield) Ltd v *Caddies* [1955] 1 WLR 352 and *Scottish Co-operative Wholesale Society Ltd* v *Meyer* [1959] AC 324 which were founded on by Goff LJ in support of this ground of judgment and, as to the first of them, to some extent also by Lord Denning MR, do not, with respect, appear to me to be concerned with that principle. But however that may be, I consider the *DHN Food* case to be clearly distinguishable on its facts from the present case. There the company that owned the land was the wholly owned subsidiary of the company that carried on the business. The latter was in complete control of the situation as respects anything which might affect its business, and there was no one but itself having any kind of interest or right as respects the assets of the subsidiary. Here, on the other hand, the company that carried on the business, Campbell, has no sort of control whatever over the owners of the land, Solfred and Woolfson. Woolfson holds two thirds only of the shares in Solfred, and Solfred has no interest in Campbell. Woolfson cannot be treated as beneficially entitled to the whole shareholding in Campbell, since it is not found that the one share in Campbell held by his wife is held as his nominee. In my opinion there is no basis consonant with principle upon which on the facts of this case the corporate veil can be pierced to the effect of holding Woolfson to be the true owner of Campbell's business or of the assets of Solfred.

Adams v Cape Industries plc
Injuries from inhaling asbestos
[1990] Ch 433, Court of Appeal

As the late Professor Gower put it, in this important case the Court of Appeal 'in a mammoth judgment, involving a number of issues, subjected lifting the veil to the most exhaustive treatment that it has yet received in the English (or Scottish) courts'. For a full discussion of the case see L. C. B. Gower, *Gower's Principles of Modern Company Law*, 5th ed. (London: Sweet & Maxwell, 1992), pp. 125–32.

Facts   Cape, an English company, mined asbestos in South Africa. The products were marketed in USA through a complex range of subsidiaries or associated companies including NAAC, Capasco, CPC and AMC. In a series of actions a large number of factory workers who had suffered from inhaling asbestos dust obtained judgment in a Texas court against the holding company, Cape. They sought unsuccessfully to have the judgment enforced against Cape in England, arguing that Cape was properly a party to the Texas proceedings as it had been present in the USA. The Court of Appeal held (at p. 530) that an English trading company would only be regarded by the English court as having been present abroad if it had established a fixed place of business there at its own expense for more than a minimal time and had carried on its own business there, or if its representative had carried on the English trading company's business at a fixed place of business for more than a material time. The difficult issue is whether it was the English holding company's business that was carried on and not the business of a subsidiary or representative. Three points were unsuccessfully put forward arguing that Cape had been present in the USA, the single economic unit argument (i.e., that Cape and its subsidiaries were really one economic unit), the corporate veil point (that the corporate form is a 'mere façade concealing the true facts', which could be drawn aside), and thirdly the agency argument (that the subsidiaries were mere agents making contracts for their principal, the holding company). Each of these arguments failed. Cape was held not to have been present in the USA. The actions against Cape in Texas were thus, in the eyes of the English court, not properly brought and so the judgments were not enforceable in England.

SLADE LJ (giving the judgment of the court):
The 'single economic unit' argument There is no general principle that all companies in a group of companies are to be regarded as one. On the contrary, the fundamental principle is that 'each company in a group of companies (a relatively modern concept) is a separate legal entity possessed of separate legal rights and liabilities': *The Albazero* [1977] AC 774, 807, per Roskill LJ.

   It is thus indisputable that each of Cape, Capasco, NAAC and CPC were in law separate legal entities. Mr Morison [for the plaintiffs] did not go so far as to submit that the very fact of the parent–subsidiary relationship existing between Cape and NAAC rendered Cape or Capasco present in

Illinois. Nevertheless, he submitted that the court will, in appropriate circumstances, ignore the distinction in law between members of a group of companies treating them as one, and that broadly speaking, it will do so whenever it considers that justice so demands. In support of this submission, he referred us to a number of authorities. . . .

We have some sympathy with Mr Morison's submissions in this context. To the layman at least the distinction between the case where a company itself trades in a foreign country and the case where it trades in a foreign country through a subsidiary, whose activities it has full power to control, may seem a slender one. . . . It is not surprising that in many cases such as *Harold Holdsworth & Co. (Wakefield) Ltd* v *Caddies* [1955] 1 WLR 352, *Scottish Co-operative Wholesale Society Ltd* v *Meyer* [1959] AC 324, *Revlon Inc.* v *Cripps & Lee Ltd* [1980] FSR 85 and *Istituto Chemioterapico Italiano SpA and Commercial Solvents Corporation* v *Commission* (cases 6 & 7/73) [1974] ECR 223, the wording of a particular statute or contract has been held to justify the treatment of parent and subsidiary as one unit, at least for some purposes. The relevant parts of the judgments in the *DHN* case [1976] 1 WLR 852 must, we think, likewise be regarded as decisions on the relevant statutory provisions for compensation, even though these parts were somewhat broadly expressed, and the correctness of the decision was doubted by the House of Lords in *Woolfson* v *Strathclyde Regional Council* 1978 SLT 159 in a passage which will be quoted below.

Mr Morison described the theme of all these cases as being that where legal technicalities would produce injustice in cases involving members of a group of companies, such technicalities should not be allowed to prevail. We do not think that the cases relied on go nearly so far as this. As Sir Godfray submitted, save in cases which turn on the wording of particular statutes or contracts, the court is not free to disregard the principle of *Salomon* v *A. Salomon & Co. Ltd* [1897] AC 22 merely because it considers that justice so requires. Our law, for better or worse, recognises the creation of subsidiary companies, which though in one sense the creatures of their parent companies, will nevertheless under the general law fall to be treated as separate legal entities with all the rights and liabilities which would normally attach to separate legal entities.

In deciding whether a company is present in a foreign country by a subsidiary, which is itself present in that country, the court is entitled, indeed bound, to investigate the relationship between the parent and the subsidiary. In particular, that relationship may be relevant in determining whether the subsidiary was acting as the parent's agent and, if so, on what terms. In *Firestone Tyre and Rubber Co. Ltd* v *Lewellin* [1957] 1 WLR 464 (which was referred to by Scott J [at first instance]) the House of Lords upheld an assessment to tax on the footing that, on the facts, the business both of the parent and subsidiary were carried on by the subsidiary as agent for the parent. However, there is no presumption of any such agency. There is no presumption that the subsidiary is the parent company's *alter ego*. In the court below the judge, [1990] Ch 433 at p. 484B, refused an invitation to infer that there existed an agency agreement between Cape and NAAC comparable to that which had previously existed between Cape and Capasco and that refusal is not challenged on this appeal. If a company chooses to arrange the affairs of its group in such a way that the business carried on in a particular foreign country is the business of its subsidiary and not its own, it is, in our judgment, entitled to do so. Neither in this class of case nor in any other class of case is it open to this court to disregard the principle of *Salomon* v *A. Salomon & Co. Ltd* [1897] AC 22 merely because it considers it just so to do. . . .

In the light of the set up and operations of the Cape group and of the relationship between Cape/Capasco and NAAC we see the attraction of the approach adopted by Lord Denning MR in the *DHN* case [1976] 1 WLR 852, 860C, which Mr Morison urged us to adopt: 'This group is virtually the same as a partnership in which all the three companies are partners'. In our judgment, however, we have no discretion to reject the distinction between the members of the group as a technical point. We agree with Scott J that the observations of Robert Goff LJ in *Bank of Tokyo Ltd* v *Karoon* [1987] AC 45, 64, are apposite:

> [Counsel] suggested beguilingly that it would be technical for us to distinguish between parent and subsidiary company in this context; economically, he said, they were one. But we are concerned not with economics but with law. The distinction between the two is, in law, fundamental and cannot here be bridged. . . .

The 'corporate veil' point Quite apart from cases where statute or contract permits a broad interpretation to be given to references to members of a group of companies, there is one well-recognised exception to the rule prohibiting the piercing of 'the corporate veil'. Lord Keith of Kinkel referred to this principle in *Woolfson* v *Strathclyde Regional Council* 1978 SLT 159 in the course of a speech with which Lord Wilberforce, Lord Fraser of Tullybelton and Lord Russell of Killowen agreed. With reference to the *DHN* decision [1976] 1 WLR 852, he said, at p. 161:

> I have some doubts whether in this respect the Court of Appeal properly applied the prin-ciple that it is appropriate to pierce the corporate veil only where special circumstances exist indicating that it is a mere façade concealing the true facts.

The only allegation of a façade in the plaintiffs' pleadings was that the formation and use of CPC and AMC in the

> alternative marketing arrangements of 1978 were a device or sham or cloak for grave impro-priety on the part of Cape or Capasco, namely to ostensibly remove their assets from the United States of America to avoid liability for asbestos claims whilst at the same time con-tinuing to trade in asbestos there.

In their notice of appeal (para. 2(b)) the plaintiffs referred to their contention made at the trial that CPC 'was set up to replace NAAC in such a way as to disguise the defendants continued involvement in the marketing of the group's asbestos in the United States of America'.

Scott J more or less accepted this contention. . . .

If and so far as the judge intended to say that the motive behind the new arrangements was irrelevant as a matter of law, we would respectfully differ from him. In our judgment, as Mr Morison submitted, whenever a device or sham or cloak is alleged in cases such as this, the motive of the alleged perpetrator must be legally relevant, and indeed this no doubt is the reason why the ques-tion of motive was examined extensively at the trial. The decision in *Jones* v *Lipman* [1962] 1 WLR 832 referred to below was one case where the proven motive of the individual defendant clearly had a significant effect on the decision of Russell J.

. . . The inference which we draw from all the evidence was that Cape's intention was to enable sales of asbestos from the South African subsidiaries to continue to be made in the United States while (a) reducing the appearance of any involvement therein of Cape or its subsidiaries, and (b) reducing by any lawful means available to it the risk of any subsidiary or of Cape as parent com-pany being held liable for United States taxation or subject to the jurisdiction of the United States courts, whether state or federal, and the risk of any default judgment by such a court being held to be enforceable in this country. Inference (a) was also made by the judge. Inference (b) is our own addition. . . .

The question of law which we now have to consider is whether the arrangements regarding NAAC, AMC and CPC made by Cape with the intentions which we have inferred constituted a façade such as to justify the lifting of the corporate veil so as that CPC's and AMC's presence in the United States of America should be treated as the presence of Cape/Capasco for this reason if no other.

In *Merchandise Transport Ltd* v *British Transport Commission* [1962] 2 QB 173, 206–7, Danckwerts LJ referred to certain authorities as showing:

> where the character of a company, or the nature of the persons who control it, is a relevant feature the court will go behind the mere status of the company as a legal entity, and will consider who are the persons as shareholders or even as agents who direct and control the activities of a company which is incapable of doing anything without human assistance.

The correctness of this statement has not been disputed, but it does not assist in determining whether 'the character of a company or the nature of the persons who control it' will be relevant in the present case.

Rather greater assistance on this point is to be found in *Jones* v *Lipman* [1962] 1 WLR 832. In that case the first defendant had agreed to sell to the plaintiffs some land. Pending completion the first defendant sold and transferred the land to the defendant company. The evidence showed that this company was at all material times under the complete control of the first defendant. It also showed that the acquisition by him of the company and the transfer of the land to the company had been carried through solely for the purpose of defeating the plaintiff's right to specific performance: see at p. 836. Russell J made an order for specific performance against both defendants. He held that specific performance cannot be resisted by a vendor who, by his absolute ownership and control of a limited company in which the property is vested, is in a position to cause the contract to be completed. As to the defendant company, he described it, at p. 836, as being

> the creature of the first defendant, a device and a sham, a mask which he holds before his face in an attempt to avoid recognition by the eye of equity.

Following *Jones* v *Lipman*, we agree with Mr Morison that, contrary to the judge's view, where a façade is alleged, the motive of the perpetrator may be highly material.

We were referred to certain broad dicta of Lord Denning MR in *Wallersteiner* v *Moir* [1974] 1 WLR 991, 1013, and in *Littlewoods Mail Order Stores Ltd* v *Inland Revenue Commissioners* [1969] 1 WLR 1241, 1254. In both these cases he expressed his willingness to pull aside the corporate veil, saying in the latter:

> I decline to treat the [subsidiary] as a separate and independent entity. . . . The courts can and often do draw aside the veil. They can, and often do, pull off the mask. They look to see what really lies behind. The legislature has shown the way with group accounts and the rest. And the courts should follow suit. I think that we should look at the Fork Manufacturing Co. Ltd. and see it as it really is—the wholly owned subsidiary of Littlewoods. It is the creature, the puppet, of Littlewoods, in point of fact: and it should be so regarded in point of law.

However, in *Wallersteiner* v *Moir* [1974] 1 WLR 991 Buckley LJ, at p. 1027, and Scarman LJ, at p. 1032, expressly declined to tear away the corporate veil. In the *Littlewoods* case [1969] 1 WLR 1241, 1255, Sachs LJ expressly dissociated himself from the suggestion that the subsidiary was not a separate legal entity and Karminski LJ refrained from associating himself with it. We therefore think that the plaintiffs can derive little support from those dicta of Lord Denning MR.

From the authorities cited to us we are left with rather sparse guidance as to the principles which should guide the court in determining whether or not the arrangements of a corporate group involve a façade within the meaning of that word as used by the House of Lords in *Woolfson* 1978 SLT 159. We will not attempt a comprehensive definition of those principles.

. . . These findings by themselves make it very difficult to contend that the operation of CPC involved a façade which entitles the court to pierce the corporate veil between CPC and Cape/Capasco and treat them all as one. Is the legal position altered by the facts that Cape's intention, in making the relevant arrangements (as we infer), was to enable sales of asbestos from the South African subsidiaries to be made while (a) reducing if not eliminating the appearance of any involvement therein of Cape or its subsidiaries, and (b) reducing by any lawful means available to it the risk of any subsidiary or of Cape as parent company being held liable for United States taxation or subject to the jurisdiction of the United States courts and the risk of any default judgment by such a court being held to be enforceable in this country?

We think not. Mr Morison submitted that the court will lift the corporate veil where a defendant by the device of a corporate structure attempts to evade (i) limitations imposed on his conduct by law; (ii) such rights of relief against him as third parties already possess; and (iii) such rights of relief as third parties may in the future acquire. Assuming that the first and second of these three conditions will suffice in law to justify such a course, neither of them apply in the present case. It is not suggested that the arrangements involved any actual or potential illegality or were intended to deprive anyone of their existing rights. Whether or not such a course deserves moral approval, there was nothing illegal as such in Cape arranging its affairs (whether by the use of subsidiaries or otherwise) so as to attract the minimum publicity to its involvement in the sale of Cape asbestos in the United States of America. As to condition (iii), we do not accept as a matter of law that the court is entitled to lift the corporate veil as against a defendant company which is the member of a corporate group merely because the corporate structure has been used so as to ensure that the legal liability (if any) in respect of particular future activities of the group (and correspondingly the risk of enforcement of that liability) will fall on another member of the group rather than the defendant company. Whether or not this is desirable, the right to use a corporate structure in this manner is inherent in our corporate law. Mr Morison urged on us that the purpose of the operation was in substance that Cape would have the practical benefit of the group's asbestos trade in the United States of America without the risks of tortious liability. This may be so. However, in our judgment, Cape was in law entitled to organise the group's affairs in that manner and (save in the case of AMC to which special considerations apply) to expect that the court would apply the principle of *Salomon* v *A. Salomon & Co. Ltd* [1897] AC 22 in the ordinary way.

The court went on to consider the agency argument and to dismiss the appeal, thus holding that the judgment was not enforceable against Cape.

Multinational companies and mega-litigation

The case of *Adams* v *Cape Industries plc* may leave readers with an uncomfortable feeling that the law has failed to give adequate redress for the injuries of foreign victims of asbestos inhalation against a British holding company. It may seem to be only a technicality of company law that enables a company wishing to oper-ate outside this country to shield itself from liability against genuine claims for damages abroad by strategically incorporating foreign subsidiaries. However, the principles of separate corporate personality and limited liability are so fundamen-tal to company law that the courts have quite properly held that they should not haphazardly lift the veil and hold a shareholder, the holding company, liable sim-ply because of a desire to see the injured plaintiffs compensated.

But the battle is not over, the ingenuity of claimants' lawyers ensuring that novel arguments will be found. In mass compensation claims for injury such as by tobacco or asbestos inhalation the primary problem is the cost of bringing a claim. In the US and increasingly in this jurisdiction this problem is being resolved by lawyers taking the claim on a 'no win, no fee' basis. As regards employees of sub-sidiaries bringing claims for injury suffered abroad against a holding company incorporated in this jurisdiction, the major preliminary issues relate to the conflict of laws. Does the English court have jurisdiction to hear the case and what law should decide the substantive liability of the defendant holding company? Suffice it to say that a number of recent decisions in the House of Lords and the Court of Appeal have held that claims may be brought against the holding company in the English court, (see *Connelly* v *RTZ Corporation plc* [1998] AC 854, HL; *Lubbe* v *Cape plc* [2000] 1 WLR 1545). See Muchlinski (2001) 50 ICLQ 1.

These issues are of considerable world-wide importance and are not merely a dusty academic backwater. Though lawsuits accusing subsidiaries of major corpo-rations of involvement in human rights abuses could once be regarded as a mere nuisance, today they may be a considerable threat to corporate reputation and profitability. (On the pressure for big companies to demonstrate appropriate 'cor-porate social responsibility', see 11.1.2 below.) Litigation is increasingly common and in one case in which villagers in Myanmar alleged that a California-based corporation was implicated in abuses by local troops while clearing land to enable a gas pipeline to be built, the corporation settled the case, agreeing to pay undis-closed damages to the villagers.

Ord v Belhaven Pubs Ltd
Holding companies as shareholders enjoy limited liability
[1998] BCC 607, Court of Appeal

A holding company is a shareholder and, like other shareholders, enjoys limited liability in respect of the debts of the companies whose shares it owns, that is, its subsidiary companies. The courts will not allow a plaintiff with a claim against one company in a group to substitute the holding company or other group subsidiaries as defendants to that claim merely because the group may be a single economic entity.

Facts   Belhaven was a subsidiary company which owned a pub, the Fox Inn at Stanford. In 1989 Mr and Mrs Ord, relying on Belhaven's optimistic claims regarding the turnover and profitability of the business, bought a 20-year lease of the pub and spent large sums unsuccessfully attempting to promote its success. Recession intervened and the Ords issued a writ against Belhaven claiming their losses. In 1992 and 1995 Belhaven, its holding company and another subsidiary undertook restructuring of the group. This involved transfers of assets from Belhaven to the co-subsidiary and then to the holding company. These transfers were made for consideration at book value. While it appeared that the group was run as if it were a single economic entity, there was no evidence that the directors were trying to be devious. In 1997 when the plaintiffs realised that Belhaven no longer had any substantial assets they applied for leave to substitute the holding company and another co-subsidiary as defendants. They succeeded at first instance, the judge holding that the directors had ignored the separate corporate identity of the different companies, and had acted solely in the interests of the group and in disregard of the interests of creditors and of the plaintiffs in particular. This justified lifting the corporate veil and treating the holding company as the controlling mind of the group and therefore as liable for the contingent debt. On appeal Hobhouse LJ held that the procedural basis for the application under the Rules of the Supreme Court did not allow substitution of the new defendants to the action. Further, on the company law issues he observed that the defendant company was in financial difficulties but this was not made worse by the restructurings of 1992 and 1995. There was no evidence that any assets had been transferred at undervalues nor of any improper motives for the transactions. He therefore ruled that the holding company could not be substituted as a defendant and made liable for its subsidiary's debts in the following terms. Substitution of the co-subsidiary as a defendant was also refused.

HOBHOUSE LJ: [The plaintiffs] are seeking to impose a liability upon the shareholders of a company when they dealt with the company itself. There is a liability of the company. The company was the proper party to be sued and remains liable to them, if they make out their case on the merits. What they wish to do now is to assert a liability of the shareholders. That is a liability which can only be properly characterised as a new cause of action. The only way in which it can be described as not a new cause of action is if it is recognised and established that it was wrong to sue the original defendant, but that is not this case. The original defendant was the right defendant; it is not suggested that it was the wrong defendant in 1991; it is suggested that the first time at which it might be appropriate to consider substitution was after 1992. That is a situation which just does not marry up to the scheme of the rule or of the contentions which are being advanced on behalf of the plaintiffs.

The plaintiffs are unable to establish that they are not making and seeking to present a new cause of action against the new party. If that is what they are in truth doing then, of course they should apply to join the new party and to deliver an amended pleading making claims against that new party. If they do that then they run into Limitation Act questions which may or may not prove insuperable. The course that they have adopted under the rule is not the appropriate course.

The second aspect is the factual aspect and the lifting of the corporate veil. As will be appreciated from what I have already said, the judge in the latter part of her judgment does not have proper regard to the evidence, or indeed what she has accepted in the earlier parts. She uses the words 'deliberately ignore the separate corporate identity', carrying with it an inference that something improper has been done. Nothing improper was done by the group or the companies in the group or their directors.

Similarly, she suggests that there were breaches of duty because she said they deliberately and totally disregarded their duties to the creditors. That is not the position on the evidence and is not something which she was entitled to say on the evidence.

Indeed, before us Mr Ashe [counsel for the plaintiffs] has frankly accepted that he does not put his case in that way. He says no impropriety is alleged. He does not allege that there was any breach of the provisions of the Insolvency Act, nor was there any conduct on the part of the directors (or any other person) in 1992 or 1995 which would give rise to remedies under the Companies Act 1985 or under the Insolvency Act. Therefore, he is not able to rely upon any concept of a fault or indeed of fraud in support of his contention that the corporate veil should be pierced. It will be appreciated that this immediately puts the facts of this case into a completely different category from cases such as *Wallersteiner* v *Moir* [1974] 1 WLR 991. Furthermore, he is not able to make out any case that at any stage the company was a mere façade, or that it concealed the true facts, nor that there was any sham. All the transactions that took place were overt transactions. They were conducted in accordance with the liberties that are conferred upon corporate entities by the Companies Act and they do not conceal anything from anybody. The companies were operating at material times as trading companies and they were not being interposed as shams or for some ulterior motive.

Therefore, the judge's factual basis was wrong, but she also seems to have relied to some extent on what can be described as a concept of corporate benefit, or a concept of the economic unit. Indeed, in support of this part of his argument Mr Ashe referred to the case of *Woolfson* v *Strathclyde Regional Council* 1978 SLT 159, and *DHN Ltd* v *Tower Hamlets London Borough Council* [1976] 1 WLR 852. These were both compensation cases which involved questions of valuation of interest which raised much broader criteria than those which are concerned with establishing legal liability of one corporate entity or another for alleged torts or breaches of contract.

But in any event, the matter was reviewed again by the Court of Appeal in the case of *Adams* v *Cape Industries plc* [1990] Ch 433. This case arose in a rather different context of the status of foreign judgments and jurisdiction over companies where a subsidiary in the group was trading in a particular company, and the extent to which what occurred could be attributed to the activity of trading could be attributed to other companies in the groups.

In the course of its judgment, the Court of Appeal considered both what is described as the single economic unit argument of groups of company and the stripping or piercing the corporate veil. They discussed the authorities and they clearly recognised that the concepts were extremely limited indeed. For example in relation to the idea of economic unit, they quoted ([1990] Ch 433 at p. 538G) with approval Robert Goff LJ in *Bank of Tokyo Ltd* v *Karoon* [1987] AC 45, where he said at p. 64F:

> [Counsel] suggested beguilingly that it would be technical for us to distinguish between parent and subsidiary company in this context; economically, he said they were one. But we are concerned not with economics but with law. The distinction between the two is, in law, fundamental and cannot here be bridged.

The approach of the judge in the present case was simply to look at the economic unit, to disregard the distinction between the legal entities that were involved and then to say: since the company cannot pay, the shareholders who are the people financially interested should be made to pay instead. That of course is radically at odds with the whole concept of corporate personality and limited liability and the decision of the House of Lords in *Salomon* v *Salomon & Co. Ltd* [1897] AC 22.

On the question of lifting the corporate veil they expressed themselves similarly at [1990] Ch 433 at p. 544, but it is clear that they were of the view that there must be some impropriety before the corporate veil can be pierced. It is not necessary to examine the extent or the limitation of the principle because, in the present case no impropriety is alleged. For example, they quoted (at p. 539D–E) what was said by Lord Keith in *Woolfson* concerning the *DHN* decision. I have some doubts whether in this respect the Court of Appeal properly applied the principle that it is appropriate to pierce the corporate veil only where special circumstances exist, indicating that it is a mere façade concealing the true facts.

The plaintiffs in the present case cannot bring themselves within any such principle. There is no façade that was adopted at any stage; there was not concealment of the true facts.

We pressed Mr Ashe during the course of his submissions as to whether he was making any such suggestion. He was unable to give a satisfactory reply—obviously inevitable because there was no basis for suggesting that there was any such façade, it was just the ordinary trading of a group of companies under circumstances where, as was said in the *Adams* case at p. 544F, the company is in law entitled to organise the group's affairs in the manner that it does, and to expect that the court should apply the principles of *Salomon* v *Salomon* in the ordinary way. Therefore the basis of the judge's reasoning and the attempt to support it cannot be sustained.

That leaves only the case of *Creasey* v *Breachwood Motors Ltd* [1992] BCC 638, the decision of Mr Southwell.

There may have been elements in that case of asset stripping. I do not so read the report of his judgment. But he appears to have followed a very similar train of thought to that which was followed by the judge in the present case. I do not consider it would be useful to analyse his reasoning in view of the comments that I have made about the reasoning of the judge in the present case. But it seems to me to be inescapable that the case in *Creasey* v *Breachwood* as it appears to the court cannot be sustained. It represents a wrong adoption of the principle of piercing the corporate veil and an issue of the power granted by the rules to substitute one party for the other following death or succession. Therefore in my judgment the case of *Creasey* v *Breachwood* should no longer be treated as authoritative.

It also follows from what I have said that I consider that the appeal should be allowed and the judge's order should be set aside. This case should proceed as a case against the original defendant, and the plaintiffs should make out their case against the original defendant and obtain such judgment as they are entitled to against them.

BROOKE LJ: I agree.

SIR JOHN BALCOMBE: I agree. I would merely add this. If there had been any substance in the allegations that there had been some impropriety in the handling of the group restructuring, insolvency law (and in particular I have in mind s. 423 of the Insolvency Act 1986 [transactions defrauding creditors]) makes adequate provision for dealing with that eventuality.

F. G. Rixon, 'Lifting the veil between holding and subsidiary companies'
(1986) 102 LQR 415

DHN Food Distributors Ltd carried on business as grocery and provision merchants. The premises from which the company traded were owned by a wholly owned subsidiary of the company, Bronze Investments Ltd, and the vehicles used in the business were owned by another wholly owned subsidiary, DHN Food Transport Ltd. The business premises of DHN Food Distributors having been compulsorily acquired by Tower Hamlets London Borough Council, and no suitable alternative premises being available, the company and its two subsidiaries went into voluntary liquidation.

Had the business, the business premises and the vehicles used in the business been in the one ownership, compensation would have been payable, under rules (2) and (6) of section 5 of the Land Compensation Act 1961, both for the value of the land compulsorily acquired and for disturbance of the business. In the circumstances, however, the acquiring authority paid compensation for the value of the land to the registered proprietors, Bronze Investments, but contended that no compensation for disturbance was payable since Bronze Investments had carried on no business, the business which had been disturbed being the business of DHN Food Distributors, which company, having no interest in the land, had no claim under the Land Compensation Act.

This contention succeeded before the Lands Tribunal but found no favour with the Court of Appeal, which held that the case was one in which the court was 'entitled to look at the realities of the situation and to pierce the corporate veil' (*DHN Food Distributions Ltd* v *Tower Hamlets London Borough Council* [1976] 1 WLR 852 per Goff LJ at p. 861); that the three companies 'should, for present purposes, be treated as one' (per Lord Denning MR at p. 860), as 'a single entity' (per Shaw LJ at p. 867); and that, 'as a group', the three companies were 'entitled to compensation not only for the value of the land, but also compensation for disturbance' (per Lord Denning MR at p. 860).

Lord Denning MR said (at p.860):

> We all know that in many respects a group of companies are treated together for the purpose of general accounts, balance sheet, and profit and loss account. They are treated as one concern. Professor Gower in *Principles of Modern Company Law*, 3rd ed. (1969), p. 216 says: 'there is evidence of a general tendency to ignore the separate legal entities of various companies within a group, and to look instead at the economic entity of the whole group'.

Goff LJ, on the other hand, was at pains to state that he 'would not at this juncture accept that in every case where one has a group of companies one is entitled to pierce the veil' and based the decision in the case, as did also Shaw LJ, on 'the facts of this particular case' (at p. 861).

When read in context, the statement of Gower quoted by Lord Denning MR is found to have been made merely by way of an aside to what Gower himself described as a 'tentative' conclusion which might 'perhaps, be drawn'. Elsewhere in his *Principles of Modern Company Law*, in a passage presumably overlooked by the Master of the Rolls, Gower stated that 'the rule that a company is distinct from its members applies equally to the separate companies of a group' (3rd ed., p. 71; [5th ed., p. 88]. Furthermore, in *Industrial Equity Ltd* v *Blackburn* (1977) 137 CLR 567 Mason J said that 'modern requirements as to consolidated or group accounts', to which Lord Denning MR referred both in *DHN Food Distributors Ltd* v *Tower Hamlets London Borough Council* [1976] 1 WLR 852 at p. 861 and in the earlier case of *Littlewoods Mail Order Stores Ltd* v *Inland Revenue Commissioners* [1969] 1 WLR 1241 at p. 1254, 'can scarcely be contended [to] operate to deny the distinct identity of each company in a group' (137 CLR 567 at p. 577).

The question for decision in *Industrial Equity Ltd* v *Blackburn* was 'whether in ascertaining the amount of profits available for distribution by a holding company by way of dividend it is correct to look at the profit of the holding company itself or to the group profit as disclosed by the consolidated accounts' (at p. 575). The Full Court of the High Court of Australia held that the principle prohibiting the payment of dividends otherwise than out of profits 'refers exclusively to the profits of the company declaring and paying the dividend', this being 'a natural consequence of the recognition of the separate personality of each company' (per Mason J at p. 577).

Mason J, with the concurrence of his four brethren, said (at p. 577):

> It has been said that the rigours of the doctrine enunciated by *Salomon* v *A. Salomon & Co. Ltd* have been alleviated by the modern requirements as to consolidated or group accounts introduced in the United Kingdom by the Companies Act 1948 and in New South Wales by the Companies Act 1961 (NSW)—see Gower, *Principles of Modern Company Law*, 3rd ed. (1969), pp. 198–9. But the purpose of these requirements is to ensure that the members of, and for that matter persons dealing with, a holding company are provided with accurate information as to the profit or loss and the state of affairs of that company and its subsidiary companies within the group.... It is for this purpose that the Companies Act treats the business group as one entity and requires that its financial results be incorporated in consolidated accounts....
>
> However, it can scarcely be contended that the provisions of the Act operate to deny the separate legal personality of each company in a group. Thus, in the absence of contract creating some additional right, the creditors of company A, a subsidiary company within a group, can look only to that company for payment of their debts. They cannot look to company B, the holding company, for payment.

(Cf. *Re Southard & Co. Ltd* [1979] 1 WLR 1198 per Templeman LJ at p. 1208.)

The decision of the Australian High Court in *Industrial Equity Ltd* v *Blackburn* is hardly consistent with the assertion of a 'general tendency to ignore the separate legal entities of various companies within a group'. No more is the tenor of the speech of Lord Keith of Kinkel in the House of Lords in *Woolfson* v *Strathclyde Regional Council* 1978 SC (HL) 90....

Further doubt is cast on *DHN Food Distributors Ltd* v *Tower Hamlets London Borough Council* by the case of *Multinational Gas and Petrochemical Co.* v *Multinational Gas and Petrochemical Services Ltd* [1983] Ch 258.

Three multinational oil companies, incorporated respectively in the United States of America, France and Japan, caused the plaintiff, Multinational Gas and Petrochemical Co. ('Multinational'), to be incorporated in Liberia to buy, transport, store and sell liquefied petroleum gas and other similar products. On the advice of tax counsel, the three oil companies procured the incorporation in England of a second wholly owned subsidiary, Multinational Gas and Petrochemical Services Ltd ('Services'), to carry on the business of Multinational under an agency agreement. The business did not prosper; on the contrary, Multinational ceased trading in circumstances which amounted to a 'financial disaster for the plaintiff's creditors' ([1983] Ch 258 at p. 265). In the course of the winding up of the company, the liquidator was advised that there was evidence that Services had acted negligently in preparing budgets, forecasts and information for Multinational and that the directors of Multinational—who, it was alleged, acted at all material times 'in accordance with the directions and at the behest of' (at p. 265) the three oil companies—had in turn been negligent in failing to appreciate the deficiencies in the material supplied by Services and had made decisions negligently. Accordingly, at the instance of the liquidator of the company, Multinational commenced an action for damages for breaches of duty of care against Services and applied for leave, under RSC Ord. 11, r. 1, to issue concurrent writs of summons against the three oil companies and the directors of Multinational and to serve notice of those writs on the defendants outside the jurisdiction.

Affirming the decision of the judge setting aside the order of the master granting leave to serve the foreign defendants outside the jurisdiction, Lawton and Dillon LJJ stated, inter alia, that Multinational was 'at law a different legal person from the subscribing oil company shareholders and was not their agent' (per Lawton LJ at p. 269; cf. Salomon v A. Salomon & Co. Ltd [1897] AC 22 per Lord Macnaghten at p. 51); that the oil companies 'as shareholders were [not] under any duty of care to the plaintiff' (per Lawton LJ at p. 269; cf. per Dillon LJ at p. 288); and that as shareholders the oil companies were not 'liable to anyone except to the extent and the manner provided by the Companies Act 1948' (per Lawton LJ at p. 269; cf. Salomon v A. Salomon & Co. Ltd per Lord Macnaghten at p. 51). And whilst May LJ dissented from the decision that the 'company law point' provided the foreign defendants with such a defence that the plaintiff's claims against them were bound to fail, he nowhere suggested that Multinational might properly be treated as one with its parent companies so as to render those companies liable for Multinational's debts.

Like Woolfson v Strathclyde Regional Council, Multinational Gas & Petrochemical Co. v Multinational Gas & Petrochemical Services Ltd can be distinguished on its facts from DHN Food Distributors Ltd v Tower Hamlets London Borough Council. However, the tenor of the judgments in Woolfson v Strathclyde Regional Council, Multinational Gas & Petrochemical Co. v Multinational Gas & Petrochemical Services Ltd and Industrial Equity Ltd v Blackburn indicates unmistakably that the decision of the Court of Appeal in DHN Food Distributors Ltd v Tower Hamlets London Borough Council was an aberration and that the principle that 'each company in a group of companies . . . is a separate legal entity possessed of separate legal rights and liabilities' is 'now unchallengeable by judicial decision' (Albacruz v Albazero [1977] AC 774 per Roskill LJ at p. 807).

In Woolfson v Strathclyde Regional Council Lord Keith, referring with approval to a passage in the judgment of Ormerod LJ in Tunstall v Steigmann [1962] 2 QB 593 at p. 602, stated that the corporate veil might be lifted only where the company was a mere 'façade'. However, neither Lord Keith nor Ormerod LJ explained the import of that term. In its figurative sense, 'façade' denotes outward appearance, especially one that is false or deceptive and imports pretence and concealment. That the corporator has 'complete control of the company' is not enough to constitute the company a mere façade (Tunstall v Steigmann per Ormerod LJ at p. 602); rather that term suggests, in the context, the deliberate concealment of the identity and activities of the corporator. Certainly the term calls to mind expressions used by the court when lifting the veil in Re Darby [1911] 1 KB 95 per Phillimore J at p. 101, 'The fraud here is that what they did through the corporation they did themselves and represented it to have been done by a corporation of some standing and position, or at any rate a corporation which was more than and different from themselves'; Gilford Motor Co. Ltd v Horne [1993] Ch 935, per Lord Hanworth MR at p. 956: '. . . this company was formed as a device, a stratagem, in order to mask the effective carrying on of a business of Mr E.B. Horne'; and Jones v Lipman [1962] 1 WLR 832 per Russell J at p. 836: 'The defendant company is . . . a mask which he holds before his face in an attempt to avoid recognition by the eye of equity': all cases in which the company was formed in order to enable the corporator to do through, and under cover of, the company what he might not do openly and in person. But whatever the precise import in this context of the term 'façade', the House of Lords has plainly discountenanced any contention that the court may 'disregard Salomon's case whenever it is just and equitable to do so' (Sugarman and Webb (1977) 93 LQR 170 at p. 174). And rightly so, it is submitted. The separate legal personality of a company, although a 'technical point' (DHN Food Distributors Ltd v Tower Hamlets London Borough Council [1976] 1 WLR 852 per Lord Denning MR at p. 860) is 'no matter of form; it is a matter of substance and reality' (Tunstall v Steigmann [1962] 2 QB 593 per Willmer LJ at p. 605) and the corporator ought not, on every occasion, to be relieved of the disadvantageous consequences of an arrangement voluntarily entered into by the corporator for reasons considered by the corporator to be of advantage to him—cf. *quod approbo non reprobo; qui sentit commodum sentire debet et onus*. In particular:

> The 'group enterprise' concept must obviously be carefully limited so that companies who seek the advantages of separate corporate personality must generally accept the corresponding burdens and limitations. (*Manley Inc.* v *Fallis* (1977) 38 CPR (2d) 74 per Lacourcière JA as quoted by Trainor J in *Schouls* v *Canadian Meat Processing Corp.* (1983) 147 DLR (3d) 81 at p. 83.)

3.4 COMPANIES AND CRIME

3.4.1 The 'directing mind and will'

There is much literature on the criminal liability of companies and many cases of which the following are but a handful. There are natural limitations on the criminal liability of a company which cannot of course commit rape or bigamy. Nor can a company be imprisoned, as a company, being an abstract person, cannot itself perform or be subjected to a physical action. We are very familiar with the idea of companies being liable for criminal offences, though the concept does not always sit easily. French lawyers in contrast tend to regard the application of criminal sanctions as the expression by the State of a moral judgment more directly appropriate for individuals. However, in England there is a mass of regulatory offences that apply to companies. Thus for example in *R* v *F. & M. Dobson Ltd* (1995) *The Times*, 8 March 1995, Court of Appeal, the manufacturer of a nut brittle sweet called 'Cock-ups' appealed against a £25,000 fine for supplying for human consumption a chocolate sweet which failed to comply with food safety requirements. The complainant's wife 'put one of the sweets into her mouth and found it not to be a sweet but the blade of a Stanley knife enrobed in chocolate'. In this case it was necessary only to prove that the company caused the criminal act, the supply of the offending item (*actus reus*), and this was not disputed.

Sometimes offences are of strict liability with no criminal intent required. For other offences criminal intention is required (*mens rea*), and sometimes guilty knowledge (e.g., that a person buying an adult video is under 18). However, as a company is an artificial legal person, it is necessary to decide whose acts or mental processes are to be attributed to the company. As appears from the following extracts the cases on 'attribution theory' have recently been coming thick and fast, apparently pointing in all different directions and causing dismay among students, especially those who still want to believe that law is a science and not an art.

The cases that follow are very varied. They consider criminal offences and defences, contempt of court and in *El Ajou* v *Dollar Land Holdings plc* [1994] 2 All ER 685 a civil claim to recover the proceeds of crime. Some cases consider what is necessary in order to prove a prima facie offence. Several others deal with 'due diligence' defences. A criminal provision may specifically state that it is a defence to show that the company had taken all reasonable precautions and exercised due diligence to avoid commission of the offence. Or a health and safety provision might require the company to take all steps as are reasonable or reasonably practicable to ensure proper safety standards. If an accident occurs, a defence of due diligence is then available. Put another way it may be necessary in order to convict the company to show that senior management had failed to establish proper safety standards.

Common themes in the cases that follow include judges attempting to construe legislation so as to second-guess Parliament's intention and enforce the policy of the provision. Another is the regular airing of the House of Lords case of *Tesco Supermarkets Ltd* v *Nattrass* [1972] AC 153. This is the case that propounds the narrowest attribution test, namely, that one attributes to the company only the acts and knowledge of its 'directing mind and will' as indicated by its constitution. Thus in simple terms, this test requires that in order to convict a company one must be able to attribute criminal acts or defaults etc. to its senior management. The next possible test is based on agency principles, to attribute to the company acts carried out by its agents with due authority. Most strict of all is to say that the company is vicariously liable in respect of all acts of employees performed 'out of and in the course of their employment'.

The courts will generally claim to select attribution tests as a matter of statutory construction, in order to promote Parliament's intention and the policy of the criminal provision. This may be to promote health and safety, to prohibit restrictive trade practices or to avoid environmental pollution. Clearly it is more difficult to convict a company if it is necessary to prove that acts or omissions by senior management led to the criminal lapses by subordinate employees. Thus, four out of the seven cases extracted or discussed below distinguish the 'directing mind and will' test in *Tesco Supermarkets Ltd* v *Nattrass*. Six cases, the exception being *Seaboard Offshore Ltd* v *Secretary of State for Transport* [1994] 1 WLR 541, take a strict approach in enforcing criminal policy. One might therefore conclude that the 'directing mind and will' principle, sometimes called the organic or alter ego theory, is not being widely applied. The comments of Hoffmann LJ in the *El Ajou* case below suggest that the organic theory is an import from Germany. (This theory transplanted from a more 'scientific' legal system than ours also appears in art. 9 of the First Company Law Directive relating to *ultra vires* and the powers of the directors and has again caused some conceptual problems; see 5.2.3.) If the 'directing mind and will' theory is a transplant then perhaps it is suffering a slow rejection in the context of criminal offences by the company. It is clear that acts of the organs of the company, primarily the board of directors, are the acts of the company. In English law when powers are then delegated to another individual it is much less easy to say that that individual is an organ of the company and so is acting as the company. English law is more happy with the concept of agency which gives a broader and more flexible approach to the problem. It also enables the courts more readily to promote the assumed policy of Parliament and to obtain the necessary convictions of companies whose ordinary employees have transgressed. (For a detailed commentary see Mayson, French and Ryan, *Company Law* at para. 19.8.)

Tesco Supermarkets Ltd v *Nattrass*
The expensive special offer
[1972] AC 153, House of Lords

In the following judgment Lord Reid considers when persons are to be regarded as the company (i.e., as its directing mind and will) as opposed to being merely its servants or agents. In the case the company was prima facie criminally liable because one of its employees acting on its behalf had committed the criminal act. However, a defence was available under the criminal provision as the criminal act was that of another person, the shop manager, and not the company itself. The senior management had exercised due diligence to avoid commission of the offence.

Facts   An assistant at a Norwich branch of Tesco had stocked the shelves with Radiant washing-powder showing the normal price while posters at the shop were advertising a lower special-offer price. The store manager failed to notice the error. The company was charged with an offence of misstating the price under the Trade Descriptions Act 1968. Section 24(1) of the Act allowed a defence where 'the commission of the offence was due to the act or default of another person' and the accused (the company in this case) had taken 'all reasonable precautions and exercised all due diligence to avoid the commission of [the] offence'. The prosecution argued that this defence was not available as the manager (as representing the company) had not done all he could to avoid the offence. The House of Lords held that (Tesco having more than 800 store managers), the manager was not the directing mind and will of the company. The company (i.e., officers at a higher level) had in fact done all they should have done to avoid the offence, and the default was that of another person, i.e., an employee. Accordingly, the company was acquitted, making prosecutions of companies in such cases very much more difficult.

LORD REID: My lords, the appellants own a large number of supermarkets in which they sell a wide variety of goods. The goods are put out for sale on shelves or stands, each article being marked with the price at which it is offered for sale. The customer selects the articles he wants, takes them to the cashier, and pays the price. From time to time the appellants, apparently by way of advertisement, sell 'flash packs' at prices lower than the normal price. In September 1969 they were selling Radiant washing-powder in this way. The normal price was 3s 11d but these packs were marked and sold at 2s 11d. Posters were displayed in the shops drawing attention to this reduction in price....

Where a limited company is the employer difficult questions do arise in a wide variety of circumstances in deciding which of its officers or servants is to be identified with the company so that his guilt is the guilt of the company.

I must start by considering the nature of the personality which by a fiction the law attributes to a corporation. A living person has a mind which can have knowledge or intention or be negligent and he has hands to carry out his intentions. A corporation has none of these: it must act through living persons, though not always one or the same person. Then the person who acts is not speaking or acting for the company. He is acting as the company and his mind which directs his acts is the mind of the company. There is no question of the company being vicariously liable. He is not acting as a servant, representative, agent or delegate. He is an embodiment of the company or, one could say, he hears and speaks through the persona of the company, within his appropriate sphere, and his mind is the mind of the company. If it is a guilty mind then that guilt is the guilt of the company. It must be a question of law whether, once the facts have been ascertained, a person in doing particular things is to be regarded as the company or merely as the company's servant or agent. In that case any liability of the company can only be a statutory or vicarious liability....

Reference is frequently made to the judgment of Denning LJ in *H.L. Bolton (Engineering) Co. Ltd* v *T.J. Graham & Sons Ltd* [1957] 1 QB 159. He said, at p. 172:

> A company may in many ways be likened to a human body. It has a brain and nerve centre which controls what it does. It also has hands which hold the tools and act in accordance with directions from the centre. Some of the people in the company are mere servants and agents who are nothing more than hands to do the work and cannot be said to represent the mind or will. Others are directors and managers who represent the directing mind and will of the company, and control what it does. The state of mind of these managers is the state of mind of the company and is treated by the law as such.

In that case the directors of the company only met once a year: they left the management of the business to others, and it was the intention of those managers which was imputed to the company.

I think that was right. There have been attempts to apply Lord Denning's words to all servants of a company whose work is brain work, or who exercise some managerial discretion under the direction of superior officers of the company. I do not think that Lord Denning intended to refer to them. He only referred to those who 'represent the directing mind and will of the company, and control what it does'.

I think that is right for this reason. Normally the board of directors, the managing director and perhaps other superior officers of a company carry out the functions of management and speak and act as the company. Their subordinates do not. They carry out orders from above and it can make no difference that they are given some measure of discretion. But the board of directors may delegate some part of their functions of management giving to their delegate full discretion to act independently of instructions from them. I see no difficulty in holding that they have thereby put such a delegate in their place so that within the scope of the delegation he can act as the company. It may not always be easy to draw the line but there are cases in which the line must be drawn. *Lennards Carrying Co. Ltd* v *Asiatic Petroleum Co. Ltd* [1915] AC 705 was one of them.

In some cases the phrase *alter ego* has been used. I think it is misleading. When dealing with a company the word *alter* is I think misleading. The person who speaks and acts as the company is not *alter*. He is identified with the company. And when dealing with an individual no other individual can be his *alter ego*. The other individual can be a servant, agent, delegate or representative but I know of neither principle nor authority which warrants the confusion (in the literal or original sense) of two separate individuals.

. . . I think that the true view is that the judge must direct the jury that if they find certain facts proved then as a matter of law they must find that the criminal act of the officer, servant or agent including his state of mind, intention, knowledge or belief is the act of the company. I have already dealt with the considerations to be applied in deciding when such a person can and when he cannot be identified with the company. I do not see how the nature of the charge can make any difference. If the guilty man was in law identifiable with the company then whether his offence was serious or venial his act was the act of the company but if he was not so identifiable then no act of his, serious or otherwise, was the act of the company itself. . . .

What good purpose could be served by making an employer criminally responsible for the misdeeds of some of his servants but not for those of others? It is sometimes argued—it was argued in the present case—that making an employer criminally responsible, even when he has done all that he could to prevent an offence, affords some additional protection to the public because this will induce him to do more. But if he has done all he can how can he do more? I think that what lies behind this argument is a suspicion that magistrates too readily accept evidence that an employer has done all he can to prevent offences. But if magistrates were to accept as sufficient a paper scheme and perfunctory efforts to enforce it they would not be doing their duty—that would not be 'due diligence' on the part of the employer.

Then it is said that this would involve discrimination in favour of a large employer like the appellants against a small shopkeeper. But that is not so. Mr Clement [the Tesco store manager] was the 'opposite number' of the small shopkeeper and he was liable to prosecution in this case. The purpose of this Act must have been to penalise those at fault, not those who were in no way to blame.

The Divisional Court decided this case on a theory of delegation. In that they were following some earlier authorities. But they gave far too wide a meaning to delegation. I have said that a board of directors can delegate part of their functions of management so as to make their delegate an embodiment of the company within the sphere of the delegation. But here the board never delegated any part of their functions. They set up a chain of command thorough regional and district supervisors, but they remained in control. The shop managers had to obey their general directions and also take orders from their superiors. The acts or omissions of shop managers were not acts of the company itself.

In my judgment the appellants established the statutory defence. I would therefore allow this appeal.

Tesco Stores Ltd v Brent London Borough Council

Miss Jones, Mr Johnnie and Stuart

[1993] 2 All ER 718, [1993] 1 WLR 1037, Queen's Bench Divisional Court

In this case the court strove to distinguish *Tesco Supermarkets Ltd v Nattrass* [1972] AC 153 in order to uphold the prohibition on selling adult videos to minors. In the earlier *Tesco* case the fact that the senior officers (though not the store manager) had taken reasonable precautions to avoid the offence, was a valid defence. In this case, however, the guilty knowledge of a check-out girl was enough to ensure the conviction of the company.

Facts   An '18' video was supplied by Miss Jones of Tesco to Stuart aged 14 (Tesco having been set up by Mr Johnnie). The Video Recordings Act 1984, s. 11(2)(b), provided a defence if the defendant 'neither knew nor had reasonable grounds to believe' that Stuart was not 18. It was argued for Tesco, the defendant that those who were the directing mind and will of the company did not know or have reasonable grounds to believe that Stuart was not 18. However, it was held that Miss Jones did, it was her knowledge that was relevant to the defence, and so Tesco was convicted on appeal.

STAUGHTON LJ: In November 1990 Mr Johnnie, a trading standards officer of the Brent London Borough Council, went to a Tesco store at Brent Park in the borough. He took with him, amongst others, a boy aged 14, whom I shall call 'Stuart'. Mr Johnnie told Stuart to go into the store, choose a video film with an '18' classification certificate from the video display cabinet and pay for it at till number 43 with a £10 note, which Mr Johnnie provided. All that Stuart did. He immediately went outside the store and handed the video film to Mr Johnnie. The cashier at till 43 was Miss Diane Jones.

On those short facts an information was preferred against Tesco Stores Ltd before the Brent justices, alleging an offence against s. 11(1) of the Video Recordings Act 1984 . . .

. . . What mattered in terms of s. 11(2)(b) was whether the accused (Tesco Stores Ltd) neither knew nor had reasonable grounds to believe that Stuart was under the age of 18. On that topic the justices did find that the video film was supplied to a person clearly under the age of 18 years. We take that to be a finding that Miss Jones did have reasonable grounds to believe that Stuart was under 18. That is accepted, and there has been no argument to the contrary.

The justices made no finding as to who comprised the directing mind and will of Tesco Stores Ltd, or whether those persons neither knew nor had reasonable grounds to believe that Stuart was aged less than 18. The justices regarded those matters as irrelevant. I do not for one moment suppose that those persons had reasonable grounds for believing anything on the topic. If it is the knowledge or information of those persons that is relevant, there was a defence to this charge. That too is accepted.

The main and almost the only question on this appeal is thus whether s. 11(2)(b) of the 1984 Act is concerned with the knowledge and information of the employee who supplies the video film or only with the knowledge and information of those who represent the directing mind and will of Tesco Stores Ltd.

Tesco Supermarkets Ltd v Nattrass [1972] AC 153 was, as it seems to me, concerned with three topics. The first was the general rule as to criminal liability of a corporate body. In the ordinary way a company is not guilty of a crime unless the criminal conduct and the guilty mind exist not merely in a servant or agent of the company of junior rank but in those who truly manage its affairs. Statutes may and sometimes do provide otherwise. There are offences for which, in derogation of the general rule, a company may incur liability through the behaviour of its servants (see [1972] AC 153 at p. 176 per Lord Morris of Borth-y-Gest citing *Mousell Bros Ltd v London and North-Western Railway Co.* [1917] 2 KB 836 at p. 844).

Secondly, it was evident in *Tesco Supermarkets Ltd v Nattrass* that the offence in question there was one which could be committed by a company through one of its junior employees acting on its behalf. Otherwise there would have been no need to consider whether the company could rely on a defence which the statute provided. . . .

The third point considered in *Tesco Supermarkets Ltd* v *Nattrass*, which was critical to the decision, was that s. 24 of the 1968 Act was concerned with the conduct of the company itself by those who managed its business. The 'person charged' in the section clearly meant the company. The words 'he', 'himself', and 'his' meant the company by its directing mind and will.

The present case is concerned with a different statute, the Video Recordings Act 1984. The offence section here is s. 11(1). Mr Stephenson for Tesco Stores Ltd concedes that this section too provides for an offence which may be committed vicariously by an employee acting in the course of his employment. The question then is whether s. 11(2), the defence section, is concerned with the knowledge and information of the company, where it is a company that is the accused, by those who manage its affairs, or whether it looks at the knowledge and information of the employee who actually supplies the video film.

In my judgment s. 11(2) of the 1984 Act is different both in language and content from s. 24 of the 1968 Act. I see no reason why it should necessarily have the same meaning as that laid down in *Tesco Supermarkets Ltd* v *Nattrass*. The language here draws no distinction between the accused and those under his control. The content is concerned with knowledge and information, not due diligence. It is, as I have already suggested, absurd to suppose that those who manage a vast company would have any knowledge or any information as to the age of a casual purchaser of a video film. It is the employee that sells the film at the check-out point who will have knowledge or reasonable grounds for belief. It is her knowledge or reasonable grounds that are relevant. Were it otherwise, the statute would be wholly ineffective in the case of a large company, unless by the merest chance a youthful purchaser were known to the board of directors. Yet Parliament contemplated that a company might commit the offence (see s. 16 of the 1984 Act).

By contrast, the single-handed shopkeeper would be less readily able to rely on the defence section, although he would fare better if he had an assistant serving at the counter while he was in the back of the shop. I cannot believe that Parliament intended the large company to be acquitted but the single-handed shopkeeper convicted . . .

I can find nothing in the authorities to prevent us holding that s. 11(2) of the 1984 Act refers to the knowledge and information of the employee through whom the company effects a supply. Accordingly, I consider that the magistrates were right to hold that *Tesco Supermarkets Ltd* v *Nattrass*, or rather the third and critical point which it decided, had no application to s. 11(2).

El Ajou v Dollar Land Holdings plc

Recovering the proceeds of fraud

[1994] 2 All ER 685, Court of Appeal

In this case the Court of Appeal acknowledged that the 'directing mind and will' theory is a constitutional question, distinguishing those who are not merely a servant or agent but whose action is that of the company itself. Thus the articles of association might identify the board of directors or a managing director as the directing mind and will, i.e., as constitutional 'organs' of the company. However, it was held that different persons may be the directing mind and will for different purposes. A company holding out or acquiescing in a person having authority to do a particular thing may cause him to be treated as its directing mind for that purpose.

Facts   This was a civil claim by which the plaintiff sought to recover £1,300,000 from Dollar Land Holdings plc (DLH). The complex facts can be simplified for present purposes as follows. Mr Ferdman, a Swiss national, had received the plaintiff's money on behalf of DLH, knowing it to be the proceeds of fraud. Though he was DLH's chairman he had no specific authority to act on the company's behalf. The question for the court was whether the knowledge of Ferdman, a director of DLH, that the money received was fraudulently disposed of in breach of trust could be imputed to DLH. If so the plaintiff would have a possible claim against DLH to assets knowingly received by it and so held on a constructive trust. The Court of Appeal concluded that Ferdman's knowledge could not be imputed to DLH on the ground that he acted as the company's agent in the transactions. However, he was to be treated for that purpose as its directing mind and will. Thus Ferdman's knowledge that the money was the proceeds of fraud could be attributed to DLH and so the claim to enforce a constructive trust on grounds of knowing receipt could succeed. Bearing in mind how difficult it is in cases of transnational fraud to bring criminal sanctions to bear, the court was clearly anxious to see the civil action for the recovery of the proceeds succeed. The result is a very wide interpretation of the directing mind and will theory, perhaps taking it far from its original narrow constitutional origins to a position more akin to the rules of agency. The case is also interesting for Hoffmann LJ's discussion of the importation of 'organic theory' into our law from Germany on which the 'directing mind' approach appears based. It is also interesting as a civil case on general principles in which the judges, though possibly wishing to achieve their own policy objective of restoring stolen property to its rightful owner, could not fall back on the presumed intentions of Parliament through interpretation of a criminal statute.

HOFFMANN LJ: This is a claim to enforce a constructive trust on the basis of knowing receipt. For this purpose the plaintiff must show, first, a disposal of his assets in breach of fiduciary duty; secondly, the beneficial receipt by the defendant of assets which are traceable as representing the assets of the plaintiff; and thirdly, knowledge on the part of the defendant that the assets he received are traceable to a breach of fiduciary duty. . . .

1. IDENTIFYING THE ASSETS BENEFICIALLY RECEIVED . . .
2. TRACING . . .
3. KNOWLEDGE

The judge correctly analysed the various capacities in which Mr Ferdman was involved in the transaction between DLH and the Canadians. First, he acted as a broker, introducing the Canadians to DLH in return for a 5 per cent commission. In this capacity he was not acting as agent for DLH but as an independent contractor performing a service for a fee. Secondly, he was authorised agent of DLH to sign the agreement with Yulara. Thirdly, he was at all material times a director and chairman of the board of DLH.

There are two ways in which Mr Ferdman's knowledge can be attributed to DLH. The first is that as agent of DLH his knowledge can be imputed to the company. The second is that for this purpose he *was* DLH and his knowledge was its knowledge [i.e., the 'directing mind and will' theory, below]. The judge rejected both.

(a) The agency theory

The circumstances in which the knowledge of an agent is imputed to the principal can vary a great deal and care is needed in analysing the cases. They fall into a number of categories which are not always sufficiently clearly distinguished. I shall mention three such categories because they each include cases on which Mr Beloff QC placed undifferentiated reliance. In fact, however, they depend upon distinct principles which have no application in this case. [The judge went on to consider agency theory at length.]

It follows that in my judgment Millett J [the judge at first instance] was right to hold that Mr Ferdman's position as agent or broker does not enable his knowledge to be imputed to DLH.

(b) The 'directing mind and will' theory

The phrase 'directing mind and will' comes from a well-known passage in the judgment of Viscount Haldane LC in *Lennards Carrying Co. Ltd* v *Asiatic Petroleum Co. Ltd* [1915] AC 705 which distinguishes between someone who is 'merely a servant or agent' and someone whose action (or knowledge) is that of the company itself. Despite their familiarity, it is worth quoting the terms in which Viscount Haldane LC said that the directing mind could be identified ([1915] AC 705 at 713).

That person may be under the direction of the shareholders in general meeting; that person may be the board of directors itself, or it may be, and in some companies it is so, that that person has an authority coordinate with the board of directors given to him under the articles of association, and is appointed by the general meeting of the company, and can only be removed by the general meeting of the company. My Lords, whatever is not known about Mr Lennard's position, this is known for certain, Mr Lennard took the active part in the management of this ship on behalf of the owners, and Mr Lennard, as I have said, was registered as the person designated for this purpose in the ship's register.

Viscount Haldane LC therefore regarded the identification of the directing mind as primarily a *constitutional* question, depending in the first instance upon the powers entrusted to a person by the articles of association. The last sentence about Mr Lennard's position shows that the position as reflected in the articles may have to be supplemented by looking at the actual exercise of the company's powers. A person held out by the company as having plenary authority or in whose exercise of such authority the company acquiesces, may be treated as its directing mind.

It is well known that Viscount Haldane LC derived the concept of the 'directing mind' from German law (see Gower, *Principles of Modern Company Law*, 5th ed. (1992), p. 194, n. 36) which distinguishes between the agents and organs of the company. A German company with limited liability (GmbH) is required by law to appoint one or more directors (Geschäftsführer). They are the company's organs and for legal purposes represent the company. The knowledge of any one director, however obtained, is the knowledge of the company (see Scholz, *Commentary on the GmbH Law*, 7th ed. (1986), s. 35). English law has never taken the view that the knowledge of a director *ipso facto* imputed to the company: see *Powles* v *Page* (1846) 3 CB 15, 136 ER 7 and *Re Carew's Estate Act (No. 2), Re* (1862) 31 Beav 39, 54 ER 1054. Unlike the German Geschäftsführer, an English director may, as an individual, have no powers whatever. But English law shares the view of German law that whether a person is an organ or not depends upon the extent of the powers which in law he has express or implied authority to exercise on behalf of the company.

Millett J did not accept that Mr Ferdman was the directing mind and will of DLH because he exercised no independent judgment. As a fiduciary he acted entirely upon the directions of the American beneficial owners and their consultant Mr Stern. All that he did was to sign the necessary documents and ensure that the company's paperwork was in order. This involved seeing that decisions which had really been taken by the Americans and Mr Stern were duly minuted as decisions of the board made in Switzerland....

The authorities show clearly that different persons may for different purposes satisfy the requirements of being the company's directing mind and will. Therefore the question in my judgment is whether in relation to the Yulara transaction, Mr Ferdman as an individual exercised powers on behalf of the company which so identified him. It seems to me that Mr Ferdman was clearly regarded as being in a different position from the other directors. They were associates of his who came and went. SAFI charged for their services at a substantially lower rate. It was Mr Ferdman who claimed in the published accounts of DLH to be its ultimate beneficial owner. In my view, however, the most significant fact is that Mr Ferdman signed the agreement with Yulara on behalf of DLH. There was no board resolution authorising him to do so. Of course we know that in fact he signed at the request of Mr Stern, whom he knew to be clothed with authority from the Americans. But so far as the constitution of DLH was concerned, he committed the company to the transaction as an autonomous act which the company adopted by performing the agreement. I would therefore hold, respectfully differing from the judge, that this was sufficient to justify Mr Ferdman being treated, in relation to the Yulara transaction, as the company's directing mind and will....

NOURSE LJ:

Directing mind and will

This doctrine, sometimes known as the alter ego doctrine, has been developed, with no divergence of approach, in both criminal and civil jurisdictions, the authorities in each being cited indifferently (sic) in the other. A company having no mind or will of its own, the need for it arises because the criminal law often requires *mens rea* as a constituent of the crime, and the civil law intention or knowledge as an ingredient of the cause of action or defence. In the oft-quoted words of Viscount Haldane LC in *Lennards Carrying Co. Ltd* v *Asiatic Petroleum Co. Ltd* [1915] AC 705 at 713:

My Lords, a corporation is an abstraction. It has no mind of its own any more than it has a body of its own; its active and directing will must consequently be sought in the person of somebody who for some purposes may be called an agent, but who is really the direct-ing mind and will of the corporation, the very ego and centre of the personality of the corporation.

The doctrine attributes to the company the mind and will of the natural person or persons who manage and control its actions. At that point, in the words of Millett J ([1993] 3 All ER 717 at 740): 'Their minds are its mind; their intention its intention; their knowledge its knowledge'. It is import-ant to emphasise that management and control is not something to be considered generally or in the round. It is necessary to identify the natural person or persons having management and control in relation to the act or omission in point. This was well put by Eveleigh J in delivering the judgment of the Criminal Division of this court in R v Andrews Weatherfoil Ltd [1972] 1 WLR 118 at 124:

It is necessary to establish whether the natural person or persons in question have the sta-tus and authority which in law makes their acts in the matter under consideration the acts of the company so that the natural person is to be treated as the company itself.

Decided cases show that, in regard to the requisite status and authority, the formal position, as regulated by the company's articles of association, service contracts and so forth, though highly relevant, may not be decisive. Here Millett J adopted a pragmatic approach. In my view he was right to do so, although it has led me, with diffidence, to a conclusion different from his own....

I would allow the appeal.

Seaboard Offshore Ltd v Secretary of State for Transport
The Safe Carrier?
[1994] 2 All ER 99, [1994] 1 WLR 541, House of Lords

In this case the House of Lords narrowly interpreted the criminal provision in the Merchant Shipping Act 1988, s. 31, requiring the owner of a ship to take all such steps as are reasonable for him to take to ensure the safe operation of the ship. Thus a company operating a ship is not vicariously liable under the section for every lapse of safety standards by the crew. The company is only criminally liable if those entrusted with the exercise of the company's powers under the 'directing mind and will' test in *Tesco Supermarkets Ltd v Nattrass* [1972] AC 153 have failed in their duty to take reasonable steps to ensure the safe operation of the ship.

Facts Seaboard Offshore Ltd. was convicted of failing to operate an offshore standby safety ves-sel, the MV Safe Carrier, in a safe manner contrary to s. 31 of the Merchant Shipping Act 1988. When the ship's electrics failed on passage to Aberdeen the engineer on board made a number of errors of judgment. Evidence showed that although he would have needed three days to familiarise him-self with the ship, he had first boarded the ship 2 hours and 50 minutes before leaving the Tyne. The House of Lords held the company was wrongly convicted as Parliament had intended that a company should only be convicted under this section if the natural persons who were to be treated as the corporation being entrusted with the exercise of its powers under its constitution had per-sonally failed in the duty to operate the ship safely. (This represents a narrow application of Tesco Supermarkets Ltd v Nattrass apparently conceiving of the directing mind and will of the company as being limited to its primary organs.) The company was not vicariously liable for any act or omission of any other officer or subordinate employee.

LORD KEITH OF KINKEL: The questions for the opinion of the High Court were stated to be:

(a) Does the law governing the criminal responsibility of corporations confirmed by the House of Lords in *Tesco Supermarkets Ltd v Nattrass* [1972] AC 153 apply to s. 31 of the Merchant Shipping Act 1988?...

The case stated came before the Divisonal Court, consisting of Staughton LJ and Buckley J [1993] 1 WLR 1025, which on 2 February 1993 quashed the conviction. The court regarded question (a) as raising the point whether or not s. 31 of the 1988 Act imposed on a shipowner vicarious liability for the acts or omissions of all its employees and expressed the opinion that it did not.... As Staughton LJ observed in the course of his judgment in the Divisional Court, it would be surprising if by the language used in s. 31 Parliament intended that the owner of a ship should be criminally liable for any act or omission by any officer of the company or member of the crew which resulted in unsafe operation of the ship, ranging from failure by the managing director to arrange repairs to a failure by the bosun or cabin steward to close portholes (see [1993] 1 WLR 1025 at 1033). Of particular relevance in this context are the concluding words of s. 31(4), referring to the taking of all such steps as are reasonable for *him* (my emphasis) to take, i.e. the owner, charterer or manager. The steps to be taken are to be such as will secure that the ship is operated in a safe manner. That conveys to me the idea of laying down a safe manner of operating the ship by those involved in the actual operation of it and taking appropriate measures to bring it about that such safe manner of operation is adhered to. Where the owner, charterer or manager is a corporation which can act only through natural persons, the natural persons who are to be treated in law as being the corporation for the purpose of acts done in the course of its business are those who by virtue of its constitution or otherwise are entrusted with the exercise of the powers of the corporation: see Lord Diplock in *Tesco Supermarkets Ltd* v *Nattrass* [1972] AC 153 at 199–200...

The justices say that they found that the respondents caused the ship to be operated in an unsafe way by only allowing the chief engineer 2 hours and 50 minutes in which to familiarise himself with the ship before sailing. They make no finding as to how it came about that the ship sailed while that was the situation, nor as to who it was who gave the instruction to sail. They had expressed the opinion that *Tesco Supermarkets Ltd* v *Nattrass* had no application to s. 31 of the 1988 Act. That was in response to a contention by the respondents that since no evidence had been adduced of any decisions taken or failed to be taken by their senior management the information ought to be dismissed. It seems, therefore, that the justices took the view that the respondents were criminally liable even though the putting to sea by the ship with a chief engineer insufficiently familiar with the engines was the fault of some employee of the company other than the senior management. That view was erroneous, and in the circumstances the conviction cannot stand.

In the judgment of the Divisional Court there is some discussion as to whether or not the offence provided for by s. 31 is one of strict liability, involving no necessary element of *mens rea*. It is not, however, helpful to seek to categorise the offence as either being or not being one of strict liability. It consists simply in failure to take steps which by an objective standard are held to be reasonable steps to take in the interests of the safe operation of a ship, and the duty which it places on the owner, charterer or manager is a personal one. The owner, charterer or manager is criminally liable if he fails personally in the duty, but is not criminally liable for the acts or omissions of his subordinate employees if he has himself taken all reasonable steps.

My lords, for these reasons I would dismiss the appeal.

Re Supply of Ready Mixed Concrete (No. 2)

By their acts shall you know them

[1995] 1 All ER 135, [1995] 1 AC 456, House of Lords

A company is guilty of contempt of court if its employees perform acts amounting to a contempt while acting in the course of employment even though in direct contravention of instructions from the company.

Facts   This case was one skirmish in a long saga in which suppliers of ready mixed concrete unlawfully made a series of agreements restricting competition and fixing prices. Employees of two companies, Pioneer Concrete and Ready Mixed Concrete met at a pub in Bicester and made a price fixing and job allocation agreement. This was unknown to and indeed prohibited by their superiors in their companies. Earlier in March 1979 the Restrictive Trade Practices Court had made orders restraining the companies from making such anti-competitive agreements. If the companies were parties to such an agreement they would be in contempt of court. The companies argued that the agreement was not their act and that they were not parties to it as they were unaware of it and had expressly forbidden it. The House of Lords took a strict approach and held that the companies were parties to the agreement and were in contempt of court. For there to be a contempt of court it is not necessary to show that the company acted through individuals who were its directing mind and will. It is sufficient to show that they acted in the course of employment even though expressly prohibited by the company.

LORD NOLAN: The principal significance of this case, and of the cases to which it refers, as it seems to me, lies in the acceptance of the proposition that even in the case of a statute imposing criminal liability, and even without any express words to that effect, Parliament may be taken to have imposed a liability on an employer for the acts of his employees, provided that those acts were carried out in the course of the employment. Further, the liability may be imposed even though the acts in question were prohibited by the employer...

The respondent companies' arguments are founded on the proposition that, for the purposes of the Act [the Restrictive Trade Practices Act 1976], the employees and their employing companies are separate persons, and that the latter are to be regarded, in isolation from the former, as the persons carrying on business in the United Kingdom. The first part of this proposition is undeniable. It is the respondent companies and not their employees against whom the court orders of 14 March 1978 and 29 March 1979 were made. But the second part of the proposition does not follow from the first, and appears to me to be untenable. A limited company, as such, cannot carry on business. It can only do so by employing human beings to act on its behalf. The actions of its employees, acting in the course of their employment, are what constitute the carrying on of business by the company. When the roll was called at the public house meeting at which the Bicester agreement was concluded the employees attending did not respond as individuals: they did so as representatives of their respective companies, fully competent as a practical matter of fact to make the agreement on behalf of their companies, and to see that it was carried out. A consensual element was required because it takes at least two parties to make a restrictive practice, but the consent required for the Bicester agreement was not that of senior management or the board: all that was needed was the consent of the employees who could and did make the agreement effective.

It follows that, at any rate for the purposes of the 1976 Act, I am unable to accept that a prohibition at some senior level against the making of an agreement or arrangement which is ignored by the employees concerned is nonetheless sufficient to prevent the employing company from becoming a party to the agreement or arrangement when made. The Act is not concerned with what the employer says but with what the employee does in entering into business transactions in the course of his employment. The plain purpose of s. 35(3) is to deter the implementation of agreements or arrangements by which the public interest is harmed, and the subsection can only achieve that purpose if it is applied to the actions of the individuals within the business organisation who make and give effect to the relevant agreement or arrangement on its behalf.

This necessarily leads to the conclusion that if such an agreement is found to have been made without the knowledge of the employer, any steps which the employer has taken to prevent it from being made will rank only as mitigation. Liability can only be escaped by completely effective preventive measures. How great a burden the devising of such measures will cast upon individual employers will depend upon the size and nature of the particular organisation. There are, of course, many areas of business life, not only in the consumer protection field, where it has become necessary for employers to devise strict compliance procedures. If the burden is in fact intolerable then the remedy must be for Parliament to introduce a statutory defence for those who can show that they have taken all reasonable preventive measures....

Mr Crystal [counsel for Pioneer Concrete] relied upon passages from the speeches of Lord Reid, Lord Morris of Borth-y-Gest and Lord Diplock in *Tesco Supermarkets Ltd* v *Nattrass* [1972] AC 153 for the proposition that in the case of a body corporate the necessary *mens rea* must be found in a natural person or persons who are the directing mind and will of the corporation. But that case was concerned with the precise terms of the statutory defence provided by the Trade Descriptions Act 1968 for those who could show that the offence in question had been committed by another person, and that the person charged had taken all reasonable precautions and exercised all due diligence to avoid the commission of the offence. The statute expressly distinguished, by s. 20(1), between 'any director, manager, secretary or other similar officer of a body corporate' and other persons who were merely its servants or agents. It was not concerned with contempt of court consisting in the breach of an injunction. I shall refer later to the speech of Lord Wilberforce in *Heaton's Transport (St Helens) Ltd* v *Transport and General Workers' Union* [1973] AC 15, and would respectfully adopt his comment that the *Tesco Supermarkets* decision does not bear upon the latter problem (see [1973] AC 15 at 109). . . .

The employees of the respondents have, by their deliberate conduct, made their employers liable for disobeying the orders of 14 March 1978 and 29 March 1979. The respondents are therefore guilty of contempt of court. Their original pleas of guilty were rightly tendered. I would allow the appeal and restore the order of the Restrictive Practices Court.

LORD TEMPLEMAN: [Rejecting the earlier finding in *Director General of Fair Trading* v *Smiths Concrete Ltd* [1992] QB 213 that it is a defence to a charge of contempt of court that the employees were acting against express instructions.] In addition to the defences and excuses put forward by the companies [in *Re Supply of Ready Mixed Concrete, Re* [1991] ICR 52], each company asserted, by way of mitigation in the case of the three companies which had pleaded guilty of contempt and by way of defence in the case of Smiths, that express instructions had been given to each employee not to participate in registrable arrangements. Smiths appealed against the finding of the Restrictive Practices Court that they were in contempt. The appeal was allowed by the Court of Appeal; see *Director General of Fair Trading* v *Smiths Concrete Ltd* [1992] QB 213 (*Smith's* case). . . .

My lords, I cannot accept this pronouncement. It would allow a company to enjoy the benefit of restrictions outlawed by Parliament and the benefit of arrangements prohibited by the courts provided that the restrictions were accepted and implemented and the arrangements were negotiated by one or more employees who had been forbidden to do so by some superior employee identified in argument as a member of the 'higher management' of the company or by one or more directors of the company identified in argument as 'the guiding will' of the company.

The decisions of the Court of Appeal in *Smiths'* case and in the instant case infringe two principles. The first principle is that a company is an entity separate from its members but, not being a physical person, is only capable of acting by its agents. The second principle is that a company, in its capacity as supplier of goods, like any other person in the capacity of taxpayer, landlord or in any other capacity, falls to be judged by its actions and not by its language. An employee who acts for the company within the scope of his employment is the company. Directors may give instructions, top management may exhort, middle management may question and workers may listen attentively. But if a worker makes a defective product or a lower manager accepts or rejects an order, he is the company. . . .

I would overrule *Smiths'* case [1992] QB 213 and allow the present appeal.

Meridian Global Funds Management Asia Ltd v *Securities Commission*
Cherry-picking attribution rules
[1995] 3 All ER 918, [1995] 2 AC 500, Privy Council

In deciding what acts are to be attributed to the company the court may choose to apply either the 'directing mind and will' theory or wider principles of agency. This choice may be made as a matter of construction of the substantive criminal provision in order to advance its terms and policy.

Facts   The New Zealand Securities Amendment Act 1988 required any person acquiring shares in a public listed company to inform the company and the stock exchange as soon as he knew or ought to have known that he or it had become a 'substantial security holder', i.e., holding 5 per cent or more of the voting shares. If a person failed to do so the Securities Commission could impose penalties. Koo, the chief investment officer of Meridian, used its money for a corrupt purpose to buy a substantial stake in a public listed company but did not notify his superiors, the company or the stock exchange. Meridian successfully appealed against a penal order imposed on it, arguing that, because Koo was not its directing mind and will it did not know that it had acquired 5 per cent of the shares in the public listed company. The Privy Council held that it was not necessary to show that Koo was Meridian's directing mind and will. Construing the legislation so that its policy was not defeated, in order to prove that the company knew that it was a substantial security holder, it was enough to prove the knowlege of the person authorised to do the deal (i.e., Koo). Koo's corrupt purpose did not affect this attribution.

LORD HOFFMANN: The phrase 'directing mind and will' comes of course from the celebrated speech of Viscount Haldane LC in *Lennards Carrying Co. Ltd* v *Asiatic Petroleum Co. Ltd* [1915] AC 705 at 713. But their lordships think that there has been some misunderstanding of the true principle upon which that case was decided. It may be helpful to start by stating the nature of the problem in a case like this and then come back to *Lennard's* case later.

Any proposition about a company necessarily involves a reference to a set of rules. A company exists because there is a rule (usually in a statute) which says that a *persona ficta* shall be deemed to exist and to have certain of the powers, rights and duties of a natural person. But there would be little sense in deeming such a *persona ficta* to exist unless there were also rules to tell one what acts were to count as acts of the company. It is therefore a necessary part of corporate personality that there should be rules by which acts are attributed to the company. These may be called 'the rules of attribution'.

The company's primary rules of attribution will generally be found in its constitution, typically the articles of association, and will say things such as 'for the purpose of appointing members of the board, a majority vote of the shareholders shall be a decision of the company' or 'the decisions of the board in managing the company's business shall be the decisions of the company'. There are also primary rules of attribution which are not expressly stated in the articles but implied by company law, such as 'the unanimous decision of all the shareholders in a solvent company about anything which the company under its memorandum of association has power to do shall be the decision of the company': see *Multinational Gas and Petrochemical Co.* v *Multinational Gas and Petrochemical Services Ltd* [1983] Ch 258, [1983] 2 All ER 565.

These primary rules of attribution are obviously not enough to enable a company to go out into the world and do business. Not every act on behalf of the company could be expected to be the subject of a resolution of the board or a unanimous decision of the shareholders. The company therefore builds upon the primary rules of attribution by using general rules of attribution which are equally available to natural persons, namely, the principles of agency. It will appoint servants and agents whose acts, by a combination of the general principles of agency and the company's primary rules of attribution, count as the acts of the company. And having done so, it will also make itself subject to the general rules by which liability for the acts of others can be attributed to natural persons, such as estoppel or ostensible authority in contract and vicarious liability in tort.

It is worth pausing at this stage to make what may seem an obvious point. Any statement about what a company has or has not done, or can or cannot do, is necessarily a reference to the rules of attribution (primary and general) as they apply to that company. Judges sometimes say that a company 'as such' cannot do anything; it must act by servants or agents. This may seem an unexceptionable, even banal remark. And of course the meaning is usually perfectly clear. But a reference to a company 'as such' might suggest that there is something out there called the company of which one can meaningfully say that it can or cannot do something. There is in fact no such thing as the company as such, no '*ding an sich*', only the applicable rules. To say that a company cannot do something means only that there is no one whose doing of that act would, under the applicable rules of attribution, count as an act of the company.

The company's primary rules of attribution together with the general principles of agency, vicarious liability and so forth are usually sufficient to enable one to determine its rights and obligations. In exceptional cases, however, they will not provide an answer. This will be the case when a rule of law, either expressly or by implication, excludes attribution on the basis of the general principles of agency or vicarious liability. For example, a rule may be stated in language primarily applicable to a natural person and require some act or state of mind on the part of that person 'himself', as opposed to his servants or agents. This is generally true of rules of the criminal law, which ordinarily impose liability only for the *actus reus* and *mens rea* of the defendant himself. How is such a rule to be applied to a company?

One possibility is that the court may come to the conclusion that the rule was not intended to apply to companies at all; for example, a law which created an offence for which the only penalty was community service. Another possibility is that the court might interpret the law as meaning that it could apply to a company only on the basis of its primary rules of attribution, i.e. if the act giving rise to liability was specifically authorised by a resolution of the board or a unanimous agreement of the shareholders. But there will be many cases in which neither of these solutions is satisfactory; in which the court considers that the law was intended to apply to companies and that, although it excludes ordinary vicarious liability, insistence on the primary rules of attribution would in practice defeat that intention. In such a case, the court must fashion a special rule of attribution for the particular substantive rule. This is always a matter of interpretation: given that it was intended to apply to a company, how was it intended to apply? Whose act (or knowledge, or state of mind) was *for this purpose* intended to count as the act etc. of the company? One finds the answer to this question by applying the usual canons of interpretation, taking into account the language of the rule (if it is a statute) and its content and policy.

The fact that the rule of attribution is a matter of interpretation or construction of the relevant substantive rule is shown by the contrast between two decisions of the House of Lords, *Tesco Supermarkets Ltd* v *Nattrass* [1972] AC 153 and *Re Supply of Ready Mixed Concrete (No. 2), Director General of Fair Trading* v *Pioneer Concrete (UK) Ltd, Re* [1995] 1 AC 456. [His lordship then considered these cases and *Lennard's* case.]

Once it is appreciated that the question is one of construction rather than metaphysics, the answer in this case seems to their lordships to be as straightforward as it did to [the judge at first instance]. The policy of s. 20 of the 1988 Act is to compel, in fast-moving markets, the immediate disclosure of the identity of persons who become substantial security holders in public issuers. Notice must be given as soon as that person knows that he has become a substantial security holder. In the case of a corporate security holder, what rule should be implied as to the person whose knowledge for this purpose is to count as the knowledge of the company? Surely the person who, with the authority of the company, acquired the relevant interest. Otherwise the policy of the Act would be defeated. Companies would be able to allow employees to acquire interests on their behalf which made them substantial security holders but would not have to report them until the board or someone else in senior management got to know about it. This would put a premium on the board paying as little attention as possible to what its investment managers were doing. Their Lordships would therefore hold that upon the true construction of s. 20(4)(e), the company knows that it has become a substantial security holder when that is known to the person who had authority to do the deal. It is then obliged to give notice under s. 20(3). The fact that Koo did the deal for a corrupt purpose and did not give such notice because he did not want his employers to find out cannot in their lordships' view affect the attribution of knowledge and the consequent duty to notify.

It was therefore not necessary in this case to inquire into whether Koo could have been described in some more general sense as the 'directing mind and will' of the company. But their lordships would wish to guard themselves against being understood to mean that whenever a servant of a company has authority to do an act on its behalf, knowledge of that act will for all purposes be attributed to the company. It is a question of construction in each case as to whether the particular rule requires that the knowledge that an act has been done, or the state of mind with which it was done, should be attributed to the company. Sometimes, as in the *Ready Mixed Concrete* case and this case, it will be appropriate. Likewise in a case in which a company was required to make a return for revenue purposes and the statute made it an offence to make a false return with intent to deceive, the Divisional Court held that the *mens rea* of the servant authorised to discharge the duty to make the return should be attributed to the company: see *Moore* v *I. Bresler Ltd* [1944] 2 All ER 515. On the other hand, the fact that a company's employee is authorised to drive a lorry does not in itself lead to the conclusion that if he kills someone by reckless driving, the company will be guilty of manslaughter. There is no inconsistency. Each is an example of an attribution rule for a particular purpose, tailored as it always must be to the terms and policies of the substantive rule.

Companies, crime and common sense

In *National Rivers Authority* v *Alfred McAlpine Homes East Ltd* [1994] 4 All ER 287, on an appeal by way of case stated, the Queen's Bench Division strongly upheld the policy of penalising environmental pollution. The company was engaged in building houses on a site through which a stream ran. A number of fish were found dead downstream of the site, killed by an escape of cement into the water from the site. A person is criminally liable 'if he causes...any polluting matter...to enter any controlled water' (Water Resources Act 1991, s. 85). The justices had dismissed a prosecution under this section on grounds that the offence is only committed by a company if committed by a person exercising its 'controlling mind or will'. The Queen's Bench Division emphatically distinguished *Tesco Supermarkets Ltd* v *Nattrass* [1972] AC 153, holding that there is an offence under the section where as a matter of common sense the company caused the pollution. Morland J stressed the policy imperative of preventing environmental pollution. Simon Brown LJ had some interesting comments on a number of other cases as follows:

> Nor, in my judgment, is any light shed on the present appeal by the recent decisions in *Seaboard Offshore Ltd* v *Secretary of State for Transport* [1993] 1 WLR 1025 and *Tesco Stores Ltd* v *Brent London Borough Council* [1993] 1 WLR 1037. In *Seaboard* the Divisional Court allowed a shipowner's appeal. Professor Smith, whilst trenchantly criticising much of the court's reasoning, nevertheless approved its conclusion:
>
> > The statute in the present case, in terms, imposes a personal duty on the owner 'to take all reasonable steps to secure that the ship is operated in a safe manner'. If the owner has taken all reasonable steps, it would seem to contradict the statute to convict him because someone else has behaved negligently. (See his commentary at [1993] Crim LR 612 at 613.)
>
> Here the corresponding duty upon the company was not 'to take all reasonable steps' to avoid pollution; rather it was not to cause pollution.
>
> In *Tesco Stores Ltd* v *Brent London Borough Council* [1993] 1 WLR 1037; just as in *Tesco* v *Nattrass*, both the company and its employee were prima facie liable under the offence section; unlike in *Tesco* v *Nattrass*, however, the Divisional Court held in *Tesco* v *Brent* that the company could not invoke the relevant defence section, there s. 11(2) of the Video Recordings Act 1984. Section 11(2), so the Divisional Court held, fell to be construed so as to attribute to the company the employee's own state of mind. Right or wrong (and Professor Smith suggests the latter (see [1993] Crim LR 612 at 625)), the decision has no bearing on the present appeal.

Safety standards at sea and ashore

In the single brief judgment in *Seaboard Offshore Ltd* v *Secretary of State for Transport* (above) the House of Lords laid down a surprisingly narrow duty to ensure the safe operation of a ship under the Merchant Shipping Act 1988. This case may be taken to apply to this section only as a matter of construction of the intention of Parliament. However, the issue is an important one. Enforcing standards will be very much more difficult if it is necessary in order to convict a company to show that lapses of safety standards by subordinate employees were the result of the failure of senior management to take reasonable steps to put in place appropriate safety systems and equipment.

Cases on other apparently similar criminal provisions may set a much broader or stricter standard for compliance by companies and their staff. For example, *R* v *British Steel plc* [1995] 1 WLR 1356 concerned a prosecution under s. 3(1) of the Health and Safety at Work Act 1974 requiring 'every employer to conduct his undertaking' so as to ensure 'so far as reasonably practicable' that employees were not exposed to health or safety risks. The prosecution of the company proceeded on the assumption that it was necessary to show defaults by senior management, the company's directing minds, a very difficult task in so large a company. The Court of Appeal upheld the conviction, however, distinguishing *Tesco Supermarkets Ltd* v *Nattrass* and saying that the directing mind test had no application to this particular offence. Construing the wording of the section, the court concluded that the possible defence of due diligence by senior management must be more narrowly interpreted in order to advance the purpose of the section and to promote a proper culture in companies of ensuring the safety of their employees.

The prosecution of companies therefore seems to present a nightmare scenario for prosecuting counsel. Is it enough with a particular offence to prove that a subordinate employee has contravened the criminal section or is it necessary in addition to show that this was the consequence of a failure by the directing minds (whoever they may be) to set up adequate systems to avoid the commission of the offence. The *Seaboard Offshore* case was cited in argument in the *British Steel* case, though the Court of Appeal made no attempt to say why on the basis of criminal provisions in very similar terms, Parliament should be presumed to regard the safety of those in peril on the sea as being less important than the safety of those in trouble at the mill. The fig leaf of statutory interpretation does not always provide a very satisfactory answer.

3.4.2 Corporate manslaughter

Whether a company can be found guilty of manslaughter raises very difficult questions. Just as a company cannot commit rape or bigamy, it seems unlikely that it can be held criminally liable for the death of an individual. However a number of highly publicised accidents, the sinking of the *Marchioness* on the Thames, of the *Herald of Free Enterprise* at Zeebrugge and the Lyme Bay canoeing tragedy, led to a strong shift in public opinion. It is not enough for the relatively junior employees directly responsible for the accident to be prosecuted for manslaughter if a failure of proper safety systems, the responsibility of top management, were a cause of the accident. The company itself should also be potentially liable for manslaughter in these circumstances.

The *Herald of Free Enterprise* case, extracted below, confirmed that a company could potentially be held liable for manslaughter, though the company was acquitted in that case. In December 1994 the company running the activity centre at Lyme Regis responsible for the deaths of four teenagers in a canoeing accident was the first company to be convicted of manslaughter and was fined £60,000. Attributing to a small private company the guilty acts of the managing director (also convicted and jailed) proved relatively simple.

Two Law Commission papers extracted below proposed the reform of the law and recommended the introduction of a special offence of corporate killing where the company's management failure in causing the death fell far below what could be reasonably expected. The topic is of special interest as it involves a close analysis of many theoretical aspects of company law. It is also topical in the context of a series of catastrophic railway accidents. The judge acquitting the railway company in

July 1999 of manslaughter in connection with the Southall train crash went on to criticise the failure to implement the Law Commission's recommendations as law. With concern heightened by the collapse of efforts to bring corporate manslaughter charges in respect of the Hatfield rail disaster, the issue increasingly became a political football. The unions pushed hard for a statutory offence of corporate manslaughter in the interest of the safety of their members, business interests resisted the whole idea and the Government prevaricated or at least proceeded cautiously, producing more drafts and consultation documents. Finally in July 2006 a Bill was presented to Parliament and corporate manslaughter was made an offence in the Corporate Manslaughter and Corporate Homicide Act 2007. (In Scotland it is called corporate homicide.)

The following readings begin with a case setting out the position at common law, followed by extracts from the Law Commission reports and finally ss. 1 and 2 of the new Act creating the offence.

R v P & O European Ferries (Dover) Ltd

The Herald of Free Enterprise

(1990) 93 Cr App R 72, Central Criminal Court

The tragedy of the capsize of the ferry at Zeebrugge with much loss of life is well known. Seven company officers and the company itself were charged with manslaughter. The very full judgment of Turner J reviewing all the authorities reaches the conclusion that a company may be convicted of manslaughter. (In the event all charges for manslaughter ultimately failed.)

TURNER J: ... The main thrust of the argument for the company in support of the submission that the four counts of manslaughter in this indictment should be quashed was not merely that English law does not recognise the offence of corporate manslaughter but that, as a matter of positive English law, manslaughter can only be committed when one natural person kills another natural person. Hence it was no accident that there is no record of any corporation or non-natural person having been successfully prosecuted for manslaughter in any English court. It was, however, accepted that there is no conceptual difficulty in attributing a criminal state of mind to a corporation. The broad argument advanced on behalf of the prosecution was that, there being no all embracing statutory definition of murder or manslaughter, there is, in principle, no reason why a corporation, or other non-natural person, cannot be found guilty of most offences in the criminal calendar. The exceptions to such a broad proposition could be found either in the form of punishment, which would be inappropriate for a corporation, or in the very personal nature of individual crimes or categories of crime such as offences under the Sexual Offences Act, bigamy and, arguably, perjury....

The prosecution advanced an alternative argument to the effect that, if it were necessary that the death be, in fact, caused by a human being, then given the modern doctrine of 'identification', as to which see below, if the perpetrator of the act who was a human being which caused death could be treated as the embodiment of the corporation, then to that extent the test would be satisfied. It is obvious, however, that this alternative argument detracts from the force of the main argument.

... [*Tesco Supermarkets Ltd* v *Nattrass* [1972] AC 153] deserves particular scrutiny for within certain of the speeches in that case are to be found the limits of this doctrine of identification. It is this doctrine which is fundamental to the true basis of corporate criminal liability which has now to be accepted is an integral part of the law of England....

Since the nineteenth century there has been a huge increase in the numbers and activities of corporations whether nationalised, municipal or commercial, which enter the private lives of all or most of 'men and subjects' in a diversity of ways. A clear case can be made for imputing to such corporations social duties including the duty not to offend all relevant parts of the criminal law. By tracing the history of the cases decided by the English courts over the period of the last 150 years, it can be seen how first tentatively and, finally confidently the courts have been able to ascribe to corporations a 'mind' which is generally one of the essential ingredients of common law and statutory offences. Indeed, it can be seen that in many Acts of Parliament the same concept has been embraced. The Parliamentary approach is, perhaps, exemplified by section 18 of the Theft Act 1968 which provides for directors and managers of a limited company to be rendered liable to conviction if an offence under section 15, 16 or 17 of the Act is proved to have been committed—and I quote: 'with the consent or connivance of any director, manager, secretary...he as well as the body corporate shall be liable to be proceeded against and punished accordingly'. Once a state of mind could be effectively attributed to a corporation, all that remained was to determine the means by which that state of mind could be ascertained and imputed to a non-natural person. That done, the obstacle to the acceptance of general criminal liability of a corporation was overcome. *Cessante ratione legis, cessat ipsa lex.* As some of the decisions in other common law countries indicate, there is nothing essentially incongruous in the notion that a corporation should be guilty of an offence of unlawful killing. I find unpersuasive the argument of the company that the old definitions of homicide positively exclude the liability of a non-natural person to conviction of an offence of manslaughter. Any crime, in order to be justiciable must have been committed by or through the agency of a human being. Consequently, the inclusion in the definition of the expression 'human being' as the author of the killing was either tautologous or, as I think more probable, intended to differentiate those cases of death in which a human being played no direct part and which would have led to forfeiture of the inanimate, or if animate non-human, object which caused the death (*deodand*) from those in which the cause of death was initiated by human activity albeit the instrument of death was inanimate or if animate non-human. I am confident that the expression 'human being' in the definition of homicide was not intended to have the effect of words of limitation as might have been the case had it been found in some Act of Parliament or legal deed. It is not for me to attempt to set the limits of corporate liability for criminal offences in English law. Examples of other crimes which may, or may not be committed by corporations will, no doubt, be decided on a case-by-case basis in conformity with the manner in which the common law has adapted itself in the past. Suffice it that where a corporation, through the controlling mind of one of its agents, does an act which fulfils the prerequisites of the crime of manslaughter, it is properly indictable for the crime of manslaughter.

Law Commission, *Involuntary Manslaughter* (Consultation Paper No. 135)
(London: HMSO, 1994)

Part IV The liability of corporations

A. Introduction

4.1 As we explained in Part I, we decided to devote special attention to corporate liability for manslaughter, because all the recent cases which have evoked demands for the use of the law of manslaughter following public disasters have involved, actually or potentially, corporate defendants. On the only occasion on which such a case has been brought to trial, the obscurities of the law of manslaughter were compounded by the obscurities of the law of corporate criminal liability. For this reason alone, we are satisfied that a real effort should be made to put the law on a clearer footing.

4.2 At the same time we should not ignore what appears to be a widespread feeling among the public that in cases where death has been caused by the acts or omissions of comparatively junior employees of a large organisation, such as the crew of a ferry boat owned by a leading public company, it would be wrong if the criminal law placed all the blame on those junior employees and did not also fix responsibility in appropriate cases on their employers who are operating, and profiting from, the service being provided to the public. If the law is able to address these concerns, consideration also needs to be given to the question whether it is the law of manslaughter, as opposed to, for example, a regulatory offence, which is the appropriate response in such cases....

4.3 This study looks at corporate liability only in the context of gross negligence manslaughter....

4.4 Before we grapple with the particular considerations which affect corporate *manslaughter*, we must first say something about the law of corporate criminal liability in general. This, of course, is the law which must be applied where it is sought to impose criminal liability on a corporation for causing death, and, so far, there have been conspicuous difficulties in the attempts made to apply it.

B. The general law of corporate liability

Background

4.5 It is trite law that a corporation is a separate legal person, but it has no physical existence and it cannot, therefore, act or form an intention of any kind except through its directors and servants. There has never been any doubt that the members or officers of a corporation cannot shelter behind the corporation and they may be successfully prosecuted as individuals for any criminal acts they may have performed or authorised. The real problem is the extent to which the corporate body itself may be criminally liable.

4.6 There appear to have been only three prosecutions of a corporation for manslaughter in the history of English law, and none of these cases resulted in a conviction. Some commentators have pointed to a number of outside factors which contribute to the low level of prosecutions brought against corporations for criminal offences generally. In this Paper, however, our concerns are devoted to studying the substantive law, the reasons for the failure, as a matter of law, of such prosecutions as are brought, and proposals for the reform of the law, if appropriate....

The principle of identification

4.14 The nature of the principle of identification, and the clear distinction between it and the doctrine of vicarious liability, was described by Lord Reid in the leading House of Lords case, *Tesco Supermarkets Ltd* v *Nattrass* [1972] AC 153 at p. 170:

> [A corporation] must act through living persons, though not always one or the same person. Then the person who acts is not speaking or acting for the company. He is acting as the company and his mind which directs his acts is the mind of the company. There is no question of the company being vicariously liable.... He is an embodiment of the company...and his mind is the mind of the company. If it is a guilty mind then that guilt is the guilt of the company.

4.15 The distinction between vicarious liability and the liability of corporations under the identification principle was also stressed in the recent case of *R* v *HM Coroner for East Kent ex parte Spooner* (1989) 88 Cr App R 10. Bingham LJ said in that case (at p. 16):

> It is important to bear in mind an important distinction. A company may be vicariously liable for the negligent acts and omissions of its servants and agents, but for a company to be criminally liable for manslaughter...it is required that the *mens rea* and *actus reus* of manslaughter should be established not against those who acted for or in the name of the company but against those who were to be identified as the embodiment of the company itself.

The controlling officers

4.16 The principle by which the controlling officers should be identified was described by Denning LJ in *H.L. Bolton (Engineering) Co. Ltd* v *T.J. Graham & Sons Ltd* [1957] 1 QB 159 at p. 172:

> A company may in many ways be likened to a human body. It has a brain and nerve centre which controls what it does. It also has hands which hold the tools and act in accordance with directions from the centre. Some of the people in the company are mere servants and agents who are nothing more than hands to do the work and cannot be said to represent the mind and will. Others are directors and managers who represent the directing mind and will of the company, and control what it does. The state of mind of these managers is the state of mind of the company and is treated by the law as such.

4.17 This dictum was approved by the majority in the House of Lords in *Tesco Supermarkets Ltd* v *Nattrass*, although the different judgments showed variations in the detailed application of the test. Lord Reid said that a company may be held criminally liable for the acts only of

...the board of directors, the managing director and perhaps other superior officers of a company [who] carry out the functions of management and speak and act as the company. ([1972] AC 153 at p. 171F.)

Viscount Dilhorne, on the other hand, said (at p. 187G) that a company should only be identified with a person

...who is in actual control of the operations of a company or of part of them and who is not responsible to another person in the company for the manner in which he discharges his duties in the sense of being under his orders.

Lord Diplock thought (at p. 200A) that the question was to be answered by

...identifying those natural persons who by the memorandum and articles of association or as a result of action taken by the directors or by the company in general meeting pursuant to the articles are entrusted with the exercise of the powers of the company.

Lord Pearson, too, thought that the constitution of the particular company should be taken into account.

4.18 The tests outlined above would, if applied strictly, produce rather different results. A company's articles of association reveal nothing about an individual officer's duties in the day-to-day running of the company. Viscount Dilhorne's test would appear to be stricter than the others, since there are very few people in a company who are not responsible to others for the manner in which they discharge their duties. However, the general principle is clear: the courts must attempt to identify the 'directing mind and will' of the corporation, the process of such identification being a matter of law (per Lord Reid at p. 170F–G).

4.19 It remains to be seen whether this principle can apply to a director or official whose appointment is invalid. There are dicta by Lord Diplock in the *Tesco Supermarkets* case (at p. 199E) suggesting that it would not apply: he stressed that 'the obvious and only place' to look in deciding whose acts are to identified with the corporation is the constitution of the corporation, its articles and memorandum of association (at pp. 199H–200A). This emphasis on the formal structure of the company would rule out anyone not validly appointed under the Companies Act 1948. This failure to take into account the realities of the situation seems to be undesirable as a matter of principle.

C. Corporate liability for manslaughter

The general theory...

4.24 The question whether a corporation could properly be charged with manslaughter came before the courts again during the litigation following the Zeebrugge ferry disaster. The coroner conducting the inquest held that a corporation could not be indicted for manslaughter. When this decision was challenged in an application for judicial review (*R v HM Coroner for East Kent ex parte Spooner* (1989) 88 Cr App R 10), Bingham LJ said (at p. 16, of the question whether a corporate body was capable of being found guilty of manslaughter):

...the question has not been fully argued and I have not found it necessary to reach a final conclusion. I am, however, tentatively of opinion that, on appropriate facts the *mens rea* required for manslaughter can be established against a corporation. I see no reason in principle why such a charge should not be established.

4.25 The question was finally decided in the criminal proceedings brought against the company which owned the ferry. In *R v P&O European Ferries (Dover) Ltd* (1990) 93 Cr App R 72, counsel for the defendant company argued first, that English law did not recognise the offence of corporate manslaughter, and, more fundamentally, that manslaughter could only be committed when one natural person killed another natural person. Turner J rejected these arguments and held that an indictment for manslaughter could lie against the company in respect of the Zeebrugge disaster. ...

4.27 Rejecting the defence argument...that a corporation, as a matter of substantive law, could not be indicted for manslaughter, Turner J referred to three leading criminal cases, and also to three other cases which introduced and developed the principle of identification in English law. As we noted at paragraph 4.11 above, the development of corporate criminal liability did not truly begin until these decisions. Before that time the criminal liability of corporations was coextensive with the vicarious liability of natural persons, in other words, restricted to certain breaches of statutory duties, criminal libel, and nuisance. The principle of identification revolutionised corporate liability since, by 'identifying' the corporation with the state of mind and actions of one of its controlling officers, it was possible to impute *mens rea* to a corporation and thereby to convict a corporation of a criminal offence requiring *mens rea*.

. . .

4.30 In conclusion he decided, in accordance with the case law which he had referred to, that where a corporation through the controlling mind of one of its agents does an act which fulfils the prerequisites of the crime of manslaughter, it is properly indictable for that crime.

The rejection of the principle of aggregation and the requirement that an individual 'controlling officer' should be guilty

4.31 Despite Turner J's ruling that an indictment for manslaughter could properly lie against a corporation, the prosecution against P&O European Ferries (Dover) Ltd ultimately failed. The judge directed the jury that, as a matter of law, there was no evidence upon which they could properly convict six of the eight defendants, including the company, of manslaughter. The principal ground for this decision in relation to the case against the company, was that, in order to convict it of manslaughter, one of the personal defendants who could be 'identified' with the company would have himself to be guilty of manslaughter. Since there was insufficient evidence on which to convict any of those personal defendants, the case against the company had to fail. In coming to this conclusion Turner J ruled against the adoption into English criminal law of the 'principle of aggregation'. This principle would have enabled the faults of a number of different individuals, none of whose faults would individually have amounted to the mental element of manslaughter, to be aggregated, so that in their totality they might have amounted to such a high degree of fault that the company could have been convicted of manslaughter.

Part V Options for Reform

G. Corporate liability for manslaughter

Introduction

5.73 We do not see any justification for applying to corporations a law of manslaughter which is different from the general law we have already expounded. That is to say, the question for this section of the Paper is how the general law of manslaughter may be applied in the particular circumstances of a corporation, and not whether standards and requirements should apply to corporations which are different from those which apply generally, that is to say to individuals. We are aware that there has been much criticism of what is alleged to be the reluctance of regulatory and prosecuting authorities to apply the general law, and in particular the health and safety laws, to corporations. However, the remedy for such lapses, if they exist, is the proper enforcement of the law which is already to hand. It is wrong and misleading to think . . . that the safety of workers can be properly or fairly protected by a system which refrains from enforcing day-to-day safety requirements, but then imposes stringent and serious penalties in the cases in which disregard of those requirements leads to or contributes to death. We invite comment on this proposition, but the rest of this Part proceeds on the basis we have indicated.

The difficulties of corporate liability

5.74 In paragraphs 4.5–4.20 above we explained the conceptual problems which have been found in attempts made by the courts to apply the criminal law to corporations. Critics have complained that the structure of the criminal law, whose concepts of *mens rea* and conscious intention or risk-taking assume the mechanisms of human, individual, choice and decision-making, are simply inept when applied to companies. This is the reason, it is suggested, for the failure to apply the criminal law effectively to damage and injury which occur in the course of companies' operations. . . .

Corporate liability and manslaughter

5.77 ... the essential difficulty which has been experienced in the present law of corporations is that of attaching liability to corporations for crimes of *conscious* wrongdoing ... But the crime of manslaughter described in this Part is not a crime of conscious wrongdoing at all; rather, it is a crime of neglect or omission, albeit neglect or omission occurring in a context of serious (objective) culpability. It is in our view much easier to say that a *corporation*, as such, has failed to do something, or has failed to meet a particular standard of conduct than it is to say that a corporation has done a positive act, or has entertained a particular subjective state of mind. The former statements can be made directly, without recourse to the intermediary step of finding a human mind and a decision-making process on the part of an individual within or representing the company; and thus the need for the identification theory, in order to bring the corporation within the subjective requirements of the law, largely falls away.

5.78 We provisionally propose, therefore, that there should be a special regime applying to corporate liability for manslaughter, in which the direct question would be whether the *corporation* fell within the criteria for liability for that offence which are described in paragraphs 5.57–5.64 above. In the following sections we set out, for critical comment, some details of how we would envisage this regime operating.

Law Commission, *Legislating the Criminal Code: Involuntary Manslaughter*

(Law Com. No. 237) (London: HMSO, 1996)

Corporate liability for manslaughter

An indictment for manslaughter now lies against a corporation

6.40 At one time it was thought that (in addition to other reasons relating to corporate liability in general) a corporation could not be guilty of manslaughter, because homicide required the killing to be done by a human being. ...

6.42 In 1987 the decision of a coroner (who had held that a corporation could not be indicted for manslaughter) was challenged in an application for judicial review. The issue was not fully argued, but Bingham LJ saw no reason in principle why such a charge could not be established and 'was tentatively of opinion' that an indictment would lie.

6.43 In 1990 the same question was argued in depth in *P & O European Ferries (Dover) Ltd*. In that case Turner J comprehensively reviewed the authorities (including some in other jurisdictions) and concluded that an indictment for manslaughter would lie today against a corporation. Although this ruling has not yet been considered at appellate level, it is plainly of great persuasive authority. ...

6.47 Rejecting the argument ... that a corporation could not, as a matter of substantive law, be indicted for manslaughter, Turner J considered in detail the subsequent authorities that had introduced and developed the principle of identification. That principle had transformed corporate liability since, by 'identifying' the corporation with the state of mind and actions of one of its controlling officers, it became possible to impute *mens rea* to a corporation and so to convict it of an offence requiring a mental element. ...

6.48 The first conviction a company of manslaughter in English legal history took place in 1994, in *R v Kite and OLL Ltd* [the Lyme Bay case, unreported]. Since the company was a one-man concern whose 'directing mind' was plainly its managing director, the company's liability was established automatically by his conviction.

The application to corporations of the substantive law of manslaughter

6.49 The prosecution against P & O European Ferries (Dover) Ltd was terminated when Turner J directed the jury that, as a matter of law, there was no evidence upon which they could properly convict six of the eight defendants, including the company, of manslaughter. The principal ground for this decision in relation to the case against the company, was that, in order to convict it of manslaughter, one of the individual defendants who could be 'identified' with the company would have himself to be guilty of manslaughter. Since there was insufficient evidence on which to convict any of those individual defendants, the case against the company had to fail....

Part VII Our provisional proposal in Consulation Paper No. 135, and our present view

The proposal

7.1 We referred in the Introduction to this report to the prevailing public concern over the difficulty of establishing criminal liability against a large company whose grossly careless failure to set up and monitor adequate systems of operating its undertaking results in death or serious injury, in some cases on a large scale.

7.2 In the light of that concern, we reviewed in Consultation Paper No. 135 the existing law relating to corporate liability for manslaughter....

7.5 We provisionally proposed the introduction of a special regime applying to corporate liability for manslaughter in which a corporation's liability would no longer be based solely on the principle of identification. Rather, 'the direct question would be whether the *corporation* fell within the criteria for liability applicable to the offence of gross negligence manslaughter (which, elsewhere in this report, we have recommended should be superseded by a new statutory offence of killing by gross carelessness).

7.6 We suggested in Consultation Paper No. 135 that the elements of such 'special regime' should be, first, that the *corporation* itself should have been aware of the risk of death or serious injury and, secondly, that its conduct fell seriously and significantly below what could reasonably have been demanded of it in dealing with the risk.

The response on consultation

7.7 On consultation, most respondents expressed the view that corporations should be held liable for manslaughter; and, of those, the majority were broadly in favour of the form of the offence that we proposed....

7.20 We agree with Turner J's comments in the *P & O* case that a 'clear case can be made for imputing to ... corporations social duties including the duty not to offend all relevant parts of the criminal law'; and that

> there is nothing essentially incongruous in the notion that a corporation should be guilty of the offence of unlawful killing.... [w]here a corporation, through the controlling mind of one of its agents, does an act which fulfils the prerequisites of the crime of manslaughter, it is properly indictable for the crime of manslaughter.

7.21 It was suggested, in the first place, that one of the Commission's aims in making the proposal—namely, that those responsible for the conduct of activities that might affect public safety should be 'kept up to the mark', is best achieved by imposing *personal* liability on those who undertake such activities. Whatever the theoretical merits of this suggestion, it does not address the difficulty that, where the inadequate management or organisation of a corporation's undertaking has caused or contributed to a death, it is often difficult in practice to identify any individual who is at fault, especially where (as is commonly the case) an omission to act is involved. The *P & O* trial, which we considered in Part VI of this Report, strikingly illustrates the point. After the judge had ruled that there was no evidence on which the jury could convict individual defendants other than members of the crew, he was bound to include the company itself within that ruling. Yet, as we have pointed out, previously the Sheen Report had concluded that 'from top to bottom' the company was 'infected with the disease of sloppiness'. There is, in our view, an overpowering argument that, on the ground of public policy, a corporation should be liable for a fatal accident caused by gross negligence in the management or organisation of its activities....

8.35 We therefore recommend

(1) that there should be a special offence of corporate killing, broadly corresponding to the individual offence of killing by gross carelessness;

(2) that (like the individual offence) the corporate offence should be committed only where the defendant's conduct in causing the death falls far below what could reasonably be expected;

(3) that (unlike the individual offence) the corporate offence should *not* require that the risk be obvious, or that the defendant be capable of appreciating the risk; and

(4) that, for the purposes of the corporate offence, a death should be regarded as having been caused by the conduct of a corporation if it is caused by a failure, in the way in which the corporation's activities are managed or organised, to ensure the health and safety of persons employed in or affected by those activities. (Recommendation 11)

Causation of death

8.36 Our proposed concept of 'management failure' is an attempt to define what, for the purposes of a corporate counterpart to the individual offence of killing by gross carelessness, can fairly be regarded as unacceptably dangerous conduct *by a corporation*. But it must of course be proved, as in the individual offence, that the defendant's conduct (which, in the present context, means the management failure) *caused* the death. To a large extent this will involve the application of the ordinary principles of causation, as in any other homicide offence. If, for example, the jury are not satisfied beyond reasonable doubt that the death would not have occurred had it not been for the management failure, the offence will not be proved. Even if the death would not otherwise have occurred, it will be open to the jury to conclude that the 'chain of causation' was broken by some unforeseeable act or event, and that the management failure was not itself a cause of the death but merely part of the events leading up to it.

CORPORATE MANSLAUGHTER AND CORPORATE HOMICIDE ACT 2007, SS. 1 AND 2

1. The offence

(1) An organisation to which this section applies is guilty of an offence if the way in which its activities are managed or organised—

    (a) causes a person's death, and

    (b) amounts to a gross breach of a relevant duty of care owed by the organisation to the deceased.

(2) The organisations to which this section applies are—

    (a) a corporation;

    (b) a department or other body listed in Schedule 1;

    (c) a police force;

    (d) a partnership, or a trade union or employers' association, that is an employer.

(3) An organisation is guilty of an offence under this section only if the way in which its activities are managed or organised by its senior management is a substantial element in the breach referred to in subsection (1).

(4) For the purposes of this Act—

    (a) "relevant duty of care" has the meaning given by section 2, read with sections 3 to 7;

    (b) a breach of a duty of care by an organisation is a "gross" breach if the conduct alleged to amount to a breach of that duty falls far below what can reasonably be expected of the organisation in the circumstances;

    (c) "senior management", in relation to an organisation, means the persons who play significant roles in—

        (i) the making of decisions about how the whole or a substantial part of its activities are to be managed or organised, or

        (ii) the actual managing or organising of the whole or a substantial part of those activities.

(5) The offence under this section is called—

    (a) corporate manslaughter, in so far as it is an offence under the law of England and Wales or Northern Ireland;

(b) corporate homicide, in so far as it is an offence under the law of Scotland.

(6) An organisation that is guilty of corporate manslaughter or corporate homicide is liable on conviction on indictment to a fine.

(7) The offence of corporate homicide is indictable only in the High Court of Justiciary.

Relevant duty of care

2. **Meaning of "relevant duty of care"**

   (1) A "relevant duty of care", in relation to an organisation, means any of the following duties owed by it under the law of negligence—

   (a) a duty owed to its employees or to other persons working for the organisation or performing services for it;

   (b) a duty owed as occupier of premises;

   (c) a duty owed in connection with—

   (i) the supply by the organisation of goods or services (whether for consideration or not),

   (ii) the carrying on by the organisation of any construction or maintenance operations,

   (iii) the carrying on by the organisation of any other activity on a commercial basis, or

   (iv) the use or keeping by the organisation of any plant, vehicle or other thing;

   (d) a duty owed to a person who, by reason of being a person within subsection (2), is someone for whose safety the organisation is responsible.

   (2) A person is within this subsection if—

   (a) he is detained at a custodial institution or in a custody area at a court or police station;

   (b) he is detained at a removal centre or short-term holding facility;

   (c) he is being transported in a vehicle, or being held in any premises, in pursuance of prison escort arrangements or immigration escort arrangements;

   (d) he is living in secure accommodation in which he has been placed;

   (e) he is a detained patient.

3.4.3 Stealing from one's own company

R v Philippou
The plundering of Sunny Tours
(1989) 89 Cr App R 290, Court of Appeal

This case allows the possibility of a person stealing from their own company, thus recognising the separate entity and property of the company. It also has the effect of protecting creditors by refusing to accept the argument that the taking of its property by its controlling directors amounts to a consent by the company. (Under the Theft Act 1968 a person is guilty of theft if they dishonestly appropriate somebody else's property.)

Facts   Philippou and Panayides were sole directors and shareholders of Sunny Tours Ltd which went into liquidation leaving unpaid debts of £11.5 million. They had withdrawn from the company's account in London £369,000 in 16 transactions to buy for themselves a property in Spain shortly before the company failed. They were charged with theft from the company. (Panayides fell ill and the case continued against Philippou.)

O'CONNOR LJ: On behalf of the Crown, Mr Dunn has submitted that, at least in this court, the matter is concluded against the appellant by the decision of this Court in *Attorney-General's Reference (No. 2 of 1982)* [1984] QB 624. The point of law referred to the court will be found at p. 635:

> Whether a man in total control of a limited liability company (by reason of his shareholding and directorship) is capable of stealing the property of the company; and whether two men in total control of a limited liability company (by reason of their shareholdings and directorships) are (while acting in concert) capable of jointly stealing the property of the company.

> . . .

Kerr LJ then set out the contentions for the defendants. He said at p. 638:

. . .

> It was submitted that since the defendants were the sole owners of the company and, through their shareholding, the sole owners of all its property, they could not, in effect, be charged with stealing from themselves. In particular, it was submitted that there was no issue to go to the jury on the ingredient of 'dishonestly'. The defendants were the sole will and directing mind of the company. The company was therefore bound to consent to all to which they themelves consented. . . .

At p. 639, Kerr LJ said:

> The basic fallacy in the submission on behalf of the defendants is the contention that, in effect, in a situation such as the present a jury is bound to be directed that, when all the members and directors of a company act in concert in appropriating the property of their company, they cannot, as a matter of law, be held to have acted dishonestly; or that, on such facts, any reasonable jury is bound to reach this conclusion. We entirely disagree with both these propositions.

> The trial judge had relied on the speeches in the House of Lords in *Tesco Supermarkets Ltd* v *Nattrass* [1972] AC 153, but Kerr LJ pointed out that the decision has no bearing on offences committed against a company. . . .

> Mr Thomas submitted that the appellant and Panayides, as sole shareholders and directors, were the mind and will of Sunny Tours. When they gave instructions to the bank to transfer money to Spain, the instructions were the instructions of the company, so that the company had consented to the transfer in the sense that the transfer could not be said to be adverse to any right of the company. But the order to the Bank is only one part of a composite transaction. The other component is the fact that the money was being used to put the block of flats into the pockets of the appellant and Panayides through the Spanish company. That component was the fact from which the jury could infer not only that the transaction was dishonest, but was intended to deprive Sunny Tours permanently of its money. For the reasons given by Kerr LJ in *Attorney-General's Reference (No. 2 of 1982)*, there was no 'consent' by the company on which the appellant can rely. His position is not improved by substituting 'authority' for consent. Once the two components are put together, the drawing of the money from the bank is shown to be adverse to the rights of the company and there was an appropriation.

> In our judgment, appropriation was correctly conceded in *Attorney-General's Reference (No. 2 of 1982)*. With great respect to the learned judges giving the majority judgments in *R* v *Roffel* [1985] VR 511, we cannot agree that the decision in *R* v *Morris* [1984] AC 320 requires us to hold that appropriation was wrongly conceded in *Attorney-General's Reference (No. 2 of 1982)*. It follows that the learned judge was right to refuse to withdraw these two counts from the jury.

NOTE: See also *Director of Public Prosecutions* v *Gomez* [1993] AC 442 affirming the above case.

3.5 TORTIOUS LIABILITY OF DIRECTORS

The circumstances of the following case, *Williams* v *Natural Life Health Foods Ltd*, resemble to some extend the recent case of *Ord* v *Belhaven Pubs Ltd* [1998] BCC 607 (3.3.4). Both cases concerned buyers of business opportunities claiming for their losses when the recession of the early 1990s intervened and the business turned out not to be the gold mine that the seller had apparently asserted it would be. In each case the seller was a company and was no longer trading or was insolvent. In the *Ord* case the plaintiff buyers sought to claim against the seller's holding company. In the *Williams* case they claimed against the director of the selling company, who, they argued, was personally responsible for the optimistic forecasts. In both cases the buyer was unsuccessful in cherry-picking a defendant worth suing; in each case the holding company and the director were held not to be liable.

Williams v *Natural Life Health Foods Ltd*

A director avoids personal liability in tort

[1998] 1 WLR 830, House of Lords

Where a defendant company becomes insolvent the plaintiffs may seek to make a director liable in its place on the grounds that the director had assumed personal liability to them. The effect of a successful claim would be to deprive a director/shareholder of the shield of limited liability to this extent. In this case it was held that the plaintiffs could not reasonably have relied upon the representations made to them so as to create a special relationship between the director and themselves. He had not therefore assumed personal responsibility to them for the matters in question and so was held not liable in tort.

Facts   Mr Mistlin successfully ran a health food shop in Salisbury. In 1986 he formed Natural Life Health Foods Ltd which offered franchises of retail health food shops. Mistlin was principal shareholder and managing director. The plaintiffs agreed with the company to take a franchise to open a shop in Rugby. They never dealt with Mistlin but with an employee of the company who produced a company brochure describing the success of Mistlin in the Salisbury shop. They were also given detailed financial projections of the likely future profitability of their shop. With this encouragement they agreed a franchise and opened their shop, but the shop was not profitable and closed causing them considerable loss. They sued the company but this went into liquidation. They then claimed against Mistlin arguing that he had assumed personal responsibility for the company's negligent advice.

LORD STEYN: In this case the identification of the applicable principles is straightforward. It is clear, and accepted by counsel on both sides, that the governing principles are stated in the leading speech of Lord Goff of Chieveley in *Henderson* v *Merrett Syndicates Ltd* [1995] 2 AC 145. First, in *Henderson's* case it was settled that the assumption of responsibility principle enunciated in *Hedley Byrne & Co. Ltd* v *Heller & Partners Ltd* [1964] AC 465 is not confined to statements but may apply to any assumption of responsibility for the provision of services. The extended *Hedley Byrne* principle is the rationalisation or technique adopted by English law to provide a remedy for the recovery of damages in respect of economic loss caused by the negligent performance of services. Secondly, it was established that once a case is identified as falling within the extended *Hedley Byrne* principle, there is no need to embark on any further inquiry whether it is 'fair, just and reasonable' to impose liability for economic loss: p. 181. Thirdly, and applying *Hedley Byrne* it was made clear that

> reliance upon [the assumption of responsibility] by the other party will be necessary to establish a cause of action (because otherwise the negligence will have no causative effect) (p. 180).

Fourthly, it was held that the existence of a contractual duty of care between the parties does not preclude the concurrence of a tort duty in the same respect.

It will be recalled that Waite LJ took the view that in the context of directors of companies the general principle must not 'set at naught' the protection of limited liability. In *Trevor Ivory Ltd* v *Anderson* [1992] 2 NZLR 517, 524, Cooke P expressed a very similar view. It is clear what they meant.

What matters is not that the liability of the shareholders of a company is limited but that a company is a separate entity, distinct from its directors, servants or other agents. The trader who incorporates a company to which he transfers his business creates a legal person on whose behalf he may afterwards act as director. For present purposes, his position is the same as if he had sold his business to another individual and agreed to act on his behalf. Thus the issue in this case is not peculiar to companies. Whether the principal is a company or a natural person, someone acting on his behalf may incur personal liability in tort as well as imposing vicarious or attributed liability upon his principal. But in order to establish personal liability under the principle of *Hedley Byrne*, which requires the existence of a special relationship between plaintiff and tortfeasor, it is not sufficient that there should have been a special relationship with the principal. There must have been an assumption of responsibility such as to create a special relationship with the director or employee himself. . . .

The touchstone of liability is not the state of mind of the defendant. An objective test means that the primary focus must be on things said or done by the defendant or on his behalf in dealings with the plaintiff. . . . The inquiry must be whether the director, or anybody on his behalf, conveyed directly or indirectly to the prospective franchisees that the director assumed personal responsibility towards the prospective franchisees. . . .

The test is not simply reliance in fact. The test is whether the plaintiff could *reasonably* rely on an assumption of personal responsibility by the individual who performed the services on behalf of the company. . . .

Returning to the particular question before the House it is important to make clear that a director of a contracting company may only be held liable where it is established by evidence that he assumed personal liability and that there was the necessary reliance. There is nothing fictional about this species of liability in tort. . . .

Mr Mistlin owned and controlled the company. The company held itself out as having the expertise to provide reliable advice to franchisees. The brochure made clear that this expertise derived from Mr Mistlin's experience in the operation of the Salisbury shop. In my view these circumstances were insufficient to make Mr Mistlin personally liable to the plaintiffs. Stripped to essentials the reasons of Langley J [the judge at first instance], the reasons of the majority in the Court of Appeal and the arguments of counsel for the plaintiffs can be considered under two headings. First, it is said that the terms of the brochure, and in particular its description of the role of Mr Mistlin, are sufficient to amount to an assumption of responsibility by Mr Mistlin. In his dissenting judgment [in the Court of Appeal] [1997] 1 BCLC 131, 156 Sir Patrick Russell rightly pointed out that in a small one-man company 'the managing director will almost inevitably be the one possessed of qualities essential to the functioning of the company'. By itself this factor does not convey that the managing director is willing to be personally answerable to the customers of the company. Secondly, great emphasis was placed on the fact that it was made clear to the franchisees that Mr Mistlin's expertise derived from his experience in running the Salisbury shop for his own account. . . . In the present case there were no personal dealings between Mr Mistlin and the plaintiffs. There were no exchanges or conduct crossing the line which could have conveyed to the plaintiffs that Mr Mistlin was willing to assume personal responsibility to them. Contrary to the submissions of counsel for the plaintiffs, I am also satisfied that there was not even evidence that the plaintiffs believed that Mr Mistlin was undertaking personal responsibility to them. Certainly, there was nothing in the circumstances to show that the plaintiffs could reasonably have looked to Mr Mistlin for indemnification of any loss. For these reasons I would reject the principal argument of counsel for the plaintiffs.

NOTE: See, however, *Merrett* v *Babb* [2001] QB 1174, where a surveyor was held liable for a negligent valuation signed by him even though the employer he was working for was incorporated (as a limited liability partnership).

4

The Disclosure Principle

4.1 THE PRIVILEGE OF LIMITED LIABILITY

This chapter is the shortest in the book but in the importance of the themes it encapsulates, not by any means the shortest on substance. One of the key pieces of jargon in company law, especially in relation to the regulation of the publicly listed share markets is the word 'disclosure'. It crops up repeatedly throughout the book and this chapter now attempts to draw together and explain the essential principles in case they become lost in the welter of detail that you, the valiant student of company law are already overwhelmed by.

There are two main reasons for the regulators' near obsession with disclosure. The most obvious one is in relation to the public share markets. If a stock market is to function properly, the companies whose shares are listed on the exchange must be required at all stages to make full disclosure of prescribed details of its financial and business affairs so that investors can make properly considered investment decisions with the benefit of all essential financial and business information that is publicly available to all. This is dealt with at 4.3 below.

Less obvious but even more fundamental a principle of company law is that as limited companies are allowed freely to trade without their members incurring liability for their debts, there is the corresponding downside that they should suffer a certain loss of privacy by publicly disclosing aspects of their affairs and financial position for the benefit of third parties dealing with them. A partnership business or an unlimited company thus do not have to file their annual accounts at the Companies Registry but limited companies must.

There is no doubt that limited liability is a considerable privilege. To be able to invest a minimal sum in a business enterprise and to be at no further risk potentially prejudices creditors. Why should they not be able to enforce their debts against the personal assets of the people who financed and now run the company? The justification for limited liability is of course to encourage enterprise and the pooling of funds in business ventures. For this privilege there has to be a price and this is exacted on behalf of creditors. The main price the entrepreneur trading with limited liability has to pay is therefore 'disclosure'. If creditors cannot enforce against the apparent wealth of the major shareholders (their land, their houses and so on), then they need to be able to assess how creditworthy is the company in whose name they are trading. They need access to a public register to be able to discover who are the owners and directors of the company and to obtain details of its financial position. Thus, as has been said, the price of limited liability is the burden of complying with a mass of statutory disclosure requirements with a consequent loss of privacy.

This chapter summarises the various categories of disclosure which are many and extensive. Even small private companies have a range of obligations including the preparation and filing of annual accounts. At one time they did not have to file their accounts as the origin of the 'private company' was an exemption from this requirement but since 1967 even private companies must file their accounts at Companies House.

In addition to routine statutory disclosure (information on business documents, registers kept at the registered office of the company, filing annual returns and accounts at the Companies Registry), public companies whose shares are listed on the London Stock Exchange have an extra burden of disclosure. To ensure that investors can make proper investment decisions and to ensure the fair working of the market a huge volume of information has to be published when the shares are first offered to the public and subsequently. (See chapter 17.)

Disclosure for stock exchange purposes is considered below at 4.3, while statutory disclosure is briefly summarised as follows.

4.2 STATUTORY DISCLOSURE

4.2.1 Information on business documents

The company name must appear on most business documents. The name must end with 'public limited company' or plc, or 'Limited' or Ltd as a warning of limited liability. The place of registration (e.g., registered in England and Wales), the company number and the address of the registered office must appear in all business letters and order forms. If there is a reference to the company's share capital, this must be to the paid-up share capital. If any business letterhead states the name of any directors, all directors' names must be stated. These are a few examples of the various requirements such as under CA 2006, Part 5, Chapter 6.

4.2.2 Information at the registered office

A wide range of information is required to be kept at the company's registered office for inspection by members of the company, and a more restricted range is open also to outsiders. For example, outsiders may inspect the registers of directors and members and copies of documents creating registrable charges on company property. Members only may inspect copies of directors' service contracts, minutes of general meetings etc. The Companies Act 2006, Part 37 specifies how companies must keep their records. For a detailed account see Mayson, French and Ryan *Company Law*, Oxford: OUP, chapter 4.4.

4.2.3 Public notification

There has long been an obligation to publish certain events in the *London* or *Edinburgh Gazette*, e.g., a liquidator in a voluntary winding up must publish the fact of his or her appointment (Insolvency Act 1986, s. 109). In addition to this there must be 'official notification' when the registrar receives or issues certain documents. This requirement was enacted to implement art. 3, para. 4, of the First EEC Directive which reflects long-standing practice in Continental jurisdictions. The Companies Act 2006, s. 1079 says that the company cannot rely on the happening of any of five events stated in the section against third parties unless they had been officially notified.

The reforms of 2006 have restructured the relevant sections which now appear below. The mention in s. 1077(1) of 'alternative means of giving public notice' is that under s. 1116 regulations are to enable notification by electronic means, i.e. on the Internet.

COMPANIES ACT 2006, SS. 1077, 1078 AND 1079

1077. Public notice of receipt of certain documents

(1) The registrar must cause to be published—
(a) in the Gazette, or
(b) in accordance with section 1116 (alternative means of giving public notice),
notice of the receipt by the registrar of any document that, on receipt, is subject to the Directive disclosure requirements (see section 1078).

(2) The notice must state the name and registered number of the company, the description of document and the date of receipt.

(3) The registrar is not required to cause notice of the receipt of a document to be published before the date of incorporation of the company to which the document relates.

1078. Documents subject to Directive disclosure requirements

(1) The documents subject to the "Directive disclosure requirements" are as follows.
The requirements referred to are those of Article 3 of the First Company Law Directive (68/151/EEC), as amended, extended and applied.
[This section lists the documents, with additional ones for public companies.]

1079. Effect of failure to give public notice

(1) A company is not entitled to rely against other persons on the happening of any event to which this section applies unless—
(a) the event has been officially notified at the material time, or
(b) the company shows that the person concerned knew of the event at the material time.

(2) The events to which this section applies are—
(a) an amendment of the company's articles,
(b) a change among the company's directors,
(c) (as regards service of any document on the company) a change of the company's registered office,
(d) the making of a winding-up order in respect of the company, or
(e) the appointment of a liquidator in a voluntary winding up of the company.

(3) If the material time falls—
(a) on or before the 15th day after the date of official notification, or
(b) where the 15th day was not a working day, on or before the next day that was,
the company is not entitled to rely on the happening of the event as against a person who shows that he was unavoidably prevented from knowing of the event at that time.

(4) "Official notification" means—
   (a) in relation to an amendment of the company's articles, notification in accordance with section 1077 (public notice of receipt by registrar of certain documents) of the amendment and the amended text of the articles;
   (b) in relation to anything else stated in a document subject to the Directive disclosure requirements, notification of that document in accordance with that section;
   (c) in relation to the appointment of a liquidator in a voluntary winding up, notification of that event in accordance with section 109 of the Insolvency Act 1986 (c. 45) or Article 95 of the Insolvency (Northern Ireland) Order 1989 (S.I.1989/2405 (N.I. 19)).

Official Custodian for Charities v Parway Estates Development Ltd
The London Gazette *is presumed to be unread*
[1984] 3 All ER 679, [1985] Ch 151, Court of Appeal

This case concludes that s. 1079 (at the time of the case, European Communities Act 1972, s. 9(4)) does not have the effect of deeming the whole world to know of the official notification of any of the items notified. Thus, for example, a third party does not have constructive notice that a company has altered its objects clause merely because this has been officially notified. The purpose of the provision is to make essential information available to the public by publication in the *Gazette*. It is not to penalise third parties. To ensure that companies do file such documents with the registrar (who, on receipt causes them to be notified), companies may not rely on the fact against third parties (e.g., if a person serves a writ on the company at its old registered office, the new one not having been gazetted, the company cannot rely on the change of registered office and claim that the writ has not been properly served).

Facts   In 1961 Parway took a lease for 107 years of valuable building land in London and spent at least £750,000 developing buildings on it. In 1979 a winding-up order was made in respect of the company which was officially notified in the London Gazette. The landlords continued to accept rent until 1981 when they did a company search. On discovering that Parway was in liquidation they refused to accept further rent. The lease gave the landlords a right to forfeit the lease if the tenant were to go into liquidation. However, this right would be lost (and the liquidator would thus be able to sell the lease) if the landlords had waived it by accepting rent knowing of the liquidation. The Court of Appeal held that the landlords had not waived the right of forfeiture since they had no actual or imputed (constructive) knowledge of the winding up at the time they accepted rent.

DILLON LJ: I turn to the case of waiver put forward in reliance on the official notifications in the *London Gazette* of the making of the winding-up order and of the appointment of the liquidator.

It is common ground that (apart from the argument based on the letter of 2 November 1976) receipt by the plaintiffs of rent after Parway had gone into liquidation cannot have operated as a waiver of the right to forfeit the lease if at the time that the rent was received the plaintiffs had had no notice that Parway had gone into liquidation.

It is also common ground that before s. 9 of the 1972 Act came into force, the registration in the companies registry and subsequently promulgation in the *London Gazette* of the fact that a company was in liquidation or of the appointment of a liquidator, did not operate as notice to all the world, and more particularly did not operate as notice to the company's landlord, that the company was in liquidation. This was decided in *Fryer v Ewart* [1901] 1 Ch 499, CA; [1902] AC 187, HL. The effect of s. 9 of the 1972 Act is therefore crucial to the argument.

Section 9 was enacted in anticipation of the entry of this country into the European Economic Community, in order to comply with EEC Council Directive 68/151, which was adopted on 9 March 1968. . . .

. . . A version of the Directive in the English language and apparently taken from the *Official Journal of the European Communities* has been put before us (see OJ S Edn 1968 (I), p. 41). In this, the provisions which have led to subs. (3) and (4) of s. 9 appear in a section headed 'Disclosure', and the relevant recital states:

> Whereas the basic documents of the company should be disclosed in order that third parties may be able to ascertain their contents and other information concerning the company, especially particulars of the persons who are authorised to bind the company.

Even without reference to the Directive, I have no doubt, on the wording of s. 9, that that section was primarily intended for the protection of persons dealing with a company rather than for the protection of the company. This is apparent not least from the opening words of subs. (1), 'In favour of a person dealing with a company in good faith', and from the opening words of subs. (4), 'A company shall not be entitled to rely against other persons on the happening of any of the following events . . .'.

The question then is whether, even so, it is implicit in subs. (4), or necessary in order to give effect to subs. (4), that, after an official notification of an event has become fully effective, all persons must be treated as having constructive notice of that event. Three matters can be urged in support of the argument, viz. (i) if an event has not been officially notified a company can still rely on it as against a person who has actual knowledge of it, and so official notification is in a sense treated as the counterpart of actual knowledge, in enabling the company to rely on the event, (ii) during the period of grace before the official notification has become fully effective, the person concerned can prevent the company relying on the event by showing that he was unavoidably prevented from knowing of the event, absence of knowledge of the event being treated in the period of grace as countervailing the official notification, and (iii) it is difficult to think of circumstances in which a company will wish to rely as against a third party on the happening of the event of its own liquidation and in which the real issue will not be the third party's knowledge of that event rather than the happening of the event itself.

This question whether official notification of a relevant event constitutes notice of that event to all the world is an important question. If indeed the notification does constitute notice to all, the very many landlords who are not in the habit of studying the *London Gazette* regularly or effecting regular searches of the files of their company tenants in the Companies Registry will be at risk of inadvertently waiving the forfeiture of leases by accepting rent after the company tenant has gone into liquidation.

The deputy judge, after considering the wording of subs. (4) and the views expressed in *Palmer's Company Law*, 23rd ed., vol. 1, pp. 184, 185–6, concluded that subs. (4) did not impute knowledge to anyone and did not impute notice to anyone. It was essentially negative in its impact. It provided that a company cannot rely on a relevant event if it is not in the *Gazette* but it did not make the positive counter proposition that a company can rely on that event, sc. it can rely on everyone having notice of that event, merely because it is in the *Gazette*. I agree with the deputy judge's analysis of the subsection and with his conclusion.

I would add two further comments. In the first place, I do not think that the link, such as it is, in subs. (4), between official notification of a relevant event and actual knowledge of the event if it has not been officially notified, requires that official notification should be treated as importing notice of the event to everyone. The object of the legislation is that persons dealing with a company should be officially given an opportunity of finding out important information concerning the company but there is no sense in hampering the company *vis-à-vis* those who have actual knowledge of the relevant event. Hence the qualification of the restriction imposed by the subsection on the company. It is not necessary to treat official notification as the equivalent of actual knowledge in all circumstances.

In the second place, among the events, other than liquidation and the appointment of a liquidator, listed in subs. (4) as events on which a company cannot rely in the absence of official notification are the making of any alteration in the memorandum of association of the company including, of course, its objects clause, and the making of any change among the company's directors. But it is plain to my mind from subs. (1) of s. 9 that a person dealing in good faith with a company is not to be treated as having constructive notice (as under the previous *ultra vires* doctrine of English law) of the terms of the company's objects clause, whether in its original form or as from time to time altered, and is not to be treated as having constructive notice of the composition from time to time of the board of directors of the company. The tenor of the section is thus against imputing constructive notice of relevant events to persons dealing with a company, while ensuring that they have an opportunity to find out information about those events.

I thus agree with the deputy judge that Parway's defence of waiver fails. . . .

4.2.4 Information at Companies House

Various returns must be made to Companies House in the 'prescribed form', that is, in the forms appearing in the current regulations. Examples are the annual return, the annual accounts, changes in the capital of the company, its memorandum or articles, registered office or directors and of any charges created by the company over its assets. Thus the public may do a 'company search' to obtain this information.

Searches used to be done by going to Companies House in London and asking for the file of original paper documents on the company in question. It is still possible to go to information centres in Cardiff, London and Edinburgh but the majority of searches are done online (www.companieshouse.gov.uk) or through specialist search agencies.

Most commonly requested are the annual return and accounts, and confirmation that the company has not gone into liquidation or receivership. (An earlier search in the *Parway* case above would have been highly beneficial!). The limitation on the value of the annual accounts is that they are merely a snapshot. Since private companies normally have nine months after the end of their 'accounting reference period' to file their accounts, the subject of the 'photo' may have deteriorated since it was taken.

4.3 STOCK EXCHANGE DISCLOSURE

To encourage investment of capital in the shares of major companies it is essential to establish an active public market for such shares. To ensure that individual shares are freely traded and find their appropriate market price it is of paramount importance that full and equal information about them is available to all investors. For public companies listed on a stock market it is therefore essential that they are obliged to make full and accurate disclosure of their affairs. In order to protect investors and to ensure the active and proper functioning of the market, the Listing Rules of the United Kingdom Listing Authority (see 17.2) are thus aimed primarily at ensuring that companies provide full information when the shares are first offered to the public and on a continuing basis. The law and practice has been influenced by the EC harmonisation programme. This was aimed at enabling shares of companies incorporated in one member state to be listed on the stock markets of other member states and at ensuring a minimum standard of investor protection across the EC. In the area of public listed companies the disclosure principle is of enormous significance and is one of the few areas in which UK law or practice has substantially influenced the EC harmonisation programme.

A major development in the 1990s has been a series of official reports on the 'corporate governance' of public listed companies. These reports have culminated in the requirement that listed companies comply with the Combined Code on Corporate Governance issued in 1998 (see 8.3). The complex web of law under the Financial Services and Markets Act 2000 and the Companies Act 2006 and the requirements of listing rules and corporate governance codes all focus substantially on the essential principle of disclosure. The delicate balance between regulatory rules, entrepreneurial acumen and disclosure obligations is well described in the opening paragraphs of the Hampel Report (Committee on Corporate Governance, *Final Report* (1988)):

> Public companies are now among the most accountable organisations in society. They publish trading results and audited accounts; and they are required to disclose much information about their operations, relationships, remuneration and governance arrangements. We strongly endorse this accountability and we recognise the contribution to it made by the Cadbury and Greenbury committees. But the emphasis on accountability has tended to obscure a board's first responsibility—to enhance the prosperity of the business over time.
>
> Business prosperity cannot be commanded. People, teamwork, leadership, enterprise, experience and skills are what really produce prosperity. There is no single formula to weld these together, and it is dangerous to encourage the belief that rules and regulations about structure will deliver success. Accountability by contrast does require appropriate rules and regulations, in which disclosure is the most important element.

Since the time of this report a decade or so ago, disclosure fever has hotted up. For example, further requirements have been introduced under the so-called 'transparency directive' (2004/109/EC), as implemented by CA 2006, Part 43, amending the Financial Services and Markets Act 2000. This makes detailed provision for rules to be made requiring companies whose shares are traded on regulated markets in the UK to disclose a wide range of information, including yearly and half-yearly reports and giving authority for the making of corporate governance rules.

The detail of such disclosure rules is beyond the scope of this book, though the disclosure theme will recur in chapter 17 on offering shares to public investors, in chapter 18 on takeovers and mergers and in chapter 19 on insider dealing and market abuse. For an undergraduate it is the broad principles that count, though an aspiring young corporate lawyer, now well versed in principle, is more likely in practice to become immersed in the dry process of producing endless disclosure documents than taking a fine point of company law to the Court of Appeal. Sadly much of company practice concerning big public companies is about checking that endless returns and disclosures comply with the rules, though at the academic stage a good grounding in the themes and theories of the law is still essential.

5

The Constitution: Memorandum of Association

When a company is incorporated it requires a constitution which basically records the purpose or purposes for which the company is incorporated, and which regulates the distribution of power in the company and its internal procedural matters. Before 1856, under the Joint Stock Companies Act 1844, a company was incorporated on the basis of a single document called the 'deed of settlement'. The Joint Stock Companies Act 1856 introduced a new constitutional framework for incorporation. Under the 1856 Act, two documents were required: the memorandum of association and the articles of association. This structure was followed in successive Companies Acts until the Companies Act 2006. Under the Companies Act 1985, the memorandum of association would state the company's name, domicile, objects, capital structure, and whether it was limited or unlimited, public or private. The articles of association, on the other hand, would deal with matters of internal management of the company, such as the procedures for a general meeting or board of directors' meeting, the appointment and removal of directors, the payment of dividends etc.

The Company Law Review Steering Group, set up by the DTI in 1998, thought that, in the interests of simplification, the distinction between the memorandum and the articles should be ended, and that there should instead be a single constitutional document as in a number of other jurisdictions (Modern Company Law for a Comparative Economy: The Strategic Framework (London: DTI, 1999), para. 5.3.11). It was suggested that this could be achieved by removing the requirement for a company to have objects and preventing any objects from having external effect. These proposals were repeated in the CLRSG's final report (Modern Company Law for a Competitive Economy: Final Report (London: DTI, 2001), para. 9.4), accepted by the Government in its White Paper published on 16 July 2002 (Modernising Company Law (Cm 5553) para. 2.2), and now adopted in CA 2006.

Under the new Act, a company's constitution includes its Articles of Association and any resolutions and agreements effecting its constitution (CA 2006, s. 17). A memorandum of association is still required for registration under the new Act, but serves a more limited purpose of stating the intention of the subscribers to form a company and to be members of the company on formation. In the case of a company limited by shares, it also states the intention of the subscribers to take at least one share each in the company. The objects clause which used to be in the memorandum of association is now moved to the articles of association and unless a company's articles specifically restrict its objects, its objects are unrestricted (CA 2006, s. 31(1)). Provisions in the memorandum of existing companies will be treated as provisions in the articles if they are of a type that will not be in the memorandum of companies formed under the 2006 Act (e.g., the objects clause) (CA 2006, s. 28). This chapter is primarily concerned with the memorandum of association. Articles of association will be dealt with in chapter 6.

5.1 FORM OF MEMORANDUM OF ASSOCIATION

The memorandum of association of a company must be in the prescribed form. The new form of memorandum is being prepared and prescribed by the Secretary of State, but it is likely to look very different from that of a company registered under the CA 1985. However, as the old-style memorandum will still exist and does not have to be replaced by an existing company with a new-style memorandum, the prescribed forms of memorandum for a private company limited by shares and a public company limited by shares under the CA 1985 respectively set out as Table B and Table F are reproduced. In practice, an old-style memorandum is a longer document because, to avoid the adverse consequences of the doctrine of *ultra vires*, it had become the practice to include a very lengthy objects clause. As mentioned, such an objects clause is now treated as part of the articles of association under the 2006 Act.

Companies (Tables A to F) Regulations 1985 (SI 1985/805), Tables B and F

TABLE B
A PRIVATE COMPANY LIMITED BY SHARES
MEMORANDUM OF ASSOCIATION

1. The company's name is 'The South Wales Motor Transport Company cyfyngedig'.

2. The company's registered office is to be situated in Wales.

3. The company's objects are the carriage of passengers and goods in motor vehicles between such places as the company may from time to time determine and the doing of all such other things as are incidental or conducive to the attainment of that object.

4. The liability of the members is limited.

5. The company's share capital is £50,000 divided into 50,000 shares of £1 each. We, the subscribers to this memorandum of association, wish to be formed into a company pursuant to this memorandum; and we agree to take the number of shares shown opposite our respective names.

Names and Addresses of Subscribers	Number of shares taken by each Subscriber
1. Thomas Jones, 138 Mountfield Street, Tredegar	1
2. Mary Evans, 19 Merthyr Road, Aberystwyth.	1
Total shares taken	2

Dated 19

Witness to the above signatures,
Anne Brown, 'Woodlands', Fieldside Road, Bryn Mawr.

TABLE F

A PUBLIC COMPANY LIMITED BY SHARES

MEMORANDUM OF ASSOCIATION

1. The company's name is 'Western Electronics Public Limited Company'.

2. The company is to be a public company.

3. The company's registered office is to be situated in England and Wales.

4. The company's objects are the manufacture and development of such descriptions of electronic equipment, instruments and appliances as the company may from time to time determine, and the doing of all such other things as are incidental or conducive to the attainment of that object.

5. The liability of the members is limited.

6. The company's share capital is £5,000,000 divided into 5,000,000 shares of £1 each. We, the subscribers of this memorandum of association, wish to be formed into a company pursuant to this memorandum; and we agree to take the number of shares shown opposite our respective names.

Names and Addresses of Subscribers	Number of shares taken by each Subscriber
1. James White, 12 Broadmead, Birmingham.	1
2. Patrick Smith, 145A Huntley House, London Wall, London EC2	1
Total shares taken	2

Dated 19

Witness to the above signatures,

Anne Brown, 13 Hute Street, London WC2.

5.2 BACKGROUND TO LEGISLATIVE REFORM

Modern Company Law for a Competitive Economy: The Strategic Framework

(London: DTI, 1999)

The company's constitution and initial registration

5.3.11 There is a case, in the interests of simplification, for ending the distinction between the Memorandum and the Articles, and providing instead for a single constitutional document as a number of other jurisdictions do. If we can do away with the requirement for a company to have objects and prevent any objects from having external effect, the special provision for the alteration of a company's objects can, arguably, fall.

5.3.12 What would appear on the register is a separate issue. The company's name, the names of the founder shareholders, the jurisdiction of registered office, the amount of authorised and subscribed share capital, and the objects (if any), should be registered in all cases. All companies must have these but they vary from company to company. This basic information could be registered on a single, standard form, which could also include space for the other particulars which are required on initial formation relating to the directors and secretary and address of registered office. The need for what is now in the Articles to be on the public register is less clear-cut. But the First Directive requires the registration of the company's constitution and we are not aware of any objections in practice to this requirement, which investors find useful.

5.3.13 The requirement for a statutory declaration ensures that the subscribers take the registration process seriously; the fact that the Registrar may rely on it also gives him comfort in granting the conclusive certificate of incorporation. We believe that companies and those dealing with them attach great importance to the conclusive character of the certificate, and would wish it to be retained. But we think that a formal statement of compliance by the subscribers, backed by penalties for the deliberate or reckless making of a false statement, could replace the statutory declaration. This alternative would also facilitate electronic registration....

The company's objects, its capacity, and the powers of the directors to bind the company

5.3.17 The 1989 reform was welcomed as a great improvement, but it has not solved all the problems. In particular, the 'general commercial company' provision has not been widely adopted as an alternative to long and complex objects clauses, since it is feared that it may not cover everything the directors might legitimately wish the company to do—e.g. participate in community initiatives, or give a guarantee to another company in the same group; and objects clauses are still relevant to determining the authority of directors when issues arise about 'good faith'. More generally, the complexity of sections 35 and 35A, and the differences in wording between them, has induced a very cautious approach. We are aware for example that some banks still expend considerable resource on checking objects clauses. Once an objects clause has been read by, for example, an employee of a bank, the bank is arguably aware of any limitation in it for all time. While this is not enough to create bad faith and thus to invalidate transactions by the board or an agent authorised by the board it is not clear what is required in addition to such knowledge, which will, in any event, invalidate the acts of an agent who is not so authorised.

5.3.18 We are therefore attracted to a radical simplification on the following lines:

- It would be made explicit that, in all relations with third parties, a company was deemed to have the capacity to do anything which a legal person, (as opposed to a natural person), was capable of doing. This would be so regardless of anything in the company's constitution;
- the requirement on companies on their formation to include an objects clause in their constitution would disappear.
- Companies would continue to be free, if they so chose, to limit the authority of their directors to bind the company, as an in-built constraint on their freedom vis-a-vis the shareholders. This could be done either by the constitution (articles), or by a shareholder resolution made under it; but no such limitation would affect rights of an independent third party dealing with the board of a company or an agent authorised by the board in good faith, even if they were aware of it. A qualification on the lines of section 322A would remain. But any such limitation should continue to have effect on directors as against shareholders.
- Existing companies could choose whether or not to retain their existing objects clauses. However, these should cease to have any effect to limit the authority of any agent of the company as against third parties, without prejudice to their limiting effect as against shareholders. Existing companies would continue to be free, like newly formed ones, to limit the authority of directors to bind the company by or under the constitution, with the same effects.
- The special minority protection in relation to resolutions to alter a company's objects would be abolished.
- The shareholders could, as now, bring proceedings to restrain the doing of an act by the directors, or a person authorised by them, which was beyond their powers as set out in the constitution or in a resolution; but this could not affect the validity of a commitment already entered into.
- The abolition of deemed notice would be implemented in full.
- The companies legislation would be silent on the authority of officers or agents of the company, below board level and persons authorised by the board, which would thus be governed by the normal rules of agency law, subject to a provision for existing companies which removes any limitation on the authority of agents by virtue of the objects clause so far as third parties are concerned.

5.3.19 In the case of public companies, it is arguable that the Second Directive requirement that the objects of the company must be stated in its constitution still applies, even where the applicable law provides that the objects clause cannot prejudice third parties. That is because the purpose of the Directive is stated to be the protection of shareholders (and indeed 'any interested person'), and not only of persons such as creditors who are actually dealing with the company. However, this question could be investigated further, and the possibility of an amendment to the Directive explored. It could also be considered whether the current requirement that a company should state its current business annually in its directors' report (perhaps modified by proposals, yet to be considered, on reporting…) is sufficient to fulfil the Directive requirement. If not, we would favour requiring public companies to state their objects on formation or registration as such; provision should be made that such objects can have no effect on third parties, thus ensuring that if there is to be any limitation on directors' authority in the company's constitution it has to be spelled out as such, either in the articles or by specific resolution. Since such a provision is likely to be exclusive, setting limits, rather than inclusive, setting out everything that might conceivably be needed, the problems of prolix objects clauses should disappear.

Modern Company Law for a Competitive Economy: Final Report

(London: DTI, 2001)

CHAPTER 9 COMPANY FORMATION

9.1 Draft clauses for a future Companies Bill have been prepared covering the formation and status of companies formed under the new legislation together with a number of related provisions. These are included among the clauses, and covered by explanatory notes, set out in Chapter 16. They reflect the proposals in *Company Formation and Capital Maintenance*, modified in the light of responses to that document.

9.2 We recommend that the law should provide for the formation of new companies of each of the types available now—a private company limited by shares or by guarantee; an unlimited private company; and a public company limited by shares. The ability of a single person to form a company, which now applies only in the case of a private company, would be extended to a public company.

9.3 We recommend that the law should specify the liability of the members when a company of each type is wound up. Otherwise the members would have no liability for the company's debts. (The present law starts from the proposition that the liability of the members is unlimited on a winding up, and then limits it. But the end result is the same.)

9.4 We recommend that companies formed under the new legislation should not have a separate memorandum and articles of association. Instead, the constitution should be in a single document. When the founder members (in present terminology, the subscribers to the memorandum) apply to form a company, they would have to deliver to the Registrar the proposed constitution, along with additional information set out in the Act. This would include: the proposed name of the company; whether it is to be situated in England and Wales (or Wales) or Scotland; the address of the registered office; details of the share capital (or guarantee); the names of the founder members; and details of the first directors and of the secretary if there is to be one. There should be a power for the Secretary of State to vary by order the information required. Apart from the move away from the separate memorandum and articles, there would be one significant change from the present law. The details of share capital given by companies with shares would no longer be of authorised share capital—a concept which would disappear from the statute—but of the share capital to be allotted to members on formation.

9.5 This information would have to be accompanied by a formal statement by a director or secretary that the material delivered met the legal requirements, and that the company was formed for a lawful purpose. This would replace the requirement in the present law for a statutory declaration. The directors and secretary would have to confirm their agreement to serve as such, and the directors would also have to confirm that they had read the new statement of directors' duties (see Annex C).

9.6 When the Registrar has received this information, and is satisfied that all the statutory requirements are met, it should be his duty to issue a certificate of incorporation. As now, this would be conclusive evidence that a company with the name and other characteristics stated in the certificate had been formed.

9.7 There would be provision for the Secretary of State to prescribe model constitutions for companies of each type (apart from an unlimited company with no share capital). As at present, companies would be free to adopt a model constitution in whole or in part, or to propose a constitution of their own. If a constitution failed to provide for a matter covered in the relevant model constitution, the model constitution would, as in the present law, apply to that matter by default, unless specifically excluded.

9.8 The members of a company would be able to change the constitution by special resolution, but would also be able, if they all agreed, to 'entrench' certain provisions by providing that they might only be changed by unanimity, or by a majority higher than the 75 per cent needed for a special resolution. Where the company was formed with its situation as 'Wales', entitling it to deliver certain information in Welsh, it would in future be able by special resolution to change its situation to 'England and Wales'. This is not now possible.

9.9 Where a new company is formed as a public company, additional requirements would continue to apply. As well as a certificate of incorporation, a new public company would need a trading certificate before it could commence business or borrow money. To obtain the trading certificate, it would, as now, have to have an initial share capital equal at least to the 'authorised minimum' of £50,000 nominal value, with a quarter of the nominal value and the whole of any premium paid up. These implement requirements of the Second Directive.

9.10 Companies formed under the new legislation would have unlimited capacity. Those doing business with such a company would no longer need to concern themselves with the question whether the company has the capacity to enter into a transaction, whether or not the company has an 'objects clause' in its constitution. Provisions would also be included, similar to those in the present law, clarifying the law on when the directors are deemed to have authority to bind the company, or to authorise others to do so. (It is intended that the special position of charitable companies on these two points will be preserved.)

9.11 The clauses on company formation in Chapter 16 are drafted to apply only to companies formed under the new legislation. It will be necessary later to prepare detailed transitional provisions which determine the extent to which these provisions are to apply to companies already in existence when the new legislation enters into force. But we have made clear in *Company Formation and Capital Maintenance* (paragraph 2.15) that we do not intend that such companies should have to re-register under the new legislation.

Modernising Company Law: The White Paper
(London: DTI, July 2002. Cm 5553)

2 Improving Governance: Shareholders and Decision-making
Nature of the company's constitution and its powers

2.2 The Government agrees with the Review that neither 'objects clauses'—the clause in a company's memorandum of association that defines its purpose—nor the split between the memorandum and articles in general serve a useful purpose any longer and should be removed. Instead companies should have a constitution in a single document. That constitution would be capable of containing an objects clause but, in the new structure, this would have only internal effect as between the directors and the members.

2.3 The members of a company will be able to amend the constitution by special resolution. They will also be able—if they all agree—to make it more difficult to make changes, by requiring a higher majority or even unanimity. As now, anyone doing business with the company in good faith will not need to worry about the details of the company's constitution.

New model constitutions for private and public companies

2.4 The Review considered the current model articles for companies limited by shares (widely known as Table A) to be out of date and unnecessarily complex. It recommended that separate model constitutions be prepared in simpler, clearer language for public and private companies, recognising their different needs. It also proposed a number of changes of substance. An illustrative draft of the model constitution for private companies limited by shares was included in the Review's Final Report.

2.5 The Government agrees with the recommendations of the Review, and intends to provide separate new model constitutions for private and public companies with the Bill. As the Review noted, it is not possible to draft a definitive model constitution until the Bill itself has been fully prepared.

6

The Constitution: Articles of Association

As mentioned in chapter 5, under the Companies Act 1985, a company could divide its constitutional rules between its memorandum and articles, and the terms of the memorandum could be amended in some respects after formation. Under the CA 2006, the memorandum will be a simple document stating the intention of the subscribers to form a company and to be members of the company on formation and, in the case of a company limited by shares, the intention of the subscribers to take at least one share each in the company. Everything else will be in the articles of association which will be the main constitutional document. The Constitution of a company is defined to include its articles of association and any resolution or agreement affecting its constitution. As the definition of constitution is expressed to be non-exhaustive, other documents clearly of constitutional relevance are also part of the constitution, for example the certificate of incorporation which summarises key information regarding the company such as whether the company is private or public limited.

Articles of association are rules governing the internal affairs of the company and form a statutory contract between the company and its members, and between each of the members in their capacity as members. The Table A of 1985 reproduced at 1.7 is the classic old form of articles applicable by default to companies incorporated before the enactment of new default articles under the CA 2006. Table A of CA 1985 will continue to apply to existing companies. However, existing companies are free to adopt new model articles (CA 2006, s. 19(3)).

Under CA 2006, the Secretary of State may by regulations prescribe model articles of association for companies registered under the new Act (s. 19(1)). A company may adopt all or any of the provisions of model articles (s. 19(3)). A company must register its articles of association, unless it is a limited company to which model articles apply (s. 18(2)). If the articles are not registered, or if articles are registered, in so far as they do not exclude or modify the relevant model articles, the relevant model articles form part of the company's articles (s. 20(1)).

COMPANIES ACT 2006, SS. 18 TO 20

18. Articles of association

(1) A company must have articles of association prescribing regulations for the company.

(2) Unless it is a company to which model articles apply by virtue of section 20 (default application of model articles in case of limited company), it must register articles of association.

(3) Articles of association registered by a company must—

(a) be contained in a single document, and

(b) be divided into paragraphs numbered consecutively.

(4) References in the Companies Acts to a company's "articles" are to its articles of association.

19. Power of Secretary of State to prescribe model articles

(1) The Secretary of State may by regulations prescribe model articles of association for companies.

(2) Different model articles may be prescribed for different descriptions of company.

(3) A company may adopt all or any of the provisions of model articles.

(4) Any amendment of model articles by regulations under this section does not affect a company registered before the amendment takes effect.

"Amendment" here includes addition, alteration or repeal.

(5) Regulations under this section are subject to negative resolution procedure.

20. Default application of model articles

(1) On the formation of a limited company—

    (a) if articles are not registered, or

    (b) if articles are registered, in so far as they do not exclude or modify the relevant model articles,

the relevant model articles (so far as applicable) form part of the company's articles in the same manner and to the same extent as if articles in the form of those articles had been duly registered

(2) The "relevant model articles" means the model articles prescribed for a company of that description as in force at the date on which the company is registered.

6.1 THE OBJECTS CLAUSE AND *ULTRA VIRES*

A company's memorandum of association frequently contained a lengthy objects clause. (For companies incorporated under CA 2006, such clauses are moved to the articles of association.) The objects clause states the capacity of the company. The primary purpose of this is to protect investors in a company. (The other purpose is to protect the outside public—those who might be creditors of the company.) A shareholder who invests money in a company is entitled to know the objects of the company for which the money will be used. An investor in a company whose object is to build railway carriages wants to be sure that the directors will not risk company money in a more speculative new venture not covered by the company's objects clause, such as financing the construction of a railway. Thus the company should not carry out acts or enter into transactions which are beyond the company's objects clause being *ultra vires*. A shareholder may therefore obtain an injunction to prevent the company from entering into an *ultra vires* transaction. If the transaction has been carried out, any shareholder may obtain damages for the company against the wrongdoing directors. It is primarily a mechanism which enables shareholders to control the activities of directors by preventing them from undertaking an *ultra vires* business, or by subsequently obtaining a remedy for the company. This aspect of the law of *ultra vires* is sometimes called the internal effects of the rule, that is, as between the shareholders and the directors of the company. The external aspect of the doctrine has an impact on the question of whether the contract is binding as between the company and a third party.

6.1.1 The external effect of objects clause

Externally, the objects clause protects the company's creditors who enter into transaction with the company that are within the objects clause. Where the transactions are *ultra vires*, they are void at common law and could not be ratified by the company even by unanimous votes. In *Ashbury Railway Carriage & Iron Co. Ltd v Riche* (1875) LR 7 HL 653 the company was incorporated 'to make and sell, or lend on hire, railway carriages and wagons, and all kinds of railway plant, fittings, machinery, and rolling stock; to carry on the business of mechanical engineers and general contractors; to purchase and sell, as merchants, timber, coal, metals, or other materials; and to buy and sell any such materials on commission, or as agents'. Under the articles of association, 'an extension of the company's business beyond or for other than the objects or purposes expressed or implied in the memorandum of association shall take place only in pursuance of a special resolution'. The company entered into an agreement with Riche to provide finance for the construction of a railway in Belgium, but later repudiated the agreement. When sued for damages, the company successfully pleaded that the agreement was *ultra vires* the company's memorandum. The House of Lords held that the agreement was *ultra vires* and could not be ratified even unanimously by the shareholders.

The doctrine of *ultra vires* had an impact on the binding relationship between the company and third parties who entered into *ultra vires* transactions with the company. As an *ultra vires* transaction was a nullity, and could not be ratified or adopted retrospectively by shareholders, the company was able to refuse to perform its obligations under the contract. This was so even if the third party entered into the transaction in good faith because the third party was taken to have constructive notice of the objects clause, having access to this information by making a search at the Companies Registry (*Ernest v Nicholls* (1857) 6 HL Cas 401; *Royal British Bank v Turquand* (1856) 6 El & Bl 327: see 8.2.1). The response of lawyers was to draft objects clauses as widely as possible to avoid transactions being found to be void. While the courts have in general applied the doctrine of *ultra vires* rigorously, in some cases they have attempted to water down the harshness the doctrine would cause by accepting a broad construction of clauses intended to broaden the scope of the company's capacity. For example, in *Cotman v Brougham* [1918] AC 514, the House of Lords recognised the practice of listing a wide variety of objects with a concluding paragraph to the effect that each clause was to be treated as an individual or independent objects clause and not to be construed restrictively as ancillary to a main objects clause. This enabled the court to find, in favour of a third party, that a transaction was covered by a subsidiary objects clause even though it was not within the main objects of the company. Here, the memorandum of association of Essequibo Rubber and Tobacco Estates Ltd (Essequibo) contained a wide variety of objects. The objects clause concluded with a declaration that every subclause should be construed as a substantive clause and not be limited or restricted by reference to any other subclause, and should not be deemed to be subsidiary or auxiliary merely to the objects mentioned in any other subclause. The company, whose business was to acquire rubber and tobacco estates, underwrote shares in the Anglo-Cuban Oil, Bitumen, and Asphalt Co. Ltd. Later both companies went into liquidation and Essequibo was placed by the liquidator of Anglo-Cuban Oil on the list of contributories in respect of these shares. In this action, the liquidator of Essequibo applied for the removal of its name from the list of contributories on the ground that the underwriting was *ultra vires*, but failed.

In *Bell Houses Ltd* v *City Wall Properties Ltd* [1966] 2 QB 656 the Court of Appeal recognised a 'subjective objects clause'. The objects of the plaintiff company were to carry on business as general, civil and engineering contractors and in particular to construct houses. By clause 3(c) of its memorandum the company was empowered 'to carry on any other trade or business whatsoever which can, in the opinion of the board of directors, be advantageously carried on by the company in connection with or as ancillary to any of the above businesses or the general business of the company'. It was held that it was *intra vires* for the company, in return for a fee of £20,000, to introduce the defendant company to a financier who was able to lend it £1 million for its business.

In *Evans* v *Brunner, Mond and Co. Ltd* [1921] 1 Ch 359 Eve J accepted the validity of a provision at the end of the company's objects clause which gave the company or its directors power to do 'all such other things as are incidental or conducive to the attainment' of the company's objects. This catch-all provision is quite often adopted by companies.

6.1.2 The 1972 reform of *ultra vires*

The problems caused by the doctrine of *ultra vires* were long recognised. The Cohen Committee (Cmnd 6659 (1945), para. 12) recommended the abolition of *ultra vires* but made no recommendation for the modification of the doctrine of constructive notice which was closely related to the doctrine of *ultra vires*. The Jenkins Committee (Cmnd 1749 (1962), para. 42), while it recommended that the doctrine of constructive notice should be replaced by a set of statutory rules, did not recommend the abolition of the doctrine of *ultra vires*. Reform was not, however, carried out until the UK's accession to the EEC in 1972. To comply with art. 9 of the First EEC Company Law Directive, s. 9(1) of the European Communities Act 1972 (replaced by CA 1985, s. 35) was passed to protect any person dealing in good faith with the company from the effects of a transaction not being within the capacity of the company.

6.1.3 The 1989 reform

The CA 1985, s. 35 was thought to be most unsatisfactory. It applied only to transactions 'decided on by the directors', and only operated in favour of persons who dealt in good faith with the company. The doctrine of constructive notice as against third parties also remained intact.

In 1986, Professor D.D. Prentice published his report which, in 1989, led to the modification of CA 1985, s. 35, which basically provided that the validity of an act done by a company should not be called into question on the ground of lack of capacity by reason of anything in the company's memorandum. (For a detailed analysis of the new s. 35, see Eilis Ferran, 'The reform of the law on corporate capacity and directors' and officers' authority: part 1' (1992) 13 Co Law 124.)

In addition, CA 1985, s. 3A (as added by CA 1989, s. 110(1)), permitted a company to adopt a clause which allows it 'to carry on business as a general commercial company'.

6.1.4 The new law

In an attempt to simplify the constitution of a company, the Company Law Review Steering Group proposed the repeal of s. 3A and that object clauses should no longer be compulsory for private companies (see *Modern Company Law for a Competitive Economy: Company Formation and Capital Maintenance* (URN 99/1145) (London: DTI, 1999), para. 2.17; *Modern Company Law for a Competitive Economy: Final Report*, Vol. 1 (URN 01/942) (London: DTI 2001), para. 9.10). These proposals are now enacted into law under the CA 2006. As mentioned in chapter 5, the objects clause which used to be in the memorandum of association is now moved to the articles of association and unless a company's articles specifically restrict its objects, its objects are unrestricted (CA 2006, s. 31(1)). Thus, for companies formed under the CA 2006, it is no longer necessary to have any objects clause. The doctrine of *ultra vires* would be irrelevant to such companies. However, for a company that adopts an objects clause to limit the capacity of the company, whilst the doctrine of *ultra vires* is irrelevant for creditors, it remains relevant internally whether a transaction is *ultra vires* the company's objects clause in deciding whether its directors have acted beyond their powers and authorities. Thus, old cases on the interpretation of various objects clause discussed above remain relevant in this regard.

As for the capacity of a company, the position remains unchanged. Section 39 of the CA 2006, restating CA 1985, s. 35, provides that the validity of a company's acts is not to be questioned on the ground of lack of capacity because of anything in the constitution. It replaces s. 35(1) and (4) of the 1985 Act. Sections 35(2) and (3) are abolished as redundant under the 2006 Act because (i) under the 2006 Act, a company may have unrestricted objects (and where it has restricted objects, the directors' powers are also restricted) and (ii) there is a specific duty on directors to abide by the company constitution under s. 171 (see 12.4.1 below).

6.2 ULTRA VIRES AND ABUSE OF POWERS

Cases on *ultra vires* are often difficult, and are sometimes entangled with questions of lack of authority of directors, breaches of fiduciary duty and other procedural irregularities under the articles.

It is implicit that one of the duties of the directors is to work within the constitution of the company and only to act *intra vires*. It follows that, if they do undertake an *ultra vires* transaction, it is not only beyond the capacity of the company, but it is also beyond the authority of the directors as agents of the company. The usual consequences of the absence of authority in making a contract on behalf of a principal therefore apply (see 8.2).

Despite the broad drafting of objects clauses, the doctrine still remained a trap for the unwary in a number of circumstances. For example, the practice of using an 'independent objects clause' as in *Cotman v Brougham* cannot convert what is intrinsically a power into an object. Thus, in *Re Introductions Ltd* [1970] Ch 199, Introductions Ltd asked the bank to borrow money for the purpose of pig breeding. The bank had a copy of the memorandum of association limiting the company's objects to tourism. The memorandum also contained an objects clause which empowered the company to borrow money with a statement to the effect that each objects clause should be treated independently. When the company went insolvent, the bank sought to enforce the transaction arguing that the 'objects clause' which empowered borrowing should be construed independently, and when so construed, the borrowing for pig breeding would be *intra vires* the company. It was held that borrowing money was a power and not an object: borrowing is not an end in itself and must be for some *intra vires* purpose of the company. As the power in this case was exercised for an *ultra vires* purpose, and the bank was aware of the purpose, the transaction was unenforceable by the bank.

In the leading case of *Rolled Steel Products (Holdings) Ltd v British Steel Corporation*, extracted below, it was concluded that such a transaction did not involve questions of *ultra vires*. The real issue was not the capacity of the company, but the abuse of a power by the directors. The principle is stated thus: if the directors were in breach of their fiduciary duty to the company in entering into the transaction, and if this were known to the third party, then the company could avoid the transaction. As the transaction was not beyond the capacity of the company it was not void but voidable, and so the company could ratify it. (Ratification can waive a breach of duty or supply a want of directors' authority; at common law it cannot cure a company's lack of capacity.)

Rolled Steel Products (Holdings) Ltd v British Steel Corporation
Powers exercised in breach of directors' duties
[1986] Ch 246, Court of Appeal

Where directors exercise a power of the company (such as granting security) the transaction is within the capacity of the company, though if it were done in breach of fiduciary duty to the knowledge of the third party, the company may avoid the transaction. This case also affirmed the long-established rule that a company had implied powers to do anything reasonably incidental to its declared objects, unless such act was expressly prohibited by the memorandum (*Attorney-General v Great Eastern Railway Co.* (1880) 5 App Cas 473). Thus, a trading company must always have an implied power to borrow money for the purposes of its trading business.

Facts   Shenkman was a director of Rolled Steel and its majority shareholder. He also owned all the share capital of Scottish Steel Sheet Ltd. Scottish Steel Sheet Ltd owed over £800,000 to Colville Ltd, a company controlled by the defendant company, British Steel Corporation. Rolled Steel executed a guarantee of Scottish Steel Sheet Ltd's liabilities to Colville Ltd and granted a debenture over all its assets in favour of Colville Ltd. (Rolled Steel did not apparently benefit from this, though Shenkman, as owner of Scottish Steel Sheet Ltd, of course did.) When Colville Ltd demanded payment from Rolled Steel under the guarantee, and the latter failed to make payment, Colville Ltd appointed a receiver of Rolled Steel. Rolled Steel brought this action against British Steel Corporation and the receiver to recover the sums paid out by the receiver on the grounds that the guarantee and the debenture were gratuitous and contrary to the interest of Rolled Steel. They argued that they were ultra vires and that all those involved knew that Shenkman only issued the security to support his other company, Scottish Steel Sheet Ltd. Under clause 3(K) of its memorandum, Rolled Steel had power to grant security or give guarantees for the indebtedness of 'any such persons, firms or companies as may seem expedient'.

BROWNE-WILKINSON LJ: ... (1) To be *ultra vires* a transaction has to be outside the capacity of the company, not merely in excess or abuse of the powers of the company. (2) The question whether a transaction is outside the capacity of the company depends solely upon whether, on the true construction of its memorandum of association, the transaction is capable of falling within the objects of the company as opposed to being a proper exercise of the powers of the company. (3) Notwithstanding the fact that the provision authorising the company to enter into the particular transaction is found in the objects clause and there is a provision requiring each paragraph to be construed as a separate object, such provision may be merely a power, and not an object, if either it is incapable of existing as a separate object or it can only be construed as a power ancillary to the other objects in the strict sense. (4) If a transaction falls within the objects, and therefore the capacity, of the company, it is not *ultra vires* the company and accordingly it is not absolutely void. (5) If a company enters into a transaction which is *intra vires* (as being within its capacity) but in excess or abuse of its powers, such transaction will be set aside at the instance of the shareholders. (6) A third party who has notice—actual or constructive—that a transaction, although *intra vires* the company, was entered into in excess or abuse of the powers of the company cannot enforce such transaction against the company and will be accountable as constructive trustee for any money or property of the company received by the third party. (7) The fact that a power is expressly or impliedly limited so as to be exercisable only 'for the purposes of the company's business' (or other words to that effect) does not put a third party on inquiry as to whether the power is being so exercised, i.e., such provision does not give him constructive notice of excess or abuse of such power.

Applying those principles to the present case, in my judgment, no question of *ultra vires* arises. ...

SLADE LJ: The statutory requirement that the objects of a company shall be specified in the memorandum marks one important difference between objects and powers. In my judgment, however, whether a particular transaction, carried out in purported exercise of an express or implied power contained in a company's memorandum of association, is within the capacity of the company must still depend on the true construction of that memorandum.

Correctly, therefore, in my opinion, [counsel for the defendants'] argument has focused attention in the present context on the wording of the memorandum of the plaintiff. His first submission has been that the guarantee was *intra vires* the plaintiff as a matter of corporate capacity because the provisions of clause 3(K) of the plaintiff's memorandum, read together with the closing words of that clause, set out a separate independent object which the plaintiff was capable of carrying on as such, and that the execution of the guarantee fell within that provision.

If this submission as to the construction of clause 3(K) were well-founded, I think the suggested conclusion would follow and that, while the relevant transactions might have involved breaches of duty on the part of the directors of the plaintiff, there would be no possible question of their having been beyond its corporate capacity. ...

The question whether clause 3(K) of the plaintiff's memorandum contains a separate independent object of the company is purely one of construction of that memorandum. The decision of the House of Lords in *Cotman v Brougham* [1918] AC 514 requires that, in answering it, full force must be given, so far as possible, to the provision at the end of clause 3 of the memorandum, which directs that each subclause shall be construed independently of the other subclauses. I accept Mr Heyman's submission that clause 3(K) must be treated as containing a substantive object unless either (i) the subject-matter of this subclause is by its nature incapable of constituting a substantive object (as was the power to borrow in *Introductions Ltd v National Provincial Bank Ltd* [1970] Ch 199) or (ii) the wording of the memorandum shows expressly or by implication that the subclause was intended merely to constitute an ancillary power only: see, for example, the observations of Buckley J in the latter case at first instance [1968] 2 All ER 1221, 1224.

Mr Heyman has submitted, and I agree, that there is no reason in principle why a company should not be formed for the specific purpose, *inter alia*, of giving guarantees whether gratuitous or otherwise, rather unusual though such an object might be.

Attention, however, has to be directed to the particular wording of clause 3(K). The authority to give guarantees and become security conferred by the second limb of the subclause is not an unrestricted authority. It is merely an authority to give guarantees or become security for 'any such persons, firms or companies'. The six words just quoted echo the words of the first limb of the subclause, which authorise the company to

> lend and advance money or give credit to such persons, firms, or companies and on such terms as may seem expedient, and in particular to customers of and others having dealings with the company.

The phrase 'as may seem expedient' necessarily implies that there is some criterion by which expediency is to be tested. The only possible criterion, in my opinion, can only mean 'as may seem expedient for the furtherance of the objects of the company'. The references in clause 3(K) to the giving of credit and to customers of and persons having dealings with the company make it additionally clear that the subclause in its context was intended to comprise merely a series of ancillary powers. It follows that, in my opinion, the powers to give guarantees and become security, which are the relevant powers in the present case, are not to be construed as independent objects of the plaintiff and the judge was right in so holding. Correspondingly, I think he was right to reject the defendants' argument that the relevant transactions were *intra vires* the plaintiff, in so far as that argument was based on the hypothesis that the powers conferred by clause 3(K) were independent objects of the plaintiff.

What, then, is the position if, as I have concluded, the power to give guarantees and to become security are to be regarded as mere powers ancillary to the objects of the plaintiff? Even on this footing, the plaintiff in executing the guarantee and the debenture was performing acts of a nature which, at least seemingly, it was expressly authorised by clause 3(K) and (L) of its memorandum to perform. The particular exercises of these powers were, on the face of them, well *capable of* falling within the objects of the plaintiff.

The judge, as I have read his judgment, accepted that these transactions were capable of falling within the scope of the wording of the powers conferred on the plaintiff by its memorandum. Nevertheless, he considered that there is a general principle of company law that a transaction, which ostensibly falls within the scope of the wording of a company's memorandum but is in fact entered into for some purpose not authorised by that memorandum, will be *ultra vires* the company in what he called the 'wider sense' and will confer rights on another party only if he can show that he dealt with the company in good faith and did not have notice that the transaction was entered into for an unauthorised purpose [1982] Ch 478, 499. It was primarily on the basis of this principle that the judge ultimately held the defendants in the present case liable to restore the moneys which they had received.

As Lord Selborne said in *Ashbury Railway Carriage and Iron Co. Ltd* v *Riche* (1875) LR 7 HL 653, 693:

> a statutory corporation, created by Act of Parliament for a particular purpose, is limited, as to all its powers, by the purposes of its incorporation as defined in that Act.

Strict logic might therefore appear to require that any act purported to be done by a company in purported exercise of powers ancillary to its objects conferred on it by its memorandum of association, whether express or implied, (e.g., a power to borrow) would necessarily and in every case be beyond its capacity and therefore wholly void if such act was in fact performed for purposes other than those of its incorporation. However, the practical difficulties resulting from such a conclusion for persons dealing with a company carrying on a business authorised by its memorandum would be intolerable. As Buckley J put it, in regard to a power to borrow, in *Re David Payne & Co. Ltd* [1904] 2 Ch 608, 613:

> A corporation, every time it wants to borrow, cannot be called upon by the lender to expose all its affairs, so that the lender can say, 'Before I lend you anything, I must investigate how you carry on your business, and I must know why you want the money, and how you apply it,

and when you do have it I must see you apply it in the right way.' It is perfectly impossible to work out such a principle.

The *David Payne* decision, in my opinion, indicates the proper alternative approach. In that case, the company concerned had express power under its memorandum of association 'to borrow and raise money for the purposes of the company's business'. It borrowed money and issued a debenture to secure the loan. Its liquidator claimed that the debenture was *ultra vires* and void because there was evidence that the borrowing had not in fact been made for the purposes of the company's business. Buckley J in his judgment considered the force of the phrase 'for the purposes of the company's business'. He asked the question, at p. 612:

is it a condition attached to the exercise of the power that the money should be borrowed for the purposes of the business, or is that a matter to be determined as between the shareholders and the directors?

In the course of answering this question he said, at p. 612:

A corporation cannot do anything except for the purposes of its business, borrowing or anything else; everything else is beyond its power, and is *ultra vires*. So that the words 'for the purposes of the company's business' are a mere expression of that which would be involved if there were no such words.

This passage has been frequently echoed in later cases and, perhaps not surprisingly, has on occasions been read as referring to the capacity of the company. However, I think that in using the phrase '*ultra vires*' in this particular context Buckley J can only have meant '*ultra vires* the directors'. This, in my opinion, is made clear by what followed. He accepted that, if the phrase 'for the purpose of the company's business' was a condition attached to the exercise of the power, a loan would be *ultra vires* and void if the condition had not been complied with. He did not, however, regard it as such a condition: in his view it did no more than state the obvious. In these circumstances, his conclusion was, at p. 613:

If this borrowing was made, as it appears to me at present it was made, for a purpose illegitimate so far as the borrowing company was concerned, that may very well be a matter on which rights may arise as between the shareholders and directors of that company. It may have been a wrongful act on the part of the directors. But I do not think that a person who lends to the company is by any words such as these required to investigate whether the money borrowed is borrowed for a proper purpose or an improper purpose. The borrowing being effected, and the money passing to the company, the subsequent application of the money is a matter in which the directors may have acted wrongly; but that does not affect the principal act, which is the borrowing of the money.

In these circumstances, he held, at p. 614, that the defendants:

who have paid this money and taken this debenture without notice that the money was going to be applied as it was, are not affected by anything arising in regard to that.

. . . Vaughan Williams and Cozens-Hardy LJJ expressly approved the manner in which Buckley J had approached the problem. Vaughan Williams LJ expressly, at p. 615, and the other members of the court implicitly rejected the borrower's first argument that, since the debenture was not issued to raise money for the purposes of the company, it was *ultra vires* altogether 'in such a sense that nothing could make it right'. All three members of the court considered that the plaintiff company could succeed if, but only if, it showed that, at the time of the loan, the lending company knew that the money was going to be applied by the borrowers for an improper purpose and that this had not been proved.

The one crucially important point to which Buckley J and the Court of Appeal in *David Payne* did not expressly advert is the basis upon which the lenders would have lost their security if they had known of the improper purpose for which the moneys lent were going to be applied. The basis is, in my opinion, this. The directors of the borrowing company in fact had no authority from the company to take the loan and grant the debenture because these transactions were not effected for the purposes of the company. Nevertheless, as a general rule, a company incorporated under the

Companies Acts holds out its directors as having ostensible authority to do on its behalf anything which its memorandum of association expressly or by implication gives the company the capacity to do. In *David Payne* the company's memorandum gave it the capacity to borrow. As a matter of construction of the company's memorandum, the court was not prepared to construe the words 'for the purposes of the company's business' as limiting its corporate capacity but construed them simply as limiting the authority of the directors. In the absence of notice to the contrary, the lenders would thus have been entitled to assume, on the authority of the principle in *Turquand's* case [*Royal British Bank* v *Turquand* (1856) 6 El & Bl 327] and on more general principles of the law of agency, that the directors of the borrowing company were acting properly and regularly in the internal management of its affairs and were borrowing for the purposes of the company's business: see, for example, *Re Hampshire Land Co.* [1896] 2 Ch 743, a decision of Vaughan Williams J which was cited in the *David Payne* case [1904] 2 Ch 608, and *Bowstead on Agency*, 14th ed. (1976), pp. 241–2 and the cases there cited. However, a party dealing with a company cannot rely on the ostensible authority of its directors to enter into a particular transaction if it knows they in fact have no such authority because it is being entered into for improper purposes. Neither the rule in *Turquand's* case nor more general principles of the law of agency will avail him in such circumstances: see *Bowstead on Agency*, 14th ed., p. 243. The various passages in the judgments in both courts in the *David Payne* case which refer to the extent of the lender's obligation, if any, to inquire as to the purposes for which the loan is to be used, in my opinion, are not directed at all to the corporate capacity of the borrowing company; they are directed to the right of the lender to rely on the ostensible authority of the borrower's directors.

In *Re Introductions Ltd* [1970] Ch 199 the Court of Appeal again had to consider the validity of debentures granted by a company as security for a loan. The company under its memorandum of association had a general ancillary power to borrow money and to issue debentures to secure its repayment. But this power was not an independent object of the company. As Harman LJ put it, at p. 210, 'borrowing is not an end in itself and must be for some purpose of the company'. The power was not expressed in terms to be exercisable only 'for the purposes of the company' but, following the reasoning of Buckley J in *Re David Payne & Co. Ltd* [1904] 2 Ch 608, 612, the court held that the words necessarily had to be implied. The company had borrowed money from a bank and granted debentures to secure the loan. But the only business carried on by it was that of pig-breeding which was a purpose not authorised by its memorandum of association. On the liquidation of the company a question arose as to the validity of the debentures. Harman LJ, who gave the leading judgment, after deciding that the power to borrow conferred by the memorandum was a mere ancillary power not an independent object, proceeded to cite, at p. 210, the following passage from the speech of Lord Parker of Waddington in *Cotman* v *Brougham* [1918] AC 514, 521:

> A person who deals with a company is entitled to assume that a company can do everything which it is expressly authorised to do by its memorandum of association, and need not investigate the equities between the company and its shareholders.

This passage, it will be seen, closely echoes some of the language used by Buckley J in his judgment in the *David Payne* case [1904] 2 Ch 608 and is, I think, an expression of the rule in *Turquand's* case (1856) 6 El & Bl 327 and the more general principles of agency to which I have already referred. Harman LJ went on to say [1970] Ch 199, 210:

> I would agree that, if the bank did not know what the purpose of the borrowing was, *it need not inquire* [the emphasis is mine] but it did know, and I can find nothing in *Cotman* v *Brougham* to protect it notwithstanding that knowledge.

The words 'it need not inquire', in my opinion, make it clear that Harman LJ did not regard the borrowing as having been beyond the *capacity* of the company. However, he then went on to point out that the *David Payne* decision [1904] 2 Ch 608 shows that the protection afforded by the principle stated by Lord Parker affords no protection to a lender who knows that the money is intended to be misapplied. The absence of any express provision in the company's memorandum of association requiring the loan to be applied for the purposes of the company, in his judgment, did not improve the bank's position, since such a provision would fall to be implied anyway. He concluded, at p. 211:

> This borrowing was not for a legitimate purpose of the company: the bank knew it, and, *therefore*, [the emphasis is mine] cannot rely on its debentures.

As I read his judgment, therefore, Harman LJ reached his decision that the bank could not rely on the debentures following the *ratio* of the *David Payne* decision, that is to say, not because they had been granted by the company in excess of its corporate capacity, but because the bank knew that the directors of the company, in purporting to grant them, had exceeded the authority conferred on them by the company by entering into the transaction for purposes other than the company's corporate purpose.

Russell LJ [1970] Ch 199, 211, in a very short judgment, reached the same conclusion but by rather a different route from that of Harman LJ. As I read his judgment, his view was that the borrowing and execution of the debentures were *ultra vires* the company as a matter of corporate capacity because it was an implicit condition attached to the power to borrow contained in the company's memorandum that moneys should not be borrowed for use *in an undertaking* ultra vires *the company*. Since the sole undertaking of that company was the pig-breeding business, which was beyond the company's corporate capacity, the loans taken for use in that business were likewise inevitably beyond its corporate capacity. I read Russell LJ's decision as being limited to the facts of that particular case and not in any way conflicting with my interpretation of the *David Payne* decision.

It follows that, in my opinion, the decisions of this court in *David Payne* [1904] 2 Ch 608 and *Introductions Ltd* [1970] Ch 199, on their true analysis, lend no support to the plaintiff's submission that the relevant transactions in the present case were beyond the corporate capacity of the plaintiff simply because they were effected for improper purposes not authorised by its memorandum of association. . . .

My conclusions from these authorities on these questions of principle may be summarised as follows. (1) The basic rule is that a company incorporated under the Companies Acts only has the capacity to do those acts which fall within its objects as set out in its memorandum of association or are reasonably incidental to the attainment or pursuit of those objects. Ultimately, therefore, the question whether a particular transaction is within or outside its capacity must depend on the true construction of the memorandum.

(2) Nevertheless, if a particular act (such as each of the transactions of 22 January 1969 in the present case) is of a category which, on the true construction of the company's memorandum, is *capable* of being performed as reasonably incidental to the attainment or pursuit of its objects, it will not be rendered *ultra vires* the company merely because in a particular instance its directors, in performing the act in its name, are in truth doing so for purposes other than those set out in its memorandum. Subject to any express restrictions on the relevant power which may be contained in the memorandum, the state of mind or knowledge of the persons managing the company's affairs or of the persons dealing with it is irrelevant in considering questions of corporate capacity.

(3) While due regard must be paid to any express conditions attached to or limitations on powers contained in a company's memorandum (e.g., a power to borrow only up to a specified amount), the court will not ordinarily construe a statement in a memorandum that a particular power is exercisable 'for the purposes of the company' as a condition limiting the company's corporate capacity to exercise the power; it will regard it as simply imposing a limit on the authority of the directors: see the *David Payne* case [1904] 2 Ch 608.

(4) At least in default of the unanimous consent of all the shareholders, . . . the directors of a company will not have *actual* authority from the company to exercise any express or implied power other than for the purposes of the company as set out in its memorandum of association.

(5) A company holds out its directors as having *ostensible* authority to bind the company to any transaction which falls within the powers expressly or impliedly conferred on it by its memorandum of association. Unless he is put on notice to the contrary, a person dealing in good faith with a company which is carrying on an *intra vires* business is entitled to assume that its directors are properly exercising such powers for the purposes of the company as set out in its memorandum.

Correspondingly, such a person in such circumstances can hold the company to any transaction of this nature.

(6) If, however, a person dealing with a company is on notice that the directors are exercising the relevant power for purposes other than the purposes of the company, he cannot rely on the ostensible authority of the directors and, on ordinary principles of agency, cannot hold the company to the transaction.

In the present case I construe the words 'as may seem expedient' in clause 3(K) of the plaintiff's memorandum not as limiting the corporate capacity of the plaintiff but as simply imposing a limit on the authority of its directors. To adapt the wording of Harman LJ in the *Introductions Ltd* case [1970] Ch 199 following the *David Payne* decision [1904] 2 Ch 608, the guarantee and *pro tanto* the debenture were not executed for a legitimate purpose of the plaintiff; Colvilles and British Steel Corporation knew it and, therefore, cannot rely on the guarantee and *pro tanto* the debenture. All this results from the ordinary law of agency, not from the corporate powers of the plaintiff. The relevant transactions in the present case, in my opinion, were not beyond its corporate capacity . . .

To sum up, my conclusions on the *ultra vires* point are these. The relevant transactions of 22 January 1969 were not beyond the corporate capacity of the plaintiff and thus were not *ultra vires* in the proper sense of that phrase. However, the entering into the guarantee and, to the extent of the sum guaranteed, the debenture was beyond the authority of the directors, because they were entered into in furtherance of purposes not authorised by the plaintiff's memorandum. Despite this lack of authority, they might have been capable of conferring rights on Colvilles if Colvilles had not known of this lack of authority. Colvilles, however, did have such knowledge and so acquired no rights under these transactions.

6.3 GRATUITOUS TRANSACTIONS

Companies frequently make gratuitous payments either as a donation or gift, or act as guarantor or give security for the indebtedness of another company in the group or an outsider. It used to be thought that a company did not have the capacity to enter into wholly gratuitous transactions which were thus *ultra vires*. The relevant tests were stated as follows: (1) Is the transaction reasonably incidental to the carrying on of the company's business? (2) Is it a bona fide transaction? and (3) Is it done for the benefit of and to promote the prosperity of the company? (*Re Lee, Behrens & Co. Ltd* [1932] 2 Ch 46). These tests were, however, not applied in *Charterbridge Corporation Ltd* v *Lloyds Bank Ltd* [1970] Ch 62 where it was held that where there was an express provision in the company's objects clause which authorised the transaction (e.g., to pay pensions or give guarantees) that was the end of the matter. This was later approved by the Court of Appeal in *Re Horsley & Weight Ltd* [1982] Ch 442 and *Rolled Steel Products (Holdings) Ltd* v *British Steel Corporation* [1986] Ch 246. Thus, gratuitous transactions are not *per se ultra vires*. The question of capacity depends on the construction of the objects clause. If gratuitous transactions are covered by the objects clause but are improperly paid, this is merely a breach of the directors' fiduciary duty. The transaction will be binding on the company unless the recipient is aware of the breach, in accordance with the principle in the *Rolled Steel* case.

Re Horsley & Weight Ltd
The power to grant pensions
[1982] Ch 442, Court of Appeal

Facts In recognition of Mr Horsley's long service to the company, the directors, who owned all the shares between them, arranged for a pension policy at the company's expense for the benefit of Mr Horsley. Later the company was compulsorily wound up and the liquidator sought a declaration that the purchase of the pension policy was ultra vires. (For a fuller statement of the facts and a further extract from the case see 11.6.)

BUCKLEY LJ: I will first consider the *ultra vires* point. The Companies Act 1948, section 2, requires the memorandum of association of a company incorporated under the Act to state the objects of the company. A company has no capacity to pursue any objects outside those which are so stated. It does not follow, however, that any act which is not expressly authorised by the memorandum is *ultra vires* the company. Anything reasonably incidental to the attainment or pursuit of any of the express objects of the company will, unless expressly prohibited, be within the implied powers of the company. It has now long been a common practice to set out in memoranda of association a great number and variety of 'objects', so called, some of which (for example, to borrow money, to promote the company's interests by advertising its products or services, or to do acts or things conducive or incidental to the company's objects) are by their very nature incapable of standing as independent objects which can be pursued in isolation as the sole activity of the company. Such 'objects' must, by reason of their very nature, be interpreted merely as powers incidental to the true objects of the company and must be so treated notwithstanding the presence of a separate objects clause: *Introductions Ltd v National Provincial Bank Ltd* [1970] Ch 199. Where there is no separate objects clause, some of the express 'objects' may upon construction fall to be treated as no more than powers which are ancillary to the dominant or main objects of the company: see, for example, *Re German Date Coffee Co.* (1882) 20 ChD 169.

Ex hypothesi an implied power can only legitimately be used in a way which is ancillary or incidental to the pursuit of an authorised object of the company, for it is the practical need to imply the power in order to enable the company effectively to pursue its authorised objects which justifies the implication of the power. So an exercise of an implied power can only be *intra vires* the company if it is ancillary or incidental to the pursuit of an authorised object. So also, in the case of express 'objects' which upon construction of the memorandum or by their very nature, are ancillary to the dominant or main objects of the company, an exercise of any such powers can only be *intra vires* if it is in fact ancillary or incidental to the pursuit of some such dominant or main object.

On the other hand, the doing of an act which is expressed to be, and is capable of being, an independent object of the company cannot be *ultra vires*, for it is by definition something which the company is formed to do and so must be *intra vires*. I shall use the term 'substantive object' to describe such an object of a company.

The question, therefore, is whether paragraph (o) of clause 3 of the company's memorandum of association in the present case contains a substantive object or merely an ancillary power. Having regard to the presence of the separate objects clause, the former of these alternatives must be the case unless the subject-matter of paragraph (o) is of its nature incapable of constituting a substantive object . . .

[Counsel for the liquidator], relying principally on the judgment of Eve J in *Re Lee, Behrens & Co. Ltd* [1932] 2 Ch 46, submits that, properly construed, paragraph (o) should be read as conferring merely an ancillary power. . . .

[His lordship referred to *Re Lee, Behrens & Co. Ltd* and the test laid down by Eve J in that case.]

[Counsel for the liquidator] submits that that passage from the judge's judgment is applicable to the present case and provides, as he submits, an aid to construction of any memorandum of association which contains a paragraph such as we have in clause 3(o) of the company's memorandum. It is true that Eve J's observation expressly refers to both express and implied powers, but in relation to the former it was no more than an *obiter dictum*. It is worthy of note that the judge uses the words 'power', not the word 'object'. [Counsel for the liquidator], however, submits that the decision indicates that a capacity to grant pensions to employees or ex-employees, or to directors or ex-directors, is of its nature a power enabling the company to act as a good employer in the course of carrying on its business, and as such is an incidental power which must be treated as though it were expressly subject to a limitation that it can only be exercised in circumstances in which a grant of a pension will benefit the company's business. I do not feel able to accept that contention. Paragraph (o) must be read as a whole. It includes not only pensions and other disbursements which will benefit directors, employees and their dependants, but also making grants for charitable, benevolent or public purposes or objects. The objects of a company do not need to be commercial; they can be charitable or philanthropic; indeed, they can be whatever the original incorporators wish, provided that they are legal. Nor is there any reason why a company should not part with its funds gratuitously or for non-commercial reasons if to do so is within its declared objects.

[Counsel for the liquidator] relies upon the finding of Oliver J [at first instance] that there is no evidence that the company did or could derive any benefit or that the question was considered by anyone connected with the transaction. He says that the provision of the pension must accordingly be accepted as having been purely gratuitous, that is to say, a gift which could and did confer no consequent benefit upon the company. Accepting this to have been the case, the transaction nonetheless falls, in my view, precisely within the scope of paragraph (o) and, in my judgment, the purposes referred to in that paragraph are such as to be capable of subsisting as substantive objects of the company and, having regard to the separate objects clause, must be so construed. For these reasons the liquidator fails, in my view, on the *ultra vires* point.

6.4 CONTRACTUAL EFFECT OF THE CONSTITUTION

Once registered, under CA 2006, s. 33, the constitution constitutes a contract between the members and the company, and between the members *inter se* (*Wood* v *Odessa Waterworks Co.* (1889) 42 ChD 636; *Hickman* v *Kent or Romney Marsh Sheep-Breeders' Association* [1915] 1 Ch 881).

COMPANIES ACT 2006, S. 33

33. Effect of company's constitution

(1) The provisions of a company's constitution bind the company and its members to the same extent as if there were covenants on the part of the company and of each member to observe those provisions.

(2) Money payable by a member to the company under its constitution is a debt due from him to the company. In England and Wales and Northern Ireland it is of the nature of an ordinary contract debt.

Thus a member may enforce a personal right under that contract such as the right to a dividend or a right to vote at general meetings. It should, however, be noted, first, that the court will not interfere with matters of pure internal irregularities which the majority can ratify (*Grant* v *United Kingdom Switchback Railways Co.* (1888) 40 ChD 135). Secondly, s. 33 of CA 2006 gives the constitution contractual effect only in respect of the members' rights and obligations *qua* member (*Eley* v *Positive Government Securities Life Assurance Co. Ltd* (1876) 1 ExD 88; *Beattie* v *E. & F. Beattie Ltd* [1938] Ch 708). Thus, if an article provides that someone should be the company's director or solicitor, he cannot rely on the article as giving him a right to be the company's director or solicitor even if he is a member. This is because the article concerns him only in his capacity as an 'outsider' (i.e., a director or a solicitor), not as a member. However, in *Quin & Axtens Ltd* v *Salmon* [1909] AC 442, as the extract below shows, the House of Lords was prepared to give effect to articles of association even though this had the effect of enforcing rights given to certain members in their capacity as directors.

The contractual effect of the constitution has been the subject-matter of much academic debate. Lord Wedderburn takes the view that every member has a personal right, under s. 33 of CA 2006, to see that the company is run according to the articles, except those already identified as concerning internal procedures only (K.W. Wedderburn [1957] CLJ 194, [1958] CLJ 93 extracted below). In Prentice's view, only those articles 'definitive of the power of the company to function' have contractual effect (G.N. Prentice, 'The enforcement of "outsider" rights' (1980) 1 Co Law 179). Goldberg puts it slightly differently saying that a member of a company has a contractual right to have any of the affairs of the company conducted by the particular organ of the company specified in the Act or the company's memorandum or articles (G.D. Goldberg, 'The enforcement of outsider rights under section 20(1) of the Companies Act 1948' (1972) 35 MLR 362 and 'The controversy on the section 20 contract revisited' (1985) 48 MLR 158). Drury takes a 'relational approach'. He argues that the contract between the company and its shareholders is a long-term relationship and that the rights of a shareholder under the company contract are not absolute, but can be understood only when considered in relation to the rights of the other shareholders under that contract (Robert Drury [1986] CLJ 219).

In its report, *Shareholder Remedies* (Law Com. No. 246, 1997) (extracted in 6.3.3), the Law Commission, having consulted widely on the reform of s. 33 of CA 2006 (or what was s. 14 of CA 1985), recommended that no reform was necessary.

It has recently been held that in the absence of special provisions in the articles or some collateral agreement between the company and its members, neither the company nor its directors owed any direct legal duties to its members as such. Thus, no terms can be implied which would have the effect of making the company or its directors contractually liable to its members for the way it carried out its functions: *Towcester Racecourse Co. Ltd* v *The Racecourse Association Ltd* [2003] 1 BCLC 260.

Wood v *Odessa Waterworks Co.*

Dividends as a personal right

(1889) 42 ChD 636, Chancery Division

The articles of association are enforceable by a shareholder against the company and other shareholders.

Facts   The articles empowered the directors with the approval of the general meeting to declare 'a dividend to be paid to the members'. The directors recommended that instead of paying a dividend, members should be given debenture-bonds bearing interest repayable at par, by annual drawings, extending over 30 years. The recommendation was approved by the company in general meeting by an ordinary resolution. The plaintiff successfully sought an injunction restraining the company from acting on the resolution on the ground that it breached the articles.

STIRLING J: The question, simply, is whether it is within the power of a majority of the shareholders to insist against the will of a minority that the profits which have been actually earned shall be divided, not by the payment of cash, but by the issue of debenture-bonds of the company bearing interest at £5 per cent and repayable at par by an annual drawing extending over 30 years. It is to be inferred from the terms in which the bonds are offered for subscription that the company cannot issue them in the open market except at a discount of at least £10 per cent. Now the rights of the shareholders in respect of a division of the profits of the company are governed by the provisions in the articles of association. By s. 16 of the Companies Act 1862, the articles of association 'bind the company and the members thereof to the same extent as if each member had subscribed his name and affixed his seal thereto, and there were in such articles contained a covenant on the part of himself, his heirs, executors, and administrators, to conform to all the regulations contained in such articles, subject to the provisions of this Act'. Section 50 of the Act provides the means for altering the regulations of the company contained in the articles of association by passing a special resolution, but no such resolution has in this case been passed or attempted to be passed; and the question is, whether this is a matter as to which the majority of the shareholders can bind those shareholders who dissent. The articles of association constitute a contract not merely between the shareholders and the company, but between each individual shareholder and every other; and the question which I have just stated must, in my opinion, be answered in the negative if there be in the articles a contract between the shareholders as to a division of profits, and the provisions of that contract have not been followed… That then brings me to consider whether that which is proposed to be done in the present case is in accordance with the articles of association of the company. Those articles provide… that the directors may, with the sanction of a general meeting, declare a dividend to be paid to the shareholders. Prima facie that means to be paid in cash. The debenture-bonds proposed to be issued are not payments in cash; they are merely agreements or promises to pay: and if the contention of the company prevails a shareholder will be compelled to accept in lieu of cash a debt of the company payable at some uncertain future period. In my opinion that contention ought not to prevail.

Hickman v Kent or Romney Marsh Sheep-Breeders' Association

The contract between the company and its members

[1915] 1 Ch 881, Chancery Division

In this case Astbury J held that an article constitutes a contract between the members. In the judgment Astbury J also took the opportunity to review the authorities, and thought that cases such as *Eley v Positive Government Securities Life Assurance Co. Ltd* (1876) 1 ExD 88 supported the proposition that an outsider right was not enforceable under s. 33.

Facts The defendant sheep-breeders' association was a non-profit-making company incorporated in 1895. Under art. 49 of its articles of association, any disputes between the association and its members should be referred to arbitration. The plaintiff brought this action to court, in breach of art. 49, claiming an injunction to restrain the association from expelling him from membership, damages for refusing to register his sheep, and a declaration that he was entitled to have his sheep registered. The court granted the association a stay of proceedings on the ground that art. 49 was binding as between the company and its members under what is now CA 2006, s. 33.

ASTBURY J: In the present case the defendants contend, first, that article 49, dealing as it does with the members of the association, in their capacity of members only, constitutes a submission within the meaning of the Arbitration Act, or, secondly, that the contract contained in the plaintiff's application for membership and the association's acceptance of it amounts to such a submission. The plaintiff contests both these propositions, and independently of the particular dispute in this case, the arguments, especially upon the first of these contentions, have raised questions of far-reaching importance.

I will first deal with the question as to the effect of art. 49.

[His Lordship read what is now s. 33 of CA 2006.]

It is laid down in textbooks of the highest repute that the articles are not a contract between the member and the company; that the articles are no contract with the company but a contract with the other members; and that the articles are a contract only as between the members *inter se* in respect of their rights as shareholders: *Buckley on Companies*, 9th ed., pp. 27, 51, 206; that the exact nature of this covenant, that is the covenant referred to in [s. 33], has given rise to considerable discussion and is even now very difficult to define; but it is now settled that it is not equivalent to a contract between the company on the one part and the members on the other, on which either a member can sue the company or the company can sue a member: *Lindley on Companies*, 6th ed., p. 456. Other writers have formed a different conclusion, and the construction of the language of this section has long been the subject of controversy: *Palmer's Company Precedents*, 11th ed., pt. 1, pp. 632–6; *Hamilton's Company Law*, 3rd ed., p. 219; *Gore-Browne on Joint Stock Companies*, 32nd ed., pp. 40, 41.

The principal authorities in support of the view that the articles do not constitute a contract between the company and its members are *Re Tavarone Mining Co., Pritchard's Case* (1873) LR 8 Ch App 956, *Melhado v Porto Alegre, New Hamburgh, & Brazilian Railway Co.* (1874) LR 9 CP 503, *Eley v Positive Government Security Life Assurance Co. Ltd* (1876) 1 ExD 20 and 88, and *Browne v La Trinidad* (1887) 37 Ch D 1.

[His Lordship referred to *Pritchard's Case* and *Melhado v Porto Alegre etc. Railway Co.*]

In *Eley v Positive Government Security Life Assurance Co. Ltd* the articles of association contained a clause in which it was stated that the plaintiff, a solicitor, should be the solicitor to the company and transact its legal business. The articles were registered and the company incorporated, and 11 months later the plaintiff became a member. The plaintiff was not appointed solicitor by any resolution of the directors, nor by any instrument bearing the seal of the company, but he acted as such for a time. Subsequently the company ceased to employ him and he brought an action for breach of contract against the company for not employing him as its solicitor. The first count of the declaration stated (1 ExD 20 at p. 22) that it was agreed by and between the plaintiff and the defendants that the plaintiff should be employed by the defendants as, and appointed by them to the office of, solicitor of the company. During the argument (at p. 23) it was contended that the contract declared on was not the contract purported to be contained in the articles. Amphlett B said (at p. 26).

> The articles, taken by themselves, are simply a contract between the shareholders *inter se*, and cannot, in my opinion, give a right of action to a person like the plaintiff, not a party to the articles, although named therein. If authority were wanted for this proposition, the cases cited in the argument, *Pritchard's Case* and *Melhado v Porto Alegre etc. Railway Co.*, are, in my opinion, quite conclusive on the subject.

Subsequently he said (at p. 28):

> For these reasons, I think that there was no contract at all between the plaintiff and the company to the effect stated in the declaration.

Cleasby B confined his judgment to the last points raised in the case and said (at p. 30):

> I am of opinion that clause 118 of the articles cannot by itself be taken to operate as a contract between the solicitor and the company.

Kelly CB said (at p. 30):

> I forbear to pronounce any opinion as to whether these articles, with the fact of the subsequent employment, constitute a contract on the terms contained in them, because, were I to so hold, there would be a difficult question behind, whether it was not *ultra vires* for the directors to attempt to bind the company to employ a solicitor to transact, for all his life, all the legal business of the company. Passing by this, I come to consider the objection raised under the 4th section of the Statute of Frauds. I do not see how any one can doubt that this agreement was not to be performed within a year. It was for the life of the plaintiff, subject to a defeasance on the possibility of his being guilty of some misconduct. But, assuming, as I think we must, that this was not to be performed in a year, the question arises, whether there is any memorandum or note in writing of it signed by the defendants. The signatures affixed to the articles were *alio intuitu*, and it can hardly be suggested that the directors had any idea that, in signing the articles, they were signing a note of this contract.

This case went to the Court of Appeal and Lord Cairns LC said (1 ExD 88 at p. 89):

> I wish to say, in the first place, that in my opinion a contract of the kind suggested to exist in this case ought not to receive any particular favour from the court. The statement is that Baylis was endeavouring to form a joint stock insurance company upon a new principle, and applied to the plaintiff to make advances to meet the expenses of getting up the company, and it was arranged between them that in the event of the company being formed the plaintiff should be appointed permanent solicitor to the company. That is to say, a bargain is made between a professional man and Baylis which, so far as the case is concerned, does not appear to have been communicated to those who were invited to join the company, that if the former will advance money for the formation of the company, he shall be appointed permanent solicitor, and the company shall be obliged to employ him as their professional adviser. When the articles are prepared, they are so by the plaintiff, and in them he inserts a clause which no doubt informs those who signed the articles of the arrangement, but does not appear to have been brought to the notice of those who joined from receiving circulars. This, I repeat, is not a proceeding which the court would encourage in any way. I also wish to reserve my judgment as to whether a clause of this kind is obnoxious to the principles by which the courts are governed in deciding on questions of public policy.

Then a little lower down he said:

> This case was first rested on the 118th article. Articles of association, as is well known, follow the memorandum, which states the objects of the company, while the articles state the arrangement between the members. They are an agreement *inter socios*, and in that view, if the introductory words are applied to art. 118, it becomes a covenant between the parties to it that they will employ the plaintiff. Now, so far as that is concerned, it is *res inter alios acta*, the plaintiff is no party to it. No doubt he thought that by inserting it he was making his employment safe as against the company; but his relying on that view of the law does not alter the legal effect of the articles. This article is either a stipulation which would bind the members, or else a mandate to the directors. In either case it is a matter between the directors and shareholders, and not between them and the plaintiff.

[Astbury J referred to *Browne* v *La Trinidad* and continued:]

Now in these four cases the article relied upon purported to give specific contractual rights to persons in some capacity other than that of shareholder, and in none of them were members seeking to enforce or protect rights given to them as members, in common with the other corporators. The actual decisions amount to this. An outsider to whom rights purport to be given by the articles in his capacity as such outsider, whether he is or subsequently becomes a member, cannot sue on those articles treating them as contracts between himself and the company to enforce those rights. Those rights are not part of the general regulations of the company applicable alike to all shareholders and can only exist by virtue of some contract between such person and the company, and the subsequent allotment of shares to an outsider in whose favour such an article is inserted does not enable him to sue the company on such an article to enforce rights which are *res inter alios acta* and not part of the general rights of the corporators as such. . . .

The wording of [s. 33] is difficult to construe or understand. A company cannot in the ordinary course be bound otherwise than by statute or contract and it is in this section that its obligation must be found. As far as the members are concerned, the section does not say with whom they are to be deemed to have covenanted, but the section cannot mean that the company is not to be bound when it says it is to be bound, as if, etc., nor can the section mean that the members are to be under no obligation to the company under the articles in which their rights and duties as corporators are to be found. Much of the difficulty is removed if the company be regarded, as the framers of the section may very well have so regarded it, as being treated in law as a party to its own memorandum and articles.

It seems clear from other authorities that a company is entitled as against its members to enforce and restrain breaches of its regulations. See, for example, *MacDougall* v *Gardiner* (1875) 1 ChD 13, *Pender* v *Lushington* (1877) 6 ChD 70, and *Imperial Hydropathic Hotel Co., Blackpool* v *Hampson* (1882) 23 ChD 1. In the last case Bowen LJ said: 'The articles of association, by s. 16 [of the Companies

Act 1862], are to bind all the company and all the shareholders as much as if they had all put their seals to them'.

It is also clear from many authorities that shareholders as against their company can enforce and restrain breaches of its regulations, and in many of these cases judicial expressions of opinion appear, which, in my judgment, it is impossible to disregard. . . .

In *Wood* v *Odessa Waterworks Co.* (1889) 42 ChD 636, which was an action by the plaintiff on behalf of himself and all other shareholders against the company, Stirling J said (at p. 642): 'The articles of association constitute a contract not merely between the shareholders and the company, but between each individual shareholder and every other'.

In *Salmon* v *Quin & Axtens Ltd* [1909] 1 Ch 311 Farwell LJ, referring to this last statement, said (at p. 318): I think that that is accurate subject to this observation, that it may well be that the court would not enforce the covenant as between individual shareholders in most cases'. . . .

It is difficult to reconcile these two classes of decisions and the judicial opinions therein expressed, but I think this much is clear, first, that no article can constitute a contract between the company and a third person; secondly, that no right merely purporting to be given by an article to a person, whether a member or not, in a capacity other than that of a member, as, for instance, as solicitor, promoter, director, can be enforced against the company; and, thirdly, that articles regulating the rights and obligations of the members generally as such do create rights and obligations between them and the company respectively. . . .

In the present case, the plaintiff's action is, in substance, to enforce his rights as a member under the articles against the association. Article 49 is a general article applying to all the members as such, and, apart from technicalities, it would seem reasonable that the plaintiff ought not to be allowed in the absence of any evidence filed by him to proceed with an action to enforce his rights under the articles, seeing that the action is a breach of his obligation under article 49 to submit his disputes with the association to arbitration.

Quin & Axtens Ltd v *Salmon*

Enforcing a right of management veto

[1909] 1 Ch 311, Court of Appeal; [1909] AC 442, House of Lords

The House of Lords gave effect to articles of association even though this had the effect of enforcing rights given to a member in his capacity as a director. Lord Wedderburn in his seminal article (extracted below) argues that this supports his view that every member has a personal right, under s. 33, to see that the company is run according to the articles, since the articles constitute a contract between the company and its members. In his view, a member can bring a personal claim to enforce this right even if that has the effect of enforcing rights conferred on him or anyone else otherwise than as a member, so long as he sues as a member. He distinguishes *Beattie* v *E. & F. Beattie Ltd* [1938] Ch 708 on the ground that the appellant there was sued as a director not as a member. (This view is supported by R. Gregory, 'The section 20 contract' (1981) 44 MLR 526.)

Facts   *Under art. 75 of the articles of Quin & Axtens Ltd, the business of the company was to be managed by the directors 'subject to such regulations (being not inconsistent with the provisions of the articles) as may be prescribed by the company in general meeting'. Article 80 provided that no resolution of the directors on certain important matters would be valid if either of two named managing directors voted against the resolution. The plaintiff, one of the two managing directors, voted against such a resolution to acquire and let premises but the company purported to ratify the resolution by a simple majority. He therefore brought an action against the company and the directors involved for an injunction restraining them from acting on the resolution.*

In the Court of Appeal

FARWELL LJ:...The articles, by s. 16 of the Act of 1862 [CA 2006, s. 33], are made equivalent to a deed of covenant signed by all the shareholders. The Act does not say with whom that covenant is entered into, and there have no doubt been varying statements by learned judges, some of them saying it is with the company, some of them saying it is both with the company and with the share-holders. Stirling J in *Wood* v *Odessa Waterworks Co.* (1889) 42 ChD 636 says (at p. 642): 'The articles of association constitute a contract not merely between the shareholders and the company, but between each individual shareholder and every other'. I think that that is accurate subject to this observation, that it may well be that the court would not enforce the covenant as between individual shareholders in most cases....

...In the present case Mr Salmon did so dissent according to the terms of that article, and there-fore the veto therein provided came into operation. That was met by the company being called together by a requisition of seven shareholders and by passing general resolutions for the acquisition of this property and the letting of the vacant premises. It is said that those resolutions are of no effect, and I am of opinion that that contention is right.

In the House of Lords

LORD LOREBURN LC: My lords, I do not see any solid ground for complaint against the judgment of the Court of Appeal.

The bargain made between the shareholders is contained in articles 75 and 80 of the articles of association, and it amounts for the purpose in hand to this, that the directors should manage the business; and the company, therefore, are not to manage the business unless there is provision to that effect. Further the directors cannot manage it in a particular way—that is to say, they cannot do certain things if Mr Salmon or Mr Axtens objects. Now I cannot agree with Mr Upjohn [counsel for the company] in his contention that the failure of the directors upon the objection of Mr Salmon to grant these leases of itself remitted the matter to the discretion of the company in general meeting. They could still manage the business, but not altogether in the way they desired.

Next, in regard to the second point I think it is really too clear for argument that the business in question was business within the meaning of the 75th article.

The only question of substance to my mind is the third contention of Mr Upjohn when he said that the word 'regulations' as employed in the 75th article includes at all events, if it is not equivalent to, directions whether general or particular as to the transaction of the business of the company. Now it may be a question for argument, but for my own part I should require a great deal of argument to satisfy me that the word 'regulations' in this article does not mean the same thing as articles, having regard to the language of the first of these articles of association [which provided: 'The regulations contained in Table A of the First Schedule to the Companies Act 1862, shall not apply to this company, but the following shall be the regulations of the Articles of Association 196 company']. But, whether that be so or not, it seems to me that the regulations or resolutions which have been passed are of themselves inconsistent with the provisions of these articles, and therefore this appeal fails, and I move your lordships that the appeal be dismissed with costs.

Lords Macnaghten, James of Hereford and Shaw of Dunfermline concurred.

NOTE: In *Beattie* v *E.&F. Beattie Ltd* [1938] Ch 708, in proceedings brought against a director, who was also a member of the company, alleging breach of duty, the director sought to rely on a clause in the articles of association obliging all disputes between the company and a member to be referred to arbitration. The county court held that the director was not entitled to rely on the article because it did not constitute a contract between the company and the defendant director in his capacity as director. The decision was affirmed by the Court of Appeal. Greene MR delivered the main judgment which endorsed Astbury J's view in *Hickman* v *Kent or Romney Marsh Sheep-Breeders' Association* [1915] 1 Ch 881, saying that the contractual force given to the articles of association by what is now the Companies Act 1985, s. 14, was limited to such provisions of the articles as apply to the relationship of the members in their capacity as members. However, he pointed out that there might be something to be said for the argument that a member had a right to say to the company, when it was in dispute with a director: ' "You, the company, are bound by your contract with me in the articles to refer this dispute to arbitration, and I call upon you so to do." ', though that was not the right the director there was seeking to enforce (at 722). In a subsequent Privy Council decision in an Indian case, *Ram Kissendas Dhanuka* v *Satya Charan Law* (1949) LR 77 Ind App 128 (which has hitherto received very little attention), Lord Greene (as he had then become) granted a declaration that managing agents, appointed by the articles of association, were not validly removed from such office by an ordinary resolution of the company in general meeting which did not comply with the terms of the articles which required an extraordinary resolution. This later case provides a modern example of a shareholder's right to enforce the articles of association even if such enforcement has the effect of indirectly protecting an outsider's right under the articles, though it does not resolve the outsider rights controversy. For a note on this case see [1989] JBL 144 (P. StJ. Smart).

K. W. Wedderburn, Shareholders' rights and the rule in *Foss* v *Harbottle*

[1957] CLJ 194, [1958] CLJ 93

'Personal rights' may be of two kinds, those which do, and those which do not, spring from the 'contract under section 20' [now CA 2006, s. 33], i.e., from the articles of association.[1] Of those which do not, some are statutory.[2] . . .

Personal rights derived from the articles Of greater interest here, however, are the personal rights arising from the contract under section 20—a 'contract of the most sacred character' as it has been called.[3] In order properly to appreciate the problem which arises, it is necessary to indicate the extent to which the individual shareholder has been allowed by the courts to enforce such contractual rights against the company, particularly because in most of the relevant cases there is no breath of discussion concerning the rule in *Foss* v *Harbottle*. Usually cited are cases where the rule was expressly held to have no application, such as *Edwards* v *Halliwell*,[4] where the court said that each member had a personal right to prevent irregular alterations in rates of contribution to the trade union, and *Pender* v *Lushington*,[5] in which the right of a shareholder to vote according to the articles was enforced: 'whether he votes with the majority or the minority, he is entitled to have his vote recorded—an individual right in respect of which he has a right to sue.' But the cases go much further than this, as the following illustrations show. They have recognised not merely the member's contractual rights in general terms under the articles,[6] and the right to enforce his rights as member,[7] but, in particular, personal rights, obtained from the articles, to transfer shares and to vote;[8] to protect preferential rights and class interests, such as the right to have shares offered to him;[9] to be registered and to enforce delivery of a share certificate in accordance with the articles;[10]

1 In some cases there may be an overlap which makes it difficult to apply this distinction; see a recent example: *Wigram Family Settled Estates Ltd* v *Inland Revenue Commissioners* [1957] 1 All ER 311, 318, 320.

2 E.g., *Mutter* v *Eastern & Midlands Railway Co.* (1888) 38 ChD 92; *Nelson* v *Anglo-American Land Mortgage Agency Co.* [1897] 1 Ch 130 (shareholder's right to inspect register).

3 *Clark* v *Workman* [1920] 1 IR 107, 110.

4 [1950] 2 All ER 1064: it is interesting to observe that in the judgments there one can find every 'exception' except *ultra vires*.

5 Jessel MR (1877) 6 ChD 70, 81.

6 E.g., *Borland's Trustee* v *Steel Brothers & Co. Ltd* [1901] 1 Ch 279; *Bisgood* v *Henderson's Transvaal Estates Ltd* [1908] 1 Ch 743.

7 *Hickman* v *Kent or Romney Marsh Sheep-Breeders' Association* [1915] 1 Ch 881 at p. 902; and see *Beattie* v *E. & F. Beattie Ltd* [1938] Ch 708, 721–2.

8 *Pender* v *Lushington* (1877) 6 ChD 70; *Moffatt* v *Farquhar* (1877) 7 ChD 591; *Marks* v *Financial News Ltd* (1919) 35 TLR 681; *Cannon* v *Trask* (1875) LR 20 Eq 669.

9 E.g., *Staples* v *Eastman Photographic Materials Co.* [1896] 2 Ch 303; *Greenhalgh* v *Arderne Cinemas Ltd* [1945] 2 All ER 719, [1946] 1 All ER 512; *James* v *Buena Ventura Nitrate Grounds Syndicate Ltd* [1806] 1 Ch 456.

10 *Moodie* v *W. & J. Shepherd (Bookbinders) Ltd* [1949] 2 All ER 1044, HL; *Burdett* v *Standard Exploration Co.* (1899) 16 TLR 112.

to enforce a declared dividend as a legal debt,[11] and if none is declared, at least to prevent dividends from being distributed otherwise than in accordance with the articles;[12] to prevent an irregular forfeiture;[13] to prevent directors holding office in breach of the articles;[14] and other 'procedural' irregularities.[15] Similarly, a member has a *personal* right to prevent alterations in the articles which would constitute a 'fraud' on the minority;[16] and probably has a similar right to enforce proper notice of meetings and business to be conducted at them.[17] It is true that cases of this character illustrate mainly rights to obtain a declaration or injunction; and it may be that a member cannot obtain a money judgment against his company, while he is a member, except in respect of a dividend which has become a debt due to him.[18] In any case, the nature of the remedies available does not affect the fact that these are all cases where the court did interfere to prevent irregularities, *intra vires* the company but in breach of the articles, at the instance of a member personally.

This line of argument is not weakened by the fact that many of these actions were in form representative actions. On the contrary, it is strengthened; for the plaintiff shareholders surely pursued their remedies as representative plaintiffs just because their fellow members, or a class of them, shared an interest in the matter.[19] Thus in *Edwards* v *Halliwell* [1950] 2 All ER 1064, *Catesby* v *Burnett* [1916] 2 Ch 325, *Wood* v *Odessa Waterworks Co.* (1889) 42 ChD 636, *Pender* v *Lushington* (1877) 6 ChD 70 and *Salmon* v *Quin & Axtens Ltd* [1909] 1 Ch 311, [1909] AC 442, as in many others, a representative form was employed. Indeed, it is surely the key to *Salmon's* case that it *was* employed. It cannot have been the case in *Salmon* that the plaintiff was trying to protect his unique right to dissent from the directors' decision, a 'right of veto . . . vested in the member by the articles alone'.[20] As *member*, he had no right of veto; the articles purported to give that right to him in his capacity as *managing director* and not as member. Article 80, indeed, clearly distinguished that capacity from his capacity as member.[21] Salmon sued as a shareholder to protect a right personal to him, but common to all the members. Hence the representative action. What was that right? It could not be a right vested in him *qua* managing director. In such a capacity (as an 'outsider') he could not enforce the contract arising from the articles. It is, therefore, obvious that Salmon enforced the

11 See *Godfrey Phillips Ltd* v *Investment Trust Corporation Ltd* [1953] Ch 449, 457; *Wall* v *London & Provincial Trust Ltd* [1920] 2 Ch 582; *Foster* v *Coles and M.B. Foster and Sons Ltd* (1906) 22 TLR 555; *Evling* v *Israel and Oppenheimer Ltd* [1918] 1 Ch 101.

12 See last note, and *Wood* v *Odessa Waterworks Co.* (1889) 42 ChD 636; *Fawcett* v *Laurie* (1860) 1 Dr & Sm 192; *Oakbank Oil Co.* v *Crum* (1882) 8 App Cas 65. Some of the 'dividend' cases involve both (i) enforcement of the contract in the articles, and (ii) the rule prohibiting dividends out of capital: e.g., *Mosely* v *Koffyfontein Mines Ltd* [1911] 1 Ch 73; [1911] AC 409.

13 *Johnson* v *Lyttle's Iron Agency* (1877) 5 ChD 687; *Sweny* v *Smith* (1869) LR 7 Eq 324; *Goulton* v *London Architectural Brick & Tile Co.* [1877] WN 141 (a 'procedural' irregularity).

14 *Catesby* v *Burnett* [1916] 2 Ch 325.

15 See the injunction that *was* granted in *Spencer* v *Kennedy* [1926] Ch 125, 135. *Henderson* v *Bank of Australasia* (1890) 45 ChD 330; *Breay* v *Browne* (1897) 41 SJ 159, 160.

16 *Greenhalgh* v *Arderne Cinemas Ltd* [1951] Ch 286 (reviewing previous cases). The right to sue is *personal*, although, oddly enough, the only two *successful* actions were both representative: *Dafen Tinplate Co. Ltd* v *Llanelly Steel Co. (1907) Ltd* [1920] 2 Ch 124; *Brown* v *British Abrasive Wheel Co. Ltd* [1919] 1 Ch 290.

17 *Baillie* v *Oriental Telephone & Electric Co. Ltd* [1915] 1 Ch 503; *Tiessen* v *Henderson* [1899] 1 Ch 861; *Kaye* v *Croydon Tramways Co.* [1898] 1 Ch 358, are curious cases if this is not the explanation. See, too, *Great Western Railway Co.* v *Rushout* (1852) 5 De G & Sm 290; *Smith* v *Duke of Manchester* (1883) 24 ChD 611; and *Re Direct East & West Junction Railway Co.* (1855) 3 Eq Rep 479.

18 [This has since been settled by CA 1985, s. 111A.]

19 *Sweny* v *Smith* (1869) LR 7 Eq 324 at p. 333. The practice plainly avoids multiplicity of actions.

20 See the article set out, [1909] 1 Ch at p. 313. The relevant parts read: 'No resolution of . . . the directors having for its object . . . [various matters including purchase and sale of premises] . . . or any matter affecting the rights of either of them, the said William Raymond Axtens and Joseph Salmon, *as holders of ordinary shares* of the company, shall be valid or binding unless . . . notice . . . shall have been given to each of the *managing directors*, the said William Raymond Axtens and Joseph Salmon, and neither of them shall have dissented . . .' (italics supplied).

21 Gower, *Modern Company Law* (1954), p. 484.

right of a member *to have the articles observed* by the company. What other right could members have? It is true that the proposition to which this conclusion gives rise apparently conflicts with the rule in *Hickman's* case that 'outsider'-rights can never be enforced by reliance upon the articles.[22] The proposition is that a member can compel the company not to depart from the contract with him under the articles, even if that means indirectly the enforcement of 'outsider'-rights vested either in third parties or himself, so long as, but only so long as, he sues *qua* member and not *qua* 'outsider'. This explanation of *Salmon's* case has not escaped later judges. Sir Wilfred Greene MR, in *Beattie* v *E. & F. Beattie Ltd*,[23] decided that case on the ground that the director-member there had not put his case in this way; but he clearly recognised that such a formulation is possible. Such a right to *call upon the company to observe the articles* is the right and the only right in this respect which is common to all the members, under this article', he said.[24] If this view is correct, the law surrounding *Hickman's* case is more complicated and more odd than has often been thought; but a line of authority, brooded over by *Salmon's* case, supports the view.[25]

The conflict between Salmon's case and the rule   At every point, however, a general application of this view conflicts with the rule in *Foss* v *Harbottle* [see chapter 13] as understood in the cases discussed earlier in this article. It clashes with the view, so forcefully put by James LJ in *MacDougall* v *Gardiner*,[26] that the member does *not* have the right to complain of 'irregularities' even if they contravene the articles. It derogates from the propositions made about majority ratifications of unauthorised directors' acts; such ratification is easily understood on ordinary agency principles where the directors purport to contract with outsiders as in *Grant* v *United Kingdom Switchback Railways Co.* (1888) 40 ChD 135; but when, as in that case, the majority are allowed to validate not merely an absence of authority but also a breach of a procedure laid down by the articles, the clash with *Salmon's* case arises again. Similarly, we can easily be led to the view that each shareholder has a right of action to prevent the company from allowing persons to act as directors in contravention of the articles,[27] the argument expressly rejected in *Mozley* v *Alston* itself;[28] and this, it is suggested, is the real cause of the feeling of uneasiness which that case has caused to certain judges.[29]

. . .

The truth is that in each case a line has to be drawn through the articles. On one side stand clauses breach of which cannot be ratified; on the other stand those in the grip of the ordinary majority. There has, as yet, been little satisfactory assistance afforded by the case law as to the way of finding out on which side of the line a particular article will fall. It is, therefore, suggested that matters of 'internal management' ought to be confined to matters already covered by judicial pronouncements. This, at best, will leave anomalies. Why should the right to vote be personally

22 The second proposition of Astbury J [1915] 1 Ch 900.

23 [1938] Ch 708, especially at p. 722. It is true that he saw 'great difficulty' because of the rule in *Foss* v *Harbottle*, but he did not go further into the matter. See, too, *Woodlands Ltd* v *Logan* [1948] NZLR 230, 236.

24 [1938] Ch 708 at p. 722: an article for arbitration of disputes between company and member; member was disputant in capacity of director.

25 The only case known to the writer to contain any lengthy discussion of the consequences of it is *Australian Coal and Shale Employees' Federation* v *Smith* (1937) 38 SR (NSW) 48, Jordan CJ. It is true that earlier cases such as *Eley* v *Positive Government Security Life Assurance Co.* (1876) 1 ExD 20, 88, are against the proposition advanced. But they do not seem to involve plaintiffs putting their case in the way suggested; and in any case, even if they did, they could not stand with *Salmon's* case as interpreted above.

26 (1875) 1 ChD pp. 22–3; and see *Foster* v *Foster* [1916] 1 Ch 532.

27 *Catesby* v *Burnett* [1916] 2 Ch 325 (no mention of *Foss* v *Harbottle* by Eve J or Gore Brown KC or Maugham KC).

28 See (1847) 1 Ph 789, 796, 799. The 'personal right' argument was expressly advanced. It might be argued that the internal statutory arrangements may not in that case have constituted a contract in the manner of the articles under s. 20; but this would be a last-ditch distinction!

29 E.g., Swinfen Eady LJ in *Baillie* v *Oriental Telephone & Electric Co. Ltd* [1915] 1 Ch 503 at p. 518, where he reduces its importance as much as he can; and compare the doubts which beset Romer J in *Cotter* v *National Union of Seamen* [1929] 2 Ch 58 at p. 70, which have the same sort of cause.

enforceable when the right to call for an effective poll is not?[30] But it will also follow *Salmon's* case in recognising that each member has a prima facie right to enforce by injunction and declaration 'in aid of his legal right,'[31] *every* provision of the contract found in the articles; that he has not merely particular, personal rights under that contract, but the personal right to see that that contract is observed—subject only to those matters of 'internal management' on which the courts have seen fit to displace his contractual rights in favour of majority rule. . . .

6.5 EXTRINSIC CONTRACTS

Contracts outside the memorandum and articles are sometimes called extrinsic contracts. Where there is an extrinsic contract between the company and a director (such as for employment), an article may be expressly or impliedly incorporated into the extrinsic contract. In this event, any rights given by the article can be enforced under the contract without relying on s. 33 of the CA 2006. Where there is no specific contract, but an article, for example, provides for the employment of the director, the court may imply an extrinsic contract (*Re New British Iron Co., ex parte Beckwith* [1898] 1 Ch 324).

As will be seen in 6.3, a company can alter its articles at any time. Thus, the terms of the articles which are incorporated into an extrinsic contract by reference, expressly or impliedly, can be altered from time to time but not retrospectively (*Swabey* v *Port Darwin Gold Mining Co.* (1889) 1 Meg 385). The power to alter the articles cannot be excluded even by an extrinsic contract. However, it may be a breach of contract for the company to alter its articles and act upon them in such a way as to affect the contract (*Southern Foundries (1926) Ltd* v *Shirlaw* [1940] AC 701 extracted at 11.7.3).

Swabey v *Port Darwin Gold Mining Co.*
The effect of altering the articles
(1889) 1 Meg 385, Court of Appeal

Facts   Under the articles the directors were entitled to be paid a fee of £200 per annum. Later the company passed a special resolution altering the articles so that the directors were entitled to receive thereafter £5 per month. The plaintiff successfully claimed fees at the old rate which had accrued prior to the alteration.

LORD HALSBURY LC: 724; I am unable to agree with the conclusion at which Mr Justice Stephen has arrived. The argument which has been addressed to us proceeds upon the erroneous basis of treating the articles as a contract, and that as there is a power given by the Act to alter the articles, the contract they contained could be put an end to and varied by the altering resolution. The articles do not themselves constitute a contract, they are merely the regulations by which provision is made for the way the business of the company is to be carried on. A person who acts as director with those articles before him enters into a contract with the company to serve as a director, the remuneration to be at the rate contemplated by the articles. The person who does this has before him, as one of the stipulations of the contract, that it shall be possible for his employer to alter the terms upon which he is to serve, in which case he would have the option of continuing to serve, if he

---

30 *Pender* v *Lushington* (1877) 6 ChD 70 and *MacDougall* v *Gardiner* (1875) 1 ChD 13.
31 Wynn-Parry J, *Godfrey Phillips Ltd* v *Investment Trust Corporation Ltd* [1953] Ch 449 at p. 457.

thought proper, at the reduced rate of remuneration. Those terms, however, could be altered only as to the future. In so far as the contract on those terms had already been carried into effect, it is incapable of alteration by the company.

LORD ESHER MR: I am of the same opinion. The articles do not themselves form a contract, but from them you get the terms upon which the directors are serving. It would be absurd to hold that one of the parties to a contract could alter it as to service already performed under it. The company has power to alter the articles, but the directors would be entitled to their salary at the rate originally stated in the articles up to the time the articles were altered.

6.6 ALTERATION OF ARTICLES

Under s. 21 of the CA 2006, a company may by special resolution alter its articles. A company may also alter its articles by unanimous consent without a meeting or resolution (*Cane* v *Jones* [1980] 1 WLR 1451). See also CA 2006, s. 288, written resolutions of private companies.

COMPANIES ACT 2006, S. 21

21. Amendment of articles

(1) A company may amend its articles by special resolution.

6.6.1 Bona fide for the benefit of the company as a whole

The power to alter a company's articles must be exercised bona fide for the benefit of the company as a whole (*Allen* v *Gold Reefs of West Africa Ltd* [1900] 1 Ch 656). A member cannot challenge an alteration which was carried out bona fide for the benefit of the company as a whole, even if such an alteration has affected the member's personal rights as long as the altered article was intended to apply indiscriminately to all members (*Greenhalgh* v *Arderne Cinemas Ltd* [1951] Ch 286). The court will generally accept the majority's subjective bona fide view of whether the alteration is for the benefit of the company as a whole, provided that the alteration is not so 'oppressive' or 'extravagant' that no reasonable person could really consider it to be for the benefit of the company (*Shuttleworth* v *Cox Bros & Co. (Maidenhead) Ltd* [1927] 2 KB 9). The application of the test can be seen from the cases extracted below.

Allen v *Gold Reefs of West Africa Ltd*
An alteration applying to all members
[1900] 1 Ch 656, Court of Appeal

An alteration of articles which gave the company a lien on fully paid shares in respect of debts owed by members was held to be made bona fide for the benefit of the company as a whole. The fact that the complaining minority shareholder was the only person practically affected at the time by the alteration, though raising suspicion as to the bona fides of the company, did not affect the validity of the alteration. The altered articles were intended to apply to all holders of fully paid shares and the complaining shareholder happened to be the only holder of fully paid up shares who at the time was in arrears of calls.

(Today such a case would probably be brought under CA 2006, s. 994, though the result of the case may still be the same. For CA 2005, s. 994, see 13.2.4. Such an article is perhaps not unfairly prejudicial to the complaining shareholder because it is only fair that the company should have a lien over shares as security for debts owed by members to the company.)

Facts   *The articles gave the company a lien for all debts owing by members to the company 'upon all shares (not being fully paid) held by such members'. Zuccani was the only holder of fully paid shares although he also held shares which were not fully paid. The company altered its articles by deleting the words 'not being fully paid', thus extending the lien to fully paid shares. In this action, Zuccani's executor unsuccessfully challenged the validity of the alteration.*

LINDLEY MR: The articles of a company prescribe the regulations binding on its members: Companies Act 1862, s. 14 [now CA 2006, ss. 18 and 19]. They have the effect of a contract (see [CA 2006, s. 33]); but the exact nature of this contract is even now very difficult to define. Be its nature what it may, the company is empowered by the statute to alter the regulations contained in its articles from time to time by special resolutions ([CA 2006, s. 21]); and any regulation or article purporting to deprive the company of this power is invalid on the ground that it is contrary to the statute: *Walker* v *London Tramways Co.* (1879) 12 ChD 705.

The power thus conferred on companies to alter the regulations contained in their articles is limited only by the provisions contained in the statute and the conditions contained in the company's memorandum of association. Wide, however, as the language of [CA 2006, s. 21] is, the power conferred by it must, like all other powers, be exercised subject to those general principles of law and equity which are applicable to all powers conferred on majorities and enabling them to bind minorities. It must be exercised, not only in the manner required by law, but also bona fide for the benefit of the company as a whole, and it must not be exceeded. These conditions are always implied, and are seldom, if ever, expressed. But if they are complied with I can discover no ground for judicially putting any other restrictions on the power conferred by the section than those contained in it. How shares shall be transferred, and whether the company shall have any lien on them, are clearly matters of regulation properly prescribed by a company's articles of association. This is shown by Table A.…Speaking, therefore, generally, and without reference to any particular case, the section clearly authorises a limited company, formed with articles which confer no lien on fully paid-up shares, and which allow them to be transferred without any fetter, to alter those articles by special resolution, and to impose a lien and restrictions on the registry of transfers of those shares by members indebted to the company.

But then comes the question whether this can be done so as to impose a lien or restriction in respect of a debt contracted before and existing at the time when the articles are altered. Again, speaking generally, I am of opinion that the articles can be so altered, and that, if they are altered bona fide for the benefit of the company, they will be valid and binding as altered on the existing holders of paid-up shares, whether such holders are indebted or not indebted to the company when the alteration is made. But, as will be seen presently, it does not by any means follow that the altered article may not be inapplicable to some particular fully paid-up shareholder. He may have special rights against the company, which do not invalidate the resolution to alter the articles, but which may exempt him from the operation of the articles as altered.

The conclusion thus arrived at is based on the language of [CA 2006, s. 21], which, as I have said already, the court, in my opinion, is not at liberty to restrict. This conclusion, moreover, is in conformity with such authorities as there are on the subject…

But, although the regulations contained in a company's articles of association are revocable by special resolution, a special contract may be made with the company in the terms of or embodying one or more of the articles, and the question will then arise whether an alteration of the articles so embodied is consistent or inconsistent with the real bargain between the parties. A company cannot break its contracts by altering its articles, but, when dealing with contracts referring to revocable articles, and especially with contracts between a member of the company and the company respecting his shares, care must be taken not to assume that the contract involves as one of its terms an article which is not to be altered.

It is easy to imagine cases in which even a member of a company may acquire by contract or otherwise special rights against the company, which exclude him from the operation of a subsequently altered article. Such a case arose in *Swabey* v *Port Gold Mining Co.* (1889) 1 Meg 385, where it was held that directors, who had earned fees payable under a company's articles, could not be deprived of them by a subsequent alteration of the articles, which reduced the fees payable to directors.

I take it to be clear that an application for an allotment of shares on the terms of the company's articles does not exclude the power to alter them nor the application of them, when altered, to the shares so applied for and allotted. To exclude that power or the application of an altered article to particular shares, some clear and distinct agreement for that exclusion must be shewn, or some circumstances must be proved conferring a legal or equitable right on the shareholder to be treated by the company differently from the other shareholders.

This brings me to the last question which has to be considered, namely, whether there is in this case any contract or other circumstance which excludes the application of the altered article to Zuccani's fully paid-up vendor's shares.

First, let us consider the shares. I am unable to discover any difference in principle between one fully paid-up share and another. Whether a share is paid for in cash or is given in payment for property acquired by the company appears to me quite immaterial for the present purpose. In either case the shareholder pays for his share, and in either case he takes it subject to the articles of association and power of altering them, unless this inference is excluded by special circumstances.

Next let us consider whether a vendor who makes no special bargain except that he is to be paid in fully paid-up shares is in any different position from other allottees of fully paid-up shares. I fail to see that he is, unless he stipulates that his shares shall be specially favoured. Zuccani bargained for fully paid-up shares and he got them. The imposition of a lien on them did not render them less fully paid-up than they were before. They remained what they were. Zuccani did not bargain that the regulations relating to paid-up shares should never be altered, or that, if altered, his shares should be treated differently from other fully paid-up shares. I cannot see that the company broke its bargain with him in any way by altering its regulations or by enforcing the altered regulations as it did. I have already drawn attention to clause 5 of the memorandum of association [which provided that shares might be issued 'with such preference, privileges or priority over or postponement to the remaining or any other shares of the company in respect of dividends or otherwise as may be determined']. Having regard to its plain language no allottee of shares, whether a vendor or an ordinary applicant, can justly complain of injustice or even hardship if his rights under the original articles are modified to his disadvantage. Every allottee was told by the memorandum that his rights as a shareholder were subject to alteration, and no allottee acquired any rights except on these terms unless, of course, some special bargain was made with him. If Zuccani had not been indebted to the company, could he have successfully maintained that the company had no power to alter the articles and so make his shares liable to a lien and consequently less marketable than before? I take it that it is clear that he could not. But I arrive at this conclusion only because the bargain with him has not been broken. Zuccani's indebtedness to the company confers on him, or his executors, no rights against it. But it is his indebtedness which creates the embarrassment from which they seek to escape. The fact that Zuccani's executors were the only persons practically affected at the time by the alterations made in the articles excites suspicion as to the bona fides of the company. But, although the executors were the only persons who were actually affected at the time, that was because Zuccani was the only holder of paid-up shares who at the time was in arrear of calls. The altered articles applied to all holders of fully paid shares, and made no distinction between them. The directors cannot be charged with bad faith.

After carefully considering the whole case, and endeavouring in vain to discover grounds for holding that there was some special bargain differentiating Zuccani's shares from others, I have come to the conclusion that the appeal from the decision of the learned judge, so far as it relates to the lien created by the altered articles, must be allowed.

Sidebottom v Kershaw, Leese & Co. Ltd
An alteration to prevent competition
[1920] 1 Ch 154, Court of Appeal

An alteration, which was made to require any shareholder who competed with the company's business to transfer his shares at their fair value to nominees of the directors, was held to be bona fide for the benefit of the company as a whole.

(Again this case might now be disposed of more easily under s. 994 of the CA 2006 although the result may still be the same as the alteration does not appear to be unfairly prejudicial on its facts.)

Facts   The defendant company altered its articles to empower the directors to buy out at a fair price the shares of any member who competed with the company's business. The plaintiffs, who carried on a competing business, failed in their attempt to challenge the validity of the alteration. It was claimed that the real target of the alteration was a member called Mr Bodden, not the plaintiffs.

LORD STERNDALE MR: . . . Now it does not seem to me to matter, as to the validity of this altered article, whether it was introduced with a view of using it against the plaintiff firm or not, except to this extent, that it might be that if it had been introduced specially for the purpose of using it against the plaintiffs' firm some question of bona fides might possibly have arisen, because it might have been argued that it was introduced to do them harm, and not to do the company good. That is the only way in which it seems to me to be relevant. The same seems to me to be the case with regard to the position of Mr Bodden. If the alteration were proposed with the intention of injuring Mr Bodden only, or getting Mr Bodden out of the company only, without any reasonable ground, and not for the benefit of the company, then again there would be, as it seems to me, a lack of bona fides, and in that way and in that way only Mr Bodden's position is of importance. I quite agree with what was said in argument by the respondents' counsel, that if by reason of the relative position of Mr Bodden and the defendant company's directors this was invalid against Mr Bodden, it is invalid altogether. The question is whether it is invalid. It introduces a new power which did not exist in the original articles at all—a power to buy out on the terms mentioned in the article any shareholder who was engaged in a competing business. It is necessary to look at what the powers of alteration of the articles of association are. They are contained in [CA 1985, s. 9] and it seems to me—and I am fortified in this opinion by, and in fact I found it upon, the words of Lindley MR in *Allen* v *Gold Reefs of West Africa* [1900] 1 Ch 656—that subject to the limitation which I shall mention a company can, under the powers of [s. 9], introduce into its altered article anything that could have been in the original articles . . . the limitations have been variously stated; but in my opinion they all come down to the same thing, which is expressed by Lindley MR in the same case, where he says: '. . . if [the articles] are altered bona fide for the benefit of the company, they will be valid . . .'. . . . There are two objections to this alteration: one is a very broad one indeed. It is that whatever alterations a company may be empowered to make in its articles varying the terms upon which its members may hold their shares, it cannot alter its articles so as to provide a means of what was called 'expelling', as in this case, by buying out a particular member and making him cease to be a member. I cannot find that such an exception as that is anywhere stated in any of the authorities as existing, but I am also bound to say that I think Mr Jenkins [counsel for the plaintiffs] was right when he said that none of the cases cited to us are dealing with matters of direct expulsion as it is called, or direct buying out such as exists in this case, but there is no doubt—in fact I think it is established by *Phillips* v *Manufacturers' Securities Ltd* (1917) 116 LT 290—that a power such as this is a perfectly valid power in the case of original articles, and it seems to me that prima facie if it could be in the original articles, it could be introduced into the altered articles provided only it is done bona fide for the benefit of the company as a whole. Therefore, in my opinion, it comes back to the same thing. The introduction into an altered article of a power of buying a person out or expelling him can only be held invalid if the alteration is not made bona fide for the benefit of the company. . . .

A second argument was addressed to us, which was this: I think Mr Jenkins rather deprecated it being put in this form, but in my opinion this is what it came to: An alteration cannot be for the benefit of the company as a whole if in fact it is a detriment to one of the members of the company, because the company as a whole means the whole body of corporators and every individual corporator, and if one of them has detriment occasioned to him by the alteration, it cannot be for the benefit of the company as a whole. I must say that I find it very difficult to follow that argument, but it seems to me to be exactly met by *Allen* v *Gold Reefs of West Africa Ltd* [1900] 1 Ch 656, because undoubtedly the alteration that was made there was not for the benefit of the shareholder, of whom the plaintiff, Mr Allen, was the executor, because it made his fully paid-up shares subject to a lien to which they were not subject before, and thereby, as I have pointed out, made it possible to get rid of Mr Allen, or Mr Allen's testator, altogether by compulsorily buying up his shares if the debt were not satisfied.

In my opinion, the whole of this case comes down to rather a narrow question of fact, which is this: When the directors of this company introduced this alteration giving power to buy up the shares of members who were in competing businesses did they do it bona fide for the benefit of the company or not? It seems to me quite clear that it may be very much to the benefit of the company to get rid of members who are in competing businesses. To a certain extent it is provided by art. 123 that the members are not to have too much knowledge of the affairs of the company, because although they may attend a meeting and hear the balance sheet and the report of the directors read, they may not have a copy of either of them, or take extracts from them. That the learned Vice-Chancellor [at first instance] has held to be a perfectly good article. There is no appeal on it, and I say nothing about it. It is a provision no doubt that prevents members having quite as full a knowledge of the business of the company as they would have in the absence of such an article, but I think there can be no doubt that a member of a competing business or an owner of a competing business who is a member of the company has a much better chance of knowing what is going on in the business of the company, and of thereby helping his own competition with it, than if he were a non-member; and looking at it broadly, I cannot have any doubt that in a small private company like this the exclusion of members who are carrying on competing businesses may very well be of great benefit to the company. That seems to me to be precisely a point which ought to be decided by the voices of the business men who understand the business and understand the nature of competition, and whether such a position is or is not for the benefit of the company. I think, looking at the alteration broadly, that it is for the benefit of the company that they should not be obliged to have amongst them as members persons who are competing with them in business, and who may get knowledge from their membership which would enable them to compete better.

That brings me to the last point. It is said that that might be so were it not for the fact that the directors and the secretary have said, 'This is directed against Mr Bodden', and therefore it is not done bona fide for the benefit of the company, but it is done to get rid of Mr Bodden. If it were directed against Mr Bodden from any malicious motive I should agree with that—the thing would cease to be bona fide at once; but these alterations are not as a rule made without some circumstances having arisen to bring the necessity of the alteration to the minds of the directors. I do not read this as meaning anything more than this: 'It was the position of Mr Bodden that made us appreciate the detriment that there might be to the company in having members competing with them in their business, and we passed this, and our intention was, if it became necessary, to use it in the case of Mr Bodden; that is what we had in our minds at the time; but we also had in our minds that Mr Bodden is not the only person who might compete, and therefore we passed this general article in order to enable us to apply it in any case where it was for the good of the company that it should be applied.' It is a question of fact. I come to the conclusion of fact to which I think the Vice-Chancellor came, that the directors were acting perfectly bona fide; that they were passing the resolution for the benefit of the company; but that no doubt the occasion of their passing it was because they realised in the person of Mr Bodden that it was a bad thing to have members who were competing with them. . . .

For these reasons I think this is a valid article. I think the alteration was within the competence of the company, and therefore this appeal must be allowed with costs here and below.

Shuttleworth v *Cox Bros & Co. (Maidenhead) Ltd*
Inserting a power to remove directors
[1927] 2 KB 9, Court of Appeal

An alteration to add an additional event disqualifying directors was held to be for the benefit of the company as a whole. (Such an alteration is potentially unfairly prejudicial under CA 2006, s. 994, depending on the circumstances in which the altered article is used.)

Facts   The plaintiff on 22 occasions within 22 months failed to account for the company's money he received. Under the existing articles, there was no ground to remove him. The articles were accordingly altered by inserting an article that on a request in writing signed by all the other directors a director should resign. The plaintiff was later duly requested to resign pursuant to the altered articles. The plaintiff unsuccessfully claimed that his dismissal was wrongful and that the alteration was invalid.

SCRUTTON LJ: In my view the plaintiff's failure to account for 22 items continuing up to and after the writ, all of which were ultimately admitted, was a very serious default in the management of the company; the directors considered this alteration of the articles under careful advice, with no precipitation, and with a genuine desire to remedy the evil, which was forced upon them, of having a man, whom they could admittedly have dismissed with notice from the post of manager, still sitting with them as a director in spite of his laxity in the management of the business entrusted to him; and I can see no evidence to justify the . . . finding [at first instance] that their determination was taken maliciously, or with any desire to spite the plaintiff, or from any motive but that of doing what they thought best in the interest of the company. If there was no evidence of lack of good faith, the other finding . . . makes an end of this appeal. That finding is that the alteration of the article was for the benefit of the company. . . .

   That would apparently conclude this case but for one point which Mr Porter [counsel for the plaintiff] raised—namely, that art. 22 in its original form constituted a contract between the company and the plaintiff, that he should be a permanent director for life, except in the events specified in that article, a contract which could not be varied without the consent of both parties; and that the plaintiff never consented to the article in its altered form. That argument would be sound if he could show a contract outside the articles; for then an alteration of the articles would not affect the contract. A good example of that principle is *Nelson* v *James Nelson & Sons Ltd* [1914] 2 KB 770. . . .

   Then Mr Porter advanced an argument based on an expression of Peterson J. in *Dafen Tinplate Co. Ltd* v *Llanelly Steel Co. (1907) Ltd* [1920] 2 Ch 124. He contended that the question is not what the shareholders think, but what the court thinks is for the benefit of the company . . . that the court must be satisfied that the alteration of the articles is genuinely for the benefit of the company. . . . To adopt that view would be to make the court the manager of the affairs of innumerable companies instead of the shareholders themselves. I think it is a mistaken view, based on a misunderstanding of an expression used by Lindley MR in *Allen's* case [1900] 1 Ch 656 at p. 671 and by Lord Sterndale MR in *Sidebottom's* case [1920] 1 Ch 154 at p. 167. Speaking of the power of altering articles, Lindley MR said: 'It must be exercised, not only in the manner required by law, but also bona fide for the benefit of the company as a whole'. The important words are 'exercised bona fide for the benefit of the company'. I do not read those words as importing two conditions, (1.) that the alteration must be found to be bona fide, and (2.) that, whether bona fide or not, it must be in the opinion of the court for the benefit of the company. I read them as meaning that the shareholders must act honestly having regard to and endeavouring to act for the benefit of the company. In *Sidebottom's* case Lord Sterndale MR, after putting the question: 'Did they do it bona fide for the benefit of the company?' proceeds to comment on the judgment of Astbury J in [*Brown* v *British Abrasive Wheel Co. Ltd* [1919] 1 Ch 290], and says that the learned judge

   found as a fact that the majority shareholders . . . were not doing this for the benefit of the company or in the interests of the company at large, but entirely for their own benefit, and in their own interests. If that finding be right, and as to that I say nothing, it was not bona fide; it was not done for the benefit of the company, but for the benefit of themselves.

As I understand him, the Master of the Rolls is contrasting the acts of those, who honestly endeavour to decide and to act for the benefit of the company as a whole, with the conduct of others who act with a view to the interest of some of the shareholders and against that of others. Now when persons, honestly endeavouring to decide what will be for the benefit of the company and to act accordingly, decide upon a particular course, then, provided there are grounds on which reasonable men could come to the same decision, it does not matter whether the court would or would not come to the same decision or a different decision. It is not the business of the court to manage the affairs of the company. That is for the shareholders and directors. The absence of any reasonable ground for deciding that a certain course of action is conducive to the benefit of the company may be a ground for finding lack of good faith or for finding that the shareholders, with the best motives, have not considered the matters which they ought to have considered. On either of these findings their decision might be set aside. But I should be sorry to see the court go beyond this and take upon itself the management of concerns which others may understand far better than the court does. So with regard to the passage, relied on by Mr Porter, from the judgment in the *Dafen Tinplate Co.'s* case [1920] 2 Ch 124 at p. 140, I can only say, if Peterson J means that, whatever the honest decision of the shareholders may be, it is the opinion of the court, and not that of the shareholders, which is to prevail, I disagree with that interpretation of the words of Lindley MR in *Allen's* case [1900] 1 Ch 656 at p. 671. If the learned judge merely means that the court will interfere where the decision of the shareholders, though honest, is such that no reasonable men could have come to it upon proper materials, I do not object to that explanation, and I should be prepared to act accordingly; but as reported I think the test laid down by the learned judge is erroneous for the reasons I have given. I think the appeal fails and must be dismissed.

Greenhalgh v *Arderne Cinemas Ltd*
Altering rights of pre-emption
[1951] Ch 286, Court of Appeal

Here, pre-emption rights in the articles were altered so as to permit a transfer of shares to any person including a non-member with the sanction of an ordinary resolution. The alteration was held bona fide and valid even though the minority lost their rights of pre-emption.

(This is perhaps the best example of alteration of articles held bona fide for the benefit of the company which might, perhaps with additional factors, be held to be unfairly prejudicial to minority shareholders under CA 2006, s. 994. This is because in practice the minority not only lost the right of pre-emption, but also did not obtain the power to permit a transfer to outsiders conferred on the majority by the new articles. The effect of the alteration was not similar to that in *Allen* v *Gold Reefs of West Africa Ltd* which would apply to all holders of fully paid shares regardless of the whim of the majority. In *Greenhalgh*, the minority could only have the same advantage as the majority if the majority joined them in voting for an ordinary resolution. The loss of rights of pre-emption and the practical advantage that they had been deprived of by a simple alteration of articles was arguably unfair to the minority.)

Facts   Under the articles, existing members had a right of pre-emption if any member wanted to sell his shares. Mr Mallard, who owned a controlling interest in the company, wanted to sell his shares to Mr Sheckman who was not a member. To achieve this, he procured the alteration of the articles so as to enable any member with the sanction of an ordinary resolution passed at any general meeting of the company to transfer his shares to any person named in such resolution. The plaintiff unsuccessfully sought a declaration that the alteration was invalid.

EVERSHED MR: The burden of the case is that the resolution was not passed bona fide and in the interests of the company as a whole, and there are, as Mr Jennings [counsel for the plaintiff] has urged, two distinct approaches.

The first line of attack is this, and it is one to which, he complains, Roxburgh J paid no regard: this is a special resolution and, on authority, Mr Jennings says, the validity of a special resolution depends upon the fact that those who passed it did so in good faith and for the benefit of the company as a whole. The cases to which Mr Jennings referred are *Sidebottom* v *Kershaw, Leese & Co. Ltd* [1920] 1 Ch 154, Peterson J's decision in *Dafen Tinplate Co. Ltd* v *Llanelly Steel Co. (1907) Ltd* [1920] 2 Ch 124, and, finally, *Shuttleworth* v *Cox Brothers & Co. (Maidenhead) Ltd* [1927] 2 KB 9. Certain principles, I think, can be safely stated as emerging from those authorities. In the first place, I think it is now plain that 'bona fide for the benefit of the company as a whole' means not two things but one thing. It means that the shareholder must proceed upon what, in his honest opinion, is for the benefit of the company as a whole. The second thing is that the phrase, 'the company as a whole', does not (at any rate in such a case as the present) mean the company as a commercial entity, distinct from the corporators: it means the corporators as a general body. That is to say, the case may be taken of an individual hypothetical member and it may be asked whether what is proposed is, in the honest opinion of those who voted in its favour, for that person's benefit.

I think that the matter can, in practice, be more accurately and precisely stated by looking at the converse and by saying that a special resolution of this kind would be liable to be impeached if the effect of it were to discriminate between the majority shareholders and the minority shareholders, so as to give to the former an advantage of which the latter were deprived. When the cases are examined in which the resolution has been successfully attacked, it is on that ground. It is therefore not necessary to require that persons voting for a special resolution should, so to speak, dissociate themselves altogether from their own prospects and consider whether what is thought to be for the benefit of the company as a going concern. If, as commonly happens, an outside person makes an offer to buy all the shares, prima facie, if the corporators think it a fair offer and vote in favour of the resolution, it is no ground for impeaching the resolution that they are considering their own position as individuals.

Accepting that, as I think he did, Mr Jennings said, in effect, that there are still grounds for impeaching this resolution: first, because it goes further than was necessary to give effect to the particular sale of the shares; and, secondly, because it prejudiced the plaintiff and minority share-holders in that it deprived them of the right which, under the subsisting articles, they would have of buying the shares of the majority if the latter desired to dispose of them.

What Mr Jennings objects to in the resolution is that if a resolution is passed altering the articles merely for the purpose of giving effect to a particular transaction, then it is quite sufficient (and it is usually done) to limit it to that transaction. But this resolution provides that anybody who wants at any time to sell his shares can now go direct to an outsider, provided that there is an ordinary reso-lution of the company approving the proposed transferee. Accordingly, if it is one of the majority who is selling he will get the necessary resolution. This change in the articles, so to speak, franks the shares for holders of majority interests but makes it more difficult for a minority shareholder, because the majority will probably look with disfavour upon his choice. But, after all, this is merely a relaxation of the very stringent restrictions on transfer in the existing article, and it is to be borne in mind that the directors, as the articles stood, could always refuse to register a transfer. A minor-ity shareholder, therefore, who produced an outsider was always liable to be met by the directors (who presumably act according to the majority view) saying, 'We are sorry, but we will not have this man in'.

Although I follow the point, and it might perhaps have been possible to do it the other way, I think that this case is very far removed from the type of case in which what is proposed, as in the *Dafen* case, is to give a majority the right to expropriate a minority shareholder, whether he wanted to sell or not, merely on the ground that the majority shareholders wanted the minority man's shares.

As to the second point, I felt at one time sympathy for the plaintiff's argument, because, after all, as the articles stood he could have said: 'Before you go selling to the purchaser you have to offer your shares to the existing shareholders, and that will enable me, if I feel so disposed, to buy, in effect, the whole of the shareholding of the Arderne company'. I think that the answer is that when a man comes into a company, he is not entitled to assume that the articles will always remain in a particular form; and that, so long as the proposed alteration does not unfairly discriminate in the way which I have indicated, it is not an objection, provided that the resolution is passed bona fide, that the right to tender for the majority holding of shares would be lost by the lifting of the restriction. I do not think that it can be said that that is such a discrimination as falls within the scope of the principle which I have stated.

6.6.2 Effect of shareholders' agreement on power to alter articles

Russell v *Northern Bank Development Corporation Ltd*
Shareholders may agree not to alter the articles
[1992] 1 WLR 588, House of Lords

This case held that although a company cannot forgo its right to alter its articles, a shareholders' agreement outside the articles as to how members will exercise their voting rights on a resolution to alter the memorandum is not necessarily void. It follows that shareholders can make a binding agreement amongst themselves as to how they should vote in relation to alteration of the company's articles.

Facts Tyrone Brick Ltd (TBL) entered into a shareholders' agreement with its four shareholders to the effect that, under clause 3, 'No further share capital shall be created or issued in the company or the rights attaching to the shares already in issue in any way altered . . . without the written consent of each of the parties hereto'. Notice was later given to hold an extraordinary general meeting to consider a proposed increase in the company's share capital. The plaintiff applied for an injunction to restrain the defendants from voting on the resolution. The application was rejected by the trial judge and the Court of Appeal in Northern Ireland. The plaintiff's appeal to the House of Lords was allowed.

LORD JAUNCEY OF TULLICHETTLE: The issue between the parties in this House was whether clause 3 of the agreement constituted an unlawful and invalid fetter on the statutory power of TBL to increase its share capital or whether it was no more than an agreement between the shareholders as to their manner of voting in a given situation. Both parties accepted the long-established principle that 'a company cannot forgo its right to alter its articles' (*Southern Foundries (1926) Ltd* v *Shirlaw* [1940] AC 701, at p. 739 per Lord Porter), a principle that was earlier stated in *Allen* v *Gold Reefs of West Africa Ltd* [1900] 1 Ch 656 at p. 671 per Lindley MR:

> . . . the company is empowered by the statute to alter the regulations contained in its articles from time to time by special resolutions (sections 50 and 51 [of the Companies Act 1862]); and any regulation or article purporting to deprive the company of this power is invalid on the ground that it is contrary to the statute: *Walker* v *London Tramways Co.* (1879) 12 ChD 705.

Murray J [at first instance] and MacDermott LJ [dissenting in the Court of Appeal] both considered that this principle applied also to the right of a company to alter its memorandum and I agree that this must be the case. Mr McCartney for the plaintiff advanced a number of arguments to the effect that the agreement in no way contravened the above principle inasmuch as it was merely an agreement between shareholders outside the scope of company legislation which in no way fettered the statutory power of TBL to alter its memorandum and articles. Mr Girvan, on the other hand [for the defendants], submitted that the agreement was not only a voting arrangement between shareholders *inter se* but was tantamount to an article of association which constituted a restriction on the power of TBL to alter its share capital.

My lords, while a provision in a company's articles which restricts its statutory power to alter those articles is invalid an agreement *dehors* the articles between shareholders as to how they shall exercise their voting rights on a resolution to alter the articles is not necessarily so. In *Welton* v *Saffery* [1897] AC 299 at p. 331, which concerned an *ultra vires* provision in the articles of association authorising the company to issue shares at a discount, Lord Davey said:

> Of course, individual shareholders may deal with their own interests by contract in such way as they may think fit. But such contracts, whether made by all or some only of the shareholders, would create personal obligations, or an *exceptio personalis* against themselves only, and would not become a regulation of the company, or be binding on the transferees of the parties to it, or upon new or non-assenting shareholders. There is no suggestion here of any such private agreement outside the machinery of the Companies Acts.

I understand Lord Davey there to be accepting that shareholders may lawfully agree *inter se* to exercise their voting rights in a manner which, if it were dictated by the articles, and were thereby binding on the company, would be unlawful.

I turn to examine the agreement in more detail. It appears from the narrative clauses that the agreement was intended to regulate the relationship between the shareholders with regard to the management and control of TBL. Clause 1 provides that the terms of the agreement was intended to regulate the relationship between the shareholders with regard to the management and control of TBL. Clause 1 provides that the terms of the agreement shall have precedence '*between the shareholders* over the articles of association' (the emphasis is mine). It further provides that where there is a conflict between the provisions of the agreement and the articles parties shall cooperate where necessary to have the articles amended to take account of the provisions of the agreement. It further provides that no further share capital shall be created or issued in TBL without the written consent of the parties to the agreement. TBL was incorporated under a previous name on 13 July 1979 and the agreement was executed on 14 December of that year. Since that date no attempt has been made to amend the articles for the purposes of clause 1, but I do not find that in any way surprising because clause 3 affects only existing shareholders and does not purport to bind other persons who may at some future date become shareholders in TBL by allotment or transfer. Clause 3 at least so far as shareholders are concerned constitutes an agreement collateral to the provisions of regulation 44 of Table A and is, as MacDermott LJ has concluded, neither in substitution for nor in conflict with that regulation.

However, it must be remembered that the agreement was executed not only by the shareholders but also by TBL. In *Bushell* v *Faith* [1969] 2 Ch 438 one of the articles of a private company provided that in the event of a resolution being proposed at a general meeting of the company for the removal of a director any share held by him should carry three votes per share. The issued capital of the company was equally divided between three persons and an attempt by two shareholders to remove the third from the office of director failed because his 300 votes outnumbered the 200 of the two other shareholders. It was held that the article in question was not invalidated by section 184 of the Companies Act 1948 which empowered a company by ordinary resolution to remove a director. Russell LJ said at pp. 447–8:

> Mr Dillon [counsel for the plaintiff] argued by reference to section 10 [of the Companies Act 1948], and the well-known proposition that a company cannot by its articles or otherwise deprive itself of the power by special resolution to alter its articles or any of them. But the point is the same one. An article purporting to do this is ineffective. But a provision as to voting rights which has the effect of making a special resolution incapable of being passed, if a particular shareholder or group of shareholders exercises his or their voting rights against a proposed alteration is not such a provision. An article in terms providing that no alteration shall be made without the consent of X is contrary to section 10 and ineffective. But the provision as to voting rights that I have mentioned is wholly different, and it does not serve to say that it can have the same result.

Both parties sought to derive comfort from this dictum. Mr McCartney relied on it as demonstrating that a provision as to the exercise of voting rights, even although it had the effect of preventing a resolution being passed, was nevertheless valid. Mr Girvan argued that the effect of clause 3 was the same as that of an article containing a provision that 'no alteration should be made without the consent of X'.

I do not doubt that if clause 3 had been embodied in the articles of association so as to be binding on all persons who were or might become shareholders in TBL it would have been invalid but it was, of course, not so embodied. To my mind the significant part of this dictum for the purposes of this appeal is the words 'articles or otherwise' occurring in the first sentence thereof. These words appear to recognise that it is not only fetters on the power to alter articles of association imposed by the statutory framework of a company which are obnoxious.

Turning back to clause 3 of the agreement it appears to me that its purpose was twofold. The shareholders agreed only to exercise their voting powers in relation to the creation or issue of shares in TBL if they and TBL agreed in writing. This agreement is purely personal to the shareholders who executed it and as I have already remarked does not purport to bind future shareholders. It is, in my view, just such a private agreement as was envisaged by Lord Davey in *Welton* v *Saffery*. . . .

6.6.3 Reform

The enforcement of a shareholder's contractual rights under the articles of association was examined by the Law Commission. Unfortunately, this did not include an examination of the issue of 'outsider' rights, the Law Commission merely saying in its consultation paper, that *Hickman* v *Kent or Romney Marsh Sheep-Breeders' Association* [1915] 1 Ch 881 was difficult to reconcile with some of the earlier cases (see Law Commission, *Shareholder Remedies* (Law Commission Consultation Paper No. 142) (London: Stationery Office, 1996), paras 1.9 and 2.20). The following extract from the Law Commission's report shows the problems identified by the Law Commission, and their explanation why no reform of s. 33 was needed.

Law Commission, *Shareholder Remedies*
(Law Commission Report No. 246)
(London: Stationery Office, 1997)

7.3 We drew attention to two potential problems in respect of the rights arising under s. 14 [now s. 33]. The first is that s. 14 does not expressly state that the company is bound by its own articles. However, our view was that it is clear on the wording of the section that the company is bound; the only point is that it is not deemed to have executed the articles under seal. As the only practical consequence of this is in relation to the limitation period for actions against the company, and as we were not aware of any particular difficulties to which this gave rise, our provisional view was that there was no reason to amend s. 14 in this respect.

7.4 The vast majority of respondents agreed with our provisional view and we therefore remain of the view that there should be no amendment to s. 14 to provide that the company is also deemed to have executed the memorandum and articles of association under seal.

7.5 The second potential problem to which we drew attention was the difficulty in identifying enforceable personal rights conferred by the articles. As we explained in the consultation paper, there are restrictions on a member's ability to bring a personal action to enforce the provisions of the articles of association. There are two aspects to this which we examined.

7.6 First, it seems to be generally accepted that the statutory contract only confers rights on a member in his capacity as member (sometimes referred to as 'insider rights') not in any 'outsider' capacity such as his position as a solicitor or director of the company. We took the view that examination of these 'outsider' rights was beyond the terms of reference of the project, but in any event we considered that there would normally be a contract between the company and the member in his other capacity so that there would be no need for him to seek to rely on the provisions of s. 14.

7.7 Secondly, the courts have classified breaches of certain constitutional provisions as 'internal irregularities' for which no personal action will lie. This restriction stems from the majority rule and proper plaintiff principles discussed above. The courts have held that if the internal affairs of the company are not being properly managed, then the company is the proper person to complain; there is no use in having litigation 'the ultimate end of which is only that a meeting has to be called and then ultimately the majority gets its wishes'. But there are cases where shareholders have been entitled to bring claims based on irregularities in voting procedures, such as the wrongful exclusion of proxy votes which would otherwise have resulted in the defeat of a resolution. Similarly, in cases involving defective notices of meetings, or inadequate notice of certain resolutions, the courts have allowed personal actions to proceed. It was the potential difficulty in identifying membership rights to which the 'internal irregularities' restriction did not apply to which we drew attention in the consultation paper.

7.8 Our provisional view, having had preliminary discussions with a number of interested parties, was that no hardship was being caused by any such difficulty. Moreover, we considered that there could never be a comprehensive definition of what constitutes a personal membership right under section 14, since regard has to be had to the terms of the particular articles in question and to the circumstances of the alleged breach.

7.9 We did, however, canvass the possibility of a non-exhaustive list of personal rights enforceable under s. 14 to be included in the section. This would set out the rights which the courts have to date allowed shareholders to enforce by personal action, but make it clear that the fact that these rights can be enforced by personal action does not mean that there are not others that can be enforced by the same means.

7.10 We provisionally considered that this would not be a useful addition to the statute for a number of reasons. First, the list could not state every breach of the articles which could give rise to a personal action, and so cases would still arise which were not expressly mentioned. Secondly, breaches of the articles vary from the trivial to the grave. Where they are trivial, we did not want to encourage litigation, and considered that setting out examples in a statute might have just this effect. The list would not reflect the exercise by the court of its discretion to refuse to give remedies for breaches of personal rights, for example, where a meeting had been improperly convened and another could be properly convened and take the same steps. We also reiterated our provisional view that there was no evidence of hardship being caused by the absence of a list, and noted that in practice actions to enforce personal rights appeared to be effectively eclipsed by proceedings under s. 459 (now CA 2006, s. 994), in which the remedies available are far wider.

7.11 The vast majority of respondents agreed that no hardship was being caused by any difficulty in identifying personal rights conferred by the articles. A large majority also rejected the proposal that there should be a statutory non-exhaustive list of personal rights enforceable under s. 14. The reasons given were similar to those set out in the previous paragraph. In the light of the responses to the consultation paper, we remain of the view that there should not be a statutory non-exhaustive list of personal rights enforceable under s. 14.

7.12 Accordingly, we do not recommend any reform of s. 14 of the Companies Act 1985.

The Steering Group, however, took a rather different view. In *Developing the Framework*, they proposed that s. 33 be replaced with a new provision setting out the extent to which individual shareholders and members are entitled to enforce the constitution against the company and that the contractual character of the rights be abolished (para. 4.90). The extract below explains why.

Modern Company Law for a Competitive Economy: Developing the Framework
(London: DTI, March 2000)

THE COMPANY'S CONSTITUTION AND PERSONAL RIGHTS

4.72 Questions on the scope of rights of minorities raise the fundamental issue of the juridical nature of a company's constitution. This is at present defined by the obscure and misleading provisions of section 14(1) [now s 33]. It is therefore convenient to look at this first, together with the extent of the personal rights which it confers, although other rights and remedies, notably section 459 [now s 994], have proved far more important in practice. We have considered whether it is necessary for the Review to examine the issues surrounding section 14, particularly since the Law Commission decided that they were best left unresolved. We explain below why we have decided that the Review, under its different terms of reference, should examine and consult again on them once we have explained to the reader what they are.

4.73 The general limitations on minority action do not, in any event, affect rights which are classified as personal to the shareholder concerned in the sense that they are his personally, rather than rights which he is to be regarded as having agreed to enjoy collectively via the company. We discuss below how such rights are to be identified but we note here that they include a right to restrain the commission of *ultra vires* acts. It is clear that a member may bring a personal action to restrain the company from acting beyond its corporate capacity and we have already made proposals to retain this rule, in modified form. It is much less clear whether an action (whether personal or derivative) may always be brought to prevent a breach of the company's articles (such as an act which is beyond the powers of the directors given by the articles), but we discuss this below.

What are Personal Rights? Section 14(1)

4.74 The essential question which arises in this context is therefore 'what rights can the shareholder, or even a third party, assert as his own under the constitution?'

4.75 Section 14(1), the key provision on this question, provides:

Subject to the provisions of this Act, the memorandum and articles, when registered, bind the company and its members to the same extent as if they respectively had been signed and sealed by each member, and contained covenants on the part of each member to observe all the provisions of the memorandum and of the articles.

4.76 A similar section has been part of the Act since 1856. It does not provide that the company is deemed to have signed and sealed the articles and memorandum (so that it is bound to the members, in the same way as they are to it and each other); but this is widely, though not universally, accepted.

4.77 The language is antique but the effect appears to be a statutory contract securing the important continuing effect of the constitution—new members will be bound by it, and have the benefit of it, without the need for separate agreement.

4.78 Appearances are however very deceptive in this case. While the effect is to give the essential flexibility and continuity (an effect which must be retained in any re-enactment of the section), the provision gives rise to notorious uncertainties and does nothing to resolve the critical question of what rights are personal to a shareholder; this has to be settled by reference to obscure and inconsistent case law. The following areas of difficulty arise:

• Contractual character—should the constitution be treated as a contract?
• Definition—how can the rights which are personally enforceable be defined?
• Parties—who can enforce them?
• Exceptions—should there be exclusion from such enforceability for 'irregularities'?
• Pre-emptive actions—should there be a special rule for actions seeking to restrain breaches before the event, rather than seeking remedies afterwards?

We first examine the current position on these issues and then the case for change.

Contractual Character of the Constitution—Flexibility

4.79 The section 14 contract is subject to the provisions of the Act, so that any contrary provision (for example, a power to issue shares at a discount) is of no effect. However the contract does give the draftsman of a constitution considerable flexibility in determining how risk, control and profit are to be allocated. We consider this flexibility should be maintained to the maximum. Our proposals in Chapter 3 retain a central role for the constitution in determining members' rights.

Contractual Character—Reality

4.80 But many of the normal contract law rules do not apply to the section 14 contract: the courts will not imply provisions into it to give it business efficacy; nor order rectification; nor rescind for misrepresentation. The only way in which the contract can be modified is under the Act (though it can be overridden by unanimity).

Definition of Personal Rights

4.81 It is clear that a member can enforce certain core individual rights, for example, the right to vote or receive dividends lawfully declared in his favour. But one would expect, in accordance with the principles outlined above, that a right held 'in common' with other members (eg the right to insist that the company is managed in accordance with its constitution) should only be enforceable collectively. However the cases conflict on this, particularly on breaches of the duty of compliance and to act for a proper purpose (see Chapter 3 above). One view is that they are personally enforceable. It would follow that breaches of them cannot be ratified; yet the case law suggests, rightly in our view, that they should be ratifiable by the general meeting.

Parties—Who Can Enforce the Constitution?

4.82 The contract has effect between the company and its members, and between the members themselves. Thus it does not directly confer rights on a third party.

4.83 Nor, in spite of the apparent effect of section 14, can even the parties always enforce it. Otherwise the principles set out above about the subordination of the individual wishes of members to the collective constitutional regime would be infringed. It is impossible to determine which provisions may be enforced with certainty from the cases. However a distinction has been drawn between 'outsider' rights and membership rights, the former not being personally enforceable even by a member. An example of an outsider right would apparently be a provision in a company's articles that a named person be appointed the company's solicitor, or a director be appointed on certain terms. Because such rights do not relate to membership as such, they probably cannot be enforced even by an intended beneficiary who happens to be a member. But it is sometimes argued that since directors are bound by the duty of compliance to comply with the articles, they should also be entitled to enforce them as directors; there is court authority for this view and it may well be the law (though directors will anyway have the same rights under their contracts of employment if the articles are incorporated).

4.84 The issue has also been raised with us of whether former members remain able to enforce their rights under the constitution in relation to events which took place when they were members and whether successors in title by operation of law acquire such rights with the share. We are not aware of any authority on these questions.

'Irregularities'

4.85 The courts have considered that breaches of certain provisions relating to the conduct of general meetings are mere 'internal irregularities', for which no personal action will lie even though they satisfy the other requirements for such action. What such irregularities are is very difficult to determine from the cases. But they are mainly concerned with irregularities in meetings and their essence is that where the action is trivial or the matter could be readily remedied by recalling the majority there is no case for upholding the personal right. Such an exception is consistent with the principles of freedom from interference, and of efficiency and cost-effectiveness mentioned above.

Pre-emptive Actions

4.86 There may be a difference between a member's right to restrain a breach of the constitution, or of a duty under it, before the event and an attempt to enforce it after the event. This is certainly the position with *ultra vires* acts.

The Case for Reforming Section 14 and Restating the Nature of the Constitution

4.87 The Law Commission took the view that while these issues were real in theory, the problems in practice were not sufficient to justify reform. Their reasons were: that it was clear on the wording of the section that a company is bound by its articles; that it seemed to be accepted that the statutory contract only confers rights on a member in his capacity as a member (but 'outsider rights' were in any event beyond their terms of reference); that the uncertainty over the definition of irregularities was causing 'no hardship'; that a comprehensive definition of personal rights was not feasible and a non-exhaustive list would encourage litigation in trivial cases and would not reflect the court's discretion to refuse a remedy in cases of irregularity, and that here again there was no evidence of hardship caused by the uncertainties.

4.88 Our position is different. As part of a comprehensive review of the whole of core company law we must examine the legal basis of the company constitution and a re-enactment of section 14 in some form will be required. We, like the Law Commission, attach great importance to accessibility of the law and bringing it up to date. Our terms of reference cover all the relevant considerations and are not constrained as were the Law Commission's. In our view the law on these issues is not clear and should be clearly stated in the new Act. We would suggest that they should be resolved along the lines set out below.

Should the Constitution be a Contract?

4.89 Since the deemed contract under section 14 is not a normal contract, there may well be a case for abandoning the idea of a contract altogether. The main purpose of the fiction appears to be to define the remedies and limitation periods available in an action to enforce it, although it is important to retain the concept that the member accepts that he is bound by the constitution when he agrees to become a member. It would arguably make more sense to address the issue of remedies directly. Thus the statute could make clear (so far as possible) not only the extent of the enforceable individual rights to which the constitution gives rise, but also the remedies. Obviously the normal range of court remedies should be available. Although damages (calculated under the rules for breach of contract rather than the rules for tort or delict) should also be available in appropriate circumstances, it seems clear that a member should not be able to recover damages where the company is insolvent, and that such individual claims should in principle rank after those of creditors but ahead of claims of other contributors (cf section 178(6)). There should presumably be no action by an individual member to the extent that an action by the company lies, since he should neither recover twice in damages nor obtain other relief which in principle should be subject to the same limitations as would apply to an action by the company. The contractual fiction also arguably makes clear that all members are deemed to have accepted the constitution by agreeing to become members. But if the legislation operated on the basis of statutory obligation this point could, perhaps, be made clear in the drafting.

4.90 We are inclined to the view that section 14 is so misleading that it would be desirable to lay down such a statutory provision explaining the extent to which individual shareholders and members are entitled to enforce the constitution against the company and that the contractual character of the rights should be abolished.

Definition of Personal Rights under the Constitution

4.91 Should a member have a personal right to enforce **all** provisions in a company's constitution—eg to enforce outsider rights or provisions relating to the conduct of directors' meetings? Clearly not, in our view—this would infringe the proper plaintiff and majority rule principles. But nor would we support the rule that rights under a company's constitution can **never** be enforced by the individual member. It seems clear that some rights are so specific and individual that it is entirely proper for a beneficiary to enforce them on his own behalf, with no risk of damage to the collective integrity of the association. Since some, but not all, of the rights should be enforceable personally it follows that a definition of those which are is required.

4.92 So how is the law to draw the distinction? It would be desirable to establish a principled approach to what characterises those core rights. One possibility would be to attempt an exhaustive listing of such rights, but, like the Law Commission, we are not convinced that it would be possible to produce such a list. It would be rigid and in borderline cases would depend on circumstances and interpretation of the constitution.

4.93 It is clear under the present law that the following rights are all enforceable by personal action, notwithstanding any decision of the company to the contrary: the right to be entered on the register of members; to transfer shares; to vote and participate in meetings of members; to receive any dividends properly declared or capital payments validly determined upon; and to exercise pre-emption rights. We suggest that this list should be included in non-exhaustive form in the legislation.

4.94 We would also suggest that rights should be excluded where breach does not involve any individual harm to the particular member, but only an indirect harm suffered as a result of damage done to the company as a whole; the legislation should provide this as a supplementary criterion for determining whether particular rights should be regarded as personal.

Parties—Who can Enforce Personal Rights?

4.95 We suggest the simple rule that the constitution should be enforceable by the company and by members as such. On the question whether directors as well as members should be able to enforce their rights under the constitution, we suggest that directors' rights as directors should be enforceable personally only under a director's service contract (including the letter of appointment in the case of a non-executive director), and not under the constitution.

4.96 On the position of ex-members who were members at the time of the alleged breach, and of persons to whom shares are transferred by operation of law (personal representatives, trustees in bankruptcy), it seems clear that a member who disposes of his shares should no longer have any rights of action (except for accrued claims on a debt), although the question whether the transferee acquires any rights of action appears not to have been definitively settled. It can perhaps be left to the courts.

Irregularities

4.97 On whether there should be a separate category of 'irregularities' which do not give rise to personal rights, we incline to the view that it should be made clear that it is open to the courts to dismiss an action on a personal right which satisfies the other criteria where the breach is trivial, or could readily be remedied by proper action by the company (eg to reconvene a meeting at which the shareholder's vote was not counted and where there was a clear majority against him).

Personal Rights for 'Pre-Emptive' Actions

4.98 A final question is whether the position should be different if the shareholder brings an action to restrain a breach in advance rather than suing after the event. As we have seen, there is some suggestion that his position is more favourable in the former case. We are inclined to suggest that this distinction is an unnecessary complication and cuts across the principles of the solution proposed. But we would be interested in views on this.

4.99 The fact that an obligation imposed under the constitution is not personally enforceable in this way does not, of course, mean that there is no remedy. The company will be able to enforce the obligation, or in a suitable case to waive or ratify; enforcement may be achievable by the individual shareholder bringing a derivative action in the name of the company; and under section 459 the court has an overriding discretion to provide a personal remedy where any breach of the constitution gives rise to unfair prejudice. Both the section 459 remedy and the derivative action may be available even if the company has purported to waive or ratify. We now set out questions for consultation immediately, for convenience in the context of the argument, before turning to these provisions; but we believe all these issues are best considered in the context of a scheme of rights and remedies for minority shareholders seen as a whole. We would therefore encourage respondents to bear the overall framework in mind when answering these questions.

The proposal proved controversial as the Steering Group explained in *Completing the Structure,* extracted below.

Modern Company Law for a Competitive Economy: Completing the Structure
(London: DTI, Nov. 2000)

Personal Rights

5.64 Currently the juridical nature of the company's constitution is laid down by section 14. This section, which is more than 150 years old, is obscurely drafted and refers to some outmoded concepts. It clearly cannot just be re-enacted and no one supports that approach. We proposed that a number of uncertainties about the legal effect of the constitution should be cleared up, that the juridical character of the constitution should be changed from a contractual to a statutory one, and that the personal rights of shareholders which derive from it should be defined in a non-exhaustive fashion (i.e. that there should be a list of them where they are already well established, together with a criterion to assist the courts in recognising further such rights). The latter two of these suggestions proved controversial while the proposed resolution of uncertainties was very widely welcomed.

Resolution of Uncertainties

5.65 We propose therefore that the replacement for section 14 should make it clear that the constitution confers mutual rights, obligations and powers between the company and its members (including between one individual member and another). The old-fashioned fiction under English law that it is a deed under seal and debts under it are 'specialty debts' should be replaced with the normal six year period of limitation and with the effect that the rights and obligations created arise by operation of law under the Act. (For whether these rights and obligations should be treated as contractual in character or as statutory rights and obligations, see below.)

5.66 We proposed that it should be made clear that:
- the constitution conferred rights only on members as members;
- it should not confer rights on former members;
- the court had power to dismiss actions to enforce personal rights where the matter was trivial or where no material difference could be achieved (e.g. because a re-holding of a meeting with proper recognition of the member's personal rights of participation and voting would produce the same result); and
- the extent of a shareholder's personal rights should be the same whether the action was brought in advance of the breach alleged or afterwards.

5.67 Of these, the first two proposals were supported by almost all responses, but there was concern about the effect on third party rights in Scotland. We propose that this should be covered by drafting which ensures that the position is not altered. The last two items are covered in the discussion of the definition of personal rights below.

Juridical Character of the Constitution—Statutory or Contractual?

5.68 All the legal professional bodies opposed the proposal to remove the contractual character of the constitution and replace it with a statutory one. Many of the supporters (who constituted a substantial majority) expressed concern about the need to achieve certainty and clarity and about the difficulty in that regard of fundamental change in the juridical approach. Many expressed concern that there should be clarity about the remedies available, but others believed that adoption of the statutory approach might lead to undue rigidity.

5.69 The present contractual character of the constitution under section 14 is in any case severely qualified under the Act. Many of the normal incidents of contractual relations and remedies available to the parties do not apply. Once this is recognised the issue becomes one of ensuring that the present rules apply subject only to the changes we are proposing. Arguably whether the relationships created are described as contractual or statutory becomes a matter of nomenclature rather than substance. Whether a modified contract, which we recognise may well be the best means of capturing the consensual character of relationships under the constitution, or explicit statutory powers and obligations are the best way of achieving the objective becomes a matter of drafting. We propose to suggest that the desired result should be explained to the draftsman and the best way of expressing it then explored in drafting.

Definition of Personal Rights

5.70 Our other main proposal in this field was that the current uncertainty about what rights were enjoyed by members personally under the constitution could be partially resolved, though not fully answered, in the new Act. This, we suggested, could be done:

- first, by listing those rights which were incontrovertibly available in this way non-exhaustively, so that rights listed would qualify as such, without excluding the existence of others; and
- second, by offering a principle, or criterion, by reference to which it could be determined whether other rights were personal or not.

5.71 So we proposed that rights to be entered in the register of members, to transfer shares, to vote and participate in meetings, to receive properly declared and determined distributions and to pre-emption, should be defined as personal, together with any other right breach of which gave rise to direct harm to the member rather than indirect, or collective, harm to the company as a whole.

5.72 This proposal was quite widely supported, but not by the legal professions, who argued that better remedies exist (e.g. under section 459), that there are no practical problems, and that what personal rights are available to particular shareholders depends on particular constitutional arrangements. It was also argued that legislation was unnecessary, the value of enumerating in statute the rights already recognised as personal questionable, and the technical effect of the proposals, for example on class rights unclear. Others argued that our proposed approach failed to address the problems, because the list of personal rights now recognised is arbitrary and it would leave in place obscure and inconsistent case law in the remaining field.

5.73 We are not persuaded that the fact that other remedies are available removes the need to clarify and define so far as possible the personal rights of shareholders. We do however accept that the non-exhaustive list approach is unsatisfactory. We now propose a much simpler approach— that all obligations imposed by the constitution should be enforceable by individual members unless the contrary is provided in the constitution. This would be subject to the 'trivial or fruitless' exception (see paragraph 5.66 above). The effect would be that a shareholder could obtain specific enforcement of a constitutional obligation unless or until the constitution was amended to remove the source of the breach. However he would only be entitled to damages for loss suffered in his personal capacity, as opposed to derivative loss suffered as a result of damage to the company. Loss would be recoverable only in respect of the period between the breach and any amendment of the constitution to remove the source of the breach. Ratification of the breach, where valid, could not, consistently with the nature of the right as a personal right, remove the entitlement to such damages for the period that the obligation remained in place.

5.74 We have considered whether this change in the effect of company constitutions should apply both to companies formed after the coming into operation of our proposals and to those already in existence, or whether the present law should remain in force for the latter, to preserve vested rights. We are inclined to the view that it should apply to both. Leaving the present law in place for existing companies would create two classes of companies with constitutions with radically different effects, which is clearly undesirable. If the period before the new legislation comes into force on this question is sufficiently long it should be possible for companies that wish to exclude personal enforcement by individual members of rights under their constitutions to adopt provisions to do so. (Nor would such a proposal strictly speaking affect existing obligations; it would rather clarify the extent of their enforceability.) However we would be grateful for comments on this proposal and the transitional question.

As a result, the Steering Group offered a different approach: all obligations imposed by the constitution should be enforceable by individual members both against the company and other members unless the contrary was provided in the constitution, unless the breach in question was trivial or the remedy fruitless. The Steering Group reaffirmed this approach in its final report.

Modern Company Law for a Competitive Economy: Final Report
(London: DTI, 2001)

Definition of personal rights

7.34 Our proposal in *Developing the Framework* to list non-exclusively the rights enjoyed by members personally, and offer a principle or criterion by reference to which it could be determined whether other rights were personal was widely supported, but not by the legal professions. Accordingly, in *Completing the Structure* we offered a different approach, namely that all obligations imposed by the constitution should be enforceable by individual members both against the company and other members unless the contrary was provided in the constitution, unless the breach in question was trivial or the remedy fruitless. The majority of responses favoured this, and we therefore recommend it. However, a number of points were raised.

7.35 Fears were expressed that it would encourage litigation, and, for example, enable shareholders unhappy with the board's performance to challenge accounts which were marginally defective, on grounds that there has been a breach by the directors of their obligation in the constitution to prepare them in accordance with the Act. This is a theoretical possibility; but such action would almost certainly fall within the 'trivial or fruitless' exception; and the courts' discretion as to whether the case should proceed ought to be sufficient to exclude vexatious claims.

7.36 The question was raised of how any exclusion of personal remedies in the constitution would interact with the remedy under section 459. We do not intend that any such exclusion should restrict that remedy. Provision will be needed to make it clear that any exclusion permitted in the constitution relates only to enforcement of the provision *as part of the constitution*; and that it does not prevent a member from arguing that its appearance in the constitution amounts to evidence of agreement between the members that it would be observed, for the purpose of determining whether the test in *O'Neill v Phillips* (which we discuss below) is satisfied. In addition, our proposal was criticised on grounds that exclusionary articles were likely to become the norm, with the result that shareholders would find themselves even worse off than they currently are under section 14. While we accept that this is a possibility, we consider that the advantage in terms of clarity of our proposal outweighs this possible disadvantage. For those forming companies, our approach would allow the maximum of flexibility, while for those subsequently becoming members, the extent of their personal rights would be apparent on the face of the constitution. So far as attempts are made subsequently to alter the constitution to the detriment of particular members, the provisions of section 459 and our proposals on the restriction of majority powers would apply.

7.37 It was also suggested that our proposal would blur the distinction between rights which are personal and those which are properly the company's, and in particular give rise to the possibility of double recovery. We discuss this at paragraph 7.51.

7.38 Almost all respondents who expressed a view were in favour of our proposal that personal rights should be enforceable against other members as well as the company. It was, however, suggested that the long-term effect of this proposal would be to encourage the inclusion in articles of provisions which would otherwise be included in shareholders' agreements, with the result that they would become lengthier and more complicated. We believe that current practice in relation to shareholders' agreements is likely to continue, because of their privacy and immutability without unanimous agreement.

7.39 We also proposed that where the constitution was breached, any amendment to remove the source of the breach should operate prospectively but not have effect to remove the member's right to damages in respect of loss incurred between the breach and the amendment; and that ratification of the breach would not remove that entitlement. Responses were almost unanimously in favour of this, and accordingly we recommend it. As to the question of where a member's claim for damages against the company should rank on insolvency, we recommend that it should be subordinate to the rights of unsecured creditors but that it should be taken into account for the purpose of final adjustment of the rights of the members among themselves, as under the current section 74(2)(f) of the Insolvency Act 1986.

7.40 As regards the transitional implementation of our proposal, we suggested that it should apply both to existing companies and those formed after the new legislation comes into force; but that sufficient time should be allowed prior to commencement for existing companies to amend their constitutions. We invited comments on this suggestion. Responses were almost unanimously in favour of it and accordingly we so recommend.

However, the government did not take up the proposal in its subsequent White Paper and the CA 2006.

7

The General Meeting

The two 'organs' of the company are the members in general meeting and the board of directors. The company's constitution is contained in the memorandum and articles of association, a contract between the current members which they can change from time to time. This constitution and the general law decide what role the members are to play in the affairs of the company. The law intervenes to a considerable extent in setting procedural rules for the general meeting as it is concerned to ensure that the company functions properly as a micro-democracy and that the directors are accountable to the members. This is achieved by making formal requirements for the calling of meetings and for the essential process of decision making. While you may find that studying these procedures induces sleep, unfortunately they are the key to understanding how companies function and the issues that are dealt with in many of the cases.

This chapter will require you to work through the important sections set out below which define the different types of resolutions and establish how meetings are called and votes concluded. It will go on to examine the common law principle that a unanimous decision of the members of the company binds the company, and will then review the trend towards simplifying formal procedures for private companies, culminating in the recent reform of the law.

It is essential first to grasp that if you are a member of a company you have a right to a vote in general meeting, but also that, unless you hold a majority of the shares, you may be on the losing side and be out-voted. The law's prime concern is to ensure that this will only be done fairly and by due process. If it were otherwise, people would be reluctant to participate in companies and the economy would be damaged.

The board of directors has a dominant position in controlling the business of the company as typically, an article such as Table A 1985, art. 70 (reproduced at 1.7 above), delegates the management of the business of the company to the board of directors. As the general meeting has few, if any, opportunities to intervene in management, its functions are only occasional. Nonetheless, the ultimate control of the company resides in the general meeting, primarily based on the power of the general meeting to appoint or remove directors. (See 11.7 below.) Other than that it has only formal, though important functions.

The primary of these is the annual general meeting, a forum at which the board presents to the members its conduct of the affairs of the company for the year for their questioning and approval. The normal business at an annual general meeting includes reappointment of retiring directors, the appointment of auditors, and the approval of the directors' reports, the accounts, and any recommended dividend.

However, since the new Act of 2006, only public companies are now obliged to hold an AGM.

The other specific power of the general meeting, whether at an annual general meeting or an extraordinary general meeting is changing the constitution by a special resolution. Thus, an objects clause or the articles, for example, can be altered by a 75 per cent majority of those voting.

The final point to remember is the different reality between public and private companies. In a publicly listed company, the shareholders are passive investors such as vast pension funds and the directors are professional managers. In a typical owner-managed private company such as a small building firm, the members and the directors are one and the same. In reality they are not sitting around in suits but are out there on site laying bricks in all weathers. The board room is a dirty portakabin and not a penthouse up on level twenty two, and in their day-to-day work they rarely if ever have to consider whether what they are doing is done in their role as a member or a director.

7.2 PROCEDURES

The articles of most companies allow the proceedings of directors to be informal, and for them to conduct their meetings as they see fit. However, the procedure of general meetings is more formalised with detailed requirements specified by the Act, the articles, and the common law. For example, alteration of the memorandum or articles by less than unanimous consent must be by special resolution.

The following sections introduce the requirements for written resolutions and resolutions in general meeting, for ordinary and special resolutions and resolutions at a meeting passed as a show of hands or on a poll.

COMPANIES ACT 2006, PART 13

281. Resolutions

(1) A resolution of the members (or of a class of members) of a private company must be passed—
   (a) as a written resolution in accordance with Chapter 2, or
   (b) at a meeting of the members (to which the provisions of Chapter 3 apply).
(2) A resolution of the members (or of a class of members) of a public company must be passed at a meeting of the members (to which the provisions of Chapter 3 and, where relevant, Chapter 4 apply).
(3) Where a provision of the Companies Acts—
   (a) requires a resolution of a company, or of the members (or a class of members) of a company, and
   (b) does not specify what kind of resolution is required,
   what is required is an ordinary resolution unless the company's articles require a higher majority (or unanimity).
(4) Nothing in this Part affects any enactment or rule of law as to—
   (a) things done otherwise than by passing a resolution,
   (b) circumstances in which a resolution is or is not treated as having been passed, or
   (c) cases in which a person is precluded from alleging that a resolution has not been duly passed.

282. Ordinary resolutions

(1) An ordinary resolution of the members (or of a class of members) of a company means a resolution that is passed by a simple majority.

(2) A written resolution is passed by a simple majority if it is passed by members representing a simple majority of the total voting rights of eligible members (see Chapter 2).

(3) A resolution passed at a meeting on a show of hands is passed by a simple majority if it is passed by a simple majority of—

(a) the members who, being entitled to do so, vote in person on the resolution, and

(b) the persons who vote on the resolution as duly appointed proxies of members entitled to vote on it.

(4) A resolution passed on a poll taken at a meeting is passed by a simple majority if it is passed by members representing a simple majority of the total voting rights of members who (being entitled to do so) vote in person or by proxy on the resolution.

(5) Anything that may be done by ordinary resolution may also be done by special resolution.

283. Special resolutions

(1) A special resolution of the members (or of a class of members) of a company means a resolution passed by a majority of not less than 75%.

(2) A written resolution is passed by a majority of not less than 75% if it is passed by members representing not less than 75% of the total voting rights of eligible members (see Chapter 2).

(3) Where a resolution of a private company is passed as a written resolution—

(a) the resolution is not a special resolution unless it stated that it was proposed as a special resolution, and

(b) if the resolution so stated, it may only be passed as a special resolution.

(4) A resolution passed at a meeting on a show of hands is passed by a majority of not less than 75% if it is passed by not less than 75% of—

(a) the members who, being entitled to do so, vote in person on the resolution, and

(b) the persons who vote on the resolution as duly appointed proxies of members entitled to vote on it.

(5) A resolution passed on a poll taken at a meeting is passed by a majority of not less than 75% if it is passed by members representing not less than 75% of the total voting rights of the members who (being entitled to do so) vote in person or by proxy on the resolution.

(6) Where a resolution is passed at a meeting—

(a) the resolution is not a special resolution unless the notice of the meeting included the text of the resolution and specified the intention to propose the resolution as a special resolution, and

(b) if the notice of the meeting so specified, the resolution may only be passed as a special resolution.

7.3 CALLING MEETINGS

COMPANIES ACT 2006, PART 13, CHAPTER 2

302. Directors' power to call general meetings

The directors of a company may call a general meeting of the company.

303. Members' power to require directors to call general meeting

(1) The members of a company may require the directors to call a general meeting of the company.

(2) The directors are required to call a general meeting once the company has received requests to do so from—

(a) members representing at least the required percentage of such of the paid-up capital of the company as carries the right of voting at general meetings of the company (excluding any paid-up capital held as treasury shares); or

(b) in the case of a company not having a share capital, members who represent at least the required percentage of the total voting rights of all the members having a right to vote at general meetings.

(3) The required percentage is 10% unless, in the case of a private company, more than twelve months has elapsed since the end of the last general meeting—

(a) called in pursuance of a requirement under this section, or

(b) in relation to which any members of the company had (by virtue of an enactment, the company's articles or otherwise) rights with respect to the circulation of a resolution no less extensive than they would have had if the meeting had been so called at their request, in which case the required percentage is 5%.

(4) A request—

(a) must state the general nature of the business to be dealt with at the meeting, and

(b) may include the text of a resolution that may properly be moved and is intended to be moved at the meeting.

(5) A resolution may properly be moved at a meeting unless—

(a) it would, if passed, be ineffective (whether by reason of inconsistency with any enactment or the company's constitution or otherwise),

(b) it is defamatory of any person, or

(c) it is frivolous or vexatious.

(6) A request—

(a) may be in hard copy form or in electronic form, and

(b) must be authenticated by the person or persons making it.

306. Power of court to order meeting

(1) This section applies if for any reason it is impracticable—

(a) to call a meeting of a company in any manner in which meetings of that company may be called, or

(b) to conduct the meeting in the manner prescribed by the company's articles or this Act.

(2) The court may, either of its own motion or on the application—

(a) of a director of the company, or

(b) of a member of the company who would be entitled to vote at the meeting,

order a meeting to be called, held and conducted in any manner the court thinks fit.

307. Notice required of general meeting

(1) A general meeting of a private company (other than an adjourned meeting) must be called by notice of at least 14 days.

(2) A general meeting of a public company (other than an adjourned meeting) must be called by notice of—

(a) in the case of an annual general meeting, at least 21 days, and

(b) in any other case, at least 14 days.

308. Manner in which notice to be given

Notice of a general meeting of a company must be given—

(a) in hard copy form,

(b) in electronic form, or

(c) by means of a website (see section 309),

or partly by one such means and partly by another.

The various statutory procedures are, of course, intended to ensure the right of every member to attend at a general meeting, and to contribute to and hear debate on the issues and to vote. The following case addressed some of these issues under earlier legislation.

Re Sticky Fingers Restaurant Ltd

A Stone gets satisfaction

[1992] BCLC 84, Chancery Division

This case is an example of how the court's power to order a meeting to be called may be used to break the deadlock caused by a dispute in the company.

Facts   Bill Wyman (of the Rolling Stones) held 66 shares and Mr Mitchell 34 shares in the company. The company's business was a restaurant in Phillimore Gardens, Kensington, displaying Wyman's rock memorabilia. Various disputes arose. Mitchell filed a s. 459 petition (now CA 2006, s. 994) alleging that the conduct of the affairs of the company was unfairly prejudicing his interest. It was then virtually agreed that Wyman would buy Mitchell's shares. However, Mitchell was refusing to attend any meetings. As the quorum for both board and general meeting was two, the formal affairs of the company could not proceed (though a manageress was successfully operating the restaurant). Wyman applied to the court for an order under CA 1985 s. 371 calling a general meeting at which he could appoint two additional directors. (The court's power under s.371 is now found in CA 2006, s. 306.)

MERVYN DAVIES J: So it is that the parties are virtually agreed on a sale of the Mitchell shares, and yet the s. 459 petition cannot be said to be disposed of. In the meantime, it is said that the company is without any effective board or the possibility of any effective company meeting. Thus, on 29 April 1991 Mr Wyman convened a board meeting for 2 May. The meeting was to consider the management of the restaurant pending the outcome of the petition, to appoint a Mr Gold and a Mr Wilkinson as additional directors and a requisition for an extraordinary general meeting. The meeting was abortive because Mr Mitchell did not attend so there was no quorum. There was then an attempt to hold an extraordinary general meeting. By notice dated 22 May 1991, notice of an extraordinary general meeting was given for 13 June. The purpose was to appoint Messrs Gold and Wilkinson as directors. Mr Mitchell did not attend, and so the proposed appointments could not be considered; there being no quorum.

It is in these circumstances that Mr Wyman makes his s. 371 application to the effect that the court order a company meeting for the purpose of appointing two additional directors; and that the court direct that if Mr Wyman finds himself alone at the meeting he alone will be deemed to constitute a 'meeting'. Thus, the quorum difficulty hitherto experienced will be overcome. In this way, it may be that the company will have a board of four so that effective control of the company can resume. In this way too, it may well be that Mr Mitchell will be removed as a director.

The difficulty, as I see it, arises from the fact that (a) it may be proper to use s. 371 to overcome the difficulty of achieving a quorum, but (b) it is not a proper use of s. 371 to use it indirectly to secure the removal of a director while a s. 459 petition is pending. As to (a), see *Re H.R. Paul & Son Ltd* (1974) 118 SJ 166, and *Re Opera Photographic Ltd* [1989] 1 WLR 634. In those cases, apart from other differences with this case, there was not the complication of a subsisting s. 459 petition.

I start from the basis that here there is no effective board of the company. Mr Weaver QC, for Mr Wyman, drew attention to the need for there to be an effective board pending disposal of the petition. But, he said, the relations between the two directors have broken down. They are at loggerheads. Mr Mitchell has adopted the tactic of absenting himself from meetings. Mr Weaver said the need for a board was there, despite the fact that the restaurant is managed by the manageress, with Mr Langham [a person agreed to by the two sides] authorised to sign cheques required in the course of business . . .

I turn to the consideration of the discretion conferred by s. 371. It seems to me that discretion ought to be exercised so as to enable an effective board to be brought into being. It cannot be right that Mr Mitchell's quorum tactics should be allowed to stop the company having its accounts, VAT difficulties, etc. dealt with. It may be many months before the s. 459 petition is heard. On the other hand, it would not be right for Mr Wyman, by using s. 371 for the purposes of constituting an effective board, to be given the opportunity of harming Mr Mitchell, e.g. by causing him to be dismissed as a director, or by being excluded from any participation in the affairs of the company pending the outcome of the petition proceedings.

I think the right course to take is to accede to [the application], but to qualify the order in this way. The order will provide that any director appointed pursuant to the order will be restrained from acting as such director, unless and until there is delivered to Mr Mitchell's solicitors an undertaking signed by the director to the effect that, pending the outcome of the s. 459 petition proceedings, he will not (a) at any meeting vote in such fashion as to dismiss Mr Mitchell from his directorship, or to exclude him from his rights and duties as such director, or to diminish such rights or duties in any way, and (b) interfere with Mr Mitchell's day-to-day conduct of the restaurant business so long as Mr Mitchell conducts such business as he has done in the past, and (c) vote to effect any alteration in the constitution or capital of the company.

7.4 VOTING

As typified by Table A, 1985, art. 58, voting may be by show of hands, or on request to the chairman, by poll, in which case each member receives one vote per share. (Some companies, however, have different classes of shares which give a privileged class more votes per share than the ordinary shares.) Voting is by ordinary resolution when a resolution is passed by a simple majority, that is, by an affirmative vote of at least 50 per cent plus one vote of those voting. In the case of a special resolution it is passed by an affirmative vote of at least 75 per cent. These percentages are of those attending and voting in person or by proxy and not as a percentage of all of the members or the votes that could possibly be cast. This voting pattern leads to the important principle of majority rule, a principle which leaves minorities in a weak position. It will be noted though that a shareholder holding more than 25 per cent of the votes would have 'negative control' enabling a special resolution to be blocked.

COMPANIES ACT 2006, S. 284

284. Votes: general rules

(1) On a vote on a written resolution—
    (a) in the case of a company having a share capital, every member has one vote in respect of each share or each £10 of stock held by him, and
    (b) in any other case, every member has one vote.
(2) On a vote on a resolution on a show of hands at a meeting—
    (a) every member present in person has one vote, and
    (b) every proxy present who has been duly appointed by a member entitled to vote on the resolution has one vote.
(3) On a vote on a resolution on a poll taken at a meeting—
    (a) in the case of a company having a share capital, every member has one vote in respect of each share or each £10 of stock held by him, and
    (b) in any other case, every member has one vote.
(4) The provisions of this section have effect subject to any provision of the company's articles.

Northern Counties Securities Ltd v *Jackson & Steeple Ltd*

Directors voting in different capacities

[1974] 2 All ER 625, [1974] 1 WLR 1133, Chancery Division

The judgment includes some useful dicta confirming that though directors voting on the board owe a fiduciary obligation to the company, when voting as shareholders in general meeting they owe no such obligation and may exercise their right to vote, a usual right to property, as they think fit and in their own interest.

WALTON J: Counsel for the plaintiffs argued that, in effect, there are two separate sets of persons in whom authority to activate the company itself resides. Quoting the well-known passages from Lord Haldane in *Lennard's Carrying Co. Ltd* v *Asiatic Petroleum Co. Ltd* [1915] AC 705 he submitted that the company as such was only a juristic figment of the imagination, lacking both a body to be kicked and a soul to be damned. From this it followed that there must be some one or more human persons who did, as a matter of fact, act on behalf of the company, and whose act therefore must, for all practical purposes, be the acts of the company itself. The first of such bodies was clearly the body of directors, to whom under most forms of articles (see art. 80 of Table A [art. 70 in the 1985 version of Table A], or art. 36 of the defendant company's articles which is in similar form) the management of the business of the company is expressly delegated. Therefore, their acts are the company's acts; and if they do not, in the present instance, cause the company to comply with the undertakings given by it to the court, they are themselves liable for contempt of court.' . . .

. . . I think that in a nutshell the distinction is this. When a director votes as a director for or against any particular resolution in a directors' meeting, he is voting as a person under a fiduciary duty to the company for the proposition that the company should take a certain course of action. When a shareholder is voting for or against a particular resolution he is voting as a person owing no fiduciary duty to the company who is exercising his own right of property to vote as he thinks fit. The fact that the result of the voting at the meeting (or a subsequent poll) will bind the company cannot affect the position that in voting he is voting simply as an exercise of his own property rights.

Perhaps another (and simpler) way of putting the matter is that a director is an agent, who casts his vote to decide in what manner his principal shall act through the collective agency of the board of directors; a shareholder who casts his vote in general meeting is not casting it as an agent of the company in any shape or form. His act, therefore, in voting as he pleases cannot in any way be regarded as an act of the company.

7.5 WRITTEN RESOLUTIONS OF PRIVATE COMPANIES

The reality of practice in private companies contrasts strongly with that in large public companies. In the case of a private company, most, if not all of the shares will be voted if there is a contentious issue at a general meeting. An actual majority of the shares is, therefore, probably necessary to control the company. (A minority interest is thus worth proportionately little as it carries no management control and is probably unsaleable.) In a large public company where shares are held by many thousands of passive shareholders who may not cast their votes at general meetings, a substantial minority holding of shares, perhaps as low as 10 per cent or 15 per cent, may control the general meeting, and the composition of the board.

Public companies carry out the formal requirements of general meetings to the letter, sending out formal notices and going through all the motions of the meeting, at which the only item of interest is probably the refreshments afterwards. Private companies generally do not bother to hold general meetings. As the members and the directors are the same people, they may not distinguish in their own minds between meetings of directors and of shareholders. They just concentrate on running the business. However, when there is a formal transaction to enter into, such as opening a bank account, borrowing money from the bank, or issuing a mortgage, then formalities are necessary.

If a general meeting is held, it is common for all members to attend the meeting, and to sign the minutes stating that they dispense with due notice of the meeting. Where the outcome of the meeting is clear, it is normal for somebody such as the solicitor or accountant to draw up formal minutes before the meeting which all of the shareholders then sign. However, the shareholders may sometimes pass a resolution without actually holding a meeting. It is an important principle of company law that the unanimous assent of all the members to an *intra vires* matter is binding on the company, even where a special resolution would otherwise be required (see the following case). It is only where the views of a minority member are to be overridden that the formal process of notification and a meeting is necessary to pass a resolution. Thus, if the members are all directors and the board of directors unanimously resolve on a matter, this amounts to the unanimous decision of the company as if it were in general meeting.

Articles such as Table A, 1985, art. 53 have long permitted the members to transact business by written resolution. However, as part of a move towards de-regulation of private companies, the government introduced in the Companies Act 1989 a new provision, which specifically enabled private companies to make unanimous resolutions in writing and so to dispense with a meeting. The current law is now found in CA 2006, Part 13, Chapter 2, from which brief extracts appear below. The major reform found in CA 2006, s. 292(2) is that a written resolution does not now have to be unanimous. Thus a member can be outvoted without the right to being heard at a meeting, though there is now a right to have circulated to members a short statement on the issues concerned.

Cane v Jones

Unanimity of members is sovereign

[1981] 1 All ER 533, [1980] 1 WLR 1451, Chancery Division

This case indicates that the unanimous assent of all the members may be effective to alter or override articles of association. The procedural safeguards of a special resolution are only necessary where not all of the members assent to the alteration.

Facts   This case concerned a family company, Kingsway Petrol Station Ltd, set up in 1946 by two brothers, Percy and Harold Jones. Percy and his offspring held half the shares and Harold and his offspring held the other half. However, the articles gave the chairman a casting vote on the board and in general meeting. So as not to disturb the equal balance of control between each side of the family, a written agreement was signed by all shareholders in 1967 which stated that the chairman should not exercise the casting vote. When the family later came to blows, Percy's side successfully claimed that the 1967 agreement was effective to override the articles and restrict the use of the chairman's casting vote.

MICHAEL WHEELER QC (sitting as a deputy High Court judge): The position now is therefore that both sides agree that Percy and Harold are the only two directors. Percy's side claim that *he* is the chairman with the casting vote, but Harold's side claim that there is no chairman's casting vote, or alternatively that there is no chairman.

Now as to the arguments about the effect of the 1967 agreement. Counsel for the plaintiff contends that it operated as an alteration of the articles on what was conveniently called in argument 'the *Duomatic* principle' based on *Re Duomatic Ltd* [1969] 2 Ch 365, and the principle is, I think, conveniently summarised in a short passage in the judgment of Buckley J in that case, [1969] 2 Ch 365 at p. 373, where he says:

    . . . I proceed on the basis that where it can be shown that all shareholders who have a right to attend and vote at a general meeting of the company assent to some matter which a general meeting of the company could carry into effect, that assent is as binding as a resolution in general meeting would be.

Applying that principle to the present case, counsel for the plaintiff says that the agreement of all the shareholders embodied in the 1967 agreement had the effect, so far as requisite, of overriding the articles. In other words, it operated to deprive the chairman for the time being of the right to use his casting vote except, perhaps, in so far as an independent chairman contemplated by clause 1 might need to do. I should add here that it is quite clear that Percy, who was actually chairman of the company at the time, was well aware of the terms of the 1967 agreement.

For the first and third defendants, counsel has two answers to counsel's argument for the plaintiff: first, that on its true interpretation in relation to a special or extraordinary resolution the *Duomatic* principle only applies if there has been (i) a resolution and (ii) a meeting; and that here he says, with some truth, there was neither a resolution nor a meeting of the four shareholders; second, he stresses that the agreement does not in terms purport to alter the articles at all . . .

The first of counsel's two arguments for the first and third defendants (namely that there must be a 'resolution' and a 'meeting') does not appear to have been raised in any of the three reported cases which were concerned with special or extraordinary resolutions. But it is not an argument to which I would readily accede because in my judgment it would create a wholly artificial and unnecessary distinction between those powers which can, and those which cannot, be validly exercised by all the corporators acting together.

For my part I venture to differ from counsel for the first and third defendants on the first limb of his argument, namely that articles can *only* be altered by special resolution. In my judgment, s. 10 of the Act is merely laying down a procedure whereby *some only* of the shareholders can validly alter the articles; and, if, as I believe to be the case, it is a basic principle of company law that all the corporators, acting together, can do anything which is *intra vires* the company, then I see nothing in s. 10 to undermine this principle. I accept that the principle requires all the corporators to 'act together'; but with regard to this I respectfully adopt what Astbury J said in *Parker and Cooper Ltd* v *Reading* [1926] Ch 975 at p. 984:

> Now the view I take of both these decisions [*Re Express Engineering Works Ltd* [1920] 1 Ch 466 and *Re George Newman & Co.* [1895] 1 Ch 674] is that where the transaction is *intra vires* and honest, and especially if it is for the benefit of the company, it cannot be upset if the assent of all the corporators is given to it. I do not think it matters in the least whether that assent is given at different times or simultaneously.

Some light is also, I think, thrown on the problem by s. 143(4) of the 1948 Act. Section 143 deals with the forwarding to the Registrar of Companies of copies of every resolution or agreement to which the section applies, and subs. (4) reads as follows:

> This section shall apply to—(a) special resolutions; (b) extraordinary resolutions; (c) resolutions which have been agreed to by all the members of a company, but which, if not so agreed to, would not have been effective for their purpose unless, as the case may be, they had been passed as special resolutions or as extraordinary resolutions.

It may be, as counsel for the plaintiff suggested, that a document which is framed as an agreement can be treated as a 'resolution' for the purposes of para. (c). (I should add in passing that a copy of the 1967 agreement was never, as far as I am aware, sent to the Registrar of Companies for registration.) It may be that there is a gap in the registration requirements of s. 143. But be that as it may, the fact that the 1967 agreement was drafted as an agreement and not as a resolution, and that the four signatories did not sign in each other's presence does not in my view prevent that agreement overriding *pro tanto*, and so far as necessary, the articles of the company; in my judgment counsel for the first and third defendants' first argument fails and unless he can show that the 1967 agreement has been superseded, the chairman of the company has no casting vote at board or general meetings.

COMPANIES ACT 2006, PART 13, CHAPTER 2

288. Written resolutions of private companies

(1) In the Companies Acts a "written resolution" means a resolution of a private company proposed and passed in accordance with this Chapter.

(2) The following may not be passed as a written resolution—
   (a) a resolution under section 168 removing a director before the expiration of his period of office;
   (b) a resolution under section 510 removing an auditor before the expiration of his term of office.

(3) A resolution may be proposed as a written resolution—
   (a) by the directors of a private company (see section 291), or
   (b) by the members of a private company (see sections 292 to 295).

(4) References in enactments passed or made before this Chapter comes into force to—
   (a) a resolution of a company in general meeting, or
   (b) a resolution of a meeting of a class of members of the company, have effect as if they included references to a written resolution of the members, or of a class of members, of a private company (as appropriate).

(5) A written resolution of a private company has effect as if passed (as the case may be)—
   (a) by the company in general meeting, or
   (b) by a meeting of a class of members of the company,
   and references in enactments passed or made before this section comes into force to a meeting at which a resolution is passed or to members voting in favour of a resolution shall be construed accordingly.

291. Circulation of written resolutions proposed by directors

(1) This section applies to a resolution proposed as a written resolution by the directors of the company.

(2) The company must send or submit a copy of the resolution to every eligible member.

292. Members' power to require circulation of written resolution

(1) The members of a private company may require the company to circulate a resolution that may properly be moved and is proposed to be moved as a written resolution.

(2) Any resolution may properly be moved as a written resolution unless—
   (a) it would, if passed, be ineffective (whether by reason of inconsistency with any enactment or the company's constitution or otherwise),
   (b) it is defamatory of any person, or
   (c) it is frivolous or vexatious.

(3) Where the members require a company to circulate a resolution they may require the company to circulate with it a statement of not more than 1,000 words on the subject matter of the resolution.

299. Publication of written resolution on website

(1) This section applies where a company sends—
   (a) a written resolution, or
   (b) a statement relating to a written resolution, to a person by means of a website.

(2) The resolution or statement is not validly sent for the purposes of this Chapter unless the resolution is available on the website throughout the period beginning with the circulation date and ending on the date on which the resolution lapses under section 297.

7.6 DEREGULATION OF PRIVATE COMPANIES

For some time governments have been anxious to reduce the burden of regulations particularly on small companies. Unnecessary red tape and bureaucracy reduce the economic efficiency of business and of the economy. Abolition of the statutory audit for many companies with a small turnover is a recent practical example (see 16.2.2).

One of the earlier reports preparatory to this policy was the white paper, *Lifting the Burden*, since when, as has been seen, it has become a dominant theme of company law reform.

Lifting the Burden
(Cmnd 9571) (London: HMSO, 1985)

1.7 On . . . deregulation, the government believe that despite considerable efforts to get the balance right the scales are still tipped too far against business. For the best of motives, regulations have grown over the years to a stage where many of them are too heavy a drain on our national resources. To the extent that regulations go further than necessary, they will lower profits for firms or raise prices, or both. Output and employment will tend to be lower. Regulations can also stifle competition and deter new firms from entering the market or prevent others from expanding. Too many people in central and local government spend too much of their time regulating the activities of others. Some regulations were framed a century and more ago, have been added to or amended, and now bear little relevance to the modern business world. Other regulations are too complex and confusing even to professional advisers (and sometimes to the people who administer them, too). Many regulations are necessary and it is, of course, government's responsibility to ensure that flexibility and freedom are not abused by those who would flout the proper interests of customers, consumers and employees. We must maintain our quality of life. But we have to strike the right balance.

Modernising Company Law: The White Paper
(London: DTI, July 2002. CM 5553)

The effort to deregulate and to lift the burden of unnecessary procedural formalities from private companies came to a head in the recent reforms of company law. Now that you have worked through some of the key sections of the new law, the following passages from the White Paper give you further background and explanation as to how some of the reforms were arrived at. It starts by mentioning the need for new 'Table A' model articles for both private and public companies.

2 Improving Governance: Shareholders and Decision-making

New Model Constitutions for Private and Public Companies

2.4 The Review considered the current model articles for companies limited by shares (widely known as Table A) to be out of date and unnecessarily complex. It recommended that separate model constitutions be prepared in simpler, clearer language for public and private companies, recognising their different needs. It also proposed a number of changes of substance. An illustrative draft of the model constitution for private companies limited by shares was included in the Review's Final Report.

2.5 The Government agrees with the recommendations of the Review, and intends to provide separate new model constitutions for private and public companies with the Bill. As the Review noted, it is not possible to draft a definitive model constitution until the Bill itself has been fully prepared.

Members' Decisions—Meetings and Resolutions

2.6 One of the purposes of company law is to create a framework within which a company can take decisions. The division of powers between the members and the directors is a matter partly for statute and partly for the company's constitution. A typical arrangement, reflected in Table A (regulation 70) is that, 'subject to the provisions of the Act, the memorandum and articles, and to any directions given by special resolution, the business of the company shall be managed by the directors, who shall exercise all the powers of the company'. But it is open to the company's constitution to provide for members to retain more powers in their own hands. There are some powers—for instance to amend the company's constitution—which are reserved by statute to the members.

2.7 With very few exceptions, the Act is not concerned with the way in which directors' decisions are taken. This is a matter for the constitution and the common law. But statute contains detailed provision on how members may take decisions, and those provisions apply in some cases in default of, and in others to the exclusion of, provisions in the company's constitution.

2.8 The main, and until recently the only way provided in statute for members to take decisions has been the general meeting. All companies were required by law to hold an Annual General Meeting (AGM) every year, and could hold additional general meetings known as Extraordinary General Meetings (EUMs). Members' decisions generally took the form of resolutions passed at those meetings—although it was common for companies' articles to provide for a written resolution procedure, which required unanimity (see Table A, regulation 53). In addition, the common law unanimous consent rule operated to enable certain decisions to be taken unanimously, without recourse to the statutory or constitutional procedures.

2.9 In the Companies Act 1989 private companies were given the opportunity of opting out of the obligation to hold AGMs. It also established a written procedure by which resolutions may be passed by members of private companies without a meeting if they are approved unanimously (see paragraphs 2.26–30). This applies notwithstanding any provision contained in their articles enabling them to do so. It does not affect the operation of the common law unanimous consent rule.

Meetings

2.10 At present, the general rule is that companies must hold an AGM at least once every calendar year, and may hold other meetings—EGMs—as required. Private companies may dispense with AGMs, but only if all the members agree.

2.11 The Bill will remove the requirement for private companies to hold AGMs. It will also remove the requirements to lay the accounts and re-appoint the auditors annually at a general meeting (usually the AGM). Most private companies will therefore no longer be automatically obliged to hold AGMs which are, for most of them, an unnecessary formality that carries out no business of substance.

. . .

2.13 For public companies, the requirement to hold an AGM is to be retained . . .

2.14 For all companies we propose to retain the power for a sufficient body of the members to require the directors to call an EGM. We also propose to retain the power of the court to order a meeting, on an application from the company itself, a director or a member.

. . .

2.18 It is not always convenient for members to attend an AGM or EGM. The Government believes that it is important that even when they cannot attend a general meeting members should be able to exercise their rights, for example by giving instructions in advance to a proxy. Accordingly the Government proposes to enhance the existing powers of proxies so that in future any proxy for a shareholder will be able to speak, vote on a show of hands as well as on a poll, and join with others in demanding a poll. In addition the Government accepts the Review's recommendation that companies should also be able to allow members directly to demand a poll in advance of a meeting and vote on that poll without needing to attend or appoint a proxy. The maximum threshold for demanding a poll will remain at five members entitled to vote or 10 per cent of the votes, whichever is the lower.

2.19 In line with the Review's recommendations, we also propose a new right for a sufficient body of members to require a scrutiny of any poll. The scrutiny would cover the activity both of the company and its registrar, and examine the procedure for establishing the admissibility of votes and proxies, the voting procedure and the procedure for counting votes. The scrutiny would be conducted by a registered auditor, though not necessarily the company's own auditor, and the object would be to give an opinion on whether the procedure for the recording and counting of proxies and votes was adequate to ensure that the statement of votes cast was accurately stated. The scrutiny would have to be completed within a month of the meeting and the scrutineer's report sent to the members.

Resolution

2.20 At present, an ordinary resolution proposed at a meeting may be passed by a majority of those members present and voting. Special and extraordinary resolutions require a majority of at least three quarters of the votes cast on the resolution.

2.21 As recommended by the Review, the Bill will effectively abolish the extraordinary reso-lution as a separate category. Where the Act requires an extraordinary resolution and an enhanced majority is justified, we propose to replace it with a requirement for a special resolution. Where the constitution of an existing company requires an extraordinary resolution, we propose that this should be understood in future as a requirement for a special resolution.

2.22 We propose to replace the present minimum notice period of 21 days for both special and extraordinary resolutions with one of 14 days for special resolutions, bringing it into line with our proposal for the minimum notice for general meetings (see paragraphs 2.16–17 above).

2.23 In two specific cases—the removal of a director and the removal or non-reappointment of an auditor—the present law provides for a special procedure requiring notice to be given to the person affected. We propose to retain similar provisions.

2.24 The Government also proposes to retain the right of a sufficient body of members to require the directors to circulate a members' resolution to an AGM and to circulate a members' statement relating to any resolution to any general meeting. At present, the circulation of such material is at the members' expense. The Review proposed, and the Government agrees, that in future mem-bers' resolutions and statements received in time to be circulated with the notice of the meeting should be circulated to all members at the company's expense.

2.25 The Government also believes that the requirement on companies to register all special resolutions at Companies House, together with certain other specified categories of resolution, should be retained.

Written Resolutions

2.26 The Act assumed that the formal general meeting was the principal, if not the only, means by which members take decisions. In 1989, a statutory written procedure was introduced for pri-vate companies, to be used where there is unanimity among the members. This requirement for unanimity means that many small companies must hold a general meeting even where the large majority of members is content to reach a decision without one. The Government agrees with the Review that this is an undesirable and unnecessary regulatory burden on private companies.

2.27 The draft Bill therefore provides a procedure whereby private companies may pass a writ-ten ordinary resolution with a simple majority of the eligible votes and a written special resolution with 75 per cent of the eligible votes. We believe that this reform will enable most small compan-ies to make decisions quickly and efficiently. This step, combined with the proposal to remove the requirement for private companies to hold AGMs (see paragraph 2.11 above), will relieve many small companies from the burden of having to hold formal general meetings.

2.28 The Government's aim has been to maintain the simplicity of the current written procedure while also ensuring that all members receive adequate information about written resolutions. In particular, we believe that companies should send proposed resolutions to all members at the same time, as far as is practicable. While it will be possible for a resolution to be agreed by the requisite majority before some of the members have seen the resolution, the Bill is designed to give full information to all members entitled to take part in the decision-making process and to prevent companies from deliberately excluding some members.

2.29 The Act allows many of the most important communications between companies and their members to be made electronically. All types of electronic communication covered by the Electronic Communications Act 2000 are permitted, where there is agreement between the company and the member. In particular, such communications need not be in legible form or even capable of being reduced to legible form; the company and the member may agree to oral communication, for example, for giving notice of meetings or the appointment of proxies.

2.30 However, the Government believes that to allow such flexibility for written resolutions would undermine the simplicity of the process. The legislation has, therefore, been drafted to allow electronic communications to be used only where the resolution can be received in legible form, or a form (agreed between a company and the member in question) which can be converted by the recipient into legible form. For example, a resolution may be proposed through an e-mail, text on a website or a text message on a mobile phone, but not through an oral telephone call, an audio file on a website or by sending an audiotape.

Unanimous Consent

2.31 One other way in which a company can take decisions, which is recognised in common law rather than in statute, is through the unanimous consent rule. The rule is of particular use to small companies, which often act informally, as it prevents many unanimous decisions of their members being invalidated through a mere procedural irregularity.

2.32 The Review considered two questions on the unanimous consent rule. Should the effect of the common law rule be preserved? If so, should it be codified in statute? The Review strongly recommended preservation of the rule, and, while the majority of those consulted were against codification, it recommended that the rule should be codified.

2.33 The Government agrees that the rule should be preserved. It clearly provides a useful and informal way for small companies to take decisions.

2.34 The Government has explored possible methods for codifying the rule. However, this further work has tended to suggest that the benefits of codification (clarity and certainty) would be outweighed by the disadvantages that would result from loss of flexibility. We would have to specify how the rule applied to every particular provision both in the Bill and in other legislation relating to company decision-making, rather than applying, as the courts can, broader principles based upon what is just and equitable.

2.35 As a result codification would probably not mean, as the Review hoped, a clarification and extension of the rule. Instead the Government believes it would risk leading to rigidity and restrictions. In addition, a number of the formal decision-making processes in the Bill have set timetables which activate related requirements. In order to codify any rule in such a case, the codification would need to make it absolutely clear when unanimity is first achieved. This would mean that every member would have to positively agree, rather than merely acquiesce by doing nothing. This would reduce the scope of the current rule, where acquiescence by doing nothing might in some circumstances be permitted. We believe companies benefit from this flexibility. Moreover, the Bill will afford companies a simple and convenient decision-making mechanism in the new written procedure. Accordingly, while we agree that it is essential to preserve the common law rule, we do not propose to codify it.

8

The Board of Directors

A company as such is an artificial person; an abstract creation of the law. There must be some organ or agent to act on behalf of the company. The powers of management must either be given to the board of directors or the shareholders in general meeting. The starting-point is the articles of association which determine which organ has the powers of management (*Automatic Self-Cleansing Filter Syndicate Co. Ltd* v *Cuninghame* [1906] 2 Ch 34). However, some functions are reserved by the Companies Acts to either the general meeting or the board, e.g., the power to alter the articles is specially reserved to the general meeting under CA 2006, s. 21, and the duty to prepare annual accounts is reserved to the board of directors under CA 2006, s. 399.

8.1 SEPARATION OF POWERS

Subject to the Companies Acts, a company may adopt any form of articles to distribute the powers of management. In most cases, a standard article (similar to the former art. 70 of Table A, 1985) is adopted, or as we have seen in chapter 6, it may apply automatically under CA 2006, s. 20(1). Under art. 70, the general powers of management are given to the board of directors. This is likely to remain the same under the new model articles of association under the CA 2006. For many years, even before 1985, the former art. 70 was used by most companies, and is the one litigated in all the leading cases.

TABLE A, ART. 70

70. Subject to the provisions of the Act, the memorandum and the articles and to any directions given by special resolution, the business of the company shall be managed by the directors who may exercise all the powers of the company. No alteration of the memorandum or articles and no such direction shall invalidate any prior act of the directors which would have been valid if that alteration had not been made or that direction had not been given. The powers given by this regulation shall not be limited by any special power given to the directors by the articles and a meeting of directors at which a quorum is present may exercise all powers exercisable by the directors.

The former art. 70 is expressed to be subject to the articles of association, the Companies Acts, and any special resolution. Thus under art. 70, shareholders in general meeting can interfere with the business of the board only by special resolution. But otherwise in the absence of contrary provisions in the articles, the

Companies Acts or any special resolution, the board of directors generally has the power to act on behalf of the company in running the business.

Article 70 replaced art. 80 of the 1948 Table A which still applies to many companies. This provided that the business of the company should be managed by the directors who may exercise all the powers of the company subject to such 'regulations' (not being inconsistent with the provisions of the articles) as may be prescribed by the company in general meeting. Questions arose, however, as to whether the shareholders in general meeting have a general power to interfere with the board's power by ordinary resolution. There has been much judicial and academic discussion on this issue (see, e.g., *John Shaw & Sons (Salford) Ltd* v *Shaw* [1935] 2 KB 113, CA; *Marshall's Valve Gear Co. Ltd* v *Manning Wardle & Co. Ltd* [1909] 1 Ch 267; Goldberg (1970) 33 MLR 177; Sullivan (1977) 93 LQR 569; MacKenzie (1983) 4 Co Law 99) and it has more recently been considered by Harman J in the following case.

Breckland Group Holdings Ltd v London & Suffolk Properties Ltd
Limiting interference by the shareholders
[1989] BCLC 100, Chancery Division

In this case, Harman J declined to follow *Marshall's Valve Gear Co. Ltd* v *Manning Wardle & Co. Ltd* [1909] 1 Ch 267 even though the facts of it were very similar to that case. Thus, whether a company adopts art. 80 of the 1948 Table A or art. 70 of the 1985 Table A, it is now settled that the general meeting can only interfere with the board's exercise of the power of management by special resolution.

It should be noted that the power to litigate is one of the general powers of management; i.e., it is vested in the board of directors. Thus, its exercise by the directors cannot be controlled by the members in general meeting by ordinary resolution (*John Shaw & Sons (Salford) Ltd* v *Shaw* [1935] 2 KB 113, CA). Harman J has clearly rejected the view taken in *Marshall's Valve Gear Co. Ltd* v *Manning Wardle & Co. Ltd* [1909] 1 Ch 267 that the general meeting could institute proceedings by ordinary resolution on behalf of the company if the directors neglected or refused to do so.

Facts   London & Suffolk Properties Ltd was controlled by two companies, Breckland Group Holdings Ltd and Crompton Enterprises Ltd. Proceedings were started by Crompton in the name of London & Suffolk against Avery who was the principal shareholder of Breckland and the managing director of London & Suffolk. The action was commenced without a board resolution of London & Suffolk. A board meeting of London & Suffolk was fixed for 3 August at which a resolution was to be proposed to adopt and ratify the action. Breckland successfully sought, inter alia, an injunction restraining Crompton from further pursuing the action.

HARMAN J: The question whether articles of association in the form of art. 80, which applies to this company, are such as to allow a general meeting to give directions to directors about the conduct of the business of a company has long been known to be a vexed subject. The decision of Jessel MR, one of the greatest of all equity judges, in *Pender* v *Lushington* (1877) 6 ChD 70, is as always with that great judge, trenchant, clear and to the point. He firmly holds that in that case he ought not, there being an action started without any proper authorisation on behalf of the company, to strike out the name of the company on the ground that the action was unauthorised, but he ought to stand the matter over to let a general meeting be called to decide whether the company's name was to be used or not. However, that matter does not appear to have turned on the terms of the articles of association there, and I cannot find in the citation of facts in the report of that case any reference to an article in terms anything like art. 80 in this case.

There is then the well-known decision of Neville J in *Marshall's Valve Gear Co. Ltd* v *Manning Wardle & Co. Ltd* [1909] 1 Ch 267, where he purported to distinguish *Automatic Self-Cleansing Filter Syndicate Co. Ltd* v *Cuninghame* [1906] 2 Ch 34, and decided, in a case where there was an article in almost precisely the same terms as art. 80, that the general meeting was entitled to decide what should be done about an action brought without due authority. That decision was reached in November 1908, and in December of that same year *Salmon* v *Quin & Axtens Ltd* [1909] 1 Ch 311 came before a two-judge Court of Appeal with distinguished members sitting, Cozens-Hardy MR and Farwell LJ. In that case the argument seeking to upset the decision below included a straight attack on the *Marshall's Valve Gear* case. It was said to be distinguishable because there was a matter of personal interest involved, but also that Neville J had taken his view inconsistently with the principles in the *Automatic Self-Cleansing Filter* case. The judgment of Farwell LJ, who delivered the first judgment, sets the matter out very clearly, and particularly adopts the observations of Buckley LJ in *Gramophone and Typewriter Ltd* v *Stanley* [1908] 2 KB 89 at p. 105 (see [1909] 1 Ch 311 at p. 319). Farwell LJ held that the resolutions to be proposed to a general meeting were inconsistent with art. 80. It was an attempt to alter the terms of the contract constituted by the articles by a simple resolution instead of by a special resolution. Farwell LJ went on to say that the case was entirely governed, if not by the decision, at any rate by the reasoning of the Lords Justices in the *Automatic Self-Cleansing* case, and he cited Buckley LJ in *Gramophone and Typewriter Ltd* v *Stanley* [1908] 2 KB 89 at pp. 105–6:

> . . . even a resolution of a numerical majority at a general meeting of the company cannot impose its will upon the directors when the articles have confided to them the control of the company's affairs. The directors are not servants to obey directions given by the shareholders as individuals; they are not agents appointed by and bound to serve the shareholders as their principals. They are persons who may by the regulations be entrusted with the control of the business, and if so entrusted they can be dispossessed from that control only by the statutory majority which can alter the articles.

Farwell LJ went on to say ([1909] 1 Ch 311 at pp. 319–20):

> Any other construction might, I think, be disastrous, because it might lead to an interference by a bare majority very inimical to the interests of the minority who had come into a company on the footing that the business should be managed by the board of directors.

That sentence appears to me to be directly applicable to what has happened in this particular case. The decision in *Salmon* v *Quin & Axtens Ltd* was approved by the House of Lords sub nom. *Quin & Axtens Ltd* v *Salmon* [1909] AC 442 without the respondents even being called on, and Lord Loreburn LC delivered an unreserved short judgment saying ([1909] AC 442 at p. 443):

> The bargain made between the shareholders is contained in arts 75 and 80 of the articles of association, and it amounts for the purpose in hand to this, that the directors should manage the business; and the company, therefore, are not to manage the business unless there is provision to that effect.

Lord Macnaghten went so far as to say that he thought the judgment of the Court of Appeal was perfectly right (at p. 444). That encomium on Farwell LJ's judgment is one which many would have been glad to have had for themselves from such a source.

Thus one has in my view observations which are not stated to be expressly overruling Neville J's decision but are inevitably wholly in conflict with it. I would cite only briefly also the well-known decision in *John Shaw & Sons (Salford) Ltd* v *Shaw* [1935] 2 KB 113 at p. 134, where Greer LJ observed:

> A company is an entity distinct alike from its shareholders and its directors. Some of its powers may, according to its articles, be exercised by directors, certain other powers may be reserved for the shareholders in general meeting. If powers of management are vested in the directors, they and they alone can exercise these powers. The only way in which the general body of the shareholders can control the exercise of the powers vested by the articles in the directors is by altering their articles.

That is entirely to the same effect and is of course a citation from a judge of high authority on the Queen's Bench side of the law.

Thus, as it seems to me, there is little doubt that the law is that, where matters are confided by articles such as art. 80 to the conduct of the business by the directors, it is not a matter where the general meeting can intervene. Counsel for the defendants sought to distinguish the cases by saying that in the cases which have been referred to the directors had come to one decision and the general meeting sought to overrule them and come to an opposite decision. In my belief that factor or distinction which undoubtedly exists is not a distinction which in law affects the principles which I have to try and apply. The principle, as I see it, is that art. 80 confides the management of the business to the directors and in such a case it is not for the general meeting to interfere. It is *a fortiori* when the shareholders coming together have specifically resolved some matters be required to have their joint consent and have confided that matter particularly to the directors. That seems to me to reinforce the general proposition which I derive from the authorities cited.

Thus, as it seems to me, the action was, as is admitted, wrongly brought: it cannot at present be known whether the board will adopt it or ratify it on 3 August. If the board do not adopt it, a general meeting would have no power whatever to override that decision of the board and to adopt it for itself. Thus at the moment there can be no certainty whatever as to what would happen. It seems to me that in those circumstances I ought to restrain further steps in this action pending a decision whether the company will by its proper organ, that is the board, adopt it. It may do so. If so, it will be valid and ratified and adopted from its initiation.

NOTES

1. SPECIFIC POWERS GIVEN TO THE BOARD BY ARTICLES OTHER THAN ONE SIMILAR TO THE FORMER ART. 70

Other than an article similar to the former art. 70, the company may adopt articles which give the board specific powers, e.g., an article (similar to art. 84 of Table A) giving the board the power to appoint one of them to be managing director. In such a case, it seems clear that the power is not subject to any interference by the shareholders in general meeting (*Thomas Logan Ltd v Davis* (1911) 104 LT 914).

2. REVERSION OF POWERS TO THE MEMBERS

If the board is given powers of management but is unable to act, such powers will reside with the general meeting (*Alexander Ward & Co. Ltd v Samyang Navigation Co. Ltd* [1975] 1 WLR 673). To quote Warrington J in *Barron v Potter* [1914] 1 Ch 895:

If directors having certain powers are unable or unwilling to exercise them—are in fact a non-existent body for the purpose—there must be some power in the company to do itself that which under other circumstances would be otherwise done. The directors in the present case being unwilling to appoint additional directors under the power conferred on them by the articles, in my opinion, the company in general meeting has power to make the appointment.

3. EFFECT OF SHAREHOLDERS' AGREEMENT

Whilst the power of management is generally distributed by the company's articles, its actual exercise may be restricted by shareholders' agreements. Thus a shareholders' agreement between all the shareholders may regulate participation in management, the right to be bought out and voluntary liquidation, or may require unanimous decisions on major matters of policy (see 6.6.2).

8.2 DIRECTORS' POWERS TO BIND THE COMPANY

The distribution of management functions as between the general meeting and the board of directors was considered in 8.1. Now it is necessary to consider the circumstances in which the board or individual directors may commit the company to a binding contract. As the board is the management organ, a resolution of the board will generally bind the company. The following paragraphs examine circumstances where a board resolution may possibly not bind the company, and secondly where something less than a board resolution (such as the signature of a single director) may or may not bind the company.

8.2.1 Constitutional limits on the board's powers

The articles of association may limit the powers of the board by, for example, putting an upper limit on the amount it can borrow, or by prohibiting the purchase of land without the approval of the members in general meeting. The question is whether a third party in good faith can rely on a transaction with a company which has not complied with such an article. At common law, the matter has traditionally been dealt with by the rule in *Turquand's* case, the 'internal management rule'. While a third party would have constructive notice of the relevant article, there would be no public document indicating whether an ordinary resolution had been passed. (In contrast, a special resolution has to be filed at the Companies Registry.) It was held in *Turquand's* case that the third party need not enquire whether an ordinary resolution has been obtained as this is a matter of internal management and the company was bound. While *Turquand's* case (extracted below) is itself unmemorable, the rule is still occasionally cited. However, with the possible abolition of constructive notice (see 4.2.6) and the enactment of CA 2006, s. 40, its importance is diminished.

CA 2006, s. 40 (extracted below), implements art. 9(2) of the First Company Law Directive of the EEC (see 5.2.3). Its purpose is to ensure that third parties entering into contracts with a company are protected and are not prejudiced by any limits on the powers of the management organs of the company. Section 40 therefore substantially supplements, even supplants, the protection given by *Turquand's* rule. The section protects a third party dealing with a company in good faith against any 'limitation under the company's constitution' on the power of the board to bind the company or to authorise others to do so. Thus, for example, as in *Turquand's* case, if the board transacts without having obtained the specific approval of the general meeting, the company is bound.

Two points should be noted. First, the section refers to the powers of the board as a whole. It does not apparently cure a limitation on the power of a managing director or a committee of directors, or a mere absence of authority of an individual director. Secondly, the section does not comprehensively spell out what may amount to 'a limitation under the company's constitution'. Subsection (3) does, however, extend the obvious meaning of the company's constitution (i.e., the memorandum and articles) by including resolutions in general meeting and shareholders' agreements. If, for example, a general meeting (relying on an article similar to the former Table A, art. 70) by special resolution directs the board not to buy Russian goods, or if a shareholders' agreement prescribes that land may only be bought with the unanimous agreement of all the members, a contract with a third party in good faith which is in breach of either of these limitations will bind the company.

Royal British Bank v *Turquand*
The internal management rule
(1856) 6 El & Bl 327, Exchequer Chamber

The Court of Exchequer Chamber held that a bond for a sum which required the authorisation of the general meeting by ordinary resolution under the company's constitution was nevertheless valid in favour of a third party as it was entitled to assume that such an authorisation had been obtained, even though in fact it had not.

Facts   The Royal British Bank sued Turquand as the liquidator of a mining and railway company for the repayment of money borrowed on a bond signed by the company's two directors and the secretary under the company seal. The company argued unsuccessfully that the bond was not valid because under its constitution, the directors had power to borrow only such sums as had been authorised by an ordinary resolution of the company, and in this case, no such resolution had been passed.

JERVIS CJ: I am of opinion that the judgment of the Court of Queen's Bench ought to be affirmed. I incline to think that the question which has been principally argued both here and in that court does not necessarily arise, and need not be determined. My impression is (though I will not state it as a fixed opinion) that the resolution set forth in the replication goes far enough to satisfy the requisites of the deed of settlement. The deed allows the directors to borrow on bond such sum or sums of money as shall from time to time, by a resolution passed at a general meeting of the company, be authorised to be borrowed: and the replication shews a resolution, passed at a general meeting, authorising the directors to borrow on bond such sums for such periods and at such rates of interest as they might deem expedient, in accordance with the deed of settlement and the Act of Parliament; but the resolution does not otherwise define the amount to be borrowed. That seems to me enough. If that be so, the other question does not arise. But whether it be so or not we need not decide; for it seems to us that the plea, whether we consider it as a confession and avoidance or a special *non est factum*, does not raise any objection to this advance as against the company. We may now take for granted that the dealings with these companies are not like dealings with other partnerships, and that the parties dealing with them are bound to read the statute and the deed of settlement. But they are not bound to do more. And the party here, on reading the deed of settlement, would find, not a prohibition from borrowing, but a permission to do so on certain conditions. Finding that the authority might be made complete by a resolution, he would have a right to infer the fact of a resolution authorising that which on the face of the document appeared to be legitimately done.

COMPANIES ACT 2006, S. 40

40. Power of directors to bind the company
(1) In favour of a person dealing with a company in good faith, the power of the directors to bind the company, or authorise others to do so, is deemed to be free of any limitation under the company's constitution.
(2) For this purpose—
    (a) a person 'deals with' a company if he is a party to any transaction or other act to which the company is a party;
    (b) a person dealing with a company— (i) is not bound to enquire as to any limitation on the powers of the directors to bind the company or authorise others to do so, (ii) is presumed to have acted in good faith unless the contrary is proved, and (iii) is not to be regarded as acting in bad faith by reason only of his knowing that an act is beyond the powers of the directors under the company's constitution.
(3) The references above to limitations on the directors' power under the company's constitution include limitations deriving—

(a) from a resolution of the company or of any class of shareholders, or

(b) from any agreement between the members of the company or of any class of shareholders.

(4) This section does not affect any right of a member of the company to bring proceedings to restrain the doing of an action that is beyond the powers of the directors. But no such proceedings lie in respect of an act to be done in fulfilment of a legal obligation arising from a previous act of the company.

(5) This section does not affect any liability incurred by the directors, or any other person, by reason of the directors' exceeding their powers.

8.2.2 Transactions by individual directors or committees

Articles of association generally permit delegation of board powers to a committee of directors or to a managing director. This is more fully discussed at 11.5. In theory delegation involves a revocable transfer of powers to the delegate who may in general exercise his or her own discretion as to how those powers are exercised. A managing director in sole charge of running the business is the obvious example.

Practically similar but theoretically distinct is the authorisation of an agent such as a director or employee to act on behalf of the company. Here the agent does not personally assume the relevant power but is wholly accountable to his or her principal, the company, to act as directed by the company and within the authority which the company has conferred. This is merely an aspect of the law of contract which enables an agent authorised by a principal to make a binding contract on behalf of the principal with a third party. Likewise, an individual director or other person may be authorised by the board to act on behalf of the company. Where a director or other agent acts within the actual authority expressly or impliedly conferred on him or her, the company is bound. In the absence of authority the company prima facie is not bound. However, it is an unmeritorious argument for a company to attempt to avoid a contract on grounds that its own director or other agent acted beyond authority. The courts have therefore developed the principle that if the company has held out the agent, or enabled the agent to appear, to be authorised, then the company is bound. In this case, there is said to be 'apparent authority'. Because of the company's action there is the appearance of authority and so it cannot raise the defence that the agent was not actually authorised. The following cases deal with these issues.

Freeman & Lockyer v Buckhurst Park Properties (Mangal) Ltd

Diplock defines apparent authority

[1964] 1 All ER 630, [1964] 2 QB 480, Court of Appeal

Diplock LJ makes clear the distinction between actual authority and apparent (or ostensible) authority. If there is no actual authority the company is not bound. However, exceptionally if the company has represented to a third party that a director is authorised, when the director is not, and the third party has relied upon this, the company may be bound. The company has made the director appear to be authorised; hence 'apparent authority' which in reality is no authority at all.

Facts The defendant company was formed to buy and resell a large estate. The second defendant was never appointed, but acted as, the managing director. He ran the day-to-day affairs of the company on his own. After a deal for the resale of the land had fallen through, the second defendant decided to develop the estate for housing. He engaged the plaintiffs, a firm of architects, to apply for planning permission. The defendant company refused to pay the plaintiffs' fees for this work on the ground that the second defendant had no authority to engage them on behalf of the company. Even though he acted as if he was a managing director he was in fact a mere director with no extended authority. The plaintiffs successfully sued the company for the fees.

DIPLOCK LJ: We are concerned in the present case with the authority of an agent to create contractual rights and liabilities between his principal and a third party whom I will call 'the contractor'. This branch of the law has developed pragmatically rather than logically, owing to the early history of the action of assumpsit and the consequent absence of a general *jus quaesitum tertii* in English law. But it is possible (and for the determination of this appeal I think it is desirable) to restate it on a rational basis. It is necessary at the outset to distinguish between an 'actual' authority of an agent on the one hand, and an 'apparent' or 'ostensible' authority on the other. Actual authority and apparent authority are quite independent of one another. Generally they co-exist and coincide, but either may exist without the other and their respective scopes may be different. As I shall endeavour to show, it is on the apparent authority of the agent that the contractor normally relies in the ordinary course of business when entering into contracts.

An 'actual' authority is a legal relationship between principal and agent created by a consensual agreement to which they alone are parties. Its scope is to be ascertained by applying ordinary principles of construction of contracts, including any proper implications from the express words used, the usages of the trade, or the course of business between the parties. To this agreement the contractor is a stranger; he may be totally ignorant of the existence of any authority on the part of the agent. Nevertheless, if the agent does enter into a contract pursuant to the 'actual' authority, it does create contractual rights and liabilities between the principal and the contractor. It may be that this rule relating to 'undisclosed principals', which is peculiar to English law, can be rationalised as avoiding circuity of action, for the principal could in equity compel the agent to lend his name in an action to enforce the contract against the contractor, and would at common law be liable to indemnify the agent in respect of the performance of the obligations assumed by the agent under the contract.

An 'apparent' or 'ostensible' authority, on the other hand, is a legal relationship between the principal and the contractor created by a representation, made by the principal to the contractor, intended to be and in fact acted on by the contractor, that the agent has authority to enter on behalf of the principal into a contract of a kind within the scope of the 'apparent' authority, so as to render the principal liable to perform any obligations imposed on him by such contract. To the relationship so created the agent is a stranger. He need not be (although he generally is) aware of the existence of the representation. The representation, when acted on by the contractor by entering into a contract with the agent, operates as an estoppel, preventing the principal from asserting that he is not bound by the contract. It is irrelevant whether the agent had actual authority to enter into the contract.

In ordinary business dealings the contractor at the time of entering into the contract can in the nature of things hardly ever rely on the 'actual' authority of the agent. His information as to the authority must be derived either from the principal or from the agent or from both, for they alone know what the agent's actual authority is. All that the contractor can know is what they tell him, which may or may not be true. In the ultimate analysis he relies either on the representation of the principal, i.e., apparent authority, or on the representation of the agent, i.e., warranty of authority. The representation which creates 'apparent' authority may take a variety of forms of which the commonest is representation by conduct, i.e., by permitting the agent to act in some way in the conduct of the principal's business with other persons. By so doing the principal represents to anyone who becomes aware that the agent is so acting that the agent has authority to enter on behalf of the principal into contracts with other persons of the kind which an agent so acting in the conduct of his principal's business has normally 'actual' authority to enter into.

In applying the law, as I have endeavoured to summarise it, to the case where the principal is not a natural person, but a fictitious person, viz., a corporation, two further factors arising from the legal characteristics of a corporation have to be borne in mind. The first is that the capacity of a corporation is limited by its constitution, i.e., in the case of a company incorporated under the Companies Act, by its memorandum and articles of association [see now CA 1985 s. 35]; the second is that a corporation cannot do any act, and that includes making a representation, except through its agent....

The second characteristic of a corporation, viz., that unlike a natural person it can only make a representation through an agent, has the consequence that, in order to create an estoppel between the corporation and the contractor, the representation as to the authority of the agent which creates his 'apparent' authority must be made by some person or persons who have 'actual' authority from the corporation to make the representation. Such 'actual' authority may be conferred by the constitution of the corporation itself, as, for example, in the case of a company, on the board of directors, or it may be conferred by those who under its constitution have the powers of management on some other person to whom the constitution permits them to delegate authority to make representations of this kind. It follows that, where the agent on whose 'apparent' authority the contractor relies has no 'actual' authority from the corporation to enter into a particular kind of contract with the contractor on behalf of the corporation, the contractor cannot rely on the agent's own representation as to his actual authority. He can rely only on a representation by a person or persons who have actual authority to manage or conduct that part of the business of the corporation to which the contract relates. The commonest form of representation by a principal creating an 'apparent' authority of an agent is by conduct, viz., by permitting the agent to act in the management or conduct of the principal's business. Thus, if in the case of a company the board of directors who have 'actual' authority under the memorandum and articles of association to manage the company's business permit the agent to act in the management or conduct of the company's business, they thereby represent to all persons dealing with such agent that he has authority to enter on behalf of the corporation into contracts of a kind which an agent authorised to do acts of the kind which he is in fact permitted to do normally enters into in the ordinary course of such business. The making of such a representation is itself an act of management of the company's business. Prima facie it falls within the 'actual' authority of the board of directors, and unless the memorandum or articles of the company either make such a contract *ultra vires* the company or prohibit the delegation of such authority to the agent [see now CA 1985, ss. 35, 35A and 35B], the company is estopped from denying to anyone who has entered into a contract with the agent in reliance on such 'apparent' authority that the agent had authority to contract on behalf of the company.

If the foregoing analysis of the relevant law is correct, it can be summarised by stating four conditions which must be fulfilled to entitle a contractor to enforce against a company a contract entered into on behalf of the company by an agent who had no actual authority to do so. It must be shown: (a) that a representation that the agent had authority to enter on behalf of the company into a contract of the kind sought to be enforced was made to the contractor; (b) that such representation was made by a person or persons who had 'actual' authority to manage the business of the company either generally or in respect of those matters to which the contract relates; (c) that he (the contractor) was induced by such representation to enter into the contract, i.e., that he in fact relied on it; and (d) that under its memorandum or articles of association the company was not deprived of the capacity either to enter into a contract of the kind sought to be enforced or to delegate authority to enter into a contract of that kind to the agent. [CA 1985, ss. 35, 35A and 35B may have rendered requirement (d) redundant.]

The confusion which, I venture to think, has sometimes crept into the cases is, in my view, due to a failure to distinguish between these four separate conditions, and in particular to keep steadfastly in mind (first) that the only 'actual' authority which is relevant is that of the persons making the representation relied on, and (second) that the memorandum and articles of association of the company are always relevant (whether they are in fact known to the contractor or not) to the questions (i) whether condition (b) is fulfilled, and (ii) whether condition (d) is fulfilled, and (but only if they are in fact known to the contractor) may be relevant (iii) as part of the representation on which the contractor relied.

In each of the relevant cases the representation relied on as creating the 'apparent' authority of the agent was by conduct in permitting the agent to act in the management and conduct of part of the business of the company. Except in *Mahony* v *East Holyford Mining Co. Ltd* (1875) LR 7 HL 869, the conduct relied on was that of the board of directors in so permitting the agent to act. As they had, in each case, by the articles of association of the company full 'actual' authority to manage its business, they had 'actual' authority to make representations in connection with the management of its business, including representations as to who were agents authorised to enter into contracts on the company's behalf. The agent himself had no 'actual' authority to enter into the contract, because there had not been compliance with the formalities prescribed by the articles for conferring it on him. In *British Thomson-Houston Co. Ltd* v *Federated European Bank Ltd* [1932] 2 KB 176, where a guarantee was executed by a single director, it was contended that a provision in the articles, requiring a guarantee to be executed by two directors, deprived the company of capacity to delegate to a single director authority to execute a guarantee on behalf of the company, i.e., that condition (d) *ante* was not fulfilled: but it was held that other provisions in the articles empowered the board to delegate the power of executing guarantees to one of their number, and this defence accordingly failed.

In *Mahony's* case no board of directors or secretary had in fact been appointed, and it was the conduct of those who, under the constitution of the company, were entitled to appoint them which was relied on as a representation that certain persons were directors and secretary. Since they had 'actual' authority to appoint these officers, they had 'actual' authority to make representations as to who the officers were. In both these cases the constitution of the company, whether it had been seen by the contractor or not, was relevant in order to determine whether the persons whose representations by conduct were relied on as creating the 'apparent' authority of the agent had 'actual' authority to make the representations on behalf of the company. In *Mahony's* case, if the persons in question had not been persons who would normally be supposed to have such authority by someone who did not in fact know the constitution of the company, it may well be that the contractor would not have succeeded in proving condition (c), viz, that he relied on the representations made by those persons, unless he proved that he did in fact know the constitution of the company....

The cases where the contractor's claim failed, viz, *J.C. Houghton & Co.* v *Nothard, Lowe and Wills Ltd* [1927] 1 KB 246, *Kreditbank Cassel GmbH* v *Schenkers Ltd* [1927] 1 KB 826, and *Rama Corporation Ltd* v *Proved Tin & General Investments Ltd* [1952] 2 QB 147 were all cases where the contract sought to be enforced was not one which a person occupying the position in relation to the company's business, which the contractor knew that the agent occupied, would normally be authorised to enter into on behalf of the company. The conduct of the board of directors in permitting the agent to occupy that position, on which the contractor relied, thus did not of itself amount to a representation that the agent had authority to enter into the contract sought to be enforced, i.e., condition (a) was not fulfilled. The contractor, however, in each of these three cases sought to rely on a provision of the articles, giving to the board power to delegate wide authority to the agent, as entitling the contractor to treat the conduct of the board as a representation that the agent had had delegated to him wider powers than those normally exercised by persons occupying the position in relation to the company's business which the agent was in fact permitted by the board to occupy. Since this would involve proving that the representation on which he in fact relied as inducing him to enter into the contract comprised the articles of association of the company as well as the conduct of the board, it would be necessary for him to establish, first, that he knew the contents of the articles (i.e., that condition (c) was fulfilled in respect of any representation contained in the articles) and, secondly, that the conduct of the board in the light of that knowledge would be understood by a reasonable man as a representation that the agent had authority to enter into the contract sought to be enforced, i.e., that condition (a) was fulfilled. The need to establish both these things was pointed out by Sargant LJ in *Houghton's* case (at pp. 266 and 267), in a judgment which was concurred in by Atkin LJ; but his observations, as I read them, are directed only to a case where the contract sought to be enforced is not a contract of a kind which a person occupying the position which the agent was permitted by the board to occupy would normally be authorised to enter into on behalf of the company....

In the present case the findings of fact by the county court judge are sufficient to satisfy the four conditions, and thus to establish that the second defendant had 'apparent' authority to enter into contracts on behalf of the defendant company for their services in connection with the sale of the company's property, including the obtaining of development permission with respect to its use.

The judge found that the board knew that the second defendant had throughout been acting as managing director in employing agents and taking other steps to find a purchaser. They permitted him to do so, and by such conduct represented that he had authority to enter into contracts of a kind which a managing director or an executive director responsible for finding a purchaser would in the normal course be authorised to enter into on behalf of the defendant company. Condition (a) was thus fulfilled. The articles of association conferred full powers of management on the board. Condition (b) was thus fulfilled. The plaintiffs, finding the second defendant acting in relation to the defendant company's property as he was authorised by the board to act, were induced to believe that he was authorised by the defendant company to enter into contracts on behalf of the company for their services in connection with the sale of the company's property, including the obtaining of development permission with respect to its use. Condition (c) was thus fulfilled. The articles of association, which contained powers for the board to delegate any of the functions of management to a managing director or to a single director, did not deprive the company of capacity to delegate authority to the second defendant, a director, to enter into contracts of that kind on behalf of the company. Condition (d) was thus fulfilled. I think that the judgment was right, and would dismiss the appeal.

Hely-Hutchinson v Brayhead Ltd

Actual authority may be implied

[1967] 3 All ER 98, [1968] 1 QB 549, Court of Appeal

This case shows that the actual authority of a director may be implied. Implied actual authority may be inferred from the conduct of the board in acquiescing in the agent acting without express authority from the board.

Facts   Mr Richards was the chairman of Brayhead Ltd. He acted as its chief executive and de facto managing director, and frequently entered into contracts on behalf of the company with the knowledge and acquiescence of the board. He gave a guarantee on behalf of the company in respect of sums owed by a company which later went into liquidation. The plaintiff successfully sought to enforce the guarantee against the company on the ground that the board had acquiesced in Richards acting as the company's chief executive, and giving the guarantee fell within the authority normally attaching to that position.

LORD DENNING MR: I need not consider at length the law on the authority of an agent, actual, apparent or ostensible. That has been done in the judgments of this court in the case of *Freeman & Lockyer* v *Buckhurst Park Properties (Mangal) Ltd* [1964] 2 QB 480. It is there shown that actual authority may be express or implied. It is *express* when it is given by express words, such as when a board of directors pass a resolution which authorises two of their number to sign cheques. It is *implied* when it is inferred from the conduct of the parties and the circumstances of the case, such as when the board of directors appoint one of their number to be managing director. They thereby impliedly authorise him to do all such things as fall within the usual scope of that office. Actual authority, express or implied, is binding as between the company and the agent, and also as between the company and others, whether they are within the company or outside it.

Ostensible or apparent authority is the authority of an agent as it *appears* to others. It often coincides with actual authority. Thus, when the board appoint one of their number to be managing director, they invest him not only with implied authority, but also with ostensible authority to do all such things as fall within the usual scope of that office. Other people who see him acting as managing director are entitled to assume that he has the usual authority of a managing director. But sometimes ostensible authority exceeds actual authority. For instance, when the board appoint the managing director, they may expressly limit his authority by saying he is not to order goods worth more than £500 without the sanction of the board. In that case his *actual* authority is subject to the £500 limitation, but his *ostensible* authority includes all the usual authority of a managing director. The company is bound by his ostensible authority in his dealings with those who do not know of the limitation. He may himself do the 'holding out'. Thus, if he orders goods worth £1,000 and signs himself 'Managing Director for and on behalf of the company', the company is bound to the other party who does not know of the £500 limitation (see *British Thomson-Houston Co. Ltd* v *Federated European Bank Ltd* [1932] 2 KB 176, which was quoted for this purpose by Pearson LJ in *Freeman & Lockyer* v *Buckhurst Park Properties (Mangal) Ltd* [1964] 2 QB 480 at p. 499). Even if the other party happens himself to be a director of the company, nevertheless the company may be bound by the ostensible authority. Suppose the managing director orders £1,000 worth of goods from a new director who has just joined the company and does not know of the £500 limitation, not having studied the minute book, the company may yet be bound. That is the sort of case envisaged by Lord Simonds in *Morris* v *Kanssen* [1946] AC 459 at p. 475 and considered by Roskill J in the present case ([1968] 1 QB 549 at p. 564).

Apply these principles here. It is plain that Mr Richards had no express authority to enter into these two contracts on behalf of the company: nor had he any such authority implied from the nature of his office. He had been duly appointed chairman of the company but that office in itself did not carry with it authority to enter into these contracts without the sanction of the board; but I think that he had authority implied from the conduct of the parties and the circumstances of the case. The judge did not rest his decision on implied authority, but I think that his findings necessarily carry that consequence. The judge finds that Mr Richards acted as *de facto* managing director of Brayhead. He was the chief executive who made the final decision on any matter concerning finance. He often committed Brayhead to contracts without the knowledge of the board and reported the matter afterwards. The judge said ([1968] 1 QB 549 at p. 564):

> ... I have no doubt that Mr Richards was, by virtue of his position as *de facto* managing director of Brayhead, or, as perhaps one might more compendiously put it, as Brayhead's chief executive, the man who had, in Diplock LJ's words, 'actual authority to manage', and he was acting as such when he signed those two documents.

Later the judge said (at p. 571):

> ... the board of Brayhead knew of and acquiesced in Mr Richards acting as *de facto* managing director of Brayhead.

The judge held that Mr Richards had ostensible or apparent authority to make the contract, but I think that his findings carry with them the necessary inference that he had also actual authority, such authority being implied from the circumstance that the board by their conduct over many months had acquiesced in his acting as their chief executive and committing Brayhead to contracts without the necessity of sanction from the board.

Egyptian International Foreign Trade Co. v Soplex Wholesale Supplies Ltd

The usual authority of a bank officer

[1985] BCLC 404, Court of Appeal

Although this case concerns the apparent authority of a manager of a bank who was not a director, the agency principles are the same.

Facts The plaintiff entered into a contract to buy cement from the first defendant (Soplex). *P. S. Refson & Co. Ltd* (Refson), Soplex's banker, guaranteed that it would pay $575,000 to the plaintiff if the cement did not arrive by a certain date or, if on arrival, it was defective. Mr Booth, the manager of the bank's documentary credits department (responsible for financing imports), signed the guarantee on its behalf. On delivery the cement was defective and the plaintiff sought payment from the bank under the guarantee. The bank refused to pay and the plaintiff brought these proceedings. The bank's defence was that Mr Booth had no actual authority to sign the documents of guarantee for the bank. The issue was whether the bank had clothed him with apparent authority to do so.

BROWNE-WILKINSON LJ: In deciding this issue, the judge [at first instance] directed himself by reference to the well-known judgment of Diplock LJ in *Freeman & Lockyer* v *Buckhurst Park Properties (Mangal) Ltd* [1964] 2 QB 480 at p. 505, viz that, there being no actual authority, a third party could only rely on the apparent authority of an agent if the principal had held out the agent as possessing authority to enter into such a transaction; that the commonest form of holding out is by permitting the agent to act in the conduct of the principal's business which constitutes a representation that the agent has authority to enter into contracts of a kind 'which an agent authorised to do acts of a kind which he is in fact permitted to do usually enters into the ordinary course of such business'. As to the scope of such apparent authority, the judge relied on certain dicta indicating that the apparent authority covers transactions in which 'normally' such officer would have power to act or which are 'within what would ordinarily be expected to be' the scope of the authority of such an agent. However, the judge accepted that, in determining what was 'usual' or 'normal', he had to take into account the kind of business carried on by the principal, the role of the office holder in that business, current business practices and all other material circumstances....

It is important to bear in mind that the doctrine of holding out is a form of estoppel. As such, the starting-point is that the principal must be shown to have made a representation, which the third party could and did reasonably rely on, that the agent had the necessary authority. The relevant inquiry, therefore, in all cases is whether the acts of the principal constitute a representation that the agent had a particular authority and were reasonably so understood by the third party. This requires the court to consider the principal's conduct *as a whole*. In many cases, the holding out or representation by the company consists solely of the fact that the company has invested the agent with a particular office, e.g., 'managing director' or 'secretary'. For example, in a case such as *British Bank of the Middle East* v *Sun Life Assurance Co. of Canada (UK) Ltd* [1983] BCLC 73, the only holding out by the defendants to the third party was to invest someone with the title 'branch manager', which enabled him so to describe himself in correspondence relied on by the third party: in such a case, the only representation which the third party can reasonably rely on is the representation that that person has the powers normally or usually enjoyed by a branch manager. Therefore, in such a case, the only relevant inquiry is as to the powers normally enjoyed by branch managers in general. But where, as in the present case, the holding out is alleged to consist of a course of conduct wider than merely describing the agent as holding a particular office, although the authority normally found in the holder of such an office is very material, it must be looked at as part and parcel of the whole course of the principal's conduct in order to decide whether the totality of the principal's actions constitute a holding out of the agent as possessing the necessary authority.

...It is not right in this case simply to inquire what is the normal authority of documentary credit managers in general. Nor is it right to start by seeking to establish the normal authority of documentary credit managers in general and then looking to see whether there are any additional factors which alter the position. The only correct approach is the one adopted by the judge, which is to consider the whole of Refson's conduct to determine whether it amounted to a holding out by Refson of Mr Booth as having the necessary authority.

[His Lordship examined the evidence in detail and continued:]

When the whole picture is looked at in the round, there was, in my judgment, ample evidence to justify the judge's finding that, in signing the undertaking, Mr Booth was acting within the authority that he had been held out by Refson as possessing and that the plaintiffs were entitled to, and did, rely on such representation. It is quite impossible to overrule the conclusion of the judge on these factual issues, he having had the advantage of seeing the participants in the witness-box and getting the 'feel' of the case in a way which is not possible on appeal. Even without these advantages, for myself I have no doubt that the judge reached the right conclusion on the basis of the bare words used by the witnesses.

...Counsel for Refson submitted that a principal cannot be held liable as a result of the agent holding himself out as possessing an authority he does not in fact possess: he relied on remarks to that effect in the *Freeman & Lockyer* case [1964] 2 QB 480 at p. 505, *Attorney-General for Ceylon* v *Silva* [1953] AC 416 at p. 479, *British Bank of the Middle East* v *Sun Life Assurance Co. of Canada (UK) Ltd* [1983] BCLC 73 and *Armagas Ltd* v *Mundogas Ltd* [1986] AC 717. As at present advised, I am not satisfied that the principle to be derived from those cases is as wide as counsel for Refson suggests: they were all cases or dicta dealing with the position where the agent had neither authority to enter into the transaction nor authority to make representations on behalf of the principal. It is obviously correct that an agent who has no actual or apparent authority either (a) to enter into a transaction or (b) to make representations as to the transaction cannot hold himself out as having authority to enter into the transaction so as to affect the principal's position. But, suppose a company confers actual or apparent authority on X to make representations and X erroneously represents to a third party that Y has authority to enter into a transaction; why should not such a representation be relied on as part of the holding out of Y by the company? By parity of reasoning, if a company confers actual or apparent authority on A to make representations on the company's behalf but no actual authority on A to enter into the specific transaction, why should a representation made by A as to his authority not be capable of being relied on as one of the acts of holding out? There is substantial authority that it can be: see *British Thomson-Houston Co. Ltd* v *Federated European Bank Ltd* [1932] 2 KB 176 esp. at p. 182 (where the only holding out was an erroneous representation by the agent that he was managing director); the *Freeman & Lockyer* case [1964] 2 QB 480 at p. 499 per Pearson LJ; *Hely-Hutchinson* v *Brayhead Ltd* [1968] 1 QB 549 at p. 583, per Lord Denning MR. If, as I am inclined to think, an agent with authority to make representations can make a representation that he has authority to enter into a transaction, then the judge was entitled to hold, as he did, that Mr Booth, as the representative of Refson in charge of the transaction, had implied or apparent authority to make the representation that only one signature was required and that this representation was a relevant consideration in deciding whether Refson had held out Mr Booth as having authority to sign the undertaking. However, since it is not necessary to decide this point for the purposes of this appeal, I express no concluded view on it.

NOTE: In *First Energy (UK) Ltd* v *Hungarian International Bank Ltd* [1993] BCLC 1409 a senior bank manager in a local branch in Manchester wrote a letter to the plaintiff company offering to provide it with finance. He did not have any actual authority to sanction the credit facility. However, the Court of Appeal held that although he did not have authority to sanction such facility, he was 'clothed with ostensible authority', because of his position, to inform the plaintiff that the head office had approved of the facility, and so when the offer was accepted the bank was bound by it. The plaintiff was entitled to rely on the bank manager's communication as it would not have been reasonable to expect it to check with the bank's head office in London whether approval had been given.

8.3 CORPORATE GOVERNANCE

This chapter has examined how formal company law traditionally distributes management powers and authority to the various organs and agents of the company. While company law has the twin purposes of facilitating commerce and at the same time regulating companies, the law is perhaps not the most effective means of promoting good management practice in companies. Especially for public listed companies, further initiatives have been needed to improve the functioning of the boards of companies within the existing legal structures.

In May 1991 a committee was set up by the Financial Reporting Council, the London Stock Exchange and the accountancy profession 'to address the financial aspects of corporate governance'. The committee, known as the Cadbury Committee after its chairman, Sir Adrian Cadbury, produced a report entitled *The Financial Aspects of Corporate Governance* on 1 December 1992. The central recommendation was that boards of all listed companies should comply with a Code of Best Practice. This has now been replaced by the Combined Code on Corporate Governance which sets out the standards of good practice in relation to issues such as board composition and development, remuneration, accountability and audit, and relations with shareholders.

It is now a continuing obligation of official listing that companies have regard to the Code. The Listing Rules require them to include in their annual report and accounts a statement as to how they apply the principles in the Code and whether they have complied with it during the year in question, or where they do not, provide an explanation for non-compliance (the 'comply or explain' approach).

As will be seen in chapter 11 (section 3), one of the key features of the Combined Code is the use of non-executive directors as custodians of the governance process. However, concerns about non-executive directors' inability to monitor the board and management led to the publication of two reports under the chairmanship respectively of Derek Higgs and Sir Robert Smith in January 2003. The Higgs Report set out guidance for non-executive directors and chairmen and made proposals for the Combined Code to require a greater proportion of independent, better-informed individuals on the board, greater transparency and accountability in the boardroom, formal performance appraisals, and closer relationships between non-executive directors and shareholders (see also 11.3). Sir Robert Smith's Report on Audit Committees set out the key elements of the audit committee's role of reinforcing the auditor's independence and of maintaining the integrity of the company's financial statements. It provided guidance on matters such as the supply of non-audit services by the company's auditor, increased transparency and resources for the committee. These recommendations were welcomed by the government and resulted in the revised Combined Code published by the Financial Reporting Council in July 2003. The Smith Guidance was revised in October 2005.

Following a recommendation in Chapter 10 of the Higgs Report, the Tyson Report published in June 2003 was commissioned to look at how companies might draw on broader pools of talent with varied and complementary skills, experience and perspective to enhance board effectiveness. A review of the implementation of the Combined Code was carried out in 2005 and a small number of further changes were incorporated into an updated version of the Combined Code published in June 2006 (extracted below).

In addition, the Turnbull guidance was also published in 1999 to provide guidance to companies on how to apply the section of the Combined Code dealing with internal control. It set out best practice on internal control for listed companies and assisted them in applying section C.2 of the Combined Code. The guidance was updated in October 2005 by a group set up by the Financial Reporting Council in July 2004 and chaired by Douglas Flint, in the light of experience in implementing the guidance and developments in the UK and internationally.

The Myner's Report published in 2001 dealt with the role of institutional investors in corporate governance. It noted the sub-optimal level of intervention by institutional investors and proposed that institutional investors should be under an obligation, as in the US, to monitor and attempt to influence the boards of companies where there was a reasonable expectation that such activity would enhance the value of the portfolio investments, including the exercise of the right to vote at shareholder meetings. The institutional investors have adopted statements of principles (a voluntary code of practice) implementing many of the recommendations in the Myner's Report.

The following extracts speak for themselves. First reproduced is para. 12.43(A) of the Listing Rules of the Financial Services Authority (which is now the United Kingdom Listing Authority) requiring a statement of compliance from companies. The second extract is from a recent Law Commission paper summarising the history of the corporate governance reports of the 1990s. This is followed by introductory paragraphs to the Cadbury Report and then the revised Combined Code itself. (Further extracts from the Cadbury Report are found in chapter 11 on non-executive directors and remuneration committees and in chapter 16 on audit, audit committees and auditors' liability.) The Higgs and Smith Reports and the Turnbull Guidance are also extracted.

Financial Services Authority—The Listing Rules

12.43A In the case of a company incorporated in the United Kingdom, the following additional items must be included in its annual report and accounts:

(a) a narrative statement of how it has applied the principles set out in Section 1 of the Combined Code, providing explanation which enables its shareholders to evaluate how the principles have been applied;

(b) a statement as to whether or not it has complied throughout the accounting period with the Code provisions set out in Section 1 of the Combined Code. A company that has not complied with the Code provisions, or complied with only some of the Code provisions or (in the case of provisions whose requirements are of a continuing nature) complied for only part of an accounting period, must specify the Code provisions with which it has not complied, and (where relevant) for what part of the period such non-compliance continued, and give reasons for any noncompliance...

Law Commission, *Company Directors: Regulating Conflicts of Interests and Formulating a Statement of Duties*
(Consultation Paper No. 153)
(London: Stationery Office, 1998)

Cadbury Report

1.30 The Committee on the Financial Aspects of Corporate Governance (known after its chairman, Sir Adrian Cadbury, as 'the Cadbury Committee') was formed in May 1991 by the Financial Reporting Council, the Stock Exchange and the accountancy profession. Its final report ('the Cadbury Report'), incorporating a Code of Best Practice for all listed companies ('the Cadbury Code of Best Practice'), was published on 1 December 1992. Recommendations of the Cadbury Committee were underpinned by a disclosure requirement to the Listing Rules.

Greenbury Report

1.31 The Study Group on Directors' Remuneration, chaired by Sir Richard Greenbury ('the Greenbury Committee'), was formed on the initiative of the Confederation of British Industry ('CBI') in January 1995 in response to widespread concern about the level of directors' remuneration, in particular following the privatisation of a series of public utility companies. Its terms of reference were to identify good practice in determining directors' remuneration and prepare a code of such practice for use by UK plc's. Its report ('the Greenbury Report') was published on 17 July 1995.

Hampel Report

1.32 The Committee on Corporate Governance, known as 'the Hampel Committee' after its chairman, Sir Ronald Hampel, was established in November 1995 on the initiative of the Chairman of the Financial Reporting Council. It produced a preliminary report in August 1997 and a final report ('the Hampel Report') in January 1998. Its sponsors were the Stock Exchange, the CBI, the Institute of Directors, the Consultative Committee of Accountancy Bodies, the National Association of Pension Funds and the Association of British Insurers. Its remit extended only to listed companies. The Committee was *inter alia* to keep under review the role of directors, executive and non-executive, recognising the need for board cohesion and the common legal responsibilities of all directors and to address as necessary the role of shareholders in corporate governance issues.

1.33 The Committee's final report stated that the Committee intended to produce a set of principles and code embracing its work and that of the Cadbury and Greenbury Committees and that compliance with this code would be underpinned by the Listing Rules. The objective of the new principles and code would be to secure sufficient disclosure so that investors and others could assess companies' performance and governance practice and respond in an informed way. In January 1998, the Hampel Committee delivered its code to the Stock Exchange.

The Stock Exchange's Combined Code of Corporate Governance

1.34 Following publication of the Hampel Report, a consolidated Code for corporate governance, combining the Cadbury and Greenbury Codes with the recommendations of the Hampel Committee, was adopted by the Stock Exchange (the 'Combined Code'). The Combined Code is appended to but does not form part of the Listing Rules. The Code is also published by the Exchange as a free-standing document.

1.35 Paragraphs (a) and (b) of Rule 12.43A of the Listing Rules require companies to make a statement in their annual report and accounts in relation to their compliance with the Combined Code. The Listing Rules also require some aspects of this compliance statement to be reviewed by the auditors. This statement must explain how the company has applied the principles in the Code, and give an explanation of why it has failed to comply with any of its provisions during any part of the relevant accounting period.

Report of the Committee on the Financial Aspects of Corporate Governance (The 'Cadbury Report')

(London: Gee, 1992)

The Setting for the Report

1.1 The country's economy depends on the drive and efficiency of its companies. Thus the effectiveness with which their boards discharge their responsibilities determines Britain's competitive position. They must be free to drive their companies forward, but exercise that freedom within a framework of effective accountability. This is the essence of any system of good corporate governance.

1.2 The Committee's recommendations are focused on the control and reporting functions of boards, and on the role of auditors. This reflects the Committee's purpose, which was to review those aspects of corporate governance specifically related to financial reporting and accountability. Our proposals do, however, seek to contribute positively to the promotion of good corporate governance as a whole.

1.3 At the heart of the Committee's recommendations is a Code of Best Practice designed to achieve the necessary high standards of corporate behaviour. The London Stock Exchange intend to require all listed companies registered in the United Kingdom, as a continuing obligation of listing, to state whether they are complying with the Code and to give reasons for any areas of non-compliance. This requirement will enable shareholders to know where the companies in which they have invested stand in relation to the Code. The obligation will be enforced in the same way as all other listing obligations. This may include, in appropriate cases, the publication of a formal statement of censure. . . .

1.5 By adhering to the Code, listed companies will strengthen both their control over their businesses and their public accountability. In so doing, they will be striking the right balance between meeting the standards of corporate governance now expected of them and retaining the essential spirit of enterprise.

1.6 Bringing greater clarity to the respective responsibilities of directors, shareholders and auditors will also strengthen trust in the corporate system. Companies whose standards of corporate governance are high are the more likely to gain the confidence of investors and support for the development of their businesses.

1.7 The basic system of corporate governance in Britain is sound. The principles are well-known and widely followed. Indeed the Code closely reflects existing best practice. This sets the standard which all listed companies need to match.

1.8 Our proposals aim to strengthen the unitary board system and increase its effectiveness, not to replace it. In law, all directors are responsible for the stewardship of the company's assets. All directors, therefore, whether or not they have executive responsibilities, have a monitoring role and are responsible for ensuring that the necessary controls over the activities of their companies are in place—and working.

1.9 Had a Code such as ours been in existence in the past, we believe that a number of the recent examples of unexpected company failures and cases of fraud would have received attention earlier. It must, however, be recognised that no system of control can eliminate the risk of fraud without so shackling companies as to impede their ability to compete in the market-place.

1.10 We believe that our approach, based on compliance with a voluntary code coupled with disclosure, will prove more effective than a statutory code. It is directed at establishing best practice, at encouraging pressure from shareholders to hasten its widespread adoption, and at allowing some flexibility in implementation. We recognise, however, that if companies do not back our recommendations, it is probable that legislation and external regulation will be sought to deal with some of the underlying problems which the report identifies. Statutory measures would impose a minimum standard and there would be a greater risk of boards complying with the letter, rather than with the spirit, of their requirements.

1.11 The Committee is clear that action by boards of directors and auditors on the financial aspects of corporate governance is expected and necessary. We are encouraged by the degree to which boards are already reviewing their structures and systems in the light of our draft recommendations. The adoption of our recommendations will mark an important step forward in the continuing process of raising standards in corporate governance.

Introduction

Reasons for setting up the Committee

2.1 The Committee was set up in May 1991 by the Financial Reporting Council, the London Stock Exchange and the accountancy profession to address the financial aspects of corporate governance....Its sponsors were concerned at the perceived low level of confidence both in financial reporting and in the ability of auditors to provide the safeguards which the users of company reports sought and expected. The underlying factors were seen as the looseness of accounting standards, the absence of a clear framework for ensuring that directors kept under review the controls in their business, and competitive pressures both on companies and on auditors which made it difficult for auditors to stand up to demanding boards.

2.2 These concerns about the working of the corporate system were heightened by some unexpected failures of major companies and by criticisms of the lack of effective board accountability for such matters as directors' pay....

Corporate governance

2.5 Corporate governance is the system by which companies are directed and controlled. Boards of directors are responsible for the governance of their companies. The shareholders' role in governance is to appoint the directors and the auditors and to satisfy themselves that an appropriate governance structure is in place. The responsibilities of the board include setting the company's strategic aims, providing the leadership to put them into effect, supervising the management of the business and reporting to shareholders on their stewardship. The board's actions are subject to laws, regulations and the shareholders in general meeting.

2.6 Within that overall framework, the specifically financial aspects of corporate governance (the Committee's remit) are the way in which boards set financial policy and oversee its implementation, including the use of financial controls, and the process whereby they report on the activities and progress of the company to the shareholders.

2.7 The role of the auditors is to provide the shareholders with an external and objective check on the directors' financial statements which form the basis of that reporting system. Although the reports of the directors are addressed to the shareholders, they are important to a wider audience, not least to employees whose interests boards have a statutory duty to take into account.

2.8 The Committee's objective is to help to raise the standards of corporate governance and the level of confidence in financial reporting and auditing by setting out clearly what it sees as the respective responsibilities of those involved and what it believes is expected of them. . . .

Companies to whom directed

3.1 The Code of Best Practice . . . is directed to the boards of directors of all listed companies registered in the UK, but we would encourage as many other companies as possible to aim at meeting its requirements.

Code Principles

3.2 The principles on which the Code is based are those of openness, integrity and accountability. They go together. Openness on the part of companies, within the limits set by their competitive position, is the basis for the confidence which needs to exist between business and all those who have a stake in its success. An open approach to the disclosure of information contributes to the efficient working of the market economy, prompts boards to take effective action and allows shareholders and others to scrutinise companies more thoroughly.

3.3 Integrity means both straightforward dealing and completeness. What is required of financial reporting is that it should be honest and that it should present a balanced picture of the state of the company's affairs. The integrity of reports depends on the integrity of those who prepare and present them.

3.4 Boards of directors are accountable to their shareholders and both have to play their part in making that accountability effective. Boards of directors need to do so through the quality of the information which they provide to shareholders, and shareholders through their willingness to exercise their responsibilities as owners.

3.5 The arguments for adhering to the Code are twofold. First, a clear understanding of responsibilities and an open approach to the way in which they have been discharged will assist boards of directors in framing and winning support for their strategies. It will also assist the efficient operation of capital markets and increase confidence in boards, auditors and financial reporting and hence the general level of confidence in business.

3.6 Second, if standards of financial reporting and of business conduct more generally are not seen to be raised, a greater reliance on regulation may be inevitable. Any further degree of regulation would, in any event, be more likely to be well directed, if it were to enforce what has already been shown to be workable and effective by those setting the standard. . . .

The Combined Code on Corporate Governance
(Financial Reporting Council, June 2006)

SECTION 1 COMPANIES
A. DIRECTORS
A.1 The Board
Main Principle

Every company should be headed by an effective board, which is collectively responsible for the success of the company.

Supporting Principles

The board's role is to provide entrepreneurial leadership of the company within a framework of prudent and effective controls which enables risk to be assessed and managed. The board should set the company's strategic aims, ensure that the necessary financial and human resources are in place for the company to meet its objectives and review management performance. The board should set the company's values and standards and ensure that its obligations to its shareholders and others are understood and met.

All directors must take decisions objectively in the interests of the company.

As part of their role as members of a unitary board, non-executive directors should construct-ively challenge and help develop proposals on strategy. Non-executive directors should scrutinise the performance of management in meeting agreed goals and objectives and monitor the reporting of performance. They should satisfy themselves on the integrity of financial information and that financial controls and systems of risk management are robust and defensible. They are responsible for determining appropriate levels of remuneration of executive directors and have a prime role in appointing, and where necessary removing, executive directors, and in succession planning.

Code Provisions

A.1.1 The board should meet sufficiently regularly to discharge its duties effectively. There should be a formal schedule of matters specifically reserved for its decision. The annual report should include a statement of how the board operates, including a high level statement of which types of decisions are to be taken by the board and which are to be delegated to management.

A.1.2 The annual report should identify the chairman, the deputy chairman (where there is one), the chief executive, the senior independent director and the chairmen and members of the nom-ination, audit and remuneration committees. It should also set out the number of meetings of the board and those committees and individual attendance by directors.

A.1.3 The chairman should hold meetings with the non-executive directors without the execu-tives present. Led by the senior independent director, the non-executive directors should meet without the chairman present at least annually to appraise the chairman's performance (as described in A.6.1) and on such other occasions as are deemed appropriate.

A.1.4 Where directors have concerns which cannot be resolved about the running of the com-pany or a proposed action, they should ensure that their concerns are recorded in the board min-utes. On resignation, a non-executive director should provide a written statement to the chairman, for circulation to the board, if they have any such concerns.

A.1.5 The company should arrange appropriate insurance cover in respect of legal action against its directors.

A.2 Chairman and chief executive

Main Principle

There should be a clear division of responsibilities at the head of the company between the running of the board and the executive responsibility for the running of the company's busi-ness. No one individual should have unfettered powers of decision.

Supporting Principle

The chairman is responsible for leadership of the board, ensuring its effectiveness on all aspects of its role and setting its agenda. The chairman is also responsible for ensuring that the direct-ors receive accurate, timely and clear information. The chairman should ensure effective com-munication with shareholders. The chairman should also facilitate the effective contribution of non-executive directors in particular and ensure constructive relations between executive and non-executive directors.

Code Provisions

A.2.1 The roles of chairman and chief executive should not be exercised by the same individual. The division of responsibilities between the chairman and chief executive should be clearly established, set out in writing and agreed by the board.

A.2.2[1] The chairman should on appointment meet the independence criteria set out in A.3.1 below. A chief executive should not go on to be chairman of the same company. If exceptionally a board decides that a chief executive should become chairman, the board should consult major shareholders in advance and should set out its reasons to shareholders at the time of the appointment and in the next annual report.

A.3 Board balance and independence

Main Principle

The board should include a balance of executive and non-executive directors (and in particular independent non-executive directors) such that no individual or small group of individuals can dominate the board's decision taking.

Supporting Principles

The board should not be so large as to be unwieldy. The board should be of sufficient size that the balance of skills and experience is appropriate for the requirements of the business and that changes to the board's composition can be managed without undue disruption.

To ensure that power and information are not concentrated in one or two individuals, there should be a strong presence on the board of both executive and non-executive directors.

The value of ensuring that committee membership is refreshed and that undue reliance is not placed on particular individuals should be taken into account in deciding chairmanship and membership of committees.

No one other than the committee chairman and members is entitled to be present at a meeting of the nomination, audit or remuneration committee, but others may attend at the invitation of the committee.

Code provisions

A.3.1 The board should identify in the annual report each non-executive director it considers to be independent.[2] The board should determine whether the director is independent in character and judgement and whether there are relationships or circumstances which are likely to affect, or could appear to affect, the director's judgement. The board should state its reasons if it determines that a director is independent notwithstanding the existence of relationships or circumstances which may appear relevant to its determination, including if the director:
- has been an employee of the company or group within the last five years;
- has, or has had within the last three years, a material business relationship with the company either directly, or as a partner, shareholder, director or senior employee of a body that has such a relationship with the company;
- has received or receives additional remuneration from the company apart from a director's fee, participates in the company's share option or a performance-related pay scheme, or is a member of the company's pension scheme;
- has close family ties with any of the company's advisers, directors or senior employees;
- holds cross-directorships or has significant links with other directors through involvement in other companies or bodies;

1 Compliance or otherwise with this provision need only be reported for the year in which the appointment is made.

2 A.2.2 states that the chairman should, on appointment, meet the independence criteria set out in this provision, but thereafter the test of independence is not appropriate in relation to the chairman.

- represents a significant shareholder; or
- has served on the board for more than nine years from the date of their first election.

A.3.2 Except for smaller companies,[3] at least half the board, excluding the chairman, should comprise non-executive directors determined by the board to be independent. A smaller company should have at least two independent non-executive directors.

A.3.3 The board should appoint one of the independent non-executive directors to be the senior independent director. The senior independent director should be available to shareholders if they have concerns which contact through the normal channels of chairman, chief executive or finance director has failed to resolve or for which such contact is inappropriate.

A.4 Appointments to the Board

Main Principle

There should be a formal, rigorous and transparent procedure for the appointment of new directors to the board.

Supporting Principles

Appointments to the board should be made on merit and against objective criteria. Care should be taken to ensure that appointees have enough time available to devote to the job. This is particularly important in the case of chairmanships.

The board should satisfy itself that plans are in place for orderly succession for appointments to the board and to senior management, so as to maintain an appropriate balance of skills and experience within the company and on the board.

Code Provisions

A.4.1 There should be a nomination committee which should lead the process for board appointments and make recommendations to the board. A majority of members of the nomination committee should be independent non-executive directors. The chairman or an independent non-executive director should chair the committee, but the chairman should not chair the nomination committee when it is dealing with the appointment of a successor to the chairmanship. The nomination committee should make available[4] its terms of reference, explaining its role and the authority delegated to it by the board.

A.4.2 The nomination committee should evaluate the balance of skills, knowledge and experience on the board and, in the light of this evaluation, prepare a description of the role and capabilities required for a particular appointment.

A.4.3 For the appointment of a chairman, the nomination committee should prepare a job specification, including an assessment of the time commitment expected, recognising the need for availability in the event of crises. A chairman's other significant commitments should be disclosed to the board before appointment and included in the annual report. Changes to such commitments should be reported to the board as they arise, and included in the next annual report. No individual should be appointed to a second chairmanship of a FTSE 100 company.[5]

A.4.4 The terms and conditions of appointment of non-executive directors should be made available for inspections.[6] The letter of appointment should set out the expected time commitment.

---

3 A smaller company is one that is below the FTSE 350 throughout the year immediately prior to the reporting year.

4 The requirement to make the information available would be met by including the information on a website that is maintained by or on behalf of the company.

5 Compliance or otherwise with this provision need only be reported for the year in which the appointment is made.

6 The terms and conditions of appointment of non-executive directors should be made available for inspection by any person at the company's registered office during normal business hours and at the AGM (for 15 minutes prior to the meeting and during the meeting).

Non-executive directors should undertake that they will have sufficient time to meet what is expected of them. Their other significant commitments should be disclosed to the board before appointment, with a broad indication of the time involved and the board should be informed of subsequent changes.

A.4.5 The board should not agree to a full time executive director taking on more than one non-executive directorship in a FTSE 100 company nor the chairmanship of such a company.

A.4.6 A separate section of the annual report should describe the work of the nomination committee, including the process it has used in relation to board appointments. An explanation should be given if neither an external search consultancy nor open advertising has been used in the appointment of a chairman or a non-executive director.

A.5 Information and professional development

Main Principle

The board should be supplied in a timely manner with information in a form and of a quality appropriate to enable it to discharge its duties. All directors should receive induction on joining the board and should regularly update and refresh their skills and knowledge.

Supporting Principles

The chairman is responsible for ensuring that the directors receive accurate, timely and clear information. Management has an obligation to provide such information but directors should seek clarification or amplification where necessary.

The chairman should ensure that the directors continually update their skills and the knowledge and familiarity with the company required to fulfil their role both on the board and on board committees. The company should provide the necessary resources for developing and updating its directors' knowledge and capabilities.

Under the direction of the chairman, the company secretary's responsibilities include ensuring good information flows within the board and its committees and between senior management and non-executive directors, as well as facilitating induction and assisting with professional development as required.

The company secretary should be responsible for advising the board through the chairman on all governance matters.

Code Provisions

A.5.1 The chairman should ensure that new directors receive a full, formal and tailored induction on joining the board. As part of this, the company should offer to major shareholders the opportunity to meet a new non-executive director.

A.5.2 The board should ensure that directors, especially non-executive directors, have access to independent professional advice at the company's expense where they judge it necessary to discharge their responsibilities as directors. Committees should be provided with sufficient resources to undertake their duties.

A.5.3 All directors should have access to the advice and services of the company secretary, who is responsible to the board for ensuring that board procedures are complied with. Both the appointment and removal of the company secretary should be a matter for the board as a whole.

A.6 Performance evaluation

Main Principle

The board should undertake a formal and rigorous annual evaluation of its own performance and that of its committees and individual directors.

Supporting Principle

Individual evaluation should aim to show whether each director continues to contribute effectively and to demonstrate commitment to the role (including commitment of time for board and

committee meetings and any other duties). The chairman should act on the results of the performance evaluation by recognising the strengths and addressing the weaknesses of the board and,
where appropriate, proposing new members be appointed to the board or seeking the resignation
of directors.

Code Provision

A.6.1 The board should state in the annual report how performance evaluation of the board, its
committees and its individual directors has been conducted. The non-executive directors, led by
the senior independent director, should be responsible for performance evaluation of the chairman, taking into account the views of executive directors.

A.7 Re-election

Main Principle

**All directors should be submitted for re-election at regular intervals, subject to continued
satisfactory performance. The board should ensure planned and progressive refreshing of
the board.**

Code Provisions

A.7.1 All directors should be subject to election by shareholders at the first annual general meeting after their appointment, and to re-election thereafter at intervals of no more than three years.
The names of directors submitted for election or re-election should be accompanied by sufficient
biographical details and any other relevant information to enable shareholders to take an informed
decision on their election.

A.7.2 Non-executive directors should be appointed for specified terms subject to re-election
and to Companies Acts provisions relating to the removal of a director. The board should set out to
shareholders in the papers accompanying a resolution to elect a non-executive director why they
believe an individual should be elected. The chairman should confirm to shareholders when proposing re-election that, following formal performance evaluation, the individual's performance continues to be effective and to demonstrate commitment to the role. Any term beyond six years (e.g. two
three-year terms) for a non-executive director should be subject to particularly rigorous review,
and should take into account the need for progressive refreshing of the board. Non-executive directors may serve longer than nine years (e.g. three three-year terms), subject to annual re-election.
Serving more than nine years could be relevant to the determination of a non-executive director's
independence (as set out in provision A.3.1).

B. REMUNERATION

B.1 The Level and Make-up of Remuneration

Main Principles

**Levels of remuneration should be sufficient to attract, retain and motivate directors of the
quality required to run the company successfully, but a company should avoid paying more
than is necessary for this purpose. A significant proportion of executive directors' remuneration should be structured so as to link rewards to corporate and individual performance.**

Supporting Principle

The remuneration committee should judge where to position their company relative to other companies. But they should use such comparisons with caution, in view of the risk of an upward ratchet
of remuneration levels with no corresponding improvement in performance. They should also be
sensitive to pay and employment conditions elsewhere in the group, especially when determining
annual salary increases.

Code Provisions

Remuneration policy

B.1.1 The performance-related elements of remuneration should form a significant proportion of the total remuneration package of executive directors and should be designed to align their interests with those of shareholders and to give these directors keen incentives to perform at the highest levels. In designing schemes of performance-related remuneration, the remuneration committee should follow the provisions in Schedule A to this Code.

B.1.2 Executive share options should not be offered at a discount save as permitted by the relevant provisions of the Listing Rules.

B.1.3 Levels of remuneration for non-executive directors should reflect the time commitment and responsibilities of the role. Remuneration for non-executive directors should not include share options. If, exceptionally, options are granted, shareholder approval should be sought in advance and any shares acquired by exercise of the options should be held until at least one year after the non-executive director leaves the board. Holding of share options could be relevant to the determination of a non-executive director's independence (as set out in provision A.3.1).

B.1.4 Where a company releases an executive director to serve as a non-executive director elsewhere, the remuneration report[7] should include a statement as to whether or not the director will retain such earnings and, if so, what the remuneration is.

Service Contracts and Compensation

B.1.5 The remuneration committee should carefully consider what compensation commitments (including pension contributions and all other elements) their directors' terms of appointment would entail in the event of early termination. The aim should be to avoid rewarding poor performance. They should take a robust line on reducing compensation to reflect departing directors' obligations to mitigate loss.

B.1.6 Notice or contract periods should be set at one year or less. If it is necessary to offer longer notice or contract periods to new directors recruited from outside, such periods should reduce to one year or less after the initial period.

B.2 Procedure

Main Principle

There should be a formal and transparent procedure for developing policy on executive remuneration and for fixing the remuneration packages of individual directors. No director should be involved in deciding his or her own remuneration.

Supporting Principles

The remuneration committee should consult the chairman and/or chief executive about their proposals relating to the remuneration of other executive directors. The remuneration committee should also be responsible for appointing any consultants in respect of executive director remuneration. Where executive directors or senior management are involved in advising or supporting the remuneration committee, care should be taken to recognise and avoid conflicts of interest.

The chairman of the board should ensure that the company maintains contact as required with its principal shareholders about remuneration in the same way as for other matters.

Code Provisions

B.2.1 The board should establish a remuneration committee of at least three, or in the case of smaller companies[8] two, independent non-executive directors. In addition the company chairman

---

7 As required under the Directors' Remuneration Report Regulations 2002.
8 See footnote 3.

may also be a member of, but not chair, the committee if he or she was considered independent on appointment as chairman. The remuneration committee should make available[9] its terms of reference, explaining its role and the authority delegated to it by the board. Where remuneration consultants are appointed, a statement should be made available[10] of whether they have any other connection with the company.

B.2.2 The remuneration committee should have delegated responsibility for setting remuneration for all executive directors and the chairman, including pension rights and any compensation payments. The committee should also recommend and monitor the level and structure of remuneration for senior management. The definition of 'senior management' for this purpose should be determined by the board but should normally include the first layer of management below board level.

B.2.3 The board itself or, where required by the Articles of Association, the shareholders should determine the remuneration of the non-executive directors within the limits set in the Articles of Association. Where permitted by the Articles, the board may however delegate this responsibility to a committee, which might include the chief executive.

B.2.4 Shareholders should be invited specifically to approve all new long-term incentive schemes (as defined in the Listing Rules) and significant changes to existing schemes, save in the circumstances permitted by the Listing Rules.

C. ACCOUNTABILITY AND AUDIT

C.1 Financial Reporting

Main Principle

The board should present a balanced and understandable assessment of the company's position and prospects.

Supporting Principle

The board's responsibility to present a balanced and understandable assessment extends to interim and other price-sensitive public reports and reports to regulators as well as to information required to be presented by statutory requirements.

Code Provisions

C.1.1 The directors should explain in the annual report their responsibility for preparing the accounts and there should be a statement by the auditors about their reporting responsibilities.

C.1.2 The directors should report that the business is a going concern, with supporting assumptions or qualifications as necessary.

C.2 Internal Control[11]

Main Principle

The board should maintain a sound system of internal control to safeguard shareholders' investment and the company's assets.

Code Provision

C.2.1 The board should, at least annually, conduct a review of the effectiveness of the group's system of internal controls and should report to shareholders that they have done so. The review should cover all material controls, including financial, operational and compliance controls and risk management systems.

---

9 See footnote 4.

10 See footnote 4.

11 The Turnbull guidance suggests means of applying this part of the Code. Copies are available at www.frc.org.uk/corporate/internalcontrol.cfm.

C.3 Audit Committee and Auditors[12]

Main Principle

The board should establish formal and transparent arrangements for considering how they should apply the financial reporting and internal control principles and for maintaining an appropriate relationship with the company's auditors.

Code provisions

C.3.1 The board should establish an audit committee of at least three, or in the case of smaller companies[13] two, members, who should all be independent non-executive directors. The board should satisfy itself that at least one member of the audit committee has recent and relevant financial experience.

C.3.2 The main role and responsibilities of the audit committee should be set out in written terms of reference and should include:

- to monitor the integrity of the financial statements of the company, and any formal announcements relating to the company's financial performance, reviewing significant financial reporting judgements contained in them;
- to review the company's internal financial controls and, unless expressly addressed by a separate board risk committee composed of independent directors, or by the board itself, to review the company's internal control and risk management systems;
- to monitor and review the effectiveness of the company's internal audit function;
- to make recommendations to the board, for it to put to the shareholders for their approval in general meeting, in relation to the appointment, re-appointment and removal of the external auditor and to approve the remuneration and terms of engagement of the external auditor;
- to review and monitor the external auditor's independence and objectivity and the effectiveness of the audit process, taking into consideration relevant UK professional and regulatory requirements;
- to develop and implement policy on the engagement of the external auditor to supply non-audit services, taking into account relevant ethical guidance regarding the provision of non-audit services by the external audit firm; and to report to the board, identifying any matters in respect of which it considers that action or improvement is needed and making recommendations as to the steps to be taken.

C.3.3 The terms of reference of the audit committee, including its role and the authority delegated to it by the board, should be made available.[14] A separate section of the annual report should describe the work of the committee in discharging those responsibilities.

C.3.4 The audit committee should review arrangements by which staff of the company may, in confidence, raise concerns about possible improprieties in matters of financial reporting or other matters. The audit committee's objective should be to ensure that arrangements are in place for the proportionate and independent investigation of such matters and for appropriate follow-up action.

C.3.5 The audit committee should monitor and review the effectiveness of the internal audit activities. Where there is no internal audit function, the audit committee should consider annually whether there is a need for an internal audit function and make a recommendation to the board, and the reasons for the absence of such a function should be explained in the relevant section of the annual report.

C.3.6 The audit committee should have primary responsibility for making a recommendation on the appointment, reappointment and removal of the external auditors. If the board does not accept

---

12 The Smith guidance suggests means of applying this part of the Code. Copies are available at www.frc.org.uk/corporate/combinedcode.cfm

13 See footnote 3

14 See footnote 4.

the audit committee's recommendation, it should include in the annual report, and in any papers recommending appointment or re-appointment, a statement from the audit committee explaining the recommendation and should set out reasons why the board has taken a different position.

C.3.7 The annual report should explain to shareholders how, if the auditor provides non-audit services, auditor objectivity and independence is safeguarded.

D. RELATIONS WITH SHAREHOLDERS

D.1 Dialogue with Institutional Shareholders

Main Principle

There should be a dialogue with shareholders based on the mutual understanding of objectives. The board as a whole has responsibility for ensuring that a satisfactory dialogue with shareholders takes place.[15]

Supporting Principles

Whilst recognising that most shareholder contact is with the chief executive and finance director, the chairman (and the senior independent director and other directors as appropriate) should maintain sufficient contact with major shareholders to understand their issues and concerns.

The board should keep in touch with shareholder opinion in whatever ways are most practical and efficient.

Code Provisions

D.1.1 The chairman should ensure that the views of shareholders are communicated to the board as a whole. The chairman should discuss governance and strategy with major shareholders. Non-executive directors should be offered the opportunity to attend meetings with major shareholders and should expect to attend them if requested by major shareholders. The senior independent director should attend sufficient meetings with a range of major shareholders to listen to their views in order to help develop a balanced understanding of the issues and concerns of major shareholders.

D.1.2 The board should state in the annual report the steps they have taken to ensure that the members of the board, and in particular the non-executive directors, develop an understanding of the views of major shareholders about their company, for example through direct face-to-face contact, analysts' or brokers' briefings and surveys of shareholder opinion.

D.2 Constructive Use of the AGM

Main Principle

The board should use the AGM to communicate with investors and to encourage their participation.

Code Provisions

D.2.1 At any general meeting, the company should propose a separate resolution on each substantially separate issue, and should in particular propose a resolution at the AGM relating to the report and accounts. For each resolution, proxy appointment forms should provide shareholders with the option to direct their proxy to vote either for or against the resolution or to withhold their vote. The proxy form and any announcement of the results of a vote should make it clear that a 'vote withheld' is not a vote in law and will not be counted in the calculation of the proportion of the votes for and against the resolution.

D.2.2 The company should ensure that all valid proxy appointments received for general meetings are properly recorded and counted. For each resolution, after a vote has been taken, except where taken on a poll, the company should ensure that the following information is given at the

---

15 Nothing in these principles or provisions should be taken to override the general requirements of law to treat shareholders equally in access to information.

meeting and made available as soon as reasonably practicable on a website which is maintained by or on behalf of the company:

- the number of shares in respect of which proxy appointments have been validly made;
- the number of votes for the resolution;
- the number of votes against the resolution; and
- the number of shares in respect of which the vote was directed to be withheld.

D.2.3 The chairman should arrange for the chairmen of the audit, remuneration and nomination committees to be available to answer questions at the AGM and for all directors to attend.

D.2.4 The company should arrange for the Notice of the AGM and related papers to be sent to shareholders at least 20 working days before the meeting.

SECTION 2 INSTITUTIONAL SHAREHOLDERS

E. INSTITUTIONAL SHAREHOLDERS[16]

E.1 Dialogue with companies

Main Principle

Institutional shareholders should enter into a dialogue with companies based on the mutual understanding of objectives.

Supporting Principles

Institutional shareholders should apply the principles set out in the Institutional Shareholders' Committee's "The Responsibilities of Institutional Shareholders and Agents—Statement of Principles",[17] which should be reflected in fund manager contracts.

E.2 Evaluation of Governance Disclosures

Main Principle

When evaluating companies' governance arrangements, particularly those relating to board structure and composition, institutional shareholders should give due weight to all relevant factors drawn to their attention.

Supporting Principle

Institutional shareholders should consider carefully explanations given for departure from this Code and make reasoned judgements in each case. They should give an explanation to the company, in writing where appropriate, and be prepared to enter a dialogue if they do not accept the company's position. They should avoid a box-ticking approach to assessing a company's corporate governance. They should bear in mind in particular the size and complexity of the company and the nature of the risks and challenges it faces.

E.3 Shareholder Voting

Main Principle

Institutional shareholders have a responsibility to make considered use of their votes.

Supporting Principles

Institutional shareholders should take steps to ensure their voting intentions are being translated into practice.

---

16 Agents such as investment managers, or voting services, are frequently appointed by institutional shareholders to act on their behalf and these principles should accordingly be read as applying where appropriate to the agents of institutional shareholders.

17 Available at www.investmentuk.org/news/research/2005/topic/corporate_governance/isc0905.pdf

Institutional shareholders should, on request, make available to their clients information on the proportion of resolutions on which votes were cast and non-discretionary proxies lodged.

Major shareholders should attend AGMs where appropriate and practicable. Companies and registrars should facilitate this.

Review of the role and effectiveness of non-executive directors, Derek Higgs (Higg's Report)
January 2003, The Stationery Office

SUMMARY OF RECOMMENDATIONS

The board

- The board is collectively responsible for promoting the success of the company by leading and directing the company's affairs. A description of the role of the board is proposed for incorporation into the Combined Code (the Code) (Box opening Chapter 4).
- The number of meetings of the board and of its main committees should be stated in the annual report, together with the attendance of individual directors (paragraph 4.8). A description should be included in the annual report of how the board operates (paragraph 4.8).
- The board should be of an appropriate size (paragraph 4.10). At least half the members of the board, excluding the chairman, should be independent non-executive directors (paragraph 9.5). There should also be a strong executive representation on the board (paragraph 8.6).

The chairman

- The chairman has a pivotal role in creating the conditions for individual director and board effectiveness. The Review describes the role of the chairman (Chapter 5) and some of the attributes and behaviours of an effective chairman (Annex D).
- The roles of chairman and chief executive should be separated (paragraph 5.3) and the division of responsibilities between the chairman and chief executive set out in writing and agreed by the board (paragraph 5.5).
- A chief executive should not become chairman of the same company (paragraph 5.7). At the time of appointment the chairman should meet the test of independence set out in the Review (paragraph 5.8).

Role of the non-executive director

- A description of the role of the non-executive director is proposed for incorporation into the Code (Box opening Chapter 6). Guidance is offered for non-executive directors on how to maximise their effectiveness (Annex C).
- The non-executive directors should meet as a group at least once a year without the chairman or executive directors present and the annual report should include a statement on whether such meetings have occurred (paragraph 8.8).
- Prior to appointment, potential new non-executive directors should carry out due diligence on the board and on the company to satisfy themselves that they have the knowledge, skills, experience and time to make a positive contribution to the board. Guidance on pre-appointment due diligence is offered (Annex G).

The senior independent director

- A senior independent director should be identified who meets the test of independence set out in the Review. The senior independent director should be available to shareholders, if they have concerns that have not been resolved through the normal channels of contact with the chairman or chief executive (paragraphs 7.4 to 7.5).

Independence

- All directors should take decisions objectively in the interests of the company (paragraph 9.10).
- A definition of independence is proposed for incorporation into the Code (paragraph 9.11).

Recruitment and appointment

- There should be a nomination committee of the board to conduct the process for board appointments and make recommendations to the board (paragraph 10.9).
- The nomination committee should consist of a majority of independent non-executive directors. It may include the chairman of the board, but should be chaired by an independent non-executive director. A statement should be made in the annual report setting out the composition, terms of reference, and activities of the nomination committee and the process used for appointments (paragraph 10.9). A summary of the principal duties of the nomination committee is offered (Annex F).
- The nomination committee should evaluate the balance of skills, knowledge and experience on the board and prepare a description of the role and capabilities required for a particular appointment (paragraph 10.9).
- On appointment, non-executive directors should receive a letter setting out what is expected of them (paragraph 10.9). A specimen letter of appointment is offered (Annex H).
- The nomination committee should provide support to the board on succession planning (paragraph 10.13).
- Chairmen and chief executives should consider implementing executive development programmes to train and develop suitable individuals in their companies for future director roles (paragraph 10.14).
- The board should set out to shareholders why they believe an individual should be appointed to a non-executive director role and how they meet the requirements of the role (paragraph 10.11).
- Proposals are made to broaden the pool of candidates for non-executive director appointments, including more executive directors and senior executives from other companies and directors of private companies, as well as advisors and those from other backgrounds (paragraphs 10.25 to 10.31).
- A small group of business leaders and others will be set up to identify how to bring to greater prominence candidates for non-executive director appointment from the non-commercial sector (paragraph 10.32).
- The Review offers guidance on the process for the appointment of a new chairman (paragraph 10.35).

Induction and professional development

- A comprehensive induction programme should be provided to new non-executive directors (paragraph 11.1) and is the responsibility of the chairman, supported by the company secretary (paragraph 11.4). The Review provides an induction checklist (Annex I).
- The chairman should address the developmental needs of the board as a whole with a view to enhancing its effectiveness. Resources should be provided for developing and refreshing the knowledge and skills of directors (paragraph 11.14).
- The performance of the board, its committees and its individual members, should be evaluated at least once a year. The annual report should state whether such performance reviews are taking place and how they are conducted (paragraph 11.22).
- Supported by the company secretary, the chairman should assess what information is required by the board (paragraph 11.26). Non-executive directors should satisfy themselves that they have appropriate information of sufficient quality to make sound judgements (paragraph 11.27).
- The company secretary should be accountable to the board as a whole, through the chairman, on all governance matters (paragraph 11.31).

Tenure and time commitment

- A non-executive director should normally be expected to serve two three-year terms, although a longer term will exceptionally be appropriate (paragraph 12.5).
- On appointment, non-executive directors should undertake that they will have sufficient time to meet what is expected of them, taking into account their other commitments (paragraph

12.13). If a non-executive director is offered appointments elsewhere, the chairman should be informed before any new appointment is accepted (paragraph 12.14).
- The nomination committee should annually review the time required of non-executive directors. The performance evaluation should assess whether non-executive directors are devoting enough time to fulfil their duties (paragraph 12.14).
- A full time executive director should not take on more than one non-executive directorship, nor become chairman, of a major company. No individual should chair the board of more than one major company (paragraph 12.19).

Remuneration

- The remuneration of a non-executive director should be sufficient to attract and fairly compensate high quality individuals. It may comprise an annual fee, a meeting attendance fee, and an additional fee for the chairmanship of committees (paragraph 12.24). Non-executive directors should have the opportunity to take part of their remuneration in the form of shares (paragraph 12.26).
- Non-executive directors should not hold options over shares in their company. If, exceptionally, some payment is made by means of options, shareholder approval should be sought in advance and any shares acquired by exercise of the options should be held until one year after the non-executive director leaves the board (paragraph 12.27).
- Where a company releases an executive director to serve as a non-executive director elsewhere, it should include in its remuneration policy report whether or not the director will retain the related remuneration and, if so, its amount (paragraph 12.28).

Resignation

- Where a non-executive director has concerns about the way in which a company is being run or about a course of action proposed by the board, these should be raised with the chairman and their fellow directors. Non-executive directors should ensure their concerns are recorded in the minutes of the board meetings if they cannot be resolved (paragraph 12.31).
- On resignation, a non-executive director should inform the chairman in writing, for circulation to the board, of the reasons for resignation (paragraph 12.32).

Audit and remuneration committees

- Sir Robert Smith's recommendations on audit committees, published today, are endorsed (paragraph 13.7).
- The remuneration committee should comprise at least three members, all of whom should be independent non-executive directors. It should have published terms of reference (paragraph 13.11). The Review offers a summary of the principal duties of the remuneration committee (Annex E).
- The remuneration committee should have delegated responsibility for setting remuneration for all executive directors and the chairman. The committee should also set the level and structure of compensation for senior executives. The committee should be responsible for appointing remuneration consultants (paragraph 13.12).
- No one non-executive director should sit on all three principal board committees (audit, nomination and remuneration) simultaneously (paragraph 13.2).

Liability

- Guidance is provided for incorporation into the Code on the position of a non-executive director, which may be relevant to the determination of liability (paragraph 14.8).
- The Review invites the Lord Chancellor's Department to consider steps to promote active case management in cases applying to directors (paragraph 14.11).
- The Government is recommended to consider the principles set out by the Company Law Review in considering criminal sanctions in relation to directors (paragraph 14.12).
- A company should be able to indemnify a director in advance against the reasonable cost of defending proceedings from the company itself, without trying to establish in advance the prospects of success of the case (paragraph 14.16).

- Companies should provide appropriate directors' and officers' insurance and supply details of their insurance cover to potential non-executive directors before they are appointed (paragraph 14.19).
- The City of London Law Society and the Institute of Chartered Secretaries and Administrators (ICSA), together with the Association of British Insurers (ABI) and the British Insurance Brokers' Association (BIBA), have agreed to draw up guidance on insurance for directors for companies to use in obtaining appropriate directors' and officers' insurance (paragraph 14.20).

Relationships with shareholders

- All non-executive directors, and in particular chairmen of the principal board committees, should attend the Annual General Meeting (AGM) to discuss issues that are raised in relation to their role (paragraph 15.10).
- The senior independent director should attend sufficient of the regular meetings of management with a range of major shareholders to develop a balanced understanding of the themes, issues and concerns of shareholders. The senior independent director should communicate these views to the non-executive directors and, as appropriate, to the board as a whole (paragraph 15.15).
- Boards should recognise that non-executive directors may find it instructive to attend meetings with major investors from time to time and should be able to do so if they choose. Moreover, non-executive directors should expect to attend such meetings if requested by major investors in the company (paragraph 15.16).
- On appointment, meetings should be arranged for non-executive directors with major investors, as part of the induction process (paragraph 15.17).
- A company should state what steps it has taken to ensure that the members of the board, and in particular the non-executive directors, develop a balanced understanding of the views of major investors (paragraph 15.18).
- The Review endorses the Government's approach to more active engagement by institutional shareholders with the companies in which they invest, and the Institutional Shareholder Committee's (ISC) code of activism. Institutional investors should attend AGMs where practicable (paragraph 15.24).

Smaller listed companies

- The recommendation that no one individual should sit on all three principal board committees at the same time should not apply to smaller listed companies. With this exception, there should be no differentiation in the Code's provisions for larger and smaller companies. It may take more time for smaller listed companies to comply fully with the Code and it is recognised that some of its provisions may be less relevant or manageable for smaller companies (paragraph 16.8).

Making change happen

- Most of the recommendations are for changes to the Code. These are consolidated in Annex A. It is hoped that the Financial Reporting Council (FRC) and the Financial Services Authority (FSA) will wish to take forward the Review's proposals and that the resulting changes will be introduced as soon as practicably possible, preferably for reporting years starting on or after 1 July 2003.
- To determine the extent to which behaviour has changed as a result of these proposals, it is recommended that the Government and the FRC review progress in two years' time on the proposals made by the Review (paragraph 17.11).

Guidance on Audit Committees (The Smith Guidance)
(FRC, Oct 2005)

AUDIT COMMITTEES—COMBINED CODE GUIDANCE

1. Introduction

1.1. This guidance is designed to assist company boards in making suitable arrangements for their audit committees, and to assist directors serving on audit committees in carrying out their role.

1.2. The paragraphs in bold are taken from the Combined Code (Section C3). Listed companies that do not comply with those provisions should include an explanation as to why they have not complied in the statement required by the Listing Rules.

1.3. Best practice requires that every board should consider in detail what arrangements for its audit committee are best suited for its particular circumstances. Audit committee arrangements need to be proportionate to the task, and will vary according to the size, complexity and risk profile of the company.

1.4. While all directors have a duty to act in the interests of the company the audit committee has a particular role, acting independently from the executive, to ensure that the interests of shareholders are properly protected in relation to financial reporting and internal control.

1.5. Nothing in the guidance should be interpreted as a departure from the principle of the unitary board. All directors remain equally responsible for the company's affairs as a matter of law. The audit committee, like other committees to which particular responsibilities are delegated (such as the remuneration committee), remains a committee of the board. Any disagreement within the board, including disagreement between the audit committee's members and the rest of the board, should be resolved at board level.

1.6. The Code provides that a separate section of the annual report should describe the work of the committee. This deliberately puts the spotlight on the audit committee and gives it an authority that it might otherwise lack. This is not incompatible with the principle of the unitary board.

1.7. The guidance contains recommendations about the conduct of the audit committee's relationship with the board, with the executive management and with internal and external auditors. However, the most important features of this relationship cannot be drafted as guidance or put into a code of practice: a frank, open working relationship and a high level of mutual respect are essential, particularly between the audit committee chairman and the board chairman, the chief executive and the finance director. The audit committee must be prepared to take a robust stand, and all parties must be prepared to make information freely available to the audit committee, to listen to their views and to talk through the issues openly.

1.8. In particular, the management is under an obligation to ensure the audit committee is kept properly informed, and should take the initiative in supplying information rather than waiting to be asked. The board should make it clear to all directors and staff that they must cooperate with the audit committee and provide it with any information it requires. In addition, executive board members will have regard to their common law duty to provide all directors, including those on the audit committee, with all the information they need to discharge their responsibilities as directors of the company.

1.9. Many of the core functions of audit committees set out in this guidance are expressed in terms of 'oversight', 'assessment' and 'review' of a particular function. It is not the duty of audit committees to carry out functions that properly belong to others, such as the company's management in the preparation of the financial statements or the auditors in the planning or conducting of audits. To do so could undermine the responsibility of management and auditors. Audit committees should, for example, satisfy themselves that there is a proper system and allocation of responsibilities for the day-to-day monitoring of financial controls but they should not seek to do the monitoring themselves.

1.10. However, the high-level oversight function may lead to detailed work. The audit committee must intervene if there are signs that something may be seriously amiss. For example, if the audit committee is uneasy about the explanations of management and auditors about a particular financial reporting policy decision, there may be no alternative but to grapple with the detail and perhaps to seek independent advice.

1.11. Under this guidance, audit committees have wide-ranging, time-consuming and sometimes intensive work to do. Companies need to make the necessary resources available. This includes suitable payment for the members of audit committees themselves. They—and particularly the audit committee chairman—bear a significant responsibility and they need to commit a significant extra amount of time to the job. Companies also need to make provision for induction and training for new audit committee members and continuing training as may be required.

1.12. This guidance applies to all companies to which the Code applies—i.e. UK listed companies. For groups, it will usually be necessary for the audit committee of the parent company to review issues that relate to particular subsidiaries or activities carried on by the group. Consequently, the board of a UK-listed parent company should ensure that there is adequate cooperation within the group (and with internal and external auditors of individual companies within the group) to enable the parent company audit committee to discharge its responsibilities effectively.

2 Establishment and role of the audit committee; membership, procedures and resources

Establishment and role

2.1 The board should establish an audit committee of at least three, or in the case of smaller companies two, members.

2.2 The main role and responsibilities of the audit committee should be set out in written terms of reference and should include:
+ to monitor the integrity of the financial statements of the company and any formal announcements relating to the company's financial performance, reviewing significant financial reporting judgements contained in them;
+ to review the company's internal financial controls and, unless expressly addressed by a separate board risk committee composed of independent directors or by the board itself, the company's internal control and risk management systems;
+ to monitor and review the effectiveness of the company's internal audit function;
+ to make recommendations to the board, for it to put to the shareholders for their approval in general meeting, in relation to the appointment of the external auditor and to approve the remuneration and terms of engagement of the external auditor;
+ to review and monitor the external auditor's independence and objectivity and the effectiveness of the audit process, taking into consideration relevant UK professional and regulatory requirements;
+ to develop and implement policy on the engagement of the external auditor to supply non-audit services, taking into account relevant ethical guidance regarding the provision of non-audit services by the external audit firm;

and to report to the Board, identifying any matters in respect of which it considers that action or improvement is needed, and making recommendations as to the steps to be taken.

Membership and appointment

2.3 All members of the committee should be independent non-executive directors. The board should satisfy itself that at least one member of the audit committee has recent and relevant financial experience.

2.4 The chairman of the company should not be an audit committee member.

2.5 Appointments to the audit committee should be made by the board on the recommendation of the nomination committee (where there is one), in consultation with the audit committee chairman.

2.6 Appointments should be for a period of up to three years, extendable by no more than two additional three-year periods, so long as members continue to be independent.

Meetings of the audit committee

2.7 It is for the audit committee chairman, in consultation with the company secretary, to decide the frequency and timing of its meetings. There should be as many meetings as the audit committee's role and responsibilities require. It is recommended there should be not fewer than three meetings during the year, held to coincide with key dates within the financial reporting and audit cycle.[1] However, most audit committee chairmen will wish to call more frequent meetings.

2.8 No one other than the audit committee's chairman and members is entitled to be present at a meeting of the audit committee. It is for the audit committee to decide if non-members should attend for a particular meeting or a particular agenda item. It is to be expected that the external audit lead partner will be invited regularly to attend meetings as well as the finance director. Others may be invited to attend.

2.9 Sufficient time should be allowed to enable the audit committee to undertake as full a discussion as may be required. A sufficient interval should be allowed between audit committee meetings and main board meetings to allow any work arising from the audit committee meeting to be carried out and reported to the board as appropriate.

2.10 The audit committee should, at least annually, meet the external and internal auditors, without management, to discuss matters relating to its remit and any issues arising from the audit.

2.11 Formal meetings of the audit committee are the heart of its work. However, they will rarely be sufficient. It is expected that the audit committee chairman, and to a lesser extent the other members, will wish to keep in touch on a continuing basis with the key people involved in the company's governance, including the board chairman, the chief executive, the finance director, the external audit lead partner and the head of internal audit.

Resources

2.12 The audit committee should be provided with sufficient resources to undertake its duties.

2.13 The audit committee should have access to the services of the company secretariat on all audit committee matters including: assisting the chairman in planning the audit committee's work, drawing up meeting agendas, maintenance of minutes, drafting of material about its activities for the annual report, collection and distribution of information and provision of any necessary practical support.

2.14 The company secretary should ensure that the audit committee receives information and papers in a timely manner to enable full and proper consideration to be given to the issues.

2.15 The board should make funds available to the audit committee to enable it to take independent legal, accounting or other advice when the audit committee reasonably believes it necessary to do so.

Remuneration

2.16 In addition to the remuneration paid to all non-executive directors, each company should consider the further remuneration that should be paid to members of the audit committee to recompense them for the additional responsibilities of membership. Consideration should be given to the time members are required to give to audit committee business, the skills they bring to bear and the onerous duties they take on, as well as the value of their work to the company. The level of remuneration paid to the members of the audit committee should take into account the level of fees paid to other members of the board. The chairman's responsibilities and time demands will

---

1 For example, when the audit plans (internal and external) are available for review and when interim statements, preliminary announcements and the full annual report are near completion.

generally be heavier than the other members of the audit committee and this should be reflected in his or her remuneration.

Skills, experience and training

2.17 It is desirable that the committee member whom the board considers to have recent and relevant financial experience should have a professional qualification from one of the professional accountancy bodies. The need for a degree of financial literacy among the other members will vary according to the nature of the company, but experience of corporate financial matters will normally be required. The availability of appropriate financial expertise will be particularly important where the company's activities involve specialised financial activities.

2.18 The company should provide an induction programme for new audit committee members. This should cover the role of the audit committee, including its terms of reference and expected time commitment by members; and an overview of the company's business, identifying the main business and financial dynamics and risks. It could also include meeting some of the company staff.

2.19 Training should also be provided to members of the audit committee on an ongoing and timely basis and should include an understanding of the principles of and developments in financial reporting and related company law. In appropriate cases, it may also include, for example, under-standing financial statements, applicable accounting standards and recommended practice; the regulatory framework for the company's business; the role of internal and external auditing and risk management.

2.20 The induction programme and ongoing training may take various forms, including attend-ance at formal courses and conferences, internal company talks and seminars, and briefings by external advisers.

3. Relationship with the board

3.1 The role of the audit committee is for the board to decide and to the extent that the audit committee undertakes tasks on behalf of the board, the results should be reported to, and consid-ered by, the board. In doing so it should identify any matters in respect of which it considers that action or improvement is needed, and make recommendations as to the steps to be taken.

3.2 The terms of reference should be tailored to the particular circumstances of the company.

3.3 The audit committee should review annually its terms of reference and its own effectiveness and recommend any necessary changes to the board.

3.4 The board should review the audit committee's effectiveness annually.

3.5 Where there is disagreement between the audit committee and the board, adequate time should be made available for discussion of the issue with a view to resolving the disagreement. Where any such disagreements cannot be resolved, the audit committee should have the right to report the issue to the shareholders as part of the report on its activities in the annual report.

4 Role and responsibilities

Financial reporting

4.1 The audit committee should review the significant financial reporting issues and judgements made in connection with the preparation of the company's financial statements, interim reports, preliminary announcements and related formal statements.

4.2 It is management's, not the audit committee's, responsibility to prepare complete and accurate financial statements and disclosures in accordance with financial reporting standards and applicable rules and regulations. However the audit committee should consider significant accounting policies, any changes to them and any significant estimates and judgements. The man-agement should inform the audit committee of the methods used to account for significant or unusual transactions where the accounting treatment is open to different approaches. Taking into account the external auditor's view, the audit committee should consider whether the company has adopted appropriate accounting policies and, where necessary, made appropriate estimates and judgements. The audit committee should review the clarity and completeness of disclosures in the financial statements and consider whether the disclosures made are set properly in context.

4.3 Where, following its review, the audit committee is not satisfied with any aspect of the proposed financial reporting by the company, it shall report its views to the board.

4.4 The audit committee should review related information presented with the financial statements, including the operating and financial review, and corporate governance statements relating to the audit and to risk management. Similarly, where board approval is required for other statements containing financial information (for example, summary financial statements, significant financial returns to regulators and release of price sensitive information), whenever practicable (without being inconsistent with any requirement for prompt reporting under the Listing Rules) the audit committee should review such statements first.

Internal controls and risk management systems

4.5 The audit committee should review the company's internal financial controls (that is, the systems established to identify, assess, manage and monitor financial risks); and unless expressly addressed by a separate board risk committee comprised of independent directors or by the board itself, the company's internal control and risk management systems.

4.6 The company's management is responsible for the identification, assessment, management and monitoring of risk, for developing, operating and monitoring the system of internal control and for providing assurance to the board that it has done so. Except where the board or a risk committee is expressly responsible for reviewing the effectiveness of the internal control and risk management systems, the audit committee should receive reports from management on the effectiveness of the systems they have established and the conclusions of any testing carried out by internal and external auditors.

4.7 Except to the extent that this is expressly dealt with by the board or risk committee, the audit committee should review and approve the statements included in the annual report in relation to internal control and the management of risk.

Whistleblowing

4.8 The audit committee should review arrangements by which staff of the company may, in confidence, raise concerns about possible improprieties in matters of financial reporting or other matters. The audit committee's objective should be to ensure that arrangements are in place for the proportionate and independent investigation of such matters and for appropriate follow-up action.

The internal audit process

4.9 The audit committee should monitor and review the effectiveness of the company's internal audit function. Where there is no internal audit function, the audit committee should consider annually whether there is a need for an internal audit function and make a recommendation to the board, and the reasons for the absence of such a function should be explained in the relevant section of the annual report.

4.10 The need for an internal audit function will vary depending on company specific factors including the scale, diversity and complexity of the company's activities and the number of employees, as well as cost/benefit considerations. Senior management and the board may desire objective assurance and advice on risk and control. An adequately resourced internal audit function (or its equivalent where, for example, a third party is contracted to perform some or all of the work concerned) may provide such assurance and advice. There may be other functions within the company that also provide assurance and advice covering specialist areas such as health and safety, regulatory and legal compliance and environmental issues.

4.11 When undertaking its assessment of the need for an internal audit function, the audit committee should also consider whether there are any trends or current factors relevant to the company's activities, markets or other aspects of its external environment, that have increased, or are expected to increase, the risks faced by the company. Such an increase in risk may also arise from internal factors such as organisational restructuring or from changes in reporting processes or underlying information systems. Other matters to be taken into account may include adverse trends evident from the monitoring of internal control systems or an increased incidence of unexpected occurrences.

4.12 In the absence of an internal audit function, management needs to apply other monitoring processes in order to assure itself, the audit committee and the board that the system of internal control is functioning as intended. In these circumstances, the audit committee will need to assess whether such processes provide sufficient and objective assurance.

4.13 The audit committee should review and approve the internal audit function's remit, having regard to the complementary roles of the internal and external audit functions. The audit committee should ensure that the function has the necessary resources and access to information to enable it to fulfil its mandate, and is equipped to perform in accordance with appropriate professional standards for internal auditors.[2]

4.14 The audit committee should approve the appointment or termination of appointment of the head of internal audit.

4.15 In its review of the work of the internal audit function, the audit committee should, inter alia:

+ ensure that the internal auditor has direct access to the board chairman and to the audit committee and is accountable to the audit committee;
+ review and assess the annual internal audit work plan;
+ receive a report on the results of the internal auditors' work on a periodic basis;
+ review and monitor management's responsiveness to the internal auditor's findings and recommendations;
+ meet with the head of internal audit at least once a year without the presence of management; and
+ monitor and assess the role and effectiveness of the internal audit function in the overall context of the company's risk management system.

The external audit process

4.16 The audit committee is the body responsible for overseeing the company's relations with the external auditor.

Appointment

4.17 The audit committee should have primary responsibility for making a recommendation on the appointment, reappointment and removal of the external auditors. If the board does not accept the audit committee's recommendation, it should include in the annual report, and in any papers recommending appointment or reappointment, a statement from the audit committee explaining its recommendation and should set out reasons why the board has taken a different position.

4.18 The audit committee's recommendation to the board should be based on the assessments referred to below. If the audit committee recommends considering the selection of possible new appointees as external auditors, it should oversee the selection process.

4.19 The audit committee should assess annually the qualification, expertise and resources, and independence (see below) of the external auditors and the effectiveness of the audit process. The assessment should cover all aspects of the audit service provided by the audit firm, and include obtaining a report on the audit firm's own internal quality control procedures.

---

2 Further guidance can be found in the Institute of Internal Auditors' Code of Ethics and the International Standards for the Professional Practice of Internal Auditing Standards.

4.20 If the external auditor resigns, the audit committee should investigate the issues giving rise to such resignation and consider whether any action is required.

Terms and Remuneration

4.21 The audit committee should approve the terms of engagement and the remuneration to be paid to the external auditor in respect of audit services provided.

4.22 The audit committee should review and agree the engagement letter issued by the external auditor at the start of each audit, ensuring that it has been updated to reflect changes in circumstances arising since the previous year. The scope of the external audit should be reviewed by the audit committee with the auditor. If the audit committee is not satisfied as to its adequacy it should arrange for additional work to be undertaken.

4.23 The audit committee should satisfy itself that the level of fee payable in respect of the audit services provided is appropriate and that an effective audit can be conducted for such a fee.

Independence, including the provision of non-audit services

4.24 The audit committee should have procedures to ensure the independence and objectivity of the external auditor annually, taking into consideration relevant UK professional and regulatory requirements. This assessment should involve a consideration of all relationships between the company and the audit firm (including the provision of non-audit services). The audit committee should consider whether, taken as a whole and having regard to the views, as appropriate, of the external auditor, management and internal audit, those relationships appear to impair the auditor's judgement or independence.

4.25 The audit committee should seek reassurance that the auditors and their staff have no family, financial, employment, investment or business relationship with the company (other than in the normal course of business). The audit committee should seek from the audit firm, on an annual basis, information about policies and processes for maintaining independence and monitoring compliance with relevant requirements, including current requirements regarding the rotation of audit partners and staff.

4.26 The audit committee should agree with the board the company's policy for the employment of former employees of the external auditor, paying particular attention to the policy regarding former employees of the audit firm who were part of the audit team and moved directly to the company. This should be drafted taking into account the relevant ethical guidelines governing the accounting profession. The audit committee should monitor application of the policy, including the number of former employees of the external auditor currently employed in senior positions in the company, and consider whether in the light of this there has been any impairment, or appearance of impairment, of the auditor's judgement or independence in respect of the audit.

4.27 The audit committee should monitor the external audit firm's compliance with applicable United Kingdom ethical guidance relating to the rotation of audit partners, the level of fees that the company pays in proportion to the overall fee income of the firm, office and partner, and other related regulatory requirements.

4.28 The audit committee should develop and recommend to the board the company's policy in relation to the provision of non-audit services by the auditor. The audit committee's objective should be to ensure that the provision of such services does not impair the external auditor's independence or objectivity. In this context, the audit committee should consider:
+ whether the skills and experience of the audit firm make it a suitable supplier of the non audit service;
+ whether there are safeguards in place to ensure that there is no threat to objectivity and independence in the conduct of the audit resulting from the provision of such services by the external auditor;
+ the nature of the non-audit services, the related fee levels and the fee levels individually and in aggregate relative to the audit fee; and
+ the criteria which govern the compensation of the individuals performing the audit.

4.29 The audit committee should set and apply a formal policy specifying the types of non-audit work:

+ from which the external auditors are excluded;
+ for which the external auditors can be engaged without referral to the audit committee; and
+ for which a case-by-case decision is necessary.

In addition, the policy may set fee limits generally or for particular classes of work.

4.30 In the third category, if it is not practicable to give approval to individual items in advance, it may be appropriate to give a general pre-approval for certain classes for work, subject to a fee limit determined by the audit committee and ratified by the board. The subsequent provision of any service by the auditor should be ratified at the next meeting of the audit committee.

4.31 In determining the policy, the audit committee should take into account relevant ethical guidance regarding the provision of non-audit services by the external audit firm, and in principle should not agree to the auditor providing a service if, having regard to the ethical guidance, the result is that:

+ the external auditor audits its own firm's work;
+ the external auditor makes management decisions for the company;
+ a mutuality of interest is created; or
+ the external auditor is put in the role of advocate for the company.

The audit committee should satisfy itself that any safeguards required by ethical guidance are implemented.

4.32 The annual report should explain to shareholders how, if the auditor provides non-audit services, auditor objectivity and independence is safeguarded.

Annual audit cycle

4.33 At the start of each annual audit cycle, the audit committee should ensure that appropriate plans are in place for the audit.

4.34 The audit committee should consider whether the auditor's overall work plan, including planned levels of materiality, and proposed resources to execute the audit plan appears consistent with the scope of the audit engagement, having regard also to the seniority, expertise and experience of the audit team.

4.35 The audit committee should review, with the external auditors, the findings of their work. In the course of its review, the audit committee should:

+ discuss with the external auditor major issues that arose during the course of the audit and have subsequently been resolved and those issues that have been left unresolved;
+ review key accounting and audit judgements; and
+ review levels of errors identified during the audit, obtaining explanations from management and, where necessary the external auditors, as to why certain errors might remain unadjusted.

4.36 The audit committee should also review the audit representation letters before signature by management and give particular consideration to matters where representation has been requested that relate to non-standard issues.[3] The audit committee should consider whether the information provided is complete and appropriate based on its own knowledge.

4.37 As part of the ongoing monitoring process, the audit committee should review the management letter (or equivalent). The audit committee should review and monitor management's responsiveness to the external auditor's findings and recommendations.

---

3 Further guidance can by found in the Auditing Practices Board's Statement of Auditing Standard 440 "Management Representations".

4.38 At the end of the annual audit cycle, the audit committee should assess the effectiveness of the audit process. In the course of doing so, the audit committee should:
+ review whether the auditor has met the agreed audit plan and understand the reasons for any changes, including changes in perceived audit risks and the work undertaken by the external auditors to address those risks;
+ consider the robustness and perceptiveness of the auditors in their handling of the key accounting and audit judgements identified and in responding to questions from the audit committees, and in their commentary where appropriate on the systems of internal control;
+ obtain feedback about the conduct of the audit from key people involved, e.g. the finance director and the head of internal audit; and
+ review and monitor the content of the external auditor's management letter, in order to assess whether it is based on a good understanding of the company's business and establish whether recommendations have been acted upon and, if not, the reasons why they have not been acted upon.

5 Communication with shareholders

5.1 The terms of reference of the audit committee, including its role and the authority delegated to it by the board, should be made available. A separate section in the annual report should describe the work of the committee in discharging those responsibilities.

5.2 The audit committee section should include, inter alia:
+ a summary of the role of the audit committee;
+ the names and qualifications of all members of the audit committee during the period;
+ the number of audit committee meetings;
+ a report on the way the audit committee has discharged its responsibilities; and
+ the explanation provided for in paragraph 4.29 above.

Internal Control: Revised Guidance For Directors on the Combined Code (The Turnbull Guidance)

(FRC, Oct 2005)

One—Introduction
The importance of internal control and risk management

1 A company's system of internal control has a key role in the management of risks that are significant to the fulfilment of its business objectives. A sound system of internal control contributes to safeguarding the shareholders' investment and the company's assets.

2 Internal control (as referred to in paragraph 19) facilitates the effectiveness and efficiency of operations, helps ensure the reliability of internal and external reporting and assists compliance with laws and regulations.

3 Effective financial controls, including the maintenance of proper accounting records, are an important element of internal control. They help ensure that the company is not unnecessarily exposed to avoidable financial risks and that financial information used within the business and for publication is reliable. They also contribute to the safeguarding of assets, including the prevention and detection of fraud.

4 A company's objectives, its internal organisation and the environment in which it operates are continually evolving and, as a result, the risks it faces are continually changing. A sound system of internal control therefore depends on a thorough and regular evaluation of the nature and extent of the risks to which the company is exposed. Since profits are, in part, the reward for successful risk-taking in business, the purpose of internal control is to help manage and control risk appropriately rather than to eliminate it.

Objectives of the guidance

5 This guidance is intended to:

- reflect sound business practice whereby internal control is embedded in the business processes by which a company pursues its objectives;
- remain relevant over time in the continually evolving business environment; and
- enable each company to apply it in a manner which takes account of its particular circumstances.

The guidance requires directors to exercise judgement in reviewing how the company has implemented the requirements of the Combined Code relating to internal control and reporting to shareholders thereon.

6 The guidance is based on the adoption by a company's board of a risk-based approach to establishing a sound system of internal control and reviewing its effectiveness. This should be incorporated by the company within its normal management and governance processes. It should not be treated as a separate exercise undertaken to meet regulatory requirements.

Internal control requirements of the Combined Code

7 Principle C.2 of the Code states that 'The board should maintain a sound system of internal control to safeguard shareholders' investment and the company's assets'.

8 Provision C.2.1 states that 'The directors should, at least annually, conduct a review of the effectiveness of the group's system of internal control and should report to shareholders that they have done so. The review should cover all material controls, including financial, operational and compliance controls and risk management systems'.

9 Paragraph 9.8.6 of the UK Listing Authority's Listing Rules states that in the case of a listed company incorporated in the United Kingdom, the following items must be included in its annual report and accounts:

- a statement of how the listed company has applied the principles set out in Section 1 of the Combined Code, in a manner that would enable shareholders to evaluate how the principles have been applied;
- a statement as to whether the listed company has:
  - complied throughout the accounting period with all relevant provisions set out in Section 1 of the Combined Code; or
  - not complied throughout the accounting period with all relevant provisions set out in Section 1 of the Combined Code and if so, setting out:
    (i) those provisions, if any, it has not complied with;
    (ii) in the case of provisions whose requirements are of a continuing nature, the period within which, if any, it did not comply with some or all of those provisions; and
    (iii) the company's reasons for non-compliance.

10 The Preamble to the Code makes it clear that there is no prescribed form or content for the statement setting out how the various principles in the Code have been applied. The intention is that companies should have a free hand to explain their governance policies in the light of the principles, including any special circumstances which have led to them adopting a particular approach.

11 The guidance in this document applies for accounting periods beginning on or after 1 January 2006, and should be followed by boards of listed companies in:

- assessing how the company has applied Code Principle C.2;
- implementing the requirements of Code Provision C.2.1; and
- reporting on these matters to shareholders in the annual report and accounts.

12 For the purposes of this guidance, internal controls considered by the board should include all types of controls including those of an operational and compliance nature, as well as internal financial controls.

Groups of companies

13 Throughout this guidance, where reference is made to 'company' it should be taken, where applicable, as referring to the group of which the reporting company is the parent company. For groups of companies, the review of effectiveness of internal control and the report to the shareholders should be from the perspective of the group as a whole.

The Appendix

14 The Appendix to this document contains questions which boards may wish to consider in applying this guidance.

Two—Maintaining a sound system of internal control

Responsibilities

15 The board of directors is responsible for the company's system of internal control. It should set appropriate policies on internal control and seek regular assurance that will enable it to satisfy itself that the system is functioning effectively. The board must further ensure that the system of internal control is effective in managing those risks in the manner which it has approved.

16 In determining its policies with regard to internal control, and thereby assessing what constitutes a sound system of internal control in the particular circumstances of the company, the board's deliberations should include consideration of the following factors:

- the nature and extent of the risks facing the company;
- the extent and categories of risk which it regards as acceptable for the company to bear;
- the likelihood of the risks concerned materialising;
- the company's ability to reduce the incidence and impact on the business of risks that do materialise; and
- the costs of operating particular controls relative to the benefit thereby obtained in managing the related risks.

17 It is the role of management to implement board policies on risk and control. In fulfilling its responsibilities management should identify and evaluate the risks faced by the company for consideration by the board and design, operate and monitor a suitable system of internal control which implements the policies adopted by the board.

18 All employees have some responsibility for internal control as part of their accountability for achieving objectives. They, collectively, should have the necessary knowledge, skills, information, and authority to establish, operate and monitor the system of internal control. This will require an understanding of the company, its objectives, the industries and markets in which it operates, and the risks it faces.

Elements of a sound system of internal control

19 An internal control system encompasses the policies, processes, tasks, behaviours and other aspects of a company that, taken together:

- facilitate its effective and efficient operation by enabling it to respond appropriately to significant business, operational, financial, compliance and other risks to achieving the company's objectives. This includes the safeguarding of assets from inappropriate use or from loss and fraud and ensuring that liabilities are identified and managed;
- help ensure the quality of internal and external reporting. This requires the maintenance of proper records and processes that generate a flow of timely, relevant and reliable information from within and outside the organisation;
- help ensure compliance with applicable laws and regulations, and also with internal policies with respect to the conduct of business.

20 A company's system of internal control will reflect its control environment which encompasses its organisational structure. The system will include:

- control activities;
- information and communications processes; and
- processes for monitoring the continuing effectiveness of the system of internal control.

21 The system of internal control should:
- be embedded in the operations of the company and form part of its culture;
- be capable of responding quickly to evolving risks to the business arising from factors within the company and to changes in the business environment; and
- include procedures for reporting immediately to appropriate levels of management any significant control failings or weaknesses that are identified together with details of corrective action being undertaken.

22 A sound system of internal control reduces, but cannot eliminate, the possibility of poor judgement in decision-making; human error; control processes being deliberately circumvented by employees and others; management overriding controls; and the occurrence of unforeseeable circumstances.

23 A sound system of internal control therefore provides reasonable, but not absolute, assurance that a company will not be hindered in achieving its business objectives, or in the orderly and legitimate conduct of its business, by circumstances which may reasonably be foreseen. A system of internal control cannot, however, provide protection with certainty against a company failing to meet its business objectives or all material errors, losses, fraud, or breaches of laws or regulations.

Three—Reviewing the effectiveness of internal control
Responsibilities

24 Reviewing the effectiveness of internal control is an essential part of the board's responsibilities. The board will need to form its own view on effectiveness based on the information and assurances provided to it, exercising the standard of care generally applicable to directors in the exercise of their duties. Management is accountable to the board for monitoring the system of internal control and for providing assurance to the board that it has done so.

25 The role of board committees in the review process, including that of the audit committee, is for the board to decide and will depend upon factors such as the size and composition of the board; the scale, diversity and complexity of the company's operations; and the nature of the significant risks that the company faces. To the extent that designated board committees carry out, on behalf of the board, tasks that are attributed in this guidance document to the board, the results of the relevant committees' work should be reported to, and considered by, the board. The board takes responsibility for the disclosures on internal control in the annual report and accounts.

The process for reviewing effectiveness

26 Effective monitoring on a continuous basis is an essential component of a sound system of internal control. The board cannot, however, rely solely on the embedded monitoring processes within the company to discharge its responsibilities. It should regularly receive and review reports on internal control. In addition, the board should undertake an annual assessment for the purposes of making its public statement on internal control to ensure that it has considered all significant aspects of internal control for the company for the year under review and up to the date of approval of the annual report and accounts.

27 The board should define the process to be adopted for its review of the effectiveness of internal control. This should encompass both the scope and frequency of the reports it receives and reviews during the year, and also the process for its annual assessment, such that it will be provided with sound, appropriately documented, support for its statement on internal control in the company's annual report and accounts.

28 The reports from management to the board should, in relation to the areas covered by them, provide a balanced assessment of the significant risks and the effectiveness of the system of internal

control in managing those risks. Any significant control failings or weaknesses identified should be discussed in the reports, including the impact that they have had, or may have, on the company and the actions being taken to rectify them. It is essential that there be openness of communication by management with the board on matters relating to risk and control.

29 When reviewing reports during the year, the board should:
- consider what are the significant risks and assess how they have been identified, evaluated and managed;
- assess the effectiveness of the related system of internal control in managing the significant risks, having regard in particular to any significant failings or weaknesses in internal control that have been reported;
- consider whether necessary actions are being taken promptly to remedy any significant failings or weaknesses; and
- consider whether the findings indicate a need for more extensive monitoring of the system of internal control.

30 Additionally, the board should undertake an annual assessment for the purpose of making its public statement on internal control. The assessment should consider issues dealt with in reports reviewed by it during the year together with any additional information necessary to ensure that the board has taken account of all significant aspects of internal control for the company for the year under review and up to the date of approval of the annual report and accounts.

31 The board's annual assessment should, in particular, consider:
- the changes since the last annual assessment in the nature and extent of significant risks, and the company's ability to respond to changes in its business and the external environment;
- the scope and quality of management's ongoing monitoring of risks and of the system of internal control, and, where applicable, the work of its internal audit function and other providers of assurance;
- the extent and frequency of the communication of the results of the monitoring to the board (or board committee(s)) which enables it to build up a cumulative assessment of the state of control in the company and the effectiveness with which risk is being managed;
- the incidence of significant control failings or weaknesses that have been identified at any time during the period and the extent to which they have resulted in unforeseen outcomes or contingencies that have had, could have had, or may in the future have, a material impact on the company's financial performance or condition; and
- the effectiveness of the company's public reporting processes.

32 Should the board become aware at any time of a significant failing or weakness in internal control, it should determine how the failing or weakness arose and reassess the effectiveness of management's ongoing processes for designing, operating and monitoring the system of internal control.

Four—The board's statement on internal control

33 The annual report and accounts should include such meaningful, high-level information as the board considers necessary to assist shareholders' understanding of the main features of the company's risk management processes and system of internal control, and should not give a misleading impression.

34 In its narrative statement of how the company has applied Code Principle C.2, the board should, as a minimum, disclose that there is an ongoing process for identifying, evaluating and managing the significant risks faced by the company, that it has been in place for the year under review and up to the date of approval of the annual report and accounts, that it is regularly reviewed by the board and accords with the guidance in this document.

35 The disclosures relating to the application of Principle C.2 should include an acknowledgement by the board that it is responsible for the company's system of internal control and for

reviewing its effectiveness. It should also explain that such a system is designed to manage rather than eliminate the risk of failure to achieve business objectives, and can only provide reasonable and not absolute assurance against material misstatement or loss.

36 In relation to Code Provision C.2.1, the board should summarise the process it has applied (where applicable, through its committees) in reviewing the effectiveness of the system of internal control and confirm that necessary actions have been or are being taken to remedy any significant failings or weaknesses identified from that review. It should also disclose the process it has applied to deal with material internal control aspects of any significant problems disclosed in the annual report and accounts.

37 Where a board cannot make one or more of the disclosures in paragraphs 34 and 36, it should state this fact and provide an explanation. The Listing Rules require the board to disclose if it has failed to conduct a review of the effectiveness of the company's system of internal control.

38 Where material joint ventures and associates have not been dealt with as part of the group for the purposes of applying this guidance, this should be disclosed.

Five—Appendix

Assessing the effectiveness of the company's risk and control processes

Some questions which the board may wish to consider and discuss with management when regularly reviewing reports on internal control and when carrying out its annual assessment are set out below. The questions are not intended to be exhaustive and will need to be tailored to the particular circumstances of the company.

This Appendix should be read in conjunction with the guidance set out in this document.

Risk assessment

- Does the company have clear objectives and have they been communicated so as to provide effective direction to employees on risk assessment and control issues? For example, do objectives and related plans include measurable performance targets and indicators?
- Are the significant internal and external operational, financial, compliance and other risks identified and assessed on an ongoing basis? These are likely to include the principal risks identified in the Operating and Financial Review.
- Is there a clear understanding by management and others within the company of what risks are acceptable to the board?

Control environment and control activities

- Does the board have clear strategies for dealing with the significant risks that have been identified? Is there a policy on how to manage these risks?
- Do the company's culture, code of conduct, human resource policies and performance reward systems support the business objectives and risk management and internal control system?
- Does senior management demonstrate, through its actions as well as it policies, the necessary commitment to competence, integrity and fostering a climate of trust within the company?
- Are authority, responsibility and accountability defined clearly such that decisions are made and actions taken by the appropriate people? Are the decisions and actions of different parts of the company appropriately co-ordinated?
- Does the company communicate to its employees what is expected of them and the scope of their freedom to act? This may apply to areas such as customer relations; service levels for both internal and outsourced activities; health, safety and environmental protection; security of tangible and intangible assets; business continuity issues; expenditure matters; accounting; and financial and other reporting.
- Do people in the company (and in its providers of outsourced services) have the knowledge, skills and tools to support the achievement of the company's objectives and to manage effectively risks to their achievement?
- How are processes/controls adjusted to reflect new or changing risks, or operational deficiencies?

Information and communication

- Do management and the board receive timely, relevant and reliable reports on progress against business objectives and the related risks that provide them with the information, from inside and outside the company, needed for decision-making and management review purposes? This could include performance reports and indicators of change, together with qualitative information such as on customer satisfaction, employee attitudes etc.
- Are information needs and related information systems reassessed as objectives and related risks change or as reporting deficiencies are identified?
- Are periodic reporting procedures, including half-yearly and annual reporting, effective in communicating a balanced and understandable account of the company's position and prospects?
- Are there established channels of communication for individuals to report suspected breaches of law or regulations or other improprieties?

Monitoring

- Are there ongoing processes embedded within the company's overall business operations, and addressed by senior management, which monitor the effective application of the policies, processes and activities related to internal control and risk management? (Such processes may include control self-assessment, confirmation by personnel of compliance with policies and codes of conduct, internal audit reviews or other management reviews).
- Do these processes monitor the company's ability to re-evaluate risks and adjust controls effectively in response to changes in its objectives, its business, and its external environment?
- Are there effective follow-up procedures to ensure that appropriate change or action occurs in response to changes in risk and control assessments?
- Is there appropriate communication to the board (or board committees) on the effectiveness of the ongoing monitoring processes on risk and control matters? This should include reporting any significant failings or weaknesses on a timely basis.
- Are there specific arrangements for management monitoring and reporting to the board on risk and control matters of particular importance? These could include, for example, actual or suspected fraud and other illegal or irregular acts, or matters that could adversely affect the company's reputation or financial position.

9

Shares and Share Capital

9.1 THE NATURE OF SHARES

The assets of a company are owned by the company and a shareholder has no property interest in them. Owning an ordinary share confers on its holder a complex bundle of rights and benefits including generally a right to vote, a right to dividends when declared, and a return of contributed capital and of any surplus assets on winding up. The specific rights actually conferred depend on the precise terms of issue of the class of shares such as ordinary or preference shares. Registration of a share in the name of a shareholder makes that shareholder a member of the company and a party to the contract contained in the memorandum and articles of association (see chapter 6).

Many of the cases in this chapter concern the underlying nature and characteristics of shares. For example, the process of valuing shares (see 9.5) necessitates an analysis of the specific rights and benefits that those particular shares confer on their holder.

The following extract from an article by Professor Pennington explores the nature or definition of shares in companies.

Robert Pennington, 'Can shares in companies be defined?'
(1989) 10 Co Law 140

Shares in registered companies Judicial decisions during and since the second half of the 19th century have made it clear beyond question that shareholders or members of a company registered under the Companies Acts have no legal or equitable interest in any part of the company's property or assets, and the company is the sole and beneficial owner of all the property vested in it. Companies can hold their assets in trust for other persons if the trust is expressly created or arises by implication or constructively under a rule of equity, but there is no such trust implied or imposed constructively by a rule of law or equity in favour of shareholders or members of the company as such. Shares are treated as personal property despite the ownership of land by the company, and as personal property they can be the subject of transactions and dispositions in the same way as other species of personal property....

The legal nature of shares in a registered company An examination of the legal antecedents of shares in companies registered under the Companies Acts helps to ascertain the rules of law and equity which are applicable to them at the present time, but it provides little material for an abstract definition of shares. This is because the courts have usually been able to solve the practical questions which have come before them without feeling the need to base their decisions on definitions, and it has usually sufficed for the courts to refer to the substantive rules of law or equity which provides the solution to those problems. The farthest the courts have ventured, except in one case (Borland's Trustee v Steel Brothers & Co. Ltd [1901] 1 Ch 279), has been to categorise shares as 'property', which is useful in indicating that transactions in shares will be legally recognised if they are possible in respect of other species of property, and to describe shares as 'choses in action' or 'things in action', which can be deceptive if taken to mean anything more than shares are classified as intangible movables, and it certainly does not mean that shares are analogous to debts.

The one decided case in which the court was compelled to provide something close to a definition of shares was one in which a provision in the company's articles of association that the shares of a shareholder who became bankrupt should be made available for purchase by the other shareholders at a certain price, was challenged on the ground that the provision infringed the rules against perpetuities and against restrictions on the alienation of property. To succeed with such a contention the plaintiff had to convince the court that shares must be treated as money or funds settled by the investor on the terms and conditions set out in the company's articles of association, which took effect in the same way as a deed constituting a trust and defining the beneficial interests in it. Farwell J rejected this contention in the following words:

> A share according to the plaintiff's argument, is a sum of money which is dealt with in a particular manner by what are called executory limitations. To my mind it is nothing of the sort. A share is the interest of a shareholder in the company measured by a sum of money, for the purpose of liability in the first place, and of interest in the second, but also consisting of a series of mutual covenants entered into by all the shareholders *inter se* in accordance with s. 16 of the Companies Act 1862 [now the Companies Act 2006, s. 33(1)]. The contract contained in the articles of association is one of the original incidents of the share. A share is not a sum of money settled in the way suggested, but is an interest measured by a sum of money and made up of various rights contained in the contract, including the right to a sum of money of a more or less amount. [*Borland* v *Steel* [1901] 1 Ch 279 at p. 288.]

The concept of a share in this decision is clear. The so-called statutory contract [CA 2006, s. 33(1)] obliges both the company and its members to conform to the terms and conditions contained in the company's memorandum and articles of association in respect of shares. This gives rise to contractual rights and obligations of each member as regards the company and every other member. The aggregate of these rights and obligations of a member is his shareholding, and when divided between the shares he holds, they constitute his shares. In fact, a concept of shares in these terms is incomplete, because many of the important rights and obligations of a member of a registered company under the present law are conferred or imposed on him, not by the statutory contract, but directly by the Companies Act 1985, itself. Nevertheless, if account is taken of such statutory rights and obligations and they are aggregated with the member's rights and obligations under the statutory contract, the whole complex of member's rights and obligations constitutes his shareholding. It follows, therefore, that because such rights and obligations are the components of shares, and not distinct items of property or limitations imposed on a separate item of property (i.e. the funds paid to the company in consideration of the issue of shares), shares cannot themselves be subject to rules of law which invalidate certain dispositions of property, such as the rule against perpetuities. Dispositions of shares which already exist are, of course, subject to those rules of law, because shares are items of property, but the constituent contractual and statutory rights which together make up shares cannot be.

Although Farwell J's decision provides a useful description of the nature of shares and a guide to the manner in which they must be treated in applying legal principles to them, the decision does not supply an abstract definition which encapsulates all the distinctive features of shares and excludes everything which is not true of them. The accepted American description of a share as 'a profit sharing contract, one of a series of units of interest and participation, authorised by the charter of a corporation, by which capital is obtained in consideration of a proportional right to participate in dividend and their distributions' (*Ballantine on Corporations*, rev. ed., 1946, para. 198; Henn and Alexander, *Law of Corporations*, 3rd ed., para. 157) is for the same reasons not a definition either, nor is the accepted French description of shares as 'the rights of a shareholder in a company with a share capital as opposed to his economic interest in it' (Ripert and Roblot, *Traité élémentaire de droit commercial*, 12th ed., para. 1147), nor the accepted German description of a share as 'the collective proprietory and membership rights inherent in a member's participation in a company (Godin-Welhelmi, *Aktiengesetz*, 3rd ed. vol. 1, p. 12). The truth of the matter is that for practical purposes Farwell J's description of shares suffices, and it is more important in applying the law to ascertain the legal rules governing the rights and liabilities of a holder of shares and the nature and formalities of transactions in shares which the law recognises, than to devise an unobjectionable definition of shares....

9.2 ISSUE AND TRANSFER OF SHARES

Traditionally shares are issued by the directors. (At common law an issue of shares for an improper purpose, such as to defeat a takeover bid, may be avoided by court action (see 12.4.1). They may issue and 'allot' shares if they are authorised to do so by the articles or by a resolution of the company (see CA 2006, s. 551 below). In private companies the directors are often given a mandate to issue shares which is renewed when necessary. (See, for example, art. 2(d) of the articles reproduced at 1.6.)

A principal feature of private companies is that they may not offer shares to the public (see 17.1). Offerings of shares by public companies are extensively regulated for the purpose of protecting investors (see chapter 17). Shares may be issued for cash or in return for property. For example, on a public company takeover offer, the bidding company usually issues its own shares in return for the shares that it is acquiring in the target company rather than paying for them in cash (see 18.1). Where a public company issues its shares in return for property (other than shares), that property must be formally valued to ensure that the capital is properly subscribed (see 10.2.2).

COMPANIES ACT 2006, PART 17

551. Power of directors to allot shares etc: authorisation by company

(1) The directors of a company may exercise a power of the company—
    (a) to allot shares in the company, or
    (b) to grant rights to subscribe for or to convert any security into shares in the company,
  if they are authorised to do so by the company's articles or by resolution of the company.
(2) Authorisation may be given for a particular exercise of the power or for its exercise generally, and may be unconditional or subject to conditions.

542. Nominal value of shares

(1) Shares in a limited company having a share capital must each have a fixed nominal value.
(2) An allotment of a share that does not have a fixed nominal value is void.
(3) Shares in a limited company having a share capital may be denominated in any currency, and different classes of shares may be denominated in different currencies.
But see section 765 (initial authorised minimum share capital requirement for public company to be met by reference to share capital denominated in sterling or euros).

617. Alteration of share capital of limited company

(1) A limited company having a share capital may not alter its share capital except in the following ways.
(2) The company may—
    (a) increase its share capital by allotting new shares in accordance with this Part, or
    (b) reduce its share capital in accordance with Chapter 10.

Shareholders may acquire their shares by subscribing for a new issue of shares that are allotted to them by the company, or they may take a transfer of shares from an existing member. Shares of companies listed on the Stock Exchange are freely transferable. It is the essential nature of a public share market that this is so. However, with a private company there are invariably restrictions on the transfer of shares. The personal nature of a private business requires appropriate control on the admission of new members. These restrictions may take the form of pre-emption rights contained in the articles. An example of these is found in art. 14 of the sample articles at 1.6. From these it will be seen that pre-emption provisions may be long and complex. Usually a member wishing to sell shares must notify the board and the shares are then offered to the existing members in proportion to their respective holdings. The difficult question is the appropriate price to be paid and a valuation is therefore usually certified by the company's auditors. Only if the existing members do not wish to acquire the shares at that price may they be offered to outsiders. (On pre-emption rights see also CA 2006, Part 17, Chapter 3.)

The other restriction on the transfer of shares in private companies is that the articles may give the directors discretion to refuse to register a transfer of shares to any outsider. To obtain registration a transferee submits the share certificate and a share transfer form signed by the seller to the board for approval and registration of the transferee's name in the register of members. At this point the board has a discretion to refuse to register the transfer, thus refusing admission of the new member. However, this discretion is a fiduciary power to be used bona fide and for the benefit of the company as appears from the following case.

Under the new s. 771 that appears below, the company must now give a transferee reasons for refusing to register the transfer.

Re Smith & Fawcett Ltd

The discretion to refuse to register transfers

[1942] Ch 304, Court of Appeal

A discretion to refuse to register transfers of shares may be absolute and uncontrolled so long as it is exercised bona fide in the company's interests.

Facts   The articles of the company said, 'The directors may at any time in their absolute and uncontrolled discretion refuse to register any transfer of shares'. Smith and Fawcett were the sole directors and each held 50 per cent of the issued shares. Fawcett died. Smith and a newly appointed second director refused to register Fawcett's shares in the name of his executors. Smith offered to register half of them and to buy the rest himself. The court, in the absence of evidence of mala fides, refused to intervene in the exercise by the directors of their discretion.

LORD GREENE MR: The principles to be applied in cases where the articles of a company confer a discretion on directors with regard to the acceptance of transfers of shares are, for the present purposes, free from doubt. They must exercise their discretion bona fide in what they consider—not what a court may consider—is in the interests of the company, and not for any collateral purpose. They must have regard to those considerations, and those considerations only, which the articles on their true construction permit them to take into consideration, and in construing the relevant provisions in the articles it is to be borne in mind that one of the normal rights of a shareholder is the right to deal freely with his property and to transfer it to whomsoever he pleases. When it is said, as it has been said more than once, that regard must be had to this last consideration, it means, I apprehend, nothing more than that the shareholder has such a prima facie right, and that right is not to be cut down by uncertain language or doubtful implications. The right, if it is to be cut down, must be cut down with satisfactory clarity. It certainly does not mean that articles, if appropriately framed, cannot be allowed to cut down the right of transfer to any extent which the articles on their true construction permit. Another consideration which must be borne in mind is that this type of article is one which is for the most part confined to private companies. Private companies are in law separate entities just as much as are public companies, but from the business and personal point of view they are much more analogous to partnerships than to public corporations. Accordingly, it is to be expected that in the articles of such a company the control of the directors over the membership may be very strict indeed. There are, or may be, very good business reasons why those who bring such companies into existence should give them a constitution which confers on the directors powers of the widest description.

The language of the article in the present case does not point out any particular matter as being the only matter to which the directors are to pay attention in deciding whether or not they will allow the transfer to be registered. The article does not, for instance, say, as is to be found in some articles, that they may refuse to register any transfer of shares to a person not already a member of the company or to a transferee of whom they do not approve. Where articles are framed with some such limitation on the discretionary power of refusal as I have mentioned in those two examples, it follows on plain principle that if the directors go outside the matters which the articles say are to be the matters and the only matters to which they are to have regard, the directors will have exceeded their powers....

There is nothing, in my opinion, in principle or in authority to make it impossible to draft such a wide and comprehensive power to directors to refuse to transfer as to enable them to take into account any matter which they conceive to be in the interests of the company, and thereby to admit or not to admit a particular person and to allow or not to allow a particular transfer for reasons not personal to the transferee but bearing on the general interests of the company as a whole—such matters, for instance, as whether by their passing a particular transfer the transferee would obtain too great a weight in the councils of the company or might even perhaps obtain control. The question, therefore, simply is whether on the true construction of the particular article the directors are limited by anything except their bona fide view as to the interests of the company. In the present case the article is drafted in the widest possible terms, and I decline to write into that clear language any limitation other than a limitation, which is implicit by law, that a fiduciary power of this kind must be exercised bona fide in the interests of the company. Subject to that qualification, an article in this form appears to me to give the directors what it says, namely, an absolute and uncontrolled discretion.

COMPANIES ACT 2006

544. Transferability of shares

(1) The shares or other interest of any member in a company are transferable in accordance with the company's articles.

768. Share certificate to be evidence of title

(1) In the case of a company registered in England and Wales or Northern Ireland, a certificate under the common seal of the company specifying any shares held by a member is prima facie evidence of his title to the shares.

770. Registration of transfer

(1) A company may not register a transfer of shares in or debentures of the company unless—
    (a) a proper instrument of transfer has been delivered to it, or
    (b) the transfer—
        (i) is an exempt transfer within the Stock Transfer Act 1982 (c. 41), or
        (ii) is in accordance with regulations under Chapter 2 of this Part.

771. **Procedure on transfer being lodged**

(1) When a transfer of shares in or debentures of a company has been lodged with the company, the company must either—
    (a) register the transfer, or
    (b) give the transferee notice of refusal to register the transfer, together with its reasons for the refusal,
    as soon as practicable and in any event within two months after the date on which the transfer is lodged with it.

(2) If the company refuses to register the transfer, it must provide the transferee with such further information about the reasons for the refusal as the transferee may reasonably request. This does not include copies of minutes of meetings of directors.

776. **Duty of company as to issue of certificates etc on transfer**

(1) A company must, within two months after the date on which a transfer of any of its shares, debentures or debenture stock is lodged with the company, complete and have ready for delivery—
    (a) the certificates of the shares transferred,
    (b) the debentures transferred, or
    (c) the certificates of the debenture stock transferred.

9.3 CLASS RIGHTS

Companies may issue classes of shares such as ordinary or preference shares with different rights attaching to them. There may be non-voting shares and shares with multiple voting rights; or, as in *Bushell* v *Faith* [1970] AC 1099 (see 11.7.2), shares may carry extra voting rights on a particular resolution, so as to effectively protect a director from removal from office. One of the questions that has come before the courts is how a solvent company's surplus assets (i.e., after debts are paid and capital is returned to members) are to be distributed between the ordinary and preference shareholders on winding up. The matter is primarily one of construing the terms of issue of the shares defining their rights, generally found in the articles. In *Birch* v *Cropper* which follows, the articles were silent and so the House of Lords opted for equality between shareholders of both classes in distributing surplus assets. In the later *Scottish Insurance* case extracted below the House of Lords set its face against the preference shareholders receiving more than a return of capital and the accumulated unpaid dividends they were expressly entitled to. Only the ordinary shareholders were held entitled to surplus assets. Such a preference share comes to look much like an investment in debenture stock enabling the company to repay capital and a fixed return at any time but giving no further entitlement to a stake in the fortunes of the company.

The final issue referred to here is the question of the variation of class rights. The general principle is that rights attaching to a class of shares should not be altered by the holders of another class of shares, i.e., the consent of a resolution of holders of the class in question is necessary to approve the alteration. The variation of class rights is dealt with in CA 2006, Part 17, Chapter 9. Articles may also stipulate that an alteration of rights requires the consent of members of the class. Often at issue is whether an event, such as an issue of further shares not removing voting rights but diluting the voting power of the class, amounts to an alteration or affects the rights of the preference shareholders. This issue is considered in *White* v *Bristol Aeroplane Co. Ltd* below, which took a narrow view of what required the consent of the preference shareholders.

The following sections outline the rules on variation of class rights and the older cases follow below.

COMPANIES ACT 2006, PART 17, CHAPTER 9

629. Classes of shares

(1) For the purposes of the Companies Acts shares are of one class if the rights attached to them are in all respects uniform.

630. Variation of class rights: companies having a share capital

(1) This section is concerned with the variation of the rights attached to a class of shares in a company having a share capital.

(2) Rights attached to a class of a company's shares may only be varied—
  (a) in accordance with provision in the company's articles for the variation of those rights, or
  (b) where the company's articles contain no such provision, if the holders of shares of that class consent to the variation in accordance with this section.

(3) This is without prejudice to any other restrictions on the variation of the rights.

(4) The consent required for the purposes of this section on the part of the holders of a class of a company's shares is—
  (a) consent in writing from the holders of at least three-quarters in nominal value of the issued shares of that class (excluding any shares held as treasury shares), or
  (b) a special resolution passed at a separate general meeting of the holders of that class sanctioning the variation.

(5) Any amendment of a provision contained in a company's articles for the variation of the rights attached to a class of shares, or the insertion of any such provision into the articles, is itself to be treated as a variation of those rights.

(6) In this section, and (except where the context otherwise requires) in any provision in a company's articles for the variation of the rights attached to a class of shares, references to the variation of those rights include references to their abrogation.

633. Right to object to variation: companies having a share capital

(1) This section applies where the rights attached to any class of shares in a company are varied under section 630 (variation of class rights: companies having a share capital).

(2) The holders of not less in the aggregate than 15% of the issued shares of the class in question (being persons who did not consent to or vote in favour of the resolution for the variation) may apply to the court to have the variation cancelled.

For this purpose any of the company's share capital held as treasury shares is disregarded.

Birch v *Cropper*

A presumption of equality between shareholders

[1886–90] All ER Rep 628, (1889) 14 App Cas 525, House of Lords

In the absence of express provision, the entitlements of different classes of shares were presumed to be equal.

Facts   The Bridgewater Navigation Co. Ltd was voluntarily wound up, leaving a surplus of assets after paying all debts and returning capital to members. Under the articles dividends were payable in proportion to the amounts paid up on the shares but the articles did not specify how surplus

assets were to be distributed on winding up. The preference shares were fully paid up but the ordinary shares were only partly paid up. In the absence of any express provision as to the application of surplus assets on winding up, each class of shareholders sought a more favourable distribution of the surplus. It was held that the surplus assets were distributable among ordinary and preference shareholders in equal proportions.

LORD MACNAGHTEN: The question before your lordships is this. In the liquidation of a company limited by shares, what is the proper mode of distributing assets not required for payment of debts and liabilities, or for the costs of the winding up, or for the adjustment of the rights of the contributories among themselves, so far, at any rate, as such rights have hitherto been understood and recognised? As incidental to that question, your lordships have to consider whether the mode of distribution can be in any way affected by one or more of the following circumstances: (i) That the shares of the company were paid up unequally, some being fully paid-up, others being paid up only in part. (ii) That the fully paid-up shares were issued separately as preference shares, carrying a preferential dividend of 5 per cent without any further right to participate in the profits of the business. (iii) That by the regulations of the company dividends on the company's shares were payable in proportion to the amounts paid up thereon.

The answer, as it seems to me, must depend on the principle applicable to companies limited by shares, and on the provisions contained in the Companies Act, 1862. . . . Every person who becomes a member of a company limited by shares of equal amount becomes entitled to a proportionate part in the capital of the company, and, unless it be otherwise provided by the regulations of the company, entitled, as a necessary consequence, to the same proportionate part in all the property of the company, including its uncalled capital. He is liable in respect of all moneys unpaid on his shares to pay up every call that is duly made upon him. But he does not by such payment acquire any further or other interest in the capital of the company. His share in the capital is just what it was before. His liability to the company is diminished by the amount paid. His contribution is merged in the common fund; and that is all.

When the company is wound up new rights and liabilities arise. The power of the directors to make calls is at an end; but every present member, so far as his shares are unpaid, is liable to contribute to the assets of the company to an amount sufficient for the payment of its debts and liabilities, the costs of winding up, and such sums as may be required for the adjustment of the rights of the contributories among themselves. . . .

The ordinary shareholders say that the preference shareholders are entitled to a return of their capital, with 5 per cent interest up to the day of payment, and to nothing more. That is treating them as if they were debenture-holders liable to be paid off at a moment's notice. Then they say that at the utmost the preference shareholders are only entitled to the capital value of a perpetual annuity of 5 per cent upon the amounts paid up by them. That is treating them as if they were holders of irredeemable debentures; but they are not debenture-holders at all. For some reason or other, the company invited them to come in as shareholders, and they must be treated as having all the rights of shareholders, except so far as they renounced those rights on their admission to the company. There was an express bargain made as to their rights in respect of profits arising from the business of the company. But there was no bargain—no provision of any sort—affecting their rights as shareholders in the capital of the company.

Then the preference shareholders say to the ordinary shareholders: 'We have paid up the whole of the amount due on our shares; you have paid but a fraction on yours. The prosperity of a company results from its paid-up capital; distribution must be in proportion to contribution. The surplus assets must be divided in proportion to the amounts paid up on the shares.' That seems to me to be ignoring altogether the elementary principles applicable to joint-stock companies of this description. I think it rather leads to confusion to speak of the assets which are the subject of this application as 'surplus assets', as if they were an accretion or addition to the capital of the company capable of being distinguished from it, and open to different considerations. They are part and parcel of the property of the company—part and parcel of the joint stock or common fund—which at the date of the winding up represented the capital of the company. It is through their shares in the capital, and through their shares alone, that members of a company limited by shares become entitled to participate in the property of the company. The shares in this company were all of the same amount. Every contributory who held a preference share at the date of the winding up must have taken that share, and must have held it on the terms of paying up all calls duly made upon him in respect thereof. In paying up his share in full he has done no more than he contracted to do. Why should he have more than he bargained for? Every contributory who was the holder of an ordinary share at the date of the winding up took his share and held it, on similar terms. He has done all he contracted to do; why should he have less than his bargain? When the preference shareholders and the ordinary shareholders are once placed on exactly the same footing in regard to the amounts paid up upon their shares, what is there to alter rights which were the subject of express contract?

Then it was said on behalf of the preference shareholders that the provision for payment of dividends in proportion to the amount paid up on the shares leads to an inference that the distribution of surplus assets was to be made in the same proportion. I do not think that it leads to any inference of the kind. It is a very common provision nowadays, though it is not what you find in Table A; and it is a very reasonable provision, because during the continuance of the company, and while it is a going concern, it prevents any sense of dissatisfaction on the part of those who have paid more on their shares than their fellow shareholders of a different issue. But when it has come to an end I cannot see how it can be used to regulate or disturb rights with which it had nothing to do even while it was in force.

I am, therefore, of opinion that the judgment of the Court of Appeal must be varied, and that it should be declared that,...the assets of the company remaining undistributed...ought to be distributed among all the shareholders in proportion to their shares.

Scottish Insurance Corporation Ltd v Wilsons & Clyde Coal Co. Ltd

Nationalisation of the coal industry

[1949] AC 462, House of Lords

This case denied the preference shareholders anything more than a return of capital and a 7 per cent cumulative dividend.

Facts   The colliery assets of a coal mining company had been transferred to the National Coal Board under the Coal Industry Nationalisation Act 1946 in return for compensation. The company, no longer trading, intended to go into liquidation, but first proposed to reduce its capital by paying off the 7 per cent cumulative preference shares. The preference shareholders unsuccessfully objected to the reduction on grounds that it deprived them of the opportunity to share in a distribution of surplus assets on liquidation (i.e., after paying off all debts and returning capital). The articles stated that on winding up, the preference shares would rank before the ordinary shares 'to the extent of repayment of the amounts called up and paid thereon'. The House of Lords held that the preference shareholders were not entitled to surplus assets and that the reduction of capital was not unfair.

LORD SIMONDS: In the formal case which they have presented to the House the element of unfairness on which the appellants insist is that the reduction deprives them of their right to participate in the surplus assets of the company on liquidation and leaves the ordinary stockholders in sole possession of those assets. But in their argument both in the Court of Session and before your lordships they have further relied on the fact that they have been deprived of a favourable 7 per cent investment which they cannot hope to replace and might have expected to continue to enjoy. They further contend that the deprivation of these rights, which would in any case have been an unmerited hardship, is rendered the more unfair because it is likely to be followed at an early date by liquidation of the company or, as it is less accurately expressed, because it is itself only a step in the liquidation of the company.

...Reading these articles as a whole with such familiarity with the topic as the years have brought, I would not hesitate to say, first, that the last thing a preference stockholder would expect to get (I do not speak here of the legal rights) would be a share of surplus assets, and that such a share would be a windfall beyond his reasonable expectations and, secondly, that he had at all times the knowledge, enforced in this case by the unusual reference in art. 139 to the payment off of the preference capital, that at least he ran the risk, if the company's circumstances admitted, of such a reduction as is now proposed being submitted for confirmation by the court. Whether a man lends money to a company at 7 per cent or subscribes for its shares carrying a cumulative preferential dividend at that rate, I do not think that he can complain of unfairness if the company, being in a position lawfully to do so, proposes to pay him off.

...It is clear from the authorities, and would be clear without them, that, subject to any relevant provision of the general law, the rights *inter se* of preference and ordinary shareholders must depend on the terms of the instrument which contains the bargain that they have made with the company and each other. This means, that there is a question of construction to be determined and undesirable though it may be that fine distinctions should be drawn in commercial documents such as articles of association of a company, your lordships cannot decide that the articles here under review have a particular meaning, because to somewhat similar articles in such cases as *Re William Metcalfe & Sons Ltd* [1933] Ch 142 that meaning has been judicially attributed. Reading the relevant articles, as a whole, I come to the conclusion that arts 159 and 160 are exhaustive of the rights of the preference stockholders in a winding up. The whole tenor of the articles, as I have already pointed out, is to leave the ordinary stockholders masters of the situation. If there are 'surplus assets' it is because the ordinary stockholders have contrived that it should be so, and, though this is not decisive, in determining what the parties meant by their bargain, it is of some weight that it should be in the power of one class so to act that there will or will not be surplus assets.

White v Bristol Aeroplane Co. Ltd

Whether a new share issue 'affected' the rights of preference shareholders

[1953] Ch 65, Court of Appeal

Facts   *The company proposed a bonus issue of new ordinary and preference shares to the existing ordinary shareholders of the company. A consequence of the issue was that the proportionate voting power of the existing preference shareholders within that class of shares would be reduced to below 50 per cent. Article 68 stated that class rights could not be 'affected, modified, varied, dealt with, or abrogated in any manner' without a resolution of a meeting of that class of shareholders. No such meeting of preference shareholders was to be held to approve the share issue. The plaintiff preference shareholder unsuccessfully argued that a resolution approving the issue was required as the issue 'affected' the rights of the preference shareholders.*

EVERSHED MR: . . . the question shortly is: will the effect of this proposed distribution, if carried out, be to 'affect' the rights of the preference stockholders? . . .

It is necessary, first, to note—although on this matter Mr Gray [counsel for the plaintiff preference stockholder] has not argued to the contrary—that what must be 'affected' are the rights of the preference stockholders. The question then is—and, indeed, I have already posed it—are the rights . . . 'affected' by what is proposed? It is said in answer—and I think rightly said—no, they are not; they remain exactly as they were before; each one of the manifestations of the preference stockholders' privileges may be repeated without any change whatever after, as before, the proposed distribution. It is no doubt true that the enjoyment of, and the capacity to make effective, those rights is in a measure affected; for as I have already indicated, the existing preference stockholders will be in a less advantageous position on such occasions as entitle them to register their votes, whether at general meetings of the company or at separate meetings of their own class. But there is to my mind a distinction, and a sensible distinction, between an affecting of the rights and an affecting of the enjoyment of the rights, or of the stockholders' capacity to turn them to account . . .

. . . I have no doubt, as I have already indicated, that upon a sufficient analysis what is here suggested will 'affect' the preference stockholders 'as a matter of business'; but we are concerned with the question whether the rights of the preference stockholders are 'affected', not as a matter of business, but according to the articles, that is, according to their meaning construed under the rules of construction and as a matter of law. . . .

ROMER LJ: . . . The plaintiff's case is that the rights attached to the class of preference stockholders whom he represents are being 'affected' within the meaning of article 68 of the company's articles of association; and plainly, therefore, the first question to be asked is: of what do those rights consist?—because until that is known it is impossible to form a view whether they are being affected.

The rights attached to a class of shares within the meaning of such an article as this, are those attached by the resolutions creating such shares or by the articles of association of the company as amended from time to time by any relevant resolution; and accordingly, regard must be had to such resolutions and to the constitution of the company for the purpose of finding out what the rights of the preference stockholders are.

The rights attaching to the preference stockholders are those which are conferred by articles 62 and 83; and the only relevant article for present purposes is article 83. Under that article it is provided, as my lord has already stated, that on a poll every member present in person or by proxy shall have one vote for every share held by him, or in the case of the preference stock, one vote for every £1 of preference stock held by him. It is suggested that, as a result of the proposed increase of capital, that right of the preference stockholders will in some way be 'affected'; but I cannot see that it will be affected in any way whatever. The position then will be precisely the same as now—namely, that the holder of preference stock will have on a poll one vote for every £1 of preference stock held by him. It is quite true that the block vote, if one may so describe the total voting power of the class, will, or may, have less force behind it, because it will *pro tanto* be watered down by reason of the increased total voting power of the members of the company; but no particular weight is attached to the vote, by the constitution of the company, as distinct from the right to exercise the vote, and certainly no right is conferred on the preference stockholders to preserve anything in the nature of an equilibrium between their class and the ordinary stockholders or any other class.

During the course of the discussion I asked Mr Gray [counsel for the plaintiff preference stockholder] whether it would not be true to say that the logical result of his argument would be that the rights of ordinary shareholders would be affected by the issue of new ordinary capital on the ground that every one of the considerations on which he was relying would be present in such a case. The votes of the existing shareholders would be diminished in power; and they would have other people with whom to share the profits, and, on a winding up, to share the capital assets. In answer to that he was constrained, I think rightly, to say that was so. But in my opinion it cannot be said that the rights of ordinary shareholders would be affected by the issue of further ordinary capital; their rights would remain just as they were before, and the only result would be that the class of persons entitled to exercise those rights would be enlarged; and for my part I cannot help thinking that a certain amount of confusion has crept into this case between rights on the one hand, and the result of exercising those rights on the other hand. The rights, as such, are conferred by resolution or by the articles, and they cannot be affected except with the sanction of the members on whom those rights are conferred; but the results of exercising those rights are not the subject of any assurance or guarantee under the constitution of the company, and are not protected in any way. It is the rights, and those alone, which are protected, and for the reasons which my lord has given, and in view of what I have myself said, the rights of the preference stockholders will not, in my judgment, be affected by the proposed resolutions.

9.4 VALUATION OF SHARES

The legal principles on which shares are valued are of great practical importance in themselves. The topic is also of wider significance as valuation of a share or block of shares necessitates analysis of the rights and benefits that its ownership confers on the shareholder.

The contrast between the market pricing of shares of public companies listed on the Stock Exchange and the valuation of private company shares also underlines the practical and theoretical distinctions between the two types of company. The price of listed company shares is to be found in the daily official list of the Stock Exchange, and is also published in the leading national broadsheet newspapers. The principle of the market is that the price should be derived from the market forces of supply and demand with investors making their choice of investment on the basis of full and equal information (see chapter 17). The price so arrived at may not always reflect a fully rational assessment of the company's underlying profitability, prospects and net worth. A speculative element is often present, such as, for example, an expectation that an artificially high demand for the company's shares may be created by a prospective takeover bid, thus driving up the price.

Compared with unlisted companies, marketability itself adds to the value of listed company shares. Indeed one of the purposes of 'going public' (i.e., 'floating' the company on the Stock Exchange) is to create marketability as well as speculative opportunities. An article in *The Times* (15 December 1993) made the point well. 'A surge in...flotations shows the dramatic divergence of public and private company valuations. Anyone trying to sell an unquoted building materials company would be hard pressed to receive more than 12 times historic earnings. If floated, the same company's shares could easily trade at twice that.' At this point the principal shareholders may become paper millionaires as their newly marketable shares appreciate in value.

Valuation of private company shares is far more prosaic. Such companies are truly private and transfer of their shares is restricted by the articles. There is thus no market and no active trading in the shares to enable a market price to be established. The shares therefore have to be valued and a sale price negotiated according to various principles or assumptions. While such valuations are more an art than a science, certain of the principles applied are said to be matters of law. However, the experts in this field are the accountants whose judgment and practices are respected by the courts.

There is a distinction between valuing a business or company as a whole and valuing an individual block of shares. A business may be valued as a whole on the basis of its profitability. As mentioned in the article quoted above, the valuation may traditionally be calculated as a multiple of the annual profits of the business. A further element of valuing a business is to value its underlying assets. If it is making profits the assets will be valued on a going concern basis at their full market value plus a possible element of goodwill. If the business is loss-making it will not be valued as a going concern in which case there will be no goodwill element. The assets will be valued at a discount on the assumption that they will have to be sold off piecemeal on a liquidator's sale in which they are unlikely to achieve their full value.

In broad terms a valuation may be either for commercial or for tax purposes. Perhaps a lender is taking the shares as security, or the court is making a purchase order under CA 2006, s. 996 as a remedy for unfair prejudice. Or members are acquiring an outgoing or deceased member's shares under pre-emption rights in the articles. Alternatively the shares are to be valued for capital gains tax, inheritance tax or stamp duty purposes. In reaching a valuation the basis for valuation stipulated by the pre-emption right or the precise terms of the tax legislation are of first importance. A decision of the court in an individual case may relate solely to those particular articles or tax legislation and be limited in its application accordingly.

When it comes to valuing an individual share or block of shares as opposed to the whole issued capital of a company further considerations apply. For example, rather than valuing the business as a whole and dividing this by the proportionate number of shares to be sold, a valuer may concentrate on finding a capital value based on the historical and prospective dividend yield of those shares. As an asset yielding an income, the shares will be valued accordingly. As private companies do not always pay dividends this approach may not be relevant however. Other bases which need not concern us here include earnings per share, the net present value of anticipated capital appreciation and discounted cash flow (on which see Gregory and Hicks [1995] JBL 56).

It also becomes necessary in valuing a block of shares to consider the precise nature of the rights and benefits attaching to shares of that class. The size of the block of shares to be sold is also highly relevant. Shares carrying more than 25 per cent of the votes can be used to block a special resolution, while 75 per cent can pass a special resolution (e.g., to alter the articles or wind up). More than 50 per cent will carry control of the company. In a private company, control of the general meeting enables the controllers to appoint themselves as directors, to earn salaries and benefits in kind which they award themselves (rather than declaring dividends), and to run the business of the company. A minority shareholder has little more than the right to be outvoted, to watch company earnings being soaked up by directors' salaries and to sit in impotent silence, except at the annual general meeting where the chairman may refuse to answer his questions. A minority holding of shares in a private company may therefore be almost worthless. On the contrary a block of shares carrying control or giving an existing shareholder the margin to obtain control may be especially valuable and so be sold at a premium to a pro rata valuation.

The question is whether as a matter of law a valuer should value at a premium a block of shares conferring control, and conversely a minority holding at a discount to a pro rata valuation. This question admits no easy answer. In *Dean v Prince*, extracted below, an auditor's valuation of 70 per cent of the shares on a pro rata basis with no control premium was regarded as fair by the Court of Appeal. Where a court makes an order on a s. 994 petition (the unfair prejudice remedy) that the majority buy the shares of the petitioning minority shareholder, the court fixes a fair value for the shares to be transferred. A line of cases has laid down with some precision when a valuation for this purpose should be pro rata or at a discount (see 13.2.3).

For companies listed on the Stock Exchange, the Takeover Code also deals with the inequity that a bidder for control of a listed company may pay a premium to obtain control. In the absence of regulation the consequent speculative surge in the share price would then collapse once this objective has been achieved. Those who succeeded in selling reap the benefit while the remainder are excluded. As a result, under r. 9 of the Code a person who obtains 30 per cent of the shares of a target company must make a 'mandatory offer' for the remaining issued shares of the company (see 18.2.3). Thus it is not permitted to offer a premium price to a limited number of sellers and then to stop buying. As a result the control premium if any is minimised or is in effect shared among all the remaining shareholders. Excess speculative pressure on the share price at the point at which control is acquired is also moderated.

Valuing a block of shares in a private company also necessitates analysis of any restrictions on transfer in the articles. For example, articles often give the directors an absolute discretion to refuse to register a transfer of shares to an outsider without giving reasons. (See, e.g., art. 14(f) reproduced at 1.7 above.) Thus the shares are not freely marketable and this must affect their value. Pre-emption rights may require a seller of shares to offer them to the other members at a fair value fixed by the auditors, sometimes expressly on a pro rata basis without premium or discount. (See, e.g., art. 24(c) reproduced at 1.7 above.) Again the value of the shares would seem to be circumscribed by this provision. Restrictions on transfer and price-fixing arrangements make the concept of finding a market value of those particular shares as between a willing buyer and a willing seller something of an enigma.

The following cases consider some of these issues. While the courts have attempted to lay down certain principles for valuation of shares it probably remains fair to say that valuation is not a science but an art, that the accountants are the professional artists and the lawyers merely enthusiastic amateurs.

Commissioners of Inland Revenue v Crossman

Valuing shares for estate duty purposes

[1937] AC 26, House of Lords

In this case shares in a private company were to be valued for estate duty purposes at the price they would fetch 'if sold in the open market at the time of the death of the deceased' (Finance Act 1894, s. 7(5)). The difficulty with finding an open-market value under such legislation is that if there are restrictions on transfer of the shares (such as a right of pre-emption for members to buy the shares at a value fixed by the auditors) then there can be no open-market value of those particular shares. The following brief extract, though part of a dissenting judgment, expresses the conundrum particularly well.

LORD RUSSELL OF KILLOWEN: A share in a limited company is a property the nature of which has been accurately expounded by Farwell J in *Borland's Trustee* v *Steel Brothers & Co. Ltd*. It is the interest of a person in the company, that interest being composed of rights and obligations which are defined by the Companies Act and by the memorandum and articles of association of the company. A sale of a share is a sale of the interest so defined, and the subject-matter of the sale is effectively vested in the purchaser by the entry of his name in the register of members. It may be that owing to provisions in the articles of association the subject-matter of the sale cannot be effectively vested in the purchaser because the directors refuse to and cannot be compelled to register the purchaser as shareholder. The purchaser could then secure the benefit of the sale by the registered shareholder becoming a trustee for him of the rights with an indemnity in respect of the obligations. In the case of the sale of such a share the risk of a refusal to register might well be reflected in a smaller price being obtainable than would have been obtained had there been no such risk. The share was property with that risk as one of its incidents.

But a further restriction may exist, as in the present case. The articles may stipulate that a shareholder must first give existing shareholders the chance of buying his shares at a price fixed and not competitive. In such a case a sale to an outsider of the shareholder's interest in the company must and can only be made subject to that obligation, which is one of the incidents which attach to and are part of the subject-matter of the sale; and the sale to the outsider must necessarily include as an incident of the subject-matter of the sale, the right to receive the fixed price if the right of pre-emption is exercised by the other shareholders. The consequence is that by reason of the nature and incidents of the subject-matter of the sale, neither Sir William Paulin nor his executors, at the time of the death, could have sold these shares in the open market to any one otherwise than subject to the right of pre-emption at the fixed price. The result of the existence of this right of pre-emption must inevitably be that no one at an actual sale in the open market would be prepared to offer more than the fixed price if even that.

Dean v *Prince*

Challenging the auditor's 'fair' valuation

[1954] Ch 409, Court of Appeal

The following judgment of Lord Denning illustrates the homespun approach of judges to valuation of shares. In this case the court had to consider the principles on which an auditor should find a 'fair value' of private company shares. For various and somewhat tenuous reasons the judges of the Court of Appeal held that the controlling interest should not be valued at a premium in this instance, though the case lays down no general rule to this effect. Secondly, as the company was 'trembling on the brink of insolvency' it should be valued on a break-up basis and not as a going concern.

Facts Dean, Prince and Cowen were shareholders and directors of a loss-making light engineering company in Sheffield. Dean, who held a majority of the shares, died. The articles contained an obligation on the surviving directors (not a right) to buy the shares of the deceased at a valuation certified as 'fair' by the auditor acting as an expert. Dean's widow contested the auditor's valuation before Harman J who overturned the valuation. The Court of Appeal then upheld the auditor's original valuation.

DENNING LJ: The task of the auditor here was to act as an expert and not as an arbitrator; and, as an expert, he was to certify what, in his opinion, was the fair value of the shares. The draftsman of the article obviously was aware that there is a special virtue in an expert's valuation. The reason is because it is so much a matter of opinion that it is very difficult to say it was wrong. But difficult as it is, nevertheless if the courts are satisfied that the valuation was made under a mistake, they will hold it not to be binding on the parties.

. . . For instance, if the expert added up his figures wrongly; or took something into account which he ought not to have taken into account, or conversely: or interpreted the agreement wrongly: or proceeded on some erroneous principle. In all these cases the court will interfere. Even if the court cannot point to the actual error, nevertheless, if the figure itself is so extravagantly large or so inadequately small that the only conclusion is that he must have gone wrong somewhere, then the court will interfere in much the same way as the Court of Appeal will interfere with an award of damages if it is a wholly erroneous estimate. . . .

In this case Harman J has upset the valuation on the ground that the auditor failed to take into account some factors and proceeded on wrong principles. I will take the points in order:

1 The right to control the company Harman J said that the auditor should have taken into account the fact that the 140 shares were a majority holding and would give a purchaser the right to control the company. I do not think that the auditor was bound to take that factor into account. Test it this way: suppose it had been Prince who had died, leaving only 30 shares. Those 30 shares, being a minority holding, would fetch nothing in the open market. But does that mean that the other directors would be entitled to take his shares for nothing? Surely not. No matter which director it was who happened to die, his widow should be entitled to the game price per share, irrespective of whether her husband's holding was large or small. It seems to me that the fair thing to do would be to take the whole 200 shares of the company and see what they were worth, and then pay the widow a sum appropriate to her husband's holding. At any rate if the auditor was of opinion that that was a fair method, no one can say that he was wrong. The right way to see what the whole 200 shares were worth, would be to see what the business itself was worth: and that is what the auditor proceeded to do.

2 Valuation of the business 'as a going concern' Harman J seems to have thought that the auditor should have valued the business as a going concern. I do not think that the auditor was bound to do any such thing. The business was a losing concern which had no goodwill: and it is fairly obvious that, as soon as Mrs Dean had sold the 140 shares to the other two directors—as she was bound to do—she would in all probability call in the moneys owing to herself and to her husband amounting to over £2,000. The judge said that she was not likely to press for the moneys because that would be 'killing the goose that laid the eggs', but he was wrong about this; because as soon as she sold the shares, she would have got rid of the goose and there was no reason why she should not press for the moneys. She was an executrix and the company's position was none too good. It had only £1,200 in the bank to meet a demand for £2,200. In these circumstances the auditor was of opinion that there was a strong probability of the company having to be wound up: and he rejected the going-concern basis. For myself, I should have thought he was clearly right, but at any rate no one can say that his opinion was wrong.

3 Valuation of the assets of the business Once the going-concern basis is rejected, the only possible way of valuing the business is to find out the value of the tangible assets. Harman J thought that the assets should have been valued as a whole *in situ*. It was quite likely, he said, that 'some one could have been found who would make a bid for the whole thing, lock, stock and barrel'. But the judge seems to have forgotten that no one would buy the assets *in situ* in this way unless he could also buy the premises; and the company had no saleable interest in the premises. In respect of part of the premises the company had only a monthly tenancy: in respect of the rest the company had only a contract for the purchase of the premises on paying £200 a year for 25 years. It had no right to assign this contract; and its interest was liable to be forfeited if it went into liquidation, either compulsory or voluntary; and the probability was, of course, that, if it sold all the assets, it would go into liquidation, and hence lose the premises. The company could, therefore, only sell the assets without the premises. That is how the auditor valued them and no one can say that he was wrong in so doing.

4 Valuation on a 'break-up' basis The auditor instructed the valuer, Colonel Riddle, to value the plant and machinery at the break-up value as loose chattels on a sale by auction. Harman J thought that that was a wrong basis because it was equivalent to a forced sale. I would have agreed with the judge if the business had been a profitable concern. The value of the tangible assets would then have been somewhere in the region of £4,000 or £5,000, being either the balance sheet figure of £4,070 or Pressley's figure of £4,835. But the business was not a profitable concern. It was a losing concern: and it is a well-known fact that a losing concern cannot realise the book value of its assets. There is an element to be taken into account which is sometimes spoken of as 'negative goodwill'. It comes about in this way: if a business is making a loss, that shows that its assets, regarded as an entity, are not a good investment. A purchaser will decline, therefore, to buy on that basis. He will only buy on a piecemeal basis, according to what the various assets taken individually are worth: and it is obvious that on a sale of assets piecemeal, the vendor will suffer heavy losses as compared with the book figures. The auditor was therefore quite justified in asking the valuer to value the assets as loose chattels sold at an auction. At any rate, if he honestly formed that opinion, no one can say that he was wrong.

5 The special purchaser Harman J thought that someone could have been found to buy the 140 shares who would use his majority holding to turn out the two directors, and reorganise the factory and put in his own business. In other words, that the shares would have a special attraction for some person (namely, the next-door neighbour) who wanted to put his own business into these premises. I am prepared to concede that the shares might realise an enhanced value on that account: but I do not think that it would be a fair price to ask the directors to pay. They were buying these shares—under a compulsory sale and purchase—on the assumption that they would continue in the business as working directors. It would be unfair to make them pay a price based on the assumption that they would be turned out. If the auditor never took that possibility into account, he cannot be blamed; for he was only asked to certify the fair value of the shares. The only fair value would be to take a hypothetical purchaser who was prepared to carry on the business if it was worthwhile so to do, or otherwise to put it into liquidation. At any rate if that was the auditor's opinion, no one can say that he was wrong.

I have covered, I think, all the grounds on which Harman J upset the valuation. I do not think they were good grounds. I would, therefore, allow the appeal and uphold the valuation.

10

Maintenance of Capital and Dividends

10.1 THE MEANING OF MAINTENANCE OF CAPITAL

The principle of maintenance of capital is perhaps one of the areas most misunderstood by students of company law. This is partly because the word 'capital' has very different meanings in every day usage, in accounting terminology and in company law. Also the phrase 'maintenance of capital' is itself highly misleading. The central idea is that as shareholders enjoy limited liability, the creditors of a limited company should be given the assurance that the share capital the company has issued, has in fact been fully paid in by its shareholders and that this capital will not later be returned to them.

However, there is no rule that a company must maintain its capital by maintaining its assets at a level at least equivalent to the amount of capital originally contributed by the shareholders and the assets, or 'net worth' of a company may often dwindle to less than the amount of its issued capital.

Thus the essence of the misnamed 'maintenance of capital' principle is twofold. First, the members must pay in or be committed to pay in the full amount of the capital payable on the shares for which they subscribe, i.e., the capital must first be raised. Then it must be 'maintained' in the sense that it must not be repaid to the members. The members thus may not withdraw their capital from the company, though they may receive dividends lawfully declared out of 'profits' and if they work for the company they may be paid duly awarded salary. Though the members' liability is limited, the creditors are thus entitled to assume that the amount of issued capital the members have agreed to pay in is indeed paid or payable and that it is not returned to the members. Clearly, however, the assets of the company may be depleted by business losses and no legal principle can guard against that.

The maintenance of capital principle is thus not a guarantee or assurance that the creditors will be paid everything that the company owes them. The paid-in capital is not kept in a box or set aside in a special account for the creditors. It is used in the business of the company and may be lost in the process. Stated at its simplest, the legal principle is therefore that the members may not plunder the company of the capital they have paid in which must be retained by the company and used commercially.

The essence for understanding this area of the law is to appreciate that it is substantially based on accounting concepts. The word 'capital', as has been said, has many meanings in different contexts. A young couple may buy a house on mortgage to start building up their 'capital'. Accountants refer to the fixed or circulating capital of a company, the fixed capital being the permanent assets such as its business premises. In revenue law and for other purposes there is a distinction between receipts that are 'income' and those that are 'capital' receipts, but in the present company law context 'capital' means something completely different. The share capital of a company is not the sum of its assets. The paid-up share capital is the total amount of shares allotted to its members, including the par value of the shares and in practice any premium paid if shares are issued at a price above the par value. The capital is thus represented as a figure shown in the 'capital account' of the company's accounts which records the amounts paid for shares issued when the company was first formed, and for shares issued subsequently.

This historical figure remains unchanged in the accounts, but as time goes by, it may become less and less related to the reality of the assets held by the company. There are many substantial companies having an issued capital of only £100 as they have grown into companies with substantial assets, just as there are many with a substantial issued capital whose net assets have fallen well below the amount of that capital. Nonetheless the figure shown in the capital account must remain the same unless for example the company follows the formal process for a reduction of capital (see 10.7). In the case of public companies there is an obligation under CA 2006, s. 656, to call an extraordinary general meeting if the assets fall to below half the called up capital, which gives the members an opportunity to express their views, though there is no obligation to take any action. (*The Times* of 23 November 1993 reported two such cases of EGMs being called. These were Queens Moat Houses plc, owner of a major hotel chain and Ferranti International plc, both in severe financial difficulty.) Otherwise, where there are trading losses, there is absolutely no obligation to maintain the assets of the company at a level equivalent to the amount of the issued share capital.

The rules prohibiting a return of capital are primarily intended to prohibit the actual outflow of cash or assets to the members. Thus a company may not buy its own shares as this means returning to members cash it has received by way of capital. However, it is also a prohibited reduction of capital to debit the capital account, thereby reducing the historical figure in the capital account. For example, if a company's capital is no longer represented by assets, it may wish to reduce that figure to reflect more accurately the reduced net worth of the company (though as has been said there is no necessity to do this as the two are not necessarily linked). To reduce the capital in this purely accounting sense will not involve a return of cash to members, but it is nonetheless strictly regulated by the Act. Under CA 2006, Part 17, Chapter 10, a public company will have to apply to the court and a private company must jump through a number of legal hoops, even though there is no actual return of cash or assets to the members.

To summarise, therefore, the requirement to 'maintain' the issued capital is first and foremost a practical obligation not to return cash or assets to members that amounts to a return of share capital, and secondly it is a formal accounting requirement that the historical figure in the capital account must not be reduced other than as permitted by the Act.

The rules are extensive but they are perhaps the minimum the law can do to protect creditors from members bleeding the company dry by withdrawing their capital investment from it. In recent years the rules have been relaxed in some respects possibly prejudicing creditors, though they were never fully effective to guarantee creditworthiness. The essence of contributions of capital is not as a guarantee fund for creditors; it is the shareholders' irretrievable stake in the company which will be put at risk in the running of the business and may well be lost.

The principle of capital maintenance is also doomed to failure as a means of protecting creditors because, while there are restrictions on loans to directors, the directors who work in the company are free to pay themselves fees and salary almost at will. The exceptions to this are very few and courts in general will not look into the adequacy of consideration given by such employees for the pay they have received. They will not generally enquire as to whether the salary is reasonable. (See *Re Halt Garage (1964) Ltd* [1982] 3 All ER 1016 and *Re Horsley & Weight Ltd* [1982] Ch 442 at 11.6 below.)

For these and other reasons, the recent review of company law has reduced the extent of the rules on capital maintenance as they were burdensome for small businesses without producing a sufficient benefit in protecting creditors. See *Modern Company Law for a Competitive Economy: The Strategic Framework*, chapter 5.4, *Consultation Document 3: Company Formation and Capital Maintenance*, and *Consultation Document 6: Capital Maintenance: Other Issues*.

The elements of the current rules relating to maintenance of capital are as follows:

(a) A company may not issue shares at a discount.
(b) Distributions or 'dividends' on shares may only be paid out of 'profits'. Clearly investors require a return on their investment even though they cannot withdraw their capital. The difficult issue is defining the profits that are available for distribution as dividends.
(c) A company may not purchase its own shares. Substantial exceptions to this rule are now allowed.
(d) A public company may not give 'financial assistance' for the purchase of its own shares. If, for example, it lends money indefinitely to a person to buy shares, the company risks the possibility that the loan is never repaid in which case the capital has not been paid in.
(e) A company may not own shares in its holding company.
(f) Share capital cannot be reduced, though a public company can apply to the court to reduce its capital, while a private company can resolve to reduce its capital by special resolution, supported by a declaration of solvency made by the directors.

These elements will now be considered in turn.

10.2 NO ISSUE AT A DISCOUNT

CA 2006, s. 580(1), reads, 'A company's shares must not be allotted at a discount'. If the subsection is contravened s. 580(2) requires the allottee nonetheless to pay up the amount of the discount plus interest. The rule reflects the principle that the members must at least pay the full nominal amount for their shares. It means that shares cannot be issued at a discount to their nominal or par value. A share of £1 cannot be issued for 50p. The rule does not, however, prohibit the issue of shares at a discount to their market value. For example, the £1 shares in a company that has successfully traded for some years may now have a market value of £3. There is nothing to prevent the company making a rights issue of new shares for only £2 each to encourage all the members to take up the issue.

The principle that shares should not be issued at a discount is an old one and was first established by the following case.

Ooregum Gold Mining Co. of India Ltd v Roper

Where shares were below par

[1892] AC 125, House of Lords

Facts   The market value of the shares of the company was less than their nominal value. As it was thus not feasible to issue them for the full nominal amount, the company issued new £1 shares for 5 shillings (25p) each, the remaining 15 shillings (75p) being credited as fully paid up.

LORD HALSBURY LC: My lords, the question in this case has been more or less in debate since 1883, when Chitty J decided that a company limited by shares was not prohibited by law from issuing its shares at a discount. That decision was overruled, though in a different case, by the Court of Appeal in 1888, and it has now come to your lordships for final determination.

My lords, the whole structure of a limited company owes its existence to the Act of Parliament, and it is to the Act of Parliament one must refer to see what are its powers, and within what limits it is free to act. Now, confining myself for the moment to the Act of 1862, it makes one of the conditions of the limitation of liability that the memorandum of association shall contain the amount of capital with which the company proposes to be registered, divided into shares of a *certain fixed amount*. It seems to me that the system thus created by which the shareholder's liability is to be limited by the amount unpaid upon his shares, renders it impossible for the company to depart from that requirement, and by any expedient to arrange with their shareholders that they shall not be liable for the amount unpaid on the shares, although the amount of those shares has been, in accordance with the Act of Parliament, fixed at a certain sum of money. It is manifest that if the company could do so the provision in question would operate nothing.

I observe in the argument it has been sought to draw a distinction between the nominal capital and the capital which is assumed to be the real capital. I can find no authority for such a distinction. The capital is fixed and certain, and every creditor of the company is entitled to look to that capital as his security.

It may be that such limitations on the power of a company to manage its own affairs may occasionally be inconvenient, and prevent its obtaining money for the purposes of its trading on terms so favourable as it could do if it were more free to act. But, speaking for myself, I recognise the wisdom of enforcing on a company the disclosure of what its real capital is, and not permitting a statement of its affairs to be such as may mislead and deceive those who are either about to become its shareholders or about to give it credit.

I think, with Fry LJ in *Re Almada and Tirito Company* (1888) 38 ChD 415, that the question which your lordships have to solve is one which may be answered by reference to an inquiry: What is the nature of an agreement to take a share in a limited company? and that that question may be answered by saying, that it is an agreement to become liable to pay to the company the amount for which the share has been created. That agreement is one which the company itself has no authority to alter or qualify, and I am therefore of opinion that... the company were prohibited by law, upon the principle laid down in *Ashbury Railway Carriage & Iron Co. Ltd v Riche* (1875) LR 7 HL 653, from doing that which is compendiously described as issuing shares at a discount.

10.2.1 Issues in kind—private companies

The rule that shares may not be issued at a discount is clear where shares are being issued for cash. However, where shares in private companies are issued other than for cash, the rule may be honoured more in the breach than in the observance. Shares may be issued 'in kind', for example, in return for assets or services. Or, particularly in a public company takeover, new shares may be issued in return for shares in the target company. Thus the members of the target company are issued new shares in the company in return for their shares in the target.

The danger is that the consideration given in return for the issue of shares may be worth less than the nominal value of those shares. For private companies there is, however, no general obligation to obtain formal valuations of the assets. The result may be that shares are in fact issued at a discount. An example is *Salomon* v *A. Salomon & Co. Ltd* [1897] AC 22 where Mr Salomon transferred an overvalued business to the company in return for fully paid-up shares. The leading case is *Re Wragg Ltd*.

Re Wragg Ltd
A coach and horses through the 'no discount' rule
[1897] 1 Ch 796, Court of Appeal

Facts   Messrs Martin and Wragg carried on business as coach and omnibus proprietors. They formed a company and transferred the business assets to the company in return for fully paid shares. When the company failed, the liquidator, alleging that the business was overvalued, unsuccessfully claimed a further capital contribution on grounds that the shares were not in fact fully paid up.

LINDLEY LJ: I understand the law to be as follows. The liability of a shareholder to pay the company the amount of his shares is a statutory liability, and is declared to be a specialty debt (Companies Act 1862, s. 16), and a short form of action is given for its recovery (s. 70). But specialty debts, like other debts, can be discharged in more ways than one—e.g., by payment, set-off, accord and satisfaction, and release—and, subject to the qualifications introduced by the doctrine of *ultra vires*, or, in other words, the limited capacity of statutory corporations, any mode of discharging a specialty debt is as available to a shareholder as to any other specialty debtor. It is, however, obviously beyond the power of a limited company to release a shareholder from his obligation without payment in money or money's worth. It cannot give fully paid-up shares for nothing and preclude itself from requiring payment of them in money or money's worth (*Re Eddystone Marine Insurance Co.* [1893] 3 Ch 9); nor can a company deprive itself of its right to future payment in cash by agreeing to accept future payments in some other way. . . .

From this it follows that shares in limited companies cannot be issued at a discount. By our law the payment by a debtor to his creditor of a less sum than is due does not discharge the debt; and this technical doctrine has also been invoked in aid of the law which prevents the shares of a limited company from being issued at a discount. But this technical doctrine, though often sufficient to decide a particular case, will not suffice as a basis for the wider rule or principle that a company cannot effectually release a shareholder from his statutory obligation to pay in money or money's worth the amount of his shares. That shares cannot be issued at a discount was finally settled in the case of the *Ooregum Gold Mining Co. of India* v *Roper* [1892] AC 125, the judgments in which are strongly relied upon by the appellant in this case. It has, however, never yet been decided that a limited company cannot buy property or pay for services at any price it thinks proper, and pay for them in fully paid-up shares. Provided a limited company does so honestly and not colourably, and provided that it has not been so imposed upon as to be entitled to be relieved from its bargain, it appears to be settled by *Re Heyford Co., Pell's Case* (1869) LR 18 Eq 222, LR 5 Ch App 11 and the others to which I have referred, of which *Anderson's Case* (1877) 7 ChD 75, is the most striking, that agreements by limited companies to pay for property or services in paid-up shares are valid and binding on the companies and their creditors. The legislature in 1867 appears to me to have distinctly recognised such to be the law, but to have required in order to make such agreements binding that they shall be registered before the shares are issued. [This provision of the Companies Act 1867 was subsequently repealed.]

... if a company owes a person £100, the company cannot by paying him £200 in shares of that nominal amount discharge him, even by a registered contract, from his obligation as a shareholder to pay up the other £100 in respect of those shares. That would be issuing shares at a discount. The difference between such a transaction and paying for property or services in shares at a price put upon them by a vendor and agreed to by the company may not always be very apparent in practice. But the two transactions are essentially different, and whilst the one is *ultra vires* the other is *intra vires*. It is not law that persons cannot sell property to a limited company for fully paid-up shares and make a profit by the transaction. We must not allow ourselves to be misled by talking of value. The value paid to the company is measured by the price at which the company agrees to buy what it thinks it worth its while to acquire. Whilst the transaction is unimpeached, this is the only value to be considered.

... In my judgment the law is settled, and cannot be declared wrongly settled by this Court, at any rate. If it is to be altered, the decisions which have settled it must be declared wrong by the House of Lords, or the law must be altered by Act of Parliament.

10.2.2 Issues in kind—public companies

The rules (found in Part 17, Chapter 6 of the Act of 2006) are stricter for public companies and require a non-cash consideration to be valued before allotment.

COMPANIES ACT 2006, SS. 593 AND 597

593. Public company: valuation of non-cash consideration for shares

(1) A public company must not allot shares as fully or partly paid up (as to their nominal value or any premium on them) otherwise than in cash unless—
   (a) the consideration for the allotment has been independently valued in accordance with the provisions of this Chapter,
   (b) the valuer's report has been made to the company during the six months immediately preceding the allotment of the shares, and
   (c) a copy of the report has been sent to the proposed allottee.

597. Copy of report to be delivered to registrar

(1) A company to which a report is made under section 593 as to the value of any consideration for which, or partly for which, it proposes to allot shares must deliver a copy of the report to the registrar for registration.

10.3 DIVIDENDS

10.3.1 Profits available for distribution

If capital is not to be returned to members, any dividend payable to members as a return on their investment must be paid only out of 'profits'. In simplistic terms, only the surplus earned over and above the capital can be distributed to the members.

The typical procedure for declaration of dividends (see, for example, Table A, 1985, arts. 102 and 103 at 1.7 above) is that the directors recommend an annual dividend as a maximum amount and the members, usually at the annual general meeting, approve that dividend. The directors may also pay an interim dividend, in public companies generally every six months.

A public listed company's reputation depends on its ability to pay regular dividends. Failure to do so is taken to indicate management failure and depresses the share price. Even in years when a loss is announced a dividend may be paid, based on accumulated profits from previous years. In private companies, for tax reasons, dividends on shares are rarely paid and it is common practice for the major shareholders to take their income as salary or directors' fees, though this means that minority shareholders derive no income from their shares. However, there is no obligation on a company to distribute all of its profits to its members who have no right to sue for payment of a dividend (*Burland* v *Earle* [1902] AC 83), unless it has been actually declared.

To stop companies returning capital to its members, the law requires that dividends on its shares be only distributed out of 'available profits'. This does not mean that the directors check the company's bank statements to see if there is any cash available. On the contrary the law lays down complex legal and accounting rules by which distributable profits are to be calculated. These rules are now found in Part 23 of the Act of 2006 and the following sections introduce some of its key principles.

COMPANIES ACT 2006, SS. 829, 830 AND 831

829. Meaning of "distribution"

(1) In this Part "distribution" means every description of distribution of a company's assets to its members, whether in cash or otherwise, subject to the following exceptions.

(2) The following are not distributions for the purposes of this Part—

    (a) an issue of shares as fully or partly paid bonus shares;

    (b) the reduction of share capital—

        (i) by extinguishing or reducing the liability of any of the members on any of the company's shares in respect of share capital not paid up, or

        (ii) by repaying paid-up share capital;

    (c) the redemption or purchase of any of the company's own shares out of capital (including the proceeds of any fresh issue of shares) or out of unrealised profits in accordance with Chapter 3, 4 or 5 of Part 18;

    (d) a distribution of assets to members of the company on its winding up.

General rules

830. Distributions to be made only out of profits available for the purpose

(1) A company may only make a distribution out of profits available for the purpose.

(2) A company's profits available for distribution are its accumulated, realised profits, so far as not previously utilised by distribution or capitalisation, less its accumulated, realised losses, so far as not previously written off in a reduction or reorganisation of capital duly made.

831. Net asset restriction on distributions by public companies

(1) A public company may only make a distribution—

    (a) if the amount of its net assets is not less than the aggregate of its calledup share capital and undistributable reserves, and

    (b) if, and to the extent that, the distribution does not reduce the amount of those assets to less than that aggregate.

10.3.2 The consequences of an unlawful distribution

First, the directors who authorised an illegal distribution are liable to repay the money to the company, unless they justifiably relied on the accuracy of the accounts.

Re Exchange Banking Co., Flitcroft's Case
The liability of directors
(1882) 21 ChD 519, Court of Appeal

Facts *The directors of the company for several years presented to the general meeting reports and balance sheets in which various debts owing to the company which they knew to be bad, were shown as assets. The directors paid dividends based on these accounts. The liquidator of the company successfully claimed to recover from the directors.*

JESSEL MR: A limited company by its memorandum of association declares that its capital is to be applied for the purposes of the business. It cannot reduce its capital except in the manner and with the safeguards provided by statute, and looking at Companies Act 1877, it clearly is against the intention of the legislature that any portion of the capital should be returned to the shareholders without the statutory conditions being complied with. A limited company cannot in any other way make a return of capital, the sanction of a general meeting can give no validity to such a proceeding, and even the sanction of every shareholder cannot bring within the powers of the company an act which is not within its powers. If, therefore, the shareholders had all been present at the meetings, and had all known the facts, and had all concurred in declaring the dividends, the payment of the dividends would not be effectually sanctioned. One reason is this—there is a statement that the capital shall be applied for the purposes of the business, and on the faith of that statement, which is sometimes said to be an implied contract with creditors, people dealing with the company give it credit. The creditor has no debtor but that impalpable thing the corporation, which has no property except the assets of the business. The creditor, therefore, I may say, gives credit to that capital, gives credit to the company on the faith of the representation that the capital shall be applied only for the purposes of the business, and he has therefore a right to say that the corporation shall keep its capital and not return it to the shareholders, though it may be a right which he cannot enforce otherwise than by a winding-up order. It follows then that if directors who are quasi trustees for the company improperly pay away the assets to the shareholders, they are liable to replace them. It is no answer to say that the shareholders could not compel them to do so. I am of opinion that the company could in its corporate capacity compel them to do so, even if there were no winding-up. They are liable to pay, and none the less liable because the liquidator represents, not only shareholders, but creditors. The body of the shareholders no doubt voted for a declaration of dividend on the faith of the misrepresentation of the directors, so that there really was no ratification at all. It is impossible to say to what extent the company and the shareholders may have been injured by these proceedings. It may be that this reduction of capital has been the cause of the ruin of the company, in which case the shareholders as such may have a right to complain of what has been done. It is not necessary, therefore, to refer to previous decisions to show the principle on which the directors are held liable. If it be necessary to resort to the doctrine of implied contract *Evans* v *Coventry* (1) is in point. The order of the Vice-Chancellor will therefore be affirmed, but with this variation, that the directors in each case are to be declared jointly and severally liable and not only jointly liable.

Secondly, by CA 2006, s. 847, a member may be liable to repay an unlawful dividend.

COMPANIES ACT 2006, S. 847

847. Consequences of unlawful distribution

(1) This section applies where a distribution, or part of one, made by a company to one of its members is made in contravention of this Part.

(2) If at the time of the distribution the member knows or has reasonable grounds for believing that it is so made, he is liable—

    (a) to repay it (or that part of it, as the case may be) to the company, or

    (b) in the case of a distribution made otherwise than in cash, to pay the company a sum equal to the value of the distribution (or part) at that time.

(3) This is without prejudice to any obligation imposed apart from this section on a member of a company to repay a distribution unlawfully made to him.

(4) This section does not apply in relation to—

    (a) financial assistance given by a company in contravention of section 678 or 679, or

    (b) any payment made by a company in respect of the redemption or purchase by the company of shares in itself.

Thirdly, s. 847(3) allows the possibility that a member receiving an unlawful dividend may be liable in other ways to repay a dividend. The following case shows that the member may be liable to the company as a constructive trustee. This adds significantly to s. 847 in that if the member is insolvent, the company will be able to sue for a real remedy under the trust (and potentially recover 100 per cent of the unlawful dividend). Under s. 847, however, it would be necessary to prove the debt in the winding up or bankruptcy of an insolvent member, probably recovering only a tiny proportion of the debt.

Precision Dippings Ltd v *Precision Dippings Marketing Ltd*

Recovery from members as constructive trustees

[1986] Ch 447, Court of Appeal

Facts *The company was wholly owned by the defendant company, 'Marketing'. The company paid a cash dividend of £60,000 to Marketing which exhausted all the company's cash. Just under a year later the company failed and went into creditors' voluntary liquidation. The liquidators successfully sought to recover the dividend from the member (i.e., Marketing, the holding company). The grounds were that the accounts by reference to which the dividends were paid had been qualified by the auditors' report and the auditors had not at the time of the dividend certified that the qualification was not material as required by the Act. The dividend was not therefore lawfully paid out of profits. The court held Marketing liable as a member to repay the dividend not on the basis of the earlier equivalent of s.847, but as a constructive trustee.*

DILLON LJ: The payment of the dividend of £60,000 was therefore an *ultra vires* act by the company, just as if it had been paid out of capital or in any other circumstances in which under any of the other provisions of [CA 2006, s. 829] and the following sections there were not profits available for dividend.

In those circumstances, can Marketing have any defence to the company's claim for repayment of the £60,000 with interest? [His lordship then quoted the rule now found in CA 2006, s. 847, see the preceding extract, and continued:]

There can be no doubt that because Mr Wynne-Jones and Mr King were the only shareholders in and directors of Marketing and were also the only directors of the company, Marketing must be taken to have known all the facts. But it did not in fact know the terms of [the Companies Act, which requires the accounts relevant to the distribution to be duly audited etc.].

It do not find it necessary to examine the wording of [s. 847] since by subsection (2) the provisions of [s. 847] are declared to be without prejudice to any other obligation imposed on a member to repay a distribution unlawfully made to him. I would put the position quite shortly. The payment of the £60,000 dividend to Marketing was an *ultra vires* act on the part of the company. Marketing when it received the money had notice of the facts and was a volunteer in the sense that it did not give valuable consideration for the money. Marketing accordingly held the £60,000 as a constructive trustee for the company: see *Rolled Steel Products (Holdings) Ltd* v *British Steel Corporation* [1986] Ch. 246 per Slade LJ at p. 298 and per Browne-Wilkinson LJ at p. 303. That situation did not change before the company went into liquidation.

10.4 PURCHASE BY A COMPANY OF ITS OWN SHARES

10.4.1 The basic rule

The old case of *Trevor* v *Whitworth* (1887) 12 App Cas 409, HL, established that a company may not purchase its own shares. Such a purchase would return to the seller of the shares the capital that has been paid up on the shares. This principle is now found in CA 2006, s. 658.

COMPANIES ACT 2006, S. 658

658. General rule against limited company acquiring its own shares

(1) A limited company must not acquire its own shares, whether by purchase, subscription or otherwise, except in accordance with the provisions of this Part.

(2) If a company purports to act in contravention of this section—

 (a) an offence is committed by—

  (i) the company, and

  (ii) every officer of the company who is in default, and

 (b) the purported acquisition is void.

10.4.2 Reforming the basic rule

During the late 1970s it was realised that the basic rule was stricter than in other jurisdictions. The following green paper concluded that the rule should be relaxed, especially to encourage investment in small companies by allowing members wishing to recover their investment in shares to be paid out by the company. Where such a buy-back involves a reduction of capital, safeguards for creditors are required. The following extract explains the background to aspects of the current law.

The Purchase by a Company of its Own Shares

(Cmnd 7944) (London: HMSO, 1980)

Part I Background

1. Broadly speaking company law in the United Kingdom does not permit a limited company to buy its own shares. The main reasons for this have been that such purchases could reduce the capital of the company available for the protection of those who deal with the company and to prevent companies 'trafficking' in their shares. However, many other countries permit such purchases and increasing interest has been shown in this country in replacing the present general prohibition

with provisions which, whilst providing for the maintenance of the company's capital, would also give companies the opportunity to buy their own shares, to the benefit both of companies and of shareholders . . .

4. The government attaches particular importance to the principal economic arguments in favour of a relaxation of the present law. For private companies, a change should make investment and participation in such companies more attractive, by providing shareholders with a further means of disposing of their shares and by permitting the remaining members to maintain control and ownership of the business. Different considerations apply to companies whose shares are dealt in on a market. Public companies with surplus cash resources could find it useful to be able to buy their own shares and thus return surplus resources to shareholders, thereby removing the pressure on such companies to employ those surplus resources in uneconomic ways, and enabling shareholders to deploy the resources to better effect.

5. Any changes in the law would need to be accompanied by safeguards for the interests of creditors, shareholders and others interested in the company, who could otherwise be prejudiced if the company was able freely to reduce its capital.

6. So far as public companies are concerned, any relaxations in the law would also have to be consistent with the provisions of the EC Second Directive on company law.

. . .

Part II By Professor L.C.B. Gower, Research Adviser on Company Law to the Department of Trade

The case for considering extension of the power to acquire the company's shares

9. Until recently there has been little public interest in the possibility of a further extension of the power for a company to acquire its own shares. The Jenkins Committee, having taken evidence from America that 'the power enjoyed by companies in the United States has not led to abuse and is useful for a number of purposes' (Cmnd 1749 of 1962, para. 167) nevertheless reported as follows:

> 168. In our view, if the Companies Act were amended to give a limited company a general power to buy its own shares it would be necessary to introduce stringent safeguards to protect both creditors and shareholders. We think it would be possible to devise effective safeguards and we do not think they need to be unduly complicated. On the other hand, we have received no evidence that British companies need this power and the relatively few witnesses who offered any evidence on this matter were almost unanimous in opposing the introduction of a general power for companies to buy their own shares. The power might occasionally be useful when a minority of the members of a small company whose shares were not readily marketable wished to retire from the company and the other members were unable or unwilling to buy their shares at a fair price; we doubt if such a power would often be exercised for this purpose since it would usually give rise to a surtax assessment in respect of past profits of the company still undistributed and, in cases where tax difficulties can be overcome, a quasi-purchase of the shares of the company can be, and in practice is, carried out by the machinery of a reduction of capital by repaying those shares at a premium. We have therefore reached the conclusion that there is no justification for the general abrogation of the familiar rule that a limited company may not buy its own shares; indeed, we think that the rule should be expressly stated in the Act . . .

In other words an extension was rejected not on the ground that it would be unduly difficult or lead to abuse but rather on the ground that nearly everybody was happy with the *status quo*.

10. This attitude has continued to prevail until very recently when there has been some pressure for a wider power. For example, the Committee under the chairmanship of Sir Harold Wilson which is reviewing the working of the City's financial institutions has, in an *Interim Report on the Financing of Small Firms* (Cmnd 7503 of 1979), advocated that consideration should be given to permitting such firms to issue redeemable equity shares as a means of enabling them to raise needed capital without parting permanently with family control (p. 12, para. 17). The Association of Independent

Businesses, in a well-argued memorandum to the Department of Trade, has pointed out that a shareholder needing to sell all or part of his equity in a small unlisted company may be unable to find a buyer other, perhaps, than a financial institution or public company and that this is one of the factors leading to excessive concentration of industry and commerce. The Association argues that if a company were permitted to buy its own shares a greater number of unlisted independent companies would be able to continue in separate existence and that additional investment in them would be encouraged. Others have suggested that larger companies with surplus liquid assets might more usefully employ them in informal reductions of capital by buying up their shares rather than by looking round for outlets for further diversification.

11. The main advantages which have been claimed for allowing companies to buy their own shares are the following:
   (a) It may enable the company to buy out a dissident shareholder.
   (b) It facilitates the retention of family control.
   (c) It provides a means whereby a shareholder, or the estate of a deceased shareholder, in a company whose shares are not listed can find a buyer.
   (d) It is particularly useful in relation to employee share schemes in enabling the shares of employees to be repurchased on their ceasing to be employed by the company.
   (e) It may help with the marketing of shares by enabling the company to give a subscriber an option to resell to the company.
   (f) It enables companies to purchase their shares for use later in stock option plans or acquisition programmes.
   (g) If redeemable shares are quoted at below the redemption price it enables the company to save money by buying up in advance of the redemption date (a practice which our companies can, and do, adopt in the case of debentures but cannot in the case of redeemable preference shares).
   (h) It permits the evolution of the open-ended investment company or mutual fund instead of having to operate through the mechanism of a unit trust.
   (i) It provides a company with surplus cash with a further means of using it advantageously.
   (j) It can be used to support the market for the shares if this is thought to be unduly depressed, thus preserving for the shareholders the value of their shares as marketable securities.
   (k) If the company not only buys its shares but trades in the treasury shares thus acquired it may make money thereby.

12. It is not suggested that all the above advantages are necessarily desirable; (j) in particular may be regarded as objectionable as leading to market-rigging and (k), trafficking in its own shares, is not self-evidently a desirable corporate activity. But some—particularly (b), (c) and (d)—clearly are valuable, especially in the case of closely held companies and it is in relation to such companies that the power is mainly used in the USA. Even in these cases, however, the power is clearly capable of abuse; for example by enabling the management to maintain its own control or to gain control and to use the company's money in doing so.

10.4.3 Exceptions to the basic rule

The current law provides that a company may purchase its own shares subject to the extensive rules in Part 18. The primary principle is that this should be done by paying for the shares out of 'distributable profits'. As these profits could have been paid out to the members as dividends but are now no longer available for this purpose as they have been used for the share purchase, the purchase out of distributable profits has caused no additional prejudice to creditors.

A further exception (which was nearly abolished in the recent reform process), is that private companies may purchase their shares out of capital (i.e., not out of available profits), subject to various detailed protections for creditors.

COMPANIES ACT 2006, PART 18

690. Power of limited company to purchase own shares

(1) A limited company having a share capital may purchase its own shares (including any redeemable shares), subject to—

    (a) the following provisions of this Chapter, and

    (b) any restriction or prohibition in the company's articles.

(2) A limited company may not purchase its own shares if as a result of the purchase there would no longer be any issued shares of the company other than redeemable shares or shares held as treasury shares.

692. Financing of purchase of own shares

(1) A private limited company may purchase its own shares out of capital in accordance with Chapter 5.

(2) Subject to that—

    (a) a limited company may only purchase its own shares out of—

        (i) distributable profits of the company, or

        (ii) the proceeds of a fresh issue of shares made for the purpose of financing the purchase, and

    (b) any premium payable on the purchase by a limited company of its own shares must be paid out of distributable profits of the company, subject to subsection (3).

709. Power of private limited company to redeem or purchase own shares out of capital

(1) A private limited company may in accordance with this Chapter, but subject to any restriction or prohibition in the company's articles, make a payment in respect of the redemption or purchase of its own shares otherwise than out of distributable profits or the proceeds of a fresh issue of shares.

(2) References below in this Chapter to payment out of capital are to any payment so made, whether or not it would be regarded apart from this section as a payment out of capital.

714. Directors' statement and auditor's report

(1) The company's directors must make a statement in accordance with this section.

(2) The statement must specify the amount of the permissible capital payment for the shares in question.

(3) It must state that, having made full inquiry into the affairs and prospects of the company, the directors have formed the opinion—

    (a) as regards its initial situation immediately following the date on which the payment out of capital is proposed to be made, that there will be no grounds on which the company could then be found unable to pay its debts, and

    (b) as regards its prospects for the year immediately following that date, that having regard to—

        (i) their intentions with respect to the management of the company's business during that year, and

        (ii) the amount and character of the financial resources that will in their view be available to the company during that year, the company will be able to continue to carry on business as a going concern (and will accordingly be able to pay its debts as they fall due) throughout that year.

10.5 FINANCIAL ASSISTANCE

10.5.1 The reasons for prohibiting 'financial assistance'

It has been seen that a company may not as a general rule buy its own shares as to do so involves a return of capital to members. A related but distinct principle previously found in CA 1985, s. 151, and now defined in CA 2006, s. 677 is that a company may not provide anyone with 'financial assistance' for the purchase of its own shares.

This area of statute law (first enacted as CA 1929, s. 45) is highly complex and has probably given Parliamentary drafters and practitioners more headaches than any other area of company law. It was for some time under review by the government, and as at October 1988 the DTI had 'finalised proposals for amending legislation when Parliamentary time allows' (*Companies in 1997–98* (London: Stationery Office, 1998, p. 3)). However, it was subjected to further scrutiny by the DTI review of core company law (see 1.2) and now the revised rules have finally been enacted, the principle reform being that the prohibition no longer applies to private companies.

Unlawful financial assistance is defined in s. 677 and may occur in the following situations:

(a) The company lends or gives money to someone to buy shares in the company.
(b) The company lends money to someone who has bought shares with bank finance, the loan being used to pay off the bank finance.
(c) The company releases a debtor from liability to the company to assist the debtor to buy shares in the company.
(d) The company guarantees or provides security for a bank loan to be used by someone to buy shares in the company.
(e) A company buys assets from a person at an overvalue to enable that person to buy shares in the company. (See, e.g., *Belmont Finance Corporation Ltd* v *Williams Furniture Ltd* (No. 2) [1980] 1 All ER 393.)

All of these examples, while not a reduction of issued share capital as such, may constitute a misuse of company funds and threaten the assets of the company. A particular situation is where an individual or company seeks to acquire a controlling interest in the shares of a target company; i.e., a takeover. It is financial assistance if the bidder intends, having got control of the company, to use the assets of the company to pay for or secure payment of the price of the shares.

Generally it is of course perfectly normal to use an asset one is purchasing, such as a house, as security for a loan to pay the price. Thus one can mortgage the house to the bank. If one is buying shares one can deposit the shares with the bank as formal or informal security for the loan. But if, for example, one buys all the shares in a company whose sole asset is a house, it is unlawful financial assistance (a criminal offence) to use the house as security for the bank loan which provided the funds to buy the shares. Such technical distinctions perplex clients and caused many problems for small business proprietors when the law applied to private companies.

The original reasons for prohibition of financial assistance are set out below in extracts from the reports of the Greene and Jenkins committees in 1925 and 1962.

Report of the Company Law Amendment Committee
(London: HMSO, 1925)

Company providing money for the purchase of its own shares

30. A practice has made its appearance in recent years which we consider to be highly improper. A syndicate agrees to purchase from the existing shareholders sufficient shares to control a company, the purchase money is provided by a temporary loan from a bank for a day or two, the syndicate's nominees are appointed directors in place of the old board and immediately proceed to lend to the syndicate out of the company's funds (often without security) the money required to pay off the bank. Thus in effect the company provides money for the purchase of its own shares. This is a typical example although there are, of course, many variations. Such an arrangement appears to us to offend against the spirit if not the letter of the law which prohibits a company from trafficking in its own shares and the practice is open to the gravest abuses.

Recommendation

31. We recommend that companies should be prohibited from directly or indirectly providing any financial assistance in connection with a purchase (made or to be made) of their own shares by third persons, whether such assistance takes the form of loan, guarantee, provision of security, or otherwise. This should not apply in the case of companies whose ordinary business includes the lending of money, to money lent in the ordinary course of such business, or to schemes by which a company puts up money in the hands of trustees for purchasing shares of the company to be held for the benefit of employees or to loans direct to employees for the same purpose.

Report of the Company Law Committee
(Cmnd 1749) (London: HMSO, 1962)

173. We do not think that the practice whereby a company provides financial assistance for the acquisition of its own shares necessarily offends against the rule that a limited company may not buy its own shares, and, had s. 54 of the Companies Act 1948 been designed merely to extend that rule, we should have felt some doubt whether it was worth retaining. The reason why a limited company may not buy its own shares is that in doing so it would part outright with the consideration for the purchase and thereby reduce its capital. A company which lends money to a person to buy its shares simply changes the form of its assets and if the borrower is able to repay the loan the company's capital remains intact. If, in the circumstances, the assistance given to the purchaser is improper and the company suffers loss, the directors who are parties to the transaction will be liable for misfeasance. In our view, however, the purpose of the section is to prevent the abuses which are likely to, and indeed do, arise when the practice is followed. If people who cannot provide the funds necessary to acquire control of a company from their own resources, or by borrowing on their own credit, gain control of a company with large assets on the understanding that they will use the funds of the company to pay for their shares it seems to us all too likely that in many cases the company will be made to part with its funds either on inadequate security or for an illusory consideration. If the speculation succeeds, the company and therefore its creditors and minority shareholders may suffer no loss, although their interests will have been subjected to an illegitimate risk; if it fails, it may be little consolation for creditors and minority shareholders to know that the directors are liable for misfeasance. In recent times there have been some flagrant abuses of this kind to the serious detriment, particularly, of minority shareholders. We therefore think that section 54 should be retained and strengthened.

Wallersteiner v Moir
Circular cheques and puppet companies
[1974] 3 All ER 217, [1974] 1 WLR 991, Court of Appeal

The following extract dealing with the old CA 1948, s. 54, looks briefly at the general problems leading to prohibition of financial assistance and summarises an offending transaction. (The background to the case appears to 3.3.2.)

LORD DENNING MR: Section 54(1) of the Companies Act 1948 says:

> ...it shall not be lawful for a company to give...any financial assistance...in connection with a purchase...made or to be made by any person of or for any shares in the company, or...in its holding company.

That section was first introduced in the Companies Act 1929. It was enacted so as to deal with a mischief which was described by Lord Greene MR in *Re VGM Holdings Ltd* [1942] Ch 235 at p. 239:

> Those whose memories enable them to recall what had been happening after the last war for several years will remember that a very common form of transaction in connection with companies was one by which persons—call them financiers, speculators, or what you will—finding a company with a substantial cash balance or easily realisable assets such as war loan, bought up the whole or the greater part of the shares of the company for cash and so arranged matters that the purchase money which they then became bound to provide was advanced to them by the company whose shares they were acquiring, either out of its cash balance or by realisation of its liquid investments. That type of transaction was a common one, and it gave rise to great dissatisfaction and, in some cases, great scandals.

Lord Greene MR spoke those words in the year 1942. Since that time financiers have used more sophisticated methods. You have only to look at such cases as *Steen* v *Law* [1964] AC 287 and *Selangor United Rubber Estates Ltd* v *Cradock (No. 3)* [1968] 1 WLR 1555 to see the devices which they use. Circular cheques come in very handy. So do puppet companies. The transactions are extremely complicated, but the end result is clear. You look to the company's money and see what has become of it. You look to the company's shares and see into whose hands they have got. You will then soon see if the company's money has been used to finance the purchase. The present case is an excellent example. In March 1962 Hartley Baird Ltd was a public company. Ten million of its shares, worth £500,000, were held by Camp Bird Ltd. Camp Bird had charged them to the Pearl Assurance Co. Ltd to secure a loan of £125,000. It would have cost an honest buyer £625,000 to get them for his own benefit, free of the charge.

By September 1962 Dr Wallersteiner (in the name of his creature, the Rothschild Trust) had acquired all those shares for his own benefit and free of any charge. But he had not paid a penny for them. He had done it by two means: (1) by loans which Hartley Baird made to him (in the name of his company, IFT of Nassau); (2) by commissions which he said he had earned in the name of the Liechtenstein company. Those loans to IFT were for £284,981 11s 4d and £50,000. They were repayable by IFT by instalments over the succeeding years. One or two instalments were paid, but none thereafter. IFT has no assets. So the sums have been lost to Hartley Baird.

It is clear that those loans by Hartley Baird to IFT greatly assisted the acquisition of the shares by Rothschild Trust; and that Dr Wallersteiner was the moving spirit behind it. In those circumstances to my mind Dr Wallersteiner was guilty of misfeasance, apart altogether from s. 54 of the Companies Act 1948. It was a misfeasance of the same quality as that which took place in *Re VGM Holdings Ltd*. But it was also a plain breach of s. 54. What is the remedy for such breach? By s. 54(2) the company and every officer who is in default is liable to a fine not exceeding £100. That is a trifling sanction. In *Essex Aero Ltd* v *Cross* (17 November 1961, Bar Library Transcript No. 388 of 1961) Harman LJ said: '. . . the section was not enacted for the company's protection but for that of its creditors...the company cannot enforce it'. I do not agree. I think the section was passed so as to protect the company from having its assets misused. If it is broken, there is a civil remedy by way of an action for damages. Every director who is a party to a breach of s. 54 is guilty of a misfeasance and breach of trust; and is liable to recoup to the company any loss occasioned to it by the default. That is shown by *Steen* v *Law* and *Selangor United Rubber Estates Ltd* v *Cradock (No. 3)*: see also *Halsbury's Laws of England*, 4th ed., vol. 7 (1974), para 208. In those cases defaulters were held liable for the loss. So should Dr Wallersteiner be held liable here.

Modern Company Law for a Competitive Economy: Final Report
(London: DTI, 2001)

Capital Maintenance
2.29 The capital maintenance provisions of the Act are complex. In normal circumstances, they are of limited practical relevance to the smallest companies, which will have only insignificant share capital. However, as companies grow and attract external equity investment, the capital maintenance provisions can become increasingly relevant. We have proposed a range of reforms to the capital maintenance regime that will, we believe, be welcome to public and private companies alike. Two are worthy of mention here as of special importance to private companies.

2.30 We recommend that the provisions of the current Act on financial assistance for the acquisition of own shares should no longer apply at all to private companies. These provisions are among the most difficult of the Act, and in many cases it is all but impossible for a company to assess whether a proposed course of action is lawful or not. The provisions are arbitrary in their effect on private companies, and innocuous transactions may be rendered unlawful by criminal law requirements that are often unenforceable and by civil sanctions of wide and damaging effect. There are alternative remedies designed to deal with threats to creditors which are likely in most circumstances to be more effective. This unnecessary burden should be lifted from private companies.

10.5.2 Prohibition of financial assistance

It is a criminal offence (CA 2006, s. 680) for a company or its subsidiary to give financial assistance directly or indirectly for the purchase of the company's shares. Section 677 defines 'financial assistance' and section 678(2) sets out the 'principal purpose' exception. Thus financial assistance given in good faith and in the interests of the company is not prohibited if its principal purpose is not the acquisition of shares or is 'only an incidental part of some larger purpose of the company'. This exception has been considered by the House of Lords in *Brady* v *Brady* extracted below.

For contravention of the prohibition against giving financial assistance the company and officers in default are liable to a fine, though the legislation does not spell out the civil consequences of contravention. It has been held that parties receiving funds with knowledge of the directors' breach of duty or in circumstances where they ought to have known of the breach are liable as constructive trustees (*Belmont Finance Corporation Ltd* v *Williams Furniture Ltd (No. 2)* [1980] 1 All ER 393, CA, *Selangor United Rubber Estates Ltd* v *Cradock (No. 3)* [1968] 1 WLR 1555). In *Heald* v *O'Connor*, extracted below, it was held that on the doctrine of illegality the transaction underlying the financial assistance, as well as attracting criminal sanctions, is also void and unenforceable.

Brief extracts from the new law now follow.

COMPANIES ACT 2006, Part 18, Chapter 2

677. Meaning of "financial assistance"

(1) In this Chapter "financial assistance" means—

 (a) financial assistance given by way of gift,

 (b) financial assistance given—

  (i) by way of guarantee, security or indemnity (other than an indemnity in respect of the indemnifier's own neglect or default), or

  (ii) by way of release or waiver,

 (c) financial assistance given—

  (i) by way of a loan or any other agreement under which any of the obligations of the person giving the assistance are to be fulfilled at a time when in accordance with the agreement any obligation of another party to the agreement remains unfulfilled, or

  (ii) by way of the novation of, or the assignment (in Scotland, assignation) of rights arising under, a loan or such other agreement, or

 (d) any other financial assistance given by a company where—

  (i) the net assets of the company are reduced to a material extent by the giving of the assistance, or

  (ii) the company has no net assets.

678. Assistance for acquisition of shares in public company

(1) Where a person is acquiring or proposing to acquire shares in a public company, it is not lawful for that company, or a company that is a subsidiary of that company, to give financial assistance directly or indirectly for the purpose of the acquisition before or at the same time as the acquisition takes place.

(2) Subsection (1) does not prohibit a company from giving financial assistance for the acquisition of shares in it or its holding company if—

 (a) the company's principal purpose in giving the assistance is not to give it for the purpose of any such acquisition, or

 (b) the giving of the assistance for that purpose is only an incidental part of some larger purpose of the company,

and the assistance is given in good faith in the interests of the company.

680. Prohibited financial assistance an offence

(1) If a company contravenes section 678(1) or (3) or section 679(1) or (3) (prohibited financial assistance) an offence is committed by—

 (a) the company, and

 (b) every officer of the company who is in default.

Brady v Brady

A family feud and the principal-purpose exception

[1988] 2 All ER 617, [1989] AC 755, House of Lords

This case illustrates how a highly complex commercial deal may be bedevilled by the prohibition on giving financial assistance, then found in CA 1985, s. 151 which applied both to public and private companies. It indicates why it was desirable to disapply the prohibition in respect of private companies and it illustrates the application of the 'principal purpose' exception. The House of Lords considered the 'principal purpose' exception, interpreting it narrowly and holding that the transaction did not fall within the exception. The following extract considers this aspect of the case. The House of Lords ultimately concluded that the litigation was unnecessary as the transaction could lawfully have been effected under the exemptions for private companies contained in the sections.

Facts   Brothers Bob and Jack carried on family businesses of road haulage and the manufacture and distribution of drinks through a private company, T. Brady & Sons Ltd (called 'Brady' in the extract below) and its subsidiaries. By the early 1980s Jack and Bob were unable to work together and were not on speaking terms. The businesses suffered. After some initial litigation it was decided that the businesses should be split up, Jack taking the haulage side and Bob the drinks business together with an equality payment to balance the difference in values. A complex scheme was devised to achieve this under which a new company, Motoreal Ltd, to be controlled by Jack, was to receive assets from Brady to help pay for shares acquired by it in Brady. Bob refused to put the agreement into effect and Jack sued for specific performance. This action was resisted on the ground that the transaction involved unlawful financial assistance. Jack argued unsuccessfully that the transaction was exempted by s. 153(2)(a) on the ground that the company's principal purpose was not the financial assistance which was merely part of the larger purpose of resolving the deadlock between the brothers.

LORD OLIVER OF AYLMERTON: My lords, it follows from what I have said that if the appellants' claim is to be successfully resisted at all, it can only be on the ground that the transaction proposed infringes the provisions of s. 151 of the 1985 Act. . . . The acquisition of the Brady shares by Motoreal has already taken place and has given rise to the issue of the loan stock to Activista. The proposed transfer therefore falls within the provisions of s. 151(2) and it is not in dispute that it does indeed constitute the provision of assistance by Brady to reduce Motoreal's liability incurred in the course of that acquisition. The appellants, however, rely on the provisions of s. 153(2). . . . As already mentioned, the appellants' case failed in the Court of Appeal because the assistance given by Brady was not, in the view of the majority (albeit for different reasons), in the interests of the company and therefore failed to satisfy para. (*b*) of the subsection. Both the trial judge and all three members of the Court of Appeal held, however, that para. (*a*) was satisfied, although Nourse LJ evidently felt some doubt on that question.

My lords, I have found myself unable to share the views of the majority of the Court of Appeal with regard to para. (*b*). The words 'in good faith in the interests of the company' form, I think, a single composite expression and postulate a requirement that those responsible for procuring the company to provide the assistance act in the genuine belief that it is being done in the company's interest. In the circumstances of this case, where failure to implement the final stage of the scheme for the division of the two sides of Brady's business is likely to lead back to the very management deadlock that it was designed to avoid and the probable liquidation of Brady as a result, the proposed transfer is not only something which is properly capable of being perceived by Brady's directors as calculated to advance Brady's corporate and commercial interests and the interests of its employees but is indeed, viewed objectively, in the company's interest. . . . As it was, when the matter came before the court, there was clear evidence that the interests of creditors not only were not jeopardised by the proposal but that, in the view of the company's auditors, their position would, indeed, be improved in the long term once the reorganisation was completed. I do not, therefore, for my part, entertain any doubt that para. (*b*) is satisfied or, since we are in fact looking at something which has not yet occurred, that it is at least capable of being satisfied.

Where I part company both from the trial judge and from the Court of Appeal is on the question of whether para. (*a*) can, on any reasonable construction of the subsection, be said to have been satisfied. As O'Connor LJ observed the section is not altogether easy to construe (see [1988] BCLC 20 at p. 25). It first appeared as part of s. 42 of the Companies Act 1981 and it seems likely that it was introduced for the purpose of dispelling any doubts resulting from the query raised in *Belmont Finance Corporation Ltd v Williams Furniture Ltd (No. 2)* [1980] 1 All ER 393 whether a transaction entered into partly with a genuine view of the commercial interests of the company and partly with a view to putting a purchaser of shares in the company in funds to complete his purchase was in breach of s. 54 of the Companies Act 1948. The ambit of the operation of the section is, however, far from easy to discern, for the word 'purpose' is capable of several different shades of meaning.

This much is clear, that para. (*a*) is contemplating two alternative situations. The first envisages a principal and, by implication, a subsidiary purpose. The inquiry here is whether the assistance given was principally in order to relieve the purchaser of shares in the company of his indebtedness resulting from the acquisition or whether it was principally for some other purpose, for instance the acquisition from the purchaser of some asset which the company requires for its business. That is the situation envisaged by Buckley LJ in the course of his judgment in the *Belmont Finance* case as giving rise to doubts. That is not this case, for the purpose of the assistance here was simply and solely to reduce the indebtedness incurred by Motoreal on issuing the loan stock. The alternative situation is where it is not suggested that the financial assistance was intended to achieve any other object than the reduction or discharge of the indebtedness but where that result (i.e. the reduction or discharge) is merely incidental to some larger purpose of the company. Those last three words are important. What has to be sought is some larger overall corporate purpose in which the resultant reduction or discharge is merely incidental. The trial judge found Brady's larger purpose to be that of freeing itself from the deadlock and enabling it to function independently and this was echoed in the judgment of O'Connor LJ where he observed that the answer 'embraces avoiding liquidation, preserving its goodwill and the advantages of an established business' (see [1988] BCLC 20 at p. 26). Croom-Johnson LJ found the larger purpose in the reorganisation of the whole group. My lords, I confess that I have not found the concept of a 'larger purpose' easy to grasp, but if the paragraph is to be given any meaning that does not in effect provide a blank cheque for avoiding the effective application of s. 151 in every case, the concept must be narrower than that for which the appellants contend.

The matter can, perhaps, most easily be tested by reference to s. 153(1)(*a*), where the same formula is used. Here the words are 'or the giving of the assistance for that purpose [i.e. the acquisition of shares] is but an incidental part of some larger purpose of the company'. The words 'larger purpose' must here have the same meaning as the same words in subs. (2)(*a*). In applying subs. (1)(*a*) one has, therefore, to look for some larger purpose in the giving of financial assistance than the mere purpose of the acquisition of the shares and to ask whether the giving of assistance is a mere incident of that purpose. My lords, 'purpose' is, in some contexts, a word of wide content but in construing it in the context of the fasciculus of sections regulating the provision of finance by a company in connection with the purchase of its own shares there has always to be borne in mind the mischief against which s. 151 is aimed. In particular, if the section is not, effectively, to be deprived of any useful application, it is important to distinguish between a purpose and the reason why a purpose is formed. The ultimate reason for forming the purpose of financing an acquisition may, and in most cases probably will, be more important to those making the decision than the immediate transaction itself. But 'larger' is not the same thing as 'more important' nor is 'reason' the same as 'purpose'. If one postulates the case of a bidder for control of a public company financing his bid from the company's own funds, the obvious mischief at which the section is aimed, the immediate purpose which it is sought to achieve is that of completing the purchase and vesting control of the company in the bidder. The reasons why that course is considered desirable may be many and varied. The company may have fallen on hard times so that a change of management is considered necessary to avert disaster. It may merely be thought, and no doubt would be thought by the purchaser and the directors whom he nominates once he has control, that the business of the company will be more profitable under his management than it was heretofore. These may be excellent reasons but they cannot, in my judgment, constitute a 'larger purpose' of which the provision of assistance is merely an incident. The purpose and the only purpose of the financial assistance is and remains that of enabling the shares to be acquired and the financial or commercial advantages flowing from the acquisition, whilst they may form the reason for forming the purpose of providing assistance, are a by-product of it rather than an independent purpose of which the assistance can properly be considered to be an incident.

Now of course in the instant case the reason why the reorganisation was conceived in the first place was the damage being occasioned to the company and its shareholders by reason of the management deadlock, and the deadlock was the reason for the decision that the business should be split in two, so that the two branches could be conducted independently. What prompted the particular method adopted for carrying out the split was the commercial desirability of keeping

Brady in being as a corporate entity. That involved, in effect, Jack buying out Bob's interest in Brady and it was, presumably, the fact that he did not have free funds to do this from his own resources that dictated that Brady's own assets should be used for the purpose. No doubt the acquisition of control by Jack was considered, at any rate by Jack and Robert, who were and are Brady's directors, to be beneficial to Brady. Indeed, your lordships have been told that the business has thriven under independent management. But this is merely the result, and no doubt the intended result, of Jack's assumption of control and however one analyses the transaction the only purpose that can be discerned in the redemption of loan stock is the payment in tangible form of the price payable to enable the Brady shares to be acquired and ultimately vested in Jack or a company controlled by him. The scheme of reorganisation was framed and designed to give Jack and Robert control of Brady for the best of reasons, but to say that the 'larger purpose' of Brady's financial assistance is to be found in the scheme of reorganisation itself is to say only that the larger purpose was the acquisition of the Brady shares on their behalf. For my part, I do not think that a larger purpose can be found in the benefits considered to be likely to flow or the disadvantages considered to be likely to be avoided by the acquisition which it was the purpose of the assistance to facilitate. The acquisition was not a mere incident of the scheme devised to break the deadlock. It was the essence of the scheme itself and the object which the scheme set out to achieve. In my judgment, therefore, s. 153(2)(a) is not satisfied and if the matter rested there the appeal ought to fail on that ground.

That is a conclusion which I reach with a measure of regret, for the bargain between the appellants and the respondents was freely negotiated and the respondents' attempt to resile from it is not immediately attractive. . . .

A further consequence of the prohibition of financial assistance is that the underlying transaction or transactions may be void for illegality. The practical impact of a complex commercial arrangement being discovered to be unlawful and therefore unenforceable is thus enormous and a nightmare for commercial practitioners. A number of conflicting cases (e.g., *Victor Battery Co. Ltd* v *Curry's Ltd* [1946] Ch 242) suggested that the civil impact of the section was limited. However, *Heald* v *O'Connor* held that underlying transactions are void. Indeed it was the primary assumption in *Brady* v *Brady* that an agreement to provide unlawful financial assistance is unenforceable.

Heald v O'Connor

A debenture providing unlawful financial assistance is void

[1971] 2 All ER 1105, [1971] 1 WLR 497, Chancery Division

Facts The plaintiffs sold to the defendant all the shares in D.E. Heald (Stoke-on-Trent) Ltd for £35,000. In a rather peculiar arrangement which was blatantly unlawful financial assistance, it was agreed that £25,000 (effectively part of the purchase price for the shares) was to remain outstanding as a loan to the defendant purchaser.

This loan was secured by a debenture granting a floating charge on the assets of the company and which acknowledged that the company owed £25,000 to the plaintiff vendors of the shares. This indebtedness in turn was guaranteed by the defendant. When the company defaulted in making the repayments on the loan, the plaintiff vendors sued the purchaser on the guarantee. The purchaser successfully argued that the debenture (i.e., the company's indebtedness and the security) was void as unlawful financial assistance. It was also held that the purchaser was not liable on the guarantee as a guarantee of an unenforceable debt guarantees nothing and so is also unenforceable.

FISHER J: The defendant says that the company gave by means of the provision of security, financial assistance for the purpose of or in connection with the purchase by the defendant of its shares. The defendant says that this not only rendered the company liable to a fine of £100 but made the debenture illegal and void and that the guarantee also is, therefore, void and unenforceable. . . .

I proceed to consider the question of law on the assumption that the debenture was given to secure the repayment of the sum of £25,000 lent by the plaintiffs to the defendant in order to enable him to pay for the shares, and that without such security the plaintiffs would not have been willing to make the loan. On this assumption I am satisfied that the company did give financial assistance within the words of s. 54(1) [of the Companies Act 1948]. Some meaning has to be given to the words in the subsection 'give...financial assistance' by means of 'the provision of security', and the meaning must be such as to cover some matter not already covered by the other words 'loan' and 'guarantee'. It seems to me that a usual way, and maybe the only way, in which a company could give financial assistance by means of the provision of a security in circumstances which would not amount to the giving of financial assistance by means of a loan or guarantee would be by entering into a debenture such as the one in the present case.

Is the debenture for this reason illegal and void? In *Victor Battery Co Ltd* v *Curry's Ltd* [1946] Ch 242 Roxburgh J held that a debenture given by a company as security for moneys lent to enable a person to purchase shares in the company was not illegal and void. He was impressed by the apparent injustice if the debenture were held to be illegal; the company which had contravened the section would benefit and the lender would suffer a loss which might greatly exceed the maximum penalty of £100. He held that the word 'security' in s. 54 must mean a 'valid security', and he said:

> The section provides, not that it shall not be lawful for a company to provide a security in order to give financial assistance, but that it shall not be lawful for a company by means of the provision of security to give any financial assistance. In my judgment, 'security' prima facie means 'valid security', although I do not say that it must mean that. Moreover, the words of the section are not 'purport to give financial assistance' but 'give financial assistance' and I cannot see how an invalid debenture could give any financial assistance. If, then, the section is, as I hold it is, referring to the provision of valid security and is treating the security as valid at the moment of the commission of the offence by the borrower, what is there to invalidate it subsequently? The section punishes the borrowing company on the footing that the security provided was and remains valid. Therefore, those principles of law to which [counsel] on behalf of the plaintiff company referred me, cannot be imported, and I cannot believe that the legislature intended them to be imported, as they appear to lead to the extravagant consequences which I have indicated.

The reasoning and conclusion of Roxburgh J in that case have been questioned in *Palmer on Company Law*, and in three Commonwealth decisions: *Dressy Frocks Pty Ltd* v *Bock* (1951) 51 SR (NSW) 390, *Shearer Transport Co. Pty Ltd* v *McGrath* [1956] VLR 316, and *E.H. Dey Ltd* v *Dey* [1966] VR 464, and more recently by Ungoed Thomas J in *Selangor United Rubber Estates Ltd* v *Cradock (No. 3)* [1968] 1 WLR 1555. I am impressed by these criticisms and I propose to adopt them and to find in the contrary sense to Roxburgh J. The reasoning which leads me to that decision is set out in the reports of those cases and I need not repeat it.

In summary, my reasoning is as follows. By the provision of a security in the circumstances of the *Victor Battery* case and of this case, the company undoubtedly gives financial assistance to the purchaser of the shares whether the security is valid or not. All that is necessary to make the financial assistance effective is that the lender should believe the security to be valid and on the strength of it make the loan. The apparent injustice which is the common result of the statutory prohibition of these particular kinds of transaction is not sufficient warranty for declining to apply the well-settled principle of law. The application of this principle in such circumstances as the present is likely to deter potential lenders from lending money on security which might be held to contravene the Act and is likely to be more efficacious in achieving the policy of the section than the very small maximum penalty on the company.

10.6 A COMPANY MAY NOT OWN SHARES IN ITS HOLDING COMPANY

To take an extreme example, suppose Smith forms Holdings Ltd and subscribes for its whole share capital of £100. Holdings Ltd forms Subsidiary Ltd and uses the £100 to subscribe for its whole share capital of £100. Subsidiary Ltd then (unlawfully) buys from Smith all his shares in Holdings Ltd, paying £100 for them. A return of capital to Smith would result, as well as two companies owning each other, each with an illusory capital.

COMPANIES ACT 2006, S. 136

136. Prohibition on subsidiary being a member of its holding company

(1) Except as provided by this Chapter—
   (a) a body corporate cannot be a member of a company that is its holding company, and
   (b) any allotment or transfer of shares in a company to its subsidiary is void.
(2) The exceptions are provided for in—
   section 138 (subsidiary acting as personal representative or trustee), and
   section 141 (subsidiary acting as authorised dealer in securities).

10.7 REDUCTION OF SHARE CAPITAL

If a company reduces its share capital, this may prejudice creditors, especially if it involves an actual return of cash to the members. As part of the maintenance of capital principal, there are therefore strict rules on capital reductions.

Under CA 1985, ss. 135 and 136, companies, both public and private, were required to apply to the court for an order confirming a special resolution to reduce capital. As this is an expensive procedure for small businesses, the reforms of 2006 now exempt private companies from the requirement for court approval.

While public companies still have to apply to the court to confirm a reduction of capital, in the case of private companies, all that is now required for a reduction of capital is a special resolution supported by a solvency declaration made by the directors.

The following brief extracts indicate the outlines of the rules on reduction of capital.

COMPANIES ACT 2006, PART 17, CHAPTER 10

641. Circumstances in which a company may reduce its share capital

(1) A limited company having a share capital may reduce its share capital—
   (a) in the case of a private company limited by shares, by special resolution supported by a solvency statement (see sections 642 to 644);
   (b) in any case, by special resolution confirmed by the court (see sections 645 to 651).
(4) In particular, a company may—
   (a) extinguish or reduce the liability on any of its shares in respect of share capital not paid up, or

(b) either with or without extinguishing or reducing liability on any of its shares—
  (i)   cancel any paid-up share capital that is lost or unrepresented by available assets, or
  (ii) repay any paid-up share capital in excess of the company's wants.

643. Solvency statement

(1) A solvency statement is a statement that each of the directors—
  (a) has formed the opinion, as regards the company's situation at the date of the statement, that there is no ground on which the company could then be found to be unable to pay (or otherwise discharge) its debts; and
  (b) has also formed the opinion—
    (i)   if it is intended to commence the winding up of the company within twelve months of that date, that the company will be able to pay (or otherwise discharge) its debts in full within twelve months of the commencement of the winding up; or
    (ii) in any other case, that the company will be able to pay (or otherwise discharge) its debts as they fall due during the year immediately following that date.

(4) If the directors make a solvency statement without having reasonable grounds for the opinions expressed in it, and the statement is delivered to the registrar, an offence is committed by every director who is in default.

645. Application to court for order of confirmation

(1) Where a company has passed a resolution for reducing share capital, it may apply to the court for an order confirming the reduction.
(2) If the proposed reduction of capital involves either—
  (a) diminution of liability in respect of unpaid share capital, or
  (b) the payment to a shareholder of any paid-up share capital,
  section 646 (creditors entitled to object to reduction) applies unless the court directs otherwise.

646. Creditors entitled to object to reduction

(1) Where this section applies (see section 645(2) and (4)), every creditor of the company who at the date fixed by the court is entitled to any debt or claim that, if that date were the commencement of the winding up of the company would be admissible in proof against the company, is entitled to object to the reduction of capital.

648. Court order confirming reduction

(1) The court may make an order confirming the reduction of capital on such terms and conditions as it thinks fit.
(2) The court must not confirm the reduction unless it is satisfied, with respect to every creditor of the company who is entitled to object to the reduction of capital that either—
  (a) his consent to the reduction has been obtained, or
  (b) his debt or claim has been discharged, or has determined or has been secured.

11

The Position of Directors

Chapters 7 and 8 of this book considered the constitutional role of the general meeting and the board of directors as the two functional 'organs' of the company, while this and the next chapter now consider the position of directors and their duties in more detail.

11.1.1 The traditional view

In understanding the position of directors it is important to appreciate the historic and current realities in which company law has developed. It should be noted that directors are officers of the company but not necessarily employees. The limited company as originally envisaged was a public corporation pooling funds for a large number of passive investors and the directors were generally officers taking a fee and attending periodic board meetings. In current business jargon such directors would be called non-executive directors. The day-to-day running of the company was largely entrusted to employees as an administrative function.

In the modern context of a public company with a listing on the Stock Exchange, there are possibly tens of thousands of shareholders, a small number of whom vote at general meetings to appoint the board of directors. The board then employs professional managers, some of whom are themselves directors. The board therefore consists of employees, generally called executive directors, and also those who do not work for the company but merely attend board meetings, who are called non-executive directors.

The net result is effectively a two-tier structure in which the members appoint the directors as officers, and the board of directors then appoints executive directors as full-time employees. The peculiarity therefore is that the board offers jobs to its own members.

In private companies (the local garage or builder or small manufacturer) the realities are somewhat different. In this case it is the major shareholders who appoint themselves as directors. As such they work full-time in the company and operate as executive directors with formal or informal contracts of employment. As owners of the company they more often than not take business profits as salary rather than as dividend. While there are sometimes non-executive directors, these are most likely to be grandmother or uncle Charlie, rather than a specialised professional.

In thinking why the law has developed in the way it has, or in considering how the law applies in a particular case, it is therefore important to consider what sort of company is involved. It is also important to consider the type or role of the particular director in question.

Directors therefore are officers of the company and sometimes also employees. As directors they owe strict trustee-like fiduciary obligations to the company requiring a high standard of honesty, but relatively undemanding standards of competence. They are not the agents of the shareholders in running the business of the company. Because the law is intrinsically conservative it adapts to new phenomena such as companies and directors by reference to its existing experience. Thus the obligations of directors, though they are not trustees, have developed by analogy to trustees. As Bowen LJ commented in *Imperial Hydropathic Hotel Co., Blackpool* v *Hampson* (1882) 23 ChD 1 at p. 12:

> ...when persons who are directors of a company are from time to time spoken of by judges as agents, trustees, or managing partners of the company, it is essential to recollect that such expressions are used not as exhaustive of the powers or responsibilities of those persons, but only as indicating useful points of view from which they may for the moment and for the particular purpose be considered—points of view at which they seem for the moment to be either cutting the circle or falling within the category of the suggested kind. It is not meant that they belong to the category, but that it is useful for the purpose of the moment to observe that they fall *pro tanto* within the principles which govern that particular class.

As will be seen from this chapter and chapter 12 on duties of directors, there are few if any prior qualifications required of directors. No special professional skills have generally been required of directors by the law, though with the recent impact of the cases on director disqualification and CA 2006 s. 174 now requiring a director to exercise reasonable care, carried out with the skill and experience that may reasonably be expected of a person performing his functions, it appears that the required standard of competence is set for an upgrade. Nonetheless, shareholders are free to appoint whoever they wish as directors, and often appoint themselves.

Directors owe strict standards of honesty to the company but may not be answerable for their own intrinsic incompetence. Only recently has the law begun to have regard to the possible impact on creditors of management incompetence (see, e.g., IA 1986, s. 214). Rules for listing of public companies on the Stock Exchange also impose further specific obligations on directors in the interests of investors and the market generally. Statutory provisions for the public disqualification of directors of all categories of companies (see 11.7) are a recent phenomenon. Thus a director of a company that has gone into insolvent liquidation may be disqualified if his or her conduct makes him or her 'unfit to be concerned in the management of a company'.

The overall picture therefore is of the courts traditionally treating directors as having a trustee-like function to manage the property and business of the company. This has been followed by increasing regulation by statute and the share markets of directors' obligations in the broader public interest. Statute has also extensively enacted provisions duplicating or extending specific aspects of the existing law on fiduciary duties (see, for example, CA 2006, Part 10, Chapters 3 to 6). Statutory provisions have also been enacted to protect creditors and in the case of disqualification to protect the public generally against abuse of the corporate form. Market regulation of the listed share markets through the Stock Exchange listing rules etc. (see chapters 17 and 18) are of first importance in ensuring proper practice by directors of listed companies.

The range of obligations of directors and their regulation is therefore complex. The following extract from an article by Professor Sealy is of great value in understanding the present-day case law on the position of directors.

L. S. Sealy, 'The director as trustee'

[1967] CLJ 83

Over two centuries ago, in the first reported case of its kind (*Charitable Corporation* v *Sutton* (1742) 2 Atk 400), Lord Hardwicke held the 'committee-men' or directors of the Charitable Corporation guilty of 'breaches of trust', for which they had to account to the corporation. The concept of the director as a trustee persists through the cases and the textbooks to this day, but its origin is ill-explained and its modern relevance imperfectly understood. Why is the director called a trustee? Is it because he once was a trustee in the full technical sense? In what respects does the position of a director resemble, and in what respects does it differ from that of a trustee? How far has the law acknowledged these differences? Is the law, in so far as it is based on trust principles, adequate to ensure the proper discharge by directors of their responsibilities?

The origin of the concept The view is widely held that the concept had its origin in the fact that, in the earliest companies, the director *was* a trustee in the full technical sense. It is claimed that, during the 150 years or so when most companies were unincorporated, established by a deed of settlement with practically no official recognition, the deed invariably or usually constituted the directors trustees of the funds and property of the undertaking, so that the courts naturally called them to account on this strict basis. Later, it is suggested, this practice persisted, even when, as a result of general incorporation, property was owned by the company in its own right; and also by analogy, it is said, the directors of chartered and statutory corporations were deemed to be trustees.

There is no support at all for this theory in the old books and reports, and it is submitted that it is wrong. . . .

It is submitted that there is no hidden mystery, no missing link lying undiscovered in the prehistory of company law, behind the trustee appellation: the real mystery is why the old label has survived in modern usage. In the limited legal vocabulary of the day, there was no other word which the judges would wish to use. It was sufficient for them to reason that the directors had accepted an appointment or 'trust'; therefore, they were 'trustees' and accountable for 'breaches of trust'. The 'trustee' in a strict sense, in whom property is legally vested for the benefit of others, was not separately identified until well into the nineteenth century, when the expression 'fiduciary' was eventually accepted to differentiate true trusts from those other relationships, like that between a director or a promoter and his company, which in some degree resemble them.

It was natural and, indeed, inevitable that those seeking redress against defaulting directors should go to the courts of Chancery, which had long had a monopoly of the jurisdiction in partnership matters. There were the advantages of better accounting facilities, of discovery, the representative suit (virtually developed for this purpose) and the general superiority of equitable remedies. As events proved, the range and flexibility of the principles of fiduciary obligation were adequate to cope with most of the problems which arose. We should not forget, however, that all fiduciary principles are trust principles, and it is on these trust principles that directors' liability is traditionally determined. On the other hand, there are clear differences in *function* between the office of company director and that of trustee—differences which have become more marked with changes in commercial practice—and these the law has, for the most part, duly recognised. When Vaughan Williams J said: 'A director is in no sense a trustee' (*Re Kingston Cotton Mill (No. 2)* [1896] 1 Ch 331 at p. 345), he was stressing these differences; but when Bacon V-C said: 'I should say they are trustees and nothing else' (*Re Exchange Banking Co., Flitcroft's Case* (1882) 21 ChD 519 at p. 525), he was thinking of the legal principles involved. Each was correct; but neither was seeing more than one half of the picture.

In the remainder of this article we shall examine more closely these points of similarity and these differences: how far the trust principles were appropriate to deal with the company director; and in what respects they have required modification.

Special features of the director's position

Property   The most obvious point of resemblance between trustees and directors is that they each have control of a fund in which others are beneficially interested. This common feature outweighed any objections based on the technical ownership of the legal estate; indeed, such objections do not appear in the reports until quite a late stage, and they have never in fact distracted the courts from the central fiduciary principle. In an incorporated body, the legal title is in the corporation itself; in an unincorporated company, it is in trustees who have no say at all in matters of management; while in the case of a trust, it is in the trustees themselves. But in each case *control* of the property—the power to dispose of the legal estate—is in the hands of the fiduciaries; the property may be applied for unauthorised as well as for authorised purposes, and the obligation to account for the due discharge of their responsibilities is the same. Accordingly, it is on trust principles that directors are accountable for their handling of the company's property and, like trust property, assets wrongfully alienated may be followed into other hands and even traced into other forms.

Discretion and risk   The normal function of trustees is to conserve a fund and to dispose of it in accordance with the directions of the settlor. The law of trusts does not allow a trustee a very wide discretion in what he does: often fixed rules, either of law or of court practice, fetter his activities and prescribe within close limits the proper course for him to take. He must be careful to preserve the trust property and avoid exposing it to unnecessary risks, and here he can look to the law to direct him as to the kind of investments a trustee may make. If he wishes to realise trust property, the law will dictate for him the conditions of sale. In these matters, the courts have the experience and the facilities to supervise his activities. But it has always been recognised that none of these rules applies to company directors. The conduct of their enterprise is entirely a matter for their judgment as businessmen, and the courts have never been willing or competent to review the exercise of this kind of discretion on the merits of the case. Commercial ventures are all in some degree speculative, and companies must encounter risks. It is not the director's concern to avoid risks, but to decide whether a risk is worth taking, and what the risk is worth. Again, a trustee's primary duties are imperative: only when he has carried them out to the court's satisfaction can he claim to be quit. But a director's role is almost wholly discretionary: on the one hand, it is up to him to decide whether his company shall undertake any venture at all; on the other hand, so long as his company's business continues, he can never claim that his work is done. These differences of function have meant that the trust rules cannot be applied literally to the director. It has been possible in some cases to modify them to fit his different situation; but all too often, where they have been abandoned as wholly inappropriate, no clear alternative rules have been developed in their place.

11.1.2 Corporate social responsibility

Vast modern companies, especially 'multinationals' with an international reach have huge power and influence and their practices can have both positive and negative impacts on modern society. In response, a movement has recently arisen demanding that big companies behave with due 'corporate social responsibility' ('CSR') towards other 'stakeholders' such as their employees, customers and suppliers and towards wider interests such as the community and the environment. A substantial corporate social responsibility 'industry' has quickly emerged and the government has responded positively towards it. See, for example, www.csr. gov.uk.

However, in law, as has been explained, directors have trustee-like duties to the company only, that is to the general body of shareholders. Their obligation is to keep their eye on the bottom line, to ensure good profits and a regular flow of dividends, and as the jargon goes, to maximise 'shareholder value'. The problem therefore is that if they owe no legal duty towards other interests potentially affected by the policies of the company, how can good corporate social responsibility be assured.

The outlook is not hopeless, however, as the cases have long held that directors can for example make political or charitable donations if they bona fide believe that these will benefit the company. Likewise the directors of The Body Shop can spend the company's money supporting environmental causes if they honestly believe it benefits the company's reputation and increases sales to customers who hug trees.

On the 'risk' side, if an oil company that disposes of a massive North Sea oil drilling rig in a way that lobby groups say is environmentally unsafe, if a manufacturer of branded trainers uses cheap 'sweat shop' labour in poor countries or if a dominant supermarket chain drives small retailers out of business, leaving the high street a desert of boarded up shops, they may suffer a loss of reputation and of market share and profitability. Thus the pressure of opinion and self-interest may force them to take these issues more seriously. How therefore can the regulation of public companies induce the directors of these commercial giants to behave with due corporate social responsibility in a way that makes them focus beyond their apparently crude and narrow duty of creating value for shareholders?

First, the Company Law Review debated this question as a major philosophical issue of company law reform and came up with a catchy phrase, that directors should be required to promote 'enlightened shareholder value'. The Government eagerly accepted the idea and the White Paper of March 2005, referring to the proposed codification of the duties of directors in the new Act, had this to say (at para. 3.3).

> The statement of duties will be drafted in a way which reflects modern business needs and wider expectations of responsible business behaviour. The CLR proposed that the basic goal of directors should be the success of the company for the benefit of its members as a whole; but that to reach this goal, directors would need to take a properly balanced view of the implications of decisions over time and foster effective relations with employees, customers and suppliers, and in the community more widely. The Government strongly agrees that this approach, which the CLR called "enlightened shareholder value", is most likely to drive long-term company performance and maximize overall competitiveness and wealth and welfare for all. It will therefore be reflected in the statement of directors' duties, and in new reporting arrangements for quoted companies under the Operating and Financial Review Regulations.

Thus CA 2006, s. 172, now requires the directors, in promoting the success of the company, to have regard to employees, suppliers, customers, the community and environment and to the desirability of maintaining a reputation for high standards of business conduct. (See chapter 12.) This is clearly a step forward, though none of those interests have a right to sue if the directors fail to 'have regard to' their interests and equally it is hard to see the company's members going to law to enforce these soft obligations either. Nonetheless, stating them expressly in the law is of value and increases the clout of lobby groups seeking to assure due corporate social responsibility. Naming and shaming and the power of collective coercion through the media can thus make a more positive contribution when it is backed up by the spirit and the letter of the law.

Also important in the area of CSR is a second innovation. When it comes to regulating the big listed companies, the standard response of British regulators is to

maximise the obligation of 'disclosure', that is to give investors as much information as possible about the companies and so expose them to the full glare of public
scrutiny. As is stated towards the end of the paragraph from the White Paper, to
make the policies of companies as transparent as possible, they should be required
to publicly report on a range of issues relating to CSR. Thus under CA 2006, s. 417,
the directors report which is drawn up annually must include what is now called
a 'business review', providing extensive information about environmental matters
and social and community issues. While such a report, could simply be a plausible
whitewash, nonetheless these issues are now brought to the forefront and the board
is obliged to confront them and to develop and disclose appropriate policies.

If one response is to increase disclosure, another regulatory knee jerk is to draw
up codes of practice and guidelines as to the information that should be disclosed.
The following is a brief extract from a report by The Association of British Insurers
who have drawn up such guidelines. (Insurance companies as sellers of life assurance etc, hold huge portfolios of shares as 'institutional investors', and so are crucially involved in 'monitoring corporate performance'.) The extract introduces
some of the jargon surrounding CSR and gives a feel for this new development in
the law and practice of public companies.

In conclusion, it could rightly be said that if the sole 'trusteeship' of directors
is to benefit the shareholders, there can be no such thing as genuine corporate
philanthropy or altruism. Thus, if the directors are induced to enhance corporate
reputation through good CSR and successfully avoid the risk of public relations disasters ('They tested the new cosmetics on beagles!'), then they and their shareholders will simply get richer and richer. Nonetheless, these developments in the law
and practice do probably generate a net social benefit by requiring boards publicly
to genuflect towards CSR, and they are, one hopes, something more than a cynical
attempt to present the acceptable face of capitalism.

RISK, RETURNS AND RESPONSIBILITY
Association of British Insurers, February 2004

- Corporate responsibility has advanced rapidly since the mid-1990s, and especially since the
  ABI published guidelines on corporate disclosure in 2001, designed to help institutional investors monitor corporate performance. But in general, financial markets have been slow to integrate the concepts, into their assessments of risk and returns.
- Companies have responded to the guidelines by beginning to publish useful information for
  investors, but more is needed from smaller public companies and more focus is required on
  what is material to each company, rather than general issues.
- Early attempts to gauge the 'business case' for corporate responsibility focused on revenue
  and cost benefits. But there is now greater awareness of the importance of risk as well as
  returns, including risk to reputation. Social, cultural, demographic and technological changes
  mean that social and environmental risks are now more significant than in the past and more
  volatile.
- Growing awareness of the importance of corporate responsibility is a global trend, with
  significant developments in many markets, including Australia, South Africa and the US.
  The European Union has taken a close interest and created a Forum to advise on necessary
  action. . . .
- UK pension funds have been encouraged to address social, ethical and environmental (SEE)
  issues since the amendment to the Pensions Act came into force in 2000, but have been slow to
  translate statements of principle into specific mandates for investment managers. . . .

- Many studies have found direct financial benefits for companies embracing corporate responsibility. Although the evidence is not conclusive, it strongly suggests benefits in areas such as corporate reputation, consumer acceptance, employee loyalty and environmental management. . . .

INTRODUCTION—THE RISE OF CORPORATE RESPONSIBILITY AND ITS IMPORTANCE TO FINANCIAL MARKETS

Corporate responsibility (CR) has risen rapidly up the agendas of governments, business and the financial world since the mid-1990s. But the broad concept has embraced a variety of ideas and been driven by a range of interests and objectives. As a result, a common understanding has been slow to emerge, especially about the connections between corporate and social objectives and the differences between moral obligation and financial interests.

A consensus has now emerged in which corporate responsibility is concerned with core aspects of business behaviour—about the way a business makes money, rather than what it does with the profits afterwards (e.g. charitable donations). The UK's minister for CSR, Stephen Timms, has put it like this:

> 'What we are talking about here is beyond philanthropy. CSR is not an add-on. It must be about the very way we do business both at home and overseas.'

This does not mean there has been any dilution in a public company's responsibility to shareholders, which remains paramount. But it recognises that businesses also have relationships with other stakeholders and society at large, and shareholder value will he affected it a company neglects these relationships. Value may be destroyed directly, most dramatically through a loss of revenues because of a reputational crisis: indirectly, because of difficulties recruiting people or excessive costs of regulatory compliance: or may be threatened by increased risks to reputation, to licenses, or to product acceptability. The converse is that more responsible companies will be able to enhance value by building reputation, by understanding social impacts better and by managing risks effectively. Chief executives have increasingly endorsed CR, concerned about the general decline of trust in business and the potential for impact on their own companies. For example, when asked about the prospects for CR in a potentially difficult economic climate, fewer than one in five of a global sample said that CR and sustainability would have a lower profile. The vast majority said they were actively working on values and ethics in their companies; about three-quarters on operational environmental impacts and employment issues such as diversity: and around half on human rights, work/life balance and product environmental impacts. As the report commented: 'More than ever before, CEOs are saying substantially is an integral part of value creation, not an add-on or a simple cost item'.

The World Business Council for Sustainable Development (WBCSD) has drawn attention to the risks and opportunities in the drive for sustainable development. Among the developments it highlighted are:

- new markets from growing populations in developing countries
- the threat from poor health in many of these markets, especially from HIV/Aids
- environmental threats from growing populations and consumption
- the challenge of preserving stocks of fish and other species
- the ageing population, in the developed world
- the demand from society for greater accountability and transparency

Business leaders are also concerned about the reluctance of investors take account of these issues. For example, the World Economic Forum will publish a report on investors and CR in Spring 2004.

Financial markets have generally been sceptical of the potential benefits and risks of CR, typically seeing the growing ethical fund sector as a profitable but insignificant niche and wider issues of corporate responsibility as having little relevance to mainstream analysts and fund managers. That scepticism has slowly been eroded, however, as corporate governance scandals have highlighted the importance of integrity and broad management issues, and as greater clarity has emerged about the connections between corporate responsibility and shareholder value in individual sectors and companies.

From the Myners Report and the changes to the Combined Code in the UK to a United Nations statement on companies' human rights obligations, the past two years have seen a torrent of initiatives which have helped companies to understand their responsibilities better and should help shareholders and financial analysts integrate these matters into investment decisions.

In the UK, the government has decided to require leading companies to publish an expanded Operating and Financial Review (OFR) in which directors will report strategic issues, including social and Investing in the Future, Business in the Community 2001 environmental factors which are material for shareholder value. [In CA 2006, s. 417, now called the business review.] . . .

. . . financial markets need to pay more attention to corporate responsibility—all companies are not affected equally, some respond more effectively than others. Clearly, understanding which are most affected and which are most effective presents important investment opportunities.

11.2 DEFINITIONS

COMPANIES ACT 2006, SS. 250 AND 251

250. "Director"

In the Companies Acts "director" includes any person occupying the positionof director, by whatever name called.

251. "Shadow director"

(1) In the Companies Acts "shadow director", in relation to a company, means a person in accordance with whose directions or instructions the directors of the company are accustomed to act.
(2) A person is not to be regarded as a shadow director by reason only that the directors act on advice given by him in a professional capacity.
(3) A body corporate is not to be regarded as a shadow director of any of its subsidiary companies for the purposes of—
    Chapter 2 (general duties of directors),
    Chapter 4 (transactions requiring members' approval), or
    Chapter 6 (contract with sole member who is also a director),
by reason only that the directors of the subsidiary are accustomed to act in accordance with its directions or instructions.

Shadow directors might include a major shareholder who refuses a board appointment to avoid personal liability but who nonetheless persistently orchestrates the company's puppet directors from the shadows. This might happen also where a person is a bankrupt and so disqualified from being a director of a company. Another example is where a subsidiary company always follows the instructions of its holding company and so, except as stated in s. 251(3), the latter will be a shadow director of the subsidiary. A number of provisions of the Act are expressed to apply equally to shadow directors as to directors formally appointed as such. For instance s. 223 requires members' approval for certain contracts between the company and a director and it applies also to shadow directors. A similar definition of shadow director also appears in IA 1986, s. 251 and so shadow directors are made liable for wrongful trading under IA 1986, s. 214 as if they were directors.

Executive directors are full-time employees of the company, while non-executive directors are purely officers without a contract of full time employment. As will be seen from 11.3 which follows, there is a strong movement to encourage appointment of non-executive directors in publicly held companies.

The chairman of the board may be a non-executive director. His role is to chair meetings of the board (art. 91 of the traditional Table A of 1985 reproduced at 1.7 above) and also general meetings (Table A, art. 42). Table A allows the chairman of a general meeting considerable powers, including a casting vote where a vote is tied (art. 50) and a number of important discretions in running the meeting (e.g., art. 47). The chairman's declaration that a special resolution has been passed by a show of hands is conclusive (CA 2006, s. 320), and minutes of a meeting signed by the chairman are evidence of the proceedings (CA 2006, s. 249(1)).

The managing director is a full-time employee to whom some or all of the powers of management of the board are delegated (Table A, art. 72). Some companies prefer to call their managing director a chief executive, a commercial term meaning much the same thing though not yet assimilated into company law. The chairman and managing director may, as a matter of company law, be the same person. However, the Cadbury Committee (*Report of the Committee on the Financial Aspects of Corporate Governance* (London: Gee, 1992), para. 4.9) recommends as follows for listed companies:

Given the importance and particular nature of the chairman's role, it should in principle be separate from that of the chief executive. If the two roles are combined in one person, it represents a considerable concentration of power. **We recommend**, therefore, that there should be a clearly accepted division of responsibilities at the head of a company, which will ensure a balance of power and authority, such that no one individual has unfettered powers of decision. Where the chairman is also the chief executive, it is essential that there should be a strong and independent element on the board.

11.3 NON-EXECUTIVE DIRECTORS

An important development in the management practice of companies listed on the London Stock Exchange is the recent requirement found in The Combined Code on Corporate Governance (see 8.3) that companies should appoint an 'effective board' having 'a balance of executive and non-executive directors (and in particular independent non-executive directors) such that no individual or small group of individuals can dominate the board's decision making'.

This distinction between executive and non-executive directors is not a legal one but is a business term reflecting current management practice in larger companies. Executive directors, as full-time employees of the company, run its affairs from day to day while non-executives do not work for the company but, having valuable expertise such as in management, finance or human resources, accept non-executive directorships with a number of companies and regularly attend their board meetings.

Broadly speaking, non-executives contribute both to the development of management strategy and monitor the activity of the executive directors. They should bring an element of objectivity and independence to decision making, especially where a conflict of interest could arise between the executive directors and other interests. They may for example, take a supervisory role on behalf of particular groups of shareholders and can moderate the self-perpetuating power that executive directors tend to accrue. Non-executives also have a valuable role to play on board committees such as the audit committee and the remuneration committee which is responsible for setting directors' pay.

A series of reports named after their chairmen (Cadbury, Greenbury, Hampel and Higgs) have examined aspects of corporate governance, including the appropriate role of non-executive directors and how they should be selected and appointed, especially in relation to their independence and their recommendations have been formalised by periodic amendments to the Combined Code on Corporate Governance.

The recent Higgs Report (Review of the Role and Effectiveness of Non-Executive Directors, January 2003, see 8.3 and www.dti.gov.uk) had this to say about their role.

6.5 Executive and non-executive directors have the same general legal duties to the company. However, as the non-executive directors do not report to the chief executive and are not involved in the day-to-day running of the business, they can bring fresh perspective and contribute more objectively in supporting as well as constructively challenging and monitoring the management team.

6.6 Non-executive directors must constantly seek to establish and maintain their own confidence in the conduct of the company, in the performance of the management team, the development of strategy, the adequacy of financial controls and risk management, the appropriateness of remuneration and the appointment and replacement of key personnel and plans for management development and succession. The role of the non-executive director is therefore both to support executives in their leadership of the business and to monitor and supervise their conduct.

The following paragraphs from the report of the Cadbury committee are the ground breaking recommendations that initiated the formal requirement in the Code that non-executive directors be appointed to the boards of listed companies as a necessary part of good corporate governance.

Report of the Committee on the Financial Aspects of Corporate Governance ('The Cadbury Report')
(London: Gee, 1992)

Non-executive directors

4.10 The Committee believes that the calibre of the non-executive members of the board is of special importance in setting and maintaining standards of corporate governance. The emphasis in this report on the control function of non-executive directors is a consequence of our remit and should not in any way detract from the primary and positive contribution which they are expected to make, as equal board members, to the leadership of the company.

4.11 Non-executive directors should bring an independent judgment to bear on issues of strategy, performance, resources, including key appointments, and standards of conduct. **We recommend** that the calibre and number of non-executive directors on a board should be such that their views will carry significant weight in the board's decisions. To meet our recommendations on the composition of subcommittees of the board, all boards will require a minimum of three non-executive directors, one of whom may be the chairman of the company provided he or she is not also its executive head. Additionally, two of the three should be independent in the terms set out in the next paragraph.

4.12 An essential quality which non-executive directors should bring to the board's delibera-tions is that of independence of judgment. **We recommend** that the majority of non-executives on a board should be independent of the company. This means that apart from their directors' fees and shareholdings, they should be independent of management and free from any business or other relationship which could materially interfere with the exercise of their independent judg-ment. It is for the board to decide in particular cases whether this definition is met. Information about the relevant interests of directors should be disclosed in the directors' report.

4.13 On fees, there is a balance to be struck between recognising the value of the contribution made by non-executive directors and not undermining their independence. The demands which are now being made on conscientious non-executive directors are significant and their fees should reflect the time which they devote to the company's affairs. There is, therefore, a case for paying for additional responsibilities taken on, for example, by chairmen of board committees. In order to safeguard their independent position, we regard it as good practice for non-executive directors not to participate in share option schemes and for their service as non-executive directors not to be pensionable by the company.

4.14 Non-executive directors lack the inside knowledge of the company of the executive dir-ectors, but have the same right of access to information as they do. Their effectiveness turns to a considerable extent on the quality of the information which they receive and on the use which they make of it. Boards should regularly review the form and the extent of the information which is provided to all directors.

4.15 Given the importance of their distinctive contribution, non-executive directors should be selected with the same impartiality and care as senior executives. **We recommend** that their appointment should be a matter for the board as a whole and that there should be a formal selec-tion process, which will reinforce the independence of non-executive directors and make it evident that they have been appointed on merit and not through any form of patronage. We regard it as good practice for a nomination committee (dealt with below) to carry out the selection process and to make proposals to the board.

4.16 Companies have to be able to bring about changes in the composition of their boards to maintain their vitality. Non-executive directors may lose something of their independent edge, if they remain on a board too long. Furthermore, the make-up of a board needs to change in line with new challenges. **We recommend**, therefore, that non-executive directors should be appointed for specified terms. Their letter of appointment should set out their duties, term of office, remu-neration and its review. Reappointment should not be automatic, but a conscious decision by the board and the director concerned.

4.17 Our emphasis on the qualities to be looked for in non-executive directors, combined with the greater demands now being made on them, raises the question of whether the supply of non-executive directors will be adequate to meet the demand. When companies encourage their execu-tive directors to accept appointments on the boards of other companies, the companies and the individuals concerned all gain. A policy of promoting this kind of appointment will increase the pool of potential non-executive directors, particularly if the divisional directors of larger companies are considered for non-executive posts, as well as their main board colleagues.

11.4 APPOINTMENT OF DIRECTORS

There are a number of things you cannot legally do until you reach the age of 16 and one of them is be appointed a director, a restriction introduced by CA 2006, s. 157. It is for the members in general meeting to appoint and remove directors in accordance with the articles of the company (see, e.g., Table A arts. 73 to 79 at 1.7). Subject to the new age requirement, they can choose whoever they like and in the case of private companies they usually appoint themselves. There are thus no prior qualifications to be appointed a director, though huge official effort is put into disqualifying a handful of 'rogue directors' who have shown themselves to be unfit and have run their company into insolvency (see 11.8).

Until the Act of 2006, it was also possible to appoint companies as directors of another company. Thus, for example, a private company might have as its sole directors two companies incorporated in the British Virgin Islands. In 1962, the Jenkins committee stated its opinion that companies should be prohibited from being directors and a brief extract from its report appears below. Forty years on, the White Paper of 2002 reached the same conclusion and ultimately CA 2006, s. 155, now rules, slightly differently, that at least one director must be a natural person. The pace of law reform can sometimes grind exceeding slow!

Report of the Company Law Committee
(Cmnd 1749) (London: HMSO, 1962)

84. The Report of the Patton Committee on Company Law Amendment in Northern Ireland (paragraph 17) says:—

In our view the responsibility of directors for wrongful acts contemplated by the Companies Acts has been the responsibility of natural persons and this has been lost sight of. . . .

It is important that it should be known who is responsible for the conduct of a company. . . . A corporation cannot officiate as a director except by delegating its duty to some of its directors or some officer or servant. The person to whom these duties are delegated may change from day to day. Except by examining the minutes there is no means of finding out who at any particular time is exercising the functions of director when a corporation is director of a company.

We agree with the views expressed by the Patton Committee and recommend that corporate bodies and Scottish firms should be prohibited from being directors.

MODERNISING COMPANY LAW
(White Paper, DTI: London, July 2002)

Corporate Directors

3.32 At present any legal person can be a company director—an individual, another company, a limited liability partnership, a local authority, etc. The only prohibition is on individuals of unsound mind, although minors are technically not capable of signing the requisite consent. At present about 2 per cent of all directors, i.e. about 64,000, are corporate bodies.

3.33 Few countries other than the Netherlands and some offshore financial centres permit corporate directors on the same basis as individuals. Some, for example Australia, New Zealand, Canada and Singapore, have only recently introduced prohibitions. France permits corporate directors but requires each to appoint an individual as its permanent representative with whom it is jointly responsible for any misconduct or negligence. Most US states, including Delaware and Maryland, require directors to be individuals.

3.34 A corporate director can act only through one or more individuals who represent it, or otherwise act on its behalf. The duties of directors need to apply to such individuals—and they need to know that they apply. If the directors are not individuals it can be difficult—both for the general public and for regulators—to determine who is actually controlling a company. Moreover, it can be difficult to apply sanctions against corporate directors. The Government believes that there would be real benefits and relatively little inconvenience from prohibiting corporate directors. It therefore proposes to:

- prohibit corporate directors for companies formed under the Bill;
- prohibit the appointment of corporate directors to existing companies; and
- after a transitional period of, say, three years, prohibit all corporate directors.

COMPANIES ACT 2006, SS. 154 AND 155

154. Companies required to have directors
   (1) A private company must have at least one director.
   (2) A public company must have at least two directors.

155. Companies required to have at least one director who is a natural person
   (1) A company must have at least one director who is a natural person.
   (2) This requirement is met if the office of director is held by a natural person as a corporation sole or otherwise by virtue of an office.

Morris v *Kanssen*

CA 1985, s. 285, does not validate a non-appointment

[1946] AC 459, House of Lords

In this case the House of Lords dealt with a rule now found in CA 2006, s. 161 (Validity of acts of directors), that the acts of a director are valid notwithstanding any defect that may afterwards be discovered in his appointment.

Facts   Cromie and Strelitz 'concocted a scheme to get rid of Kanssen', the other shareholder. They falsely entered a minute of the board that Strelitz had been appointed as a director and built an edifice of deception on this uncertain foundation. The House of Lords held that there was not a 'defect' in Strelitz's appointment, but a total non-appointment which was not validated by the section.

LORD SIMONDS: It is in these circumstances that the question arises whether the section or article can be called in aid by Morris in order to validate . . . the allotment to him of shares or the appointment of him as a director. Do the facts that I have stated establish a defect in the appointment or qualification of Cromie or Strelitz? There is, as it appears to me, a vital distinction between (a) an appointment in which there is a defect or, in other words, a defective appointment, and (b) no appointment at all. In the first case it is implied that some act is done which purports to be an appointment but is by reason of some defect inadequate for the purpose; in the second case there is not a defect, there is no act at all. The section does not say that the acts of a person acting as director shall be valid notwithstanding that it is afterwards discovered that he was not appointed a director. Even if it did, it might well be contended that at least a purported appointment was postulated. But it does not do so, and it would, I think, be doing violence to plain language to construe the section as covering a case in which there has been no genuine attempt to appoint at all. These observations apply equally where the term of office of a director has expired, but he nevertheless continues to act as a director, and where the office has been from the outset usurped without the colour of authority . . . . The point may be summed up by saying that the section and the article, being designed as machinery to avoid questions being raised as to the validity of transactions where there has been a slip in the appointment of a director, cannot be utilised for the purpose of ignoring or overriding the substantive provisions relating to such appointment.

11.5 DELEGATION OF DIRECTORS' POWERS

11.5.1 Delegation to committees

Typically articles such as Table A, 1985, art. 72 say that, 'The directors may delegate any of their powers to any committee consisting of one or more directors'. With larger companies the use of specialist committees is an important feature of corporate practice. For example, the Cadbury report recommended (see para. 4.42 of the extract from the report at 11.6 below) that companies appoint remuneration committees consisting mainly of non-executive directors to recommend to the board the remuneration of the executive directors. The report also recommended the appointment of audit committees (see the extract from the report at 16.2.2 below) responsible for overseeing the audit process for the company.

A group of directors may be appointed as a committee in authorising them to deal with a specific issue such as a single transaction. For example, a bank lending money to a company may be satisfied as to the authority of the directors signing the loan documentation only if it receives a certified copy of a board resolution resolving that any two directors (or two named directors) are constituted as a committee of the board for the purpose of committing the company to the loan and signing the documentation.

An example of a committee operating in this way appears in *Guinness plc* v *Saunders* [1990] 2 AC 663 (see 11.6) where three directors were constituted as a committee of the board with authority to settle the terms of the offer for all the share capital of Distillers Co. plc and to complete the documentation. The court held, interpreting the articles of association, that a payment authorised by the committee and paid to one of its number was recoverable by the company because the articles required payments to directors to be decided upon by the full board.

11.5.2 Delegation to managing directors

Typically Table A, 1985, art. 72, says that the directors may 'delegate to any managing director or any director holding any other executive office such of their powers as they consider desirable to be exercised by him'. This article correctly implies that a managing director may be invested with a wide range of powers. This may amount to a total delegation to him of all the board's powers of management of the business of the company. As art. 72 states, such extensive delegation may be revoked or altered. Alternatively a person may be cloaked with the title of managing director but with relatively limited powers. Thus it is not enough for a board to resolve to appoint a director as managing director; it should also stipulate with reasonable precision the extent of his actual authority. However, if a person is described as a managing director but is given limited authority, the company may not be able to plead lack of actual authority against an innocent third party if the managing director acts beyond his actual authority. If he or she has been held out as being authorised, then the company will be bound (see, e.g., *Freeman & Lockyer* v *Buckhurst Park Properties (Mangal) Ltd* at 8.2.2 above).

The question of whether a managing director is entitled to damages on termination of his contract of employment in a number of circumstances is considered at 11.7.3 below.

The following case indicates that appointment as 'managing director' entitles the appointee to no general or minimal range of powers or duties.

Harold Holdsworth & Co. (Wakefield) Ltd v Caddies

The office of 'managing director' implies no specific duties

[1955] 1 All ER 725, [1955] 1 WLR 352, House of Lords

This case turns on the construction of an agreement to appoint a managing director. Under the agreement the company was held to be entitled to limit the managing director's duties according to its own wishes. The case suggests that there are no minimum duties or settled functions implicit in appointment as a managing director. (Clearly, however, the withdrawal from a managing director of all duties would be in breach of an agreement to appoint him as such.)

Facts   *Mr Caddies was sole shareholder and managing director of a textile company. In 1947 he sold all its shares to the appellant company, H.H. Ltd. By an agreement in 1949 he was appointed as managing director of H.H. Ltd on a full-time basis for five years. Under clause 1 of the agreement it was stated that he should perform the duties in relation to the business of the company and the businesses of its subsidiaries 'which may from time to time be assigned to or vested in him by the board of directors of the company'. There were three such subsidiaries, one of them the textile company of which he was already managing director. Following differences, the board of H.H. Ltd resolved that he confine his duties to the affairs of the textile company only, thus substantially excluding him from management of H.H. Ltd. In the House of Lords (Lord Keith of Avonholm dissenting) it was held that this was not a repudiation of the agreement that he be managing director of H.H. Ltd.*

EARL JOWITT: My lords, the appellants are a limited company carrying on business as worsted yarn spinners at Balne Mills, Wakefield, Yorkshire. . . .

My lords, in the view which I take . . . I am clearly of the opinion that the resolution did not constitute any breach of the agreement. I think that, on the true construction of clause 1 of the agreement of 1949, the respondent was to perform such duties and exercise such powers in relation to the business of the appellant company, and to perform such duties and exercise such powers in relation to the business of the Textile Company and the other subsidiaries, as might from time to time be vested in him by the appellant company's board. In directing the respondent on May 10, 1950, to confine his attention to the Textile Company, the board of the appellant company were, in my opinion, merely exercising the right given to them by the agreement.

The Lord President (Lord Cooper) took a different view, because he considered that the appointment of managing director was

> a well-recognised title in company administration, carrying responsibilities of a familiar nature and involving sundry obligations and liabilities under the Companies Act. The [respondent] was not appointed to perform such duties, if any, as the board might assign to him.

The Lord President, having formed this view, no doubt considered that the resolution which called on the respondent to devote his whole time to the affairs of the Textile Company prevented him from carrying out those responsibilities, obligations and liabilities which, on this view, he had the right to perform for the appellant company, by virtue of his office as their managing director. My lords, with the greatest respect for the Lord President, I do not think that the respondent, by the mere fact that he was appointed managing director of the appellant company, had any responsibilities, obligations or liabilities which would prevent the appellant company ordering him to devote his full time to a subsidiary, and I am of the opinion that the appellant company had, by clause 1 of the agreement, expressly preserved their right to call on the respondent to devote his time to the affairs of the Textile Company if they judged this course desirable.

Being of the opinion that there was no relevant breach of contract averred, I think the action should have been dismissed without proof, and, accordingly, I would allow the appeal.

11.6 REMUNERATION OF DIRECTORS

The problem stated simply is that directors may pay themselves too much at the expense of the members and ultimately of creditors. Table A, art. 82, states that the directors are 'entitled to such remuneration as the company may by ordinary resolution determine'. However, either their votes may control the general meeting or an apathetic membership may rubber-stamp the remuneration they recommend for themselves. If the proper procedure has been followed it becomes difficult to argue that the payment is in breach of duty or is an improper return of capital.

Excessive drawing of salary may at its extreme amount to directors dipping their hands into the till. In private companies, excessive salary in particular prejudices minority shareholders who are unable to complain. It is also potentially detrimental to creditors if the company's solvency is doubtful and excessive salaries may even be the cause of a company's failure. English commercial law, however, offers few opportunities to liquidators to challenge the appropriateness of the directors' salaries. The courts in general will not review the commercial value of salaries awarded to directors if paid according to the correct procedures.

Equity treats directors as if trustees and starts from the opposite viewpoint that they are prohibited from benefiting from their position unless the 'trust deed', (in this case the articles of association) allows. Articles such as Table A, 1985, art. 82, always do permit directors to be paid and invariably permit payment of pensions. If a director has done work for which he is not strictly entitled to remuneration, the courts may permit payment of a *quantum meruit* or an equitable allowance. However, as in the *Guinness* case below this will not be permitted if there is a clear conflict of interest.

Of the cases that follow, the first two concern liquidators attempting to recover payments to directors. In *Re Halt Garage (1964) Ltd* [1982] 3 All ER 1016, which is summarised in the extract from *Rolled Steel Products (Holdings) Ltd* v *British Steel Corporation* below, the court considered whether salary was recoverable which was paid to directors at a time when the company was loss-making and insolvency was approaching. To a very limited extent it was held to have been improperly paid. In *Re Horsley & Weight Ltd* the court refused to question the commercial substance of a pension arrangement paid not long before the company went insolvent. General principles of law thus offer few opportunities to liquidators to question remuneration paid before winding up. Liquidators therefore may have to look to other statutory provisions such as IA 1986, s. 214, the wrongful trading provision (see 20.12). As to minority shareholders, their opportunity to complain is limited by the rule in *Foss* v *Harbottle* which holds that only the company (i.e., ultimately the majority shareholders) may bring an action against the directors and not the minority. Their only remedy may be under CA 2006, s. 994 (see 13.2.3).

The leading case in the area is *Guinness plc* v *Saunders* which reviews the equitable principles on conflicts of interest in relation to directors' remuneration.

As usual where the common law is inadequate to remedy a mischief, the legislature has intervened. The principle means is through disclosure (see Chapter 4). Thus there must be disclosed in the accounts of the company certain limited information about directors' remuneration, directors' service contracts must be kept available for inspection by members (CA 2006, s. 228) and directors' service contracts can only be awarded for more than five years if approved by the company in general meeting (CA 2006, s. 189). These provisions impose an element of accountability on directors in respect of their terms of service including their remuneration.

Time and again generous pay awards for individual directors of publicly listed companies have proved controversial and have attracted criticism in the media. This is especially so where directors are given substantial compensation on leaving office when their company has performed badly, an apparent reward for management failure to the prejudice of shareholders. The issue is politically sensitive but governments have been reluctant to intervene, regarding it as a private matter for investors. The question therefore is whether the law enables shareholders to make the directors sufficiently accountable in respect of their own pay awards. Once again the law has been amended by extending the disclosure principle and now gives shareholders a more active role in approving directors' pay. Brought into force in August 2000, a new provision now found in CA 2006, ss. 420 to 428, requires boards of 'quoted companies' (i.e., listed companies, see s. 385) to prepare a directors' remuneration report for approval by the company in general meeting giving details of their remuneration packages and incentives including pensions and retirement benefits.

There are further non-statutory means of regulation in the case of publicly listed companies and the Cadbury report recommended an organisational means of avoiding conflicts of interest on directors' pay. Thus the establishment by publicly listed companies of a remuneration committee wholly or mainly of non-executive directors is intended to bring an independent approach to settling the pay of executive directors. The Greenbury Committee on directors' remuneration (mentioned in an extract from a Law Commission report at 8.3 above) reported in July 1995 and its recommendations were incorporated into the Listing Rules.

Rolled Steel Products (Holdings) Ltd v British Steel Corporation

Vinelott J discusses Re Halt Garage (1964) Ltd—Querying the amount of directors' pay
[1982] 3 All ER 1057, [1982] Ch 478, Chancery Division

In *Re Halt Garage (1964) Ltd* [1982] 3 All ER 1016, it was concluded that directors were entitled to continue to pay themselves salary at a time when their company was not making profits prior to its ultimate insolvency. The case confirms that there is little restraint upon the directors paying themselves disproportionate amounts even though this may prejudice creditors. As is usual, the courts do not assess whether payments were reasonable or for the objective benefit of the company but may ask a series of formalistic questions. Was the correct procedure for awarding remuneration followed, e.g., by the members in general meeting (including probably the directors) voting by ordinary resolution pursuant to a power in the articles to pay fees or salary? Was there a fraud on creditors or minority shareholders (whatever that may mean)? Was the payment genuinely directors' remuneration or was it a disguised return of capital (an equally vague concept)? If these questions are answered in the negative then the payments cannot, it appears, be questioned by the company or a liquidator.

Facts The liquidator of Halt Garage (1964) Ltd brought a misfeasance summons against its two directors, Mr and Mrs Charlesworth, under what is now IA 1986, s. 212, they having continued to draw salary while the company was in terminal decline and at a time when Mrs Charlesworth was ill and unlikely ever to resume her duties. It was held that it was for the company and not the court to decide what it was proper to pay Mr Charlesworth. As regards Mrs Charlesworth, it was said that a company may reward a director for undertaking the responsibility of this office even though not actively involved in the company. The court, however, ordered that payments in excess of reasonable remuneration amounting to a disguised gift of capital or improper payment of dividend could be recovered from her.

The familiar hands-off approach of the courts to the commercial adequacy of a payment or consideration leaves judges impotent unless they strain to reach a just conclusion using technical and unsatisfactory distinctions in their reasoning. This case is another example of this difficulty.

The extract that follows is not from the judgment in Re Halt Garage (1964) Ltd but is taken from comments on the case by Vinelott J giving judgment at first instance in Rolled Steel Products (Holdings) Ltd v British Steel Corporation. The later appeal decision in the Rolled Steel case is extracted at 5.2.2 above and apparently refers to the Halt Garage decision with approval.

VINELOTT J: *Re Halt Garage (1964) Ltd* [1982] 3 All ER 1016 concerned a claim made by the liquidator of a company, which was being compulsorily wound up, to recover remuneration paid to the directors of the company, a Mr and Mrs Charles-worth, in the accounting years (which ended on 30 May), 1967/68, 1968/69, 1969/70 and 1970/71. The application was made under s. 333 of the Companies Act 1948. Mr and Mrs Charlesworth were the only shareholders of the company. The remuneration paid to them as directors for the years 1967/68 and 1968/69 had been approved by the company in general meeting and it was conceded by the liquidator that, in the light of *Re Duomatic Ltd* [1969] 2 Ch 365, the remuneration paid in the last two years also fell to be treated as if it had been sanctioned by the company in general meeting. In the year 1967/68 the company traded at a loss but it had a reserve on profit and loss account distributable as dividend greater than the remuneration paid in that year. In the year 1968/69 and subsequent years there was a deficit on profit and loss account even after taking into account the reserve on profit and loss account for the earlier years and, accordingly, the sums paid to the directors by way of remuneration in those years could not be treated as paid out of moneys which, if the remuneration had not been paid, could have been distributed to Mr and Mrs Charlesworth by way of dividend. It was conceded by counsel who appeared for the liquidator that while a company 'has divisible profits remuneration may be paid on any scale which the shareholders are prepared to sanction within the limits of available profits'. The question was whether the remuneration paid in the last three years, when there were no distributable profits, to the extent that it exceeded reasonable remuneration, could be recovered by the liquidator. The proposition contended for by the liquidator was that any disposition of a company's assets made otherwise than for full consideration was invalid unless the disposition satisfied the test set out in the judgment of Eve J in *Re Lee, Behrens & Co. Ltd* [1932] 2 Ch 46 and that, to the extent that the disposition was made otherwise than out of the profits available for distribution by way of dividend, the invalidity could not be cured by the sanction of the company in general meeting. I should mention that the company's articles incorporated reg. 76 of part I of Table A in sch. 1 to the Companies Act 1948.

The judgment of Oliver J contains an exhaustive review of the decisions cited by Eve J in the *Lee, Behrens & Co.* case, of the cases in which the decision in the *Lee, Behrens & Co.* case has been followed, in particular *Parke v Daily News Ltd* [1962] Ch 927, *Re W. & M. Roith Ltd* [1967] 1 WLR 43 and *Ridge Securities Ltd v Inland Revenue Commissioners* [1964] 1 WLR 479 and of *Re Introductions Ltd*

[1968] 1 All ER 1221, [1970] Ch 199 and *Charterbridge Corporation Ltd v Lloyds Bank Ltd* [1970] Ch 62. He summarised his conclusions in these terms ([1982] 3 All ER 1016 at pp. 1034–5):

> I must therefore attempt, although I do so with some unease, some analysis of what I conceive to be the principles which underlie the cases. Part of the difficulty, I think, arises from the fact that Eve J in *Re Lee, Behrens & Co.* combined together, in the context of an inquiry as to the effective exercise of directors' powers, two different concepts which have since been regarded as a single composite test of the corporate entity's capacity. In fact, however, as it seems to me at any rate, only one of the three tests postulated in *Lee, Behrens & Co.* is truly applicable to that question. The court will clearly not imply a power, even if potentially beneficial to the company, if it is not reasonably incidental to the company's business (see *Tomkinson v South-Eastern Railway Co.* (1887) 35 ChD 675) and express powers are to be construed as if they were subject to that limitation (see *Re Introductions Ltd,* particularly the judgment of Russell LJ ([1970] Ch 199 at p. 211). But the test of bona fides and benefit to the company seems to me to be appropriate, and really only appropriate, to the question of the propriety of an exercise of a power rather than the capacity to exercise it.
>
> The cases really divide into two groups: those such as *Hampson v Price's Patent Candle Co.* (1876) 45 LJ Ch 437, *Hutton v West Cork Railway Co.* (1883) 23 ChD 654, *Henderson v Bank of Australasia* (1888) 40 ChD 170 and *Parke v Daily News Ltd,* where the question was not so much that of the company's capacity to do a particular act as that of the extent to which a majority in general meeting could force a particular measure on a dissentient minority; and those such as *Lee, Behrens & Co.* itself, *Re W. & M. Roith Ltd, Ridge Securities v IRC* and the *Charterbridge* case, where the question was as to the validity of an exercise of the powers, express or implied, by directors. Although the test of benefit to the company was applied in both groups of cases, I am not at all sure that the phrase 'the benefit of the company' was being employed in quite the same sense in each.
>
> In the latter group, where what was in question was whether an exercise of powers by directors was effective, the benefit regarded seems to have been that of the company as a corporate entity (see the phrase 'to promote the prosperity of the company') whereas in the former it was, I think, used in the same sense as that in which it was used in the line of cases dealing with, for instance, the power of the majority to alter the articles of association.

Then after citing from *Allen v Gold Reefs of West Africa Ltd* [1900] 1 Ch 656 at p. 671 and *Greenhalgh v Arderne Cinemas Ltd* [1951] Ch 286 at p. 291, he continued:

> In my judgment the true rationale of this group of cases is not that what was proposed was *ultra vires* in the sense that it could not be confirmed by a general meeting where there was no dissentient minority, but that they were concerned with a very different question, namely the circumstances in which the court will interfere to prevent a majority from overriding the rights of a dissentient minority to have the company's property administered in accordance with its constitution. I think that, in truth, neither group properly falls to be regarded as exemplifying applications of the *ultra vires* doctrine. Both, as it seems to me, more properly belong to the sphere of abuse of power, and part of the confusion has, I think, arisen from the fact that in *Hutton's* case, which contains the classical judgment of Bowen LJ always cited in this context, the determination of the question of the majority's power to bind the minority did, because the affairs of the company were being conducted under, and only under, the provisions of a special Act conferring very limited powers, necessarily also involve a consideration of the extent of those powers, which was, indeed, a true *ultra vires* question.

Later, having pointed out that there is no rule that directors' remuneration is payable only out of divisible profits, he stated his conclusion as to the application of the principles he had explained to the payment of remuneration in the following terms (at p. 1039):

> I do not think that in circumstances such as those in the instant case the authorities compel the application to the express power of a test of benefit to the company which, certainly construed as Plowman J held that it should be construed, would be largely meaningless. The real test must, I think, be whether the transaction in question was a genuine exercise of the power. The motive is more important than the label. Those who deal with a limited company

do so on the basis that its affairs will be conducted in accordance with its constitution, one of the express incidents of which is that the directors may be paid remuneration. Subject to that, they are entitled to have the capital kept intact. They have to accept the shareholders' assessment of the scale of that remuneration, but they are entitled to assume that, whether liberal or illiberal, what is paid is genuinely remuneration and that the power is not used as a cloak for making payments out of capital to the shareholders as such.

It may well be that one way of ascertaining the true nature of the payment made in pur-ported exercise of such an express power is by subjecting it to the three tests postulated in the *Lee, Behrens & Co.* case, but it cannot, I think, be conclusive that the court, looking at the matter with hindsight, concludes that a particular application was not beneficial to the company as a corporate entity or that the shareholders in considering it did not have that in mind. If benefit in that sense were the conclusive test, it is difficult to see how the directors in *Hutton's* case could have been paid for their past services in connection with the winding up. Such a payment, as I have pointed out, could not have been of any possible benefit to the company which was in the course of winding up. Yet both Cotton and Bowen LJJ clearly contemplated that this could quite properly be paid.

This last sentence is a reference to the last paragraph of the judgment of Bowen LJ in the *Hutton* case (1883) 23 ChD 654 at p. 678, as to which Oliver J had earlier observed that it showed that Bowen LJ—

clearly contemplated that there was nothing necessarily improper or wrong with paying rea-sonable remuneration, albeit it could not be said to be for the benefit of the company, since the business at that time was defunct and the services which the directors had rendered were past. ([1982] 3 All ER 1016 at 1028.)

Turning to the facts of that case Oliver J held that the payments to Mr Charlesworth were not so blatantly excessive or unreasonable as to compel the conclusion that the payments were not really remuneration but gratuitous distributions to a shareholder out of capital dressed up as remuner-ation. As regards the payments to Mrs Charlesworth (who in the last three years was so seriously ill that 'she was able to contribute nothing to the company's prosperity beyond, perhaps, the occa-sional discussion with her husband and the formal signature of documents' (see [1982] 3 All ER 1016 at p. 1021)) he held that payments in excess of a modest weekly sum could not be regarded 'as being anything more than disguised gifts out of capital' (see [1982] 3 All ER 1016 at p. 1044). He therefore held that the liquidator succeeded to that extent.

Re Horsley & Weight Ltd
Challenging a director's pension
[1982] 3 All ER 1045, [1982] Ch 442, Court of Appeal

This decision of the Court of Appeal shortly before *Rolled Steel* was an important step in asserting that, for example, a power to grant pensions is a substantive object and not a mere incidental power. A grant of a pension is therefore *intra vires* and it is irrelevant whether the pension would benefit the prosperity of the company. (On this issue, see a further extract at 5.2.2.) In this and other ways it limits the opportunity of the company or a liquidator to question a transaction such as a pension on grounds that it is excessive or disproportionate or not proper in com-mercial terms. Again the courts refuse to review the commercial substance of the transaction.

Facts   *The company's objects clause included a clause enabling the grant of pensions to employ-ees and directors. Mr Campbell-Dick and Mr Horsley were directors and the sole shareholders. (Their wives were inactive directors.) In 1975 the two directors bought a substantial pension policy for a fifth director who was about to retire. They did so in good faith and there was no evidence to suggest that they should have appreciated the negative impact on creditors. In 1977 the company*

went into insolvent liquidation and the liquidator unsuccessfully brought an action against the two
directors for misfeasance. The following extract discusses whether the unauthorised payment by
the two directors (i.e., without a formal board resolution) was validated by an implicit ratification,
they being the sole shareholders. (It further concludes that directors owe no general duty to keep
the capital of the company intact but must expend the company's property for intra vires purposes
and must not make unauthorised returns of capital to members.)

BUCKLEY LJ: I now turn to the second head of counsel for the liquidator's argument, viz that the purchase of the pension was effected by Mr Campbell-Dick and Mr Frank Horsley without the authority of the board of directors or of the company in general meeting, and was an act of misfeasance which was not validated as against the company's creditors by virtue of the fact that Mr Campbell-Dick and Mr Frank Horsley were the only shareholders. Ignoring for the moment that Mr Campbell-Dick and Mr Frank Horsley were the only shareholders, the transaction in question was indeed carried out by them without the sanction of any board resolution, whether antecedent, contemporary or by way of subsequent ratification. It was an unauthorised act which they were, as two only of the company's five directors, incompetent to carry out on the company's behalf. It therefore cannot stand unless it has in some way been ratified. The question is whether the fact that Mr Campbell-Dick and Mr Frank Horsley were the only shareholders of the company has the effect of validating the transaction.

Counsel for the liquidator has submitted that there is a general duty incumbent on directors of a company, whether properly described as owed to creditors or not, to preserve the company's capital fund (which he identifies as those assets which are not distributable by way of dividend) and not to dispose of it otherwise than for the benefit or intended benefit of the company. He submits that creditors dealing with the company are entitled to assume that directors will observe that duty; and that creditors, although they are not entitled to interfere in the day-to-day management of a company which is not in liquidation, are entitled through a liquidator to seek redress in respect of a breach of the duty. Consequently counsel for the liquidator submits, the members of the company cannot, even unanimously, deprive the creditors of any remedy so available to them.

On this part of the case counsel for the liquidator mainly relies on *Re Exchange Banking Co.,*
Flitcroft's Case (1882) 21 ChD 519. In that case dividends were declared and paid at a time when the directors of the company knew, but the shareholders did not know, that there were no profits available out of which to pay them, with the consequence that the dividends were paid out of contributed capital. The directors were held liable to repay to the company the amounts distributed in dividends notwithstanding that the dividends had been declared by resolutions of the company in general meeting. It was held that the company in general meeting had not ratified the improper payment of the dividends because the shareholders were ignorant of the circumstances which rendered the dividends improper; but it was also held that, even if all the shareholders individually had assented to the payments, this would not have relieved the directors from liability, or have bound the company, because the payments were illegal and *ultra vires* the company and so were incapable of ratification by the shareholders. The facts of that case were very different from those of the present case and the principles applicable were, in my opinion, also different. A company cannot legally repay contributed capital to the contributors otherwise than by way of an authorised reduction of capital. Nothing of that kind occurred in the present case. There is nothing in the statute or in the general law which prevents a company or its directors expending contributed capital in doing anything which is an authorised object of the company. In the present case the cost of effecting the pension policy was, in my view, incurred in the course of carrying out an express object of the company.

It is a misapprehension to suppose that the directors of a company owe a duty to the company's creditors to keep the contributed capital of the company intact. The company's creditors are entitled to assume that the company will not in any way repay any paid-up share capital to the shareholders except by means of a duly authorised reduction of capital. They are entitled to assume that the company's directors will conduct its affairs in such a manner that no such unauthorised repayment will take place. It may be somewhat loosely said that the directors owe an indirect duty to the creditors not to permit any unlawful reduction of capital to occur, but I would regard it as more accurate to say that the directors owe a duty to the company in this respect and that, if the company is put into liquidation when paid-up capital has been improperly repaid, the liquidator owes a duty to the creditors to enforce any right to repayment which is available to the company. On the other hand, a company, and its directors acting on its behalf, can quite properly expend contributed capital for any purpose which is *intra vires* the company. As I have already indicated, the purchase of the pension policy was, in my view, *intra vires* the company. It was not, however, within the powers of Mr Campbell-Dick and Mr Frank Horsley acting not as members of the board of directors but as individual directors. Unless the act was effectually ratified it cannot bind the company. They were, however, the only two shareholders. A company is bound in a matter which is *intra vires* the company by the unanimous agreement of its members (per Lord Davey in *Salomon* v *A. Salomon & Co. Ltd* [1897] AC 22 at p. 57; and see *Re Express Engineering Works Ltd* [1920] 1 Ch 466) even where that agreement is given informally (see *Parker and Cooper Ltd* v *Reading* [1926] Ch 975). That both Mr Campbell-Dick and Mr Frank Horsley assented to the transaction in question in the present case is beyond dispute. They both initialled the proposal form and they both signed the cheques for the premiums. Their good faith has not been impugned, nor, in my view, does the evidence support any suggestion that in effecting the policy they did not honestly apply their minds to the question whether it was a fair and proper thing for the company to do in the light of the company's financial state as known to them at the time. In my judgment, their assent made the transaction binding on the company and unassailable by the liquidator.

Guinness plc v Saunders

Conflicts of interest in paying directors

[1990] 1 All ER 652, [1990] 2 AC 663, House of Lords

This important House of Lords case decided that the director concerned was not entitled to reasonable remuneration on a *quantum meruit* or to an equitable allowance for special services rendered to the company, as his personal interests conflicted irreconcilably with his duty as a director. A payment of £5.2 million made to him by a committee of three directors (including himself) and not authorised by the full board as required by art. 91 could not be retained and was held by him on constructive trust.

In practical terms the case is about directors' remuneration. More generally it considers in depth the obligation of directors not to allow a potential conflict of interest nor to profit from their position other than as permitted by the company's articles and the general law of companies. (As such it should be read in conjunction with the conflict of interest cases at 12.3.2 and 12.3.3.) It is also an illustration of how fiduciary principles of trust law are applied to directors. (For academic commentary see Beatson and Prentice (1990) 106 LQR 365, Hopkins [1990] CLJ 220 and McCormack (1991) 12 Co Law 90.)

Tom Ward, an American attorney was a non-executive director of Guinness. His role was to solicit American investment in Guinness shares in order to support its share price in the bid for Distillers shares. That things went horribly wrong came to light in the DTI investigation and led to the criminal prosecutions and the action for recovery from Ward of his sweetener of £5.2 million.

Facts   Guinness plc was bidding for (and successfully acquired) all the shares of Distillers Co. plc. Following a resolution of the board, the chief executive, Mr Saunders, and two non-executive directors, Mr Roux and Mr Ward, were constituted as a committee of the board with authority to settle the terms of the offer for Distillers and to complete any documentation. After the success of the bid Ward submitted an invoice for £5.2 million for advice and services given to Guinness in the course of the bid. The invoice was paid by the company. After the scandalous circumstances of the bid came into the open, Guinness claimed to recover the payment. Ward asserted that the committee had agreed on behalf of Guinness to pay 0.2 per cent of the ultimate value of the bid. Thus he argued, the £5.2 million was properly paid for his personal services in negotiating the deal over a period of about 14 weeks.

The case illustrates the typical formality of the law. The courts deal with the question not on the basis of whether the payment was commercially fair or appropriate. On the face of the judgments the court had to assume that Ward and the committee acted in good faith and that the payment was a proper reward for the services. In reality one feels that the judges were at pains to find any possible technical grounds which would enable Guinness to recover payment. Thus they concluded that the money was recoverable as the payment had not been authorised by the board as the articles require (Ward as an insider being on notice of this). Secondly they held that he was not entitled to an equitable allowance for his services as he was in a conflict of interest position. (His supposed role was to negotiate for and advise the company whether to go ahead with the bid and on what terms. However, he would only receive commission if the bid was accepted. The more that Guinness, his client, paid for Distillers the larger would be his commission; an irreconcilable conflict.)

The extract from Lord Templeman's judgment is long but pure genius and undoubtedly good for you. It illustrates first, how the courts interpret articles of association. Secondly, the judgment surveys some fundamental equitable principles, usefully citing a series of authoritative passages from leading texts. Thirdly, it goes on to review a number of important Court of Appeal decisions on remuneration and conflicts of interest.

LORD TEMPLEMAN: My lords, the appellant, Mr Ward, admits receiving £5.2 million, the money of the respondent company, Guinness plc (Guinness), at a time when Mr Ward was a director of Guinness. Payment of this sum to Mr Ward was, he says, remuneration authorised by Mr Saunders, Mr Roux and Mr Ward, who formed a committee of the board of directors of Guinness. It is admitted by Mr Ward that payment was not authorised by the board of directors. In these proceedings Guinness claim £5.2 million from Mr Ward and in this application, Guinness seek an order for immediate payment on the grounds that the articles of association of Guinness and the facts admitted by Mr Ward show that the payment to Mr Ward was unauthorised and must be repaid. . . .

Thus Mr Ward admits receipt of £5.2 million from Guinness and pleads an agreement by Guinness that he should be paid this sum for his advice and services in connection with the bid. Mr Ward admits that payment was not authorised by the board of directors of Guinness.

The articles of association of Guinness provide:

Remuneration of directors

90. The board shall fix the annual remuneration of the directors provided that without the consent of the company in general meeting such remuneration (excluding any special remuneration payable under art. 91 and art. 92) shall not exceed the sum of £100,000 per annum. . . .

91. The board may, in addition to the remuneration authorised in art. 90, grant special remuneration to any director who serves on any committee or who devotes special attention to the business of the company or who otherwise performs services which in the opinion of the board are outside the scope of the ordinary duties of a director. . . .

Articles 90 and 91 of the articles of association of Guinness depart from the Table A articles recommended by statute, which reserve to a company in general meeting the right to determine the remuneration of the directors of the company. But by art. 90 the annual remuneration which the directors may award themselves is limited and by art. 91 special remuneration for an individual director can only be authorised by the board. A committee, which may consist of only two or, as in the present case, three members, however honest and conscientious, cannot assess impartially the value of its work or the value of the contribution of its individual members. A director may, as a condition of accepting appointment to a committee, or after he has accepted appointment, seek the agreement of the board to authorise payment for special work envisaged or carried out. The shareholders of Guinness run the risk that the board may be too generous to an individual director at the expense of the shareholders but the shareholders have, by art. 91, chosen to run this risk and can protect themselves by the number, quality and impartiality of the members of the board who will consider whether an individual director deserves special reward. Under art. 91 the shareholders of Guinness do not run the risk that a committee may value its own work and the contribution of its own members. Article 91 authorises the board, and only the board, to grant special remuneration to a director who serves on a committee.

It was submitted that art. 2 alters the plain meaning of art. 91. In art. 2 there are a number of definitions each of which is expressed to apply 'if not inconsistent with the subject or context'. The expression 'the board' is defined as:

> The directors of the company for the time being (or a quorum of such directors assembled at a meeting of directors duly convened) or any committee authorised by the board to act on its behalf.

The result of applying the art. 2 definition to art. 91, it is said, is that a committee may grant special remuneration to any director who serves on a committee or devotes special attention to the business of the company or who otherwise performs services which in the opinion of the committee are outside the scope of the ordinary duties of a director. In my opinion, the subject and context of art. 91 are inconsistent with the expression 'the board' in art. 91 meaning anything except the board. Article 91 draws a contrast between the board and a committee of the board. The board is expressly authorised to grant special remuneration to *any* director who serves on *any* committee. It cannot have been intended that any committee should be able to grant special remuneration to any director, whether a member of the committee or not. The board must compare the work of an individual director with the ordinary duties of a director. The board must decide whether special remuneration shall be paid in addition to or in substitution for the annual remuneration determined by the board under art. 90. These decisions could only be made by the board surveying the work and remuneration of each and every director. Article 91 also provides for the board to decide whether special remuneration should take the form of participation in profits; the article could not intend that a committee should be able to determine whether profits should accrue to the shareholders' funds or be paid out to an individual director. The remuneration of directors concerns all the members of the board and all the shareholders of Guinness. Article 2 does not operate to produce a result which is inconsistent with the language, the subject and the context of art. 91. Only the board possessed power to award £5.2 million to Mr Ward ...

Since, for the purposes of this application, Guinness concede that Mr Ward performed valuable services for Guinness in connection with the bid, counsel on behalf of Mr Ward submits that Mr Ward, if not entitled to remuneration pursuant to the articles, is, nevertheless, entitled to be awarded by the court a sum by way of *quantum meruit* or equitable allowance for his services. Counsel submits that the sum awarded by the court might amount to £5.2 million or a substantial proportion of that sum; therefore Mr Ward should be allowed to retain the sum of £5.2 million which he has received until, at the trial of the action, the court determines whether he acted with propriety and, if so, how much of the sum of £5.2 million he should be permitted to retain; Mr Ward is anxious for an opportunity to prove at a trial that he acted with propriety throughout the bid. It is common ground that, for the purposes of this appeal, it must be assumed that Mr Ward and the other members of the committee acted in good faith and that the sum of £5.2 million was a proper reward for the services rendered by Mr Ward to Guinness.

My lords, the short answer to a *quantum meruit* claim based on an implied contract by Guinness to pay reasonable remuneration for services rendered is that there can be no contract by Guinness to pay special remuneration for the services of a director unless that contract is entered into by the board pursuant to art. 91. The short answer to the claim for an equitable allowance is the equitable principle which forbids a trustee to make a profit out of his trust unless the trust instrument, in this case the articles of association of Guinness, so provides. The law cannot and equity will not amend the articles of Guinness. The court is not entitled to usurp the functions conferred on the board by the articles.

Snell's Principles of Equity (28th ed., 1982), first published in 1868, contains the distilled wisdom of the author and subsequent editors, including Sir Robert Megarry, on the law applicable to trusts and trustees. It is said (p. 244):

With certain exceptions, neither directly nor indirectly may a trustee make a profit from his trust.... The rule depends not on fraud or *mala fides*, but on the mere fact of a profit made.

Palmer's Company Law (24th ed., 1987), first published in 1898, contains the distilled wisdom of the authors and subsequent editors concerning the law applicable to companies and directors. It is said (vol. 1, pp. 943–4, para. 63–13):

Like other fiduciaries directors are required not to put themselves in a position where there is a conflict (actual or potential) between their personal interests and their duties to the company.... the position of a director, *vis-à-vis* the company, is that of an agent who may not himself contract with his principal, and... is similar to that of a trustee who, however fair a proposal may be, is not allowed to let the position arise where his interest and that of the trust may conflict.... he is, like a trustee, disqualified from contracting with the company and for a good reason: the company is entitled to the collective wisdom of its directors, and if any director is interested in a contract, his interest may conflict with his duty, and the law always strives to prevent such a conflict from arising.

The application of these principles to remuneration in the case of a trustee is described by *Snell*, p. 252 as follows:

As the result of the rule that a trustee cannot make a profit from his trust, trustees and executors are generally entitled to no allowance for their care and trouble. This rule is so strict that even if a trustee or executor has sacrificed much time to carrying on a business as directed by the trust, he will usually be allowed nothing as compensation for his personal trouble or loss of time.

The application of these principles to remuneration in the case of a director is described by *Palmer*, p. 902, para. 60–38 as follows:

Prima facie, directors of a company cannot claim remuneration, but the articles usually provide expressly for payment of it... and, where this is the case, the provision operates as an authority to the directors to pay remuneration out of the funds of the company; such remuneration is not restricted to payment out of profits.

The following also appears (p. 903, para. 60–40):

The articles will also usually authorise the payment by the directors to one of their number of extra remuneration for special services. Where such provision is made, it is a condition precedent to a director's claim for additional remuneration that the board of directors shall determine the method and amount of the extra payment; it is irrelevant that the director has performed substantial extra services and the payment of additional remuneration would be reasonable.

...

Equity forbids a trustee to make a profit out of his trust. The articles of association of Guinness relax the strict rule of equity to the extent of enabling a director to make a profit provided that the board of directors contracts on behalf of Guinness for the payment of special remuneration or decides to award special remuneration. Mr Ward did not obtain a contract or a grant from the board of directors. Equity has no power to relax its own strict rule further than and inconsistently with the express relaxation contained in the articles of association. A shareholder is entitled to compliance with the articles. A director accepts office subject to and with the benefit of the provisions of the articles relating to directors. No one is obliged to accept appointment as a director. No director can be obliged to serve on a committee. A director of Guinness who contemplates or accepts service on a committee or has performed outstanding services for the company as a member of a committee may apply to the board of directors for a contract or an award of special remuneration. A director who does not read the articles or a director who misconstrues the articles is nevertheless bound by the articles. Article 91 provides clearly enough for the authority of the board of directors to be obtained for the payment of special remuneration.... the law will not imply a contract between Guinness and Mr Ward for remuneration on a *quantum meruit* basis awarded by the court when the articles of association of Guinness stipulate that special remuneration for a director can only be awarded by the board.

It was submitted on behalf of Mr Ward that Guinness, by the committee consisting of Mr Saunders, Mr Ward and Mr Roux, entered into a voidable contract to pay remuneration to Mr Ward and that since Mr Ward performed the services he agreed to perform under this voidable contract there could be no *restitutio integrum* and the contract cannot be avoided. This submission would enable a director to claim and retain remuneration under a contract which a committee purported to conclude with him, notwithstanding that the committee had no power to enter into the contract. The fact is that Guinness never did contract to pay anything to Mr Ward. The contract on which Mr Ward relies is not voidable but non-existent. In support of a *quantum meruit* claim, counsel for Mr Ward relied on the decision of Buckley J in *Re Duomatic Ltd* [1969] 2 Ch 365. In that case a company sought and failed to recover remuneration received by a director when the shareholders or a voting majority of the shareholders had sanctioned or ratified the payment. In the present case there has been no such sanction or ratification either by the board of directors or by the shareholders. Mr Ward also relied on the decision in *Craven-Ellis* v *Canons Ltd* [1936] 2KB 403. In that case the plaintiff was appointed managing director of a company by an agreement under the company's seal which also provided for his remuneration. By the articles of association each director was required to obtain qualification shares within two months of his appointment. Neither the plaintiff nor the other directors obtained their qualification shares within two months or at all and the agreement with the managing director was entered into after they had ceased to be directors. The plaintiff having done work for the company pursuant to the terms of the agreement was held to be entitled to the remuneration provided for in the agreement on the basis of a *quantum meruit*. In *Craven-Ellis's* case the plaintiff was not a director, there was no conflict between his claim to remuneration and the equitable doctrine which debars a director from profiting from his fiduciary duty, and there was no obstacle to the implication of a contract between the company and the plaintiff entitling the plaintiff to claim reasonable remuneration as of right by an action in law. Moreover, as in *Re Duomatic Ltd*, the agreement was sanctioned by all the directors, two of whom were beneficially entitled to the share capital of the company. In the present case Mr Ward was a director, there was a conflict between his interest and his duties, there could be no contract by Guinness for the payment of remuneration pursuant to art. 91 unless the board made the contract on behalf of Guinness and there was no question of approval by directors or shareholders.

In support of a claim for an equitable allowance, reference was made to the decision . . . in *Phipps* v *Boardman* [1964] 1 WLR 993 [affirmed [1967] 2 AC 46]. . . . *Phipps* v *Boardman* decides that in exceptional circumstances a court of equity may award remuneration to the trustee. Therefore, it is argued, a court of equity may award remuneration to a director. As at present advised, I am unable to envisage circumstances in which a court of equity would exercise a power to award remuneration to a director when the relevant articles of association confided that power to the board of directors. Certainly, the circumstances do not exist in the present case. It is in this respect that s. 317 of the Companies Act 1985 is relevant. By that section:

(1) It is the duty of a director of a company who is in any way, whether directly or indirectly, interested in a contract or proposed contract with the company to declare the nature of his interest at a meeting of the directors of the company. . . .

(7) A director who fails to comply with this section is liable to a fine.

In *Hely-Hutchinson* v *Brayhead Ltd* [1968] 1 QB 549 the Court of Appeal held that s. 317 renders a contract voidable by a company if the director does not declare his interest. Section 317 does not apply directly to the present case because there was no contract between Guinness and Mr Ward. But s. 317 shows the importance which the legislature attaches to the principle that a company should be protected against a director who has a conflict of interest and duty. There is a fundamental objection to the admission of any claim by Mr Ward. . . . The objection is that by the agreement with the committee, which is the foundation of Mr Ward's claim to any relief, he voluntarily involved himself in an irreconcilable conflict between his duty as a director and his personal interests. Both before and after 19 January 1986 Mr Ward owed a duty to tender to Guinness impartial and independent advice untainted by any possibility of personal gain. Yet by the agreement, which Mr Ward claims to have concluded with the committee and which may have been in contemplation by Mr Ward even before 19 January 1986, Mr Ward became entitled to a negotiating fee payable by Guinness if, and only if, Guinness acquired Distillers and, by the agreement, the amount of the negotiating fee depended on the price which Guinness ultimately offered to the shareholders of Distillers. If such an agreement had been concluded by the board of directors, it would have been binding on Guinness under art. 91 but foolish in that the agreement perforce made Mr Ward's advice to Guinness suspect and biased. But at least the conflict would have been revealed to the board.... I agree with my noble and learned friend Lord Goff that for the purposes of this appeal it must be assumed that Mr Ward acted in good faith, believing that his services were rendered under contract binding on the company, and that in that mistaken belief Mr Ward may have rendered services to Guinness of great value and contributed substantially to the enrichment of the shareholders of Guinness. Nevertheless, the failure of Mr Ward to realise that he could not properly use his position as director of Guinness to obtain a contingent negotiating fee of £5.2 million from Guinness does not excuse him or enable him to defeat the rules of equity which prohibit a trustee from putting himself in a position in which his interests and duty conflict and which insist that a trustee or any other fiduciary shall not make a profit out of his trust.

NOTE: The civil action in this case was of course only a sideshow in the Guinness affair. The illegal share support scheme allegedly involving unlawful financial assistance (explained at 10.5.1 above) is but one of the other company law issues which surfaced. The affair was one of the most highly publicised of the financial scandals arising out of the boom of the late 1980s. It led to a DTI investigation and what the *Independent* referred to as 'the City fraud trial of the century'. The trial led to the conviction of four directors including Ernest Saunders, Guinness's chairman, on charges including theft and false accounting. Prison sentences actually served proved to be relatively modest. However, the affair was not yet finally over. In September 1994 the European Commission of Human Rights ruled that his conviction was unfair and this was confirmed by the European Court of Human Rights in December 1996 (*Saunders* v *United Kingdom* (1996) 23 EHRR 313). The use by the prosecution at Saunders's trial of statements given under compulsion during the DTI investigation infringed his right not to incriminate himself.

11.7 REMOVAL OF DIRECTORS

11.7.1 The mechanics of removal of directors

It is a long-standing principle that the controlling majority of members of a company may appoint all its directors and may also remove them at will. Where the directors are not the major shareholders of the company, this principle is important in ensuring the accountability of directors to the company.

The Cohen Committee on Company Law Amendment (Cmd 6659), 1945, remarked that it was not unusual for articles to provide for removal of directors only by an extraordinary resolution, i.e., by a 75 per cent majority. A section was therefore enacted in 1947 to ensure that directors could be removed by ordinary resolution notwithstanding anything to the contrary in the articles or in any agreement between the director and the company.

Sometimes articles may say that a director vacates office if a written request is made by all the other directors that he or she should resign. Such an article is effective and as the following case suggests, this may be so even where there is a suspicion of an ulterior motive in the removal. The decision is a little surprising in this respect, though it perhaps re-asserts the reality that the members (or in this case the directors) must be free to remove a director with whom they cannot work or in whom they have lost confidence. Just as the law will not enforce an employment contract by specific performance, the aggrieved director must probably look to his remedy in damages rather than try to challenge the removal.

Samuel Tak Lee v Chou Wen Hsien

Removal by notice from co-directors

[1984] 1 WLR 1202, Privy Council appeal from Hong Kong

The articles of the company required that a director vacate office if requested to do so in writing by all his or her co-directors. While this is a fiduciary power to be exercised in the best interests of the company, removal may still be effective even though some of the directors acted from an ulterior motive.

Facts   Lee was one of eight directors of Ocean-Land Development Ltd, a holding company with 32 subsidiary and associated companies. Management was harmonious for 10 years until 1982. Lord Brightman's judgment notes:

> In earlier years a representative of the Hong Kong and Shanghai Banking Corporation served as a director. He resigned in September 1980 on his retirement from the corporation. He was not replaced by another representative of the corporation. The plaintiff [Lee] felt that Ocean-Land thereby lost someone whom he regarded as a wholly independent director. Until then harmony seems to have prevailed on the board.

(A nice plug for non-executive directors.) In 1982 Lee became suspicious about certain transactions concerning subsidiaries including sale of the company's shareholding in Prat Development Ltd. This he claimed had been sold at an undervalue to a company he suspected of being beneficially owned by Mr Chou, chairman and managing director of Ocean-Land and by his brother, the vice-chairman and deputy managing director. Lee asked for access to various accounts but his requests were not complied with. He asked for a board meeting to be convened, but before the date of the meeting he received without warning a notice signed by all his co-directors requesting him to resign pursuant to art. 73(d). This article stated that the office of a director shall be vacated if requested in writing by all his co-directors to resign.

The decision of the Privy Council confirmed the removal of Lee as a director largely on grounds of commercial certainty that a company must be capable of ascertaining precisely who its directors are. Implicit is the point that if all the directors are unable to work with one of their number then his removal is inevitable. What is left undecided is what kind of ulterior motive on the part of the directors would invalidate a notice to vacate office or when and on what basis a claim for wrongful removal might arise.

LORD BRIGHTMAN: Their lordships are in agreement with the majority of the Court of Appeal that the power given by art. 73 to directors to expel one of their number from the board is fiduciary, in the sense that each director concurring in the expulsion must act in accordance with what he believes to be the best interests of the company, and that he cannot properly concur for ulterior reasons of his own. It does not, however, follow that a notice will be void and of no effect, and that the director sought to be expelled will remain a director of the board, because one or more of the requesting directors acted from an ulterior motive. Their lordships have not been referred to any reported case directly in point. The decision of Farwell J in *Re Bodega Co. Ltd* [1904] 1 Ch 276 provides the nearest analogy, but is only of limited assistance. While it emphasises the automatic operation of an article similar to art. 73, the bona fides of the continuing directors were not there in issue.

To hold that bad faith on the part of any one director vitiates the notice to resign and leaves in office the director whose resignation is sought, would introduce into the management of the company a source of uncertainty which their lordships consider is unlikely to have been intended by the signatories to the articles and by others becoming shareholders in the company. In order to give business sense to art. 73(d), it is necessary to construe the article strictly in accordance with its terms without any qualification, and to treat the office of director as vacated if the specified event occurs. If this were not the case, and the expelled director challenged the bona fides of all or any of his co-directors, the management of the company's business might be at a standstill pending the resolution of the dispute by one means or another, in consequence of the doubt whether the expelled director ought or ought not properly to be treated as a member of the board. Their lordships therefore take the view that the plaintiff's claim, as spelt out in the endorsement on the writ, in argument before the Court of Appeal, and in his printed case, inevitably fails at this point.

It is not strictly necessary to deal with the plaintiff's third submission, to the effect that if art. 73(d) confers a fiduciary power and a request made in breach of that duty is of no effect, the wrongly expelled director is nevertheless entitled to maintain an action in his own name to restore himself to office and is not bound to sue, if at all, in a derivative action on behalf of the company to repair a wrong done to the company. Without developing the matter at length, their lordships agree with the Court of Appeal that, on the two hypotheses stated, the ordinary principles of *Foss* v *Harbottle* (1843) 2 Hare 461 would preclude such an action.

11.7.2 Attempts to entrench directors

Entrepreneurs who set up companies may wish to take steps to ensure that they are appointed as directors and that they retain office come what may. Obviously the way to achieve this is to hold a majority of the shares or voting rights, though this is not always possible. An alternative is to reach an agreement with one's co-shareholders outside the articles. An example of this is given at 1.7 above (stage (e)) where the four partners in the firm of builders each become minority shareholders in the new company, J. B. Baker & Co. Ltd. They therefore draw up a shareholders' agreement which states that each of them will vote in favour of appointing the others as director and will not vote to remove them from the board. Shareholders' agreements appear generally to be enforceable (see 6.3.2 above) and are an effective way of supplementing the articles and general company law.

One other way of entrenching directors, now no longer possible, was to name them in the memorandum of association and to declare this provision unalterable. Another way was to name them in the articles and then their opponents would have to be able to pass a special resolution on a 75 per cent majority to alter the article and remove the directors. Companies Act 1985, s. 303, was intended to ensure that, just as directors could be appointed on a simple majority vote, they could also be made accountable and removed by a simple majority. Now under CA 2006, s. 22, the policy is that if by unanimous decision you, as members of a private company, want to constrain yourselves and subsequent members from removing directors by procedures even 'more restrictive' than a special resolution, then the law is not going to stop you. However, for listed public companies anything more restrictive than an ordinary resolution would not comply with the listing requirements.

The leading case on this area was *Bushell* v *Faith* and an extract now follows. Before reading it, you should be bear in mind that CA 2006, s. 168, which replaces CA 1985, s. 303, no longer says that a director of a company can be removed by ordinary resolution 'notwithstanding anything in its articles'. (See 11.7.3 below.) These words are deleted from the section and so *Bushell* v *Faith* is no longer of direct authority in this area. Nonetheless, it is a major House of Lords decision which should be read as a vivid illustration of the approach of the courts to statutory interpretation in the field of company law. It indicates that, as in the *Salomon* case, the courts interpret legislation literally according to the words of the section as enacted by Parliament and will not allow a broader interpretation in order to promote a purpose or policy that the section is evidently intended to promote. Though s. 303 was clearly intended to ensure that directors could be removed by a simple majority, the House of Lords allowed a clever device to circumvent this rule.

Bushell v Faith

Two sisters fail to sack their brother director
[1970] AC 1099, House of Lords

In this case a special article was successful in protecting a director from removal even though CA 1985, s. 303, said that a director of a company can be removed from office by ordinary resolution 'notwithstanding anything in its articles'. The case is a fascinating instance of how the courts may refuse to take a purposive approach to construction of a statute but take the safer course of interpreting it literally. In this case the House of Lords knew that Parliament by s. 303 intended directors to be removable by a simple majority. Lord Reid recognised that the device in the articles was an attempt to evade the effect of the section. He also said that legislation must be construed in the light of the mischief the Act was designed to meet. Nonetheless he reluctantly approved the effectiveness of the article protecting the director from removal. In short Parliament had done its task of drafting the section inadequately. Even the highest appeal court could not rewrite the section to achieve its obvious purpose as to do so would challenge the established principle that members may attach such voting rights to shares as they think fit. To vary that principle on an *ad hoc* basis without wider consideration might have unforeseen consequences. Such a review of policy would be for Parliament and not the courts which invariably choose the safer literal interpretation of the statute.

Facts   Bush Court (Southgate) Ltd had three shareholders, a brother and two sisters, each holding 100 shares. The two sisters purported to remove their brother as a director by casting 200 votes on a resolution against his 100. He challenged the removal on the grounds of art. 9 which said that on a resolution to remove a director from office 'any shares held by that director shall on a poll in respect of such resolution carry the right to three votes per share' (thus defeating the resolution to remove by 300 to 200). The House of Lords (Lord Morris of Borth-y-Gest dissenting) held that the brother had not been validly removed as a director. (All directors were thus entrenched as the article was effective and could not be altered by a special resolution unless all three voted in favour. Whether the sisters could issue more shares to themselves to destroy the brother's negative control would depend on the articles and the proper purposes doctrine.)

LORD DONOVAN: My lords, the issue here is the true construction of s. 184 of the Companies Act, 1948 [later CA 1985, s. 303] and I approach it with no conception of what the legislature wanted to achieve by the section other than such as can reasonably be deduced from its language.

Clearly it was intended to alter the method by which a director of a company could be removed while still in office. It enacts that this can be done by the company by ordinary resolution. Furthermore, it may be achieved notwithstanding anything in the company's articles, or in any agreement between the company and the director.

Accordingly any case (and one knows there were many) where the articles prescribed that a director should be removable during his period of office only by a special resolution or an extraordinary resolution, each of which necessitated *inter alia* a three-to-one majority of those present and voting at the meeting, is overridden by s. 184. A simple majority of the votes will now suffice; an ordinary resolution being, in my opinion, a resolution capable of being carried by such a majority. Similarly any agreement, whether evidenced by the articles or otherwise, that a director shall be a director for life or for some fixed period is now also over-reached.

The field over which s. 184 operates is thus extensive for it includes, admittedly, all companies with a quotation on the Stock Exchange.

It is now contended, however, that it does something more; namely, that it provides in effect that when the ordinary resolution proposing the removal of the director is put to the meeting each shareholder present shall have one vote per share and no more: and that any provision in the articles providing that any shareholder shall, in relation to *this* resolution, have 'weighted' votes attached to his shares, is also nullified by s. 184. A provision for such 'weighting' of votes which applies generally, that is as part of the normal pattern of voting, is accepted by the appellant as unobjectionable: but an article such as the one here under consideration which is special to a resolution seeking the removal of a director falls foul of s. 184 and is overridden by it.

Why should this be? The section does not say so, as it easily could. And those who drafted it and enacted it certainly would have included among their numbers many who were familiar with the phenomenon of articles of association carrying 'weighted votes'. It must therefore have been plain at the outset that unless some special provision were made, the mere direction that an ordinary resolution would do in order to remove a director would leave the section at risk of being made inoperative in the way that has been done here. Yet no such provision was made, and in this Parliament followed its practice of leaving to companies and their shareholders liberty to allocate voting rights as they pleased.

When, therefore, it is said that a decision in favour of the respondent in this case would defeat the purpose of the section and make a mockery of it, it is being assumed that Parliament *intended* to cover every possible case and block up every loophole. I see no warrant for any such assumption. A very large part of the relevant field is in fact covered and covered effectively. And there may be good reasons why Parliament should leave some companies with freedom of manoeuvre in this particular matter. There are many small companies which are conducted in practice as though they were little more than partnerships, particularly family companies running a family business; and it is, unfortunately, sometimes necessary to provide some safeguard against family quarrels having their repercussions in the boardroom. I am not, of course, saying that this is such a case: I merely seek to repel the argument that unless the section is construed in the way the appellant wants, it has become 'inept' and 'frustrated'.

LORD REID: My lords, with some reluctance I agree with the majority of your lordships that this appeal must be dismissed. Article 9 of the articles of association of this company is obviously designed to evade s. 184(1) of the Companies Act 1948, which provides that a company may by ordinary resolution remove a director notwithstanding anything in its articles. The extra voting power given by that article to a director, whose removal from office is proposed, makes it impossible in the circumstances of this case for any resolution for the removal of any director to be passed if that director votes against it. . . .

My lords, when construing an Act of Parliament it is a canon of construction that its provisions must be construed in the light of the mischief which the Act was designed to meet. In this case the mischief was well known; it was a common practice, especially in the case of private companies, to provide in the articles that a director should be irremovable or only removable by an extraordinary resolution; in the former case the articles would have to be altered by special resolution before the director could be removed and of course in either case a three-quarters majority would be required. In many cases this would be impossible, so the Act provided that notwithstanding anything in the articles an ordinary resolution would suffice to remove a director. That was the mischief which the section set out to remedy; to make a director removable by virtue of an ordinary resolution instead of an extraordinary resolution or making it necessary to alter the articles.

An ordinary resolution is not defined nor used in the body of the Act of 1948 though the phrase occurs in some of the articles of Table A in the first schedule to the Act. But its meaning is, in my opinion, clear. An ordinary resolution is in the first place passed by a bare majority on a show of hands by the members entitled to vote who are present personally or by proxy and on such a vote each member has one vote regardless of his shareholding. If a poll is demanded then for an ordinary resolution still only a bare majority of votes is required. But whether a share or class of shares has any vote upon the matter and, if so, what is its voting power upon the resolution in question depends entirely upon the voting rights attached to that share or class of shares by the articles of association.

I venture to think that Ungoed-Thomas J overlooked the importance of art. 2 of Table A which gives to the company a completely unfettered right to attach to any share or class of shares special voting rights upon a poll or to restrict those rights as the company may think fit. Thus, it is commonplace that a company may and frequently does preclude preference shareholders from voting unless their dividends are in arrear or their class rights are directly affected. It is equally commonplace that particular shares may be issued with specially loaded voting rights which ensure that in all resolutions put before the shareholders in general meeting the holder of those particular shares can always be sure of carrying the day, aye or no, as the holder pleases....

Parliament has never sought to fetter the right of the company to issue a share with such rights or restrictions as it may think fit. There is no fetter which compels the company to make the voting rights or restrictions of general application and it seems to me clear that such rights or restrictions can be attached to special circumstances and to particular types of resolution. This makes no mockery of s. 184; all that Parliament was seeking to do thereby was to make an ordinary resolution sufficient to remove a director. Had Parliament desired to go further and enact that every share entitled to vote should be deprived of its special rights under the articles it should have said so in plain terms by making the vote on a poll one vote one share. Then, what about shares which had no voting rights under the articles? Should not Parliament give them a vote when considering this completely artificial form of ordinary resolution? Suppose there had here been some preference shares in the name of Mr Faith's wife, which under the articles had in the circumstances no vote; why in justice should her voice be excluded from consideration in this artificial vote?

I only raise this purely hypothetical case to show the great difficulty of trying to do justice by legislation in a matter which has always been left to the corporators themselves to decide.

I agree entirely with the judgment of the Court of Appeal, and would dismiss this appeal.

LORD MORRIS OF BORTH-Y-GEST (dissenting): My lords, it is provided by s. 184(1) that a company may by ordinary resolution remove a director before the expiration of his period of office. The company may do so notwithstanding anything to the contrary in its articles. So if an article provided that a director was irremovable he could nevertheless be removed if an ordinary resolution to that effect was passed. So also if an article provided that a director could only be removed by a resolution carried by a majority greater than a simple majority he would nevertheless be removed if a resolution was passed by a simple majority.

Some shares may, however, carry a greater voting power than others. On a resolution to remove a director shares will therefore carry the voting power that they possess. But this does not, in my view, warrant a device such as art. 9 introduces. Its unconcealed effect is to make a director irremovable. If the question is posed whether the shares of the respondent possess any added voting weight the answer must be that they possess none whatsoever beyond, if valid, an *ad hoc* weight for the special purpose of circumventing s. 184. If art. 9 were writ large it would set out that a director is not to be removed against his will and that in order to achieve this and to thwart the express provision of s. 184 the voting power of any director threatened with removal is to be deemed to be greater than it actually is. The learned judge thought that to sanction this would be to make a mockery of the law. I think so also.

I would allow the appeal.

QUESTION. ASSERTING GIRL POWER.

Could the sisters have removed their brother from the board despite the decision in the House of Lords? Would the following be effective under the articles of the company? The sisters propose a single resolution to remove the brother and one sister from the board. The brother votes against with 300 votes. Both sisters vote in favour with 400 votes (100 + 300 votes). The resolution is carried thus removing both brother and sister from the board.

The new CA 2006, s. 168, says that a director can be removed by ordinary resolution at a meeting notwithstanding anything in an agreement with him only, but no longer 'notwithstanding anything in its articles' (see below). Although s. 21(1) allows articles to be amended by special resolution on a 75 per cent majority, s. 22(1) now states that 'entrenched provisions' in the articles can provide that the articles may specify provisions that may only be amended or repealed by procedures that are 'more restrictive' than on a vote for a special resolution. Such a provision for entrenchment can only be made in the articles on formation of the company or by unanimous agreement of the members; s. 22(2). Putting in the articles a provision for entrenchment of a particular article (such as for the removal of directors), can thus now only be done in accordance with s. 22(2). Any other attempt to make changing an article 'more restrictive' is presumably of no effect and the article could be removed by a special resolution. Again, an article inserted by unanimous agreement appointing a particular director for life and declaring the article unalterable could later be removed by unanimous agreement and presumably even by special resolution as it is not within the wording of s. 22(1).

COMPANIES ACT 2006, SS. 168 AND 169

168. Resolution to remove director

(1) A company may by ordinary resolution at a meeting remove a director before the expiration of his period of office, notwithstanding anything in any agreement between it and him.
(2) Special notice is required of a resolution to remove a director under this section or to appoint somebody instead of a director so removed at the meeting at which he is removed.
(5) This section is not to be taken—
   (a) as depriving a person removed under it of compensation or damages payable to him in respect of the termination of his appointment as director or of any appointment terminating with that as director, or
   (b) as derogating from any power to remove a director that may exist apart from this section.

169. Director's right to protest against removal

(1) On receipt of notice of an intended resolution to remove a director under section 168, the company must forthwith send a copy of the notice to the director concerned.

11.7.3 Other restraints on removal of directors

In private companies which are owned by a group of people who appoint themselves as directors and run the company together, it might be unfair to remove one of them from office as director. If there is an expectation of participation in management and employment then a failure of relationships leading to expulsion may offer the aggrieved party little opportunity for a remedy except to petition the court for a winding-up order on the just and equitable ground under IA 1986, s. 122(1)(g). Alternatively, removal, perhaps coupled with other factors, may be unfairly prejudicial to his interests as a shareholder and so enable him to petition the court for a remedy under CA 2006, s. 994. The likely order is that his shares be bought out by the other shareholders at the court's valuation. (See 13.2.3.) It has to be realised therefore that in small companies which are akin to partnerships, removal of a director may be unfair and may lead to legal repercussions. The right of removal in such companies has to be exercised with restraint having regard to wider considerations of fairness to the individual to be removed.

The other important consideration is that where the director is also an employee, removal may probably amount to a breach of contract. Especially where the director has a fixed-term contract, the cost of damages payable by the company may be a significant restraint on his or her removal. The following cases deal with some of the contractual issues in relation to removal of directors, all of them involving managing directors.

Southern Foundries (1926) Ltd v Shirlaw

Freedom to alter the articles

[1940] AC 701, House of Lords

A company remains free to alter its articles and to act upon a new article to remove a director but may be liable for breach of contract.

Facts In 1933 the company appointed Shirlaw as managing director for 10 years. The articles provided that a managing director's appointment would terminate if he ceased to be a director. Article 105 enabled removal of a director before expiry of his term of office. In 1935 Federated Foundries Ltd acquired all the shares in the company. The company's articles were replaced by new articles which enabled Federated, the controlling shareholder, to remove any director of the company. Shirlaw was removed from office under this article. In a majority decision of the House of Lords, two Law Lords dissenting, he was awarded substantial damages for breach of contract.

LORD ATKIN: My lords, the question in this case is whether the appellant company have broken their contract with the respondent made in December 1933, that he should hold the office of managing director for 10 years. The breach alleged is that under the articles adopted by the company, after the agreement, the respondent was removed from the position of director of the company by the Federated Foundries Ltd. There can be no doubt that the office of managing director could only be held by a director, and that upon the holder of the office of managing director ceasing for any cause to be a director the office would be *ipso facto* vacated.... Thus the contract of employment for the term of 10 years was dependent upon the managing director continuing to be a director. This continuance of the directorship was a concurrent condition. The arrangement between the parties appears to me to be exactly described by the words of Cockburn CJ in *Stirling v Maitland* (1864) 5 B & S 840 at p. 852: 'If a party enters into an arrangement which can only take effect by the continuance of an existing state of circumstances'; and in such a state of things the Lord Chief Justice said: 'I look on the law to be that...there is an implied engagement on his part that he shall do nothing of his own motion to put an end to that state of circumstances, under which alone the arrangement can be operative'. That proposition in my opinion is well-established law. Personally I should not so much base the law on an implied term, as on a positive rule of the law of contract that conduct of either promiser or promisee which can be said to amount to himself 'of his own motion' bringing about the impossibility of performance is in itself a breach. If A promises to marry B and before performance of that contract marries C, A is not sued for breach of an implied contract not to marry anyone else, but for breach of his contract to marry B. I think it follows that if either the company of its own motion removed the respondent from the office of director under art. 105, or if the respondent caused his office of director to be vacated by giving one month's notice of resignation under art. 89, either of them would have committed a breach of the agreement in question.... I agree, therefore, with the trial judge, with the majority of the Court of Appeal, and with I believe all your lordships in thinking that if during the term the respondent had given a notice of resignation, or if the company had exercised its power of removal under art. 105, either would have committed a breach of the contract.

LORD PORTER: The general principle therefore may, I think, be thus stated. A company cannot be precluded from altering its articles thereby giving itself power to act upon the provisions of the altered articles—but so to act may nevertheless be a breach of contract if it is contrary to a stipulation in a contract validly made before the alteration.

Nor can an injunction be granted to prevent the adoption of the new articles and in that sense they are binding on all and sundry, but for the company to act upon them will none the less render it liable in damages if such action is contrary to the previous engagements of the company. If, therefore, the altered articles had provided for the dismissal without notice of a managing director previously appointed, the dismissal would be *intra vires* the company but would nevertheless expose the company to an action for damages if the appointment had been for a term of (say) 10 years and he were dismissed in less.

Once it is established that the appointment is for a time certain and the dismissal before its termination, the result follows, and I do not understand the appellants to contend to the contrary.

Read v *Astoria Garage (Streatham) Ltd*
Appointed managing director subject to the articles
[1952] Ch 637, Court of Appeal

The terms of articles for appointment and dismissal of a managing director may, in the absence of a specific contractual term, enable the company to dismiss the managing director lawfully without giving reasonable notice.

Facts Article 38 gave the directors a discretion to appoint a managing director and said that the appointment would be determined 'if he ceases for any cause to be a director, or if the company in general meeting resolve that his tenure of the office of managing director … be determined'. In 1932 Read was appointed managing director at £7 a week. In 1949 the directors resolved to terminate his employment. Read unsuccessfully claimed damages for breach of contract on grounds that he had not been given reasonable notice.

JENKINS LJ: There remains … the claim in respect of the alleged wrongful dismissal of the plaintiff from his office of managing director. There is no record anywhere of any terms on which the plaintiff was appointed managing director beyond the minute of resolution No. 4 which was passed at the first meeting of directors and the articles of association of the company.

It is argued by counsel for the plaintiff that, notwithstanding the provisions of art. 68, there was a contract between the plaintiff and the defendant company in the nature of a contract of general hiring—a plain contract of employment, one of the terms of which was that the plaintiff's employment should not be determined by the defendant company except by reasonable notice. The learned judge came to the conclusion that the terms of the plaintiff's appointment were not such as to entitle him to any notice in the event of the company choosing, under art. 68, to resolve in general meeting that his tenure of office as managing director be determined, and, in my judgment, the learned judge was clearly right. …

Counsel for the plaintiff said alternatively that, even if the appointment made by the resolution of the board must be taken as, in effect, incorporating the provisions of art. 68, nevertheless the provisions of the article as so incorporated must be held to be subject to an implied term that the plaintiff's employment could not be determined without reasonable notice. For my part, I see no ground for implying any such term. Indeed, to imply one comes back to saying over again that the appointment was not on the terms of art. 68, but on some other and different terms, including a term as to reasonable notice. I see no ground for implying any such term in the absence of any contract outside the article and the resolution, and in the absence, moreover, of any provision about it in the resolution itself.

We were also referred to *Southern Foundries (1926) Ltd* v *Shirlaw* [1940] AC 701, a decision of the House of Lords. In that case the majority of their lordships held the managing director concerned to be entitled to damages. That is, however, an entirely different case from the present one, for two reasons. In the first place, there was a contract of service between the company and the managing director *dehors* the articles of association, and, in the second place, the contract was sought to be determined by a power which was not present in the articles of association of the company as they stood at the date of the contract, but was inserted in the articles by subsequent alteration. In my view, therefore, the case was wholly different from the present case, and it does not seem to me that any assistance can be obtained from it for the present purpose. …

In my view, on the facts of this case, the position was simply that the plaintiff was appointed to be a managing director in accordance with the Companies Act 1929, Table A, art. 68, with such tenure of office as was provided for by that article, and had no special right to receive any particular notice of the termination of his employment in the event of the company deciding to determine it and doing so by a resolution in general meeting. Accordingly, in my view, the learned judge came to a right conclusion on the plaintiff's second claim, and in the result the appeal fails on both points, and should be dismissed.

11.8 DISQUALIFICATION OF DIRECTORS

Recent governments have presented the disqualification of directors as being an important means of dealing with 'rogue directors' of companies that have failed leaving their debts unpaid. The number of grounds on which directors may be disqualified has gradually increased and the law is found in a special Act, the Company Directors Disqualification Act 1986 (CDDA 1986). The following are the principal grounds for disqualification.

First, directors are automatically disqualified from being directors if they are undischarged bankrupts. Secondly, the court may disqualify them for persistent default in filing returns at the Companies Registry. Thirdly, they may be disqualified if they have been convicted of an indictable offence in connection with management etc. of a company, and fourthly under section 6 if, following the insolvency of their company they are shown to be unfit to be concerned in the management of a company. (CDDA 1986, sch. 1 lists the matters to which the court is to have regard in determining whether a director is unfit.) In the case of company insolvency the official receiver, or the insolvency practitioner acting as liquidator or administrative receiver is obliged to submit a report to the Secretary of State on the conduct of every director of the failed company. These reports are considered by the Disqualification Unit of the Insolvency Service which deals with section 6 cases and where appropriate an application for disqualification is made to the court. The Registrar of Companies keeps a register of disqualified directors and there are only a few thousand names on the register. (The register can be searched on their website at http://www.companieshouse.gov.uk.)

By the late 1990s the number of section 6 disqualification orders began to exceed a thousand a year, a relatively modest cull, though the cost of proceedings in court is high. A report published by the National Audit Office in 1999 (*Company Director Disqualification—A Follow-up Report*) notes that in 1997/98 the Insolvency Service obtained the disqualification of 1,297 directors and that its costs of so doing were £22 million. The report, however, estimates the future losses to creditors likely to be saved by disqualifying those unfit directors as being only £11 million. While this is not the only possible benefit of disqualification, the direct benefit to creditors seems a small return for a substantial expenditure of public funds. (See further, Hicks (1999) 15 Insol Law & Practice 112 and (2001) JBL 433.) However, the cost of disqualification is now falling as the Insolvency Act 2000, inserting a new s. 1A in the Act, now provides that an undertaking by an unfit director to the Secretary of State not to be a director or to take part in management etc. has the same effect as a disqualification order. As a full hearing in open court is not required, cost savings are achieved. It is argued below, however that the burden for directors of resisting a disqualification order may unfairly pressurise them into giving a disqualification undertaking.

The extract from the research report that now follows surveys the effectiveness of disqualification for unfitness following company insolvency and makes proposals for reform. The cases then extracted establish a tariff for disqualification sentencing and suggest that the duty imposed by the Act to participate fully in management, to supervise colleagues and to be sufficiently competent in the subject matter of the company's line of business is stricter than the traditional standards of the common law.

Andrew Hicks, *Disqualification of Directors: No Hiding Place for the Unfit?* (ACCA Research Report No. 59)
(London: Association of Chartered Certified Accountants, 1998)

Under section 6 of the Company Directors' Disqualification Act 1986, the Insolvency Service of the DTI, on proof that a director's conduct in the management of an insolvent company shows him or her to be unfit, may obtain an order of the court disqualifying that person from being a director or concerned in the management of limited companies for a period of between two and 15 years. The broad objective is the protection of creditors and the commercial public generally, curbing the abuse of limited liability and improving standards in running businesses. In the relatively few years that disqualification for unfitness has been on the statute books, it has proved to be surprisingly controversial. Media attention has focused on rogue directors of fly-by-night companies who take easy credit and then leave many unpaid creditors. The imagery of the so-called 'phoenix company', where the directors of the failed company buy its assets and recommence a substantially similar business with a new corporate entity, has proved particularly appealing and newsworthy.

Ministers have made extravagant claims for the effectiveness of energetic enforcement, citing substantially increased numbers of disqualification orders in recent years. *The Times* of 22 August 1996 quoted the then Minister, John Taylor, as saying that the Insolvency Service was on a mission to rid the business world of unfit directors. 'There will be no hiding place for those who abrogate or neglect their responsibility. It is not possible to slip through the net.' The Labour minister has continued in the same style, a DTI press release in June 1997, headed 'Griffiths goes gunning against cowboy directors' saying, 'Let there be no doubt—war has been declared on the cowboy director'. In January 1998 a press release announced, 'Griffiths launches hotline to name and shame defiant directors'.

Yet most commentators have been lukewarm about the effectiveness of disqualification. *The Times*, for example on 17 January 1998, referring to the disqualification of Terry Venables, said the DTI 'needs reminding that this sanction is a limp lettuce leaf'. Professor Cheffins has written, 'It must remain a matter for speculation whether expanding the scope for director disqualification has yielded a net social benefit'. A recent editorial in a leading insolvency journal asks whether the government is brave enough to tackle the problem of creditor protection or will instead 'be content to bathe in the dubious glory of director disqualification statistics' (1998 Insolvency Law and Practice 186). Speaking in New York recently, the Secretary of State for Trade and Industry, Peter Mandelson, is reported as saying that failed entrepreneurs should be encouraged to take new business risks (*The Times*, 14 October 1998). In the drive for competitiveness British business culture needs to be changed so that business failure is not stigmatised; the government's job is to create and encourage 'serial entrepreneurs'. While this viewpoint is not inconsistent with the need to restrain those who behave improperly, it does represent an interesting change of emphasis.

A report by the National Audit Office entitled *The Insolvency Service Executive Agency: Company Director Disqualification* (18 October 1993) was highly critical of aspects of the mechanics and effectiveness of disqualification under section 6. The report (at para. 1.4) usefully describes the objectives of the Insolvency Service Agency under the Act as follows.

- To protect the commercial world and the public at large by effective action against the abuse of limited liability through disqualification of individuals for periods, determined by the court, of between two and 15 years.
- Further, by deterrents and by the promulgation of orders made by the courts, to contribute to fostering the integrity of markets generally and improving the standards of company stewardship, in particular, but without inhibiting genuine enterprise and entrepreneurial management.

The report of the Cork committee (*Insolvency Law and Practice*, Cmnd 8558, 1982) saw the reinvigoration of disqualification for unfitness, together with the new device of wrongful trading, as an important means of providing protection and compensation for creditors following the failure of limited companies.... Other than the report of the National Audit Office, which is primarily a value-for-money report on the effectiveness of the Insolvency Service Agency, there has been no broad survey of the impact and effectiveness of disqualification under section 6. The purposes of this research paper are thus: to assess the effectiveness of the disqualification legislation in protecting the public interest and in raising the standards of conduct of directors of limited companies; to review its role in relation to other relevant legislation; and to propose reforms.

[Research conclusions]

The vast majority of limited companies are owner-managed small businesses. The result of limited liability is that the person setting up and managing the company is not personally liable for its debts, unless personal guarantees are given. It is against those who abuse the considerable privilege of limited liability that disqualification for unfitness is primarily targeted. Abuse of limited liability generally consists of the improper use of the company's assets and unfairly prejudicing the interests of creditors. Disqualification is not primarily directed at simple management incompetence, the purpose of limited liability being to encourage entrepreneurial risk-taking and to protect entrepreneurs from their honest mistakes and inadequacies.

Most disqualification actions are brought against directors who are owner-managers of their own small businesses and who are part of a self-employed culture. Unfortunately, disqualification has the least impact on this type of director as, once disqualified, they are relatively likely to be able to find work or to set up in business again in their own name. Furthermore, it is very easy to incorporate a company and there is no qualification required to be a director. As a result, disqualifying a few thousand small company directors is a limited control on the access of the potentially unfit to the privilege of trading with limited liability. On the other hand, disqualification is a more effective sanction against the professionally qualified or experienced director who is an employed executive, for whom a possible disqualification is a major threat. Policy should, therefore, give more emphasis to the conduct of directors of the larger failed companies rather than pursuing ever-increasing numbers of disqualifications, many of which are of directors of relatively small companies.

It appears that while much attention has been given to the extreme problem of 'phoenix' companies, the more widespread abuse of limited liability may arise from those companies that borrow too optimistically and offer floating charges and personal guarantees to the bank. Over-borrowing, failed risk-taking and personal security give directors an increasing incentive to keep trading in order to avoid a collapse of their livelihood and being made personally liable for the company's debts. It is at this point that they are most likely to treat creditors unfairly and behave in manner which is unfit.

The general effectiveness of disqualification is limited. Given a population of perhaps three million directors and of many more millions who could readily become directors the protective benefit of even a thousand short disqualifications annually is limited. The deterrent effect of disqualification is weak, though it is stronger against the more professional executives. Disqualification is also ineffective in promoting best practice towards creditors, as the law does not provide any clear and accessible statement of any such principles that may have been established by the legislation and the courts.

When companies fail or are struck off, the level of investigation of the conduct of directors varies and in some cases there is no investigation at all; investigation depends on there being sufficient assets in the company and proactive creditors willing to initiate a winding up. Directors may now apply for the company to be struck off, thereby avoiding a winding up and any investigation of their conduct, a procedure that should be reviewed in case it is being used to the detriment of creditors.

If a director who has been disqualified takes part in management in breach of the order, he or she may be penalised by prosecution for a criminal offence. Infringements by disqualified directors are difficult to detect, an intrinsic limitation on the effectiveness of disqualification. In recent years, while huge effort has gone into achieving disqualifications, there have only been a handful of prosecutions of disqualified directors. Improved publicity on the Companies House web site and the recent introduction of a disqualified directors hotline, inviting the public to report the disqualified taking part in management, could prove effective. While Companies House routinely checks names of current directors against the register of disqualifications, there is no check against the names of those who have been made bankrupt. Yet being an undischarged bankrupt disqualifies a person from taking part in management of a company. There are tens of thousands of undischarged bankrupts who will thus not be apprehended if they return their name as a company director to Companies House. The questionnaire surveys of disqualified directors and of insolvency practitioners also suggest that there is a relatively high level of infringement of section 6 disqualification orders and that the chances of being caught are thought to be low. Increasing the number of disqualifications, without adequate enforcement, is, however, futile. A full review of enforcement is therefore now essential to assure the effectiveness and credibility of disqualification.

Reforms of disqualification for unfitness

While imposing a statutory duty on insolvency practitioners (IPs) to report unfit directors of failed companies to the Disqualification Unit of the DTI has, in general, been a successful experiment, achieving consistency in the standards of such reporting is extremely difficult. IPs seem to be unclear as to the legal nature of the prima facie case of unfitness which they must identify before reporting a director as being unfit. The law should be reformed to require them instead to report whenever they identify any matter which is significant for determining unfitness, thus reflecting what appears already to be their current practice. Expecting a consistent prediction from them that, despite instances of unfit conduct by a director, it would not be prima facie in the public interest to disqualify is unrealistic and impracticable. More unfit returns would then be received by the Disqualification Unit of the DTI. The Unit is then best placed to tot up the matters of unfit conduct consistently, using any wider information available to them and to decide whether there is a prima facie case of unfitness that should be brought in the public interest....

The mandatory requirement to disqualify the unfit for at least two years has the result that the courts will not consider the current suitability of a director to manage a company but must disqualify even if it is no longer in the public interest to do so. Abolition of this mandatory requirement should therefore be considered. On the other hand, where a director is found currently to be unfit a long disqualification may be justified. Sentencing guidelines which currently lead to short disqualifications should be reviewed if necessary by legislation. The powers of the High Court should also be extended to disqualification for an indefinite period, thus maximising the protective effect in serious cases and putting the onus on the individual to apply for leave to undertake a particular management role.

For a whole range of reasons, the courts are not best adapted to assessing the fitness of individuals to take part in the management of companies. Disqualification trials have thus become a costly and artificial exercise which determine not whether the person is currently a risk to the public but whether they have, in the past, infringed the required technical standards of unfitness. The public resources and expertise of the DTI are arrayed against the individual who often feels that access to justice is denied. It is therefore proposed that a Director Disqualification Tribunal should be established to hear applications for disqualification for unfitness. It should also hear applications for leave to take part in management by those disqualified on all grounds including bankruptcy. A tribunal with informal proceedings more in the nature of a professional disciplinary hearing, should have many advantages. It would be better able to consider what is only partially a legal issue and offer a fairer trial and better access to justice. It should also be better able to advance consistently the policy of the legislation.

To improve the ability of the legislation to promote best practice towards creditors, a Directors' Code for Creditors should be drawn up, pulling together the principles found in the legislation and developed through case law. The courts would be required to judge an individual's conduct against this code when deciding whether a director is unfit. The code, which should be supplied to all directors by Companies House, would answer the criticism that there are at present no accessible best practice guidelines to assist the well-intentioned director. Its dissemination would also enhance the moral justification of a disqualification where the code is clearly infringed.

Any call for automatic disqualification on corporate insolvency or for disqualification by administrative means and not by an independent court or tribunal should be resisted. The current proposal [see NOTE below] that legislation be introduced to allow disqualifications to be made without a court hearing where the respondent so 'agrees' is not a desirable reform. The burden on the individual of resisting an application by the DTI is so great that consent to a disqualification can hardly be refused and is almost inevitable. Such a process could therefore be oppressive and could appear to be anti-enterprise. The better way to relieve the courts of the pressure of disqualification cases is the swifter and more accessible process of the Director Disqualification Tribunal proposed above.

Other approaches to the regulation of companies

Much attention has been given to the disqualification of unfit directors of failed companies, but the disqualification, under section 2, of those convicted of criminal offences in connection with the management of a company has had a relatively low profile. Criminality is a substantial reason for disqualifying and attention should be given to reviewing sentencing policy in this respect in order to achieve more disqualifications. Consideration could also be given to reforms enabling a disqualification where the offence was not in connection with management of a company, where a conviction occurred outside this jurisdiction, and where an offence has been committed but has not led to a conviction.

There may be other, better and more cost-effective ways of deterring misconduct and establishing best practice than the disqualification of unfit directors. The criminal law should be reviewed to ensure that it can properly perform the punitive function that disqualification is sometimes seen as performing. New, strict-liability offences and civil penalties which penalise the misuse of corporate property to the detriment of creditors could be highly effective, being easier to prove than the broad and uncertain test of unfitness. However, care has to be taken not to discourage valid enterprise and risk-taking and that business failure is not unfairly stigmatised....

Requiring errant directors to compensate creditors has not only a deterrent and a formative effect: it also provides some redress for wrong caused. Yet despite trading at risk to creditors being the most common default alleged against unfit directors, none of the disqualified directors who answered the questionnaire had a wrongful trading or other claim made against them. The laws enabling compensation to be recovered from directors should be reviewed. This could include the possibility of a disqualifying court making a compensation order and of the Insolvency Service providing resources in a number of possible ways for pursuing wrongful trading or other compensation claims.

The ease of incorporating companies and recent deregulation to make them more efficient has made limited liability accessible to huge numbers of small businesses, some of whose directors are not prepared to undertake the consequential responsibilities to creditors. If fewer of these businesses traded as limited companies, the incidence of abuse of limited liability would fall. A compulsory minimum capital would be a modest entry fee which would give pause for thought before setting up a limited company. The development of a new, unlimited, corporate vehicle (such as an incorporated partnership or the 'business corporation' proposed in my previous research paper for ACCA) would also diminish the number of limited companies formed by smaller businesses. The small business sector would then have a real choice between a simple unlimited corporate form for whose debts the proprietors are liable or the limited company which inevitably means more regulation and special responsibilities to creditors. Disqualification would then be more justifiable as it would withdraw from the abuser of limited liability that privilege only but not the legitimate opportunity to use a corporate business structure without limited liability.

NOTE: This proposal has now been enacted by the Insolvency Act 2000 as a new s. 1A of the CDDA, which enables the Secretary of State to accept an undertaking by a director not to act as a director etc. for an 'agreed' period of up to 15 years. Many uncontested disqualification cases are now being dealt with more cheaply and, one hopes, more quickly under this procedure. New s. 8A enabling a person subject to a disqualification undertaking to apply to the court for a variation of the undertaking means that giving an undertaking does not finally burn one's boats. Even so it does not in any way relieve those who feel that they should not be disqualified from the excessive burden of challenging the State machine and establishing their fitness to take part in management. Many individuals may be highly aggrieved as they will feel pressurised to sign a disqualification undertaking by the high cost of defending a disqualification application and by the fear of an order for costs being made against them if their defence is unsuccessful.

Re Sevenoaks Stationers (Retail) Ltd

Disqualification for unfitness

[1991] BCLC 325, [1991] Ch 164, Court of Appeal

This case attempts to set principles for disqualification for unfitness based on a tariff for cases of greater and lesser seriousness.

Facts   Mr Cruddas was a director of five companies which went insolvent leaving debts of £559,000 unpaid. Though he was a chartered accountant, in Dillon LJ's view 'absence of proper financial control, which was Mr Cruddas's responsibility, was the main reason for the failure of the five companies with such large deficiencies'. The accounts of the companies had not been properly audited and the accounting records of one of them were not properly kept. Proven allegations of mismanagement against Mr Cruddas are set out in the following extract. The Court of Appeal reduced the period of disqualification from seven to five years. (Non-payment of Crown debts was also regarded as a serious default but this will no longer be of significance as the Crown's preference in respect of PAYE, VAT and National Insurance contributions collected by an employer has been abolished. See 20.8.)

DILLON LJ: Mr Michael Cruddas, a chartered accountant, appeals against an order made by Harman J on 15 November 1989 ([1990] BCLC 668) under s. 6 of the Company Directors Disqualification Act 1986 whereby the judge disqualified him for a period of seven years from being, without the leave of the court, a director of a company or in any way concerned or taking part in the promotion formation or management of a company. . . .

   The main point urged for Mr Cruddas on this appeal was however that the period of seven years' suspension imposed by the judge was too long. In that regard this appeal has an importance beyond its own facts, since it is the first appeal against a disqualification order which has come to this court. . . .

   I would for my part endorse the division of the potential 15-year disqualification period into three brackets, which was put forward by Mr Keenan for the official receiver to Harman J in the present case and has been put forward by Mr Charles for the official receiver in other cases, viz: (i) The top bracket of disqualification for periods over 10 years should be reserved for particularly serious cases. These may include cases where a director who has already had one period of disqualification imposed on him falls to be disqualified yet again. (ii) The minimum bracket of two to five years' disqualification should be applied where, though disqualification is mandatory, the case is, relatively, not very serious. (iii) The middle bracket of disqualification for from six to ten years should apply for serious cases which do not merit the top bracket.

   I will come back to the appropriate bracket and period of disqualification when I have considered the facts and other issues. . . .

   The term 'Crown debts' has become a term of art on applications for the disqualification of directors under s. 6 or under the legislation which preceded the 1986 Act. It denotes debts due from the company in question to the Crown in respect of PAYE, national insurance contributions and

VAT, but not debts due to the Crown in respect of other matters (such as development grants). The judgments at first instance of judges in the Chancery Division appear to show a considerable difference in approach to the significance of Crown debts, as so interpreted, in relation to the disqualification of directors. One of the matters we have to consider on this appeal is the correctness of the explanations of law in certain judgments, and the correctness of Harman J's assessment of the significance of the Crown debts in the present case.

It is beyond dispute that the purpose of s. 6 is to protect the public, and in particular potential creditors of companies, from losing money through companies becoming insolvent when the directors of those companies are people unfit to be concerned in the management of a company.

The test laid down in s. 6, apart from the requirement that the person concerned is or has been a director of a company which has become insolvent, is whether the person's conduct as a director of the company or companies in question 'makes him unfit to be concerned in the management of a company'. These are ordinary words of the English language and they should be simple to apply in most cases. It is important to hold to those words in each case.

The judges of the Chancery Division have, understandably, attempted in certain cases to give guidance as to what does or does not make a person unfit to be concerned in the management of a company. Thus in *Re Lo-Line Electric Motors Ltd* [1988] Ch 477 at p. 486 Browne-Wilkinson V-C said:

> Ordinary commercial misjudgment is in itself not sufficient to justify disqualification. In the normal case, the conduct complained of must display a lack of commercial probity, although I have no doubt in an extreme case of gross negligence or total incompetence disqualification could be appropriate.

Then he said that the director in question—

> has been shown to have behaved in a commercially culpable manner in trading through limited companies when he knew them to be insolvent and in using the unpaid Crown debts to finance such trading. ([1988] Ch 477 at p. 492.)

Such statements may be helpful in identifying particular circumstances in which a person would clearly be unfit. But there seems to have been a tendency, which I deplore, on the part of the Bar and possibly also on the part of the Official Receiver's Department, to treat the statements as judicial paraphrases of the words of the statute which fall to be construed as a matter of law in lieu of the words of the statute. The result is to obscure that the true question to be tried is a question of fact, what used to be pejoratively described in the Chancery Division as 'a jury question'. . . .

This is not a case in which it was alleged that Mr Cruddas had, in the colloquial phrase, 'ripped off' the public and pocketed the proceeds. On the contrary, and as the judge found, he had lost a lot of his own money which he had put into Rochester and Retail. There was evidence that Mr Cruddas had remortgaged his home to raise money to pay creditors of the companies, and he claimed to have lost from £200,000 to £250,000 of his own money. . . .

I turn next to the question of Crown debts . . .

Mr Cruddas made a deliberate decision to pay only those creditors who pressed for payment. The obvious result was that the two companies traded, when in fact insolvent and known to be in difficulties at the expense of those creditors who, like the Crown, happened not to be pressing for payment. Such conduct on the part of a director can well, in my judgment, be relied on as a ground for saying that he is unfit to be concerned in the management of a company. But what is relevant in the Crown's position is not that the debt was a debt which arose from a compulsory deduction from employees' wages or a compulsory payment of VAT, but that the Crown was not pressing for payment, and the director was taking unfair advantage of that forbearance on the part of the Crown, and, instead of providing adequate working capital, was trading at the Crown's expense while the companies were in jeopardy. It would be equally unfair to trade in that way and in such circumstances at the expense of creditors other than the Crown. . . .

Taking that view of the Crown debts in Rochester and Retail and adding to it (i) that there were never any audited accounts of any of the five companies, let alone registered accounts (ii) the inadequacy of the accounting records of Retail (iii) the loan by Retail to Rochester (iv) the payment of debts of Hoo Paper by Hoo Waste Paper (v) the guarantee given by Sevenoaks Stationers for liabilities of Hoo Paper (vi) the continued trading while insolvent and known to be in difficulties of Rochester and Retail and (vii) the extent of the deficiency in each company after a relatively short period of trading, I have no doubt at all that it is amply proved that Mr Cruddas is unfit to be concerned in the management of a company. His trouble is not dishonesty, but incompetence or negligence in a very marked degree and that is enough to render him unfit; I do not think it is necessary for incompetence to be 'total', as suggested by the Vice-Chancellor in *Re Lo-Line Electric Motors Ltd*, to render a director unfit to take part in the management of a company.

Re Westmid Packing Services Ltd

A pillar of the community

[1998] 2 All ER 124, Court of Appeal

This important Court of Appeal case states that a board of directors of a company has a collective responsibility based on the individual responsibility of each director to inform himself about its affairs and to join with his co-directors in supervising and controlling them. Directors who allow one director to dominate them and to use them in an improper and dishonest course of conduct of which they are unaware are liable to be found to be unfit and disqualified. The court also stated that as a finding of unfitness is based solely on past misconduct, and as such a finding makes a disqualification order of at least two years mandatory, a disqualification order may be made where the person has in the intervening period conducted himself properly and so is evidently no longer a danger to the public.

Facts　Mr Griffiths was the controlling shareholder and the driving force behind the company. He was a 'pillar of the community' and his two co-directors were impressed by him and trusted him. He treated them more like employees than directors and excluded them from full participation and access to accounts and other important management information. However, when the company failed it became apparent that Griffiths was a rogue. He was disqualified for nine years and they for the minimum period of two years. The Secretary of State appealed, seeking to increase their period of disqualification The court dismissed this appeal saying that the Judge's exercise of his discretion had not been wrong in principle. It went on to comment on the purposes for which disqualification orders are made. It also indicated that wider indicators of current fitness (in this case the current success of the two respondents in responsibly directing a company with the leave of the court) may not be adduced to prove their fitness in order to resist a disqualification order, but may be relevant in mitigating the length of the disqualification.

LORD WOOLF MR:　That is sufficient to dispose of this appeal. But we wish to ensure that our dismissal of the Secretary of State's respondent's notice does not convey the wrong message. We also wish to give some general guidance as to what is relevant and admissible evidence for the purpose of determining the length of the disqualification period, and for the purposes of any application under s.17 of the Act [by a disqualified person seeking leave to be a director of a specific company].

(1) It is of the greatest importance that any individual who undertakes the statutory and fiduciary obligations of being a company director should realise that these are inescapable personal responsibilities. The appellants may have been dazzled, manipulated and deceived by Mr Griffiths but they were in breach of their own duties in allowing this to happen. They can count themselves fortunate to have received the minimum period of disqualification and to have had the benefit of immediate orders under s. 17 of the Act....

(3) In *Re Lo-Line Electric Motors Ltd* [1988] Ch 477 Browne-Wilkinson V-C said that the primary purpose of s. 300 of the Companies Act 1985 [the predecessor of s. 6 of the Company Directors Disqualification Act 1986] was to protect the public against the future conduct of companies by persons whose past records as directors of insolvent companies showed them to be a danger to creditors and others. That statement has often been approved by this court. But there is often a

considerable time lag between the conduct complained of, its discovery and the disqualification proceedings actually coming to court.... One result of delay when it does occur is that there are occasions when disqualification must be ordered even though, by reason of the director's recognition of his previous failings and the way he has conducted himself since the conduct complained of, he is in fact no longer a danger to the public at all. In such cases it is no longer necessary for the director to be kept 'off the road' for the protection of the public, but other factors come into play in the wider interests of protecting the public, i.e. a deterrent element in relation to the director himself and a deterrent element as far as other directors are concerned. Despite the fact that the courts have said disqualification is not a 'punishment', in truth the exercise that is being engaged in is little different from any sentencing exercise. The period of disqualification must reflect the gravity of the offence. It must contain deterrent elements. That is what sentencing is all about, and that is what fixing the appropriate period of the disqualification is all about. What Vinelott J (in *Re Pamstock Ltd* [1994] 1 BCLC 716 at 73 7) called 'tunnel vision', i.e. concentration on the facts of the offence, is necessary when considering whether a director is unfit. In relation to the period of disqualification the facts of the offence are still obviously important but many other factors ought (and in reality do) come into play....

(7) ...A wide variety of matters—including the former director's age and state of health, the length of time he has been in jeopardy, whether he has admitted the offence, his general conduct before and after the offence, and the periods of disqualification of his co-directors that may have been ordered by other courts—may be relevant and admissible in determining the appropriate period of disqualification.

Nick Leeson and the Barings debacle

The story of how Nick Leeson, the 'rogue trader' dealing on behalf of Barings Bank in derivatives on the Singapore International Monetary Exchange, brought about the collapse of this centuries-old bank with losses of almost a billion pounds is now the subject of a major film. While Barings in London thought Leeson was making massive profits he was in fact losing money on a huge scale. When he contacted London to say 'please send more dosh' to support his trading, the directors transmitted funds in Monopoly money figures ending with large numbers of noughts. The bank went bust, Leeson got the Go to Jail card and some of the directors tried to pass Go and collect their annual bonuses.

The directors faced disciplinary proceedings before the Securities and Futures Authority, which imposed various sanctions including in some cases restrictions on their employment in the City. The bank went into administration and the administrator made returns to the Insolvency Service detailing the directors' alleged unfit conduct. Two disqualification orders were made unopposed, five were made under the *Carecraft* procedure and three directors defended the application for disqualification. They were accused of failing to monitor Leeson, failing to monitor appropriate limits on trading risks, failing to question how such high profits were being made and having inadequate compliance systems in place, such as allowing Leeson to run his own 'back office' in Singapore. (Thus he was able to operate the accounts for his own trading and so could hide his continuing mistakes.)

In *Re Barings plc (No. 5)* [1999] 1 BCLC 433 Jonathan Parker J, in a 180-page judgment, disqualified all three directors. He held that their failures, including failing to heed warnings of malpractice, were 'incompetence' of a sufficiently high degree to justify disqualification. 'If a manager does not properly understand the business he is seeking to manage he will be unable to take informed management decisions in relation to it.' While directors may delegate functions to employees, adequate systems and a certain level of supervision are essential in order to avoid a finding of unfitness. He concluded that the following general propositions can be derived from the authorities as to the directors' duties:

(i) Directors have, both collectively and individually, a continuing duty to acquire and maintain a sufficient knowledge and understanding of the company's business to enable them properly to discharge their duties as directors.

(ii) Whilst directors are entitled (subject to the articles of association of the company) to delegate particular functions to those below them in the management chain, and to trust their competence and integrity to a reasonable extent, the exercise of the power of delegation does not absolve a director from the duty to supervise the discharge of the delegated functions.

(iii) No rule of universal application can be formulated as to the duty referred to in (ii) above. The extent of the duty, and the question whether it has been discharged, must depend on the facts of each particular case, including the director's role in the management of the company.

On 25 February 2000 the Court of Appeal ([2000] 1 BCLC 523) confirmed the first-instance decision in every respect. They concluded that Baker's conduct involved a serious abdication of responsibility by a senior director of the principal operating subsidiary of a major public company. He had taken insufficient steps to understand the nature of the business Leeson was carrying on. He had failed to heed even clear warning signals and had simply hoped for the best. It was plain that he had not performed his duty and although he was not the only director at fault, that could not excuse the effect of his own conduct.

While it may be that the Barings directors did not exhibit sufficient competence to trust them with management of a major bank, the consequence is that they were disqualified from being a director of each and every small high street business in the country. As *The Times* put it (4 March 1998), 'the latest blackballed Barings bosses were punished for incompetence, failing to monitor Nick Leeson and ignoring warning signs, such as disgracefully high profits. Fair enough. But if such tests were applied rigorously, swathes of Britain's boardrooms would be emptied at a stroke.' The difficulty for the courts is deciding at what point 'mere incompetence' becomes such an improper abrogation of responsibility that it is an abuse of the privilege of limited liability and so justifies a disqualification. But it has to be remembered that the whole purpose of limited liability is to protect entrepreneurs against the risks of setting up a business, including the consequences of their own mistakes. Incompetence alone should therefore rarely be sufficient grounds for a disqualification order.

12

Directors' Duties

As has been seen in chapter 8, the board of directors has general powers of management and is subject to very limited control by the shareholders in general meeting. To prevent abuse of powers, directors are subject to certain duties imposed by law. As explained at 11.1, directors owe strict trustee-like duties to the company in exercising these powers, including fiduciary duties to be explained below. They also owe a duty of care and skill. These duties were developed by judges over the years on a case by case basis. However, cases on directors' fiduciary duties and duty of care and skills had become complex and sometimes inconsistent. As a result, after lengthy discussion by the Law Commission and the Steering Group (see extract in 12.2), the Government finally enacted a statutory statement of the directors' fiduciary duties and duty of care and skill in Part 10 Chapter 2 (ss. 170–177) of CA 2006.

In addition to the fiduciary duties and the duty of care and skill, a wide range of statutory provisions also impose various duties on directors, e.g., to keep proper books of account, to lay profit and loss accounts and balance sheets before the company's general meeting, to make a director's report etc. But to further supplement the fiduciary duty to avoid conflict of interest, Part X of the Companies Act 1985 was enacted to regulate dealings by directors with the company. However, Part X was widely perceived as being extremely detailed, fragmented, excessive and in some respects a defective means of regulating directors. Many criticisms were made of its provisions to the DTI by directors and other users of company law. Again, after some lengthy discussion by the Law Commission and the Steering Group, Part X was substantially revised and replaced by Part 10, Chapters 3 to 6 (ss. 182–231) of CA 2006.

12.1 GUIDING PRINCIPLES FOR THE NEW LAW

The principles relating to directors' duties of care and skill and fiduciary duties have been developed on a case-by-case basis by the court without a set of coherent, and well-thought-out guiding principles suitable for the development of company law as a whole. Indeed such a process is not possible with the common law judicial process whereby legal principles are formulated and reshaped incrementally. Part X of the Companies Act 1985 was of course a legislative product, but was not seemingly informed by such guiding principles, or if it were, such principles were not clearly articulated. In reforming the law, the Law Commission stood back from the detail and complexity of the law, and the problems which they sought to address, and asked in somewhat abstract terms what policy approach the law should seek to adopt and came up with a list of guiding principles which now form the basis of the new law. Before we examine the new law on directors' duties in detail, it would be useful for readers to bear in mind those guiding principles and the relevant economic considerations which are now extracted.

Law Commission and Scottish Law Commission, *Company Directors: Regulating Conflicts of Interests and Formulating a Statement of Duties*
(Consultation Paper No. 153)
(London: Stationery Office, 1998)

Part 2 Guiding principles for reform

Guiding principles for directors' dealings and duties?

2.17 We suggest for consideration by consultees that the following are the key principles that should apply in the area of core company law covered by this project:

(1) *A principle of separate but interdependent roles for shareholders and directors:* We provisionally consider that any reform of the law in this area should recognise that the roles of shareholders and directors are separate but interdependent. Of course the precise roles may be varied by the articles in some companies such as joint venture companies or in practice where the shareholders are all directors and the distinction between their two roles is blurred. But the law should start from the recognition that usually directors and shareholders have quite separate roles in the company. Directors manage the business while shareholders monitor their stewardship. However the roles of shareholders and directors are *mutually interdependent* and the law should strike an appropriate *balance* between their respective interests. Shareholders are not in a position to control the activities of directors on a day-to-day basis, and this means that the law has to impose some restrictions on the activities of directors. On the other hand management must also have freedom from unnecessary shareholder interference. This freedom is one of the principles identified in the Law Commission's Shareholder Remedies project. In the context of shareholder remedies, this principle was left to be mediated through the courts. That is less likely to be the route available in this context and therefore care has to be taken to see that where it is absent there are other mechanisms to subject directors to appropriate scrutiny and sanctions.

(2) *Law as facilitator principle:* Law in this area should facilitate and not impede the conduct of proper business transactions. . . .

(3) *Appropriate sanctions principle:* There must be a flexible range of sanctions and consideration should be given to whether the existing sanctions for any particular breach are effective and realistic. . . .

(4) *A company-specific principle:* The rules which emanate from this project must be tested against the different sorts of companies to which they apply and where the appropriate different rules should be devised for different types of company. This raises the question of how companies are appropriately classified in this area.

(5) *An inclusive principle:* In Part X [of the Companies Act 1985] generally and in the formulation of directors' duties under the general law, due regard must be paid, to the extent to which the law from time to time allows this, to the obligation of directors to consider other constituency interests apart from those of shareholders. In this respect, the law must have an in-built elasticity to permit organic growth and development.

(6) *A usability principle:* The law in this area must be accessible, comprehensible, clear and consistent with common sense. It must also meet business needs and be built on a proper understanding of how business works.

(7) *A certainty principle*: The prescriptive rules of Part X must be clear and certain so that directors can be advised or decide for themselves without difficulty whether a particular transaction falls within their ambit or not. There is rather a special need for certainty in this area because generally there is no time to go to court to determine the question of law: the opportunity which it was desired to pursue will no longer be capable of being pursued if the parties have to wait for a court decision. But the principle of certainty as we see it has to be applied with caution. First, the existence of prescriptive rules can sometimes be self-defeating: because they are construed very literally, it is often possible, with a little ingenuity, to 'drive a coach and horses' through them. In circumstances such as these the courts have sometimes, but not often, been prepared to recharacterise the transaction and in tax law the courts have gone further and devised rules to disregard artificial transactions. Second, it is also the case that even in the Companies Acts Parliament has had to include provisions which are very general and imprecise such as 'shadow director', 'subsidiary undertaking', 'financial assistance', directors' 'interests' in transactions. While therefore we see that in general the rules of Part X should be abundantly clear in their scope, we consider that users of company law must recognise that there are going to be situations where, from the nature of the subject matter, this is not achievable.

(8) *An 'enough but not excessive' principle*: Part X must strike the right balance between necessary regulation and freedom for directors to make business decisions. It should not be criticised simply for failing to deal with every possible permutation of facts or eventuality. Part X should ideally seek to regulate in those areas and in those ways in which legal regulation call be effective. If consultees agree with this statement in principle, we invite them to give us their views as to how effective regulation might be achieved. It may be difficult to apply the ideal without research which may not be currently available. This ideal also leads to the question of what legal doctrines should be developed and/or legislated for to achieve the most effective regulatory result.

(9) *A principle of ample but efficient disclosure*: Disclosure, like sunlight in Justice Brandeis's famous phrase, is the best disinfectant. It is one of the best ways of achieving high standards, since, although directors are not prohibited from doing that which they have to disclose, they will not in general be willing to see disclosed that which, though not illegal, may subject them to criticism. On the other hand disclosure carries its own cost, both direct and indirect, and the consequences of information being available in the public domain. Care must be taken to ensure that the costs of disclosure do not outweigh its utility.

(10) *The principle of efficiency and cost effectiveness*: As with the law relating to shareholders' remedies, the law in the field covered by this project too must be made as efficient and cost-effective as can be achieved in the circumstances. Thus in the context of disclosure it is important to bear in mind not merely the need to avoid the risk of information overload, but also the waste of costs and management resources which may result from an obligation to disclose information to shareholders which shareholders do not need to perform their function. Such waste tends to diminish a company's ability to perform well and to be competitive.

(11) *The commercial judgment principle*: There are areas of company law in which the courts pass judgment on what are essentially, commercial matters, such as whether putting a company into administration is likely to lead to its survival as a going concern. But the general principle, in a review of an act said to have constituted a breach of duty, should be that the courts do not substitute their judgment for that of the directors made in good faith. In the context of this project the rationale for such a principle may be more a need to provide the right incentives to directors to take proper commercial risks, than because the courts would not be able to review the commercial wisdom of the decision. On the other hand there will be circumstances where despite this general approach the court has to reject the view of the directors, for instance because they acted for an irrelevant purpose.

(12) *The principle of sanctity of contract*: [A person is bound by the terms of the agreement that he made and the court is not given power to relieve him from that contract.] There are, however, examples within the scope of this project where the company is relieved of a contract because

some mandatory rule in Part X or the general law is not complied with. In addition the court has power under s. 727 of the Companies Act 1985 in limited circumstances to relieve a director from the consequences of breach of duty. The matter can be approached on the basis that these points only illustrate the principle. The starting point is that the law will generally uphold contractual relationships....

Part 3 Economic considerations

Conclusions

3.92 The main conclusions of this part may be restated:

(1) The contribution of this economic analysis has been threefold: to identify economic rationales for the existing body of law; to identify possible outcomes of legal reform; and to indicate the main areas in which further, empirical research would be desirable.

(2) Company law can be seen as having a number of economic purposes, in particular: (1) promoting efficient bargaining between corporate actors; (2) protecting the interests of third parties (such as creditors) who may be affected by negative externalities, that is to say, unbargained for costs which are imposed upon them by transactions between others; and (3) providing incentives for cooperation, thereby promoting innovation and competitiveness.

(3) The underlying principle of legal regulation in this area should be the achievement of procedural fairness in the regulation of self-dealing and other conflicts of duty and interest, that is to say the specification of the conditions under which disclosure, approval, release and ratification are needed in order to avoid liability, rather than an outright prohibition on all conflicts of duty and interest.

(4) A restatement of the fiduciary duties of directors should make some reference to the possibility of the avoidance of liability through disclosure, approval, release and ratification.

(5) There is a case for constituting the fiduciary principle in the form of a *penalty default rule* which places the onus of avoiding liability through disclosure ratification etc. on the fiduciary.

(6) Absolute prohibitions on certain types of transactions can be justified only where there is a significant risk that the transactions in question would give rise to a negative externality or unbargained for effect imposed upon a third party (such as harm to the interests of creditors. sufficient to outweigh the gains to the internal corporate actors) or where they would harm a significant public interest (such as the need to maintain market integrity).

(7) The guiding principle for disclosure should be to ensure that each organ of the company (board, shareholders) receives from management the information which it needs to have in order to be confident that it has carried out its monitoring function. Hence, the shareholders must have sufficient information to enable them to decide whether the directors are acting in good faith in the best interests of the company. Two further factors place a limit on efficient disclosure; firstly, the need for confidentiality, that is to say, the problem that excessive disclosure of information may destroy the value of that information; and, secondly, the costs incurred in the process of dissemination.

(8) On this basis, the provisions of Part X do not constitute a consistent approach to the imposition of disclosure and ratification requirements. In particular, the rules governing shareholders' approval for certain terms of service contracts do not reveal a coherent scheme, since the basis on which certain terms but not others are singled out for approval is not apparent. This means that the regulatory intent of the legislation can be avoided through contracting, which in itself may be costly.

(9) These considerations suggest that there may be merit in moving towards a general principle of disclosure to the shareholders of information concerning self-dealing and other conflicts of duty and interest and directors' contracts. Shareholder approval and/or ratification etc. would be required only in a smaller number of cases, where there was a danger of the depletion of corporate

assets from particular types of transactions or where the agreed division of powers between the board and the shareholders was in danger of being undermined.

(10) Under the present state of both English and Scots law, the existence of a restitutionary element in civil damages for breach of fiduciary duty by directors can be justified as providing an efficient incentive against disloyalty.

(11) A role for criminal sanctions in the enforcement of fiduciary duties may be defended on economic grounds. However, this point is subject to certain qualifications: first, the limits of criminal liability must be clearly set, and, secondly, low-level sanctions, such as fines, are probably appropriate.

(12) Conversely, there would be a strong case for decriminalisation in respect of Part X of the Companies Act 1985 if more effective alternative means were to be found for monitoring and detecting illicit self-dealing, such as lower-cost civil litigation by shareholders, or for improved internal monitoring (for example, by non-executive directors).

(13) If the standard of care for directors' duties of care and skill is raised, possible problems are that directors may be deterred from taking normal business risks, in particular if there are limits to the availability of insurance; non-executive directors may be unable to overcome insider domination by executive directors and officers; and internal systems of communication, through which the board ensures internal compliance with its general instructions, may break down, in each case preventing the board from acting as an effective monitor of employees' performance.

(14) To avoid possible adverse effects, consideration should be given to the adoption, within a restatement of the duty of care, of a general 'business judgment' defence, the effect of which would be to provide some protection with regard to decisions within the range of normal business risks. A role for more specific limits on directors' personal liability, in the form of checklists for compliance with due diligence, could also be considered.

12.2 A STATUTORY STATEMENT OF DUTIES?

In the Law Commissions' Report extracted below, the Commissions consider the question of whether there should be a statutory statement of directors' duties.

Law Commission and Scottish Law Commission, *Company Directors: Regulating Conflicts of Interests and Formulating a Statement of Duties* (Law Com. No. 261)
(London: Stationery Office, 1999)

Part 4 A statutory statement of directors' duties?

Full or partial codification

Consultation issues

4.4 In the Paper, we proposed two main options for codifying directors' duties: *full codification* or *partial codification*.

4.5 *Full codification* would be a statutory statement of all a director's fiduciary duties as well as his duty of care and skill. It would be an exhaustive statement and would entirely replace the general law.

4.6 *Partial codification* would be a statement of the main, settled duties, including the director's duty of care. It would not be exhaustive. The general law would continue to apply in those areas not covered by statute. It would, however, be superseded in relation to the duties set out in the statement.

4.7 We discussed in the Paper how *full codification* might make the law more consistent, certain, accessible and comprehensible. However, we noted that some duties are not well-settled. It might therefore be difficult to state them in statutory form. For example, a director is in breach of duty if he misappropriates information which he has received and should have reported to his board. But the courts have not defined the circumstances in which he ought to report. The Paper observed that views are likely to differ on what those circumstances should be. To put duties that were not yet well-settled into statutory form might well restrict the ability of the law to develop. Importantly, with any codification, the approach of those who use it and advise on its meaning is likely to change from one of looking at the policy or principle behind the decided cases to one of statutory interpretation of the wording used. Likewise 'the court's task is diverted into one of statutory construction' (Lord Millett).

4.8 This was an argument that was also advanced against codification of a director's duty of care. We explained how the standard of care which the director must show in carrying out his functions has evolved over the century to adapt to changing commercial circumstances. To set the standard out in statute would freeze it at the time of enactment. We also observed, though, that stating it in statutory form would clarify the law and make it more certain.

4.9 If the statutory statement of duties covers only those duties that are settled and if the general law continues to apply in those areas not expressly governed by statute *(partial codification)*, a director might be confused to discover that he was subject to other duties not set out in the statement. However, it was noted that the statement could be drafted to make it clear that a director was subject to other duties. This is the position in some of the common law jurisdictions.

An additional statutory statement

4.10 We also considered a statutory statement of a director's principal duties which would be in addition to the general law. However, we have not pursued this option. It would be open to the strong objection that the director would find himself subject to two overlapping regimes covering the same subject matter, one under the general law and one under statute.

Drafting of statement: general or detailed?

4.11 In the Paper we explained that the statement of a director's duties could be drafted in detail setting out all the circumstances in which duties might conceivably arise. Alternatively it could be framed as a general statement of broader principles.

4.12 The main argument in favour of a detailed statement is that it might make the law more accessible to directors and might help to make it more consistent and certain, reducing the scope for judicial development. The argument against it is the converse: the flexibility of the law would be lost.

4.13 By contrast the advantage of a statement expressed in broad and general language is that it would leave some scope for flexibility and development. The corollary is that the statement would be less certain and less accessible. It would in many cases need to be scrutinised and explained by legal advisers to see how it applied to a particular case. An example of this style is the draft statement set out in Appendix A to the Paper, which also forms Appendix A to this report.

Questions for consultees

4.14 We asked consultees whether there should be *full* or *partial codification* or an additional statutory statement. We also asked which of the fiduciary duties described in the Paper could be considered as settled, and whether there was any objection to a statutory statement of the duty of care without a statutory statement of the fiduciary duties of directors.

Summary of respondents' views

4.15 Most respondents were not in favour of *full codification*. One of the most common arguments against it was that in an effort to retain some flexibility and allow for judicial development, the duties would have to be stated widely and in general terms. The general language would require interpretation by the courts: directors without ready access to legal advice (the main beneficiaries of the exercise) would, therefore, have no better idea of their duties. One respondent said that a lack of precision could give considerable scope to those looking for grounds upon which to defend disqualification proceedings or offer mitigation.

4.16 The duties might, of course, be drafted in a more detailed and specific way. Most respondents thought that this would reduce the likelihood of directors reading the statement, particularly if legalistic language was used. Again, it was considered that this would not improve the accessibility of the law to lay directors. Many respondents emphasised that if directors' duties were set out in detail, the law might be too rigid and would lack the present flexibility to cope with and reflect continuing developments. It was also felt that once the duties were embodied in legislation, there was a danger that directors and their legal advisers would merely comply with the letter of the law as opposed to its spirit.

4.17 It was generally thought that codification was only possible for duties that were well-settled and were not contentious. Many respondents argued that there are only a number of fiduciary duties within this category (such as the duty to act in good faith in what the director considers to be the company's interests). Other duties were dynamic and subject to constant commercial development (such as the duty not to misuse corporate opportunities). One respondent thought that, due to their dynamic nature, directors' fiduciary duties could never be effectively put into statutory form, and consequently any statement would be vague and incomplete.

4.18 There was also concern that a codifying statute (whether framed as a general or detailed statement) might produce an unexpected result, which could then only be remedied by further legislation.

4.19 Not all respondents were against *full codification*. A number of respondents, including the Law Society of Scotland, the Stock Exchange and KPMG, indicated varying levels of support for this option. Several respondents, such as the Stock Exchange, thought that a full binding statement of duties was the best option in terms of the accessibility and certainty of the law (particularly for lay directors). Most in favour of codification thought that the statement should be in general terms. The courts would then be able to expand and 'flesh out' the duties.

4.20 The argument put forward in the Paper that codification may be impossible if there are differences of opinion was criticised by KPMG. They asked how directors and others are expected to understand and comply with the law if experts could not reach agreement about it. The difficulty of achieving *full codification* was no reason not to attempt it. Moreover, it could be argued that the common law has not been satisfactory in identifying the duties of directors. The courts can only develop the law as and when appropriate cases come before them. A more systematic and comprehensive approach to this area might, therefore, be beneficial.

4.21 A smaller majority of respondents also opposed *partial codification*. Many of the disadvantages and concerns identified in respect of *full codification* were said to apply equally to a partial binding statement. A common criticism was that although *partial codification* might maintain the flexibility of the law, it would also render it more uncertain by having some duties in a statutory statement and some under the general law. A partial binding statement was a potentially misleading substitute for a complete statement. It would not inform the director of the full range, extent and scope of his duties. A member of the judiciary commented that the director would not know what was omitted. This would defeat the object of certainty and accessibility which it was intended to provide. Two respondents were concerned that a director might use a statement of duties to support his case that he had done everything he reasonably needed to if the statement made no reference to duties in the area in which the director stood accused of misconduct.

4.22 However, there were a number of respondents who favoured *partial codification*, including the Institute of Chartered Accountants of Scotland, PIRC, PricewaterhouseCoopers and academics, such as Professor Wooldridge, Professor Parkinson and Professor Cheffins. The main reason for support was that it would best achieve a balance between certainty and flexibility. Setting out the main duties in statute would emphasise their seriousness. If done by general principles, codified duties could still be developed by the courts. This was the experience of Canada where there is *partial codification* of the main duties. Many respondents in favour of this option felt that *partial codification* might also be complemented by referring to the statement on prescribed forms or by non-binding explanatory material (such as pamphlets).

4.23 By contrast to the general views against codification (whether full or partial), a large majority of respondents were in favour of having a director's duty of skill and care set out in statute. It was felt that this would be generally useful and would clarify the standard of the duty. Of those who did not support this, most felt that there was no clear advantage when the common law had developed effectively and was also more flexible, particularly as the standard would have to apply to directors in different types of companies. A large majority of respondents also did not object to having a statutory statement of the duty of care without a statutory statement of fiduciary duties.

4.24 Generally respondents thought that an additional statutory statement would not be helpful. It was felt that a statutory statement that did not replace the general law but was in addition to it would be highly unsatisfactory and very misleading. Having a second layer of duties would be an additional burden without offering any obvious benefit. It was also considered that (as with *full* and *partial codification*) there were dangers that the statement might become inflexible and quickly outdated.

Summary of responses of directors: the empirical research

4.25 61 per cent of all directors surveyed in the empirical research thought that it would be helpful for the Appendix A statement to be set out in the Act, even though it would only be a partial statement of directors' duties. Respondents in non-listed companies, closed companies and companies with few non-executive directors were significantly more likely to approve of this suggestion.

4.26 Around a quarter of directors considered that the statement was likely to be of either great assistance or very great assistance. Approval was higher among directors of smaller, non-listed and closed companies as well as companies without non-executive directors. This is consonant with the suggestion that in larger and listed companies, where use is made of non-executive directors, internal corporate governance procedures already deal effectively with many of the issues raised in the statement. In addition these companies will usually have company secretaries and in-house legal staff who can give advice. However, in companies without such procedures, it would appear that the statement would play a valuable informative and guiding role.

Commentary on arguments against codification

4.27 We agree with the majority of our respondents that *full codification* is undesirable. The law governing directors' duties is dynamic. It continues to develop. For example, the courts have recently had to determine the duties of a director who has resigned, but who then uses commercial opportunities connected with the company's business for his own benefit. They have also considered the duties which directors owe when there are groups or classes of shareholders whose interests conflict. We expect that the law will need to continue to evolve incrementally as circumstances require. The commercial context is constantly changing. It is important that the law retains the capacity to develop.

4.28 For this reason we think that a *full codification* of directors' duties would not be desirable. To set out in statute duties that were still developing might restrict their ability to adapt to changing circumstances. However, not all duties are evolving. Many are settled. To state the settled duties in statutory form might increase the accessibility of the law.

4.29 We also agree with respondents' general view that an additional statutory statement would not be helpful. To have a statutory statement in addition to existing law could be misleading and therefore the law would not become more certain or accessible. This option would appear to add further complexity while offering little benefit. We therefore reject this option.

4.30 Partial codification of directors' fiduciary duties was not favoured by the majority of our respondents, but a slightly smaller majority did support the codification of a director's duty of care.

An explanation may, however, lie in the way in which the issues were presented. In relation to the duty of care, the codification issue was raised with respect to a particular duty. Respondents may have shared our view of the development of the modern law, and concluded with us that once the appropriate standard of care has been settled codification presents little difficulty. In relation to other duties, the partial codification issue was presented more generally, and could have included duties the boundaries of which are less well developed in the common law. The issue, therefore, may be less about the principle of partial codification, where the content of the duties is reasonably settled, than the identification of the duties which fall into that category.

4.31 We think that *partial codification* could be a valuable piece of law reform. We discuss below why we consider that the main arguments against a *partial codification*—loss of flexibility, uncertainty of its extent and no gain in accessibility—can be rebutted. We then explain why there are other reasons that make the case for *partial codification* a powerful one, namely the coherence of company law and the international dimension.

Loss of flexibility?

4.32 We do not accept the argument that there will necessarily be a loss of flexibility if any part of the law is codified. As was recently noted by the Joint Committee on Parliamentary Privilege on the question of whether to codify case law on parliamentary privilege, this is not the case if the law sets out general principles.

4.33 Concepts such as 'good faith in the interests of the company' and 'conflict of interest' which might be included in a *partial codification* are relatively easily understood. The difficulty which often arises is the application of such concepts to particular facts. If in a *partial codification* the duties are formulated using general language which addresses the principles on which detailed duties are based and avoids the level of detail which specifies the circumstances in which the duties arise, any loss of flexibility may not be significant. A distinction may be drawn between the meaning of a term such as 'conflict of interest' or 'reasonable care' and its content. While the meaning of the concept is understood, the content of a duty may vary in different circumstances and be developed by the judiciary over time. The more abstract the rule, the less useful it is to the director or legal adviser who seeks to apply it to the facts of a particular case. Nevertheless, the benefit of *partial codification* is that the general statement of duties is available in the Act.

4.34 Although Appendix A was drafted as a non-binding explanatory statement, it contains the level of detail which we envisage in a *partial codification*. Indeed a comparison between the duty of care in the non-binding explanatory statement and draft s. 309A (also in Appendix A of the Paper), shows a very similar level of detail. Many of the words in this statement, such as 'the interests of the company' and 'the company's property, information or opportunities', are capable of significant judicial interpretation.

4.35 We had asked consultees whether they considered that the draft statement in Appendix A set out the principal duties of directors under the general law. The consensus on consultation was that it did set out the principal duties. Furthermore, over 80 per cent of directors in the empirical survey also thought that the statement was about right in terms of content. This does not mean that Appendix A could not be improved and we would expect that the outcome of the debates in the Company Law Review may affect the content of the statement. For example, it could contain a duty to act honestly, on the basis that this would impose an objective standard of behaviour (which the requirement to act in good faith does not) and is a concept which can be given a dynamic interpretation.

4.36 Some respondents were concerned that the statement could be interpreted in a novel, unanticipated way. It will, however, be clear from the Act that the intention of our *partial codification* is to state the principal duties and not to alter them in any respect. As with any Act of Parliament, the courts should give effect to the meaning of the words used by Parliament. In the event of any ambiguity in the statutory statement, the courts could have regard to the general law that the statute was intended to codify.

4.37 More problematic is the possibility that the statutory statement might become out of step with changing commercial circumstances. Primary legislation would then be necessary to amend it. The Strategic Framework Document has noted that the difficulties in bringing forward primary legislation quickly might mean that company law becomes outdated. It discussed, therefore, whether the DTI could take powers in primary legislation to amend the Act by statutory instrument. It was noted that this would aid flexibility, although difficult constitutional issues were involved, notably the lack of detailed Parliamentary scrutiny inherent in secondary legislation. It is for that reason that we do not recommend amending primary legislation on directors' duties by statutory instrument. The duties are fundamental to the relationship between a director and his company and merit the higher level of scrutiny. We note that the Strategic Framework Document invited views on new institutional arrangements to ensure effective continuing reforms. If there were such arrangements, it would assist in the updating of a statutory statement of duties.

Uncertainty about extent of duties?

4.38 To ensure that the duties which are not codified are preserved, the statutory statement would make it clear that to the extent that there were other duties, they would not be affected by the statement of duties. It was argued with some force that such a statement would be unhelpful and misleading: a director would not know the extent of his duties.

4.39 We are not persuaded by this argument for four reasons. First, the director will know what his *main* duties are. Secondly, codification has been done in a similar way before and it has not given rise to great difficulties. Thirdly, we think that there are other ways of bringing to a director's attention a fuller range of his duties, notably the use of pamphlets. Fourthly, the statutory statement would be drafted to make it clear that a director was subject to other duties.

Accessibility?

4.40 Many respondents were concerned that the attempt to improve accessibility by codifying the law would prove to be illusory. The statement would still need to be interpreted by lawyers.

4.41 This is undoubtedly true, but it seems to us an insufficient reason not to *improve* the accessibility. As Lord Herschell noted in *Bank of England* v *Vagliano Brothers* [1891] AC 107 at p. 145, the singular benefit of a codifying statute is there is no longer a need to '[roam] over a vast number of authorities in order to discover what the law [is], extracting it by a minute critical examination of the prior decisions'. Moreover, the majority of the directors surveyed in our empirical research thought that a statement set out in Appendix A was helpful, even though it was only partial. Furthermore, in the important area of directors' duties, the law should aim to educate and inform directors, and not merely impose liabilities on them.

Coherence of company law

4.42 The provisions of Part X of the Act are intended to fortify the inhibitions on directors when their duties conflict with their interest. There are, for example, obligations to obtain approval from shareholders, even where this is not required by the company's articles. And yet the Act does not contain the seminal principle, that a director should act in good faith in what he considers to be the interests of the company, nor does it give any indication that the general law has rules which apply when a director has an interest in a transaction which may conflict with that of his company. The absence of a statutory statement of duties makes it difficult, therefore, to understand the law in relation to directors' duties. For example, s. 309 of the Act, which deals with the position of employees, is grafted onto the rule of law that the directors owe a duty to act in what they consider to be the best interests of the company.

International dimension

4.43 Company law is used internationally: companies are often owned or run by persons who are not citizens of the country in which the company is registered. As awareness of corporate governance continues to increase, it is becoming the norm for the company law of the developed nations to have a statutory statement of the duties of directors. We consider that a modern UK Companies Act would look odd without one. If the Act is, as envisaged by the DTI's objectives in launching the

Company Law Review, to provide an internationally competitive framework for business, so that the UK continues to be an attractive place to do business, then in our view it needs a statement of a director's main duties.

Certainty and the Human Rights Act 1998

4.44 We have considered whether the case for codification is likely to be strengthened by the coming into effect of the Human Rights Act 1998, and with it the direct application of the European Convention on Human Rights. The Law Commission has discussed elsewhere the principle of 'certainty' as developed by the Strasbourg Court in the context of criminal proceedings, and the relevance of this principle to the case for codification of the criminal law. In the criminal law, art. 7 of the Convention has been held to encompass the principle that 'an offence must be clearly defined in the law'; a requirement which is satisfied:

> ... where the individual can know from the wording of the relevant provision and, if need be, with the assistance of the courts' interpretation of it, what acts and omissions will make him criminally liable. (*SW* v *United Kingdom* (1996) 21 EHRR 363 at p. 399, para. 35.)

4.45 Civil rights and obligations are not subject to art. 7, although they are subject to art. 6(1) which guarantees 'a fair and public hearing' in their determination.

4.46 Breach of directors' duties may lead, not merely to remedies in favour of other parties, but also to action by public authorities and the possibility of disqualification. It has been argued that, for the purpose of the Convention, the serious consequences of disqualification proceedings justify treating them as criminal. Under the Convention, the term 'criminal' is an 'autonomous concept', which does not necessarily bear the same meaning as in domestic law. The Court of Appeal, however, has preferred the view that, even under this extended approach, such proceedings are not criminal in nature, being regulatory rather than penal. (*R* v *Secretary of State for Trade and Industry, ex parte McCormick* [1998] BCC 379 per Staughton LJ at p. 395).

4.47 Accordingly, the case for codification, total or partial, must be made without specific reliance on principles of certainty under the Convention. However, the Commissions are under a statutory duty to promote codification of the law where appropriate. With or without help from Strasbourg, the arguments for certainty and accessibility in this area of the law, derived from general principles, can only be reinforced by consideration of the potentially serious consequences of breach.

Recommendation

4.48 For the reasons set out above, we think that *partial codification* would modernise the law. It would make company law more coherent and more accessible. *Accordingly, we recommend that:*

(1) *there should be a statutory statement of a director's main fiduciary duties and his duty of care and skill, being those duties which are set out in Appendix A;*

(2) *the statement should so far as possible be drafted in broad and general language as in Appendix A; and*

(3) *it should not be exhaustive i.e. it should state that a director is subject to other duties which have not been codified.*

Statutory statement without operative effect

4.49 We have recommended that we should have a statutory statement that replaces the general law in the areas it covers. We can, therefore, deal briefly with the suggestion made in the Paper for a statutory statement of directors' duties which would have no legal effect and which would merely be for guidance. There are some fundamental arguments against it. First, the statement and the general law as developed by the courts may diverge over time. Secondly, the traditional view is that a statute should not contain explanatory material.

4.50 Most respondents rejected this option. Most saw little point in having a statutory statement for information only. Indeed one respondent argued that a statement for guidance only was bizarre and inconsistent with the concept of law. We agree that this would be inappropriate.

4.51 Most respondents preferred the idea of producing guidance in the form of pamphlets or a non-binding statement in prescribed forms. It is to this that we now turn.

A non-binding statement of the main duties of directors in certain prescribed forms

Consultation issue

4.52 We discussed in the Paper other, non-statutory ways of presenting a statement of directors' duties. We considered the role of a statement without legal effect that could be contained in certain prescribed forms. This would be a way of informing a director of his main duties, but would preserve the flexibility of the general law. We set out in Appendix A of the Paper a statement of the duties to illustrate this option. We have already referred to this above (para. 4.13).

4.53 We asked consultees whether a director should sign that he has read the statement when he submits the return confirming that he has been appointed as a director; whether each director should be required to sign that he has read the statement when the company submits its annual return; and whether the statement should be annexed to the company's articles and be included in the directors' report attached to the company's annual accounts.

Summary of respondents' views

4.54 A large majority of respondents favoured the inclusion of a non-binding statement in prescribed forms. Inclusion of the statement on form 288a (intimation of change of director) was seen as the most practical way to bring the duties to directors' attention. Many respondents, such as the CBJ, ICAEW, Serious Fraud Office, the Commercial Bar Association and the Law Society of England and Wales, were attracted to the idea of complementing this statement with explanatory pamphlets as part of an overall education package for directors.

4.55 Some considered that the statement should also appear on forms 10(2) (intimation of the first director of a company) and 680(1) (for companies incorporated under an Act of Parliament). A few respondents supported its inclusion in the directors' report, although others thought that this would add unnecessary length to the annual accounts. Attaching the statement to the company's articles had limited support: most respondents took the view that articles are already sufficiently long and confusing and, in any event, most directors never read them. There was also little support for inclusion in the annual return. Most respondents felt that it would be impractical to require each director to sign the annual return.

4.56 Respondents recognised that it might be difficult to make the statement comprehensible and succinct, while also giving sufficient information. The Stock Exchange wondered whether a more basic statement such as 'Remember you have fiduciary duties' might be more effective. Others thought that it should concentrate on more practical duties such as the duty to keep proper accounting records.

Summary of responses of directors: the empirical research

4.57 88 per cent of the directors surveyed supported the proposal that they should sign that they had read the statement of duties when confirming their appointment. The directors surveyed were significantly less in favour of the other proposals for publicising the statement, although there was some support for annexing it to the company's articles of association.

Recommendation

4.58 We have explained above why we have recommended *partial codification* of a director's principal duties. This significantly changes the context of the debate over a statement on prescribed forms. As (on our recommendations) there will be a statutory statement of the main duties with legal effect, it would make little sense to produce a non-binding statement covering the same ground on prescribed forms. Instead the educational aspect of having a statement on prescribed forms can be combined with the *partial codification* by using the statutory statement of a director's main duties. The only question then is which forms should contain the statement.

4.59 In the light of the responses from our respondents and the empirical research, we consider that when a director signs a form 10(2) or form 288a he should sign that he has read the statutory statement of duties. We think that the statement should be set out in the form itself, as many directors are unlikely to follow up a reference to the legislation.

4.60 As respondents and directors surveyed were less in favour of the inclusion of the statement in the articles, directors' report, annual return or other statutory return, we recommend that only forms 10(2) and 288a should contain the statement.

4.61 *We recommend that forms 10(2) and 288a should contain the statutory statement of duties and that when a director signs the forms he should acknowledge that he has read this statement.*

Non-binding authoritative pamphlets (question 100)

Consultation issue

4.62 We also explored another possible form of non-binding material, namely an authoritative pamphlet summarising the duties of directors. We noted that a pamphlet of this kind could be used in addition to a statutory statement of directors' duties. Various private bodies issue pamphlets on directors' duties, and there are also a number of books written for directors. But, at present, apart from a pamphlet issued by Companies House describing a directors' duties in very general terms, which is sent out on request, there is no pamphlet issued by an official source of which we are aware.

4.63 We envisaged that such a pamphlet would need the support of the DTI and, amongst others, the IoD, the Institute of Chartered Secretaries and Administrators, the Federation of Small Businesses, the Law Societies and accountancy bodies. We suggested that Companies House could send out a copy of the pamphlet at certain times, for example, to a person appointed as director or secretary and to those who had applied for registration of the company.

Summary of respondents' views

4.64 A large majority of respondents supported the preparation of pamphlets setting out the duties together with explanations and practical examples. However, it was stressed by some respondents that care would need to be taken to ensure that any such pamphlet was treated only as guidance and not as a comprehensive, binding statement of the law. There was also concern that the pamphlet should be regularly updated. Some respondents, such as the Stock Exchange, thought that many directors—particularly of small companies—would probably not read them. Another criticism was that if there were omissions in the pamphlet, this might offer a defence to a claim that a duty had not been complied with.

Recommendation

4.65 We consider that since Companies Acts and related legislation are complex and impose heavy liabilities on those who breach the law, the government should take steps to provide information about directors' duties to directors in a comprehensible form. It might be helpful if the pamphlets contain practical examples by way of illustration. Any pamphlet would have to be kept up to date, and there would have to be resources and a mechanism for this.

4.66 Any pamphlet would state that it was not a comprehensive or binding statement of the law and that it should be read in conjunction with other duties and responsibilities which directors owe under statute and the general law. Such a caveat would make it difficult for a director to rely on an omission in the pamphlet as a defence to a breach of his duties.

4.67 *Accordingly, we recommend that the DTI should consider the most effective way of producing and distributing a pamphlet explaining a director's duties.*

Summary of recommendations under this Part

4.68 *To summarise, our recommendations under this Part are that there should be a statutory statement of a director's main fiduciary duties and a director's duty of care and skill; that this statement should be set out on forms 10(2) and 288a; that when a director signs such a form he should acknowledge that he has read this statement; and that the DTI should consider how pamphlets explaining a director's duties might be made available to directors.*

The Law Commission's recommendations were taken up by the Steering Group in their consultation papers *Developing the Framework* and *Completing the Structure* through to their *Final Report* (extracted below). The Government welcomed the recommendations and prepared draft legislative provisions (extracted below) for consultation in its White Paper which provided the basis for the relevant new provisions in the CA 2006.

Modern Company Law for a Competitive Economy: Final Report
(London: DTI, July 2001)

Directors' Duties—Codification, or Legislative Restatement

3.5 The emphasis on improved disclosure needs to be accompanied by clarity about the rules governing decision-making by directors. These rules set the basic standards of directors' accountability. There is a wide demand from company directors themselves for clarity on what the law requires of them here. The case law already provides such rules, laying down the directors' duties: *obedience* to the company constitution and decisions adopted under it binding on them; *loyalty* to the purposes of the company in securing the interests of its members; *independence* of judgement; *avoidance of conflicts of interest; fairness* between members; and *care, skill and diligence* in the performance of their duties. But the duties in their present form are widely misunderstood, and unclear or imperfect in a number of areas.

3.6 The case for and against providing a clear restatement of directors' duties has been examined by the Law Commissions and has been set out by us in *Developing the Framework* and *Completing the Structure.*

3.7 We continue to recommend such a legislative statement. We do so for three main reasons:

- it will provide greater clarity on what is expected of directors and make the law more accessible. We believe that this will in turn help to improve standards of governance. Areas where authoritative guidance and clarification are widely sought include the issues of: for whose benefit directors are to run the company; the appropriate time horizons for decision-making; the nature of the standards of care and skill demanded of directors; and the position of stakeholders other than shareholders;
- it will enable defects in the present law to be corrected in important areas where it no longer corresponds to accepted norms of modern business practice: this is particularly so in relation to the duties of conflicted directors and the powers of the company in respect of such conflicts (we deal with this in more detail below); and
- it is a key element in addressing the question of 'scope'—i.e. in whose interests should companies be run—in a way which reflects modern business needs and wider expectations of responsible business behaviour.

3.8 On this final point, our proposed statement of the duty of loyalty makes clear the obligation of each director to act to serve the purposes of the company as laid down in the constitution and as set for it by its members collectively: that is, it sets as the basic goal for directors the success of the company in the collective best interests of shareholders. But it also requires them to recognise, as the circumstances require, the company's need to foster relationships with its employees, customers and suppliers, its need to maintain its business reputation, and its need to consider the company's impact on the community and the working environment. As we emphasised in Chapter 1, we believe that these factors are of growing importance for companies in a modern economy. Just as companies should be required to provide an account of these factors in their annual reports where relevant to their business, so the need to take account of them should be reflected in the way in which directors' duties are expressed.

3.9 The need for clear, accessible and authoritative guidance for directors on which they may safely rely, on the basis that it will bind the courts and thus be consistently applied, combined with the need to clarify the law in the areas of uncertainty and to make good the defects, makes us all the more convinced that the case for a legislative restatement of directors' duties, or codification, it well founded.

3.10 Our 'trial draft' of a statement of directors' duties was almost unanimously welcomed. We are encouraged by the views of the Parliamentary draftsman that such a statement can be effectively drafted in an accessible form which is also fit for the statute book. Counsel's draft is now set out with a commentary in Annex C to this Report.

3.11 The statement sets out the duty of obedience (i.e. to obey the constitution and to exercise powers for their proper purpose); the duty of loyalty, as outlined above (including the need to act fairly as between shareholders); the duty to exercise independence of judgement, and to exercise care, skill and diligence. The statement also sets out the duties of directors to have regard to the interests of creditors where there is a risk of insolvency, and directors' duties in relation to conflicts of interests. In these two areas we are introducing new or revised proposals which we believe may significantly improve the overall outcome. We therefore address these two issues in some detail here. (The commentary which accompanies the draft statement in Annex C provides a more comprehensive explanation of how the statement addresses each of the duties, including those not covered in detail in this Chapter. It also deals with a number of more detailed but nonetheless important points, such as the relative priorities of the duties—i.e. which duty prevails if they appear to lead to incompatible conclusions.)

A Duty in Relation to Creditors

3.12 In providing a high level statement of directors' duties, it is important to draw to directors' attention that different factors may need to be taken into consideration where the company is insolvent or threatened by insolvency. To fail to do so would risk misleading directors by omitting an important part of the overall picture. When we consulted on our initial draft statement we noted that including in the statement itself a specific duty in relation to creditors, which would displace, partially or entirely, the normal shareholder-oriented loyalty duty at the onset of insolvency, raised a number of technical problems. We were also concerned that such inclusion risked cutting across insolvency law. We proposed to resolve the issue by including a separate warning to directors that special principles become relevant where a company is threatened by insolvency.

3.13 While many supported this approach, and it remains feasible, arguments were voiced in favour of including in the statement a duty towards creditors, applicable in cases where insolvency was imminent. There was also criticism that the responsibility of company management not to abuse limited liability had been given insufficient attention. By simplifying and clarifying the law and removing unnecessary restrictions we are making such limited liability more accessible for business. Furthermore, we now believe that the technical difficulties can be resolved. With all these factors in mind, we now propose that there be incorporated in the statutory statement principles requiring directors to have regard to the interests of creditors in relation to threatened insolvency.

3.14 The key issue then is: when should the normal rule, that a company is to be run in the interests of its members, or shareholders, be modified by an obligation to have regard also to the interests of creditors, or, in an extreme case, by an obligation to override the interests of members entirely, to the extent necessary to ensure creditors have the best protection?

3.15 While a company is solvent there is always some risk that insolvency may occur unexpectedly. The resulting risk to creditors is the essence of limited liability. But as insolvency becomes more imminent, the normal synergy between the interests of members, who seek the preservation and enhancement of the assets, and of creditors, whose interests are protected by that process, progressively disappears. As the margin of assets reduces, so the incentive on directors to avoid risky strategies which endanger the assets of members also reduces; the worse the situation gets, the less members have to lose and the more one-sided the case becomes for supporting risky, perhaps desperate, strategies.

3.16 The present law provides two solutions to this. The first is section 214 of the Insolvency Act 1986, which makes directors liable to contribute towards the funds available to creditors in an insolvent winding up, where they ought to have recognised that *the company had no reasonable prospect of avoiding insolvent liquidation* and then failed to take all reasonable steps to minimise the loss to creditors. We believe that this rule should be included in the restatement, so as to make clear the point at which the normal duty of loyalty, to run the company to promote its success for the benefit of members, is displaced. The draft in Annex C does this (see paragraph 9 of the draft Schedule).

3.17 However, arguably directors should also be bound to take a balanced view of the risks to creditors at an earlier stage in the onset of insolvency. Such a principle has been recognised in some Australasian case law and in one case in our Court of Appeal. It would require directors, where they know or ought to recognise that there is a *substantial probability of an insolvent liquidation*, to take such steps as they believe, in their good faith judgement, appropriate to reduce the risk, without undue caution and thus continuing also to have in mind the interests of members. The greater the risk of insolvency in terms of probability and extent, the more directors should take account of creditors' needs and the less those of members. At the point where there is no reasonable prospect of avoiding insolvent liquidation the interests of creditors become overriding under the first (section 214) test.

3.18 Such a rule may be regarded as of considerable merit, at least in principle. It reflects what good directors should do. Without it, directors would apparently, at least, be bound to act in the ultimate interests of members until all reasonable prospect of avoiding shipwreck had been lost. Yet even where insolvency is less than inevitable but the risk is substantial, directors should, at least in theory, consider the interests of members and creditors together.

3.19 The counter argument is that in practice such a 'balanced judgement' test will have a 'chilling' effect, bringing with it the risk that directors may run down or abandon a going concern at the first hint of insolvency. The balanced judgement demanded is a difficult and indeterminate one. Fears of personal liability may lead to excessive caution. Small company directors in particular may feel driven to take expensive professional advice which may well be likely to err on the side of caution, with personal liabilities involved. Liquidation can, where there are means of saving the going concern, be as damaging to creditors as to shareholders. Break-up destroys value and employment. Arguably the first, 'no reasonable prospect', test will, in practice, influence directors to act more cautiously on the approach of insolvency.

3.20 These are valid concerns. That case law already imposes such a duty is not a sufficient reason for retaining it unless we can be confident that it will not in practice lead to failure of viable businesses. The concerns can to some extent be met in the framing of the appropriate principle. The balanced judgement required would need to be expressed subjectively as subject to the good faith assessment of the director; but it would be defined by the scope of the competing interests of the members' and the creditors' claims, both of which are legally defined. We would also purpose that, if this principle were to be adopted, the law should be clarified by providing that the duty only arises when the directors ought in the exercise of due care and skill to recognise that a failure to meet the company's liabilities is more probable than not. Directors could thus safely be advised that it is only the greater than even probability of such failure which they need to take account of—which might be some comfort when faced with normal day-to-day business risk. Moreover, where the business is threatened with insolvency there are procedures short of full liquidation open to directors which both provide protection for creditors and preserve the going concern. Creditors' agreement to such procedures should remove the liability. Some of us believe that with these clarifications, and bearing in mind this context, the common law rule is soundly based and should be included in the statement. To reflect the views of these members a draft is included in Annex C, on an illustrative basis only (paragraph 8 of the draft Schedule). Others of us believe, however, that even as drafted the principle gives inadequate guidance to directors and depends on their being able to discern an intermediate stage on the path to insolvency which is not identifiable in reality. In the view of these members the break from a going concern to an insolvent basis of trading is normally so abrupt and rapid in practice that references to calculating the probabilities and to 'sliding scales' of risk and benefit are unhelpful and potentially misleading. The incorporation of the section 214 rule in the statement will, in their view, be sufficient in practice and would avoid the serious disadvantages of the broader and less precise principle. The advantages and disadvantages of such a principle are very much a matter of commercial judgement, on which we have not been able to reach an agreed view nor, in the time available, to consult on the basis of a clear draft. We recommend that the DTI should do so.

Personal Exploitation of Corporate Opportunities

3.21 The other key issue of principle which we need to address here is the process for addressing directors' conflicts of interest, and in particular which company body—the board or the shareholders—should have the authority to permit a director to exploit for his personal benefit or for the benefit of some other person a business opportunity which he has encountered as a director. Such exploitation would, of course, otherwise be a breach of the duty on conflicts of interest.

3.22 In theory there are at least three kinds of case: where the company *cannot* exploit the opportunity itself in any event; where the company *has already decided to abandon* the opportunity; and where the company *does not wish* to exploit it and is *content for the director* to do so. The present law is that in all cases—even those where the company could not take advantage of the opportunity itself—a director wishing to pursue the opportunity on his own account must first obtain the members' authorisation, unless some alternative procedure is properly provided under the constitution. The requirement for member approval in all cases seems unduly strict compared with what most people would regard as reasonable standards of business and ethical behaviour, and we understand that there may be widespread ignorance and disregard of the requirement in practice. There are arguments in principle for allowing a director to exploit opportunities which the company could not pursue or which it has abandoned, without the need for shareholder authorisation. But in practice it is often difficult to distinguish clearly between the different types of opportunity, and all bring with them a danger of board collusion.

3.23 The possibility of collusion would point to preserving the requirement for such cases to be authorised by the members. But there are strong arguments that such a requirement is impractical an onerous, is inconsistent with the principle that it is for the board to make business assessments, and stifles entrepreneurial activity. It is also argued that in practice independent board approval may be stricter than member approval in many small companies where the general meeting is dominated by the controlling powers of a few directors. (But see our proposal for disqualifying interested members from voting on such resolutions, at paragraph 7.46, below.) We therefore consulted on a number of options for providing a more effective mechanism for addressing these issues, particularly in the case of private companies.

3.24 We believe that in the case of private companies, the arguments are sufficiently strong to support the conclusion that statute should (subject to any stricter rule in the company's constitution, or adopted by agreement) allow the company's rights to be waived by the board, acting independently of any conflicted director. (We considered also allowing a director to escape liability where he could prove that the company could not have exploited the opportunity in question; but such cases raise major factual uncertainties and we have concluded that board authorisation is the minimum desirable safeguard in all cases.)

3.25 It is important that this provision should be subject to appropriate safeguards. First, authorisation should only be given by directors who are genuinely independent, in the sense that they have no interest, direct or indirect, in the transaction. Second, the transaction should subsequently be disclosed in the company's annual report and accounts. Third, the authorisation should be specific to the proposal.

3.26 Furthermore, in our original draft proposal we suggested allowing the constitution, of both private and public companies, to make provision for such authorisation in any way. For example, it could have allowed exploitation of opportunities up to a certain amount, or of a certain kind, or even, to take an extreme example, with permission of the company secretary. It is doubtful under present law whether these would be valid under section 310 (see paragraph 6.2 below), but under our proposal whatever is authorised under the statement of directors' duties would be exempt from liability. We now believe that, apart from approval by the members, the only mechanism for such authorisation should be specific approval by an independent board, and that in the case of a public company board approval should only be permitted if explicitly provided for in the constitution. This is a new proposal, though it follows logically from the development of the policy in the light of consultees' views.

3.27 We believe that these proposals now strike the right balance between, on the one hand, encouraging efficient business operations and the take-up of new business opportunities—if the approval procedures are unwieldy and disproportionate there is a real risk that opportunities will simply be discarded—and, on the other, providing effective protection against abuse.

Modernising Company Law: The White Paper
(London: DTI, July 2002. Cm 5553)

Directors' Duties

General Duties Owed to the Company

3.2 The Act contains many specific provisions about responsibilities of directors. A company's constitution will also define their functions. But general rules about directors' propriety of conduct and standards of skill and care are laid down by complex and inaccessible case law. The duties are not therefore readily accessible to the layman. Indeed, a 1999 survey of members of the Institute of Directors showed that many company directors were not clear about what their general duties were or to whom they were owed.

3.3 The Review considered to whom directors should owe duties and consulted on this issue on several occasions. Its conclusion, with which the Government agrees, was that the basic goal for directors should be the success of the company in the collective best interests of shareholders, but that that directors should also recognise, as the circumstances require, the company's need to foster relationships with its employees, customers and suppliers, its need to maintain its business reputation, and its need to consider the company's impact on the community and the working environment.

3.4 The Review, building on the recommendations of a 1999 report by the Law Commissions, *Company Directors: Regulating Conflicts of Interest and Formulating a Statement of Duties*, recommended the codification of directors' common law duties—though without changing the essential nature of those duties—and the Final Report included a draft statutory statement restating the general principles governing the conduct of directors.

3.5 The Government agrees that:
- directors' general duties to the company should be codified in statute largely as proposed in the Final Report—but with some changes, explained in paragraphs 3.8–3.14 below. This statement of duties will replace the existing common law and also section 309 of the Act;
- the basic objective of directors, and the matters to which they should have regard when acting in furtherance of it, should be broadly as described in paragraph 3.3 above; and
- all the directors of a company should be subject to the same set of general duties, regardless of any particular duties they might have under service agreements as employees.

3.6 This approach—reflected in the draft at Schedule 2 in Volume II, which is essentially the version in the Review's Final Report (except for the removal of the final two paragraphs it had suggested—see 3.8 et seq. below)—balances a number of different elements. In particular, the duty in paragraph 2 of the Schedule to the draft Bill makes clear that directors must consider both the short and long term consequences of their actions, where relevant, and take into account where practicable relevant matters such as their relationships with employees and the impact of the business on the community and on the environment. At the same time the reference to practicability recognises that business decisions are often constrained by time limits or by the availability of information. In addition, the draft duties make clear that a director must exercise the care, skill and diligence of a reasonably diligent person with both the knowledge, skill and experience which may reasonably be expected of a director in his or her position and any additional knowledge, skill and experience which the particular director has.

3.7 The Government is currently considering how the text of the draft duties might be improved, and will consult in detail on a revised draft in due course. We would therefore welcome any detailed comments respondents may have on the drafting of clause 19 and Schedule 2 in Volume II, particularly from practitioners and those currently occupying the position of company director.

. . .

Directors' Duties in Relation to Creditors

3.8 The Review proposed incorporating in the statutory statement a duty based on section 214 of the Insolvency Act 1986 which provides that where a company has gone into liquidation, the court, on the application of the liquidator, can declare that the director should make a contribution to its assets if, once there was no reasonable prospect of avoiding insolvency, he failed to take every step with a view to minimising the potential loss to the company's creditors.

3.9 In addition, it raised the possibility of also including a duty on directors in circumstances where the company was likely to become insolvent which would require them to strike a balance between the risk of the company becoming insolvent and promoting its success for the benefit of the members. However, the Review acknowledged fears that a duty framed in this way would 'have a chilling effect, bringing with it the risk that directors may run down or abandon a going concern at the first hint of insolvency'. It concluded that the advantages and disadvantages of such a principle were finely balanced and did not reach a final view on the point.

3.10 The Government has carefully considered both suggestions but has concluded in both cases that the weight of the argument is against the inclusion of any duties in relation to creditors in the statutory statement.

3.11 As noted above, the arguments against the retention of the second suggestion were outlined by the Review itself. Directors would need to take a finely balanced judgement, and fears of personal liability might lead to excessive caution. This would run counter to the 'rescue culture' which the Government is seeking to promote through the Insolvency Act 2000 and the Enterprise Bill now before Parliament.

3.12 The inclusion of a special duty where there is no reasonable prospect of avoiding insolvency was suggested mainly for presentational reasons. It was not intended to alter the law (although arguably it might result in some improvement or clarification at the margins). It would, however, de-couple the obligations imposed by section 214 of the Insolvency Act 1986 from the remedies under that Act in the case of registered companies. Its inclusion in the statutory statement would therefore be incongruous, particularly given that the Government is proposing to provide a comprehensive code of remedies in the Bill for all of the other duties in the Schedule.

3.13 It is important to emphasise that there is no question about the need for section 2.14; but to incorporate it in the statement would unhelpfully conflate company and insolvency law. Directors have duties and obligations under many headings apart from company law (for example in relation to health and safety). The Government does not believe it appropriate to single out one requirement from insolvency law and include it within the codification of common law duties owed by directors to companies. To the extent that these obligations need to be drawn to directors' attention, it is considered that the comprehensive guidance on directors' statutory duties referred to in paragraph 3.17 below should include references to relevant provisions in the insolvency legislation.

3.14 An alternative approach to the question of creditors might be to include mention of them, perhaps by reference to the company's obligations to them, in the notes setting out the factors which, where they are relevant, directors must take into account in complying with duty in paragraph 2 of Schedule 2 in Volume II. The Government believes that this proposal is worth further consideration. However, such an approach would not achieve the effect intended by the Review in putting forward the duty in paragraph 8 of the Schedule included in the Review's Final Report.

...

How Should Directors Be Made Aware of Their Duties?

3.15 The Review recommended that directors should be required to sign a statement to the effect that they had read and understood the statutory statement of duties. There are obvious attractions in drawing the new, codified statement to all directors' attention in this way. However, it could also give a false impression that it was a comprehensive statement of directors' responsibilities. For example, it would not cover directors' obligations to make returns to Companies House.

3.16 There are also some technical problems with the Review's approach. The duties would be binding whether or not directors sign the statement, so signing would have no significant legal effect.

3.17 The Government therefore proposes instead to build on the current practice of Companies House of sending all new directors a leaflet setting out the requirements on directors to file accounts, make returns and provide other information to Companies House. In future all new directors would receive plain language guidance (also available in minority languages) summarising the main legal requirements placed on directors by company and insolvency legislation. This guidance would cover the statutory statement of duties, requirements to provide information to Companies House, and key provisions in the Bill such as the prohibition on fraudulent trading, as well as relevant aspects of insolvency law. It could be produced in a similar format to employment law guidance (and also made available on the web, through Business Links etc). There could be at least two versions of the guidance, one aimed at directors of (mostly smaller) private companies and another at directors of public companies.

Codification of Civil Remedies for Breach of Directors' Duties

3.18 The Review suggested that it would also be desirable to codify civil remedies for breach of directors' duties, although it noted that this is a difficult and complex area of law. If a workable scheme can be devised, the Government will publish draft clauses for consultation.

Directors' Conflicts of Interests

3.19 Part X of the Act underpins a directors' fiduciary duties to his company by regulating possible conflicts of interest. The provisions were introduced to tackle abuses which the general law had failed to prevent.

3.20 The Government shares the overall recommended by the Review, which built on a report from the Law Commissions (see paragraph 3.4). We will consult on draft clauses in this area in due course.

Payments to Directors

3.21 One of the most significant and obvious conflicts of interest which directors face is in the setting of their remuneration. The current Table A provides that the board may determine the remuneration of the managing and executive directors. The Government agrees this is the right approach, and also believes that it is essential that there is effective disclosure and accountability to shareholders in this area.

3.22 The Government issued a consultative document in July 1999 which made a number of recommendations with a view to strengthening transparency and accountability in this area in respect of quoted companies. A further consultation document was issued in December 2001, inviting comments on the details of these proposals. We have subsequently laid a statutory instrument before Parliament which, when it comes into force, will require quoted companies to:

- publish a report on directors' remuneration as part of the company's annual reporting cycle;
- disclose within the report details of individual directors' remuneration packages, the company's remuneration policy, and the role of the board and remuneration committee in this area; and
- put an annual resolution to shareholders on the remuneration report.

3.23 The Government does not believe that it is appropriate to require such a formal approval procedure in respect of unquoted companies.

Political Donations by Companies

3.24 Directors may also face a conflict of interest over political donations by companies, since a director's personal wishes or interests may conflict with his duty to the company. For that reason, the Act requires both the disclosure of donations in excess of £200 and—in line with a recommendation by the Committee on Standards in Public Life—prior shareholder authorisation of political donations above an annual threshold of £5,000.

3.25 The Government intends, for the most part, to retain in the Bill the recent amendments to the Act made by the Political Parties, Elections and Referendums Act 2000. It will, however, consider the case for further amendments in the light of the experience of companies and their members in implementing the new requirements and will consult on any proposals for changes in due course.

The Role of Codes of Best Practice

3.26 Operating at a number of levels, the corporate governance framework in Great Britain affects the ways in which directors run companies. There are some areas—particularly those relating to conflicts of interest—where Parliament has taken the view that it is appropriate to impose requirements on companies. In other areas, again primarily relating to conflicts of interest, the Listing Authority has imposed requirements on listed companies.

3.27 There is also, however, widespread agreement that there is an important role for a generally accepted code of best practice; in the United Kingdom, the Combined Code on Corporate Governance has fulfilled this role since 1998. There are, in addition, some areas where institutional investors have chosen to supplement the Combined Code with their own best practice guidance. Examples include the policy document *Responsible Voting* which was issued jointly by the Association of British Insurers and the National Association of Pension Funds in 1999.

3.28 The consensus that emerged from those who commented to the Review was that it would be unhelpful or inappropriate to put the provisions of the Combined Code into legislation. The main reasons given were that the case for flexibility in company governance structures was very strong; the definitional problems in the field were very severe; and shareholder control was a more appropriate mechanism for regulating such matters.

3.29 The Government believes that all the components of the corporate governance framework will continue to be important. In particular, it takes the view that, whilst legislative and regulatory requirements have an essential role, there will also be a continuing need for a code of best practice and other guidance. There is also a vital need for regular, systematic contact between directors and shareholders.

3.30 The Combined Code derives its strength from the widespread support which it has received from business and City organisations. The Government believes that it is very important that the Code continues to have this broad business and City support. (Responsibility for future reviews of the Code is discussed in paragraphs 5.11–5.13 below.)

3.31 The Review examined some areas covered by the Code. In particular, it considered the role of non-executive directors. The Government believes that non-executive directors can play a key role in the governance of companies, both in respect of accountability and business prosperity. It has therefore asked Derek Higgs to build on the work of the Review and of the Myners report on institutional investors by undertaking a short, independent review of the role and effectiveness of non-executive directors in the UK.

Corporate Directors

3.32 At present any legal person can be a company director—an individual, another company, a limited liability partnership, a local authority, etc. The only prohibition is on individuals of unsound mind, although minors are technically not capable of signing the requisite consent. At present about 2 per cent of all directors, i.e. about 64,000, are corporate bodies.

3.33 Few countries other than the Netherlands and some offshore financial centres permit corporate directors on the same basis as individuals. Some, for example Australia, New Zealand, Canada and Singapore, have only recently introduced prohibitions. France permits corporate directors but requires each to appoint an individual as its permanent representative with whom it is jointly responsible for any misconduct or negligence. Most US states, including Delaware and Maryland, require directors to be individuals.

3.34 A corporate director can act only through one or more individuals who represent it, or otherwise act on its behalf. The duties of directors need to apply to such individuals—and they need to know that they apply. If the directors are not individuals it can be difficult—both for the general public and for regulators—to determine who is actually controlling a company. Moreover, it can be difficult to apply sanctions against corporate directors. The Government believes that there would be real benefits and relatively little inconvenience from prohibiting corporate directors. It therefore proposes to:
- prohibit corporate directors for companies formed under the Bill;
- prohibit the appointment of corporate directors to existing companies; and
- after a transitional period of, say, three years, prohibit all corporate directors.

3.35 This issue was not addressed during the course of the Review, and we would welcome views.

. . .

COMPANIES BILL 2003, CLAUSE 19

19. General principles by which directors are bound
(1) Schedule 2 sets out—
  (a) the general principles applying to a director of a company in the performance of his functions as director; and
  (b) the general principles—
    (i) applying to a director of a company in relation to his entering into transactions with the company, and
    (ii) applying to a director or former director in relation to the use of property, information and opportunities of the company and to benefits from third parties;
  and has effect in place of the corresponding equitable and common law rules.
(2) A director of a company owes a duty to the company to comply with that Schedule, and a former director owes a duty to the company to comply with paragraphs 6 and 7 of that Schedule.
(3) Nothing in that Schedule authorises the contravention by a director (or former director) of any prohibition or requirement imposed on him by or under any other enactment or rule of law.

SCHEDULE 2   **Section 19**

GENERAL PRINCIPLES BY WHICH DIRECTORS ARE BOUND

Obeying the constitution and other lawful decisions

1. A director of a company must act in accordance with—
    (a) the company's constitution, and
    (b) decisions taken under the constitution (or by the company, or any class of members, under any enactment or rule of law as to means of taking company or class decisions), and must exercise his powers for their proper purpose.

Promotion of company's objectives

2. A director of a company must in any given case—
    (a) act in the way he decides, in good faith, would be most likely to promote the success of the company for the benefit of its members as a whole (excluding anything which would breach his duty under paragraph 1 or 5); and
    (b) in deciding what would be most likely to promote that success, take account in good faith of all the material factors that it is practicable in the circumstances for him to identify.

NOTES
(1) In this paragraph, 'the material factors' means—
     (a) the likely consequences (short and long term) of the actions open to the director, so far as a person of care and skill would consider them relevant; and
     (b) all such other factors as a person of care and skill would consider relevant, including such of the matters in Note (2) as he would consider so.
(2) Those matters are—
     (a) the company's need to foster its business relationships, including those with its employees and suppliers and the customers for its products or services;
     (b) its need to have regard to the impact of its operations on the communities affected and on the environment;
     (c) its need to maintain a reputation for high standards of business conduct;
     (d) its need to achieve outcomes that are fair as between its members.
(3) In Note (1) a 'person of care and skill' means a person exercising the care, skill and diligence required by paragraph 4.
(4) A director's decision as to what constitutes the success of the company for the benefit of its members as a whole must accord with the constitution and any decisions as mentioned in paragraph 1.

Delegation and independence of judgement

3. A director of a company must not, except where authorised to do so by the company's constitution or any decisions as mentioned in paragraph 1—
    (a) delegate any of his powers; or
    (b) fail to exercise his independent judgement in relation to any exercise of his powers.

NOTE: Where a director has, in accordance with this Schedule, entered into an agreement which restricts his power to exercise independent judgement later, this paragraph does not prevent him from acting as the agreement requires where (in his independent judgement, and according to the other provisions of this Schedule) he should do so.

Care, skill and diligence

4. A director of a company must exercise the care, skill and diligence which would be exercised by a reasonably diligent person with both—
    (a) the knowledge, skill and experience which may reasonably be expected of a director in his position; and
    (b) any additional knowledge, skill and experience which he has.

Transactions involving conflict of interest

5. A director of a company must not—
    (a) in the performance of his functions as director, authorise, procure or permit the company to enter into a transaction, or
    (b) enter into a transaction with the company,
    if he has an interest in the transaction which he is required by this Act to disclose to any persons and has not disclosed the interest to them to the extent so required.

Personal use of the company's property, information or opportunity

6. A director or former director of a company must not use for his own or anyone else's benefit any property or information of the company, or any opportunity of the company which he became aware of in the performance of his functions as director, unless—
    (a) the use has been proposed to the company and the company has consented to it by ordinary resolution; or
    (b) the company is a private company, the use has been proposed to and authorised by the board, and nothing in the constitution invalidates that authorisation; or
    (c) the company is a public company, its constitution includes provision enabling the board to authorise such use if proposed, and the use has been proposed to and authorised by the board in accordance with the constitution.

NOTES

1. In this paragraph 'the board' means the board of directors acting without the participation of any interested director.
2. This paragraph does not apply to a use to which the director has a right under a contract or other transaction that he has entered into with the company, or that he has in the performance of his functions authorised, procured or permitted the company to enter into.

Benefits from third parties

7. A director or former director of a company must not accept any benefit which is conferred because of the powers he has as director or by way of reward for any exercise of his powers as director, unless the benefit is conferred by the company or—
    (a) acceptance of the benefit has been proposed to the company and the company has consented to it by ordinary resolution; or
    (b) the benefit is necessarily incidental to the proper performance of any of his functions as director.

12.3 SCOPE AND NATURE OF GENERAL DUTIES

Directors' fiduciary duties and the duty of care and skill are now described as their general duties and are specified in CA 2006, ss. 170–177. These duties are based on certain common law rules and equitable principles and are to be interpreted and applied in the same way as common law rules or equitable principles. Thus, it is expressly stipulated in the new Act that regard must be had to the corresponding common law rules and equitable principles in interpreting and applying the general duties. These duties, in line with the common law principles, are owed by a director to the company (CA 2006, s. 170; *Percival* v *Wright* [1902] 2 Ch 421) which means the shareholders (present and future) as a whole (*Re Pantone 485 Ltd* [2002] BCLC 266). Only in very limited circumstances capable of generating fiduciary obligations (e.g., in takeovers, see 18.3; see also *Platt* v *Platt* [1999] 2 BCLC 745) do they owe duties to the members personally: *Peskin* v *Anderson* [2001] 1 BCLC 372,

CA. Neither do they owe any direct fiduciary duty to an individual creditor (*Yukong Line Ltd* v *Rendsburg Investments Corporation (No. 2)* [1998] 1 WLR 294). Note, however, that when a company becomes insolvent, the directors must act in the interest of the company's creditors and not its shareholders (*Re Pantone 485 Ltd* [2002] BCLC 266).

COMPANIES ACT 2006, S. 170

170. Scope and nature of general duties

(1) The general duties specified in sections 171 to 177 are owed by a director of a company to the company.

(2) A person who ceases to be a director continues to be subject—

    (a) to the duty in section 175 (duty to avoid conflicts of interest) as regards the exploitation of any property, information or opportunity of which he became aware at a time when he was a director, and

    (b) to the duty in section 176 (duty not to accept benefits from third parties) as regards things done or omitted by him before he ceased to be a director.

To that extent those duties apply to a former director as to a director, subject to any necessary adaptations.

(3) The general duties are based on certain common law rules and equitable principles as they apply in relation to directors and have effect in place of those rules and principles as regards the duties owed to a company by a director.

(4) The general duties shall be interpreted and applied in the same way as common law rules or equitable principles, and regard shall be had to the corresponding common law rules and equitable principles in interpreting and applying the general duties.

(5) The general duties apply to shadow directors where, and to the extent that, the corresponding common law rules or equitable principles so apply.

12.4 GENERAL DUTIES

12.4.1 Duty to act within powers

A director must (a) act in accordance with the company's constitution and (b) only exercise powers for the purposes for which they are conferred (s. 171); (a) is a duty of long standing and recognised in s. 35(3) CA 1985, and (b) is the well-known proper purpose rule (*Hogg* v *Cramphorn Ltd*; *Horward Smith Ltd* v *Ampol Petroleum Ltd*).

Hogg v *Cramphorn Ltd*
A share issue for an improper purpose
[1967] Ch 254, Chancery Division

This case concerned an allotment of shares by the directors to prevent a takeover in the honest belief that the takeover would not be in the interest of the company. The court held that the fiduciary power to issue shares had been exercised for an improper purpose, i.e., to prevent a takeover, and not for a purpose for which the power was given to the directors. The shares allotted were therefore not validly issued. It was not enough that the directors issued the shares in the honest belief that this was in the interest of the company. The power must have been exercised for its proper purpose. (Until *Howard Smith Ltd* v *Ampol Petroleum Ltd* extracted below, judges in the Commonwealth (see, for example, *Teck Corporation Ltd* v *Millar* (1972) 33 DLR (3d) 288, British Columbia; *Mills* v *Mills* (1938) 60 CLR 150, Australia) appeared to have rejected this approach. They seemed to favour the view that even if the effect of an allotment was to manipulate voting power, the allotment was valid as long as the directors had acted bona fide in the interest of the company in making the allotment.)

Facts   To prevent a takeover bid by Baxter, the directors devised a scheme under which 5,707 unissued preference shares carrying 10 votes per share on a poll were allotted to trustees for the company's employees. This effectively prevented the takeover by Baxter. In this action, a shareholder successfully challenged the validity of the allotment.

BUCKLEY J: I now turn to what has been the main matter of debate in this case, which is whether the allotment of the 5,707 shares was an improper use by the directors of their discretionary and fiduciary power under art. 10, to decide to whom these unissued shares should be allotted. Mr Instone [counsel for the plaintiff shareholder] has submitted that the allotment was made with the primary object of preventing Mr Baxter from obtaining control of the company and ousting the then existing board of directors and that the allotment was accordingly a breach of the directors' fiduciary duties and should be set aside on the authority of *Piercy* v *S. Mills & Co. Ltd* [1920] 1 Ch 77. In this connection, I should, I think, ignore the fact that the directors were incompetent to attach to the shares the special voting rights which they purported to attach to them.

It is common ground that the scheme of which this allotment formed part was formulated to meet the threat, as the directors regarded it, of Mr Baxter's offer. The trust deed would not have come into existence, nor would the 5,707 shares have been issued as they were, but for Mr Baxter's bid and the threat that it constituted to the established management of the company. It is also common ground that the directors were not actuated by any unworthy motives of personal advantage, but acted as they did in an honest belief that they were doing what was for the good of the company. Their honour is not in the least impugned, but it is said that the means which they adopted to attain their end were such as they could not properly adopt.

I am satisfied that Mr Baxter's offer, when it became known to the company's staff, had an unsettling effect upon them. I am also satisfied that the directors and the trustees of the trust deed genuinely considered that to give the staff through the trustees a sizeable, though indirect, voice in the affairs of the company would benefit both the staff and the company. I am sure that Colonel Cramphorn [the chairman and managing director] and also probably his fellow directors firmly believed that to keep the management of the company's affairs in the hands of the existing board would be more advantageous to the shareholders, the company's staff and its customers than if it were committed to a board selected by Mr Baxter. The steps which the board took were intended not only to ensure that if Mr Baxter succeeded in obtaining a shareholding which, as matters stood, would have been a controlling shareholding, he should not secure control of the company, but also, and perhaps primarily, to discourage Mr Baxter from proceeding with his bid at all . . .

Accepting as I do that the board acted in good faith and that they believed that the establishment of a trust would benefit the company, and that avoidance of the acquisition of control by Mr Baxter would also benefit the company, I must still remember that an essential element of the scheme, and indeed its primary purpose, was to ensure control of the company by the directors and those whom they could confidently regard as their supporters. Was such a manipulation of the voting position a legitimate act on the part of the directors? . . .

Unless a majority in a company is acting oppressively towards the minority, this court should not and will not itself interfere with the exercise by the majority of its constitutional rights or embark upon an inquiry into the respective merits of the views held or policies favoured by the majority and the minority. Nor will this court permit directors to exercise powers, which have been delegated to them by the company in circumstances which put the directors in a fiduciary position when exercising those powers, in such a way as to interfere with the exercise by the majority of its constitutional rights; and in a case of this kind also, in my judgment, the court should not investigate the rival merits of the views or policies of the parties. Thus, in *Fraser* v *Whalley* (1864) 2 Hem & M 10 Page Wood V-C said: 'I say nothing on the question whether the policy advocated by the directors, or that which I am told is to be pursued by Savin, is the more for the interest of the company', and in *Piercy* v *S. Mills & Co. Ltd* [1920] 1 Ch 77, Peterson J said that he had no concern whatever with the merits of the dispute. It is not, in my judgment, open to the directors in such a case to say, 'We genuinely believe that what we seek to prevent the majority from doing will harm the company and therefore our act in arming ourselves or our party with sufficient shares to outvote the majority is a conscientious exercise of our powers under the articles, which should not be interfered with'.

Such a belief, even if well-founded, would be irrelevant. A majority of shareholders in general meeting is entitled to pursue what course it chooses within the company's powers, however wrong-headed it may appear to others, provided the majority do not unfairly oppress other members of the company. These considerations lead me to the conclusion that the issue of the 5,707 shares, with the special voting rights which the directors purported to attach to them, could not be justified by the view that the directors genuinely believed that it would benefit the company if they could command a majority of the votes in general meetings. The fact that, as I have held, the directors were mistaken in thinking that they could attach to these shares more than one vote each is irrelevant. The power to issue shares was a fiduciary power and if, as I think, it was exercised for an improper motive, the issue of these shares is liable to be set aside.

Howard Smith Ltd v Ampol Petroleum Ltd

Allotments for improper purposes again

[1974] AC 821, Privy Council

This case is rather similar to *Hogg* v *Cramphorn Ltd*. It was an appeal from the Supreme Court of New South Wales to the Privy Council which gave the Privy Council an opportunity to review the whole question of the 'proper purpose' doctrine. The Supreme Court of New South Wales held that the shares had been allotted for an improper purpose and was therefore void. An appeal to the Privy Council was dismissed.

Facts   Ampol Petroleum Ltd and Bulkships Ltd together owned 55 per cent of the issued share capital of R.W. Miller (Holdings) Ltd. Ampol and Howard Smith Ltd were making competing takeover bids for Miller. The directors of Miller favoured Howard Smith's higher bid but there was no prospect of this bid succeeding because Ampol and Bulkships would not accept Howard Smith's offer. The evidence showed that Miller was in need of further capital. The directors of Miller resolved to allot new shares to Howard Smith for two purposes, first, so as to raise the capital needed, and secondly to reduce the holding of Ampol and Bulkships to a minority one so as to enable Howard Smith's bid to succeed. In this action, Ampol challenged the validity of the allotment.

LORD WILBERFORCE: The directors, in deciding to issue shares, forming part of Millers' unissued capital, to Howard Smith, acted under clause 8 of the company's articles of association. This provides, subject to certain qualifications which have not been invoked, that the shares shall be under the control of the directors, who may allot or otherwise dispose of the same to such persons on such terms and conditions and either at a premium or otherwise and at such time as the directors may think fit. Thus, and this is not disputed, the issue was clearly *intra vires* the directors. But, *intra vires* though the issue may have been, the directors' power under this article is a fiduciary power: and it remains the case that an exercise of such a power though formally valid, may be attacked on the ground that it was not exercised for the purpose for which it was granted. It is at this point that the contentions of the parties diverge. The extreme argument on one side is that, for validity, what is required is bona fide exercise of the power in the interests of the company: that once it is found that the directors were not motivated by self-interest—i.e. by a desire to retain their control of the company or their positions on the board—the matter is concluded in their favour and that the court will not inquire into the validity of their reasons for making the issue. All decided cases, it was submitted, where an exercise of such a power as this has been found invalid, are cases where directors are found to have acted through self-interest of this kind.

On the other side, the main argument is that the purpose for which the power is conferred is to enable capital to be raised for the company, and that once it is found that the issue was not made for that purpose, invalidity follows...

In their lordships' opinion neither of the extreme positions can be maintained. It can be accepted, as one would only expect, that the majority of cases in which issues of shares are challenged in the courts are cases in which the vitiating element is the self-interest of the directors, or at least the purpose of the directors to preserve their own control of the management; see *Fraser* v *Whalley* (1864) 2 Hem & M 10; *Punt* v *Symons & Co. Ltd* [1903] 2 Ch 506; *Piercy* v *S. Mills & Co. Ltd* [1920] 1 Ch 77; *Ngurli Ltd* v *McCann* (1953) 90 CLR 425 and *Hogg* v *Cramphorn Ltd* [1967] Ch 254, 267.

Further it is correct to say that where the self-interest of the directors is involved, they will not be permitted to assert that their action was bona fide thought to be, or was, in the interest of the company; pleas to this effect have invariably been rejected (e.g. *Fraser* v *Whalley* and *Hogg* v *Cramphorn Ltd*)—just as trustees who buy trust property are not permitted to assert that they paid a good price.

But it does not follow from this, as the appellants assert, that the absence of any element of self-interest is enough to make an issue valid. Self-interest is only one, though no doubt the commonest, instance of improper motive: and, before one can say that a fiduciary power has been exercised for the purpose for which it was conferred, a wider investigation may have to be made. This is recognised in several well-known statements of the law...

On the other hand, taking the respondents' contention, it is, in their lordships' opinion, too narrow an approach to say that the only valid purpose for which shares may be issued is to raise capital for the company. The discretion is not in terms limited in this way: the law should not impose such a limitation on directors' powers. To define in advance exact limits beyond which directors must not pass is, in their lordships' view, impossible. This clearly cannot be done by enumeration, since the variety of situations facing directors of different types of company in different situations cannot be anticipated. No more, in their lordships' view, can this be done by the use of a phrase—such as 'bona fide in the interest of the company as a whole', or 'for some corporate purpose'. Such phrases, if they do anything more than restate the general principle applicable to fiduciary powers, at best serve, negatively, to exclude from the area of validity cases where the directors are acting sectionally, or partially: i.e. improperly favouring one section of the shareholders against another...

In their lordships' opinion it is necessary to start with a consideration of the power whose exercise is in question, in this case a power to issue shares. Having ascertained, on a fair view, the nature of this power, and having defined as can best be done in the light of modern conditions the, or some, limits within which it may be exercised, it is then necessary for the court, if a particular exercise of it is challenged, to examine the substantial purpose for which it was exercised, and to reach a conclusion whether that purpose was proper or not. In doing so it will necessarily give credit to the bona fide opinion of the directors, if such is found to exist, and will respect their judgment as to matters of management; having done this, the ultimate conclusion has to be as to the side of a fairly broad line on which the case falls...

The main stream of authority, in their lordships' opinion, supports this approach. In *Punt* v *Symons & Co. Ltd* Byrne J expressly accepts that there may be reasons other than to raise capital for which shares may be issued. In the High Court [of Australia] case of *Harlowe's Nominees Pty Ltd* v *Woodside (Lakes Entrance) Oil Co. NL* (1968) 121 CLR 483, an issue of shares was made to a large oil company in order, as was found, to secure the financial stability of the company. This was upheld as being within the power although it had the effect of defeating the attempt of the plaintiff to secure control by buying up the company's shares...

Their lordships were referred to the recent judgment of Berger J in the Supreme Court of British Columbia, in *Teck Corporation Ltd* v *Millar* (1972) 33 DLR (3d) 288. This was concerned with the affairs of Afton Mines Ltd in which Teck Corporation Ltd, a resource conglomerate, had acquired a majority shareholding. Teck was indicating an intention to replace the board of directors of Afton with its own nominees with a view to causing Afton to enter into an agreement (called an 'ultimate deal') with itself for the exploitation by Teck of valuable mineral rights owned by Afton. Before this could be done, and in order to prevent it, the directors of Afton concluded an exploitation agreement with another company 'Canex'. One of its provisions, as is apparently common in this type of agreement in Canada, provided for the issue to Canex of a large number of shares in Afton, thus displacing Teck's majority. Berger J found, at p. 328:

> their [sc. the directors'] purpose was to obtain the best agreement they could while.... still in control. Their purpose was in that sense to defeat Teck. But, not to defeat Teck's attempt to obtain control, rather it was to foreclose Teck's opportunity of obtaining for itself the ultimate deal. That was. . . no improper purpose.

His decision upholding the agreement with Canex on this basis appears to be in line with the English and Australian authorities to which reference has been made....

By contrast to the cases of *Harlowe* and *Teck*, the present case, on the evidence, does not, on the findings of the trial judge, involve any considerations of management, within the proper sphere of the directors. The purpose found by the judge is simply and solely to dilute the majority voting power held by Ampol and Bulkships so as to enable a then minority of shareholders to sell their shares more advantageously. So far as authority goes, an issue of shares purely for the purpose of creating voting power has repeatedly been condemned: *Fraser* v *Whalley*; *Punt* v *Symons & Co. Ltd*; *Piercy* v *S. Mills & Co. Ltd* ('merely for the purpose of defeating the wishes of the existing majority of shareholders') and *Hogg* v *Cramphorn Ltd*. In the leading Australian case of *Mills* v *Mills* (1938) 60 CLR 150, it was accepted in the High Court that if the purpose of issuing shares was solely to alter the voting power the issue would be invalid. And, though the reported decisions, naturally enough, are expressed in terms of their own facts, there are clear considerations of principle which support the trend they establish. The constitution of a limited company normally provides for directors, with powers of management, and shareholders, with defined voting powers having power to appoint the directors, and to take, in general meeting, by majority vote, decisions on matters not reserved for management. Just as it is established that directors, within their management powers, may take decisions against the wishes of the majority of shareholders, and indeed that the majority of shareholders cannot control them in the exercise of these powers while they remain in office (*Automatic Self-Cleansing Filter Syndicate Co. Ltd*. v *Cuninghame* [1906] 2 Ch 34), so it must be unconstitutional for directors to use their fiduciary powers over the shares in the company purely for the purpose of destroying an existing majority, or creating a new majority which did not previously exist. To do so is to interfere with that element of the company's constitution which is separate from and set against their powers. If there is added, moreover, to this immediate purpose, an ulterior purpose to enable an offer for shares to proceed which the existing majority was in a position to block, the departure from the legitimate use of the fiduciary power becomes not less, but all the greater. The right to dispose of shares at a given price is essentially an individual right to be exercised on individual decision and on which a majority, in the absence of oppression or similar impropriety, is entitled to prevail. Directors are of course entitled to offer advice, and bound to supply information, relevant to the making of such a decision, but to use their fiduciary power solely for the purpose of shifting the power to decide to whom and at what price shares are to be sold cannot be related to any purpose for which the power over the share capital was conferred upon them. That this is the position in law was in effect recognised by the majority directors themselves when they attempted to justify the issue as made primarily in order to obtain much-needed capital for the company. And once this primary purpose was rejected, as it was by Street J, there is nothing legitimate left as a basis for their action, except honest behaviour. That is not, in itself, enough.

Their lordships therefore agree entirely with the conclusion of Street J that the power to issue and allot shares was improperly exercised by the issue of shares to Howard Smith.

NOTE: In *Bishopsgate Investment Management Ltd* v *Maxwell (No. 2)* [1994] 1 All ER 261, CA, Mr Ian Maxwell, as director, was held to be in breach of his fiduciary duty to act bona fide in the interests of the company and not for an improper purpose, when he signed various stock transfers transferring for no consideration the shares held by the company as trustee of a number of pension funds to another company of which he was also a director.

12.4.2 Duty to promote the success of the company

Directors must act bona fide in a way that would promote the success of the company for the benefit of its members as a whole (s. 172). This means that they must act in what they think, not what the court thinks, is for the benefit of its members as a whole (cf *Regentcrest plc (in liq)* v *Cohen* [2001] 2 BCLC 80). This is similar to the well-known duty to act bona fide in the interest of the company (Re Smith & Fawcett Ltd [1942] Ch 304). However, s. 172 now provides a list of factors including other stakeholders' interests the director must take into account when discharging this duty. This appears to be wider than the factors (primarily shareholders' interests) which directors were traditionally required to consider under case law. Thus, cases on directors' duty to act bona fide in the interest of the company must be read with caution. The duty to act for the benefit of its members as a whole prima facie includes a duty to inform the company of any activity, actual or threatened, which damages those interests: cf *British Midland Tool Ltd* v *Midland International Tooling Ltd* [2003] 2 BCLC 523, at 560.

Section 172 further provides that the duty to promote the success of the company is subject to any enactment or rule of law requiring directors in certain circumstances to consider or act in the interests of creditors of the company. This appears to have preserved cases such as *Liquidator of West Mercia Safetywear Ltd* v *Dodd* [1988] BCLC 250 which require directors to consider the creditors' interests as insolvency approaches, even though such a duty is not owed to the creditors (*Yukong line Ltd* v *Rendsburg Investments Corporation (No 2)* [1998] 1 WLR 294).

COMPANIES ACT 2006, S. 172

172. Duty to promote the success of the company

(1) A director of a company must act in the way he considers, in good faith, would be most likely to promote the success of the company for the benefit of its members as a whole, and in doing so have regard (amongst other matters) to—

   (a) the likely consequences of any decision in the long term,

   (b) the interests of the company's employees,

   (c) the need to foster the company's business relationships with suppliers, customers and others,

   (d) the impact of the company's operations on the community and the environment,

   (e) the desirability of the company maintaining a reputation for high standards of business conduct, and

   (f) the need to act fairly as between members of the company.

(2) Where or to the extent that the purposes of the company consist of or include purposes other than the benefit of its members, subsection (1) has effect as if the reference to promoting the success of the company for the benefit of its members were to achieving those purposes.

(3) The duty imposed by this section has effect subject to any enactment or rule of law requiring directors, in certain circumstances, to consider or act in the interests of creditors of the company.

12.4.3 Duty to exercise independent judgement

Directors owe a duty to exercise independent judgment (s. 173(1)). This means that they must not fetter the exercise of their powers or discretion—the no-fettering rule (*Boulting* v *Association of Cinematograph, Television and Allied Technicians* [1963] 2 QB 606). However, they are not in breach of this duty if they act in accordance with an agreement duly entered by the company that restricts the future exercise of discretion by its directors, or if they act in a way authorised by the company's constitution (s. 173(2)). This appears to preserve the rule in *Thorby* v *Goldberg* (1964) 112 CLR 597 which was applied in *Cabra Estates Plc* v *Fulham Football Club* [1994] BCLC 363.

12.4.4 Duty to exercise reasonable care, skill and diligence

A director must exercise the care, skill and diligence that would be exercised by a reasonably diligent person with (a) the general knowledge, skill and experience that may reasonably be expected of a person carrying out the functions carried out by the director and (b) the general knowledge, skill and experience of that director (s. 174).

COMPANIES ACT 2006, S. 174

174. Duty to exercise reasonable care, skill and diligence

(1) A director of a company must exercise reasonable care, skill and diligence.
(2) This means the care, skill and diligence that would be exercised by a reasonably diligent person with—
  (a) the general knowledge, skill and experience that may reasonably be expected of a person carrying out the functions carried out by the director in relation to the company, and
  (b) the general knowledge, skill and experience that the director has.

This is a codification of the common law duty of care and skill. There was some confusion as to whether the common law duty of care and skill as formulated in *Re Brazilian Rubber Plantations & Estates Ltd* and *Re City Equitable Fire Insurance Co Ltd* (extracted below) was, as sometimes believed, a subjective one, or whether it was a dual objective/subjective test which set a minimal objective standard of care and skill. Hoffmann J expressed, in *Norman* v *Theodore Goddard* [1991] BCLC 1028 at pp. 1030–1 and *Re D'Jan of London Ltd* [1993] BCC 646 at p. 648, the view that the common law test of a director's duty of care was the same as that stated in s. 214(4) of the Insolvency Act 1986 (see Hicks (1994) 110 LQR 390 extracted below), which was a dual subjective/objective test. The Law Commissions agreed that Hoffmann J's view represented the law and should be set out in statute. In the extract below the Law Commissions also considered the possibility of changing the law to either subjective, dual subjective/objective or objective but recommended that the present law (i.e., dual subjective/objective test) should be adopted. This section was enacted to give effect to the Law Commissions' recommendation to remove the uncertainty on the test.

The Company Directors Disqualification Act 1986 should encourage directors to act more responsibly and to show a greater degree of competence in management. (For detail on grounds for disqualification see 11.8.) Potential liability under the Insolvency Act 1986, s. 214 (the wrongful trading provision), also means that directors must take 'every step' to minimise losses to creditors when insolvent liquidation is unavoidable if they are to avoid personal liability. (For detail on wrongful trading see 20.12.)

Re Brazilian Rubber Plantations & Estates Ltd

Directors of rubber company who knew nothing about rubber

[1911] 1 Ch 425, Chancery Division

In this case, Neville J laid down a semi-subjective standard of duty of care and skill to be measured according to the expertise the directors had.

Facts   *A rubber company made serious financial losses in a ruinous speculation in rubber plantations in North Brazil. The directors of the company who had no expertise in the business of rubber plantations were sued on grounds of negligence.*

NEVILLE J: I have to consider what is the extent of the duty and obligation of directors towards their company. It has been laid down that so long as they act honestly they cannot be made responsible in damages unless guilty of gross negligence. There is admittedly a want of precision in this statement of a director's liability. In truth, one cannot say whether a man has been guilty of negligence, gross or otherwise, unless one can determine what is the extent of the duty which he is alleged to have neglected. A director's duty has been laid down as requiring him to act with such care as is reasonably to be expected from him, having regard to his knowledge and experience. He is, I think, not bound to bring any special qualifications to his office. He may undertake the management of a rubber company in complete ignorance of everything connected with rubber, without incurring responsibility for the mistakes which may result from such ignorance; while if he is acquainted with the rubber business he must give the company the advantage of his knowledge when transacting the company's business. He is not, I think, bound to take any definite part in the conduct of the company's business, but so far as he does undertake it he must use reasonable care in its despatch.

Such reasonable care must, I think, be measured by the care an ordinary man might be expected to take in the same circumstances on his own behalf. He is clearly, I think, not responsible for damages occasioned by errors of judgment.

NOTE: Neville J said that a director 'is not, I think, bound to take any definite part in the conduct of the company's business'. Hoffmann LJ in *Bishopsgate Investment Management Ltd v Maxwell (No. 2)* [1994] 1 All ER 261, CA, whilst saying that 'the existence of a duty to participate must depend upon how the particular company's business is organised and the part which the director could reasonably have been expected to play', has observed that 'in the older cases the duty of a director to participate in the management of a company is stated in very undemanding terms. The law may be evolving in response to changes in public attitudes to corporate governance, as shown by the enactment of the provisions consolidated in the Company Directors Disqualification Act 1986' (see 11.8), and, one might add, the Cadbury Report (extracted at 8.3).

Re City Equitable Fire Insurance Co. Ltd

'A daring and unprincipled scoundrel'

[1925] Ch 407, Chancery Division

In this case, Romer J in his much-cited judgment laid down the directors' duty of care and skill at common law. A close examination of the judgment reveals a degree of objectivity in the standards: a basic objective standard of reasonable care such as might be expected of an ordinary person acting on his or her own behalf (a standard of care based on that of trustees), plus a subjective standard that a director need not exhibit greater skill than can be expected of a person of his or her knowledge and experience.

Facts   *The company suffered a great financial loss as a result of fraud by the chairman, Bevan. The liquidator brought this action against other directors for negligently failing to detect the fraud. Two of the directors were in the end found negligent, but were saved by a clause in the articles of association which exempted directors from liability for negligence except losses caused by their own 'wilful neglect or default'. Such clauses were subsequently outlawed by the Companies Act 1929 (see now the Companies Act 1985, s. 310).*

ROMER J: It has sometimes been said that directors are trustees. If this means no more than that directors in the performance of their duties stand in a fiduciary relationship to the company, the statement is true enough. But if the statement is meant to be an indication by way of analogy of what those duties are, it appears to me to be wholly misleading. I can see but little resemblance between the duties of a director and the duties of a trustee of a will or of a marriage settlement. It is indeed impossible to describe the duty of directors in general terms, whether by way of analogy or otherwise. The position of a director of a company carrying on a small retail business is very different from that of a director of a railway company. The duties of a bank director may differ widely from those of an insurance director, and the duties of a director of one insurance company may differ from those of a director of another. In one company, for instance, matters may normally be attended to by the manager or other members of the staff that in another company are attended to by the directors themselves. The larger the business carried on by the company the more numerous, and the more important, the matters that must of necessity be left to the managers, the accountants and the rest of the staff. The manner in which the work of the company is to be distributed between the board of directors and the staff is in truth a business matter to be decided on business lines. . . .

In order, therefore, to ascertain the duties that a person appointed to the board of an established company undertakes to perform, it is necessary to consider not only the nature of the company's business, but also the manner in which the work of the company is in fact distributed between the directors and the other officials of the company, provided always that this distribution is a reasonable one in the circumstances, and is not inconsistent with any express provisions of the articles of association. In discharging the duties of his position thus ascertained a director must, of course, act honestly; but he must also exercise some degree of both skill and diligence. To the question of what is the particular degree of skill and diligence required of him, the authorities do not, I think, give any very clear answer. . . . The care that he is bound to take has been described by Neville J in [*Re Brazilian Rubber Plantations and Estates Ltd* [1911] 1 Ch 425] as 'reasonable care' to be measured by the care an ordinary man might be expected to take in the circumstances on his own behalf. In saying this Neville J was only following what was laid down in *Overend Gurney & Co.* v *Gibb* (1872) LR 5 HL 480 as being the proper test to apply, namely: 'Whether or not the directors exceeded the powers entrusted to them, or whether if they did not so exceed their powers they were cognisant of circumstances of such a character, so plain, so manifest, and so simple of appreciation, that no men with any ordinary degree of prudence, acting on their own behalf, would have entered into such a transaction as they entered into?'

There are, in addition, one or two other general propositions that seem to be warranted by the reported cases: (1) A director need not exhibit in the performance of his duties a greater degree of skill than may reasonably be expected from a person of his knowledge and experience. A director of a life insurance company, for instance, does not guarantee that he has the skill of an actuary or of a physician. In the words of Lindley MR: 'If directors act within their powers, if they act with such care as is reasonably to be expected from them, having regard to their knowledge and experience, and if they act honestly for the benefit of the company they represent, they discharge both their equitable as well as their legal duty to the company': *Lagunas Nitrate Co.* v *Lagunas Syndicate* [1899] 2 Ch 392 at p. 435. It is perhaps only another way of stating the same proposition to say that directors are not liable for mere errors of judgment. (2) A director is not bound to give continuous attention to the affairs of his company. His duties are of an intermittent nature to be performed at periodical board meetings, and at meetings of any committee of the board upon which he happens to be placed. He is not, however, bound to attend all such meetings, though he ought to attend whenever, in the circumstances, he is reasonably able to do so. (3) In respect of all duties that, having regard to the exigencies of business, and the articles of association, may properly be left to some other official, a director is, in the absence of grounds for suspicion, justified in trusting that official to perform such duties honestly. In the judgment of the Court of Appeal in *Re National Bank of Wales Ltd* [1899]

2 Ch 629 the following passage occurs (at p. 673) in relation to a director who had been deceived by the manager, and managing director, as to matters within their own particular sphere of activity:

> Was it his duty to test the accuracy or completeness of what he was told by the general manager and the managing director? This is a question on which opinions may differ, but we are not prepared to say that he failed in his legal duty. Business cannot be carried on upon principles of distrust. Men in responsible positions must be trusted by those above them, as well as by those below them, until there is reason to distrust them. We agree that care and prudence do not involve distrust; but for a director acting honestly himself to be held legally liable for negligence, in trusting the officers under him not to conceal from him what they ought to report to him, appears to us to be laying too heavy a burden on honest business men.

> . . .

> These are the general principles that I shall endeavour to apply in considering the question whether the directors of this company have been guilty of negligence. . . .

Andrew Hicks, 'Directors' liability for management errors'
(1994) 110 LQR 390

Two recent first-instance decisions herald a possible reconsideration of the common law duties of care and skill of company directors. The cases are *Norman v Theodore Goddard* [1991] BCLC 1028 and *Re D'Jan of London Ltd* [1993] BCC 646.

The traditional interpretation of the old case law is that directors are only liable for gross errors of judgment amounting to negligence. Furthermore, there is no general professional standard of expertise required of directors. Thus for example Farrar's *Company Law* (3rd ed., 1991 at p. 397) commenting on the leading case of *Re City Equitable Fire Insurance Co. Ltd* [1925] Ch 407, states that the degree of skill required 'is a subjective test with no minimum reasonable amount of skill being required. Under such a test the less knowledge and experience a director has, the less skill is expected of him, and the less likely he is to be liable when something goes wrong.'

It is debatable whether such a minimalistic standard can really represent the law, especially in the closing years of the twentieth century. (The standard of care expected of a trust corporation has, however, been held to be higher than that owed by the ordinary prudent businessman: *Bartlett v Barclays Bank Trust Co. Ltd* [1980] 1 Ch 515.) It seems nevertheless that while actions are commonly brought against directors for breach of fiduciary duty, neither members nor liquidators are sufficiently confident to sue directors in respect of errors of judgment. There is therefore an absence of recent cases, with the law either uncertain or unable to supply an adequate remedy.

In the two cases referred to, Hoffmann J concluded that the relevant test of a director's duty is not merely a subjective test. In *Norman v Theodore Goddard* he propounded an objective requirement that a director must possess the skill 'that may reasonably be expected from a person undertaking those duties', adding by way of example, 'A director who undertakes the management of the company's properties is expected to have reasonable skill in property management, but not in offshore tax avoidance'. He went on, without calling for argument on the point, to assume that counsel's proposition was correct that the appropriate test of the common law duty of care is that set out in s. 214 of the Insolvency Act 1986.

More recently in *Re D'Jan of London Ltd*, Hoffmann LJ, sitting as an additional judge in the Chancery Division, has stated again that 'the duty of care owed by a director at common law is accurately stated in s. 214(4) of the Insolvency Act 1986'. In this case, Mr D'Jan was held prima facie liable to the company for loss caused by the company's insurers repudiating liability on a fire policy, he having signed an incorrectly completed proposal form without first reading it. This breach of duty was described by Hoffmann LJ as not a gross breach, but 'the kind of thing that could happen to any busy man'.

The striking feature of subsection (4) of s. 214 (the wrongful trading provision), is that it includes an objective element. The standard required by the section is that of the 'reasonably diligent person having both (a) the general knowledge, skill and experience that may reasonably be expected of a person carrying out the same functions as are carried out by that director in relation to the company, and (b) the general knowledge, skill and experience that that director has'. The section requires a director to satisfy this part objective, part subjective standard in concluding that there is no reasonable prospect of the company avoiding insolvent liquidation and in taking every step to minimise the potential loss to the company's creditors. The statutory objective test thus applies very late in the day when insolvency is predictable. Hoffmann LJ's conclusion is that the effect of the common law is to demand the same objective standard throughout the life of the company. In the one case he refers to an objective standard of skill as set out in s. 214. In the second case he refers to an objective standard of care. The two standards are conceptually separate though difficult to segregate, as the appropriate level of care may depend on the required standard of skill. However it may be applied, the clear requirement of an objective standard of competence is a striking development.

At first sight, these two cases from an influential commercial judge thus seem to be a major departure from conventional perceptions of the law. If they conflict with the findings in the *City Equitable* case, it has to be remembered that Romer J's three principles neatly encapsulated in that case were only laid down at first instance. They were not directly relevant when limited aspects of the case went to the Court of Appeal. However, it is submitted that Hoffmann LJ's findings are not in conflict with the earlier decision. First, *City Equitable* and most of the earlier cases on which it was based were dealing primarily with the duties of what are now called non-executive directors in companies run by powerful managing or executive directors. The duties of a director concerned in day-to-day management in today's more professional context may clearly be stricter.

Secondly, *City Equitable* has perhaps been misrepresented by writers over-stressing the quaint subjective standard of the 'amiable lunatic'. If the lengthy judgment rather than the headnote is actually read, substantial objective elements are clearly apparent. Romer J accepted as the primary test that of Neville J in *Re Brazilian Rubber Plantations & Estates Ltd* [1911] 1 Ch 425 at p. 437. The necessary standard is that of 'reasonable care ... measured by the care an ordinary man ought to be expected to take in the circumstances on his own behalf' (i.e., running his own business affairs). Romer J's well-known three propositions were expressed to be 'in addition' to this basic objective test. The first proposition is the subjective one that 'A director need not exhibit in the performance of his duties a greater degree of skill than may reasonably be expected from a person of his knowledge or experience'. This has been taken to mean that if the members appoint a half-wit as a director, he may only be judged by what one can reasonably expect of a half-wit. However the next sentence of the judgment qualifies the subjective test with the words 'A director of a life insurance company, for instance, does not guarantee that he has the skill of an actuary or of a physician'. This example indicates that the subjective test of skill does not allow the standard of care to be reduced to the level of the half-wit. Romer J was setting out a dual standard, first the minimum and irreducible objective standard of the reasonable care of the ordinary man acting on his own behalf; and secondly, the subjective test that relieves him if he does not have highly specialised expertise. Romer J's subjective test is not intended to reduce the standard of care below that of the reasonable ordinary businessman. It relieves the director if he is not an actuary or a physician or an expert in offshore tax avoidance, but presumably holds him to that higher standard if he was appointed as having that expertise. This interpretation is wholly borne out by Romer J's treatment of the actual allegations of negligence which, throughout the judgment, he deals with on the assumption of objective irreducible standards of proper Directors' Duties 364 management. Such a conclusion suggests that *City Equitable* has been widely misread and that Hoffmann LJ's application of the double test in s. 214 may be appropriate.

Bearing in mind the age of most of the cases and the different commercial circumstances in which they were heard, one cannot, however, derive any coherent statement of the law from them. As Romer J himself said (at p. 426), the practical duties of a director in one company will differ fundamentally from those of a director in a different company. The responsibilities of individual directors within the same company also may vary greatly. As Knox J said in the s. 214 case of *Re Produce Marketing Consortium Ltd* (No. 2) [1989] BCLC 520 at p. 550C, the objective standard required of a director depends on the particular company and its business and 'will be much less extensive in a small company in a modest way of business, with simple accounting procedures and equipment, than it will be in a large company with sophisticated procedures'.

The old cases also tend to use the terms 'care' and 'skill' interchangeably, which, with the additional complication of 'diligence', may have led to some confusion. Whereas one cannot expect all directors to possess a comprehensive portfolio of skills, one can expect them all to be reasonably careful. For example, in *Dorchester Finance Ltd* v *Stebbing* [1989] BCLC 498 at p. 501 Foster J suggests that the law imposes an objective standard of 'care', that of the ordinary man acting on his own behalf. The standard of 'skill' however is said to be subjective, that which 'may reasonably be expected from a person with his knowledge and experience'. Whether care, skill and diligence can fully be segregated in this way, as has been suggested above, is doubtful.

One can only conclude that the recent decisions of Hoffmann LJ indicate the uncertain and undeveloped state of the law in this area. But they suggest that courts may not in future be prepared to accept the minimalistic standard of competence said to be tolerated by the law in the first quarter of this century.

NOTE: In Australia, in *Daniels* v *Anderson* (1995) 13 ACLC 614, the New South Wales Court of Appeal held that directors must take reasonable steps to place themselves in a position to guide and monitor the management of the company. This decision raises uncertainty as to the circumstances in which a director can delegate his responsibilities to others and rely on them. What is clear is that directors who are wholly inactive or passive run the high risk of being found negligent.

Law Commission and Scottish Law Commission, *Company Directors: Regulating Conflicts of Interests and Formulating a Statement of Duties* (Law Com. No. 261)

(London: Stationery Office, 1999)

Part 5 *A director's duty of care and skill: setting the standard*

Introduction

5.1 We have recommended above that a director's main duties should be set out in statute. We have explained how our basic intention is to state the existing law and not to alter it. However, in one respect we had considered the possibility of *changing* the content of one of the director's core duties, namely the standard of care and skill. In the Paper we invited consultees' comments on three possible options for the standard of a director's duty of care and skill, namely a subjective, a dual objective/subjective or an objective test. We also asked consultees whether the duty should be codified or left as general law. We provisionally considered that a dual objective/subjective test, which in our view currently represented the law, should be set out in statute.

5.2 We consider these options and respondents' views. We then examine whether a statutory statement of a director's duty of care should be complemented by a statutory business judgment rule and by provisions dealing with delegation to and reliance on third parties.

Consultation issues: the standard of a director's duty of care

A subjective test

5.3 One option for a statutory statement of a director's duty of care was for a director to owe a duty to his company to exercise the care, diligence and skill that would be exercised by a reasonable person having his knowledge and experience. This is effectively the traditional view of the standard of care. Account would be taken of the responsibilities of the individual director and the circumstances of the particular company. A subjective standard would be low if the director has little knowledge and experience, although for directors with special expertise it would be higher than a purely objective standard.

5.4 We explained that a subjective standard might be appropriate because management is not a profession. Directors do not require particular skills to discharge their duties. A company might appoint a person as a director for some attribute he possesses, knowing that he lacks skill in business matters.

5.5 However, we noted that many areas of business do require specialised skills and knowledge beyond those possessed by the layman. Moreover a subjective standard would be out of line with the duties generally imposed on persons who agree to provide services (particularly where they are paid) and would also be out of step with many other jurisdictions that require directors to act as reasonable, competent businessmen.

A dual objective/subjective test

5.6 The second option we discussed was for a director to owe a duty to his company to exercise the care, diligence and skill that would be exercised by a reasonable person in the same circumstances having both (a) the knowledge and experience that may reasonably be expected of a person in the same position as the director, and (b) the director's knowledge and experience. This requires the conduct of directors to be judged both objectively and subjectively by reference to their own personal characteristics.

5.7 For illustrative purposes we appended to the Paper a draft clause imposing a dual objective/subjective standard. We explained that it was important that the standard of care set out in statute should take account of the responsibilities of directors of different types and in different situations, for example the difference between what executive and non-executive directors are expected to do. The test therefore looks at the notional knowledge and experience that may reasonably be expected of a person *in the same position* as the director. This involves taking account of the particular role which the director is expected to take on in the particular company. We also proposed that the same standard should apply to each of the duties of skill, care and diligence.

5.8 This test is based on that in s. 214(4) of the Insolvency Act 1986, which imposes a liability on directors to contribute to the assets of the company if they have caused their company to trade at a time when it could not avoid entering into insolvent liquidation. The courts have recently used this section as a basis for the standard of care which a director must show under the common law. Our view was that this statement now represents the law and would be followed by the higher courts.

5.9 In the Paper we explained our provisional preference was for a dual objective/subjective test. We considered that all directors should be subject to a general standard of care. A director should not be able to rely on his own lack of knowledge or experience to avoid liability. We thought that it was only fair that a director with some special expertise should be bound to exercise it. Accordingly, it was our view that the subjective limb could operate only as a requirement in addition to the objective standard and could not be used by the director to avoid being subject to the minimum standard of care required by every director. We also noted that it would be sensible to base the standard on s. 214(4). Not only would directors then have the same duties during the life of the company and as it approached insolvent liquidation, but the courts had also had over 12 years' experience in interpreting this section.

5.10 However, we did note that there were fears that a dual standard might lead to an increase in the number of claims against directors and that this might deter people from acting as directors (particularly as non-executive directors) or lead to over-cautious behaviour. We referred to the existence of a market in … insurance and concluded that there was an expectation that the market for this kind of insurance will increase with greater awareness of the responsibilities of directors.

An objective test

5.11 The third option was for a director to owe a duty to his company to exercise the care, diligence and skill that would be exercised by a reasonable person having the knowledge and experience which may reasonably be expected of a person in the same position as the director without taking account of any special expertise that the particular director possesses.

5.12 We pointed out a number of problems with this purely objective standard. It would ignore the special qualifications that a director has, even if they were the reason why the company appointed him. An objective standard would also mean that the standard would change when the company approached insolvent liquidation.

Summary of respondents' views

5.13 There was little support amongst respondents for a subjective test. One respondent said that this would be appropriate for an owner-manager whose role as a director would be secondary to his role as an owner. It was pointed out, though, that this would not be acceptable for a director of a plc and that it would be undesirable to draw a distinction between the two types of companies.

5.14 Indeed most respondents thought that a subjective test would produce too low a standard for modern business. It was considered that in the absence of a formal assessment of a person's fitness to become a director, the public interest demanded that directors should be subject to at least an objective standard. This might afford some protection to shareholders and creditors. (It was noted, however, that many executive directors owe duties under their contracts of employment that impose objective standards.)

5.15 Instead the vast majority of respondents favoured the dual objective/subjective test. This included the IoD. Many agreed with our view that this was the current common law position. The dual test was widely regarded as the best way to account for the differing levels of knowledge and experience possessed by directors. Some respondents suggested that our illustrative clause needed to be more carefully drafted to ensure that it took into account both the functions to be performed by the individual director and the size and type of company. We agree that this is important.

5.16 A number of respondents argued that the test should be the same as that in s. 214(4) of the Insolvency Act 1986. This was thought to be a workable formula. If a different standard were introduced, there would be two overlapping yet distinct duties in the same area. However, some respondents considered that there was no incoherence in a different duty arising on impending insolvency: a director would then owe duties to creditors in addition to those owed to the company.

5.17 There was little support for a purely objective test. It was thought that a director with special skills should be expected to use them. An objective test would be too low for skilled directors. Those who supported this option did so largely because they were concerned about the position of non-executive directors. It was thought that a dual objective/subjective test would discourage non-executive directors from taking up office or from taking risks. The fact that a director is a non-executive would be something that would be taken into account under this standard in any event.

Summary of responses of directors: the empirical research

5.18 The dual objective/subjective test was favoured by around half of the directors surveyed. Just under a third supported the subjective test. Support for the subjective test was significantly more likely in 'closed' companies where the directors, together, held a majority of the shares. However, even among this group, a majority of the respondents favoured the objective/subjective test. The interview component of the empirical research also suggested that setting out the dual test in statute would probably not in itself lead to an increase in litigation by institutional shareholders against directors.

Recommendation

5.19 The Commissions provisionally supported codification of the dual objective/subjective standard. Respondents clearly supported setting this dual test out in statute. It is important that regard should be had to the functions of the particular directors and the circumstances of the particular company. The wording of the standard would be a matter for parliamentary counsel in due course. We consider that the statutory statement should supersede the general law.

5.20 *Accordingly, we recommend that (1) a director's duty of care, skill and diligence to his company should be set out in statute; (2) the standard should be judged by a twofold objective/subjective test; and (3) regard should be had to the functions of the particular director and the circumstances of the company.*

Should there be a statutory business judgment rule?

Consultation issue

5.21 In relation to commercial decisions in general, the courts take the view that it would be wrong 'to substitute [their] opinion for that of the management, or indeed to question the correctness of the management's decision . . . if bona fide arrived at'.

5.22 In many states of the USA the courts have adopted a business judgment rule. The basic rule is that a director who makes a business judgment in good faith fulfils his duty of care if (1) he is not interested in the subject of the business judgment; (2) he is informed about the subject to the extent he reasonably believes to be appropriate; and (3) he rationally believes that the business judgment is in the best interests of the corporation. The American Law Institute described the rule as a 'judicial gloss on duty of care standards that sharply reduces exposure to liability' and explained that the standard in (3) 'is intended to provide directors . . . with a wide ambit of discretion'.

5.23 We noted in the Paper how the Australian government had recently proposed a statutory business judgment rule similar to this. This may have been due, in part, to recent case law such as *Daniels* v *Anderson* (1995) 16 ACSR 607, which has increased concern in Australia about the liability of directors. The government was concerned that uncertainty over the extent of this liability might be encouraging risk-averse business behaviour. Although the government noted that the courts already declined to review the merits of business decisions, it thought that a statutory business judgment rule would create a presumption in favour of a director's judgment that would lead to greater certainty.

5.24 We noted that the UK courts do not currently review the commercial decisions made by directors in good faith or judge them with the wisdom of hindsight. In this context we thought that the best argument for introducing a statutory business judgment rule was if empirical research showed that directors were concerned about a statutory statement of the duty of care, or if there was evidence that such a rule would help raise the standard of behaviour by directors.

5.25 On the assumption that the director's duty of care was made statutory, we asked consultees whether there should be a statutory principle of non-interference by the courts in commercial decisions made in good faith, and, if so, whether it should be similar to that proposed in Australia or stated by the American Law Institute.

Summary of respondents' views

5.26 A small majority of respondents were against the introduction of a business judgment rule into statute. Most recognised that the courts already respect commercial decisions under the general law and did not see any reason to codify this. The principle would be best left to be developed by the courts. Some argued that it was implicit in the duty of care and that the courts would see it as such. A number of respondents also noted that the UK was less litigious than either the USA or Australia: a flood of litigation following the introduction of a statutory duty of care was considered unlikely.

5.27 Those in favour based their support largely on the need to clarify the law and to relieve concerns that a statutory duty would raise the standard of care and lead to defensive management.

Recommendation

5.28 The courts currently do not judge directors with the wisdom of hindsight and do not 'second-guess' directors on commercial matters. There is nothing to suggest that this long-established judicial approach would not apply. It would in any event be difficult to formulate a business judgment principle without either narrowing it or making it too rigid. The examples reviewed in the Paper suggest that there is no simple way of embodying the principle in the statutory form.

5.29 We had considered in the Paper that the main reason for introducing a statutory business judgment rule would be if there was evidence that directors were concerned about the dual objective/subjective standard. Those respondents who favoured its introduction thought that this might be the case. However, our empirical research did not reveal particular concern among directors about this. *Accordingly, we do not recommend a statutory business judgment rule.*

Should there be statutory provisions dealing with delegation to and reliance on third parties?

Consultation issue

5.30 Currently the general law sets out when a director may properly delegate his responsibilities to third parties and rely on third parties. These rules have been codified in some common law jurisdictions. For example the New Zealand Companies Act 1993 provides that the board of directors remains responsible for the exercise of powers it delegates *unless* the board (a) believed on reasonable grounds at all times before the exercise of the power that the delegate would exercise the power in conformity with the duties imposed on the directors of the company; and (b) has properly monitored the exercise of the power by the delegate. It further provides that a director may rely on information given by an employee, expert, professional adviser or another director in relation to matters within their competence or responsibility, provided that the director acted in good faith, made proper enquiries and had no grounds for suspicion.

5.31 We noted in the Paper that the Australian government is consulting on the introduction of draft legislation similar to this. The government was concerned about the implications of *Daniels v Anderson* (1995) 16 ACSR 607), which concerned the monitoring of management by the board. With the complexity of modern business this is an important and difficult area. The court had stressed in that case that a director could not blindly rely on the judgments of others, but must take positive steps to satisfy himself that the company was being properly run. As with the business judgment rule discussed above (paras 5.21–5.29), there is fear that this decision may lead to an over-conservative business approach.

5.32 The courts in this country have also recently had to consider the responsibility of a director who delegates. In *Re Barings plc* (unreported, applied by Jonathan Parker J in *Re Barings plc (No. 5)* [1999] 1 BCLC 433 at p. 487) Sir Richard Scott V-C confirmed that the overall responsibility of a director is not delegable. He said that the degree of personal blameworthiness that may attach to the individual with the overall responsibility, on account of a failure by those to whom he has delegated, must depend on the facts of each particular case. For example it might be that personal responsibility would attach because the system in which the failure occurred was inadequate. Similarly, in *Re Westmid Packing Services Ltd* [1998] 2 All ER 124 Lord Woolf MR said (at p. 130) that each individual director owes duties to the company to inform himself about its affairs and to join with his co-directors in supervising and controlling them. A proper degree of delegation and division of responsibility was of course permissible, and often necessary, but not total abrogation of responsibility.

5.33 Unless the empirical research showed that there were similar concerns in the UK, we considered that there was probably no reason for supposing that the present judge-made law was not working satisfactorily. We asked consultees whether there should be a statutory provision that set out the circumstances in which a director may delegate his powers to others and rely on information provided by others without incurring liability.

Summary of respondents' views

5.34 The majority of respondents were not in favour of such a statutory provision. Most preferred this issue to be left to the courts to develop on a case-by-case basis. Some thought that the present law was clear and satisfactory. It was pointed out that providing specifically for all the circumstances in which a director may delegate or rely on others might cause difficulties in interpretation and, therefore, might not help advisers and courts.

5.35 Few reasons were given by those who supported a statutory provision. One respondent thought that it might be useful as part of a general statement of the rights and liabilities of non-executive directors. Another supported it on the grounds of certainty and clarity, although the difficulty in drafting the provisions was recognised.

Recommendation

5.36 We consider that the law in relation to this area is still developing. We see real problems in setting out in statute detailed circumstances in which a director can properly rely on a third party. We think that any such rules are likely to be too restrictive and to fail to deal with a situation in which a director should be able to rely on another.

5.37 As our empirical research did not reveal undue concern amongst directors on the question of delegation and reliance under the present law, we agree with the majority of our respondents and *recommend that there should not be a statutory provision setting out the circumstances in which a director may delegate his powers to others and rely on information provided by others without incurring liability.*

Summary of recommendations under this Part

5.38 *To summarise, our recommendations under this Part are (1) that a director's duty of care, skill and diligence to his company should be set out in statute; (2) that the standard should be judged by a twofold objective/subjective test; (3) that regard should be had to the functions of the particular director and the circumstances of the company; and (4) that there should not be a statutory business judgment rule or statutory provisions dealing with delegation of a director's powers to others or reliance on information provided by others.*

12.4.5 Duty to avoid conflicts of interest

COMPANIES ACT 2006, S. 175

175. Duty to avoid conflicts of interest

(1) A director of a company must avoid a situation in which he has, or can have, a direct or indirect interest that conflicts, or possibly may conflict, with the interests of the company.

(2) This applies in particular to the exploitation of any property, information or opportunity (and it is immaterial whether the company could take advantage of the property, information or opportunity).

(3) This duty does not apply to a conflict of interest arising in relation to a transaction or arrangement with the company.

(4) This duty is not infringed—

(a) if the situation cannot reasonably be regarded as likely to give rise to a conflict of interest; or

(b) if the matter has been authorised by the directors.

(5) Authorisation may be given by the directors—

(a) where the company is a private company and nothing in the company's constitution invalidates such authorisation, by the matter being proposed to and authorised by the directors; or

(b) where the company is a public company and its constitution includes provision enabling the directors to authorise the matter, by the matter being proposed to and authorised by them in accordance with the constitution.

(6) The authorisation is effective only if—

(a) any requirements as to the quorum at the meeting at which the matter is considered is met without counting the director in question or any other interested director, and

(b) the matter was agreed to without their voting or would have been agreed to if their votes had not been counted.

(7) Any reference in this section to a conflict of interest includes a conflict of interest and duty and a conflict of duties.

A director must not place himself in a situation where his interest may conflict with the interests of the company (s. 175(1)). This duty applies to the exploitation of any property, information or opportunity of the company (s. 175(2)). This replaces the well known no-conflict rule (*Aberdeen Railway Co v Blaikie Bros*). An example where this rule applies is where a director sells his own property to the company (as in *Aberdeen Railway Co.* v *Blaikie Bros* extracted below), in which case the director cannot retain the benefit of the contract which is voidable at the instance of the company unless the contract has been ratified or approved by the shareholders in general meeting after full disclosure by the director of the nature of his interest in the contract (see 12.5 below and *DEG-Deutsche Investitions* v *Konshy* [2002] 1 BCLC 478). A director's duty is to obtain the lowest possible price for the company and this duty conflicts with the director's personal interest in selling property to the company at the highest possible price. (See *J.J. Harrison (Properties) Ltd* v *Harrison* [2002] 1 BCLC 162 for an example of a director buying his company's property at an undervalue.)

Aberdeen Railway Co. v Blaikie Bros

Selling chairs to your company

[1843–60] All ER Rep 249, House of Lords

Facts   *The railway company agreed to buy chairs from a partnership, Blaikie Bros. A member of the partnership was also a director of the company. When the partners sought to enforce the contract the defendant company successfully claimed that the contract was voidable.*

LORD CRANWORTH LC: This, therefore, brings us to the general question, whether a director of a railway company is or is not precluded from dealing on behalf of the company with himself or with a firm in which he is a partner. The directors are a body to whom is delegated the duty of managing the general affairs of the company. A corporate body can only act by agents, and it is, of course, the duty of those agents so to act as best to promote the interests of the corporation whose affairs they are conducting. Such an agent has duties to discharge of a fiduciary character towards his principal, and it is a rule of universal application that no one having such duties to discharge shall be allowed to enter into engagements in which he has or can have a personal interest conflicting or which possibly may conflict with the interests of those whom he is bound to protect. So strictly is this principle adhered to that no question is allowed to be raised as to the fairness or unfairness of a contract so entered into. It obviously is, or may be, impossible to demonstrate how far in any particular case the terms of such a contract have been the best for the cestui que trust which it was impossible to obtain. It may sometimes happen that the terms on which a trustee has dealt or attempted to deal with the estate or interests of those for whom he is a trustee have been as good as could have been obtained from any other person; they may even at the time have been better. But still so inflexible is the rule that no inquiry on that subject is permitted.

   The English authorities on this subject are numerous and uniform. The principle was acted on by Lord King in *Keech* v *Sandford* (1726) Sel Cas t King 61, and by Lord Hardwicke, in *Whelpdale* v *Cookson*, and the whole subject was considered by Lord Eldon on a great variety of occasions. It is sufficient to refer to what fell from that very able and learned judge in *Ex parte James* (1803) 8 Ves Jr 337. It is true that the questions have generally arisen on agreements for purchases or leases of land, and not, as here, on a contract of a mercantile character. But this can make no difference in principle. The inability to contract depends not on the subject-matter of the agreement, but on the fiduciary character of the contracting party, and I cannot entertain a doubt of its being applicable to the case of a party who is acting as manager of a mercantile or trading business for the benefit of others no less than to that of an agent or trustee employed in selling land.

   Was, then, Mr Blaikie so acting in the case now before us? If he was, did he, while so acting, contract, on behalf of those for whom he was acting, with himself? Both these questions must obviously be answered in the affirmative. Mr Blaikie was not only a director, but, if that was necessary, the chairman of the directors. In that character it was his bounden duty to make the best bargains he could for the benefit of the company. While he filled that character, viz, on February 6, 1846, he entered into a contract on behalf of the company with his own firm for the purchase of a large quantity of chairs at a certain stipulated price. His duty to the company imposed on him the obligation of obtaining these iron chairs at the lowest possible price. His personal interest would lead him in an entirely opposite direction—would induce him to fix the price as high as possible. This is the very evil against which the rule in question is directed; and I see nothing whatever to prevent its application here. I observe that Lord Fullerton seemed to doubt whether the rule would apply where the party whose act or contract is called in question, is only one of a body of directors not a sole trustee or manager. But, with all deference, this appears to me to make no difference. It was Mr Blaikie's duty to give to his co-directors, and through them to the company, the full benefit of all the knowledge and skill which he could bring to bear on the subject. He was bound to assist them in getting the articles contracted for at the cheapest possible rate. As far as related to the advice he should give them, he put his interest in conflict with his duty, and whether he was the sole director, or only one of many, can make no difference in principle. The same observation applies to the fact, that he was not the sole person trading with the company. He was one of the firm of Blaikie Brothers with whom the contract was made, and so was interested in driving as hard a bargain with the company as he could induce them to make.

Conflicts of interest can also arise when a director makes a profit from his position. Thus, s. 175(1) also replaces the well-known no-profit rule in *Regal (Hastings)* and *Cook* v *Deeks*. As directors owe trustee-like duties, it is not surprising that, unless expressly allowed, they must not profit from their position. This is an application of the leading trust case of *Keech* v *Sandford* (1726) Sel Cas t King 61. If the directors make a personal profit as a result of their office or of any information or corporate opportunity that comes to them by reason of their office, they are required to account for the profit to the company. The rule, by analogy with trust law, is absolutely strict and does not depend on fault or lack of good faith. The reasons for this strictness are to discourage temptation and because the company may easily approve the transaction and allow the director to keep the profit by a resolution of disinterested members by majority or by unanimous consent of the company (CA 2006, s. 239).

Section 175(2) also makes it clear that it is immaterial whether the company could take advantage of the property, information or opportunity. This reaffirms the decision in *Regal (Hastings)* v *Gulliver* (extracted below) but is contrary to the Canadian case of *Peso Silver Mines Ltd* v *Cropper* (1966) 58 DLR (2d) 1, which took the view that if the board had rejected the opportunity bona fide and for sound business reasons the directors could then take the opportunity for themselves and the Privy Council's decision in *Queensland Mines Ltd* v *Hudson* (1978) 52 ALJR 399, that if the director had disclosed the contract to and discussed it with the board and they had resolved not to pursue the contract further, the director was entitled to take up the contract personally and retain any profit.

Regal (Hastings) Ltd v Gulliver
The high-water mark of the no-profit rule
[1942] 1 All ER 378, [1967] 2 AC 134, House of Lords

This case shows that although the liability of directors may not be quite the same as that of trustees, the principle that a person in a fiduciary position is not allowed to make a profit out of the position applies equally to directors. Thus, four directors of Regal (Hastings) Ltd, who made an incidental profit by reason of and in the course of the execution of their office as directors, were required to account for the profit notwithstanding that they had acted bona fide throughout. The directors' liability did not depend on fraud or lack of good faith. It was conceded by Lord Porter that the result would mean that the new owners of Regal (Hastings) would receive a windfall. This in fact amounted to a reduction in the price they paid for their shares. The no-profit rule was thus vigorously enforced almost to the point of absurdity.

Facts   Regal (Hastings) Ltd owned a cinema. A subsidiary, Hastings Amalgamated Cinemas Ltd (Amalgamated), was set up to buy long leases of two other cinemas so that all three could be sold as a going concern. The owner of the two cinemas was only willing to grant the leases if Amalgamated's fully paid-up capital was £5,000 or if the directors would give personal guarantees for the rent. The directors of Regal were not prepared to give personal guarantees and Regal could not contribute capital of more than £2,000 for the shares in Amalgamated. In the end it was decided that four directors, Bobby, Griffiths, Bassett and Bentley, would themselves subscribe for 2,000 shares. The chairman, Gulliver, found outside subscribers for 500 shares, and the company's solicitor, Garton, took the remaining 500 shares. The deal went through. Amalgamated acquired the leases. All the shares in Regal and the individually held shares in Amalgamated were then sold and the four directors made a useful profit on selling those shares. The new controllers caused Regal to bring an action and successfully required the directors to account for their profit to Regal.

LORD RUSSELL OF KILLOWEN: We have to consider the question of the respondents' liability on the footing that, in taking up these shares in Amalgamated, they acted with bona fides, intending to act in the interest of Regal.

Nevertheless, they may be liable to account for the profits which they have made, if, while standing in a fiduciary relationship to Regal, they have by reason and in course of that fiduciary relationship made a profit . . .

The rule of equity which insists on those, who by use of a fiduciary position make a profit, being liable to account for that profit, in no way depends on fraud, or absence of bona fides; or upon such questions or considerations as whether the profit would or should otherwise have gone to the plaintiff, or whether the profiteer was under a duty to obtain the source of the profit for the plaintiff, or whether he took a risk or acted as he did for the benefit of the plaintiff, or whether the plaintiff has in fact been damaged or benefited by his action. The liability arises from the mere fact of a profit having, in the stated circumstances, been made. The profiteer, however honest and well-intentioned, cannot escape the risk of being called upon to account.

The leading case of *Keech v Sandford* (1726) Sel Cas t King 61 is an illustration of the strictness of this rule of equity in this regard, and of how far the rule is independent of these outside considerations . . .

My lords, I have no hesitation in coming to the conclusion, upon the facts of this case, that these shares, when acquired by the directors, were acquired by reason, and only by reason of the fact that they were directors of Regal, and in the course of their execution of that office.

It now remains to consider whether in acting as directors of Regal they stood in a fiduciary relationship to that company. Directors of a limited company are the creatures of statute and occupy a position peculiar to themselves. In some respects they resemble trustees, in others they do not. In some respects they resemble agents, in others they do not. In some respects they resemble managing partners, in others they do not . . .

In the result, I am of opinion that the directors standing in a fiduciary relationship to Regal in regard to the exercise of their powers as directors, and having obtained these shares by reason and only by reason of the fact that they were directors of Regal and in the course of the execution of that office, are accountable for the profits which they have made out of them. The equitable rule laid down in *Keech v Sandford* and *Ex parte James* (1803) 8 Ves Jr 337, and similar authorities applies to them in full force. It was contended that these cases were distinguishable by reason of the fact that it was impossible for Regal to get the shares owing to lack of funds, and that the directors in taking the shares were really acting as members of the public. I cannot accept this argument. It was impossible for the cestui que trust in *Keech v Sandford* to obtain the lease, nevertheless the trustee was accountable. The suggestion that the directors were applying simply as members of the public is a travesty of the facts. They could, had they wished, have protected themselves by a resolution (either antecedent or subsequent) of the Regal shareholders in general meeting. In default of such approval, the liability to account must remain. The result is that, in my opinion, each of the respondents Bobby, Griffiths, Bassett and Bentley is liable to account for the profit which he made on the sale of his 500 shares in Amalgamated.

The case of the respondent Gulliver, however, requires some further consideration, for he has raised a separate and distinct answer to the claim. He says: 'I never promised to subscribe for shares in Amalgamated. I never did so subscribe. I only promised to find others who would be willing to subscribe. I only found others who did subscribe. The shares were theirs. They were never mine. They received the profit. I received none of it.' If these are the true facts, his answer seems complete. The evidence in my opinion establishes his contention...

As regards Gulliver, this appeal should, in my opinion, be dismissed.

There remains to consider the case of Garton. He stands on a different footing from the other respondents in that he was not a director of Regal. He was Regal's legal adviser; but, in my opinion, he has a short but effective answer to the plaintiffs' claim. He was requested by the Regal directors to apply for 500 shares. They arranged that they themselves should each be responsible for £500 of the Amalgamated capital, and they appealed, by their chairman, to Garton to subscribe the balance of £500 which was required to make up the £3,000. In law his action, which has resulted in a profit, was taken at the request of Regal, and I know of no principle or authority which would justify a decision that a solicitor must account for profit resulting from a transaction which he has entered into on his own behalf, not merely with the consent, but at the request of his client.

LORD PORTER: My lords, I am conscious of certain possibilities which are involved in the conclusion which all your lordships have reached. The action is brought by the Regal company. Technically, of course, the fact that an unlooked-for advantage may be gained by the shareholders of that company is immaterial to the question at issue. The company and its shareholders are separate entities. One cannot help remembering, however, that in fact the shares have been purchased by a financial group who were willing to acquire those of the Regal and the Amalgamated at a certain price. As a result of your lordships' decision that group will, I think, receive in one hand part of the sum which has been paid by the other. For the shares in Amalgamated they paid £3 16s 1d per share, yet part of that sum may be returned to the group, though not necessarily to the individual shareholders by reason of the enhancement in value of the shares in Regal—an enhancement brought about as a result of the receipt by the company of the profit made by some of its former directors on the sale of Amalgamated shares. This, it seems, may be an unexpected windfall, but whether it be so or not, the principle that a person occupying a fiduciary relationship shall not make a profit by reason thereof is of such vital importance that the possible consequence in the present case is in fact as it is in law an immaterial consideration...

The legal proposition may, I think, be broadly stated by saying that one occupying a position of trust must not make a profit which he can acquire only by use of his fiduciary position, or, if he does, he must account for the profit so made. For this proposition the cases of *Keech v Sandford* (1726) Sel Cas t King 61 and *Ex parte James* (1803) 8 Ves Jr 337 are sufficient authority...

Directors, no doubt, are not trustees, but they occupy a fiduciary position towards the company whose board they form. Their liability in this respect does not depend upon breach of duty but upon the proposition that a director must not make a profit out of property acquired by reason of his relationship to the company of which he is director. It matters not that he could not have acquired the property for the company itself—the profit which he makes is the company's, even though the property by means of which he made it was not and could not have been acquired on its behalf...

My lords, these observations apply generally to the action, but the cases of Gulliver and Garton stand on a somewhat different footing. As to them, there are additional and special considerations to be kept in mind. I need not set them out or refer to them further than by saying that I find myself in agreement with the reasoning and conclusion of my noble and learned friend, Lord Russell of Killowen.

Cook v Deeks

Appropriating a corporate opportunity

[1916] 1 AC 554, Privy Council

This is a classic case of directors usurping a corporate opportunity that belongs to the company and so making a personal profit. The Privy Council held that the contract had come to the profiteers in their capacity and by virtue of their position as directors, and as such it belonged in equity to the company. The directors' profit-making represented a misappropriation of company property and was therefore not ratifiable by the wrongdoers. (Note, however, that under CA 2006, s. 239, the transaction could be ratified by disinterested shareholders by majority or by the company by unanimous consent.)

Facts   The Toronto Construction Co. Ltd was very successful in obtaining construction contracts from the Canadian Pacific Railway Co. Three of the four directors and shareholders, Deeks, Deeks and Hinds, fell out with Cook, who was also a director and shareholder. Later, when a large Canadian Pacific Railway contract came available for tender by the Toronto Construction Co., the three direct-ors formed a new company to take the contract, and so as to exclude Cook. A resolution was later passed by the three directors as shareholders of the Toronto Construction Co., inter alia, to declare that the company claimed no interest in the contract.

LORD BUCKMASTER (giving the judgment of the Privy Council): Two questions of law arise out of this long history of fact. The first is whether, apart altogether from the subsequent resolutions, the company would have been at liberty to claim from the three defendants the benefit of the contract which they had obtained from the Canadian Pacific Railway Co.; and the second, which only arises if the first be answered in the affirmative, whether in such event the majority of the shareholders of the company constituted by the three defendants could ratify and approve of what was done and thereby release all claim against the directors …

It is quite right to point out the importance of avoiding the establishment of rules as to directors' duties which would impose upon them burdens so heavy and responsibilities so great that men of good position would hesitate to accept the office. But, on the other hand, men who assume the complete control of a company's business must remember that they are not at liberty to sacrifice the interests which they are bound to protect, and, while ostensibly acting for the company, divert in their own favour business which should properly belong to the company they represent.

Their lordships think that, in the circumstances, the defendants T.R. Hinds and G.S. and G.M. Deeks were guilty of a distinct breach of duty in the course they took to secure the contract, and that they cannot retain the benefit of such contract for themselves, but must be regarded as holding it on behalf of the company.

There remains the more difficult consideration of whether this position can be made regular by resolutions of the company controlled by the votes of these three defendants. The Supreme Court [of Ontario] have given this matter the most careful consideration, but their lordships are unable to agree with the conclusion which they reached.

In their lordships' opinion the Supreme Court has insufficiently recognised the distinction between two classes of case and has applied the principles applicable to the case of a director selling to his company property which was in equity as well as at law his own, and which he could dispose of as he thought fit, to the case of a director dealing with property which, though his own at law, in equity belonged to his company. The cases of *North-West Transportation Co.* v *Beatty* (1887) 12 App Cas 589 and *Burland* v *Earle* [1902] AC 83 both belonged to the former class. In each, direct-ors had sold to the company property in which the company had no interest at law or in equity. If the company claimed any interest by reason of the transaction, it could only be by affirming the sale, in which case such sale, though initially voidable, would be validated by subsequent ratification. If the company refused to affirm the sale the transaction would be set aside and the parties restored to their former position, the directors getting the property and the company receiving back the purchase price. There would be no middle course. The company could not insist on retaining the property while paying less than the price agreed. This would be for the Court to make a new contract between the parties. It would be quite another thing if the director had originally acquired the property which he sold to his company under circumstances which made it in equity the property of the company. The distinction to which their lordships have drawn attention is expressly recognised by Lord Davey in *Burland* v *Earle* and is the foundation of the judgment in *North-West Transportation Co.* v *Beatty*, and is clearly explained in the case of *Jacobus Marler Estates* v *Marler* (1913) 85 LJ PC 167...

If, as their lordships find on the facts, the contract in question was entered into under such circumstances that the directors could not retain the benefit of it for themselves, then it belonged in equity to the company and ought to have been dealt with as an asset of the company. Even supposing it be not *ultra vires* of a company to make a present to its directors, it appears quite certain that directors holding a majority of votes would not be permitted to make a present to themselves. This would be to allow a majority to oppress the minority. To such circumstances the cases of *North-West Transportation Co.* v *Beatty* and *Burland* v *Earle* have no application. In the same way, if directors have acquired for themselves property or rights which they must be regarded as holding on behalf of the company, a resolution that the rights of the company should be disregarded in the matter would amount to forfeiting the interest and property of the minority of shareholders in favour of the majority, and that by the votes of those who are interested in securing the property for themselves. Such use of voting power has never been sanctioned by the courts, and, indeed, was expressly disapproved in the case of *Menier* v *Hooper's Telegraph Works* (1874) LR 9 Ch App 350.

Industrial Development Consultants Ltd v *Cooley*

An 'opportunity' that never belonged to the company

[1972] 1 WLR 443, Birmingham Assizes

In this case a director who took a contract personally was held accountable for his profit even though it was clear that the other party was not prepared to offer the contract to the company. Roskill J here took an orthodox *Regal (Hastings)* approach which is to look at the capacity of the profiteer. The director was held liable for the profit even though the company could not in any event have obtained it for itself.

Facts   The defendant was the managing director of the plaintiff company. He entered into negotiations with the Eastern Gas Board for a contract for the company. The Gas Board indicated that it would offer the contract only to him personally, not to the company. The defendant promptly resigned, ostensibly on grounds of ill-health, and personally took up the contract from the Gas Board. The court held him liable for the profit he made.

ROSKILL J: The first matter that has to be considered is whether or not the defendant was in a fiduciary relationship with his principals, the plaintiffs. Mr Davies [counsel for the defendant] argued that he was not because he received this information which was communicated to him privately. With respect, I think that argument is wrong. The defendant had one capacity and one capacity only in which he was carrying on business at that time. That capacity was as managing director of the plaintiffs. Information which came to him while he was managing director and which was of concern to the plaintiffs and was relevant for the plaintiffs to know, was information which it was his duty to pass on to the plaintiffs because between himself and the plaintiffs a fiduciary relationship existed...

It seems to me plain that throughout the whole of May, June and July 1969 the defendant was in a fiduciary relationship with the plaintiffs. From the time he embarked upon his course of dealing with the Eastern Gas Board, irrespective of anything which he did or he said to Mr Hicks [chairman of the plaintiff company], he embarked upon a deliberate policy and course of conduct which put his personal interest as a potential contracting party with the Eastern Gas Board in direct conflict with his pre-existing and continuing duty as managing director of the plaintiffs. That is something which for over 200 years the courts have forbidden...

Therefore, I feel impelled to the conclusion that when the defendant embarked on this course of conduct of getting information on June 13, using that information and preparing those documents over the weekend of June 14/15 and sending them off on June 17, he was guilty of putting himself into the position in which his duty to his employers, the plaintiffs, and his own private interests conflicted and conflicted grievously. There being the fiduciary relationship I have described, it seems to me plain that it was his duty once he got this information to pass it to his employers and not to guard it for his own personal purposes and profit. He put himself into the position when his duty and his interests conflicted. As Lord Upjohn put it in *Phipps v Boardman* [1967] 2 AC 46 at p. 127: 'It is only at this stage that any question of accountability arises'.

Does accountability arise? It is said: 'Well, even if there were that conflict of duty and interest, nonetheless, this was a contract with a third party in which the plaintiffs never could have had any interest because they would have never got it'. That argument has been forcefully put before me by Mr Davies.

The remarkable position then arises that if one applies the equitable doctrine upon which the plaintiffs rely to oblige the defendant to account, they will receive a benefit which… it is unlikely they would have got for themselves had the defendant complied with his duty to them. On the other hand, if the defendant is not required to account he will have made a large profit, as a result of having deliberately put himself into a position in which his duty to the plaintiffs who were employing him and his personal interests conflicted. I leave out of account the fact that he dishonestly tricked Mr Hicks into releasing him on June 16 although Mr Brown [counsel for the plaintiff company] urged that that was another reason why equity must compel him to disgorge his profit. It is said that the plaintiffs' only remedy is to sue for damages either for breach of contract or maybe for fraudulent misrepresentation. Mr Brown has been at pains to disclaim any intention to claim damages for breach of contract save on one basis only, and he has disclaimed specifically any claim for damages for fraudulent misrepresentation. Therefore, if the plaintiffs succeed they will get a profit which they probably would not have got for themselves had the defendant fulfilled his duty. If the defendant is allowed to keep that profit he will have got something which he was able to get solely by reason of his breach of fiduciary duty to the plaintiffs.

When one looks at the way the cases have gone over the centuries it is plain that the question whether or not the benefit would have been obtained but for the breach of trust has always been treated as irrelevant…

In one sense the benefit in this case did not arise because of the defendant's directorship; indeed, the defendant would not have got this work had he remained a director. However, one must, as Lord Upjohn pointed out in *Phipps v Boardman* [1967] 2 AC 46 at p. 125, look at the passages in the speeches in *Regal (Hastings) Ltd v Gulliver* [1967] 2 AC 134 having regard to the facts of that case to which those passages and those statements were directed. I think Mr Brown was right when he said that it is the basic principle which matters. It is an overriding principle of equity that a man must not be allowed to put himself in a position in which his fiduciary duty and his interests conflict. The variety of cases where that can happen is infinite. The fact that there has not previously been a case precisely of this nature with precisely similar facts before the courts is of no import. The facts of this case are, I think, exceptional and I hope unusual. They seem to me plainly to come within this principle.

The duty to avoid conflict of interests does not apply where the director enters into a transaction or arrangement with the company (s. 175(3)) as such transaction or arrangement is regulated by s. 177 or s. 182 of the CA 2006. This is a departure from the old law which also applied to such transaction or arrangement (cf *Aberdeen Railway*). Where the director enters into a transaction or arrangement with a third party in a conflict of interest situation, he is not in breach of his duty if the transaction or arrangement has been approved by the board (s. 175(4)). This is also a departure from the old law (cf. *Cook v Deeks*).

What constitutes an opportunity for the purposes of s. 175 will remain a contentious point, as is the case under the old common law. It would appear that the position remains that where the director has not obtained for himself a maturing business opportunity, it is not a breach of fiduciary duty for him to form an intention to set up business in competition with his company after his directorship has ceased (see *Balston Ltd* v *Headline Filters Ltd* [1990] FSR 385). Likewise, where the director is offered better terms of service by another company, it is not a breach of his duties to resign from his present employment and accept the better offer. This is so even if the other company was at the same time also negotiating to buy out the director's original company so long as the director is not involved in the negotiation. There will be no conflict of interest as what the other company is seeking to obtain from the director is an asset which belongs to the director (i.e., the client goodwill which attached to him as the person who had, over many years, managed his clients' investments) and which he is free to exploit for himself on leaving his present employment (see *Framlington Group plc* v *Anderson* [1995] 1 BCLC 475 below).

In appropriate circumstances a director who has been effectively excluded from the management may work for a competing company (*In Plus Group Ltd* v *Pyke* [2002] BCLC 201, CA). A director is free to resign his directorship at any time notwithstanding the damage that the resignation may cause the company (*CMS Dolphin Ltd* v *Simonet* [2001] 2 BCLC 704 at 733). By resigning his directorship he will put an end to his fiduciary obligations to the company so far as any future activity by himself is concerned provided that it does not involve the exploitation of confidential information or business opportunity available to him by virtue of his directorship (*British Midland Tool Ltd* v *Midland International Tooling Ltd* [2003] 2 BCLC 523 at 560). The general fiduciary duties of a director or an employee does not prevent a person from forming the intention, whilst a director, to set up in competition after his directorship or employment ceased nor does it prevent him from taking any preliminary steps to investigate or forward that intention provided he did not engage in any actual competitive activity whilst the directorship or employment continued (*Coleman Taymar Ltd* v *Oakes* [2001] 2 BCLC 749). A director who wishes to engage in a competing business and not to disclose his intentions to the company ought to resign his office as soon as his intention has been irrevocably formed and he has launched himself in the actual taking of preparatory steps (*British Midland Tool Ltd*).

Whilst s. 175(2) has adopted the orthodox rule in *Regal (Hastings)* contrary to the more flexible Canadian approach, it seems that cases such as *Island Export Finance Ltd* v *Umunna* and *Framlington Group plc* v *Anderson* remain valid as examples of situations which cannot reasonably be regarded as likely to give rise to a conflict of interest under s. 175(4)(a)—in *Umunna*, the managing director had resigned, prior to the transaction complained of, due to dissatisfaction with the company, and in *Anderson*, the directors did not take part in the negotiation.

Island Export Finance Ltd v *Umunna*
A more flexible approach to 'corporate opportunities'
[1986] BCLC 460, Queen's Bench Division

This is quite an important first-instance decision because in this case, Hutchinson J endorsed the more flexible approach preferred by Laskin J in the Supreme Court of Canada in *Canadian Aero Service Ltd* v *O'Malley* (1973) 40 DLR (3d) 371. This approach, while accepting the orthodox view, would take into account other factors such as the office or position held, the nature of the corporate opportunity, its ripeness etc. (See Hutchinson J's judgment extracted below where Laskin J's approach was referred to.) Hutchinson J's endorsement of Laskin J's approach may well open the way to a more flexible view of corporate opportunities in English company law.

Facts   Umunna was the managing director of IEF Ltd. In 1976 he secured a contract for IEF Ltd from the Cameroon postal authorities. In 1977, he resigned as managing director due to dissatisfaction with the company. He subsequently obtained orders for his own company from the Cameroon postal authorities. IEF Ltd unsuccessfully brought this action alleging that Umunna was in breach of his fiduciary duty even after his resignation.

HUTCHISON J: The plaintiff's case is based on the assertion that in approaching the Postal Department in the Cameroons and obtaining the two 1977 orders Mr Umunna was in breach of the fiduciary duty that he owed as a director of the plaintiff company. Counsel for the plaintiff began by referring me to *Regal (Hastings) Ltd* v *Gulliver* [1967] 2 AC 134.... He contends (and counsel for the defendants does not dispute this) that the case is authority for the proposition that directors of a company are in a fiduciary position and their liability to account does not depend on proof of bad faith and arises quite irrespective of whether the company could itself have taken advantage of the opportunity of which the directors availed themselves, or of the question whether in the event the company benefited from what they did. The rule is a strict one, to the effect that where directors have obtained a benefit only by reason of the fact that they were directors and in the course of the execution of their office, they are accountable for any profits which they have made...

Counsel for the plaintiff seeks to extend the principle by means of the following submission. He contends that a director is liable to account to the company if he learns of an opportunity or business advantage whilst he is working for the company and by virtue of his fiduciary position, and then uses the opportunity or exploits the advantage for his own benefit either while he is still working for the company or after the termination of his appointment. However, he recognises a limitation which applies in those cases where the use of the opportunity occurs after termination of the appointment, conceding that in such cases the director is liable only if (a) he had such use or exploitation in contemplation whilst a director, or (b) the opportunity fairly belongs to the company, for example if the company was actively pursuing the opportunity through the director before termination.

In support of this extended principle counsel for the plaintiff relies on the decision of the Supreme Court of Canada in the case of *Canadian Aero Service Ltd* v *O'Malley* (1973) 40 DLR (3d) 371. It is necessary to look with some care at this important decision...

This was...a case in which the two defendants had for some years been working up a detailed and complex project which had almost come to fruition, of which they had a particular knowledge, and which plainly they planned while still employed by Canaero to make away with if possible. It is clear that but for the work they had done and the knowledge they had acquired while employed, they would not have been able in the name of their new company and its associates to submit a tender only a month after that new company was incorporated...

Laskin J [said] (at p. 382):

An examination of the case law in this court and in the courts of other like jurisdictions on the fiduciary duties of directors and senior officers shows the pervasiveness of a strict ethic in this area of the law. In my opinion, this ethic disqualifies a director or senior officer from usurping for himself or diverting to another person or company with whom or with which he is associated a maturing business opportunity which his company is actively pursuing; he is also precluded from so acting even after his resignation where the resignation may fairly be said to have been prompted or influenced by a wish to acquire for himself the opportunity sought by the company, or where it was his position with the company rather than a fresh initiative that led him to the opportunity which he later acquired.

Counsel for the defendants submitted that this decision does not accord with the law of England, which does not recognise any fiduciary duty after termination. He contended that there was no English authority which held that it did, suggesting that one of the cases relied on by counsel for the plaintiff, the decision of Roskill J in *Industrial Development Consultants Ltd* v *Cooley* [1972] 1 WLR 443, was not in truth an authority for such a proposition because the breach of duty found really related to the actions of the defendant while still employed. In a sense, this is true, but the fact remains that the case is one in which the contract was obtained after the defendant had left the plaintiff's employment though (the judge found) as a result of work which he did while still the plaintiff's managing director. Essentially, the assertion of counsel for the defendants that there is no continuing fiduciary duty after termination of employment is based on the absence of any English case which positively asserts that there is such a duty: and certainly he has been unable to point to any case which asserts that there is not.

It seems to me that counsel's bold submission cannot be right, amounting as it does to the contention that a director, provided he *does* nothing contrary to his employers' interests while employed, may with impunity conceive the idea of resigning so that he may exploit some opportunity of the employers and, having resigned, proceed to exploit it for himself. Such a suggestion has only to be stated to be seen to be unsustainable, and in my judgment counsel for the plaintiff is right when he says that it conflicts with the dictum in one of the earliest cases in this line of authority, cited and relied on in the Canaero case, namely *Ex Parte James* (1803) 8 Ves Jr 337 where Lord Eldon LC said (at p. 352), speaking of the fiduciary in that case (who was a solicitor purchasing at a sale):

> With respect to the question now put, whether I will permit Jones to give up the office of solicitor, and to bid, I cannot give that permission. If the principle is right, that the solicitor cannot buy, it would lead to all the mischief of acting up to the point of sale, getting all the information that may be useful to him, then discharging himself from the character of solicitor, and buying the property ... On the other hand I do not deny, that those interested in the question may give the permission.

The submission of counsel for the defendants is that the decision in Canaero can be explained or justified by reference to the law relating to the misuse of confidential information. The nature of the information there exploited was, he suggests, truly confidential and could be protected as such even after the termination of employment. Moreover, he submits that the decision could have been justified on the basis that the directors had abused their position while still employees of Canaero, at which time they met, discussed the project which they later carried into operation, and incorporated the company through which they did it, using the expertise they had acquired in the plaintiff's service. Furthermore, counsel submits that there is no authority for the proposition that the fiduciary duty of agents or trustees continues after their office has terminated. While in a sense this may be correct, if it is intended to mean that immediately on termination an agent or trustee is completely unfettered in the use he may make of information acquired during his period of office, it seems to me to be self-evidently wrong.

It appears to me, if I may say so with respect, that the judges in the Canaero case were absolutely right to conclude that on the facts of that case there was a breach of fiduciary duty by the defendants: and that in so holding they were consistently applying the principles laid down in the line of authorities of which *Regal (Hastings) Ltd* v *Gulliver* is an example. I do, however, question whether in stating the principle (40 DLR (3d) 371 at p. 382) they do not put the matter somewhat too widely in the last three lines of the passage I have cited. The words in question are: '... or where it was his position with the company rather than a fresh initiative that led him to the opportunity which he later acquired'.

It is to be noted that this passage begins with the word 'or', and that it would seem that the phrase 'that led him to the opportunity which he later acquired' has been deliberately chosen rather than the phrase 'that led him to acquire the opportunity'. Thus, it seems to me that, literally construed, this last part of the formulation could justify holding former directors accountable for profits wherever information acquired by them as such led them to the source from which they subsequently, perhaps as the result of prolonged fresh initiative, acquired business. If it is intended to mean that, it is far more widely stated than the facts of the case require: but I do not believe that that is what was intended.

It is, in this context, instructive to read two paragraphs in *Canadian Aero Service* (1973) 40 DLR (3d) 371 at p. 390. The first emphasises what an extreme case Canaero was and the second contains a passage much relied on, in my judgment rightly, by counsel for the defendants:

> In holding that on the facts found by the trial judge there was a breach of fiduciary duty by [the defendants] which survived their resignations I am not to be taken as laying down any rule of liability to be read as if it were a statute. The general standards of loyalty, good faith and avoidance of conflict of duty and self-interest to which the conduct of a director or senior officer must conform, must be tested in each case by many factors which it would be reckless to attempt to enumerate exhaustively. Among them are the factor of position or office held, the nature of the corporate opportunity, its ripeness, its specificness and the director's or managerial officer's relation to it, the amount of knowledge possessed, the circumstances in which it was obtained and whether it was special or, indeed, even private, the factor of time in the continuation of fiduciary duty where the alleged breach occurs after termination of the relationship with the company, and the circumstances under which the relationship was terminated, that is whether by retirement or resignation or discharge.

In this context counsel for the defendants rightly stresses the fundamental principles relating to contracts in restraint of trade. It would, it seems to me, be surprising to find that directors alone, because of the fiduciary nature of their relationship with the company, were restrained from exploiting after they had ceased to be such any opportunity of which they had acquired knowledge while directors. Directors, no less than employees, acquire a general fund of knowledge and expertise in the course of their work, and it is plainly in the public interest that they should be free to exploit it in a new position. It is one thing to hold them accountable when, in the graphic words of Laskin J (at p. 391), 'they entered the lists in the heat of the maturation of the project, known to them to be under active government consideration when they resigned from Canaero and when they proposed to bid on behalf of Terra'; but it is an altogether different thing to hold former directors accountable whenever they exploit for their own or a new employer's benefit information which, while they may have come by it solely because of their position as directors of the plaintiff company, in truth forms part of their general fund of knowledge and their stock-in-trade . . .

It appears to me that, on the basis of the findings I have made, the plaintiff's claim fails for a variety of reasons. I would summarise them as follows: (a) The hope of obtaining further orders for postal caller boxes could not in any realistic sense be said to be 'a maturing business opportunity'. (b) Neither when Mr Umunna resigned nor when he succeeded in obtaining the two June 1977 orders was the plaintiff actively pursuing the matter. (c) It cannot in any true sense be said that, at the time he resigned, Mr Umunna had in contemplation the exploitation of the Cameroons postal box business. As I have already indicated, the highest that it can be put is that, if asked, he would undoubtedly have replied that that was a potential source of business which he might be minded to pursue. It was certainly not his motive for resigning, and it cannot possibly be said that his resignation was 'prompted or influenced by a wish to acquire for himself the opportunity sought by the company'.

NOTE: See also *Bhullar* v *Bhullar* [2003] 2 BCLC 241, CA where Jonathan Parker LJ held that the no conflict or no profit rule was universal and inflexible. He said the test was whether 'reasonable men, looking at the facts would think there was a real sensible possibility of conflict' and where a director exploited a commercial opportunity for his own benefit, the relevant question was not whether the company had some kind of beneficial interest in the opportunity but whether the director's exploitation of the opportunity was such as to attract the application of the rule.

Framlington Group plc v Anderson
[1995] 1 BCLC 475, Chancery Division

In the absence of restrictive covenants in the contract of employment, directors are entitled to leave their present employment to join a competing company, and are entitled to bring with them the client goodwill which attached to them and to exploit it. They are not under a duty to inform their current employer of the terms of their new employment. Where their employer is at the same time negotiating to sell its business to their new employer, they are not under a duty to assist their current employer in obtaining the best price, especially where they are not involved in the negotiation.

Facts   FIM agreed to sell part of its private client fund management business to Rathbone after its three directors who managed its private client fund business had been offered employment by Rathbone. The negotiation was conducted by Mr Loach, managing director of FIM's parent company, Framlington plc, and Mr Ingall, chief executive of Rathbone. The three directors did not, and were indeed specifically told not to, take part in the negotiation. They were offered generous terms of employment, including holdings of shares in Rathbone, which were not known to FIM until after the sale of its business to Rathbone. Framlington plc and FIM brought an action claiming that the three directors were accountable for the shares as secret profits.

BLACKBURNE J: [His lordship referred to *Boardman* v *Phipps* [1967] 2 AC 46 at p. 123 per Lord Upjohn, *Boulting* v *Association of Cinematograph, Television and Allied Technicians* [1963] 2 QB 606 at pp. 637–8 per Upjohn LJ, *Bell* v *Lever Brothers Ltd* [1932] AC 161 at p. 194 per Lord Blanesburgh, and *Balston Ltd* v *Headline Filters Ltd* [1990] FSR 385 at p. 412 per Falconer J and continued:]

Wherein then lies the conflict? What is the specific interest of FIM which is in conflict with the three managers' conduct in negotiating for themselves a generous remuneration package with Rathbone at the time that Mr Loach was in negotiation with Mr Ingall?

It is not suggested, although initially in the correspondence it was, that the consideration shares represented a payment to the three managers for an asset which belonged to FIM or that they acquired them by the use of some property or confidential information of FIM which came to them as directors of FIM. The shares were paid in consideration of an asset of the three managers which they were willing to bring to Rathbone—an asset which belonged to them and which, on leaving the Framlington group's employment they were free to exploit for themselves, namely, the client goodwill which attached to them as the persons who had, over many years, managed their clients' investments. The consideration shares were the price which the three were willing to accept in return for binding themselves under five-year service contracts to make that goodwill available to Rathbone and for restricting their freedom, after the termination of their service contracts, to exploit that client goodwill for themselves or for others.

Nor is it suggested, or can be suggested, that the three managers diverted to themselves some kind of maturing business opportunity which should have been made available to the plaintiffs of the kind which featured in *Industrial Development Consultants Ltd* v *Cooley* [1972] 1 WLR 443 to which I was referred. The opportunity which the plaintiffs had of extracting a payment from Rathbone in consideration of a transfer by FIM to Rathbone of one of its assets, namely its client goodwill in the private client investment management business which the three managers had been managing, was one that Mr Loach, on behalf of the group, was free to exploit and did exploit.

It is not suggested, and cannot be, that the consideration shares represented some kind of secret bribe or commission for having introduced Rathbone to the Framlington group. The many authorities to which I was referred on that topic did not seem to me to be in point. The consideration shares were payment for securing the long-term service of the three managers and with it their client goodwill.

Nor can it be suggested that the three managers were not free to negotiate whatever price they could from Rathbone for their future services to that company. The fact that the consideration for so doing took one form (a regular salary, in-service benefits and equity participation in the employer calculated by reference to the value of funds transferred) rather than another (a salary, in-service benefits and an annual profit bonus dependent upon profits achieved, or participation in an executive share option scheme) was, in itself, entirely a matter for the three managers. I mention this because at times during his submissions Mr Pymont [counsel for the plaintiffs] appeared to be contending that a director contemplating joining a new employer was under an obligation to disclose to the company of which he is a director any unusually generous terms (such as a large capital payment) that the new employer is offering to pay him to secure his services. I cannot see why.

One of the duties with which the three managers' interest is said to have been in conflict was their duty, as it is put in para. 3A of the statement of claim, 'to assist FIM in obtaining the best price reasonably obtainable' for what FIM was negotiating to sell to Rathbone. I do not consider that

that did form any part of the three managers' duty. Nor, to make the point clear, do I consider that in failing (if they did) to assist FIM to obtain the best price reasonably obtainable for what FIM was negotiating to sell to Rathbone, the three acted in breach of any general duty to act bona fide in FIM's interests. What precisely a director's duty is within a company must depend, as Hoffmann J observed in *Bishopsgate Investment Management Ltd* v *Maxwell (No. 2)* [1994] 1 All ER 261 at 264 (when commenting on whether a director is under a duty to participate in the management of a company) 'upon how the particular company's business is organised and the part which the director could reasonably have been expected to play'.

In this case there was no evidence to indicate what part, apart from managing clients' investments, each of the three managers was expected to play within FIM and I am not willing to assume, without more, that each was under the particular duty alleged. But the point is academic because it is clear that, as regards the sale to Rathbone, the three were instructed by Mr Loach speaking on behalf of Framlington plc (the sole beneficial shareholder of FIM) not to take part in the sale negotiations with Mr Ingall. I reject any suggestion that, because neither Mr Anderson nor Mr Lanyon informed Mr Loach of all of the terms which Mr Ingall was then offering to them if they were willing to join Rathbone, that instruction can be ignored. Knowing that they would be joining Rathbone, Mr Loach clearly realised that it would be quite impossible for those two to be involved in negotiating the price which Rathbone should pay to the Framlington group to secure the latter's cooperation to a smooth transfer to Rathbone of the private client business. Furthermore, it seems to me that the three did assist FIM to obtain the best price reasonably obtainable for its private client business because, as I have earlier related, the three, without being under the least obligation to do so, entered into deeds of non-solicitation with FIM on completion of the sale agreement on 13 January 1992. That there should be such deeds in order to protect what remained of FIM's business after the sale to Rathbone was a part of the bargain struck by the plaintiffs with Rathbone embodied in the sale agreement.

Nor do I consider that the negotiations by the three with Mr Ingall at a time when the group was in negotiation with Rathbone, of the remuneration package that they could expect to receive on joining Rathbone was in itself, with or without disclosure to FIM, a breach of any general duty of good faith owed by them to FIM. In the absence of some special circumstance (for example a prohibition in a service contract) a director commits no breach of his fiduciary duty to the company of which he is a director merely because, while a director, he takes steps so that, on ceasing to be a director (and, if he is one, an employee of that company), he can immediately set up in business in competition with that company or join a competitor of it. Nor is he obliged to disclose to that company that he is taking those steps. See *Balston Ltd* v *Headline Filters Ltd* [1990] FSR 385 at 412.

In any event Mr Loach made it clear to Mr Anderson and Mr Lanyon that he was not concerned with the remuneration terms that they might negotiate with Rathbone. Those terms included the acquisition of the consideration shares in return for entering into the five-year service contracts. It is not suggested that Mr Loach's attitude differed in this respect once Mr Clarke had decided to join Rathbone and had told Mr Loach of that fact. Since I do not consider that Mr Loach's remark was in any way improperly induced I do not see how it lies in the plaintiffs' mouths to say that the three should not have taken that remark at face value which, on the facts, they plainly did.

The fact, if fact it was, that Rathbone set a ceiling on the amount it was willing to pay to acquire the goodwill in the private client investment management business which attached partly to FIM and partly to the three managers so that whatever the three managers were able to negotiate was likely to be at the expense of what Mr Loach could negotiate for the plaintiffs did not, in my judgment, involve any breach of duty or obligation in equity on the part of the three managers. Specifically I see no reason why a director cannot, without committing any breach of his duty of good faith, seek to drive as hard a bargain as he able with his future employer over the terms on which he is to be employed and the fact, if fact it be, that the result of so doing may be that the employer is deprived of assets which that employer might otherwise have devoted to trading with or acquiring an asset from the company of which the director is still then a director seems to me to be of no consequence. If Mr Loach had thought that the price which Mr Ingall was willing to pay for the transfer to Rathbone of the private client business was too little he was free to reject it. He did not, presumably because he came to the view, uninfluenced on the evidence by anything the three managers said or did, that, in all the circumstances, it was acceptable in amount.

Were it otherwise it is difficult to see what the three managers could do. Supposing the three had agreed their remuneration package with Rathbone before any question of a sale by the group to Rathbone had arisen. What are the three to do once the group decides to negotiate a sale of its interest to Rathbone? Disclosing to the group what they have agreed is not likely to affect the amount that Rathbone is willing to pay to the group but even if it might, it is difficult to see on what basis, in these circumstances, the three are accountable to FIM for the fruits of what they have negotiated. I cannot see that the fact that, at the time the group embarks upon its negotiation with Rathbone, no deal has been struck between the three managers and Rathbone makes any difference.

Rathbone plainly needed to secure the services of the three managers otherwise the sum it was willing to pay the group might turn out to be largely if not wholly wasted: unless Rathbone secured their services, the three would be free to go elsewhere and take with them as many of the private clients as they could. I am quite unable to see why, merely because at the time a deal was being negotiated between the group and Rathbone the three were in negotiation with Rathbone over the terms of their remuneration package, the three are accountable to FIM for the undisclosed part of what they eventually negotiated when, if they had not embarked on their negotiations until after 1 November 1991, or had concluded a binding agreement with Rathbone before the group had decided to offer the private client business to Rathbone, they would not....

What is crucial, to my mind, is that the three managers were not involved in the negotiations between the Framlington group and Rathbone. That distinguishes the case from *Furs Ltd* v *Tomkies* (1936) 54 CLR 583, which bears a superficial similarity to this case....

In the result I can find no basis upon which the three managers can be made to account to the plaintiffs for the consideration shares and the action therefore falls to be dismissed.

NOTE: See also *Dranez Anstalt* v *Hayek* [2002] 1 BCLC 693 which basically affirms the *Framlington* decision although it was not referred to in the judgment.

12.4.6 Duty not to accept benefits from third parties

COMPANIES ACT 2006, S. 176

176. Duty not to accept benefits from third parties
(1) A director of a company must not accept a benefit from a third party conferred by reason of—
   (a) his being a director, or
   (b) his doing (or not doing) anything as director.
(2) A "third party" means a person other than the company, an associated body corporate or a person acting on behalf of the company or an associated body corporate.
(3) Benefits received by a director from a person by whom his services (as a director or otherwise) are provided to the company are not regarded as conferred by a third party.
(4) This duty is not infringed if the acceptance of the benefit cannot reasonably be regarded as likely to give rise to a conflict of interest.
(5) Any reference in this section to a conflict of interest includes a conflict of interest and duty and a conflict of duties.

A director must not accept a benefit from a third party conferred by reason of his position as director or anything he does or does not do as director (s. 176). This codifies the no-profit rule which prohibits the exploitation of the position of director for personal benefit. The acceptance of a benefit giving rise to an actual or potential conflict of interest also falls within s. 175. However, this duty not to accept benefits from third parties cannot be condoned by board authorisation, but such acceptance of benefit can be authorised by the company (s. 180(4)).

12.5 LIABILITY AS CONSTRUCTIVE TRUSTEES

Where there is a breach of a director's fiduciary duty, the director who holds the benefit as a result of the breach is required to hold it as a constructive trustee. Any person who knowingly assists in the breach or receives the benefit of it is also required to hold it as a constructive trustee for the company.

Belmont Finance Corporation Ltd v *Williams Furniture Ltd (No. 2)*
Constructive trusteeships
[1980] 1 All ER 393, Court of Appeal

A third party who receives company property with the knowledge that it has been applied for an improper purpose or in breach of directors' fiduciary duties is liable to account for it to the company as a constructive trustee.

Facts   City owned all the shares in Belmont. The case essentially involved two complex transactions: (a) the directors of Belmont caused it to pay £500,000 to some third parties for a piece of property; (b) those third parties paid City £489,000 for all the shares in Belmont. It was found that these transactions were illegal for breach of a statutory provision (now CA 1985, s. 151) prohibiting financial assistance by a company for the purchase of its own shares. The issue was whether City was liable as constructive trustee for the £489,000 which it had received with knowledge of the circumstances.

BUCKLEY LJ: I now come to the constructive trust point. If a stranger to a trust (a) receives and becomes chargeable with some part of the trust fund or (b) assists the trustees of a trust with knowledge of the facts in a dishonest design on the part of the trustees to misapply some part of a trust fund, he is liable as a constructive trustee (*Barnes* v *Addy* (1874) LR 9 Ch App 244 per Lord Selborne LC at pp. 251–2).

A limited company is of course not a trustee of its own funds: it is their beneficial owner; but in consequence of the fiduciary character of their duties the directors of a limited company are treated as if they were trustees of those funds of the company which are in their hands or under their control, and if they misapply them they commit a breach of trust (*Re Lands Allotment Co.* [1894] 1 Ch 616 per Lindley LJ at p. 631 and Kay LJ at p. 638). So, if the directors of a company in breach of their fiduciary duties misapply the funds of their company so that they come into the hands of some stranger to the trust who receives them with knowledge (actual or constructive) of the breach, he cannot conscientiously retain those funds against the company unless he has some better equity. He becomes a constructive trustee for the company of the misapplied funds....

In the present case, the payment of the £500,000 by Belmont... being an unlawful contravention of [CA 1985, s. 151], was a misapplication of Belmont's money and was in breach of the duties of the directors of Belmont. £489,000 of the £500,000 so misapplied found their way into the hands of City with City's knowledge of the whole circumstances of the transaction. It must follow, in my opinion, that City is accountable to Belmont as a constructive trustee of the £489,000 under the first of Lord Selborne LC's two heads.

There remains the question whether City is chargeable as a constructive trustee under Lord Selborne LC's second head on the ground that Belmont's directors were guilty of dishonesty... and that City with knowledge of the facts assisted them in that dishonest design. As I understand Lord Selborne LC's second head, a stranger to a trust notwithstanding that he may not have received any of the trust fund which has been misapplied will be treated as accountable as a constructive trustee if he has knowingly participated in a dishonest design on the part of the trustees to misapply the fund; he must himself have been in some way a party to the dishonesty of the trustees. It follows from what I have already held that the directors of Belmont were guilty of misfeasance but not that they acted dishonestly. [His lordship accordingly ruled that City was not liable for the whole £500,000 on this ground.]

Royal Brunei Airlines Sdn Bhd v Tan
Dishonestly assisting breach of trust
[1995] 3 All ER 97, [1995] 2 AC 378, PC

A stranger who dishonestly assists a breach of trust or fiduciary obligations by the trustee or fiduciary is liable personally as a constructive trustee. It is not necessary to show that the breach was dishonest or fraudulent on the part of the trustee or fiduciary.

Facts   Royal Brunei Airlines appointed Borneo Leisure Travel, a private limited company, as its agent to sell passenger and cargo transportation. BLT was required under the agreement to hold the moneys received from such sales on trust for the airline and to pay them to it within 30 days. BLT paid all such moneys into its current account for the conduct of its business. When BLT was insolvent later, the airline brought an action against BLT's managing director and principal shareholder, Tan Kok Ming, for unpaid money alleging that he was liable as a constructive trustee because he had knowingly assisted in a fraudulent and dishonest breach by BLT. The High Court of Brunei upheld the claim, but the Court of Appeal of Brunei allowed the appeal. The airline successfully appealed to the Privy Council.

LORD NICHOLLS OF BIRKENHEAD: The proper role of equity in commercial transactions is a topical question. Increasingly plaintiffs have recourse to equity for an effective remedy when the person in default, typically a company, is insolvent. Plaintiffs seek to obtain relief from others who were involved in the transaction, such as directors of the company or its bankers or its legal or other advisers. They seek to fasten fiduciary obligations directly onto the company's officers or agents or advisers, or to have them held personally liable for assisting the company in breaches of trust or fiduciary obligations.

This is such a case. An insolvent travel agent company owed money to an airline. The airline seeks a remedy against the travel agent's principal director and shareholder. Its claim is based on the much-quoted dictum of Lord Selborne LC, sitting in the Court of Appeal in Chancery, in *Barnes* v *Addy* (1874) LR 9 Ch App 244 at 251–2:

> That responsibility [of a trustee] may no doubt be extended in equity to others who are not properly trustees, if they are found . . . actually participating in any fraudulent conduct of the trustee to the injury of the *cestui que trust*. But . . . strangers are not to be made constructive trustees merely because they act as the agents of trustees in transactions within their legal powers, transactions, perhaps of which a court of equity may disapprove, unless those agents receive and become chargeable with some part of the trust property, or unless they assist with knowledge in a dishonest and fraudulent design on the part of the trustees.

In the conventional shorthand the first of these two circumstances in which third parties (non-trustees) may become liable to account in equity is 'knowing receipt', as distinct from the second where liability arises from 'knowing assistance'. Stated even more shortly, the first limb of Lord Selborne LC's formulation is concerned with the liability of a person as a *recipient* of trust property or its traceable proceeds. The second limb is concerned with what, for want of a better compendious description, can be called the liability of an *accessory* to a trustee's breach of trust. Liability as an accessory is not dependent upon receipt of trust property. It arises even though no trust property has reached the hands of the accessory. It is a form of secondary liability in the sense that it only arises where there has been a breach of trust. In the present case the plaintiff relies on the accessory limb. The particular point in issue arises from the expression 'a dishonest and fraudulent design on the part of the trustees'.

[His lordship read the facts, referred to the decisions of the trial judge and the Court of Appeal of Brunei and continued:]

Delivering the judgment of the [Court of Appeal of Brunei], Fuad P stated:

As long-standing and high authority shows, conduct which may amount to a breach of trust, however morally reprehensible, will not render a person who has knowingly assisted in the breach of trust liable as a constructive trustee, if that conduct falls short of dishonesty.

This view of the state of the law has the support of the English Court of Appeal. In *Selangor United Rubber Estates Ltd* v *Cradock (No. 3)* [1968] 1 WLR 1555 at 1591 Ungoed-Thomas J held that the expression 'dishonest and fraudulent design' was to be understood according to the principles of a court of equity. That approach was emphatically rejected by the Court of Appeal in *Belmont Finance Corporation Ltd* v *Williams Furniture Ltd* [1979] Ch 250 at 267. Buckley LJ observed that the rule as formulated by Lord Selborne LC had stood for more than 100 years, and that to depart from it would introduce an undesirable degree of uncertainty to the law over what degree of unethical conduct would suffice if dishonesty was not to be the criterion. Goff LJ agreed that it would be dangerous and wrong to depart from 'the safe path of the principle as stated by Lord Selborne' to the 'uncharted sea of something not innocent... but still short of dishonesty' (see [1979] Ch 250 at 274).

In short, the issue on this appeal is whether the breach of trust which is a prerequisite to accessory liability must itself be a dishonest and fraudulent breach of trust by the trustee.

The honest trustee and the dishonest third party

It must be noted at once that there is a difficulty with the approach adopted on this point in the *Belmont* case. Take the simple example of an honest trustee and a dishonest third party. Take a case where a dishonest solicitor persuades a trustee to apply trust property in a way the trustee honestly believes is permissible but which the solicitor knows full well is a clear breach of trust. The solicitor deliberately conceals this from the trustee. In consequence, the beneficiaries suffer a substantial loss. It cannot be right that in such a case the accessory liability principle would be inapplicable because of the innocence of the trustee. In ordinary parlance, the beneficiaries have been defrauded by the solicitor. If there is to be an accessory liability principle at all, whereby in appropriate circumstances beneficiaries may have direct recourse against a third party, the principle must surely be applicable in such a case, just as much as in a case where both the trustee and the third party have been dishonest. Indeed, if anything, the case for liability of the dishonest third party seems stronger where the trustee is innocent, because in such a case the third party alone was dishonest and that was the cause of the subsequent misapplication of the trust property.

The position would be the same if, instead of *procuring* the breach, the third party dishonestly *assisted* in the breach. Change the facts slightly. A trustee is proposing to make a payment out of the trust fund to a particular person. He honestly believes he is authorised to do so by the terms of the trust deed. He asks a solicitor to carry through the transaction. The solicitor well knows that the proposed payment would be a plain breach of trust. He also well knows that the trustee mistakenly believes otherwise. Dishonestly he leaves the trustee under his misapprehension and prepares the necessary documentation. Again, if the accessory principle is not to be artificially constricted, it ought to be applicable in such a case.

These examples suggest that what matters is the state of mind of the third party sought to be made liable, not the state of mind of the trustee. The trustee will be liable in any event for the breach of trust, even if he acted innocently, unless excused by an exemption clause in the trust instrument or relieved by the court. But *his* state of mind is essentially irrelevant to the question whether the *third party* should be made liable to the beneficiaries for the breach of trust. If the liability of the third party is fault-based, what matters is the nature of his fault, not that of the trustee. In this regard dishonesty on the part of the third party would seem to be a sufficient basis for his liability, irrespective of the state of mind of the trustee who is in breach of trust. It is difficult to see why, if the third party dishonestly assisted in a breach, there should be a further prerequisite to his liability, namely that the trustee also must have been acting dishonestly. The alternative view would mean that a dishonest third party is liable if the trustee is dishonest, but if the trustee did not act dishonestly that of itself would excuse a dishonest third party from liability. That would make no sense.

[His lordship referred to earlier authorities, discussed the questions whether a third party should never be made liable for assisting a breach of trust or should be strictly liable, or whether his liability should be fault-based and concluded in favour of the third option and said that the predominant view was that it should be based on 'dishonesty', and continued:]

Dishonesty

Before considering this issue further it will be helpful to define the terms being used by looking more closely at what dishonesty means in this context. Whatever may be the position in some criminal or other contexts (see, for instance, *R v Ghosh* [1982] QB 1053), in the context of the accessory liability principle acting dishonestly, or with a lack of probity, which is synonymous, means simply not acting as an honest person would in the circumstances. This is an objective standard. At first sight this may seem surprising. Honesty has a connotation of subjectivity, as distinct from the objectivity of negligence. Honesty, indeed, does have a strong subjective element in that it is a description of a type of conduct assessed in the light of what a person actually knew at the time, as distinct from what a reasonable person would have known or appreciated. Further, honesty and its counterpart dishonesty are mostly concerned with advertent conduct, not inadvertent conduct. Carelessness is not dishonesty. Thus for the most part dishonesty is to be equated with conscious impropriety.

However, these subjective characteristics of honesty do not mean that individuals are free to set their own standards of honesty in particular circumstances. The standard of what constitutes honest conduct is not subjective. Honesty is not an optional scale, with higher or lower values according to the moral standards of each individual. If a person knowingly appropriates another's property, he will not escape a finding of dishonesty simply because he sees nothing wrong in such behaviour.

In most situations there is little difficulty in identifying how an honest person would behave. Honest people do not intentionally deceive others to their detriment. Honest people do not knowingly take others' property. Unless there is a very good and compelling reason, an honest person does not participate in a transaction if he knows it involves a misapplication of trust assets to the detriment of the beneficiaries. Nor does an honest person in such a case deliberately close his eyes and ears, or deliberately not ask questions, lest he learn something he would rather not know, and then proceed regardless. However, in the situations now under consideration the position is not always so straightforward. This can best be illustrated by considering one particular area: the taking of risks.

Taking risks

All investment involves risk. Imprudence is not dishonesty, although imprudence may be carried recklessly to lengths which call into question the honesty of the person making the decision. This is especially so if the transaction serves another purpose in which that person has an interest of his own.

This type of risk is to be sharply distinguished from the case where a trustee, with or without the benefit of advice, is aware that a particular investment or application of trust property is outside his powers, but nevertheless he decides to proceed in the belief or hope that this will be beneficial to the beneficiaries or, at least, not prejudicial to them. He takes a risk that a clearly unauthorised transaction will not cause loss. A risk of this nature is for the account of those who take it. If the risk materialises and causes loss, those who knowingly took the risk will be accountable accordingly. This is the type of risk being addressed by Peter Gibson J in *Baden* v *Sociét générale pour favoriser le développement du commerce et de l'industrie en France SA* [1993] 1 WLR 509 at 574, when he accepted that fraud includes taking 'a risk to the prejudice of another's rights, which risk is known to be one which there is no right to take' (quoting from the Court of Appeal judgment in *R v Sinclair* [1968] 1 WLR 1246 at 1249).

This situation, in turn, is to be distinguished from the case where there is genuine doubt about whether a transaction is authorised or not. This may be because the trust instrument is worded obscurely, or because there are competing claims as in *Carl-Zeiss-Stiftung* v *Herbert Smith & Co. (No. 2)* [1969] 2 Ch 276, or for other reasons. The difficulty here is that frequently the situation is neither clearly white nor clearly black. The dividing edge between what is within the trustee's powers and what is not is often not clear cut. Instead there is a gradually darkening spectrum which can be described with labels such as clearly authorised, probably authorised, possibly authorised, wholly unclear, probably unauthorised and, finally, clearly unauthorised.

The difficulty here is that the differences are of degree rather than of kind. So far as the trustee himself is concerned the legal analysis is straightforward. Honesty or lack of honesty is not the test for his liability. He is obliged to comply with the terms of the trust. His liability is strict. If he departs from the trust terms he is liable unless excused by a provision in the trust instrument or relieved by the court. The analysis of the position of the accessory, such as the solicitor who carries through the transaction for him, does not lead to such a simple, clear cut answer in every case. He is required to act honestly, but what is required of an honest person in these circumstances? An honest person knows there is doubt. What does honesty require him to do?

The only answer to these questions lies in keeping in mind that honesty is an objective standard. The individual is expected to attain the standard which would be observed by an honest person placed in those circumstances. It is impossible to be more specific. Knox J captured the flavour of this, in a case with a commercial setting, when he referred to a person who is 'guilty of commercially unacceptable conduct in the particular context involved': see *Cowan de Groot Properties Ltd v Eagle Trust plc* [1992] 4 All ER 700 at 761. Acting in reckless disregard of others' rights or possible rights can be a tell-tale sign of dishonesty. An honest person would have regard to the circumstances known to him, including the nature and importance of the proposed transaction, the nature and importance of his role, the ordinary course of business, the degree of doubt, the practicability of the trustee or the third party proceeding otherwise and the seriousness of the adverse consequences to the beneficiaries. The circumstances will dictate which one or more of the possible courses should be taken by an honest person. He might, for instance, flatly decline to become involved. He might ask further questions. He might seek advice, or insist on further advice being obtained. He might advise the trustee of the risks but then proceed with his role in the transaction. He might do many things. Ultimately, in most cases, an honest person should have little difficulty in knowing whether a proposed transaction, or his participation in it, would offend the normally accepted standards of honest conduct.

Likewise, when called upon to decide whether a person was acting honestly, a court will look at all the circumstances known to the third party at the time. The court will also have regard to personal attributes of the third party such as his experience and intelligence, and the reason why he acted as he did.

Before leaving cases where there is real doubt, one further point should be noted. To inquire, in such cases, whether a person dishonestly assisted in what is later held to be a breach of trust is to ask a meaningful question, which is capable of being given a meaningful answer. This is not always so if the question is posed in terms of 'knowingly' assisted. Framing the question in the latter form all too often leads one into tortuous convolutions about the 'sort' of knowledge required, when the truth is that 'knowingly' is inapt as a criterion when applied to the gradually darkening spectrum where the differences are of degree and not kind.

[His lordship thought that as a general proposition, beneficiaries cannot reasonably expect that all the world dealing with their trustees should owe them a duty to take care lest the trustees are behaving dishonestly. He also rejected 'unconscionable conduct' as the basis for liability in assisting a breach of trust.]

The accessory liability principle

Drawing the threads together, their lordships' overall conclusion is that dishonesty is a necessary ingredient of accessory liability. It is also a sufficient ingredient. A liability in equity to make good resulting loss attaches to a person who dishonestly procures or assists in a breach of trust or fiduciary obligation. It is not necessary that, in addition, the trustee or fiduciary was acting dishonestly, although this will usually be so where the third party who is assisting him is acting dishonestly. 'Knowingly' is better avoided as a defining ingredient of the principle, and in the context of this principle the *Baden* scale of knowledge is best forgotten.

NOTES

1. In *Twinsectra Ltd* v *Yardley* [2002] 2 All ER 377, HL, it was held that although dishonesty meant dishonesty according to the ordinary standards of reasonable and honest people, it was necessary to show that the third party should realise that his conduct was dishonest according to those standards. There is therefore an element of subjectivity for liability to arise.

2. In the case of a third party knowingly receiving the company property transferred to him in breach of a director's fiduciary obligations, it is not necessary to show that the third party has acted dishonestly in knowingly receiving the company property. But it is necessary to show that he has knowledge that the company property was traceable to a breach of fiduciary duty. The recipient's state of knowledge must be such as to make it unconscionable for him to retain the benefit of the receipt (*BCCI (Overseas) Ltd* v *Akindele* [2001] Ch 437, CA).

3. Where a company's money is paid away by one of its directors to another company, in breach of the director's fiduciary duty, a claim against an employee of that other company in relation to the money has to be one of knowing assistance, not one of knowing receipt, unless the employee can be properly regarded as the alter ego of that other company (*Houghton* v *Fayers* [2000] 1 BCLC 511).

4. An action to recover the company property or the proceeds of the property received by a director in breach of his fiduciary duties is not statute-barred by the Limitation Act 1980, s. 21(3): *J.J. Harrison (Properties) Ltd* v *Harrison* [2002] 1 BCLC 162, CA.

12.6 RELIEF FROM LIABILITY

12.6.1 Introduction

Although directors' general duties are strict, there are a number of ways in which directors may be relieved from liability.

(a) Where conduct by a director amounting to negligence, default, breach of duty or breach of trust is ratifiable, it can be ratified by a resolution of the disinterested members of the company by majority or unanimous consent (s. 239 CA 2006). This changes the rule in *North-West Transportation Co. Ltd* v *Beatty* (1887) 12 App Cas 589, Privy Council where it was held that a director who owned shares in the company could vote in the general meeting as a member for his own personal interest.

(b) Section 239 does not affect any other enactment or rule of law imposing additional requirements for valid ratification or any rule of law as to acts that are incapable of being ratified by the company. Thus as required by equitable rules, the director must make full disclosure to the company before ratification. Furthermore, ratification by majority will not be effective if the directors have wrongfully misappropriated company assets (see, e.g., *Cook* v *Deeks* extracted at 12.3.2) unless by unanimous consent.

(c) CA 2006, s. 182, requires directors also to disclose interests in contracts with the company, but this time to the board itself. This is an additional and distinct requirement which imposes criminal sanctions only for its breach but does not expressly affect the validity of the contract. However, in *Guinness plc* v *Saunders* [1990] 2 AC 663, Lord Templeman said (at p. 694) that 'In *Hely-Hutchinson* v *Brayhead*

Ltd [1968] 1 QB 549, the Court of Appeal held that s. 317 of CA 1985 (which is replaced by s. 182 CA 2006) renders a contract voidable by a company if the director does not declare his interest'. On the other hand, Lord Goff of Chieveley in a fuller discussion said (at p. 697):

> I cannot see that a breach of s. 317 . . . had itself any effect upon the contract. . . . As a matter of general law, to the extent that there was failure . . . to comply with [the] duty of disclosure under the relevant article . . . the contract . . . was no doubt voidable under the ordinary principles of the general law. (Emphasis added.)

More recently, Dillon LJ in *Lee Panavision Ltd* v *Lee Lighting Ltd* [1992] BCLC 22, at p. 33, said that he would hesitate to hold that a technical breach of s. 317 (for example, although the terms of the relevant service contract were not disclosed to a formal board meeting they were known to all the directors) renders a contract voidable, but he declined to express any view on the construction and effect of art. 85 (see the next point) in the light of s. 317. In *Runciman* v *Walter Runciman plc* [1992] BCLC 1084, Simon Brown J was more willing to hold that 'there is ample authority for the proposition that non-compliance with a requirement such as that imposed here by art. 85(1) leaves the contract voidable at the option of the company' (citing *Hely-Hutchison* v *Brayhead Ltd* [1968] 1 QB 549 and *Guinness plc* v *Saunders* [1990] 2 AC 663). However, he also shared the view that where the breach of s. 317 is technical, the contract is not necessarily voidable (at pp. 1095–7).

COMPANIES ACT 2006, S. 182

182. Declaration of interest in existing transaction or arrangement

(1) Where a director of a company is in any way, directly or indirectly, interested in a transaction or arrangement that has been entered into by the company, he must declare the nature and extent of the interest to the other directors in accordance with this section.

This section does not apply if or to the extent that the interest has been declared under section 177 (duty to declare interest in proposed transaction or arrangement).

(2) The declaration must be made—
   (a) at a meeting of the directors, or
   (b) by notice in writing (see section 184), or
   (c) by general notice (see section 185).

(3) If a declaration of interest under this section proves to be, or becomes, inaccurate or incomplete, a further declaration must be made.

(4) Any declaration required by this section must be made as soon as is reasonably practicable. Failure to comply with this requirement does not affect the underlying duty to make the declaration.

(5) This section does not require a declaration of an interest of which the director is not aware or where the director is not aware of the transaction or arrangement in question.

For this purpose a director is treated as being aware of matters of which he ought reasonably to be aware.

(6) A director need not declare an interest under this section—
   (a) if it cannot reasonably be regarded as likely to give rise to a conflict of interest;
   (b) if, or to the extent that, the other directors are already aware of it (and for this purpose the other directors are treated as aware of anything of which they ought reasonably to be aware); or
   (c) if, or to the extent that, it concerns terms of his service contract that have been or are to be considered—
      (i) by a meeting of the directors, or
      (ii) by a committee of the directors appointed for the purpose under the company's constitution.

(d) As it would be wholly impracticable for a resolution of the company in general meeting to be obtained every time a possible conflict of interest arises, articles of association often include a blanket waiver enabling directors to contract with the company. For example, the former Table A, art. 85 (reproduced at 1.7) imposes a *third* disclosure requirement, saying that a director may transact with the company if he or she has disclosed his or her interest to the board. However, by the former art. 94, a director who is interested in a matter may not generally vote on the matter nor be counted in the quorum (art. 95). General disclosure of a continuing interest under art. 86 is a common practice to enable companies to function smoothly. These articles are likely to be retained in the new model articles.

Disclosure must be in full compliance with the article, otherwise, the transaction is still liable to be set aside. Thus disclosure to a committee will not be sufficient when disclosure to the board is required. As already seen in 11.6, one of the more recent examples of conflict of interest by directors is the landmark case of *Guinness plc* v *Saunders*.

(e) The waters are, however, muddied by CA 2006, s. 232 (extracted and considered below), which says that provisions in the articles or in any contract exempting an officer from liability for breach of duty are void. (Section 234 of the CA 2006, however, enables companies to pay for directors' liability insurance which indemnifies directors against any liability they may incur.)

(f) CA 2006, s. 1157 (extracted below), gives the court a broad discretion to relieve directors who have 'acted honestly and reasonably . . . and ought fairly to be excused' from liability for their negligence or breach of duty.

12.6.2 CA 2006, s. 232

Under CA 2006, s. 232, any provision in the articles or in any contract with the company which exempts a director from liability for breach of duty is void. This raises the question whether an article similar to the former art. 85 of Table A is void under s. 232. There has been a great deal of academic discussion on this until it was addressed for the first time judicially by Vinelott J in *Movitex Ltd* v *Bulfield* [1988] BCLC 104.

COMPANIES ACT 2006, S. 232

232. Provisions protecting directors from liability

(1) Any provision that purports to exempt a director of a company (to any extent) from any liability that would otherwise attach to him in connection with any negligence, default, breach of duty or breach of trust in relation to the company is void.

(2) Any provision by which a company directly or indirectly provides an indemnity (to any extent) for a director of the company, or of an associated company, against any liability attaching to him in connection with any negligence, default, breach of duty or breach of trust in relation to the company of which he is a director is void, except as permitted by—

    (a) section 233 (provision of insurance), •

    (b) section 234 (qualifying third party indemnity provision), or

    (c) section 235 (qualifying pension scheme indemnity provision).

(3) This section applies to any provision, whether contained in a company's articles or in any contract with the company or otherwise.

(4) Nothing in this section prevents a company's articles from making such provision as has previously been lawful for dealing with conflicts of interest.

Movitex Ltd v *Bulfield*
Reconciling art. 85 with s. 310
[1988] BCLC 104, Chancery Division

The facts of this case are not relevant for our purpose. The issue Vinelott J had to consider was whether an article similar to art. 85 was valid under s. 310 of the CA 1985 (or what is now s. 232 of the CA 2006). He concluded that the no-profit or no-conflict rule merely *disables* the director from dealing with the company and obtaining a profit. It does not impose a *duty* on the director. Therefore, art. 85, which excludes or modifies the application of the no-profit or no-conflict rule, does not infringe s. 310.

VINELOTT J: The argument advanced on behalf of Movitex can be shortly summarised as follows. The self-dealing rule is founded on and exemplifies the wider principle that 'no one who has a duty to perform shall place himself in a situation to have his interests conflicting with that duty' (see *Broughton* v *Broughton* (1855) 5 De G M& G 160 at p. 164 per Lord Cranworth). To that should be added for completeness 'nor to have his duty to one conflicting with his duty to another' (see *Re Haslam & Hier-Evans* [1902] 1 Ch 765). So, it is said, the fiduciary owes a duty to the person whose interest he is bound to protect not to place himself in a position in which duty and interest or duty and duty are in conflict. If he does place himself in such a position in relation to a particular transaction, the beneficiary may have the transaction set aside or compel the fiduciary to account for any profit he has made or, if no profit has been realised but if restitution of the property is none the less impractical or inequitable, to make compensation. So, it is said, to the extent that a provision in the articles of a company permits a director to enter into a transaction in which one of their number has an interest or owes a duty to another the provision is one 'for exempting' the director from a liability which under the general law would otherwise attach to him in respect of a breach of his duty not to place himself in a position of conflict.

This argument, if sound, would have very startling consequences, for it would give rise to inconsistency between s. 205 [now CA 1985, s. 310] on the one hand and arts 78 and 84 of Table A [see now arts 85 and 94], which correspond in their general purport though not in detail with arts 98 to 100 of Movitex's articles, on the other hand. Whether s. 205 would then override or be overridden by arts 78 and 84 of Table A read in conjunction with s. 8(2) of the 1948 Act [now CA 1985, s. 8(2)], is a question which does not directly arise. The articles of Movitex exclude the regulations in Table A and arts 98 to 100 of Movitex's articles, though similar in their general purport to arts 78 and 84, cannot be said to be a mere repetition of them. But it would be at the lowest very paradoxical to find that s. 205 conflicts with arts 78 and 84. The legislature in enacting the 1948 Act must have contemplated that the modifications of the self-dealing rule in arts 78 and 84 do not infringe s. 205. Accordingly, if s. 205 is fairly capable of a construction which avoids that conflict, that construction must clearly be preferred to one which does not.

This problem has attracted the attention of the authors and editors of some of the leading textbooks. The solution advanced by the editors of *Gore Brown on Companies* (43rd ed.) is that a provision may, without infringing s. 205, reduce or abrogate a duty owed by a director, provided it does not exempt the director from liability for breach of it. That solution fails, I think, to give effect to the words, 'for exempting', and leads to the absurd result that an article could, without infringing s. 205, modify a director's duty to use reasonable skill and care in the conduct of the company's affairs and so avoid a liability for damages for breach of duty which would otherwise arise, a conclusion which seems to me manifestly in conflict with the purpose of the section. Counsel for the defendants (Mr Stubbs QC) took me through a number of early cases in which the scope and effect of an article modifying a director's duty to a company and exempting him from breach of that duty has been considered by the courts and in particular the decision of Romer J and of the Court of Appeal in *Re City Equitable Fire Insurance Co. Ltd* [1925] Ch 407 and to the report of the Greene Committee which led to the inclusion in the Companies Act 1929 of s. 152, the legislative predecessor of s. 205. If I may say so without disrespect to counsel's very thorough argument, it does not follow that because the purpose of s. 152 was to nullify articles similar to the article on which the directors successfully relied in the *City Equitable Fire Insurance* case that that section and s. 205 should be construed as invalidating only an article in those or similar terms. A patch may be intentionally wider than the visible hole to which it is applied.

There is so far as the researches of counsel have been able to discover no guidance to be found in any reported case....

The true solution is, I think, to be found in a passage in the judgment of Megarry V-C in *Tito* v *Waddell (No. 2)* [1977] Ch 106. [His lordship quoted Megarry V-C's judgment (at pp. 248–9)]:

> In this case, the question becomes one of whether a trustee as such can properly be said to be under a 'duty' not to purchase the trust property, and under a 'duty' not to purchase a beneficiary's interest in the trust property without making proper disclosure, and so on. If the answer is yes, then of course there is much logical force in the contention that a breach of these duties is a breach of trust within the Limitation Act 1939, s. 19(2), and so is subject to the six-years period of limitation. The problem is essentially one of classification.
>
> Now it is true that some textbooks set out the rules about self-dealing and fair-dealing as part of the duties and discretions of trustees.... Some books avoid any problems of classification by setting out the rules in a separate self-contained chapter.... But *Halsbury's Laws of England*, 3rd ed., vol. 38 (1962), pp. 961–6, includes both the self-dealing rule and the fair-dealing rule under the head of 'Disabilities of trustees' and not 'Duties of trustees'; and it is this that appears to me to be the true view.... In my judgment, what equity does is to subject trustees to particular disabilities in cases falling within the self-dealing and fair-dealing rules....
>
> This way of regarding the matter is reinforced by considering those who fall within the scope of the fair-dealing rule. This applies, of course, not only to trustees, but also to many others, such as agents, solicitors and company directors. If a breach of the fair-dealing rule by a trustee were to be treated as a breach of trust to which the six-years period under the Limitation Act 1939 would apply, while a breach of the rule by one of the others were to be free from the six-years period, the result would indeed be anomalous. A possible line of escape from the anomaly would be to treat agents, solicitors and the rest as constructive trustees for this purpose, so that all would be subject to the six-years period; but I should be reluctant to resort to such an artificiality unless driven to it.
>
> Another aspect of the matter, producing the same result, is that the fair-dealing rule is essentially a rule of equity that certain persons (including trustees) are subject to certain consequences if they carry through certain transactions without, where appropriate, complying with certain requirements. The rule seems to me to be a general rule of equity and not a specific part of the law of trusts which lays down the duties of a trustee. Trusteeship is merely one of the categories of relationship which brings a person within the rule. There are many things that a trustee may do or omit to do which will have consequences for him as a trustee without the act or omission amounting to a breach of trust. I do not think that it could be said that a trustee is under a duty as trustee not to become bankrupt, so that his bankruptcy will constitute a breach of trust: yet his bankruptcy may be a ground for removing him from his trusteeship.

Looked at in the light of this analysis of the self-dealing rule, the explanation of the apparent conflict between s. 205 and arts 78 and 84 becomes clear. The true principle is that if a director places himself in a position in which his duty to the company conflicts with his personal interest or his duty to another, the court will intervene to set aside the transaction without inquiring whether there was any breach of the director's duty to the company. That is an overriding principle of equity. The shareholders of the company, in formulating the articles, can exclude or modify the application of this principle. In doing so they do not exempt the director from or from the consequences of a breach of a duty owed to the company.

12.6.3 CA 2006, s. 1157

The court may relieve directors for breach of duty if they have acted honestly and reasonably and ought fairly to be excused.

COMPANIES ACT 2006, S. 1157

1157. Power of court to grant relief in certain cases

(1) If in proceedings for negligence, default, breach of duty or breach of trust against—

   (a) an officer of a company, or

   (b) a person employed by a company as auditor (whether he is or is not an officer of the company),

it appears to the court hearing the case that the officer or person is or may be liable but that he acted honestly and reasonably, and that having regard to all the circumstances of the case (including those connected with his appointment) he ought fairly to be excused, the court may relieve him, either wholly or in part, from his liability on such terms as it thinks fit.

(2) If any such officer or person has reason to apprehend that a claim will or might be made against him in respect of negligence, default, breach of duty or breach of trust—

   (a) he may apply to the court for relief, and

   (b) the court has the same power to relieve him as it would have had if it had been a court before which proceedings against him for negligence, default, breach of duty or breach of trust had been brought.

(3) Where a case to which subsection (1) applies is being tried by a judge with a jury, the judge, after hearing the evidence, may, if he is satisfied that the defendant (in Scotland, the defender) ought in pursuance of that subsection to be relieved either in whole or in part from the liability sought to be enforced against him, withdraw the case from the jury and forthwith direct judgment to be entered for the defendant (in Scotland, grant decree of absolvitor) on such terms as to costs (in Scotland, expenses) or otherwise as the judge may think proper.

12.7 STATUTORY DUTIES

It should not be thought that the common law and equity are the only source of directors' duties and obligations. A glance at the legislation will make it clear that the accumulation of statutory regulation enacted in the last sixty years, is immense. An obvious example is CA 2006, Part 10, Chapters 3 to 6 (replacing Part X, CA 1985). This enacts a range of obligations and prohibitions many of which amount to enactment or extension of existing duties of directors as they apply in specific circumstances. The main themes relate to directors and persons connected with them dealing with the company, whether making contracts generally, buying assets from or selling assets to the company, or taking loans from the company. Loans to directors are specifically prohibited and constitute a criminal offence, and, for public companies, loans to persons connected with the directors are also prohibited. Some sections impose an obligation of disclosure on pain of criminal sanctions, such as s. 182 (extracted below) obliging directors to disclose interests in contracts. Disclosure is not necessary where other directors are already aware of the transaction. This incorporates the rule in *MacPherson v European Strategic Bureau* [1999] 2 BCLC 203, Chancery Division.

A sole director does not have to comply with the disclosure requirement in a private company (CA 2006, s. 186, which changes the rule in *Neptune (Vehicle Washing Equipment) Ltd* v *Fitzgerald* [1996] Ch 274). Other sections pass power back to the general meeting by requiring approval of particular transactions by resolution of the company in general meeting. An example in another part of the Act is ss. 549 to 551 giving the general meeting an element of control over the issue of shares (see 9.2). Another example is ss. 190 to 231 which require certain 'substantial property transactions involving directors' to be first approved by the company in general meeting, failing which the company may avoid the transaction. This amounts to a statutory enactment of a specific trustee-like obligation and operates in addition to existing equitable rules (see s. 195(8)). Sections 182 and 190 are reproduced below by way of example.

A whole range of other statutory rules supplement the common law duties of directors to the company. They also add further duties to creditors, to minority shareholders and, in the case of publicly listed companies, to the public share markets in general.

The legislation on disqualification of directors, enabling unfit directors to be disqualified following company insolvency, tends to ensure that directors act as fit and proper persons in managing companies (see 11.8). The wrongful trading provision (IA 1986, s. 214) creates a duty to creditors by imposing possible personal liability on directors who do not take every step to minimise losses when insolvent liquidation is predictable (see 20.12). It was the specific intention of this legislation to promote responsible decision-making in the face of insolvency as well as to obtain compensation for creditors. The CA 2006, s. 994 giving minorities a right to a remedy if their interests have been unfairly prejudiced, should tend to create a case-law code of acceptable practice of controlling directors towards minority shareholders (see 13.2.3). A final example is the legislation prohibiting insider dealing (see chapter 19). Thus if a director (or others) with inside information deals in the shares in his or her company, a criminal offence may be committed. While this may be a victimless crime in that the company does not suffer loss, it is easy to recognise the related principle of penalising insiders who wrongfully profit from their position within or relating to a company.

COMPANIES ACT 2006, SS. 182 AND 190

182. Declaration of interest in existing transaction or arrangement

(1) Where a director of a company is in any way, directly or indirectly, interested in a transaction or arrangement that has been entered into by the company, he must declare the nature and extent of the interest to the other directors in accordance with this section.

This section does not apply if or to the extent that the interest has been declared under section 177 (duty to declare interest in proposed transaction or arrangement).

(2) The declaration must be made—
   (a) at a meeting of the directors, or
   (b) by notice in writing (see section 184), or
   (c) by general notice (see section 185).

(3) If a declaration of interest under this section proves to be, or becomes, inaccurate or incomplete, a further declaration must be made.

(4) Any declaration required by this section must be made as soon as is reasonably practicable.

Failure to comply with this requirement does not affect the underlying duty to make the declaration.

(5) This section does not require a declaration of an interest of which the director is not aware or where the director is not aware of the transaction or arrangement in question.

For this purpose a director is treated as being aware of matters of which he ought reasonably to be aware.

(6) A director need not declare an interest under this section—

  (a) if it cannot reasonably be regarded as likely to give rise to a conflict of interest;

  (b) if, or to the extent that, the other directors are already aware of it (and for this purpose the other directors are treated as aware of anything of which ought reasonably to be aware); or

  (c) if, or to the extent that, it concerns terms of his service contract that have been or are to be considered—

    (i) by a meeting of the directors, or

    (ii) by a committee of the directors appointed for the purpose under the company's constitution.

190. Substantial property transactions requirement of members' approval

(1) A company may not enter into an arrangement under which—

  (a) a director of the company or of its holding company, or a person connected with such a director, acquires or is to acquire from the company (directly or indirectly) a substantial non-cash asset, or

  (b) the company acquires or is to acquire a substantial non-cash asset (directly or indirectly) from such a director or a person so connected,

unless the arrangement has been approved by a resolution of the members of the company or is conditional on such approval being obtained.

For the meaning of "substantial non-cash asset" see section 191.

(2) If the director or connected person is a director of the company's holding company or a person connected with such a director, the arrangement must also have been approved by a resolution of the members of the holding company or be conditional on such approval being obtained.

(3) A company shall not be subject to any liability by reason of a failure to approval required by this section.

(4) No approval is required under this section on the part of the members of a body corporate that—

  (a) is not a UK-registered company, or

  (b) is a wholly-owned subsidiary of another body corporate.

(5) For the purposes of this section—

  (a) an arrangement involving more than one non-cash asset, or

  (b) an arrangement that is one of a series involving non-cash assets,

shall be treated as if they involved a non-cash asset of a value equal to the aggregate value of all the non-cash assets involved in the arrangement or, as the case may be, the series.

(6) This section does not apply to a transaction so far as it relates—

  (a) to anything to which a director of a company is entitled under his service contract, or

  (b) to payment for loss of office as defined in section 215 (payments requiring members' approval).

12.7.1 Background to the Reforms in Part 10, CA 2006

Parts 6 to 15 of the Law Commission and Scottish Law Commission's report, *Company Directors: Regulating Conflicts of Interests and Formulating a Statement of Duties* (Law Com. No. 261), review the responses the Commissions received to their proposals (in Consultation Paper No. 153) for simplifying and modernising the provisions of Part X of the Companies Act 1985, which reforms are now in Part 10 of the CA 2006 discussed above. The introduction and the recommendations in the executive summary are extracted here to provide some historical background to the new Part 10, CA 2006.

Law Commission and Scottish Law Commission *Company Directors: Regulating Conflicts of Interests and Formulating a Statement of Duties* (Law Com. No. 261)

(London: Stationery Office, 1999)

Section B: Part X of the Companies Act

Part 6 Introduction to Section B; major repeal of Part X

Introduction

6.1 In this Section we consider Part X of the Act. Part X underpins a director's fiduciary duties to his company in that it regulates possible conflicts of interests. For example, it regulates a director's service contract and payments for loss of office; it requires a director to disclose any personal interest in company transactions; it restricts certain transactions between a company and a director or a person connected with him; it requires a director to disclose interests in shares in the company; and it restricts loans made by a company to a director. In the main Part X regulates conflicts of interest by requiring compliance with specified procedures....

6.2 We have described in Part 1 above why Part X needs to be reformed. In the Paper we proposed three main options, which were:
(1) whether large parts of Part X should be repealed;
(2) whether Part X should be disapplied where appropriate self-regulatory rules exist; or
(3) whether substantive amendments should be made to Part X.

Repeal

6.3 We discuss the question of repeal in this Part. We asked consultees for views on whether large parts of Part X could be repealed. This would clearly place greater reliance on the general law and our proposals for increasing awareness of and accessibility to the general law are discussed in Parts 4 and 5 above. However, our provisional view was that large parts of Part X should *not* be repealed. We consider that the provisions of Part X provide protection which is often superior to that of the general law. The majority of respondents supported this and we have not altered our provisional view through consultation. Accordingly, our recommendation below is that the relevant sections be retained.

Self-regulation

6.4 We described the extent to which self-regulation covers the same ground as Part X and asked consultees for views on whether Part X should be disapplied where appropriate self-regulatory rules exist. As noted in Part 1, we have agreed with the DTI that the role of self-regulation should not be dealt with in this report, and we have therefore not discussed it in general terms.

Substantive amendment

6.5 Our third option was for substantive amendments to be made to Part X. Respondents were in favour of this and, in light of our recommendation that these provisions should be retained, most of this Section consists of a discussion of our proposed substantive amendments. In Parts 7 to 14, we consider individual sections or groups of related sections in turn.

6.6 At the end of this Section we also consider our proposal for the introduction of a single code of civil remedies and effects into Part X.

Major repeal of Part X

6.7 In the Paper we set out the option of repealing a number of significant provisions in Part X. If these provisions were repealed, reliance would be placed on more general principles of law to regulate the transactions which the provisions now cover. The sections in question were:

sections 312–316 (compensation for loss of office etc.);

section 319 (the period of directors' service contracts);

sections 320–322 (substantial property transactions); and

sections 330–344 (loans and similar transactions).

6.8 Several of these provisions (sections 312–316, 319, 320–322) governed transactions which are now subject to considerable self-regulation where the company in question is a listed company. On the other hand private companies and many public limited companies are not subject to the Listing Rules or the AIM Rules and are regulated only by the Act and the general law.

6.9 The principal argument in favour of repeal of these provisions is that it would simplify Part X by removing complex legal provisions on which directors require legal advice. Removal of these provisions, which contain a number of loopholes, would allow the remaining provisions of Part X to be expressed more coherently and Part X as a whole to be simplified. Reliance on the principles of the general law would be assisted if there were a statutory statement of the duties of directors under the general law.

6.10 The principal argument against repeal of these provisions is that they provide protection which is superior to that offered by the general law. The provisions were enacted to prevent abuses which the general law had failed to prevent. We are not aware of any evidence that the development of the general law has removed the need for the protection which these provisions give. Self-regulation does not apply to private companies and many public limited companies. Repeal of the provisions and reliance on the general law would mean that the criminal sanctions and civil remedies which are now available under these provisions would no longer be available. The prohibitions in ss. 330–342 against loans and similar transactions provide protection not only to shareholders in a company but also to the company's creditors. Reliance on the general law to regulate directors would not provide that protection to the company's creditors unless the general law were to develop so as to impose duties on directors in relation to a company's creditors.

6.11 In the Paper we expressed the view that the arguments against repeal appeared to outweigh those in favour but invited consultees' views.

Summary of respondents' views

6.12 A significant majority of respondents did not favour repeal of these provisions. It was suggested that there was no basis for confidence that the general law would prevent the abuses which caused these provisions to be enacted. Some company lawyers emphasised that they found it helpful to be able to refer to clearer statutory rules rather than general principles when advising directors in situations where there was a conflict of interest. A minority supported repeal of some or all of these provisions and reliance on disclosure to shareholders. One respondent pointed out that Canada had no equivalent to the provisions of Part X but placed reliance on a partial codification of directors' duties and on the general law. Other respondents expressed concern that repeal of these provisions would send the wrong message to directors.

Recommendation

6.13 Having considered the responses we accept that it would not be appropriate to repeal the sections referred to in paragraph 6.7 above. We agree with the respondents who considered that the provisions provide protection to shareholders and creditors in addition to that provided by the general law. If the Company Law Review takes forward our work on the rewriting of Part X, there may be scope to simplify the restrictions in ss. 312–316 and 330–344. *Accordingly, we recommend that sections 312–316, 319, 320–322 and 330–344 should not be repealed.*

Limited repeals

6.14 In the Paper we also discussed the option of more limited repeals of particular statutory provisions. We expressed the provisional view that four sections or subsections could be repealed. These provisions were ss. 311, 318(5), 318(11) and 323. Discussion of the repeal of these sections can be found in the text dealing with general improvements to these sections or related sections, and in particular at paragraphs 7.96 to 7.99, 9.12 to 9.17 and 11.3 to 11.7. We consider that ss. 311, 318(5) and (11) and 323 may safely be repealed.

Executive summary

Part X of the Companies Act 1985

We recommend:

- The retention of most of the provisions of Part X in order to supplement the protection provided by the general law.
- Further disclosure in a company's annual accounts of compensation paid to individual directors for loss of office.
- Limitation on the interests which a director requires to disclose to the board and the introduction of civil remedies for non-disclosure.
- A reduction from five to three years of the period of duration of a director's service contract which requires shareholder approval and extension of statutory control to rolling contracts.
- The amendment of s. 320 to allow a company to agree a substantial property transaction with a director by a contract which is conditional on the company first obtaining shareholder approval.
- The extension of the prohibitions on loans and similar transactions in ss. 330–337 to all companies and the retention of existing exemptions from prohibitions.
- The repeal of ss. 311, 318(5) and (11), 323 and 327.
- The introduction of a coherent code of civil remedies.

The Steering Group's views on Part X are set out in the extract below. The Government's White Paper makes, however, no mention of them.

Modern Company Law for a Competitive Economy: Final Report
(London: DTI, July 2001)

Part X—Sections 312 to 317

6.8 Turning to Part X of the Act (conflicted directors) we set out our proposals on sections 312 to 316 (payments to directors in connection with loss of office, etc.) in paragraphs 4.9 and 4.10 of *Completing the Structure*. In paragraphs 4.11 to 4.16 we made firm proposals on section 317 (directors' interests in company transactions—disclosure to fellow directors). There is now substantial agreement on our proposals for defining the materiality of interests justifying disclosure. It was, however, suggested that to allow directors to escape their obligations if they could prove that other directors were 'properly aware' of the interest might be insufficient to enable a director to proceed with confidence and might also be open to abuse, which would be best met by imposing the burden of proof on a director seeking to take advantage of this 'safe harbour'. It was in fact always our intention that the onus of proving such knowledge should be on the director; but we accept that there is a case for allowing this to be discharged by proof that he had in due time notified his fellow directors in writing.

6.9 We have already indicated in paragraph 4.9 of this Report that in private companies where there is only one director the obligation to notify the board of his interest in company transactions should be removed.

Directors' Contracts of Employment

6.10 Paragraphs 4.17 to 4.20 of *Completing the Structure* covered directors' contracts of employment. We suggested extension of section 318, which requires directors' service contracts to be open to inspection by members, by requiring disclosure of ancillary provisions (as proposed by the Law Commissions) but with a confidentiality exception, the invocation of which should be subject to scrutiny by the auditors. We also suggested that members should be entitled to receive copies of such contracts (or of a memorandum of their terms if they were not in writing) on demand and on payment of a reasonable fee to cover expenses. Concern was expressed that the requirement might be evaded by excluding key provisions or by fixing an unreasonable fee. Both concerns can be met in the drafting. Otherwise there was very wide support for both proposals. Auditors were uneasy at the prospect of having to vet invocation of the confidentiality exception. Here again, the drafting will need to ensure that the auditors need only be satisfied that there is reasonable evidence on which such a judgment could be reached. Where confidentiality has been invoked this would be required to be disclosed in the annual report.

6.11 It was also suggested that terms of engagement for NEDs should be subject to similar disclosure. This was originally suggested by the Law Commissions, and we agree.

6.12 On the maximum permitted duration of directors' contracts of employment, which is mainly of importance in setting the maximum compensation for loss of employment, we proposed a normal limit of one year, but with flexibility to contract for three years on first employment, both limits to be subject to extension by members' resolution. The great majority of responses had supported the reduction of the present five year maximum to three, but there was quite strong opposition to the reduction to one year, except as a matter of Combined Code ('comply or explain') requirement. In particular it was pointed out that if there are genuine market forces at work here they will only reassert themselves in some other way—for example by offers of excessive remuneration on the shorter contracts. Others believed that, if the general meeting waiver provision allowed a general waiver or authorisation of the board to approve longer periods, that was too lax, or even that the one year and three year maxima were too high. Others suggested that this new rule could prove a competitive disadvantage for British companies in the market for management skills, if (as indeed we believe to be the case) it is significantly tighter than the requirements in other jurisdictions. Yet other believed that the proposal was sensible for public companies, but not for closely-held private ones. In our view the shareholder authorisation provision should be flexible so that where shareholders are convinced that there are genuine competitive issues they can provide an appropriate waiver. Such authorisation will be readily achievable in closely-held companies in appropriate cases. We agree with those who emphasised the importance of any such exempted contracts being subject to appropriate disclosure in the annual report throughout their duration.

6.13 While we maintain our view that the one year and three year limits we have proposed set the right pattern, further questions arise as to the extent to which they should be capable of relaxation by the members or under the constitution, and how widely expressed any resulting authority conferred by the members should be permitted to be. Section 319 does not currently permit a more general prior disapplication of the limit (as opposed to approval of a specific proposed contractual term), either by ordinary resolution or by provision in the constitution. (A constitutional disapplication would of course require an initial special resolution for existing companies.) It was clear that a number of respondents supported our proposal for reduction of the normal maximum term to one year only on the basis that it would be possible for companies, in general meeting or by their constitutions, to authorise their boards to allow longer terms in appropriate cases. Having considered the balance of the arguments on this, we believe that such advance authorisation by special resolution should be possible, subject to the requirements that terms in excess of three years should require specific approval by ordinary resolution as currently required by section 319 and that any authority conferred should have a maximum duration of five years, so that the issue would require periodic re-examination by the members. Disclosure, with a justification, of any terms in excess of one year should remain a requirement under the Combined Code. This would be in addition to the disclosure of the terms proposed under paragraph 6.10.

6.14 This proposal for limiting contractual periods led us to consider possible evasion by specific covenants for severance payments, separate from compensation for early dismissal. We proposed that, again subject to members' specific waiver, such covenants should be void to the extent that they provided for more compensation than would be available by way of compensation for the loss of the balance of the one year or three year terms, as appropriate. There was quite wide misunderstanding of our proposal, some believing the effect would be to interfere with the courts' powers to quantify loss on breach of contract, or that it would remove a right to compensation for loss of bonuses or other payments in excess of basic salary, or that entitlements under statute should be included within the capped amount (e.g. redundancy payment rights); we had intended none of these. Subject to these points of clarification the proposal was supported by almost all, except those who opposed the basic proposition on employment terms from which it stems. We accordingly maintain it. The effect will be that where the general meeting has authorised longer terms to be agreed within the three year limit the measure of compensation allowed would be adjusted accordingly.

Directors' Dealing in Share Options, and Loans Secured on Shares

6.15 The very recent report of the DTI Inspectors on Mirror Group Newspapers plc recommends (paragraphs 23.97 and 23.98) that directors' dealings in options (section 323) and the securing by directors of loans on their companies' shares should be subjected to additional regulation. The justification for these proposals appears to be concern about market manipulation. Indeed it was for this very reason (i.e. that the matter was not one for companies legislation) that we proposed the repeal of section 323. They therefore appear to be a matter for the FSA and HM Treasury, rather than for us. On section 330 to 344 (loans, quasi-loans and credit transactions), our main outstanding proposal in *Completing the Structure* was provision for additional exemption by member resolution, (see *Completing the Structure* paragraph 4.21). This was very widely supported.

6.16 Our remaining proposals on Part X are set out in *Completing the Structure* (paragraph 4.21).

13

Majority Rule and Protection of Minorities

13.1.1 Majority rule and minority remedies

All powers of a company are in theory exercised by one or other of its own organs: the shareholders in general meeting or the board of directors. Each of these bodies generally makes its decision by majority vote. This democratic principle of majority rule means that those who control more than half of the votes on the board or at a shareholders' meeting (and, indeed, those who command a good deal less than a majority of the votes but manage to exercise *de facto* control), thus have substantial power. It is obvious that the law must provide some remedies in cases where such majority power has been abused. At common law minority shareholders who are unhappy with a decision of the majority can bring a claim only if that decision is illegal or *ultra vires* the memorandum of association, or infringes the member's personal rights conferred by the Companies Act or the articles of association. Problems arise where the alleged wrong is done to the company or is an act which the majority is entitled to ratify. In those cases the minority can get very little help as the courts are extremely reluctant to interfere on their behalf. At common law, in order to redress the wrong the claim had to be brought by the company itself under the rule in *Foss* v *Harbottle* (1843) 2 Hare 461. Where the wrongdoers are in control of the voting in the board and the general meeting, a claim against themselves is improbable. However, the judiciary have made some attempts to combat this injustice that may arise in applying the rule in *Foss* v *Harbottle*. Thus there is an exception to this rule where the decision of the majority is said to be a 'fraud on the minority'.

The rule in *Foss* v *Harbottle* springs from two related concepts: (a) that a company is a legal entity distinct from its shareholders; and (b) that a company cannot function effectively unless the will of the majority generally prevails. Under this rule, a minority shareholder is often at risk. In some respects shareholders of public companies are in a better position in that they are able to realise their investment if need be. Furthermore, listed companies are subject to stock market control. Bad publicity of the majority's unfair conduct towards the minority may affect the company's profitability and share value. For minority shareholders in an unlisted company, there is no such readily available market. Publicity is unlikely to affect substantially the majority's conduct of the company's affairs but may make it even more difficult for the minority to realise their shares in the company. Even if the minority could find a buyer, the price they would get for their shares is likely to be depressed. There may also be restrictions in the company's articles making it difficult for a member to transfer shares.

For shareholders who want to resort to litigation, for example, where the directors are persistently in breach of duty to the company, there are a number of possibilities. First, as an exception to the rule in *Foss* v *Harbottle*, a shareholder may now bring a statutory derivative claim under the procedures in Part 11 of the CA 2006. This was enacted to give effect to the recommendations of the Law Commission. It does not replace the rule in *Foss* v *Harbottle*, but simply provides a statutory procedure for a derivative action. Under this Part, a derivative claim will be available for any actual or proposed act or omission involving negligence, default, breach of duty or breach of trust by a director (s 260(3)). This is wider than the old common law derivative action where the claimant had to show that the breach or default amounted to 'fraud on the minority', a concept which was fraught with difficulties. Under the CA 2006, the claimant has to show a prima facie case in order to get the permission of the court to proceed. The court will first consider the case based on the evidence filed by the applicant only, without requiring evidence from the defendant. If the applicant cannot establish a prima facie case, the application will be dismissed. If a prima facie case is established, the court may then require evidence to be provided by the company, before the substantive action begins. A list of the matters which the court must take into account is provided by s 260 in considering whether to give permission and the circumstances where the court must refuse permission. This new procedure was designed to overcome the problems caused by the old common law derivative action where the claimant had to show the wrongdoer in control which was not easy to do as the well-known case of *Prudential Assurance* v *Newman (No 2)* shows (extracted at 13.2.5 below).

In addition to a shareholder, a person who is not a member but to whom shares have been transferred or transmitted by operation of law, for example a trustee in bankruptcy or personal representative of a deceased member's estate, can also bring a derivative claim (s. 260(5)). As in many countries, the statutory derivative claim replaces the common law derivative action.

It should be noted that the purpose of a derivative claim by minority shareholders is to obtain a remedy for the company, possibly against defaulting directors. However, it may be that these shareholders would prefer to obtain a remedy for themselves. The modern remedy for individual shareholders is now contained in CA 2006, s. 994, which replaces CA 1985, s. 459. The new s. 994 is substantially the same as the old s. 459 thus cases on s. 459 will continue to be relevant.

Section 459 of the CA 1985 was enacted to replace CA 1948, s. 210. Prior to the enactment of CA 1948, s. 210, minority shareholders were often forced to use the 'sledgehammer' device of petitioning for the winding up of the company under what is now s. 122(1)(g) of the Insolvency Act 1986. This remedy was drastic and inflexible and not always appropriate. Following the recommendations of the Cohen Committee (Cmd 6659, para. 60), s. 210 of the CA 1948 was passed in an attempt to provide a remedy for the minority against oppressive conduct by the majority and as an alternative to s. 122(1)(g). Section 210, however, soon became a dead letter as it was too restrictively applied. As a result, it was replaced by CA 1980, s. 75, which adopted the changes proposed by the Jenkins Committee. The provisions in s. 75 were subsequently contained in CA 1985, ss. 459 to 461, as amended by CA 1989. Section 459 allowed a member of a company to petition on the ground of unfair prejudice. There was an explosion of litigation under the section and the section presumably also enabled many more disputes to be settled out of court. With the comparatively liberal interpretation of s. 459 by the judiciary, cases on the rule in *Foss* v *Harbottle* and its exceptions became less significant.

The popularity of s. 459 as a remedy for the minority, however, caused some problems which attracted certain criticism. These mainly related to the complexity of the proceedings as petitioners often found it necessary to make wide-ranging allegations of unfairly prejudicial conduct occurring throughout the history of the company. This prolonged the hearing and increased the cost of the petition. The Law Commission in its report on shareholder remedies (No. 246) addressed the issue and made some proposals for reform (see 13.2.5) which were taken up by the Steering Group. However, none of these recommendations was enacted into law. Section 994 simply restates s. 459.

Foss v *Harbottle*

None of the minority's business

(1843) 2 Hare 461, Chancery Division

This case is authority for the principle that where there is a wrong done to the company, the company is the proper plaintiff. A minority shareholder cannot bring a claim.

Facts Two shareholders brought this action against the company's directors and promoters alleging, inter alia, that they had sold land to the company at an exorbitant price. They brought this action on behalf of themselves and all other shareholders except the defendants. It was held that the conduct complained of was a wrong done to the company and that only the company could sue.

WIGRAM V-C: The Victoria Park Co. is an incorporated body, and the conduct with which the defendants are charged in this suit is an injury not to the plaintiffs exclusively; it is an injury to the whole corporation by individuals whom the corporation entrusted with powers to be exercised only for the good of the corporation. And from the case of *Attorney-General* v *Wilson* (1840) Cr & Ph 1 (without going further) it may be stated as undoubted law that a bill or information by a corporation will lie to be relieved in respect of injuries which the corporation has suffered at the hands of persons standing in the situation of the directors upon this record. This bill, however, differs from that in *Attorney-General* v *Wilson* in this—that, instead of the corporation being formally represented as plaintiffs, the bill in this case is brought by two individual corporators, professedly on behalf of themselves and all the other members of the corporation, except those who committed the injuries complained of—the plaintiffs assuming to themselves the right and power in that manner to sue on behalf of and represent the corporation itself.

It was not, nor could it successfully be, argued that it was a matter of course for any individual members of a corporation thus to assume to themselves the right of suing in the name of the corporation. In law the corporation and the aggregate members of the corporation are not the same thing for purposes like this; and the only question can be whether the facts alleged in this case justify a departure from the rule which, prima facie, would require that the corporation should sue in its own name and in its corporate character, or in the name of someone whom the law has appointed to be its representative....

The first objection taken in the argument for the defendants was that the individual members of the corporation cannot in any case sue in the form in which this bill is framed. During the argument I intimated an opinion, to which, upon further consideration, I fully adhere, that the rule was much too broadly stated on the part of the defendants. I think there are cases in which a suit might properly be so framed. Corporations like this, of a private nature, are in truth little more than private partnerships; and in cases which may easily be suggested it would be too much to hold that a society of private persons associated together in undertakings, which, though certainly beneficial to the public, are nevertheless matters of private property, are to be deprived of their civil rights, *inter se*, because, in order to make their common objects more attainable, the Crown or the legislature may have conferred upon them the benefit of a corporate character. If a case should arise of injury to a corporation by some of its members, for which no adequate remedy remained, except that of a suit by individual corporators in their private characters, and asking in such character the protection of those rights to which in their corporate character they were entitled, I cannot but think that the principle so forcibly laid down by Lord Cottenham in *Wallworth* v *Holt* (1841) 4 My & Cr 619 at p. 635; see also *Adley* v *Whitstable Co.* (1810) 17 Ves Jr 315 at p. 320 per Lord Eldon) and other cases would apply, and the claims of justice would be found superior to any difficulties arising out of technical rules respecting the mode in which corporations are required to sue.

But, on the other hand, it must not be without reasons of a very urgent character that established rules of law and practice are to be departed from, rules which, though in a sense technical, are founded on general principles of justice and convenience; and the question is whether a case is stated in this bill entitling the plaintiffs to sue in their private characters....

...it is only necessary to refer to the clauses of the Act to show that, whilst the supreme governing body, the proprietors at a special general meeting assembled, retain the power of exercising the functions conferred upon them by the Act of Incorporation, it cannot be competent to individual corporators to sue in the manner proposed by the plaintiffs on the present record.

NOTE: The rule in *Foss* v *Harbottle* was considered in *Johnson* v *Gore Wood and Co.* [1999] PNLR 426, where the Court of Appeal laid down the following principles after reviewing authorities including: *Prudential Assurance Co. Ltd* v *Newman Industries Ltd (No. 2)* [1982] Ch 204; *Heron International Ltd* v *Lord Grade* [1983] BCLC 244; *R.P. Howard Ltd* v *Woodman Matthews and Co.* [1983] BCLC 117; *George Fischer (Great Britain) Ltd* v *Multi Construction Ltd* [1995] 1 BCLC 260; *Christensen* v *Scott* [1996] 1 NZLR 273; *Barings plc* v *Coopers and Lybrand* [1997] 1 BCLC 427; *Gerber Garment Technology Inc.* v *Lectra Systems Ltd* [1997] RPC 443; *Stein* v *Blake* [1998] 1 All ER 724; *Watson* v *Dutton Forshaw Motor Group Ltd* (1999) LTL 17/8/99. The House of Lords have basically affirmed these principles (see [2001] 1 BCLC 313) (see also *Day* v *Cook* [2002] 1 BCLC 1, CA).

1. The rule in *Foss* v *Harbottle* provides the starting point that A cannot bring an action against B to recover damages for an injury done by B to C.

2. Where the shareholder's loss is not separate and distinct from but is reflective of the direct loss suffered by the company as a result of the defendant's conduct, then no personal loss from the diminution in the market value of the shares arises and accordingly the shareholder has no right of action: *Prudential Assurance*.

3. The gloss on this is, that the defendant's conduct can cause loss in two directions—one, arising as a shortfall of assets or profits, being a loss to the coffers of the company; the other being a loss to his own pocket as when he is induced to part with his shares at an undervalue: the *Heron* distinction.

4. If the duty is owed to the shareholder only and *ex hypothesi* the company has no cause of action, then the shareholder can recover such losses, if not too remote, as he can prove to have been caused by the defendant's conduct no matter that the losses arise through loss of dividends or his share of profits in the company or a fall in the value of his shares: *George Fischer* and *Gerber*.

5. If the defendants are in breach of a different duty of care owed to the shareholder distinct from a duty owed to the company, the shareholder, who accordingly has a right of action independent from the company, cannot be disentitled from suing merely because there is an overlap in recoverable damages: the *Barings* point.

6. The synthesis of the propositions derived from the *Barings* point and the *Heron* distinction seems to be that liability may well depend upon whether there are different duties (and it may be

with different conduct constituting the breach of the duty) and/or whether different kinds of damage arise from such breach.

Edwards v *Halliwell*

The Foss v Harbottle exceptions

[1950] 2 All ER 1064, Court of Appeal

In this case Jenkins LJ identified four 'exceptions' to the rule in *Foss* v *Harbottle*: (a) where the act complained of was *ultra vires*; (b) where there was fraud on the minority and the wrongdoers were in control; (c) where the act complained of was a violation of a requirement in the articles for a special majority; and (d) where the act complained of was an invasion of members' personal rights as members. This case is a classic example of the third exception. It should be noted, however, that Jenkins LJ himself made it clear that exceptions (a), (c) and (d) are not true exceptions. They are cases where the rule in *Foss* v *Harbottle* simply has no application.

Facts   Under the constitution of the defendant trade union, contributions by members could only be altered by a two-thirds majority in a ballot of the membership. A general meeting of delegates passed a resolution increasing the contributions of members, without taking a ballot. The two plaintiffs, members of the union, successfully sued the union and members of its executive committee for a declaration that the resolution was invalid.

JENKINS LJ: The rule in *Foss* v *Harbottle* (1843) 2 Hare 461, as I understand it, comes to no more than this. First, the proper plaintiff in an action in respect of a wrong alleged to be done to a company or association of persons is prima facie the company or the association of persons itself. Secondly, where the alleged wrong is a transaction which might be made binding on the company or association and on all its members by a simple majority of the members, no individual member of the company is allowed to maintain an action in respect of that matter for the simple reason that, if a mere majority of the members of the company or association is in favour of what has been done, then *cadit quaestio*. No wrong had been done to the company or association and there is nothing in respect of which anyone can sue. If, on the other hand, a simple majority of members of the company or association is against what has been done, then there is no valid reason why the company or association itself should not sue. In my judgment, it is implicit in the rule that the matter relied on as constituting the cause of action should be a cause of action properly belonging to the general body of corporators or members of the company or association as opposed to a cause of action which some individual member can assert in his own right.

The cases falling within the general ambit of the rule are subject to certain exceptions. It has been noted in the course of argument that in cases where the act complained of is wholly *ultra vires* the company or association the rule has no application because there is no question of the transaction being confirmed by any majority. It has been further pointed out that where what has been done amounts to what is generally called in these cases a fraud on the minority and the wrongdoers are themselves in control of the company, the rule is relaxed in favour of the aggrieved minority who are allowed to bring what is known as a minority shareholders' action on behalf of themselves and all others. The reason for this is that, if they were denied that right, their grievance could never reach the court because the wrongdoers themselves, being in control, would not allow the company to sue. Those exceptions are not directly in point in this case, but they show, especially the last one, that the rule is not an inflexible rule and it will be relaxed where necessary in the interests of justice.

There is a further exception which seems to me to touch this case directly. That is the exception noted by Romer J in *Cotter* v *National Union of Seamen* [1929] 2 Ch 58. He pointed out that the rule did not prevent an individual member from suing if the matter in respect of which he was suing was one which could validly be done or sanctioned, not by a simple majority of the members of the company or association, but only by some special majority, as, for instance, in the case of a limited company under the Companies Act, a special resolution duly passed as such. As Romer J pointed out, the reason for that exception is clear, because otherwise, if the rule were applied in its full rigour, a company which, by its directors, had broken its own regulations by doing something without a special resolution which could only be done validly by a special resolution could assert that it alone was the proper plaintiff in any consequent action and the effect would be to allow a company acting in breach of its articles to do *de facto* by ordinary resolution that which according to its own regulations could only be done by special resolution. That exception exactly fits the present case inasmuch as here the act complained of is something which could only have been validly done, not by a simple majority, but by a two-thirds majority obtained on a ballot vote. In my judgment, therefore, the reliance on the rule in *Foss* v *Harbottle* in the present case may be regarded as misconceived on that ground alone.

I would go further. In my judgment, this is a case of a kind which is not even within the general ambit of the rule. It is not a case where what is complained of is a wrong done to the union, a matter in respect of which the cause of action would primarily and properly belong to the union. It is a case in which certain members of a trade union complain that the union, acting through the delegate meeting and the executive council in breach of the rules by which the union and every member of the union are bound, has invaded the individual rights of the complainant members, who are entitled to maintain themselves in full membership with all the rights and privileges appertaining to that status so long as they pay contributions in accordance with the tables of contributions as they stood before the purported alterations of 1943, unless and until the scale of contributions is validly altered by the prescribed majority obtained on a ballot vote. Those rights, these members claim, have been invaded. The gist of the case is that the personal and individual rights of membership of each of them have been invaded by a purported, but invalid, alteration of the tables of contributions. In those circumstances, it seems to me the rule in *Foss* v *Harbottle* has no application at all, for the individual members who are suing sue, not in the right of the union, but in their own right to protect from invasion their own individual rights as members.

Pender v *Lushington*

Voting as a personal right

(1877) 6 ChD 70, Court of Appeal

This case provides an example of a personal claim, the fourth 'exception' to the rule in *Foss* v *Harbottle* as identified by Jenkins LJ in *Edwards* v *Halliwell* extracted above. (It is interesting to note that Jessel MR said that the action could be brought either in the company's name by the minority shareholder, or in the minority shareholder's name. Does this indicate that an invasion of a member's right can also be a wrong done to the company?)

Facts   The company's articles entitled every member to one vote for every 10 shares with a maximum of 100 votes in all. Pender had registered his substantial shareholding in the names of several nominees so as to exceed the limit of 100 votes. At a general meeting the chairman declared lost a resolution proposed by Pender because he refused to accept the nominees' votes. Pender brought a representative action against the directors, naming the company as a co-plaintiff, on behalf of himself, the shareholders and the company.

JESSEL MR: In all cases of this kind, where men exercise their rights of property, they exercise their rights from some motive adequate or inadequate, and I have always considered the law to be that those who have the rights of property are entitled to exercise them, whatever their motives may be for such exercise....

This being so, the arguments which have been addressed to me as to whether or not the object for which the votes were given would bring about the ruin of the company, or whether or not the motive was an improper one which induced these gentlemen to give their votes, or whether or not their conduct shows a want of appreciation of the principles on which this company was founded, appear to me to be wholly irrelevant....

I now come to the subordinate question, not very material in the view I take of the case, namely, whether you have the right plaintiffs here. The plaintiffs may be described as three, though they are really two. There is, first, Mr Pender himself, on behalf of himself; next, as the representative of the class of shareholders who voted with him, whose votes I hold to have been improperly rejected; and, next, there is the Direct United States Cable Co. It is said that the company ought not to have been made plaintiffs.

The reasons given were reasons of some singularity, but there is no doubt of this, that under the articles the directors are the custodians of the seal of the company, and the directors, who in fact are defendants, have certainly not given any authority to the solicitor for the plaintiffs on this record to institute this suit in the name of the company as plaintiffs. It is equally clear, if I am right in the conclusion to which I have come as to the impropriety of the decision of the chairman in rejecting these votes, that it is a case in which the company might properly sue as plaintiffs to restrain the directors from carrying out a resolution which had not been properly carried, and then comes the question whether I ought or ought not to allow the company now to remain as plaintiffs.

The first point to be considered is this: Supposing there was no objection to the right of a general meeting to direct an action to be brought, could I, even in that case, allow the company to sue? I think I could. In that case the general meeting, having a right to direct an action to be brought, would act by the majority of the members. The majority wish their rights to be protected. A meeting could be called, and, if the court was satisfied that the majority would direct an action to be brought, the company's name would not be taken away. In the meantime the court must act....

But what is the court to do in the meantime, if it is satisfied that a real majority decided in favour of bringing an action? Surely it must do something in the meantime, and it follows, I think, from that portion of the judgment, that in the meantime the court ought to grant the injunction to keep things *in statu quo*....

In the meantime, whether this is an action in the name of the shareholders or in the name of the company, in either case I think there should be an injunction....

But there is another ground on which the action may be maintained. This is an action by Mr Pender for himself. He is a member of the company, and whether he votes with the majority or the minority he is entitled to have his vote recorded—an individual right in respect of which he has a right to sue. That has nothing to do with the question like that raised in *Foss* v *Harbottle* (1843) 2 Hare 461 and that line of cases. He has a right to say, 'Whether I vote in the majority or minority, you shall record my vote, as that is a right of property belonging to my interest in this company, and if you refuse to record my vote I will institute legal proceedings against you to compel you'. What is the answer to such an action? It seems to me it can be maintained as a matter of substance, and that there is no technical difficulty in maintaining it.

13.1.2 Statutory derivative claims

COMPANIES ACT 2006, SS. 260 TO 264

260. Derivative claims

(1) This Chapter applies to proceedings in England and Wales or Northern Ireland by a member of a company—
   (a) in respect of a cause of action vested in the company, and
   (b) seeking relief on behalf of the company.
   This is referred to in this Chapter as a "derivative claim".
(2) A derivative claim may only be brought—
   (a) under this Chapter, or
   (b) in pursuance of an order of the court in proceedings under section 994 (proceedings for protection of members against unfair prejudice).
(3) A derivative claim under this Chapter may be brought only in respect of a cause of action arising from an actual or proposed act or omission involving negligence, default, breach of duty or breach of trust by a director of the company.

The cause of action may be against the director or another person (or both).

(4) It is immaterial whether the cause of action arose before or after the person seeking to bring or continue the derivative claim became a member of the company.

(5) For the purposes of this Chapter—

(a) "director" includes a former director;

(b) a shadow director is treated as a director; and

(c) references to a member of a company include a person who is not a member but to whom shares in the company have been transferred or transmitted by operation of law.

261. Application for permission to continue derivative claim

(1) A member of a company who brings a derivative claim under this Chapter must apply to the court for permission (in Northern Ireland, leave) to continue it.

(2) If it appears to the court that the application and the evidence filed by the applicant in support of it do not disclose a prima facie case for giving permission (or leave), the court—

(a) must dismiss the application, and

(b) may make any consequential order it considers appropriate.

(3) If the application is not dismissed under subsection (2), the court—

(a) may give directions as to the evidence to be provided by the company, and

(b) may adjourn the proceedings to enable the evidence to be obtained.

(4) On hearing the application, the court may—

(a) give permission (or leave) to continue the claim on such terms as it thinks fit,

(b) refuse permission (or leave) and dismiss the claim, or

(c) adjourn the proceedings on the application and give such directions as it thinks fit.

262. Application for permission to continue claim as a derivative claim

(1) This section applies where—

(a) a company has brought a claim, and

(b) the cause of action on which the claim is based could be pursued as a derivative claim under this Chapter.

(2) A member of the company may apply to the court for permission (in Northern Ireland, leave) to continue the claim as a derivative claim on the ground that—

(a) the manner in which the company commenced or continued the claim amounts to an abuse of the process of the court,

(b) the company has failed to prosecute the claim diligently, and

(c) it is appropriate for the member to continue the claim as a derivative claim.

(3) If it appears to the court that the application and the evidence filed by the applicant in support of it do not disclose a prima facie case for giving permission (or leave), the court—

(a) must dismiss the application, and

(b) may make any consequential order it considers appropriate.

(4) If the application is not dismissed under subsection (3), the court—

(a) may give directions as to the evidence to be provided by the company, and

(b) may adjourn the proceedings to enable the evidence to be obtained.

(5) On hearing the application, the court may—

(a) give permission (or leave) to continue the claim as a derivative claim on such terms as it thinks fit,

(b) refuse permission (or leave) and dismiss the application, or

(c) adjourn the proceedings on the application and give such directions as it thinks fit.

263. Whether permission to be given

(1) The following provisions have effect where a member of a company applies for permission (in Northern Ireland, leave) under section 261 or 262.

(2) Permission (or leave) must be refused if the court is satisfied—

(a) that a person acting in accordance with section 172 (duty to promote the success of the company) would not seek to continue the claim, or

    (b) where the cause of action arises from an act or omission that is yet to occur, that the act or omission has been authorised by the company, or

    (c) where the cause of action arises from an act or omission that has already occurred, that the actor omission—

        (i)   was authorised by the company before it occurred, or

        (ii) has been ratified by the company since it occurred.

(3) In considering whether to give permission (or leave) the court must take into account, in particular—

    (a) whether the member is acting in good faith in seeking to continue the claim;

    (b) the importance that a person acting in accordance with section 172 (duty to promote the success of the company) would attach to continuing it;

    (c) where the cause of action results from an act or omission that is yet to occur, whether the actor omission could be, and in the circumstances would be likely to be—

        (i)   authorised by the company before it occurs, or

        (ii) ratified by the company after it occurs;

    (d) where the cause of action arises from an act or omission that has already occurred, whether the act or omission could be, and in the circumstances would be likely to be, ratified by the company;

    (e) whether the company has decided not to pursue the claim;

    (f) whether the act or omission in respect of which the claim is brought gives rise to a cause of action that the member could pursue in his own right rather than on behalf of the company.

(4) In considering whether to give permission (or leave) the court shall have particular regard to any evidence before it as to the views of members of the company who have no personal interest, direct or indirect, in the matter.

(5) The Secretary of State may by regulations—

    (a) amend subsection (2) so as to alter or add to the circumstances in which permission (or leave) is to be refused;

    (b) amend subsection (3) so as to alter or add to the matters that the court is required to take into account in considering whether to give permission (or leave).

(6) Before making any such regulations the Secretary of State shall consult such persons as he considers appropriate.

(7) Regulations under this section are subject to affirmative resolution procedure.

264. Application for permission to continue derivative claim brought by another member

(1) This section applies where a member of a company ("the claimant")—

    (a) has brought a derivative claim,

    (b) has continued as a derivative claim a claim brought by the company, or

    (c) has continued a derivative claim under this section.

(2) Another member of the company ("the applicant") may apply to the court for permission (in Northern Ireland, leave) to continue the claim on the ground that—

    (a) the manner in which the proceedings have been commenced or continued by the claimant amounts to an abuse of the process of the court,

    (b) the claimant has failed to prosecute the claim diligently, and

    (c) it is appropriate for the applicant to continue the claim as a derivative claim.

(3) If it appears to the court that the application and the evidence filed by the applicant in support of it do not disclose a prima facie case for giving permission (or leave), the court—

    (a) must dismiss the application, and

    (b) may make any consequential order it considers appropriate.

(4) If the application is not dismissed under subsection (3), the court—

    (a) may give directions as to the evidence to be provided by the company, and

    (b) may adjourn the proceedings to enable the evidence to be obtained.

> (5) On hearing the application, the court may—
>   (a) give permission (or leave) to continue the claim on such terms as it thinks fit,
>   (b) refuse permission (or leave) and dismiss the application, or
>   (c) adjourn the proceedings on the application and give such directions as it thinks fit.

It is now no longer necessary for a claimant to show that the act complained of is a fraud on the minority. Old cases on fraud on the minority (which includes misappropriation of corporate property (*Menier* v *Hooper's Telegraph Works* (1874) LR 9 Ch App 350), *mala fide* abuse of power (*Estmanco (Kilner House) Ltd* v *Greater London Council* [1982] 1 All ER 437, [1982] 1 WLR 2), or discrimination against a section of the membership or errors of judgment from which the directors themselves benefit (*Daniels* v *Daniels* [1978] Ch 406)) will now be covered by the new section, but the new section will also cover cases which were not fraud on the minority, e.g., pure negligence.

Wrongdoer in control will cease to be a definitive factor for the court to decide whether the derivative action should proceed. Whilst the court is required to consider the views of the members who have no personal interest, direct or indirect, in the matter (i.e., to see if there is wrongdoer in control), it is only one of the factors to be considered.

Other relevant factors include whether the claimant is bringing the claim in good faith. This reflects the Court of Appeal's decision in *Barrett* v *Duckett* [1995] 1 BCLC 243 which held that the shareholder would be allowed to sue on behalf of the company if he was bringing the claim bona fide for the benefit of the company for wrongs to the company for which no other remedy was available, and that if the claim was brought for an ulterior purpose or if another adequate remedy was available, the court would not allow the derivative claim to proceed.

In *Barrett* v *Duckett*, Mrs Barrett and Mr Duckett each owned half of the shares in the company, Travel Ltd. Mrs Barrett brought a derivative action against Mr Duckett, his wife, the company, and another company owned and controlled by Mr and Mrs Duckett. She claimed that Mr and Mrs Duckett had set up another company so as to divert business from Travel to it, and that business had been diverted. She also claimed that Mr Duckett had taken money from the company and he and his wife had paid themselves excessive remuneration. The defendants applied by motions to strike out the derivative action arguing that Mrs Barrett was not the proper plaintiff. Mrs Barrett argued that as she only owned 50 per cent of the shares she could not compel the company to sue. The defendants also argued that she had an alternative remedy and therefore should not be allowed to bring a derivative action. The alternative remedy was, they argued, that Mr Duckett had presented a winding-up petition, and if a winding-up order was made the question of proceedings against Mr Duckett could be considered by the liquidator. (The point was not apparently made that a remedy might have been available under CA 1985, s. 459.)

Following the *Prudential* case, Sir Mervyn Davies, sitting as a High Court judge at first instance ([1993] BCC 778), refused to strike out a derivative action as a prima facie case had been made out. It was said that a prima facie case was established if (a) the company was entitled to the relief claimed, and (b) if the minority had no other remedy. A possible winding-up order, which would give the liquidator power to consider any proceedings against the wrongdoers, was thought not to be an alternative remedy.

Mr Duckett's appeal to the Court of Appeal was allowed, and Mrs Barrett's derivative action was struck out. The Court of Appeal conceded that Mr Duckett's petition for a winding-up order might be viewed with suspicion as an attempt to create a situation where Mrs Barrett was no longer at the mercy of Mr Duckett. However, the court thought that such a suspicion was negatived by the facts that (a) Mr Duckett's petition came after a long period of deadlock, (b) he followed advice from an insolvency practitioner in a well-known firm of accountants, and (c) the petition preceded not only the commencement of the derivative action, but also any intimation that the action would be commenced. Thus, the court concluded that the winding-up petition provided an alternative remedy which rendered the derivative action inappropriate. The court also found that Mrs Barrett was not pursuing the action bona fide in the interests of the company but was pursuing it for personal reasons associated with the divorce of her daughter from Mr Duckett.

13.1.3 Indemnity for costs

The new law does not make provisions dealing with indemnity for costs. Indeed, the Law Commission and the Steering Group made no specific recommendations either. The court already has the power to make an indemnity order for costs. In *Wallersteiner* v *Moir (No. 2)* the court held that a minority shareholder who brings a derivative suit may have a right to an indemnity from the company in respect of costs if the proceeding were brought in good faith and reasonably. Thus, provided the authority of the court is obtained in advance, minority plaintiffs are reasonably safe from having to pay the costs of an unsuccessful claim themselves. But they will have to take the risk of paying for counsel's opinion, which the court may require before sanctioning further proceedings at the company's expense. In determining whether such an order is to be made the court has to decide whether an independent board of directors or shareholders would in the circumstances have properly authorised a claim in the name of the company. The minority may also have to persuade other shareholders at any shareholders' meeting which the court may require to be summoned. If further proceedings are not sanctioned by the meeting or the court, any costs incurred will have to be paid by the minority if the claim fails. (If the claim succeeds costs will be awarded against the defendant directors.) The facts of the *Wallersteiner* case and an extract on the corporate veil point are given at 3.3.1.

Wallersteiner v Moir (No. 2)
Who pays the costs?
[1975] QB 373, Court of Appeal

LORD DENNING MR: Now that the principle [that where there is a fraud on the minority and the wrongdoers are in control, the minority can bring an action on behalf of the company against the wrongdoers] is recognised, it has important consequences which have hitherto not been perceived. The first is that the minority shareholder, being an agent acting on behalf of the company, is entitled to be indemnified by the company against all costs and expenses reasonably incurred by him in the course of the agency. This indemnity does not arise out of a contract express or implied, but it arises on the plainest principles of equity. It is analogous to the indemnity to which a trustee is entitled from his cestui que trust who is *sui iuris*. ... Seeing that, if the action succeeds, the whole benefit will go to the company, it is only just that the minority shareholder should be indemnified against the costs he incurs on its behalf. If the action succeeds, the wrongdoing director will be ordered to pay the costs: but if they are not recovered from him, they should be paid by the company. And all the additional costs (over and above party and party costs) should be taxed on a common fund basis and paid by the company. The solicitor will have a charge on the money recovered...through his instrumentality: see s. 73 of the Solicitors Act 1974.

But what if the action fails? Assuming that the minority shareholder had reasonable grounds for bringing the action—that it was a reasonable and prudent course to take in the interests of the company—he should not himself be liable to pay the costs of the other side, but the company itself should be liable, because he was acting for it and not for himself. In addition, he should himself be indemnified by the company in respect of his own costs even if the action fails. It is a well-known maxim of the law that he who would take the benefit of a venture if it succeeds ought also to bear the burden if it fails. *Qui sentit commodum sentire debet et onus.* This indemnity should extend to his own costs taxed on a common fund basis.

In order to be entitled to this indemnity, the minority shareholder soon after issuing his writ should apply for the sanction of the court in somewhat the same way as a trustee does....In a derivative action, I would suggest this procedure: the minority shareholder should apply *ex parte* to the master for directions, supported by an opinion of counsel as to whether there is a reasonable case or not. The master may then, if he thinks fit, straightaway approve the continuance of the proceedings until close of pleadings, or until after discovery or until trial (rather as a legal aid committee does). The master need not, however, decide it *ex parte*. He can, if he thinks fit, require notice to be given to one or two of the other minority shareholders—as representatives of the rest—so as to see if there is any reasonable objection. (In this very case another minority shareholder took this very point in letters to us.) But this preliminary application should be simple and inexpensive. It should not be allowed to escalate into a minor trial. The master should simply ask himself: is there a reasonable case for the minority shareholder to bring at the expense (eventually) of the company? If there is, let it go ahead.

NOTE: Now under the Civil Procedure Rules 1998, r. 19.9(7), the claimant may include in his application for permission to continue with his derivative claim an application for an order that the company must indemnify him against any liability in respect of costs incurred in the claim.

13.2 THE STATUTORY REMEDIES

13.2.1 Legislative background

The difficulties faced by minority shareholders at common law under the rule in *Foss* v *Harbottle* (1843) 2 Hare 461 and the unsatisfactory relief under what is now s. 122(1)(g) of the Insolvency Act 1986 (see 13.2.2) resulted in the enactment of s. 210 of the Companies Act 1948 as was recommended by the Cohen Committee (extract below). Section 210 was intended to provide more flexible remedies free from the restrictions of the *Foss* v *Harbottle* rule and the harshness of a winding-up order. However, it soon became a dead letter and there were only two successful cases under the section in the UK: *Re H. R. Harmer Ltd* [1959] 1 WLR 62 and *Scottish Co-operative Wholesale Society* v *Meyer* [1959] AC 324 (extract below).

Changes recommended by the Jenkins Committee (extract below) led to the repeal of s. 210 and the enactment of CA 1980, s. 75, which was later contained in CA 1985, ss. 459 to 461. This is now replaced by ss. 994 to 998 CA 2006.

13.2.2 Just and equitable winding up

Where in a 'quasi-partnership company' relationships have irretrievably broken down, a member may petition under s. 122(1)(g) of the Insolvency Act 1986 for the company to be wound up on the ground that it is just and equitable to do so. This was a relatively popular remedy in the days when an action at common law was the only alternative. It was also frequently used in conjunction with, and as alternative to, s. 459 of the CA 1985 (now replaced by s. 994 of the CA 2006) until the practice direction (Chancery Division: 101/90) (now replaced by Practice Direction 49B (supplementing the Civil Procedure Rules 1998), para. 9) which draws attention to the undesirability of including as a matter of course a prayer for winding up as an alternative to relief under s. 459. The undesirability of including a winding-up prayer as a matter of course lies in the fact that under s. 127 (extract at 20.6.1) any disposition of the company's property or transfer of shares etc. made after the commencement of the winding up of the company is void. Winding up by the court commences on presentation of the petition (Insolvency Act 1986, s. 129(2)). Thus, as soon as a prayer for winding up is included in the petition, the company would be paralysed because no business transaction relating to the company's property can be entered into as it would be void in the event of a winding-up order being made. For the relationship between ss. 459 and 122(1)(g) see S. H. Goo (1994) 15 Co Law 184.

A winding-up order will be refused if the court is also of the opinion that some other remedy, for example, relief under CA 2006, s. 994, is available to the petitioners and that they are acting unreasonably in seeking to have the company wound up instead of pursuing that other remedy (Insolvency Act 1986, s. 125(2)). The availability of relief under s. 994 has perhaps placed some limitations on the application of s. 122(1)(g). Other limitations are procedural. Under IA 1986, s. 124, only a contributory who has had shares allotted to him or held by him and registered in his name for at least six months during the 18 months before the commencement of the winding up may apply for a winding up order under s. 122(1)(g). A contributory who has not held shares for the requisite period of time may petition under s. 122(1)(g) only if the number of members is reduced below two or the shares have devolved on him through the death of a former holder. A contributory is any person who is liable to contribute to the assets of a company in the event of its being wound up (Insolvency Act 1986, s. 79). A fully paid-up member who is not liable to contribute has to show that he has a tangible interest in the winding up (*Re Rica Gold Washing Co.* (1879) 11 ChD 36). A petitioner must also come with clean hands, and so a petition may be rejected if the matters complained of were largely due to the petitioner's own misconduct (*Ebrahimi* v *Westbourne Galleries Ltd* [1973] AC 360 at p. 387, per Lord Cross of Chelsea). A petitioner under CA 2006, s. 994, does not have to come with clean hands although the petitioner's conduct will be taken into account.

As will be seen, s. 994 enables an individual to recover his investment by being bought out by the respondents, who are often the majority who conduct the company's affairs in an unfairly prejudicial manner. Much the same can also be achieved under s. 122(1)(g) by winding up the company. Although this sounds a drastic remedy it does not necessitate a termination of the business. The liquidator can sell the business as a going concern, perhaps to the existing shareholders, so that no economic activity or jobs are lost. However, as the Cohen Committee pointed out (Cmnd 6659, at para. 60, see extract below), in practice the only available purchaser may be that very majority whose oppression has driven the minority to seek redress. Thus the value for the minority's shareholding received after paying the company's debts and the costs of winding up is likely to be small.

INSOLVENCY ACT 1986, SS. 122(1)(G) AND 125(2)

122. Circumstances in which company may be wound up by the court

(1) A company may be wound up by the court if—

...

    (g) the court is of the opinion that it is just and equitable that the company should be wound up.

125. Powers of court on hearing of petition

(2) If the petition is presented by members of the company as contributories on the ground that it is just and equitable that the company should be wound up, the court, if it is of opinion—

    (a) that the petitioners are entitled to relief either by winding up the company or by some other means, and

    (b) that in the absence of any other remedy it would be just and equitable that the company should be wound up,

shall make a winding-up order; but this does not apply if the court is also of the opinion both that some other remedy is available to the petitioners and that they are acting unreasonably in seeking to have the company wound up instead of pursuing that other remedy.

Ebrahimi v *Westbourne Galleries Ltd*
The oriental carpet shop
[1973] AC 360, House of Lords

The circumstances in which it would be just and equitable to wind up a company are extremely wide. In this case, Lord Wilberforce (at p. 379E-G) suggested that a company can be wound up on the just and equitable ground not only where there is a breach of rights and obligations defined by the Companies Act and the articles of association, but also where there is a breach of equitable rights, obligations and legitimate expectations. This is the case if the company was formed or continued on the basis of a personal relationship, involving mutual confidence, or if there is an agreement or understanding giving members equitable rights, obligations or expectations (in *Ebrahimi* v *Westbourne Galleries*, that all or some of the members participate in the conduct of the business), or if there is a restriction on the transfer of shares in the company.

Facts   Nazar and Ebrahimi ran a business in oriental carpets as partners for over a decade. They then formed a company, Westbourne Galleries Ltd, to take over the business. They were equal shareholders and the only directors. Later Nazar's son joined the company as a shareholder and director. Ebrahimi was in the minority on the board and at the general meeting. There was a disagreement between the parties, and as a result, Ebrahimi was removed from the board. Ebrahimi petitioned for relief under CA 1948, s. 210, or alternatively s. 222(f) (now IA 1986, s. 122(1)(g)).

LORD WILBERFORCE: My lords, the petition was brought under s. 222(f) of the Companies Act 1948, which enables a winding up order to be made if 'the court is of the opinion that it is just and equitable that the company should be wound up' [now Insolvency Act 1986, s. 122(1)(g)]. This power has existed in our company law in unaltered form since the first major Act, the Companies Act 1862. Indeed, it antedates that statute since it existed in the Joint Stock Companies Winding up Act 1848. For some 50 years, following a pronouncement by Lord Cottenham LC [*Re Agriculturist Cattle Insurance Co. ex parte Spackman* (1849) 1 Mac & G 170, 174] in 1849, the words 'just and equitable' were interpreted so as only to include matters *eiusdem generis* as the preceding clauses of the section, but there is now ample authority for discarding this limitation. There are two other restrictive interpretations which I mention to reject. First, there has been a tendency to create categories or headings under which cases must be brought if the clause is to apply. This is wrong. Illustrations may be used, but general words should remain general and not be reduced to the sum of particular instances. Secondly, it has been suggested, and urged upon us, that (assuming the petitioner is a shareholder and not a creditor) the words must be confined to such circumstances as affect him in his capacity as shareholder. I see no warrant for this either. No doubt, in order to present a petition, he must qualify as a shareholder, but I see no reason for preventing him from relying upon any circumstances of justice or equity which affect him in his relations with the company, or, in a case such as the present, with the other shareholders.

One other signpost is significant. The same words 'just and equitable' appear in the Partnership Act 1892, s. 25, as a ground for dissolution of a partnership and no doubt the considerations which they reflect formed part of the common law of partnership before its codification. The importance of this is to provide a bridge between cases under s. 222 (f) of the Act of 1948 and the principles of equity developed in relation to partnerships.

The winding-up order was made following a doctrine which has developed in the courts since the beginning of this century. As presented by the appellant, and in substance accepted by the learned judge, this was that in a case such as this the members of the company are in substance partners, or quasi-partners, and that a winding up may be ordered if such facts are shown as could justify a dissolution of partnership between them. The common use of the words 'just and equitable' in the company and partnership law supports this approach. Your lordships were invited by the respondents' counsel to restate the principle on which this provision ought to be used; it has not previously been considered by this House. The main line of his submission was to suggest that too great a use of the partnership analogy had been made; that a limited company, however small, essentially differs from a partnership; that in the case of a company, the rights of its members are governed by the articles of association which have contractual force; that the court has no power or at least ought not to dispense parties from observing their contracts; that, in particular, when one member has been excluded from the directorate, or management, under powers expressly conferred by the Companies Act and the articles, an order for winding up, whether on the partnership analogy or under the just and equitable provision, should not be made. Alternatively, it was argued that before the making of such an order could be considered the petitioner must show and prove that the exclusion was not made bona fide in the interests of the company.

[His lordship referred to various authorities, including *Re Yenidje Tobacco Co. Ltd* [1916] 2 Ch 426, *Loch* v *John Blackwood Ltd* [1924] AC 783, and continued:]

My lords, in my opinion these authorities represent a sound and rational development of the law which should be endorsed. The foundation of it all lies in the words 'just and equitable' and, if there is any respect in which some of the cases may be open to criticism, it is that the courts may sometimes have been too timorous in giving them full force. The words are a recognition of the fact that a limited company is more than a mere legal entity, with a personality in law of its own: that there is room in company law for recognition of the fact that behind it, or amongst it, there are individuals, with rights, expectations and obligations *inter se* which are not necessarily submerged in the company structure. That structure is defined by the Companies Act and by the articles of association by which shareholders agree to be bound. In most companies and in most contexts, this definition is sufficient and exhaustive, equally so whether the company is large or small. The 'just and equitable' provision does not, as the respondents suggest, entitle one party to disregard the obligation he assumes by entering a company, nor the court to dispense him from it. It does, as equity always does, enable the court to subject the exercise of legal rights to equitable considerations; considerations, that is, of a personal character arising between one individual and another, which may make it unjust, or inequitable, to insist on legal rights, or to exercise them in a particular way.

It would be impossible, and wholly undesirable, to define the circumstances in which these considerations may arise. Certainly the fact that a company is a small one, or a private company, is not enough. There are very many of these where the association is a purely commercial one, of which it can safely be said that the basis of association is adequately and exhaustively laid down in the articles. The superimposition of equitable considerations requires something more, which typically may include one, or probably more, of the following elements: (i) an association formed or continued on the basis of a personal relationship, involving mutual confidence—this element will often be found where a pre-existing partnership has been converted into a limited company; (ii) an agreement, or understanding, that all, or some (for there may be 'sleeping' members), of the shareholders shall participate in the conduct of the business; (iii) restriction upon the transfer of the members' interest in the company—so that if confidence is lost, or one member is removed from management, he cannot take out his stake and go elsewhere. . . .

My lords, this is an expulsion case, and I must briefly justify the application in such cases of the just and equitable clause. The question is, as always, whether it is equitable to allow one (or two) to make use of his legal rights to the prejudice of his associate(s). The law of companies recognises the right, in many ways, to remove a director from the board. Section 184 of the Companies Act 1948 [now CA 2006, s. 168] confers this right upon the company in general meeting whatever the articles may say. Some articles may prescribe other methods: for example, a governing director may have the power to remove (compare *Re Wondoflex Textiles Pty Ltd* [1951] VLR 458). And quite apart from removal powers, there are normally provisions for retirement of directors by rotation so that their re-election can be opposed and defeated by a majority, or even by a casting vote. In all these ways a particular director-member may find himself no longer a director, through removal, or non-re-election: this situation he must normally accept, unless he undertakes the burden of proving fraud or *mala fides*. The just and equitable provision nevertheless comes to his assistance if he can point to, and prove, some special underlying obligation of his fellow member(s) in good faith, or confidence, that so long as the business continues he shall be entitled to management participation, an obligation so basic that, if broken, the conclusion must be that the association must be dissolved. And the principles on which he may do so are those worked out by the courts in partnership cases where there has been exclusion from management (see *Const* v *Harris* (1824) Turn & R 496 at p. 525) even where under the partnership agreement there is a power of expulsion (see *Blisset* v *Daniel* (1853) 10 Hare 493; *Lindley on Partnership*, 13th ed. (1971), pp. 331, 595).

I come to the facts of this case. It is apparent enough that a potential basis for a winding-up order under the just and equitable clause existed. The appellant after a long association in partnership, during which he had an equal share in the management, joined in the formation of the company. The inference must be indisputable that he, and Mr Nazar, did so on the basis that the character of the association would, as a matter of personal relation and good faith, remain the same. He was removed from his directorship under a power valid in law. Did he establish a case which, if he had remained in a partnership with a term providing for expulsion, would have justified an order for dissolution? This was the essential question for the judge. Plowman J [at first instance] dealt with the issue in a brief paragraph in which he said [1970] 1 WLR 1378 at p. 1389:

> . . . while no doubt the petitioner was lawfully removed, in the sense that he ceased in law to be a director, it does not follow that in removing him the respondents did not do him a wrong. In my judgment, they did do him a wrong, in the sense that it was an abuse of power and a breach of the good faith which partners owe to each other to exclude one of them from all participation in the business upon which they have embarked on the basis that all should participate in its management. The main justification put forward for removing him was that he was perpetually complaining, but the faults were not all on one side and, in my judgment, this is not sufficient justification. For these reasons, in my judgment, the petitioner, therefore, has made out a case for a winding-up order.

Reading this in the context of the judgment as a whole, which had dealt with the specific complaints of one side against the other. I take it as a finding that the respondents were not entitled, in justice and equity, to make use of their legal powers of expulsion and that, in accordance with the principles of such cases as *Blisset* v *Daniel*, the only just and equitable course was to dissolve the association.

To my mind, two factors strongly support this. First, Mr Nazar made it perfectly clear that he did not regard Mr Ebrahimi as a partner, but did regard him as an employee. But there was no possible doubt as to Mr Ebrahimi's status throughout, so that Mr Nazar's refusal to recognise it amounted, in effect, to a repudiation of the relationship. Secondly, Mr Ebrahimi, through ceasing to be a director, lost his right to share in the profits through directors' remuneration, retaining only the chance of receiving dividends as a minority shareholder. It is true that an assurance was given in evidence that the previous practice (of not paying dividends) would not be continued, but the fact remains that Mr Ebrahimi was thenceforth at the mercy of the Messrs Nazar as to what he should receive out of the profits and when. He was, moreover, unable to dispose of his interest without the consent of the Nazars. All these matters lead only to the conclusion that the right course was to dissolve the association by winding up.

NOTES

1. This landmark decision of the House of Lords has made an important contribution to the minority shareholder's remedy. Not only has Lord Wilberforce's 'equitable considerations' approach widened the category of cases where an order for just and equitable winding up can be ordered, it has also been transplanted by Hoffmann J, in *Re A Company (No. 00477 of 1986)* [1986] BCLC 376, into the machinery of unfair prejudice remedy under s. 994 which is now accepted by the House of Lords in *O'Neill* v *Phillips* [1999] 1 WLR 1092 extracted below.

2. The petitioner sought an order under CA 1948, s. 210, in the first instance but petitioned for a just and equitable winding-up order in the alternative. The petition under s. 210 was unsuccessful. Today, as Hoffmann J has adopted Lord Wilberforce's approach in the context of CA 2006, s. 994, it would appear that a case for unfair prejudice could be made out. The court could make an appropriate order, such as a purchase order, without having the company wound up.

3. Other circumstances where winding up is just and equitable are cases where a member can show a justifiable loss of confidence in the probity of the majority (*Loch* v *John Blackwood Ltd* [1924] AC 783), where there is a total deadlock in the management of the affairs of the company (*Re Yenidje Tobacco Co. Ltd* [1916] 2 Ch 426), or where the main objects for which the company was formed cannot now be achieved (*Re German Date Coffee Co.* (1882) 20 ChD 169). Deadlock is rare as the chairman will often have a casting vote to break the deadlock at board level, and if this does not solve the problem, the matter may be resolved by the general meeting (*Barron* v *Potter* [1914] 1 Ch 895).

13.2.3 The old 'oppression' remedy

It was realised that just and equitable winding up did not always provide a sufficient remedy for minority shareholders. The views of the Cohen Committee (reporting in 1945) that a special remedy was required where minorities suffer 'oppression' are extracted below. Thus the Companies Act 1948, s. 210, was passed to enable any member to complain that the affairs of the company were being conducted in a manner oppressive to some of the members including himself to petition the court, which could make such order as it thought fit by way of relief.

The two cases that follow are rare examples of the old s. 210 oppression remedy working effectively in practice. They remain relevant to the current law as examples of how a court may interpret its wide discretion under s. 994 to resolve company disputes. However, s. 210 was not regarded as a success and in 1962 the Jenkins Committee, whose views are extracted below, recommended that a new remedy be accorded where unfairly prejudicial conduct was proven. This recommendation found itself in force as the CA 1985, s. 459, which is replaced by s. 994 of the CA 2006.

Report of the Committee on Company Law Amendment
(Cohen Committee)
(Cmnd 6659, 1945)

58. *Restrictions on transfer of shares.*—It has been represented to us that the provisions which are inserted in the articles of a private company for the restriction of the transfer of the shares have caused hardship especially where the legal representatives of minority shareholders have to raise money to pay estate duties. The directors of the company, who are usually the principal shareholders, sometimes exercise their power to refuse to register transfers to outsiders, with the result that executors, who must realise their testators' shares in order to pay estate duty, have to sell to the directors or persons approved by them at prices much lower than the values at which the shares are assessed by the Board of Inland Revenue in valuing the estate of the deceased for purpose of estate duty. This difficulty is not in law peculiar to private companies since there is no legal impediment to a public company having in its articles a provision subjecting transfer of shares to the approval of the directors though Stock Exchanges do not accept it where leave to deal is required. This restriction is valued as a means of keeping a family business under the control of the family and we see no sufficient reason for its removal, particularly if our suggestion in paragraph 60 is adopted.

59. *Excessive remuneration of directors.*—Another abuse which has been found to occur is that the directors absorb an undue proportion of the profits of the company in remuneration for their services so that little or nothing is left for distribution among the shareholders by way of dividend. This may happen where, for example, two persons trading in partnership form their business into a limited company and one partner dies, leaving his share to his widow who takes no active part in the business. At present the only remedy open to the minority shareholder is to commence an action to restrain the company from paying the remuneration on the ground that such payment is a fraud on the minority, since the court would not make a winding-up order in view of the alternative remedy.

60. *Oppression of minorities.*—We have carefully examined suggestions intended to strengthen the minority shareholders of a private company in resisting oppression by the majority. The difficulties to which we have referred in the two preceding paragraphs are, in fact, only illustrations of a general problem. It is impossible to frame a recommendation to cover every case. We consider that a step in the right direction would be to enlarge the power of the court to make a winding-up order by providing that the power shall be exercisable notwithstanding the existence of an alternative remedy. In many cases, however, the winding up of the company will not benefit the minority shareholders, since the break-up value of the assets may be small, or the only available purchaser may be that very majority whose oppression has driven the minority to seek redress. We, therefore, suggest that the court should have, in addition, the power to impose upon the parties to a dispute whatever settlement the court considers just and equitable. This discretion must be unfettered, for it is impossible to lay down a general guide to the solution of what are essentially individual cases. We do not think that the court can be expected in every case to find and impose a solution; but our proposal will give the court a jurisdiction which it at present lacks, and thereby at least empower it to impose a solution in those cases where one exists.

Scottish Co-operative Wholesale Society Ltd v *Meyer*
Oppressive conduct by a holding company
[1958] 3 All ER 66, [1959] AC 324, House of Lords

This is the only House of Lords decision on CA 1948, s. 210, and in it the Law Lords took a liberal approach to interpreting the section. It was held that by substituting the interests of a subsidiary company to those of its holding company the subsidiary company's directors had acted in a manner oppressive towards the minority shareholders of the subsidiary. This remains a very valuable case to study even though s. 210 was replaced by CA 1985, s. 459, because the decision would probably still be the same under s. 459.

Facts   The Scottish Co-operative Wholesale Society formed a subsidiary company, Scottish Textile & Manufacturing Co. Ltd to manufacture rayon material. The Scottish Co-operative formed the subsidiary because it could not obtain the necessary licence without the experience of the petitioners Meyer and Lucas, who were the minority shareholders and directors of Scottish Textile. Scottish Co-operative owned the majority shares in Scottish Textile and appointed three of its directors as nominees on the board of Scottish Textile. Later when a licence was no longer required owing to the lifting of licensing control, the Scottish Co-operative decided to transfer the subsidiary's business to one of its own departments. The nominee directors of Scottish Textile participated in this decision which was wholly opposed to the company's best interests. The petitioners successfully sought an order under CA 1948, s. 210, for the purchase of their shares.

LORD DENNING: Such being 'the matters complained of' by the respondents, it is said 'Those are all complaints about the conduct of the society. How do they touch the real issue—the manner in which the affairs of the company were being conducted?' The answer is, I think, by their impact on the nominee directors. It must be remembered that we are here concerned with the manner in which the affairs of the company were being conducted. That is, with the conduct of those in control of its affairs. They may be some of the directors themselves, or, behind them, a group of shareholders who nominate those directors or whose interests those directors serve. If those persons—the nominee directors or the shareholders behind them—conduct the affairs of the company in a manner oppressive to the other shareholders, the court can intervene to bring an end to the oppression.

What, then, is the position of the nominee directors here? Under the articles of association of the company, the society was entitled to nominate three out of the five directors, and it did so. It nominated three of its own directors and they held office, as the articles said, 'as nominees' of the society. These three were, therefore, at one and the same time directors of the society—being three out of 12 of that company—and also directors of the company—three out of five there. So long as the interests of all concerned were in harmony, there was no difficulty. The nominee directors could do their duty by both companies without embarrassment. But, so soon as the interests of the two companies were in conflict, the nominee directors were placed in an impossible position. Thus, when the realignment of shareholding was under discussion, the duty of the three directors to the company was to get the best possible price for any new issue of its shares (see per Lord Wright in *Lowry v Consolidated African Selection Trust, Ltd* [1940] AC 648 at p. 679) whereas their duty to the society was to obtain the new shares at the lowest possible price—at par, if they could. Again, when the society determined to set up its own rayon department, competing with the business of the company, the duty of the three directors to the company was to do their best to promote its business and to act with complete good faith towards it; and, in consequence, not to disclose their knowledge of its affairs to a competitor, and not even to work for a competitor, when to do so might operate to the disadvantage of the company (see *Hivac Ltd v Park Royal Scientific Instruments Ltd* [1946] Ch 169) whereas they were under the self-same duties to the society. It is plain that, in the circumstances, these three gentlemen could not do their duty by both companies, and they did not do so. They put their duty to the society above their duty to the company in this sense, at least, that they did nothing to defend the interests of the company against the conduct of the society. They probably thought that, 'as nominees' of the society, their first duty was to the society. In this they were wrong. By subordinating the interests of the company to those of the society, they conducted the affairs of the company in a manner oppressive to the other shareholders.

It is said that these three directors were, at most, only guilty of inaction—of doing nothing to protect the company. But the affairs of a company can, in my opinion, be conducted oppressively by the directors doing nothing to defend its interests when they ought to do something—just as they can conduct its affairs oppressively by doing something injurious to its interests when they ought not to do it. The question was asked: What could these directors have done? They could, I suggest, at least on behalf of the company, have protested against the conduct of the society. They could have protested against the setting up of a competing business. . . .

Your Lordships were referred to *Bell* v *Lever Brothers Ltd* ([1932] AC 161 at p. 195), where Lord Blanesburgh said that a director of one company was at liberty to become a director also of a rival company. That may have been so at that time. But it is at the risk now of an application under s. 210 if he subordinates the interests of the one company to those of the other.

So I would hold that the affairs of the company were being conducted in a manner oppressive to the respondents. . . .

One of the most useful orders mentioned in the section—which will enable the court to do justice to the injured shareholders—is to order the oppressor to buy their shares at a fair price; and a fair price would be, I think, the value which the shares would have had at the date of the petition, if there had been no oppression. Once the oppressor has bought the shares, the company can survive. It can continue to operate. That is a matter for him. It is, no doubt, true that an order of this kind gives to the oppressed shareholders what is, in effect, money compensation for the injury done to them; but I see no objection to this. The section gives a large discretion to the court, and it is well exercised in making an oppressor make compensation to those who have suffered at his hands.

True it is that in this, as in other respects, your lordships are giving a liberal interpretation to s. 210. But it is a new section designed to suppress an acknowledged mischief. When it comes before this House for the first time it is, I believe, in accordance with long precedent—and particularly with the resolution of all the judges in *Heydon's Case* (1584) 3 Co Rep 7a—that your lordships should give such construction as shall advance the remedy. And that is what your lordships do today.

I would dismiss the appeal.

Re H. R. Harmer Ltd

A father oppresses his sons

[1958] 3 All ER 689, [1959] 1 WLR 62, Court of Appeal

This is an important Court of Appeal decision on CA 1948, s. 210, in which the petitioners were successful. As with the *Meyer* case, the outcome of this case would probably be the same under CA 2006, s. 994. Its most interesting feature is the wide and flexible remedy ordered by Roxburgh J which was approved by the Court of Appeal.

Facts   Old Mr Harmer, who was the founder of the firm (well-known stamp dealers), made a gift of a majority of shares to his sons, but retained voting control in general meeting. He continued to run the business as if it were his own and to disregard the wishes of his sons, who were shareholders and co-directors. He committed the company to business ventures without obtaining proper authorisation and procured the appointment of directors who submissively did his bidding. As a result of his autocratic and unbusinesslike behaviour, it became impossible for the business to be carried on successfully. Roxburgh J held that a case of oppression under CA 1948, s. 210, had been made out. It was irrelevant that the misconduct was not for financial gain but simply due to the father's overwhelming desire for power and control. He ordered, *inter alia*, that 'the company should contract for the services of the father as philatelic consultant at a named salary, that the father should not interfere in the affairs of the company otherwise than in accordance with the valid decision of the board of directors, and that he should be appointed president of the company for life, but that this office should not impose any duties or rights or powers'. Old Mr Harmer appealed.

JENKINS LJ: The question remains whether, on these facts, the petitioners were rightly granted the relief which Roxburgh J thought fit to grant under s. 210. On this issue counsel for the father made, in effect, the following submissions. In stating them I am not attempting to quote his words; I merely give the general effect of his argument, as I understood it. First, he said that the sons should not be heard to complain since they acquired their shares through the generosity of their father, who, having built up the business, proceeded to turn it into a company and to hand over a major part of the beneficial interest in the form of shares to his sons virtually by way of gift. As to this, the sons did at all events pay for their preference shares, and if they had not paid anything, two of them at all events had long been working in the business, while the third gave up his career in the Colonial Office in order to take up employment in the business. Moreover, the question of consideration appears to me to be irrelevant, a mere matter of prejudice. Suppose the transaction was a mere matter of gift, the gift, if valid (and there is no suggestion that it was not) must surely have conferred the same rights as if the transaction had been for full consideration. The second point taken by counsel for the father was that the sons knew full well when the company was formed that the father was to retain control by means of his predominant holding of B shares so long as he lived. I agree, but I cannot concur with counsel in adducing from this that the sons must be taken to have assumed that the father would exercise his control irregularly by doing what he thought fit without reference to the board or in defiance of the board's decisions. Then counsel's third submission was that what was done by the father was not oppressive of the rights of the sons as members, but merely oppressive of their rights as directors. I cannot accept this. It appears to me that the sons as members, and not merely as directors, were oppressed by the singular conduct of the father. The oppression must, no doubt, be oppression of members as such, but it does not follow that the fact that the oppressed members are also directors is a disqualifying circumstance when the question of relief under s. 210 arises. I think that there may well be oppression from the point of view of member-directors where a majority shareholder (that is to say, a shareholder with a preponderance of voting power) proceeds, on the strength of his control, to act contrary to the decisions of, or without the authority of, the duly constituted board of directors of the company. Fourthly, counsel for the father said that the acts complained of might have been restrained by injunction in so far as they were acts done without the authority of the board. As to this, I do not think that a wrongdoer in this field can well complain that the person wronged might have chosen another remedy. Then fifthly, counsel said that the acts complained of were not in their result oppressive, because it cannot be demonstrated that the company suffered any loss from any of them. I cannot agree. The acts complained of were, I should say for the most part, calculated to damage the company in one way or the other. Sixthly, counsel said that the acts complained of might have been lawfully done by calling a general meeting and passing the requisite resolutions, ordinary or special. As to this, I think that the sons were at least entitled to require that the proper procedure should be applied. Then seventhly, counsel said that this is not a case of discrimination between different shareholders or classes of shareholders. I agree, but see no reason for holding that s. 210 is necessarily confined to cases of discrimination, although it is to be expected that cases calling for its application would most usually take that form. Finally, counsel submitted that the father got no pecuniary benefit out of what he did. That is not literally true, but even if it were, I do not think that it is essential to a case of oppression that the alleged oppressor is oppressing in order to obtain pecuniary benefit. If there is oppression, it remains oppression even though the oppression is due simply to the controlling shareholder's overweening desire for power and control and not with a view to his own pecuniary advantage. The result rather than the motive is the material thing.

[His lordship referred to arguments of the counsel for the petitioners and continued:]

Having given the best consideration I can to this not altogether easy case, I have come to the same conclusion, preferring the reasoning of counsel for the petitioners to that of counsel for the father and accepting the reasoning and conclusion of the learned judge. I am fortified in this view by the consideration that it has obviously become increasingly difficult, nay really impossible, for the business of this company to be carried on successfully as matters stood before the order of Roxburgh J and that it is plainly in the best interests of all parties that an order in these terms, or substantially in these terms, should be made. No criticism of any importance of the form of the order made by Roxburgh J has been made good before us. For these reasons I would dismiss this appeal.

The next company law committee to consider the matter made the following observations about s. 210 and recommended a reform which became CA 1985, s. 459.

Report of the Company Law Committee

(Jenkins Committee)

(Cmnd 1749, 1962)

203. …if [s. 210] is to afford effective protection, it must extend to cases in which the acts complained of fall short of actual illegality.

204. In *Elder* v *Elder and Watson Ltd* 1952 SC 49, it was said by Lord Cooper (at p. 55) with reference to the meaning of oppression in s. 210 'the essence of the matter seems to be that the conduct complained of should at the lowest involve a visible departure from the standards of fair dealing, and a violation of the conditions of fair play on which every shareholder who entrusts his money to a company is entitled to rely'. This statement accords with our own view as to the intention underlying s. 210 as originally framed, namely that it was meant to cover complaints not only to the effect that the affairs of the company were being conducted in a manner oppressive (in the narrower sense) to the members concerned but also to the effect that those affairs were being conducted in a manner unfairly prejudicial to the interests of those members. …

205. As the Cohen Committee observed in paragraph 60 of their report, it is impossible to frame a recommendation to cover every case, and we do not propose to attempt to do so. But we may perhaps usefully mention as illustrative of the situations in which action under s. 210 might be appropriate those in which directors appoint themselves to paid posts with the company at excessive rates of remuneration…Other possibilities are the issue of shares to directors and others on advantageous terms. …

212. We recommend that: …

(c) it should be made clear that s. 210 extends to cases where the affairs of the company are being conducted in a manner unfairly prejudicial to the interests of some part of the members and not merely in an 'oppressive' manner.

13.2.4 The unfair prejudice remedy

Under the CA 2006, s. 994, which replaces s. 459 of the CA 1985, a member may petition the court for a remedy if the company's affairs have been conducted in a manner unfairly prejudicial to members' interests. The essence of s. 994 is to provide a remedy where a complaint exists concerning the way in which a company's affairs are being conducted through the use of, or failure to use, corporate powers in relation to the conduct of the company's affairs, as provided by the company's constitution (*Re Legal Costs Negotiators Ltd* [1999] 2 BCLC 171, in which it was held that a shareholder's refusal to sell his shareholding was a private matter and could not be a ground for a petition under this section). Unfair prejudice is wider than and replaced the concept of oppression in the old Companies Act 1948, s. 210. Both unfairness and prejudice must be established. It is not necessary to show that the act complained of is improper or illegal and an exercise of a legal right may have an unfairly prejudicial effect. As the following extracts show, the court has now taken a new approach in dealing with minority shareholders' complaints, and is prepared to look at any alleged prejudicial conduct from an objective point of view, to take into account any relevant circumstances and to give the section its natural meaning without any technical gloss. (The Law Commission in its report on shareholder remedies (No. 246) has proposed that the words 'unfairly prejudicial' should not be defined: see paras. 4.9–4.13.) In deciding whether an act is unfairly prejudicial, the court will take into account factors such as the petitioner's conduct, prior knowledge of the matters complained of (see *Bermuda Cablevision Ltd* v *Colica Trust Co. Ltd* [1998] AC 198, PC), any offer made to buy out the petitioner, the motive of the oppressor, any delay in petitioning, and other relevant factors.

In the early days of s. 994, it was thought that the petitioner must have unfairly suffered prejudice to an interest as a member only (and not, e.g., as a director). This requirement has since been relaxed in that the court is prepared to recognise that members may have different interests arising out of common understanding or agreement which is not stated in the articles, e.g., there may be an understanding that all shareholders will be involved in the management in a quasi-partnership company (*Re A Company (No. 00477 of 1986)* [1986] BCLC 376; *O'Neill* v *Phillips* [1999] 1 WLR 1092 extracted below). But where there is no such common understanding or agreement, or where the articles make detailed provision for any departing members to sell their shares at a fair price, the position may be different— there may be no legitimate expectation or equitable restraints in such cases that all shareholders will be involved in the management merely from the fact that it is a quasi-partnership company. Likewise in a public company case, the court is unlikely to look at any shareholders' agreement outside the constitution.

Section 994 has proved to be a powerful weapon for minority shareholders, particularly in the case of quasi-partnerships. In such companies, minorities who are excluded from management participation or who unfairly suffer loss as a result of wrongdoing by directors or majority shareholders may get relief under the section.

Under s. 996, the court is empowered to make any order it thinks fit. The most commonly sought remedy is an order that the petitioner's shares be bought. When this order is made a key issue is the basis and date for valuation of the shares.

Where appropriate, the court may order a third party to be joined as a respondent and be required to buy out the petitioner. Thus, in *Re Little Olympian Each-Ways Ltd (No. 3)* [1995] 1 BCLC 636, where the company's assets had been sold at an undervalue by those in *de facto* control to a company controlled by them, Evans-Lombe J made a purchase order against that other company. Charles Aldous QC (sitting as a deputy judge of the High Court) said, in *Lowe* v *Fahey* [1996] 1 BCLC 262, that s. 461(1) (which is replaced by s. 996 of the CA 2006) conferred a very wide jurisdiction on the court and thus where the alleged unfairly prejudicial conduct involved the diversion of company funds, a petitioner was entitled to seek an order under the section for payment to the company itself not only against members, former members or directors allegedly involved in the unlawful diversion, but also against third parties who had knowingly received or improperly assisted in the wrongful diversion. He added that where the court had jurisdiction under s. 461 to make an order in favour of the company, it should not strike out the petition simply because it was legally aided (on the ground that where such a claim is pursued by writ legal aid would not be available), but should first consider whether the petition should be struck out if the petitioner was not legally aided.

In appropriate circumstances, the court may also make an order requiring the majority shareholders to sell their shares to the petitioners (e.g., *Re Brenfield Squash Racquets Club Ltd* [1996] 2 BCLC 184).

While the court has jurisdiction to make an order for the equivalent of interest to be included in the purchase price, this power should be exercised cautiously; the petitioner should produce clear and persuasive evidence on which the court could decide what amount of interest to allow: *Profinance Trust SA* v *Gladstone* [2002] 1 BCLC 141, CA.

The court has no jurisdiction, however, unlike in derivative actions, to make an order requiring the company to indemnify the petitioner as to costs (see *Re Sherborne Park Residents Co. Ltd* [1987] BCLC 82). Furthermore, in general, the company's funds should not be used to finance the costs of the petition (see *Re Crossmore Electrical and Civil Engineering Ltd* [1989] BCLC 137). However, where it was necessary and expedient in the interests of the company as a whole for the company to participate in the proceedings, such costs could be properly incurred (see *Re A Company (No. 1126 of 1992)* [1994] 2 BCLC 146).

Where no relief would meet the justice of the case, the court may refuse to grant any relief. Where it would be appropriate to wind up the company (e.g., the company is completely dormant), the court may allow the petition to be amended so as to seek winding up on just and equitable grounds, with a view to a winding-up order being obtained after complying with the requirements concerning advertising (*Re Full Cup International Trading Ltd* [1995] BCC 682).

Often the respondent would seek to strike out an unfair prejudice petition on the basis that it is an abuse of the court process. In determining whether the petition should be struck out, it is proper to assume that the pleaded allegations would be established if the matter goes to trial, as long as the basic propositions of law on which the allegations are based are clearly arguable (*North Holdings Ltd* v *Southern Tropics Ltd* [1999] 2 BCLC 625, CA).

COMPANIES ACT 2006, SS. 994 TO 996

994. Petition by company member

(1) A member of a company may apply to the court by petition for an order under this Part on the ground—

    (a) that the company's affairs are being or have been conducted in a manner that is unfairly prejudicial to the interests of members generally or of some part of its members (including at least himself) or

    (b) that an actual or proposed act or omission of the company (including an act or omission on its behalf) is or would be so prejudicial.

(2) The provisions of this Part apply to a person who is not a member of a company but to whom shares in the company have been transferred or transmitted by operation of law as they apply to a member of a company.

(3) In this section, and so far as applicable for the purposes of this section in the other provisions of this Part, 'company' means—

    (a) a company within the meaning of this Act, or

    (b) a company that is not such a company but is a statutory water company within the meaning of the Statutory Water Companies Act 1991.

995. Petition by Secretary of State

(1) This section applies to a company in respect of which—

    (a) the Secretary of State has received a report under section 437 of the Companies Act 1985 (inspector's report);

    (b) the Secretary of State has exercised his powers under section 447 or 448 of that Act (powers to require documents and information or to enter and search premises);

    (c) the Secretary of State or the Financial Services Authority has exercised his or its powers under Part 11 of the Financial Services and Markets Act 2000 (information gathering and investigations); or

(d) the Secretary of State has received a report from an investigator appointed by him or the Financial Services Authority under that Part.or section 44(2) to (6) of the Insurance Companies Act 1982; and

(2) If it appears to the Secretary of State that in the case of such a company—

(a) the company's affairs are being or have been conducted in a manner that is unfairly prejudicial to the interests of members generally or of some part of its members, or

(b) an actual or proposed act or omission of the company (including an act or omission on its behalf) is or would be so prejudicial,

he may apply to the court by petition for an order under this Part.

(3) The Secretary of State may do this in addition to, or instead of, presenting a petition for the winding up of the company.

(4) In this section, and so far as applicable for the purposes of this section in the other provisions of this Part, 'company' means any body corporate that is liable to be wound up under the Insolvency Act 1986 or the Insolvency (Northern Ireland) Order 1989 (SI 1989/2405 (NI 19)).

996. Powers of the court under this Part

(1) If the court is satisfied that a petition under this Part is well founded, it may make such order as it thinks fit for giving relief in respect of the matters complained of.

(2) Without prejudice to the generality of subsection (1), the court's order may—

(a) regulate the conduct of the company's affairs in the future;

(b) require the company—(i) to refrain from doing or continuing an act complained of, or (ii) to do an act that the petitioner has complained it has omitted to do;

(c) authorise civil proceedings to be brought in the name and on behalf of the company by such person or persons and on such terms as the court may direct;

(d) require the company not to make any, or any specified, alterations in its articles without the leave of the court;

(e) provide for the purchase of the shares of any members of the company by other members or by the company itself and, in the case of a purchase by the company itself, the reduction of the company's capital accordingly.

O'Neill v *Phillips*

The House of Lords considers s. 459

[1999] 1 WLR 1092

Lord Hoffmann, in this first House of Lords decision on s. 459 (now CA 2006, s. 994), has reviewed the judicial interpretation of the section in the last decade or so. He held that ordinarily unfairness to a member requires a breach of the terms on which it has been agreed that the affairs of the company shall be conducted, though in certain circumstances it might be unfair for those conducting the affairs of the company to rely on their strict legal powers. However, he disapproved the finding of the Court of Appeal, holding that as the respondent Phillips had not agreed to give the petitioner O'Neill a right to take up more shares when certain targets were met, nor made any unconditional promise about the sharing of profits, it was not unfairly prejudicial for Phillips to remove O'Neill from acting as managing director nor to stop paying O'Neill an extra profit share. Lord Hoffmann further held that a member of a company who had not been excluded from participation in its management was not entitled to require the other to buy him out whenever a breakdown of confidence or trust occurred.

Facts   The company, wholly owned by the respondent Phillips at the time, employed the petitioner O'Neill as a manual worker in 1983. Phillips was impressed by O'Neill's energy and ability and promoted him rapidly. In January 1985, Phillips gave O'Neill 25 per cent of the shares and appointed him a director. In May that year, Phillips informally expressed the hope that O'Neill would take over the management of the company and on that basis would allow him to draw 50 per cent of the company's profits. O'Neill did take over the running of the business and was credited with half the profits. There were discussions later with a view to O'Neill obtaining a 50 per cent shareholding when certain targets were reached. These were, however, not formalised or finalised. The company began to have financial problems, and in August 1991 Phillips decided to resume personal command of the business. In November, in a meeting at which he admitted he 'ranted and raved', Phillips told O'Neill that as he was no longer managing director, he would no longer receive 50 per cent of the profits. O'Neill issued a petition under s. 459 alleging unfairly prejudicial conduct which involved two complaints: (a) Phillips's termination of equal profit-sharing and (b) his repudiation of the alleged agreement for the allotment of more shares.

LORD HOFFMANN: My Lords, this appeal raises, for the first time in your Lordships' House, a question on the scope of the remedy which Part XVII (ss. 459–61) of the Companies Act 1985 provides for a member of a company, typically holding a minority of the shares, who considers that the company's affairs are being conducted in a manner unfairly prejudicial to his interests. . . .

3 The petition

In the end...the allegations of unfairly prejudicial conduct came down to two complaints. The first was Mr Phillips's termination of equal profit-sharing and the second was his repudiation of the alleged agreement for the allotment of more shares. The judge rejected these and dismissed the petition on two grounds. One was that it fails on the facts. . . .

The judge's second ground for dismissing the petition was that the prejudice to Mr O'Neill's interests from the reduction in his profit-share and refusal to give him more shares was not suffered in his capacity as a shareholder, as a member of the company. The profit-share was his remuneration for acting as managing director and the additional shares were likewise a reward and incentive for working for the company. They did not derive from his previously having had a 25 per cent shareholding. On the contrary, that too had been a reward for his services as an employee. Mr O'Neill's membership of the company was therefore irrelevant to the expectations which he claimed it would be unfair to deny. They would have been exactly the same if he had not previously held any shares at all.

4 The Court of Appeal

The Court of Appeal allowed the appeal and ordered Mr Phillips to buy Mr O'Neill's shares. Nourse LJ gave the judgment. He said, [1997] 2 BCLC 739 at p. 767, that although there was no concluded agreement about giving him more shares, he had a 'legitimate expectation' that he would receive them when the targets were reached. Likewise, he had a legitimate expectation of receiving 50 per cent of the profits. It was therefore unfairly prejudicial of Mr Phillips to deny these expectations without giving Mr O'Neill 'notice and an opportunity to defend himself' or offering to buy his shares at a fair value: p. 770. The Court of Appeal made the important additional finding, at p. 767, that Mr O'Neill had been in effect 'forced out of the company'. In view of the denial of his legitimate expectations, he could no longer be expected to remain with the company and 'was bound to engage himself elsewhere'.

Nourse LJ also rejected the judge's second reason. One took, he said, a broad view of the interests of a member. They were not necessarily limited to his strict legal rights. So, for example, a member who had subscribed for shares on the understanding that he would take part in the management of the company might have an interest as member in his continuing participation, though this was not a right attached to his shares under the articles of the company. Nourse LJ considered that there was no other relevant capacity in which the unfair prejudice of which Mr O'Neill complained could have been suffered. He did not expressly deal with the possibility that it might have been as an employee. It must of course be borne in mind that whereas the judge was considering only the prejudice arising from the termination of the profit-sharing and share allocation arrangements, the Court of Appeal was taking a more global view and treating them as part of conduct by which Mr O'Neill was deprived of all participation in the affairs of the company by a kind of constructive expulsion.

5 'Unfairly prejudicial'

In s. 459 Parliament has chosen fairness as the criterion by which the court must decide whether it has jurisdiction to grant relief. It is clear from the legislative history (which I discussed in *Re Saul D. Harrison and Sons Plc, Re* [1995] 1 BCLC 14, 17–20) that it chose this concept to free the court from technical considerations of legal right and to confer a wide power to do what appeared just and equitable. But this does not mean that the court can do whatever the individual judge happens to think fair. The concept of fairness must be applied judicially and the content which it is given by the courts must be based upon rational principles. As Warner J said in *Re J.E. Cade and Son Ltd, Re* [1992] BCLR 213, 227: 'The court . . . has a very wide discretion, but it does not sit under a palm tree'.

Although fairness is a notion which can be applied to all kinds of activities, its content will depend upon the context in which it is being used. Conduct which is perfectly fair between competing businessmen may not be fair between members of a family. In some sports it may require, at best, observance of the rules, in others ('it's not cricket') it may be unfair in some circumstances to take advantage of them. All is said to be fair in love and war. So the context and background are very important.

In the case of s. 459, the background has the following two features. First, a company is an association of persons for an economic purpose, usually entered into with legal advice and some degree of formality. The terms of the association are contained in the articles of association and sometimes in collateral agreements between the shareholders. Thus the manner in which the affairs of the company may be conducted is closely regulated by rules to which the shareholders have agreed. Secondly, company law has developed seamlessly from the law of partnership, which was treated by equity, like the Roman *societas*, as a contract of good faith. One of the traditional roles of equity, as a separate jurisdiction, was to restrain the exercise of strict legal rights in certain relationships in which it considered that this would be contrary to good faith. These principles have, with appropriate modification, been carried over into company law.

The first of these two features leads to the conclusion that a member of a company will not ordinarily be entitled to complain of unfairness unless there has been some breach of the terms on which he agreed that the affairs of the company should be conducted. But the second leads to the conclusion that there will be cases in which equitable considerations make it unfair for those conducting the affairs of the company to rely upon their strict legal powers. Thus unfairness may consist in a breach of the rules or in using the rules in a manner which equity would regard as contrary to good faith.

This approach to the concept of unfairness in s. 459 runs parallel to that which your Lordships' House, in *Ebrahimi* v *Westbourne Galleries Ltd* [1973] AC 360, adopted in giving content to the concept of 'just and equitable' as a ground for winding up. After referring to cases on the equitable jurisdiction to require partners to exercise their powers in good faith, Lord Wilberforce said, at p. 379:

> The words ['just and equitable'] are a recognition of the fact that a limited company is more than a mere legal entity, with a personality in law of its own: that there is room in company law for recognition of the fact that behind it, or amongst it, there are individuals, with rights, expectations and obligations inter se which are not necessarily submerged in the company structure. That structure is defined by the Companies Act [1948] and by the articles of association by which shareholders agree to be bound. In most companies and in most contexts, this definition is sufficient and exhaustive, equally so whether the company is large or small. The 'just and equitable' provision does not, as the respondents [the company] suggest, entitle one party to disregard the obligation he assumes by entering a company, nor the court to dispense him from it. It does, as equity always does, enable the court to subject the exercise of legal rights to equitable considerations; considerations, that is, of a personal character arising between one individual and another, which may make it unjust, or inequitable, to insist on legal rights, or to exercise them in a particular way.

I would apply the same reasoning to the concept of unfairness in s. 459. The Law Commission, in its Report on Shareholder Remedies (1997) (Law Com. No. 246), p. 43, para. 4.11, expresses some concern that defining the content of the unfairness concept in the way I have suggested might unduly limit its scope and that 'conduct which would appear to be deserving of a remedy may be left unremedied...'. In my view, a balance has to be struck between the breadth of the discretion given to the court and the principle of legal certainty. Petitions under s. 459 are often lengthy and expensive. It is highly desirable that lawyers should be able to advise their clients whether or not a petition is likely to succeed. Lord Wilberforce, after the passage which I have quoted, said that it would be impossible 'and wholly undesirable' to define the circumstances in which the application of equitable principles might make it unjust, or inequitable (or unfair) for a party to insist on legal rights or to exercise them in particular way. This of course is right. But that does not mean that there are no principles by which those circumstances may be identified. The way in which such equitable principles operate is tolerably well settled and in my view it would be wrong to abandon them in favour of some wholly indefinite notion of fairness.

I should make it clear that the parallel I have drawn between the notion of 'just and equitable' as explained by Lord Wilberforce in *Ebrahimi* v *Westbourne Galleries Ltd* and the notion of fairness in s. 459 does not mean that conduct will not be unfair unless it would have justified an order to wind up the company. There was such a requirement in s. 210 of the Companies Act 1948 but it was not repeated in s. 459. As Mummery J observed in *Re A Company (No. 00314 of 1989), Re* [1991] BCLC 154, 161, the grant of one remedy will not necessarily require proof of conduct which would have justified a different remedy:

> Under ss. 459 to 461 the court is not...faced with a death sentence decision dependent on establishing just and equitable grounds for such a decision. The court is more in the position of a medical practitioner presented with a patient who is alleged to be suffering from one or more ailments which can be treated by an appropriate remedy applied during the course of the continuing life of the company.

The parallel is not in the conduct which the court will treat as justifying a particular remedy but in the principles upon which it decides that the conduct is unjust, inequitable or unfair.

An example of such equitable principles in action is *Blisset* v *Daniel* (1853) 10 Hare 493 to which Lord Wilberforce referred in *Ebrahimi* v *Westbourne Galleries Ltd* [1973] AC 360, 381. Page Wood V-C held that upon the true construction of the articles, two-thirds of the partners could expel a partner by serving a notice upon him without holding any meeting or giving any reason. But he held that the power must be exercised in good faith. He said, 10 Hare 493, 523, that 'the literal construction of these articles cannot be enforced' and, after citing from the title '*De Societate*' in Justinian's *Institutes*, went on, at pp. 523–4:

> It must be plain, that you can neither exercise a power of this description by dissolving the partnership, nor do any other act for purposes contrary to the plain general meaning of the deed, which must be this—that this power is inserted, not for the benefit of any particular parties holding two-thirds of the shares, but for the benefit of the whole society and partnership.

In the Australian case of *Re Wondoflex Textiles Pty Ltd, Re* [1951] VLR 458, 467, Smith J also contrasted the literal meaning of the articles with the true intentions of the parties:

> It is also true, I think, that, generally speaking, a petition for winding up, based upon the partnership analogy, cannot succeed if what is complained of is merely a valid exercise of powers conferred in terms by the articles....To hold otherwise would enable a member to be relieved from the consequences of a bargain knowingly entered into by him....But this, I think, is subject to an important qualification. Acts which, in law, are a valid exercise of powers conferred by the articles may nevertheless be entirely outside what can fairly be regarded as having been in the contemplation of the parties when they became members of the company; and in such cases the fact that what has been done is not in excess of power will not necessarily be an answer to a claim for winding up. Indeed, it may be said that one purpose of [the just and equitable provision] is to enable the court to relieve a party from his bargain in such cases.

I cite these references to 'the literal construction of these articles' contrasted with good faith and 'the plain general meaning of the deed' and 'what the parties can fairly have had in contemplation' to show that there is more than one theoretical basis upon which a decision like *Blisset v Daniel* can be explained. Nineteenth-century English law, with its division between law and equity, tradition-ally took the view that while literal meanings might prevail in a court of law, equity could give effect to what it considered to have been the true intentions of the parties by preventing or restraining the exercise of legal rights. So Smith J speaks of the exercise of the power being valid 'in law' but its exer-cise not being just and equitable because contrary to the contemplation of the parties. This way of looking at the matter is a product of English legal history which has survived the amalgamation of the courts of law and equity. But another approach, in a different legal culture, might be simply to take a less literal view of 'legal' construction and interpret the articles themselves in accord-ance with what Page Wood V-C called 'the plain general meaning of the deed'. Or one might, as in Continental systems, achieve the same result by introducing a general requirement of good faith into contractual performance. These are all different ways of doing the same thing. I do not suggest there is any advantage in abandoning the traditional English theory, even though it is derived from arrangements for the administration of justice which were abandoned over a century ago. On the contrary, a new and unfamiliar approach could only cause uncertainty. So I agree with Jonathan Parker J when he said in *Re Astec (BSR) plc, Re* [1998] 2 BCLC 556, 588:

> in order to give rise to an equitable constraint based on 'legitimate expectation' what is required is a personal relationship or personal dealings of some kind between the party seeking to exercise the legal right and the party seeking to restrain such exercise, such as will affect the conscience of the former.

This is putting the matter in very traditional language, reflecting in the word 'conscience' the ecclesiastical origins of the long-departed Court of Chancery. As I have said, I have no difficulty with this formulation. But I think that one useful cross-check in a case like this is to ask whether the exercise of the power in question would be contrary to what the parties, by words or conduct, have actually agreed. Would it conflict with the promises which they appear to have exchanged? In *Blisset v Daniel* the limits were found in the 'general meaning' of the partnership articles them-selves. In a quasi-partnership company, they will usually be found in the understandings between the members at the time they entered into association. But there may be later promises, by words or conduct, which it would be unfair to allow a member to ignore. Nor is it necessary that such promises should be independently enforceable as a matter of contract. A promise may be binding as a matter of justice and equity although for one reason or another (for example, because in favour of a third party) it would not be enforceable in law.

I do not suggest that exercising rights in breach of some promise or undertaking is the only form of conduct which will be regarded as unfair for the purposes of s. 459. For example, there may be some event which puts an end to the basis upon which the parties entered into association with each other, making it unfair that one shareholder should insist upon the continuance of the asso-ciation. The analogy of contractual frustration suggests itself. The unfairness may arise not from what the parties have positively agreed but from a majority using its legal powers to maintain the association in circumstances to which the minority can reasonably say it did not agree: *non haec in foedera veni.* It is well recognised that in such a case there would be power to wind up the company on the just and equitable ground (see *Virdi v Abbey Leisure Ltd* [1990] BCLC 342) and it seems to me that, in the absence of a winding up, it could equally be said to come within s. 459. But this form of unfairness is also based upon established equitable principles and it does not arise in this case.

6 Legitimate expectations

In *Re Saul D. Harrison and Sons plc, Re* [1995] 1 BCLC 14, 19, I used the term 'legitimate expectation', borrowed from public law, as a label for the 'correlative right' to which a relationship between com-pany members may give rise in a case when, on equitable principles, it would be regarded as unfair for a majority to exercise a power conferred upon them by the articles to the prejudice of another member. I gave as an example the standard case in which shareholders have entered into associ-ation upon the understanding that each of them who has ventured his capital will also participate in the management of the company. In such a case it will usually be considered unjust, inequitable or unfair for a majority to use their voting power to exclude a member from participation in the management without giving him the opportunity to remove his capital upon reasonable terms. The aggrieved member could be said to have had a 'legitimate expectation' that he would be able to participate in the management or withdraw from the company.

It was probably a mistake to use this term, as it usually is when one introduces a new label to describe a concept which is already sufficiently defined in other terms. In saying that it was 'correlative' to the equitable restraint, I meant that it could exist only when equitable principles of the kind I have been describing would make it unfair for a party to exercise rights under the articles. It is a consequence, not a cause, of the equitable restraint. The concept of a legitimate expectation should not be allowed to lead a life of its own, capable of giving rise to equitable restraints in circumstances to which the traditional equitable principles have no application. That is what seems to have happened in this case.

7 Was Mr Phillips unfair?

The Court of Appeal found that by 1991 the company had the characteristics identified by Lord Wilberforce in *Ebrahimi* v *Westbourne Galleries Ltd* [1973] AC 360 as commonly giving rise to equitable restraints upon the exercise of powers under the articles. They were (1) an association formed or continued on the basis of a personal relationship involving mutual confidence; (2) an understanding that all, or some, of the shareholders shall participate in the conduct of the business; and (3) restrictions on the transfer of shares, so that a member cannot take out his stake and go elsewhere. I agree. It follows that it would have been unfair of Mr Phillips to use his voting powers under the articles to remove Mr O'Neill from participation in the conduct of the business without giving him the opportunity to sell his interest in the company at a fair price. Although it does not matter, I should say that I do not think that this was the position when Mr O'Neill first acquired his shares in 1985. He received them as a gift and an incentive and I do not think that in making that gift Mr Phillips could be taken to have surrendered his right to dismiss Mr O'Neill from the management without making him an offer for the shares. Mr O'Neill was simply an employee who happened to have been given some shares. But over the following years the relationship changed. Mr O'Neill invested his own profits in the company by leaving some on loan account and agreeing to part being capitalised as shares. He worked to build up the company's business. He guaranteed its bank account and mortgaged his house in support. *Re H.R. Harmer Ltd, Re* [1959] 1 WLR 62 shows that shareholders who receive their shares as a gift but afterwards work in the business may become entitled to enforce equitable restraints upon the conduct of the majority shareholder.

The difficulty for Mr O'Neill is that Mr Phillips did not remove him from participation in the management of the business. After the meeting on 4 November 1991 he remained a director and continued to earn his salary as manager of the business in Germany. The Court of Appeal held that he had been constructively removed by the behaviour of Mr Phillips in the matter of equality of profits and shareholdings. So the question then becomes whether Mr Phillips acted unfairly in respect of these matters.

To take the shareholdings first, the Court of Appeal said that Mr O'Neill had a legitimate expectation of being allotted more shares when the targets were met. No doubt he did have such an expectation before 4 November and no doubt it was legitimate, or reasonable, in the sense that it reasonably appeared likely to happen. Mr Phillips had agreed in principle, subject to the execution of a suitable document. But this is where I think that the Court of Appeal may have been misled by the expression 'legitimate expectation'. The real question is whether in fairness or equity Mr O'Neill had a right to the shares. On this point, one runs up against what seems to me the insuperable obstacle of the judge's finding that Mr Phillips never agreed to give them. He made no promise on the point. From which it seems to me to follow that there is no basis, consistent with established principles of equity, for a court to hold that Mr Phillips was behaving unfairly in withdrawing from the negotiation. This would not be restraining the exercise of legal rights. It would be imposing upon Mr Phillips an obligation to which he never agreed. Where, as here, parties enter into negotiations with a view to a transfer of shares on professional advice and subject to a condition that they are not to be bound until a formal document has been executed, I do not think it is possible to say that an obligation has arisen in fairness or equity at an earlier stage.

The same reasoning applies to the sharing of profits. The judge found as a fact that Mr Phillips made no unconditional promise about the sharing of profits. He had said informally that he would share the profits equally while Mr O'Neill managed the company and he himself did not have to be involved in day-to-day business. He deliberately retained control of the company and with it, as the judge said, the right to redraw Mr O'Neill's responsibilities. This he did without objection in August 1991. The consequence was that he came back to running the business and Mr O'Neill was no longer managing director. He had made no promise to share the profits equally in such circumstances and it was therefore not inequitable or unfair for him to refuse to carry on doing so. The Court of Appeal seems to have contemplated that Mr Phillips might have been entitled to do what he did if he had given Mr O'Neill notice of his intentions and treated him more politely at the meeting on 4 November 1991. But these matters cannot affect the question of whether a change in the profit-sharing arrangements was a breach of faith.

It follows in my opinion that there was no basis for the Court of Appeal's finding that Mr O'Neill had been driven out of the company. He may have decided that he had lost confidence in Mr Phillips and that he could no longer work with him. After Christmas 1992 Mr Phillips said that he recognised that Mr O'Neill had come to this conclusion and that there was no way in which he could put their relationship together again. But Mr O'Neill's decision was not the result of anything wrong or unfair which Mr Phillips had done.

8 No-fault divorce?

Mr Hollington, who appeared for Mr O'Neill, said that it did not matter whether Mr Phillips had done anything unfair. The fact was that trust and confidence between the parties had broken down. In those circumstances it was obvious that there ought to be a parting of the ways and the unfairness lay in Mr Phillips, who accepted this to be the case, not being willing to allow Mr O'Neill to recover his stake in the company. Even if Mr Phillips was not at fault in causing the breakdown, it would be unfair to leave Mr, O'Neill locked into the company as a minority shareholder.

Mr Hollington's submission comes to saying that, in a 'quasi-partnership' company, one part-ner ought to be entitled at will to require the other partner or partners to buy his shares at a fair value. All he need do is to declare that trust and confidence has broken down. In the present case, trust and confidence broke down, first, because Mr Phillips failed to do certain things which, on the judge's findings, he had never promised to do; secondly, because Mr O'Neill wrongly thought that Mr Phillips had committed various improprieties; and finally because, as the judge said [1997] 2 BCLC 739, 742, he was 'inclined to see base motives in everything that Mr Phillips did'. Nevertheless it is submitted that fairness requires that Mr [Phillips] or the company ought to raise the necessary liquid capital to pay Mr O'Neill a fair price for his shares.

I do not think that there is any support in the authorities for such a stark right of unilateral with-drawal. There are cases, such as *Re A Company, Re a (No. 006834 of 1988)* [1989] BCLC 365, in which it has been said that if a breakdown in relations has caused the majority to remove a shareholder from participation in the management, it is usually a waste of time to try to investigate who caused the breakdown. Such breakdowns often occur (as in this case) without either side having done any-thing seriously wrong or unfair. It is not fair to the excluded member, who will usually have lost his employment, to keep his assets locked in the company. But that does not mean that a member who has not been dismissed or excluded can demand that his shares be purchased simply because he feels that he has lost trust and confidence in the others. I rather doubt whether even in partnership law a dissolution would be granted on this ground in a case in which it was still possible under the articles for the business of the partnership to be continued. And as Lord Wilberforce observed in *Ebrahimi v Westbourne Galleries Ltd* [1973] AC 360, 380, one should not press the quasi-partnership analogy too far: 'A company, however small, however domestic, is a company not a partnership or even a quasi-partnership'.

The Law Commission Report on Shareholder Remedies to which I have already referred considered whether to recommend the introduction of a statutory remedy 'in situations where there is no fault' (para. 3.65) so that members of a quasi-partnership could exit at will. They said, at p. 39, para. 3.66:

> In our view there are strong economic arguments against allowing shareholders to exit at will. Also, as a matter of principle, such a right would fundamentally contravene the sanctity of the contract binding the members and the company which we considered should guide our approach to shareholder remedies.

The Law Commission plainly did not consider that s. 459 already provided a right to exit at will and I do not think so either.

9 Capacity in which prejudice suffered

The judge, it will be recalled, gave as one of his reasons for dismissing the petition the fact that any prejudice suffered by Mr O'Neill was in his capacity as an employee rather than as a shareholder. The Court of Appeal's rejection of this reason was, I think, influenced by its view that Mr O'Neill had been constructively expelled. In a case of expulsion, where the equitable restraint on the exercise of the power is based upon the terms upon which the petitioner became or continued as a member of the company, the prejudice will be suffered in the capacity of a member. It is the terms, agreement, or understanding on which he became associated as a member which generates the restraint on the power of expulsion. But the judge was considering only the prejudice suffered through not getting a half-share in the profits or the additional shares. It is somewhat unreal to deal with the capacity in which prejudice was suffered in these respects when there was no entitlement in law or equity in the first place. But assuming there had been a contractual obligation, I would not exclude the possibility that prejudice suffered from the breach of that obligation could be suffered in the capacity of shareholder. As I have said, the initial gift of 25 shares in 1985 did not in my view change the essential relationship between the parties. Mr Phillips remained controlling shareholder and Mr O'Neill remained an employee who had some shares. If at that stage Mr Phillips had promised another 25 shares and then broken his promise, I do not think that Mr O'Neill would have suffered prejudice in his capacity as an existing shareholder. I agree with the judge that the case would have been no different if Mr O'Neill had had no shares and Mr Phillips had broken a promise to give him 50. On the other hand, once Mr O'Neill had invested his own money and effort in the company, the situation may have changed. A promise to give Mr O'Neill more shares or a larger share in the profits may well have been based not merely upon his position as an employee but on the fact that he already had a stake in the company. As cases like *R and H Electrical Ltd v Haden Bill Electrical Ltd* [1995] 2 BCLC 280 show, the requirement that prejudice must be suffered as a member should not be too narrowly or technically construed. But the point does not arise because no promise was made.

10 The offer to buy

Mr Ralls who appeared for Mr Phillips, submitted that even if his conduct had been unfairly prejudicial, the petition should have been dismissed because he had made an offer to buy the shares at a fair price, which was the whole of the relief to which Mr O'Neill would have been entitled. In view of the conclusion I have reached about the absence of unfair prejudice, with which I understand your Lordships to agree, this point does not need to be decided. Nevertheless, the effect of an offer to buy the shares as an answer to a petition under s. 459 is a matter of such great practical importance that I would invite your Lordships to consider it.

The petition was presented on 22 January 1992 and points of defence were delivered on 16 March 1992. The points of defence contained no offer to buy but asked that Mr Phillips or the company should be 'at liberty' to buy the shares

> at a fair value to be fixed by the court upon such basis as to the court shall seem just and equitable and depending upon its finding in respect of the various issues between the parties disclosed on the pleadings herein.

This plainly contemplated that the petition would go to full hearing and be decided on the merits. There was then considerable delay and a number of interlocutory hearings. On 28 November 1994, pursuant to an undertaking given to the court Mr Phillips made an offer in terms scheduled to a consent order of that date. The offer was to purchase at a price to be agreed or in default fixed by a chartered accountant as valuer on the basis that the value was one-quarter of the fair value of the entire issued share capital. The offer was rejected on various grounds, one being that it made no provision for Mr O'Neill's costs. The result was that the petition went to a full hearing.

The judge, who dismissed the petition, did not find it necessary to deal with the offer. The Court of Appeal accepted the argument that Mr O'Neill was justified in rejecting it because it did not provide for his costs.

In my opinion the Court of Appeal was right. The offer is only material to the outcome at the trial if the court considers that the petitioner is otherwise entitled to succeed. So the fact that he was made an earlier offer of the relief to which the court has now held him entitled after trial can logically go only to the question of costs. If the petitioner was offered everything to which he has been held entitled, the respondent may, as in the case of a *Calderbank* letter (*Calderbank* v *Calderbank* [1976] Fam 93), be entitled to say that the costs after the date of that offer should be borne by the successful petitioner, who ought to have accepted the offer and brought the litigation to an end. On the other hand, it seems to me that in the case of a petition which has been on foot for nearly three years, a petitioner who, we are assuming, has a well founded case will not obtain everything to which he is entitled unless there is an offer of costs. Mr Ralls said that no such offer was made because there had been some orders for the petitioner to pay the costs of interlocutory applications in any event and Mr Phillips took the view that on balance the petitioner would not be entitled to any costs. But Mr O'Neill was not to be expected to guess what the results of a taxation would be. Mr Phillips could have offered to pay the costs less any which had been awarded to him by interlocutory order. I therefore agree that the offer was inadequate.

In the present case, Mr Phillips fought the petition to the end and your Lordships have decided that he was justified in doing so. But I think that parties ought to be encouraged, where at all possible, to avoid the expense of money and spirit inevitably involved in such litigation by making an offer to purchase at an early stage. This was a somewhat unusual case in that Mr Phillips, despite his revised views about Mr O'Neill's competence, was willing to go on working with him. This is a position which the majority shareholder is entitled to take, even if only because he may consider it less unattractive than having to raise the capital to buy out the minority. Usually, however, the majority shareholder will want to put an end to the association. In such a case, it will almost always be unfair for the minority shareholder to be excluded without an offer to buy his shares or make some other fair arrangement. The Law Commission Report on Shareholder Remedies, at pp. 30–7, paras 3.26–56 has recommended that in a private company limited by shares in which substantially all the members are directors, there should be a statutory presumption that the removal of a shareholder as a director, or from substantially all his functions as a director, is unfairly prejudicial conduct. This does not seem to me very different in practice from the present law. But the unfairness does not lie in the exclusion alone but in exclusion without a reasonable offer. If the respondent to a petition has plainly made a reasonable offer, then the exclusion as such will not be unfairly, prejudicial and he will be entitled to have the petition struck out. It is therefore very important that participants in such companies should be able to know what counts as a reasonable offer.

In the first place, the offer must be to purchase the shares at a fair value. This will ordinarily be a value representing an equivalent proportion of the total issued share capital, that is, without a discount for its being a minority holding. The Law Commission (paragraphs 3.57–62) has recommended a statutory presumption that in cases to which the presumption of unfairly prejudicial conduct applies, the fair value of the shares should be determined on a pro rata basis. This too reflects the existing practice. This is not to say that there may not be cases in which it will be fair to take a discounted value. But such cases will be based upon special circumstances and it will seldom be possible for the court to say that an offer to buy on a discounted basis is plainly reasonable, so that the petition should be struck out.

Secondly, the value, if not agreed, should be determined by a competent expert. The offer in this case to appoint an accountant agreed by the parties or in default nominated by the President of the Institute of Chartered Accountants satisfied this requirement. One would ordinarily expect the costs of the expert to be shared but he should have the power to decide that they should be borne in some different way.

Thirdly, the offer should be to have the value determined by the expert as an expert. I do not think that the offer should provide for the full machinery of arbitration or the halfway house of an expert who gives reasons. The objective should be economy and expedition, even if this carries the possibility of a rough edge for one side or the other (and both parties in this respect take the same risk) compared with a more elaborate procedure. This is in accordance with the terms of the draft reg. 119 (exit right) [for Table A] recommended by the Law Commission: see Appendix C to the report, p. 133.

Fourthly, the offer should, as in this case, provide for equality of arms between the parties. Both should have the same right of access to information about the company which bears upon the value of the shares and both should have the right to make submissions to the expert, though the form (written or oral) which these submissions may take should be left to the discretion of the expert himself.

Fifthly, there is the question of costs. In the present case, when the offer was made after nearly three years of litigation, it could not serve as an independent ground for dismissing the petition, on the assumption that it was otherwise well founded, without an offer of costs. But this does not mean that payment of costs need always be offered. If there is a breakdown in relations between the parties, the majority shareholder should be given a reasonable opportunity to make an offer (which may include time to explore the question of how to raise finance) before he becomes obliged to pay costs. As I have said, the unfairness does not usually consist merely in the fact of the break-down but in failure to make a suitable offer. And the majority shareholder should have a reasonable time to make the offer before his conduct is treated as unfair. The mere fact that the petitioner has presented his petition before the offer does not mean that the respondent must offer to pay the costs if he was not given a reasonable time.

11 Conclusion
I would allow the appeal and dismiss the petition.

Re Saul D. Harrison and Sons plc
Test of unfairness
[1995] 1 BCLC 14, Court of Appeal

Hoffmann LJ explains the concept of unfair prejudice and points out that for the purposes of s. 459, unfairness must be judged in a commercial context. Neill LJ usefully extracts from decided cases the guidelines applicable to the concept.

Facts   The petitioner held about 8 per cent of the class C shares in a family-run company which was established by her great-grandfather in 1891. She alleged, inter alia, that the directors (her cousins) had allowed the company to continue trading at a loss in order to pay themselves excessive remu-neration, instead of closing it down and distributing its substantial assets to the shareholders. The director successfully sought to strike out the petition. The appeal by the petitioner was dismissed by the Court of Appeal.

HOFFMANN LJ: 'Unfairly prejudicial' is deliberately imprecise language which was chosen by Parliament because its earlier attempt in s. 210 of the Companies Act 1948 to provide a similar remedy had been too restrictively construed. The earlier section had used the word 'oppressive', which the House of Lords in *Scottish Co-operative Wholesale Society Ltd* v *Meyer* [1959] AC 324 said meant 'burdensome, harsh and wrongful'. This gave rise to some uncertainty as to whether 'wrongful' required actual illegality or invasion of legal rights. The Jenkins Committee on Company Law, which reported in 1962, thought that it should not. To make this clear, it recommended the use of the term 'unfairly prejudicial', which Parliament somewhat tardily adopted in s. 75 of the Companies Act 1980. This section is reproduced (with minor amendment) in the present s. 459 of the Companies Act 1985.

Mr Purle, who appeared for the petitioner, said that the only test of unfairness was whether a reasonable bystander would think that the conduct in question was unfair. This is correct, so far as it goes, and has some support in the cases. Its merit is to emphasise that the court is applying an objective standard of fairness. But I do not think that it is the most illuminating way of putting the matter. For one thing, the standard of fairness must necessarily be laid down by the court. In explaining how the court sets about deciding what is fair in the context of company manage-ment, I do not think that it helps a great deal to add the reasonable company watcher to the already substantial cast of imaginary characters which the law uses to personify its standards of justice in different situations. An appeal to the views of an imaginary third party makes the concept seem more vague than it really is. It is more useful to examine the factors which the law actually takes into account in setting the standard.

In deciding what is fair or unfair for the purposes of s. 459, it is important to have in mind that fairness is being used in the context of a commercial relationship. The articles of association are just what their name implies: the contractual terms which govern the relationships of the shareholders with the company and each other. They determine the powers of the board and the company in general meeting and everyone who becomes a member of a company is taken to have agreed to them. Since keeping promises and honouring agreements is probably the most important element of commercial fairness, the starting point in any case under s. 459 will be to ask whether the conduct of which the shareholder complains was in accordance with the articles of association. . . .

Although one begins with the articles and the powers of the board, a finding that conduct was not in accordance with the articles does not necessarily mean that it was unfair, still less that the court will exercise its discretion to grant relief. . . . So trivial or technical infringements of the articles were not intended to give rise to petitions under s. 459.

Not only may conduct be technically unlawful without being unfair it can also be unfair without being unlawful. In a commercial context, this may at first seem surprising. How can it be unfair to act in accordance with what the parties have agreed? As a general rule, it is not. But there are cases in which the letter of the articles does not fully reflect the understandings upon which the shareholders are associated. Lord Wilberforce drew attention to such cases in a celebrated passage of his judgment in *Ebrahimi* v *Westbourne Galleries Ltd* [1973] AC 360 at 379, which discusses what seems to me the identical concept of injustice or unfairness which can form the basis of a just and equitable winding up:

> The words [just and equitable] are a recognition of the fact that a limited company is more than a mere judicial entity, with a personality in law of its own: that there is room in company law for recognition of the fact that behind it, or amongst it, there are individuals, with rights, expectations and obligations *inter se* which are not necessarily submerged in the company structure. That structure is defined by the Companies Act 1948 and by the articles of association by which the shareholders agree to be bound. In most companies and in most contexts, this definition is sufficient and exhaustive, equally so whether the company is large or small. The 'just and equitable' provision does not, as the respondents suggest, entitle one party to disregard the obligation he assumes by entering a company, nor the court to dispense him from it. It does, as equity always does, enable the court to subject the exercise of legal rights to equitable considerations; considerations, that is, of a personal character arising between one individual and another, which may make it unjust, or inequitable, to insist on legal rights or to exercise them in a particular way.

Thus the personal relationship between a shareholder and those who control the company may entitle him to say that it would in certain circumstances be unfair for them to exercise a power conferred by the articles upon the board or the company in general meeting. I have in the past ventured to borrow from public law the term 'legitimate expectation' to describe the correlative 'right' in the shareholder to which such a relationship may give rise. It often arises out of a fundamental understanding between the shareholders which formed the basis of their association but was not put into contractual form, such as an assumption that each of the parties who has ventured his capital will also participate in the management of the company and receive the return on his investment in the form of salary rather than dividend. These relationships need not always take the form of implied agreements with the shareholder concerned; they could enure for the benefit of a third party such as a joint venturer's widow. But in *Ebrahimi* v *Westbourne Galleries Ltd* Lord Wilberforce went on to say:

> It would be impossible, and wholly undesirable, to define the circumstances in which these considerations may arise. Certainly the fact that the company is a small one, or a private company, is not enough. There are very many of these where the association is a purely commercial one, of which it can safely be said that the basis of association is adequately and exhaustively laid down in the articles. The superimposition of equitable considerations requires something more.

Thus in the absence of 'something more', there is no basis for a legitimate expectation that the board and the company in general meeting will not exercise whatever powers they are given by the articles of association.

In this case, as the judge emphasised, there is nothing more. The petitioner was given her shares in 1960 pursuant to a reorganisation of the share capital which vested the entire control of the company in the A shareholders and the board whom they appointed. This scheme is binding upon her and there are no special circumstances to modify its effects. Although the petition speaks of the petitioner having various 'legitimate expectations', no grounds are alleged for saying that her rights are not 'adequately and exhaustively' laid down by the articles. And in substance the alleged 'legitimate expectations' amount to no more than an expectation that the board would manage the company in accordance with their fiduciary obligations and the terms of the articles and the Companies Act....

NEILL LJ: The scope of the protection afforded by s. 459 and by the remedies available under s. 461 is clearly intended to be more extensive than that provided by s. 210 of the 1948 Act. At this stage, however, the precise boundaries of the protection are unclear and they will have to be worked out on a case by case basis. Nevertheless it seems to me that it is already possible to collect from the cases decided under the 1948 Act and under the 1985 Act the following guidelines as to the correct approach to the concept of 'unfairly prejudicial' in s. 459.

(1) The words 'unfairly prejudicial' are general words and they should be applied flexibly to meet the circumstances of the particular case. I have in mind the warning which Lord Wilberforce gave in *Ebrahimi* v *Westbourne Galleries Ltd* [1973] AC 360 at 374 in relation to the words 'just and equitable':

> Illustrations may be used, but general words should remain general and not be reduced to the sum of particular instances.

It is also relevant to bear in mind that whereas a winding-up order on just and equitable grounds will terminate the existence of the company a wider range of remedies is available under s. 461. In *Re A Company, (No. 00314 of 1989)* [1991] BCLC 154 at 161 Mummery J put the matter as follows:

> Under ss. 459 to 461 the court is not, therefore, faced with a death sentence decision dependent on establishing just and equitable grounds for such a decision. The court is more in the position of a medical practitioner presented with a patient who is alleged to be suffering from one or more ailments which can be treated by an appropriate remedy applied during the course of the continuing life of the company.

(2) On the other hand, as Hoffmann J pointed out in *Re A Company (No. 007623 of 1984), Re* [1986] BCLC 362 at 367 in relation to a s. 459 petition:

> ...the very width of the jurisdiction means that unless carefully controlled it can become a means of oppression.

These words have been echoed in later cases.

(3) The relevant conduct (of commission or omission) must relate to the affairs of the company of which the petitioner is a member: see Peter Gibson J in *Re a Company (No. 005685 of 1988) (No. 2)* [1989] BCLC 427 at 437.

(4) The conduct must be both prejudicial (in the sense of causing prejudice or harm to the relevant interest) and also unfairly so: conduct may be unfair without being prejudicial or prejudicial without being unfair, and it is not sufficient if the conduct satisfies only one of these tests: see Peter Gibson J [1989] BCLC 427 at 437.

(5) In construing the word 'unfairly' in this context it will be necessary to take account not only of the legal rights of the petitioner, but also consider whether there are any equitable considerations such as the petitioner's legitimate expectations to be weighed in the balance.

(6) For the purpose of determining the legal rights of the petitioner one turns to the memorandum and articles of the company because the articles constitute the contract between the

company and the member in respect of his rights and liabilities as a shareholder. Furthermore, it is to be remembered that the management of a company is entrusted to the directors, who have to exercise their powers in the interests of the company as a whole.

(7) In order to establish unfairness it is clearly not enough to show that some managerial decision may have prejudiced the petitioner's interest. A shareholder on joining a company will be deemed to have accepted the risk that in the wider interests of the company decisions may be taken which will prejudice his own interests. Thus it may be necessary for the directors to take steps which are prejudicial to some of the members in order to secure the future prosperity of the company or even its survival: cf. *Nicholas* v *Soundcraft Electronics Ltd* [1993] BCLC 360 at 372 per Ralph Gibson LJ.

(8) Though it is open to the court to find that serious mismanagement of a company's business constitutes conduct that is unfairly prejudicial to the interests of the shareholders the court will normally be very reluctant to accept that managerial decisions can amount to unfairly prejudicial conduct: see *Re Elgindata Ltd, Re* [1991] BCLC 959 at 993.

(9) A shareholder can legitimately complain, however, if the directors exceed the powers vested in them or exercise their powers for some illegitimate or ulterior purpose.

(10) Though in general members of a company have no legitimate expectations going beyond the legal rights conferred on them by the constitution of the company, additional legitimate expectations may be superimposed in certain circumstances. These may arise from agreements or understandings between the members or between the members and the directors. Thus I am satisfied that the concept of fairness in the phrase 'unfairly prejudicial' is capable of introducing considerations similar to those explained by Lord Wilberforce in the *Westbourne Galleries* case ([1973] AC 360 at 379) where he said that the 'just and equitable' provision in s. 222(f) of the Companies Act 1948 enabled the court to subject the exercise of legal rights to equitable considerations. Lord Wilberforce continued [1973] AC 360 at 379):

> ... considerations, that is, of a personal character arising between one individual and another, which may make it unjust, or inequitable, to insist on legal rights, or to exercise them in a particular way.
>
> It would be impossible, and wholly undesirable, to define the circumstances in which these considerations may arise. Certainly the fact that a company is a small one, or a private company, is not enough. There are very many of these where the association is a purely commercial one, of which it can safely be said that the basis of association is adequately and exhaustively laid down in the articles. The superimposition of equitable considerations requires something more, which typically may include one, or probably more, of the following elements: (i) an association formed or continued on the basis of a personal relationship, involving mutual confidence—this element will often be found where a pre-existing partnership has been converted into a limited company; (ii) an agreement, or understanding, that all, or some (for there may be 'sleeping' members), of the shareholders shall participate in the conduct of the business; (iii) restriction upon the transfer of the members' interests in the company—so that if confidence is lost, or one member is removed from management, he cannot take out his stake and go elsewhere.

NOTES

1. In *Re a Company (No. 00477 of 1986)* [1986] BCLC 376, Hoffmann J had to decide the interest of a member qua member. He was able to adopt Lord Wilberforce's 'equitable consideration' approach to look beyond the memorandum and articles of association to find out the 'interest' of a member in a quasi-partnership. Following this approach, a pre-incorporation understanding or agreement may give rise to a legitimate expectation or interest of shareholders. There, the petitioners held all the shares in A Ltd. They later sold them to O plc in return for an issue of shares in O plc. The understanding was that the relationship between them and the controlling shareholders in O plc would be a 'partnership'. They now petitioned against the controlling shareholders of O plc on the ground that the dismissal of Mr S, one of the

petitioners, in breach of his service contract with O plc, was contrary to their agreement and unfairly prejudicial. They also alleged that the conduct of the controlling shareholders had unfairly affected the value of the petitioners' shares in O plc. The respondents applied unsuccessfully for the petition to be struck out arguing that the allegations constituted wrongs to them as vendors of shares and to Mr S as an employee but did not affect them as members of O plc.

2. In *Re A Company (No. 003160 of 1986)* [1986] BCLC 391, Mr F, a shareholder in the company, was discharged as an employee. His shares were temporarily registered in his wife's name. The issue was whether the wife as a shareholder could complain about the unfair exclusion by the majority of her husband. This depended on whether she had an interest that her husband would not be excluded from employment in the business. Taking the 'equitable consideration' approach, the court was prepared even to find that a shareholder had an interest to see that someone other than herself was not excluded from management. For other cases involving exclusion from management see *Re Cumana Ltd, Re* [1986] BCLC 430, CA, *Re London School of Electronics Ltd, Re* [1986] Ch 211, *Re Bird Precision Bellows Ltd, Re* [1984] Ch 419, and *Re A Company (No. 00477 of 1986), Re* [1986] BCLC 376; *Whyte* 1984 SLT 330; *Re Haden Bill Electrical Ltd, Re* [1995] 2 BCLC 280; *Quinlan v Essex Hinge Co. Ltd* [1996] 2 BCLC 417. Where the articles allow a shareholder director's contract of employment with the company to be terminated on notice, relief is unlikely to be granted under the section to prevent the implementation of the notice (*Wright, Petitioners* [1997] BCC 198).

3. Where the majority has offered to buy out the minority's shares to be valued by an independent valuer, a petition under s. 994 would normally be regarded as an abuse of the process because the offer would normally have given the petitioner all the relief he could realistically expect to obtain on his petition: see, e.g., *Re A Company (No. 003843 of 1986)* [1987] BCLC 562; *Re A Company (No. 003096 of 1987)* (1987) 4 BCC 80; *Re A Company (No 006834 of 1988)* [1989] BCLC 365. However, if there is a risk that the independent valuer's valuation of the petitioner's interest in the company might apply a discount, it would not be unreasonable for the petitioner to refuse the offer (*Re A Company (No. 00330 of 1991)* [1991] BCLC 597, applying *Virdi v Abbey Leisure Ltd* [1990] BCLC 342, CA), unless the terms of the offer have eliminated the risk (*Re A Company (No. 00836 of 1995)* [1996] BCLC 192).

4. Where there is evidence that the auditors had failed to act independently when valuing the petitioner's shares, it would not be wrong to petition under s. 994: *Re Benfield Greig Group plc* [2002] 1 BCLC 65, CA.

5. Where the petitioner and the respondent offer to buy each other out, the court has to decide which of them has a realistic prospect and reasonable likelihood of being able to pay the price likely to be decided upon by an independent expert valuer: *West v Blanchet* [2000] 1 BCLC 795.

6. Section 994 does not provide a member of a quasi-partnership company who wishes voluntarily to sever his connection with the company for personal reasons with the means of forcing the other members to buy his shares at their full undiscounted value when he has no contractual right to do so: *Re Phoenix Office Supplies Ltd* [2003] 1 BCLC 76, CA.

Re London School of Electronics Ltd

Misappropriation of assets

[1986] Ch 211, Chancery Division

This case is analogous to the common law cases of misappropriation of company assets. Here, the majority's conduct in taking the students of the company with them was thought to be unfairly prejudicial. The effect of this and other cases may be to render common law derivative actions less attractive than a petition under s. 994 in future cases of misappropriation of company assets.

The other important feature of the case is the way in which the petitioner's shares, ordered to be purchased by the respondents, were valued.

Facts *The company, London School of Electronics Ltd, ran courses in electronics. It was owned as to 25 per cent by the petitioner who was a director of the company. City Tutorial College Ltd, which ran a tutorial college, owned the remaining shares. CTC was in turn mainly owned by Athanasiou and George. The petitioner was employed by CTC as a teacher. Later relationships between the parties broke down. A resolution was passed to remove the petitioner as a director of LSE. Athanasiou and George also transferred most of LSE's students to courses run by CTC. They further made an agreement with an American university to grant recognition for a BSc degree course to CTC, rather than LSE. The petitioner having left CTC and LSE, set up a rival institution, LCEE, in the same centre as CTC, taking with him some 12 LSE students. He petitioned successfully under CA 1980, s. 75 (now CA 2006, s. 994) for a purchase order of his shares in LSE.*

NOURSE J: The combined effect of subs. (1) and (3) [of CA 1980, s. 75; now CA 1985, ss. 459(1) and 461(1)] is to empower the court to make such order as it thinks fit for giving relief, if it is first satisfied that the affairs of the company are being or have been conducted in a manner which is unfairly prejudicial to the interests of some part of the members. The conduct of the petitioner may be material in a number of ways, of which the two most obvious are these. First, it may render the conduct on the other side, even if it is prejudicial, not unfair: cf. *Re R.A. Noble & Sons (Clothing) Ltd* [1983] BCLC 273. Secondly, even if the conduct on the other side is both prejudicial and unfair, the petitioner's conduct may nevertheless affect the relief which the court thinks fit to grant under subs. (3). In my view there is no independent or overriding requirement that it should be just and equitable to grant relief or that the petitioner should come to the court with clean hands.

Mr Oliver [counsel for the company] then submitted that on a view of the facts as a whole the affairs of the company were not conducted in a manner which was unfairly prejudicial to the interests of the petitioner as a member of the company. He relied in particular on the injury caused to the company by the petitioner, whilst still a director, in deliberately taking away a dozen or so students and enrolling them with LCEE. He also relied on the nine grounds of complaint specified in the letter of 17 June 1983, although it must be said that those matters were not much investigated in the evidence. Mr Oliver submitted that in all the circumstances the conduct of CTC, even if it was prejudicial, was not unfair.

While I have no doubt that during the academic year 1982/83 the petitioner proved himself to be difficult and unreliable, perhaps lazy, in the discharge of his teaching and related duties, there was in my view no adequate justification for the decision of CTC to transfer to itself students who had completed their first year of the BSc course in electronics and to register with itself all new students for that course. . . .

In my judgment it was CTC's decision to appropriate the BSc students to itself which was the effective cause of the breakdown in the relationship of mutual confidence between the quasi-partners. Furthermore, that was clearly conduct on the part of CTC which was both unfair and prejudicial to the interests of the petitioner as a member of the company. It is possible, although I do not so decide, that CTC would have been entitled to relieve the petitioner of his teaching duties before June 1983. It is even possible, although it is much less likely, that CTC, had it gone through the appropriate formalities, could have properly removed the petitioner as a director of the company. But none of that is to say that CTC was entitled to take the extreme step of determining to deprive the petitioner of his 25 per cent interest in the profits attributable to the BSc students. Furthermore, I do not think that the petitioner's removal of a dozen or so students to LCEE in August and September can have any effect on the question of unfair prejudice. It was Mr Athanasiou and Mr George who had unfairly brought about the petitioner's departure from the company and his remaining a director was little more than a technicality. His removal of the students is certainly something which will have consequences later in the case. It did not in my view have the effect of rendering the prejudicial conduct no longer unfair.

In the circumstances I hold that the petitioner is entitled to an order under s. 75 requiring CTC to purchase his shares. That makes it necessary for me to go on and consider three further questions. First, at what date ought the shares to be valued? Secondly, ought the valuation to be made on the footing that the students which the petitioner removed to LCEE remained with the company or ought they to be left out of account? Thirdly, ought the price to be fixed pro rata according to the value of shares as a whole or ought it to be discounted on the ground that the petitioner's shares constitute a minority in number?

If there were to be such a thing as a general rule, I myself would think that the date of the order or the actual valuation would be more appropriate than the date of the presentation of the petition or the unfair prejudice. Prima facie an interest in a going concern ought to be valued at the date on which it is ordered to be purchased. But whatever the general rule might be it seems very probable that the overriding requirement that the valuation should be fair on the facts of the particular case would, by exceptions, reduce it to no rule at all. That that is so is already suggested by such authorities as there are on this question. In *Scottish Co-operative Wholesale Society Ltd* v *Meyer* [1959] AC 324 the shares were ordered to be purchased at the value which they would have had at the date of the petition if there had been no oppression. In *Re Jermyn Street Turkish Baths Ltd* [1970] 1 WLR 1194 the order of Pennycuick J discloses that the assets, undertaking and goodwill of the company were to be valued on an inquiry as at the date of the master's certificate. In *Re a Company (No. 002567 of 1982)* [1983] 1 WLR 927 Vinelott J held that the shares of a petitioner who had unreasonably rejected previous fair offers to purchase them ought to be valued at the date of the valuation and not at the date when he had been excluded from participation in the affairs of the company. However, Vinelott J said that he could conceive of many cases where, in an application under s. 75, fairness would require that the valuation should relate back to an earlier date such as, in that case, the exclusion of the petitioner: see p. 937. That observation was approved by Mervyn Davies J in *Re OC (Transport) Services Ltd* [1984] BCLC 251 at p. 258, where he held that the facts required the valuation to be made at a date earlier than the date of the petition, in fact at the date when the unfair prejudice had occurred. Finally, in *Bird Precision Bellows Ltd* [1984] Ch 419 the valuation was made as at the date of a consent order that the shares should be purchased at such price as the court should thereafter determine. That case is not of any real assistance on this point, because the date was no doubt implicit in the terms of the consent order.

In the present case I have held that the conduct which was unfairly prejudicial to the interests of the petitioner as a member of the company was CTC's decision to appropriate the BSc students to itself. Had that conduct not taken place the petitioner would effectively have become entitled to 25 per cent of the profits attributable to the BSc students. Since those profits would not have been earned until the academic year 1983/84, it would not in my view be fair to value the petitioner's shares as at 3 June 1983. He is at the least entitled to have them valued at some date during the academic year 1983/84 and, since no other date has been suggested, the date of the presentation of the petition—10 February 1984—is as good as any other. Ought I to go further and order a valuation as at today's date or the actual date of valuation, i.e., at a date during the academic year 1984/85? It is not clear to me on the evidence whether there has been a significant increase in the number of BSc students this year. I suspect that there may have been. The more important point is that Mr Athanasiou and Mr George have now been able to acquire a greater academic standing for the course in this country. I find that that has been entirely due to their own efforts and owes nothing to the petitioner and, moreover, that it is unlikely that it would have been achieved if the petitioner had remained with the company. It would therefore be unfair to Mr Athanasiou and Mr George to order a valuation as at today's date. I shall direct that the petitioner's shares be valued as at 10 February 1984.

I am also in no doubt that the valuation ought to be made on the footing that the students which the petitioner removed to LCEE remained with the company . . . since the whole object of the exercise is that the petitioner should be bought out on the footing that the unfair prejudice had never occurred, in which event both he and the students would have remained with the company.

Finally, it is clear that the price must be fixed pro rata according to the value of the shares as a whole and not discounted: see *Re Bird Precision Bellows Ltd* [1984] Ch 419. Mr Oliver argued that this was a case where the petitioner had made a constructive election to sever his connection with the company and thus to sell his shares, but that argument falls with the findings of fact which I have already made.

The parties are agreed that the valuation should be made out of court. Having now decided the outstanding questions in dispute, I hope that it will be possible for there to be an agreed order referring the matter to a valuer.

Re Blue Arrow plc

Unfair prejudice in a public company

[1987] BCLC 585, Chancery Division

This is one of the rare s. 994 cases which involve public companies. Here the court was less willing to look beyond the memorandum and articles of association to take account of agreements or understandings between the shareholders. Thus, a shareholder was unable to complain of unfairly prejudicial conduct when she was removed from her office as a permanent president.

Facts   The petitioner was made a permanent non-executive president of the company when the company went public on the Unlisted Securities Market. She was later removed from the position.

VINELOTT J: Counsel for the petitioner (Mr Heslop QC) has put forward three grounds in support of the petition. The first is that, it is said, her right to remain as president is a class right, and in support of that submission he referred me to a decision of Scott J in *Cumbrian Newspapers Group* v *Cumberland and Westmorland Herald Newspaper and Printing Co. Ltd* [1987] Ch 1. I can see nothing in that case which supports the proposition that a right conferred on an individual by the articles of a company to remain as president until removed in general meeting, and which is unrelated to any shareholding, can, by any stretch, be described as a class right. A class right is a right attaching, in some way, to a category of the shares of the company. So far as that decision is material at all, it seems to me plainly against the submission advanced by counsel for the petitioner. The right claimed, to remain as president, falls, to my mind, quite clearly within the second of the three categories distinguished by Scott J (see [1987] Ch 1 at p. 16). The article did not confer any right on the petitioner as a member of the company. She would in fact retain the right, even if she sold all her shares; and moreover the office is not an exclusive one.

The second ground is that if the article is looked at in the light of the whole of the history, it becomes clear, it is said, that the petitioner has a legitimate expectation that she will remain president, unless and until she is removed by the machinery provided, that is by resolution of the members, and that an alteration to the articles which gives the power to the directors transgresses that legitimate expectation.

As was pointed out by Hoffmann J in *Re a Company (No 00477 of 1986)* [1986] BCLC 376, the interests of a member are not limited to his strict legal rights under the constitution of the company. There are wider equitable considerations which the court must bear in mind in considering whether a case falls within s. 459 in particular in deciding what are the legitimate expectations of a member. If I may say so, I respectfully accept that approach, but it is to my mind impossible, on the face of the allegations in the petition, to apply it here. Of course, the petitioner had a legitimate expectation that the affairs of the company would be properly conducted within the framework of its constitution. I wholly fail to understand how it can be said that the petitioner had a legitimate expectation that the articles would not be altered by special resolution in a way which enabled her office to be terminated by some different machinery. No doubt there are cases where a legitimate expectation may be inferred from arrangements outside the ambit of the formal constitution of the company, but it must be borne in mind that this is a public company, a listed company, and a large one, and that the constitution was adopted at the time when the company was first floated on the Unlisted Securities Market. Outside investors were entitled to assume that the whole of the constitution was contained in the articles, read, of course, together with the Companies Acts. There is in these circumstances no room for any legitimate expectation founded on some agreement or arrangement made between the directors and kept up their sleeves and not disclosed to those placing the shares with the public through the Unlisted Securities Market.

As regards these two grounds, therefore, I think that the petition, on its face, is so hopeless that the only right course is to strike it out.

Re Bird Precision Bellows Ltd

Valuation of shares

[1984] 3 All ER 444, [1984] Ch 419, Chancery Division; [1985] 3 All ER 523, [1986] Ch 658, Court of Appeal

The following extracts show the decision of Nourse J in the Chancery Division and Oliver LJ's endorsement of it in the Court of Appeal. Nourse J's approach in determining the basis and date for valuation has become a much-quoted view. (On valuation see also *Re London School of Electronics* extracted above, the article by Gregory and Hicks that follows and 9.5.)

Facts   *The two petitioners were minority shareholders of a small quasi-partnership company. They were removed by the controlling shareholder as directors at an extraordinary general meeting. They petitioned under CA 1980, s. 75 (now CA 2006, s. 994) for a purchase order.*

In the Chancery Division

NOURSE J: The question in this case is whether the price of shares in a small private company which were ordered to be purchased pursuant to s. 75 of the Companies Act 1980 [now CA 1985, s. 461] should be fixed pro rata according to the value of the shares as a whole or should be discounted on the ground that they constitute a minority in number....

Although both s. 210 [of the Companies Act 1948] and s. 75 are silent on the point, it is axiomatic that a price fixed by the court must be fair. While that which is fair may often be generally predicated in regard to matters of common occurrence, it can never be conclusively judged in regard to a particular case until the facts are known. The general observations which I will presently attempt in relation to a valuation of shares by the court under s. 75 are therefore subject to that important reservation.

Broadly speaking, shares in a small private company are acquired either by allotment on its incorporation or by transfer or devolution at some later date. In the first category it is a matter of common occurrence for a company to be incorporated in order to acquire an existing business or to start a new one, and in either event for it to be a vehicle for the conduct of a business carried on by two or more shareholders which they could, had they wished, have carried on in partnership together. [Often referred to as a quasi-partnership.] In the second category, irrespective of the nature of the company, it s a matter of common occurrence for a shareholder to acquire shares from another at a price which is discounted because they represent a minority holding. It seems to me that some general observations can usefully be made in regard to each of these examples....

I would expect that in a majority of cases where purchase orders are made under s. 75 in relation to quasi-partnerships the vendor is unwilling in the sense that the sale has been forced on him. Usually he will be a minority shareholder whose interests have been unfairly prejudiced by the manner in which the affairs of the company have been conducted by the majority. On the assumption that the unfair prejudice has made it no longer tolerable for him to retain his interest in the company, a sale of his shares will invariably be his only practical way out short of a winding up. In that kind of case it seems to me that it would not merely not be fair, but most unfair, that he should be bought out on the fictional basis applicable to a free election to sell his shares in accordance with the company's articles of association, or indeed on any other basis which involved a discounted price. In my judgment the correct course would be to fix the price pro rata according to the value of the shares as a whole and without any discount, as being the only fair method of compensating an unwilling vendor of the equivalent of a partnership share. Equally, if the order provided... for the purchase of the shares of the delinquent majority, it would not merely not be fair, but most unfair, that they should receive a price which involved an element of premium.

Of the other, I would expect more rare, cases in which the court might make a purchase order in relation to a quasi-partnership the arguments of counsel for the respondents require me to mention one. Suppose the case of a minority shareholder whose interests had been unfairly prejudiced by the conduct of the majority, but who had nevertheless so acted as to deserve his exclusion from the company. It is difficult to see how such a case could arise in practice, because one would expect acts and deserts of that kind to be inconsistent with the existence of the supposed conduct of the majority. Be that as it may, the consideration of that possibility has been forced on me by the agreement for the price to be determined by the court without any admission of unfairly prejudicial conduct on the part of the respondents. As will appear, counsel for the respondents submitted that the petitioners did act in such a way as to deserve their exclusion from the company. He further submitted that it would therefore be fair for them to be bought out on the basis which would have been applicable if they had made a free election to sell their shares pursuant to the articles, i.e. at a discount. Assuming at present that the respondents can establish the necessary factual basis, I think that the further submission of counsel for the respondents is correct. A shareholder who deserves his exclusion has, if you like, made a constructive election to sever his connection with the company and thus to sell his shares. . . .

Next, I must consider the example from the second category of cases in which, broadly speaking, shares in a small private company are acquired. It is not of direct relevance for present purposes, but I mention it briefly in order finally to refute the suggestion that there is any rule of universal application to questions of this kind. In the case of the shareholder who acquires shares from another at a price which is discounted because they represent a minority it is to my mind self-evident that there cannot be any universal or even a general rule that he should be bought out under s. 75 on a more favourable basis, even in a case where his predecessor has been a quasi-partner in a quasi-partnership. He might himself have acquired the shares purely for investment and played no part in the affairs of the company. In that event it might well be fair, I do not know, that he should be bought out on the same basis as he himself had bought, even though his interests had been unfairly prejudiced in the mean time. *A fortiori*, there could be no universal or even a general rule in a case where the company had never been a quasi-partnership in the first place.

In summary, there is in my judgment no rule of universal application. On the other hand, there is a general rule in a case where the company is at the material time a quasi-partnership and the purchase order is made in respect of the shares of a quasi-partner. Although I have taken the case where there has in fact been unfairly prejudicial conduct on the part of the majority as being the state of affairs most likely to result in a purchase order, I am of the opinion that the same consequences ought usually to follow in a case like the present where there has been an agreement for the price to be determined by the court without any admission as to such conduct. It seems clear to me that, even without such conduct, that is in general the fair basis of valuation in a quasi-partnership case, and that it should be applied in this case unless the respondents have established that the petitioners acted in such a way as to deserve their exclusion from the company.

In the Court of Appeal

OLIVER LJ: [Counsel for the respondents] suggests that an order made under s. 75(4) [now CA 1985, s. 461(2)] is simply an order for a purchase, without any discretion in the court to give directions which might have the effect of increasing or reducing the value of the shares in the open market, as shares in a private company. If the shares with which the purchase order is concerned are a majority holding, they are to be valued as such; if they are a minority holding, they are to be valued as such, and in his submission the court is not entitled to look behind the company and to reflect, in the order for purchase or for sale, the actual relationship between the parties. According to this approach, any agreement which has been made between the parties as to the basis on which they were to participate in the company's affairs, or as to the way in which the company's affairs were to be conducted, any contribution which the petitioner may have made to the company's success, any absence of any contribution at all by the respondent, apart from the mere fact of his shareholding, is to be ignored. The court, in other words, is to be rigidly restricted, if it is to make an order under subs. (4)(d) [now CA 1985, s. 461(2)(d)] at all, to making an order for a purchase at a market price of the holding being purchased, to be arrived at only by the ordinary valuation principles, which will take into account the proportionate size of the holding in relation to the issued capital as a whole and to the control of the company.

For my part I find myself quite unable to accept this submission. It seems to me that the whole framework of the section, and of such of the authorities as we have seen, which seem to me to support this, is to confer on the court a very wide discretion to do what is considered fair and equitable in all the circumstances of the case, in order to put right and cure for the future the unfair prejudice which the petitioner has suffered at the hands of the other shareholders of the company; and I find myself quite unable to accept that that discretion in some way stops short when it comes to the terms of the order for purchase in the manner in which the price is to be assessed.

NOTES

1. The court could interfere to rectify a mistake made by a valuer if the fault did not derive from a question of judgment or opinion but from the instructions of the parties: see *Macro v Thompson (No. 2)* [1997] 1 BCLC 626, CA.

2. Where the competent experts on each side have taken different approaches in their expert evidence on the valuation of shares, it would be inappropriate to use the strike-out jurisdiction to reject the expert evidence of one as incredible without a full hearing (*Guinness Peat Group plc v British Land Co. plc* [1999] BCC 536, CA).

3. Where preferential shareholders are ordered to sell their shares to the petitioner, the fair price may be subject to a discount as they do not undertake anywhere near as much risk as the ordinary shareholders (*Re Planet Organic Ltd* [2000] 1 BCLC 366).

Andrew Hicks with Alan Gregory, 'Valuation of shares: a legal and accounting conundrum'

[1995] JBL 56

Minority unfair prejudice actions   Under s. 459 of the Companies Act 1985 a member may petition the court for an order on the ground that the petitioner's interests have been, are being or will be unfairly prejudiced by the conduct of the company's affairs. A considerable body of case law has built up on what constitutes unfairly prejudicial conduct. Under s. 461 the court may make such order as it thinks fit for giving relief including the purchase of the shares of any member of the company by other members or by the company itself. Here the crucial question for the courts and for the parties negotiating a buy-out in the shadow of the courts is the basis and amount of valuation.

Two principal issues present themselves.[1] First, where as is generally the case, the petitioner's interest to be valued and purchased is a minority holding, is a discounted or a pro rata valuation to apply? Secondly, given that the unfairly prejudicial conduct has probably depressed the value of the shares,[2] at what times are the shares to be valued or what assumptions are to be made to take account of such depreciation.

The first principle stated by the Court of Appeal in *Re Bird Precision Bellows Ltd* [1986] Ch 658 is that the court has 'a very wide discretion to do what is considered fair and equitable in all the circumstances of the case, in order to put right and cure for the future the unfair prejudice which the petitioner has suffered' (at p. 669). Such an approach tends to militate against establishing strict principles for valuation as the basis of a fair value may vary from case to case.

However, on a valuation by the court Nourse J at first instance [in *Re Bird Precision Bellows Ltd* [1984] Ch 419] stated (at p. 436A) that the question of whether a discount is applicable is a matter of law for the court. One of the relevant circumstances is whether or not the company is a 'quasi-partnership',[3] and the petitioner a quasi-partner. Where the petitioner was not a quasi-partner, there is no rule of universal application. Where a shareholder buys shares from another shareholder (even from a quasi-partner) at a discounted price being a minority interest, and he bought

---

1 Other issues also of course arise. For example in a case where a petitioner went into a company on the understanding that he would be employed and paid a salary and that would be the principal way in which he would share in its profitability, a fair value for his shares must reflect the fact that this expectation has been frustrated: *Re a Company (No. 007623 of 1984)* [1986] BCLC 362 at p. 369.

2 It is possible, however, to prove unfair prejudice without showing that the conduct alleged has diminished the value of the shares. See *Re Elgindata Ltd* [1991] BCLC 959.

3 Defined in *Ebrahimi v Westbourne Galleries Ltd* [1973] AC 360, HL, as a company formed or continued on the basis of a personal relationship, including mutual confidence, it being agreed that all or some of the shareholders shall participate in the management of the business, and there being restrictions on the transfer of the member's interest in the company.

for investment only,[4] then there is no rule that he should be bought out on a pro rata basis. The amount of the discount on the minority interest is then a question of valuation. Even more will this apply if the company was not a quasi-partnership. However, Oliver LJ in the Court of Appeal commented that it would be an odd result if the valuation led to the petitioner receiving less than he would be entitled to on a sale under the articles [1986] Ch 658 at pp. 675–6. As pre-emption clauses often stipulate for valuation on a pro rata basis, a court might choose a pro rata valuation in such an instance. It would be a strange policy if, having unfairly treated a minority, the majority were able to acquire his shares for less than on a buy-out under the articles.[5]

Where the company is a quasi-partnership Nourse J said that in most cases the petitioner is an unwilling seller in the sense that the sale has been forced upon him. In such a case it would be unfair on the petitioner to value the shares on a discounted basis ([1984] Ch 419 at p. 430). A minority shareholder should be given a pro rata valuation as being the only fair way of compensating an unwilling vendor of a partnership share. If it were the delinquent majority whose shares were to be bought out by the minority,[6] it would equally be unfair if the shares were to be valued at a premium.

If a minority shareholder whose interests were unfairly prejudiced nevertheless deserved to be excluded,[7] or if a quasi-partner were excluded from management, but then for some years did not petition for an order,[8] then a discounted valuation may be appropriate.

On the other hand it has to be noted that where an expert valuer certifies a valuation under pre-emption rights in the articles or a shareholders' agreement it may be left to him to decide whether to apply a discount or not. He may for example take account of the fact that the majority shareholder ordered to buy out the minority is an involuntary buyer deriving no immediate benefit from the purchase. If the expert valuer certifies a figure without giving any reasons it will be impossible to know the basis on which the valuation was made, and so it will not be possible to challenge the valuation on appeal.[9] Even where reasons are given as *Dean v Prince* [1954] Ch 409 indicates, an honest valuation is hard to overturn.

The second principal issue is that, given that the unfairly prejudicial conduct may have depreciated the value of the shares, at what date or on what assumptions should the valuation be made? First, the court has a broad discretion to fix a price that is fair. In the 'oppression' case of *Scottish Co-operative Wholesale Society Ltd* v *Meyer* [1959] AC 324 under s. 210 of the Companies Act 1948, the House of Lords stated the fair price to be the value of the shares at the date of the petition assuming there to have been no oppression. If impropriety on the part of the respondent has occurred, such as by misfeasance or misappropriation, a valuer may write back into the accounts any sums he considers to have been improperly disbursed.[10] Where the valuation is not on an assets basis, the company's earnings or distributable profits may be notionally adjusted for example to offset the loss caused by the majority paying themselves excessive salaries.[11]

4 A recent example of this is *Re Elgindata Ltd* [1991] BCLC 959.

5 That it is an appropriate policy to provide disincentives to majority shareholders to unfairly prejudice the interests of minorities and to encourage them to make out of court offers is stressed in the articles by Prentice in (1986) 102 LQR 174 and (1988) Oxford J Legal Stud 55 at p. 82.

6 An unlikely event; see *Re a Company (No. 006834 of 1988)* [1989] BCLC 365.

7 In the unlikely event of a minority shareholder proving unfair prejudice but nonetheless deserving his exclusion from the company, then a discount may be appropriate; see Nourse J [1984] Ch 419 at p. 431. It has also been held in *Howie* v *Crawford* [1990] BCC 330 that an arbitrator valuing shares under a pre-emption agreement at a 'fair market price' was wrong in applying no discount. The *market* price normally though not invariably depends on the proportion of shares to be sold. In *Re Castleburn Ltd* (1989) 5 BCC 652 it was held that on valuations under articles requiring a certificate of fair value on a sale by a 'willing vendor to a willing purchaser' one would expect a discount for a minority holding. The precise wording of pre-emption agreements therefore has to be taken carefully into account.

8 *Re DR Chemicals Ltd* (1988) 5 BCC 39.

9 *Re a Company (No. 006834 of 1988)* [1989] BCLC 365; *Re Castleburn Ltd* (1989) 5 BCC 652.

10 *Re a Company (No. 003843 of 1986)* [1987] BCLC 562; *Re a Company (No. 006834 of 1988)* [1989] BCLC 365.

11 See Prentice (1988) Oxford J Legal Stud 55 at p. 84 citing *Sandford* v *Sandford Courier Service Pty Ltd* (1987) 11 ACLR 373.

The matter however remains complex and depends on what is fair in the circumstances. In *Re Cumana Ltd* [1986] BCLC 430 the Court of Appeal said (at p. 436) that if the majority shareholder deliberately took steps to depreciate the value of the shares in anticipation of a petition being presented, it would be permissible to value the shares at a date before such action was taken. In the event the court held that the shares should be valued on evidence of the company's 'maintainable profits' at the date of the petition. This is the date on which a petitioner elects to treat the unfair conduct as destroying the basis on which he agreed to be a shareholder and becomes entitled to the proceeds of sale. In the *Cumana* case the shares had depreciated between the date of the petition and of judgment. However valuation on the petition date caused no injustice to the majority who could have and perhaps should have offered to acquire the petitioner's shares at the time his relationship with them broke down and he left the company.[12]

Where the value of the shares increases after the date of the petition it is possible that a fair valuation should be at the date of judgment or of the valuation itself. Clearly any contribution made by the petitioner which is only reflected in the share valuation after the date of the petition should enure to the benefit of the petitioner. However the petitioner should not be entitled to benefit to the extent that this increase in value is attributable to the efforts of the majority.[13]

It is therefore difficult to generalise as to the date for valuation. Nourse J in *Re London School of Electronics Ltd* [1986] Ch 211 suggested (at p. 224) that as a general rule the date of the order or the actual valuation was more appropriate than the date of the petition or the unfair prejudice itself. However, he said, the overriding principle of fairness would by exceptions reduce it to no rule at all. In the *London School of Electronics Ltd* case Nourse J in fact ordered valuation at the date of the petition. In some cases fairness may dictate that the valuation date relate back to an earlier date such as the exclusion of the petitioner from the company.[14] The options for the court in pursuit of fairness are therefore many. Valuation may thus be at an early time prior to the unfairly prejudicial conduct, the time of exclusion from the company, the date of the petition or of judgment or of the actual valuation. Specific assumptions may also be made, such as that the unfairly prejudicial conduct depreciating the value of the shares did not occur. Each case has to be taken on its facts and to attempt to generalise as to the basis for a valuation date is therefore not a useful exercise.

13.2.5 Background to legislative changes under CA 2006

The law on minority shareholders' protection prior to CA 2006 was weak and unsatisfactory. The Law Commission commented that the rule in *Foss* v *Harbottle* and its exceptions were 'complex and obscure', whilst proceedings for unfair prejudice often involved 'complex factual investigation and resulted in costly and cumbersome litigation, which was particularly detrimental to smaller companies' (e.g., in *Re Elgindata Ltd* [1991] BCLC 959 the hearing lasted 43 days, costs totalled £320,000 and the shares, originally purchased for £40,000 were finally valued at only £24,600). The readings that follow explain the difficulties in common law derivative actions and the proposals of the Law Commission and the position taken by the Steering Group. Not all the proposals by the Law Commission and the Steering Group were enacted into law in the end, as we have seen above.

12 See comments of Prentice, op. cit. (note 11) at p. 86.

13 See *Re London School of Electronics Ltd* [1986] Ch 211. This point is not uncontroversial. A minority shareholder usually expects to benefit from the efforts of the majority and would have taken that benefit if he had not been forced to sell out.

14 See e.g. *Re OC (Transport Services) Ltd* [1984] BCLC 251 at p. 258, and *Re London School of Electronics Ltd*. See also dicta of Vinelott J in *Re a Company (No. 002567 of 1982)* [1983] 1 WLR 927 at p. 937D.

Prudential Assurance Co. Ltd v *Newman Industries Ltd (No. 2)*

Have I got a right to sue?

[1980] 2 All ER 841, [1981] Ch 257, Chancery Division;

[1982] 1 All ER 354, [1982] Ch 204, Court of Appeal

This was an extremely lengthy and expensive trial on the preliminary procedural issue of whether a minority shareholder had *locus standi* to bring a derivative action. The trial itself lasted for almost 80 days costing three-quarters of a million pounds. The Court of Appeal expressed concern at the length of the trial and the mounting costs in such proceedings from which nobody really benefited.

Facts   *The plaintiff was a large institutional investor which owned 3 per cent of the shares in Newman. It sought to bring a derivative action against two directors of Newman, Bartlett and Laughton for allegedly defrauding Newman of over £440,000. Bartlett and Laughton were not majority shareholders and therefore had no de iure voting control. The transaction by which Bartlett and Laughton had allegedly defrauded the company had been approved by the company in general meeting. The plaintiff claimed that the shareholders in general meeting had been misled into approving the transaction.*

In the Chancery Division

VINELOTT J:

Fraud

[Having discussed Lord Davey's dicta in *Burland* v *Earle* [1902] AC 83 and other authorities including *Pavlides* v *Jensen* [1956] Ch 565, *Daniels* v *Daniels* [1978] Ch 406, his lordship continued:]

   Thus the authorities show that the exception applies not only where the allegation is that directors who control a company have improperly appropriated to themselves money, property or advantages which belong to the company or, in breach of their duty to the company, have diverted business to themselves which ought to have been given to the company, but more generally where it is alleged that directors though acting 'in the belief that they were doing nothing wrong' (per Lord Lindley MR in *Alexander* v *Automatic Telephone Co.* [1900] 2 Ch 56 at p. 65) are guilty of a breach of duty to the company (including their duty to exercise proper care) and as a result of that breach obtain some benefit. In the latter case it must be unnecessary to allege and prove that the directors in breaking their duty to the company acted with a view to benefiting themselves at the expense of the company; for such an allegation would be an allegation of misappropriation of the company's property. On the other hand, the exception does not apply if all that is alleged is that directors who control a company are liable to the company for damages for negligence it not being shown that the transaction was one in which they were interested or that they have in fact obtained any benefit from it. It is not easy to see precisely where the line between these cases is to be drawn. For instance, is an action to be allowed to proceed if the allegation is that the controlling director is liable to the company for damages for negligence and that as a result of his negligence a benefit has been obtained by his wife or a friend or by a company in which he has a substantial shareholding? In *Pavlides* v *Jensen* would it have been enough if, in addition to the allegation of negligence, it had been alleged that Portland Tunnel had a substantial shareholding in the Cyprus company and therefore benefited indirectly? It is also not easy to see what principle underlies the distinction. Whether the claim is for property improperly withheld or for damages for negligence or breach of fiduciary duty and, in the latter case, whether those controlling the company have or have not obtained some benefit, the reason for the exception is the same, namely that the claim is brought against persons whose interests conflict with the interest of the company. It may be said, in a perfectly intelligible sense, to be a fraud on the minority that those against whom the claim would be brought are in a position to procure, and, if the derivative claim is not brought, will procure that the company's claim, however strong it may appear to be, will not be enforced. Counsel for Mr Bartlett, very frankly, admitted that he could not put forward any valid ground of distinction between a case where the claim by the company is of a proprietary nature and one where it is for damages only, nor between a claim for damages for negligence where the loss to the company is matched by a benefit to those in control and a claim for damages for negligence where the loss to the company is either not matched by any benefit to anybody or is not matched by a benefit to those in control. However, counsel for Mr Bartlett also conceded that the claim by the Prudential is a claim founded on acts of a 'fraudulent character', whatever meaning is attributed to those words. I have endeavoured to state the principle which underlies the first limb of the exception, because the second limb cannot be construed in isolation from it, but it is unnecessary for me to decide precisely where the boundary limiting the category of cases which permit of a minority shareholders' action is to be drawn and it would be wrong for me to attempt to do so.

Control The central issue in this case is whether a derivative action can be brought against defendants who do not have voting control of the company on whose behalf the derivative claim is brought and, if it can, in precisely what circumstances such a claim will be allowed to proceed.

[His lordship referred to, *inter alia, Atwool* v *Merryweather* (1867) LR 5 Eq 464 n, *Edwards* v *Halliwell* [1950] 2 All ER 1064, *Russell* v *Wakefield Waterworks Co.* (1875) LR 20 Eq 474 and continued:]

If the rule and the exception cannot be confined within the rigid formulation expressed in terms of voting control by the persons against whom relief is sought on behalf of the company, then the question whether a given case falls within the exception can only be answered by reference to the principle which underlies the rule and the exception to it. Counsel for Mr Bartlett submitted, I think rightly, that the principle which underlies the rule is that it would be wrong to allow a minority shareholder to bring proceedings joining the company as defendant and claiming against other defendants relief on behalf of the company for a wrong alleged to have been done to it if the majority of the members of the company take the view that it is not in the interests of the company that the proceedings should be pursued. Indeed, it would be so plainly wrong that it might be said that, in a broad sense, the court would have no jurisdiction to allow the wishes of the minority to override the wishes of the majority in that way. The principle which underlies the exception to the rule is that in ascertaining the view of the majority whether it is in the interests of the company that the claim be pursued, the court will disregard votes cast or capable of being cast by shareholders who have an interest which directly conflicts with the interests of the company. Those are general principles of substantive law and are not mere rules of procedure. But in any derivative action the plaintiff must allege in his statement of claim some ground which, if established at the trial, would bring the case within the exception and justify an order that the company recover damages or property from the other defendants: see *Birch* v *Sullivan* [1957] 1 WLR 1247. Thus the question whether an action falls within the exception will normally be tested at an early stage. So, if the defendants against whom relief is sought on behalf of the company control the majority of votes the action will be allowed to proceed whether a resolution that no action should be brought by the company has been passed or not; so also, if the persons against whom relief is sought do not control a majority of the votes but it is shown that a resolution has been passed and passed only by the use of their votes. By contrast if a resolution has been passed that no proceedings should be started by the company or if the matter has not been put to the shareholders in general meeting and if no good reason is advanced in the statement of claim why the wishes of the majority should not be given effect the action will be struck out or, possibly, in the latter case, stood over while a general meeting is called (as in *East Pant Du United Lead Mining Co. Ltd* v *Merryweather* (1864) Hem & M 254).

But there are an infinite variety of possible circumstances which fall within these two extremes. If shareholders having a majority of votes in general meeting are nominees the court will look behind the register to the beneficial owners to see whether they are the persons against whom relief is sought: see *Pavlides* v *Jensen* [1956] Ch 565 at p. 577. There seems no good reason why the court should not have regard to any other circumstances which show that the majority cannot be relied on to determine in a disinterested way whether it is truly in the interests of the company that proceedings should be brought. For instance, some shareholders able to exercise decisive votes may have been offered an inducement to vote in favour of the wrongdoers. . . . Moreover, today it would be uncommon for any large number of shareholders to attend and vote in person at a general meeting of a large public company and (an instance suggested by counsel for Mr Bartlett) directors alleged to be liable to the company might be able to determine the outcome of a resolution in general meeting in their own favour by the use of proxy votes. Similarly, most modern articles confide to the directors the management of the business of the company (see e.g., art. 80 of Table A of sch. 1 to the Companies Act 1948 [art. 70 of the 1985 version of Table A]) and it is possible that an article in these terms vests in the directors a discretion whether proceedings should be commenced by the company which cannot be overridden by resolution in general meeting (see *Buckley on the Companies Acts*, 13th ed. (1957), p. 860, and *John Shaw & Sons (Salford) Ltd* v *Shaw* [1935] 2 KB 113 at p. 134, where an earlier passage in Buckley (11th ed. (1930), p. 723) in the same terms was approved in the Court of Appeal). If directors who have an interest direct or indirect in the question whether proceedings should be commenced refuse to submit that question to the shareholders in general meeting the majority could in theory remove the directors but might only be able to ensure that the question whether proceedings should be commenced is properly considered by a disinterested board by taking that extreme step, which, in turn, they might consider would involve damage to the company greater than any benefits to be derived from the action against the directors. Counsel for Mr Bartlett at the end of his very clear and helpful argument summarised the principle that underlies the exception to the rule in these terms: it applies wherever the persons against whom the action is sought to be brought on behalf of the company are shown to be able 'by any means of manipulation of their position in the company' to ensure that the action is not brought by the company. That broad formulation I accept, provided that the means of manipulation of the defendant's position in the company are not too narrowly defined.

In the Court of Appeal

CUMMING-BRUCE, TEMPLEMAN and BRIGHTMAN LJJ: It is commonly said that an exception to the rule in *Foss* v *Harbottle* arises if the corporation is 'controlled' by persons implicated in the fraud complained of, who will not permit the name of the company to be used as plaintiffs in the suit: see *Russell* v *Wakefield Waterworks Co.* (1875) LR 20 Eq 474 at p. 482. But this proposition leaves two questions at large. First, what is meant by 'control', which embraces a broad spectrum extending from an overall absolute majority of votes at one end to a majority of votes at the other end made up of those likely to be cast by the delinquent himself plus those voting with him as a result of influence or apathy. Second, what course is to be taken by the court if, as happened in *Foss* v *Harbottle*, in the *East Pant Du* case and in the instant case, but did *not* happen in *Atwool* v *Merryweather*, the court is confronted by a motion on the part of the delinquent or by the company seeking to strike out the action? For at the time of the application the existence of the fraud is unproved. It is at this point that a dilemma emerges. If, on such an application, the plaintiff can require the court to assume as a fact every allegation in the statement of claim, as in a true demurrer, the plaintiff will frequently be able to outmanoeuvre the primary purpose of the rule in *Foss* v *Harbottle* by alleging fraud and 'control' by the fraudster. If on the other hand the plaintiff has to prove fraud and 'control' before he can establish his title to prosecute his action, then the action may need to be fought to a conclusion before the court can decide whether or not the plaintiff should be permitted to prosecute it. In the latter case the purpose of the rule in *Foss* v *Harbottle* disappears. Either the fraud has not been proved, so *cadit quaestio*; or the fraud has been proved and the delinquent is accountable unless there is a valid decision of the board or a valid decision of the company in general meeting, reached without impropriety or unfairness, to condone the fraud. . . .

. . . we have no doubt whatever that the judge erred in dismissing the summons of 10 May 1979. He ought to have determined as a preliminary issue whether the plaintiffs were entitled to sue on behalf of Newman by bringing a derivative action. It cannot have been right to have subjected the company to a 30-day action (as it was then estimated to be) in order to enable him to decide whether the plaintiffs were entitled in law to subject the company to a 30-day action. Such an approach defeats the whole purpose of the rule in *Foss* v *Harbottle* and sanctions the very mischief that the rule is designed to prevent. By the time a derivative action is concluded, the rule in *Foss* v *Harbottle* can have little, if any, role to play. Either the wrong is proved, thereby establishing conclusively the rights of the company, or the wrong is not proved, so *cadit quaestio*. In the present case a board, of which all the directors save one were disinterested, with the benefit of the Schroder–Harman report, had reached the conclusion before the start of the action that the prosecution of the action was likely to do more harm than good. That might prove a sound or an unsound assessment, but it was the commercial assessment of an apparently independent board. Obviously the board would not have expected at that stage to be as well-informed about the affairs of the company as it might be after 36 days of evidence in court and an intense examination of some 60 files of documents. But the board clearly doubted whether there were sufficient reasons for supposing that the company would at the end of the day be in a position to count its blessings, and clearly feared, as counsel said, that it might be killed by kindness. Whether in the events which have happened Newman (more exactly the disinterested body of shareholders) will feel that it has all been well worth while, or must lick their wounds and render no thanks to those who have interfered in their affairs, is not a question which we can answer. But we think it is within the bounds of possibility that, if the preliminary issue had been argued, a judge might have reached the considered view that the prosecution of this great action should be left to the decision of the board or of a specially convened meeting of the shareholders, albeit less well informed than a judge after a 72-day action.

So much for the summons of 10 May. The second observation which we wish to make is merely a comment on the judge's decision that there is an exception to the rule in *Foss* v *Harbottle* whenever the justice of the case so requires. We are not convinced that this is a practical test, particularly if it involves a full-dress trial before the test is applied. On the other hand we do not think that the right to bring a derivative action should be decided as a preliminary issue on the hypothesis that all the allegations in the statement of claim of 'fraud' and 'control' are facts, as they would be on the trial of a preliminary point of law. In our view, whatever may be the properly defined boundaries of the exception to the rule, the plaintiff ought at least to be required before proceeding with his action to establish a prima facie case (i) that the company is entitled to the relief claimed and (ii) that the action falls within the proper boundaries of the exception to the rule in *Foss* v *Harbottle*. On the latter issue it may well be right for the judge trying the preliminary issue to grant a sufficient adjournment to enable a meeting of shareholders to be convened by the board, so that he can reach a conclusion in the light of the conduct of, and proceedings at, that meeting. . . .

The rule in *Foss* v *Harbottle* is founded on principle but it also operates fairly by preserving the rights of the majority. We were invited to give judicial approval to the public spirit of the plaintiffs who, it was said, are pioneering a method of controlling companies in the public interest without involving regulation by a statutory body. In our view the voluntary regulation of companies is a matter for the City. The compulsory regulation of companies is a matter for Parliament. We decline to draw general conclusions from the exceptional circumstances of the present case. But the results of the present action give food for thought. The judge thought it possible that Newman had suffered damage amounting to £440,000 by the fraud of Mr Bartlett and Mr Laughton. Counsel for Newman submitted in the court below that damage to Newman by the prosecution of the action exceeded the benefits liable to be derived from the action. The costs of the proceedings at the end of the trial were said in newspaper reports to be in the region of £¾m. . . .

If this appeal succeeds the burden of the costs on the Prudential will be enormous. The innocent shareholders of Newman . . . and the Prudential may well wonder, whether this appeal succeeds or not, if there is not something to be said after all for the old-fashioned rule in *Foss* v *Harbottle*.

Law Commission, *Shareholder Remedies*
(Law Com. No. 246)
(London: Stationery Office, 1997)

Part I Introduction
Problems identified in the consultation paper

1.4 In the consultation paper we identified two main problems. The first is the obscurity and complexity of the law relating to the ability of a shareholder to bring proceedings on behalf of his company. He may wish to do so to enforce liability for a breach by one of the directors of his duties to the company. Generally it is for the company itself, acting in accordance with the will of the majority of its members, to bring any such proceedings. This is as a result of principles commonly known as the rule in *Foss* v *Harbottle*. However, if the wrongdoing director(s) control the majority of votes they may prevent legal proceedings being brought. There are therefore exceptions to the rule which enable a minority shareholder to bring an action to enforce the company's rights. But our provisional view was that the law relating to these exceptions is rigid, old-fashioned and unclear. We pointed out that it is inaccessible save to lawyers specialising in this field because, to obtain a proper understanding of it, it is necessary to examine numerous reported cases decided over a period of 150 years. We also explained that the procedure is lengthy and costly, involving a preliminary stage which in one case took 18 days of court time to resolve.

1.5 The second main problem which we identified in the consultation paper relates to the efficiency and cost of the remedy which is most widely used by minority shareholders to obtain some personal remedy in the event of unsatisfactory conduct of a company's business. This is the remedy for unfairly prejudicial conduct contained in ss. 459–461 of the Companies Act 1985. Although the remedy can be used in companies of any size and for unfairly prejudicial conduct of any kind, we pointed out that it is often used where there is a breakdown in relations between the owner-managers of small private companies and one of them is prevented from taking part in management. The dissatisfied shareholder can obtain a variety of types of relief but the most popular is a court order requiring the majority shareholder(s) to purchase his shares. As at 3 August 1997, there were some 1,080,671 private companies in Great Britain. Our statistical survey of petitions filed under s. 459 at the High Court in London has indicated that 97% of petitions related to private companies and 93% of petitions related to companies with 10 or fewer members. 76% of petitions involved companies where all or most of the shareholders were involved in the management, and 64% of petitions included an allegation of exclusion from management.

1.6 Our provisional view was that proceedings under s. 459 are costly and cumbersome. Unfair prejudice cases which go to trial often last weeks rather than days, and the costs of the litigation can be substantial. There is also a significant cost on the taxpayer.

1.7 We expressed the view that small owner-managed companies are particularly affected by this problem. This is because the case law on s. 459 enables members of those types of companies to resort to this remedy more easily than members of other types of companies; and because the consequent delays and lost management time are particularly detrimental to such companies. While the dispute between the shareholders is continuing, the companies' business can be brought to a standstill.

1.8 A third problem which we examined in the consultation paper is the enforcement of shareholders' contractual rights under the articles of association. This includes the extent to which a shareholder can insist on the affairs of the company being conducted in accordance with the articles of association. However, our provisional view was that no hardship was being caused by any difficulty in identifying personal rights conferred by the articles.

Guiding principles

1.9 In the consultation paper we set out six guiding principles for our proposals in relation to the reform of the law and procedure relating to shareholder remedies. These were as follows:

(i) *Proper plaintiff*
   Normally the company should be the only party entitled to enforce a cause of action belonging to it. Accordingly, a member should be able to maintain proceedings about wrongs done to the company only in exceptional circumstances.

(ii) *Internal management*
   An individual member should not be able to pursue proceedings on behalf of a company about matters of internal management, that is, matters which the majority are entitled to regulate by ordinary resolution.

(iii) *Commercial decisions*
   The court should continue to have regard to the decision of the directors on commercial matters if the decision was made in good faith, on proper information and in the light of the relevant considerations, and appears to be a reasonable decision for the directors to have taken. In those circumstances the court should not substitute its own judgment for that of the directors.

(iv) Sanctity of contract

A member is taken to have agreed to the terms of the memorandum and articles of association when he became a member, whether or not he appreciated what they meant at the time. The law should continue to treat him as so bound unless he shows that the parties have come to some other agreement or understanding which is not reflected in the articles or memorandum. Failure to do so will create unacceptable commercial uncertainty. The corollary of this is that the best protection for a shareholder is appropriate protection in the articles themselves.

(v) Freedom from unnecessary shareholder interference

Shareholders should not be able to involve the company in litigation without good cause, or where they intend to cause the company or the other shareholders embarrassment or harm rather than genuinely pursue the relief claimed. Otherwise the company may be 'killed by kindness', or waste money and management time in dealing with unwarranted proceedings. The importance of this principle increases if the circumstances in which the individual shareholders can bring derivative actions are enlarged. Nuisance or other litigation of this nature has to be identified on a case by case basis. This means that the requisite control has to be exercised by the courts, with increased powers if necessary.

(vi) Efficiency and cost-effectiveness

All shareholder remedies should be made as efficient and cost effective as can be achieved in the circumstances. This is largely a matter for the courts and the report prepared by Lord Woolf on the civil justice system in England and Wales, but it has to be considered whether any additional powers are needed in the case of shareholder litigation.

1.10 We went on to say that we provisionally considered that all save the first two of these principles were applicable to all kinds of shareholder remedies. The first two were relevant only to derivative actions. The fifth had only limited relevance to proceedings under s. 459, since, in general, such proceedings do not require the company to take an active role (although, in small owner-managed companies, s. 459 proceedings may well result in lost management time). However, if a member seeks a winding up order as an alternative to relief under s. 459 in circumstances in which this is unjustified, then the relevance of the fifth principle was increased.

1.11 Applying these principles, we reached three basic provisional conclusions. The first of these was that, within proper bounds, the rule in *Foss* v *Harbottle* should be replaced by a simpler and more modern procedure if a satisfactory procedure could be devised. The second was that the court must have all necessary powers to streamline minority shareholder litigation so that it is less costly and complicated. The third was that we should provide a 'self-help' remedy (or range of remedies) to avoid the need for shareholders to resort to the court to resolve disputes.

1.12 There was virtually unanimous support for these principles from those who commented on consultation. (Indeed, perhaps not surprisingly, consultees were unanimous in approving the sixth principle.) In the light of this clear expression of opinion we have applied these principles in framing our recommendations in this report. Thus a key feature of the new structure for shareholder remedies recommended in this report is strong judicial control. In some contexts, the control consists of the exercise of a discretion (or residual discretion) conferred by procedural rules or statute which for good reason has to be open-textured to deal with the variety of cases that come within it. In other contexts in the field of shareholder remedies, such as the derivative action, we have so far as we can specifically pointed the court to the relevant considerations which are derived from the guiding principles as set out above. One of the advantages in controlling the derivative action by a rule of court is that the form of the rule can be strengthened, extended or clarified if that proves necessary to achieve the policy behind the guiding principles. Again, in the light of this strong expression of opinion, we have it in mind that, in so far as the court is free to decide how to exercise its control over shareholder actions, it too would apply the same policy.

Provisional recommendations

1.13 In the light of the principles and conclusions set out above, we proposed three main approaches in the consultation paper to deal with the problems identified. First, we proposed that there should be a new derivative action governed by rules of court which would replace the main exception to the rule in *Foss* v *Harbottle*. More modern, flexible and accessible criteria for leave to bring a derivative action would replace the current 'fraud on the minority' exception. It was suggested that not only would this be desirable in itself, in simplifying and modernising the derivative action, but it may also encourage members to bring this claim rather than the wide-ranging proceedings under s. 459 in appropriate cases. The proposal for a new derivative action is also in line with international developments, notably in Australia, Canada, Hong Kong, Japan, South Africa and New Zealand.

1.14 Secondly, we proposed that the courts should be given all necessary powers to streamline shareholder litigation so that it is less costly and complicated. A range of case management techniques was put forward. Some of these involved new powers drawn from the reforms recommended in the Woolf Report; others involved greater use of existing powers. Although this approach is clearly relevant to all shareholder proceedings, it is in dealing with the often cumbersome and factually complex claims which are brought under s. 459 that we considered that effective case management would be of particular benefit.

1.15 One option which we canvassed to assist in streamlining shareholder litigation (although no provisional recommendation was made) was the introduction of a new remedy for small owner-managed companies. This would be directed at the situation where a shareholder entitled to management participation is wrongly excluded, and provide a more focused alternative to proceedings under s. 459.

1.16 Thirdly, we proposed a 'self-help' approach which would seek to avoid the need to bring legal proceedings at all. Three draft regulations were set out in the consultation paper which we suggested could be inserted into Table A: a shareholders' exit article for smaller private companies; an arbitration article; and a valuation procedure article.

1.17 A number of other suggestions for reform were also canvassed.

Response to consultation and summary of main recommendations

1.18 We received 109 responses to the consultation paper. The vast majority of these agreed with our identification of the two main problems, and our approach to reform. In particular, there was widespread support for the increased use of effective case management techniques to deal with the length and cost of proceedings under s. 459, and the introduction of new articles of association to try to avoid disputes arising which have to be brought before the courts.

1.19 The proposals for a new unfair prejudice remedy for smaller companies received a mixed response and, as explained below, we do not favour the introduction of such a remedy. However, we do recommend the introduction into ss. 459–461 of presumptions that, in certain circumstances, there has been unfairly prejudicial conduct and that, where a purchase order is made, the shares should be valued on a pro rata basis. Although this is a rather different approach, we consider that it can achieve much the same as the proposed new remedy without some of the disadvantages.

1.20 A number of other reforms canvassed in respect of proceedings under s. 459 received support from respondents, notably proposals for a limitation period and for the addition of winding up to the remedies available to the court on a finding of. unfairly prejudicial conduct.

1.21 The vast majority of respondents agreed that the operation of the rule in *Foss* v *Harbottle* is unsatisfactory. Some concerns were expressed about the proposals for a new derivative action, and in particular whether they were really necessary when derivative actions are brought so rarely in practice. Nevertheless, for the reasons given below, we still consider that it would be desirable for a new derivative procedure to be introduced along the lines of the provisional recommendations. However, in the light of the responses received, we do recommend some changes to the proposals put forward in the consultation paper.

1.22 Respondents agreed with the provisional view that no hardship is being caused by difficulties in identifying personal rights conferred by the articles and we maintain our view that no reform is necessary in this respect.

1.23 Accordingly, our main final recommendations are as follows:

(i)   the problems of the excessive length and cost of many proceedings brought under s. 459 should be dealt with primarily by active case management by the courts;

(ii) there should be presumptions in proceedings under s. 459 that in certain circumstances (a) conduct will be presumed to be unfairly prejudicial, and (b) where the court grants a purchase order in favour of the petitioner the shares will be valued on a pro rata basis;

(iii) a number of other amendments should be made to proceedings under s. 459, notably that there should be a limitation period in respect of claims under the section and that winding up should be added to the remedies available;

(iv) a draft regulation should be included in Table A to encourage parties to sort out areas of potential dispute at the outset so as to avoid the need to bring legal proceedings;

(v)   there should be a new derivative procedure with more modem, flexible and accessible criteria for determining whether a shareholder should be able to pursue the action;

(vi) there is no need for reform in relation to the enforcement of the rights of shareholders under the articles of association....

Part 3 A new additional unfair prejudice remedy for smaller companies

3.27 Under [proposals based on suggestions made by respondents to the consultation paper] ss. 459–461 would be amended to raise presumptions that, in certain circumstances: (a) unless the contrary is shown, the affairs of the company have been conducted in a manner which is unfairly prejudicial to the petitioner; and (b) where the court orders his shares to be bought out, the appropriate order (unless the court otherwise orders) is that the shares should be valued on a pro rata basis....the main feature of the presumptions is that the petitioner has been excluded from the management of the company.

3.28 This approach has the advantages of providing some degree of certainty for the parties on the position which the court is likely to take....It should also mean that cases can be dealt with more quickly when proceedings are in fact issued. For example, assuming the relevant circumstances are made out, the respondent will have to show good reason why the presumptions should not apply, and this will limit the factual allegations which the court will have to consider. Alternatively, if the respondent has made (or makes during the course of the proceedings) a fair offer for the purchase of the petitioner's shares without a discount, then save in exceptional circumstances (and subject to the question of costs), the petition should be dismissed.

3.29 On the other hand, this proposal will allow the court the flexibility, in an appropriate case, to find, for example, that the petitioner's exclusion from management was not in fact unfair, or that the appropriate basis on which the petitioner's shares should be valued for a purchase order is on a discounted or some other basis. Also, this approach will not involve the introduction of a new remedy, and so will not give rise to the problem [that litigants might choose to pursue two remedies simultaneously].

3.30 Accordingly, we recommend that there should be legislative provision for presumptions in proceedings under ss. 459–461 that, in certain circumstances, (a) where a shareholder has been excluded from participation in the management of the company, the conduct will be presumed to be unfairly prejudicial by reason of the exclusion; and (b), if the presumption is not rebutted and the court is satisfied that it ought to order a buy-out of the petitioner's shares, it should do so on a pro rata basis.

Part 6 A new derivative action

Introduction

6.1 In this part we are concerned with the law relating to the ability of a shareholder to bring proceedings to enforce a cause of action vested in the company (a derivative action). We explained in the consultation paper that there were two related principles which restrict a member's ability to bring such proceedings. The first is the majority rule principle developed as a result of the court's historical reluctance to become involved in disputes over the internal management of business ventures. The second is the proper plaintiff principle which has been described as '…the elementary principle that A cannot, as a general rule, bring an action against B to recover damages or secure other relief on behalf of C for an injury done by B to C'. As a company is a separate legal entity, it is the proper plaintiff where it has suffered injury. These principles were applied in the case of *Foss v Harbottle* (1843) 2 Hare 461 and are often applied by the courts as 'the rule in *Foss* v *Harbottle*'.

6.2 However, these restrictions are not absolute. If they were, they would mean that where a wrong has been done to the company by or with the support of the majority shareholders, there could never be any redress. There are cases, therefore, when the rule will not apply and an individual shareholder will be able to bring an action. These were set out by the Court of Appeal in *Edwards v Halliwell* [1950] 2 All ER 1064 and restated in *Prudential Assurance Co. Ltd* v *Newman Industries Ltd (No. 2)* [1982] Ch 204 ('*Prudential*') in the following terms:

(1) The proper plaintiff in an action in respect of a wrong alleged to be done to a corporation is, prima facie, the corporation.

(2) Where the alleged wrong is a transaction which might be made binding on the corporation and on all its members by a simple majority of the members, no individual member of the corporation is allowed to maintain an action in respect of that matter because, if the majority confirms the transaction, *cadit quaestio* [the question is at an end]; or, if the majority challenges the transaction, there is no valid reason why the company should not sue.

(3) There is no room for the operation of the rule if the alleged wrong is *ultra vires* the corporation, because the majority of members cannot confirm the transaction.

(4) There is also no room for the operation of the rule if the transaction complained of could be validly done or sanctioned only by a special resolution or the like, because a simple majority cannot confirm a transaction which requires the concurrence of a greater majority.

(5) There is an exception to the rule where what has been done amounts to fraud and the wrongdoers are themselves in control of the company.

6.3 We noted that only the fifth limb of the restatement in *Prudential* was a true 'exception' to the rule in *Foss* v *Harbottle*, in that it permitted a shareholder to bring a derivative action (i.e. an action to enforce the company's cause of action) in spite of the majority rule and proper plaintiff principles. The third and fourth limbs were really situations where the principles had no application; actions under those limbs can be brought by a shareholder as a personal action in his own right, and need not be brought as a derivative action.

6.4 Our view was that the basic approach to the right to bring a derivative action was a sound one: an individual shareholder should only be able to bring such an action in exceptional circumstances. This approach is also reflected in the first, second and fifth guiding principles set out in paragraph 1.9 above (proper plaintiff, internal management, and freedom from unnecessary shareholder interference). But we considered that the rule was complicated and unwieldy. It could only be found in case law, much of it decided many years ago; the meaning of terms such as 'wrongdoer control' were not clear; and there were situations which appeared to fall outside the fraud on the minority exception when it might be desirable for a member to be able to bring an action. We also expressed concern at the way in which a member was required to prove standing to bring an action as a preliminary issue by evidence which shows a prima facie case on the merits, and noted that this could easily result in a mini trial which increases the length and cost of litigation. We therefore put forward proposals for a new procedure for derivative actions.

6.5 The substance of our proposal was that the new derivative action would be available to any member if the case fell within the following situation:

that, if the company were the applicant, it would be entitled to any remedy against any person as a result of any breach or threatened breach by any director of the company of any of his duties to the company.

6.6 But this would be subject to tight judicial control at all stages. In particular, an applicant would be required to seek leave from the court by close of pleadings to continue the action and in considering whether to grant leave the court would take account of all the circumstances. Our view was that, for the most part, primary legislation was not required and that this reform should be achieved by rules of court....

International developments

6.8 We noted in the consultation paper a number of international developments with regard to the derivative action. Eight of the 10 provinces of Canada have since 1975 replaced the rule in *Foss* v *Harbottle* with a requirement that the shareholder obtain leave of the court. In Australia and Hong Kong there are legislative proposals for a statutory derivative action. The proposals in Australia (as in Canada) would also replace the fifth limb of the rule in *Foss* v *Harbottle* and require the shareholder to obtain leave from the court. The court would decide whether a derivative action should be commenced on the basis of statutory criteria. The Companies Act 1993 of New Zealand introduced a statutory derivative action. There is a statutory derivative action in South Africa by virtue of the Companies Act No. 61 of 1973. In 1993, Japan changed its law so as to facilitate derivative actions.

6.9 Thus the introduction of a clear set of rules for the derivative action in this country would follow the lead given in other leading jurisdictions. In an age of increasing globalisation of investment and growing international interest in corporate governance, greater transparency in the requirements for a derivative action is in our view highly desirable.

The need for a new derivative action

6.10 The vast majority of respondents considered that the operation of the rule in *Foss* v *Harbottle* was unsatisfactory, and agreed with the problems which we had identified. However, a number of these did express reservations about the need for a new derivative procedure along the lines proposed. Three particular points were made. First, it was said that the derivative action was of such little relevance in practice that there was no point in reforming it. Secondly, some respondents expressed concerns about the adverse consequences of making the derivative action more widely available. Thirdly, several others commented that the proposed new procedure was unlikely to be simpler or more efficient than the current law.

6.11 Dealing with the first point, we accept that, as a matter of practice, derivative actions are brought far less frequently than proceedings under s. 459, but we do not accept that this means that no reform should be made. There are still cases where a derivative action is the only or most appropriate route to take. Whilst we noted the tendency of applicants to bring s. 459 proceedings in respect of matters which could have given rise to a derivative action, we do not consider that the two should be entirely assimilated. They are different in principle—one gives rise to a personal right which the shareholder can enforce, the other relates to the company's cause of action—and although they may cover some of the same ground, this will not always be the case. As was pointed out on consultation, s. 459 has largely become an exit remedy, and what is needed is a remedy for those who want to stay in the company. We consider that a separate and distinct right to bring a derivative action should remain. Section 461(2)(c) provides a means of bringing a derivative action but as we observed in the consultation paper, this has not worked satisfactorily because the court cannot make this order unless it is satisfied that unfair prejudice has occurred and that an order under s. 461(2)(c) is the appropriate relief.

6.12 We highlighted the problems with the current procedure with which respondents agreed and these need to be addressed. We consider that the derivative procedure should be rationalised and modernised in accordance with our provisional recommendations. As we noted in the consultation paper, this may also have the added advantage of encouraging some parties to bring claims as derivative actions which they might otherwise have brought under s. 459; these are likely to be more focused than the wide-ranging proceedings under s. 459.

6.13 So far as the second point is concerned, we do not accept that the proposals will make significant changes to the availability of the action. In some respects, the availability may be slightly wider; in others it may be slightly narrower. But in all cases the new procedure will be subject to tight judicial control. As indicated in the previous paragraph, it may be that some claims will be brought under the new procedure instead of under s. 459, but for the reasons given we consider that this is desirable. We do not anticipate that there will be a large overall increase in litigation, but we consider that where litigation is brought, the new procedure will assist in making sure that it is dealt with fairly and efficiently.

6.14 We disagree with the third point. We consider that the proposals will put the derivative action on a much clearer and more rational basis. They will give courts the flexibility to allow cases to proceed in appropriate circumstances, while giving advisers and shareholders the necessary guidance on the matters which the court will take into account in deciding whether to grant leave.

6.15 Accordingly, we recommend that there should be a new derivative procedure with more modern, flexible and accessible criteria for determining whether a shareholder can pursue the action.

NOTES
1. The Court of Appeal has echoed the Law Commission's suggestions of the need for active case management. It has urged the court to exercise its powers under the new Civil Procedure Rules 1998. In particular, the registrar is urged to give directions to enable petitions to come on for trial as efficiently, quickly and inexpensively as possible. For example, where the issue is the basis of the valuation, the identification of the problem and the trial of a preliminary issue directed to it should remove that obstacle to an agreement. If the issue is the identity of the valuer, the obstacle may be removed by the court itself appointing an expert to value the shares (*North Holdings Ltd* v *Southern Tropics Ltd* [1999] 2 BCLC 625, CA).
2. In an attempt to give effect to the new Civil Procedure Rules to cut cost and minimise the length of court hearings, it has been suggested that when a s. 459 petition comes before the registrar, the registrar should consider giving directions requiring the parties and/or their advisers to meet with a view to narrowing the issues, identifying what issues are really important, what issues are really in dispute and how those issues are to be resolved or proved, and resolving and narrowing any other matters which in the context of the particular petition could reasonably be expected to be narrowed. Only if they cannot agree should the matter be referred to the court (*Re Rotadata Ltd* [2000] 1 BCLC 122).

Modern Company Law for a Competitive Economy: Final Report
(London: DTI, July 2001)

Arbitration for Shareholder Disputes

4.10 In *Completing the Structure*, we noted that consultation had shown significant demand for action to reduce the burden of litigation in shareholder disputes. We noted that the creation of ADR (including arbitration) schemes was the key to solving the problem, and that, if tailor-made schemes were available, it would be easier for both those involved in disputes and the courts to seek or encourage access to them; in such circumstances, a statutory presumption in favour of ADR or cost sanctions against those who unreasonably failed to use ADR would probably prove unnecessary. We said that we would hold discussions with ADR providers with a view to further consideration in this Report.

4.11 We have held discussions with some of the main ADR providers, including the Centre for Dispute Resolution, the Chartered Institute of Arbitrators and the Faculty of Mediation and ADR of the Academy of Experts. We have also spoken to the Law Society, which has expressed an interest in facilitating ADR for shareholder disputes. The main conclusion that we have drawn is that the facilities exist to offer companies and shareholders the means to resolve their disputes quickly and with the minimum necessary costs. We believe that two main steps must be taken to enhance confidence in ADR and encourage its take-up:
  • first, awareness and accessibility of ADR should be greatly increased, so that participants will choose it at the earliest stage as an alternative to litigation. We believe that the ADR providers already have many of the resources necessary to make available methods such as

mediation which could defuse and resolve many disputes before they escalate. We recommend that the Government use its own resources, such as the Small Business Service, and those of non-government bodies, such as the legal profession and trade associations, to set up a programme of publicity and referral machinery to ADR before disputes reach the stage of litigation; and

• second, where cases have reached the stage of litigation, the parties must be encouraged to take a step back and use ADR wherever possible. We believe that the new civil procedure rules provide the means for the courts to apply such encouragement and we recommend that this approach should be proactively used in appropriate cases. If the Government undertakes the programme that we have suggested above, confidence of litigants in all forms of ADR will be increased. However, it is at the stage of litigation that we believe it is necessary to improve confidence in arbitration in particular. If one or more arbitration schemes exist that are respected by the courts and the legal profession, the use of arbitration will be seen as an increasingly attractive option, especially where a dispute has progressed beyond the scope of other forms of ADR. We recommend that the Government work with arbitration providers in order to establish an arbitration scheme designed specifically for shareholder disputes.

4.12 If these steps are taken, we believe that encouragement in the Act through a statutory presumption or costs sanctions will not be necessary.

...

The Unfair Prejudice Remedy (section 459)

7.41 In paragraphs 5.75 to 5.79 of *Completing the Structure*, we considered the scope of the remedy contained in section 459, continuing the discussion in *Developing the Framework*, where we had expressed views against presumptions of unfair prejudice in certain circumstances and against making winding up available under the section. There was no support for either proposal, so in *Completing the Structure*, we concentrated on the question of whether the scope of the remedy as set out in *O'Neill* v *Phillips* was adequate. Although the majority of views expressed in responses to *Developing the Framework* were in favour of reversing *O'Neill* and thereby extending the scope of the remedy, after careful consideration we came down against this. In particular, we agreed with the House of Lords that the basis for a claim should be a departure from an agreement, broadly defined, between those concerned, to be identified by their words or conduct. This is necessary in the interests of certainty and the containment of the scope of section 459 actions. Concern was again expressed that in complex circumstances there might be genuine unfairness, which would not amount to breach of agreement or equitable principle. But we remain convinced that this is the correct approach. Accordingly, we recommend against reversing *O'Neill* v *Phillips*.

7.42 In paragraphs 5.80 and 5.81 of *Completing the Structure* we said that the case was not made out for specific remedies based on unfairness in relation to unfair refusals to register transfers of shares. The general duties of the directors would apply, and a refusal would only be lawful if the decision was reached in good faith to promote the success of the company for the benefit of its members as a whole. We did, however, propose that directors who refuse such a transfer should be required to give reasons.

7.43 The majority were in favour of this proposal, although a considerable number, mainly from the legal professions, were against it. It was suggested that such a requirement would fuel litigation; and that it would represent a fundamental change to the rules on which companies have operated, particularly small family businesses. It was argued that the introduction of such a right would be an infringement of the rights of existing members, and that it would be inappropriate to restrict the right of members of small companies, particularly those with finely balanced memberships, to decide what happens on death or bankruptcy of a member (in relation to transfers by personal representatives and trustees in bankruptcy). Questions were also raised as to whether the requirement would be effective, on grounds that it would simply encourage the production of formulaic reasons. Finally, it was suggested that the requirement would lead to directors having to obtain expensive legal advice; and that it would inhibit the incorporation of companies that in economic reality are partnerships.

7.44 We are not persuaded. Our proposal is not directed at creating a new substantive right. Rather, it is aimed at transparency. Without such a provision, there may be no realistic way, short of challenging the refusal in the courts, in which those disadvantaged by it can ascertain whether or not it was in breach of the directors' duties. In the small family company situation referred to above, it could be perfectly legitimate for the directors to refuse to register a transfer to a hostile outsider whom they judged likely to disrupt the company's activities. Equally, it could be legitimate to decline to register a transfer which resulted in a shift in the balance of control, if they considered that that could endanger the company's success: see paragraph 2 of the draft statement of duties in Annex C. Accordingly we recommend that where there is a discretion to refuse registration of a transfer of shares, the directors should be obliged to give reasons at the same time as they notify their refusal under section 183(5).

7.45 We also asked whether, if a duty to give reasons were to be imposed, it should apply in relation to all companies or just those incorporated after commencement. Those who supported the proposal were almost unanimous in the view that it should apply to all companies. The case for the rule is good for all companies and it is not desirable to create regimes which operate only for new ones. We accordingly so recommend.

Derivative Actions (or, in Scotland, 'Shareholders' Actions')

7.46 In *Completing the Structure* we proceeded on the basis (recommended by the Law Commission and adopted in *Developing the Framework*) that (*inter alia*) derivative actions would be restricted to breaches of directors' duties, including the duty of care and skill; and that they would be put on a statutory footing. We also adopted the proposals in *Developing the Framework* regarding ratification, i.e. that the validity of a decision by the members of the company to ratify a wrong on the company or by the board not to pursue the wrong would depend on whether the necessary majority was reached without the support of the wrongdoers or those under their influence. These proposals drew heavily on the earlier work done by the Law Commission; and indeed all of our work on this aspect of the Review has been greatly assisted by the results of their deliberations on the subject of shareholder remedies. Nothing which has been said in the context of the various consultations has altered our view that these proposals, which form the background to the discussion on other limits on majority power which follows, are the best approach to this difficult issue and accordingly we recommended them.

7.47 One respondent to *Completing the Structure* raised a general concern about derivative actions in relation to the duty of care and skill, arguing that this would cause more problems than it would solve, not least because the courts were likely to adopt a restrictive approach on the general principle that the board were responsible for management. The same respondent also suggested that problems may arise where there is a clear breach of duty by a director, but the board takes a commercial decision not to pursue it. As to the former, we consider that the fact that the courts are likely (quite properly) to restrict the availability of a remedy does not touch the question of whether it should exist at all. As to the latter, we are not convinced that such situations are likely to be problematic. If an untainted majority of the board takes the decision, in compliance with their duties, then it should stand. If not, then whether an action should proceed would be determined in accordance with the principles discussed below.

7.48 In *Developing the Framework* we suggested that where a wrong had not been ratified, nor a decision not to sue lawfully taken, the best test of whether the action should proceed was whether the minority's views were the best available evidence of what was in the best interests of the company. Reactions to this proposal were mixed, and in paragraph 5.87 of *Completing the Structure* we suggested conferring on the court a discretion to consider all the circumstances in determining whether a derivative action should proceed, and in doing so to pay particular regard to the issue of whether it was in the best interests of the company in accordance with the criterion set out in the principles on directors' duties in paragraph 1b of the trial draft (see paragraph 2 of the draft in Annex C).

7.49 As regards the question of whether the criteria to be applied when considering such actions should be laid down by statutory instrument or dealt with by rules of court, we took the view that there may be a case for leaving the remaining issues to the court's discretion; but that any criteria should be the same both in England and Wales and in Scotland; and that a power should be provided to enable the standards body to make further rules.

7.50 We continue to take the view that in the first instance these matters are best left to the courts. In view of the importance of the rights in question, and the need to ensure consistency of approach so far as possible between the two jurisdictions, we continue to take the view that a rule-making power should be provided. However, since these rules will affect substantive rights, we consider that the Secretary of State should be given the necessary power, rather than the Standards Board.

7.51 On the need for provision to ensure that a shareholder should not recover damage suffered by the company, other than at the suit of the company, our inclination was that as this was the current state of the law, no further provision was required. However, we held over the question whether it was necessary to put the matter beyond doubt pending the outcome of court proceedings, including the House of Lords decision in *Johnson v Gore Wood*. The outcome of that case was consistent with our view. The approach adopted by the courts is in our view the appropriate one; accordingly our recommendation is against legislation.

Other Limits on Majority Power

7.52 In *Developing the Framework* we flagged for further discussion the question of whether, apart from the limits on the powers of the appropriate majority to ratify directors' wrongs and the constraints imposed by section 459, there should be any other limits on the power of the majority to control the company. In *Completing the Structure* we considered the current law on this issue and the ways in which it could be improved, including on special resolutions changing the company's constitution and class rights, other special resolutions, ordinary resolutions, and blocking minorities.

7.53 On special resolutions altering the constitution or altering class rights, we noted that the current law (the '*Greenhalgh* rule') was that the relevant decision must be taken in the best interest of the members of the company, or the class, as the case may be, as a whole. We remarked that the law was unclear beyond that, and that there were almost no decisions applying these principles to other resolutions. We also considered the Australian case of *Gambotto* which held unlawful an alteration to the articles depriving a minority shareholder of a 'proprietary right' because it did not satisfy the higher test of protecting the company from harm.

7.54 We rejected *Gambotto*, but considered that there was a case for maintaining the *Greenhalgh* rule in the areas in which it now clearly applies. As regards resolutions facilitating or condoning wrongs, we proposed that those members with an interest, or subject or substantial influence by a person with an interest, in the relevant wrong should be disqualified from voting, whether as a member of a relevant majority or blocking minority. We took the view that no special provision should be made covering the consequences of unlawful resolutions other than the invalidation of the resolution itself.

7.55 Support for the principle that resolutions to change the constitution, or at class meetings to change class rights, should be subject to the requirement that the decision be taken in good faith in the interests of the members as a whole was almost unanimous. However, a few respondents raised concerns as to the clarity of the approach in *Greenhalgh*, and its appropriateness where there were two conflicting factions of shareholders. It was suggested that a statutory formulation of the rule risked creating a situation where the constitution could not be altered where such a conflict existed; and that accordingly this was an area which the courts should be left to develop.

7.56 Those who disagreed with our approach in principle did so on grounds that shareholders should be free to exercise their votes as they wish in their own selfish interests, and that a provision along the lines of the proposal would be intolerable in situations where venture capitalists were given special class rights specifically to protect their own interests above those of the company and the other shareholders. As our proposal was to preserve the existing position as set out in the relevant case law, rather than to introduce new restrictions, and we have received no evidence that the present rules cause such difficulty, we do not think that these objections are well founded.

7.57 We did not, in *Completing the Structure*, discuss the possibility of seeking to codify the restriction in legislation. However, codification of the directors' duties does raise the issue of codification in this context. In particular, we have, in paragraph 2 of the proposed draft statement of directors' duties, introduced a formulation of the 'members as a whole' for whose benefit the directors conduct the affairs of the company which may not be perfectly aligned with the present state of the law in this area. While agreeing that a statutory statement of the restriction will require careful thought, a failure to make such provision could give rise to a misalignment between the 'members as a whole' in respect of whom the directors owe their duties, and those in relation to which the shareholders must consider their actions. Further questions arise on the interaction with the directors' duty to act fairly as between the members, and the restriction of the majority in this context from discriminating to the disadvantage of the minority.

7.58 The effect of this principle is essentially that members should vote in what they honestly believe is in the interest of their company, in the sense of the interests of members as fellow members in the association. There would be merit in codifying the principle so as to align it with paragraph 2 of the statement and the basic test of company success. As under the present law, this criterion is a subjective one, and such decisions will continue to be very difficult to challenge unless it is evident that members are riding roughshod over the interests of other members for selfish purposes which have nothing to do with the success of the business. What we would wish such codification to make clear is that the issue is not whether the decision is in the interest of each individual member—it may even be contrary to the interests of a substantial group of members and discriminatory (though any such discrimination will need to be considered). The test is simply whether the majority honestly believe that their vote is best calculated to promote the success of the company for the benefit of its members as a whole—the same requirement as is to be applied to the directors under paragraph 2 of the statement of directors' duties. To that extent, it will differ from the rule as currently understood.

7.59 Responses were almost unanimously in favour of our rejection of the imposition of a further constraint along the lines of *Gambotto*. However, one of the respondents who objected to the *Greenhalgh* approach suggested that such a restriction should be imposed as an alternative to it. Bearing in mind the views of the overwhelming majority of respondents, we recommend that resolutions to change the constitution, or at class meetings to change class rights, should be subject to the requirement that the decision should be taken in good faith with a view to promoting the success of the company in the interests of the members, or the class as the case may be, as a whole; and that no further restriction should be imposed. Further, we recommend that the rule should be codified in a way which aligns it with paragraph 2 in the statement of directors' duties. These requirements should be enforceable by the aggrieved minority, their remedy being to have the resolution declared invalid—i.e. there should be no right to damages.

7.60 We do not consider that an extension of the approach set out in paragraph 7.59 to other types of resolution would be justified. In *Completing the Structure*, we proposed a different rule, namely that members with an interest or subject to substantial influence by a person with an interest in a wrong should not have their votes counted on any resolution to facilitate or condone it, whether as a member of a relevant majority or blocking minority. This approach was also supported by the great majority of respondents, and we therefore recommend that it should be adopted. However, it was suggested that difficulties would arise in establishing whether a member is subject to 'substantial influence'. In addition, the view was expressed that the proposal would be unworkable in practice, for example where a director improperly exploits an opportunity and the rest of the board are negligent in allowing him to do so; or where the wrongdoing directors are the only shareholders. We believe the detailed definition of 'substantial influence' can be dealt with in the drafting. There may be a case for a presumption of influence for certain kinds of related parties (cf. section 346 of the Act). However, at the margin we recognise that the definition will need to be interpreted by the courts. As to those situations where the untainted majority of the board are simply negligent—in principle, this would not affect a decision to ratify; but in such a case, a separate action for breach of the duty of care and skill might lie against them. But we agree that in general, where all the members are implicated in the wrongdoing the disqualification should not apply.

7.61 We also proposed no special sanction for breach of these provisions, beyond invalidation of the resolution. Once again, responses were almost unanimously in favour of this approach and we recommend that it should be adopted. However, in our view, the discounting of a person's vote should not affect his ability to be counted toward the quorum.

7.62 The effect of these proposals would be to make it clear that the majority is, subject of course to the constitution, free to exercise its powers as it wishes, apart from the cases we have mentioned above—i.e. in sum, cases of breach of an agreement, actual or implied, amounting to unfairly prejudicial conduct for the purposes of section 459 as interpreted in the light of *O'Neill v Phillips*; cases involving changes in the articles or class rights; and resolutions ratifying or condoning wrongs. It has to be recognised that this may lead in some cases to outcomes which are prejudicial or unfair in some sense to the majority and for which there would be no remedy. We generally believe that in the interests of certainty it is not desirable to recognise in law some further standard of fairness or unconscionability against which majority decisions are to be assessed. However, one member of the Steering Group has expressed reservations as to whether any resolution should be regarded as a resolution ratifying or condoning a wrong other than a resolution for this express purpose, and whether our recommendations should remove the means of challenging resolutions in certain circumstances in which a minority shareholder can now challenge them, given that our proposals would exclude the application of the concept of fraud on the minority. We have not been able to find a solution to these arguments. Accordingly these are matters which are likely to require further consideration by the DTI.

14

Groups of Companies

The readings that follow this introduction enigmatically conclude that there is no English law of groups. For this reason the chapter will cross-refer to many aspects of the law that only incidentally have an impact on groups of companies. The justification for having a chapter on groups, however, is that as they are such a major and unavoidable feature of company law and practice, it would be a serious omission if they did not receive separate attention. (See 3.3.4 on groups in the context of 'lifting the veil'.)

While 'group of companies' may be strictly defined for certain legal purposes, this discussion also refers more generally to companies in common ownership or under common management control. Where an individual or family owns all the shares in a number of companies, this is not technically a group though the effect of a single economic entity under unified management may be similar.

The principal terminology is that a parent or holding company and its subsidiaries, both wholly-owned and not wholly-owned, together constitute a group. These terms originated as business rather than legal terms but the Companies Acts have provided some complex definitions of them for certain very specific purposes such as the company's obligations relating to accounts. These definitions must be closely read, remembering that as in Alice in Wonderland, a word in a statute means precisely what the parliamentary draftsman says it means, no more and no less. For an Index of Defined Expressions, see Schedule 8 of the CA 2006 which is an essential research tool when reading the Act. Particular words or expressions are very precisely defined and sometimes have that meaning for the purposes of the Act as a whole but sometimes for a specific part of the Act only. To take an example that Lewis Carroll would be proud of, the term 'quoted company' has no fewer than three separate definitions for the purposes of different parts of the Act.

The terms 'holding company', 'subsidiary' and 'wholly-owned subsidiary' are defined by CA 2006, s. 1159 (below), together with a further two pages of verbiage in Schedule 6 to the Act. For the purposes of CA 2006, Part 15 (Accounts and Reports), 'group' means 'a parent undertaking and its subsidiary undertakings' (CA 2006, s. 474(1)), and these terms are defined in CA 2006, s. 1162 and Schedule 7. Under s. 399 'parent companies' that are 'not subject to the small company regime' are obliged to prepare and file group accounts, and by s. 1173(1) parent company is defined as meaning 'a company that is a parent undertaking (see s. 1162 and Schedule 7)'. (Remember the Preface to this book that warned you against trying to learn the content of company law!)

Mention of these statutory definitions is only incidental to the broader purposes of this chapter but the above summary and the following example indicate how very complex such definitions can be, remembering that s. 1159 must also be read together with the further sub-definitions in Schedule 6.

COMPANIES ACT 2006, S.1159

1159. Meaning of "subsidiary" etc

(1) A company is a "subsidiary" of another company, its "holding company", if that other company—
   (a) holds a majority of the voting rights in it, or
   (b) is a member of it and has the right to appoint or remove a majority of its board of directors, or
   (c) is a member of it and controls alone, pursuant to an agreement with other members, a majority of the voting rights in it,
   or if it is a subsidiary of a company that is itself a subsidiary of that other company.
(2) A company is a "wholly-owned subsidiary" of another company if it has no members except that other and that other's wholly-owned subsidiaries or persons acting on behalf of that other or its wholly-owned subsidiaries.
(3) Schedule 6 contains provisions explaining expressions used in this section and otherwise supplementing this section.
(4) In this section and that Schedule "company" includes any body corporate.

A group of companies as defined in the Act or several companies in common ownership may often be managed under a unified management policy as a single economic entity. An example is the fictitious small group of private building companies operated by the Baker family described at 1.7, stage (k). In this case the brothers are all directors of all the companies and probably treat the group as a single economic entity. They do not conceive of any subsidiary as having separate interests of its own. When the original trading company became a holding company on the incorporation of the four wholly owned subsidiary companies, the brothers' perception of the business as a single economic entity probably did not change. (In fact they probably continued to think of it as their business and not the company's!) In reality nothing of substance apparently changed. They continued to run the business as a single economic entity out of the same premises and using the same equipment, but with some incidental accounting and legal complications foisted on them by their professional advisers.

A group of companies which includes a public company listed on the Stock Exchange may likewise be managed with a unified management structure or policy. As groups get larger, the directors throughout the group may not be the same and the unity of management may become looser. This is especially so where the group has been assembled by taking over other previously independent companies. Such an acquired company, as a previously independent economic entity, may be less easy to integrate fully into the group. At the furthest extreme a holding company may acquire shares solely as an investment and may not intend to integrate the subsidiary into the group at all, but may leave it as a separate economic entity with little control of policy.

Another phenomenon is the so-called 'multinational' group of companies whose operations spread perhaps throughout the globe. An example of one such group with a worldwide presence is Shell which adopted a decentralised management policy, subsequently restructured in 1995 and again in 2005. The following notes taken from Shell's 1987 Annual Report and Fig 14.1 show that Royal Dutch Petroleum Co. at that time held 60 per cent and the 'Shell' Transport and Trading Co. plc 40 per cent of the shares of the principal Dutch, UK and American subsidiaries. These in turn have a vast number of subsidiaries operating in more than 100 countries. It is thus truly a multinational group of companies.

What has to be appreciated therefore is that it is misleading to think of a single company as being the typical trading vehicle for anything but the smallest of incorporated businesses. On the other hand the ways in which groups of companies or controlling shareholdings are organised are many and varied and are often

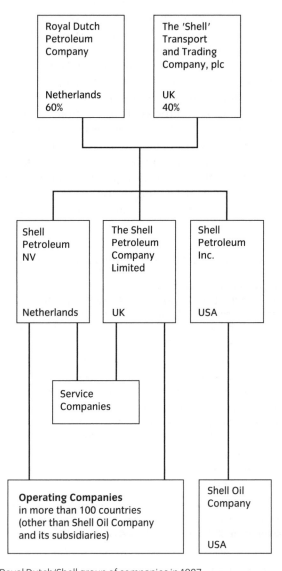

Figure 14.1 The Royal Dutch/Shell group of companies in 1987

immensely complex. It is such tangled webs of interests that often lead to legal problems.

The reasons why groups of companies are so common are mentioned in the readings that follow. Probably, just as an individual about to take the risk of starting a business may wish to limit his liability, so also may a company form a subsidiary to start up a new business. When a new business is set up as a subsidiary company, this gives to the ultimate individual shareholders of the holding company a double layer of limited liability. Not only are their personal assets safe from failure of the new company, the business assets owned by the holding company are also protected from its possible failure.

The aim of operating as a group may thus be to separate assets from potential liabilities and risks. To take an extreme example, a publishing company might incorporate a new subsidiary to publish each issue of a scurrilous satirical magazine so that if any libel writ is received the subsidiary is sacrificed and the holding company's assets preserved. A shipping line may incorporate a company to own each new ship. These shipowning companies probably do not actively trade, but the ships are operated by a series of undercapitalised operating companies. Thus, for example, if a ship incurs massive uninsured liability for an oil spill, the operating company only is liable and the assets of the group are protected from risk. Again the Baker brothers (see 1.7 above) as builders may incorporate a company to undertake each speculative development of a house. If on completion of the house the market has collapsed and it can only be sold at a loss, the damage to the overall business of the group is limited. (However, just as major individual shareholders may be asked to guarantee bank lending, so also the banks will probably demand cross-guarantees and security from the companies in the group holding valuable assets.)

The Royal Dutch/Shell Group of Companies Annual Report 1987

The Royal Dutch/Shell group of companies has grown out of an alliance made in 1907 between Royal Dutch Petroleum Co. and the 'Shell' Transport and Trading Co. plc, by which the two companies agreed to merge their interests on a 60 : 40 basis while keeping their separate identities. Today the title describes a group of companies engaged in the oil, natural gas, chemicals, coal and metals businesses throughout the greater part of the world.

Parent companies   As parent companies, Royal Dutch Petroleum Co. and the 'Shell' Transport and Trading Co. plc do not themselves directly engage in operational activities. They are public companies, one domiciled in the Netherlands, the other in the United Kingdom.

The parent companies directly or indirectly own the shares in the group holding companies but are not themselves part of the group. They appoint directors to the boards of the group holding companies, from which they receive income in the form of dividends.

Shareholdings   There are some 325,000 shareholders of Royal Dutch and some 300,000 of Shell Transport. Shares of one or both companies are listed and traded on stock exchanges in eight European countries and in the USA.

Service companies   The main business of the service companies is to provide advice and services to other group and associated companies, excluding Shell Petroleum Inc. and its subsidiaries. The service companies are variously located in the Netherlands or the UK.

Group holding companies   Shell Petroleum NV and the Shell Petroleum Co. Ltd between them hold all the shares in the service companies and, directly or indirectly, all group interests in the operating companies other than those held by Shell Petroleum Inc.

Operating companies Operating companies are engaged in various branches of the oil and natural gas, chemicals, coal, metals and other businesses in many countries. The management of each operating company is responsible for the performance and long-term viability of its own operations, but can draw on the experience of the service companies and, through them, of other operating companies.

14.2 THE LEGAL ISSUES

Having sketched the broad practical background to groups of companies, what are the legal issues that arise? In short the principal problems arise when the interests of a subsidiary are subordinated to those of the holding company or of the group as a whole. In this situation the subsidiary company as a separate entity of course suffers loss with the following consequences. First, its minority shareholders, if any, are prejudiced. Secondly, creditors of the subsidiary are prejudiced in that it has suffered loss and so will be less able to pay its debts. Furthermore, because of the principle of limited liability the holding company is not liable to creditors for its subsidiary's debts. The readings that follow graphically illustrate these problems that may arise from group trading. As mentioned they conclude that the issue is not dealt with by any special legal provision for groups which are only incidentally governed by the law which applies to companies generally.

To take a few examples, if directors of a subsidiary, without the approval of its members, act in a way that prejudices its interest (such as by guaranteeing another group company's bank loan) they are ultimately liable, perhaps at the suit of a liquidator, for breach of fiduciary duty. If the lender is aware that the guarantee was given in breach of fiduciary duty, it may be unable to take the benefit of the guarantee. (See *Rolled Steel Products (Holdings) Ltd* v *British Steel Corporation* [1986] Ch 246 extracted in 5.2.2.) If the subsidiary transfers its assets to other group companies at an undervalue or pays off debts owed to the holding company in preference to other creditors these transactions may in certain circumstances be overturned by the liquidator under general provisions of the Insolvency Act 1986 (see 20.11). If minority shareholders of a subsidiary complain that the conduct of the holding company has been unfairly prejudicial to their interests, they may petition the court for a remedy under CA 2006, s. 994. If a holding company continues actively to direct and operate a subsidiary at a time when it ought to have concluded that there was no reasonable prospect of the subsidiary avoiding going into insolvent liquidation, then the holding company may be treated as a shadow director of the subsidiary. Under IA 1986, s. 214, the holding company is potentially liable for wrongful trading and may be ordered to contribute to the assets of the subsidiary (see 20.12). These are just a few examples of how the general law of companies deals with the problems arising from the operation of groups of companies.

Also relevant to groups is the debate on 'lifting the veil of incorporation', considered earlier at 3.3. From this it seems that the courts are prepared in very exceptional cases to lift the veil where there is an abuse of the corporate form. In theory also (but unlikely in practice) a holding company may be liable for its subsidiary's debts if it can be shown that the subsidiary was carrying on business as the agent of the holding company and that the debt is therefore that of the holding company as principal. However, the trend of the cases at present is to confirm the separate entity of companies as a fundamental principle in the absence of legislation. Preserving this certainty is perhaps to be welcomed at a time of growing complexity in the law. At 3.3.4 above, several cases are set out, including *Adams v Cape Industries plc* [1990] Ch 433 which strongly indicate this trend, though as as is suggested by the note of the end of 3.3.4 on multinational companies and mega-litigation, the big international groups are not always successful in shielding themselves from liability.

The readings that follow are long, but clear and informative. As will be seen the Cork Committee wrestled with the possibilities of reform of the law as it applies to groups but drew back, not only because of the complexities but because their remit was limited to insolvency law. Reforming the law of groups would have much wider implications. The extract from the Cork Report and the one that follows by Professor Prentice add some valuable background about the extent of the problems thrown up by groups of companies.

Insolvency Law and Practice: Report of the Review Committee (The 'Cork Report')
(Cmnd 8558) (London: HMSO, 1982)

Group trading

General

1922. Group activity in the sense of the conduct of various businesses by a holding company through a number of subsidiaries is a twentieth-century phenomenon. The principles of our company law and of our insolvency law were developed in the nineteenth century. It is not surprising, therefore, that some of the basic principles of company and insolvency law fit uneasily with the modern commercial realities of group enterprise....

1924. We have received a large number of submissions on the subject of group trading and the state of the law...has been most powerfully criticised. It is clearly the view of many of those who gave evidence to us that it is unsatisfactory and offensive to the ordinary canons of commercial morality that a parent company should allow its wholly owned subsidiary to fail, or that a company should be permitted by other companies in the same group, and particularly by its ultimate parent, to take commercial advantage from its membership of the group, without there being incurred by those other companies any countervailing obligations.

1925. The legal position is that each company in a group is a separate legal entity, and the directors of any one company are not entitled to sacrifice the interests of that company to the interests of the group as a whole. Even in the case of a parent company with wholly owned subsidiaries where the ultimate shareholding interest in all the companies in the group is the same, the existence of separate groups of creditors of each company requires the directors of each company to have separate regard to its particular interests.

1926. In practice, however, the affairs of companies in a group are often conducted by management by reference to the interests of the group as a whole. The control which the parent company has over the composition of the board of each of the subsidiaries and the series of common directorships which this often entails mean that transactions between companies in the group can be, and often are, conducted on a basis which is not arm's length. Assets may be transferred between group companies at lower than market value. Loans may be made without interest or at less than market rates. Guarantees may be given by one group company of another group company's obligations for no charge and without reference to the interests of the guaranteeing company. Dividends may be paid from a subsidiary to the parent without regard to the cash requirements of the subsidiary.

1927. Not only are such transactions—and there are countless other examples—commonplace, but in a number of areas of law, and particularly taxation law, recognition is given to the group concept. One company in a group may be made liable for the VAT of the whole of the group; one company in the group may be made responsible for tax liabilities primarily attaching to other companies in the group; trading losses incurred by one company in the group may be made available to other companies for the purpose of obtaining group relief: and so on.

1928. It has seemed to a large number of those who gave evidence to us that, given the command which the parent company has in practice over the affairs of the subsidiary, it is absurd and unreal to allow the commercial realities to be disregarded and the technical legal separate status to predominate once a subsidiary has gone into insolvency.

1929. There are two principal questions which arise in insolvency as regards groups of companies. First, whether or not one or more of the other companies in the group should be made responsible for the external debts of the company which is insolvent. Secondly, how should the claims of other group companies in the winding up of an insolvent group company be treated? We take these questions separately, but it will be readily apparent that they are interrelated.

Liabilities to external creditors

1930. The strength of the case of those who seek a change in the law—and a radical change at that—can be seen if a simple and perhaps extreme example is taken.

1931. A wholly owned subsidiary company is undercapitalised. It relies virtually wholly on moneys lent by the parent. Its affairs are conducted by and in the interest of the parent and they are mismanaged. There is a history of transactions between subsidiary and parent which, although not individually or collectively susceptible to attack at law, have, cumulatively, advantaged the parent and disadvantaged the subsidiary. All profits earned by the subsidiary have been paid up to the parent by way of dividend and the moneys needed by the subsidiary to conduct its business lent back by the parent.

1932. The subsidiary, at the instance of the parent, has obtained substantial credit by relying on its membership of the group of companies headed by the parent. The subsidiary indicates its membership of the group on its letter heading and advertises its membership on all documents and billings by showing a device or logo distinctive of the group.

1933. The subsidiary becomes insolvent and goes into liquidation. The parent company declines all liability for its subsidiary's debts to external creditors, and competes with them by submitting a proof in respect of its loan. The result is that, out of the total funds realised by the liquidator for distribution among the creditors, a substantial proportion goes to the parent company.

1934. We recognise that a law which permits such an outcome is undoubtedly a defective law. We have, consequently, looked anxiously at the many different proposals put to us for reform. . . .

1938. Our proposals in relation to wrongful trading (ch. 44) will effect a major change in the law. A parent company will be exposed to liability for the debts of its subsidiary in circumstances where the parent company has exercised managerial functions in the subsidiary and become party to the wrongful trading of the subsidiary. Such liability will be imposed, for example, where the parent company has given instructions to the board or to members of the board of the subsidiary as a result of which the business of the subsidiary has been carried on wrongfully. . . .

1946. It appears to us that there may be difficulty in the introduction of any changes in the law. Creditors of a parent company, for instance, if it is to become responsible for the debts of all of its subsidiaries, will find that upon an insolvent liquidation of the group they are forced to share the worth of the solvent subsidiaries with the creditors of the insolvent subsidiaries. This would create a significant alteration in the position of the existing creditors of a parent company (for instance, long-term creditors) and, being a change having a retrospective significance, might require intricate transitional provisions. . . .

1952. It is impossible to divorce the position in insolvency from the position prior to insolvency, and we have reluctantly come to the conclusion that we should not recommend a fundamental change in company law by means of proposals to effect a change in insolvency law. The matter is of such importance and of such gravity that there should be the widest possible review of the different considerations, with a view to the introduction of reforming legislation within the foreseeable future. We would wish to see such a revision undertaken as a matter of urgency.

Intercompany indebtedness

1953. Creditors of an insolvent subsidiary company, already angered by the unexpected failure of its parent company to meet the subsidiary's liabilities to them, are unlikely to be mollified by the discovery that the parent company proposes to prove in competition with them in respect of a substantial debt owing to it; or by the discovery that the failure of the subsidiary has been caused or aggravated by the application of its assets, at the instigation of the parent company, for the benefit of other companies in the group which have since become insolvent, with the result that all or part of those assets are irrecoverable.

1954. So long as each company in a group is treated as a separate legal entity, distinct from every other company in the group, and with its own distinct class of creditors, the problems created by the existence of intercompany debts require a solution to be found. These are the debts owed by the company in liquidation to other companies in the group, which are entitled to prove for them in competition with the external creditors; and the debts owed to the company in liquidation by other companies in the group, which may or may not themselves be insolvent.

1955. Such debts may represent trading balances arising from intercompany trading within the group; or they may arise from loans and subventions made by other companies in the group to support continued trading by the borrowing company. The parent company may have adopted a policy of channelling subsidiaries' profits upwards by way of dividend to the parent, leaving the operating subsidiaries' working capital to be financed by loans and subventions from other companies in the group, repayable on demand, and provable in a liquidation in competition with debts owed to external creditors.

1956. Intercompany debts may also arise from the practice of using all available money and assets in the group, not solely for the benefit of the company to which they belong, but wherever they may be put to the best commercial use in the interests of the group as a whole, balancing the books at the insistence of the auditors by loans and 'intercompany balances'. . . .

Misapplication of the company's assets

1968. A parent company is normally in a position to give directions to the board of its subsidiary, and to ensure that those directions are carried out. This is made easier when, as is often the case, the board of the subsidiary consists of or includes persons who are also on the board of the parent company.

1969. Notwithstanding the directions of the parent company, the directors of the subsidiary are bound to apply its property for the benefit of the subsidiary, and not for the benefit of the parent company or other companies in the group. Failure to observe this fundamental principle of company law will often lead to a misapplication of the subsidiary's property, for which the directors will, in theory at least, be personally liable.

1970. Where the company is a wholly owned subsidiary, and the directors have acted at the instigation of the parent company, this does not matter, provided that the company remains solvent. The creditors are not prejudiced; and the shareholders cannot complain of anything done at their own direction or with their own consent. Where the company is insolvent, or becomes insolvent in consequence of what has been done, the creditors will have been prejudiced, and the liquidator may wish to bring proceedings for their benefit, not only against the directors, but also against the parent company in order to recover the assets which have been misapplied.

1971. As the law stands, however, it seems that the liquidator of a wholly owned subsidiary cannot complain of anything done at the direction or with the consent of the parent company, the only shareholder of the subsidiary, even if the company was insolvent, unless the act was *ultra vires* the subsidiary. In some cases, it may be possible to escape this conclusion by treating the misapplication as constituting an unlawful dividend or return of capital to the shareholders; but in many cases this is not possible, particularly where the act complained of is the assumption of liabilities or the giving of a guarantee.

Dan D. Prentice, 'A survey of the law relating to corporate groups in the United Kingdom'

in E. Wymeersch (ed.), *Groups of Companies in the EC*

(Berlin: Walter de Gruyter, 1993)

I. The phenomenon of groups

1. Although English company law does not possess a specific law of corporate groups in the way, for example, that German law does, the phenomenon of groups clearly exists and there is a range of significant legal consequences flowing from the fact that commercial activity is carried on in group form.... The absence of any overarching legal principle to deal with corporate groups does, however, mean that the system of regulation is fragmented and highly complex.

2. What is clear, is that the carrying on of business in group form is a salient feature of English commercial life. There is tentative evidence to suggest that the use of the group form may be more widespread in the United Kingdom than in other comparable economies. It is essential to appreciate the complexity of group structures within the United Kingdom as any proposal for change must be evaluated against this background. There is no exhaustive survey of the group phenomenon in the United Kingdom, but a survey has been carried out of the group structure of companies within The Times 1000 UK top industrial, quoted companies concentrating on the companies lying in the 1–100 and 401–500 size bands. This revealed:...that the top 50 companies had over 10,000 subsidiaries and that the arithmetical average for each company is 230. This survey, however, fails to present anything like a complete picture of the group phenomenon as many unlisted, private companies will also make use of the group structure.

3. Also of importance in examining the structure of groups, is the level within the group at which a subsidiary operates, that is, the distance at which sub-subsidiaries are removed from the ultimate holding company. This becomes an issue of some importance if the question arises as to the liability of a 'parent company' for the obligations of its subsidiary; some company in the chain of companies has to be identified as the parent. As was stated in the report of the Cork Committee: 'Should it be the ultimate holding company, or should it be an intermediate holding company?' The statistics on this phenomenon indicate that a pyramid structure is not uncommon [e.g., 44 of the top 50 companies had, on average, 28 sub-sub-sub-subsidiaries].

4. There is no completely satisfactory explanation for the widespread use of the group form in the United Kingdom. The following factors provide some explanation:
(i) easy access to the corporate form, in the sense that there are few hurdles put in the way of obtaining corporate status, makes the company a convenient and relatively cheap method for carrying on business;
(ii) the strictness with which the courts adhere to the corporate entity doctrine, and their reluctance to pierce the corporate veil, entails that a subsidiary can be used as a convenient device for shielding a parent company against risk. Limited liability is seen as an important and legitimate device for encouraging entrepreneurial activity and it is felt that it should be made equally available to companies and individuals;
(iii) the philosophy of English company managers does not seem to encourage the rationalising of business structures; why this should be so is far from clear;
(iv) there never has been any prohibition on one company holding shares in another. And, even though up until 1980 it was necessary for a public company to have at least seven

shareholders, as a shareholder could act as a nominee of a third party, this meant that a public company could be the subsidiary of another company through the use of nominees;

(v) the chronology of the development of various interrelated legal doctrines is also of importance. Limited liability preceded the development of the group structure and, initially, it was not fully appreciated that the use of the group form created 'two levels of limited liability sheltering the parent corporation as well as the shareholders of the parent'. . . .

5. A group of companies will obviously exist where there is the relationship of parent and subsidiary between them. Under the Companies Act 1985 (as amended by the Companies Act 1989) a parent–subsidiary relationship will be taken to exist if one company (the parent) (i) holds a majority of the voting rights in another, (ii) is a member of the other and has a right to appoint or remove a majority of the board or the other, or (iii) is a member of it and controls alone or with the agreement of others a majority of the voting rights in the company. But this is only one of the many ways in which as a matter of economic reality group activity may arise. For example, it could arise from interlocking directorates, and holdings of less than 50 per cent of a company's voting shares will often guarantee control of a company particularly where ownership of the remaining shares is dispersed. Tricker, in examining the phenomenon of 'associated companies', which were defined as companies in which one company held an equity interest in another of at least 10 per cent but less than 50 per cent of the other company's equity shares [found, e.g., that 39 companies, all in the top 50, had on average 34 associated companies].

6. Somewhat related to the associated company phenomenon, are *cross-holdings* and *circular holdings*. A cross-holding occurs where, for example, three companies 'with a common board of directors or with boards which agree to act in concert' each have a holding of 26 per cent of the votes of each of the other companies. This assures *de iure* control of each company. . . .

7. The virtual economic equivalence of a group structure can also be produced by joint venture arrangements and there is some tentative evidence to suggest that these are often used.

8. Lastly, the above discussion has assumed that for a group to exist there has in some way to be control of *one company* by another company. But the effects of the group form can just as equally be produced where an individual (or a small group of individuals) controls two or more companies. The reported cases indicate that there is a high level of abuse of the corporate form in this type of situation (normally involving private companies) with a common controller misusing the assets of one company he controls to benefit another company which he also controls. . . .

11. Despite the concern expressed by the Cork Committee, there has not been, however, a strong demand in the United Kingdom for the introduction of a law which would deal in a comprehensive way with the issues and problems arising from group activity. The reason for this may be attributable to legal culture. English statutory law is extremely pragmatic: instead of laying down broad principles to deal with all contingencies, issues are dealt with on an individual and an *ad hoc* basis. It has been observed, rightly it is submitted, that most English 'legislation is drafted in the form of specific rules, *ad hoc* solutions to particular problems'. This emphasis on the particular and the specific in the drafting of legislation is also motivated by a desire to obtain a high degree of certainty as regards the scope of legislation. It is a feature of English legal culture that lawyers, particularly those in the commercial field, are very hostile to commercial legislation containing open-textured concepts. Thus a concept such as that of 'control', without further detailed specification, is something to which they would take strong objection. It will also be seen that many of the problems associated with the group form are not unique to the group form of trading but arise from the use of the limited liability company to carry on trading. Accordingly, these problems have been dealt with by principles which apply to all aspects of company law and this has accordingly reduced the need for a special law to deal with groups.

II. The creation, transparency and operation of groups

12. English law facilitates, or at least puts no substantial obstacles, in the way of the creation of groups although, as will be seen later, there is a tension between legal theory and commercial practice in relation to the operation of groups. There is also a high degree of transparency with respect to the affairs of groups.

1. Creation of a group

13. It is permissible for one company to hold shares in another. The statutory requirement that all companies must possess at least two shareholders does not preclude the creation of a 'wholly owned subsidiary' as one of the shareholders can act as nominee for the other. A subsidiary is forbidden from being a member of its holding company. This prohibition does not apply where the subsidiary holds the shares as a personal representative or a trustee. The justification for this prohibition is threefold: (i) it precludes a parent company from trafficking in its own shares, (ii) it prevents the dilution of a parent company's capital and (iii) where the shares carry votes, it prevents the directors of a parent company from using these votes to keep themselves in control. . . .

2. Transparency of groups

14. English company law requires extensive disclosure by persons who have an interest in the shares of a public company (Companies Act 1985, part VI). Where a person acquires an interest in 3 per cent or more of the 'relevant share capital' of a public company, or ceases to be interested, then he must make disclosure of that interest, or of any alterations to it, within two days of the obligation arising. 'Relevant share capital' is defined as capital 'carrying rights to vote in all circumstances'. This obligation to disclose an interest in shares is also extended to cover the interests in shares of a person's spouse, infant child, or a company which a person controls. Also, where persons acting in concert acquire shares in a public company, disclosure must be made of the shares acquired pursuant to the arrangement between them. . . .

19. Cross-guarantees', 'group set-off' and 'automated end-of-day transfers', three not uncommon banking transactions, illustrate the way in which a group is often treated as a single economic entity. To enter into these transactions, a company must have a specific power in its constitution to enable it to guarantee or grant security with respect to the debts of a third party and this applies even to companies within a group. Invariably, however, commercial companies will have such an explicit power in their constitution.

   (i) *cross-guarantees*: often in the context of a bank loan to a member of a group, whether it is the parent company or a subsidiary that is borrowing the money, the other members of the group will guarantee the repayment of the loan and these cross-guarantees will be entered into by all the members of the group to guarantee each other's debts. . . .

20. Where the various members of a group are solvent (thus there will be no issue of creditor protection), it is possible to a large extent to reconcile legal theory and commercial practice where the affairs of the component members of a group are conducted in the interests of the group. It can be argued with considerable plausibility that the interests of the various members of a group are virtually synonymous with the interests of the group itself so that what is for the benefit of the group is also for the benefit of its individual members. In this way legal theory and commercial practice are to a large extent—although not completely—reconciled. Of course, in many situations the directors of a company which is part of a group will fail to consider the interests of the individual company but will act on the instructions of the parent company. However, where the company is solvent this failure to consider separately the interests of the company will not affect the validity of the transaction between the company and the third party provided 'an intelligent and honest man in the position of a director of the company concerned, could, in the whole of the existing circumstances have reasonably believed that the transactions were for the benefit of the company' (*Charterbridge Corporation Ltd* v *Lloyds Bank Ltd* [1970] Ch 62).

21. Inevitably there will be situations where it will not be possible to equate the interests of the individual members of the group with those of the group and, where this is the case, it will be improper for the directors of any group member to act so as to further the group's interests if this is not also in the interests of the individual group member. Such a transaction would be voidable (not void) and a third party dealing with the company without notice that the directors were acting improperly would be able to enforce the transaction against the company.

22. As was stated above, it is a requirement of English company law that the directors of each company within a group must only enter into transactions that are in the interests of that company and must not subordinate its interests to those of the group. This raises the difficult question of determining what are the 'interests of a company', particularly when one is dealing with a wholly owned subsidiary. English law does not present a particularly clear answer to this question, and probably the answer will vary with the context. Where a company is solvent, the interests of the company are normally taken as those of its shareholders. Thus in *Brady* v *Brady* [1988] BCLC 20, CA, it was stated that:

> The interests of the company, an artificial person, cannot be distinguished from the inter-ests of the persons who are interested in it. Who are those persons? Where a company is both going and solvent, first and foremost come the shareholders, present and no doubt future as well. How material are the interests of the creditors in such a case? Admittedly existing creditors are interested in the assets of the company as the only source for the sat-isfaction of their debts. But in a case where the assets are enormous and the debts minimal it is reasonable to suppose that the interests of the creditors ought not to count for very much. Conversely, where the company is insolvent, or even doubtfully solvent, the interests of the company are in reality the interests of existing creditors alone.

The interests of the company cannot, however, be equated absolutely with those of the sharehold-ers; as the dictum from *Brady* makes clear, where a company has substantial creditors then they will have prior claims and the interests of the company will not be those of the shareholders. In fact if the company is insolvent, the shareholders will cease to have any continued interest in the com-pany. . . .

1. Taxation

25. There are a wide range of situations in which the tax regime lays down special rules for the taxation of the profits of companies that are part of a group. The underlying policy of these rules is to treat the group as a single economic entity for tax purposes so that the fact that the economic activities of the group are conducted through separate legal entities rather than in divisional form should not affect the overall incidence of tax. . . .

2. Accounts

27. English company law has for long recognised the concept of consolidated accounts by which companies that are part of a group have to file consolidated accounts. Up until 1989, group was defined in formal, *de iure* terms of parent and subsidiary. This meant that if one company could control another without the other being its subsidiary as defined in the 1985 Act, no consolidated accounts had to be filed. It was possible by appropriate drafting to set up what were 'controlled non-subsidiaries' with the consequence that consolidated accounts did not have to be filed since the statutory definition of parent–subsidiary had not been satisfied. The obligation to implement the Seventh Directive on consolidated accounts was made use of as an opportunity to deal with this practice and, more generally, as part of regulatory attempts to come to terms with off balance sheet financing.

IV. The protection of creditors

37. An issue of some concern within the United Kingdom relates to the liability of a parent for the debts of its subsidiaries. . . .

40. Before examining in any detail these liability and disability rules, it is proposed to examine the reasons why English law has opted for a system which imposes liability on a parent company only where it is shown to have 'abused' its position rather than imposing liability solely because of its status as a parent company. The English system of regulation is seen as providing a necessary degree of flexibility in the organisation of the affairs of a group and also avoiding what are seen to be some of the policy difficulties associated the imposition of liability because of the fact that a group form exists. The following is a list of such policy considerations that have been invoked to justify the present approach.

(i) First, the limited liability company is seen as a mechanism for limiting the extent to which an entrepreneur is exposed to risk and it is felt that this facility should be available to a company in the same way that it is available to an individual. Obviously the privilege of limited liability can be abused, but the mere fact that risk is 'hived off' is not in itself considered evidence of abuse. It is considered that company law should be sufficiently flexible to enable a company to arrange its activities to limit its risk by the use of subsidiary companies but that it should not be able to use this device so as to impose unreasonable risks on others. As was stated by the Cork Committee when dealing with the question of the liability of a parent company for the liabilities of its subsidiaries:

> The availability of a limitation on liability may bear significantly on the readiness of an already prosperous company to enter upon a new enterprise. It may quite properly take the view that in the interests of its own shareholders, it should limit its risk. A change in the law [to make a parent company because of its status answerable for its subsidiary's liabilities] may, therefore, affect entrepreneurial activity, whether on a large or a small scale, in commerce and industry.

(ii) Secondly, difficult problems as regards the treatment of various classes of creditors arise if a parent is to answerable for the liabilities of its subsidiary. Such liability would entail that the whole of the assets of the group would, in the last resort, be made available to meet the liabilities of any individual member of the group. If a creditor deals with a group member on the basis that that member's assets are to be made exclusively available to meet its own debts, any form of group liability could result in such a creditor finding that the creditors of other group members possessed a potential claim on these assets. This could be seen as unfair to a creditor who dealt with a member of a group with adequate assets to pay its own debts but which is dragged into a group insolvency. . . .

(iii) Thirdly, imposing liability on a parent company for the debts of a subsidiary is considered to give rise to some special problems in the case of a subsidiary which is not wholly owned. If such liability is imposed, this could provide the minority shareholders in the subsidiary with a windfall. The potential liability of the parent company could be seen as operating virtually as a guarantee for which the subsidiary would not have to pay and this would benefit the minority shareholders in the subsidiary; this would in effect result, by operation of law, in a wealth transfer from the shareholders in the parent to the minority shareholders in the subsidiary for which the former were not compensated.

(iv) Finally, if a parent company is to be made answerable for the debts of its subsidiary, difficult questions arise in determining the extent of such liability where a new member joins or an existing member leaves the group. For example, where a member leaves a group, does the liability of the parent cease at this point or does it in some way continue?

Piercing the corporate veil

. . .

44. Given that the cases do not reflect a principled jurisprudence the following broad comments can be made. It is probably not realistic to expect any significant judicial creativity in this field. This is partly due to (a) the extent to which the corporate entity doctrine is entrenched in English company law (a doctrine which predates the evolution of the group form), (b) judicial conservatism, and (c) policy considerations which are considered to make this an area which is more suitable for legislative than judicial intervention. Given the complex issues raised by group liability, it is probably more appropriate that they should be dealt with by the legislature. In adhering to the entity doctrine in the context of groups, the courts have been influenced by precedent and legal doctrine rather than, for example, any form of economic theory that departure from the entity doctrine would be undesirable because it would impose an unreasonable risk on a parent company.

Wrongful trading: section 214 of the Insolvency Act 1986

. . .

50. There are a number of important features of s. 214 which need to be emphasised in so far as it relates to the liability of a parent company for the debts of its subsidiary:

(i)   s. 214 will only apply where a parent company is shown to have acted as a shadow director. This will be a matter of evidence and such a status (i.e. being a shadow director) is not, for example, automatically assumed where one company has majority control of another company, or even where the other company is its wholly owned subsidiary. However, in many situations it will be difficult for a parent to deny that it does not control its subsidiary's affairs. As companies are legally required to maintain extensive records of their affairs (minutes of meetings, accounts, etc.), it will be difficult for a parent company to conceal the reality of control if it is at all being exercised. In the case of a wholly owned subsidiary, or where the directors of the parent company also act as the subsidiary's directors, the inference of control will be virtually irrebuttable.

(ii) (as the section is confined to situations where the company goes into insolvent liquidation, it is obviously designed primarily to protect creditors and not shareholders. Thus it does not deal with the situation where a parent company causes damage to its subsidiary to the prejudice of minority shareholders in the subsidiary but which does not ultimately result in the insolvent liquidation of the subsidiary.

(iii) liability under s. 214 is not absolute…there is no liability where the director (or shadow director) shows that he 'took every step with a view to minimising the potential loss to the company's creditors'. There are no decisions spelling out what this defence entails, but it is reasonably clear that the standard imposed is a demanding one. However, the possibility of this defence does mean that a parent which has acted as a shadow director of its subsidiary is not made automatically liable for the debts of its insolvent subsidiary. . . .

V. The protection of minority shareholders

59. It is clear that the group structure presents the possibility that the interests of minority shareholders, particularly in subsidiaries, could be prejudiced. A parent company may operate the affairs of its subsidiary so as to maximise the overall welfare of the group and this could cause prejudice to minority shareholders in a particular subsidiary company. For example, a subsidiary might be forced to sell to another group member at less than the fair market price for its goods. Alternatively, and more subtly, the parent in allocating economic opportunities may prefer a wholly owned subsidiary at the expense of one that is partly owned.

64. Section 459 of the Companies Act 1985 contains a far-reaching provision dealing with minority shareholder oppression. . . . [Now CA 2006, s. 994.]

65. A good example of how the section could be used to protect the interests of a minority shareholder in a group situation is provided by *Scottish Co-operative Wholesale Society Ltd v Meyer* [1959] AC 324. In that case the parent company deliberately ran down the affairs of its subsidiary as part of [a scheme] to force the minority shareholder to sell his shares to the parent company. The directors of the subsidiary, who were the nominees of the parent, did nothing to protect the interests of the subsidiary. The court granted the minority shareholder relief on the grounds that the failure of the directors of the subsidiary to take steps to protect the interests of the subsidiary constituted oppression and the minority shareholder was entitled to relief. . . .

Conclusion

68. The group form is a widespread phenomenon of English commercial life and English company law places no significant impediments in the way of carrying on business in group form. There is, however, some tension between the corporate entity doctrine—requiring the separate and independent recognition of each group member—and commercial reality which on occasions (perhaps more often than not) will result in the group being operated as a single economic entity. There is no reliable data indicating whether the interests of member companies in a group are systematically subordinated to the overall interests of the group. Even if one makes the not implausible assumption that this is indeed the case, it does not follow that the affairs of each member of the group would necessarily be conducted differently from how they would have been conducted had they been treated as independent companies. Even though the affairs of each group member may be conducted so as to maximise the economic welfare of the group 'each corporation [may] be operated as a separate profit centre in order to assure that the profits of the group will be maximised': thus group maximisation of profits is achieved by maximising the profits of the individual members of the group.

69. It is recognised that the group form of trading can give rise to problems, particularly as regards the protection of creditors and minority shareholders. There is less agreement, however, as to whether these problems are uniquely associated with groups but instead are simply a consequence of the use of the corporate form to carry on business with its principle of majority control. On this latter hypothesis, if these abuses are remedied then this would also deal with them in so far as they are associated with groups. To a large extent, this has been the policy adopted by English law, with the result that there has not been felt to be a need to deal with the special problems of groups. This approach has led to the issues of creditor and minority shareholder protection being addressed, but not that relating to the facilitation of group activity, that is, creating structures that enable the group to be conducted as such.

15

Borrowing and Security

15.1.1 Financing

The financing of private companies is obviously very different from that of public companies. A public company may apply for a listing of its shares on the Stock Exchange. On the other hand private companies are not permitted to offer their shares to or solicit investment from the public.

Private company promoters can, therefore, only raise share capital from the immediate family and other private connections. The availability of 'venture capital' (finance available for investment in private company shares from specialised corporate investors) is increasing but is still the exception. Otherwise private companies have to rely on commercial borrowing from banks and the like. Many companies, private and public alike, borrow substantial amounts from banks and are often required to give security for that borrowing. The law and practice relating to these transactions is of immense academic and practical importance, and it is rare for commercial practitioners not to be deeply involved in it during their career.

Strangely, in the area of borrowing and security the company law textbooks tend to concentrate on the loan capital raised by public companies. This is an area of law encountered by only a few City practitioners. As explained below in 15.1.2, public companies sometimes offer loan or debenture stocks to the public, and these are listed on the Stock Exchange, and are traded just like ordinary shares. By the time this introduction has been read, it is hoped that the student will have disentangled and have understood the practical distinction between private borrowings from banks and the issue of loan capital to the public.

One source of confusion in this area is the use of the term 'debenture'. This usually refers to a loan secured in one form or another. It is more of a commercial term than a legal term of art, though it does sometimes have a technical meaning. For example, CA 2006, s. 738, says that the word 'debenture' in the Act 'includes debenture stock, bonds and any other securities of a company, whether or not constituting a charge on the assets of the company'. If one looks at the root of the word and removes a few letters, one is left with the word 'debt'. In broad terms, 'debenture' thus means a written acknowledgement of indebtedness. When a company borrows from a bank it usually signs a debenture document, which sets out the terms of the loan and usually the security offered. An example is reproduced at 1.7 above.

A public company may also 'issue debentures to the public', meaning the listed loan stocks already mentioned. The term 'debenture' is, therefore, very loosely used, and care has to be taken to check in what particular context the reference is made.

Another confusing term is the word 'security'. In one sense a mortgage is a security in that it secures payment of a debt. In a totally different sense shares or loan stocks issued by a company are, in the commercial world, described as 'securities' though there is no security in the earlier sense.

In the following case the court held that a particular loan instrument was not a promissory note, but a debenture and so attracted a higher rate of stamp duty under the then current Stamp Duty Act.

British India Steam Navigation Co.* v *Commissioners of Inland Revenue
(1881) 7 QBD 165

LINDLEY J: Now, what the correct meaning of 'debenture' is I do not know. I do not find anywhere any precise definition of it. We know that there are various kinds of instruments commonly called debentures. You may have mortgage debentures, which are charges of some kind on property. You may have debentures which are bonds; and, if this instrument were under seal, it would be a debenture of that kind. You may have a debenture which is nothing more than an acknowledgment of indebtedness. And you may have a thing like this, which is something more; it is a statement by two directors that the company will pay a certain sum of money on a given day, and will also pay interest half-yearly at certain times and at a certain place, upon production of certain coupons by the holder of the instrument. I think any of these things which I have referred to may be debentures within the Act.

15.1.2 Public offers of debentures

As well as offering ordinary shares to the public (known as equity share capital), public companies may offer loan stocks and debenture stocks to the public (known as loan capital). These may be listed on the Stock Exchange, and their prices quoted in the daily official list. They are issued by the company and are bought as a transferable investment. A certain value of loan or debenture stock is bought (in units of say £100) and the buyer receives a certificate. An investor may resell at any time and the trading process is very similar to buying or selling public company shares. As a more conservative investment, loans or debentures are, however, less actively traded.

The holder of loan or debenture stock is a creditor and not a member and receives interest on the amount of the stock. Investors will buy them as a safe investment in which the capital value will fluctuate relatively little. The capital value will of course fall if the ability of the company to repay comes into doubt. A loan or debenture stock offering a high fixed interest rate would, on the other hand, appreciate in value at a time when interest rates are falling.

Debentures offered to the public are fully subject to the financial services legislation and are subject to the Listing Rules. These rules, which are considered at chapter 17, refer to listed loan capital as 'debt securities', which they define as 'debentures, debenture or loan stock, bonds and notes, whether secured or unsecured'.

Public companies commonly issue debt securities, but the proportion of these to equity share capital is in total relatively small. In respect of all UK and Irish registered companies listed on the Stock Exchange, the proportion of the total market value of all debt securities to equities is generally about 1 : 20.

An example of a company that has issued debt securities is Bass plc, for which the daily official list showed four different ones quoted. One of these was a 4.5 per cent unsecured loan stock 1992/97. An investor in this loan stock would therefore receive annual interest of 4.5 per cent and the current holder was repaid the capital amount by the company between the years 1992 and 1997. Bass has also issued a 10234 per cent debenture stock 2016 (i.e., redeemable or repayable in the year 2016). This debenture stock is secured as the word 'debenture' indicates, while in contrast a 'loan stock' is not secured (though it is still called a debt security). The *Stock Exchange Official Yearbook 1992–1993* states for Bass plc, 'All debenture stocks except 10234 per cent debenture stock 2016 rank *pari passu* and are secured by trust deeds of 31 Oct. 1969, 31 Jul. 1970, 14 Jan. 1971 and 20 Jul. 1981 (to Prudential Assurance Co. Ltd) as a first floating charge on undertaking and assets of the company and 26 charging subsidiaries'. Under the terms of these trust deeds, all the assets of the company are charged by way of floating charge to the Prudential, which as trustee for the creditors (i.e., investors) supervises the possible enforcement of the security. The debentures and presumably their security rank *pari passu*; that means equally in priority. Thus in the unlikely event that the company were to fail to repay the debt and go into administrative receivership, the receiver would apply the assets of the company in paying off all the debenture holders equally according to the amount of the debentures that they each hold.

15.1.3 Bank borrowing

Arranging bank finance is one of the most important formal transactions that a private company enters into. Banks often demand that a private company give them a floating charge to secure repayment as well as mortgages over their land and premises. It is only highly creditworthy companies that can borrow substantial sums without giving security. This security is usually conferred by a debenture document such as the one reproduced at 1.7. As stated in clause 1 of that debenture, these are usually repayable on demand. If the bank is concerned that the borrower company is getting into financial difficulty, it can then demand repayment of all outstanding principal and interest. If the company is unable immediately to repay, clause 6 of the debenture document entitled the bank to appoint an administrative receiver to enforce the security. This now obsolescent remedy is explained further in 15.4.

The bank may also demand that the major shareholders (who are probably also directors) sign a personal guarantee. This is an agreement that if the company fails to repay the loan, they will be personally liable for its repayment. They may also be asked to put up further personal security, such as a mortgage on their homes. The effect of this is to remove the shield of limited liability in respect of the company's principal creditor. If the company fails and its assets are less than its indebtedness to the bank, these guarantors will be personally liable. As a result, small company proprietors are often overwhelmed by this debt on the failure of their company and then go into bankruptcy.

Where the borrower company is one of a group, it is common for collateral security to be given by other companies in the group. If a loan is made to an undercapitalised subsidiary, the lender cannot recover any shortfall from a wealthy holding company. The latter, as a separate legal person enjoys limited liability (see chapter 14). Banks often, therefore, demand that the holding company guarantee the loan to the subsidiary or offer actual security. Various legal difficulties arise where one subsidiary guarantees or secures the borrowing of another subsidiary as the transaction does not benefit the guarantor subsidiary. The directors of that subsidiary are not therefore acting for its benefit, but are acting in the interest of the borrower subsidiary. They are therefore in breach of fiduciary duty to the guarantor subsidiary, and certain legal consequences flow from this (see the *Rolled Steel* case at 5.2.2).

The following extract is from the Cork Report, which is still an invaluable source of practical and technical information on insolvency law and practice. The extract describes the importance of bank finance for companies, though the references to the floating charge are now primarily of historical interest. See 15.3.

Insolvency Law and Practice: Report of the Review Committee (The 'Cork Report')
(Cmnd 8558) (London: HMSO, 1982)

Secured creditors

1473. One notable change in commercial life which has taken place during the present century …is the increase in the extent to which working capital for commerce and industry is raised by means of secured loans from commercial lenders.

1474. In the nineteenth century, it was usual for the greater part of the capital required for any business to be provided by those who were engaged in carrying it on or, in the case of the larger enterprises, by investors who were willing to risk their own savings. The individual, trading alone or in partnership, did so without the benefit of imited liability; he invested his own, or his family's money in the business and avoided borrowing from commercial lenders. The joint stock company, trading with limited liability, obtained its working capital from investors to whom it issued its share capital, often in the form of partly paid shares; if further capital was needed, it called upon its shareholders to provide it. If investors sought a fixed return for their money they subscribed for preference shares and, like other investors in the enterprise, were subordinated to the claims of creditors if it failed.

1475. A very different picture is presented today. The small trader tends nowadays to carry on business through the medium of a company with limited liability; though he usually does so as much for tax reasons as from any desire to avoid personal liability. The company's share capital is often small, and may be nominal in amount; it seldom provides a significant proportion of the company's working capital. The greater part of this is borrowed, usually by way of overdraft from a bank, at a variable rate of interest, repayable on demand, and often guaranteed by the principal directors and shareholders, their guarantees being supported by charges on their personal assets. The small businessman is thus still personally liable without limitation of liability, at least to his major creditor, but he trades with much of his working capital borrowed from a secured commercial lender.

1476. In the case of the larger corporate enterprise partly paid shares have virtually disappeared and new issues of preference shares are seldom made. Working capital is provided partly by share capital and reserves and to a major extent by borrowing. Such capital is often raised by way of overdraft facilities from a bank, repayable on demand and secured by a floating charge on the whole, or substantially the whole, of the company's undertaking. In recent years, companies' borrowing requirements have increasingly been met by fixed-term advances, similarly secured.

1477. …a significant part of the working capital of the corporate sector, particularly that part of it which consists of loan finance provided by the banking community, is raised upon the security of floating charges; and it is thought that the greater part of the materials in course of processing and of the ordinary stock in trade of the corporate sector is subject to them. [Since the Enterprise Act 2002, this will no longer be the case. See 15.3.]

1478. These changes have had a major impact upon the financial consequences of any commercial insolvency. They have resulted in the withdrawal of an increasing proportion of the debtor's assets from the claims of the general body of creditors. The creditor who stipulates for security does so with the specific object of minimising his loss or avoiding it altogether in the event of the debtor's insolvency. By taking security he acquires a proprietary interest in the mortgaged assets; only the equity of redemption remains the property of the debtor and available, in the event of his insolvency, for the general body of his creditors. On the debtor's failure, the secured creditor may resort to his security, which he is usually free to realise for his own benefit and at a time of his own choosing without reference to and independently of the insolvency, and without regard to the effect upon other creditors.

15.1.4 Types of security

The most familiar form of security is the mortgage on land. This is an attractive security because land does not generally depreciate and cannot be destroyed or disappear. Because of the system of transfer of title by documents, the mortgage can be protected by deposit of title deeds and registration of the mortgage (see 15.2.1). The use of goods as security raises more difficult problems which are mentioned in 15.2.

A mortgage may be a legal mortgage, created by a mortgage document granting to the lender a legal interest in specified property as security for the loan. The security enables the lender, on the insolvency of the debtor or borrower, to appropriate the specific property and sell it to pay off the debt, free of the claims of other creditors. Thus the secured creditor is probably paid off in full while unsecured creditors may recover little or nothing in the debtor's liquidation.

An equitable mortgage is an agreement for a mortgage or an uncompleted mortgage such as a mere deposit of title documents (no longer recognised in the case of land after 27 September 1989). It may also be a mortgage of an equitable interest. Equitable mortgages were not recognised by the law but are only enforceable in equity. An example is the floating, as opposed to fixed, security. A mortgage of a house is a fixed security as the house is specified in the mortgage document. A floating security is not fixed upon a specific asset but upon a changing class of assets. (Floating charges are dealt with in 15.3 and have in effect been abolished.) The term 'charge' is used to denote any form of security interest.

Another source of financing is to offer book debts or invoices as security. The term book debts refers to debts owed to the company in the ordinary course of business which are entered in the books of the company. A company dealing in machine tools, for example, may sell on 60 days' credit. The total unpaid invoices over a 60-day period may be very substantial and can be used as security for finance. Alternatively, immediate cash can be raised by an outright assignment of book debts to a finance company, the amount paid being at a discount to the face value of the debts.

The following extract from the Diamond Report helpfully describes the broader functions of security and distinguishes security interests properly so called granting a property interest to the creditor from those such as retention of title which do not (considered below at 15.2.3).

A. L. Diamond, *A Review of Security Interests in Property*

(London: Department of Trade and Industry, 1981)

Security interests

The nature of security

3.1 There are two types of security. One type is often known as personal security. This is where a person who is not otherwise liable under a contract between the debtor and the creditor enters into a separate contract with the creditor under which he assumes some form of liability to ensure that the creditor does not lose (or loses less than he otherwise might) if the debtor fails to perform his contractual obligations. The debtor's contractual obligations may involve the payment of money, but this is not necessarily the case: they may require the performance of any kind of act. Personal security may take the form of a guarantee, caution or indemnity, or may be known as a performance bond. This report is not concerned with this form of security.

3.2 The other type of security is security over property. This is a right relating to property, the purpose of which is to improve the creditor's chance of getting paid or of receiving whatever else the debtor is required to do by way of performance of the contract. It is this type of security—security over property other than land—which is the subject-matter of this report. Such security may be possessory, where the creditor takes possession of the subject-matter of the security, or non-possessory.

The purpose of security

3.3 As stated in the last paragraph, the purpose of security is to improve the creditor's chance of obtaining performance of the contract with the debtor. In particular, the taking of security may have any one or more of the following effects:

(a) *Coercion*   In most situations the last thing the creditor wants is to have to enforce his security. His prime objective is that the contract he has entered into with the debtor should be performed. The debtor's fear that the security may be enforced, or a threat by the creditor to enforce the security, will often be enough to ensure that a debtor who is having difficulty in fulfilling all his contracts will give priority to performance in favour of the secured creditor.

(b) *Insolvency*   If the debtor is unable to meet all his obligations, the creditor with security will usually be in a better position than unsecured creditors, for he will be able to look to the security which, if it has sufficient value, will enable him to receive money on its disposal. In some situations the agreement creating the right by way of security will entitle the creditor to appoint a receiver in specified circumstances.

(c) *Execution or diligence*   Another creditor may, usually after obtaining a judgment against the debtor, attempt to seize the debtor's property by way of execution or diligence, or a landlord may, without obtaining a judgment, distrain on the debtor's goods or sequestrate the debtor's goods for rent. The holder of security will hope to exercise his rights against the property subject to the security and to prevent seizure by or on behalf of the other creditor.

(d) *Sale*   If the debtor purports to sell the subject-matter of the security interest, the question arises whether the holder of the security interest can assert his rights as against the buyer or whether he can, in the alternative or in addition, lay claim to the proceeds of the sale in the debtor's hands.

(e) *General*   The above may be summed up in Professor Goode's words:

'All forms of real security...confer on the secured creditor at least two basic real rights: the right of pursuit, and the right of preference. The secured party can follow his asset, and its products and proceeds, into the hands of any third party other than one acquiring an overriding title by virtue of some exception to the *nemo dat* rule; and the secured party is entitled to look to the proceeds of the asset to satisfy the debt due to him in priority to the claims of other creditors. (R.M. Goode, *Commercial Law* (Harmondsworth: Penguin 1982), p. 733.)

Professor Goode continues:

Other real rights are available for the enforcement of the security, depending on the nature of the security interest. These are: the retention or recovery of possession of the asset; sale of the asset; foreclosure; and an order vesting legal title in the secured creditor.

Security interest

3.4 It is necessary to say something about my use of the term 'security interest'. I use it to encompass two types of interest in or relating to property.

(i) The first type arises where the debtor (or someone else), as owner of property (or as the holder of some other interest in property), creates in favour of the creditor an interest in the property, or a right to look to the property, to secure the debtor's obligations. The interest created may be the transfer of full legal ownership or the creation or transfer of some lesser right. The interest may be variously described as a mortgage, charge, floating charge, security, pledge or lien.

(ii) The second type is where rights in property are created or retained by the creditor for the same purpose. For example, although a hire-purchase agreement takes the form of a letting of goods on hire, and the debtor has merely an option to purchase those goods, it is generally acknowledged today that the real objective of the parties is a sale of the goods from the creditor to the debtor, the debtor paying by instalments. Neither the creditor nor the debtor looks on the agreement as a true hiring, the agreement taking the form it does to enable the creditor to repossess the goods if the debtor defaults and to get the goods back from a purchaser if the debtor wrongly sells them (*Helby* v *Matthews* [1895] AC 471). In this type of transaction I have throughout this report referred to the creditor's ownership, retained under the hire-purchase agreement until the price is paid in full and the option to purchase exercised, as a security interest. Similarly, I regard the seller's title retained under a conditional sale agreement or a retention of title clause as a security interest.

3.5 I realise that by including the creditor's interests referred to in subparagraph (ii) above within the category of 'security interests' I am departing from what is usually thought to be the present state of the law. The conventional distinction in English law is between real rights created by the debtor, such as a mortgage or charge, and rights retained by the creditor, such as retention of title. In strict law the latter are not rights by way of security. This was clearly established in England and Wales by the House of Lords in a case dealing with a retention of title clause, *McEntire* v *Crossley Brothers Ltd* [1895] AC 457.

15.2 REGISTRATION OF CHARGES

15.2.1 Perfection of security

The Companies Act 1985 required most mortgages, charges and other security interests created by a company to be perfected by registration at the Companies Registry. Third parties are thus able to obtain details of them in order to assess the general creditworthiness of the company and to check whether a particular asset is encumbered. The Act goes on to say that failure to register within the specified time of 21 days makes the security, though not the debt, void and unenforceable in certain respects. Precise details of this and the particular charges that are registrable appear from the sections extracted below.

The purpose of perfection of security is to enable the secured lender to assert the security rights against a third party. A third party who buys property subject to a perfected security will be obliged to pay off the amount secured to the holder of the security, even though it was the seller who was the debtor and created the security. So that this is not unjust to the third party, the law requires the security to be perfected by statutory registration which puts the world on notice. Somebody buying a major asset, such as land, from a company (or wanting to check its credit-worthiness) will thus do a search at the Companies Registry to see if there is a debt secured for example by mortgage against that asset.

The classic form of mortgage is that of land where the mortgage is created by formal documentation and the title documents are deposited with the secured creditor. (However, since the Law of Property (Miscellaneous Provisions) Act 1989, s. 2 came into effect, a deposit of title deeds is no longer effective to create an equit-able mortgage.) It is much more difficult to perfect a security over chattels as these can be freely disposed of by delivery, and transfer of ownership does not require documentation.

The effect of registration of a charge at Companies House is to give constructive notice of the security to third parties taking a charge over the company's property. Registration is thus a notification of the whole world and validates the security against third parties.

The history of the reform of legislation on registration of charges has been a long and difficult one. The CA 1989 enacted a series of new provisions on registration of company charges but these were not brought into force and have been repealed. Reform was further considered in the consultation document, *Modern Company Law for a Competitive Economy, No. 7, Registration of Company Charges* (October 2000). Finally, the Law Commission issued a report entitled *Registration of Security Interests: Company Charges and Property Other Than Land*, LC 295 in August 2005 in which they proposed a simple online registration system and removal of the exist-ing 21-day time limit for filing the electronic notice.

15.2.2 The mechanics of registration

Only the categories of charges listed in CA 2006, s. 860, require registration. However, the list is comprehensive omitting few possibilities only, such as a charge on shares owned by the company. Section 870 sets out the 21-day time limit for registration of charges, a requirement etched into the consciousness of commercial practitioners as the section enables a liquidator to ignore an unregistered charge and to sell the secured assets for the benefit of the unsecured creditors. Section 401 puts subsequent lenders on notice of charges duly registered.

COMPANIES ACT 2006, PART 25

860. Charges created by a company

(1) A company that creates a charge to which this section applies must deliver the prescribed particulars of the charge, together with the instrument (if any) by which the charge is cre-ated or evidenced, to the registrar for registration before the end of the period allowed for registration.

(7) This section applies to the following charges—

(a) a charge on land or any interest in land, other than a charge for any rent or other periodical sum issuing out of land,

(b) a charge created or evidenced by an instrument which, if executed by an individual, would require registration as a bill of sale,

(c) a charge for the purposes of securing any issue of debentures,

(d) a charge on uncalled share capital of the company,

(e) a charge on calls made but not paid,

(f) a charge on book debts of the company,

(g) a floating charge on the company's property or undertaking,

(h) a charge on a ship or aircraft, or any share in a ship,

(i) a charge on goodwill or on any intellectual property.

870. The period allowed for registration

(1) The period allowed for registration of a charge created by a company is—

(a) 21 days beginning with the day after the day on which the charge is created, or

(b) if the charge is created outside the United Kingdom, 21 days beginning with the day after the day on which the instrument by which the charge is created or evidenced (or a copy of it) could, in due course of post (and if despatched with due diligence) have been received in the United Kingdom.

869. Register of charges to be kept by registrar

(1) The registrar shall keep, with respect to each company, a register of all the charges requiring registration under this Chapter.

(7) The register kept in pursuance of this section shall be open to inspection by any person.

874. Consequence of failure to register charges created by a company

(1) If a company creates a charge to which section 860 applies, the charge is void (so far as any security on the company's property or undertaking is conferred by it) against—

(a) a liquidator of the company,

(b) an administrator of the company, and

(c) a creditor of the company,

unless that section is complied with.

(2) Subsection (1) is subject to the provisions of this Chapter.

(3) Subsection (1) is without prejudice to any contract or obligation for repayment of the money secured by the charge; and when a charge becomes void under this section, the money secured by it immediately becomes payable.

15.2.3 Retention of title

It will be seen therefore that registration is an essential but quite complex procedure necessary to perfect and validate most forms of security given by companies over their assets. However, creditors of companies have also attempted to create devices equivalent to security without the necessity for registration. The most common circumstance is that unpaid sellers of goods may wish to secure payment on the goods sold, thus entitling them to recover the goods from the buyer on default in payment. The most successful of these devices is hire-purchase, which enables the 'seller' to pursue the goods 'sold' not only against the defaulting 'buyer' but also against an innocent sub-purchaser.

Also free of the need to register is the retention of title clause in the commercial sale of goods. When a seller delivers goods on credit to the buyer, but retains title to them (i.e., general ownership) until payment, if the buyer becomes insolvent, the seller can recover any of the goods that have not been paid for. The buyer's receiver or liquidator is not entitled to them as they are not the property of the insolvent buyer. The seller can thus recover and resell the goods rather than having to prove for a minimal dividend in the winding up or bankruptcy of the buyer. Though the primary purpose of retention of title is to secure payment of the price, it has been repeatedly held that the agreement does not require registration as a charge if title is claimed only to the goods sold (see *Clough Mill Ltd* v *Martin* extracted below). The law does not regard it as a registrable security if the seller continues ownership of the goods after delivery to the buyer. Thus simple reservation of title is not registrable as a charge. However, certain extended claims may be registrable. If, for example, the buyer processes the goods sold to create a new product (as in *Re Bond Worth Ltd* [1980] Ch 228 extracted at 15.3.1) that product is the property of the buyer. Any rights over it reserved by the seller until such time only as the price has been paid are treated as a registrable security. As registration of every such sale contract is not practicable, claims to new products seem doomed to failure. In the sale contract a seller may also assert that the proceeds of resale of the goods do not belong to the buyer but that the seller is entitled to trace them into the hands of the buyer or to collect payment from the sub-buyer. Such a claim, being determinable on the payment to the seller of the price for the goods, was held in *Compaq Computer Ltd* v *Abercorn Group Ltd* (extracted below) to be a registrable charge.

Clough Mill Ltd v Martin

Retention of title to the goods sold is not a registrable charge

[1984] 3 All ER 982, [1985] 1 WLR 111, Court of Appeal

Clough Mill Ltd sold yarn on credit terms to HF Ltd. By the first sentence of condition 12 of the sale contract the seller retained ownership until payment in full. If payment was overdue the seller was entitled to recover and resell the yarn. The fourth sentence read, 'If any of the [yarn] is incorporated or used as material for other goods before such payment the property in the whole such goods shall be and remain with the seller until such payment has been made'. While Clough Mill was still unpaid, Martin was appointed as receiver of the buyer company. The matter at issue was what rights Clough Mill as seller had to the unused yarn.

The Court of Appeal held that the first sentence was enforceable by the seller as title to the yarn was effectively retained, even though the fourth sentence constituted a registrable charge over new products made with the yarn. (The seller was not attempting to recover new products in this case.)

OLIVER LJ: Counsel for the receiver relies on the proposition of law to be found in the judgment of Slade J in *Re Bond Worth Ltd* [1980] Ch 228 at p. 248 expressed thus:

> ... any contract which, by way of security for the payment of a debt, confers an interest in property defeasible or destructible on payment of such debt, or appropriates such property for the discharge of the debt, must necessarily be regarded as creating a mortgage or charge, as the case may be.

The operative word here, however, is 'confers' and the whole of Slade J's judgment in that case was based on the fact, as he found, that the legal title to the goods had passed to the buyer. That was in the context of a clause which, in terms, sought to reserve only to the seller the 'beneficial' interest and to seek to apply it to the condition now under consideration is to assume the very thing that is sought to be proved.

Of course, where the legal title has passed, security can be provided by a charge created by the new legal owner. But it is not a necessary incident of the seller's securing his position that he should pass the legal title. The whole question is: how has his position been secured? If in fact he has retained the legal title to the goods, then by definition the buyer cannot have charged them in his favour.

SIR JOHN DONALDSON MR: So far as is material in deciding this appeal, I am in complete agreement with the judgment of Robert Goff LJ. Section 95 of the Companies Act 1948 provides [similarly to the current s. 874]:

> (1) ... every charge created...by a company...shall, so far as any security on the company's property...is conferred thereby, be void against the liquidator and any creditor of the company...

Accordingly s. 95 can only apply if (a) the company creates a charge and (b) that charge *confers* a security on *the company's property*.

The appellants' demands on the receiver related solely to unused and unsold yarn and it is quite clear that, if the first sentence of condition 12 had stood alone, s. 95 would have had no application. The agreement between the appellants and the buyers involved the appellants *retaining* property in the goods. It did not involve the buyers *conferring* a charge on any property, still less on their own property.

The argument that the object of the exercise was to give the appellants security for the price of the yarn does not of itself advance the matter. Just as it is possible to increase the amount of cash available to a business by borrowing, buying on hire-purchase or credit sale terms, factoring book debts or raising additional share capital, all with different legal incidents, so it is possible to achieve security for an unpaid purchase price in different ways, with different legal consequences. The parties have chosen not to use the charging method in relation to unused yarn.

Fortunately we do not have to decide whether the fourth sentence creates a charge to which s. 95 would apply. I say 'fortunately', because this seems to me to be a difficult question. If the incorporation of the yarn in, or its use as material for, other goods leaves the yarn in a separate and identifiable state, I see no reason why the appellants should not retain property in it and thereby avoid the application of s. 95. However, in that situation I should have thought that the buyers were clearly purporting to create a charge on the 'other goods', which would never have been the appellants' goods. I say 'purporting', because those goods might themselves remain the property of another supplier in consequence of the inclusion of the equivalent of the first sentence of condition 12 in the relevant sale contract. If, on the other hand, the incorporation of the yarn created a situation in which it ceased to be identifiable and a new product was created consisting of the yarn and the other material, it would be necessary to determine who owned that product. If, and to the extent that, the answer was the buyers, it seems to me that the fourth sentence would create a charge.

For present purposes I am content to assume that in some circumstances the fourth sentence would indeed give rise to a charge to which s. 95 would apply, but they are not the circumstances which exist in the instant appeal and I see no reason to distort the plain language of the first sentence on the false assumption that the parties must be deemed to have intended that the same legal framework should apply both before and after the yarn was made up into other goods.

Compaq Computer Ltd v *Abercorn Group Ltd*

Claims to the proceeds of resale

[1991] BCC 484, [1993] BCLC 602, Chancery Division

This case contains a useful summary of the law of retention of title in respect of claims to the goods sold, and where the buyer has resold the goods, in respect of the original seller's claim to the proceeds of resale.

MUMMERY J: The accumulation of decisions on retention of title clauses since the *Romalpa* case (*Aluminium Industrie Vaassen BV* v *Romalpa Aluminium Ltd* [1976] 1 WLR 676) makes it possible to state some well-settled principles without the need to refer in detail to the facts and legal discussion in individual cases. The authorities exhibit a wide variety of factual situations. There is, for example, the relatively straightforward case of a clause retaining title to goods pending payment of the purchase price and compliance with other conditions, where those goods remain unchanged and identifiable in the possession of the buyer. A more complicated case is where the goods in which title has been retained by the seller have, after delivery to the buyer but before payment of the price, been mixed with other goods or incorporated with other goods into manufactured articles. This case is concerned with the even more complex situation where the seller has not been paid the price of the goods or other sums owing to him, and the buyer has sold the goods to a subpurchaser who has either paid the price of the goods to the original buyer or is under a contractual obligation to pay for those goods....

It appears from the authorities that the following general points are relevant to the preliminary points of law on the charge issue.

(1) The broad purpose of an agreement that a seller retains title to goods pending payment of the purchase price and other moneys owing to him is to protect the seller from the insolvency of the buyer in circumstances where the price and other moneys remain unpaid. The seller's aim in insisting on a retention of title clause is to prevent the goods and the proceeds of sale of the goods from becoming part of the assets of an insolvent buyer, available to satisfy the claims of the general body of creditors.

(2) It does not, however, follow that this purpose predetermines the legal form of protection agreed upon or its legal consequences. The question is: how has the position of the seller been secured? On the one hand it may be held that, on the true construction of the particular agreement, the seller has retained full legal and beneficial title in physical goods. In those circumstances the court cannot hold that the buyer has created a charge on such goods in favour of the seller. It is not legally possible for the buyer to charge in favour of the seller a title or interest which the buyer has not got. On the other hand if, on the true construction of the agreement, the legal title to the goods has passed from the seller to the buyer, the court may conclude that the legal consequence of the agreement is that the position of the seller is in fact secured by a charge created in his favour over the goods by the buyer: compare *Clough Mill Ltd* v *Martin* [1985] 1 WLR 111 at pp. 122E–123D with *Re Bond Worth Ltd* [1980] Ch 228 at p. 248.

(3) In determining whether any given agreement creates a charge, equity looks to the substance and reality of the transaction. What on the face of it may appear to be an out-and-out disposition of a legal or equitable interest in property by way of assignment or conveyance or an out-and-out disposition of a beneficial interest in property by way of trust, may in fact be by way of security only, with a right of redemption and, therefore, in the nature of a charge: see, for example, *Re Kent & Sussex Sawmills Ltd* [1947] Ch 177 at p. 181, and *Re Welsh Irish Ferries Ltd* [1986] Ch 471 at p. 478.

(4) An unpaid seller, who contends for a direct claim (other than by way of charge) to the proceeds of sale of goods subsold by the original buyer, cannot establish an equitable right to or to trace the proceeds simply by relying on the retention of title to the physical goods subsold. There is no equity to trace into a mixed fund in the absence of a fiduciary relationship. The unpaid seller must establish that there was a fiduciary relationship between himself and the original buyer affecting the proceeds of sale.

(5) The existence of a fiduciary relationship in this context depends on whether the parties have agreed terms, either expressly or by implication, which, when construed in the context of the whole agreement and the surrounding circumstances of the individual case, are appropriate to create such a relationship.

(6) The relationships of bailor and bailee and principal and agent are normally fiduciary, but not necessarily so. Contractual or juridical labels are not conclusive of the nature of the relationship. In the *Romalpa* case the fiduciary relationship of bailment was conceded by counsel and there was a finding that there was a relationship of agency with an implied power of sale on account of the unpaid seller and a fiduciary obligation to account fully to him for all the proceeds of sale. Later cases illustrate how the existence of a fiduciary relationship in the cases of bailment or agency may be negatived by contractual terms inconsistent with the existence of fiduciary obligations. For example, it has been held that there was no implied fiduciary relationship where the buyer was expressly allowed credit for a fixed period and could make subsales of the goods during the period

of credit and use the proceeds of sales effected within that period as he wished, nor where the buyer was permitted to mix the proceeds of sale with his own money and then deal with them as he pleased in his business. Such provisions are more consistent with the relationships of buyer and seller and of debtor and creditor than with a fiduciary relationship.

15.3 FLOATING CHARGES

15.3.1 Nature of floating charges

The once mighty floating charge has recently been brought low. The Enterprise Act 2002, s. 250, enacting a new Part III, Chapter IV to the Insolvency Act 1986, effective from 15 September 2003, has made any new floating charge ineffective as the lender may no longer appoint an administrative receiver to enforce payment of the debt. However, the old law is not yet dead as floating charges created before that date are not affected by the reform and as Part III exempts from the section a number of floating charges relating to capital market arrangements, public-private partnership projects etc as defined. It is thus still necessary to recognise a floating charge when you see one, though like elephants, floating charges are recognisable but hard to define.

The following brief words in a debenture document (similar to para. 3(b) of the bank debenture reproduced at 1.6) create a floating charge, and in the past were effective to give the lender unparalleled rights of security over all the free assets of the company:

The company hereby charges with the payment or discharge of all moneys to be paid by the company by way of a first floating charge all the undertaking and assets of the company whatsoever and wheresoever both present and future.

The floating charge was the creation of commercial lawyers and of the courts of equity. It is not something created by statute. While a fixed mortgage is suitable as security over a substantial asset that the borrower will not dispose of, a floating charge was able to cover any or all of the assets of the company. A floating charge could be a charge on a varying class of assets such as a floating charge on book debts, for example, but more usually it was over all the undertaking and assets of the company. What distinguishes a floating charge from a fixed charge is the understanding that the borrower is free to deal with or dispose of the assets in the ordinary course of business. Buckley LJ in *Evans v Rival Granite Quarries Ltd* [1910] 2 KB 979 at p. 999 concluded also that a floating charge is a present security:

A floating charge is not a future security; it is a present security, which presently affects all the assets of the company expressed to be included in it.... A floating security is not a specific mortgage of the assets, plus a licence to the mortgagor to dispose of them in the course of his business, but is a floating mortgage applying to every item comprised in the security, but not specifically affecting any item until some event occurs or some act on the part of the mortgagee is done which causes it to crystallise into a fixed security.

It is these features which determine that a charge is a floating and not a fixed charge, whether the parties or documents call it a fixed or floating charge. If the borrower was in default in paying the loan (or commits other defaults specified in the debenture document) the lender could intervene and cause the floating charge to become fixed upon the assets in the secured class, usually by appointing an administrative receiver who took possession of the secured assets. However, under a new s. 72A of the Insolvency Act 1986 (inserted by Enterprise Act 2002, s. 250), a holder of a floating charge created after the new law was brought into force may no longer appoint an administrative receiver. Thus administrative receivership is prospectively 'abolished', precluding any new floating charges being created, though administrative receivers will continue to be validly appointed to enforce payment of existing loans made before the law was reformed. Under the new law, the lender may now instead appoint an 'administrator' (Enterprise Act 2002, Schedule B1 para. 14). See 15.4.2 and Mayson, French and Ryan, *Company Law* (Oxford, OUP, 2007) at 20.3.

The following extracts from the Cork Report and from *Re Bond Worth Ltd* describe the principal features of the floating charge.

Insolvency Law and Practice: Report of the Review Committee
(The 'Cork Report')
(Cmnd 8558) (London: HMSO, 1982)

Receivership

100. Bankruptcy of individuals, and the winding up of companies are primarily concerned with the realisation of the uncharged assets, and the distribution of their proceeds among the unsecured creditors. Receivership is concerned with the realisation of the assets of a company which are subject to a floating charge, and the payment of the proceeds to the holder of the charge in or towards discharge of his security. Secured creditors normally resort to their security, which they are usually free to realise outside and independently of the bankruptcy or winding up, and without regard to the effect upon the unsecured creditors. If the security is deficient, they are entitled to be treated as unsecured creditors to the extent of the deficiency, and to that extent participate in the bankruptcy or winding up.

101. English law has long since developed convenient and flexible forms of security over land and intangible property such as stocks and shares. However, it has developed no convenient and readily available form of chattel mortgage with the exceptions, first of the security bill of sale, a cumbrous and hazardous instrument applicable only to individuals and not to companies, secondly, of the agricultural charge grantable only by farmers to bankers, and thirdly, and most important, of the floating charge. By a historical accident, the floating charge is peculiar to companies; it cannot effectively be created by an individual (except in the case of a farmer).

102. The floating charge was devised by the Court of Chancery in the 1860s, and its validity was first recognised by the Court of Appeal in Chancery in a case in 1870. It is a creature of equity. It has three principal characteristics:
   (a) it is a charge on a class of assets of a company both present and future;
   (b) those assets are of a kind which, in the ordinary course of the business of a company, would be changing from time to time; and
   (c) it is contemplated that, until some step is taken by or on behalf of those interested in the charge, the company may carry on its business in the ordinary way, and dispose of all or any of those assets in the ordinary course of business.

103. A floating charge is, therefore, an equitable charge on present and future assets. It does not attach to any specific property, but constitutes a charge upon assets which are constantly varying. It is commonly given over the whole of the undertaking of the borrowing company. Even in such a

case, however, the company remains free to deal with and dispose of its property without consulting the holder of the charge. Upon the happening of an event set out in the deed constituting the charge, or on the appointment of a receiver (whether by the court or by the holder of the charge under a power contained in it) or on the winding up of the company, the floating charge is said to 'crystallise'. The company ceases to be free to deal with or dispose of the assets then subject to the charge, which from then on becomes indistinguishable from a fixed charge on those specific assets.

104. The floating charge possesses great advantages, and it was quickly adopted by the financial community. It permits the easy creation of security upon the entire undertaking of the borrowing company, thus conferring the maximum security upon the lender, while at the same time permitting the borrowing company complete freedom to deal with and dispose of its assets in the ordinary course of business. So widespread has the use of the floating charge become, that today it is thought that the greater part of the loan finance obtained by the corporate sector, particularly in the case of the finance obtained from the banking community, is raised upon the security of such charges; and that the greater part of the materials in course of processing and of the ordinary stock in trade of the corporate sector is subject to them.

Re Bond Worth Ltd

A seller seeks to secure payment of the price
[1980] Ch 228, Chancery Division

The following extract is a useful comment on the nature of the floating charge, and cites several classic and much-quoted judicial definitions. The wider significance of the case is that a commercial sale agreement may inadvertently create a floating charge.

Facts   *Fibres were sold on credit to Bond Worth Ltd to be woven into carpets. A 'retention of title' agreement stated that ownership of the fibre would remain with the seller and the seller would have equitable ownership of the carpets produced from the fibre until the price of the fibre had been paid. Bond Worth Ltd went into receivership (i.e., the bank lender enforced its floating charge). The seller unsuccessfully claimed the carpets from the receiver. It was held that ownership had passed to the buyer. As the buyer was free to deal with the carpets in the ordinary course of business, the seller had a floating equitable charge over the carpets as security for the purchase price. However, as this charge had not been registered (see 15.2) it was void against the liquidator. (The seller could therefore not enforce the security but would have to prove in the buyer's liquidation as an unsecured creditor.)*

SLADE J: There is, however, one type of charge (and I think one type only) which, by its very nature, leaves a company at liberty to deal with the assets charged in the ordinary course of its business, without regard to the charge, until stopped by a winding up or by the appointment of a receiver or the happening of some other agreed event. I refer to what is commonly known as a 'floating charge'....Such a charge remains unattached to any particular property and leaves the company with a licence to deal with, and even sell, the assets falling within its ambit in the ordinary course of business, as if the charge had not been given, until it is stopped by one or other of the events to which I have referred, when it is said to 'crystallise'; it then becomes effectively fixed to the assets within its scope.

Romer LJ in *Re Yorkshire Woolcombers Association Ltd* [1903] 2 Ch 284, gave the following description of a floating charge at p. 295:

> I certainly do not intend to attempt to give an exact definition of the term 'floating charge' nor am I prepared to say that there will not be a floating charge within the meaning of the Act, which does not contain all of the three characteristics that I am about to mention, but I certainly think that if a charge has the three characteristics that I am about to mention, it is a floating charge. (1) If it is a charge on a class of assets of a company present and future;

(2) if that class is one which, in the ordinary course of the business of the company, would be changing from time to time; and (3) if you find that by the charge it is contemplated that, until some future step is taken by or on behalf of those interested in the charge, the company may carry on its business in the ordinary way as far as concerns the particular class of assets I am dealing with.

This description of a floating charge shows that it need not extend to all the assets of the company. It may cover assets merely of a specified category or categories....

Romer LJ himself disclaimed any intention of saying that there could not be a floating charge within the meaning of the Companies Acts which did not contain all the three characteristics that he mentioned.

The critical distinction in my judgment is that between a specific charge on the one hand and a floating charge on the other. Vaughan Williams LJ pointed out in the *Woolcombers* case that it is quite inconsistent with the nature of a specific charge, though not of a floating charge, that the mortgagor is at liberty to deal with the relevant property as he pleases. He said, at p. 294:

I do not think that for a 'specific security' you need have a security of a subject-matter which is then in existence. I mean by 'then' at the time of the execution of the security; but what you do require to make a specific security is that the security whenever it has once come into existence, and been identified or appropriated as a security, shall never thereafter at the will of the mortgagor cease to be a security. If at the will of the mortgagor he can dispose of it and prevent its being any longer a security, although something else may be substituted more or less for it, that is not a 'specific security'.

When that case went on appeal to the House of Lords, under the name *Illingworth* v *Houldsworth* [1904] AC 355, Lord Macnaghten drew the distinction between a specific charge and a floating charge in the following terms, at p. 358:

A specific charge, I think, is one that without more fastens on ascertained and definite property or property capable of being ascertained and defined; a floating charge, on the other hand, is ambulatory and shifting in its nature, hovering over and so to speak floating with the property which it is intended to affect until some event occurs or some act is done which causes it to settle and fasten on the subject of the charge within its reach and grasp.

...

Accordingly in the end I answer question (c) above [the legal effect of the retention of title clause] by saying that in my judgment the effect of the retention of title clause was to create floating equitable charges over the four categories of charged assets, for the purpose of securing payment of the purchase prices due under the relevant orders, and to constitute Bond Worth a trustee of such assets for the purpose of such security, but for no other purpose.

15.4 ADMINISTRATIVE RECEIVERSHIP

15.4.1 A brief description

The following briefly describes how a bank or other creditor holding a floating charge created before the restrictions enacted by the Enterprise Act 2002, s. 250 came into effect, enforces its security. Pursuant to its contractual rights under the debenture document it may appoint a receiver, who is called an 'administrative receiver' (see below) where the floating charge is over all or substantially all of the assets of the company. The bank may appoint following a default by the borrower. Or if the bank anticipates default, it is usually entitled to demand repayment and immediately to appoint when the borrower inevitably fails to repay. The bank chooses an administrative receiver from the ranks of local insolvency practitioners anxiously waiting for the work. The insolvency practitioner must be authorised under IA 1986, part XIII (see IA 1986, s. 230(2)) and will generally be a member of a private firm of accountants. The appointment is made in accordance with the debenture document and is usually effected by a simple written document. An insolvency practitioner will not accept the appointment unless there are sufficient assets subject to the charge to pay his or her costs and expenses and to give a reasonable pay-out to the bank. That morning, to their surprise, the directors of the company will be notified that an administrative receiver has been appointed, who is taking possession of the company's premises and assets. The administrative receiver's powers supersede those of the directors and the receiver has total control of the assets of the company. The appointment is then notified to the Registrar of Companies.

One of the administrative receiver's first acts will be to instruct solicitors to advise whether his or her appointment is valid. If, for example, the directors who entered into the debenture on behalf of the company were not authorised to sign it, if the debenture was not duly executed by the company, if it was not properly registered with the Registrar of Companies, if no event had occurred entitling the bank to enforce the floating charge, or if for any other reason the floating charge was void or unenforceable, then the appointment will be invalid. The administrative receiver could then be liable for intermeddling in the affairs of the company.

The administrative receiver's first practical move will be to secure the assets of the company before they 'walk'. This will be done by changing the locks, locking up the premises, turning away surplus employees, taking inventories and posting security guards. The administrative receiver will have to make a quick decision as to whether to close down the business or businesses entirely. Sometimes existing contracts only, such as for construction of a ship or a house, may be completed. Otherwise a business which is potentially viable may be sold as a going concern. For example, factory premises with all plant and equipment and with skilled and experienced employees and managers in post may be worth significantly more than the sum of the parts if the business is sold on a break-up basis. The administrative receiver, in taking over from the directors, is empowered to run the business, pending a sale. As agent of the company, a receiver may sack employees and otherwise cut outgoings. Frantic negotiations will take place with potential purchasers for an early sale of the business.

The administrative receiver writes to all creditors. To ordinary creditors especially this will come as a bombshell as they will be aware that the bank, having secured rights over all the assets of the company, will be entitled to the company's assets in priority to them. As the bank has rights of security over the company's assets, ordinary creditors will be unable to enforce any claims against those assets. When writing to unpaid suppliers of goods, the administrative receiver also invites them to submit claims that they have retained title to any identifiable goods still in the possession of the company. The administrative receiver also examines all company documentation, and takes legal advice as to whether any assets do not belong to the company or are subject to the prior claims of any other secured lender.

If it is not possible to sell as a going concern, the business will be closed and the assets sold off piecemeal on a break-up basis. The use of auction sales is very common for this purpose. The administrative receiver thus generates sufficient cash to pay off the costs and expenses of the administrative receivership, to pay off the preferential creditors (see IA 1986, s. 40), to set aside the prescribed percentage of the assets (currently £5,000 plus 20 per cent of the remainder, up to a maximum of £600,000) which Insolvency Act 1986, s. 176A, requires to be paid to unsecured creditors and finally to pay to the bank or other debenture holder sufficient to discharge the capital and interest owing. Sometimes there is a shortfall, in which case the bank is not paid in full. The bank may then look to any guarantor for payment. Where there are few if any assets remaining to the company after completion of the receivership, the company will effectively be defunct. When it becomes apparent that annual returns etc. are not being filed, the Registrar of Companies will take steps to strike the company off the register. If there are sufficient assets remaining to interest creditors, either the members may resolve to wind up or, on the application of a creditor, the court will order that the company be wound up. A liquidator will then be appointed to do whatever is necessary to complete the job of realising the assets of the company, and distributing the proceeds to the ordinary creditors. They will probably be paid a very small proportion of their debts, but will have been lucky to receive anything more.

As the following paragraphs from the Cork Report describe, an administrative receivership in effect precludes a winding up in the usual case where there are no assets left once the receivership costs, the preferential creditors and the floating chargee have been paid. (With the recent abolition of the Crown's preference, the preferential debts are now much less significant. See 20.8)

Insolvency Law and Practice: Report of the Review Committee
(The 'Cork Report')
(Cmnd 8558) (London: HMSO, 1982)

1479. Where the security consists of a floating charge over the entire undertaking of a corporate debtor, the whole of the assets fall to be realised outside the winding up. Parliament has intervened by requiring the receiver to pay the claims of preferential creditors in priority to the debt secured by the floating charge; but if the proceeds are insufficient to discharge both the preferential debts and the debt due to the holder of the floating charge, there is nothing for the unsecured creditors and any ultimate winding up of the company is an empty formality.

1480. With the increase in the burden of the preferential debts in recent years, and the proliferation of floating charges, this outcome has become sufficiently common to cause much dissatisfaction in the commercial community. It has led many creditors to resort to devices like the reservation of title clause in self-defence; and it discourages ordinary creditors from resorting to proceedings for liquidation or from playing a full part in administering the liquidation where one has taken place. It has, as much as any other single factor, brought the law of insolvency into disrepute....

432. A floating charge normally extends over all the assets and undertakings of the company granting the charge. The powers conferred on the receiver in a well-drawn charge are extensive. In practice, virtually everything is withdrawn from the ordinary unsecured creditors in a winding up. Often they are left with nothing but an empty shell and the right, not easy to exercise, to call the receiver or the debenture holder to account. On the other hand, the holder of the floating charge may himself be left partly unpaid as the figures never balance so finely. It cannot therefore be suggested that it is a position the holder of the charge regards lightly.

433. Once a receiver is appointed, the assets are realised by the receiver and not by the liquidator, and wholly outside the winding up. It thus sometimes appears, to the layman, as if receivership were an alternative to winding up, with none of the safeguards provided by the latter. This is,

however, not so. The rights of the holder of a floating charge are conferred by the debtor, not by the general law, and are conferred for the purpose of enabling the holder of the charge to realise his security. The empty nature of the winding up where a floating charge exists is simply the consequence of a creditor's security which extends to the whole or substantially the whole of the debtor's assets.

434. In the instrument creating a floating charge, there is normally an express power to appoint a receiver, not merely over the income of the mortgaged property (as in the case of the statutory power conferred by the Law of Property Act 1925 and commonly incorporated in fixed charges) but over the property itself; that is, all the assets and the undertaking of the company. The express powers will normally include powers to sell the charged assets, and to bring proceedings and execute conveyances in the name of the company.

435. A floating charge may be, and occasionally is, granted over a limited category of assets; though the great majority of floating charges are granted over the whole, or substantially the whole, of the assets of the company.

15.4.2 Critical evaluation

The following extract from the Cork Report argued that although receivers of all the assets of companies may be very effective in rescuing and reselling businesses, the floating charge was also capable of causing serious injustice to ordinary creditors. But reform was a long time coming. Apart from introducing the requirement that only an authorised insolvency practitioner can be appointed as an administrative receiver (which professionalises the process but makes it more expensive), very little was done in the Insolvency Act to address these difficult issues. (See, however, Insolvency Act 1986, ss. 48 and 49 giving certain protection to unsecured creditors in response to para. 438 of the Report, quoted below. Since late 2003, the new s. 176A of the IA 1986, mentioned above, requires an administrative receiver to set aside a prescribed percentage of the assets for ordinary creditors. Finally, CA 2006, s. 1282, adds a new s. 176Z in the IA 1986 to the effect that the expenses of a winding up are payable out of the assets subject to a floating charge. Administrative receivership is thus now less likely to preclude a winding up.)

Insolvency Law and Practice: Report of the Review Committee
(The 'Cork Report')
(Cmnd 8558) (London: HMSO, 1982)

495. Elsewhere in this Report we have made a number of criticisms of the present law relating to floating charges, and we shall put forward various proposals for reform. There is, however, one aspect of the floating charge which we believe to have been of outstanding benefit to the general public and to society as a whole; we refer to the power to appoint a receiver and manager of the whole property and undertaking of a company. This power is enjoyed by the holder of any well-drawn floating charge, but by no other creditor. Such receivers and managers are normally given extensive powers to manage and carry on the business of the company. In some cases, they have been able to restore an ailing enterprise to profitability, and return it to its former owners. In others, they have been able to dispose of the whole or part of the business as a going concern. In either case, the preservation of the profitable parts of the enterprise has been of advantage to the employees, the commercial community, and the general public....

437. Many of the complaints which we have received have been concerned with the low level of distributions to unsecured creditors in a winding up where there is a floating charge, and with such

injustices (as they have been represented to us) as the right of the receiver to retain goods for which the supplier has not been paid. Such complaints are due to the nature and extent of the security constituted by the floating charge itself....

438. The most frequent complaint which we have received is of the lack of information once a receiver has been appointed. This is a complaint which we have received, not only from creditors, but also from shareholders. Another widely felt grievance is the belief that the receiver has too much regard for the interests of the holder of the charge, and that insufficient attention is paid to the interests of the other creditors and the shareholders....

105. At the same time, the floating charge has serious disadvantages, and is capable of working great injustice. It is sufficient for present purposes to mention three of the problems to which it gives rise:

(a) it enables a company, apparently in possession of assets of great value, to obtain credit from suppliers and others, and to continue to trade on borrowed money, while the semblance of wealth on the strength of which such credit is obtained is falsified by the existence of the charge, which is capable of being enforced at any moment;

(b) there is scope for the dishonest director, who is often the principal shareholder in the case of a small trading company, and who is in the best position to judge the true financial position of the company, to avoid the loss of the capital invested by him in the venture, by obtaining a floating charge in his own favour and thus gaining priority over the unsecured and often unsuspecting trade creditors with whom he has been dealing; and

(c) the common practice of giving a floating charge over the entire undertaking of the company means that, in the event of insolvency, the whole of the assets fall to be realised outside the winding up.

If the proceeds are insufficient to discharge the debt due to the holder of the charge and there is nothing left for the unsecured creditors, the winding up of the company becomes an empty formality. In the case of most major enterprises, it will be found that the assets will fall to be realised not by the liquidator but by the receiver.

106. These features of the floating charge have given rise to a widespread and long-standing sense of grievance in the commercial community. It was voiced as long ago as 1905 by Buckley J in *Re London Pressed Hinge Co. Ltd* [1905] 1 Ch 576 at pp. 581 and 583:

> The cases are numerous in which the undertaking of a limited company is so loaded with debentures that the profits are barely sufficient, or perhaps not sufficient, to keep down the debenture interest, and that, if the company is wound up, there is nothing for any one but the debenture holders. In short, the facts often are that the undertaking is substantially carried on only for the benefit of the debenture holders who have a floating security over it. In this state of facts money is lent or goods consigned to the company in respect of which a debt accrues to a creditor, and so long as the security floats, as it is termed, and no receiver is appointed, the creditor has a possibility or expectation of being paid by the company, for, as between the company and the debenture holders, the former may pay in the ordinary course of business. But directly a receiver is appointed, this expectation of the creditor is intercepted. He may have lent his money, or consigned his goods, to the company last week: but if he has the audacity to ask payment and to enforce his legal remedies to obtain it, the debenture holder obtains a receiver in a proceeding to which the execution creditor is not a party, and thus closes the door against him, taking his money or his goods as part of the security, and leaving the creditor who supplied the money or the goods to go unpaid. I regret to be driven to the conclusion that, as the law stands, those are the rights of a debenture holder entitled to a floating charge....
>
> It is an injustice arising from the nature as defined by the authorities of a floating security. The mischief arises from the fact that the law allows a charge upon all future property. The subject, however, is one which, I think, urgently requires attention.... It is not for me to say whether the matter requires the attention of the legislature.

107. The matter for wonder is that such a device should ever have been invented by a court of equity. It is not easy to discern on what principle of equity the holder of a floating charge should obtain security over goods for which his money has not paid, in priority to the claim of the unpaid supplier of the goods. The subject had already received some attention from the legislature before 1905, and was to do so from time to time thereafter. Already, the Act of 1898 had introduced the concept of preferential debts, to be paid out of assets collected by the receiver in priority to the debt secured by the floating charge. In 1906 the Loreburn Committee made recommendations for change, while recognising that the floating charge had become an integral part of corporate financing and could not be abolished. There was, however, a powerful note of dissent which recommended the outright abolition of the floating charge.

108. As the result of that Committee's Report, the Companies (Consolidation) Act 1908 invalidated (*inter alia*) any floating charge, in the event of a subsequent liquidation of the company, unless it had been registered within a period of 21 days after its creation; and similarly invalidated any floating charge within three months of the commencement of the winding up, unless the company was solvent immediately after the creation of the floating charge, and except to the amount of any cash paid to the company at the time of or subsequently to the creation and in consideration for the floating charge. This last period was progressively increased to six months in 1929 and to 12 months in 1948.

109. These legislative provisions have done little to alleviate the widespread feeling of grievance generated by the floating charge, and we have received more evidence both oral and written on this one subject from those whom we have consulted than on any other. The mischief has not been met, as is sometimes asserted, by the requirement of registration. The register gives very inadequate information to a trade creditor. Most floating charges secure repayment of a bank overdraft, the amount of which fluctuates daily. It is impossible to discover the amount secured by the floating charge from the register, or even from the company's last balance sheet. Quite apart from the fact that the latter will usually be out of date to a greater or smaller degree, it will be unlikely to disclose contingent liabilities, such as the guarantees of the overdrafts of associated companies, which may be secured by the floating charge. Moreover, much trade credit is involuntary. Services are necessarily performed, and goods supplied, on normal credit terms. To demand immediate payment for services rendered or goods supplied would be quite impracticable.

110. Like our predecessors in 1906, we accept that the floating charge has become so fundamental a part of the financial structure on which the commercial and industrial system of the United Kingdom depends that its abolition can no longer be contemplated. But we are satisfied that a major measure of reform is overdue and can no longer be delayed. One of the most difficult questions to which we have tried to find a solution is how best to reconcile the legitimate safeguards to those who are required to provide adequate finance to commerce and industry, with justice to the ordinary unsecured trade creditor who is an involuntary supplier of goods, materials or services on credit.

The floating charge finally founders

It was not until the end of the 1990s that a fundamental review of the law relating to the 'rescue' of companies in financial difficulty took place. The conclusion broadly stated has been to replace administrative receivership with a newly reformed administration procedure. (See Mayson, French and Ryan, *Company Law*, (Oxford, OUP, 2007 at 11.6.3 and 20.3.)

The reasons for 'abolishing' the floating charge were that administrative receivership is not an official collective insolvency procedure for the benefit of all creditors but is a contractual remedy benefiting a single powerful secured lender, often a bank. It is not a procedure recognised in other jurisdictions and creates difficulties for harmonisation of insolvency laws within the EU. The process is expensive and the administrative receiver has limited duties to take into account the interests of other creditors or to be accountable to them. This is because the administrative receiver's main aim is to pay off the bank that appointed him and to realise sufficient of the insolvent company's assets to pay his own professional fees. Finally, it was thought that the existence of a floating charge made it too easy for banks to appoint an administrative receiver and close down a company that was still trading without due regard to its interest or that of other stakeholders such as employees.

16

Accounts and Audit

16.1 THE DUTY TO KEEP ACCOUNTS

Broadly the Companies Act 2006 requires directors to ensure that accounting records are kept from day to day, that annual accounts and reports in a specific form are drawn up every year, and in the case of the largest companies that they be audited by a duly qualified statutory auditor. Copies must be sent to every member, approved and signed by the directors and in the case of public companies presented to the members in general meeting, and finally be filed with the Registrar of Companies. This is an area of the law where size matters. Thus small companies as defined have lesser obligations in the form and extent of the annual accounts they have to prepare and the exemptions from the obligation to audit the annual accounts now mean that only the largest companies have to have their accounts audited. (See 16.2.1.)

The provisions on accounts and audit are some of the more complex and important parts of the Companies Act, though they are hardly 'lawyers' law'. Nonetheless they are hotly debated and often come under the media spotlight whenever there are major corporate failures or financial scandals such as the collapse of major companies, Enron and Worldcom in the USA. Just as accountants can be some of the most exciting people you are ever likely to meet, the provisions of the Act on accounts are also a stimulating area that reward close study. Looked at more broadly, as they impose strict obligations on the directors in the management of the company's money they are perhaps the must important way in which the directors are quite literally made accountable to the members. Furthermore, the production and publication of annual accounts at Companies House is the principal price the law exacts for the privilege of limited liability. The members will not be liable for the debts of the company, but third parties are at least able to inspect the last set of filed accounts, a snap shot of the company's financial position which can be helpful in deciding if the company is creditworthy or not.

Recent developments in the law are that in addition to the directors' report to be prepared by all companies (s. 415), companies that are not 'small companies' must also produce a 'business report' as required pursuant to the EU Accounts Modernisation Directive (2003/51/EEC). This is intended to help members to assess how well directors have performed their duty under s. 172 to promote the success of the company.

Responding to the problem of directors apparently taking too much pay and benefits, the usual panacea of 'disclosure' is again seen in the requirement first introduced in 2002 for quoted companies to produce a directors' remuneration report, detailing not only the usual statistics on remuneration but also details of individual named directors' remuneration packages, the company's remuneration policy and the role of the board and the remuneration committee in this area. The policy is that executive pay is not a matter for government but it is for the shareholders to control the fat-cat tendency and accordingly they should have access to all essential information on this score.

The following highly selective extracts introduce the main terminology and the broad outlines of the law. You should note how often much of the detail is left to be filled in by regulations to be made by the Secretary of State

---

COMPANIES ACT 2006, PART 15, ACCOUNTS AND REPORTS

380. Scheme of this Part

(1) The requirements of this Part as to accounts and reports apply in relation to each financial year of a company.

(2) In certain respects different provisions apply to different kinds of company.

(3) The main distinctions for this purpose are—

    (a) between companies subject to the small companies regime (see section 381) and companies that are not subject to that regime; and

    (b) between quoted companies (see section 385) and companies that are not quoted.

382. Companies qualifying as small: general

(1) A company qualifies as small in relation to its first financial year if the qualifying conditions are met in that year.

(2) A company qualifies as small in relation to a subsequent financial year—

    (a) if the qualifying conditions are met in that year and the preceding financial year;

    (b) if the qualifying conditions are met in that year and the company qualified as small in relation to the preceding financial year;

    (c) if the qualifying conditions were met in the preceding financial year and the company qualified as small in relation to that year.

(3) The qualifying conditions are met by a company in a year in which it satisfies two or more of the following requirements—

1. Turnover	Not more than £5.6 million
2. Balance sheet total	Not more than £2.8 million
3. Number of employees	Not more than 50

386. Duty to keep accounting records

(1) Every company must keep adequate accounting records.

(2) Adequate accounting records means records that are sufficient—

    (a) to show and explain the company's transactions,

    (b) to disclose with reasonable accuracy, at any time, the financial position of the company at that time, and

    (c) to enable the directors to ensure that any accounts required to be prepared comply with the requirements of this Act (and, where applicable, of Article 4 of the IAS Regulation).

(3) Accounting records must, in particular, contain—

    (a) entries from day to day of all sums of money received and expended by the company and the matters in respect of which the receipt and expenditure takes place, and

    (b) a record of the assets and liabilities of the company.

393. Accounts to give true and fair view

(1) The directors of a company must not approve accounts for the purposes of this Chapter unless they are satisfied that they give a true and fair view of the assets, liabilities, financial position and profit or loss—

    (a) in the case of the company's individual accounts, of the company;

(b) in the case of the company's group accounts, of the undertakings included in the consolidation as a whole, so far as concerns members of the company.

394. Duty to prepare individual accounts

The directors of every company must prepare accounts for the company for each of its financial years.

Those accounts are referred to as the company's "individual accounts".

395. Individual accounts: applicable accounting framework

(1) A company's individual accounts may be prepared—
    (a) in accordance with section 396 ("Companies Act individual accounts"), or
    (b) in accordance with international accounting standards ("IAS individual accounts").
This is subject to the following provisions of this section and to section 407 (consistency of financial reporting within group).

396. Companies Act individual accounts

(1) Companies Act individual accounts must comprise—
    (a) a balance sheet as at the last day of the financial year, and
    (b) a profit and loss account.
(2) The accounts must—
    (a) in the case of the balance sheet, give a true and fair view of the state of affairs of the company as at the end of the financial year, and
    (b) in the case of the profit and loss account, give a true and fair view of the profit or loss of the company for the financial year.
(3) The accounts must comply with provision made by the Secretary of State by regulations as to—
    (a) the form and content of the balance sheet and profit and loss account, and
    (b) additional information to be provided by way of notes to the accounts.

399. Duty to prepare group accounts

(1) This section applies to companies that are not subject to the small companies regime.
(2) If at the end of a financial year the company is a parent company the directors, as well as preparing individual accounts for the year, must prepare group accounts for the year unless the company is exempt from that requirement.

404. Companies Act group accounts

(1) Companies Act group accounts must comprise—
    (a) a consolidated balance sheet dealing with the state of affairs of the parent company and its subsidiary undertakings, and
    (b) a consolidated profit and loss account dealing with the profit or loss of the parent company and its subsidiary undertakings.
(2) The accounts must give a true and fair view of the state of affairs as at the end of the financial year, and the profit or loss for the financial year, of the undertakings included in the consolidation as a whole, so far as concerns members of the company.

412. Information about directors' benefits: remuneration

(1) The Secretary of State may make provision by regulations requiring information to be given in notes to a company's annual accounts about directors' remuneration.
(2) The matters about which information may be required include—
    (a) gains made by directors on the exercise of share options;
    (b) benefits received or receivable by directors under long-term incentive schemes;
    (c) payments for loss of office (as defined in section 215);
    (d) benefits receivable, and contributions for the purpose of providing benefits, in respect of past services of a person as director or in any other capacity while director;
    (e) consideration paid to or receivable by third parties for making available the services of a person as director or in any other capacity while director.

414. Approval and signing of accounts

(1) A company's annual accounts must be approved by the board of directors and signed on behalf of the board by a director of the company.

415. Duty to prepare directors' report

(1) The directors of a company must prepare a directors' report for each financial year of the company.

416. Contents of directors' report: general

(1) The directors' report for a financial year must state—
   (a) the names of the persons who, at any time during the financial year, were directors of the company, and
   (b) the principal activities of the company in the course of the year.
(4) The Secretary of State may make provision by regulations as to other matters that must be disclosed in a directors' report.
   Without prejudice to the generality of this power, the regulations may make any such provision as was formerly made by Schedule 7 to the Companies Act 1985.

417. Contents of directors' report: business review

(1) Unless the company is subject to the small companies' regime, the directors' report must contain a business review.
(2) The purpose of the business review is to inform members of the company and help them assess how the directors have performed their duty under section 172 (duty to promote the success of the company).
(3) The business review must contain—
   (a) a fair review of the company's business, and
   (b) a description of the principal risks and uncertainties facing the company.
(4) The review required is a balanced and comprehensive analysis of—
   (a) the development and performance of the company's business during the financial year, and
   (b) the position of the company's business at the end of that year, consistent with the size and complexity of the business.
(5) In the case of a quoted company the business review must, to the extent necessary for an understanding of the development, performance or position of the company's business, include—
   (a) the main trends and factors likely to affect the future development, performance and position of the company's business; and
   (b) information about—
      (i) environmental matters (including the impact of the company's business on the environment),
      (ii) the company's employees, and
      (iii) social and community issues, including information about any policies of the company in relation to those matters and the effectiveness of those policies; and
   (c) subject to subsection (11), information about persons with whom the company has contractual or other arrangements which are essential to the business of the company.
   If the review does not contain information of each kind mentioned in paragraphs (b)(i), (ii) and (iii) and (c), it must state which of those kinds of information it does not contain.
(6) The review must, to the extent necessary for an understanding of the development, performance or position of the company's business, include—
   (a) analysis using financial key performance indicators, and
   (b) where appropriate, analysis using other key performance indicators, including information relating to environmental matters and employee matters.
   "Key performance indicators" means factors by reference to which the development, performance or position of the company's business can be measured effectively.

420. Duty to prepare directors' remuneration report

(1) The directors of a quoted company must prepare a directors' remuneration report for each financial year of the company.

421. Contents of directors' remuneration report

(1) The Secretary of State may make provision by regulations as to—
   (a) the information that must be contained in a directors' remuneration report,
   (b) how information is to be set out in the report, and
   (c) what is to be the auditable part of the report.

423. Duty to circulate copies of annual accounts and reports

(1) Every company must send a copy of its annual accounts and reports for each financial year to—
   (a) every member of the company,
   (b) every holder of the company's debentures, and
   (c) every person who is entitled to receive notice of general meetings.

430. Quoted companies: annual accounts and reports to be made available on website

(1) A quoted company must ensure that its annual accounts and reports—
   (a) are made available on a website, and
   (b) remain so available until the annual accounts and reports for the company's next financial year are made available in accordance with this section.

437. Public companies: laying of accounts and reports before general meeting

(1) The directors of a public company must lay before the company in general meeting copies of its annual accounts and reports.

441. Duty to file accounts and reports with the registrar

(1) The directors of a company must deliver to the registrar for each financial year the accounts and reports required by—
   section 444 (filing obligations of companies subject to small companies regime),
   section 445 (filing obligations of medium-sized companies),
   section 446 (filing obligations of unquoted companies), or
   section 447 (filing obligations of quoted companies).
(2) This is subject to section 448 (unlimited companies exempt from filing obligations).

16.2 AUDITORS

16.2.1 Appointment and qualification

For limited companies, filing of their annual accounts at the Companies Registry and the consequential loss of privacy over their financial affairs is a fundamental obligation which arises from the privilege of limited liability. People dealing with the company are not able to sue its members but at least they have a right to see the company's last annual accounts on a public register before committing themselves to a deal. The principle that these accounts have been audited as being true and fair by a duly qualified and independent auditor is then a valuable assurance to anyone searching the register that the accounts have indeed been properly drawn up. In addition, an audit gives a similar assurance to the company's members that they can rely on the annual accounts as a correct statement of the financial position of the company in which they have invested their money.

In practice, the company will appoint a firm of accountants to be its auditors and the bulk of audit work is done by the inner circle of large accountancy firms whose names are well known. To be an auditor, an individual must be a member of a 'recognised supervisory body' such as the Institute of Chartered Accountants of England and Wales (ICAEW) or the Association of Chartered Certified Accountants (ACCA), and be duly qualified and registered as an auditor with them.

Until relatively recently, the Companies Acts obliged all limited companies to have their annual accounts audited but in order to reduce the burden of costs for small businesses, small companies (defined in CA 2006, s. 382) are now exempt from the requirement. This size definition of small companies is now set at the maximum permitted by the rules of the EU and in consequence only the largest of companies are now in fact required to have their annual accounts audited. However, to balance the loss of regular audit for minorities in small companies, s. 476 now allows members holding 10 per cent of the company's issued share capital to require the company to obtain an audit.

The following extracts introduce the broad outlines of the audit requirement.

COMPANIES ACT 2006, PART 42 AND PART 16

1209. Main purposes of Part

The main purposes of this Part are—
(a) to secure that only persons who are properly supervised and appropriately qualified are appointed as statutory auditors, and
(b) to secure that audits by persons so appointed are carried out properly, with integrity and with a proper degree of independence.

1212. Individuals and firms: eligibility for appointment as a statutory auditor

(1) An individual or firm is eligible for appointment as a statutory auditor if the individual or firm—
(a) is a member of a recognised supervisory body, and
(b) is eligible for appointment under the rules of that body.

1214. Independence requirement

(1) A person may not act as statutory auditor of an audited person if one or more of subsections (2), (3) and (4) apply to him.
(2) This subsection applies if the person is—
(a) an officer or employee of the audited person, or
(b) a partner or employee of such a person, or a partnership of which such a person is a partner.
(3) This subsection applies if the person is—
(a) an officer or employee of an associated undertaking of the audited person, or
(b) a partner or employee of such a person, or a partnership of which such a person is a partner.
(4) This subsection applies if there exists, between—
(a) the person or an associate of his, and
(b) the audited person or an associated undertaking of the audited person, a connection of any such description as may be specified by regulations made by the Secretary of State.

475. Requirement for audited accounts

(1) A company's annual accounts for a financial year must be audited in accordance with this Part unless the company—

(a) is exempt from audit under—
section 477 (small companies), or
section 480 (dormant companies);
or

(b) is exempt from the requirements of this Part under section 482 (nonprofit-making companies subject to public sector audit).

476. Right of members to require audit

(1) The members of a company that would otherwise be entitled to exemption from audit under any of the provisions mentioned in section 475(1)(a) may by notice under this section require it to obtain an audit of its accounts for a financial year.

(2) The notice must be given by—
(a) members representing not less in total than 10% in nominal value of the company's issued share capital, or any class of it, or
(b) if the company does not have a share capital, not less than 10% in number of the members of the company.

477. Small companies: conditions for exemption from audit

(1) A company that meets the following conditions in respect of a financial year is exempt from the requirements of this Act relating to the audit of accounts for that year.

(2) The conditions are—
(a) that the company qualifies as a small company in relation to that year,
(b) that its turnover in that year is not more than £5.6 million, and
(c) that its balance sheet total for that year is not more than £2.8 million.

(3) For a period which is a company's financial year but not in fact a year the maximum figure for turnover shall be proportionately adjusted.

16.2.2 The audit process

The obligation of the auditors in making their report is found in CA 2006, s. 495, while their duties are defined in s. 498 extracted below. The traditional view of the primary purpose of the annual audit is described below in extracts from two of the speeches in the House of Lords in the case of *Caparo Industries plc* v *Dickman*. The Cadbury Report dealt extensively with the importance of audit. Some of its more general comments are extracted below, followed by its recommendation that listed companies appoint an audit committee. This is a committee of the board responsible for all aspects of audit, including appointing and dealing with the auditor, and generally monitoring the company's own internal accounting and financial controls. (The background to the Cadbury Report is discussed at 8.3 followed by the text of the Combined Code on Corporate Governance, of which part D deals with accountability and audit.)

COMPANIES ACT 2006, SS. 495 AND 498

495. Auditor's report on company's annual accounts

(1) A company's auditor must make a report to the company's members on all annual accounts of the company of which copies are, during his tenure of office—
(a) in the case of a private company, to be sent out to members under section 423;
(b) in the case of a public company, to be laid before the company in general meeting under section 437.

(2) The auditor's report must include—

   (a) an introduction identifying the annual accounts that are the subject of the audit and the financial reporting framework that has been applied in their preparation, and

   (b) a description of the scope of the audit identifying the auditing standards in accordance with which the audit was conducted.

(3) The report must state clearly whether, in the auditor's opinion, the annual accounts—

   (a) give a true and fair view—

      (i) in the case of an individual balance sheet, of the state of affairs of the company as at the end of the financial year,

      (ii) in the case of an individual profit and loss account, of the profit or loss of the company for the financial year,

      (iii) in the case of group accounts, of the state of affairs as at the end of the financial year and of the profit or loss for the financial year of the undertakings included in the consolidation as a whole, so far as concerns members of the company;

   (b) have been properly prepared in accordance with the relevant financial reporting framework; and

   (c) have been prepared in accordance with the requirements of this Act (and, where applicable, Article 4 of the IAS Regulation).

Expressions used in this subsection that are defined for the purposes of Part 15 (see section 474) have the same meaning as in that Part.

(4) The auditor's report—

   (a) must be either unqualified or qualified, and

   (b) must include a reference to any matters to which the auditor wishes to draw attention by way of emphasis without qualifying the report.

498. Duties of auditor

(1) A company's auditor, in preparing his report, must carry out such investigations as will enable him to form an opinion as to—

   (a) whether adequate accounting records have been kept by the company and returns adequate for their audit have been received from branches not visited by him, and

   (b) whether the company's individual accounts are in agreement with the accounting records and returns, and

   (c) in the case of a quoted company, whether the auditable part of the company's directors' remuneration report is in agreement with the accounting records and returns.

(2) If the auditor is of the opinion—

   (a) that adequate accounting records have not been kept, or that returns adequate for their audit have not been received from branches not visited by him, or

   (b) that the company's individual accounts are not in agreement with the accounting records and returns, or

   (c) in the case of a quoted company, that the auditable part of its directors' remuneration report is not in agreement with the accounting records and returns,

   the auditor shall state that fact in his report.

(3) If the auditor fails to obtain all the information and explanations which, to the best of his knowledge and belief, are necessary for the purposes of his audit, he shall state that fact in his report.

Caparo Industries plc v Dickman

The primary purpose of audit

[1989] QB 653, Court of Appeal; [1990] 2 AC 605, House of Lords

In the Court of Appeal

BINGHAM LJ: The members, or shareholders, of the company are its owners. But they are too numerous, and in most cases too unskilled, to undertake the day-to-day management of that which they own. So responsibility for day-to-day management of the company is delegated to directors. The shareholders, despite their overall powers of control, are in most companies for most of the time investors and little more. But it would of course be unsatisfactory and open to abuse if the shareholders received no report on the financial stewardship of their investment save from those to whom the stewardship had been entrusted. So provision is made for the company in general meeting to appoint an auditor, whose duty is to investigate and form an opinion on the adequacy of the company's accounting records and returns and the correspondence between the company's accounting records and returns and its accounts: The auditor has then to report to the company's members (among other things) whether in his opinion the company's accounts give a true and fair view of the company's financial position. In carrying out his investigation and in forming his opinion the auditor necessarily works very closely with the directors and officers of the company. He receives his remuneration from the company. He naturally, and rightly, regards the company as his client. But he is employed by the company to exercise his professional skill and judgment for the purpose of giving the shareholders an independent report on the reliability of the company's accounts and thus on their investment. 'No doubt he is acting antagonistically to the directors in the sense that he is appointed by the shareholders to be a check upon them' (*Re Kingston Cotton Mill Co.* [1896] 1 Ch 6 per Vaughan Williams J at p. 11). The auditor's report must be read before the company in general meeting and must be open to inspection by any member of the company:. It is attached to and forms part of the company's accounts:[this is no longer true]. A copy of the company's accounts, including the auditor's report, must be sent to every member:. Any member of the company, even if not entitled to have a copy of the accounts sent to him, is entitled to be furnished with a copy of the company's last accounts on demand and without charge:

In the House of Lords

LORD OLIVER OF AYLMERTON: My lords, the primary purpose of the statutory requirement that a company's accounts shall be audited annually is almost self-evident. The structure of the corporate trading entity, at least in the case of public companies whose shares are dealt with on an authorised Stock Exchange, involves the concept of a more or less widely distributed holding of shares rendering the personal involvement of each individual shareholder in the day-to-day management of the enterprise impracticable, with the result that management is necessarily separated from ownership. The management is confided to a board of directors which operates in a fiduciary capacity and is answerable to and removable by the shareholders who can act, if they act at all, only collectively and only through the medium of a general meeting. Hence the legislative provisions requiring the board annually to give an account of its stewardship to a general meeting of the shareholders. This is the only occasion in each year upon which the general body of shareholders is given the opportunity to consider, to criticise and to comment upon the conduct by the board of the company's affairs, to vote upon the directors' recommendation as to dividends, to approve or disapprove the directors' remuneration and, if thought desirable, to remove and replace all or any of the directors. It is the auditors' function to ensure, so far as possible, that the financial information as to the company's affairs prepared by the directors accurately reflects the company's position in order, first, to protect the company itself from the consequences of undetected errors or, possibly, wrongdoing (by, for instance, declaring dividends out of capital) and, secondly, to provide shareholders with reliable intelligence for the purpose of enabling them to scrutinise the conduct of the company's affairs and to exercise their collective powers to reward or control or remove those to whom that conduct has been confided....

It is argued on behalf of the respondent that there is to be discerned in the legislation an additional or wider commercial purpose, namely that of enabling those to whom the accounts are addressed and circulated, to make informed investment decisions, for instance, by determining whether to dispose of their shares in the market or whether to apply any funds which they are individually able to command in seeking to purchase the shares of other shareholders. Of course, the provision of any information about the business and affairs of a trading company, whether it be contained in annual accounts or obtained from other sources, is capable of serving such a purpose just as it is capable of serving as the basis for the giving of financial advice to others, for arriving at a market price, for determining whether to extend credit to the company, or for the writing of financial articles in the press. Indeed it is readily foreseeable by anyone who gives the matter any thought that it might well be relied on to a greater or less extent for all or any of such purposes.

It is, of course, equally foreseeable that potential investors having no proprietary interest in the company might well avail themselves of the information contained in a company's accounts published in the newspapers or culled from an inspection of the documents to be filed annually with the Registrar of Companies (which includes the audited accounts) in determining whether or not to acquire shares in the company. I find it difficult to believe, however, that the legislature, in enacting provisions clearly aimed primarily at the protection of the company and its informed control by the body of its proprietors, can have been inspired also by consideration for the public at large and investors in the market in particular.

Report of the Committee on the Financial Aspects of Corporate Governance (The 'Cadbury Report')

(London: Gee, 1992)

Importance of audit

5.1 The annual audit is one of the cornerstones of corporate governance. Given the separation of ownership from management, the directors are required to report on their stewardship by means of the annual report and financial statements sent to the shareholders. The audit provides an external and objective check on the way in which the financial statements have been prepared and presented, and it is an essential part of the checks and balances required. The question is not whether there should be an audit, but how to ensure its *objectivity* and *effectiveness*.

5.2 Audits are a reassurance to all who have a financial interest in companies, quite apart from their value to boards of directors. The most direct method of ensuring that companies are accountable for their actions is through open disclosure by boards and through audits carried out against strict accounting standards. . . .

5.4 A further problem is the lack of understanding of the nature and extent of the auditors' role. This is the so-called 'expectations gap'—the difference between what audits do achieve, and what it is thought they achieve, or should achieve. The expectations gap is damaging not only because it reflects unrealistic expectations of audits but also because it has led to disenchantment with their value in the wake of the *Caparo* judgment. . . .

5.5 Steps have already been taken, within the last three years, to strengthen the audit system through the establishment of a new regulatory framework. The Financial Reporting Council and its associated bodies—the Accounting Standards Board, the Urgent Issues Task Force, and the Financial Reporting Review Panel—have been set up to improve and tighten accounting standards, to deal with problem areas as they emerge, and to examine departures by individual companies from the statutory requirements and accounting standards. The new statutory regime for regulating auditors requires all auditors to satisfy a supervisory body as to their competence, experience and training, and to be subject to regular monitoring. The arrangements for setting auditing standards have also been reformed with the establishment of the Auditing Practices Board.

5.6 The new system has only recently been established and its full impact has yet to be felt. In the following paragraphs we endorse the steps that are being taken and recommend additional action to strengthen public confidence in the audit approach.

Professional objectivity

5.7 The central issue is to ensure that an appropriate relationship exists between the auditors and the management whose financial statements they are auditing. Shareholders require auditors to work with and not against management, while always remaining professionally objective—that is to say, applying their professional skills impartially and retaining a critical detachment and a consciousness of their accountability to those who formally appoint them. Maintaining such a professional and objective relationship is the responsibility both of boards of directors and of auditors, as is that of taking appropriate action if the basis for that relationship no longer holds.

5.8 An essential first step must be the development of more effective accounting standards. Accounting standards provide important reference points against which auditors exercise their professional judgment. Their position is strengthened if standards do not allow alternative accounting treatments. The work of the Accounting Standards Board is well in hand and has our full support.

5.9 A second step should be the formation by every listed company of an audit committee which gives the auditors direct access to the non-executive members of the board. Shareholders look to the audit committee to ensure that the relationship between the auditors and management remains objective and that the auditors are able to put their views in the event of any difference of opinion with management....

Ways to increase effectiveness and value of the audit
The 'expectations gap'

5.13 An essential first step is to be clear about the respective responsibilities of directors and auditors for preparing and reporting on the financial statements of companies, in order to begin to narrow the 'expectations gap'.

5.14 The auditors' role is to report whether the financial statements give a true and fair view, and the audit is designed to provide a reasonable assurance that the financial statements are free of material misstatements. The auditors' role is *not* (to cite a few of the misunderstandings) to prepare the financial statements, nor to provide absolute assurance that the figures in the financial statements are correct, nor to provide a guarantee that the company will continue in existence....

Fraud

5.23 The prime responsibility for the prevention and detection of fraud (and other illegal acts) is that of the board, as part of its fiduciary responsibility for protecting the assets of the company. The auditor's responsibility, as defined in auditing guidance, is 'properly to plan, perform and evaluate his audit work so as to have a reasonable expectation of detecting material misstatements in the financial statements'.

5.24 One problem for the auditors is that by its very nature fraud, if it involves forgery, collusion or management override of control systems, is hard to detect. It is no solution, as some have suggested, simply to place a duty on the auditor to detect material fraud because he will never be in a position to guarantee that no such fraud has taken place. A higher level of safeguard against some categories of fraud can be attempted by carrying out a more extensive audit, but at a cost. The question is whether that extra cost is justified.

5.25 Another problem for the auditors is when they suspect that top management itself is implicated in the fraud, without having the necessary evidence to back up their suspicions. They are not in a strong enough position to confront management, nor have they a case to report to the appropriate authorities.

5.26 These are not easy problems to resolve, but an effective and independent-minded audit committee is an essential safeguard. It has an important role to play in considering whether any extra work should be undertaken in addition to the normal audit procedures to investigate defences against fraud, and in reviewing reports on the adequacy of internal control systems. The audit committee also provides a forum in which auditors can discuss at board level any concern they may have about the possibility of fraud by senior management. It can then commission whatever investigations are necessary to resolve the matter.

5.27 One proposal made to the Committee was that auditors should have a duty to report fraud to the appropriate authorities. The auditor's duty is normally to report fraud to senior management.... Where, however, he no longer has confidence that senior management will deal adequately with the matter, he is encouraged by professional guidance to report fraud to the proper authorities. Lord Justice Bingham, in his recent report on BCCI, has recommended that in the case of banks it would be better for there to be a statutory duty, and the government, in accepting the recommendation, has announced that a similar approach will be extended to the rest of the regulated sector (namely building societies, insurance, and investment business).

The Code of Best Practice

4.3 The board should establish an audit committee of at least 3 non-executive directors with written terms of reference which deal clearly with its authority and duties.

Appendix 4 Audit committees

1 In the main body of the report the Committee recommends that all listed companies which have not already done so should establish an audit committee, and places great emphasis on the importance of properly constituted audit committees in raising standards of corporate governance.

2 Many UK companies already have an audit committee, and a recent research study ('Audit Committees in the United Kingdom', published by the ICAEW, April 1992) has found a steady growth in their number. Audit Committees are now established in 53 per cent of the top 250 industrial firms in the Times 1000, and the figure rises to 66 per cent if unlisted companies and foreign subsidiaries are excluded from the calculation. Most major UK listed financial institutions have also formed an audit committee.

3 Audit committees are well established in the United States, where they have been a listing requirement of the New York Stock Exchange since 1978. A 1989 study revealed that 97 per cent of major corporations had them. In Canada, they are a legal requirement.

4 If they operate effectively, audit committees can bring significant benefits. In particular, they have the potential to:
  (a) improve the quality of financial reporting, by reviewing the financial statements on behalf of the board;
  (b) create a climate of discipline and control which will reduce the opportunity for fraud;
  (c) enable the non-executive directors to contribute an independent judgment and play a positive role;
  (d) help the finance director, by providing a forum in which he can raise issues of concern, and which he can use to get things done which might otherwise be difficult;
  (e) strengthen the position of the external auditor, by providing a channel of communication and forum for issues of concern;
  (f) provide a framework within which the external auditor can assert his independence in the event of a dispute with management;
  (g) strengthen the position of the internal audit function, by providing a greater degree of independence from management;
  (h) increase public confidence in the credibility and objectivity of financial statements.

16.2.3 Liability of auditors to the company

Auditors owe duties to the company by statute (see s. 498 extracted in 16.2.2) and at common law. Lindley LJ in *Re London and General Bank (No. 2)* [1895] 2 Ch 673 said (at p. 683):

An auditor... is not an insurer; he does not guarantee that the books do correctly show the true position of the company's affairs; he does not even guarantee that his balance sheet is accurate according to the books of the company.... [but] he must be honest—i.e., he must not certify what he does not believe to be true, and he must take reasonable care and skill before he believes that what he certifies is true. What is reasonable care in any particular case must depend upon the circumstances of that case.

The auditor's duty to the company is described in the following extracts from nineteenth and twentieth century cases.

Re Kingston Cotton Mill Co. (No. 2)

Auditors' duty to the company

[1896] 2 Ch 279, Court of Appeal

Facts   *The liquidator of the company claimed against the auditors as accounts audited by them grossly overstated the value of stock-in-trade. (This led to an apparent profit which had been wrongfully distributed as dividends.) For the value of stock the auditors had relied on the certificate of a director and manager. By deducting stock sold during the year from stock held during the year, it would have been apparent that the value of stock at year end was overvalued. It was held that the auditors were not in breach of their duty of care and skill, and were entitled to rely on the director, a man of competence and high reputation. The following extract describes the duties of an auditor to the company.*

LOPES LJ: But in determining whether any misfeasance or breach of duty has been committed, it is essential to consider what the duties of an auditor are. They are very fully described in *Re London and General Bank* [1895] 2 Ch 673, to which judgment I was a party. Shortly they may be stated thus: It is the duty of an auditor to bring to bear on the work he has to perform that skill, care, and caution which a reasonably competent, careful, and cautious auditor would use. What is reasonable skill, care, and caution must depend on the particular circumstances of each case. An auditor is not bound to be a detective, or, as was said, to approach his work with suspicion or with a foregone conclusion that there is something wrong. He is a watchdog, but not a bloodhound. He is justified in believing tried servants of the company in whom confidence is placed by the company. He is entitled to assume that they are honest, and to rely upon their representations, provided he takes reasonable care. If there is anything calculated to excite suspicion he should probe it to the bottom; but in the absence of anything of that kind he is only bound to be reasonably cautious and careful.

In the present case the accounts of the company had been for years falsified by the managing director, Jackson, who subsequently confessed the frauds he had committed. . . . Jackson deliberately overstated the quantities and values of the cotton and yarn in the company's mills. He did this for many years. . . . Jackson had been so successful in falsifying the accounts that what he had done was never detected or even suspected by the directors. . . . Jackson was a trusted officer of the company in whom the directors had every confidence; there was nothing on the face of the accounts to excite suspicion, and I cannot see how in the circumstances of the case it can be successfully contended that the auditors are wanting in skill, care, or caution in not testing Jackson's figures.

It is not the duty of an auditor to take stock; he is not a stock expert; there are many matters in respect of which he must rely on the honesty and accuracy of others. He does not guarantee the discovery of all fraud. I think the auditors were justified in this case in relying on the honesty and accuracy of Jackson, and were not called upon to make further investigation. It is not unimportant to bear in mind that the learned judge has found the directors justified in relying on the figures of the managing director.

The duties of auditors must not be rendered too onerous. Their work is responsible and laborious, and the remuneration moderate. . . . Auditors must not be made liable for not tracking out ingenious and carefully laid schemes of fraud when there is nothing to arouse their suspicion, and when those frauds are perpetrated by tried servants of the company and are undetected for years by the directors. So to hold would make the position of an auditor intolerable.

Fomento (Sterling Area) Ltd v Selsdon Fountain Pen Co. Ltd

A mere adder-upper and subtractor?

[1958] 1 All ER 11, [1958] 1 WLR 45, House of Lords

In this case auditors were appointed for the specific task of verifying the amount of royalties payable to a patent owner by a manufacturer licensed to make pens etc. to the licensor's patented design. The case is not therefore about the typical function of auditing annual accounts, but the following is nonetheless a useful description of aspects of the duties of an auditor.

LORD DENNING: What is the proper function of an auditor? It is said that he is bound only to verify the sum, the arithmetical conclusion, by reference to the books and all necessary vouching material and oral explanations; and that it is no part of his function to inquire whether an article is covered by patents or not. I think this is too narrow a view. An auditor is not to be confined to the mechanics of checking vouchers and making arithmetical computations. He is not to be written off as a professional 'adder-upper and subtractor'. His vital task is to take care to see that errors are not made, be they errors of computation, or errors of omission or commission, or downright untruths. To perform this task properly, he must come to it with an inquiring mind—not suspicious of dishonesty, I agree—but suspecting that someone may have made a mistake somewhere and that a check must be made to ensure that there has been none. I would not have it thought that *Re Kingston Cotton Mill Co. (No. 2)* [1896] 2 Ch 279 relieved an auditor of his responsibility for making a proper check. But the check, to be effective, may require some legal knowledge, or some knowledge of patents or other specialty. What is he then to do? Take, for instance, a point of law arising in the course of auditing a company's accounts. He may come on a payment which, it appears to him, may be unlawful, in that it may not be within the powers of the corporation, or improper in that it may have no warrant or justification. He is, then, not only entitled but bound to inquire into it and, if need be, to disallow it. . . . It may be, of course, that he has sufficient legal knowledge to deal with it himself, as many accountants have, but, if it is beyond him, he is entitled to take legal advice on the principle stated in *Bevan* v *Webb* [1901] 2 Ch 59 at p. 75, that 'permission to a man to do an act, which he cannot do effectually without the help of an agent, carries with it the right to employ an agent'. So, also, with an auditor who is employed for the purpose of checking the royalties payable. It is part of his duty to use reasonable care to see that none has been omitted which ought to be included. He is not bound to accept the *ipse dixit* of the licensee that there are no other articles which attract royalty. He is entitled to check the accuracy of that assertion by inquiring the nature of any other articles, which, it appears to him, may come within the patented field. If he cannot be sure, of his own knowledge, whether they attract royalty or not, he can take the advice of a patent agent, just as, within the legal sphere, he can take the advice of a lawyer.

16.2.4 Liability of auditors to third parties

Far more difficult is the question of possible liability to third parties in the tort of negligence. The disclosure doctrine itself ensures that audited accounts are available to outsiders such as prospective purchasers of shares, or potential creditors assessing the company as a credit risk. The *Caparo* case extracted below holds that no general duty of care is owed to third parties purchasing shares in a takeover bid and that the auditors were not liable when the buyers allegedly relied on the audit report and subsequently suffered loss. Before reading the technicalities of the *Caparo* decision, the following extract from the Cadbury Report neatly encapsulates the practical difficulties of opening up liability to third parties generally.

Report of the Committee on the Financial Aspects of
Corporate Governance (The Cadbury Report)
(London: Gee, 1992)

Auditors' liability

   5.31 In the *Caparo* judgment, the House of Lords laid down that auditors owed a legal duty of care to the company and to the shareholders collectively, but not to the shareholders as individuals nor to third parties. It was established in particular that in the absence of special features, no duty of care was owed to subscribers to new shares (whether existing shareholders or not), purchasers or intending purchasers of shares from third parties including those conducting takeover bids, bankers or other lenders, or persons doing business with the company.

5.32 …The case has aroused controversy because it exposed two widely held misconceptions:
(a) that the audit report is a guarantee as to the accuracy of the accounts, and perhaps even as to the soundness of the company;
(b) that anyone (including investors and creditors) can rely on the audit, not only in a general sense but also very specifically by being able to sue the auditors if they are negligent.

In deciding the case, the House of Lords studied with great care the complex issues involved in balancing the interests of the parties involved and the public interest in having a fair, viable and affordable system. The size of auditors' potential liabilities, the difficulties in defining wider liability in any fair yet practicable way, and the likely difficulties in establishing whether third-party losses were in fact due to reliance on the accounts were among the principal concerns underlying the conclusions reached by the House of Lords. Bearing in mind the wide range of users of accounts, the Committee is unable to see how the House of Lords could have broadened the boundaries of the auditors' legal duty of care without giving rise (in the words of Cardozo CJ deciding a case in 1931 and frequently quoted since) 'to a liability in an indeterminate amount for an indeterminate time to an indeterminate class'. Nor, in consequence, do we recommend that the legal position with regard to civil liability laid down by *Caparo* should be altered by statute at the present time.

5.33 In coming to this conclusion, we recognise that the current position is a source of concern to both auditors and investors. There are two main reasons:
(a) the scale of existing litigation against auditors or former auditors. Auditors are fully liable in negligence to the companies they audit and their shareholders collectively, and *Caparo* has not changed this. The size of settlements has been increasing in Britain and auditors are concerned that this trend may continue;
(b) the belief of some that, notwithstanding *Caparo*, auditors should in principle be liable to those (such as individual investors and creditors) who rely on audited accounts. Auditors are naturally concerned about the increased litigation that would result if their liability were extended to other accounts users. They are also concerned about increased litigation that could arise from adapting the audit to meet changing needs and expectations—a process which the Committee's report itself is intended to encourage.

Caparo Industries plc v Dickman

Auditors' liability to purchasers of shares

[1990] 2 AC 605, House of Lords

This leading case deals with important issues in the law of tort. In the context of company law it refuses to extend the liability of auditors to third parties generally. In tort the principle is that a person (e.g., an auditor) making a negligent statement is liable only if he owes a duty of care to the person who relied on it and suffered loss. The auditor owes a duty, first, if it was reasonably foreseeable that the plaintiff would suffer loss; and secondly if there was a relationship of sufficient proximity between the plaintiff and defendant (e.g., the auditor knew that the statement would be passed to the defendant individually or as a member of a class of persons in connection with a particular transaction or type of transaction, and that the plaintiff would be very likely to rely on it in deciding whether or not to transact). Thirdly, the court must consider that the imposition of the duty is fair and reasonable. The House of Lords, however, recognised that such tests overlap, are little more than labels and are not capable of accurately defining whether liability is established or not. An element of policy in the court's decision inevitably exists, and in this case was opposed to extending the liability of auditors to third parties. (See also *Al-Nakib Investments (Jersey) Ltd* v *Longcroft* [1990] 1 WLR 1390 in which the *Caparo* case is applied.)

Facts   The defendants were partners in Touche Ross, the firm of accountants who audited the accounts of Fidelity plc. Caparo owned shares in Fidelity and subsequently made a takeover bid, acquiring all the remaining shares of Fidelity. Caparo unsuccessfully sued the auditors claiming that it had paid too much for the shares because the auditors were allegedly negligent in certifying the accounts as true and fair by showing a profit of £1.2 million when there had in reality been a loss of £0.4 million.

The following extract gives a flavour of the reasoning of the House of Lords in rejecting the claim against the auditors.

LORD BRIDGE OF HARWICH: What emerges is that, in addition to the foreseeability of damage, necessary ingredients in any situation giving rise to a duty of care are that there should exist between the party owing the duty and the party to whom it is owed a relationship characterised by the law as one of 'proximity' or 'neighbourhood' and that the situation should be one in which the court considers it fair, just and reasonable that the law should impose a duty of a given scope upon the one party for the benefit of the other. But it is implicit in the passages referred to that the concepts of proximity and fairness embodied in these additional ingredients are not susceptible of any such precise definition as would be necessary to give them utility as practical tests, but amount in effect to little more than convenient labels to attach to the features of different specific situations which, on a detailed examination of all the circumstances, the law recognises pragmatically as giving rise to a duty of care of a given scope. Whilst recognising, of course, the importance of the underlying general principles common to the whole field of negligence, I think the law has now moved in the direction of attaching greater significance to the more traditional categorisation of distinct and recognisable situations as guides to the existence, the scope and the limits of the varied duties of care which the law imposes. We must now, I think, recognise the wisdom of the words of Brennan J in the High Court of Australia in *Sutherland Shire Council* v *Heyman* (1985) 60 ALR 1 at pp. 43–4, where he said:

> It is preferable, in my view, that the law should develop novel categories of negligence incrementally and by analogy with established categories, rather than by a massive extension of a prima facie duty of care restrained only by indefinable 'considerations which ought to negative, or to reduce or limit the scope of the duty or the class of person to whom it is owed'.

One of the most important distinctions always to be observed lies in the law's essentially different approach to the different kinds of damage which one party may have suffered in consequence of the acts or omissions of another. It is one thing to owe a duty of care to avoid causing injury to the person or property of others. It is quite another to avoid causing others to suffer purely economic loss....

The salient feature of all these cases [which his lordship had discussed] is that the defendant giving advice or information was fully aware of the nature of the transaction which the plaintiff had in contemplation, knew that the advice or information would be communicated to him directly or indirectly and knew that it was very likely that the plaintiff would rely on that advice or information in deciding whether or not to engage in the transaction in contemplation. In these circumstances the defendant could clearly be expected, subject always to the effect of any disclaimer of responsibility, specifically to anticipate that the plaintiff would rely on the advice or information given by the defendant for the very purpose for which he did in the event rely on it. So also the plaintiff, subject again to the effect of any disclaimer, would in that situation reasonably suppose that he was entitled to rely on the advice or information communicated to him for the very purpose for which he required it. The situation is entirely different where a statement is put into more or less general circulation and may foreseeably be relied on by strangers to the maker of the statement for any one of a variety of different purposes which the maker of the statement has no specific reason to anticipate. To hold the maker of the statement to be under a duty of care in respect of the accuracy of the statement to all and sundry for any purpose for which they may choose to rely on it is not only to subject him, in the classic words of Cardozo CJ to 'liability in an indeterminate amount for an indeterminate time to an indeterminate class' (see *Ultramares Corporation* v *Touche* (1931) 174 NE 441 at p. 444) it is also to confer on the world at large a quite unwarranted entitlement to appropriate for their own purposes the benefit of the expert knowledge or professional expertise attributed to the maker of the statement. Hence, looking only at the circumstances of these decided cases where a duty of care in respect of negligent statements has been held to exist, I should expect to find that the 'limit or control mechanism... imposed upon the liability of a wrongdoer towards those who have suffered economic damage in consequence of his negligence' (*Candlewood Navigation Corporation Ltd* v *Mitsui OSK Lines Ltd* [1986] AC 1 at p. 25) rested in the necessity to prove, in this category of the tort of negligence, as an essential ingredient of the 'proximity' between the plaintiff and the defendant, that the defendant knew that his statement would be communicated to the plaintiff, either as an individual or as a member of an identifiable class, specifically in connection with a particular transaction or transactions of a particular kind (e.g. in a prospectus inviting investment) and that the plaintiff would be very likely to rely on it for the purpose of deciding whether or not to enter upon that transaction or upon a transaction of that kind. ...

These considerations amply justify the conclusion that auditors of a public company's accounts owe no duty of care to members of the public at large who rely upon the accounts in deciding to buy shares in the company. If a duty of care were owed so widely, it is difficult to see any reason why it should not equally extend to all who rely on the accounts in relation to other dealings with a company as lenders or merchants extending credit to the company. A claim that such a duty was owed by auditors to a bank lending to a company was emphatically and convincingly rejected by Millett J in *Al Saudi Banque* v *Clarke Pixley* [1990] Ch 313. The only support for an unlimited duty of care owed by auditors for the accuracy of their accounts to all who may foreseeably rely upon them is to be found in some jurisdictions in the United States of America where there are striking differences in the law in different States. In this jurisdiction I have no doubt that the creation of such an unlimited duty would be a legislative step which it would be for Parliament, not the courts, to take.

The audit firms' lobby for change has been powerful as they felt aggrieved that if one of their company clients goes insolvent, those who suffer loss may then, instead of suing its directors, sue them as its auditors for vast sums as they are the potential defendants with the deepest pockets. They argued that even if they were negligent in failing to warn of the forthcoming financial crisis in the company, it was not they who caused the failure and so in all fairness they should only bear a proportion of the loss, relative to their share of the blame. They thus wanted to be allowed to 'cap' their liability by agreement with the company.

The Government was duly persuaded that in respect of auditors' liability to the client company only, agreements should be allowed which limit an auditor's liability to such amount as is just and equitable, having regard to the relative extent of their responsibility for the damage incurred. However, 'the company could not agree in advance a monetary limit to the auditor's liability. This means there would be no scope for maxima set as cash sums, or expressed in accordance with a quantifiable formula (for example, as a multiple of the audit fee)'. (White Paper: Company Law Reform, Cm 8458, 17 March 2005, para. 3.5.)

The new provisions for liability limitation agreements are found in the CA 2006, Part 16, supplemented by regulations made under s. 535. The following brief extracts give an outline of the new law.

COMPANIES ACT 2006, PART 16, CHAPTER 6

532. Voidness of provisions protecting auditors from liability

(1) This section applies to any provision—

    (a) for exempting an auditor of a company (to any extent) from any liability that would otherwise attach to him in connection with any negligence, default, breach of duty or breach of trust in relation to the company occurring in the course of the audit of accounts, or

    (b) by which a company directly or indirectly provides an indemnity (to any extent) for an auditor of the company, or of an associated company, against any liability attaching to him in connection with any negligence, default, breach of duty or breach of trust in relation to the company of which he is auditor occurring in the course of the audit of accounts.

(2) Any such provision is void, except as permitted by—

    (a) section 533 (indemnity for costs of successfully defending proceedings), or

    (b) sections 534 to 536 (liability limitation agreements).

(3) This section applies to any provision, whether contained in a company's articles or in any contract with the company or otherwise.

(4) For the purposes of this section companies are associated if one is a subsidiary of the other or both are subsidiaries of the same body corporate.

534. Liability limitation agreements

(1) A "liability limitation agreement" is an agreement that purports to limit the amount of a liability owed to a company by its auditor in respect of any negligence, default, breach of duty or breach of trust, occurring in the course of the audit of accounts, of which the auditor may be guilty in relation to the company.

(2) Section 532 (general voidness of provisions protecting auditors from liability) does not affect the validity of a liability limitation agreement that—

    (a) complies with section 535 (terms of liability limitation agreement) and of any regulations under that section, and

    (b) is authorised by the members of the company (see section 536).

535. Terms of liability limitation agreement

(1) A liability limitation agreement—

    (a) must not apply in respect of acts or omissions occurring in the course of the audit of accounts for more than one financial year, and

    (b) must specify the financial year in relation to which it applies.

(2) The Secretary of State may by regulations—

    (a) require liability limitation agreements to contain specified provisions or provisions of a specified description;

    (b) prohibit liability limitation agreements from containing specified provisions or provisions of a specified description.

"Specified" here means specified in the regulations.

536. Authorisation of agreement by members of the company

(1) A liability limitation agreement is authorised by the members of the company if it has been authorised under this section and that authorisation has not been withdrawn.

537. Effect of liability limitation agreement

(1) A liability limitation agreement is not effective to limit the auditor's liability to less than such amount as is fair and reasonable in all the circumstances of the case having regard (in particular) to—

    (a) the auditor's responsibilities under this Part,

    (b) the nature and purpose of the auditor's contractual obligations to the company, and

    (c) the professional standards expected of him.

Auditors' liability—watch this space

The question of the liability of auditors is often a lively issue. While the accountancy profession heaved a sigh of relief at the *Caparo* decision, they have not had it all their own way since. In another case (*ADT Ltd* v *BDO Binder Hamlyn* [1996] BCC 808) a firm of accountants was held liable to a third party for an award of £105 million. The firm, BDO Binder Hamlyn, had audited the accounts of Britannia

Security Services Ltd, for which ADT, the electronic security group, was making a takeover offer in 1980. One of the partners of BDO Binder Hamlyn orally confirmed to ADT at a meeting that he stood by the audited accounts. ADT went ahead with its takeover of Britannia and successfully claimed its losses from BDO Binder Hamlyn when it turned out that Britannia's accounts were negligently audited and that Britannia was worth very much less than its audited accounts indicated. By orally confirming the accounts the auditor assumed responsibility to ADT for their reliability. BDO Binder Hamlyn entered an appeal but in February 1997 withdrew it and settled for payment of £50 million, an amount said to be within its insurance cover. Similar litigation against auditors has followed the collapse of the Maxwell business empire and of Barings Bank. (See also Mayson, French and Ryan, *Company Law*, 8.10.)

Accounting firms by tradition practise as partnerships. Each of the partners is thus jointly and severally liable without any limitation for the debts of the firm (Partnership Act 1890, s. 9). With such huge potential liabilities they fear not only for the future of the firm itself but also the inevitable personal bankruptcy and the loss of their homes if the firm is overwhelmed by debt. As one accountant put it, the law means that if an audit partner commits a cock-up in Bristol, a tax partner in Aberdeen potentially loses his house. They also complain that when something goes wrong, accountancy firms are chosen as deep-pocketed defendants even though they may only have partially contributed by their negligence to the loss being incurred by the plaintiff. If, for example, in completing an audit they negligently fail to spot errors in the accounts or to detect fraud, it is the careless or fraudulent insiders who are primarily at fault. They have argued strongly for a change to the law of joint and several liability, so that they would only incur liability proportionate to their contribution to the loss incurred, as is the case in the US. However, the Law Commission in a recent report (*Joint and Several Liability*, 1996) rejected such a major change in the law, to accountants' considerable and vociferous disappointment.

It is of course standard practice for accountants to protect themselves by taking out liability insurance and it is a professional requirement to do so. However, it is generally not possible to obtain cover for the whole of their potential exposure, which may be immense.

It was never permissible to put a contractual limit on an auditor's liability to the company client as this was prohibited by CA 1985, s. 310. The success of the audit profession in being allowed to enter into 'liability limitation argreements' with the company, placing an important though uncertain limit on their liability, just described above, thus came as a major vindication. However, the remaining issue of their possible liability to third parties remains open.

Accounting firms could alternatively incorporate their auditing functions as limited companies, thus protecting the partners' personal assets if not the accounting practice itself. Some have done so, including KPMG Audit plc. However, relatively few firms have chosen to incorporate, many fighting shy of the obligation of companies to disclose their accounts, concerned at an adverse tax regime and preferring the management structure of a partnership. The ideal would therefore be a partnership-style vehicle conferring limited liability on the partners but enjoying the possible advantages of taxation as a partnership. Indeed in 1993 the American State of Delaware created such a limited liability partnership for exactly that purpose. The legislature of Jersey (a jurisdiction separate from the UK and not a member of the EC) passed its own Limited Liability Partnerships (Jersey) Law in late 1996. Jersey's purpose was to earn the financial spin-offs of major UK accountancy (and possibly other) firms registering as Jersey LLPs. Not to be outdone in facilitating business, the DTI promoted the enactment of the Limited Liability Partnerships Act 2000 establishing the LLP, a relatively complex limited liability vehicle for partnerships. (See also the note at the end of 2.5 above.)

The law and practice concerning the liability of auditors to the company and to third parties, and how partners may shield themselves from potentially catastrophic liabilities, remains controversial. A director of Caparo, James Leek, styling himself as the 'victim' who brought and paid for the Caparo legal action (above), commented in a letter to *The Times* (28 August 1996):

Post-*Caparo*, the efforts of Cadbury and the auditing profession seem to have been directed mainly at shunting more responsibility onto the directors (including non-executives), whilst protecting themselves with limited liability companies and Channel Island registration. The result is that, whilst corporate governance may have improved, the auditors' responsibility for accounts is as shrouded in mystery and mystique as ever.

Sir Adrian Cadbury has himself written (in F.D. Padfield (ed.), *Perspectives on Company Law* (Graham & Trotman, 1995)):

It can be argued that the *Caparo* judgment is too restrictive, first, as to the classes of people to whom auditors owe a duty of care and, secondly, as to the purposes for which they are entitled to rely on a company's audit statement. The first restriction follows inevitably from the second. Indeed, there appear to be marked differences of view among the judiciary as to the purpose of the audit process. In the end, the Committee was unable to propose practical remedies for the problems raised by the *Caparo* judgment. It seems that we have to regard *Caparo* as unfinished business, both because there is another leg to the case and because the judgment is unlikely to be the last word in the matter of auditors' duty of care.

17

Offering Shares to Public Investors

Company law facilitates enterprise by allowing investors in a separate corporate entity to limit their liability or loss to the amount they invest in its shares. A secondary objective is to make shares in companies (or at least in larger companies) fully marketable. Thus although the maintenance of capital principle prevents shareholders from withdrawing their capital from the company, there should be an active public market where those shares can be freely traded and investments disposed of. Thus the raising of business capital and the trading of shares are the principal purposes of public stock exchanges.

The London Stock Exchange is one of the largest in the world and is intended to fulfil this purpose. By making shares marketable it stimulates investment in companies and thus in commerce and industry generally. Stock exchanges compete for business and London lists a large number of European stocks that can be bought and sold on its market.

For stock markets to operate efficiently there should be adequate liquidity, i.e., there should be sufficient transactions in shares to enable their market price to be established and to enable sellers to find a buyer promptly at an appropriate price. The market price should be established on the basis of undistorted supply and demand. For example, regulations should heavily penalise attempts to support the price of a share artificially by misrepresentation or by creating an impression of active trading. Holders of identical shares should be equally entitled to the same price for their shares. Thus, for example, a block of shares carrying control of a company should not sell at a premium pro rata to all the other shares in the company (see 18.2.3).

Demand for individual shares should be appropriately stimulated by ensuring that all investors have equal access to full information about the company to enable an investment decision at an appropriate price to be made. Thus when shares are offered to the public, a 'prospectus' (sometimes called 'listing particulars') must be issued free, giving a range of specified information to help prospective investors in deciding whether to apply for shares. Continuing obligations of disclosure will also be imposed on companies to ensure a flow of information to investors. The use by company 'insiders' of confidential information not publicly available to make a decision to buy or sell the company's shares is prohibited by making 'insider dealing' a criminal offence (see chapter 19). Regulation of share markets also relies on self-regulation and on the individual and financial integrity and competence of those operating in the market such as sponsors and listing agents.

In addition to ensuring free flows of capital, a major function of regulation is investor protection. Investors must be put in a position where full and accurate information is available to them to enable investment decisions to be made. Many of the principles mentioned above which contribute to the proper functioning of the market also contribute to the protection of investors.

From the point of view of larger companies, a 'flotation' of shares or 'going public' (i.e., offering shares to the public) is an important way of raising new finance. This reduces reliance on bank borrowing and may be cheaper than loan interest charges. It is also an opportunity sometimes for existing shareholders to create a market for and maximise the value of their shares, thus making substantial capital gains. (Shares in a private company are hardly marketable and may not be offered to the public. (See CA 2006, ss. 755 and 756 below.) Float the company as a public company so as to create a public market for the shares and their value may increase dramatically (see 9.5).) If it is wished to make a takeover bid for another company, an issue of shares in the bidder to the seller of shares in the target company may be used to pay for the takeover. Only shares in a publicly listed company will be acceptable as the currency for payment and so a private company will probably have to buy for cash. Finally a public 'listing' of a company's shares may add to its prestige and public profile.

Many companies listed on the Stock Exchange were not incorporated as public companies but after successful trading as a private company convert to a public company in order to offer their shares to the public. Of a total of about 2,000 public companies a tiny proportion account for the bulk of market capitalisation and turnover. As discussed at 15.1.1 private companies are largely dependent on loan finance for expansion and may not offer shares to the public.

The principal legislation that regulates the issue of shares and other investments is the Financial Services and Markets Act 2000. This builds upon and replaces most of the Financial Services Act 1986, whose origins are explained in the extracts that follow. The new Act is administered by the Financial Services Authority, which is charged with maintaining confidence in and promoting public awareness of the financial system, protecting consumers of financial services and minimising financial crime within this sector. It is also concerned with the authorisation, approval and discipline of those working within the financial services industry. (See www.fsa.gov.uk.) The following brief extracts from the legislation set out its duties.

COMPANIES ACT 2006, SS. 755 AND 756

755. Prohibition of public offers by private company

(1) A private company limited by shares or limited by guarantee and having a share capital must not—
  (a) offer to the public any securities of the company, or
  (b) allot or agree to allot any securities of the company with a view to their being offered to the public.

756. Meaning of "offer to the public"

(1) This section explains what is meant in this Chapter by an offer of securities to the public.
(2) An offer to the public includes an offer to any section of the public, however selected.
(3) An offer is not regarded as an offer to the public if it can properly be regarded, in all the circumstances, as—
  (a) not being calculated to result, directly or indirectly, in securities of the company becoming available to persons other than those receiving the offer, or
  (b) otherwise being a private concern of the person receiving it and the person making it.

(4) An offer is to be regarded (unless the contrary is proved) as being a private concern of the person receiving it and the person making it if—

(a) it is made to a person already connected with the company and, where it is made on terms allowing that person to renounce his rights, the rights may only be renounced in favour of another person already connected with the company; or

(b) it is an offer to subscribe for securities to be held under an employees' share scheme and, where it is made on terms allowing that person to renounce his rights, the rights may only be renounced in favour of—

(i) another person entitled to hold securities under the scheme, or

(ii) a person already connected with the company.

(5) For the purposes of this section "person already connected with the company" means—

(a) an existing member or employee of the company,

(b) a member of the family of a person who is or was a member or employee of the company,

(c) the widow or widower, or surviving civil partner, of a person who was a member or employee of the company,

(d) an existing debenture holder of the company, or

(e) a trustee (acting in his capacity as such) of a trust of which the principal beneficiary is a person within any of paragraphs (a) to (d).

(6) For the purposes of subsection (5)(b) the members of a person's family are the person's spouse or civil partner and children (including step-children) and their descendants.

FINANCIAL SERVICES AND MARKETS ACT 2000, SS. 1 AND 2

1. The Financial Services Authority

(1) The body corporate known as the Financial Services Authority ('the Authority') is to have the functions conferred on it by or under this Act....

2. The Authority's general duties

(1) In discharging its general functions the Authority must, so far as is reasonably possible, act in a way—

(a) which is compatible with the regulatory objectives; and

(b) which the Authority considers most appropriate for the purpose of meeting those objectives.

(2) The regulatory objectives are—

(a) market confidence;

(b) public awareness;

(c) the protection of consumers; and

(d) the reduction of financial crime.

(3) In discharging its general functions the Authority must have regard to—

(a) the need to use its resources in the most efficient and economic way;

(b) the responsibilities of those who manage the affairs of authorised persons;

(c) the principle that a burden or restriction which is imposed on a person, or on the carrying on of an activity, should be proportionate to the benefits, considered in general terms, which are expected to result from the imposition of that burden or restriction;

(d) the desirability of facilitating innovation in connection with regulated activities;

(e) the international character of financial services and markets and the desirability of maintaining the competitive position of the United Kingdom;

(f) the need to minimise the adverse effects on competition that may arise from anything done in the discharge of those functions;

(g) the desirability of facilitating competition between those who are subject to any form of regulation by the Authority.

(4) The Authority's general functions are—

(a) its function of making rules under this Act (considered as a whole);

(b) its function of preparing and issuing codes under this Act (considered as a whole);

(c) its functions in relation to the giving of general guidance (considered as a whole); and

(d) its function of determining the general policy and principles by reference to which it performs particular functions.

17.2 OFFICIAL LISTING OF SECURITIES

A public company is known as a listed company if any of its securities (i.e., shares
etc.) are listed and admitted to trading on the London Stock Exchange. (See www.
londonstockexchange.com.) The following extract now provides useful background to the procedure and advantages for a company of obtaining a public listing of shares on the London Stock Exchange.

Stock Exchange Official Yearbook 1992–1993

A listing on the London Stock Exchange

In providing a framework for private companies to 'go public' the Stock Exchange through its rules
and regulations as UK competent authority for listing sits between the providers of capital and the
users of capital. In performing the role the Exchange seeks to balance issuer needs for accessibility,
liquidity and cost effectiveness with investor needs for orderly and full disclosure of information.
The Exchange's role as competent authority is bounded by both UK and European legislation.

Three European Directives—the Admissions Directive, the Listing Particulars Directive, and the
Interim Reports Directive—were adopted into UK law, first through the Stock Exchange (Listing)
Regulations 1984 and latterly by part IV of the Financial Services Act 1986. Although the bulk of the
Directives are not contained in part IV of the Act the Stock Exchange was appointed competent
authority and was given powers to make Listing Rules. The Directives laid down minimum requirements for admission of securities to listing, the content, scrutiny and publication of listing particulars as a condition of admission to listing and the continuing obligations of issuers after admission.
The Directives make provision for the competent authority in each Member State to impose additional requirements. [Further directives have since been implemented.]

The requirements of the Listing Rules…seek to secure the confidence of investors in the conduct of the market by ensuring, firstly, that all applicants for listing are of a certain size, and have a
record of trading of adequate duration under the present management. This information, together
with information about the history, prospects and financial condition of the applicant, is set out in
formal listing particulars or equivalent offering document and is used as a reliable basis for market evaluation. Secondly, that all marketings of securities are conducted on a fair and open basis,
allowing the public access wherever appropriate; and finally that investors are treated with proper
consideration at all times by company boards even though the public may only represent a minority
of the shareholders.

The attractions of public companies and access to the public markets appear as strong as ever
despite the rigours of disclosure imposed on the management of the companies. Going public represents for a company and its management a coming of age of significant change to the company
and its associates. The motivation to attempt this transition is likely to affect not only the needs of
the business but the character and the requirements of the individuals who own and manage it.
The issue of shares on the Exchange's markets is one of the most important methods of converting
individual savings into capital investment for industry. By pooling risks and rewards among a number of investors the stock market allows companies to raise capital on better terms than would be
available from a single investor.

There are many advantages of going public; the most important are set out below.

Capital raising Companies are able to raise new equity capital, both at the time of flotation and
subsequently, by issuing shares for cash or as consideration in acquisitions. This ability to raise

equity finance provides companies with greater flexibility in financing business expansion plans, introducing new products or reducing borrowings.

The ability for existing shareholders to realise a return on their funds invested should not be underestimated. Going public provides a convenient opportunity for the original shareholders to take a profit on their hard work.

Marketability   The ability to sell shares freely provides a more satisfactory route for existing share-holders who may wish to realise some or all of their investments. The offering of shares to public investors in orderly trading provided by the Exchange's markets ensures that a fair price is struck for the shares to become more attractive to investors. Its increased marketability ensures that the multiples applied to the earnings of a public company are often higher than those of a similar private company, resulting in a higher valuation.

Once listed, shares become more acceptable to banks as security for loans, either on their own or as part of a portfolio. This provides an alternative for shareholders who do not wish necessarily to sell but need to raise money from time to time. In addition, once listed, a company may issue its shares as consideration in acquisitions, widening its financing options and allowing it to consider larger acquisition targets. Acceptance of an acquirer's paper rather than cash may have attractions to vendors both from tax considerations and by allowing them to feel they still retain an interest in the asset or business they are selling.

Visibility and prestige   The initial flotation of a company and the ongoing Stock Exchange require-ments for the publication of information necessarily means that a company becomes more visible to the public. The attention drawn to the company and its business may increase awareness of its attractions as a business or joint venture partner. A public company is generally regarded by its customers, suppliers and creditors as having a higher standing than a private company. Employees may take a pride in working in a public company rather than an individual family-owned business and a share incentive scheme may be offered to foster a sense of participation. Although perhaps less tangible, there is a general feeling that a company of a certain size and reputation should be a public company.

As already mentioned above, the principal legislation governing public share issues is the Financial Services and Markets Act 2000 repealing most of the Financial Services Act 1986. The 1986 Act owes its origins to the Gower Report (*Review of Investor Protection*, Cmnd 9125), a lengthy report commissioned to make recom-mendations on protection of investors generally. In the following extract the late Professor Gower explains the philosophy that regulation should be sufficient only to enable reasonable investors to protect themselves. The second extract is from the white paper which preceded the 1986 Act and sets out the government's objec-tives in creating the first comprehensive framework for investor protection.

Review of Investor Protection
(Cmnd 9125) (London: HMSO, 1984)

1.16 In assessing the optimum degree of regulation I have not attempted any sort of cost-benefit analysis, partly because I am not competent to undertake it and partly because I am sceptical about its practicability. I can see that it would be practicable to analyse whether markets work more or less efficiently, *qua* markets, according to the degree of regulation to which they are subject. But inevitably there is a tension between market efficiency and investor protection which often pull in different directions. It may be that the most efficient market is that which is wholly free from regu-lation but it is unlikely that such a market would afford protection to investors which anyone today would regard as adequate. One has to make a value judgment on the relative weight to be attached to market freedom and to investor protection. My judgment, as I have said, is that regulation in the interests of the latter *should be no greater than is necessary to protect reasonable people from being made fools of.* That degree of protection is essential if members of the public are to have the justified confidence to invest in productive enterprise through the wider range of opportunities now available to them. There seems to be no evidence that that degree of regulation impairs market efficiency; whether further regulation is needed to enhance market efficiency is not within my terms of reference.

Financial Services in the UK; A New Framework for Investor Protection
(Cmnd 9432) (London: HMSO, 1985)

3.1 The government's objectives in designing a new framework for investor protection are:

i. *Efficiency*—the financial services industry of the United Kingdom should be able to provide services to industry and commerce, private investors and government in the most efficient and economic way.

ii. *Competitiveness*—the industry must be competitive both domestically and internationally. Regulation must stimulate competition and encourage innovation; it must be responsive to international developments and not a cover for protectionism.

iii. *Confidence*—the system of regulation must inspire confidence in issuers and investors by ensuring that the financial services sector is, and is seen to be, a 'clean' place to do business.

iv. *Flexibility*—the regulatory framework must be clear enough to guide but not cramp structural and other change in the industry. It must have the resilience not to be overrun by events.

Principles underlying the new system

3.2 These objectives are best met by action to apply the following principles:

i. *Market forces* provide the best means of ensuring that an industry meets the needs of its customers. If market forces are to operate properly it is essential that:
  — as much *information* as possible is disclosed about the investments and services on offer to the customer; and
  — the forces of *competition* are brought to bear on practitioners and their institutions.

ii. The law should provide a *clearly understood set of general principles and rules* which facilitate:
  — raising capital in the United Kingdom;
  — investment and saving; and
  — buying and selling of investments.

iii. *Prevention* is better than cure. The regulatory framework should make fraud less likely to occur in the first place.

iv. Vigorous *enforcement* of a simplified, clear investment law is necessary to deter fraud and malpractice.

v. *Self-regulation* has a continuing and crucial contribution to make. It means commitment by practitioners to the maintenance of high standards as a matter of integrity and principle, not because they are imposed from outside. Regulation should encourage the commitment of individuals in the financial services industry to high standards. It is in the interests of both the industry and its customers that the opportunity for theft, fraud and deception in the buying and selling of securities and investment services should be minimised.

vi. If the law and the regulatory system are to be clear and fair there must be so far as this is possible *equivalence of treatment* between products and services competing in the same market. The law should not create artificial distinctions.

Caveat emptor

3.3 No regulatory system can, or should, relieve the investor of responsibility for exercising judgment and care in deciding how to invest his money. If he makes a foolish decision on the basis of adequate disclosure—venturing all his savings on an avowedly speculative and high-risk proposition which fails for straightforward commercial reasons—he cannot look to any regulator to make good the losses arising from his own misjudgement.

> 3.4 The regulatory framework outlined in this white paper gives proper prominence to this time-honoured principle of *caveat emptor*. But it recognises that *caveat emptor* alone is not enough. For investors to have the confidence to venture into the market, measures are needed to reduce the likelihood of fraud and to encourage high standards in the conduct of investment business.

The other source influencing the legislation is an extensive series of European directives on the regulation of capital markets. Their objective is the admission of securities (shares) to official stock exchange listing in each member state, offering equivalent protection to investors in each, with a view to creating a single European capital market.

Recent directives are the consolidated admissions and reporting directive known as CARD (2001/34/EC) and the prospectus directive (2003/71/EC). See also CA 2006, Part 43, implementing the 'transparency directive' (2004/109/EC) by amending the Financial Services and Markets Act 2000 to make provision for rules requiring companies whose securities are traded on regulated markets in the UK to disclose a wide range of information for the benefit of investors.

The earlier directives were implemented by the Financial Services Act 1986, now superceded by the Financial Services and Markets Act 2000, and itself already amended to implement recent directives, in particular with changes to Part VI on official listing.

The following sections from Part VI of the Act establish the Financial Services Authority as the 'competent authority' and introduce terminology such as the 'official list', 'listing particulars' and 'prospectuses'. A prospectus is a massive document also available on the company's website containing a welter of financial and other information that is required to be made publicly available to inform investors before a company can offer its shares to the public.

FINANCIAL SERVICES AND MARKETS ACT 2000, PART VI OFFICIAL LISTING

72. The competent authority

(1) On the coming into force of this section, the functions conferred on the competent authority by this Part are to be exercised by the Authority....

73. General duty of the competent authority

(1) In discharging its general functions the competent authority must have regard to—
  (a) the need to use its resources in the most efficient and economic way;
  (b) the principle that a burden or restriction which is imposed on a person should be proportionate to the benefits, considered in general terms, which are expected to arise from the imposition of that burden or restriction;
  (c) the desirability of facilitating innovation in respect of listed securities and in respect of financial instruments which have otherwise been admitted to trading on a regulated market or for which a request for admission to trading on such a market has been made;
  (d) the international character of capital markets and the desirability of maintaining the competitive position of the United Kingdom;
  (e) the need to minimise the adverse effects on competition of anything done in the discharge of those functions;
  (f) the desirability of facilitating competition in relation to listed securities and in relation to financial instruments which have otherwise been admitted to trading on a regulated market or for which a request for admission to trading on such a market has been made.
(2) The competent authority's general functions are—
  (a) its function of making rules under this Part (considered as a whole);

(b) its functions in relation to the giving of general guidance in relation to this Part (considered as a whole);

(c) its function of determining the general policy and principles by reference to which it performs particular functions under this Part.

73A. Part 6 Rules

(1) The competent authority may make rules ('Part 6 rules') for the purposes of this Part.

(2) Provisions of Part 6 rules expressed to relate to the official list are referred to in this Part as 'listing rules'.

(3) Provisions of Part 6 rules expressed to relate to disclosure of information in respect of financial instruments which have been admitted to trading on a regulated market or for which a request for admission to trading on such a market has been made, are referred to in this Part as 'disclosure rules'.

(4) Provisions of Part 6 rules expressed to relate to transferable securities are referred to in this Part as 'prospectus rules'.

74. The official list

(1) The competent authority must maintain the official list.

(2) The competent authority may admit to the official list such securities and other things as it considers appropriate....

75. Applications for listing

(1) Admission to the official list may be granted only on an application made to the competent authority in such manner as may be required by listing rules....

79. Listing particulars and other documents

(1) Listing rules may provide that securities (other than new securities) of a kind specified in the rules may not be admitted to the official list unless—

(a) listing particulars have been submitted to, and approved by, the competent authority and published; or

(b) in such cases as may be specified by listing rules, such document (other than listing particulars or a prospectus of a kind required by listing rules) as may be so specified has been published.

(2) 'Listing particulars' means a document in such form and containing such information as may be specified in listing rules....

84. Matters which may be dealt with by prospectus rules

(1) Prospectus rules may also make provision as to—

(a) the required form and content of a prospectus (including a summary);

(b) the cases in which a summary need not be included in a prospectus;

(c) the languages which may be used in a prospectus (including a summary);

(d) the determination of the persons responsible for a prospectus;

(e) the manner in which applications to the competent authority for the approval of a prospectus are to be made.

(2) Prospectus rules may also make provision as to—

(a) the period of validity of a prospectus;

(b) the disclosure of the maximum price or of the criteria or conditions according to which the final offer price is to be determined, if that information is not contained in a prospectus;

(c) the disclosure of the amount of the transferable securities which are to be offered to the public or of the criteria or conditions according to which that amount is to be determined, if that information is not contained in a prospectus;

(d) the required form and content of other summary documents (including the languages which may be used in such a document);

(e) the ways in which a prospectus that has been approved by the competent authority may be made available to the public;

    (f) the disclosure, publication or other communication of such information as the competent authority may reasonably stipulate;

    (g) the principles to be observed in relation to advertisements in connection with an offer of transferable securities to the public or admission of transferable securities to trading on a regulated market and the enforcement of those principles;

    (h) the suspension of trading in transferable securities where continued trading would be detrimental to the interests of investors;

    (i) elections under section 87 or under Article 2.1(m)(iii) of the prospectus directive as applied for the purposes of this Part by section 102c.

  (3) Prospectus rules may also make provision as to—

    (a) access to the register of investors maintained under section 87R; and

    (b) the supply of information from that register.

  (4) Prospectus rules may make provision for the purpose of dealing with matters arising out of or related to any provision of the prospectus directive.

85. Prohibition of dealing etc. in transferable securities without approved prospectus

  (1) It is unlawful for transferable securities to which this subsection applies to be offered to the public in the United Kingdom unless an approved prospectus has been made available to the public before the offer is made.

  (5) Subsection (I) applies to all transferable securities other than—

    (a) those listed in Schedule 11A;

    (b) such other transferable securities as may be specified in prospectus rules.

  (7) 'Approved prospectus' means, in relation to transferable securities to which this section applies, a prospectus approved by the competent authority of the home State in relation to the issuer of the securities.

18

Takeovers and Mergers

Until relatively recently there has been no body of law regulating what are loosely called takeovers and mergers. The ways in which companies acquire others or reorganise themselves are so many and varied that they are difficult to categorise precisely and much of the terminology (e.g., merger, amalgamation, reconstruction etc.) are essentially business terms without clear definition. The late Professor Gower in his pioneering work *Principles of Modern Company Law*, 6th ed. (1997), p. 757, explained the position as follows:

> One difficulty in dealing with [reconstructions of companies] is the looseness of English legal terminology in this area. The operations are variously described as reductions, reconstructions, reorganisations, schemes of arrangement, amalgamations, mergers, demergers, buy-outs, etc. etc. But none of those expressions is a term of art with a clearly defined meaning distinguishing one such transaction from another. In general the expression 'reconstruction', 'reorganisation', or 'scheme of arrangement' is employed when only one company is involved, the last of these terms being more commonly used when the rights of creditors are varied as well as those of the shareholders. Under an 'amalgamation' or 'merger' two or more companies are merged either by the acquisition of their undertakings and assets by one of them or by a newly incorporated company or, more commonly, by one such company acquiring a controlling shareholding in the others. In English practice most mergers are achieved through takeovers.

One of the few clearly distinct processes is the public company takeover in which one company bids to acquire another company by buying its shares. Such takeovers are subject to the City Code on Takeovers and Mergers (see 18.2.1) which for many years was a self-regulatory code of practice but which now, to implement the takeovers directive (2004/25/EC), has been made statutory under Part 8 of CA 2006. (See 18.2.1.) In addition to this newly formalised body of law, mergers and divisions of public companies are now dealt with by Part 27 of the CA 2006, enacted to implement the third Council directive, 1978/855/EEC, and the sixth Council directive, 82/891/EEC, which enable public companies to apply to the court to sanction arrangements or reconstructions concerning a merger or division.

From the economic point of view, companies may acquire others to enable them to grow in size and efficiency, to take control of a profitable competitor, or to acquire valuable markets, customers, brands or underexploited corporate assets. A takeover can also be seen as a means by which business efficiency may be enhanced through the substitution of new and more efficient management. It is thus thought to be important that the state facilitates such combinations as part of the proper functioning of market capitalism, except where a combination tends to create a monopoly or is otherwise anti-competitive. At this point UK or EC laws on competition or monopolies and mergers which deal primarily with economic issues may intervene. (See the extract by Lord Alexander at 18.2.1 below under 'Functions of the Panel'.)

In broad terms, a purchasing company can either buy from a company its business assets as a going concern or it can acquire the company itself by buying all or a controlling interest in its shares from the shareholders. Probably because stamp duties on transfer of shares have tended to be lower than on purchase of land (the principal assets of many companies), purchase of shares has generally been preferred to purchase of assets. In the case of private companies this is achieved by drawing up a share sale agreement between the acquiring company and the shareholders who are selling and these contain extensive warranties as to the state of the company and are a common feature of high street legal practice. In total contrast, a public company takeover bid where the offeror company offers a stated price for the shares of the target company is a newsworthy feature of City practice.

It should be noted that with an asset purchase the buyer company makes an offer to the directors of the target company to buy its business assets. On the other hand, with a share purchase or takeover bid, the offeror is not dealing direct with the target company itself but makes its offer to the shareholders of the target to buy their shares. Especially with public company takeovers, the shareholders are often not paid in cash but by a new issue of shares in the offeror company. The directors of the target company are required to take professional advice and to make formal recommendations to the shareholders as to whether the offer is favourable or not, but it is not they who are in a position to accept the offer. If they recommend that the offer be not accepted this is known as a hostile takeover bid. At this point, their motives for recommending rejection of the offer may come under close scrutiny. As the new owners will often sack the old board of directors, their jobs may be on the line. The question of their duties to their shareholders in making recommendations on the terms of the bid to their shareholders is considered in 18.3 below.

Where a company acquires the shares of another company the new relationship will generally be that of holding company and subsidiary. However, the very concept of a takeover may appear predatory as it involves one company swallowing up another. Both for psychological and other reasons the alternative terminology or procedure of a merger or amalgamation may be used. Thus the two merging companies may agree to form a third company for the purpose and transfer their assets to it, and then wind up. More likely the members of the merging companies may agree to transfer their shares to a new holding company in return for shares in that company. Thus the two companies are 'merged' by becoming subsidiaries under the control of a common holding company.

18.2 TAKEOVERS

18.2.1 Introduction to the Takeover Code

As part of the process of the regulation of public companies listed on the London Stock Exchange, takeover bids for such companies must comply with the City Code on Takeovers and Mergers. The code is issued, administered and enforced by the Panel on Takeovers and Mergers. This was set up for the purpose by City interests in 1968 and proved to be a unique and creative method of self-regulation. Though the Code was not legislation, in the late Professor Gower's words 'the Panel is now clearly recognised by the courts, the legislature and the government as a public body performing public functions on behalf of the State' (*Gower's Principles of Modern Company Law*, 6th ed. (1997), p. 776). Again to quote Gower, 'The basic objective of the Code is to ensure that the shareholders of the target company are treated fairly and equally and that the decision on the acceptability of the offer is made by the shareholders of the target company (and not, say, by its management)' having the benefit of 'all the information they need in order to decide whether or not to accept the bid' (p. 779).

The following extracts from the *Guinness* and *Datafin* cases contain Lord Donaldson's vivid descriptions of the role of the Panel in administering the Code, its structure, the nature of self-regulation and the process of enforcement. There then follows an extract from an authoritative but very readable lecture by the late Lord Alexander of Weedon QC, speaking and writing as chairman of the Panel. This stresses that the function of the Code is to ensure fairness to shareholders but that wider economic issues such as the anti-competitive effect of a takeover are dealt with under other UK or EC legislation. He identifies four principles on which the Code was based and describes the important daily consultative work of the Panel's executive. He finally refers to the *Datafin* and *Guinness* cases in which it was held by the Court of Appeal that decisions of the Panel as performing a public duty are subject to judicial review on grounds of procedural irregularity leading to injustice. (It should be noted however that following implementation of the take-over directive by the CA 2006 (see below), the Takeover Panel and Code are now constituted by statute and the unique and successful exercise of self-regulation has now become a formal part of the law. The merits of self-regulation as opposed to a statutory framework may long be debated at City dinner parties.)

R v Panel on Takeovers and Mergers, ex parte Guinness plc

The role of the Panel

[1990] 1 QB 146, Court of Appeal

LORD DONALDSON OF LYMINGTON MR: Part legislator, part court of interpretation, part consult-ant, part referee, part disciplinary tribunal, [the Panel's] self-imposed task is to regulate and police the conduct of takeovers and mergers in the financial markets of the United Kingdom.

Lacking a statutory base, it has to determine and declare its own terms of reference and the rules applicable in the markets, thus acting as a legislator. It has to give guidance in situations in which those involved in takeovers and mergers may be in doubt how they should act. These doubts may arise because the situation is one which is novel and not covered by the rules. The panel then acts as the conscience of the markets. This is the consultancy role. Or they may arise out of difficulty in applying the rules literally, in which case the panel interprets them in its capacity as a court of inter-pretation. I use the word 'interpret' rather than 'construe' advisedly because, as noted in the *R v Panel on Takeovers and Mergers ex parte Datafin plc* [1987] QB 815, at p. 841, the panel as legislator tends to lay down general principles on the lines of EEC legislation rather than to promulgate specific prohibitions, although such prohibitions do exist. Where it detects breaches of the rules during the course of a takeover, it acts as a whistle-blowing referee, ordering the party concerned to stop and, where it considers it appropriate, requiring that party to take action designed to nullify any advan-tage which it has obtained and to redress any disadvantage to other parties. Finally, when the dust has settled, it can take disciplinary action against those who are found to have broken the rules.

R v Panel on Takeovers and Mergers, ex parte Datafin plc
Judicial review of Panel decisions
[1987] 1 All ER 564, [1987] QB 815, Court of Appeal

DONALDSON MR: The Panel on Takeovers and Mergers is a truly remarkable body. Perched on the 20th floor of the Stock Exchange building in the City of London, both literally and metaphorically it oversees and regulates a very important part of the United Kingdom financial market. Yet it performs this function without visible means of legal support.

The panel is an unincorporated association without legal personality and, so far as can be seen, has only about 12 members. But those members are appointed by and represent the Accepting Houses Committee, the Association of Investment Trust Companies, the Association of British Insurers, the Committee of London and Scottish Bankers, the Confederation of British Industry, the Council of the Stock Exchange, the Institute of Chartered Accountants in England and Wales, the Issuing Houses Association, the National Association of Pension Funds, the Financial Intermediaries Managers and Brokers Regulatory Association, and the Unit Trust Association, the chairman and deputy chairman being appointed by the Bank of England. Furthermore, the panel is supported by the Foreign Bankers in London, the Foreign Brokers in London and the Consultative Committee of Accountancy Bodies. [The membership has since changed: see the extract from the Takeover Code in 18.2.2.]

It has no statutory, prerogative or common law powers and it is not in contractual relationship with the financial market or with those who deal in that market. According to the introduction to the City Code on Takeovers and Mergers, which it promulgates:

> The Code has not, and does not seek to have, the force of law, but those who wish to take advantage of the facilities of the securities markets in the United Kingdom should conduct themselves in matters relating to takeovers according to the Code. Those who do not so conduct themselves cannot expect to enjoy those facilities and may find that they are withheld.

[His lordship went on to quote extensively from provisions of the Code, the current version of which is reproduced in part below.]

'Self-regulation' is an emotive term. It is also ambiguous. An individual who voluntarily regulates his life in accordance with stated principles, because he believes that this is morally right and also, perhaps, in his own long-term interests, or a group of individuals who do so, are practising self-regulation. But it can mean something quite different. It can connote a system whereby a group of people, acting in concert, use their collective power to force themselves and others to comply with a code of conduct of their own devising. This is not necessarily morally wrong or contrary to the public interest, unlawful or even undesirable. But it is very different.

The panel is a self-regulating body in the latter sense. Lacking any authority *de iure*, it exercises immense power *de facto* by devising, promulgating, amending and interpreting the City Code on Takeovers and Mergers, by waiving or modifying the application of the Code in particular circumstances, by investigating and reporting on alleged breaches of the Code and by the application or threat of sanctions. These sanctions are no less effective because they are applied indirectly and lack a legally enforceable base. Thus, to quote again from the introduction to the Code:

> If there appears to have been a material breach of the Code, the executive invites the person concerned to appear before the Panel for a hearing. He is informed by letter of the nature of the alleged breach and of the matters which the Director General will present. If any other matters are raised he is allowed to ask for an adjournment. If the Panel finds that there has been a breach, it may have recourse to private reprimand or public censure or, in a more flagrant case, to further action designed to deprive the offender temporarily or permanently of his ability to enjoy the facilities of the securities markets. The Panel may refer certain aspects of a case to the Department of Trade and Industry, the Stock Exchange or other appropriate body. No reprimand, censure or further action will take place without the person concerned having the opportunity to appeal to the Appeal Committee of the Panel.

The unspoken assumption, which I do not doubt is a reality, is that the Department of Trade and Industry or, as the case may be, the Stock Exchange or other appropriate body would in fact exercise statutory or contractual powers to penalise the transgressors. Thus, for example, rr. 22 to 24 of the Stock Exchange Rules provide for the severest penalties, up to and including expulsion, for acts of misconduct, and by r. 23.1:

> Acts of misconduct may consist of any of the following ... (g) Any action which has been found by the Panel on Takeovers and Mergers (including where reference has been made to it, the Appeal Committee of the Panel) to have been in breach of the City Code on Takeovers and Mergers. The findings of the Panel, subject to any modification by the Appeal Committee of the Panel, shall not be reopened in proceedings taken under rules 22 to 24.
>
> ...

As I have said, the panel is a truly remarkable body, performing its function without visible means of legal support. But the operative word is 'visible', although perhaps I should have used the word 'direct'. Invisible or indirect support there is in abundance. Not only is a breach of the Code, so found by the Panel, *ipso facto* an act of misconduct by a member of the Stock Exchange, and the same may be true of other bodies represented on the Panel, but the admission of shares to the Official List may be withheld in the event of such a breach. This is interesting and significant for listing of securities is a statutory function performed by the Stock Exchange in pursuance of [regulations] enacted in implementation of EEC Directives.

Lord Alexander of Weedon QC, *'Takeovers: the regulatory scene'*
[1990] JBL 203

The Takeover Panel is now well into its twenty-first year. During that time, and especially in the last few years, takeover activity has much increased and become a regular feature of corporate activity. The characteristics of the financial markets of the City of London and the way in which acquisitions are pursued have changed dramatically. So, too, has the basic regulatory system, which has become far more professional, intense and is to a great extent set within a statutory framework. Since the Financial Services Act the formal control of markets and practitioners has become much more wide-ranging and detailed. The Panel, although it has a very distinct role, works closely with the other regulatory authorities, including the Department of Trade and Industry, [the London Stock Exchange plc, the Financial Services Authority and the Bank of England]. The overall success of the regulatory system depends upon the activities of all regulators, fulfilling their specific role in their own fields and in accordance with their expertise, but working in the closest cooperation with each other. It also requires that the system for compliance within individual firms is vigorously operated, and that the quality of compliance officers is as high as their task is important. The financial markets require the highest skills and increasing sophistication for their success, but even more fundamentally are dependent upon being known for the integrity and fairness of their dealings.

Functions of the Panel May I stress straight away that the Panel does not control all aspects of takeovers, but focuses primarily on ensuring fairness to shareholders. We are not concerned with the economic wisdom of the decision whether an offer for a company is high enough to be accepted. The economic merit of the takeover is for shareholders. Nor, as you are aware, do we consider aspects of public interest, notably the effect on competition ... The Panel is essentially by contrast the referee of the fair conduct of the bid.

Structure and content of the Code There are essentially four principles which underlie the Code. [Since implementation of the directive, these are now expressed more succinctly as six General Principles, as set out at 18.2.3, though in essence they are similar.] These are:

(1) That shareholders should have full information in order to enable them to consider the merits of a bid, and should have it in proper time to enable them to reach a decision. Full information may involve the avoidance of unhelpful, distracting information, which explains the restrictive approach adopted by the Panel to advertising. Shareholders are entitled to factual information, and reasoned

argument. 'Knocking copy' is a distraction. It also diminishes respect for the takeover process, and the protagonists.

(2) There should be equal treatment of all shareholders of a particular class. This is the reason why r. 9 requires a person who acquires 30 per cent or more of the voting rights of a company to make a cash offer to all other shareholders at the highest price paid by him in the previous 12 months. In this way, control of a company cannot be bought by paying a high price to the controlling shareholder, leaving the remainder a minority to those who have already achieved effective control of the company. Another example of the fair treatment principle at work is r. 11. When shares carrying 15 per cent or more of the voting rights of a company have been acquired for cash by an offeror during or within 12 months prior to the commencement of an offer period, the offer must include a cash alternative for all the shares of that class at the highest price paid by the offeror during the period. So a special deal in terms of cash cannot be offered to important shareholders leaving paper of somewhat more dubious and uncertain value to be offered to the others. In similar vein, r. 6 provides that if an offeror purchases shares in the offeree company at a price higher than the value of its offer, then that offer must be increased accordingly.

(3) A fundamental provision of the Code excludes the taking of frustrating action by the management of the target company. As United States experience shows, it is not always easy for the entrenched management of a company to differentiate between its own interests and those of its shareholders. The taking of 'poison pills', followed by actions in the courts either by the offerors or on behalf of shareholders, has been a feature of bids in the United States. It has often led to protracted legal proceedings, and can lead to shareholders being denied altogether the opportunity of considering a bid for their company. Rule 21 of the Code prevents such action being taken without the consent of the shareholders in general meetings. Rule 19.4 is another example of the anti-frustration principle. It requires that equal information must be given by an offeree company to competing offerors. So it is not possible for the offeree to give a more favoured suitor an unfair advantage by supplying it with information which is designed to enable it to pay a high and generous price, whilst at the same time depriving the less favoured rival of information and so making it harder for the latter to compete. The principle which rules out frustrating tactics prohibits a great deal of manoeuvring during takeovers, and so enables a bid to be considered on its merits. I think it is one of the fundamental strengths of the Code.

(4) The Code seeks to ensure a fair market. It is easy to use the phrase 'fair market' but the concept can be elusive. The Code works through our requirements as to disclosure seeking to secure transparency of dealings. By r. 8 it requires that dealings by an offeror or the offeree company, and any associates, during an offer period must be publicly disclosed. In addition, disclosure is required of others with significant shareholdings. For a time the requirement was that those with 5 per cent shareholdings disclosable under the Companies Act had to disclose dealings by the following day. Experience showed, however, that the market could be influenced by dealings below that level. So the Panel introduced in early 1987 its own requirement that disclosure of dealings must be made by shareholders owning or controlling 1 per cent of a company involved in a takeover. The knowledge given by such a disclosure can assist to avoid distortion of the market. The Panel considers that disclosure of dealing is a more effective way of ensuring a fair market than prohibiting dealings by any of those involved either as principals to the bid or as advisers....

The importance of flexibility Why is flexibility needed in control of takeovers when a potentially more rigid, statutory control may be apt to govern other transactions? There are some financial activities which take a predictable and relatively constant form: examples are the sale of stocks and shares, or insurance policies. They can more easily be brought within a relatively strict code, capable of legal interpretation and enforcement by the law. Even in those transactions, however, it may be important to avoid an over-detailed, legalistic structure and to search...for a 'principle-oriented' approach. But takeovers, involving as they do the quest for control of a company, provide the artist with a large canvas. The methods of achieving a successful outcome, or of defending a bid, constantly evolve and challenge both the creativity and knowledge of clever, inventive and sometimes aggressive people. Bids may be in cash, or in securities, or in a combination of both. The characteristics may differ in a market which is rising from those seen in a falling market. Methods of financing change: we have recently seen the emergence of the highly leveraged bid. The amount of information required for shareholders to be properly informed may depend very much on the characteristics of the individual bid. The Code seeks to respond to these changes, and to avoid situations where practitioners can order their affairs so as to comply with the letter of the rules whilst designing round their spirit and purpose.

As well as flexibility in interpretation, the existence of a non-statutory regime allows more rapid amendment to the Code than if it was comprised either in a statute or even in a statutory instrument.

The Panel in action   How does the Panel go about its task of advising and resolving disagreements during the course of a bid? The daily work of the Panel is carried out by the executive. Before, and during a bid, a party may, for good reason, wish to obtain guidance from the executive in confidence. Wherever it is possible this is given, but clearly there are limitations. Sometimes it would be inappropriate to form any view unless the advisers raising the issue consent to the Panel consulting any other party potentially affected. On other occasions it is possible only to give a provisional view, which may have to be reconsidered if the issue is subsequently raised by the other party. This process reflects the most positive part of the work of the Panel. When the Panel was established, it was decided that its function should not be simply, or even primarily, to pass judgment on conduct after the event. Its main work was to be done during the course of a bid, by acting as an advisory body available for consultation, and also by intervening on the application of a party or on its own initiative wherever necessary. This constructive role of umpiring the contest while it proceeds is central to the Panel's work. Parties are expected to consult in advance of action. Their financial advisers have the main responsibility to seek the Panel's view where any doubt arises as to the proper course of conduct. We have stressed that consultation with a party's own lawyers is no substitute for seeking our guidance where such doubts exist. The work of the Panel is designed to enable the bid to go smoothly, rather than simply to take corrective action after the event. It is this that makes the informal, advisory role of the executive of such very great importance.

In fulfilling this role, the members of the executive meet regularly with advisers during bids to hear argument on and resolve points of difference. The executive welcomes the attendance of senior members of companies concerned at such meetings with their advisers: it is their interests which are ultimately affected, and they are entitled both to be heard and to have the decision explained to them. The executive works informally, but sets great store by its fairness to all parties. This advisory function means that much of the work of the executive does not become public knowledge, and is unsung. In the 20 years of its history, the Panel has monitored more than 5,000 takeovers. Approximately two thirds have been agreed mergers. They involve general monitoring and sometimes advice from the Panel as to proper conduct. The one third of contested takeovers frequently gives rise to issues raised on an adversarial, sometimes highly adversarial, basis. Even then the executive's procedures are sufficiently skilled and fair that in most cases the advisers accept the decision without an appeal to the full Panel. This quiet advisory work, and resolution of disagreements, is inevitably not the stuff of newspaper reports, and so perhaps it is not so widely appreciated outside the City as it deserves to be. The executive works in a non-bureaucratic way, and at the pace and for the hours which are required by the financial markets. This is of the essence of responsible self-regulation.

The other respect in which the Panel operates within a legal framework is that we are susceptible to judicial review. In 1986, a bidder, Datafin, and its leading financial backer Prudential-Bache challenged a decision of the Panel that the other bidders, Norton Opax and the Kuwait Investment Office, were not acting in concert. A finding of concertedness could have led to important Code consequences. The Court of Appeal dismissed the complaint that the Panel had acted improperly. The application raised the issue of principle as to whether the Panel, as a self-regulating body, could be liable to judicial review. This was, incidentally, my own first exposure to the work of the Panel, as I was briefed as its counsel. I argued the case in happy ignorance of the impact which the decision would have on my own future activities! For the Court of Appeal held that the Panel was in principle subject to judicial review. Essentially this was because we are performing a public duty.

From a practical point of view, a quite vital element of the judgment of the Court of Appeal was its decision as to when the judicial discretion would be exercised to interfere with the Panel's ruling. The court held that the cases where it could intervene at all would be rare, and even then, it would generally do so by declaring the law for the future rather than seeking to disturb the decision of the Panel in a particular case. The Master of the Rolls, Sir John Donaldson, said, and it is important to highlight this,

> I wish to make it clear beyond a peradventure that in the light of the special nature of the Panel, its functions, the market in which it is operating, the time-scales which are inherent in that market and the need to safeguard the position of third parties, who may be numbered in thousands, all of whom are entitled to continue to trade upon an assumption of the validity of the Panel's rules and decisions, unless and until they are quashed by the court, I should expect the relationship between the Panel and the court to be historic rather than contemporaneous. I should expect the court to allow contemporary decisions to take their course, considering the complaint and intervening, if at all, later and in retrospect by declaratory orders which would enable the Panel not to repeat any error and would relieve individuals of the disciplinary consequences of any erroneous finding of breach of the rules.

From the vantage point of those who have to monitor takeovers, where it is critical that decisions should be given speedily and not interrupted by the process of litigation, this decision demonstrated the operation of judicial review at its most sensible and valuable. As was subsequently stressed in *R v Panel on Takeovers and Mergers ex parte Guinness plc* [1990] 1 QB 146 this is 'a supervisory or long-stop jurisdiction'. It does not involve the courts substituting their judgment for the commercial experience of the Panel. I believe that it is healthy that the Panel should be potentially amenable to the discipline of the law in judicial review proceedings. We take decisions with important consequences and, if we were to act outside our jurisdiction or to decline to operate fair procedures or to proceed in a way which could be seen to be perverse, we should be told so that we may put our affairs in order for the future. But it would seriously undermine the function of the Panel if during a takeover our rulings with which one party did not agree could be taken to the courts. Litigation brought during a takeover would, as the experience of other jurisdictions shows, often be brought for tactical reasons. As Lord Donaldson said in the *Guinness* case,

> ...contemporary intervention by the court will usually either be impossible or contrary to the public interest. Furthermore it is important that this should be known, as otherwise attempts would undoubtedly be made to undermine the authority of the Panel by tactical applications for judicial review.

This would be detrimental to the need for shareholders to be given a fair opportunity to consider the merits of an orderly conducted bid. Tactical litigation may be desirable for one or other of the parties. But it is not the true reason for the availability of legal process. Nor does it take any account of the interests of the very wide public who are not parties to the dispute but who have an interest in the bid being decided on its merits.

18.2.2 The European dimension

The public company takeover in the European context is largely a British phenomenon. With takeovers relatively unusual elsewhere within Europe, our system of regulation through the City Code has been uniquely successful. The proposal for a Thirteenth Directive on takeovers in 1990 (OJ C240, 26 September 1990, p. 7) was therefore greeted with concern, some aspects of which were expressed at the time in the following extract. In the light of the criteria for subsidiarity the proposal was reviewed and, following consultation, a new proposal was presented in November 1997 (OJ C378, 13 December 1997, p. 10). This was a 'framework' Directive establishing general principles but not attempting detailed harmonisation as in the original text. Its explanatory memorandum states that its aim was not to encourage takeovers as an end in themselves but to view them as a means to meet international competition in so far as they contribute to the expansion and reconstruction of European companies. It continues:

> The Commission also considers that it is a legitimate concern for the Union (legal basis art. 54 of the Treaty) to ensure that within the internal market shareholders of listed companies enjoy equivalent safeguards in the case of a change of control and that a certain level of transparency prevails during takeovers. Therefore, the aims of the Directive are to ensure an adequate level of protection for shareholders throughout the Union and to provide for minimum guidelines on the conduct of takeover bids.

The requirements focus on the protection of minority shareholders, the necessary degree of information and disclosure and the role of the board of the offeree company during the bid.

In April 1996 the DTI issued a consultative document in which concern is expressed about a number of issues. It is suggested that the proposal for legislation setting out principles to be followed by the supervisory body (the Panel) could lead to extensive tactical litigation. To confound a takeover, the target company might bring proceedings for judicial review against the Panel on grounds for example that it had not interpreted the statutory principles in accordance with the purpose of the Directive. Legal actions between the parties to the bid were also predicted. The DTI's expressed view was that it is in the interests of all parties that a takeover bid be concluded as early as possible, supervised by the authoritative guidance of the Panel but without the distraction of lengthy litigation. The intervention of a Directive could damage and not enhance the current non-statutory approach to regulation. It was later argued that an amendment agreed to by the European Parliament in December 2000 permitting the board of a target company to adopt certain defensive measures to a bid without first consulting their shareholders would have a detrimental effect on takeover activity in the UK. On the other hand the adoption of the Directive would be of value in opening up the market in corporate control in many continental member States.

The following extract from an article written in response to the earlier draft Directive of 1990 sets out some of the arguments.

David Calcutt, 'The work of the Takeover Panel'
(1990) 11 Co Law 203

> There are, I believe, four areas where there would be likely to be loss without compensating gain [if the non-statutory Code were replaced by legislation].
>
> First, I have already stressed the central importance in the work of the Panel of the opportunity—and indeed duty—for parties and their advisers to consult the executive in advance when there is any doubt whether or not a proposed course of conduct is in accordance with the general principles and the rules. In a system in which the regulator combines the functions of legislator, interpreter and consultant, it is easy to understand how this can work effectively. But it is difficult to see how the role of consultant could easily be incorporated into a statutorily based system.
>
> Secondly, the Takeover Code is flexible—that is, it can and will be adapted to meet the needs of changed circumstances. There must, of course, be sufficient certainty in the Code to enable businessmen to be able to take commercial decisions, but it is the spirit and purpose of the Code, not its letter, that prevails. In this way, in the wake of the Big Bang, it was possible to introduce the concept of exempt market-makers; and, similarly, the amendment of the rules relating to management

buy-outs. It is important for the Panel to be able to adapt the Code to ever-changing circumstances, and, in most cases to be able to do so rapidly. It is difficult to believe that it would be possible to adapt a statutory code with the same ease and speed.

Thirdly, the decisions of the Panel—given at the time, during the bid process—have to have sufficient certainty that they can be relied upon by those who are required to take business decisions. The relationship between the courts and the Panel was foreshadowed by the relationship between the courts and the Monopolies and Merger Commission....

The Panel, then, is not above the law, but the role of the courts is restricted to 'long-stop review'. This is something very different from the courts ever substituting their decision for the decision of the Panel.

It is understandable that those from other jurisdictions should find difficulty in appreciating how our non-statutory system—with its highly restricted access to the courts—can work. They ask, 'How can the Panel's decisions be enforced?' The Panel replies 'Enforcement has never been a problem'. All who are concerned have an interest in supporting the system. Adverse comment by the Panel is an effective deterrent in the market-place. There are arrangements for what is quaintly known as 'cold-shouldering'. And, finally, the work of the Panel is tied in, statutorily, with the work of other financial regulatory bodies, so that each derives strength and support from the other. And the order that Guinness should make £85 million available to the shareholders of Distillers does not suggest any lack of muscle.

It is difficult to think that a Panel which was placed on a statutory basis would not expose itself to a more active involvement on the part of the courts; and if this were to happen, the possibilities for delaying tactical litigation must inevitably be increased.

Fourthly—the vital ingredient of speed (this is tied in with the earlier points). If the takeover process is not to be interrupted, with the consequent possible distortion of the market, and if target companies are not to remain under siege for unduly long, then speed of action is essential at every point: the speed with which the executive can be consulted and its ruling given, the speed with which the matter can be brought to the Panel and its decision obtained, and the speed with which the Code can be adapted to meet changed circumstances. It is difficult to conceive of a statutorily based system which could move with anything approaching the speed of the Panel. And if that speed is lost, shareholder protection may be lessened, and the market would doubtless become unsettled.

When finalized, the Takeover Directive required that member states formally designate by law an authority competent to supervise bids for the purposes of the rules to be made pursuant to the Directive (2004/25/EC, article 4). The Panel and its Code were therefore required to be made statutory. A consultation document, 'Company Law—Implementation of the European Directive on Takeover Bids', published January 2005, then helped to shape the final implementation of the directive. Sections 945, 951, 955, 956 and 961 are thus now intended to limit litigation, for example by requiring parties to exhaust the Panel's appeal process before having recourse to the courts. While as in the *Datafin* case (see above 18.2.1), judicial review of Panel decisions is still available, generally this will only be available after a bid has been concluded.

As a result the apparently cosy regulation of public company takeovers by a panel of professionals appointed by City interests has come to an end and under the Act of 2006 there is now a formal legal structure in place constituting the same Panel and the same Code doing what they had always done before. If this peculiarly British form of self-regulation has thus bitten the dust, needless to say it has immediately been seamlessly reincarnated. More importantly the Directive represents a relatively rare occasion when UK company law and practice (or should one say Anglo-American style capitalism) has strongly influenced the European harmonisation process.

The extract below from the White Paper omits any mention of earlier concern about the loss of self-regulation in favor of statutory regulation but quietly notes that under the Directive, 'many of the core values of the UK system' are being adopted at the EU level. There then follows a brief miscellany of relevant provisions from the 2006 Act.

Company Law Reform: A White Paper
(London: DTI, March 2005. Cm 8458)

3.6 Company Takeovers

The Takeovers Directive—which completed the European legislative process in April 2004—lays down minimum standards for takeover regulation across the Community, and applies many of the core values of the UK system at the EU level. It will also reduce barriers to takeovers in the Community through improved shareholder protection and access to capital markets.

Takeover regulation in the UK has been overseen by the Takeover Panel, essentially on a non-statutory basis, for the past 36 years. Implementation of the Takeovers Directive requires the introduction of a statutory framework but the intention is to preserve the independence and authority of the Takeover Panel and its capacity to make and enforce rules regulating takeover activity. The Department published a consultative document—available at www.dti.gov.uk/cld/current.htm—on 20 January 2005, setting out proposals for implementing the Directive. The consultation period is open until 15 April 2005.

The Bill will include provisions to implement the Takeovers Directive and place the Takeover Panel on a statutory footing. The precise nature of these provisions will be determined in the light of the responses to consultation.

COMPANIES ACT 2006, PART 28, TAKEOVERS

942. The Panel

(1) The body known as the Panel on Takeovers and Mergers ("the Panel") is to have the functions conferred on it by or under this Chapter.

943. Rules

(1) The Panel must make rules giving effect to Articles 3.1, 4.2, 5, 6.1 to 6.3, 7 to 9 and 13 of the Takeovers Directive.

(2) Rules made by the Panel may also make other provision—

    (a) for or in connection with the regulation of—

        (i) takeover bids,

        (ii) merger transactions, and

        (iii) transactions (not falling within sub-paragraph (i) or (ii)) that have or may have, directly or indirectly, an effect on the ownership or control of companies;

    (b) for or in connection with the regulation of things done in consequence of, or otherwise in relation to, any such bid or transaction;

    (c) about cases where—

        (i) any such bid or transaction is, or has been, contemplated or apprehended, or

        (ii) an announcement is made denying that any such bid or transaction is intended.

(3) The provision that may be made under subsection (2) includes, in particular, provision for a matter that is, or is similar to, a matter provided for by the Panel in the City Code on Takeovers and Mergers as it had effect immediately before the passing of this Act.

(8) In this Chapter "the Takeovers Directive" means Directive 2004/25/EC of the European Parliament and of the Council.

945. Rulings

(1) The Panel may give rulings on the interpretation, application or effect of rules.

(2) To the extent and in the circumstances specified in rules, and subject to any review or appeal, a ruling has binding effect.

951. Hearings and appeals

(1) Rules must provide for a decision of the Panel to be subject to review by a committee of the Panel (the "Hearings Committee") at the instance of such persons affected by the decision as are specified in the rules.

952. Sanctions

(1) Rules may contain provision conferring power on the Panel to impose sanctions on a person who has—
   (a) acted in breach of rules, or
   (b) failed to comply with a direction given by virtue of section 946.

955. Enforcement by the court

(1) If, on the application of the Panel, the court is satisfied—
   (a) that there is a reasonable likelihood that a person will contravene a rule-based requirement, or
   (b) that a person has contravened a rule-based requirement or a disclosure requirement,
   the court may make any order it thinks fit to secure compliance with the requirement.

974. Meaning of "takeover offer"

(1) For the purposes of this Chapter an offer to acquire shares in a company is a "takeover offer" if the following two conditions are satisfied in relation to the offer.
(2) The first condition is that it is an offer to acquire—
   (a) all the shares in a company, or
   (b) where there is more than one class of shares in a company, all the shares of one or more classes,
   other than shares that at the date of the offer are already held by the offeror.
   Section 975 contains provision supplementing this subsection.
(3) The second condition is that the terms of the offer are the same—
   (a) in relation to all the shares to which the offer relates, or
   (b) where the shares to which the offer relates include shares of different classes, in relation to all the shares of each class.
   Section 976 contains provision treating this condition as satisfied in certain circumstances.

18.2.3 The Takeover Code

The Code consists of more than 250 pages containing rules based on six brief general principles. Extensive notes to the rules and principles add important guidance on practice and interpretation.

The following extracts from the Code are a very brief selection which nonetheless cover some important points about the Code and how it works. After describing the broad purpose of the Code, the responsibility of directors and financial advisers to ensure its proper application is stressed. The membership of the Panel representing various financial institutions is listed followed by a description of the work of the Executive. The general principles set out standards of commercial behaviour in takeovers, to be applied according to their spirit as well as their letter. The extensive rules that follow expand the general principles in non-technical language and are to be interpreted according to their spirit 'as well as their letter'. Some selective extracts from the rules are included to illustrate the working of the Code. Many of these are procedural in nature.

Rule 9 on mandatory bids applies the principle that all shareholders of an offeree company must be treated similarly by the offeror company. More specifically it applies the first general principle that shareholders of an 'offeree company' must be afforded equivalent treatment. Thus where a person (or persons acting 'in concert') acquires control of a company (meaning 30 per cent or more of the voting rights), that person or persons must make a 'general' or 'mandatory' offer to buy all the outstanding shares in the company. The offeror must offer not less than the highest price that it has paid for such shares within the preceding 12 months. Thus when a change of control occurs, shareholders have the opportunity of disposing of their shares at a proper price. The offeror cannot offer an inflated price in order to obtain control and all shareholders are equally entitled to share in the opportunity to sell out their shares at a premium price that the takeover bid presents to them. The bidder must thus be prepared to make an offer for all the shares if acquisition of control is contemplated. (The Code is regularly updated and can be found at www.thetakeoverpanel.org.uk/new.)

The City Code on Takeovers and Mergers

INTRODUCTION

1 OVERVIEW

The Panel on Takeovers and Mergers (the "Panel") is an independent body, established in 1968, whose main functions are to issue and administer the City Code on Takeovers and Mergers (the "Code") and to supervise and regulate takeovers and other matters to which the Code applies in accordance with the rules set out in the Code. It has been designated as the supervisory authority to carry out certain regulatory functions in relation to takeovers pursuant to the Directive on Takeover Bids (2004/25/EC) (the "Directive"). Its statutory functions are set out in and under Chapter 1 of Part 28 of the Companies Act 2006 (the "Act"). Rules are set out in the Code (including this Introduction, the General Principles, the Definitions and the Rules (and the related Notes and Appendices)) and the Rules of Procedure of the Hearings Committee. These rules may be changed from time to time, and rules may also be set out in other documents as specified by the Panel. Statutory rules will not apply to the Channel Islands or the Isle of Man until the provisions of Chapter 1 of Part 28 of the Act are extended to them pursuant to the Act or equivalent statutory provision is made in those jurisdictions.

Further information relating to the Panel and the Code can be found on the Panel's website at www.thetakeoverpanel.org.uk. The Code is also available on the Panel's website.

2 THE CODE

Save for sections 2(c) and (d) (which each set out a rule), this section gives an overview of the nature and purpose of the Code.

(a) Nature and purpose of the Code

The Code is designed principally to ensure that shareholders are treated fairly and are not denied an opportunity to decide on the merits of a takeover and that shareholders of the same class are afforded equivalent treatment by an offeror. The Code also provides an orderly framework within which takeovers are conducted. In addition, it is designed to promote, in conjunction with other regulatory regimes, the integrity of the financial markets. The Code is not concerned with the financial or commercial advantages or disadvantages of a takeover. These are matters for the company and its shareholders. Nor is the Code concerned with those issues, such as competition policy, which are the responsibility of government and other bodies.

The Code has been developed since 1968 to reflect the collective opinion of those professionally involved in the field of takeovers as to appropriate business standards and as to how fairness to shareholders and an orderly framework for takeovers can be achieved. Following the implementation of the Directive by means of the Act, the rules set out in the Code have a statutory basis in relation to the United Kingdom and comply with the relevant requirements of the Directive. The rules set out in the Code will also have a statutory basis in relation to the Channel Islands and the Isle of Man when the provisions of Chapter 1 of Part 28 are extended to them pursuant to the Act or equivalent statutory provision is made in those jurisdictions.

(b) General Principles and Rules

The Code is based upon a number of General Principles, which are essentially statements of standards of commercial behaviour. These General Principles are the same as the general principles set out in Article 3 of the Directive. They apply to takeovers and other matters to which the Code applies. They are expressed in broad general terms and the Code does not define the precise extent of, or the limitations on, their application. They are applied in accordance with their spirit in order to achieve their underlying purpose.

In addition to the General Principles, the Code contains a series of rules. Although most of the rules are expressed in less general terms than the General Principles, they are not framed in technical language and, like the General Principles, are to be interpreted to achieve their underlying purpose. Therefore, their spirit must be observed as well as their letter.

(c) Derogations and Waivers

The Panel may derogate or grant a waiver to a person from the application of a rule (provided, in the case of a transaction and rule subject to the requirements of the Directive, that the General Principles are respected) either:

(i) in the circumstances set out in the rule; or

(ii) in other circumstances where the Panel considers that the particular rule would operate unduly harshly or in an unnecessarily restrictive or burdensome or otherwise inappropriate manner (in which case a reasoned decision will be given).

3 COMPANIES, TRANSACTIONS AND PERSONS SUBJECT TO THE CODE

This section (except for sections 3(d) and (e)) sets out the rules as to the companies, transactions and persons to which the Code applies.

(a) Companies

(i) UK, Channel Islands and Isle of Man registered and traded companies The Code applies to all offers (not falling within paragraph (iii) below) for companies and Societas Europaea (and, where appropriate, statutory and chartered companies) which have their registered offices* in the United Kingdom, the Channel Islands or the Isle of Man if any of their securities are admitted to trading on a regulated market in the United Kingdom or on any stock exchange in the Channel Islands or the Isle of Man.

4 THE PANEL AND ITS COMMITTEES

Save for section 4(d) (which sets out a rule), this section gives an overview of the membership, functions, responsibilities and general activities of the Panel and certain of its Committees. Details of various other Committees of the Panel are available on the Panel's website.

(a) The Panel

The Panel assumes overall responsibility for the policy, financing and administration of the Panel's functions and for the functioning and operation of the Code. The Panel operates through a number of Committees and is directly responsible for those matters which are not dealt with through one of its Committees.

The Panel comprises up to 34 members:

(i) the Chairman, who is appointed by the Panel;

(ii) up to two Deputy Chairmen, who are appointed by the Panel;

(iii) up to twenty other members, who are appointed by the Panel; and

(iv) individuals appointed by each of the following bodies:—

      The Association of British Insurers

      The Association of Investment Companies

      The Association of Private Client Investment Managers and Stockbrokers

      The British Bankers' Association

      The Confederation of British Industry

      The Institute of Chartered Accountants in England and Wales

      Investment Management Association

      The London Investment Banking Association (with separate representation also for its Corporate Finance Committee and Securities Trading Committee)

      The National Association of Pension Funds.

The Chairman and the Deputy Chairmen are designated as members of the Hearings Committee. Each other Panel member appointed by the Panel under paragraphs (i) to (iii) above is designated upon appointment to act as a member of either the Panel's Code Committee or its Hearings Committee.

5 THE EXECUTIVE

This section gives an overview of the functions, responsibilities and general activities of the Executive.

The day-to-day work of takeover supervision and regulation is carried out by the Executive. In carrying out these functions, the Executive operates independently of the Panel. This includes, either on its own initiative or at the instigation of third parties, the conduct of investigations, the monitoring of relevant dealings in connection with the Code and the giving of rulings on the interpretation, application or effect of the Code. The Executive is available both for consultation and also the giving of rulings on the interpretation, application or effect of the Code before, during and, where appropriate, after takeovers or other relevant transactions.

The Executive is staffed by a mixture of employees and secondees from law firms, accountancy firms, corporate brokers, investment banks and other organisations. It is headed by the Director General, usually an investment banker on secondment, who is an officer of the Panel. The Director General is assisted by Deputy Directors General, Assistant Directors General and Secretaries, each of whom is an officer of the Panel, and the various members of the Executive's permanent and seconded staff. In performing their functions, the secondees act independently of the body which has seconded them (and not as that body's agent or delegate). Further information about the membership of the Executive is available on the Panel's website.

6 INTERPRETING THE CODE

This section sets out the rules according to which the Executive issues guidance and rulings on the interpretation, application or effect of the Code. The Executive gives guidance on the interpretation, application and effect of the Code. In addition, it gives rulings on points of interpretation, application or effect of the Code which are based on the particular facts of a case. References to "rulings" shall include any decision, direction, determination, order or other instruction made by or under rules.

GENERAL PRINCIPLES

   1. All holders of the securities of an offeree company of the same class must be afforded equivalent treatment; moreover, if a person acquires control of a company, the other holders of securities must be protected.

   2. The holders of the securities of an offeree company must have sufficient time and information to enable them to reach a properly informed decision on the bid; where it advises the holders of securities, the board of the offeree company must give its views on the effects of implementation of the bid on employment, conditions of employment and the locations of the company's places of business.

   3. The board of an offeree company must act in the interests of the company as a whole and must not deny the holders of securities the opportunity to decide on the merits of the bid.

4. False markets must not be created in the securities of the offeree company, of the offeror company or of any other company concerned by the bid in such a way that the rise or fall of the prices of the securities becomes artificial and the normal functioning of the markets is distorted.

5. An offeror must announce a bid only after ensuring that he/she can fulfil in full any cash consideration, if such is offered, and after taking all reasonable measures to secure the implementation of any other type of consideration.

6. An offeree company must not be hindered in the conduct of its affairs for longer than is reasonable by a bid for its securities.

DEFINITIONS

Acting in concert

This definition has particular relevance to mandatory offers and further guidance with regard to behaviour which constitutes acting in concert is given in the Notes on Rule 9.1.

Persons acting in concert comprise persons who, pursuant to an agreement or understanding (whether formal or informal), co-operate to obtain or consolidate control (as defined below) of a company or to frustrate the successful outcome of an offer for a company. A person and each of its affiliated persons will be deemed to be acting in concert all with each other (see Note 2 below).

Without prejudice to the general application of this definition, the following persons will be presumed to be persons acting in concert with other persons in the same category unless the contrary is established:—

(1) a company, its parent, subsidiaries and fellow subsidiaries, and their associated companies, and companies of which such companies are associated companies, all with each other (for this purpose ownership or control of 20% or more of the equity share capital of a company is regarded as the test of associated company status);

(2) a company with any of its directors (together with their close relatives and related trusts);

(3) a company with any of its pension funds and the pension funds of any company covered in (1);

(4) a fund manager (including an exempt fund manager) with any investment company, unit trust or other person whose investments such fund manager manages on a discretionary basis, in respect of the relevant investment accounts;

(5) a connected adviser with its client and, if its client is acting in concert with an offeror or with the offeree company, with that offeror or with that offeree company respectively, in each case in respect of the interests in shares of that adviser and persons controlling, controlled by or under the same control as that adviser (except in the capacity of an exempt fund manager or an exempt principal trader); and

(6) directors of a company which is subject to an offer or where the directors have reason to believe a bona fide offer for their company may be imminent.

RULES

SECTION D. THE APPROACH, ANNOUNCEMENTS AND INDEPENDENT ADVICE

RULE 1. THE APPROACH

(a) The offer must be put forward in the first instance to the board of the offeree company or to its advisers.

(b) If the offer, or an approach with a view to an offer being made, is not made by the ultimate offeror or potential offeror, the identity of that person must be disclosed at the outset.

(c) A board so approached is entitled to be satisfied that the offeror is, or will be, in a position to implement the offer in full.

RULE 2. SECRECY BEFORE ANNOUNCEMENTS; THE TIMING AND CONTENTS OF ANNOUNCEMENTS

2.1 SECRECY

The vital importance of absolute secrecy before an announcement must be emphasised. All persons privy to confidential information, and particularly price-sensitive information, concerning an offer or contemplated offer must treat that information as secret and may only pass it to another person if it is necessary to do so and if that person is made aware of the need for secrecy. All such persons must conduct themselves so as to minimise the chances of an accidental leak of information.

2.2 WHEN AN ANNOUNCEMENT IS REQUIRED

An announcement is required:—

(a) when a firm intention to make an offer (the making of which is not, or has ceased to be, subject to any pre-condition) is notified to the board of the offeree company from a serious source, irrespective of the attitude of the board to the offer;

(b) immediately upon an acquisition of any interest in shares which gives rise to an obligation to make an offer under Rule 9. The announcement that an obligation has been incurred should not be delayed while full information is being obtained; additional information can be the subject of a later supplementary announcement;

(c) when, following an approach to the offeree company, the offeree company is the subject of rumour and speculation or there is an untoward movement in its share price;

(d) when, before an approach has been made, the offeree company is the subject of rumour and speculation or there is an untoward movement in its share price and there are reasonable grounds for concluding that it is the potential offeror's actions (whether through inadequate security or otherwise) which have led to the situation;

(e) when negotiations or discussions are about to be extended to include more than a very restricted number of people (outside those who need to know in the companies concerned and their immediate advisers). An offeror wishing to approach a wider group, for example in order to arrange financing for the offer (whether equity or debt), to seek irrevocable commitments or to organise a consortium to make the offer should consult the Panel; or

(f) when a purchaser is being sought for an interest, or interests, in shares carrying in aggregate 30% or more of the voting rights of a company or when the board of a company is seeking one or more potential offerors, and:

    (i) the company is the subject of rumour and speculation or there is an untoward movement in its share price; or

    (ii) the number of potential purchasers or offerors approached is about to be increased to include more than a very restricted number of people.

2.3 RESPONSIBILITIES OF OFFERORS AND THE OFFEREE COMPANY

Before the board of the offeree company is approached, the responsibility for making an announcement can lie only with the offeror. The offeror should, therefore, keep a close watch on the offeree company's share price for any signs of untoward movement. The offeror is also responsible for making an announcement once a Rule 9 obligation has been incurred.

Following an approach to the board of the offeree company which may or may not lead to an offer, the primary responsibility for making an announcement will normally rest with the board of the offeree company which must, therefore, keep a close watch on its share price. A potential offeror must not attempt to prevent the board of an offeree company from making an announcement at any time the board thinks appropriate.

2.7 CONSEQUENCES OF A "FIRM ANNOUNCEMENT"

When there has been an announcement of a firm intention to make an offer, the offeror must normally proceed with the offer unless, in accordance with the provisions of Rule 13, the offeror is permitted to invoke a pre-condition to the posting of the offer or would be permitted to invoke a condition to the offer if the offer were made.

SECTION E. RESTRICTIONS ON DEALINGS

RULE 4

NB Notwithstanding the provisions of Rule 4, a person may be precluded from dealing or procuring others to deal by virtue of restrictions contained in the Criminal Justice Act 1993 regarding insider dealing and in the FSMA regarding market abuse. Where the Panel becomes aware of instances to which such restrictions may be relevant, it will inform the FSA.

4.1 PROHIBITED DEALINGS BY PERSONS OTHER THAN THE OFFEROR

(a) No dealings of any kind in securities of the offeree company by any person, not being the offeror, who is privy to confidential pricesensitive information concerning an offer or contemplated offer may take place between the time when there is reason to suppose that an approach or an offer is contemplated and the announcement of the approach or offer or of the termination of the discussions.

(b) No person who is privy to such information may make any recommendation to any other person as to dealing in the relevant securities.

(c) No such dealings may take place in securities of the offeror except where the proposed offer is not price-sensitive in relation to such securities.

SECTION F. THE MANDATORY OFFER AND ITS TERMS

RULE 9

9.1 WHEN A MANDATORY OFFER IS REQUIRED AND WHO IS PRIMARILY RESPONSIBLE FOR MAKING IT

Except with the consent of the Panel, when:—

(a) any person acquires, whether by a series of transactions over a period of time or not, an interest in shares which (taken together with shares in which persons acting in concert with him are interested) carry 30% or more of the voting rights of a company; or

(b) any person, together with persons acting in concert with him, is interested in shares which in the aggregate carry not less than 30% of the voting rights of a company but does not hold shares carrying more than 50% of such voting rights and such person, or any person acting in concert with him, acquires an interest in any other shares which increases the percentage of shares carrying voting rights in which he is interested,

such person shall extend offers, on the basis set out in Rules 9.3, 9.4 and 9.5, to the holders of any class of equity share capital whether voting or non-voting and also to the holders of any other class of transferable securities carrying voting rights. Offers for different classes of equity share capital must be comparable; the Panel should be consulted in advance in such cases.

An offer will not be required under this Rule where control of the offeree company is acquired as a result of a voluntary offer made in accordance with the Code to all the holders of voting equity share capital and other transferable securities carrying voting rights.

SECTION I. CONDUCT DURING THE OFFER

RULE 20. EQUALITY OF INFORMATION

20.1 EQUALITY OF INFORMATION TO SHAREHOLDERS

Information about companies involved in an offer must be made equally available to all offeree company shareholders as nearly as possible at the same time and in the same manner.

20.2 EQUALITY OF INFORMATION TO COMPETING OFFERORS

Any information, including particulars of shareholders, given to one offeror or potential offeror, whether named or unnamed, must, on request, be given equally and promptly to another offeror or bona fide potential offeror even if that other offeror is less welcome. This requirement will usually only apply when there has been a public announcement of the existence of the offeror or potential offeror to which information has been given or, if there has been no public announcement, when the offeror or bona fide potential offeror requesting information under this Rule has been informed authoritatively of the existence of another potential offeror.

18.3 DIRECTORS' DUTIES IN TAKEOVERS

A takeover offer is made by the board of the offeror company to the shareholders of the target company. How the directors of the target company then advise the shareholders on whether or not to accept a bid is especially important. Clearly in this instance the directors may be influenced by some personal partiality towards their new controllers, especially with regard to preserving their own jobs.

In general terms, directors are responsible for the proper application of the Code, and the directors of the target must obtain independent advice on the bid and inform the shareholders of that advice in addition to giving their own. It has already been seen that at common law directors may not improperly use their powers to issue shares to block a takeover bid (*Hogg* v *Cramphorn Ltd* [1967] Ch 254, see 12.3.1). General principle 3 adds that the board of the offeree 'must act in the interests of the company as a whole and must not deny the holders of securities the opportunity to decide on the merits of the bid.'

What duty, if any, do directors owe at common law to individual shareholders when advising on a bid? The following extract from a Scottish case presents the traditional view that while directors owe fiduciary duties to the company (i.e., to the general body of shareholders), they do not owe fiduciary duties to individual shareholders contemplating selling their shares. However, in advising the shareholders on a bid they may assume liability to them based on ordinary principles of law.

Dawson International plc v Coats Patons plc
Duties to individual shareholders
(1988) 4 BCC 305, Court of Session (Outer House)

LORD CULLEN: At the outset I do not accept as a general proposition that a company can have no interest in the change of identity of its shareholders upon a takeover. It appears to me that there will be cases in which its agents, the directors, will see the takeover of its shares by a particular bidder as beneficial to the company. For example, it may provide the opportunity for integrating operations or obtaining additional resources. In other cases the directors will see a particular bid as not in the best interests of the company....

I next consider the proposition that in regard to the disposal of their shares on a takeover the directors were under a fiduciary duty to the shareholders and accordingly obliged to act in such a way as to further their best interests. It is well recognised that directors owe fiduciary duties to the company. Thus the directors have the duty of fiduciaries with respect to the property and funds of the company. In terms of s. 309 of the Companies Act 1985, when discharging their functions, the directors are under a fiduciary duty to the company to have regard to *inter alia* the interests of members and employees. These fiduciary duties spring from the relationship of the directors to the company, of which they are its agents. I should observe that for the purposes of s. 309 there appears to be no reason why 'members' should not be capable of applying to future as well as to present members of the company.

In contrast I see no good reason why it should be supposed that directors are, in general, under a fiduciary duty to shareholders, and in particular current shareholders with respect to the disposal of their shares in the most advantageous way. The directors are not normally the agents of the current shareholders. They are not normally entrusted with the management of their shares. The cases and other authorities to which I was referred do not seem to me to establish any such fiduciary duty. It is contrary to statements in the standard textbooks such as *Palmer's Company Law* 3rd ed., para. 64–02. The absence of such a duty is demonstrated by the remarkable case of

Percival v *Wright* [1902] 2 Ch 421. I think it is important to emphasise that what I am being asked to consider is the alleged fiduciary duty of directors to current shareholders as sellers of their shares. This must not be confused with their duty to consider the interests of shareholders in the discharge of their duty to the company. What is in the interests of current shareholders as sellers of their shares may not necessarily coincide with what is in the interests of the company. The creation of parallel duties could lead to conflict. Directors have but one master, the company. Further it does not seem to me to be relevant to the present question to build an argument upon the rights, some of them very important rights, which shareholders have to take steps with a view to seeing that directors act in accordance with the constitution of the company and that their own interests are not unfairly prejudiced.

If on the other hand directors take it upon themselves to give advice to current shareholders, the cases cited to me show clearly that they have a duty to advise in good faith and not fraudulently, and not to mislead whether deliberately or carelessly. If they fail to do so the affected shareholders may have a remedy, including the recovery of what is truly the personal loss sustained by them as a result. However, these cases do not, in my view, demonstrate a pre-existing fiduciary duty to the shareholders but a potential liability arising out of their words or actions which can be based on ordinary principles of law. This, I may say, appears to be a more satisfactory way of expressing the position of directors in this context than by talking of a so-called secondary fiduciary duty to the shareholders.

This brings me to comment on the use made in argument of the decision of the Court of Appeal in *Heron International Ltd* v *Lord Grade* [1983] BCLC 244. It is important to note that this case was concerned with the power of directors under art. 29 of the articles of association, to decide who should be the purchaser and transferee when any shareholder desired to sell his shares. . . . I do not consider that the case is authority for the proposition that directors may not on behalf of the company agree to recommend a bid and not to encourage or cooperate with an approach from another would-be bidder without being in breach of a fiduciary duty to the current shareholders. In passing I would add that the case is also not authority for the proposition that directors are under a positive duty to recommend a bid on the basis that it is the higher bid: see *Re a Company (No. 008699 of 1985)*(1986) 2 BCC 99,024, per Hoffmann J at p. 99,031, to which I referred counsel. A comparison may be made with the case of *Clark* v *Workman* [1920] 1 IR 107. In that case directors of a private company had power under art. 139 of the articles of association to approve the transfer of shares. The directors approved the transfer of a controlling interest which involved, according to Ross J (at p. 117), 'a complete transformation of the company'. He held that the directors' action was wrongful and inconsistent with their fiduciary duty to the company in respect that the chairman had fettered himself by a promise to the transferee so that he was disqualified from acting bona fide in the interests of the company. . . .

For these reasons I reject the view that directors are under a fiduciary duty to current shareholders in regard to the disposal of their shares in a takeover.

19

Insider Dealing and Market Abuse

Few areas of company law have generated such debate and such diverse opinions as insider dealing. There is insider dealing when somebody makes a profit trading in the shares of a company with the benefit of inside information about it which is not available to other investors. The classic situation is where directors, employees or outside advisers, knowing that unexpectedly good profit figures or a takeover bid are about to be announced, then buy shares in the company in anticipation of the price going up. Under Part V of the Criminal Justice Act 1993 it is a criminal offence for an individual to deal in securities who has information as an insider relating to them (i.e., he knowingly has private information from an inside source which is 'specific or precise', and which he knows, if made public, would be likely to have a significant effect on their price). Opinions have varied widely as to whether this should be a criminal offence, should merely give rise to civil liability or, if no breach of confidence arises, not be penalised at all.

An earlier EEC Directive on insider dealing (1989/592/EEC) was replaced by the Directive on 'insider dealing and market manipulation (market abuse)', (extracted below), which was then supplemented later the same year by a further directive (2003/124/EC) on the definition and public disclosure of inside information and the definition of market manipulation. These shift the focus somewhat from criminal sanctions for insider dealing to the softer approach of imposing civil penalties both for insider dealing and market manipulation.

The following brief extract from the Directive gives some basic definitions of inside information and market manipulation and lays down the prohibitions to be made by the member states. There then follows a longer extract from *Insider Crime: the New Law* by Barry Rider and Michael Ashe, which provides a readable account of the different theories as to why the law should penalise insider dealing; is it because it is unfair, or because it causes harm to the company, is an abuse of confidence, or breaches the principal of equality of information? The writers conclude that insider dealing should be proscribed as it has an adverse impact on confidence in the integrity of the stock market generally. The extract goes on to discuss the background to the introduction of the 1993 legislation.

COUNCIL DIRECTIVE OF THE EUROPEAN PARLIAMENT AND OF THE COUNCIL OF 28
JANUARY 2003 ON INSIDER DEALING AND MARKET MANIPULATION
(MARKET ABUSE), (2003/6/EC)

Article I

For the purposes of this Directive:

1. 'Inside information' shall mean information of a precise nature which has not been made public, relating, directly or indirectly, to one or more issuers of financial instruments or to one or more financial instruments and which, if it were made public, would be likely to have a significant effect on the prices of those financial instruments or on the price of related derivative financial instruments.

   In relation to derivatives on commodities, 'inside information' shall mean information of a precise nature which has not been made public, relating, directly or indirectly, to one or more such derivatives and which users of markets on which such derivatives are traded would expect to receive in accordance with accepted market practices on those markets.

   For persons charged with the execution of orders concerning financial instruments, 'inside information' shall also mean information conveyed by a client and related to the clients pending orders, which is of a precise nature, which relates directly or indirectly to one or more issuers of financial instruments or to one or more financial instruments, and which, if it were made public, would be likely to have a significant eff on the prices of those financial instruments or on the price of related derivative financial instruments.

2. 'Market manipulation' shall mean:
   a) transactions or orders to trade:
      — which give, or are likely to give, false or misleading signals as to the supply of, demand for or price of financial instruments, or
      — which secure, by a person, or persons acting m collaboration, the price of one or several financial instruments at an abnormal or artificial level,

      unless the person who entered into the transactions or issued the orders to trade establishes that his reasons for so doing are legitimate and that these transactions or orders to trade conform to accepted market practices on the regulated market concerned;
   b) transactions or orders to trade which employ fictitious devices or any other form of deception or contrivance;
   c) dissemination of information through the media, including the Internet, or by any other means, which gives, or is likely to give, false or misleading signals as to financial instruments, including the dissemination of rumours and false or misleading news, where the person who made the dissemination knew, or ought to have known, that the information was false or misleading. In respect of journalists when they act in their professional capacity such dissemination of information is to be assessed, without prejudice to Article II, taking into account the rules governing their profession, unless those persons derive, directly or indirectly, an advantage or profits from the dissemination of the information in question.

   In particular, the following instances are derived from the core definition given in points (a), (b) and (c) above:
      — conduct by a person, or persons acting in collaboration, to secure a dominant position over the supply of or demand for a financial instrument which has the effect of fixing, directly or indirectly, purchase or sale prices or creating other unfair trading conditions,
      — the buying or selling of financial instruments at the close of the market with the effect of misleading investors acting on the basis of closing prices,
      — taking advantage of occasional or regular access to the traditional or electronic media by voicing an opinion about a financial instrument (or indirectly about its issuer) while having previously taken positions on that financial instrument and profiting subsequently from the impact of the opinions voiced on the price of that instrument, without having simultaneously disclosed that conflict of interest to the public in a proper and effective way.

The definitions of market manipulation shall be adapted so as to ensure that new patterns of activity that in practice constitute market manipulation can be included.
3. 'Financial instrument' shall mean:
   — transferable securities as defined in Council Directive 93/22 of 10 May 1993 on investment services in the securities field (1),
   — units in collective investment undertakings,
   — money-market instruments,
   — financial-futures contracts, including equivalent cashsettled instruments,
   — forward interest-rate agreements,
   — interest-rate, currency and equity swaps,
   — options to acquire or dispose of any instrument falling into these categories, including equivalent cash-settled instruments. This category includes in particular options on currency and on interest rates,
   — derivatives on commodities,
   — any other instrument admitted to trading on a regulated market in a member State or for which a request for admission to trading on such a market has been made.
4. 'Regulated market' shall mean a market as defined by Article 1(13) of Directive 93/22/EEC.
5. 'Accepted market practices' shall mean practices that are reasonably expected in one or more financial markets and are accepted by the competent authority in accordance with guidelines adopted by the Commission in accordance with the procedure laid down in Article 17(2).
6. 'Person' shall mean any natural or legal person.
7. 'Competent authority' shall mean the competent authority designated in accordance with Article 11.

In order to take account of developments on financial markets and to ensure uniform application of this Directive in the Community, the Commission, acting in accordance with the procedure laid down in Article 17(2), shall adopt implementing measures concerning points 1, 2 and 3 of this Article.

Article 2

1. Member States shall prohibit any person referred to in the second subparagraph who possesses inside information from using that information by acquiring or disposing of, or by trying to acquire or dispose of, for his own account or for the account of a third party, either directly or indirectly, financial instruments to which that information relates.

   The first subparagraph shall apply to any person who possesses that information:
   a) by virtue of his membership of the administrative, management or supervisory bodies of the issuer; or
   b) by virtue of his holding in the capital of the issuer; or
   c) by virtue of his having access to the information through the exercise of his employment, profession or duties; or
   d) by virtue of his criminal activities.

Article 3

Member States shall prohibit any person subject to the prohibition laid down in Article 2 from:

a) disclosing inside information to any other person unless
b) such disclosure is made in the normal course of the exercise of his employment, profession or duties;
c) recommending or inducing another person, on the basis of inside information, to acquire or dispose of financial instruments to which that information relates.

Article 4

Member States shall ensure that Articles 2 and 3 also apply to any person, other than the persons referred to in those Articles, who possesses inside information while that person knows, or ought to have known, that it is inside information.

Article 5

Member States shall prohibit any person from engaging in market manipulation.

Article 6

1. Member States shall ensure that issuers of financial instruments inform the public as soon as possible of inside information which directly concerns the said issuers.

    Without prejudice to any measures taken to comply with the provisions of the first sub-paragraph, Member States shall ensure that issuers, for an appropriate period, post on their Internet sites all inside information that they are required to disclose publicly.

Barry Rider and Michal Ashe, *Insider Crime: the New Law*

(Bristol: Jordans, 1993)

Background to the legislation

Introduction

Public perception of insider dealing   To many, if not most people, the phrase 'insider dealing' conjures up a picture of a slick and rather smooth 'City-type' making a 'killing' on the Stock Exchange on the basis of a 'tip' some chum of his has given him over lunch. As with most popular impressions, this picture has an element of justification and a good deal of prejudice. To the extent that many of us consider such conduct objectionable, one wonders if this is from a reaction of jealousy rather than from any deep-seated moral, let alone rational, principle. It is true that in the US, and to some degree elsewhere, a significant proportion of serious cases of insider abuse come to the attention of the authorities, not through the sophisticated endeavours and diligence of 'stock watch units', but because someone 'grouses'. Indeed, the Chief Litigation Counsel of the US Securities and Exchange Commission (SEC) has observed, not entirely tongue in cheek, that the enforcement role of his Division would have been far less impressive without the aid of hurt wives, disappointed and jilted lovers, disgruntled employees and jealous colleagues. In fact, the SEC considered this so important in policing insider dealing that US Congress, at the urging of the SEC, introduced a provision in the Insider Trading and Securities Fraud Enforcement Act 1988 empowering the SEC to pay 'bounties' to informants. The House of Commons Select Committee on Trade and Industry considered whether such an approach would be useful in the UK. However, whilst some members of the Committee inclined to the prospect of 'bounty hunters' in the Square Mile, it was generally thought to be a little too American!

   Traditionally, insider abuse has involved individuals who are connected with the management of companies, rather than the smooth operators conjured up in the popular press. Of course, this is not to say that, in fact, the incidence of insider abuse is not greater in regard to those who operate in the financial services industry and relevant professions than in the more easily identifiable relationships of management and ownership. To some extent what is considered to be insider dealing will be influenced by the philosophical basis upon which it is sought to distinguish such conduct (invariably as an object of opprobrium) from other 'normal' conduct. For the ordinary man in the street, who has neither the opportunity nor the desire to contemplate the outpourings of academics and others on this much discussed topic, insider dealing can be described as involving the deliberate exploitation of information by dealing in securities, or other property, to which the information relates, having obtained that information by virtue of some privileged relationship or position. In other words, insider dealing involves 'taking advantage' of an opportunity to profit which is not available to others and from whom, directly or indirectly, the profit will be taken. . . .

The policy of regulation   One must look, albeit briefly, at the policy justifications for regulating insider dealing. The effectiveness of insider regulation, supposing that regulation is desirable, must be determined in the light of the policy selected for justifying intervention in the first place.

   Whilst it is rare to find positive support for insider dealing outside the ranks of those seeking to justify a brand of economic liberalism which would embarrass 'Captain Morgan' let alone 'Captain

Bob', it is difficult to identify, in any empirical way, the harm which insider dealing is thought to cause. Indeed, despite all the literature and the promotion of an international anti-insider dealing crusade by the SEC little is really known about the incidents, character and quality of insider abuse. Like so many forms of questionable or questioned conduct in the financial and business sector, the picture is unclear. The incidents which are apparent tend to be thrown up, if not by accident, then by events unrelated to the systematic procedures that have been created for detection. Hence, the notion exists, rightly or wrongly, that what is seen or even perceived is only the tip of the iceberg. To adopt another metaphor, one might assume that there are insider traders in the market in the same way that, where there is long grass, one might assume the presence of elephants—at least in Africa!

Professor Henry Manne (in what is generally regarded as the most convincing defence of insider trading, *Insider Trading and the Stock Market* (New York: Free Press, 1966), referring to the widespread view that insider dealing is unfair, equated this 'unscientific' approach to one of his young law students stamping [their] foot and stating 'I don't care: it's just not right'. Fairness is a well-known and cherished concept, but one which is difficult to rationalise or to use as a reliable tool for creating, as opposed to fashioning, rights. Furthermore, it is often pointed out, at least in anonymous market transactions, that the person who happens to deal with the insider, usually as a consequence of random matching of orders, is a willing purchaser or seller at the market price at that point in time. He is in no way misled by the insider. So where is the unfairness to this person?

Is it not unfair that the insider has taken advantage of information or an opportunity which has come to him by virtue of his position or through some privileged relationship? Generally, we do not regard the mere taking of a benefit as unfair unless there is some kind of demonstrable harm. It is difficult to perceive that harm has been done to the person with whom, by chance, the insider deals, and it is equally hard to perceive that harm, in the majority of cases, has been done to the owner of the information or controller of the insider's status. Thus, whilst Professor Loss observes that one might consider the young student's retort somewhat healthier than the scepticism of that student's professor ((1970) 33 MLR 34 at p. 37), it is difficult to justify insider regulation simply on the basis that it is unfair to the person with whom the insider deals.

It could be argued (and has been—particularly in North America) that insider dealing harms the proper interests of the corporate issuer in whose shares the insider dealing takes place. Where the person who takes advantage of the information in question is also a director or officer or is in some other clearly defined relationship involving confidence and trust within the company, the potential for harm is considered to be even greater. A company which has acquired the reputation of being an 'insiders' company will, it is contended by proponents of this view, have difficulty in securing finance on competitive terms. The company will also suffer in the market as a consequence of loss of respect in the integrity of its management. It is also argued that, if insider dealing is permitted, there will be a temptation for those responsible for ensuring prompt disclosure of price-sensitive information to delay or manipulate such disclosures. The courts have been prepared to accept that the harm caused to issuers by such conduct justifies legal liability. In reality, however, most of these arguments are somewhat academic and insubstantial.

Perhaps a more telling justification of legal liability is the notion that where a person in a position of trust abuses the confidence that has been reposed in him, it is right and proper that he should be required to yield up any benefit that he has obtained by virtue of this breach of duty. The harm is in the breach of trust and specific damage beyond this is not required. Whilst such an approach is appropriate in relation to what the law regards as fiduciaries, the vast majority of those likely to be involved in insider trading will not be in a traditional, fiduciary relationship. It would seem appropriate to justify control of insider dealing on this basis only in situations where there is a pre-existing relationship of stewardship and, thus, an implicit obligation of trust. Thus, the fiduciary approach would justify depriving insiders who are fiduciaries of their unauthorised profits, but would be of limited application. Another approach is to regard the information as 'belonging' to the issuer of the securities or some other party who has a proper interest in a person not using the information for his or another's personal and unauthorised gain. According to this notion, insider trading involves a misappropriation, or almost a theft, of the inside information or the opportunity to exploit that information. To some extent this approach merely moves the debate into determining what information is considered capable of being misappropriated and in which circumstances this will arise. As a general rule, it is only where an individual is under a duty of some kind not to misuse the information that it can sensibly be argued that his taking advantage of it amounts to a misappropriation. In practical terms, this limits the approach to cases of definite fiduciary obligation. However, it is conceivable to attach the obligation to the information itself, provided that those who receive it do so in circumstances where, because of their knowledge that it is communicated to them in breach of an obligation, there is a fiduciary obligation not to misuse it. In practice, however, given the underdeveloped jurisprudence in England, relating to information as property, this approach is fraught with difficulty.

It is argued that the primary justification for insider dealing regulation is equality of information for those in the market. Whilst this notion comports with the proper desire to draw into the market as much information as possible to allow investors to reach informed and sensible decisions, it has been criticised as being naïve. It has been observed, not just by cynics, that many investment decisions are made because the investor considers that he has superior information. Indeed, the efficient market hypothesis, for what it is worth, would argue that substantial profits can only be made, on a regular basis, on information which is not available to the market. Furthermore, why should it be necessary for such information to be disclosed in the context of securities transactions when it has always been assumed that there is no similar merit in dealings on other markets? Furthermore, it may be more sensible, in order to achieve equality of information, to require issuers to make timely disclosure of all material events as a matter of law, rather than to seek equality through the random penalising of those who take advantage of informational imbalances. Some would also argue, perhaps with questionable empirical support, that insider dealing is a reasonably effective and economic means of drawing such information into the market, both through direct intervention in the market and induced trading.

In the view of the authors, however, no matter how appealing these, and the legion of other, arguments seem, the main (if not only) convincing justification for controlling insider dealing is that it has a perceived, adverse impact on confidence. It does not matter, according to this view, whether insider dealing has a detrimental effect on the operation of the markets or the fortunes of issuers because, if enough opinion-forming individuals consider that it is wrong (apropos Professor Manne's foot-stomping student), insider dealing will alienate investors and potential investors, with adverse consequences for society as a whole. Most people would agree that stock markets, whether of the traditional or electronic variety, are efficient in allocating capital. For such markets to operate effectively and without inhibition, they require confidence and respect from their own societies and, increasingly, from the international community.

In the Second Reading of the Criminal Justice Bill, Earl Ferrers observed that, 'in order to operate successfully, those markets require investors to have confidence in their fairness. Insider dealing destroys that confidence.' During discussion in the Committee Stage of the Companies Bill 1980, Mr Cecil Parkinson MP (then Secretary of State for Trade and Industry) stated that 'people who involve themselves in insider dealings are in the process of destroying confidence in the market'. Whilst other countries have played around with one or a mixture of the various theories, in the UK the justification for regulating insider abuse is based on the harm which it causes to investor confidence.

If it is felt that insider dealing is unfair and immoral, the economics, which are in any case equivocal, are not important and it is right and proper for those charged with protecting confidence in the integrity of the market to intervene. Neither is it important that scholars of jurisprudence and theologians might be minded to contend the illogicality of the common man's perception. At the end of the day, it is not scholars such as these (save for the few who have risen to become college bursars) who significantly influence the flow of funds directly to the stock market. As Professor Loss has observed, what is important in this context is the appearance of a concern to stamp out conduct which is considered abusive. Of course, where action is taken which is neither effective nor credible, such intervention does nothing to foster confidence in the integrity of the market and may bring into disrepute those seeking to vindicate the markets and even the law.

The significance of protecting the proper functioning of markets, whether in securities or other forms of property, has long been recognised and the law is considered a proper tool to achieve this. Indeed, the English common law, at a very early stage of its development, outlawed any practice or device which falsely enhanced the price of 'victuals' and other merchandise in the public markets, as being injurious to the public good. The importance of protecting the market, rather than individuals within it, has been recognised in a number of cases and, thus, to justify anti-insider dealing provisions on this basis underlines that it is the market and those depending upon the market who are harmed by such practices. This clearly shows that the notion that insider dealing is a victimless crime is a nonsense. In so far as it undermines the proper functioning of the markets, it harms all those who have a direct or indirect interest in the efficiency of the markets—in other words, everyone. The British government has traditionally sought to regulate insider dealing on the basis that it constitutes a wrong to the market and it is appropriate to utilise the criminal law to curb it. Whilst this approach may justify the intervention of legal rules, the appropriateness of which have long been recognised, it does not necessarily mean that the sledgehammer of the criminal justice system is the most suitable instrument for surgery.

The legislative background

Following a number of unsuccessful attempts to enact specific provisions rendering insider trading a criminal offence, part V of the Companies Act 1980 achieved this. The relevant provisions were re-enacted, with minor amendments, in the Company Securities (Insider Dealing) Act 1985. Whilst many of the concepts in that Act are found in the Criminal Justice Act 1993, there are a number of very significant differences. Indeed, to a large degree the present law reflects a different philosophy from the earlier enactments. Whilst the importance of maintaining confidence in the integrity of the market remains central, there is a manifest break with the tradition of regarding insider abuse as essentially a breach of attenuated fiduciary relationship. Thus...under the new law it is not necessary for the insider to be connected with either the source of the relevant information or the issuer of the securities in question; nor is it necessary for the information to be confidential in the traditional sense of that word. Such notions reflect the company law perspective and are, thus, more orientated to notions associated with breach of directors' duties, than market fairness and equality of information. The earlier UK legislation was, in so far as it strove to vindicate the integrity of the market, a curious mixture of what might be described as the 'stewardship' and 'market fraud' approaches.

   The change in form and substance of UK law is a direct result of the harmonisation of company law within the European Community. Whilst in more recent years the debate on regulation of such abuses as insider dealing and market manipulation has tended to emphasise the importance of fostering a sound and respected capital market, there is no doubt that the initiative in seeking to impose standard or equivalent regulations arose directly from the company law programme. However, the first reference which the authors have found to insider dealing regulation in the context of the European Community is in the report of a Committee of Experts, appointed by the European Commission, to consider how best to facilitate the development of an effective and efficient European capital market. In this report the Committee of Experts emphasised the importance of investors having 'at their disposal sufficient and reasonably homogeneous information on securities dealt in other markets'. Whilst the facilitation of market development was clearly recognised to be of critical importance in furthering the objectives of the Community, the institutions of the Community, until recently, attempted to deal with insider abuse primarily through the harmonisation of company law. A working party was set up as early as 1976 and there had been *ad hoc* deliberations and studies prior to this. Indeed, it was not until 1983 that the European Commission finally resolved that it would be appropriate to regulate insider abuse through an EC Directive on insider dealing rather than merely a recommendation. The text of the 'initial' final Directive was very different from the earlier discussion documents and bore a marked difference from the version which the Council finally accepted. As a result it is rather simplistic to attempt to discern an underlying philosophy other than pragmatism; although from the preamble to the Directive, it is clear that the concept of market egalitarianism remains a guiding principle. The Directive also states that 'for the market to be able to play its role effectively, every measure should be taken to ensure that the market operates smoothly'. The Directive observes that the 'smooth operation of the market depends to a large extent on the confidence it inspires in investors'. For such confidence, the Directive states that investors must be assured that they are 'on an equal footing' and will be protected against the improper use of inside information. Thus, according to the European Commission, 'by benefiting certain investors as compared with others, insider dealing is likely to undermine this confidence and may therefore prejudice the smooth operation of the market'. Even if it can be accepted that it is desirable economically, socially and politically to have smooth markets, whatever that may mean, it is highly debatable whether insider dealing is likely to ruffle markets. Indeed . . . there are arguments to the effect that insider dealing actually encourages information into the market. Furthermore, it may be questioned whether the average investor actually wants, let alone expects, to be on an equal footing in any respect, let alone in regard to the availability of information. In so far as it is possible to distil, other than in an anecdotal sense, investor motivation, it would seem that most decisions will, at least in part, be influenced by a view that one person is better informed or at least a little more perceptive than the majority. It seems unusual that Europe has now espoused the philosophy of equal access to information when, after almost half a century of experience it has been rejected in the US as not being a sensible basis for regulating insider abuse.

19.2 CRIMINAL SANCTIONS

The following extracts outline the offences of insider dealing and creating a false market. As you will appreciate on reading these provisions, criminal proof of the required knowledge or intention to constitute the offence will often be difficult to obtain.

CRIMINAL JUSTICE ACT 1993, PART V

PART V INSIDER DEALING

The offence of insider dealing

52. The offence

(1) An individual who has information as an insider is guilty of insider dealing if, in the circumstances mentioned in subsection (3), he deals in securities that are price-affected securities in relation to the information.

(2) An individual who has information as an insider is also guilty of insider dealing if—

   (a) he encourages another person to deal in securities that are (whether or not that other knows it) price-affected securities in relation to the information, knowing or having reasonable cause to believe that the dealing would take place in the circumstances mentioned in subsection (3); or

   (b) he discloses the information, otherwise than in the proper performance of the functions of his employment, office or profession, to another person.

(3) The circumstances referred to above are that the acquisition or disposal in question occurs on a regulated market, or that the person dealing relies on a professional intermediary or is himself acting as a professional intermediary.

(4) This section has effect subject to section 53.

53. Defences

(1) An individual is not guilty of insider dealing by virtue of dealing in securities if he shows—

   (a) that he did not at the time expect the dealing to result in a profit attributable to the fact that the information in question was price-sensitive information in relation to the securities; or

   (b) that at the time he believed on reasonable grounds that the information had been disclosed widely enough to ensure that none of those taking part in the dealing would be prejudiced by not having the information; or

   (c) that he would have done what he did even if he had not had the information.

(2) An individual is not guilty of insider dealing by virtue of encouraging another person to deal in securities if he shows—

    (a) that he did not at the time expect the dealing to result in a profit attributable to the fact that the information in question was price-sensitive information in relation to the securities; or

    (b) that at the time he believed on reasonable grounds that the information had been or would be disclosed widely enough to ensure that none of those taking part in the dealing would be prejudiced by not having the information; or

    (c) that he would have done what he did even if he had not had the information.

(3) An individual is not guilty of insider dealing by virtue of a disclosure of information if he shows—

    (a) that he did not at the time expect any person, because of the disclosure, to deal in securities in the circumstances mentioned in subsection (3) of section 52; or

    (b) that, although he had such an expectation at the time, he did not expect the dealing to result in a profit attributable to the fact that the information was price-sensitive information in relation to the securities.

(4) Schedule 1 (special defences) shall have effect.

(5) The Treasury may by order amend Schedule 1.

(6) In this section references to a profit include references to the avoidance of a loss.

56. 'Inside information', etc.

(1) For the purposes of this section and section 57, 'inside information' means information which—

    (a) relates to particular securities or to a particular issuer of securities or to particular issuers of securities and not to securities generally or to issuers of securities generally;

    (b) is specific or precise;

    (c) has not been made public; and

(2) For the purposes of this Part, securities are 'price-affected securities' in relation to inside information, and inside information is 'price-sensitive information' in relation to securities, if and only if the information would, if made public, be likely to have a significant effect on the price of the securities.

(3) For the purposes of this section 'price' includes value.

57. 'Insiders'

(1) For the purposes of this Part, a person has information as an insider if and only if—

    (a) it is, and he knows that it is, inside information; and

    (b) he has it, and knows that he has it, from an inside source.

(2) For the purposes of subsection (1), a person has information from an inside source if and only if—

    (a) he has it through—

        (i) being a director, employee or shareholder of an issuer of securities; or

        (ii) having access to the information by virtue of his employment, office or profession; or

    (b) the direct or indirect source of his information is a person within paragraph (a).

NOTE: DEFINING AND EXPANDING COMPLEXITY

The above sections give a limited flavour of the insider dealing legislation. To appreciate the full effect of the law, which relies extensively on defining the meaning of key phrases, it is necessary to consult Part V of the Act in its entirety. (It is included in D. French, *Statutes on Company Law 2006–2007*, 10th ed. (Oxford: Oxford University Press, 2006).)

FINANCIAL SERVICES AND MARKETS ACT 2000, S. 397

397 Misleading statements and practices

(3) Any person who does any act or engages in any course of conduct which creates a false or misleading impression as to the market in or the price or value of any relevant investments is guilty of an offence if he does so for the purpose of creating that impression and of thereby inducing another person to acquire, dispose of, subscribe for or underwrite those investments or to refrain from doing so or to exercise, or refrain from exercising, any rights conferred by those investments.

(5) In proceedings brought against any person for an offence under subsection (3) it is a defence for him to show—

(a) that he reasonably believed that his act or conduct would not create an impression that was false or misleading as to the matters mentioned in that subsection;

(b) that he acted or engaged in the conduct—

(i) for the purpose of stabilising the price of investments; and

(ii) in conformity with price stabilising rules; or

(c) that he acted or engaged in the conduct in conformity with control of information rules.

19.3 PREVENTION AND ENFORCEMENT

If insider dealing is the misuse of private information likely to have a significant effect on the price of shares, it follows that abuse will be minimised if legislation and listing rules oblige the early release of such information to the market. This aspect of the disclosure principle is discussed in the following extract from *Insider Crime: the New Law* by Rider and Ashe. Then follows FSAMA 2000, s. 96A, which specifies the information that companies issuing shares for trading on a regulated market (i.e., stock exchange) must be required to publicly disclose under 'disclosure rules relating to such shares'. (See also FSAMA, s. 73A(3).)

One of the grave difficulties of insider dealing as a criminal offence is that it is extremely difficult to bring successful prosecutions. As a result prosecutions are rare. As regards preventive measures, the Listing Rules (see 17.2) are also influential in the area of insider dealing. Apart from generally promoting disclosure, they require directors and certain employees of listed companies to comply with a code of practice for dealings in the company's shares (Listed companies are required to adopt a code no less exacting than the 'Model Code' found in the Listing Rules.) Thus for example a director should not deal in the company's shares during a 'close period', i.e., during a specified period before the company's annual or other results are announced.

Barry Rider and Michael Ashe, *Insider Crime: the New Law*
(Bristol: Jordans, 1993)

Disclosure   Insider dealing...is all about taking advantage of information which has not yet been effectively discounted by the market or, in direct personal transactions, by the person with whom the insider is dealing. If price-sensitive information which is withheld from the market is kept to a minimum, there will be less opportunity for those desirous of exploiting it. [There is a] likelihood that insiders will attempt to manipulate events so as to avoid prompt disclosure of information which they can exploit for their own ends. This is a particular problem in situations where those in a position to influence the management of a company are also substantially interested in its securities. Thus, in many developing countries it is far more common to encounter insider manipulation of information than insiders merely attempting to beat the market. If it is important to encourage as much relevant information into the market as possible to facilitate sensible investment decisions, it makes sense to require issuers to disclose, through appropriate procedures, all information which might be reasonably considered to have an impact on the price of their securities.

A company will encounter disclosure obligations at various stages of its life. When it seeks to raise capital there are certain disclosure obligations tailored to the promotion of the securities. There are also continuous disclosure obligations designed to provide all those dealing with the company with adequate information to reach sensible decisions on the terms and circumstances of their relationship. Both promotional and continuous disclosure rely significantly on the medium of financial statements which, even if accurate and comprehensive, are inherently historic in perspective. Therefore, timely disclosure is probably of greater interest to the financial markets. This involves the immediate release of information in a readily understood form to the market, and is the most efficient means of disclosure in regard to significant and unexpected events.

Promotional and continuous disclosure are governed by the requirements of company law and in the case of listed securities, the exacting requirements of the Stock Exchange. .... The Stock Exchange requires, as a condition of admission, that issuers disclose 'any information necessary to enable holders of [the company's] listed securities and the public to appraise the position of the company and avoid the creation of a false market in its listed securities' (Listing Rules, para. 9.1), in addition to a series of specifically identified matters. The Stock Exchange has procedures for the announcement of such information which is designed to facilitate prompt and effective dissemination. It also monitors compliance with this obligation as part of its ordinary market surveillance operation. It has been questioned, however, whether leaving this important obligation on issuers to the Listing Rules and not imposing a statutory obligation on those responsible for the management of the company to ensure proper adherence to the Stock Exchange's timely disclosure policy, is enough, both in terms of common sense or in relation to obligations under European Community law. ...

Another important role that disclosure has in regulating insider abuse is in the obligations that are placed upon certain insiders to report promptly dealings which may give grounds for suspicion. Thus, since the Companies Act 1948, considerable reliance has been placed on the statutory obligation which is imposed on directors to report to their companies their own interests in the securities of the company as well as the interests of their spouses and children, as a means of discouraging insider trading. [These provisions have been deleted from the Companies Act and similar requirements now apply only to public companies whose shares are traded on a regulated market.] There are other disclosure and reporting requirements in the City Code on Takeovers and Mergers and in the Listing Rules of the Stock Exchange. To what extent insider abuse is discouraged by such obligations to report dealings is not clear. In practice, it is possible to evade such provisions through the use of nominees and associates, and criminal prosecutions for non-compliance are very rare.

FINANCIAL SERVICES AND MARKETS ACT 2000, S. 96A

96A Disclosure of information requirements

(1) Disclosure rules must include provision specifying the disclosure of information requirements to be complied with by—

   (a) issuers who have requested or approved admission of their financial instruments to trading on a regulated market in the United Kingdom;

   (b) persons acting on behalf of or for the account of such issuers;

   (c) persons discharging managerial responsibilities within an issuer—

     (i) who is registered in the United Kingdom and who has requested or approved admission of its shares to trading on a regulated market; or

     (ii) who is not registered in the United Kingdom or any other EEA State but who has requested or approved admission of its shares to trading on a regulated market and who is required to file annual information in relation to the shares in the United Kingdom in accordance with Article 10 of the prospectus directive;

   (d) persons connected to such persons discharging managerial responsibilities.

(2) The rules must in particular—

   (a) require an issuer to publish specified inside information;

   (b) require an issuer to publish any significant change concerning information it has already published in accordance with paragraph (a);

   (c) allow an issuer to delay the publication of inside information in specified circumstances;

   (d) require an issuer (or a person acting on his behalf or for his account) who discloses inside information to a third party to publish that information without delay in specified circumstances;

   (e) require an issuer (or person acting on his behalf or for his account) to draw up a list of those persons working for him who have access to inside information relating directly or indirectly to that issuer; and

   (f) require persons discharging managerial responsibilities within an issuer falling within subsection (1)(c)(i) or (ii), and persons connected to such persons discharging managerial responsibilities, to disclose transactions conducted on their own account in shares of the issuer, or derivatives or any other financial instrument relating to those shares.

(3) Disclosure rules may make provision with respect to the action that may be taken by the competent authority in respect of non-compliance.

19.4 MARKET ABUSE

The principal limitation on the effectiveness of controls on insider dealing is that because of the problems of establishing sufficient evidence of an offence on the criminal burden of proof, it is very difficult to bring successful criminal prosecutions. In addition, insider dealing is only one possible way in which the public market in shares may be abused or distorted. Therefore the Financial Services and Markets Act 2000 took the opportunity to empower the new Financial Services Authority (FSA) to impose financial penalties for 'market abuse' not amounting to a criminal offence. The definition of market abuse appears below, the first three heads of which would constitute an offence of insider dealing while the remaining six are examples of market manipulation.

The new provisions have proved to be among the most controversial in the Act. Their effect is broad and general and even non-professionals not otherwise regulated by the FSA are potentially within their scope. As required by the legislation, the FSA has issued a Code on Market Conduct which further defines the nature of market abuse. The Code is highly detailed. Thus, for example, it says that it would be market abuse (improper disclosure) by X if 'X, a director at B Plc has lunch with a friend Y, who has no connection with B Plc or its advisers. X tells Y that his company has received a takeover offer that is at a premium to the current share price at which it is trading.' (The Code of Market Conduct, 1.6.) If Y, realising that the share price will go up as soon as the takeover offer is announced, then rushes off and buys some shares in B Plc, he has probably committed the offence of insider dealing. He may be lucky and not get prosecuted but the Financial Services Authority can impose a financial penalty on X for market abuse. While the example has director X opening his mouth too wide at lunchtime, it would equally be market abuse if this occurs at dinner time or even at a concert party.

One of the key controversies has been the very nature of the new system of penalties. It seems to be accepted that for the purposes of the European Convention on Human Rights, the new penalty is substantially criminal. Issues thus arise as to the appropriate protections to be afforded to those who are potentially subject to a penal sanction. The proper criminal process, for example, offers the accused the right of silence and a fair trial based upon a strict onus of proof. This will be clarified as the legislation is applied in practice by the FSA.

The following brief extracts give the flavour of the legislation.

FINANCIAL SERVICES AND MARKETS ACT 2000, SS. 118, 119 AND 123

118. Market abuse

(1) For the purposes of this Act, market abuse is behaviour (whether by one person alone or by two or more persons jointly or in concert) which—

   (a) occurs in relation to—

      (i) qualifying investments admitted to trading on a prescribed market,

      (ii) qualifying investments in respect of which a request for admission to trading on such a market has been made, or

      (iii) in the case of subsection (2) or (3) behaviour, investments which are related investments in relation to such qualifying investments, and (b) falls within any one or more of the types of behaviour set out in subsections (2) to (8).

(2) The first type of behaviour is where an insider deals, or attempts to deal, in a qualifying investment or related investment on the basis of inside information relating to the investment in question.

(3) The second is where an insider discloses inside information to another person otherwise than in the proper course of the exercise of his employment, profession or duties.

(4) The third is where the behaviour (not falling within subsection (2) or (3))—

   (a) is based on information which is not generally available to those using the market but which, if available to a regular user of the market, would be, or would be likely Financial Services and Markets Act 2000, Part VIII 599 to be, regarded by him as relevant when deciding the terms on which transactions in qualifying investments should be effected, and

   (b) is likely to be regarded by a regular user of the market as a failure on the part of the person concerned to observe the standard of behaviour reasonably expected of a person in his position in relation to the market.

(5) The fourth is where the behaviour consists of effecting transactions or orders to trade (otherwise than for legitimate reasons and in conformity with accepted market practices on the relevant market) which—

(a) give, or are likely to give, a false or misleading impression as to the supply of, or demand for, or as to the price of, one or more qualifying investments, or

(b) secure the price of one or more such investments at an abnormal or artificial level.

(6) The fifth is where the behaviour consists of effecting transactions or orders to trade which employ fictitious devices or any other form of deception or contrivance.

(7) The sixth is where the behaviour consists of the dissemination of information by any means which gives, or is likely to give, a false or misleading impression as to a qualifying investment by a person who knew or could reasonably be expected to have known that the information was false or misleading.

(8) The seventh is where the behaviour (not falling within subsection (5), (6) or (7))—

(a) is likely to give a regular user of the market a false or misleading impression as to the supply of, demand for or price or value of, qualifying investments, or

(b) would be, or would be likely to be, regarded by a regular user of the market as behaviour that would distort, or would be likely to distort, the market in such an investment, and the behaviour is likely to be regarded by a regular user of the market as a failure on the part of the person concerned to observe the standard of behaviour reasonably expected of a person in his position in relation to the market.

(9) Subsections (4) and (8) and the definition of 'regular user' in section 130A(3) cease to have effect on 30 June 2008 and subsection (1)(b) is then to be read as no longer referring to those subsections.

119. The code

(1) The Authority must prepare and issue a code containing such provisions as the Authority considers will give appropriate guidance to those determining whether or not behaviour amounts to market abuse.

(2) The code may among other things specify—

(a) descriptions of behaviour that, in the opinion of the Authority, amount to market abuse;

(b) descriptions of behaviour that, in the opinion of the Authority, do not amount to market abuse;

(c) factors that, in the opinion of the Authority, are to be taken into account in determining whether or not behaviour amounts to market abuse....

(d) descriptions of behaviour that are accepted market practices in relation to one or more specified markets;

(e) descriptions of behaviour that are not accepted market practices in relation to one or more specified markets.

123. Power to impose penalties in cases of market abuse

(1) If the Authority is satisfied that a person ('A')—

(a) is or has engaged in market abuse; or

(b) by taking or refraining from taking any action has required or encouraged another person or persons to engage in behaviour which, if engaged in by A, would amount to market abuse;

it may impose on him a penalty of such amount as it considers appropriate.

(2) But the Authority may not impose a penalty on a person if, having considered any representations made to it in response to a warning notice, there are reasonable grounds for it to be satisfied that—

(a) he believed, on reasonable grounds, that his behaviour did not fall within paragraph (a) or (b) of subsection (1); or

(b) he took all reasonable precautions and exercised all due diligence to avoid behaving in a way which fell within paragraph (a) or (b) of that subsection.

(3) If the Authority is entitled to impose a penalty on a person under this section it may, instead of imposing a penalty on him, publish a statement to the effect that he has engaged in market abuse.

20

Corporate Insolvency

It goes without saying that as company law is a recent phenomenon, the law of personal insolvency (i.e., bankruptcy law) developed long before the law of corporate insolvency. Corporate insolvency is therefore historically based on bankruptcy law. However, companies do not become bankrupt, they are 'wound up' on behalf of creditors. Until 1985 the law of bankruptcy for individual insolvents and of winding up for companies was to be found separately in the Bankruptcy Acts and the Companies Acts. Nevertheless corporate insolvency law and many of its principles and concepts was and remains closely related to and firmly founded in the law of bankruptcy.

In October 1976, recognising that insolvency law had not been reviewed for over 100 years, the Secretary of State for Trade announced the setting up of a Review Committee on Insolvency Law and Practice. With wide terms of reference to formulate a comprehensive insolvency system, the committee was established under the chairmanship of Mr (later Sir) Kenneth Cork, a prominent accountant and insolvency practitioner. The 'Cork Report', a clear and readable survey of insolvency law and its problems was published in June 1982. The government then responded with its white paper, *A Revised Framework for Insolvency Law* (Cmnd 9175), published in February 1984. The Insolvency Bill 1985 became what was then perhaps the most amended piece of legislation in Parliamentary history with over 1,200 tabled amendments. Passed as the Insolvency Act 1985, this was then consolidated with existing unamended legislation as the Insolvency Act 1986, which is the current legislation dealing with both corporate and personal insolvency. The Act puts into effect many but by no means all of the recommendations of the Cork Report and has since been amended several times. At the end of the twentieth century a more limited review led to significant reforms enacted by the Insolvency Act 2002 and the Enterprise Act 2002, mainly concerning the rehabilitation of companies in financial difficulty. But insolvency legislation does not end with the primary legislation. Almost as extensive are the Insolvency Rules 1986 (SI 1986/1925), which deal with some substantive and many procedural aspects of insolvency law. However, as law in practice consists more of procedure than principle, the Rules are of immense importance and should not be overlooked.

Many courses on company law tend to leave corporate insolvency as a makeweight topic to be rushed through in the last lecture or two if time permits. In reality it is a topic of fundamental importance to company law, both theoretically and practically. Insolvent winding up is the process by which a liquidator takes control of the company's assets and in which many fundamental company law principles are tested. It is in liquidation that limited liability and separate legal personality become significant. It is at this time that directors become fully accountable for breaches of common law and statutory duties, that the maintenance of capital rules are checked for compliance and when the effectiveness of security arrangements become crucial. A broad understanding of corporate insolvency principles and procedures is therefore an essential part of company law.

The subject brings a bewildering array of terminology. The distinctions between insolvency, bankruptcy, winding up, liquidation, and dissolution are not obvious. Students may readily confuse liquidators, administrative receivers, administrators and official receivers. A thumbnail sketch of this terminology will probably not solve all the problems, but it may resolve some. 'Insolvency' is generally a lack of solvency or liquidity, a lack of cash currently available to pay debts, i.e., when the debtor is currently unable to pay its debts as they fall due. A further test of insolvency is the 'balance sheet' test, i.e., that total liabilities exceed total assets. Thus if the company were wound up it would be ultimately unable to pay its debts in full. Nonetheless it is also possible to say that a debtor with assets exceeding liabilities is currently insolvent if it cannot raise the cash to pay its debts as they fall due. It is, however, quite common that a company can continue in business even though its liabilities exceed its total assets. Such a company may borrow for a long term from Peter to pay an immediate debt to Paul and so may be able to pay its current debts as they fall due. The fact that it would ultimately be unable to pay all its debts in full will probably not lead to a creditors' winding up if creditors are currently being paid in full. The term 'insolvent' is therefore a general one with a range of meanings. (See further 20.3 below.) Most important, however, are the specific provisions of the legislation that enable creditors to commence insolvency proceedings if the debtor is unable to pay its debts as they fall due.

A debtor which has no ready cash will be unable to pay its debts. An unsecured creditor's only means of recovering a debt will therefore be to get access to the debtor's assets. For individual (not corporate) insolvents the primary insolvency procedure to achieve this is bankruptcy. Thus from the creditor's point of view bankruptcy is merely a debt-collecting procedure. Bankruptcy is a court procedure (or court-supervised procedure) whereby the individual is adjudicated bankrupt and divested of his assets. Creditors may then make no further individual claims against the bankrupt but must prove for their debts collectively in the bankruptcy procedure. As a collective procedure creditors must await the administration of the bankrupt's estate and will receive a proportionate share of the bankrupt's assets in partial satisfaction of their debts. (This may be as little as 10, 15 or 20 per cent.) The principle is of equality between ordinary creditors; that the assets are distributed *pari passu* ('in equal steps'). The bankrupt may then be discharged from bankruptcy and thereby be released from liability for all his or her debts.

The equivalent for a company is a winding up by the court. A liquidator is appointed who 'liquidates' the company's assets (i.e., turns them into cash) and finally distributes the proceeds *pari passu* to the ordinary creditors. The insolvent company is not of course discharged from liability for its unpaid debts but is instead dissolved. *Winding up* is therefore the process of *liquidating* the assets of an *insolvent* company and finally *dissolving* the company.

In contrast to a compulsory winding up (i.e., by order of the court), an insolvent company may instead resolve to wind up by special resolution of its members. This is called a 'creditors' voluntary winding up' as, being insolvent, there will be nothing available to return capital to members.

Thus from a creditor's viewpoint both compulsory winding up and creditors' voluntary winding up may be seen as debt-collecting procedures. However, the proportion of the debt recovered is likely to be low as liabilities generally far exceed the assets available. A recent survey showed the overall return to creditors in insolvent liquidations during the year was on average only 10 per cent of the total debt (Society of Practitioners of Insolvency, *Company Insolvency in the United Kingdom 1996–97*).

Contrasted with creditors' voluntary windings up are members' voluntary windings up where creditors are paid off in full, leaving the possibility of a surplus to be repaid to members.

Administrative receivership (dealt with in 15.4) is not technically an insolvency proceeding properly so called though it looks very much like one. It is the procedure whereby an administrative receiver appointed by the holder of a floating charge, often a bank, realises some or all of the assets of the company to satisfy that one secured creditor (i.e., the bank). This is a private agreement for the realisation of security. In contrast an insolvent liquidation is a public procedure for the satisfaction of all creditors subject to the insolvency legislation.

An administration order (see 20.13.2), a creature of the Cork Report of 1982, is a rescue process whereby an 'administrator' is appointed to attempt to achieve the preservation of some or all of the business or businesses of the company. Preserving the company itself (and thus the financial interest of its shareholders) is not of first importance; what matters most is preserving economic activity: if insolvency law is too 'pro-creditor', enabling creditors to close down a company and plunder its assets without proper consideration of the viability of underlying businesses, employment and economic activity will be unnecessarily lost. Administration is thus intended to offer the opportunity to rescue companies or their businesses.

The role of the official receiver is explained below at 20.6.

20.2 THE PURPOSES OF CORPORATE INSOLVENCY LAW

The above introduction hints at some of the purposes of corporate insolvency law; for example, to achieve a fair balance between debtor and creditors; of giving creditors access to the debtor's assets as a debt-collecting process at an appropriate time, while giving an opportunity for a rescue of viable businesses where possible. The purposes are many and are convincingly expounded in the following extract from the Cork Report. There then follows an extract from the 1984 white paper in which the DTI sets out more specifically its objectives in enacting the new insolvency code to promote and regulate industry and commerce.

Insolvency Law and Practice: Report of the Review Committee
(The 'Cork Report')
(Cmnd 8558) (London: HMSO, 1982)

Principles of insolvency law

The basic objectives of insolvency law

191. It is a basic objective of the law to support the maintenance of commercial morality and encourage the fulfilment of financial obligations. Insolvency must not be an easy solution for those who can bear with equanimity the stigma of their own failure or their responsibility for the failure of a company under their management.

192. The law of insolvency takes the form of a compact to which there are three parties: the debtor, his creditors and society. Society is concerned to relieve and protect the individual insolvent from the harassment of his creditors, and to enable him to regain financial stability and to make a fresh start. It accords him this relief in return for:

(a) such contribution, not only from the realisation of his assets but also from his future earnings, as can reasonably be made by him without reducing him and his family to undue and socially unacceptable poverty and without depriving him of the incentive to succeed in his fresh start;

(b) the obligation to give an account of the reasons for his failure and, if required, to submit the conduct of his affairs to impartial investigation; and

(c) subjection to such disabilities as may be appropriate in all the circumstances.

193. In the case of an insolvent company, society has no interest in the preservation or rehabilitation of the company as such, though it may have a legitimate concern in the preservation of the commercial enterprise. None of the directors or shareholders is normally liable for the debts of the company, but their freedom from liability is granted in return for:

(a) an obligation on the part of those responsible for the management of the company's affairs to give an account of the reasons for the company's failure, and, if required, to submit their conduct of the company's affairs to impartial investigation; and

(b) subjection to such personal liability for the company's debts and such personal disabilities as may be appropriate in all the circumstances....

198. We believe that the aims of a good modern insolvency law are these:

(a) to recognise that the world in which we live and the creation of wealth depend upon a system founded on credit and that such a system requires, as a correlative, an insolvency procedure to cope with its casualties;

(b) to diagnose and treat an imminent insolvency at an early rather than a late stage;

(c) to relieve and protect where necessary the insolvent, and in particular the individual insolvent, from any harassment and undue demands by his creditors, whilst taking into consideration the rights which the insolvent (and where an individual, his family) should legitimately continue to enjoy; at the same time, to have regard to the rights of creditors whose own position may be at risk because of the insolvency;

(d) to prevent conflicts between individual creditors;

(e) to realise the assets of the insolvent which should properly be taken to satisfy his debts, with the minimum of delay and expense;

(f) to distribute the proceeds of the realisations amongst the creditors in a fair and equitable manner, returning any surplus to the debtor;

(g) to ensure that the processes of realisation and distribution are administered in an honest and competent manner;

(h) to ascertain the causes of the insolvent's failure and, if and in so far as his conduct or, in the case of a company, the conduct of its officers or agents, merits criticism or punishment, to decide what measures, if any, require to be taken against him or his associates, or such officers or agents;

(i) to recognise that the effects of insolvency are not limited to the private interests of the insolvent and his creditors, but that other interests of society or other groups in society are vitally affected by the insolvency and its outcome, and to ensure that these public interests are recognised and safeguarded;

(j) to provide means for the preservation of viable commercial enterprises capable of making a useful contribution to the economic life of the country;

(k) to devise a framework of law for the governing of insolvency matters which commands universal respect and observance, and yet is sufficiently flexible to adapt to and deal with the rapidly changing conditions of our modern world; in particular, to achieve a system that:

   (i) is seen to produce practical solutions to financial and commercial problems,

   (ii) is simple and easily understood,

   (iii) is free from anomalies and inconsistencies, and

   (iv) is capable of being administered efficiently and economically;

(l) to ensure due recognition and respect abroad for English insolvency proceedings....

232. Insolvency proceedings are inherently of a collective nature; their prime beneficiary is the general body of the insolvent's creditors, each of whom is affected, though clearly by no means necessarily to the same extent, by the common disaster. If each such creditor is denied by law the right to pursue separate remedies against the insolvent and is obliged to rely on the outcome of collective proceedings, then his interest in those proceedings ought to be, so far as consistent with the claims of his fellow creditors, as fair and reasonable as circumstances will permit, to compensate him for the loss of his individual rights....

Insolvency and society

235. It is sometimes argued that the function of insolvency law is simply the distribution of the proceeds of the insolvent's assets amongst his creditors, giving him, where appropriate, personal relief from their claims. This has never been the English approach. The policy of our insolvency laws has always been far more complex; at least two other major objectives will be found to have existed:

(a) the insolvency laws are treated by the trading community as an important instrument in the process of debt recovery: the threat or imminence of insolvency proceedings as a weapon in persuading a defaulting debtor to pay or make proposals for the settlement of a debt cannot be underestimated as it constitutes, in the majority of cases, the sanction of last resort for the enforcement of obligations;

(b) the insolvency laws, through their investigative processes, are the means by which the demands of commercial morality can be met; any disciplinary measures against the debtor which may appear necessary in the light of this investigatory process can be imposed either inside the insolvency proceedings themselves or outside, for example, by the machinery of the criminal law or by professional disciplinary bodies....

238. We believe that the investigative process is a crucial ingredient of any good modern insolvency law. Creditors and debtors alike must know that in the event of insolvency proceedings taking place there is a risk that an investigation, fully and competently carried out, will take place with a view to uncovering assets concealed from creditors, to ascertaining the validity of creditors' claim and to exposing the circumstances surrounding the debtor's failure. Anything less would, we believe, be unacceptable in a trading community such as our own and would be bound to lead to a lowering of business standards and an erosion of confidence in our insolvency law.

239. We do not mean to imply that the investigative machinery should be brought into use in every single set of insolvency proceedings. Apart from the cost, this would be impracticable and, moreover, oppressive in the majority of cases. Nonetheless, the machinery must remain available for use in appropriate cases. The conduct and activities of the debtor may exhibit reprehensible features, such as fraud, recklessness or other wrongful acts or omissions to such an extent that, irrespective of considerations of punishment, his affairs should be exposed not only to the creditors whose interests he has harmed but also to full public scrutiny.

A Revised Framework for Insolvency Law

(Cmnd 9175) (London: HMSO, 1984)

> 2. The fundamental objectives of the Department of Trade and Industry are to encourage, assist and ensure the proper regulation of British trade, industry and commerce, and to promote a climate conducive to growth and the national production of wealth. In pursuing these objectives, the principal role of the insolvency legislation is (i) to establish effective and straightforward procedures for dealing with and settling the affairs of corporate and personal insolvents in the interests of their creditors; (ii) to provide a statutory framework to encourage companies to pay careful attention to their financial circumstances so as to recognise difficulties at an early stage and before the interests of creditors are seriously prejudiced; (iii) to deter and penalise irresponsible behaviour and malpractice on the part of those who manage a company's affairs; (iv) to ensure that those who act in cases of insolvency are competent to do so and conduct themselves in a proper manner; and (v) to facilitate the reorganisation of companies in difficulties to minimise unnecessary loss to creditors and to the economy when insolvency occurs. The main task in furthering the department's objectives is to ensure that action is taken at an early stage in insolvencies under the control of the court to protect the insolvents' assets in the interests of creditors, and to investigate the affairs of insolvents where it appears that malpractice rather than misfortune has been the cause of liquidation or bankruptcy, so that undesirable commercial or individual conduct is sufficiently deterred.

20.3 STATUTORY DEFINITIONS

It will be seen from the following sections that the Insolvency Act 1986 does not give a comprehensive definition of insolvency. Section 247(1) merely states that in the 'first group of parts' (i.e., ss. 1–251 covering the bulk of corporate insolvency) 'insolvency' of a company includes company voluntary arrangements, administration and administrative receivership. (Section 247(2) states that a company goes into liquidation if it resolves to wind up or the court orders that it be wound up. Sections 86 and 129 define the time of commencement of winding up.)

As mentioned in 20.1 above the crucial trigger for winding up by the court is not any definition of 'insolvency' but inability to pay debts, which is defined in s. 123 set out below. The definition in s. 123(2) is the 'balance sheet' test that the company's liabilities (including contingent and prospective liabilities) exceed its assets. Section 123(1)(a) also deems a company unable to pay its debts if, following a formal 'statutory demand', it has for three weeks failed to pay a debt of more than £750. Serving of a statutory demand is a common means of prompting a company into paying a debt. Unless the debt is disputed the company will almost certainly pay if it can as the creditor will have grounds for a winding-up order if it does not pay within three weeks. (The entitlement of the creditor for an order to wind up is considered at 20.6.2 below.) The procedures for making a statutory demand are set out in the Insolvency Rules 1986, r. 4.4. This rule is reproduced below as an illustration of the typical function of the Insolvency Rules. It is followed by a fictitious example of a statutory demand.

INSOLVENCY ACT 1986, SS. 247 AND 123

247. 'Insolvency' and 'go into liquidation'

(1) In this Group of Parts, except in so far as the context otherwise requires, 'insolvency', in relation to a company, includes the approval of a voluntary arrangement under Part I or the appointment of an administrator or administrative receiver.

(2) For the purposes of any provision in this Group of Parts, a company goes into liquidation if it passes a resolution for voluntary winding up or an order for its winding up is made by the court at a time when it has not already gone into liquidation by passing such a resolution.

123. Definition of inability to pay debts

(1) A company is deemed unable to pay its debts—
  (a) if a creditor (by assignment or otherwise) to whom the company is indebted in a sum exceeding £750 then due has served on the company, by leaving it at the company's registered office, a written demand (in the prescribed form) requiring the company to pay the sum so due and the company has for three weeks thereafter neglected to pay the sum or to secure or compound for it to the reasonable satisfaction of the creditor; or
  (b) if, in England and Wales, execution or other process issued on a judgment, decree or order of any court in favour of a creditor of the company is returned unsatisfied in whole or in part; or
  (c) if, in Scotland, the induciae of a charge for payment on an extract decree, or an extract registered bond, or an extract registered protest, have expired without payment being made; or
  (d) if, in Northern Ireland, a certificate of unenforceability has been granted in respect of a judgment against the company; or
  (e) if it is proved to the satisfaction of the court that the company is unable to pay its debts as they fall due.
(2) A company is also deemed unable to pay its debts if it is proved to the satisfaction of the court that the value of the company's assets is less than the amount of its liabilities, taking into account its contingent and prospective liabilities.
(3) The money sum for the time being specified in subsection (1)(a) is subject to increase or reduction by order under section 416 in Part XV.

INSOLVENCY RULES 1986, RR. 4.4 TO 4.6

4.4 Preliminary

. . .

(2) A written demand served by a creditor on a company under section 123(1)(a) (registered companies) or 222(1)(a) (unregistered companies) is known in winding-up proceedings as 'the statutory demand'.

(3) The statutory demand must be dated, and be signed either by the creditor himself or by a person stating himself to be authorised to make the demand on the creditor's behalf.

4.5 Form and content of statutory demand

(1) The statutory demand must state the amount of the debt and the consideration for it (or, if there is no consideration, the way in which it arises).
(2) If the amount claimed in the demand includes—
  (a) any charge by way of interest not previously notified to the company as included in its liability; or
  (b) any other charge accruing from time to time,
  the amount or rate of the charge must be separately identified, and the grounds on which payment of it is claimed must be stated.

In either case the amount claimed must be limited to that which has accrued due at the date of the demand.

4.6 Information to be given in statutory demand

(1) The statutory demand must include an explanation to the company of the following matters—

(a) the purpose of the demand, and the fact that, if the demand is not complied with, proceedings may be instituted for the winding up of the company;

(b) the time within which it must be complied with, if that consequence is to be avoided; and

(c) the methods of compliance which are open to the company.

(2) Information must be provided for the company as to how an officer or representative of it may enter into communication with one or more named individuals, with a view to securing or compounding for the debt to the creditor's satisfaction.

In the case of any individual so named in the demand, his address and telephone number (if any) must be given.

Rule 4.5

Statutory Demand under section 123(1)(a) or 222(1)(a) of the Insolvency Act 1986

Warning
- This is an important document. This demand must be dealt with within 21 days after its service upon the company or a winding up order could be made in respect of the company.

- Please read the demand and notes carefully.

Notes for Creditor
- If the creditor is entitled to the debt by way of assignment, details of the original creditor and any intermediary assignees should be given in part B on page 3.
- If the amount of debt includes interest not previously notified to the company as included in its liability, details should be given, including the grounds upon which interest is charged. The amount of interest must be shown separately.
- Any other charge accruing due from time to time may be claimed. The amount or rate of the charge must be identifed and the grounds on which it is claimed must be stated.
- In either case the amount claimed must be limited to that which has accrued due at the date of the demand.
- If signatory of the demand is a solicitor or other agent of the creditor, the name of his/her firm should be given.

*Delete if signed by the creditor himself

Demand

To   J.G. PENTIRE & CO. LIMITED

Address   173 WEST STREET, EXETER EX7 5BY

This demand is served on you by the creditor:

Name   B & J BUILDERS (A FIRM)

Address   27 MARSH LANE

EXETER EX10 3LD

The creditor claims that the company owes the sum of £1236, full particulars of which are set out on page 2.

The creditor demands that the company do pay the above debt or secure or compound for it to the creditor's satisfaction.

Signature of individual

Name   JAMES GARTHWAITE
(BLOCK LETTERS)

Date   30 SEPTEMBER 1994

*   Position with or relationship to creditor SOLICITOR WITH STONES SOLICITORS FOR THE CREDITOR

*   I am authorised to make this demand on the creditor's behalf.

Address   STONES, NORTHERNHAY PLACE,

EXETER EX4 3QQ

Tel No.   0392-51501   Ref.   JG/WS

N.B.   The person making this demand must complete the whole of this page, page 2 and parts A and B (as applicable) on page 3.

Figure 20.1 A specimen statutory demand

Particulars of Debt.
(These particulars must include (a) when the debt was incurred, (b) the consideration for the debt (or if there is no consideration the way in which it arose) and (c) the amount due as at the date of this demand).

MONIES DUE AS SET OUT IN THE INVOICE DETAILED BELOW.

INVOICE NO.	INVOICE DATE	AMOUNT
3736	13 MAY 1994	£820
3812	17 JUNE 1994	416
		£1236

IN RESPECT OF MATERIALS SUPPLIED AND BUILDING WORK CARRIED OUT BY THE CREDITOR FOR THE DEBTOR AT THE DEBTOR'S PREMISES AT 173 WEST STREET, EXETER.

Notes for Creditor
Please make sure that you have read the notes on page 1 before completing this page.

Note:
If space is insufficient continue on reverse of page 3 and clearly indicate on this page that you are doing so.

PART A

The individual or individuals to whom any communication regarding this demand may be addressed is/are:–

Name   JAMES GARTHWAITE
(BLOCK LETTERS)

Address   STONES, NORTHERNHAY PLACE

EXETER, EX4 3QQ

Telephone number   0392–51501

Reference   JG/MS

PART B

For completion if the creditor is entitled to the debt by way of assignment

	Name	Date(s) of Assignment
Original creditor		
Assignees		

How to comply with a statutory demand

If the company wishes to avoid a winding-up petition being presented it must pay the debt shown on page 1, particulars of which are set out on page 2 of this notice, within the period of 21 days after its service upon the company. Alternatively, the company can attempt to come to a settlement with the creditor. To do this the company should:

- inform the individual (or one of the individuals) named in part A above immediately that it is willing and able to offer security for the debt to the creditor's satisfaction; or

- inform the individual (or one of the individuals) named in part A immediately that it is willing and able to compound for the debt to the creditor's satisfaction.

If the company disputes the demand in whole or in part it should:

- contact the individual (or one of the individuals) named in part A immediately.

REMEMBER!   The company has only 21 days after the date of service on it of this document before the creditor may present a winding-up petition.

20.4 INSOLVENCY PRACTITIONERS

Since the Insolvency Act 1985 a person acting as a liquidator, provisional liquidator, administrator or administrative receiver or as a supervisor of a company voluntary arrangement must be qualified to act as an insolvency practitioner (IA 1986, ss. 388 to 390). This qualification is obtained primarily by being authorised by virtue of membership of a recognised professional body such as the Institute of Chartered Accountants. In other words authorisation is primarily delegated to the professions, principally that of chartered accountancy. It is the partners of the major firms of chartered accountants that do the bulk of the work of insolvency practitioners.

Under IA 1986, s. 390(3), and part III of the Insolvency Practitioners Regulations 1990 (SI 1990/439) an insolvency practitioner is not qualified to act unless security has been given for the proper performance of his or her functions. The Regulations require a general bond for a prescribed amount plus a specific bond issued in case of each appointment equal to the amount of the insolvent's assets. Under the terms of such bonds a surety (generally a substantial insurance company) undertakes to be jointly and severally liable with the insolvency practitioner for the proper performance of his or her duties and obligations under the Act.

The government's policy of requiring professional qualifications for insolvency practitioners and of requiring fidelity insurance as recommended by the Review Committee (i.e., the Cork Committee) is set out in the following paragraphs from the white paper.

A Revised Framework for Insolvency Law
(Cmnd 9175) (London: HMSO, 1984)

Professional Standards for Insolvency Practitioners

8. It is desirable that the public should have trust in those who handle insolvencies and the government recognises that the present law which allows persons with no practical experience or relevant professional qualifications to act as trustee or liquidator, or as receiver for a debenture holder, is unsatisfactory. Further, it is only in cases under the control of the court that trustees and liquidators are required to take out fidelity insurance to protect creditors against losses to the estate through the misappropriation of funds. These deficiencies have in the past allowed a minority of practitioners to engage in questionable, if not illegal, practices to the detriment of creditors.

9. The Review Committee recommended that these deficiencies be remedied by requiring professional standards to be observed by insolvency practitioners and by extending bonding and insurance requirements to all forms of insolvency proceedings, including receivership and the administration procedure. The government accepts that there is a need for action in this area. To give creditors confidence in the persons they appoint to administer insolvent estates and to reduce the amount of supervision required by the Department of Trade and Industry, insolvency practitioners will normally have to be practising solicitors or members of accountancy bodies recognised for the purpose by the Secretary of State. They will also be obliged to obtain an insurance bond against all types of dishonesty and negligence and this requirement will extend to all the appointments which they undertake. The review committee also proposed that there should be transitional arrangements to cater for experienced but unqualified practitioners. The government agrees and provision will be made in this respect.

20.5 CREDITORS' VOLUNTARY WINDING UP

When a company is in severe financial difficulties, its members may choose to wind up the company rather than wait for a creditor to petition the court for a compulsory winding up. With a small company, it may be possible to do this relatively rapidly by passing an extraordinary resolution to wind up. It has to be remembered that the members are possibly also major creditors of the company and have an interest in the best possible payment on winding up.

A voluntary winding up (i.e., initiated by resolution of the members) is a creditors' voluntary winding up unless the directors make a statutory declaration that they are of the opinion that the company will be able to pay its debts in full within 12 months from the date of the resolution (IA 1986, ss. 89 and 90). Following the members' meeting at which it is resolved to wind up, a creditors' meeting is held which receives a statement of affairs from the directors and appoints a liquidator (ss. 98 to 100). On the appointment of the liquidator all the powers of the directors cease (s. 103).

20.6 WINDING UP BY THE COURT

20.6.1 Process and impact of winding up by the court

Winding up by the court (compulsory winding up) may occur on a number of grounds (see 20.6.2 below). Its primary function as a debt-collecting process is initiated by unpaid creditors where the company is unable to pay its debts. The petitioning creditor presents a petition to the court, which IA 1986, s. 129, deems to be the commencement of the winding up. Some days or weeks later the petition is heard in open court and if the petitioner proves that the company is unable to pay its debts, the court will order that the company be wound up. The official receiver, an official of the Department of Trade and Industry, becomes the liquidator of the company (IA 1986, s. 136(2)) and continues in office until such time as another liquidator is appointed. However, in every compulsory liquidation the official receiver has the duty to investigate the affairs of the company, the causes of its failure and the conduct of its directors. (There are many official receiver officers in towns throughout England and Wales.)

In the larger liquidations with sufficient assets to cover the costs involved, the creditors may thus under IA 1986, s. 139, appoint an insolvency practitioner, generally a chartered accountant, as liquidator to collect the assets of the company and distribute them to its creditors. Nonetheless the vast majority of cases are dealt with by the official receiver as in most cases the gross assets remaining to failed companies free of security (some office furniture, a few obsolete computers perhaps) are pathetically small.

The following are the key provisions indicating the impact of winding up by the court.

INSOLVENCY ACT 1986, SS. 127, 128, 129 AND 130

130. Consequences of winding-up order

(1) On the making of a winding-up order, a copy of the order must forthwith be forwarded by the company (or otherwise as may be prescribed) to the registrar of companies, who shall enter it in his records relating to the company.

(2) When a winding-up order has been made or a provisional liquidator has been appointed, no action or proceeding shall be proceeded with or commenced against the company or its property, except by leave of the court and subject to such terms as the court may impose.

129. Commencement of winding up by the court

(2) … the winding up of a company by the court is deemed to commence at the time of the presentation of the petition for winding up.

128. Avoidance of attachments, etc.

(1) Where a company registered in England and Wales is being wound up by the court, any attachment, sequestration, distress or execution put in force against the estate or effects of the company after the commencement of the winding up is void.…

127. Avoidance of property dispositions, etc.

In a winding up by the court, any disposition of the company's property, and any transfer of shares, or alteration in the status of the company's members, made after the commencement of the winding up is, unless the court otherwise orders, void.

Thus, when a winding-up order has been made, no proceedings may be begun or continued against the company (s. 130(2)). On commencement of winding up (i.e., presentation of the petition: s. 129(2)) certain enforcement procedures against the company are void (s. 128(1)), as is any disposal of the company's property unless the court orders otherwise (s. 127). Creditors may then only recover by proving their debts in the collective process of winding up. The purpose of preventing the disposal of property after commencement and the need for court approval of certain transactions is summarised in a dictum of Cairns LJ in the old case of *Re Wiltshire Iron Co., ex parte Pearson* (1868) LR 3 Ch App 443:

This is a wholesome and necessary provision, to prevent, during the period which must elapse before a petition can be heard, the improper alienation and dissipation of the property of a company *in extremis*. But where a company actually trading, which it is in the interest of every one to preserve, and ultimately to sell, as a going concern, is made the object of a winding-up petition which may fail or may succeed, if it were to be supposed that transactions in the ordinary course of its current trade, bona fide entered into and completed, would be avoided, and would not, in the discretion given to the court, be maintained, the result would be that the presentation of a petition, groundless or well-founded, would, *ipso facto*, paralyse the trade of the company, and great injury, without any counterbalance of advantage, would be done to those interested in the assets of the company.

The consequence of avoiding dispositions of property, in effect retrospectively, even before a winding up order has been made can have a dramatic impact on the company immediately a winding-up petition is presented. Presentation of the petition is the simple procedure of filing the petition in standard form verified by affidavit in the court registry (Insolvency Rules 1986, r. 4.7(1)). Thereupon the company may no longer deal with its property without court approval. In particular when the company's bank becomes aware of presentation of the petition it will probably close the company's account and may refuse to operate the account further. In the following case the court considered the criteria by which a court will validate a disposition of property following presentation of a winding up petition.

Denney v John Hudson & Co. Ltd

Validating a void transaction

[1992] BCLC 901, Court of Appeal

FOX LJ: The principles governing the exercise of the court's jurisdiction under [the Insolvency Act 1986, s. 127] were considered by the Court of Appeal in *Re Gray's Inn Construction Co. Ltd* [1980] 1 WLR 711 at 717–19. The leading judgment was given by Buckley LJ and was concurred in by Goff L J and Sir David Cairns. I take the following propositions to be approved by that judgment:

(1) The discretion vested in the court by [s. 127] is entirely at large, subject to the general principles which apply to any kind of discretion, and subject also to limitation that the discretion must be exercised in the context of the liquidation provisions of the statute.

(2) The basic principle of law governing the liquidation of insolvent estates, whether in bankruptcy or under the companies' legislation, is that the assets of the insolvent at the time of the commencement of the liquidation will be distributed *pari passu* among the insolvent's unsecured creditors as at the date of the bankruptcy....

(3) There are occasions, however, when it may be beneficial not only for the company but also for the unsecured creditors, that the company should be able to dispose of some of its property during the period after the petition has been presented, but before the winding-up order has been made. Thus, it may sometimes be beneficial to the company and its creditors that the company should be able to continue the business in its ordinary course.

(4) In considering whether to make a validating order, the court must always do its best to ensure that the interests of the unsecured creditors will not be prejudiced.

(5) The desirability of the company being enabled to carry on its business was often speculative. In each case the court must carry out a balancing exercise.

(6) The court should not validate any transaction or series of transactions which might result in one or more pre-liquidation creditors being paid in full at the expense of other creditors, who will only receive a dividend, in the absence of special circumstances making such a course desirable in the interest of the creditors generally. If, for example, it were in the interests of the creditors generally that the company's business should be carried on, and this could only be achieved by paying for goods already supplied to the company when the petition is presented (but not yet paid for) the court might exercise its discretion to validate payments for those goods.

(7) A disposition carried out in good faith in the ordinary course of business at a time when the parties were unaware that a petition had been presented would usually be validated by the court unless there is ground for thinking that the transaction may involve an attempt to prefer the disponee—in which case the transaction would not be validated.

(8) Despite the strength of the principle of securing *pari passu* distribution, the principle has no application to post-liquidation creditors; for example, the sale of an asset at full market value after the presentation of the petition. That is because such a transaction involves no dissipation of the company's assets for it does not reduce the value of its assets.

20.6.2 Grounds for winding up

IA 1986, s. 122, sets out the grounds for winding up. The 'just and equitable ground' (s. 122(1)(g)) is treated as a minority remedy in chapter 13. Otherwise, in the insolvency context s. 122(1)(f) is of prime importance. How it is proved that a company is unable to pay its debts appears from s. 123 set out at 20.3 above. The statutory demand for a sum exceeding £750 under s. 123(1)(a) (an example of which is shown at 20.3) is a standard means of obtaining a winding-up order. However, as appears from the *Taylors Industrial Flooring Ltd* case extracted below other proof of inability to pay debts (see s. 123(1)(e)) such as non-payment of a debt, without suffering the three-week delay of a statutory demand, may suffice.

INSOLVENCY ACT 1986, S. 122

122. Circumstances in which company may be wound up by the court

(1) A company may be wound up by the court if—

   (a) the company has by special resolution resolved that the company be wound up by the court;

   (b) being, a public company which was registered as such on its original incorporation, the company has not been issued with a certificate under section 117 of the Companies Act [CA 2006, s. 761] (public company share capital requirements) and more than a year has expired since it was so registered;

   (c) it is an old public company, within the meaning of the Consequential Provisions Act;

   (d) the company does not commence its business within a year from its incoporation or suspends its business for a whole year;

   (e) except in the case of a private company limited by shares or by guarantee the number of members is reduced below two;

   (f) the company is unable to pay its debts;

   (fa) at the time at which a moratorium for the company under section 1A comes to an end, no voluntary arrangement approved under Part I has effect in relation to the company;

   (g) the court is of the opinion that it is just and equitable that the company should be wound up.

Where a petitioner proves that the company is unable to pay its debts, the petitioner is generally entitled to a winding-up order as a matter of justice, though it remains within the court's discretion.

Only a creditor may present a creditor's petition. If the unpaid debt relied upon to found the petition is disputed on substantial grounds the petitioner has not established his standing as a creditor. Furthermore a winding-up petition is not a proper means of trying a disputed debt. To attempt to do so is an abuse of the process of the court. Presentation of the petition will be restrained by injunction, or the petition will be dismissed with costs against the petitioner.

As mentioned at 20.3, serving a statutory demand on a debtor company may prompt it to pay the debt. However, using a statutory demand and a winding-up petition to coerce a debtor company into paying a debt may be a risky course to take. An application for summary judgment under the Rules of the Supreme Court, ord. 14 is the proper procedure for enforcing payment. In *Re A Company, (No. 0012209 of 1991)* [1992] 1 WLR 351 at p. 354F, Hoffmann J said:

It does seem to me that a tendency has developed ... to present [winding-up] petitions against solvent companies as a way of putting pressure upon them to make payments of money which is bona fide disputed rather than to invoke procedures which the rules provide for summary judgment ... If ... it appears that the defence [of the company] has a prospect of success and the company is solvent, then I think that the court should give the company the benefit of the doubt and not do anything which would encourage the use of the Companies Court as an alternative to [the summary judgment] procedure.

The following cases consider these issues.

Mann v *Goldstein*

An abuse of the process of the court

[1968] 2 All ER 769, [1968] 1 WLR 1091, Chancery Division

Facts   An application was successfully made to restrain further proceedings on a winding-up petition on grounds that the debts relied upon were disputed. The provisions of CA 1948 referred to are materially the same as the current provisions of IA 1986.

UNGOED-THOMAS J: It is well-established that this court has jurisdiction to restrain the presentation or advertising of a winding-up petition and restrain all further proceedings on it. That jurisdiction is a facet of the court's inherent jurisdiction to prevent an abuse of the process of the court. It will be exercised where a winding-up application is presented or prosecuted otherwise than in accordance with the legitimate purpose of such process (see, for example, *Re a Company (No. 0089 of 1894)* [1894] 2 Ch 349).

The presentation of a petition is governed by statutory provision. Section 224 of the Companies Act, 1948, provides that an application to wind up a company shall be by petition presented, so far as material for present purposes '…by any creditor or creditors' [see now IA 1986, s. 124] The section seems to me plainly, on the face of it, exhaustive, so that a person not within its ambit cannot petition. This conclusion is in accordance with the note in *Buckley on the Companies Acts* 13th ed., p. 462, based on the observation of Wynn-Parry J in *Re H.L. Bolton Engineering Co. Ltd* [1956] Ch 577. Of course, a person not named in s. 224 as a person entitled to present a winding-up petition, does not become so named because the company is insolvent. Therefore, so far as material to our case, if the defendants are not creditors they are not entitled to present or advertise their petitions or apply for a winding-up order; they have no *locus standi*, and their petitions are bound to fail even though the company be insolvent.…

To enable the Companies Court to make the winding-up order itself, not only must the petitioner have been shown to be entitled to present the petition, but also one of the grounds specified in s. 222 of the Companies Act 1948 [now IA 1986, s. 122] must be established: and the only such ground relied on in the petition and before me was that the company is unable to pay its debts. This requirement is additional to the precondition of presenting the petition, that the petitioner must be a creditor, and is not alternative to it. The insolvency requirement, however, unlike the creditor requirement, is only a prerequisite of the order and not a prerequisite of the presentation of the petition. So if a person is entitled to present a petition, then the company's inability to pay its debts is the very matter which it is appropriate for the Companies Court to enquire into and decide in the exercise of its jurisdiction to make a winding-up order.

I come now to the allegation of lack of bona fides and to abuse of process. It seems to me that to pursue a substantial claim in accordance with the procedure provided and in the normal manner, though with personal hostility or even venom and from some ulterior motive, such as the hope of compromise or some indirect advantage, is not an abuse of the process of the court or acting *mala fide* but acting bona fide in accordance with the process. Certainly no authority suggesting otherwise has been brought to my attention. In *Re Welsh Brick Industries Ltd* [1946] 2 All ER 197 Lord Greene MR treated a bona fide claim as being a claim based on some substantial ground, when he referred to

> …considering whether or not the dispute is a bona fide dispute, or, putting it in another way, whether or not there is some substantial ground for defending the action.

So far as is material here, the winding-up process provides that the petition shall be presented by a creditor and that the winding-up order shall be on the ground that the company is unable to pay its debts. As Malins VC said in *Cadiz Waterworks Co.* v *Barnett* (1874) LR 19 Eq 182, if the court

> …sees a petition to wind up presented, not for a bona fide purpose of winding up the company, but for some collateral and sinister object, on that ground it will be dismissed with costs.

There the purpose of winding up the company is treated as a bona fide purpose in contrast with some purpose other than the winding up of the company.

What then is the course for this court to take (i) when the creditor's debt is clearly established; (ii) when it is clearly established that there is no debt; and (iii) when the debt is disputed on substantial grounds?

(i) When the creditor's debt is clearly established it seems to me to follow that this court would not, in general at any rate, interfere even though the company would appear to be solvent, for the creditor would, as such, be entitled to present a petition and the debtor would have its own remedy in paying the undisputed debt which it should pay. So, to persist in non-payment of the debt in such circumstances would itself either suggest inability to pay or that the application was an application that the court should give the debtor relief which it itself could provide, but would not provide, by paying the debt. Further, the winding-up order on the ground of inability to pay debts would be the very matter which it would be for the Companies Court to decide after presentation of the petition: and validly to present a creditor's petition which the company inexplicably would not pay could hardly, in general at any rate, be an abuse of the process of the court.

(ii) When it is clearly established that there is no debt, it seems to me similarly to follow that there is no creditor, that the person claiming to be such has no *locus standi* and that his petition is bound to fail. Once that becomes clear, pursuit of the petition would be an abuse of process, and this court would restrain its presentation or advertisement. Indeed, I understand counsel for the second defendant to concede this proposition.

(iii) When the debt is disputed by the company on some substantial ground (and not just on some ground which is frivolous or without substance and which the court should, therefore, ignore) and the company is solvent, the court will restrain the prosecution of a petition to wind up the company. As Malins VC said in *Cadiz Waterworks Co.* v *Barnett*, of a winding-up application.

...it is not a remedy intended by the legislature, or that ought ever to be applied, to enforce payment of a debt where these circumstances exist—solvency and a disputed debt.

As Jessel MR said in [*Niger Merchants Co.* v *Copper* (1877) 185 ChD 557 n]. 'When a company is solvent, the right course is to bring an action for the debt'. So, to pursue a winding-up petition in such circumstances is an abuse of the process of the court.

...For my part, I would prefer to rest the jurisdiction directly on the comparatively simple propositions that a creditor's petition can only be presented by a creditor, that the winding-up jurisdiction is not for the purpose of deciding a disputed debt (that is, disputed on substantial and not insubstantial grounds) since, until a creditor is established as a creditor he is not entitled to present the petition and has no *locus standi* in the Companies Court; and that, therefore, to invoke the winding-up jurisdiction when the debt is disputed (that is, on substantial grounds) or after it has become clear that it is so disputed is an abuse of the process of the court....

The second matter to mention is the companies' insolvency. Insolvency in connection with a winding-up petition means inability to pay debts as they fall due and not a deficiency of assets as compared with liabilities. Indeed, insolvency in that sense, of inability to pay debts as they fall due, clearly appears from Mr Mann's own affidavits. The evidence of such insolvency of both companies is altogether so conclusive to my mind that I do not propose to analyse or particularise it, especially as I do not rely on it for my conclusion but come to my conclusion despite it.

My conclusion, therefore, is, in the case of each company, for the reasons which I have given at length, that the plaintiffs are entitled to the injunctions which they claim....

Taylors Industrial Flooring Ltd v *M & H Plant Hire (Manchester) Ltd*

Avoiding the delay of a statutory demand

[1990] BCLC 216, Court of Appeal

Non-payment of an undisputed debt, even in the absence of a statutory demand, is evidence of a company's inability to pay its debts.

Facts   In this case a creditor, a plant hire company, appealed when its petition against the company, Taylors, was struck out. Part of the debt relied on was disputed but the undisputed part exceeded £750. However, a statutory demand had not been served. The petitioner merely relied as evidence that the company was unable to pay its debts under s. 122(1)(f) on the mailing of a number of unpaid invoices for plant hire to the company's address. These had not been returned by the Post Office or disputed by the company.

DILLON LJ: If there is a debt which to an extent above the statutory minimum is indisputable, then a petition can validly be presented even if the debt as claimed in the petition is for a larger sum, part of which is bona fide disputed. That was decided in *Re Tweeds Garages Ltd* [1962] Ch 406, and therefore since there is no substantial dispute in respect of the December and January supplies, it is unnecessary to consider the subsequent supplies included in the invoices delivered after the end of March (that is to say, the next month's supply). ...

There is no requirement that a creditor must serve a statutory demand. The practice for a long time has been that the vast majority of creditors who seek to petition for the winding up of companies do not serve statutory demands. The practical reason for that is that if a statutory demand is served, three weeks have to pass until a winding-up petition can be presented. If, after the petition has been presented, a winding-up order is made, the winding up is only treated as commencing at the date of the presentation of the petition; thus, if the creditor takes the course of serving a statutory demand, it would be giving the company an extra three weeks' grace in which such assets as the company may have may be dissipated in attempting to keep an insolvent business afloat, or may be absorbed into the security of a debenture holder bank. So there are practical reasons for not allowing extra time, particularly where commercial conditions and competition require promptness in the payment of companies' debts so that the creditor companies can manage their own cash flow and keep their own costs down.

The short answer to the judge's view is twofold. They run together. The first limb is that if a debt is due and an invoice sent and the debt is not disputed, then the failure of the debtor company to pay the debt is itself evidence of inability to pay. That appears from the judgment of Harman J in *Cornhill Insurance plc* v *Improvement Services Ltd* [1986] 1 WLR 114. The headnote correctly states that:

> Where a company was under an undisputed obligation to pay a specific sum and failed to do so, it could be inferred that it was unable to do so; that accordingly, the defendants could properly swear to their belief in the plaintiff company's insolvency and present a petition for its winding up.

The judge refers in passing to a statement by Vaisey J in an earlier case: 'Rich men and rich companies who did not pay their debts had only themselves to blame if it were thought that they could not pay them'. It is not right to say, as was submitted to us by counsel for the respondent (Mr Sterling) 'Well, it may be just that they do not want to pay and so you cannot from non-payment of an undisputed debt deduce inability to pay'.

The second point is that the reason for non-payment has to be substantial. It is not enough if a thoroughly bad reason is put forward honestly.

I refer to the decision of this court in *Re Welsh Brick Industries Ltd* [1946] 2 All ER 197. ... In giving the leading judgment Lord Greene MR said (at p. 198):

> The law and practice on those matters is for present purposes stated with sufficient accuracy in *Buckley on the Companies Acts*, 11th ed., pp. 356, 357, as follows: 'A winding-up petition is not a legitimate means of seeking to enforce payment of a debt which is bona fide disputed by the company. A petition presented ostensibly for a winding-up order but really to exercise pressure will be dismissed and under circumstances may be stigmatised as a scandalous abuse of the process of the court. Some years ago petitions founded on disputed debt were directed to stand over till the debt was established by action. If, however, there was no reason to believe that the debt, if established, would not be paid, the petition was dismissed. The modern practice has been to dismiss such petitions. But, of course, if the debt is not disputed on some substantial ground, the court may decide it on the petition and make the order.' I do not think that there is any difference between the words 'bona fide

disputed' and the words 'disputed on some substantial ground'. I cannot accept the proposition that, merely because unconditional leave to defend is given, that of itself must be taken as establishing that there is a bona fide dispute or that there is some substantial ground of defence.

Therefore it was necessary to consider whether there was indeed a substantial ground of defence and the judge had found that there was not. Therefore the position was that the company had not paid a debt as it fell due and had no substantial ground for opposing it. Therefore there was evidence of insolvency.

In the present case it is now conceded that the amounts of the invoices for the services supplied in December and January were, on any view, properly payable before the petition was presented. The presentation of the petition was thus in my judgment amply warranted.

Malayan Plant (Pte) Ltd v Moscow Narodny Bank Ltd

The bank may demand its umbrella back when it rains

[1980] 2 MLJ 53, Privy Council

This case discusses the question whether, having served a statutory demand and the debt remaining unpaid, the creditor is entitled to a winding-up order or whether this remains within the discretion of the court. More specifically it explores whether a bank lending money on demand may without restraint demand payment and wind up its borrower company when the latter may be commercially viable but is inevitably unable to find alternative finance at short notice.

Facts   The bank was wholly owned by the then Soviet government and had a branch in Singapore. The appellant company was substantially financed by it. When trading conditions deteriorated and the bank became concerned, it served a statutory demand for all outstanding indebtedness. The Chief Justice of Singapore made a winding-up order. The company's appeal failed in Singapore's Court of Appeal and finally reached the Privy Council.

LORD EDMUND-DAVIES: ... when the appeal reached the Court of Appeal on March 22, 1978, it was expressly conceded that the company owed the bank the full amount of $8,092,088.96 with 14 per cent interest, and the sole ground of appeal persisted in was that it would be neither just nor equitable to allow the winding-up order to remain. Reliance was sought to be placed on the fact that the relationship of bank to customer had existed between the parties for over five years. It was said that this had involved the former in making large advances which had enabled the latter to trade successfully and to have assets exceeding their liabilities, that there was no possibility of the company finding an alternative source of finance at short notice, and that the demands in December 1976 and January 1977 for repayment within three weeks of all outstanding loans and advances had placed the company in an impossible situation which had resulted from their refusal to accede to the bank's persuasion that they should trade in Russian goods. The Court of Appeal summarised the company's plea by saying that it had, in effect, asserted,

That the bank's general behaviour in this matter was not that of a good and reasonable banker, *vis-à-vis* its customer, in that it had made it too easy for the company to become indebted to it in the sum of over $8 million and, worse still, to ask the company to pay off the debt in three weeks, in one lump sum.

Holding that it was clear that the company were unable to pay its debts and that it was just and equitable to make a winding-up order, the Court of Appeal declined to interfere with the learned Chief Justice's exercise of his discretion and dismissed the appeal.

Before this Board Mr John Newey QC [counsel for the appellant company] has repeated his submission made in the Court of Appeal that the source of error has throughout been that the Chief Justice had exercised his discretion according to what counsel described as 'the Buckley concept', whereas he should have adopted the modern concept as propounded by the Court of Appeal in *Re LHF Wools Ltd* [1970] Ch 27.

It is not entirely easy to see how the petitioner's case was presented at first instance, save that it was submitted that it would be more beneficial to all creditors if there were *no* winding-up. The learned Chief Justice's notes disclose that his attention was drawn to the observations of Jessel MR in *Re Great Britain Mutual Life Assurance Society* (1880) 16 ChD 246 at p. 253 that,

> ...it is not sufficient for the respondents, upon a petition of this kind, to say, 'We dispute the claim'. They must bring forward a prima facie case which satisfies the court that there is something which ought to be tried.

There was also cited to the Chief Justice a passage from *Buckley on the Companies Acts*, 13th ed., p. 460, dealing with 'commercial insolvency, that is, of the company being unable to meet current demands upon it', and containing the following observations, which are, in the opinion of the Board, impeccable:

> In such a case it is useless to say that if its assets are realised there will be ample to pay 20 shillings in the pound: this is not the test. A company may be at the same time insolvent and wealthy. It may have wealth locked up in investments not presently realisable; but although this be so, yet if it have not assets available to meet its current liabilities it is commercially insolvent and may be wound up.

But the appellants' counsel referred the Board to an earlier passage (*not* referred to in the Chief Justice's notes) which he said contained what he described as 'the Buckley concept'. It is to be found at p. 450, and is in these words:

> A creditor who cannot obtain payment of his debt is entitled as between himself and the company *ex debito justitiae* to an order if he brings his case within the Act. He is not bound to give time. And, notwithstanding a voluntary winding up, on proving his debt and that it remains unsatisfied he will be so entitled.
>
> ...it is not a discretionary matter with the court when a debt is established, and not satisfied, to say whether the company shall be wound up or not; that is to say, if there be a valid debt established, valid both at law and in equity. One does not like to say positively that no case could occur in which it would be right to refuse it; but, ordinarily speaking, it is the duty of the court to direct the winding up.

The citation is from Lord Cranworth's speech in *Bowes v Hope Life Insurance and Guarantee Co.* (1865) 11 HL Cas 389 at p. 402, and appellants' counsel criticised it as being both too rigid and too narrow. It was contrasted with what he submitted was the preferable (or 'modern') approach adopted in the *Wools* case, where, however, Edmund Davies LJ stressed (at p. 41) what he described as the 'important qualifying words' with which Lord Cranworth had rounded off his observations, and commented, 'accordingly, we come to the position that whether or not an order should be made ... is a matter of discretion'.

In the *Wools* case the company being sought to be wound up had against the petitioner a cross-claim which was awaiting litigation in Belgium. It had a substantial chance of succeeding there and would, in the words of Harman LJ (p. 35H), 'overtop the [petitioner's] debt and wipe it out altogether'. Furthermore, the cross-claim was the solitary asset of the company. The Court of Appeal held that, in the light of all these circumstances, the learned trial judge should have stayed the hearing of the winding-up petition, and cited with approval the following observations of Lord Denning MR in *Ward v James* [1966] 1 QB 273:

> ...the courts have laid down considerations to guide judges in the exercise of their discretion, and these considerations have been changed from time to time as the years go by. They change as public policy demands. ... The cases all show that, when a statute gives discretion, the court must not fetter it by rigid rules from which a judge is never at liberty to depart.

If it is permissible to say so, the *Wools* case made no new law and it is not particularly 'modern' in its approach. It may be that the decision served a useful purpose in underlining yet again that s. 225(1) of the Companies Act 1948—which is similar to s. 221(1) of the Singapore Act—serves to vest in the court a wide discretion. Regard must, therefore, always be had to the statutory provision itself, for, as Lord Wilberforce said in *Ebrahimi v Westbourne Galleries Ltd* [1973] AC 360 at p. 374H, 'Illustrations may be used, but general words should remain general and not be reduced to the sum of particular instances'. There is no distinction in principle between a cross-claim of substance (such as in the *Wools* case) and a serious dispute regarding the indebtedness imputed against a company, which has long been held to constitute a proper ground upon which to reject a winding-up petition.

There are, of course, other grounds which, consonant with the statutory provisions, may lead the court to the same conclusion. Do any such exist in the present case? Mr Newey relied strongly on what he described as the indefensible conduct of the petitioning bank, to which reference has already been made. But no evidence of oppression or unfairness by the bank was adduced, and it has to be said that, upon the available material, it is difficult to see in what respect their conduct is open to legitimate criticism. It may be, for all one knows, that they could well have extended some indulgence to the company, but they were under no obligation to do more in that way than they had already done, and it cannot be said that they were either unjust or inequitable in failing to do so. At one stage learned counsel appeared to submit that it was an implied term of their relationship that the respondents should from time to time have advised the appellants on the prudent managing of their business, but he later disclaimed that anything of the sort was being suggested. And the relevant facts are widely different from those in the cases cited by Mr Newey where a bank was in one respect or another held not to have measured up to their duty to their customer—for example, *Cumming* v *Shand* (1860) 5 Hurl & N 95, which turned on a particular course of dealing between the parties and not simply on the banker/customer relationship; or *Buckingham* v *L.M. Bank* (1895) 12 TLR 70, where a bank closed the customer's account without proper notice; or *Woods* v *Martins Bank Ltd* [1959] 1 QB 55 where a bank manager whose advice was sought by a customer gave grossly negligent information regarding a company's stability. At the end of the day, beyond observing that to give the statutory notice demanding payment within three weeks was to ask the impossible, no concrete criticism of the respondent's conduct was advanced by learned counsel.

20.7 THE *PARI PASSU* PRINCIPLE

The *pari passu* principle is an old and fundamental principle derived from bank-ruptcy law, and like many elderly principles it is riddled with exceptions. Now found in the current insolvency legislation, the principle is that creditors should be treated equally; that the insolvent's assets should be shared proportionately between them and their debts should abate and be paid 'in equal steps'. Thus a liquidator may pay, for example, a 25 per cent 'dividend' to all ordinary creditors on finally administering the insolvent company's assets.

However, creditors are not in fact treated equally. Some, such as secured and preferential creditors, are more equal than others. Further devices such as hire-purchase, retention of title (see 15.2.3 above) and the *Quistclose* trust also have the effect of preferring such creditors to others. The legislation creates a number of important categories of preferential debt, principally for taxes collected by the business and employees' wages (see 20.8 below). As these creditors get paid first, ordinary creditors are paid less, and very possibly nothing.

English law also permits a debtor to grant to his creditor security rights over a particular asset. On the debtor's insolvency the creditor can exercise these prop-erty rights and appropriate the asset to recover the debt and the costs of recovery. The common law recognises the principle of freedom of contract and of respecting rights of property, but in so doing diminishes the principle of equal treatment of creditors.

Thus the *pari passu* principle in recent years has been reduced to a principle of equality between ordinary creditors, secured and preferential creditors having probably taken the lion's share of the assets. However, the abolition of Crown preference (see 20.8) and of the floating charge (see 15.3) should have the effect of increasing what the liquidator is able to pay out to ordinary creditors.

The following extract from an article by Professor Milman is a clear and useful account of how the *pari passu* principle, while remaining fundamental, has been eroded by the *laissez-faire* approach to the creation of security, and in contrast by the interventionist policy of favouring preferential creditors.

David Milman, 'Priority rights on corporate insolvency'
Current Issues in Insolvency Law (London: Stevens, 1991)

Security and unsecured creditors

The mid nineteenth century saw the introduction of the registered company into English law and the advent of limited liability. Priority disputes at this time tended to concentrate on one black and white issue; did the creditor enjoy security? If so, that creditor clearly had a prior claim to a particular corporate asset encompassed by the security, remembering that in those days only fixed assets were suitable subjects for security. Such priority could be justified merely by referring to the notion of freedom of contract, which in turn relied heavily on Victorian *laissez-faire* philosophy. Every creditor dealing with a limited liability company had, in theory, the freedom to stipulate that the right to insist on repayment of his debt be supported by security over the company's assets. To turn this reasoning on its head it could be further argued that a creditor who failed to arrange security took the risk of being 'trumped' on corporate insolvency by a secured creditor. Perhaps the best example of this philosophy at work comes from a case which is well known to company lawyers throughout the English-speaking world, namely *Salomon v A. Salomon & Co. Ltd*. The essence of the dispute in this case was whether the controller of a 'one-man company' could lend money to it and take security over its assets in return, thereby ensuring priority for himself over the unsecured creditors of the company. Both Vaughan Williams J (at first instance) and the Court of Appeal rejected such a possibility. A powerfully constituted House of Lords took the opposite view. Lord Macnaghten typified their attitude when he declared:

> Any member of a company, acting in good faith, is as much entitled to take and hold the company's debentures as any outside creditor. Every creditor is entitled to get and to hold the best security the law allows him to take.

This classical theory, of course, ignored the economic and practical realities faced by different groups of persons dealing with such companies. Many creditors had neither the economic power, nor indeed sufficient legal knowledge, to require that security be given.

The willingness of English law to permit companies the freedom to grant security in return for loan finance may also be justified on economic grounds in that such security lessened the risk for the borrower and thereby reduced the cost of credit. It is generally recognised that this relaxed attitude towards security did much to boost the growth of capitalism in the nineteenth century.

Supporters of the economic analysis of law could also put forward their own justification for permitting some creditors to secure priority over their fellows by this route. Thus, by analysing transaction costs, it has been argued that:

> The rule permitting debtors to encumber the assets by private agreement is therefore justifiable as a cost-saving device that makes it easier and cheaper for the debtor's creditors to do what they would do in any case.

This argument is based on the view that were creditors free to arrange their own priorities *inter se* they would probably agree to a regime very similar to that imposed by the law, because economic bargaining power would inevitably strengthen the hand of certain creditors (notably banks) at the expense of their fellows.

Once secured creditors had exercised their contractual rights to realise particular assets, unsecured creditors were entitled to share in the residue and in general ranked *pari passu inter se*— i.e. their debts would be repaid rateably, (i.e. in common proportions), as opposed to ranking in order of time, for example. This particular rule was established in the early days of bankruptcy law and was subsequently adopted by corporate insolvency law. It has been argued that it represents a pure form of distributable justice, having its origins in the equitable maxim 'Equality is Equity'. That may be so, though it does not really explain why this particular system of distribution was selected in preference to other available models. It is perhaps understandable that equitable maxims came into play because the assets of an insolvent company were often said to be held on trust for its creditors. Nevertheless, it would have been possible to opt for a regime that ranked debts for repayment according to date of accrual or according to the personal need of each individual creditor. These solutions were spurned in favour of the simplicity of *pari passu*, though some judges have been brave enough to acknowledge that it is not a panacea. In the end one suspects that the *pari passu* rule has been adopted by the courts as a convenient fall back position that avoids the necessity of making difficult choices where the legislature has failed to take the initiative.

Whatever the conceptual justification for the *pari passu* rule suffice it to say that it has provided the basic distributional matrix in corporate insolvency law for nearly 150 years....

At 20.11 below the powers of the liquidator to overturn prior transactions are examined. For example, where directors in anticipation of liquidation pay off debts owed by the company to themselves, they have intentionally put themselves in a better position than if they had had to prove for the debt in the liquidation. Empowering the liquidator to recover the payment assists equal treatment of ordinary creditors. At 20.10 it is explained that creditors may not (other than by taking security) contract out of the statutory requirements as to *pari passu* distributions.

The statutory requirements for equal distribution to creditors are found in IA 1986, s. 107, set out below, which applies to voluntary liquidations. (Insolvency Rules 1986, r. 4.181 has similar effect for compulsory liquidations.) There then follow the conclusions of the Cork Committee that although the *pari passu* principle has been 'greatly eroded' in practice, it has to remain 'the cornerstone of any new insolvency legislation'.

INSOLVENCY ACT 1986, S. 107

107. Distribution of company's property

Subject to the provisions of this Act as to preferential payments, the company's property in a voluntary winding up shall on the winding up be applied in satisfaction of the company's liabilities *pari passu* and, subject to that application, shall (unless the articles otherwise provide) be distributed among the members according to their rights and interests in the company.

Insolvency Law and Practice, Report of the Review Committee (The 'Cork Report')

(Cmnd 8558) (London: HMSO, 1982)

233. The principle of *pari passu* distribution has been greatly eroded during the last century or so until today it remains as a theoretical doctrine only, with scarcely any application in real life. In a great number of cases, insolvency results in the distribution of the assets among the preferential creditors (chiefly the revenue departments) and the holders of floating charges (often though not invariably the banks) with little if anything for the ordinary unsecured creditors. We have received widespread complaints on this score. We have been left in no doubt that, as a result, there is a general disenchantment with the existing law of insolvency, and in the commercial community a feeling

of anger at the barrenness of insolvency proceedings so far as the great majority of creditors are concerned. We believe that these criticisms are fully justified. Measures are urgently required to redress the balance before the whole system falls into even greater disrepute. . . .

Conclusions

1072. We consider that the principle of *pari passu* distribution of the insolvent's estate should continue to form a cornerstone of any new insolvency legislation and we would not advocate any qualification of this principle in an attempt to deal with the particular problems to which we have referred in this chapter. We accept that no one should be able to contract out of insolvency law, and *pari passu* distribution in particular.

1073. If for their own protection creditors, such as members of the public making payments in advance for goods or services, succeed in engrafting into their relationship with a particular debtor a trust situation creating an equitable interest, or if such a situation is created by the debtor himself prior to the insolvency, then it is no part of the insolvency law to strike down such interests unless, as mentioned in paragraph 1042 their creation took place in circumstances which require them to be set aside if the general scheme of the insolvency law is to be upheld.

1074. Again, if the construction industry, or any other group of traders, wish to achieve protection against the workings of the principle of *pari passu* distribution in insolvency, it is for them to frame their commercial arrangements and documentation so as to ensure that any property of the insolvent, such as debts due to him, is at the commencement of the insolvency made clearly subject to interests which, in equity, will prevail against a trustee or liquidator in the insolvency and which have not otherwise been created in circumstances which fall foul of the insolvency laws. We have made it clear to the representatives of the industry who have given evidence to us that we cannot express opinions as to the effectiveness or otherwise in this respect of provisions in existing standard contracts or subcontracts, nor is it for us to make suggestions as to any alteration of such provisions.

1075. Accordingly, we do not propose any amendment in principle of the existing law in this field, but we consider that the new Insolvency Act should contain general provisions, applicable to companies and individuals alike,

    (a) expressly excluding from property available for distribution among creditors property held in trust, whether the trust is express, constructive or implied, and

    (b) providing for *pari passu* distribution of available property on the lines of section 302 of the Act of 1948 [now IA 1986, s. 107 extracted above].

20.8 PREFERENTIAL DEBTS

A limitation on the *pari passu* principle is that certain debts owed by the company such as wages due to its employees are paid in full as 'preferential debts' (subject to a specified maximum) before ordinary creditors are paid anything. It has long been controversial, however, that certain debts owed to the Crown were also given preference. Thus VAT received and income tax and National Insurance contributions deducted by the company from the wages it paid were preferential in a winding up, so that the Crown was first in line to recover these from the liqidator. The Enterprise Act 2002 has now abolished this 'Crown preference', perhaps as a gesture to acknowledge that the Crown is better able to absorb the loss than ordinary creditors such as small businesses. (The Inland Revenue, for example, will now have to queue for payment along with ordinary creditors, rather than being entitled to prior payment. As the Inland Revenue will thus receive less, the other ordinary creditors should now be paid a larger proportion of the debts that they are claiming in the insolvency.)

However, the unpaid wages of employees remains an important category of preferential debt. The principle is that if the company they work for goes bust, the workers should be first in line to collect payment of their wages.

The following reading gives some of the background on preferential debts.

Insolvency Law and Practice: Report of the Review Committee (The 'Cork Report')

(Cmnd 8558) (London: HMSO, 1982)

Preferential debts

Introduction

1396. It is a fundamental objective of the law of insolvency to achieve a rateable, that is to say *pari passu*, distribution of the uncharged assets of the insolvent among the unsecured creditors. In practice, however, this objective is seldom, if ever, attained. In the overwhelming majority of cases it is substantially frustrated by the existence of preferential debts. These are unsecured debts which, by force of statute, fall to be paid in bankruptcy or winding up in priority to all other unsecured debts. Where debts are paid out of assets subject to a floating charge, preferential debts must also be paid in priority to claims for principal and interest secured by the charge.

1397. We have received a considerable volume of evidence on this subject, most of it critical of the present law, and much of it deeply hostile to the retention of any system of preferential debts. We are left in no doubt that the elaborate system of priorities accorded by the present law is the cause of much public dissatisfaction, and that there is a widespread demand for a significant reduction, and even a complete elimination, of the categories of debts which are accorded priority in an insolvency.

1398. We have, therefore, considered it our duty to re-examine the present categories of preferential debts, with a view to determining which, if any, should be retained and which, if any, curtailed or abolished. Since the existence of any preferential debt militates against the principle of *pari passu* distribution and operates to the detriment of ordinary unsecured creditors, we have adopted the approach that no debt should be accorded priority unless this can be justified by reference to principles of fairness and equity which would be likely to command general public acceptance.

Crown preference

1409. The Crown's claim to preference for unpaid tax is of great antiquity. Whatever may have been the historical basis for this privilege, only two grounds for its retention in modern times have been put forward in evidence to us. It has been represented to us that sums due in respect of unpaid tax ought to have priority, first because they are owed to the community; and secondly because the Revenue, unlike others who give credit, is an involuntary creditor.

1410. We unhesitatingly reject the argument that debts owed to the community ought to be paid in priority to debts owed to private creditors. A bad debt owed to the State is likely to be insignificant in terms of total government receipts; the loss of a similar sum by a private creditor may cause substantial hardship, and bring further insolvencies in its train. . . .

1413. We . . . are not persuaded . . . that debts due to the Crown in respect of unpaid tax ought to be paid in an insolvency in priority to other debts. In recent years, the Revenue's position has been greatly strengthened by the granting by Parliament of additional powers to raise assessments and to charge interest on unpaid or late paid tax. It has powers to impose penalties, and possesses remarkable powers to enable it to obtain information, including where necessary powers of entry, search and seizure. HM Customs and Excise enjoy even more extensive powers. It may be correct to describe the Crown as an involuntary creditor in respect of unpaid tax, but it is only fair to add that it has recourse to exceptional remedies which are not available to the ordinary creditor. . . .

1417. In our view, the ancient prerogative of the Crown to priority for unpaid tax cannot be supported by principle or expediency, and cannot stand against the powerful tide calling for fairness and reform.

1418. In certain special cases, however, such as PAYE, National Insurance contributions, value added tax and car tax, different considerations obtain. In these cases, the Crown's claim is for moneys collected by the debtor, whether by deduction or charge, and for which the debtor is accountable to the Crown; the debtor is to be regarded as a tax collector rather than a taxpayer. Unless some measure of priority were accorded to the Crown for moneys collected on its behalf, or they were to be regarded as impressed with a trust, they would go to swell the insolvent's estate to the advantage of the general body of creditors. We cannot think it right that statutory provisions enacted for the more convenient collection of the revenue should enure to the benefit of private creditors. It would be commercially impractical to treat moneys collected for the Crown as impressed with a trust, and in these special circumstances we have formed the view that the retention of a measure of Crown preference is justified. ...

1421. Criticism is often levelled at the Revenue over alleged heavy-handedness in pursuing tax debts, with the result that businesses collapse when they could have survived if they had been allowed more time in which to weather a bad patch. The Revenue's view is that if financial help is needed it should be sought from the banks or other similar sources and not by failing to pay what is due to the public purse. In practice some limited measure of flexibility is shown if there appears to be a bona fide case of short-term difficulty over finding cash to pay a tax bill. Whether permission should be given to defer a payment is very much a matter for the judgment of the individual collector, but the emphasis is on orderly staged payments being made with a view to early discharge of the whole tax debt. Collectors are alive to the special importance of securing payment of PAYE tax as quickly as possible. ...

Preference for wages

1428. The preferential treatment of employees in an insolvency in respect of their claims for unpaid wages was originally a social measure. It was introduced in an effort to ease the financial hardship caused to a relatively poor and defenceless section of the community by the insolvency of their employer. In the early days of the Bankruptcy Acts, there was no welfare State, and wages were low. Since then, the position of wage earners has been greatly improved by the introduction of unemployment pay and earnings-related benefits, severance and redundancy payments, and other social security benefits.

1429. Despite this, the Blagden Committee commented upon the hardship and distress caused to employees by the delay in making preferential payments, owing to the need to make detailed computation of the amount of the Crown's preferential claims. This has been alleviated by the Employment Protection Acts, under which a substantial part, and in the majority of cases probably the whole, of each employee's claim is paid immediately out of the Redundancy Fund.

20.9 SET-OFF

It is a general rule of law that a debtor owing say £5,000 to a creditor may 'set off' £1,000 immediately due and payable to him by the same creditor. The debtor may thus tender £4,000 in full settlement of the debt. If in this example the creditor is insolvent the traditional rule of the law of bankruptcy makes set-off a mandatory requirement in the insolvency of both individuals and companies. Thus the debtor *must* set off the amount owed by the insolvent and remains liable for the net amount, in the above example £4,000. In consequence the debt of £1,000 owed by the insolvent company has effectively been paid in full rather than *pari passu* with other ordinary creditors. Nonetheless, as has been said, in case of insolvency the rule is mandatory that the debts must be set off against each other. The following extract from the Cork Report sets out the background to the law. The present position currently found in Insolvency Rules 1986, r. 4.90 then follows.

Insolvency Law and Practice: Report of the Review Committee (The 'Cork Report')

(Cmnd 8558) (London, HMSO, 1982)

Set-off

The present law

1334. It has been a principle of the law of bankruptcy for nearly 300 years that where there are mutual debts existing between a creditor and a bankrupt, the smaller debt is to be set against the larger debt and only the balance is to be accounted for by the creditor or to be proved for in bankruptcy. The object, in the words of Parke B in *Foster* v *Wilson* (1843) 12 M & W 191, is 'to do substantial justice between the parties where a debt is really due from the bankrupt to the debtor to his estate'. It should be distinguished from the general law of set-off which applies between solvent parties and which is concerned to prevent cross-actions.

1335. The law of set-off in bankruptcy is now found in s. 31 of the [Bankruptcy] Act of 1914 [see now IA 1986, s. 323]. This section provides that where there have been mutual credits, mutual debts or other mutual dealings between the two parties and a receiving order is made against one of the parties, an account must be taken of what is due from one party to the other in respect of such dealings, and the sum due from the one party shall be set off against any sum due from the other party, and the balance of the account and no more shall be claimed or paid on either side respectively. . . .

1336. The right of set-off in bankruptcy must satisfy three conditions:
(a) there must be mutual credits, debts or other dealings and, generally speaking, the claims of each party must be such as result in money claims so that the account may be taken and a balance struck (though in *Rolls Razor Ltd* v *Cox* [1967] 1 QB 552, CA, an employee was able to set off the value of the goods of his employer, a company, entrusted to him for sale, against unpaid remuneration due to him);
(b) there must be mutuality; that is to say, the debts must be between the same persons and in the same right; and
(c) the claim must be capable of proof in the bankruptcy.

1337. By s. 317 of the [Companies] Act of 1948, the rules of set-off in bankruptcy are imported into the winding up of insolvent companies in England and Wales. The effective date at which mutual claims must exist is the date of commencement of winding up. [See now Insolvency Rules 1986, r. 4.90 extracted below.] . . .

The mandatory nature of set-off

1338. It is not possible in England (though it is in Scotland) for parties to contract out of the requirement to set off. It was held by a majority of the House of Lords in the case of *National Westminster Bank Ltd* v *Halesowen Presswork & Assemblies Ltd* [1972] AC 785 that the provisions of s. 31 are mandatory and that it is not possible for parties to contract out of them. These provisions prescribe the course to be followed in the administration of the property of the bankrupt (and, by reference, the property of insolvent companies). Lord Cross, however, who dissented, took the view that although mandatory in its terms, the section should be read as being subject to any agreement to the contrary. He said that there was no reason why, in principle, the person in whose interest it would be to invoke the rule of set-off, should not be entitled to agree in advance that in the event of the bankruptcy of the other party, he would not invoke it.

INSOLVENCY RULES 1986, R. 4.90

4.90. Mutual credit and set-off

(1) This rule applies where, before the company goes into liquidation there have been mutual credits, mutual debts or other mutual dealings between the company and any creditor of the company proving or claiming to prove for a debt in the liquidation.

(2) An account shall be taken of what is due from each party to the other in respect of the mutual dealings, and the sums due from one party shall be set off against the sums due from the other.

(3) Sums due from the company to another party shall not be included in the account taken under paragraph (2) if that other party had notice at the time they became due that a meeting of creditors had been summoned under section 98 or (as the case may be) a petition for the winding up of the company was pending.

(4) Only the balance (if any) of the account is provable in the liquidation. Alternatively (as the case may be) the amount shall be paid to the liquidator as part of the assets.

20.10 CONTRACTING OUT OF THE *PARI PASSU* RULE

The principle of equality between creditors is diminished by the granting of security and retention of title rights and by the creation of preferential debts. However, the following House of Lords case indicates that the *pari passu* rule is still alive. It was held that it is contrary to public policy for parties to attempt to contract out of an equal distribution of assets on a debtor's insolvency.

British Eagle International Airlines Ltd v *Compagnie Nationale Air France*
No contracting out of the pari passu rule
[1975] 2 All ER 390, [1975] 1 WLR 758, House of Lords

Despite the dissenting views of two of the five Law Lords in this difficult case, its conclusion that parties cannot contract out of a *pari passu* distribution of assets represents the current state of the law.

Facts   The case arises from the practice that air travellers may buy an air ticket from one airline but then travel on another airline. To avoid airlines having to reimburse each other in respect of each ticket so transferred, the International Air Transport Association (IATA) set up a clearing-house scheme. Airlines could become a member of the clearing house by agreeing to complex contractual regulations. These provided that airlines should claim net amounts (for passengers carried on tickets issued by other airlines) direct from IATA and not from the issuing airline. These sums were to be notified and paid monthly. British Eagle and Air France were both members of the scheme. On 6 November 1968 British Eagle went out of business and then resolved to wind up. British Eagle owed money to the scheme, but was owed a net £5,934 by Air France for carriage of passengers on tickets issued by Air France. The liquidator of British Eagle, ignoring the agreement, successfully sued Air France for £5,934. Air France argued without success that the agreement was binding on the liquidator and that all claims and payments must continue to be settled through the clearing house only.

LORD CROSS OF CHELSEA: I turn now to the rival contentions on the points at issue. The liquidator of British Eagle relies on s. 302 of the Companies Act 1948 [now IA 1986, s. 107 extracted in 20.7] . . . He submits that the credits to which British Eagle was entitled and the debits to which it became liable in respect of trading between 1st October and 6th November were, in substance, debts due to and from it, that to give effect to the clearing-house arrangements with regard to them would result in what were in substance debts owing to the company being applied not for the general benefit of all the creditors but exclusively for the benefit of what may be called the 'clearing-house creditors' and that this would infringe the principle embodied in the section.

To this the clearing house—through Air France—replies that what passes into the control of the liquidator on a winding-up is the property of the company subject to any rights over it created by the company in favour of others in good faith while it was a going concern; that the Interline Traffic Agreement and the rules and regulations of the clearing house constituted a bona fide commercial contract between the members of the clearing house and IATA; . . . and that the contract is as binding on the liquidator as it was on the company before it went into liquidation.

British Eagle then points out that even though there may be nothing in the Companies Act 1948 which deals expressly with a case of this sort the court can always refuse to give effect to provisions in contracts which achieve a distribution of the insolvent's property which runs counter to the principles of our insolvency legislation.

. . . The 'clearing-house' creditors are clearly not secured creditors. They are claiming nevertheless that they ought not to be treated in the liquidation as ordinary unsecured creditors but that they have achieved by the medium of the 'clearing house' agreement a position analogous to that of secured creditors without the need for the creation and registration of charges on the book debts in question. Air France argue that the position which, according to them, the clearing-house creditors have achieved, though it may be anomalous and unfair to the general body of unsecured creditors, is not forbidden by any provision in the 1948 Act, and that the power of the court to go behind agreements, the results of which are repugnant to our insolvency legislation, is confined to cases in which the parties' dominant purpose was to evade its operation. I cannot accept this argument. In *Ex parte Mackay* (1873) LR 8 Ch App 643 the charge on this second half of the royalties was—so to say—an animal known to the law which on its face put the chargee in the position of a secured creditor. The court could only go behind if it was satisfied—as was indeed obvious in that case—that it had been created deliberately in order to provide for a different distribution of the insolvent's property on his bankruptcy from that prescribed by the law. But what Air France are saying here is that the parties to the 'clearing house' arrangements by agreeing that simple contract debts are to be satisfied in a particular way have succeeded in 'contracting out' of the provisions contained in s. 302 of the 1948 Act for the payment of unsecured debts '*pari passu*'. In such a context it is to my mind irrelevant that the parties to the 'clearing house' arrangements had good business reasons for entering into them and did not direct their minds to the question how the arrangements might be affected by the insolvency of one or more of the parties. Such a 'contracting out' must, to my mind, be contrary to public policy. The question is, in essence, whether what was called in argument the 'mini liquidation' flowing from the clearing-house arrangements is to yield or to prevail over the general liquidation. I cannot doubt that on principle the rules of the general liquidation should prevail. I would therefore hold that, notwithstanding the clearing-house arrangements, British Eagle on its liquidation became entitled to recover payment of the sums payable to it by other airlines for services rendered by it during that period and that airlines which had rendered services to it during that period became on the liquidation entitled to prove for the sums payable to them.

A further context in which there may be attempts to contract out of the *pari passu* rule are debt subordination agreements. Debt subordination occurs typically in a number of situations; in issues of domestic and international subordinated loan stocks; in corporate rescues when new credit is attracted by an agreement that the new debt will be repayable in advance of existing creditors; and sometimes when a holding company makes a loan to a subsidiary which is subordinated, thus not affecting the company's creditworthiness. Debt subordination involves an agreement with a creditor or creditors that they will be subordinated to other creditors who will be paid first; i.e., will receive more than a *pari passu* settlement of their debts. It was thought that such agreements could be ineffective on insolvency as being contrary to the *pari passu* principle, but see now two recent decisions,

Re Maxwell Communications Corporation plc [1993] 1 WLR 1402 and *Re British & Commonwealth Holdings plc (No. 3)* [1992] 1 WLR 672, in which Vinelott J has held a debt subordination agreement and a debt subordination trust as effective.

20.11 OVERTURNING PRIOR TRANSACTIONS

The *pari passu* principle seeks to achieve fairness and equality between those who are unfortunate enough to be ordinary creditors at the time winding up commences. However, it would make a mockery of the rule if shortly prior to the insolvency the directors were free intentionally to prefer and pay off certain creditors, such as themselves and their families, in order to put them in a better position than the other creditors. Likewise the ordinary creditors are prejudiced if gifts have been made by management or if assets have been sold at a significant undervalue (possibly to themselves) shortly before winding up. These issues are dealt with by IA 1986, ss. 238 to 241, which enable the liquidator to recover the payment or asset by court order in certain circumstances.

The readings include extracts from the Cork Report which reviewed the then existing law, followed by the current sections of the Act which resulted. An article by Vanessa Finch explores the extent to which the legislation ensures proper practice by directors with regard to creditors' interests, including some concluding comments on disqualification. Finally a relevant case is extracted.

Insolvency Law and Practice: Report of the Review Committee (The 'Cork Report')
(Cmnd 8558) (London: HMSO, 1982)

Recovery of assets disposed of by the debtor
Introduction

1200. Most advanced systems of law recognise the need to enable certain transactions between a debtor and other parties to be set aside in appropriate circumstances, so that assets disposed of by the debtor may be recovered and made available to meet the claims of his creditors ... remedies have been provided by statute and have formed part of the law of England since the sixteenth century....

1208. In the present chapter, we shall be concerned with transactions voluntarily initiated by the debtor himself. Such cases fall into two classes:
 (a) the disposal of assets by the debtor by way of gift or other voluntary disposition, including any disposition for less than full consideration, even when there is no intent on the part of the debtor to defraud creditors (see paragraphs 1221 to 1240); and
 (b) the preferring of one creditor (or more than one) by paying to him the whole or part of his debt, or otherwise treating him more favourably than other creditors of like degree; for example, by providing security or further security for an existing debt, or by returning goods which have been delivered but not paid for, to the detriment of the general body of creditors (see paragraphs 1241 to 1277).

1209. The statutory provisions dealing with such transactions are ... directed towards achieving a *pari passu* distribution of the bankrupt's estate among his creditors. The justification for setting aside a disposition of the bankrupt's assets made shortly before his bankruptcy is that, by depleting his estate, it unfairly prejudices his creditors; and even where the disposition is in satisfaction of a debt lawfully owing by the bankrupt, by altering the distribution of his estate it makes a *pari passu* distribution among all the creditors impossible....

Gifts and other voluntary dispositions

1221. The purpose of s. 42 of the [Bankruptcy] Act of 1914 is to prevent assets from being put in the hands of the debtor's family or associates in order to preserve them from the claims of creditors....

One suggestion for reform: 'pooling' spouses' assets

1228. We have received numerous complaints that property to which the creditors might have expected to have recourse is often unavailable to them in a bankruptcy, because it is found to be held in the name of the bankrupt's wife under a title unassailable in the bankruptcy or because the business with which they have been dealing as if it were the business of the bankrupt is, in law, carried on in his wife's name. One solution which has been proposed to us is that when a trader or other person carrying on business is made bankrupt, all the assets of his or her spouse should be pooled with his or her own and made available to meet the creditor's claims, in so far as they relate to that trade or business.

1229. We reject this proposal as an unjustified interference with individual property rights, which would produce an unfair result in many cases, and which in many respects would be a reversion to outmoded concepts of matrimonial property which have long since been abandoned....

Our preferred solution: 'connected persons'

1230. This is not, however, to say that husband and wife, or persons living together as man and wife, or other closely connected persons, should in the insolvency of one of them be treated in all respects as if they were unrelated parties dealing with each other at arm's length. Special relationships call for special provision to be made. In this chapter we shall include a number of proposals designed to make it easier for assets to be recovered from persons and companies which are closely connected with the debtor.... We have set out in ch. 21 our suggested definition of 'connected persons', to which reference should be made where necessary.

Our proposals for reform

1231. We propose that s. 42 of the Act of 1914 be repealed and replaced by an entirely new section, drafted in modern language, applicable equally whether the debtor is a man or woman, and referring, not to 'settlements of property', but to 'gifts or other voluntary dispositions of money or property'....

Fraudulent preferences

1241. As has already been pointed out, the payment of a debt lawfully due, even if made by a debtor in contemplation of his impending bankruptcy, and with the deliberate intention of preferring the creditor to whom the payment is made over his other creditors, is neither illegal nor fraudulent. Where, however, the expected bankruptcy supervenes shortly afterwards, such a payment has the effect of preventing the proper distribution of the bankrupt's estate *pari passu* among the creditors.

1242. It was, therefore, natural that, even in the absence of any provision to this effect made by statute, the judges of the bankruptcy courts should have evolved a doctrine by which such payments could be recovered by the trustee for the benefit of the general body of creditors. The doctrine which they developed, and which was later given statutory form, was concerned with what has become generally known as 'fraudulent preference'....

1248. The [Bankruptcy] Act of 1869, however, introduced for the first time, as a prerequisite for establishing a voidable preference, proof that the payment or transfer was made 'with a view of giving the creditor a preference over the other creditors'. This was probably not intended to represent a departure from the law as previously established by the bankruptcy courts. Nevertheless, since 1869 the critical question in determining whether a payment by a debtor to a creditor constitutes a voidable preference has been whether the debtor made the payment *with the dominant intention* of preferring the creditor. The burden of establishing the presence of the necessary intention is on the trustee or liquidator.

1249. There is no doubt that this gives rise to a difficult and unsatisfactory inquiry. It has been represented to us that the present law makes it too difficult for recovery to be obtained in any but the clearest cases. This is largely because of the difficulty in discharging the burden of proving that the debtor, or in the case of a corporate debtor its directors, had the necessary intention, and that such intention was paramount. Various proposals have been put forward to remedy this, including reversing the burden of proof, and introducing a short period of 'absolute recovery'.

1250. In Australia, a more radical solution has been adopted, by dispensing altogether with the need to establish an intention to prefer. Under s. 122 of the Australian Bankruptcy Act 1963, enacted in consequence of the Clyne Report, the test is no longer whether the debtor made the payment *with a view to giving* a preference to the creditor, but whether the payment *had the effect* of giving a preference to the creditor....

1255. It should be observed that, whichever test is adopted, payments made in the ordinary course of business and without pressure on the part of the creditor would continue to be irrecoverable. The principal difference between the two tests lies in their approach to the creditor who, suspecting that the debtor is or may be insolvent, brings pressure to obtain payment. Such payments have never been recoverable in England; before 1869, because they were not 'voluntary', and after 1869, because, unless the pressure was not real but collusive, it negatived any intention on the part of the debtor to prefer.

1256. The majority of the Committee have therefore reached the conclusion that the requirement of an intention to prefer should be retained, and that genuine pressure by the creditor should continue to afford a defence....

1257. The whole Committee, however, is satisfied that, in the present state of the law, the task which faces the trustee or liquidator is too difficult, and that in consequence many payments which ought in fairness to be recovered are not challenged. We believe that the best solution to this problem is to reverse the burden of proof, at least in those cases where the debtor and creditor were not at arm's length.

INSOLVENCY ACT 1986, SS. 238 AND 239

238. Transactions at an undervalue (England and Wales)

(1) This section applies in the case of a company where—
    (a) the company enters administration, or
    (b) the company goes into liquidation;
    and 'the office-holder' means the administrator or the liquidator, as the case may be.
(2) Where the company has at a relevant time (defined in section 240) entered into a transaction with any person at an undervalue, the office-holder may apply to the court for an order under this section.
(3) Subject as follows, the court shall, on such an application, make such order as it thinks fit for restoring the position to what it would have been if the company had not entered into that transaction.
(4) For the purposes of this section and section 241, a company enters into a transaction with a person at an undervalue if—
    (a) the company makes a gift to that person or otherwise enters into a transaction with that person on terms that provide for the company to receive no consideration; or
    (b) the company enters into a transaction with that person for a consideration the value of which, in money or money's worth, is significantly less than the value, in money or money's worth, of the consideration provided by the company.

(5) The court shall not make an order under this section in respect of a transaction at an under-value if it is satisfied—

    (a) that the company which entered into the transaction did so in good faith and for the purpose of carrying on its business; and

    (b) that at the time it did so there were reasonable grounds for believing that the transaction would benefit the company.

239. Preferences (England and Wales)

(1) This section applies as does section 238.

(2) Where the company has at a relevant time (defined in the next section) given a preference to any person, the office-holder may apply to the court for an order under this section.

(3) Subject as follows, the court shall, on such an application, make such order as it thinks fit for restoring the position to what it would have been if the company had not given that preference.

(4) For the purposes of this section and section 241, a company gives a preference to a person if—

    (a) that person is one of the company's creditors or a surety or guarantor for any of the company's debts or other liabilities; and

    (b) the company does anything or suffers anything to be done which (in either case) has the effect of putting that person into a position which, in the event of the company going into insolvent liquidation, will be better than the position he would have been in if that thing had not been done.

(5) The court shall not make an order under this section in respect of a preference given to any person unless the company which gave the preference was influenced in deciding to give it by a desire to produce in relation to that person the effect mentioned in subsection (4)(b).

(6) A company which has given a preference to a person connected with the company (otherwise than by reason only of being its employee) at the time the preference was given is presumed, unless the contrary is shown, to have been influenced in deciding to give it by such a desire as is mentioned in subsection (5).

(7) The fact that something has been done in pursuance of the order of a court does not, without more, prevent the doing or suffering of that thing from constituting the giving of a preference.

NOTE: See also s. 240 which defines 'relevant time' for the purposes of ss. 238 and 239. Section 241 deals with orders under ss. 238 and 239. Section 241 was extensively amended by the Insolvency (No. 2) Act 1994 to ensure that subsequent purchasers in good faith and for value are not prejudiced by an earlier transaction at an undervalue or preference. The legislation had previously caused considerable problems for conveyancers as an earlier transaction could be brought into question by a liquidator within the 'relevant time', thus constituting a potential defect in title for the subsequent purchaser. The only form of protection for purchasers was title insurance. In view of the expense and inconvenience the Law Society promoted the amendment as a private members' Bill which was enacted and came into force on 26 July 1994.

Vanessa Finch, 'Directors' duties: insolvency and the unsecured creditor'
Current Issues in Insolvency Law (London: Stevens, 1991)

… What does the Insolvency Act 1986 et al. offer the unsecured creditor? Initially, he can be directed to those sections of the legislation aimed at preventing directors from diminishing the company's assets in ways which prejudice the company's general creditors and unfairly favour another party. (These sections are usually referred to as the 'avoidance provisions.') In fact these statutory attempts to preserve the corporate pool of assets can be seen as the positive side of the *pari passu* principle from the unsecured creditor's point of view. Thus there are the new provisions dealing with the setting aside of preferences and transactions at undervalue.

A 'preference' under s. 239 of the Insolvency Act 1986 occurs where a company does anything which puts a creditor in a better position than he would have been on the insolvent liquidation of the company, and the company in carrying out the act was 'influenced by a desire' to put the creditor in a more favourable position. Unless the transaction involved a 'connected person' it can only be challenged by an administrator or liquidator if it is within six months of 'the onset of insolvency'. Accepting that the 'company' here in practice means the directors, unsecured creditors can interpret s. 239 as a means of ensuring their equal treatment *by directors*. This is effectively what is important for the purposes of the section. It is not the fact of a creditor *receiving* a preference that matters, nor is the receiving creditor's knowledge a factor. The section focuses on the debtor director's *desire* to prefer.

Section 238 of the Insolvency Act 1986 (transactions at an undervalue) can also be seen to be concerned with policing directors' actions and protecting creditors against directorial misbehaviour, and, indeed, many transactions falling within s. 238 will also be vulnerable as preferences under s. 239. The transaction at undervalue section protects creditors by precluding third parties from benefiting at their expense by receiving in a two-year period prior to the company's insolvency, the company's assets for no or an inadequate consideration. The commercial basis of the directors' decision will in effect be examined by the court: for the transaction to be saved, the court will have to be convinced that the transaction was a genuine one, entered into in good faith for the purposes of the company's business *and* that at the time there were reasonable grounds for believing the transaction would benefit the company (s. 238(5)).

The advantage of this new power from the unsecured creditor's point of view is that now the question of balancing the interests of unpaid creditors against those who have received gratuitous dispositions from the company (directors) is considered directly, rather than indirectly as formerly via the *ultra vires* doctrine or breach of directors' fiduciary duty.... Unsecured creditors, however, still have to rely on the liquidator or administrator to enforce the section.

An alternative provision, focusing on the same definition of transactions at undervalue, could provide direct assistance for unsecured creditors. That is the revised s. 423 of the Insolvency Act 1986 relating to undervalue transactions entered into by the company (directors) for the purpose of putting the assets beyond the reach of a claimant or otherwise prejudicing a claimant (s. 423(3)). This section is of potent interest to individual creditors in that there is no time limit applicable, no prerequisite of winding up/administration, and the court has the power under s. 423(2) to order reimbursement to the particular party prejudiced.

The avoidance provisions in the 1986 Act are not the only statutory means of ensuring certain directorial standards towards unsecured creditors. As mentioned previously, both the Cork Report and the white paper believed that an improvement in the unsecured creditors' position could be achieved by extending and toughening up provisions on directors' personal liability and on their disqualification. Thus, it is on the resulting 1986 legislation that hopes of upgrading directors' duties of skill and care are pinned. The notoriously lax standard of prudence, *care* and *skill* demanded by the courts had evolved largely based on the argument that if shareholders chose incompetent amateurs to run their businesses, the judges would not intervene. From the unsecured creditors' point of view, however, this indulgence was hardly satisfactory. Directors whose negligence and incompetence had brought insolvency on their companies but who were nevertheless honest, were rarely held to account.

Now however there are wider grounds for disqualifying delinquent directors under the Company Directors Disqualification Act 1986. For example, directors' duties to file returns and accounts and give notices under the companies legislation have been backed up with discretionary disqualification for persistent failure, at least bolstering unsecured creditors' confidence with regard to such returns.

The most significant provision from the unsecured creditors' perspective must, however, be s. 6 of the Company Directors Disqualification Act which *requires* disqualification on the application of the Secretary of State in the case of a director whose company has become insolvent and whose conduct makes him unfit to manage.

Re MC Bacon Ltd
Whether a floating charge was a preference or a transaction at an undervalue
[1990] BCLC 324, Chancery Division

Facts   Mr Glover, Mr Creal and his son, Martin were directors of the company which imported bacon. When the company's main customer withdrew its business, Mr Creal and Mr Glover (who was 22.5 stone and suffered from arthritis and could no longer do the manual work required of a director in such a company) both decided to retire. The bank then became nervous and demanded a debenture to secure by way of floating charge the company's overdraft which was unsecured. In granting this the directors knew that the company was in financial difficulty and probably could not survive without continued support from the bank. The company went into liquidation and the bank appointed an administrative receiver under the debenture. The liquidator applied unsuccessfully to have the debenture (and hence the floating charge and administrative receivership) set aside as a voidable preference under s. 239 or as a transaction at an undervalue under s. 238. The court concluded that the company had issued the debenture, not with the intention to prefer the bank but to save its hide. The granting of the debenture was not a gift and it did receive a consideration for it. Hence the transaction fell within neither section.

MILLETT J: So far as I am aware, this is the first case under [IA 1986, s. 239] and its meaning has been the subject of some debate before me. I shall therefore attempt to provide some guidance.

The section replaces s. 44(1) of the Bankruptcy Act 1914, which in certain circumstances deemed fraudulent and avoided payments made and other transactions entered into in favour of a creditor 'with a view of giving such creditor . . . a preference over the other creditors'. Section 44(1) and its predecessors had been construed by the courts as requiring the person seeking to avoid the payment or other transaction to establish that it had been made 'with the dominant intention to prefer' the creditor.

Section 44(1) has been replaced and its language has been entirely recast. Every single word of significance, whether in the form of statutory definition or in its judicial exposition, has been jettisoned. 'View', 'dominant', 'intention' and even 'to prefer' have all been discarded. These are replaced by 'influenced', 'desire', and 'to produce in relation to that person the effect mentioned in subsection (4)(b)'.

I therefore emphatically protest against the citation of cases decided under the old law. They cannot be of any assistance when the language of the statute has been so completely and deliberately changed. It may be that many of the cases which will come before the courts in future will be decided in the same way that they would have been decided under the old law. That may be so, but the grounds of decision will be different. What the court has to do is to interpret the language of the statute and apply it. It will no longer inquire whether there was 'a dominant intention to prefer' the creditor, but whether the company's decision was 'influenced by a desire to produce the effect mentioned in subsection (4)(b)'.

This is a completely different test. It involves at least two radical departures from the old law. It is no longer necessary to establish a *dominant* intention to prefer. It is sufficient that the decision was *influenced* by the requisite desire. That is the first change. The second is that it is no longer sufficient to establish an *intention* to prefer. There must be a *desire* to produce the effect mentioned in the subsection.

This second change is made necessary by the first, for without it it would be virtually impossible to uphold the validity of a security taken in exchange for the injection of fresh funds into a company in financial difficulties. A man is taken to intend the necessary consequences of his actions, so that an intention to grant a security to a creditor necessarily involves an intention to prefer that creditor in the event of insolvency. The need to establish that such intention was dominant was essential under the old law to prevent perfectly proper transactions from being struck down. With the abolition of that requirement intention could not remain the relevant test. Desire has been substituted. That is a very different matter. Intention is objective, desire is subjective. A man can choose the lesser of two evils without desiring either.

It is not, however, sufficient to establish a desire to make the payment or grant the security which it is sought to avoid. There must have been a desire to produce the effect mentioned in the subsection, that is to say, to improve the creditor's position in the event of an insolvent liquidation. A man is not to be taken as *desiring* all the necessary consequences of his actions. Some consequences may be of advantage to him and be desired by him; others may not affect him and be matters of indifference to him; while still others may be positively disadvantageous to him and not be desired by him, but be regarded by him as the unavoidable price of obtaining the desired advantages. It will still be possible to provide assistance to a company in financial difficulties provided that the company is actuated only by proper commercial considerations. Under the new regime a transaction will not be set aside as a voidable preference unless the company positively wished to improve the creditor's position in the event of its own insolvent liquidation.

There is, of course, no need for there to be direct evidence of the requisite desire. Its existence may be inferred from the circumstances of the case just as the dominant intention could be inferred under the old law. But the mere presence of the requisite desire will not be sufficient by itself. It must have influenced the decision to enter into the transaction. It was submitted on behalf of the bank that it must have been the factor which 'tipped the scales'. I disagree. That is not what subs. (5) says; it requires only that the desire should have influenced the decision. That requirement is satisfied if it was one of the factors which operated on the minds of those who made the decision. It need not have been the only factor or even the decisive one. In my judgment, it is not necessary to prove that, if the requisite desire had not been present, the company would not have entered into the transaction. That would be too high a test.

It was also submitted that the relevant time was the time when the debenture was created. That cannot be right. The relevant time was the time when the decision to grant it was made.... But it does not matter. If the requisite desire was operating at all, it was operating throughout....

I am satisfied that throughout the period from 15 April to 29 May Mr Glover, Mr Creal and Martin knew (i) that the company was probably insolvent and might not be able to avoid an insolvent liquidation; (ii) that its continuing to trade was entirely dependent on the continued support of the bank; (iii) that if the debenture which Mr Hill [the bank manager] had asked for were not forthcoming the bank would withdraw its support; and (iv) that if the bank withdrew its support the company would be forced into immediate liquidation. I am also satisfied that they had decided to continue trading in a genuine belief that the company could be pulled round. It follows that they had no choice but to accede to the bank's request for a debenture. I accept Martin's evidence: 'It was viewed as a simple decision. Either we gave the bank a debenture or they called in the overdraft.'

That sufficiently explains the decision to grant the debenture and there is no justification for inferring any other reason. There is no evidence that either Martin or Mr Creal wanted to improve the bank's position in the event of an insolvent liquidation and there is no reason why they should. I find as a fact that in deciding to grant the debenture to the bank neither of them was motivated by any desire except the desire to avoid the calling in of the overdraft and to continue trading....

Conclusion   I dismiss the applicant's claim to set the debenture aside as a voidable preference.

3 Transaction at an undervalue   Section 238 of the 1986 Act is concerned with the depletion of a company's assets by transactions at an undervalue. Section 238(4) of the Act defines a transaction at an undervalue ...

The granting of the debenture was not a gift, nor was it without consideration. The consideration consisted of the bank's forbearance from calling in the overdraft and its honouring of cheques and making of fresh advances to the company during the continuance of the facility. The applicant relies therefore on para. (b).

To come within that paragraph the transaction must be (i) entered into by the company; (ii) for a consideration; (iii) the value of which measured in money or money's worth; (iv) is significantly less than the value; (v) also measured in money or money's worth; (vi) of the consideration provided by the company. It requires a comparison to be made between the value obtained by the company for the transaction and the value of consideration provided by the company. Both values must be measurable in money or money's worth and both must be considered from the company's point of view.

In my judgment, the applicant's claim to characterise the granting of the bank's debenture as a transaction at an undervalue is misconceived. The mere creation of a security over a company's assets does not deplete them and does not come within the paragraph. By charging its assets the company appropriates them to meet the liabilities due to the secured creditor and adversely affects the rights of other creditors in the event of insolvency. But it does not deplete its assets or diminish their value. It retains the right to redeem and the right to sell or remortgage the charged assets. All it loses is the ability to apply the proceeds otherwise than in satisfaction of the secured debt. That is not something capable of valuation in monetary terms and is not customarily disposed of for value.

In the present case the company did not suffer that loss by reason of the grant of the debenture. Once the bank had demanded a debenture the company could not have sold or charged its assets without applying the proceeds in reduction of the overdraft; had it attempted to do so, the bank would at once have called in the overdraft. By granting the debenture the company parted with nothing of value, and the value of the consideration which it received in return was incapable of being measured in money or money's worth.

Counsel for the applicant (Mr Vos) submitted that the consideration which the company received was, with hindsight, of no value. It merely gained time and with it the opportunity to lose more money. But he could not and did not claim that the company ought to have received a fee or other capital sum in return for the debenture. That gives the game away. The applicant's real complaint is not that the company entered into the transaction at an undervalue but that it entered into it at all.

In my judgment, the transaction does not fall within subs. (4), and it is unnecessary to consider the application of subs. (5) which provides a defence to the claim in certain circumstances.

4 Conclusion In my judgment, the granting of the debenture to the bank was neither a voidable preference nor a transaction at an undervalue and I dismiss the application.

20.12 FRAUDULENT AND WRONGFUL TRADING

The provisions on fraudulent and wrongful trading were enacted to prevent the abuse of limited liability by those running companies. The concern is that directors may continue to trade and incur further debts at a time when the company is in financial difficulty with the result that losses to creditors are increased. Fraudulent trading, introduced in 1929 and now found in IA 1986, s. 213, requires a dishonest 'intent to defraud creditors'. A liquidator may apply to the court for a declaration that those who were party to the fraudulent trading make a contribution to the assets of the company, i.e., partially lose their limited liability. By CA 2006, s. 993, fraudulent trading is also made a criminal offence. The heavy onus of proving dishonesty prompted the Cork Committee to recommend the new provisions for wrongful trading. The result is IA 1986, s. 214, which follows the philosophy of Cork but in some respects is stricter than the Report's proposal. The section enables the liquidator to obtain a court order that directors contribute to the assets of the company, i.e., to compensate creditors generally for the loss caused by their wrongful trading. There is no need to prove dishonesty. The liquidator must point to a moment in time (the 'point of no return') when the director 'knew or ought to have concluded that there was no reasonable prospect that the company would avoid going into insolvent liquidation' (s. 214(2)(b)). The director's obligation to predict insolvency is judged both subjectively according to the knowledge, skill and experience the director actually has, or objectively according to those qualities that he ought to possess for the position he holds in that company. This latter element most strikingly imposes (prior to insolvency at the point of no return) an objective duty not to increase creditors' losses. From this moment the director, under s. 214(3), must take 'every step' to minimise losses to creditors if he is to avoid potential personal liability.

The following readings are first, extracts from the Cork Report criticising the old fraudulent trading provision (CA 1948, s. 332) and setting out the philosophy of its wrongful trading proposals; secondly s. 213 and most of s. 214; and thirdly extracts from two articles describing the novel aspects of s. 214 but questioning whether it has had the practical impact that the Cork Committee had hoped for. Finally there follows a selection of cases on ss. 213 and 214.

Insolvency Law and Practice: Report of the Review Committee (The 'Cork Report')

(Cmnd 8558) (London: HMSO, 1982)

Fraudulent trading

1758. The concept of fraudulent trading was introduced in the Act of 1929 by way of an experiment.... It imposes both a civil and a criminal responsibility on any persons who have knowingly been parties to the carrying on of a company's business with intent to defraud creditors of the company or creditors of any other person or for any fraudulent purpose. The Jenkins Committee recommended an expansion of these provisions to include directors who could be shown to have acted 'recklessly or incompetently' in relation to the affairs of a company, but those proposals have never been implemented.

1759. The structure and detailed provisions of s. 332 [of CA 1948] have been the subject of widespread criticism. The main complaints are, first, that by its intermixture of criminal with civil liability, it imposes upon a liquidator, in any civil proceedings, an unduly stringent burden of proof in relation to the ingredient of fraud and, secondly, that its ambit is confined to situations where the company is in liquidation. It is also a common experience to find that the liquidator is inhibited from commencing civil proceedings, by the imminence or currency of criminal proceedings against the same defendants based on the same evidence....

Inadequacies of the present law

1776. Section 332 not only creates a civil and personal liability, it also creates a criminal offence. The constituent elements of the two are identical. As a result the courts have consistently refused to entertain a claim to civil liability in the absence of dishonesty and, moreover, have insisted upon a strict standard of proof. It is the general experience of those concerned with the administration of the affairs of insolvent companies that the difficulty of establishing dishonesty has deterred the issue of proceedings in many cases where a strong case has existed for recovering compensation from the directors or others involved.

1777. It is right that it should be an offence to carry on a business dishonestly; and right that, in the absence of dishonesty, no offence should be committed. Where, however, what is in question is not the punishment of an offender, but the provision of a civil remedy for those who have suffered financial loss, a requirement that dishonesty be proved is inappropriate. Compensation ought, in our view to be available to those who suffer foreseeable loss as a result, not only of fraudulent, but also of unreasonable, behaviour....

1783. Our proposals substitute an objective test. It will constitute wrongful trading for a company to incur liabilities with no reasonable prospect of meeting them; and a director will be personally liable for its debts if, being party to the company's trading, he knows or ought to have known that such trading was wrongful. In determining whether there was a reasonable prospect of the company meeting its liabilities and, if not, whether the director ought to have known this, the test will be objective, and the standard to be applied will be that of the ordinary, reasonable man....

1786. We recommend that if the directors at any time consider the company to be insolvent, they should have a duty to take immediate steps for the company to be placed in receivership, administration or liquidation. Failure to do so will normally expose any director who is party to the company's continued trading to civil liability....

The justification for the new concept

1805. A balance has to be struck. No one wishes to discourage the inception and growth of businesses, although both are unavoidably attended by risks to creditors. Equally a climate should exist in which downright irresponsibility is discouraged and in which those who abuse the privilege of limited liability can be made personally liable for the consequences of their conduct. We believe that our proposals in this chapter strike a fair balance between those two conflicting needs.We regard them as of the greatest importance, and their implementation as a matter of urgent necessity.

INSOLVENCY ACT 1986, SS. 213 AND 214

213. Fraudulent trading

(1) If in the course of the winding up of a company it appears that any business of the company has been carried on with intent to defraud creditors of the company or creditors of any other person, or for any fraudulent purpose, the following has effect.

(2) The court, on the application of the liquidator may declare that any persons who were knowingly parties to the carrying on of the business in the manner above-mentioned are to be liable to make such contributions (if any) to the company's assets as the court thinks proper.

214. Wrongful trading

(1) Subject to subsection (3) below, if in the course of the winding up of a company it appears that subsection (2) of this section applies in relation to a person who is or has been a director of the company, the court, on the application of the liquidator, may declare that that person is to be liable to make such contribution (if any) to the company's assets as the court thinks proper.

(2) This subsection applies in relation to a person if—

(a) the company has gone into insolvent liquidation;

(b) at some time before the commencement of the winding up of the company, that person knew or ought to have concluded that there was no reasonable prospect that the company would avoid going into insolvent liquidation; and

(c) that person was a director of the company at that time;

but the court shall not make a declaration under this section in any case where the time mentioned in paragraph (b) above was before 28th April 1986.

(3) The court shall not make a declaration under this section with respect to any person if it is satisfied that after the condition specified in subsection (2)(b) was first satisfied in relation to him that person took every step with a view to minimising the potential loss to the company's creditors as (assuming him to have known that there was no reasonable prospect that the company would avoid going into insolvent liquidation) he ought to have taken.

(4) For the purposes of subsections (2) and (3), the facts which a director of a company ought to know or ascertain, the conclusions which he ought to reach and the steps which he ought to take are those which would be known or ascertained, or reached or taken, by a reasonably diligent person having both—

(a) the general knowledge, skill and experience that may reasonably be expected of a person carrying out the same functions as are carried out by that director in relation to the company; and

(b) the general knowledge, skill and experience that that director has.

Andrew Hicks, 'Advising on wrongful trading'

(1993) 14 Co Law 16

An accessible remedy?   A leading academic has written that enactment of s. 214 of the Insolvency Act 1986, which introduced wrongful trading, has greatly altered the topography of company law. Significantly eroding the principle of limited liability, it 'is unquestionably one of the most important developments in company law this century' (D.D. Prentice, 'Creditor's interests and director's duties' (1990) 10 Oxford J Legal Stud 265 at p. 277).

These comments are undoubtedly true, though the precise impact is yet to be seen in practice. Wrongful trading is a far sharper weapon in the hands of the liquidator than the earlier provision for fraudulent trading. To prove fraudulent trading it is necessary to prove a fraudulent intent on the part of the director: that they continued to trade when they actually knew there was no reasonable prospect of the debts being paid. As the fraudulent trading provision remains in force, liquidators may still make a parallel claim in fraudulent trading in the hope of a punitive order, which does not appear to be available for wrongful trading. But the easier burden of proof for wrongful trading, outlined below, makes it a very much more accessible remedy on behalf of ordinary creditors than has been available before.

Directors and their advisers have long been aware of the risks of fraudulent trading. The precise impact on companies in difficulty will depend on general awareness of the new remedy and its effect. Whether it is proving to be a powerful weapon for ordinary creditors also depends on the advice liquidators receive and their determination to press claims.

Liquidators may readily decide not to bring claims unless the sums involved are high. Evidence may be difficult and expensive to collect. Proving that the directors should have predicted insolvency, except in extreme cases, may be hit and miss.

Directors of companies in financial difficulty are often in financial difficulty themselves, so it may not be worth obtaining an order against them. Orders may be difficult to enforce. Despite the prospect of an order for costs against the directors if successful, the amount of the liquidator's costs put at risk in pursuing a claim may be thought to be an unjustifiable risk to ordinary creditors' funds. All these things may deter a liquidator from making a wrongful trading claim except in the clearest case of irresponsibility, where the directors are financially substantial and the sums involved justify the costs. Further, banks holding floating charges may also be the beneficiary, as an order requires a contribution to the company's assets which in turn are subject to the security.

All these factors discourage wrongful trading claims, and may limit the impact of wrongful trading envisaged by the writer quoted above.

The new objective standard   Company law has traditionally been indulgent with directors in the standards of competence expected of them. If the members appoint a second-rate board, then they cannot demand a high standard of management from those directors. In the interest of creditors, however, wrongful trading now imposes a minimum objective standard on directors.

Section 214 says that a person who is or has been a director of a company which goes into insolvent liquidation may be ordered to contribute to the company's assets if at a time he was a director he 'knew or ought to have concluded that there was no reasonable prospect that the company would avoid going into insolvent liquidation'. Most remarkable is that by s. 214(4) what a director knew or ought to have concluded is not only what a reasonably diligent person should have known or concluded on the basis of his own subjective knowledge, skill and experience. An objective standard is also required of him according to 'the general knowledge, skill and experience that may reasonably be expected of a person carrying out the same functions as are carried out by that director in relation to the company'. Directors are judged by the higher of two standards measured either objectively according to the job or subjectively according to the person.

The recent first-instance decision of *Re Produce Marketing Consortium Ltd (No. 2)* [1989] BCLC 520 confirms that in this respect it is necessary to have regard to the particular company and its business. The qualities required will 'be much less extensive in a small company in a modest way of business, with simple accounting procedures and equipment, than it will be in a large company with sophisticated procedures' (at p. 550).

As Knox J pointed out, the Companies Act 1985 requires accounting records to be kept which disclose with reasonable accuracy at any time the financial position of the company. It may not be enough for a director to plead ignorance of accounting facts or figures if with reasonable diligence and an appropriate level of skill, he ought to have ascertained them. Thus, knowledge of disastrous financial results for the end of a particular year, which were in fact late and not yet available, was imputed to the directors. The directors were accordingly held liable for depletion of the company's assets as from the time they should have received these figures.

Directors, therefore, must not only live up to the subjective standard expected in the light of their own qualification. They must also comply with such an objective standard as is appropriate for their position in the particular company that has failed, if the latter standard is more stringent than the former.

Andrew Hicks, 'Wrongful trading—has it been a failure?'
(1993) 8 Ins L & P 134

How much is the remedy used?   Wrongful trading has a high profile. It is well-known by professional advisers who extensively use it to scare their director clients. However it may come to be seen by directors as a paper tiger.

Liquidators' formal procedures generally require the possibility of a claim to be considered and cleared off in each liquidation. In more than half of liquidations, respondents [to a survey of insolvency practitioners conducted by the author] reported actively considering a possible claim. In less than half of these some action was taken, generally negotiating for a settlement. A useful minority of these negotiations resulted in directors agreeing to make a contribution to the assets. Writs are being issued in a significant number of cases and one solicitor in the Midlands reported six current cases. Occasional contribution orders are obtained. However, as one would have guessed, the actual benefit to creditors of contributions from directors is thus very limited. Nonetheless claims are succeeding or being settled from time to time. Whether claims are successful against mere incompetents as well as against idiots and rogues can only be a matter for speculation....

It now has to be considered whether the other, and perhaps more important objective of the Cork Report has been achieved, namely improving responsible practice when insolvency is threatened....

The research suggests that wrongful trading could not have been expected to resolve the problem of directors abusing the privilege of limited liability to the detriment of creditors. However in the light of these limited expectations, in general s. 214 works well. A small but significant number of claims are being pressed against errant directors. The fact that in global terms, little is recovered on behalf of creditors does not condemn the section as a failure. The preventative influence of wrongful trading in improving responsible practice when insolvency is threatened seems to be valuable. Though it is an undramatic and unquantifiable benefit, it should be recognised and welcomed. As an additional comment it should be added that any more Draconian provisions imposing more extensive liability would ask for the premature closure of businesses and inhibit rescues. Economic activity and employees have to be considered as well as creditors. The policy objective of stressing obligations to creditors without over-penalising directors and leading to premature closures is probably appropriately balanced.

NOTE: SOME RECENT REFORMS

Liquidators considering an action on behalf of the company in liquidation against wrongdoing directors, such as on grounds of wrongful trading, have two primary problems to consider. First, whose approval for the action should they obtain, and secondly, how should the costs of the action be funded. Ordinary creditors may be aggrieved that suing the directors without their consent could be a total waste of what little money remains available to pay their debts. Very often there is no money left at all so no action is brought and the directors get off scot free.

The Enterprise Act 2002 s. 252 now 'ring-fences' a part of the company's net property available for the satisfaction of unsecured debts (see 15.4.1), which could thus potentially be made available to fund an action against the directors. Section 253 requires that the liquidator obtains the approval of the court or the liquidation committee (a committee of creditors) before an action is brought against directors. These detailed provisions represent a further attempt to fine-tune the law to make directors of failed companies more accountable to its creditors.

Re Produce Marketing Consortium Ltd (No. 2)

The first wrongful trading case

[1989] BCLC 520, Chancery Division

This is the first of the handful of cases so far reported on wrongful trading.

Facts Mr David and Mr Murphy were directors of the company which imported fruit. The company acted as agent, charging the exporters commission on the gross sale price of fruit imported. From 1981 the company traded at a loss, its position gradually and predictably worsening. Statutory accounts were not delivered in time. Mr Tough, the auditor, warned of the possibility of fraudulent or wrongful trading. The liquidator applied for a contribution order against the directors. The case appears to be an obvious example of wrongful trading, but nonetheless went to a nine-day hearing in the Chancery Division. Whether the liquidator recovered the £75,000 awarded or his costs and those of his solicitors, his QC and junior, and whether the creditors ultimately benefited is not of course recorded. The directors earning about £12,000 and £14,000 a year hardly seem worthwhile defendants. (For the significance of 27 April 1986 mentioned in the first few lines of the judgment see s. 214(2)(c).)

KNOX J: The first question is whether it appears that subs. (2) applies to Mr David and Mr Murphy. There is no question but that they were directors at all material times and that PMC has gone into insolvent liquidation. The issue is whether at some time after 27 April 1986 and before 2 October 1987, when it went into insolvent liquidation, they knew or ought to have concluded that there was no reasonable prospect that PMC would avoid going into insolvent liquidation. It was inevitably conceded by counsel for the first respondent that this question has to be answered by the standards postulated by subs. (4), so that the facts which Mr David and Mr Murphy ought to have known or ascertained and the conclusions that they ought to have reached are not limited to those which they themselves showing reasonable diligence and having the general knowledge, skill and experience which they respectively had, would have known, ascertained or reached but also those that a person with the general knowledge, skill and experience of someone carrying out their functions would have known, ascertained or reached.

This was a new provision in the Insolvency Act 1985, s. 15. It contrasts with s. 213 of the 1986 Act in relation to fraudulent trading....

Two steps in particular were taken in the legislative enlargement of the court's jurisdiction. First, the requirement for an intent to defraud and fraudulent purpose was not retained as an essential, and with it goes what Maugham J [in *Re Patrick & Lyon Ltd* [1933] Ch 786] called 'the need for actual dishonesty involving real moral blame'.

I pause here to observe that at no stage before me has it been suggested that either Mr David or Mr Murphy fell into this category.

The second enlargement is that the test to be applied by the court has become one under which the director in question is to be judged by the standards of what can reasonably be expected of a person fulfilling his functions, and showing reasonable diligence in doing so. I accept the submission of counsel for the first respondent in this connection, that the requirement to have regard to the functions to be carried out by the director in question, in relation to the company in question, involves having regard to the particular company and its business. It follows that the general knowledge, skill and experience postulated will be much less extensive in a small company in a modest way of business, with simple accounting procedures and equipment, than it will be in a large company with sophisticated procedures.

Nevertheless, certain minimum standards are to be assumed to be attained. Notably there is an obligation laid on companies to cause accounting records to be kept which are such as to disclose with reasonable accuracy *at any time* the financial position of the company at that time: see the Companies Act 1985, s. 221(1) and (2)(a) [as originally enacted; see now s. 221(1)(a)]. . . .

The knowledge to be imputed in testing whether or not directors knew or ought to have concluded that there was no reasonable prospect of the company avoiding insolvent liquidation is not limited to the documentary material actually available at the given time. This appears from s. 214(4) which includes a reference to facts which a director of a company ought not only to know but those which he ought to ascertain, a word which does not appear in subs. (2)(b). In my judgment this indicates that there is to be included by way of factual information not only what was actually there but what, given reasonable diligence and an appropriate level of general knowledge, skill and experience, was ascertainable. This leads me to the conclusion in this case that I should assume, for the purposes of applying the test in s. 214(2), that the financial results for the year ending 30 September 1985 were known at the end of July 1986 at least to the extent of the size of the deficiency of assets over liabilities.

Mr David and Mr Murphy, although they did not have the accounts in their hands until January 1987, did, I find, know that the previous trading year had been a very bad one. They had a close and intimate knowledge of the business and they had a shrewd idea whether the turnover was up or down. In fact it was badly down in that year to £526,459 and although I have no doubt that they did not know in July 1986 that it was that precise figure, I have no doubt that they had a good rough idea of what it was and in particular that it was well down on the previous year. A major drop in turnover meant almost as night follows day that there was a substantial loss incurred, as indeed there was. That in turn meant again, as surely as night follows day, a substantial increase in the deficit of assets over liabilities.

That deals with their actual knowledge but in addition I have to have regard to what they have to be treated as having known or ascertained and that includes the actual deficit of assets over liabilities of £132,870. . . .

Counsel for the first respondent was not able to advance any particular calculation as constituting a basis for concluding that there was a prospect of insolvent liquidation being avoided. He is not to be criticised for that for in my judgment there was none available. Once the loss in the year ending 30 September 1985 was incurred PMC was in irreversible decline, assuming (as I must) that the respondents had no plans for altering the company's business and proposed to go on drawing the level of reasonable remuneration that they were currently receiving.

. . . Nor, in my judgment, do the facts that the bank was throughout willing to continue its facilities and that Mr Tough, although expressing the grave warnings that he did when the accounts for the years ending 30 September 1985 and 1986 were available to him, was willing to accompany Mr David and Mr Murphy to the bank in February 1987 to see if further facilities would be granted, detract from the conclusion I have reached that Mr David and Mr Murphy ought to have concluded at the end of July 1986 that there was no reasonable prospect that PMC would avoid going into insolvent liquidation. . . .

The next question which arises is whether there is a case under s. 214(3) for saying that after the end of July 1986 the respondents took every step with a view to minimising the potential loss to the creditors of PMC as, assuming them to have known that there was no reasonable prospect of PMC avoiding insolvent liquidation, they ought to have taken. This clearly has to be answered no, since they went on trading for another year.

In my judgment the jurisdiction under s. 214 is primarily compensatory rather than penal. Prima facie the appropriate amount that a director is declared to be liable to contribute is the amount by which the company's assets can be discerned to have been depleted by the director's conduct which caused the discretion under subs. (1) to arise. But Parliament has indeed chosen very wide words of discretion and it would be undesirable to seek to spell out limits on that discretion, more especially since this is, so far as counsel were aware, the first case to come to judgment under this section. The fact that there was no fraudulent intent is not of itself a reason for fixing the amount at a nominal or low figure, for that would amount to frustrating what I discern as Parliament's intention in adding s. 214 to s. 213 in the 1986 Act, but I am not persuaded that it is right to ignore that fact totally. . . .

Taking all these circumstances into account I propose to declare that Mr David and Mr Murphy are liable to make a contribution to the assets of PMC of £75,000.

Re Purpoint Ltd

A company condemned from day one?

[1991] BCC 121, Chancery Division

One of the key issues for wrongful trading is identifying the point of no return at which insolvent liquidation is as good as inevitable. At what precise moment in time should the reasonably competent director have predicted insolvency? This case considers the position where an undercapitalised company takes on an unprofitable business and so may seem likely to fail from the very start.

VINELOTT J: The first question is as to the date when Mr Meredith ought to have known that there was no reasonable prospect that the company could avoid going into insolvent liquidation. The latest date is 28 May 1987 when Mr Meredith was warned by Adamsons that if the company continued to trade he might be personally liable for its debts. Nothing that happened thereafter would have given any reasonable director ground for hoping that the company could avoid an insolvent liquidation.

I have felt some doubt whether a reasonably prudent director would have allowed the company to commence trading at all. It had no capital base. Its only assets were purchased by bank borrowing or acquired by hire-purchase. And its working capital was contributed by a loan from Mr Froome. The business it inherited from Winnersh Printing Services Ltd had proved unprofitable and with the winding up of that company the creditors, other than the Royal Bank of Scotland, were left with an empty shell. The new company assumed the additional burden of paying a salary to Mr Meredith. However, I do not think it would be right to conclude that Mr Meredith ought to have known that the company was doomed to end in an insolvent winding up from the moment it started to trade. That would, I think, impose too high a test. Mr Meredith believed that his connections in the advertising and publicity field would enable him to introduce new business and that the failure of the old company had been due not to any want of skill or organising ability on Mr Froome's part, but on his inability to attract custom. I cannot say that that was a belief that could not have been entertained by a reasonable and prudent director conscious of his duty to persons to whom the company would incur liabilities in the ordinary course of carrying on its business.

On the other hand, in my judgment, it should have been plain to Mr Meredith by the end of 1986 that the company could not avoid going into insolvent liquidation. The company could not meet its trade debts as they fell due. In addition it owed very large Crown debts and it had no prospect whatever that it could turn its trading into profit sufficiently quickly to pay them off. . . .

. . . The purpose [of a compensation order] is to recoup the loss to the company so as to benefit the creditors as a whole. The court has no jurisdiction to direct payment to creditors or to direct that moneys paid to the company should be applied in payment of one class of creditors in preference to another. Moreover, creditors whose debts are incurred after the critical date in fact have no stronger claim than those whose debts were incurred before that date. The former class also suffers to the extent that the assets of the company are depleted by wrongful trading.

R v Grantham

Intent in fraudulent trading

[1984] QB 675, Court of Appeal

This case concludes that intent to defraud under s. 213 is established on proof of an intention dishonestly to prejudice the creditors in receiving payment of their debts. It appears that it is not necessary to show that the accused knew at the time of incurring the debts that there was no reasonable prospect that they would ever be paid. (Note how the court expressed the question at issue in the certificate at the end of the judgment.)

Facts   Grantham was convicted of fraudulent trading and appealed unsuccessfully on grounds that the trial judge had wrongly directed the jury as to the necessary intent to prove the offence.

LORD LANE CJ: IThe passages in the summing up which are relevant to this ground of appeal are as follows:

As against the individual, the individual defendant, the prosecution have to prove first that he took an active part in carrying on the business. That is the first thing. They then have to prove that in doing so he had an intention to defraud creditors and thirdly they have to prove that he was acting dishonestly.... I go on to consider the position on the assumption that in respect of the man you are considering you answer that one in the affirmative, 'He was playing an active part'. The prosecution have then got to prove that he had an intent to defraud creditors and was acting dishonestly. Members of the jury, my direction, as a matter of law, to you with regard to what is meant by intent to defraud is this. A man intends to defraud a creditor either if he intends that the creditor shall never be paid or alternatively if he intends to obtain credit or carry on obtaining credit when the rights and interests of the creditor are being prejudiced in a way which the defendant himself knows is generally regarded as dishonest.... Some fraudulent traders intend from the outset never to pay or never to pay more than a fraction of the debt. If that is true in your view in this case then the intent to defraud would be made out but a trader can intend to defraud if he obtains credit when there is a substantial risk of the creditor not getting his money or not getting the whole of his money and the defendant knows that that is the position and knows he is stepping beyond the bounds of what ordinary decent people engaged in business would regard as honest.

Members of the jury, if a man honestly believes when he obtains credit that although funds are not immediately available he will be able to pay them when the debt becomes due or within a short time thereafter, no doubt you would say that is not dishonest and there is no intent to defraud but if he obtains or helps to obtain credit or further credit when he knows there is no good reason for thinking funds will become available to pay the debt when it becomes due or shortly thereafter then, though it is entirely a matter for you this question of dishonesty, you might well think that is dishonest and there is an intent to defraud.

It is that final passage of which complaint is made. It is submitted that that direction runs counter to authorities which have emanated from the Chancery Division in respect of s. 332(1) [of CA 1948; now IA 1986, s. 213] or predecessors to that section.

The first case of relevance is *Re William C. Leitch Brothers Ltd* [1932] 2 Ch 71; Maugham J had this to say (at p. 77) about the corresponding provision of the Companies Act 1929:

In my opinion I must hold with regard to the meaning of the phrase carrying on business 'with intent to defraud creditors' that, if a company continues to carry on business and to incur debts at a time when there is to the knowledge of the directors no reasonable prospect of the creditors ever receiving payment of those debts, it is, in general, a proper inference that the company is carrying on business with intent to defraud.

The same judge in the following year, in *Re Patrick and Lyon Ltd* [1933] 1 Ch 786 reverted to the topic in the following words (at p. 790):

... I will express the opinion that the words 'defraud' and 'fraudulent purpose', where they appear in the section in question, are words which connote actual dishonesty involving, according to current notions of fair trading among commercial men, real moral blame. No judge, I think, has ever been willing to define 'fraud', and I am attempting no definition. I am merely stating what, in my opinion, must be one of the elements of the word as used in this section.

Basing himself principally on these two passages, Mr Beckman [for the appellant] submits that the judge ought to have directed the jury that it was for the prosecution to prove that the appellant knew at the time at which the debts were incurred that there was no reasonable prospect of the creditors *ever* receiving payment of their debts.

It should be noted however, in relation to the two cases just cited, that Maugham J was expressly disavowing any intention to define 'fraud'. Moreover he was not having to direct a jury in general as to the meaning of the section in question.

What the judge in the present case was doing was to direct the jury in the first passages as to the general meaning of the section and, then, in the later passage as to which complaint is made, directing the jury that it was possible for them, if they thought fit, to come to the conclusion that the appellant was acting dishonestly and fraudulently if he realised at the time when the debts were incurred that there was no reason for thinking that funds would become available to pay the debt when it became due or shortly thereafter. We do not think that the judge was in error in this direction.

Mr Beckman however relied further upon a passage in *Palmer's Company Law*, 23rd ed. (1982), vol. 1, para. 85–84, p. 1192 wherein is to be found a passage from the decision of Buckley J in *Re White and Osmond (Parkstone) Ltd* (unreported), 30 June 1960:

> In my judgment, there is nothing wrong in the fact that directors incur credit at a time when, to their knowledge, the company is not able to meet all its liabilities as they fall due. What is manifestly wrong is if directors allow a company to incur credit at a time when the business is being carried on in such circumstances that it is clear that the company will *never* be able to satisfy its creditors. However, there is nothing to say that directors who genuinely believe that the clouds will roll away and the sunshine of prosperity will shine upon them again and disperse the fog of their depression are not entitled to incur credit to help them to get over the bad time.

We have been fortunate enough to run to earth a transcript of the whole of that judgment. The judge eventually decided in favour of the trader on the basis that, although he might have been guilty of insufficient care and supervision of his business, he could not be said, in the words of Maugham J, to have been guilty of real moral blame so as to justify the judge in saying that he ought to be liable for the debts of the company without limit. In other words, he acquitted the trader of dishonesty—an essential ingredient to liability. In so far as Buckley J was saying that it is never dishonest or fraudulent for directors to incur credit at a time when, to their knowledge, the company is not able to meet all its liabilities as they fall due, we would respectfully disagree....

In the light of those considerations we conclude that the judge's directions on intent in the present case are in accordance with the law....

26 March. Certificate that a point of law of general public importance was involved in the decision, namely, 'In a prosecution under s. 332 of the Companies Act 1948 (as amended) is it sufficient to establish an intent to defraud for the prosecution to prove an intention dishonestly to prejudice the interests of creditors in receiving payment of their debts or must the prosecution prove an intention that the creditors should never be paid at all?'

Index